Short Story Criticism

Guide to Gale Literary Criticism Series

When you need to review criticism of literary works, these are the Gale series to use:

If the author's death date is:	You should turn to:
After Dec. 31, 1959 (or author is still living)	**Contemporary Literary Criticism** for example: Jorge Luis Borges, Anthony Burgess, William Faulkner, Mary Gordon, Ernest Hemingway, Iris Murdoch
1900 through 1959	**Twentieth-Century Literary Criticism** for example: Willa Cather, F. Scott Fitzgerald, Henry James, Mark Twain, Virginia Woolf
1800 through 1899	**Nineteenth-Century Literature Criticism** for example: Fedor Dostoevski, Nathaniel Hawthorne, George Sand, William Wordsworth
1400 through 1799	**Literature Criticism From 1400 to 1800** (excluding Shakespeare) for example: Anne Bradstreet, Daniel Defoe, Alexander Pope, Francois Rabelais, Jonathan Swift, Phillis Wheatley **Shakespearean Criticism** Shakespeare's plays and poetry
Antiquity through 1399	**Classical and Medieval Literature Criticism** for example: Dante, Homer, Plato, Sophocles, Vergil, the Beowulf Poet

Gale also publishes related criticism series:

Children's Literature Review

This series covers authors of all eras who have written for the preschool through high school audience.

Short Story Criticism

This series covers the major short fiction writers of all nationalities and periods of literary history.

ISSN 0895-9439

Volume 5

Short Story Criticism

Excerpts from Criticism of the
Works of Short Fiction Writers

6254

Thomas Votteler
Editor

Shannon J. Young
Associate Editor

Gale Research Inc.

DETROIT • NEW YORK • WASHINGTON, D.C.
CHICAGO • LONDON

STAFF

Thomas Votteler, *Editor*

David Segal, Robyn V. Young, Shannon J. Young, *Associate Editors*

Rogene M. Fisher, Elizabeth Parker Henry, *Assistant Editors*

Jeanne A. Gough, *Permissions & Production Manager*
Linda M. Pugliese, *Production Supervisor*
Jennifer Gale, David G. Oblender, Suzanne Powers, Maureen Puhl,
Linda M. Ross, *Editorial Associates*
Donna Craft, *Editorial Assistant*

Victoria B. Cariappa, *Research Supervisor*
H. Nelson Fields, Judy L. Gale, Maureen Richards, Mary D. Wise, *Editorial Associates*
Jill M. Ohorodnik, *Editorial Assistant*

Sandra C. Davis, *Permissions Supervisor (Text)*
Josephine M. Keene, Kimberly F. Smilay, *Permissions Associates*
Maria L. Franklin, Camille P. Robinson, Shalice Shah,
Denise M. Singleton, *Permissions Assistants*

Patricia A. Seefelt, *Permissions Supervisor (Pictures)*
Margaret A. Chamberlain, *Permissions Associate*
Pamela A. Hayes, Lillian Quickley, *Permissions Assistants*

Mary Beth Trimper, *Production Manager*
Evi Seoud, *Assistant Production Manager*

Arthur Chartow, *Art Director*
C. J. Jonik, *Keyliner*

Laura Bryant, *Production Supervisor*
Louise Gagné, *Internal Production Associate*

Copyright © 1990 Gale Research Inc.
835 Penobscot Bldg.
Detroit, MI 48226-4094

Library of Congress Catalog Card Number 88-641014
ISBN 0-8103-2554-3
ISSN 0895-9439

Printed in the United States of America

Contents

Preface

S *hort Story Criticism (SSC)* presents significant passages from criticism of the world's greatest short story writers and provides supplementary materials—biographical and bibliographical—to guide the interested reader to a greater understanding of the authors of short fiction. This series was developed in response to suggestions from librarians serving high school, college, and public library patrons who had noted a considerable number of requests for critical material on short story writers. Although major short story writers are covered in such Gale literary criticism series as *Contemporary Literary Criticism (CLC), Twentieth-Century Literary Criticism (TCLC), Nineteenth-Century Literature Criticism (NCLC),* and *Literature Criticism from 1400 to 1800 (LC),* librarians perceived the need for a series devoted solely to writers of the short story genre.

Scope of the Work

SSC is designed to serve as an introduction to major short story writers of all eras and nationalities. For example, the present volume includes commentary on O. Henry, one of the most popular and widely read American short story writers of the twentieth century; Honoré de Balzac, considered among the greatest writers of nineteenth-century France, whose vast work *La comédie humaine* consists of more than 140 short stories and novels; and Alice Walker, author of the Pulitzer Prize-winning novel *The Color Purple,* whose short story collections have extended her reputation as a gifted writer. Since these authors have inspired a great deal of relevant critical material, *SSC* is necessarily selective, and the editors have chosen the most important published criticism to aid readers and students in their research.

Ten to fifteen authors will be included in each volume, and each author entry presents a historical survey of the critical response to that author's work: some early criticism is included to indicate initial reaction, later criticism is selected to represent any rise or decline in the author's reputation, and current analyses provide a modern view. The length of an entry is intended to reflect the amount of critical attention the author has received from critics writing in English and from foreign critics in translation. Critical articles and books that have not been translated into English are excluded. Every attempt has been made to identify and include excerpts from the most significant essays on each author's work. In order to provide these important critical pieces, the editors will sometimes reprint essays that have appeared in previous volumes of Gale's literary criticism series. Such duplication, however, never exceeds twenty percent of an *SSC* volume.

Organization of the Book

An *SSC* author entry consists of the following elements:

- The **author heading** cites the author's full name, followed by birth and death dates. The unbracketed portion of the name denotes the form under which the author most commonly wrote. If the author wrote consistently under a pseudonym, the pseudonym will be listed in the author heading and the real name given in parentheses on the first line of the biographical and critical introduction.

- The **biographical and critical introduction** contains background information designed to introduce a reader to the author and to the critical debates surrounding his or her work. Parenthetical material following the introductions provides references to other biographical and critical series published by Gale, including *CLC, TCLC, NCLC,* and *LC, Children's Literature Review, Contemporary Authors, Dictionary of Literary Biography,* and *Something about the Author.*

- A **portrait of the author** is included when available. Many entries also contain illustrations of materials pertinent to an author's career, including holographs of manuscript pages, title pages, dust jackets, letters, or representations of important people, places, and events in the author's life.

- The list of **principal works** is chronological by date of first publication and lists the most important works by the author. The first section comprises short story collections, novellas, and novella collections. The second section gives information on other major works by the author. For foreign authors, the editors have provided original foreign language publication information and have selected what are considered the best and most complete English-language editions of their works.

- **Criticism** is arranged chronologically in each author entry to provide a useful perspective on changes in critical evaluation over the years. All short story, novella, and collection titles by the author featured in the entry are printed in boldface type to enable a reader to ascertain without difficulty the works discussed. Also for purposes of easier identification, the critic's name and the publication date of the essay are given at the beginning of each piece of criticism. Unsigned criticism is preceded by the title of the journal in which it appeared.

- Critical essays are prefaced with **explanatory notes** as an additional aid to students and readers using *SSC.* The explanatory notes provide several types of useful information, including: the reputation of a critic, the importance of a work of criticism, and the specific type of criticism (biographical, psychoanalytic, structuralist, etc.).

- A complete **bibliographical citation,** designed to help the interested reader locate the original essay or book, follows each piece of criticism.

- The **further reading list** appearing at the end of each author entry suggests additional materials on the author. In some cases it includes essays for which the editors could not obtain reprint rights.

Other Features

A **cumulative author index** lists all the authors who have appeared in *SSC, CLC, TCLC, NCLC, LC,* and *Classical and Medieval Literature Criticism (CMLC),* as well as cross-references to the Gale series *Children's Literature Review, Authors in the News, Contemporary Authors, Contemporary Authors Autobiography Series, Dictionary of Literary Biography, Something about the Author, Something about the Author Autobiography Series,* and *Yesterday's Authors of Books for Children.* Users will welcome this cumulated index as a useful tool for locating an author within the literary criticism series.

A **cumulative nationality index** lists all authors featured in *SSC* by nationality, followed by the number of the *SSC* volume in which they appear.

A **cumulative title index** lists in alphabetical order all short story, novella, and collection titles contained in the *SSC* series. Titles of short story collections, separately published novellas, and novella collections are printed in italics, while titles of individual short stories are printed in roman type with quotation marks. Each title is followed by the author's name and the corresponding volume and page numbers where commentary on the work may be located. English-language translations of original foreign-language titles are cross-referenced to the foreign titles so that all references to discussion of a work are combined in one listing.

A Note to the Reader

When writing papers, students who quote directly from any volume in the Literary Criticism Series may use the following general forms to footnote reprinted criticism. The first example pertains to material drawn from periodicals, the second to material reprinted from books:

[1]Henry James, Jr., "Honoré de Balzac," *The Galaxy* 20 (December 1875), 814-36; excerpted and reprinted in *Short Story Criticism,* Vol. 5, ed. Thomas Votteler (Detroit: Gale Research, 1990), pp. 8-11.

[2]F. R. Leavis, *D. H. Lawrence: Novelist* (Alfred A. Knopf, 1956); excerpted and reprinted in *Short Story Criticism,* Vol. 4, ed. Thomas Votteler (Detroit: Gale Research, 1990), pp. 202-06.

Suggestions Are Welcome

Readers who wish to suggest authors to appear in future volumes, or who have other suggestions, are cordially invited to contact the editors, either by letter or by calling Gale's toll-free number: 1-800-347-GALE.

Acknowledgments

The editors wish to thank the copyright holders of the excerpted criticism included in this volume, the permissions managers of many book and magazine publishing companies for assisting us in securing reprint rights, and Anthony Bogucki for assistance with copyright research. We are also grateful to the staffs of the Detroit Public Library, the Library of Congress, the University of Detroit Library, Wayne State University Purdy/Kresge Library Complex, and University of Michigan Libraries for making their resources available to us. Following is a list of the copyright holders who have granted us permission to reprint material in this volume of *SSC*. Every effort has been made to trace copyright, but if omissions have been made, please let us know.

COPYRIGHTED EXCERPTS IN *SSC*, VOLUME 5, WERE REPRINTED FROM THE FOLLOWING PERIODICALS:

The American Book Review, v. 4, May-June, 1982. © 1982 by *The American Book Review.* Reprinted by permission of the publisher.—*American Imago,* v. 27, Summer, 1970 for "Kafka's 'A Hunger Artist': The Ego in Isolation" by Paul Neumarkt; v. 35, Winter, 1978 for "Franz Kafka, 'A Country Doctor': The Narrator as Dreamer" by Katherine Stockholder. Copyright 1970, 1978 by The Association for Applied Psychoanalysis, Inc. Both reprinted by permission of the Wayne State University Press and the respective authors.—*Approach,* n. 49, Fall, 1963 for "Kafka's 'Metamorphosis': A Literal Reading" by Norman Friedman. Copyright 1963 by *Approach.* Reprinted from the Approach Collection, by permission of George Arents Research Library for Special Collections at Syracuse University and the author.—*The Black Scholar,* v. 12, March-April, 1981; v. 13, Spring, 1982. Copyright 1981, 1982 by *The Black Scholar.* Both reprinted by permission of the publisher.—*Book World—The Washington Post,* May 31, 1981. © 1981, *The Washington Post.* Reprinted by permission of the publisher.—*Books Abroad,* v. 39, Summer, 1965. Copyright 1965 by the University of Oklahoma Press. Reprinted by permission of the publisher.—*The Canadian Fiction Magazine,* n. 28, 1978 for "The Three Stages of Mavis Gallant's Short Fiction" by Ronald B. Hatch; n. 43, 1982 for "Home Truths: Selected Canadian Stories" by Ronald B. Hatch. Copyright © 1978, 1982 by *The Canadian Fiction Magazine.* Both reprinted by permission of the author.—*Canadian Forum,* v. LXI, February, 1982 for "A National Sense of Self" by Michael Thorpe. Reprinted by permission of the author.—*Canadian Literature,* n. 56, Spring, 1973 for "Perils of Compassion" by Peter Stevens; n. 93, Summer, 1982 for "Exiles in Time: Gallant's 'My Heart Is Broken' " by David O'Rourke; n. 111, Winter, 1986 for "From a Balloon" by Peter Buitenhuis. All reprinted by permission of the respective authors.—*The Carleton Miscellany,* v. II, Winter, 1961. Copyright 1961 by Carleton College. Reprinted by permission of the publisher.—*CLA Journal,* v. X, September, 1966. Copyright, 1966 by The College Language Association. Used by permission of The College Language Association.—*Colby Library Quarterly,* v. IX, June, 1971. Reprinted by permission of the publisher.—*College English,* v. 24, December, 1962 for " 'Death in Venice': The Disguised Self" by Eugene McNamara. Copyright © 1962 by the National Council of Teachers of English. Reprinted by permission of the publisher and the author.—*College Literature,* v. VI, Spring, 1979. Copyright © 1979 by West Chester University. Reprinted by permission of the publisher.—*Commentary,* v. 18, July, 1954 for "The Triumph of Decay" by Philip Rahv. Copyright 1954 by the American Jewish Committee. All rights reserved. Reprinted by permission of the publisher and the Literary Estate of Philip Rahv.—*Criticism,* v. VI, Spring, 1964 for "The Existentialist and the Diabolical Machine" by Douglas Angus. Copyright, 1964, Wayne State University Press. Reprinted by permission of the publisher and the author.—*Critique: Studies in Modern Fiction,* v. IV, Winter, 1963-64; v. VII, Winter, 1964-65; v. IX, 1967. Copyright © 1963, 1964, 1967 Helen Dwight Reid Educational Foundation. All reprinted with permission of the Helen Dwight Reid Educational Foundation, published by Heldref Publications, 4000 Albemarle Street, N. W., Washington, DC 20016.—*Eire-Ireland,* v. XIII, Winter, 1978. Copyright © 1978 Irish American Cultural Institute, 2115 Summit Ave., St. Paul, MN 55105. Reprinted by permission of the publisher.—*English Literature in Transition: 1880-1920,* v. 29, 1986 for "Hesitation in Kipling's 'The Phantom 'Rickshaw' " by William J. Scheick. Copyright © 1986 *English Literature in Transition: 1880-1920.* Reprinted by permission of the publisher and the author.—*Essays on Canadian Writing,* n. 33, Fall, 1986. © 1986 Essays on Canadian Writing Ltd. Reprinted by permission of the publisher.—*Freedomways,* v. 14, first quarter, 1974. Copyright © 1974 by Freedomways Associates, Inc. Reprinted by permission of *Freedomways.*—*German Life & Letters,* n.s. v. XXVIII, April, 1975. Reprinted by permission of the publisher.—*The Germanic Review,* v. XLV, November, 1970 for "The Dialectic of Decadence: An Analysis of Thomas Mann's 'Death in Venice' " by Albert Braverman and Larry David Nachman. Copyright 1970 by Helen Dwight Reid Educational Foundation. Reprinted by permission of the authors.—*The Hudson Review,* v. XXII, Autumn, 1969. Copyright © 1969 by The Hudson Review, Inc. Reprinted by permission of the publisher.—*Illinois Quarterly,* v. 41, Winter, 1978 for "Quest for Meaning: The Stories of Frank O'Connor" by Gordon Bordewyk. Copyright, Illinois State University, 1978. Reprinted by permission of the publisher and the author.—*Irish Renaissance Annual I,* v. I, 1980. © 1980 by Associated Presses, Inc. Reprinted by permission of the publisher.—*Irish Studies,* v. 1, 1980. Reprinted by permission of the publisher.—*Journal of Afro-American Issues,* v. 5, Spring, 1977. Copyright © 1977 by Educational and Community

Authors to Be Featured in *SSC,* Volumes 6 and 7

Hans Christian Andersen, 1805-1875. (Danish fairy tale writer, poet, short story writer, novelist, travel writer, autobiographer, and dramatist)—One of the most distinguished and best-loved writers of fairy tales, Andersen created an enduring legacy of lively and inventive literature that includes such tales as "Thumbelina," "The Princess and the Pea," and "The Ugly Duckling."

Isak Dinesen, 1885-1962. (Danish short story writer, autobiographer, novelist, and translator)—One of Denmark's most widely acclaimed modern writers, Dinesen is perhaps best known for her novel *Out of Africa*, and for her short fiction collections *Seven Gothic Tales* and *Winter's Tales.*

F(rancis) Scott (Key) Fitzgerald, 1896-1940. (American novelist, short story writer, essayist, scriptwriter, and dramatist)—Renowned for his classic novel *The Great Gatsby,* Fitzgerald is considered one of the most influential novelists and short story writers of the twentieth century. In such stories as "May Day," "Babylon Revisited," "The Rich Boy," and "The Diamond as Big as the Ritz," Fitzgerald depicts the prosperity, excess, and subsequent disillusionment that characterized America's Jazz Age.

Hermann Hesse, 1877-1962. (German novelist, short story writer, poet, and essayist)—Internationally revered for his novels *Demian, Steppenwolf,* and *Siddhartha,* Hesse also wrote a considerable body of short fiction, much of which has been collected in his *Stories of Five Decades.*

Doris Lessing, b. 1919. (Persian-born English novelist, short story writer, essayist, dramatist, poet, nonfiction writer, journalist, and travel writer)—Considered among the most powerful contemporary novelists, Lessing has explored many of the central ideas, ideologies, and social issues of the twentieth century. Three of her most acclaimed volumes of short fiction—*Five: Short Novels, The Habit of Loving,* and *African Stories*—focus primarily on racial concerns and the emancipation of modern women.

Liam O'Flaherty, 1896-1984. (Irish novelist, short story writer, autobiographer, and travel writer)—O'Flaherty is considered an important figure in the Irish Renaissance, a literary movement that sought inspiration in Celtic cultural tradition. Best known for novels that chronicle the Irish struggle for independence from England, O'Flaherty is also respected for short stories that vividly portray the arduous peasant life of his native Aran Islands.

Grace Paley, b. 1922. (American short story writer and essayist)—Critically acclaimed for her fiction collections *The Little Disturbances of Man, Enormous Changes at the Last Minute,* and *Later the Same Day,* Paley creates seriocomic stories noted for their authentic portrayals of working-class New Yorkers.

Mark Twain, 1835-1910. (American novelist, short story writer, journalist, essayist, autobiographer, and dramatist)—Regarded by many as the father of modern American literature, Twain is credited with freeing American fiction from the staid literary conventions of the nineteenth century. Although best known for his novel *Adventures of Huckleberry Finn,* Twain also wrote such notable stories as "The Man That Corrupted Hadleyburg," and "The Celebrated Jumping Frog of Calaveras County," which caustically satirize hypocrisy and social injustice.

Additional Authors to Appear in Future Volumes

Agnon, Shmuel Yosef
  1888-1970
Aiken, Conrad 1889-1973
Aldiss, Brian 1925-
Aleichem, Sholom 1859-1916
Asimov, Isaac 1920-
Atherton, Gertrude 1857-1948
Babel, Isaac 1894-1941?
Baldwin, James 1924-1987
Barth, John 1930-
Beattie, Ann 1947-
Beerbohm, Max 1872-1956
Bellow, Saul 1915-
Benét, Stephen Vincent
  1898-1943
Bierce, Ambrose 1842-1914?
Boccaccio, Giovanni 1313?-1375
Böll, Heinrich 1917-1985
Brentano, Clemens 1778-1842
Caldwell, Erskine 1903-
Calisher, Hortense 1911-
Camus, Albert 1913-1960
Carter, Angela 1940-
Carver, Raymond 1938-1988
Cassill, R. V. 1919-
Cervantes 1547-1616
Chandler, Raymond 1888-1959
Chaucer, Geoffrey 1345-1400
Chopin, Kate 1851-1904
Conrad, Joseph 1857-1924
Coover, Robert 1932-
Cortázar, Julio 1914-1984
Crane, Stephen 1871-1900
Dahl, Roald 1916-
Dante Alighieri 1265-1321
Davenport, Guy 1927-
de la Mare, Walter 1873-1956
Dick, Philip K. 1928-1982
Disch, Thomas M. 1940-
Doyle, Arthur Conan 1859-1930
Elkin, Stanley 1930-
Ellison, Harlan 1934-
Fast, Howard 1914-
Flaubert, Gustave 1821-1880

Forster, E. M. 1879-1970
France, Anatole (ps. of Anatole-
  François Thibault) 1844-1924
Friedman, Bruce J. 1930-
Gaines, Ernest J. 1933-
Galsworthy, John 1867-1933
García-Márquez, Gabriel 1928-
Gardner, John 1933-1982
Garland, Hamlin 1860-1940
Gass, William H. 1924-
Gide, André 1869-1951
Gilchrist, Ellen 1935-
Golding, William 1911-
Gordimer, Nadine 1923-
Gordon, Caroline 1895-1981
Grau, Shirley Ann 1929-
Greene, Graham 1904-
Grimm, Jakob Ludwig
  1785-1863
Grimm, Wilhelm Karl
  1786-1859
Hammett, Dashiell 1894-1961
Harris, Joel Chandler
  1848-1908
Harte, Bret 1836-1902
Heinlein, Robert A. 1907-
Hoffmann, E. T. A. 1776-1822
Hughes, Langston 1902-1967
Jackson, Shirley 1919-1965
James, Henry 1843-1916
James, M. R. 1862-1936
Jewett, Sarah Orne 1844-1909
Jhabvala, Ruth Prawer 1927-
King, Stephen 1947-
Knowles, John 1926-1979
Lardner, Ring 1885-1933
Laurence, Margaret 1926-1987
LeFanu, Joseph Sheridan
  1814-1873
LeGuin, Ursula K. 1929-
Machado de Assis, Joaquim
  Maria 1839-1908
Malamud, Bernard 1914-1986
Mansfield, Katherine 1888-1923

Masters, Edgar Lee 1869?-1950
McCullers, Carson 1917-1967
Maugham, W. Somerset
  1874-1965
Mérimée, Prosper 1803-1870
Oates, Joyce Carol 1938-
O'Brien, Edna 1936-
O'Faolain, Sean 1900-
Olsen, Tillie 1913-
Ozick, Cynthia 1928-
Pasternak, Boris 1890-1960
Pavese, Cesare 1908-1950
Perelman, S. J. 1904-1976
Pritchett, V. S. 1900-
Robbe-Grillet, Alain 1922-
Roth, Philip 1933-
Saki (ps. of H. H. Munro)
  1870-1916
Saroyan, William 1908-1981
Schwartz, Delmore 1913-1966
Scott, Sir Walter 1771-1832
Solzhenitsyn, Alexander 1918-
Spark, Muriel 1918-
Stafford, Jean 1915-1979
Stead, Christina 1902-1983
Stein, Gertrude 1874-1946
Steinbeck, John 1902-1983
Stevenson, Robert Louis
  1850-1894
Sturgeon, Theodore 1918-1985
Tagore, Rabindranath
  1861-1941
Taylor, Peter 1917-
Thackeray, William Makepeace
  1811-1863
Tolstoy, Leo 1828-1910
Turgenev, Ivan 1818-1883
Updike, John 1932-
Vonnegut, Kurt, Jr. 1922-
Wells, H. G. 1866-1946
West, Nathanael 1904-1940
White, E. B. 1899-1986
Zola, Émile 1840-1902

Honoré de Balzac

1799-1850

(Born Honoré Balzac; also wrote under the pseudonyms Lord R'hoone and Horace de Saint-Aubin) French novelist, short fiction writer, dramatist, essayist, and editor.

Considered one of the greatest novelists of nineteenth-century France, Balzac was an important contributor to the development of the short story genre. His literary fame rests on his vast work *La comédie humaine,* which consists of more than 140 short stories and novels, and provides a complex portrait of nineteenth-century French society. As a short fiction writer, Balzac is hailed for his intricate and perceptive psychological analyses as well as for his candid assessments of the social mores of his society. He is credited with popularizing the short story in France, and many critics contend that he played a vital role in developing the Realist movement in French literature.

Balzac was born in Tours to bourgeois parents. Neglected as a child, he lived with a wet nurse until the age of four, thereafter residing year-round at boarding schools until his family moved to Paris in 1814. Balzac wrote in detail of the loneliness he felt as a child, noting with bitterness his mother's indifference to his unhappiness. In 1819 he received his law degree but immediately announced his intention of becoming a writer. From 1819 to 1825 Balzac experimented with various literary forms, including sensationalistic short stories and novels that he submitted under various pseudonyms. He considered these endeavors stylistic exercises; they were conscious efforts to learn his craft, as well as his only means of support. In 1822 Balzac became romantically involved with Mme Laure de Berny, a woman more than twenty years his senior who gave him a confidence that he had hitherto lacked. De Berny encouraged Balzac in his literary pursuits, critiquing his stories and serving as his principal mentor throughout much of his career. In 1824 Balzac began publishing under his own name, to which he eventually added the aristocratic particle *de* in 1831. The early 1830s were crucial years in his career; he published numerous works, including such famous stories as "Une passion dans le désert," "Une épisode sous la terreur," and "Étude de femme," and he formulated the structure of *La comédie humaine.* His short story collection *Scènes de la vie privée* enhanced his popular reputation, appealing in particular to female readers, who valued his realistic and sympathetic portraits of women as vital members of society. In 1832 Balzac received a letter from a female admirer signed *l'Étrangère* (the Stranger). The writer expressed her admiration for *Scènes de la vie privée* and chided Balzac for the ironic tone in his newest novel, *La peau de chagrin.* Later she revealed her identity as Madame Hanska, the wife of a wealthy Polish count. Balzac and Madame Hanska carried on an extended liaison through letters and infrequent visits that eventually led to marriage, though not until just five months prior to Balzac's death in 1850.

Commentators on Balzac seldom fail to note his flamboyant lifestyle and working habits. Each year he produced approximately 2000 pages of printed text, rarely completing a manuscript before giving it to the printer; instead, he would send a brief outline and scrupulously compose the entire story on

successive galley proofs. To be free of distractions, he began working at midnight and continued until midday, fueled by tremendous quantities of strong black coffee. After months of this solitary, exhausting routine, Balzac would cease working and plunge into a frenzy of social activity. His ostentatious dress, extensive collection of antiques, and outlandish printer's bills kept him perennially short of money. In addition, early in his career he engaged in a series of disastrous business ventures that left him deeply in debt. Pressure from creditors and mounting financial obligations pushed Balzac to write faster, contributing to his creation of *La comédie humaine* and ultimately, scholars conclude, to his premature death of heart failure.

Despite the great length and ambitious scope of *La comédie humaine,* most commentators concur that the work should be approached as a whole. Written between 1830 and 1850, *La comédie humaine* is Balzac's greatest literary achievement. The body of the work contains three main sections: the *Études analytiques, Études philosophiques,* and the bulk of his work, the *Études de moeurs,* which Balzac further divided into the *Scènes de la vie de province, Scènes de la vie militaire, Scènes de la vie politique, Scènes de la vie de campagne,* and *Scènes de la vie privée* (an enlarged edition of the short story collection published in 1830). Referring to himself as "secretary to French society," Balzac expressed his desire to describe and interpret in detail his era by arranging human social types in the same manner the Naturalists had classified zoological species. Dividing his stories into groups that depict the various classes and their milieus, Balzac revealed his conviction that environment largely determines the actions, development, and fate of individuals. Central to this structural unity is an enormous cast of recurring characters. Some 570 of the over-2000 characters in *La comédie humaine* appear in more than one story. For many critics, this technique of repeating characters in different works at various stages in their lives strengthens the verisimilitude of Balzac's fictional world and enables him to explore the psychology of individual characters more fully than is possible in a single piece.

In his short fiction, Balzac frequently follows a formulaic narrative structure. Several of his stories open with a startling revelation that is followed by a lengthy flashback intended to establish the tenor of the story. The climax is often brief, and the story concludes with an epilogue that contains a moral or message. Balzac was primarily interested in probing the psychological motivations behind his characters' actions. As a result, plot is almost always secondary to character development. Balzac believed the short story form was ideally suited to exploring individual personality traits, particularly oddities of human nature he considered fascinating but unworthy of a novel-length work. For example, in "La chef-d'oeuvre inconnu" ("The Unknown Masterpiece"), he examines the monomania of Frenhofer, an artist who works feverishly for ten years to create his ideal of the perfect painting. In other short stories, essential characteristics of an individual are distilled into an embodiment and reflection of an entire class. When characters attempt to defy established social boundaries, the consequences are often dire, as in the story "La maison du chat-qui-pelote." In this tale, a shopkeeper's daughter rejects her parents' choice of a suitor and marries above her class. The girl's blatant disregard for prevailing social parameters insures the failure of her marriage. She returns home broken-hearted and dies in disgrace.

Balzac was one of the most popular writers of nineteenth-century France. He received numerous fan letters and was usually paid in advance for his manuscripts. In his efforts to achieve a realistic, comprehensive representation of society, Balzac included in his world not only virtue, faithfulness, and happiness, but also squalor, misery, chicanery, sexual perfidy, and greed. Ferdinand Brunetière acknowledged, "Balzac brought about a revolution . . . by doing artistic work with elements reputed unworthy of art." Many nineteenth-century commentators found this approach depressing, and despite his general popularity, Balzac was not always well-received by the press or by his literary peers. Nineteenth-century commentator J. W. Croker epitomized the critical view that Balzac's stories were unfit for publication, claiming, "A baser, meaner, filthier scoundrel never polluted society than M. de Balsac's standard of '*public morals*'."

Modern critical interest in Balzac attests to his enduring importance, and many scholars consider his contribution to the development of the short story and novel in France unsurpassed. Biographer Stephan Zweig called Balzac "the historian of his own age . . . the psychologist and physiologist, painter and physician, judge and literary creator." His popularity continues unabated, as successive generations look to his works for a universal as well as a personal view of human life.

(For further information on Balzac's life and career, see *Nineteenth-Century Literature Criticism,* Vol. 5.)

PRINCIPAL WORKS

SHORT FICTION

Scènes de la vie privée   1830; also published as *Scènes de la vie privée* [enlarged edition], 1832

Romans et contes philosophiques   (novel and short stories) 1831

*Les célibataires   1832; published in *Scènes de la vie privée* [enlarged edition]; also published as *Le curé de Tours* in *Les célibataires,* 1858
   [*The Abbé Birotteau*   (*Le Curé de Tours*), 1895-98]

Les cent contes drôlatiques: Colligez ès abbaïes de Touraine et mis en lumière par le sieur de Balzac, pour l'esbattement des Pantagruelistes et non aultres, premier dixain   1832; *deuxieme dixain*   1833; *troisieme dixain,* 1837
   [*Balzac's Contes Drôlatiques: Droll Stories Collected from the Abbeys of Touraine,* 1874]

Les nouveaux contes philosophiques   (novel and short stories)   1832

Études de moeurs au XIXe siècle. 12 vols.   (novels, novellas, and short stories)   1834-37

Histoire des treize   1834-35; published in *Études de moeurs au XIXe siècle*
   [*The Thirteen,* 1895-98]

Le livre mystique   (novels and short stories)   1835

**Les deux poètes   1837; published in *Études de moeurs au XIXe siècle*

** *Un grand homme de province à Paris*   1839
   [*A Great Man of the Provinces in Paris,* 1893]

Oeuvres complètes de M. de Balzac: La comédie humaine. 17 vols.   (novels, novellas, and short stories)   1842-48

** *Eve et David*   1843; published in *Oeuvres complètes de M. de Balzac: La comédie humaine;* also published as *Les souffrances de l'inventeur* in *Oeuvres complètes de H. de Balzac: Édition définitive,* 1879

Honorine   1844
   [*Honorine,* 1895-98]

Oeuvres complètes de H. de Balzac. 20 vols.   (novels, novellas, short stories, and dramas)   1855-63

Les célibataires   1858

Pierrette   1858; published in *Les célibataires*
   [*Pierrette,* 1895-98]

La Rabouilleuse   1858; published in *Les célibataires*
   [*A Bachelor's Establishment,* 1895-98]

Oeuvres complètes de H. de Balzac: Édition définitive. 26 vols. (novels, novellas, short stories, dramas, letters, and essays)   1869-1906

Comédie humaine. 40 vols.   (novels, novellas, and short stories)   1895-98

Oeuvres complètes de Honoré de Balzac. 40 vols.   (novels, novellas, short stories, dramas, letters, and essays) 1912-40

OTHER MAJOR WORKS

Le dernier Chouan; ou, La Bretagne en 1800   (novel)   1829; also published as *Les Chouans; ou, La Bretagne en 1799,* 1834
   [*The Chouans,* 1890]

Physiologie du mariage; ou, Méditations de philosophie éclectique sur le bonheur et le malheur conjugal   (novel) 1830

[The Physiology of Marriage, 1904]

Le peau de chagrin (novel) 1831
[*The Wild Ass's Skin,* 1895-98]

Notice biographique sur Louis Lambert (novel) 1832; published in *Les nouveaux contes philosophiques;* also published in revised form as *Histoire intellectuel de Louis Lambert* in *Le livre mystique,* 1835
[*Louis Lambert,* 1889]

Le medecin de campagne (novel) 1833
[*The Country Doctor,* 1887]

La recherche de l'absolu (novel) 1834; published in *Études de moeurs au XIXe siècle;* also published as *Balthazar Claës; ou, La recherche de l'absolu,* 1839
[*Balthazar; or, Science and Love,* 1859; also published as *The Quest of the Absolute,* 1888]

Le père Goriot: Histoire parisienne (novel) 1835
[*Daddy Goriot; or, Unrequited Affection,* 1860; also published as *Old Goriot,* 1895-98]

Séraphita (novel) 1835; published in *Le livre mystique*
[*Séraphita,* 1889]

Le lys dans la vallée (novel) 1836
[*The Lily of the Valley,* 1891]

Eugénie Grandet (novel) 1837?; published in *Études de moeurs au XIXe siècle*
[*Eugenia Grandet; or, The Miser's Daughter: A Tale of Everyday Life in the Nineteenth Century,* 1843]

La vielle fille (novel) 1837; published in *Études de moeurs au XIXe siècle*

Histoire de la grandeur et de la décadence de César Birotteau, parfumeur (novel) 1838
[*History of the Grandeur and Downfall of César Birotteau,* 1860; also published as *The Rise and Fall of César Birotteau,* 1912]

Béatrix; ou, Les amours forcés (novel) 1839
[*Béatrix,* 1895-98]

La femme de trent ans (novel) 1842; published in *Oeuvres complètes de M. de Balzac: La comédie humaine*
[*A Woman of Thirty,* 1895-98]

Ursule Mirouët (novel) 1842
[*Ursula,* 1891]

Illusions perdues (novel) 1842-48; published in *Oeuvres complètes de M. de Balzac: La comédie humaine*
[*Lost illusions,* 1895-98]

Les trois amoureux (novel) 1844; also published as *Modeste Mignon; ou, Les trois amoureux,* 1844
[*Modeste Mignon,* 1888]

Histoire des parens [sic] pauvres: La cousine Bette et Les deux musiciens (novels) 1847; also published as *Les parents pauvres.* 12 vols. 1847-48
[*Poor Relations,* 1880]

Théâtre [first publication] (dramas) 1853

Les paysans [completed by Madame Hanska] (novel) 1863; published in *Oeuvres complètes de H. de Balzac*
[*The Peasantry,* 1895-98]

Correspondance de H. de Balzac, 1819-1850 (letters) 1876
[*The Correspondence of Honoré de Balzac,* 1878]

Splendeurs et misères des courtisanes (novel) 1879; published in *Oeuvres complètes de H. de Balzac: Édition définitive*
[*A Harlot's Progress,* 1895-98; also published as *Splendors and Miseries of a Courtesan*]

Lettres à l'étrangère. 4 vols. (letters) 1899-1950

Honoré de Balzac: Letters to Madame Hanska, Born Countess Rzewuska, Afterwords Madame Honoré de Balzac, 1833-1846 (letters) 1900

The Dramatic Works of Honoré de Balzac (dramas) 1901
The Love Letters of Honoré de Balzac: 1833-1842 (letters) 1901

Les célibataires, the title of Balzac's 1832 novella, is also the title of his collection of novellas published in 1858. The novella appeared in the collection under the title *Le curé de Tours.*

**These works were collectively published as *Illusion perdues* in *Oeuvres complètes: La comédie humaine,* 1842-48.

J. W. CROKER (essay date 1836)

[*A prominent nineteenth-century British man of letters, Croker is remembered for his sarcastic literary style. In the following excerpt, he presents a scathing appraisal of the "public morals" exemplified in Balzac's short stories.*]

If we were considering the *literary merit* of [his] works, we should have much to say in praise and at least as much in censure of M. de Balsac. He has considerable powers of local description, but he considerably abuses them by idle and wearisome minutiæ. He occasionally excites great interest, but quite as often destroys all interest by the improbability and incongruity of his incidents. He is often eloquent, and sometimes pathetic; but, in his efforts after these qualities, frequently deviates into whining and bombast. But it is only as evidence of the state of *moral* feeling and *social* life in France that we have at present to deal with M. de Balsac; and in this view his evidence is indeed most important, not only on account of his acknowledged talents, but because he claims—and because the public voice has assented to his claim—to be, *par excellence,* the most accurate painter of private life and existing society. The titles of his principal works—**Scenes of Private Life, Scenes of Parisian Life, Scenes of Provincial Life**—sufficiently attest this pretension. In the preface to the **Scenes of Private Life,** he sets out with a declaration which reveals an honest and noble ambition;—

> That his works are of such a tendency, that he hopes that well-educated mothers, who unite in their own persons feminine graces to manly good sense, will not hesitate to *place his works in the hands of their daughters.*

And he has found a panegyrist—in the writer of a rather elaborate essay, originally, it seems, published in some French review, but now affixed to the fourth volume of the **Scenes of Parisian Life**—who not only extols him as one of the greatest literary geniuses that ever lived, but as the most faithful painter of manners, and, above all, as one of the *purest moralists* of the age. This critic goes so far, indeed, as to endeavour, by a formal classification and commentary, to prove that these *"splendid works,"* instead of being, as they may appear to the common reader, a series of unconnected tales of the vulgarest and most licentious character, are, in fact, a profound and well-digested course of moral philosophy, written with one great design, and deserving to be distinguished by the loftier title of **Etudes sur les Moeurs!** (p. 81)

[This] great series which M. de Balsac's admirers call the **Etudes sur les Moeurs**—the **Scènes de la Vie, Privée, Parisienne,** et **de Province,** of which we have before us twelve or fourteen volumes, and must endeavour to give some idea, still repeating our consciousness that English ears would not bear an unreserved repetition of the prurient lessons of M. de Balsac. We shall take the stories in the order in which they are presented to us, for two reasons: first, because, as *nemo repente fuit turpissimus,* his earliest tales are the least offensive; and secondly, that by taking them in order, we avoid all possible suspicion of making unfair selections.

The first of the *Scènes de la Vie privée* is entitled **"La Vendetta"** (**"Revenge"**). The only daughter of one of Buonaparte's Corsican followers, whom he has raised to rank and wealth, is, nevertheless, a pupil in a common painting school, where she makes acquaintance with a proscribed officer *de la vieille armée,* whom she persists in marrying, in spite of the advice, entreaties, and command of her affectionate parents—who had the deepest and best founded objections to the match—namely, an old family feud (*Vendetta*), exasperated by recent bloody injuries. She at first supports herself and her husband by her great talents as a painter—but she goes gradually out of fashion, and poverty comes. Her parents are inexorable; and then perish, of actual starvation—first her baby—for the sources of maternity are dry—and then she and her husband! The old parents repent when too late—the mother dies of *remorse,* and the father is left alone in the world—soon, also, to die of a broken heart, the punishment of *his cruelty.* The moral seems to be, that the father and mother were justly punished; which we admit, though the provocation was very strong; but not a censure is breathed against the cruel disobedience of the daughter, nor against a state of society which allows an admired and admirable artist to perish with her husband and child from actual hunger in the capital, as they call it, of the civilization of mankind. The picture may be true enough, but we think a *great moralist* should not have laid *all* the blame on the *Vendetta* of the insulted parents. But let that pass.

The next tale is **"Les Dangers de l'Inconduite"**—the dangers of misconduct—which are exemplified by a Countess de Restaud, who, by a long course of adultery, has given a right to her husband's name and property to children that are not his. She sells her jewels to pay the debts of her paramour; borrows, for the same purpose, large sums from an usurer, which her husband must pay; and on her death-bed she employs the most malignant artifices on her eldest child, (the only one which her husband believes to be his,) to burn a deed by which she supposes that child would receive a larger share of his father's property, to the injury of the children of the adulterous intercourse. And this story is related to a young lady and her family by a common friend of all the parties, as a means of promoting that young lady's union with the son of those amiable parents. This may be a moral lecture at Paris; but to us it looks like a lesson of corruption.

The third story, the **"Bal de Sceaux,"** is comparatively innocent, which is accounted for by its having been borrowed from a female novelist of good morals and good taste. It exhibits what the English will think a strange system of manners. At the *bal de Sceaux*—which is little better than a dance in a booth at Greenwich fair—a young lady of rank falls in love with a most fascinating youth whom she had never before seen, and the passion has reached a great height before she even discovers that to his personal beauty and accomplishments he adds great wealth and the noble name of *Longueville.* This suits the young lady exactly—for, though she can fall in love at the *bal de Sceaux,* she is an aristocrat at heart, and has resolved never to marry anything below a

Peer of France,—(the story, we suppose, must have been written before Louis Philippe's peers had brought that body more nearly to the common level)—but, alas! it turns out that, as in England—

> ——One sometimes views
> Howards and Russels *cleaning shoes*—

so a *Longueville* may keep a linendraper's shop in the Rue St. Denis. Alas! such is the fact—the hero is actually detected selling tape, and is scandalously *jilted* by his proud mistress. But mark the sequel—the haberdasher is, in *due time,* made a peer of France, and the haughty beauty is reduced to marry her own uncle or grand-uncle—we are not quite sure which. This may, perhaps, be a picture of real life in France—it would be presumptuous in *Englishmen* to deny it; but to us it seems just such a novel as the haberdasher's boy himself might have written. But these are trifles—the prelude, as it were, of M. de Balsac's admirable talent;—he is now about to take a deeper tone.

"Gloire et Malheur" is the history of a young painter who marries Augustine, a shopkeeper's daughter, and intrigues with a duchess. (pp. 83-5)

[The] moral is admirable—'a treasure of domestic affection, angelic beauty, and celestial virtue,' are not, it seems, good enough for a French painter, if he be—as every French painter must be—a *genius;* and when the man of genius betrays, insults, *beats,* and *kills* his victim—*her* friends see in it only the *last scene of a drama*—*his* friends, we presume, see only the last scene of a *farce!* and whatever little blame the *great moralist* imputes to the whole transaction falls to the lot of the poor victim, who was only a *trésor de bonté* and a *creature celeste,* when she should have been a *femme forte,* fit to wrestle with a *genius.*

"La Femme Vertueuse" is a young heiress, beautiful, accomplished, and wealthy, suitably united, by a marriage of mutual affection, to M. Grandville, a young lawyer of great promise, who, in the course of the story, rises successively to the most eminent dignities of his profession. The lady has but one fault in the world—but that, to be sure, is a fatal one—she is *pious*—something of what is in England too lightly called a *saint:* she is an excellent mother, and a most affectionate and even submissive wife, when M. Grandville does not exact from her compliances with forms of society which she thinks inconsistent with her higher duties. She willingly accompanies her husband to dinners, concerts, and even assemblies, at the houses of his friends and brother magistrates, but she has a disinclination to *operas* and *balls;* and when, in compliance with her husband's commands, she does go to a ball, she *mortally offends* him by not having danced—and above all, by having worn an unfashionable gown which—*covered her shoulders and neck.* Such *unreasonable* scruples in the mother of several children—in the wife of a judge, are quite intolerable; and this prudent magistrate threatens his too modest and too domestic wife with his eternal displeasure, if she will not admire the decencies of the opera *ballets,* and so far imitate their costume as to wear a *robe à la Grecque*—a fashion of the day, which was next to wearing no robe at all. (pp. 86-7)

And for all these and other horrors, which we suppress——no one seems to blame but *la femme vertueuse!* We shall not waste time in observations on the inconsistencies and absurdities of the details of this story, which are quite equal to its deep immorality; but there is a little circumstance relating to the author himself which we must notice. The hero of the tale begins as plain *Monsieur Grandville;* when he rises a little in life he is called 'M. *de* Grandville,' and Balsac, by printing the *feudal particle* in italics, marks and derides the aristocratic assumption. Now, is it not amusing to find that in the title-page of these very volumes—the author modestly describes himself as *Monsieur Balsac*—but when he had acquired a little fame, and published the *Médecin de Campagne,* he becomes Monsieur H. DE Balsac; and by-and-by, to all his later works, he prefixes the full aristocratic name of *Monsieur DE Balsac!* When he laughed at M. *de* Grandville, he did not foresee that he himself should become M. *de* Balsac. We take this opportunity of remarking, that although we have been told, *ad nauseam,* that the great passion of modern France is *Equality,* every publication we read, and every event we witness, and every room that anybody can enter in Paris, give the most decided contradiction to that assertion, and prove, on the contrary, that there is no nation on the face of the earth so greedy, so morbidly anxious, for anything and everything that looks like personal and aristocratical distinction. In truth, their passion for *equality* is that so admirably stated by Dr. Johnson:—'Sir, your levellers wish to level *down* as far as themselves; but they cannot bear levelling up to themselves.' This great truth was never so strongly exemplified as in the present state of society in France.

In the next story an injured wife reclaims her husband, and restores **"La Paix du Ménage"** by the (not very delicate) stratagem of obtaining from an admirer of her own—by some simulated compliances—proofs of her husband's infidelity, which she then generously lets *him* see she is *resolved not to believe.* As in this little story the husband's fault is decently veiled, and the wife's experiment is not carried to any serious extent, we are not surprised to find that M. de Balsac's admirers think it *somewhat feeble:*—'Cette scène est la plus faible de tous; et se ressent de la petitesse du cadre primitivement adopté.' If M. de Balsac, *more suo,* had blazoned all the sensual details of which the story was susceptible, and had wound up with a murder or a suicide, he would, no doubt, have been spared this severe reproach—a reproach which, as far as we are informed, he has never deserved again.

The next volume opens with two stories, also founded on adulteries; one of which is terminated by a most shocking and, we must add, powerfully managed incident of the husband's murdering the wretched paramour by building him up in the recess of a wall in which he had been concealed. This frightful story has been copied into one of our annuals, without an acknowledgment of the translator's obligations to M. de Balsac. Another tale of the same volume relates the celebrated passage of the Beresina (the horrors of which are exaggerated almost to cannibalism), and the fate of the *wife* of a general officer, who is saved by the exertions of her *lover* from the common destruction; but being separated from him in the subsequent tumult becomes the prey of a licentious soldiery, and sinks into the most disgusting species of insanity; after years of absence, the lover finds her, *wild* and *shameless,* in the forest of St. Germain—the *denouement,* of course, is that she recovers her reason just to pronounce his name and die, and he forthwith blows out his brains! And this is assuredly the least immoral story, according to our confined ideas, of the whole series.

The next volume has what appears at first sight to be three or four separate tales, but on a closer inspection these are seen to be portions of one mysterious and frightful history. We must here pause to observe that his French critic thinks it one of the greatest merits of M. de Balsac, that he re-produces the same personages—in different periods and circumstances of their lives—in his different works—'by which means,' says this panegyrist, 'he gives his novels a kind of historical connexion with each other, and spreads a greater air of reality over the whole.' The fact is indisputable, but we do not altogether believe in the assigned motive. It seems to us that M. de Balsac, writing with great haste and to produce sudden and powerful effects—both on the public and his *paymaster* the publisher—finds it more rapid and convenient to *jump,* as it were, from scene to scene, than to spend time and trouble in weaving a connected narrative. He may also think that the obscurity which these intervals leave tends to create a mysterious interest. It may be so; but it also produces inconsistencies and confusion, and we are often, as in the case of the three or four tales now more especially under consideration, not quite satisfied, nor does his French critic seem to be, as to the degree of connexion which the author means to establish between them. (pp. 87-9)

Such are some of M. de Balsac's pictures of the *vie privée* of his country—such are the scenes which his panegyrists pronounce enchanting, sublime, pure, moral, and, above all, *faithful* and *true.* We think our readers will excuse us from continuing the analysis of any more of these anecdotes of private life; particularly when we add, that in the subsequent volumes there are other stories still more atrocious, and which combine equal or greater horrors with the deeper disgust of *unutterable* sensualities; but we must say a few words on the two other series.

The first volume of the **Scènes de la Vie de Province** has five tales. Of three of them the heroines are adulteresses; in two the heroes died shocking deaths. Another is only the adventures of a *commis marchand,* or *bagman,* which are meant to be droll; but even M. de Balsac's admirers admit that the drollery is *feeble*—we should call it vulgar stuff. The fifth, called **"Les Célibataires,"** is the story of the rivalry of two priests of the cathedral of Tours: in this there is no indecency, and the intrigues and *tracassaries* of a country town are cleverly sketched; but the details exhibit a painful and discreditable state of society. (p. 91)

[In] **Scenes of Parisian life** many of the characters with which we have become acquainted in the *Père Goriot* are re-produced, but with deeper immorality and exaggerated improbabilities. They for the most part hinge on an association of conspirators called **The Thirteen.** This association is formed of villains of *all ranks,* from the *stigmatized felon* to the *titled dandy,* who, by their union, secrecy, and desperate fidelity to their chief and to each other, are represented as *all-powerful*—to save or to destroy life—to confer or to ruin fortunes: the highest society and the lowest are equally at their mercy; money, office, rank, consideration, are all at their disposal; and from poison and poniard up to naval and military armaments, no instrument of power is beyond their reach. And this is the monstrous stuff—and only not ridiculous and contemptible because it is monstrous—which forms the ground-work of M. de Balsac's most applauded scenes of Parisian life; and we can assure our readers, that of about thirty tales which these twelve or fourteen volumes contain, there are not above four or five which are not tainted, impregnated, *saturated* with every kind of crime, every kind of filth, every kind of meanness, and, we we must add, every kind of absurdity and improbability. (pp. 93-4)

J. W. Croker, in an originally unsigned essay titled "French Novels," in The Quarterly Review, Vol. LVI, No. CXI, April, 1836, pp. 65-131.

HONORÉ DE BALZAC (essay date 1842)

[*The following is Balzac's often-quoted "Avant-propos" (preface) to the first edition of his works published under the title* La comédie humaine. *In this essay Balzac defines the scope, theory, and purpose of his vast work, in which he intended to portray all elements of society and to represent a "history of manners" of contemporary France.*]

In giving the general title of **The Human Comedy** to a work begun nearly thirteen years since, it is necessary to explain its motive, to relate its origin, and briefly sketch its plan, while endeavoring to speak of these matters as though I had no personal interest in them. (p. li)

The idea of **The Human Comedy** was at first as a dream to me, one of those impossible projects which we caress and then let fly; a chimera that gives us a glimpse of its smiling woman's face, and forthwith spreads its wings and returns to a heavenly realm of phantasy. But this chimera, like many another, has become a reality; has its behests, its tyranny, which must be obeyed.

The idea originated in a comparison between Humanity and Animality.

It is a mistake to suppose that the great dispute which has lately made a stir, between Cuvier and Geoffroi Saint-Hilaire, arose from a scientific innovation. Unity of structure, under other names, had occupied the greatest minds during the two previous centuries. As we read the extraordinary writings of the mystics who studied the sciences in their relation to infinity, such as Swedenborg, Saint-Martin, and others, and the works of the greatest authors on Natural History—Leibnitz, Buffon, Charles Bonnet, etc., we detect in the *monads* of Leibnitz, in the *organic molecules* of Buffon, in the *vegetative force* of Needham, in the correlation of similar organs of Charles Bonnet—who in 1760 was so bold as to write, "Animals vegetate as plants do"—we detect, I say, the rudiments of the great law of Self for Self, which lies at the root of *Unity of Plan.* There is but one Animal. The Creator works on a single model for every organized being. "The Animal" is elementary, and takes its external form, or, to be accurate, the differences in its form, from the environment in which it is obliged to develop. (pp. li-lii)

I, for my part, convinced of this scheme of nature long before the discussion to which it has given rise, perceived that in this respect society resembled nature. For does not society modify Man, according to the conditions in which he lives and acts, into men as manifold as the species in Zoölogy! The differences between a soldier, an artisan, a man of business, a lawyer, an idler, a student, a statesman, a merchant, a sailor, a poet, a beggar, a priest, are as great, though not so easy to define, as those between the wolf, the lion, the ass, the crow, the shark, the seal, the sheep, etc. Thus social species have always existed, and will always exist, just as there are zoölogical species. If Buffon could produce a magnificent work by attempting to represent in a book the whole realm of zoölogy, was there not room for a work of the same kind on society? But the limits set by nature to the variations of animals have no existence in society. When Buffon describes the lion, he dismisses the lioness with a few phrases; but in society a wife

is not always the female of the male. There may be two perfectly dissimilar beings in one household. The wife of a shopkeeper is sometimes worthy of a prince, and the wife of a prince is often worthless compared with the wife of an artisan. The social state has freaks which Nature does not allow herself; it is nature *plus* society. The description of social species would thus be at least double that of animal species, merely in view of the two sexes. Then, among animals the drama is limited; there is scarcely any confusion; they turn and rend each other—that is all. Men, too, rend each other; but their greater or less intelligence makes the struggle far more complicated. . . . Buffon found that life was extremely simple among animals. Animals have little property, and neither arts nor sciences; while man, by a law that has yet to be sought, has a tendency to express his culture, his thoughts, and his life in everything he appropriates to his use. Though Leuwenhoek, Swammerdam, Spallanzani, Réaumur, Charles Bonnet, Müller, Haller and other patient investigators have shown us how interesting are the habits of animals, those of each kind are, at least to our eyes, always and in every age alike; whereas the dress, the manners, the speech, the dwelling of a prince, a banker, an artist, a citizen, a priest, and a pauper are absolutely unlike, and change with every phase of civilization.

Hence the work to be written needed a threefold form—men, women, and things; that is to say, persons and the material expression of their minds; man, in short, and life. (pp. lii-liv)

But how could such a drama, with the four or five thousand persons which a society offers, be made interesting? How, at the same time, please the poet, the philosopher, and the masses who want both poetry and philosophy under striking imagery? Though I could conceive of the importance and of the poetry of such a history of the human heart, I saw no way of writing it; for hitherto the most famous story-tellers had spent their talent in creating two or three typical actors, in depicting one aspect of life. It was with this idea that I read the works of Walter Scott. Walter Scott, the modern troubadour, or finder (*trouvère—trouveur*), had just then given an aspect of grandeur to a class of composition unjustly regarded as of the second rank. . . . Walter Scott raised to the dignity of the philosophy of History the literature which, from age to age, sets perennial gems in the poetic crown of every nation where letters are cultivated. He vivified it with the spirit of the past; he combined drama, dialogue, portrait, scenery, and description; he fused the marvelous with truth—the two elements of the times; and he brought poetry into close contact with the familiarity of the humblest speech. But as he had not so much devised a system as hit upon a manner in the ardor of his work, or as its logical outcome, he never thought of connecting his compositions in such a way as to form a complete history of which each chapter was a novel, and each novel the picture of a period.

It was by discerning this lack of unity, which in no way detracts from the Scottish writer's greatness, that I perceived at once the scheme which would favor the execution of my purpose, and the possibility of executing it. Though dazzled, so to speak, by Walter Scott's amazing fertility, always himself and always original, I did not despair, for I found the source of his genius in the infinite variety of human nature. Chance is the greatest romancer in the world; we have only to study it. French society would be the real author; I should only be the secretary. By drawing up an inventory of vices and virtues, by collecting the chief facts of the passions, by depicting characters, by choosing the principal incidents of social life, by composing types out of a combination of homogeneous characteristics, I might perhaps succeed in writing the history which so many historians have neglected: that of Manners. By patience and persevernance I might produce for France in the nineteenth century the book which we must all regret that Rome, Athens, Tyre, Memphis, Persia, and India have not bequeathed to us; [a] history of their social life. . . . (pp. liv-lvi)

The work, so far, was nothing. By adhering to the strict lines of a reproduction a writer might be a more or less faithful, and more or less successful painter of types of humanity, a narrator of the dramas of private life, an archaeologist of social furniture, a cataloguer of professions, a registrar of good and evil; but to deserve the praise of which every artist must be ambitious, must I not also investigate the reasons or the cause of these social effects, detect the hidden sense of this vast assembly of figures, passions, and incidents? And finally, having sought—I will not say having found—this reason, this motive power, must I not reflect on first principles, and discover in what particulars societies approach or deviate from the eternal law of truth and beauty? In spite of the wide scope of the preliminaries, which might of themselves constitute a book, the work, to be complete, would need a conclusion. Thus depicted, society ought to bear in itself the reason of its working. (pp. lvi-lvii)

As to the intimate purpose, the soul of this work, these are the principles on which it is based.

Man is neither good nor bad; he is born with instincts and capabilities; society, far from depraving him, as Rousseau asserts, improves him, makes him better; but self-interest also develops his evil tendencies. Christianity, above all, Catholicism, being—as I have pointed out in the *Country Doctor* (*Le Médecin de Campagne*)—a complete system for the repression of the depraved tendencies of man, is the most powerful element of social order.

In reading attentively the presentment of society cast, as it were, from the life, with all that is good and all that is bad in it, we learn this lesson—if thought, or if passion, which combines thought and feeling, is the vital social element, it is also its destructive element. In this respect social life is like the life of man. Nations live long only by moderating their vital energy. Teaching, or rather education, by religious bodies is the grand principle of life for nations, the only means of diminishing the sum of evil and increasing the sum of good in all society. Thought, the living principle of good and ill, can only be trained, quelled, and guided by religion. The only possible religion is Christianity. . . . Christianity created modern nationalities, and it will preserve them. Hence, no doubt, the necessity for the monarchical principle. Catholicism and Royalty are twin principles. (pp. lvii-lviii)

I write under the light of two eternal truths—Religion and Monarchy; two necessities, as they are shown to be by contemporary events, towards which every writer of sound sense ought to try to guide the country back. (p. lviii)

Some persons may, perhaps, think that this declaration is somewhat autocratic and self-assertive. They will quarrel with the novelist for wanting to be an historian, and will call him to account for writing politics. I am simply fulfilling an obligation—that is my reply. The work I have undertaken will be as long as a history; I was compelled to explain the logic of it, hitherto unrevealed, and its principles and moral purposes. (p. lix)

Now every one who, in the domain of ideas, brings his stone by pointing out an abuse, or setting a mark on some evil that it may be removed—every such man is stigmatized as immoral. The accusation of immorality, which has never failed to be cast at the courageous writer, is, after all, the last that can be brought when nothing else remains to be said to a romancer. If you are truthful in your pictures; if by dint of daily and nightly toil you succeed in writing the most difficult language in the world, the word *immoral* is flung in your teeth. Socrates was immoral; Jesus Christ was immoral; they both were persecuted in the name of the society they overset or reformed. When a man is to be killed he is taxed with immorality. . . .

When depicting all society, sketching it in the immensity of its turmoil, it happened—it could not but happen—that the picture displayed more of evil than of good; that some part of the fresco represented a guilty couple; and the critics at once raised the cry of immorality, without pointing out the morality of another portion intended to be a perfect contrast. . . . [The] time for an impartial verdict is not yet come for me. (p. lx)

Some persons, seeing me collect such a mass of facts and paint them as they are, with passion for their motive power, have supposed, but wrongly, that I must belong to the school of Sensualism and Materialism—two aspects of the same thing—Pantheism. But their misapprehension was perhaps justified—or inevitable. I do not share the belief in indefinite progress for society as a whole; I believe in man's improvement in himself. (p. lxii)

A sure grasp of the purport of this work will make it clear that I attach to common, daily facts, hidden or patent to the eye, to the acts of individual lives, and to their causes and principles, the importance which historians have hitherto ascribed to the events of public national life. The unknown struggle which goes on in a valley of the Indre between Mme. de Mortsauf and her passion is perhaps as great as the most famous of battles (*Le Lys dans la Vallée*). In one the glory of the victor is at stake; in the other it is heaven. The misfortunes of the two Birotteaus, the priest and the perfumer, to me are those of mankind (**"Le Curé de Tours"** and *Histoire de la Grandeur et de la Décadence de César Birotteau, Parfumeur*). La Fosseuse (*Médecin de Campagne*) and Mme. Graslin (*Curé de Village*) are almost the sum-total of woman. We all suffer thus every day. (pp. lxiii-lxiv)

It was no small task to depict the two or three thousand conspicuous types of a period; for this is, in fact, the number presented to us by each generation, and which **The Human Comedy** will require. This crowd of actors, of characters, this multitude of lives, needed a setting—if I may be pardoned the expression, a gallery. Hence the very natural division, as already known, into **Scenes of Private Life,** of **Provincial Life,** of **Parisian, Political, Military,** and **Country Life.** Under these six heads are classified all the studies of manners which form the history of society at large, of all its *faits et gestes,* as our ancestors would have said. These six classes correspond, indeed, to familiar conceptions. Each has its own sense and meaning, and answers to an epoch in the life of man. . . . After being informed of my plan, [the young writer Felix Davin] said that the **Scenes of Private Life** represented childhood and youth and their errors, as the **Scenes of**

Provincial Life represented the age of passion, scheming, self-interest, and ambition. Then the *Scenes of Parisian Life* give a picture of the tastes and vice and unbridled powers which conduce to the habits peculiar to great cities, where the extremes of good and evil meet. Each of these divisions has its local color—Paris and the Provinces—a great social antithesis which held for me immense resources.

And not man alone, but the principal events of life, fall into classes by types. There are situations which occur in every life, typical phases, and this is one of the details I most sought after. I have tried to give an idea of the different districts of our fine country. My work has its geography, as it has its genealogy and its families, its places and things, its persons and their deeds; as it has its heraldry, its nobles and commonalty, its artisans and peasants, its politicians and dandies, its army—in short, a whole world of its own.

After describing social life in these three portions, I had to delineate certain exceptional lives, which comprehend the interests of many people, or of everybody, and are in a degree outside the general law. Hence we have *Scenes of Political Life.* This vast picture of society being finished and complete, was it not needful to display it in its most violent phase, beside itself, as it were, either in self-defence or for the sake of conquest? Hence the *Scenes of Military Life,* as yet the most incomplete portion of my work, but for which room will be allowed in this edition, that it may form part of it when done. Finally, the *Scenes of Country Life* are, in a way, the evening of this long day, if I may so call the social drama. In that part are to be found the purest natures, and the application of the great principles of order, politics, and morality.

Such is the foundation, full of actors, full of comedies and tragedies, on which are raised the *Philosophical Studies*—the second part of my work, in which the social instrument of all these effects is displayed, and the ravages of the mind are painted, feeling after feeling; the first of this series, *The Magic Skin,* to some extent forms a link between the *Philosophical Studies* and Studies of Manners, by a work of almost Oriental fancy, in which life itself is shown in a mortal struggle with the very element of all passion.

Besides these, there will be a series of *Analytical Studies,* of which I will say nothing, for one only is published as yet—*The Physiology of Marriage.*

In the course of time I purpose writing two more works of this class. First, the Pathology of Social Life, then an Anatomy of Educational Bodies, and a Monograph on Virtue. In looking forward to what remains to be done, my readers will perhaps echo what my publishers say, "Please God to spare you!" I only ask to be less tormented by men and things than I have hitherto been since I began this terrific labor. (pp. lxiv-lxvii)

The vastness of a plan which includes both a history and a criticism of society, an analysis of its evils, and a discussion of its principles, authorizes me, I think, in giving to my work the title under which it now appears—*The Human Comedy.* Is this too ambitious? Is it not exact? That, when it is complete, the public must pronounce. (p. lxvii)

Honoré de Balzac, "Author's Introduction," in his The Works of Honoré de Balzac: The Magic Skin, The Quest of the Absolute, and Other Stories, Vols. I-II, *edited by William P. Trent, translated by Ellen*

Marriage, Thomas Y. Crowell, Co., Inc, 1900, pp. li-lxvii.

HENRY JAMES, JR.   (essay date 1875)

[*James was an American-born English novelist, short story writer, and critic who is regarded as one of the greatest novelists of the English language. His criticism is considered insightful and is informed by his sensitivity to European culture, particularly English and French literature of the late nineteenth century. James was an early, ardent admirer of Balzac's fiction. In a lecture delivered in 1905, he remarked, "I speak of him, and can only speak, as a man of his own craft, an emulous fellow-worker, who has learned from him more of the lessons of the engaging mystery of fiction than from any one else, and who is conscious of so large a debt to repay that it has been positively to be discharged in installments; as if one could never have at once all the required cash in hand." Here, James characterizes Balzac as a writer, positing that several of the author's short stories will endure longer than his novels.*]

The quantity of [Balzac's] work, when we consider the quality, seems truly amazing. There are writers in the same line who have published an absolutely greater number of volumes: Alexandre Dumas, Mme. Sand, Anthony Trollope, have all been immensely prolific; but they all weave a loose web as it were, and Balzac weaves a dense one. The tissue of his tales is always extraordinarily firm and hard; it may not at every point be cloth of gold, but it has always a metallic rigidity. It has been worked over a dozen times, and the work can never be said to belong to light literature. You have only to turn the pages of a volume of Balzac to see that, whatever may be the purity of the current, it at least never runs thin. There is none of that wholesale dialogue, chopped into fragments, which Dumas and Trollope manufacture by the yard, and which bears the same relation to real narrative architecture as a chain of stepping-stones tossed across a stream does to a granite bridge. Balzac is always definite; you can say yes or no to him as you go on. . . . Most of Balzac's shorter tales are antecedent to 1840, and his readers know how many masterpieces the list contains. **"Le Colonel Chabert"** and **"L'Interdiction"** are found in it, as well as **"La Femme Abandonnée," "La Grenadière,"** and **"Le Message,"** and the admirable little stories grouped together (in the common duodecimo edition) with **"Les Marana."** The duration of Balzac's works will certainly not be in proportion to their length. **"Le Curé de Tours,"** for all its brevity, will be read when *Le Député d'Arcis* lies unopened, and more than one literary adventurer will turn, out-wearied, from *La Peau de Chagrin,* and find consolation in **"Un Début dans la Vie."**

I know not how early Balzac formed the plan of the *Comédie Humaine;* but the general preface, in which he explains the unity of his work, and sets forth that each of his tales is a block in a single immense edifice, and that this edifice aims to be a complete portrait of the civilization of his time—this remarkable manifesto dates from 1842. (If I call it remarkable, it is not that I understand it; though so much as I have just expressed may easily be gathered from it. From the moment that Balzac attempts to philosophize, readers in the least sensible of the difference between words and things must part company with him.) He complains, very properly, that the official historians have given us no information about manners that is worth speaking of; that this omission is unpardonable, and that future ages will care much more for the testimony of the novel, properly executed, than for that of the writers who "set in order facts which are about the same in all nations, look up the spirit of laws which have fallen into disuse, elaborate theories which lead nations astray, or, like certain metaphysicians, endeavor to explain what is." Inspired by this conviction, Balzac proposed to himself to illustrate by a tale or a group of tales every phase of French life and manners during the first half of the nineteenth century. To be colossally and exhaustively complete—complete not only in the generals but in the particulars—to touch upon every salient point, to illuminate every typical feature, to reproduce every sentiment, every idea, every person, every place, every object that played a part, however minute, however obscure, in the life of the French people—nothing less than this was his programme. The undertaking was enormous, but it will not seem at first that Balzac underestimated the needful equipment. He was conscious of the necessary talent, and he deemed it possible to acquire the necessary knowledge. This knowledge was almost encyclopædic, and yet, after the vividness of his imagination, Balzac's strongest side is his grasp of actual facts. Behind our contemporary civilization is an immense and complicated machinery—the machinery of government, of police, of the arts, the professions, the trades. Among these things Balzac moved easily and joyously; they form the rough skeleton of his great edifice. There is not a little pedantry in his pretension to universal and infallible accuracy, but his accuracy, so far as we can measure it, is extraordinary, and in dealing with Balzac we must, in every direction, make our account with pedantry. He made his *cadres,* as the French say; he laid out his field in a number of broad divisions; he subdivided these, and then he filled up his moulds, pressing the contents down and packing it tight. You may read the categories on the back of the cover of the little common edition. There are the *Scènes de la Vie Privée—de la Vie de Province—de la Vie Parisienne—de la Vie Politique—de la Vie Militaire—de la Vie de Campagne;* and in a complementary way there are the *Etudes Philosophiques*—portentous name! (the picturesque *Recherche de l'Absolu* is one of these)—and the *Etudes Analytiques.* Then, in the way of subdivisions, there are *Les Célibataires, Les Parisiens en Province, Les Rivalités, Les Illusions Perdues,* the *Splendeurs et Misères des Courtisanes,* the *Parents Pauvres,* the *Envers de l'Histoire Contemporaine.* This goodly nomenclature had a retroactive effect; the idea of the *Comédie Humaine* having developed itself when the author was midway in his career, a number of its component parts are what we may call accomplices after the fact. They are pieces which dovetail into the vast mosaic as they best can. But even if the occasional disparities were more striking they would signify little, for what is most interesting in Balzac is not the achievement but the attempt. The attempt was, as he himself has happily expressed it, to "faire concurrence à l'état civil"—to start an opposition, as we should say here, to the civil registers. He created a complete social system—a hierarchy of ranks and professions which should mirror that of which the officers of the census have cognizance. Everything is there, as we find it in his pages—the king (in *Le Député d'Arcis* Louis XVIII. is introduced and makes witticisms quite *inédits*), the administration, the church, the army, the judicature, the aristocracy, the bourgeoisie, the proletariat, the peasantry, the artists, the journalists, the men of letters, the actors, the children (a little girl is the heroine of **"Pierrette,"** and an urchin the hero of **"Un Début dans la Vie"**), the shopkeepers of every degree, the criminals, the thousand irregular and unclassified members of society. All this in Balzac's hands becomes an organic whole; it moves together; it has a pervasive life; the blood circulates through it; its parts are connected by sinuous arteries.

We have seen in English literature, in two cases, a limited attempt to create a permanent stock, a standing fund, of characters. Thackeray has led a few of his admirable figures from one novel to another, and Trollope has mildly bewildered us by the repeated reappearances of his Bishop Proudies and his Archdeacon Grantleys. But these things are faint shadows of Balzac's extravagant thoroughness—his fantastic cohesiveness. A French brain alone could have persisted in making a system of all this. Balzac's *Comédie Humaine* is on the imaginative line very much what Comte's *Positive Philosophy* is on the scientific. These great enterprises are equally characteristic of the French passion for completeness, for symmetry, for making a subject *totus tercs atque rotundus*— of its intolerance of the indefinite, the unformulated. (pp. 818-20)

In addition to possessing an immense knowledge of his field, [Balzac] was conscious that he needed a philosophy—a system of opinions. On this side too he equipped himself; so far as quantity goes no man was ever better provided with opinions. Balzac has an opinion on everything in heaven and on earth, and a complete, consistent, ever available theory of the universe. "The signs of a superior mind," says M. Taine, in speaking of him, "are *vues d'ensemble*—general views"; and judged by its wealth in this direction, Balzac's should be the greatest mind the world has seen. I can think of no other mind which has stood ready to deliver itself on quite so many subjects. I doubt whether, on the whole, Aristotle had so many *vues d'ensemble* as Balzac. In Plato, in Bacon, in Shakespeare, in Goethe, in Hegel, there are shameful intermissions and lapses, ugly blank spots, ungraceful liabilities to be taken by surprise. But Balzac, as the showman of the human comedy, had measured his responsibilities unerringly, and concluded that he must not only know what everything is, but what everything should be. He is thus *par excellence* the philosophic novelist; his pages bristle with axioms, moral, political, ethical, æsthetical; his narrative groans beneath the weight of metaphysical and scientific digression. The value of his philosophy and his science is a question to be properly treated apart; I mean simply to indicate that formally in this direction he is as complete as in the others. In the front rank of course stand his political and religious opinions. These are anchored to "the two eternal truths—the monarchy and the Catholic Church." Balzac is, in other words, an elaborate conservative—a tory of the deepest dye (as we should say in English). How well, as a picturesque romancer, he knew what he was about in adopting this profession of faith, will be plain to the most superficial reader. His philosophy, his morality, his religious opinions have a certain picturesque correspondence with his political views. Speaking generally, it may be said that he had little belief in virtue and still less admiration for it. He is so vast and various that you find all kinds of contradictory things in him; he has that sign of the few supreme geniuses that, if you look long enough, he offers you a specimen of every possible mode of feeling. (pp. 820-21)

There are two writers in Balzac—the spontaneous one and the reflective one—the former of which is much the more delightful and the latter the more extraordinary. It was the reflective observer that aimed at colossal completeness and equipped himself with a universal philosophy; and it was of this one I spoke when I said just now that Balzac had little belief in virtue. Balzac's beliefs, it must be confessed, are delicate ground; from certain points of view, perhaps, the less said about them the better. His sincere, personal beliefs may be reduced to a very compact formula: he believed that it was possible to write magnificent novels, and that he was the man to do it. He believed, otherwise stated, that human life was infinitely dramatic and picturesque, and that he possessed an incomparable analytic perception of the fact. His other convictions were all derived from this, and humbly danced attendance upon it; for if being a man of genius means being all in one's productive faculty, never was there such a genius as Balzac's. A monarchical society is unquestionably more picturesque, more available for the novelist than any other, as the others have as yet exhibited themselves; and therefore Balzac was with glee, with gusto, with imagination, a monarchist. Of what is to be properly called religious feeling I do not remember a suggestion in all his many pages; on the other hand, the reader constantly encounters the handsomest compliments to the Catholic Church as a social *régime*. A hierarchy is as much more picturesque than a "congregational society" as a mountain is than a plain. . . . Balzac was willing to accept any morality that was curious and unexpected, and he found himself as a matter of course more in sympathy with a theory of conduct which takes account of circumstances and recognizes the merits of duplicity, than with the comparatively colorless idea that virtue is nothing if not uncompromising. Like all persons who have looked a great deal at human life, he had been greatly struck with most people's selfishness, and this quality seemed to him the most general in mankind. . . . If we add to this that he had a great fancy for "electricity" and animal magnetism, we have touched upon the most salient points of Balzac's philosophy. This makes, it is true, rather a bald statement of a matter which at times seems much more redundant and far-reaching; but it may be maintained that an exact analysis of his heterogeneous opinions will leave no more palpable deposit. His imagination was so fertile, the movement of his mind so constant, his curiosity and ingenuity so unlimited, the energy of his phrase so striking, he raises such a cloud of dust about him as he goes, that the reader to whom he is new has a sense of his opening up gulfs and vistas of thought and pouring forth flashes and volleys of wisdom. But from the moment he ceased to be a simple dramatist Balzac was an arrant charlatan. It is probable that no equally vigorous mind was ever at pains to concoct such elaborate messes of folly. They spread themselves over page after page, in a close, dense verbal tissue, which the reader scans in vain for some little flower of available truth. It all rings false—it is all mere flatulent pretension. It may be said that from the moment he attempts to deal with an abstraction the presumption is dead against him. About what the discriminating reader thus brutally dubs his charlatanism, as about everything else in Balzac, there would be very much more to say than this small compass admits of. (Let not the discriminating reader, by the way, repent of his brutality; Balzac himself was brutal, and must be handled with his own weapons. It would be absurd to write of him in semi-tones and innuendoes; he never used them himself.) The chief point is that he himself was his most perfect dupe; he believed in his own magnificent rubbish, and if he made it up, as the phrase is, as he went along, his credulity kept pace with his invention. This was, briefly speaking, because he was morally and intellectually so superficial. He paid himself, as the French say, with shallower conceits than ever before passed muster with a strong man. The moral, the intellectual atmosphere of his genius is extraordinarily gross and turbid; it is no wonder that the flower of truth does not bloom in it, nor any natural flower whatsoever. (pp. 822-23)

[Balzac] had a sense of this present, terrestrial life which has never been surpassed, and which in his genius overshadowed everything else. There are many men who are not especially occupied with the idea of another world, but I believe there has never been a man so completely detached from it as Balzac. This world of our senses, of our purse, of our name, of our *blason* (or the absence of it)—this palpable world of houses and clothes, of seven per cents and multiform human faces, pressed upon his imagination with an unprecedented urgency. It certainly is real enough to most of us, but to Balzac it was ideally real—charmingly, absorbingly, absolutely real. There is nothing in all imaginative literature that in the least resembles his mighty passion for *things*—for material objects, for furniture, upholstery, bricks and mortar. The world that contained these things filled his consciousness, and being, at its intensest, meant simply being thoroughly at home among them. . . . It was natural, therefore, that the life of mankind should seem to him above all an eager striving along this line—a multitudinous greed for personal enjoyment. The master-passion among these passions—the passion of the miser—he has depicted as no one else has begun to do. Wherever we look in the **Comédie Humaine** we see a miser, and he—or she—is sure to be a marvel of portraiture. In the struggle and the race it is not the sweetest qualities that come uppermost, and Balzac, watching the spectacle, takes little account of these. It is strength and cunning that are most visible—the power to climb the ladder, to scramble, to wriggle to the top of the heap, to clutch the money-bag. In human nature, viewed in relation to this end, it is force only that is desirable, and a feeling is fine only in so far as it is a profitable practical force. Strength of purpose seems the supremely admirable thing, and the spectator lingers over all eminent exhibitions of it. It may show itself in two great ways—in vehemence and in astuteness, in eagerness and in patience. Balzac has a vast relish for both, but on the whole he prefers the latter form as being the more dramatic. It admits of duplicity, and there are few human accomplishments that Balzac professes so explicit a respect for as this. He scatters it freely among his dear "gens d'église," and his women are all compounded of it. If he had been asked what was, for human purposes, the faculty he valued most highly, he would have said the power of dissimulation. He regards it as a sign of all superior people, and he says somewhere that nothing forms the character so finely as having had to exercise it in one's youth, in the bosom of one's family. In this attitude of Balzac's there is an element of affectation and of pedantry; he praises duplicity because it is original and audacious to do so. But he praises it also because it has for him the highest recommendation that anything could have—it is picturesque. Duplicity is more picturesque than honesty—just as the line of beauty is the curve and not the straight line. In place of a moral judgment of conduct, accordingly, Balzac usually gives us an æsthetic judgment. A magnificent action with him is not an action which is remarkable for its high motive, but an action with a great force of will or of desire behind it, which throws it into striking and monumental relief. It may be a magnificent sacrifice, a magnificent devotion, a magnificent act of faith; but the presumption is that it will be a magnificent lie, a magnificent murder, or a magnificent adultery. (pp. 824-25)

In all this it may seem that there has been more talk about faults than about merits, and that if it is claimed that Balzac did a great work, I should have plucked more flowers and fewer thistles. But the greatest thing in Balzac cannot be exhibited by specimens. It is Balzac himself—it is the whole attempt—it is the method. This last is his unsurpassed, his incomparable merit. That huge, all-compassing, all-desiring, all-devouring love of reality which was the source of so many of his fallacies and stains, of so much dead weight in his work, was also the foundation of his extraordinary power. The real, for his imagination, had an authority that it has never had for any other. When he looks for it in the things in which we all feel it, he finds it with a marvellous certainty of eye and proves himself the great novelist that he pretends to be. When he tries to make it prevail everywhere, explain everything, and serve as a full measure of our imagination, then he becomes simply the hugest of dupes. He is an enormous tissue of contradictions. He is at once one of the most corrupt of writers and one of the most naïf, the most mechanical and pedantic, and the fullest of *bonhomie* and natural impulse. He is one of the finest of artists and one of the coarsest. Viewed in one way, his novels are ponderous, shapeless, overloaded; his touch is graceless, virulent, barbarous. Viewed in another, his tales have more color, more composition, more grasp of the reader's attention than any others. Balzac's style would demand a chapter apart. It is the least simple style, probably, that ever was written; it bristles, it cracks, it swells and swaggers, but it is a perfect expression of the man's genius. Like his genius, it contains a certain quantity of everything, from immaculate gold to flagrant dross. He was a very bad writer, and yet unquestionably he was a very great writer. One may say briefly, that in so far as his method was an impulse it was successful, and that in so far as it was a theory it was a failure. But both in instinct and in theory he had the aid of an immense force of conviction. His imagination warmed to its work so intensely that there was nothing his volition could not impose upon it. Hallucination settled upon him, and he believed anything that was necessary in the circumstances. This accounts for all his grotesque philosophies, his heroic attempts to furnish specimens of things of which he was profoundly ignorant. He believed that he was about as creative as the Deity, and that if mankind and human history were swept away, the **Comédie Humaine** would be a perfectly adequate substitute for them. M. Taine says of him very happily that, after Shakespeare, he is our great magazine of documents on human nature. When Shakespeare is suggested I feel rather his differences from Shakespeare—feel how Shakespeare's characters stand out in the open air of the universe, while Balzac's are enclosed in a peculiar artificial atmosphere, musty in quality and limited in amount, which persuades itself with a sublime sincerity that it is a very sufficient infinite. But it is very true that Balzac may, like Shakespeare, be treated as a final authority upon human nature; and it is very probable that as time goes on he will be resorted to much less for entertainment, and more for instruction. He has against him that he lacks that slight but needful thing—charm. To feel how much he lacked it, you must read his prefaces, with their vanity, avidity, and garrulity, their gross revelation of his processes, of his squabbles with his publishers, their kitchen atmosphere. But one's last word about him is that he had incomparable power. (pp. 835-36)

Henry James, Jr., "Honoré de Balzac," in The Galaxy, *Vol. XX, No. 6, December, 1875, pp. 814-36.*

FERDINAND BRUNETIÈRE (essay date 1903)

[*An influential nineteenth-century French critic, Brunetière taught for many years at the prestigious École normale supérieure and edited and contributed frequently to the popular journal* Revue des deux mondes. *Conservative and classical in his tastes, he opposed the aesthetics of Romanticism, Impressionism, and Naturalism. Scholars regard his most important contribution to literary criticism his Darwinian-based theory of the evolution of genres, which he explicated in his* L'évolution des genres dan l'histoire de la littérature (1890). *In the following excerpt, Brunetière suggests reasons for Balzac's use of the short story and novella genres.*]

Balzac's short stories, which we call in French *nouvelles,* are, generally speaking, not the best-known or the most popular part of his work; nor are they the part best fitted to give a true and complete idea of his genius. But some of them are none the less masterpieces in their kind; they have characteristics and a significance not always possessed by their author's long novels, such as *Eugénie Grandet* or *Cousin Pons;* and finally, for this very reason, they hold in the unfinished structure of **The Human Comedy** a place which it will be interesting to try to determine.

Some of the stories were written under curious circumstances. In the first place it is to be noted that the majority date from 1830, 1831, and 1832, and therefore precede the conception and planning of **The Human Comedy.** Their value is far from being diminished by that fact. **"An Episode under the Terror"** (1830), for instance, was composed as an introduction to the **"Memoirs"** of Samson—that executioner who of all executioners in the world's history despatched the fewest criminals and yet shed the most blood; and the **"Memoirs"** themselves, which are entirely apocryphal, are also in part Balzac's own work. But, though composed in this way, to order and as a piece of hack work, **"An Episode under the Terror"** is in its artistic brevity one of Balzac's most tragic and most finished narratives. **"La Grande Bretèche"** (1832) was at first only an episode inserted among the more extended narratives of which it made part, as in the old-fashioned novel of tales within tales of which *Gil Blas* is the type; and brief as it is, Balzac nevertheless rewrote it three or four times. It is therefore anything but an improvisation. Yet no other of these short stories can give more vividly than **"La Grande Bretèche"** the impression of a work sprung at once in full completeness from its author's brain, and conceived from the very first in its indivisible unity. But, precisely, it is one of the characteristic traits of Balzac's genius that we hardly need to know when or for what purpose he wrote this or that one of his novels or stories. He bore them all within him at once—we might say that the germ of them was pre-existent in him before he had any conscious thought of objectivizing them. His characters were born in him, as though from all eternity, before he knew them himself; and before he himself suspected it, his **Human Comedy** was alive, was confusedly moving, was slowly shaping itself, in his brain. This point must be clearly seen before he can be understood or appreciated at his true value. However much interest a monograph on some animal or plant may have in itself—and that interest, no doubt, is often great—it has far more through the relation it bears to other monographs and to the whole field of knowledge of which its subject is only a fragmentary part. So it is with Balzac's novels and stories. Their interest is not limited to themselves. They bring out one another's value and significance, they illustrate and give importance to each other; they have, outside themselves, a justification for existence. This will become clear if we compare Mérimée's "Mateo Falcone," for instance, with **"A Seashore Drama"** (1835). The subject is the same: in each case it is a father who constitutes himself justiciary of the honor of his race. But while Mérimée's work, though perhaps better written or at least engraved with deeper tooling, is after all nothing but an anecdote, a sensational news-item, a story of local manners, Balzac's is bound up with a whole mass of ideas, not to say a whole social philosophy, of which it is, properly speaking, only a *chapter;* and of which **"The Conscript"** (1831) is another.

But why did Balzac confine some of his subjects within the narrow limits of the *nouvelle,* while he expanded others to the dimensions of epic, we might say, or of history? It was because, though analogies are numerous between natural history and what we may call social history or the natural history of society, yet their resemblance is not complete nor their identity absolute. There are peculiarities or variations of passion which, though physiologically or pathologically interesting, are *socially* insignificant and can be left out of account: for instance, **"A Passion in the Desert"** (1830), or **"The Unknown Masterpiece"** (1831). It is rare, in art, for the passionate pursuit of progress to result only, as with Frenhofer, in jumbling the colors on a great painter's canvas; and, even were this less rare, artists are not very numerous! So, if the writer gave to his narrative of this painful but infrequent adventure as full a development, if he diversified and complicated it with as many episodes and details as the adventures of Baron Hulot in *Cousin Bette* or those of Madame de Mortsauf in *The Lily in the Valley,* he would thereby attribute to it, *socially* or *historically,* an importance it does not possess. He would err, and would make us err with him, regarding the true proportions of things. He would represent the humanity which he was attempting to depict, in a manner far from consistent with reality. Hence may be deduced the æstetics of the *nouvelle,* and its distinction from the *conte,* and also from the *roman* or novel.

The *nouvelle* differs from the *conte* in that it always claims to be a picture of ordinary life; and it differs from the novel in that it selects from ordinary life, and depicts by preference and almost exclusively, those examples of the strange, the rare, and the extraordinary which ordinary life does in spite of its monotony nevertheless contain. It is neither strange nor rare for a miser to make all the people about him, including his wife and children, victims of the passion to which he is himself enslaved; and that is the subject of *Eugénie Grandet.* It is nothing extraordinary for parents of humble origin almost to be disowned by their children whom they have married too far above them, in another class of society; and that is the subject of *Father Goriot.* But for a husband, as in **"La Grande Bretèche,"** to wall up his wife's lover in a closet, and that before her very eyes; and, through a combination of circumstances in themselves quite out of the ordinary, for neither one of them to dare or be able to make any defence against his vengeance—this is certainly somewhat rare! Then read **"The Conscript,"** or **"An Episode under the Terror"**; the plot is no ordinary one, and perhaps, with a little exaggeration, we may say it can have occurred but once. Such, then, is the field of the *nouvelle.* Let us set off from it the fantastic, in the style of Hoffmann or Edgar Allan Poe, even though Balzac sometimes tried that also, as in *The Wild Ass's Skin,* for instance, or in **"Melmoth Converted"**; for the fantastic belongs to the field of the *conte.* But unusual events, especially such as result from an unforeseen combination of circumstances; and really tragic adventures, which, like Monsieur and Madame de Merret's in **"La Grande Bretèche"** or Cambremer's in **"A Seashore Drama,"** make human conscience hesitate to call the crime by its name; and illogical variations, deviations, or perversions of passion; and the pathology of feeling, as in **"The Unknown Masterpiece"**; and still more generally, if I may so express myself, all those things in life which are out of the usual run of life, which happen *on its margin,* and so are beside yet not outside it; all that makes

its surprises, its differences, its *startlingness,* so to speak—all this is the province of the *nouvelle,* bordering on that of the novel yet distinct from it. Out of common every-day life you cannot really make *nouvelles,* but only novels—miniature novels, when they are brief, but still novels. In no French writer of the last century, I think, is this distinction more evident or more strictly observed than it is in *The Human Comedy;* and unless I am much mistaken, this may serve to solve, or at least to throw light on, the vexed question of Honoré de Balzac's *naturalism* or *romanticism.* (pp. 306-08)

A romantic imagination, struggling to triumph over itself, and succeeding only by confining itself to the study of the model—such may be the definition of Balzac's imagination or genius; and, in a way, to justify this definition by his work we need only to distinguish clearly his *nouvelles* from his novels.

Balzac's *nouvelles* represent the share of romanticism in his work. **"La Grande Bretèche"** is the typical romantic narrative, and we may say as much of **"The Unknown Masterpiece."** The observer shuts his eyes; he now looks only within himself; he imagines "what might have been"; and he writes **"An Episode under the Terror."** It is for him a way of escape from the obsession of the real:

> The real is strait; the possible is vast.

His unbridled imagination takes free course. He works in a dream. And, since of course we can never succeed in building within ourselves perfectly water-tight compartments, entirely separating dream from memory and imagination from observation, reality does find its way into his *nouvelles* by way of exactness in detail, but their conception remains essentially or chiefly romantic; just as in his long novels, *Eugénie Grandet, A Bachelor's Establishment* (*Un Ménage de Garcon*), *César Birotteau, A Dark Affair, Cousin Pons,* and *Cousin Bette,* his observation remains naturalistic, and his imagination perverts it, by magnifying or exaggerating, yet never intentionally or systematically or to the extent of falsifying the true relations of things. Shall I dare say that by this fact he belongs to the family of Shakespeare? His long novels are his *Othello,* his *Romeo,* his *Macbeth,* his *Richard III.,* and *Coriolanus;* and his *nouvelles,* his short stories, are his *Tempest,* his *Twelfth Night,* and his *Midsummer Night's Dream.*

This comparison, which really is not a comparison but a mere analogy, such as might be drawn between Musset and Byron, may serve to bring out one more characteristic of Balzac's *nouvelles*—they are philosophic; in *The Human Comedy* it is under the title of *Philosophic Studies* that he brought together, whatever their origin, such stories as **"A Seashore Drama," "The Unknown Masterpiece,"** and even **"The Conscript."** By so doing he no doubt meant to imply that the sensational stories on which they are based did not contain their whole significance; that he was using them merely as a means of stating a problem, of fixing the reader's attention for a moment on the vastness of the mysterious or unknown by which we are, so to speak, enwrapped about.

> We might add this tragic story [he writes at the end of **"The Conscript"**] to the mass of other observations on that sympathy which defies the law of space—a body of evidence which some few solitary scholars are collecting with scientific curiosity, and which will one day serve as basis for a new science, a science which till now has lacked only its man of genius.

These are large words, it would seem, with which to point the moral of a mere historical anecdote. But if we consider them well, we shall see that, whatever we may think of this "new science," Balzac wrote **"The Conscript"** for the sole purpose of ending it with that sentence. Read, too, **"A Seashore Drama."** It is often said that "A fact is a fact"—and I scarcely know a more futile sophism, unless it be the one which consists in saying that "Of tastes and colors there is no disputing." Such is not Balzac's opinion, at any rate. He believes that a fact is more than a fact, that it is the expression or manifestation of something other or more than itself; or again, that it is a piece of evidence, a *document,* which it is not enough to have put on record, but in which we must also seek, through contrasts and resemblances, its deep ulterior meaning. And this is what he has tried to show in his *nouvelles.*

Thus we see what place they hold in *The Human Comedy.* Balzac's short stories are not, in his work, what one might be tempted to call somewhat disdainfully "the chips of his workshop." Nor are they even, in relation to his long novels, what a painter's sketches, rough drafts, and studies are to his finished pictures. He did not write them by way of practice or experiment; they have their own value, intrinsic and well-defined. It would be a mistake, also, to consider them as little novels, in briefer form, which more time or leisure might have allowed their author to treat with more fulness. He conceived them for their own sake; he would never have consented to give them proportions which did not befit them. The truth of the matter is that by reason of their dealing with the exceptional or extraordinary, they are, in a way, the element of *romantic drama* in Balzac's *Comedy;* and by reason of their philosophic or symbolic significance, they add the element of mystery to a work which but for them would be somewhat harshly illuminated by the hard light of reality. Once more, that is why he did not classify **"The Conscript"** with the *Scenes of Political Life,* or his **"A Seashore Drama"** with the *Scenes of Country Life.* That, too, is what gives them their interest and their originality. That is what distinguishes them from the stories of Prosper Mérimée, or, later, those of Guy de Maupassant. So much being made clear, it is not important now to ask whether they really have as much depth of meaning as their author claimed for them. Only in a complete study of Balzac could his *nouvelles* be adequately judged. Then their due place would be assigned to them, in the full scheme of *The Human Comedy.* (pp. 308-09)

> *Ferdinand Brunetière, "Balzac's Short Stories," in*
> The Critic, *New York, Vol. XLIII, No. 4, October,*
> *1903, pp. 306-09.*

HORATIO E. SMITH (essay date 1914)

[*In the following excerpt, Smith assesses Balzac's stories "La grande bretèche," "Une passion dans le désert," and "Jésus-Christ en Flandre."*]

Several of [Balzac's] narratives of the years 1830-32 deserve notice, and the next step will be to examine these, in chronological order, and to point out whatever is of interest from the point of view of short-story technique.

The first is **"Une passion dans le désert"** (1830). After a brief introduction, in which, apropos of wild-animal training, the tale of the old soldier is brought up, a curt sentence starts the exposition:

> Lors de l'expédition entreprise dans la haute Égypte par le général Desaix, un soldat provençal, étant tombé au pouvoir des Maugrabins, fut emmené par ces Arabes dans les déserts situés au delà des cataractes du Nil.

By the end of the first paragraph we have been told how the soldier escapes on a horse, rides the horse to death, and finds himself helpless in the middle of the desert. This is a good beginning; we are now acquainted with the hero and the setting. In view of Poe's requirement that the very first part of the narrative be constructed with an eye to the single preconceived effect of the whole, the directness with which Balzac sets out is striking, and, even if he lacks the supreme skill of the American, he achieves here, as well as in certain other cases, an able initial paragraph. Following a description of the beauty and the dreadful solitude of the desert, the despair of the soldier is put with that concision which is a prime factor in the short-story: "Le Provençal avait vingt-deux ans, il arma sa carabine." But he postpones suicide, finds a shelter, fells a palm tree so as to put a barrier at its entrance—and at this point there is a ring of foreboding in the narrator's voice:

> Quand, vers le soir, ce roi du désert tomba, le bruit de sa chute retentit au loin, et il y eut une sorte de gémissement poussé par la solitude; le soldat en frémit comme s'il eût entendu quelque voix lui prédire un malheur.

Here Balzac is employing an accredited short-story device, suggesting the characteristic tone of the narrative and thereby intensifying the totality of effect. In the night the man awakes and discovers at his side in the cave a panther. There follows a graphic and plausible enough description of the taming of the beast. The situation during the ensuing days, when the man's impulse to plunge a knife into the creature is several times blocked by her trustfulness, is made exceedingly tense, and there is a careful ordering of the incidents with a view to bringing the suspense to a head. At length, in their games, the panther suddenly shows irritation and starts to bite and is instantly killed by her companion, who at once regrets his haste in resenting what may have been simply playfulness. The narrative ends tersely: "Et les soldats qui avaient vu mon drapeau, et qui accoururent à mon secours, me trouvèrent tout en larmes."

With this dramatic close Balzac completes the requirements, and it becomes clear that at least one of his compositions possesses that harmony, resting upon a well-arranged series of incidents leading to a single decisive act, which constitutes a successful short-story. The harmony, moreover, is increased, the whole is closer knit, thanks to the fact that the soldier constantly compares the panther to womankind, and, more specifically, to a former mistress of his. Before leaving this narrative a difference in editions must be noticed. Whereas in the first edition there is the swift *dénoûment* above described, in the *édition définitive* four extra paragraphs are inserted immediately before the final solution; here the lady, to whom the story is being told, and the narrator converse about the outcome of the adventure. The resultant heightening of the suspense becomes an irritation, and the more direct culmination in the first edition is better. Furthermore, in the first edition the final sentence of the story stands, as it should, at the end of a paragraph, and the conclusion, a kind of envoy which Balzac attaches, begins with a fresh paragraph. There is no such division in the *édition définitive,* and the finality of the narrative proper is consequently less complete.

In **"Jésus-Christ en Flandre"** (1831), there is added to the main narrative an account of a vision which the author has in a church near the scene of the story, but this fragment, which originally appeared separately under the title **"L'Église,"** and which was not appended until 1845, is in no way essential and may in the present consideration be wholly disregarded. The subject is a miracle: Christ saves the lives of those who have sufficient faith to walk with him across a tempestuous sea. The preparation for the single climacteric moment when the miracle takes place is skilful. A feeling is created at the outset that the last traveler to board the ferry is no ordinary person—and that perhaps his joining the company for this trip, when a storm is brewing, is no ordinary event. Frequent repetitions of this *motif* help in holding the narrative true to its course. During the approach of the storm the reader is completely informed as to the characteristics of the passengers, so that he is ready to focus his gaze, with full appreciation, upon their behavior in face of peril. The manner in which Balzac suggests the supernatural, and his general method of presentation, call to mind what Professor Baldwin, speaking of American short-stories, terms static art. Of Poe, Professor Baldwin writes:

> he gained his own peculiar triumphs in the static—
> in a situation developed by exquisite gradation of
> such infinitesimal incidents as compose "Berenice"
> to an intense climax of emotional suggestion, rather
> than in a situation developed by gradation of events
> to a climax of action.

In Balzac's tale, the climax is certainly one of action, but the preparation consists of a deliberate adjustment of the setting with an eye to the selection of such details as will emphasize the meaning of this action; there are few events before the decisive one. In other words, the static and the kinetic are combined. The subject, I think, does not lend itself to short-story treatment as readily as that of **"Une passion dans le désert,"** yet the structure undoubtedly warrants the classification of this narrative as an example of the type under discussion, the second to be found in Balzac by 1831.

The theme of **"La grande Bretèche"** (1832) suggests that of Poe's "The Cask of Amontillado" (1846), an impeccable short-story. The unique effect, in both compositions, rests upon the narration of an act of vengeance: one man murders another by shutting him up behind a wall of solid masonry; in Poe the cause for revenge is not specified, in Balzac a husband thus punishes a lover. It must be explained at the outset that Balzac's story consists of three parts, and that for the present comparison the first two may be dismissed with a word. The interest, throughout, is in the mystery of a certain deserted house: after an introductory description sounding a note of gloom, the first part shows that the abandonment of the estate has been decreed by the will of the deceased countess, without revealing her motive, the second vaguely suggests an explanation by a reference to a Spaniard who may have been the lover, and the third part is a complete solution. The whole is harmonious, and illustrates the possibilities of a short-story based upon a process of ratiocination, as suggested by Poe, with the interest depending upon the manner in which the man who exposes the mystery accumulates and arranges his data, but it is somewhat long and detailed, with an occasional short digression. The third section, which consists of the tale of Rosalie, the maid of the countess, is more compact than the other parts, is in itself complete, and affords an excellent opportunity for comparison with the work of Poe, the master craftsman. The first and second parts con-

Portrait of Balzac by Jean-Alfred Gérard-Séguin. Balzac wrote of it: "Only the outer man is displayed—it is the beast with no trace of poetry. . . ."

tribute largely to the suspense, yet no violence is done to the structure when the third part is considered separately.

Poe's beginning illustrates admirably his principle that the initial sentence shall tend to the outbringing of the single effect of the story:

> The thousand injuries of Fortunato I had borne as
> I best could, but when he ventured upon insult I
> vowed revenge.

With Balzac, the start is direct enough, but cumbersome:

> La chambre que Madame de Merret occupait à la
> Bretèche était située au rez-de-chaussée. Un petit
> cabinet de quatre pieds de profondeur environ, pra-
> tiqué dans l'intérieur du mur, lui servait de garde-
> robe.

It will be seen later that the closet is essential to the story, but the forced and clumsy allusion to it in the second sentence is utterly different from Poe's reference, at once casual and natural, to the niche in the wall, which, in his tale, plays the corresponding rôle. The remainder of Balzac's initial paragraph is well done: he proceeds to tell how, one evening, the husband comes home late, enters his wife's chamber, and is caused to suspect, by her manner and by a noise as if a door had been shut just before his arrival, that somebody is hidden in the closet. The action is rapid: the wife swears innocence, the husband's suspicions grow, he sends for a mason and has the closet walled up during the night, and stays with his wife constantly for several weeks. Whenever there is a sound in the closet and the wife begs for mercy, he answers—and this sentence closes the narrative: "Vous avez juré sur la croix qu'il n'y avait là personne." It is clear from a remark which Balzac makes elsewhere that he valued the dramatic quality of this final scene. Certainly it is as effective as Poe's: "Against the new masonry I re-erected the old rampart of bones. For the half of a century no mortal has disturbed them. *In pace requiescat!*"

Balzac's structure is skilful, especially at the climax, but the main part of Poe's story is in two ways superior. Poe's totality of effect is enhanced by the simplicity of the plot, which is such that there are only two characters and that the action flows steadily in a single direction and ends in a swift catastrophe. In **"La grande Bretèche,"** such incidents have been chosen that the introduction of several subsidiary characters is required and the *dénoûment* is less sudden, and the result, although the unity is excellent, is second to Poe's. Again, in the "Cask of Amontillado," the unity of tone is heightened, the note of menace and the suggestion of revenge are maintained, by the introduction of such details as Montresor's drinking to the long life of Fortunato, who is to become his victim, and his reference to the family motto, *Nemo me impune lacessit.* In **"La grande Bretèche"** there is no such device, although Balzac uses it elsewhere.

Poe's is a better short-story. The point is that while Balzac has not been supremely successful—and no one would attempt to set him up as a rival to Poe—and while it has been necessary to lift this story bodily out of its context, yet this is a narrative which meets the requirements of the short-story type. (pp. 73-8)

The net result of this investigation is to demonstrate that Balzac took a lively interest in that kind of fiction of which the ultimate development is the short-story, and that he himself wrote several genuine short-stories. A more convincing case could be made out for Balzac, if I marshaled the material differently, offering first the negative evidence, and reserving for the end the presentation of those facts which make it necessary to set aside the verdict of Professor Baldwin that Balzac's "handling does not seem. . . . directive." But a chronological arrangement is more satisfactory, as being absolutely judicial, as emphasizing that Balzac was most interested in highly unified narrative during the early part of his career, at a time when it has been supposed the short-story was not born in France, and, incidentally, before Balzac became a deep-dyed realist, thus bearing out the view that the short-story is pre-eminently a form for the romanticist.

While it may be accepted as a matter of fact that several of Balzac's compositions have the general structure demanded of a narrator who desires "to produce a single narrative effect with the greatest economy of means that is consistent with the utmost emphasis," conclusions must be less precise when the more elastic requirements, such as conciseness of style, are considered. It is sure that the clean-cut exactness of Poe contributed to the success of his tales and that Balzac's clumsiness hindered effectual compression; it is sure that Balzac did not possess the gift of epithet which so distinguished Stevenson; but we promptly reach a point where the problem becomes a matter of purely subjective literary criticism, and speculation of that nature will not settle a point in literary history.

And, in any case, no one would seek to prove that Balzac was a great short-story artist; there appear to have been none in France until several decades later. But he contributed not a little to that groping after a new form which was evident before 1850. (pp. 83-4)

Horatio E. Smith, "Balzac and the Short-Story," in Modern Philology, *Vol. XII, No. 6, December, 1914, pp. 71-84.*

FREDERICK WEDMORE   (essay date 1920)

[*Wedmore was an English journalist, art critic, novelist, and essayist. In the excerpt below, he appraises several of Balzac's short stories.*]

The short stories of Balzac no more form a collection of literary masterpieces than do his lengthy and elaborately wrought novels; but there are masterpieces amongst them—several masterpieces—and it is high time that these should be more generally recognised. The widespread recognition of them is even more particularly due, now that Balzac, no longer either loathed or worshipped, can in England and France be appraised calmly: appraised with justice done. (p. 484)

It is possible to be prolix—at least to be superfluous—even in literary compositions whose form and compass actually are small; and Balzac, who tore himself to pieces, so to say, over every work that he began and finished, accomplished the feat of being wordy when there was really opportunity and call not for diffuseness, but for pregnant brevity, for the right adjective that paints the picture, for the charged phrase—for that and little more.

But if one of the questionable—I should boldly say, I think, one of the undesirable—of the characteristics of Balzac's novels is abundantly reflected in stories nominally 'short'—*conte* or *nouvelle* are the words that satisfy the average person's measure of craving for a working definition of the thing that is supposed to be before him—it is certain that the greater virtues of a brilliantly imaginative man are shown as clearly, are shown as effectively, in Balzac's briefer and less often turned-to disquisitions. The best of the Short Stories present, I think, an even more than proportionate share of his great qualities of seeing, comprehending, feeling and representing the circumstances and the characters that are his themes. Needless to say it is 'character,' more than 'circumstance,' and, broadly speaking, it is the perception and representation of character that wins for him the day. Just here and there, however—at the highest point of his achievement—it is neither circumstance nor character, neither incident nor personality, that most asserts itself as the receptive mind absorbs the labours of this Master. It is, rather, *a sense of being.* One is in the presence, not of the momentarily exciting, not in the particular circumstance hoped for or feared, but of a world that *is*—and of a world to which one is attached by how many tentacles!

As a rule in Balzac's work I think that success—patent success, the success it is impossible to forget or to ignore—belongs either to a few of the best of the long novels or to a few of the best of the really 'short' stories. Often, in the beginning of what is meant to be a short story, Balzac becomes apparently so interested in every detail, and is so inclined to revel in the excellence of the atmosphere he has created, that what was to have been the short story ends by being a pretty generous but not a really well-advised contribution to the execution of a long romance. Not enough to deal quite finally with the matter broached, but enough to imperil and certainly to deteriorate the satisfactoriness of the treatment. The definitive edition of the Master's work may include little, it may even include nothing, of which Balzac actively disapproved, but it includes a quantity by no means negligible of what it would have been much better if he had disapproved. Many pages of many of the middle-sized stories are of this character. My own observation causes me to fear that the world of Letters generally, and Balzac in particular, presents too many instances of that which is either novel too short or short story too long. The writer of prose Fiction should remember more habitually than it is his custom to do that bulk and repetition are both disadvantageous, and that it is to do us wrong 'to wind about our love with circumstance.'

By far the greater number of Balzac's score, or it may be score and a half, of what are deemed his Short Stories are to be found amongst the productions of his earlier years. He nearly always dated them, and in that practice he has been—may it be said in a parenthesis?—he has been followed by too few of those writers who have reason to hope that the First Editions of their stories may not also be the final ones.

They are early, then, the greater number of Balzac's Short Stories; yet hardly one of them belongs to a period which can fairly be described as immature. Most of those which after a prolonged acquaintance with them are found to belong emphatically to the things that last belong to the Thirties—to the Thirties not only late but early—of Balzac's century. Two of the very noblest—**"La Messe de l'Athée"** and **"Jésus-Christ en Flandre"**—which in a moment I shall be found speaking of in more or less of detail with happy admiration, belong to 1831. So indeed does **"Le Réquisitionnaire,"** which is high up in the second rank of this order of labour; and not very far from it are **"L'Interdiction"** and **"Un Drame au Bord de la Mer."** (pp. 484-86)

"L'Interdiction," as the, I fear, too scanty number of its English readers will no doubt remember, is concerned mainly with the masterly, and in every way to be praised, fashion in which one Popinot, 'le bon Popinot,' a magistrate of the Department of the Seine, deals with a villainous conspiracy to declare mad a sane and wise and singularly generous-minded gentleman—the Marquis d'Espard—greatly tried husband of a fashionable beauty who is egoist, heartless and unprincipled. Could but Judge Popinot—happily astute for all his kindly sensibility—have been successfully invited by unprincipled schemers to consider M. d'Espard as incompetent, not only the care of the two young boys who were his children, but the sometime possession of the family fortune, would have passed into the hands of his intriguing and evil-minded enemies. The story ends—or stops rather—before the case comes actually into Court; but the sagacity of Popinot has been sufficiently exercised in preliminary inquiry and interview to establish to his own certainty the rights of the matter. Alas! he has to deal with rogues and with the bribeable, and rogues and bribeables have learnt to make effective use of little technical objections and pronouncements. It is contrived that one small error on the part of the just judge shall cause him to be requested, and in truth compelled, to pass on to other and too manageable hands the trial of the matter. The man of Law who will replace him is young, ambitious, overawed by the influence of the great who may be expected to help him hereafter. And we are left persuaded of, but not reconciled to, the quite scandalous failure of justice which has been ensured. Until this last invention of the novelist's imagination all has gone well, but finally we are a little rebellious of a pessimism deeper than Mr. Hardy's—of a satire, an

irony, as pungent as M. Brieux's (in *La Robe Rouge*), but less useful.

The more popular, but more slightly considered and undoubtedly less substantive literary performance in **"La Grenadière"** suggests as to method a sufficiently striking contrast to **"L'Interdiction,"** and I will deal with it briefly, and from that point of view, a few lines further on; but there are one or two remarks that have still to be made as to **"L'Interdiction,"** and one is that the recognition of the solidity of its construction, and of the potent charm that 'le bon Popinot'—its memorable character—exercises over the reader, must not result in our forgetting how well is arranged the presentation, in this story, of Rastignac—one of Balzac's most favourite photographs of the ambitious and the self-seeking—and, again, the presentation of le Docteur Bianchon—straight man and excellent, even famous physician. In longer novels of the **Comédie Humaine,** both play parts that are more striking; but they are true to themselves here, and that is matter of importance indeed.

Yet more noteworthy in **"L'Interdiction"** is the searching analysis of the personage—I do not like in this case to employ the term 'the character'—of Madame D'Espard. Few things in any equally brief fiction are more successfully elaborate than is the portrayal of this thrice worthless woman. Then there is again Monsieur D'Espard—the very pink of maligned chivalry. And then again one comes back to Popinot: one remembers indulgently his habit of personal shabbiness—he is pre-occupied by Charity, and by administered Justice. He has no time to be smart. A plain face, an ugly face—yet as part of it, *'cette homme avait une bouche sur les lèvres de laquelle respirait une bonté divine.'* And, withal, that extraordinary penetration: that *'seconde vue judiciaire'* which one notes with admiration, but of which the processes are for ever a secret.

"La Grenadière," written at Angoulême in 1832, during one of the Master's frequent sojourns at the homes of men and women in whom Balzac recognised sympathy, has something of that grave quietude belonging to such times and circumstances as those the story moves amongst. The scene is laid most fittingly in the immediate neighbourhood of Tours, near to the famous bridge there—it is very near to the broad Loire's slowly sweeping waters. The tale's main character is a mysterious lady, full of distinction and of grace, for whom all vivid personal life, for whom all life in the wide world seems to be over. She is the mother of the one or two children; and now, in her secluded home, which fixed intention makes more secluded yet, she is that and nothing besides.

Had the tale been written in English, it might have had for title 'The Closed Book.' The work is dreamily suggestive. It is poetic, but it is not poetry. Yet it impresses. In **"The Grenadière"** the evening light gathers and fades over the landscape. The atmosphere is laden with emanations from a departing or a vanished day. (pp. 486-88)

I could have wished to have referred to, and in a certain degree to have dwelt upon, more than one other story. There is **"Le Chef d'Oeuvre Inconnu,"** which, though it drags a little, and makes nobody particularly interesting, has many a sentence upon Fine Art worth consideration, and more than one which is assuredly illuminating. I should like to have lingered for a moment in the world of **"Massimilla Doni,"** and in **"Gambara"** to have noted something of what was Balzac's attitude to Music—for Balzac, if one may use the phrases he bestowed upon another, and that other a woman, breathed the air through every one of his pores, and all his soul lived. Therefore, no Art came amiss to him. But I restrict myself to one more piece, and that is one for which Balzac has been content to make no other claim than that it is 'a naïve legend.' It is of course much more. I am referring to that notable small masterpiece of thought and feeling and performance, **"Jésus-Christ en Flandre."**

It is done in plain narrative—even more largely and more continuously in narrative than is the wont of a writer who on the whole indeed made strangely little use of dialogue, and used it not very dexterously when he used it at all. Vividness, lifelikeness, is in these scanty pages seen with not much surprise to be unquestionably not incompatible with a maintained simplicity of method. But what a firm possession has Balzac of his subject-matter! Even when he reaches the apparently miraculous the reader has no thought of questioning the truth of the events narrated.

The period of the tale is of the early Middle Age: the place, the long-stretched waters between the Flemish coast, where Ostend was not already large, and the island of Cadzant, of which Middelbourg was then the small and only port. From Middelbourg it is now time to be starting. The ferry boat fills up.

Men and women of very various, far removed ranks sort themselves, much as on a railway platform, before the third-class carriages, they would to-day. Into their places the skipper hastens them. That done he says to his oarsmen *'Ramez, ramez fort, et depêchons. La mer sourit à un mauvais grain.'* The humbler folk, accustomed to the open air, had understood by the aspect of the skies the menace that was before them. Admirable is the differentiation of this and of that passenger. They become our familiars—the thing is real, absolutely. But as they put up fervent prayers to Notre Dame de Bon Secours at Antwerp, 'She is in the Heavens,' declares a voice that seems borne in over the sea. The storm breaks upon them. Fear seizes upon every soul. The man of learning laughs at the supplications of the lowly. The seas engulf him quickly. Again from the waters the Stranger—the apparition with the luminous visage—speaks: 'Those who have faith will be saved. Let them follow me!' There is a doubt, there is a pause, there is a critical instant. But they are well through. 'In that place was built later the Convent of Mercy.' But the Stranger with the luminous visage passes soon from no one's recollection; and long, long afterwards were seen, in the arrested sands, the marks of His feet.

It is refreshing to remember that in more recent French Literature there is one *conte* in which the thought appears to be as reverent, and the manner as splendidly simple and as finely severe, as in this particular example of the work with which I have been dealing. For myself I never glance at that bright gem of Balzac's that I have just been extolling without calling to mind—however unexpectedly, so to say—Monsieur Anatole France's flawless and delightful pages in *Le Christ de l'Océan.* By the side of them one puts in imagination this or that sample of the nobly poetic patriotism of Monsieur Maurice Barrès, and reflects that whatever may be her material circumstances of the hour, happy and proud must be the land which, nearly seventy years after the death of Balzac, finds still the great traditions of an inexhaustible Literature represented as they are represented at this hour. (pp. 490-91)

Frederick Wedmore, "Balzac's Short Stories," in

The Nineteenth Century and After, *Vol. LXXXVII, No. DXVII, March, 1920, pp. 484-91.*

EDWIN PRESTON DARGAN   (essay date 1932)

[*Dargan was an American academic, biographer, and essayist. In the following excerpt from his* Honoré de Balzac: A Force of Nature, *he assesses Balzac's abilities as a short fiction writer.*]

As an advocate of Romance, Stevenson has rightly dwelt upon the charm and force of incident, especially as rendered by his masters, Sir Walter Scott and the elder Dumas. May we recall in this connection such wonderful brief touches as the death of Bothwell in the skirmish at Drumclog, and the death of Porthos in the cave at Locmaria? From Stevenson himself we are warranted in remembering the duel in *The Master of Ballantrae,* the rock on which the fugitives sunned themselves in *Kidnapped,* the auction scene in *The Wrecker.* Are there thrills like these in the **Human Comedy?**

Reader, there are! There is the wild cry of "Adieu!" uttered by the heroine who loses her lover and her sanity at the terrible crossing of the Beresina. There is the attempted carrying-off of the Duchesse de Langeais from her island-convent in the Mediterranean by the desperate band of Thirteen. There is the sudden arrest of Vautrin in *Goriot,* and the whisking-away of Lucien in the arch-criminal's coach at the end of *Lost Illusions.* There is the dreadful picture of the same Lucien writing erotic songs to pay the funeral expenses of his mistress, who is lying dead in the same room. There is the insatiable Baron Hulot, following the wicked and fascinating Valérie through the tortuous byways of Paris. Who can forget the episode when the high-hearted Laurence de Cinq-Cygne, that French counterpart of Diana Vernon, kneels at the feet of Napoleon and beseeches pardon for her conspiring cousins? Or the midnight drive of Esther Gobseck, when she passes like a lovely moonlit apparition before Nucingen and enslaves him forever?

Often the action rises to a crisis in such decisive fragments of time—the day when poor Pons is cut on the Boulevard by his last wealthy relative—the hour when Rabourdin realizes that, through the unwitting treachery of his own household, he is ruined at the peak of his unselfish ambition—the terrible moment when Henri de Marsay finds his Paquita slain by her Lesbian lover.

In one particular set of incidents we find Balzac running closely parallel to Scott. The latter, for example in *Guy Mannering* and in *The Heart of Midlothian,* is masterly at suggesting an atmosphere of suspense, the sort of breathless expectation that seizes a group of people waiting and watching for the dramatic issue of deeds to be done around them. Is not this the very atmosphere that incloses the beginning of **"Adieu,"** the pause before the conflict in *The Chouans,* the sitting-room of the old aristocratic couple in *A Dark Affair* who await tensely the perilous return of their banished sons?

On a more extended scale, one thinks of tableaux or scenes in which description often plays a good part. Philippe Bridau, disreputable, clad in his old army coat, appears before the incapable Rouget, and with a great whack of his cane on the table formidably defies him and all Issoudun. Galope-Chopine, a Chouan, is suspected of treachery; his miserable cabin is invaded by revengeful members of his band; they seize and execute him almost in the presence of his wife. At a formal dinner-party, the Princess de Cadignan falls madly in love with the noble D'Arthez, whom she had expected to bewitch. In a fantastic curiosity shop, the imaginative Raphaël de Valentin sees the forms of the past crush upon him in a semi-animate symbolism. Amid the detailed luxuries of a boudoir, Judge Popinot, that incarnation of equity, faces the fashionable Marquise d'Espard and strips her of all her gorgeous disguises, down to her small and naked soul.

Hundred of such visions must have teemed in Balzac's memory. "I have seen," says Derville, speaking for the author in a reminiscential mood, "I have seen a father perishing penniless in a garret, abandoned by his two daughters to whom he had given forty thousand francs a year." Could anything more succinctly call up the image of the dying Goriot, already developed by Balzac in a long and painful passage? Other deathbed scenes are scarcely less effective: Agathe Bridau, yearning for her absent rascal of a son; the miserly Grandet, clutching with his last gasp at the golden crucifix held before him.

There are half-a-dozen reminiscential passages of the type just illustrated by Derville. Sometimes he, or another important character, will narrate a whole story, from the point of view of an interested observer. The tale of a murder at **"The Red Inn"** is retold at a banquet, in the presence of the murderer, whose by-play almost reveals his guilty knowledge of the events in question. Dr. Bianchon describes to us the walling-up of Mme de Merret's lover by her implacable husband.

Of all these various scenes, some are approached from the romantic angle, others from the realistic; but in either case they are set forth vividly and memorably.

We recur to the vexed matter of Balzac's plots. Here something depends upon length. In the short-story field, it is usually recognized that our author has few superiors—that is, when he is willing simply to tell the story without cumbersome disquisitions. Such tales of mystery and horror as **"An Episode under the Terror"** and **"La Grande Bretèche,"** such a mirthful anecdote as **"The Illustrious Gaudissart,"** thoroughly deserve their fame for the swiftness and sureness in the narration, as well as for that cumulative power which is Balzac's special gift. And there are many others, particularly in his first two periods, which are nearly as good.

Then there is the form of the *nouvelle,* or "long short-story," the thrice-blest *nouvelle* as Henry James wistfully considered it. The form is usually frowned upon by American editors (it would run to about the length of this brochure), but it has been favored in Latin countries since the Renaissance, and all the French story-writers, such as Mérimée and Maupassant, have done it justice. Some of Balzac's most superb effects are found in this field. We have already mentioned **"Adieu,"** **"Colonel Chabert,"** **"The Red Inn."** Others equally as effective are surely **"The Curé of Tours,"** that well-centered masterpiece; **"Gobseck;"** and **"Honorine,"** for its fine characterization; and **"Pierre Grassou,"** for the humor of contrast.

In these two shorter forms, viewed purely from the fictional angle, Balzac often appears at his best. Why? Partly because he goes back to the old Aristotelian law of representing "men *in action*": the characters are at first ably set on their feet, but their subsequent movements are not arrested while the author talks. There is no time, no space, here to indulge extensively his insatiable research into social causes and the like, however well this probing may be justified elsewhere. Besides active men, the author is constantly depicting, we repeat,

both men and women *in passion.* The study of the passions from Descartes down through Rousseau, Stendhal, Balzac, has been much more of a favorite exercise with the French than with us. Consider the timidities, not only of Sir Walter Scott, but of such recent writers as James and Howells; they are eternally analyzing, but the concoction they give us is a very thin soup indeed; their characters seem bloodless, boneless, bosomless, instead of three-dimensional realities. (pp. 58-63)

Edwin Preston Dargan, in his Honoré de Balzac: A Force of Nature, *The University of Chicago Press, 1932, 87 p.*

SEÁN O'FAOLÁIN   (essay date 1948)

[*A short story writer, biographer, novelist, and critic, O'Faoláin is considered a master of the short story and one of Ireland's foremost men of letters. In the following excerpt from his critical work* The Short Story, *he briefly considers Balzac's tale* "La grande bretèche."]

Balzac was almost a pure romantic when writing **"La Grande Bretèche"** and he used therein nothing but situation to prise out his kernel. What his kernel is, who can say? As Sir Walter Raleigh put it, in writing about R. L. S., the kernel of a romantic story appeals 'to the blood . . . to the superstitions of the heart,' never to the reason, and it is true that Balzac's story appeals to we know not what fears, hates, or 'anonymous desires and pleasures' (Stevenson's words). The Comte de Merret, the bald summary would run, discovers that his wife is unfaithful to him; taken one night by surprise her Spanish lover hides in a closet; the husband, having made the Countess swear that the closet is empty, bricks it up, and to all subsequent entreaties he replies coldly that she has sworn on the cross that the closet is empty. This is elemental drama; Elizabethan in its diabolism; or else it is a fairy-tale of Beauty and the Beast, or of an Ogre and a Damsel in Distress. Like much of Balzac the theme and the figures are more than life-size, more pathetic and more cruel than normal. (Which is typical of all romantics. 'Art,' says Thomas Hardy, 'is a disproportioning of realities.') A more natural woman, a more Flaubertian woman, might have fallen into the same situation as the Countess; but since no Flaubertian man would have handled it with the diabolism of the Comte de Merret, she would not have been so angelically helpless. Balzac presumably knew this as well as anybody else. He knew that he was handling something as primitive as a folk-tale. Here, certainly, all character falls away and passion burns blue, for there is no explaining emotions so primitive. Characterisation is irrelevant here, even in the realist's outline. All one can do is re-create the mood, the atmosphere, affect our emotions and abandon rational persuasion.

It was this, I suggest, rather than the realist habit (though that, also was present) which made Balzac construct his tale in a manner that must, otherwise, be thought merely cumbersome. He first describes the abandoned château in all its mysterious gloom, isolation and decay; then the local lawyer who warns him to cease trespassing and reveals just a little of its strange story; then he describes how, in increasing curiosity, he tries to wheedle the whole tale from his landlady, and how she lifts another corner of the curtain, or, one is inclined to say, of the shroud. By this time we have heard of the death of the unhappy Comtesse de Merret, and of the unexplained disappearance of the Spanish refugee who had formerly stayed in this inn nearby. The narrator, having worked on our nerves and on our sympathy, finally prises from the maid Rosalie the secret of the Comte de Merret, and it is significant that Balzac does not recount this interview with the maid, as he has recounted his earlier interviews with the lawyer and the landlady, but, having created his atmosphere of awe, tells the story in straightforward narration. In all this from start to finish the only efforts to characterise the Comte and Comtesse are, for her, the bare adjectives 'kindhearted' and 'pleasant'; and for him, 'quick-tempered,' 'proud' and 'lively' and 'agreeable to women,' adjectives so general that they might be applied to millions of men and women. All Balzac's labour has been concentrated elsewhere, on the creation of mood in preparation for the final situation.

One cannot say that the impressiveness of this tale lies wholly in this preliminary 'softening process,' for the final tale is told with a very real dramatic power; but if we make the test of omitting all the preliminaries and going straight for the last four pages, beginning 'The room which Madame de Merret occupied at **"La Grande Bretèche"** was on the ground floor,' we will find that the effect is far less impressive. I do not say that this form of construction is neat, and I think that the realistic desire for external verisimilitude and plausibility has affected the construction, though it did not dictate it. (pp. 199-201)

Seán O'Faoláin, "On Construction," in his The Short Story, Devin-Adair, 1951, pp. 193-216.

NORMAN LINDSAY (essay date 1959)

[Lindsay was an Australian novelist, artist, essayist, and children's writer. In the following excerpt, he considers whether the Droll Stories *deserve a place among Balzac's finest fiction.]*

If Balzac used the tradition of the *Decameron* and *Heptameron* for the spirit of the **Droll Stories**, the comparison need go no further. And if he took something of their style from Rabelais and their psychology from Montaigne, he had no need for either stimulus, for the stories are a derivative of the most fecund creative power in the whole range of prose fiction. They are Balzac at his best, for he has sent the severe ordinances of form and construction which hedge about the novel to the devil of gravity. For once he has slipped the chains of the galley slave: the daemonic lash is off his back and he is free to have a lark with work. This is the rarest of rewards given to one so driven as Balzac to get work done and done with. It was the obsession of his whole being, from which he derived the monstrous conception of covering every aspect of human life in his novels. A dozen Balzacs could not have completed his forecast of the **Human Comedy** yet to be written. Even on his deathbed, when told he had only a couple of weeks of life left, he cried, "There is yet time."

A mind so satanically driven, which burned itself out at the age of fifty-two, did at least take one gay holiday from work by shifting its accent from one of dramatic intensity to one of humour. Dramatic intensity in the **Droll Stories** is never allowed to impose emotional intensity on the reader. At a crisis of drama, its stress is always lifted by a reversion to humour. **"The High Constable's Wife"** is one of the best of the stories. Its drama is superb, but its nice detachment from stress is the key in which all the stories are written. (p. 32)

[There is] a vital reality in these stories which has nothing to do with a realistic idiom, for the imageries of fantasy run riot through them. Because all passions are reduced to their stark essentials, men and women were never so alive elsewhere in fiction as they are here.

It is the women who dominate action in these stories, and who dedicate men to the service of their desires. Husbands of the nobility, ferocious and intemperate as mad bulls, are cuckolded with audacity by their ladies; citizens, cunning in the chicanery of their professions, are invariably outwitted by their wives. So in his novels, it is in the creation of his women that Balzac's greatest achievement is manifest. They are alive with desire and desirability, infused into them by Balzac's adoration for women. The images of feminine allure that he pours out in their portraiture are inexhaustible; they are complete women, from the tops of their heads to the tips of their toes; the key of their presentation is that of a lover's caress. . . .

> A lady most dazzling white, most delicately wanton, with long tresses and velvet hands, filling out her dress at the least movement, for she was gracefully plump, with a laughing mouth, and eyes moist in advance, a woman to beautify hell.

> What lovely thick hair hung over her ivory back, showing white places, fair and shining, between so many tresses.

> The Maid of Thilouse, whose arms were red and firm and her breasts hard as bastions, which kept the cold from her heart—her waist round as a young oak, fresh, clean and pretty, like a first frost, green and tender as an April bud.

> Joseph inspected the pretty white of the girl's breasts, which a modest grace covered with an old rag, and looked at them as a schoolboy looks at a rosy apple on a hot day.

> Believing herself alone with her maid, she made those little jokes that women will when undressing. 'Am I not worth 20,000 crowns tonight? Are these overpaid by a castle in Brie?'

> And saying this she gently raised her two white supports, firm as rocks, which had well sustained many assaults, seeing they had been furiously attacked, and had never softened.

> And the page noticed his lady's foot, which was delicately slippered in a little laced shoe of a blue colour, a true foot of delight—a virginal foot that merited a kiss, as a robber does the gallows; a roguish foot, a foot wanton enough to damn an archangel; an ominous foot, a devilishly enticing foot, which gave one a desire to make two new ones just like it.

There never was such a harem of vital femininities caged between the covers of a book. Peasant girls, street girls, citizens' wives, young virgins, great courtesans and great ladies of the court: to each is given an imagery drawn from the status of whatever rank of the social order she was born to. One thinks of the great army of serious-minded novelists who have sweated midnight oil to find variants for the shop-worn clichés about hair, skin, eyes, noses and mouths, to create the illusion of lovely women in cold type, searching the dictionary for synonyms of desirability which only the warm embrace of a woman's body can evoke. . . .

Fantasy must insist that desire is inexhaustible, and so it is, as an image. That image must be drawn from the flesh, even though the flesh is so swiftly exhausted of desire. But if the writer, the artist, allows the flesh to make a fool of him there, so much the worse for his art. Creation in art must have a full experience of life, but if it allows that experience to dominate creation it is creation which becomes exhausted. Physical chastity is as essential to the image of desire as experience in desire is essential to the creation of its image. A balance must be maintained between the factuality of all experience in life and the imagery by which it is re-created in art. As evidence of where that balance is maintained, and where disrupted, contrast the lives and works of Balzac and Hugo.

Balzac had few love affairs, and those only with mature women of highly cultivated minds. From them he derived his subtle knowledge of feminine psychology. In the action of work, he lived a celibate existence, shutting himself up like a monk in his cell and sometimes working eighteen hours at a stretch, keeping himself mentally alert with cups of black coffee. Between novels, he plunged into the world of affairs, squandering money earned by his novels in those wildcat schemes for making money which kept him constantly on the verge of bankruptcy, pursued by duns. From those affairs he drew his vast knowledge of finance, commercial rapacity, sociological conflict and political corruption, as well as the army of characters which people the stage of his *Human Comedy.* Biographers have failed to see in his seeming feckless behaviour over money the hard and ruthless logic which threw it away recklessly that the bare need for it should drive him back again to work. (pp. 34-5)

Most critics of Balzac's works pass the *Droll Stories* as of little consequence compared to his novels; a work tossed off as a diversion rather than a serious contribution to literature. To me, it is one of the greatest of his works. Will the illusion never be dissipated that humour is an inferior quality to gravity in art? For the very few prose works of high quality dedicated to the spirit of humour there are scores and scores of works created in a serious idiom, or, to use the cant term of critical virtuosity, "works to be taken seriously". Is the *Satyricon* not to be taken seriously? Or *Don Quixote* or *Tom Jones?* As a supreme act of creation, is Falstaff to be taken less seriously than Hamlet, or Mrs Gamp than Lady Dedlock? It seems to me that these sapient critics of works to be taken seriously are confusing the humorous with the comic.

The comic consists of satirical comment on the passing scene and is as ephemeral as the social habits, customs and conventions from which it is drawn. Almost every decade brings in some variation in an outlook on human behaviour and states of mind dictated by whatever may be the prevailing fashions and opinions of the moment. Since the era of illustrated journalism, we are able to observe that what one generation found extremely funny in these external facets of behaviour the next generation found nothing whatever to laugh at. All literature derived from the comic is destined to an abysm of dullness.

Humour is that supreme clarity of vision that sees mankind precisely as it is and not as false sentiment and human dissimulation assume it to be. It is aware of the incongruity of human behaviour as distinct from its pretensions; it sees in the idiosyncratic individual the prototype of it in the mass. It is the rarest of all gifts, for its spiritual content is a delight in the whole spectacle of life, whether that inspires laughter, horror or pity. It may not always use the idiom of humour, but its approach to the spectacle of life is always in that sane detachment from emotional histrionics which is the most

subtle expression of humour. The "serious" novel, however competently done, which lacks this detached approach to a drama of the emotions will not endure.

The *Droll Stories* compact both aspects of the approach humorous; outright comedy and dramatic intensity. That balance is maintained throughout the whole book, and for that reason it is an inexhaustible treasure-trove of entertainment.

It is preferable to leave this tribute to Balzac at the *Droll Stories.* No single essay could encompass the achievement of his great novels alone, even by discarding the greater mass of his work thrown off recklessly and indiscriminately till he found the form and outlook he was looking for. It may be a praiseworthy industry to labour through all those early experimental works, or even those blatantly turned out under the heading of potboilers, but I have never attempted to do so. (pp. 35-6)

Attention to the *Droll Stories* is stressed in this essay because they are the last great contribution to bawdy in literature—bawdy in the Elizabethan key of gusto. (p. 36)

> Norman Lindsay, "The Delicate Art of Bawdy," in Southerly, *Vol. 20, No. 1, 1959, pp. 30-7.*

ALBERT J. GEORGE   (essay date 1964)

[*George is an American academic and essayist specializing in Romance languages and literature. In the following excerpt from his* Short Fiction in France, 1800-1850, *he traces the development of Balzac's short stories within the context of the French writer's entire literary career.*]

Balzac's reputation rests so solidly on his contribution to the novel and the technique of realism that it is sometimes forgotten that he also wrote a large number of short tales. But from 1829 to 1847 he produced an impressive number of brief narratives, partly because the form interested him, partly for financial reasons. Since the newspapers and magazines were prepared to pay substantial sums for the work of popular authors, Balzac was glad to oblige, particularly since his ever-growing list of creditors made profitable work essential. However, like Stendhal, he had difficulty understanding the nature of brief stories. His talent lay in the field of the novel and the scope of his imagination was such that when he attempted a short narrative he could not concentrate effect or control incident.

Balzac's major contribution to the writing of fiction lay in his acceptance of contemporary society as the source of his material. Of all the major writers of the first part of the nineteenth century, he alone seems to have recognized the full implications of the crisis in France at the end of the Empire: the consequences of the Revolution, the first impact of the Industrial Revolution, and more particularly the dramatic rise of the middle class to power and responsibility. From a society based on birth, the country had shifted to one founded on money, and the modern world appeared. The greed for wealth and the control it represented, the acquisition of the symbols representative of success, these seemed to him the hallmark of the age. An orderly and ordered society had been transformed into a jungle; men and women lived by the law of the survival of the fittest. The meek would not inherit the earth but would be gobbled up by men like Vautrin and Rastignac who, each in his own sphere, would write the rules for the new order of gamesmanship. Balzac's vision was clear because, unlike Vigny, Musset, and Lamartine, he had had to fight his way to the top, learning the new facts the hard way. He knew no other world, and he felt compelled to etch the portrait of this one in acid of its own making.

Since he had the talent to satisfy his drive to become the historian of the new order, he organized this perception for expression in the various prose forms: the essay, novel, short fiction, and newspaper articles, both serious and humorous. By preference he chose to communicate his vision primarily in the novel, which offered sufficient space and time to satisfy his stylistic propensity to inflation. He could fit his world into its ample frame because his mind operated according to the optics of magnification. Balzac turned to the short narrative only as a professional who recognized a popular and marketable new genre.

Because Balzac's understanding of people was sociological, the short story forced him to squeeze his fictional universe into an uncomfortably small space. Like other writers of the early nineteenth century, he had to develop his own type of brief narrative, since the simple anecdote structure then available did not meet his requirements. Consequently, between 1830 and 1835 Balzac arrived at a structure for brief fiction that unfortunately hardened into a handy prescription. He began abruptly with a short opening scene calculated to hold attention, then proceeded via a flashback to sketch the antecedent facts. The rest of the plot was conceived in two or three segments, the first generally a major portrait of the leading character, the second the action resulting from the conditions previously established by the portrait. A short epilogue, moral in tone, clarified the author's intent and the allegory.

Since the portraits presupposed a special concept of man in society, the beginning of the narrative outlined the premises from which the action was deduced almost deterministically. A long preparation set up the simple plot like a syllogism. This kind of structure, fleshed out by Balzac's pictorial imagination, tended to make the work seem static, which consequently faced him with the problem of conveying a sense of the passage of time. This he did by repeated time references until he reached the last scene, where the principal action unfolded.

Most of the tales revolved around tragic themes, apart from the sex-centered *Contes drolatiques.* A fault committed by a major character in either the flashback or the first scene culminated in a crisis, at which point society claimed its payment. Yesterday's reality led to today's fall. Actually, Balzac was developing a modern conception of tragedy consistent with his view of society. Rastignac and Vautrin represent an amoral power loose in a world where human lions devour the lambs and doves of mankind. To be sure, Balzac understood the Aristotelian notion of tragedy as stemming from a personality fault that led to destruction, but he introduced another element: given the conditions of a modern, industrialized world, the very constitution of an increasingly complex society provided new sources of neuroses. Failure was conceived in other terms, with the petty and the degrading accompanying catastrophes that soiled more often than they destroyed. Man was denied the privilege of being overwhelmed in grand and courageous defiance of the gods.

Because the plots were generally inconsequential, the characters themselves had to carry the brunt of Balzac's message. These figures constitute a major contribution to modern my-

thology because so many of them verge on the stereotype. He emptied the world in his head onto his pages, peopling them with representations of the age in a perception of what the twentieth century would call the human condition. Through the courtesan, the status-hungry, the ambitious, the lawyer, the artist, and the speculator, he caught the features of many of his contemporaries. Basically he used them to formulate moral judgments but, as often happens, he succeeded better in picturing the rogue and the amorality of the cynic than in making credible the naïve and the innocent. (pp. 77-80)

The brief tale ["El Verdugo"] takes shape around the dilemma in which the recapture of Menda placed the marquis who led the rebellion. The story rests basically on the horror of the situation: the villagers and servants are hanged; the noble family is to be shot. At this point the marquis faced a dilemma: how to avoid the obliteration of his family name. Therefore, the focus shifted to the son, who might refuse to pay the price for his life, then to daughter Clara.

Balzac assumed that his readers would recall the guerrilla warfare that virtually imprisoned the French army in Spain and provoked a savage repression. He founded his narrative on the logic of the conqueror who finds himself outnumbered in a hostile land, and on the universal cliché of Spanish honor. French readers who remembered the glory of the Napoleonic epic could resent, yet sympathize with, the fate of the rebels; they could hope that a plebeian French lieutenant might wed a grandee's daughter, but they surely read with fascination the fate of the rebellious nobles. The characters derive their personality from their names, their positions, and their problems. They are stereotypes in familiar situations: a grocer's son moonstruck over an aristocratic girl, a marquis hypersensitive about family honor, an inflexible general, a son who does his ghastly duty. Told chronologically, the story moves fast because Balzac had not yet begun to amass detail and descriptions. Its form lies close to the oral anecdote, polished for literary usage.

Balzac's particular manner of conceiving short fiction is apparent in **"La Maison du chat-qui-pelote,"** dated October, 1829, and published in *Les Scènes de la vie privée.* Here the sociologist came to the fore in a tale of the love of Augustine, the younger daughter of a draper, for Thomas de Sommervieux, a painter. Balzac fashioned the story according to the pattern that became his most consistent method of organization. A detailed portrait of the draper's shop as seen by Thomas established Augustine's world and set the conditions that would ruin her marriage. The description moved over the face of the old house, disclosing M. and Mme Guillaume and the functioning of the staid establishment. The premises of the action were merely stated: the family resembled "ces débris antédiluviens retrouvés par Cuvier." The old draper ran his business shrewdly, bargained sharply, and trusted in safe investments. Life was slow, highly moral, and dedicated to the profits of commerce.

Having set the basis for his thesis, Balzac had to explain the relationship of the long introduction to subsequent events. Hence, he used a flashback to establish the plot, then distributed the story between two major scenes: the courtship and subsequent married life. In the first, when Guillaume offered his senior clerk, Joseph, a share of the business and his elder daughter's hand, the clerk listened to the clear call of reason; but sentimental Augustine persisted in following her heart over her parents' objections. By the end of a year, Augustine found that Thomas had begun to stray, whereas Virginie had settled into a "bonheur égal, sans exaltation." A short conclusion pictured a disillusioned Augustine who crept home to die in shame.

The epilogue contended that living with a genius required strong character and deep understanding in a woman. No girl, however beautiful, could be transplanted from the simple life of a shop to the hostile climate of high society and great art. Along with his portrayal of a mésalliance based on the unstable grounds of passion, Balzac could not resist moralizing as he indicated the relationship of the house to its inhabitants: "ces vieilles maisons étaient des écoles de moeurs et de probité"; he commented on interclass marriage, and discoursed on how to hold a husband. He had difficulty restraining an urge to inflate his descriptions beyond the needs of the story.

The structure enabled Balzac to juxtapose the major scenes for maximum effect: Augustine happy and Augustine heartbroken permitted even the simplest-minded to grasp his meaning. Moreover, the long preface made an essential point: that the girl's fate was inevitable, given her background. Hence Balzac wrung all possible meanings from the old house, and related the personalities of the characters to their background, station in life, and residence. Augustine's fate was the logical outcome of the opening scene, and she walked a predetermined path to catastrophe.

To clarify this intent, Balzac arranged the characters so that Joseph and Virginie acted in counterpoint to Thomas and Augustine. The clerk and his wife accepted the conditions of their *mariage de convenance* with understanding yet attained prosperity and a reasonable happiness, while Augustine met tragedy by marrying for love. Youth and inexperience foundered where age and logic prospered.

Balzac, however, paid a price for choosing so simple a scheme. The use of two scenes faced him with the problem of introducing a sense of temporal fluidity, since he had sacrificed any sense of action to pictorial composition. To overcome this handicap, he had to rely on such phrases as "three years later" and frequent references to the aging of the protagonists. Similarly, he could only state the characters in this kind of structure. Because Augustine's behavior was deduced from her social stratum, Balzac sketched her as the innocent product of a half-century of merchant tyranny, born to be a shopkeeper's wife. Thomas, Joseph, and Virginie also acted out stock parts, struck stock attitudes, each almost a caricature. Since the nature of Balzac's thesis demanded social types, he presented easily recognized faces and manipulated the plot in these terms.

The two volumes of *Scènes de la vie privée* published by Mame in April, 1830, contained—in addition to "Le Chat-qui-pelote," "La Vendetta," and "Une Double Famille"—a short portrait entitled "Gobseck." Balzac had arrived at a basic conception of his art, but in this tale he utilized a variation on the method of contrasting scenes.

The portrait of the usurer forms a story within a story told to solve a problem set in the introduction. For his major characters Balzec employed a combination of two social types common to the satires written during 1827 and 1828: Derville, the lawyer, and Gobseck, the money lender. In order to recommend the young Count de Restaud as a proper husband for the daughter of a friend, Derville tells of two calls made by Gobseck—one on the poor but honest Fanny, the other on the adulterous Countess Restaud. To thwart the

countess, Gobseck had agreed to help her dying husband by becoming administrator of his estate, a position he used to teach the young Count de Restaud respect for money.

The structure of the double scene used in the "Chat-qui-pelote" is repeated here. The introduction to Derville's story delineates in detail the personality of Gobseck, later enlarged in his antithetical meetings with Mme de Restaud and Fanny. The major episodes expose the countess ruining herself, and the countess ruined. Money, one of Balzac's favorite themes, motivates the struggle between Gobseck and the unfaithful wife, one seeking power, the other struggling to hold a lover. Gobseck wins because money has no real meaning for him and he can avoid the mistakes engendered by desperation.

Balzac carried the principle of antithesis into other details of the plot. Wealthy Gobseck chose to live simply, avoiding waste even in motion and emotion, while the wastrel countess threshed about in frantic scheming. Honest Fanny was juxtaposed to Goriot's frivolous daughter, and the moral husband helped highlight the despicable Maxime, the lover who sponged on his mistress. Even the description of Gobseck's bare apartment clashed with that of the luxurious Restaud home, in which the miser read the foreshadowing of her doom.

In a manner that later became his trademark, Balzac spent pages describing Gobseck as the necessary condition of the story, establishing those aspects of Maxime, the count and countess, upon which he based his moralizing. After the relationships were fixed, Gobseck's second sight permitted him to give the advice that motivated the tale. Since Balzac then had to avoid the jerkiness of a series of disconnected anecdotes, Derville stressed his student days, his purchase of a practice, and the long repayment of a loan. The count had to die, but slowly. The dramatic tension originated from the questions raised in the first introduction. Could Derville convince Camille's mother of M. de Restaud's respectability? In the second major scene, would Derville and Gobseck outwit the countess? Thus Balzac approached the main incidents in a leisurely way; the premises were explicitly stated and the characters well sketched before the action exploded in the last few pages.

Since the formula was still new, the elements of the narrative occasionally escaped Balzac's control. Gobseck dominated the action at first, but once the count agreed to follow his advice, Derville and the countess elbowed him from sight. He reappeared at the end, consistent with his portrait as a harsh and honest man, but the events concerned only Mme de Restaud. Recalling the melodramatic techniques of the Restoration novel, Balzac presented her as the hardhearted wife who could search a dead man's room while the corpse was still warm. Gobseck functioned both as *deus ex machina* and avenging angel; he represented the author's moral indignation in operation.

In March, 1830, Balzac introduced in "Adieu" a new theme, "le foudroiement de l'être humain," which would become the principal topic of the *Contes philosophiques.* He went back to the epic retreat from Moscow to explain how Philippe de Guez lost his beloved Stéphanie in the chaos of the Beresina retreat. He found her in a madhouse eight years later, and recreated the battle scene to shock her into sanity. She revived momentarily, then died muttering "Adieu."

In "Adieu," time played a major role in the development of the story. Philippe found Stéphanie in 1819; then the action turned back to the Empire and returned to run into 1820. Balzac's literary prescription helped him highlight the drama and prevent the action from concluding too rapidly. Since the disappearance of Stéphanie, her long travels, and the many attempts at cures could only seem probable over an extended period of time, Balzac introduced a long digression on the history of a mad peasant girl who also lived at the asylum.

The distribution of incidents called for the usual arrangement of scenes, the most dramatic of which is the flashback. Under the Imperial spell like his generation, Balzac painted a stirring portrait of the rear-guard action at the Beresina retreat which caused Stéphanie's madness. Young Philippe, on the far side of the bridge, was trying to save a wagon carrying old General de Vaudières and his young wife. In the shambles of the rout, Philippe and his men built a raft for the general and Stéphanie. "Mourir avec toi!" she cried as she saw him crowded off. Left to the dubious mercies of the Russians, Philippe watched the general fall into the river and drown. Balzac deduced her behavior from this experience instead of from the usual sociological facts. Because of her breakdown and loss of identity, she was dragged along in the wake of the retreat; because of her madness, she could only be saved by shock treatment. But she died because the cure required more strength than she possessed. Recognition of the reality she had fled years before killed her.

With such a sensational plot, Balzac could not resist catering to his taste for the romanesque. Taking a page from the romantics' book, he set one of the scenes in a picturesque ruined abbey. Stephanie's cure took the form of an antithesis: Philippe failing and Philippe successful, with an ironic twist added to defeat the hero at the very moment of triumph. His picture of the retreat emphasized its ghastly aspects: men eating horses, sabering their comrades in hysterical panic; their mad rush to scramble aboard the raft; and the burning of the bridge, which left the stragglers to the avenging Cossacks. He described the scene on the grand scale, infusing it with an epic quality.

Balzac, however, was so concerned with incident that he paid little attention to the characters. Stéphanie, the beautiful wife, then the pathetic madwoman, remains a name and a condition. Philippe functions as the man who rescues his beloved at the cost of his own freedom and remains faithful forever after. A hardened officer who can cut down his own troops to save a girl, he nonetheless faints from strong emotion. Quite properly, he commits suicide after her death, after suffering quietly for years. The other characters, even the peasant girl, only help people the story. (pp. 80-6)

In his insatiable quest for material, Balzac inevitably turned to the supernatural. The vogue for Hoffmann's tales, for the mysterious and the fantastic, offered a promising field for exploitation. He found in **"Jésus-Christ en Flandre"** (1831) a subject both to his and to the popular taste. "A une époque assez indéterminée de l'histoire brabançonne . . . ," a ferry was sailing from Cadzant to Ostend with a divided group of passengers: a bishop, a young knight, a noble demoiselle, a rich bourgeois, and, in the rear of the boat, a huddle of poor people. When a storm threatened to swamp the boat, the rich promised candles; the bishop blessed the waves while thinking of his mistress; the young knight felt certain his class-conscious God would not let him die with peasants. The ferry split open in sight of land but a golden-haired passenger walked on the water. "Ceux qui ont la foi seront sauvés; qu'ils me suivent." The plain folk followed him to safety; one,

Thomas, doubted and sank, then repented and walked. The miser was dragged down by his gold, drowned along with the servant, the knight, and the bishop. Jesus walked away, leaving on the sand footprints over which a church was built.

Balzac's understanding of his stories as a series of building blocks led him to append to the ***Romans et contes philosophiques*** an epilogue originally entitled **"L'Eglise."** A first-person account related the visit of a melancholy man to a church just after the revolution of 1830. As he stared at white-robed nuns, a huge Christ smiled maliciously, the columns danced, and he accused a woman freshly out of the cemetery of prostituting herself. Suddenly transformed, the woman showed the man thousands of cathedrals rising, hordes of men serving the poor or copying manuscripts. "On ne croit plus," the old lady cried, and Balzac closed with a profession of faith, "Je viens de voir passer le convoi d'une Monarchie, il faut défendre L'Eglise."

The opening of the story gave it a tone of fantasy, almost in Mérimée's tongue-in-cheek manner. Long ago and far away it happened. "Le narrateur y croit, comme tous les esprits superstitieux de la Flandre y ont cru." The anecdote was based on Matthew's account of the miracle of walking on water, and on the medieval legend of the divine stranger come to test a group of people. Balzac contrasted the poor to the rich, who were of little faith. With poetic license, he decided that not Peter but a doubting Thomas had to face drowning before he could believe. Resting shakily on Biblical authority, the plot combined appeal to the religious and interest in folklore, a pairing popular during the Restoration. Balzac, however, ruined the unity of the tale when he related the plot to his own religious views. The vision, reminiscent of legends like that of the Bloody Nun, formed an epitaph for a monarchy which had lost the confidence of the French. The epilogue pleaded for Catholicism on the grounds that it had fulfilled its social and cultural obligations. "Croire . . . c'est vivre." This was the miracle that could save a France which he symbolized as a sinking ship.

The added section allowed Balzac to give **"Jésus-Christ et Flandre"** a contemporary meaning at the cost of artistic integrity. The focus shifted from the figure of Christ to *I*, with no transition. The plot had little relation to the moral Balzac hung onto it; perhaps he envisioned himself as the new Messiah but, at any rate, his sorrow at the decline of monarchy did literature no favor. By turning the story into an exemplum he ruined an excellent tale enlivened by a highly active intelligence.

Balzac soon dropped fantasy for the more comfortable portrayal of historical or contemporary scenes; tales of the unusual were rapidly falling from fashion. In **"Le Chef-d'oeuvre inconnu"** he found a more congenial subject that permitted the use of a historical figure to support his ideas on art. Divided into two sections, *Gillette* and *Catherine Lescault,* the story concerns an experience of young Nicolas Poussin with the monomaniac Maître Frenhofer. For ten years Frenhofer had slaved over a mysterious unfinished painting, "La Belle Noiseuse," or Catherine Lescault. Frenhofer agreed to let Poussin see the portrait if Gillette, his mistress, would pose for him, but the finished painting turned out to be a mass of bizarre lines and colors from which stood out a beautifully executed foot. That night Frenhofer died of a broken heart after burning his picture.

The point of the narrative is a familiar one in Balzac's stories:

talent or genius, expanding uncontrolled like a cancerous growth, transformed Frenhofer into a monomaniac. As his passion blinded him to facts, he entered a dream world, and the recognition of reality killed him as it had Stéphanie in **"Adieu."** An obsession turned into the kind of consuming passion that destroyed Louis Lambert in *La Recherche de l'absolu*. The excessive use of a talent, as Balzac's own life proved, carried the seeds of its own death.

The *idée fixe*, however, also motivated the plot. Frenhofer was presented in a scene that established the master's skill, though Balzac withheld his identify for some time. In the first scene, at the painter's studio, a new mystery developed around the masterpieces his compulsion was driving him to create, but explanation of the mystery was reserved for a second act. Thus the plot falls into two sections: Frenhofer's dream, and its destruction, with a short transition on Gillette, the model, stitching them together.

As previously, Balzac needed most of his space to prepare the action. He had formed the habit of suggesting analogies between his descriptions and the works of painters, and now he welcomed the chance to air decided opinions on the world of art. He established Frenhofer's theories at the outset, "la mission de l'art n'est pas de copier la nature, mais de l'exprimer." The artist's capacity, theories, and ten years' search for perfect beauty, these were the conditions out of which the tale grew. The description, in effect, the local color so dear to the romantics, became a necessary justification of the plot. Balzac had simply to distribute the facts according to a pattern, then smash Frenhofer, like Stéphanie, with a return to sanity.

Again, so much care went into the arrangement of the story line that the characters suffered. Gillette scarcely appeared, although her name was given to half the story, functioning only to persuade Frenhofer to unveil his surrealist picture, while the other two artists, Poussin and Porbus, merely provided the means for shocking him back to reality. The emphasis fell on the monomania, on its symbol, the mysterious painting that provided the surprise ending.

So successfully did the recipe work that it became Balzac's principal and formalized manner of storytelling. It could also, he discovered, be explored more fully than previously. If the narrative were directed toward character delineation and stripped of romanesque details, if it were developed without reliance on so many contemporary tricks and mannerisms, the format could produce a bold and imaginative tale based on life-size portraiture.

Balzac tried just this when, on February 20 and 27, and March 6 and 13, 1832, he published **"La Transaction"** in *L'Artiste*. Later entitled **"Le Colonel Chabert,"** it recounted the terrible misfortunes of an Imperial hero who suffered the fate of Enoch Arden. Colonel Chabert, the man who smashed the enemy charge and won victory at Eylau, had been left for dead on the field, stripped of his uniform, and tossed into a ditch. After he dug his way out of a mound of corpses, he found himself a vagabond without a provable identity. When he could substantiate his claims his wife, by then the Countess Ferrand, denied his existence, although she did persuade the colonel to sacrifice himself to her happiness. Six months later, Derville, Chabert's lawyer, saw his client, now an old tramp, being sentenced to perpetual detention.

"Le Colonel Chabert" contains a richness of topics unusual in Balzac's short fiction. Beginning with the theme of the returned husband or, as Balzac put it, "les morts ont donc bien tort de revenir," he made avarice and social climbing the motives for the countess' behavior, pairing off her moral depravity against Chabert's generosity. Her thirst for money and position provided movement as well as another set of contrasting themes: justice versus the law. Derville thought in terms of all justice within the law, but Chabert embodied the moral indignation of man. He rose from military hero to the greater stature of champion of decency in a world where the meek inherit the suffering and the moral find their reward in hell on earth; he was transformed into the personification of self-sacrifice. By balancing the themes against each other, intermingling forms of gratitude and ingratitude, Balzac gave the plot complexity, yet the obvious antitheses made it easy to follow.

This same principle was applied to the characters. Chabert has all the virtues his wife lacks. Among the minor personages, the countess's attorney, who uses the law to obstruct justice, presents a crooked caricature of honest Derville, the latter a more distinct personality than the others since he has already acted as Chabert's lawyer. His adversary, a shadowy figure at best, stands as the stereotype of the shyster in the service of his own purse. The portrait of the countess lacks clear definition since she constitutes merely a yardstick by which the colonel can be measured.

As in **"Gobseck,"** the main characters stand forth full-length. Since the story, like the history of the miser, was intended as a study of people under stress, events were arranged to force responses from Chabert that would outline his psychological profile. After a description of Derville's study, the colonel entered, cadaverous and tormented, permitting Balzac to ask the first motivating question: was the vagabond really the great hero? From this past he deduced the present character. Then Derville, patently the author's alter ego, discussed the moral problems basic to Chabert's case, and another question arose: what would the old man do? While the attorney prepared his case, he observed Chabert loyal to old companions and Chabert vengeful. A second flashback outlined the countess' position, while another visit to the law study, where the drama really unfolded, revealed a restored and optimistic colonel. But the conquering hero became putty in the hands of the wily wife when the sight of her children and her tears persuaded him to abandon his suit, for which he paid with his identity and his sanity.

The portrait of the old soldier stands out starkly despite the fact that Balzac again strayed into unnecessary detail. Chabert's skirmish with death is recorded in grisly terms as, tossed into a ditch with a tangle of naked bodies, he had to claw his way out of the gruesome pile. When his wife tricks him, the scene relies on sentimentality and the opposition of primitive virtue and sophisticated wile. The ironic incarceration of the hero provides a brutal ending to the plot in a savage comment on civilized behavior.

Since Balzac concentrated on portraiture, he fell back on the trusted flashback and the emphasis on dates to ease the static quality of the tale. Similarly, he indulged in humor, the teasing of the bewildered colonel by the clerks and the errand boy, the kind of heedless cruelty which symbolized society's attitude, because he could not permit the incidents to precipitate a sudden climax. Twice Chabert visited Derville's study, once as supplicant, then as potential victor, and his moral decision had to be made in terms of the conditions set therein. As his plight unfolded, consistent with the premises, his picture filled in gradually through the slowly developed action.

This prescription for brief fiction produced perhaps its greatest success in **"Le Curé de Tours,"** first published as *Les Célibataires* in the second edition of the *Scènes de la vie privée* (1832). Here, in a *drame bourgeois* that recalls the *romans de moeurs* popular between 1825 and 1830, he created the pathetic picture of a man "soumis aux effets de cette grande Justice distributive . . . nommé par certains niais les *malheurs de la vie.*" He united his power of observation and a strong imagination to produce a powerful account of ambition and hate in a small town: the persecution of Abbé Birotteau, a gouty old priest who aspired only to become canon of the metropolitan chapter of Saint-Gatien in Tours and to inhabit a coveted apartment in the home of Mlle Gamard.

The action, if such it can be called, rises from the conditions of provincial life as they operate on a weak personality. The abbé Birotteau's character is not developed but stated at great length, first with a physical portrait, followed by a minute character analysis. The episodes serve to demonstrate the effect of "distributive justice" on a guileless person, covetous of creature comfort, with too much faith in the goodness of man. His doom results from an incapacity to understand evil or to cope with the harsher facts of life; his simple mind and tactlessness unwittingly generate the resentment that ruins his dream. The saga has overtones of a morality play, as do so many of Balzac's brief narratives, but with evil triumphant and the meek gobbled up by the ruthless.

The themes of the story were arranged in a more complex manner than usual, with the basic interest in ambition leading to a consideration of petty provincial rivalries that broadened into a concern for justice. Though Birotteau was abused by his landlady, then bilked of an inheritance, his noble friends abandoned him after they had advised a lawsuit. Thus, he became the agent of his own destruction, with many an assist from well-wishers, in whom Balzac pictured the degeneration of the aristocracy. The power of the Church, misused for personal reasons, brought his protectresses to heel through the machinations of that mysterious bogey of the nineteenth century, the *Congrégation*.

Through all this, Balzac wove another theme: the evils of celibacy. Mlle Gamard, unwed and hence embittered, physically and morally shriveled, was the classic *vieille fille* turned harpy who, like any other frustrated old maid, enjoyed hurting people. As the brief epilogue stated, "le célibat offre donc ce vice capital que, faisant converger les qualités de l'homme sur une seule passion, l'égoisme, il rend les célibataires ou nuisibles ou inutiles." Thus Birotteau, his rival, Troubert, and Mlle Gamard ran afoul of this "law." Since the first was an innocent, the other two pounced on him in accord with Balzac's theory of the social jungle. Egoism was for all three a dangerous monomania.

Balzac had put his favorite organization of brief fiction at the service of a major psychological portrait that illustrated his social theories and his concept of divine justice. The plot strayed little; Balzac, sure of his method, felt no need for coating a bitter didactic pill with the sugar of strange episodes. The story unrolled naturally, moved by personalities reacting to their separate ambitions, with the minor characters acting credibly as small-town busybodies. Only in the episode of Mme de Listomère's nephew, the officer whose promotion was threatened by the Congrégation, did Balzac's penchant for complications reappear. Otherwise, after a short parenthesis explaining the characters and their actions, he set up three sections: the beginning of the persecution, the expulsion of Birotteau, and the failure of a lawsuit that eventuated in the abbé's exile to a poor suburban parish. Since the process of describing the erosion of the priest's hopes would cover months, Balzac took pains to indicate time as a major ingredient of his action. The plot began with Birotteau's predecessor, with the sequence carefully specified: the next morning, eight days later, after ten days . . . it took almost twelve years of events to produce a full-length Abbé Birotteau. He was contrasted physically, mentally, and morally with Troubert, the successful competitor for the canonry, a latter-day Hildebrand with no way of using his talents for the social good. Although Troubert and Mlle Gamard were contemporary stereotypes, Balzac made them as individual as Birotteau. Only the minor characters remained faceless, with one of them, a M. de Bourbonne, helping the author explain exactly where the curate's simplicity would lead him. Thus Balzac restrained his urge to intrude, though he could not resist underscoring the moral of the tale as though he had little faith in the intelligence of the reader to grasp the implications of a *drame bourgeois*.

By the time Balzac had completed **"Le Colonel Chabert"** and **"Le Curé de Tours,"** his method had become almost settled as he began to move from brief fiction into the novel. To be sure, he would write this kind of story all his life, but not as a major interest. Lack of time, the constant pressure of commitments, rarely permitted him the leisure necessary to attain the maximum economy and effect. Moreover, the conception of the short narrative at which he had arrived fitted his understanding of the novel, and he used the same structure in both genres. Hence, the more he worked with the longer form, the less interest he had in experimenting with brief fiction. The

Portrait of Balzac's first love, Mme Laure de Berny.

kind of portrait he achieved in **"Le Colonel Chabert"** and **"Le Curé de Tours"** was precisely what he needed for the illustration of his social theories in the *Comédie humaine.* Meanwhile, as more and more he fell back on short fiction to raise money, he depended on romanesque, tortuous plots like **"La Marana,"** and memories from his pot-boiler days. Not all his productions were bad, but the good ones came more rarely.

It was in portraits like **"L'Illustre Gaudissart"** (1833) that Balzac showed how he could control his medium, given time and a sympathetic subject. He had specialized in humorous and satiric portraits during his stints on such journals as *La Silhouette* and *La Caricature,* and this type of sketch matched his talent and dream of immortalizing contemporary social types. Gaudissart represented a figure new to the nineteenth century, a gift of the expanding industrial economy: the traveling salesman. When Paris companies discovered the advantages to be gained from transforming the itinerant peddler into the sales representative of non-competing firms, they flooded the provinces with fast-talking men wise in the ways of country folk. Inevitably Balzac added this striking figure to his gallery of illustrious stereotypes.

"L'Illustre Gaudissart" is technically a full-length portrait, the plot of which ironically describes the working habits of the traveling salesman. Gaudissart, of course, has suggestions of the Titanic, the biggest and the best, "le génie de la civilisation et les inventions." Since Gaudissart could sell anything, he had risen to become the Napoleon of his trade, wooed by manufacturers, insurance companies, and even newspapers. He left for his adventure at Vouvray with superb confidence, but when the arrogant huckster encountered the cunning Vernier, the latter sent Gaudissart to sell insurance and newspaper subscriptions to a madman. To the delight of the population, the lunatic palmed off barrels of bad wine on his caller while Gaudissart sold Margaritis only a single subscription to the *Journal des enfants.* The joke almost turned to tragedy when the offended Parisian challenged Vernier to a duel, but the adversaries prudently fired wide and fell into each other's arms.

In **"Gaudissart,"** Balzac indulged his sense of humor in a manner unusual for him. The subject invited it, and he happily obliged. Gaudissart was a salesman to end all salesmen, the epitome and nadir of the species, at once the perfect specimen and his own caricature. Since he believed in his mission, he also became a pathetic comment on the dubious benefits of the new middle-class world. Using satire at no time delicate, Balzac burlesqued the nobility of commerce: "Calembours, gros rire, figure monacale, teint de cordelier, envelope rabelaisienne; vêtement, corps, esprit, figure s'accordaient pour mettre de la gaudisserie, de la gaudriole en toute sa personne. Rond en affaires, bon homme, rigoleur . . ." His consort was Jenny, a *fleuriste,* the courtesan of the new age, at whose feet he laid his conquests of subscriptions. He even talked like a feudal lord, for he did not sell, but put products "sous ma protection." The bravery of the old order had changed into the prudent canniness of the new; a different conception of honor had been provided for the bourgeoisie.

Using popular notions of provincial life, Balzac employed the age-old theme of the trickster tricked. Only Gaudissart and the madman remained unaware of the joke; the salesman plied his trade as usual, but circumstances, as in a Maupassant tale, provided the dramatic irony. The Napoleon of the hat trade met his match in a simple-minded farmer in a com-

bat whose obvious humor lent force to Balzac's comment on society. The argument leaned heavily on a familiar stock situation in which stereotypes followed immediately recognizable patterns. A new type entered an old plot, personifying urban arrogance about to get its come-uppance, the city slicker undone by the wily hick whose very provincialism endowed him with primitive virtue.

The portrait of Gaudissart unfolded as Balzac deduced him from the general introduction, and the personality of the salesman unfolded from the premises of a previously stated character. The brash Gaudissart twice came a cropper, in the encounter with the lunatic and in the comic duel. Since Balzac had become vaguely aware of the benefits derived from changing point of view, he began by talking to the reader, but then had Gaudissart explain his psychology to his mistress, Jenny, in a revelatory scene; later, when Balzac fell back on the epistolary device, the salesman entered the plot on his own. The situation that resulted provided a sharply etched comic sketch for the **Human Comedy.**

By 1834, Balzac was committing himself more and more to the novel, partly from personal taste, partly because the first quick vogue for the *conte* and the *nouvelle* was petering out. A surfeit of writers eager for quick profits had cut down the sales value of short fiction. Balzac's interest in the genre lagged, particularly since he felt he could put the lessons learned to better use in the longer form. This attitude became obvious in an anecdote like **"Un Drame au bord de la mer"** (1835), a first-person narrative concerning the spoiled, nasty son of a fisherman whose long-suffering father finally heaved him into the sea.

Balzac's interests, like those of his major characters, were assuming an almost compulsive force; he became fascinated with discovering the "natural laws" motivating the society that inhabited his vast imagination. His plots, therefore, tended to revolve around contemporary moral and religious problems, growing heavier with moral statement, as in **"La Messe de l'athée."**

After 1835, Balzac's production of short narratives dropped considerably; by this time he had ceased experimenting. His plots tended to bog down in increasing complexity, although occasionally there were flashes of his great talent, as in **"L'Interdiction"** (1836). The tale recalls the treachery of Mme Chabert and the money-hungry Comtesse de Restaud. Once again Balzac relied on his trusted method to create honest Judge Popinot, but the economy of the story suffered from dependence on coincidence, misunderstanding, and a curious change in the sentimental and the melodramatic took over as lack of time encouraged haste, making the delineation of character almost accidental and incidental. **"Facino Cane"** (1836), for instance, combined the pathetic figure of a blind musician with a fantastic tale of adultery, a strangled husband, and escape from a dungeon into a cellar that contained the secret wealth of the Venetian government. Similarly, **"Gambara"** repeated the plight of a monomaniacal artist who played cacophonic music on a Panharmonium. The narrative bulged with complications surrounding the tragedy of an unrecognized genius as Balzac became involved in a long-winded attempt to blend fiction and a dissertation on music. The genius in a slum, the faithful wife who later deserted him, the handsome young man who purported to help the less fortunate, all these, with a large dash of sentimentality, were jumbled together in unhappy juxta-position. Balzac relied too heavily on his stock arrangement to provide a neat solution for all his literary difficulties. As a result, the plot creaked along and the skeleton of his work never did fill out with any artistic flesh. Such was the case in *Massimilla Doni*, a complicated dissertation on ethereal and physical love, full of digressions, involving a host of characters in complicated and bizarre relationships. "Esprits purs qui peuvent se dépouiller ici-bas de leurs larves de chair . . ."

The old touch was disappearing as Balzac lashed himself on to meet his commitments. **"Z. Marcas"** (1840) unsuccessfully attempted a portrait as outstanding as that of Gobseck or Chabert. **"Albert Savarus"** (1842) described provincial life and the obsessively possessive love of Rosalie de Watteville, whose pursuit of Albert, worthlessly single-minded and brilliantly described, was buried in an uncontrolled mass of detail, along with essays on provincial political machinations.

But Balzac hit bottom in *La Dernière Incarnation de Vautrin* (1847), a rambling account of the master thief's conversion to virtue. The old method no longer served its purpose, although Balzac had the advantage of being able to use characters like Camusot, Popinot, Vautrin, and M. de Grandville, who by now had amassed extensive histories and full personalities. He established a story line so complicated that no character could escape its tangled web, indulged his interest in thieves' jargon, then expanded the narrative by explaining his theory of criminology. Balzac seemed to have lost his conception of brief prose, and he swamped the tale with moralizing. The genre functioned here only as a carrier for his theses, not as an autonomous art form. The more he worked with the novel, the more he tended to confuse the two media, to consider one a dehydrated version of the other. *Vautrin* seems an undeveloped novel, not conceived to benefit from the advantages of the short narrative nor adequately structured to provide the psychological motivation of the novel. In Balzac's mind, the longer form had won out after a minor debate. (pp. 89-102)

> *Albert J. George, "Stendhal, Balzac, Mérimée," in his* Short Fiction in France, 1800-1850, *Syracuse University Press, 1964, pp. 65-134.*

CHARLES AFFRON   (essay date 1966)

[*Affron is an American essayist and academic. In the following excerpt from* Patterns of Failure in "La comédie humaine," *he attributes the deficiencies of such characters as Colonel Chabert and Gobseck to the incongruity of their actions.*]

It has become increasingly evident that one can validly discuss the typical character in *La Comédie humaine.* If a lesson is to be learned from the categorization of failure, it is that the divisions are most emphatically arbitrary. They are useful only in clarification, in an effort to impose some kind of form onto the sprawling matter under analysis. The vocabulary used to describe the different examples bears, through necessity, a sameness, a ring of familiarity. The rhetorical devices used in the case of Lucien de Rubempré can be discerned in the presentations of César Birotteau and Louis Lambert. Balzac fervently believes that "there is only one animal" (Avant-propos à *La Comédie humaine*). Man is a single animal type. All men are subject to the same pressures, the same laws. The failures that result from weakness are also infected by a certain amount of blindness. The genius type might just as accurately be characterized as blind and passionate. Finally, all the failures in *La Comédie humaine* should be ascribed to the single fault of incongruence.

This incongruence is most poignantly and concisely dramatized in the case of Colonel Chabert, the one figure in *La Comédie humaine* who is physically and officially divorced from reality. The very embodiment of incongruence, he is completely cut off from time. He lives without name, without identity. As far as the world is concerned, he is a dead man and therefore can exert no will. The fact that Colonel Chabert is alive, though in some ways dead, is manifested in his physical being and in his clothing, symbolic extensions of his inner being and unmistakable signals for the reader. "His neck was tightly encircled by a miserable tie of black silk" (**"Le Colonel Chabert"**). The black necktie seems to be part of the ideal frame for this portrait of death. The brim of Chabert's hat complements this effect. "The brim of the hat which covered the old man's forehead projected a black furrow upon the upper part of his face. Through the bluntness of the contrast, this bizarre, although natural effect put into relief the white wrinkles, the cold sinuosities, the discolored sentiment of this cadaverous face." Death is written on this man's face. He has no business among the living, and the remainder of his fictional life is grim proof of his incongruence. Balzac is careful in this first, long description of the hero to emphasize his deathlike characteristics. "Finally, the absence of any movement in the body, of any warmth in the glance, harmonized with a certain expression of dolorous madness, with the degrading symptoms by which idiocy is characterized, to make of this face something deadly, that no human word could express." Colonel Chabert is not mad. His expression is simply that of a man who no longer sees as other men do. He has known death and now lives with its imprint on his face. Without a name, deprived of his official existence, which truly defined his relation to other men, he cannot survive.

Chabert's great mistake is that he attempts to return to the living. Taken for dead at the battle of Eylau, a victim of amnesia, he has ceased to exist in the eyes of the law. His wife has inherited his fortune and remarried. He attempts to reclaim his name and, in doing so, dies a second death infinitely more horrible than the first. At least at Eylau he died a hero. Before learning the final truth about his wife's baseness, he asks her: "Are the dead then wrong in coming back?" He should have known the answer. Chabert submits to many deceptions before realizing that his position is a false and impossible one. Thoroughly disgusted by the extent to which self-interest degrades humanity, a process he has witnessed most brutally in the actions of his own wife, he disowns his name and, in fact, abdicates his status in society. He therefore admits to his own incongruence. "You cannot know the extent of my disdain for this exterior life which the majority of men prize. I have suddenly been seized by a disease: disgust for humanity." Chabert has seen humanity with the kind of detachment that only a "live" dead man can enjoy, and he has learned a bitter lesson. What is incongruent to reality has lost its right to existence.

Years later, the lawyer Derville, a witness to the tragedy of Colonel Chabert, sees this wreck of a human being at the side of a road. Derville says to a friend: "That old man . . . is a poem, or as the romantics say, a drama." Truly the story of Colonel Chabert is a poem, a dramatization of failure. Balzac has created a situation in which a human being judges life from the vantage point of death. He has created a character who perfectly symbolizes his theory that fitting into reality, functioning within the framework of a given society, and reacting to its ever-changing demands are prime requisites for success, life, mere survival.

The author's values give impulse and conviction to the omnipresent rule of congruence. These values, introduced in the first chapter, are political, moral, and literary. In fact, they belong to all these categories at once. The conservatism that colors Balzac's views on government and religion reflects his desire (a noticeably frustrated one) to tie together in some way the numerous and opposing aspects of life. For fleeting moments the author deludes himself into believing that an order can be imposed upon the hydra of existence. This tendency on his part is seen in the Dantesque arrangement that *La Comédie humaine* was supposed to have taken in its final version. Although Balzac fulfills his literary plan to a great extent, the penetrating artist's eye lodged within him perceives the impracticability of his social, political, and religious ideas. This same eye does not, however, lose its avidity for order, its need to find a pattern in disorder. The artistic solution lies in the Word, while the human one is defined by the now-familiar construct wherein men must obey the most immediate demands of the moment. They must, in other words, conform to the virtually unpredictable currents of reality. The character who turns his back to the whirlpool, voluntarily or not, faces instead his own failure. (pp. 133-36)

For Balzac, failure leaves an uneradicable imprint upon human existence. He judges life by its standard; he nurtures art with its inspiration. Very conveniently, the reader is provided with an image of the author in the body of *La Comédie humaine.* Refracted through the character of Gobseck we can perceive Balzac's relationship to his fictional universe and the role that failure plays therein.

Gobseck the moneylender dominates the lives of his debtors in the same way that the author controls the destinies of his fictional children. Since gold is the true base of society, since only money is viable in Balzac's world, the source of money is the source of power; it is creativity. Gobseck's command of the world through money is os complete that it renders him omniscient. In fact, due to his special qualities, no power can challenge him. "My glance is like that of God, I see into hearts. Nothing is hidden from me. You refuse nothing to the man who ties and unties the purse-strings" (**"Gobseck"**). Life passes before the eyes of Gobseck in all its nakedness, without shame, declaiming its needs with the honesty of despair. No one but the author has this god-like vantage point. Both Gobseck and Balzac have the power of life and death over their subjects.

Gobseck has the privilege of reading into the souls of the desperate people forced to come to him. He examines men who are on the verge of failure, their nerves quivering under his clear scrutiny. "No one having any credit at the Bank comes into my shop, where the first step made from my door to my office proclaims despair, a failure ready to burst forth, and in particular a refusal of money by all the bankers. I only see stags at bay, tracked by their pack of creditors." It is in this atmosphere of crisis that failure takes on its full significance. Failure is the sum of a life. At the moment of ruin one removes the disguise, however imperfectly it has been worn, and the whole truth is revealed. Witnessing this process is an important and moving experience. Gobseck is aware of this and appreciates his position.

> Do you believe that it is a small matter to penetrate thus the most secret recesses of the human heart, to take up the life of others, to see it naked? The spectacles are always varied: hideous wounds, mortal sorrows, love scenes, miseries for which the wa-

ters of the Seine lie in wait, a young man's joys which lead to the scaffold, laughs of despair and sumptuous parties. Yesterday, a tragedy: some good-natured father asphyxiates himself because he can no longer feed his children. Tomorrow a comedy: a young man will try to play the scene of Monsieur Dimanche for me, with the variations of our time.

In this passage Balzac extracts art from failure. He idealizes the privilege of Gobseck and, in doing so, explains his own attraction to ruin. The author exultantly embraces his creation in the most crucial moment of its existence, simply because it is then so true, so real, so vibrant. It is the finale of a human comedy where all is exposed in blazing clarity, where life exhibits itself in its most extreme aspects. Balzac, an artist of despair, sees a diseased life in a hideous wound, and the drama that precedes suicide is reflected in the waters of the Seine. He hears laughter in the voice of a doomed man and then creates a life to go with that laughter.

Failure is a manifestation of the author's pessimism. In its more gruesome aspects, it is an outlet for his morbidity. Finally, it is one of the frontiers of *La Comédie humaine,* the point to which the characters inexorably march, amassing their lives on their shoulders as they go. At this frontier sits a judge with burning eyes, a man who, from this vantage point, chooses those who are fated to cross the border into the land of defeat. (pp. 140-42)

> *Charles Affron, in his* Patterns of Failure in "La comédie humaine," *Yale University Press, 1966, 148 p.*

F. W. J. HEMMINGS (essay date 1967)

[*Hemmings is an English academic, biographer, and essayist who has written several critical studies of French authors. In the preface to his* Balzac: An Interpretation of "La comédie humaine," *Hemmings defines the aim of his study as an examination of "the two terms of the dialectic underlying* La comédie humaine . . . : *individual visions, ambitions, and nostalgias acting on, colliding with, modified by the solid-seeming yet disintegrating rock of society." The following is taken from Hemmings's discussion of several short stories that he considers representative of Balzac's view of married life.*]

The title *Scènes de la vie privée* was first used by Balzac in 1830 for a two-volume collection of short stories (half a dozen in all), the purpose of which was avowedly didactic. The previous year he had scored a considerable success with a waggish and cynical treatise, *Physiologie du mariage;* the 1830 collection dealt similarly with the subject of matrimony, but soberly and rather more chastely. If certain remarks in his Preface are to be taken at face value, these stories—in which he had "attempted to depict with fidelity the events that follow marriage or precede it"—were designed to constitute a manual suitable for enlightened mothers to give to their marriageable daughters, the author believing that "it is far less imprudent to put markers at the dangerous passages in life, as watermen on the Loire drive willow branches in the sandbanks, than to leave them hidden from the eyes of the inexperienced."

In the circumstances, it is hardly surprising that such charm as these stories might once have possessed has faded, or at least taken on an irremediably period air, almost—though not quite—to the same degree as has that of Maria Edgeworth's *Moral Tales,* which they recall and which may have partly inspired them. The haughty young beauty of **"Le Bal de Sceaux,"** who rebuffs a blameless suitor because she sees him serving in a draper's shop, is hardly more than a lay figure in a moral demonstration. The ballroom setting of **"La Paix du ménage,"** in the heyday of the First Empire, glitters still, but with a spectral remoteness, and the dancers are puppets. Balzac is still at the stage of inventing, he is not yet creating.

There is one story, however, to which these strictures do not apply. Entitled, in 1830, **"Gloire et malheur,"** it was subsequently rechristened, for the first edition of *La Comédie humaine,* **"La Maison du chat-qui-pelote,"** with reference to the street sign, a cat playing rackets, hanging over the old-fashioned linen draper's establishment that is the story's principal setting. The work, slight as it is, has the great merit of presenting a convincing and warmly human picture of the mercer and his family. The life of these lower middle class people is shown as unspeakably monotonous, though not felt by them as being so; the annual stock taking is a great event, a visit to an art gallery a momentous outing. But the shopkeeper's family, narrow though their horizons are, have a poetic appeal for a stranger with an eye for the picturesque. Sommervieux, a talented young artist, catches sight of the group sitting at dinner one evening by an uncurtained window and falls in love with the prettier of the two daughters, Augustine. He executes a portrait of her and also paints a view of the shop. These pictures attract considerable attention when exhibited, and Augustine discovers she has an admirer in a sphere far removed from her own. Her parents are not easily persuaded to give their consent to the match; her father, a robust believer in commonsense marriages, has no desire to see a daughter of his "marry above her station."

In the event his apprehensions are fully justified. Augustine lacks the training to appreciate her husband's work, and inevitably Sommervieux turns away from her. Balzac is far from blaming him: "Poetry, art, and the exquisite pleasures afforded by the imagination exert indefeasible rights over lofty spirits." This arrogant claim, very typical of the romantic era, may not exonerate Sommervieux in our eyes today, but we can forget that point: it is not on the selfishness of the artist, but on the distress of the betrayed wife that Balzac wishes to fix our attention—not that he tries very hard to enlist our sympathy on her behalf. She is deservedly punished because she has used marriage to satisfy a naively ambitious dream of greatness. Her hopes of "glory" result in "unhappiness." **"La Maison du chat-qui-pelote"** is both a study of incompatibility in marriage and a warning against disregarding parental advice in one's choice of a life's partner, which is a particular case of defying the authority of the family.

Two other early stories, **"La Bourse"** and **"La Vendetta,"** introduce scenes from the lives of artists; this is explainable by the circumstance that around 1830 Balzac was frequenting the *salon* of the painter Gérard, whose other regular visitors included Delacroix, Gavarni, Ary Scheffer, and the sculptor David d'Angers, with most of whom Balzac was on terms of friendly acquaintance, even though not all of them could stand his exuberant good humor in company.

In **"La Bourse"** a young painter falls off a ladder in his studio and is helped by the girl from the flat below, who turns out to be a wholly suitable bride. The heroine of **"La Vendetta"** meets her future husband in even more romantic circumstances. (pp. 35-8)

Possibly Balzac's intention in this melodramatic tale was to warn his young female readers of the risks of marrying, even when the law is on your side, without your father's consent—particularly when your future husband lacks the resources to support you. But for the modern reader the principal interest of **"La Vendetta"** lies elsewhere: in the study of the relations between father and daughter—relations that, on the old man's side at least, are tinged with incestuous passion and in the depiction of which Balzac can be watched trying out certain scenes that were later to figure in a major masterpiece, *Le Père Goriot.* As soon as Ginevra declares her intention of getting married, and even before the Piombos realize the identity of their prospective son-in-law, Bartolomeo flies into a violent rage:

> I could not bear to see you love a man. . . . If he loved you as you deserve to be loved, it would kill me; and if he did not love you, I should stab him. . . . To love you as a father, is not that already to dwell in paradise? Who then is there worthy to be your husband?

Ginevra's answers are pert and only irritate the old man still further; but everything ends in a fit of tenderness:

> And the father played with his daughter as with a six-year-old girl, he took delight in loosening the wavy tresses of her hair, in jumping her up and down; there was a touch of insanity in the expression of his affection.

The security of the family can be threatened not only by imprudent or rebellious conduct on the part of the children; irresponsible and unreasonable displays of emotion by a parent are equally dangerous. And yet, slight though the sketch is, these two willful, intensely passionate characters (Bartolomeo had delighted in instilling something of his own ferocity in Ginevra's heart, we are told, "exactly as a lion teaches his cubs to spring on their prey") clearly captured the imagination of their creator; here again, Balzac condemns with his rational judgment, speaking with the voice of society, what he admires and responds to in his guise as advocate of the free-ranging individual.

A far more serious and poignant study of dissension within a family is provided by the history of Roger de Granville. The title of this story, in the original *Scènes de la vie privée,* was ironical: **"La Femme vertueuse;"** Balzac later changed it to **"Une double famille."** Roger makes an unwise marriage, but at least it was not contracted in defiance of his father's wishes; on the contrary. At twenty-six, with excellent prospects in the magistrature, he is urged to accept the hand of a wealthy young heiress from Bayeux, whose widowed mother, though "fearfully pious," would be flattered to see her daughter enter the aristocratic family of the Granvilles. Angélique, as the count describes her to his son, is "the prettiest girl in Bayeux, a little puss who will never give you any trouble, because she has been brought up with principles." These "principles" are those of a narrow-minded bigotry, which should guarantee that she will remain physically faithful to him. Roger would prefer something more in a wife than this negative virtue, but his father, who spent his own youth in the frivolous court circles of the *ancien régime,* smiles at his seriousness. As soon as he sets eyes on Angélique, the younger Granville hesitates no more; he commits "the cardinal error of mistaking the allurements of desire for those of love."

There follows a careful, searching, and convincing analysis

of the breakdown of a marriage when the puritanical scruples of the wife kill all joy and destroy all graciousness in the home. Balzac had quoted, at the beginning of one of the chapters of his *Physiologie du marriage,* a caustic epigram of La Bruyère: "Piety and gallantry together in a wife are too much for a husband to contend with: she should choose between the two." Angélique de Granville has chosen the former, with results almost as uncomfortable for her husband as if she had chosen the latter. Granville's position and his hopes of advancement require that he should entertain at home and, with his wife, should attend the social gatherings of the beau monde. But as soon as they move to Paris, Angélique insists on taking a house in a remote and unfashionable quarter and furnishing it tastelessly. She finds excuses to stay away from balls whenever they are invited and, when Granville tricks her into going to one, she makes herself ridiculous by covering her shoulders and refusing to dance. They quarrel, and the dispute is even referred to the Pope, who writes that she must obey her husband in all things; encouraged, however, by a fanatical confessor, she continues as before, accomplishing her bare duties as a wife with a chilly punctiliousness that satisfies no one but herself:

> The imperturbable smile into which the young woman forced her lips whenever she looked at Granville seemed to her a jesuitical formula of happiness by which she imagined herself to be fulfilling every demand of married life; her charity wounded, her beauty, lacking passion, seemed monstrous to those who knew her, and the gentlest of her speeches was irritating; she never acted in accordance with her feelings, but only in obedience to the voice of duty.

The exact discharge of her duties will, she imagines, be rewarded in the next life. The calculus of salvation is irrefutable: on the one side of the equation, the idle pleasures of the world, on the other, eternal bliss. "Is this not," asks Balzac, "egoism sanctified, the *self* beyond the tomb?"

"Une double famille" was only incidentally a criticism of a certain type of religious upbringing and religious outlook; Balzac's real target was Mme de Granville's egoism. She is not the long-suffering wife, the Christian spouse of a worldly husband that she tries to be, that perhaps she ought to be, and that Adeline Hulot will be in *La Cousine Bette.* When she discovers that Granville has sought solace outside the home and has founded a "second family" with a complaisant grisette, instead of falling on her knees and praying for her husband to be delivered from the toils of Satan, she hunts down the address of his other establishment and bursts in on him when he is with his mistress and children. Unmoved, Granville turns the tables on her, victoriously castigating her egoism by the dubious procedure of asserting the superior claims of his own:

> You have sacrificed my happiness to your salvation. . . . No woman can be a man's wife and the bride of Jesus at the same time—that would constitute bigamy: she must make up her mind and opt between a husband and a convent.

Angélique asks him what he understands by wifely love, and the answer he gives is comprehensive and not a little breathtaking:

> To yield to our whims, anticipate them, find pleasure in pain, place us higher than the world's opinion, than self-love, than religion even, and to con-

sider these sacrifices as rating no more than a pinch of incense burned in honor of the idol. That is love . . .

To which the countess retorts (with some justice, it must be admitted): "The love of opera dancers!" This kind of selfless devotion is, in fact, best illustrated in *La Comédie humaine* by the ex-prostitute Esther's feelings for Lucien de Rubempré (*Splendeurs et misères des courtisanes*).

To ensure that his lesson was fully understood, Balzac added a final episode to **"Une double famille"** showing how the count's experiment in founding a family outside the home ended in disaster. His mistress quitted him for another man who robbed her and left her to perish in want. Her son, not having had the benefit of a regular upbringing, turned to crime. Granville is shown, on the last page, reading his rightful heir a homily on the importance of studying the character of the woman one intends to marry.

Our discussion of this cycle of edifying stories must end with a brief look at a somewhat uncharacteristic work, the *Mémoires de deux jeunes mariées.* Written some twelve years later than the original *Scènes de la vie privée,* it introduces a new theme, to be examined more fully in the next chapter: the threat to marriage and the family posed by romantic love. Balzac chose an already outmoded form, the novel-by-letters, in order to trace the parallel but opposed life stories of two convent-school friends. Louise marries for love, after an ideally glamorous courtship; her Spanish teacher turns out to be a grandee in exile who blows love letters from a tube through her window, bows to her slightest caprice before and even—incredibly—after marriage, is melancholy, adoring, and faithful. Renée accepts the bridegroom her family finds for her, a man of thirty-seven, prematurely aged, lacking in energy, but docile. Louise's husband dies early, worn out by the insatiable demands she makes on his affections. She remarries but, suspecting her second husband of infidelity, dies in her turn. Meanwhile Renée has made up her mind that her mission in life is to raise a healthy family and to instill self-respect and ambition in her husband: these humdrum aims are fulfilled without much difficulty.

The *Mémoires de deux jeunes mariées* is a *roman à thèse* on the theme of "sense and sensibility," but Renée's good sense is so unbearably smug, Louise's sensibility so wildly extravagant, that the sermon is finally robbed of all effect. A few of the maxims in Renée's letters serve, however, as useful clues to Balzac's thought on the central question he was raising. It is worth observing that Renée is a student of Bonald in between her pregnancies. As she sees it, Louise is a mere child of nature; society, in thwarting nature, perfects the individual in accordance with the divine will. So "every married woman learns to her cost the social law, which at many points is incompatible with the laws of nature." The family is a hierarchical structure, not an association or a partnership. "There exists an equality between two lovers which I think can never manifest itself between husband and wife, under penalty of social disorders and irreparable harm." Passionate love is a jewel stolen by society from the treasure house of nature; by which Renée probably means that passionate love is an intruder in the social order, something transitory and unmeaningful like all natural phenomena. In any case, that passionate love can endure is a fiction invented by romantic poets. "Nature and society are in league to destroy the existence of absolute felicity, something which is contrary to nature and society alike." In her last letter, which is addressed not to

Louise (who is by now dead) but to her husband, Renée sums up the whole of this bleak philosophy in a single, uncompromising statement: "Marriage cannot be founded on passion, nor even on love." This is not just an antiromantic sally: it has its sour logic. If passion is supremely a force rooted in egoism, a manifestation of the individual libido, it clearly has no place in the social arrangement that marriage is, an arrangement designed to enable society to progress toward its own ends and not to offer a way of self-fulfillment to its particular members.

Granted that the thesis has a certain rough common sense behind it, still it has to be acknowledged that Balzac's presentation of it in these early works is crude and conspicuously devoid of humanity and true understanding. Tolstoy, a novelist as keenly aware as was Balzac of the importance of marriage as a social institution, succeeded far better in conveying the same message. In *Anna Karenina* everything that Balzac meant to say is said with a compassion, a delicacy, and a persuasive sureness of touch that one looks for in vain in those novels of *La Comédie humaine* that deal with the topic of men and women linked in marriage or trying to break free of its bonds. Partly the reason is that Balzac was unfortunately as much at pains to convince himself as to convince his reader; and partly that he, unlike Tolstoy, had no personal knowledge of the conditions he was describing. Intuition can take an author a long way, but not the whole way. (pp. 39-47)

> *F. W. J. Hemmings, in his* Balzac: An Interpretation of "La comédie humaine," *Random House, 1967, 189 p.*

PETER W. LOCK (essay date 1972)

[*In the following excerpt, Lock examines narrative function, technique, and perspective in Balzac's short stories.*]

Among the most experimental of Balzac's works are his *contes* and *nouvelles*. It should be remembered that after publishing *Les Chouans* in 1829, Balzac immediately turned to short fiction and produced the *Scènes de la vie privée* (1830) and the group of philosophical stories which were published just after *La Peau de chagrin* under the heading of *Romans et contes philosophiques* in 1831. In retrospect these series can be seen as laying the groundwork for two of the three major divisions of the *Comédie humaine* (the third division, *Les Études analytiques,* had already been prepared with the publication of the anecdotal *Physiologie du mariage* in 1829). The six *Scènes de la vie privée* demonstrate a new concern with the dramatic representation of everyday reality and reveal considerable diversity in narrative technique—from the basically 'scenic' presentation of "La Vendetta" and "La Paix du ménage" to the 'pictorial' handling of "La Maison du chat-qui-pelote" and "Une Double Famille." Balzac continued to experiment with short fiction until the end of his life, and although his greatest output was from 1830 to 1832 and coincided with the vogue of the short story in France, he nonetheless produced some 20 of his 50 short works between 1832 and 1845, among them such divergent masterpieces as "Melmoth réconcilié" (1835), "Les Secrets de la Princesse de Cadignan" (1839) and "Honorine" (1843).

A study of point of view in these 50 short works permits an assessment of the function of the narrator in the *Comédie humaine,* and leads to important conclusions concerning Balzac's attitude towards his characters and their values. In only

29 of the stories is a conventional third-person narrator used throughout; in five other works the third-person narrator predominates, but information, evaluation and judgment are yielded by means of such devices as letters "La Femme abandonnée" or summary by a character (as, for example, in "Les Marana"). In four other stories the function of the third-person narrator is reduced to providing situation or setting; the main events are related by a character who has been present as observer or as active participant (Nathan in "Un Prince de la Bohème," Derville in "Gobseck," Desplein in "La Messe de l'athée," the Consul-Général in "Honorine"). These last four works thus become basically first-person narratives and could be included with the 12 works in which some variation of the first-person narrator is adopted at the outset. In this latter group there are also important distinctions to be made however; in six of the stories the 'je' narrator (who may be unidentified as, for example, in "Les Deux Rêves" or named as in "La Grande Bretèche" recounts a story which he has learned about either from another character ("Un Drame au bord de la mer," "Une Passion dans le désert") or from an unidentified source (*Sarrasine*) or even by eavesdropping ("La Maison Nucingen"). The six remaining stories contain first-person narrators who have in some way been active in the events they relate, either from the beginning (Bianchon in "Étude de femme;" the unidentified narrator in "L'Église" and in "Le Message"), or as the action progresses ("L'Auberge rouge," "Facino Cane" and "Z. Marcas").

These groupings, though they demonstrate the diversity of approaches adopted, do not in themselves indicate the extent or the nature of the narrator's participation in the action; nor do they determine his relationship with the other characters or with the author. In "Facino Cane," for example, the unidentified narrator is endowed with powers of divination and comprehension which lead to a peculiar kind of passionate involvement in events which are merely recounted to him; whereas Bianchon in "Étude de femme" adopts an air of humorous detachment in relating a story in which he played the leading role. And at any time a first-person narrator may be far more passive and objective than the third-person narrator so frequently employed in the *Comédie humaine* to provide commentary, assessment and judgment.

Important distinctions must be made with respect to the extent of the involvement of the narrator (be he first-person or third-person) and the nature of his attitude towards events and persons. "La Paix du ménage" may be taken as an example of a work in which the narrator's role is primarily that of spectator. The story, which is told in the third person, opens with a brief preparatory summary followed by a scene and a succinct recapitulation, after which the narrator adopts the position of a neutral observer and contents himself with recording conversation, actions and gestures which reveal the personalities and motives of the characters. The scene is a society ball; the plot concerns the successful attempt of Madame de Soulanges to recover from an admirer her diamond ring which her husband had given to his mistress. The characters are engaged throughout in a battle of wits and a game of concealment and decipherment. Only rarely is the reader given an 'inside view'; for the most part he, like the narrator and the other characters, is forced to interpret words, glances and gestures in an attempt to assess the situation and to predict the outcome of the tragi-comedy. A similarly discreet stance is adopted by the narrator in such works as "El Verdugo," "Adieu," "Les Comédiens sans le savoir" and "Un

Homme d'affaires;" authorial commentary is rare, direct judgment withheld, and the stories seem to come unmediated to the reader.

The last two works contain groups of Balzac's reappearing characters whose personalities are perhaps so well known that they do not need presentation or evaluation. In other works the reappearing characters may function as narrators or as narrator-agents. Their presence adds authenticity and colour to the particular story, permits Balzac to withdraw from a position of direct responsibility, and confers the fiction of autonomy upon the created world. In **"Autre Étude de femme"** Balzac throws together a couple of dozen of his best-known characters, four of whom—de Marsay, Blondet, Montriveau and Bianchon—recount anecdotes or relate events from their own past, while the other characters provide comments and reactions as they listen to the four narrators. **"Un Prince de la Bohème"** adds a dimension to this device; as a result of listening to Nathan's account of the rakish adventures of La Palférine, one of the characters, the marquise de Rochefide, falls in love with La Palférine and her passion affects the outcome of the third part of *Béatrix*. As Claude-Edmonde Magny has pointed out, these examples reveal and affect "l'architecture cachée de l'édifice balzacien". They also show the extent to which Balzac's characters can 'take over' from their creator and achieve a seeming independence of action and existence. It is as if, having set the complex world of *La Comédie humaine* in motion and having created his enormous cast of reappearing characters, Balzac can afford to retire from the scene and, like some inscrutable divinity, watch and listen to his characters reminiscing about themselves and gossiping about one another.

By means of these narrative devices Balzac deliberately adopts a stance of apparent neutrality, and renounces his powers of intervention, overt manipulation and direct judgment. A *nouvelle* like **"La Maison du chat-qui-pelote,"** usually considered a typical Balzacian work, contains a more conventional use of the narrator who is present throughout as observer, commentator and judge. In his analysis of this work in his *Short Fiction in France*, Albert J. George provides a strong sense of the fundamental and apparently rather facile oppositions which Balzac established between the world of the draper Guillaume and that higher sphere to which Guillaume's daughter Augustine ascends as the result of her marriage to the painter de Sommervieux [see excerpt dated 1964]. The basic plot is simple: because of her anachronistic upbringing in the stagnant sub-world of "la maison Guillaume", Augustine is unable to adapt herself to her new surroundings, and, after a brief period of felicity, she is destroyed by the effects of her husband's character and mode of existence; in the final words of the story which take up and weld together a whole series of familiar Balzacian metaphors used throughout: "Les humbles et modestes fleurs, écloses dans les vallées, meurent . . . quand elles sont transplantées trop près des cieux, aux régions où se forment les orages, où le soleil est brûlant". This figurative language suggests a thematic preoccupation running deeper than the concern with 'mésalliance' which Balzac, cashing in on his recently established reputation as a diabolically inspired marriage counsellor, appeared anxious to set up at the centre of the work.

In mapping out the antipodes of the story Balzac makes it plain that the basic opposition is between the physical prison of the maison Guillaume and the liberating, heady world of Théodore. The house itself is closed, anachronistic, monastic,

tyrannical; barred and shuttered, antediluvian, empty, it is governed by Guillaume's "principles inexorables", and "pensée symétrique". The "hieroglyphics" on its walls, the dress of its inhabitants, their physiognomies, their language, their gestures, all are signs conspiring, with typically Balzacian fervour, to point inwards to the void which threatens Augustine. Yet a second series of motifs, presented from a different, more sympathetic perspective—less evident and slower to emerge—suggests in M. Guillaume not only a tenacious will to endurance, but also a prudent solicitude for his employees, probity, even "bonté naturelle". There is a third view, also, provided, indirectly by Théodore, a sensuous view compounded of the amorous and the æsthetic, which travelling the façade of the house and glimpsing the interior, sets up painterly "oppositions", creates almost supernatural illuminations, sees in Augustine "un ange exilé du ciel" and in general transposes the observed reality into a work of art, later to result in the two pictures which Théodore exhibits at the *Salon*. These divergent optics prepare for later misunderstandings of value and evaluation. A further set of uncertainties, now concerning the lovers uniquely, is opened up by the images of light and fire used in the portrait of Théodore—"grâce lumineuse," "feu sombre"—and the depiction of the dual nature of the effect of passion on Augustine: "un rayon de soleil était tombé dans cette prison", "cette pantomime [Théodore's amorous signals] jeta comme un brasier dans le corps de la pauvre fille qui se trouva criminelle, en se figurant qu'il venait de se conclure un pacte entre elle et l'artiste"; both these sets of images lead towards the final words of the text already quoted, in which the image of the sun is represented as a force of vivification and of destruction.

Taken together, all these views and images indirectly suggest value, outcome and judgment. Théodore's assessment of Augustine is revealed as superficial; inevitably she disappoints him, and he is in part guilty of her destruction. Augustine lacks the strength to survive the move from the centripetal world of her family to the centrifugal sphere of the prodigal artist; yet her predicament is real and wins sympathy from the author's delegate, an unknown admirer who, appearing in the last lines of the story, obliquely draws attention to Augustine's innocence and her weakness, both of which are present in her character and are to some extent determined by her milieu. The story ends with Augustine's death, yet there is promise of continuation. Joseph Lebas, Guillaume's chief clerk, endures by means of the double mechanism of renunciation and transformation, operations which consistently favour the prudent throughout the *Comédie humaine.* Rejected by Augustine, urged to fall in with the "pensée symétrique" of M. Guillaume, Lebas marries Augustine's tranquil sister Virginie and undertakes to preserve, with some modification, the structure which he has inherited. Unlike the older Guillaumes who are forced upon their retirement to change their milieu, and find themselves "échoués sur un rocher d'or", Lebas and Virginie "[marchent] avec leur siècle", and discover a happiness which, while lacking the intensity of Augustine's two years of passionate felicity, has the virtue of endurance, and hence merits approbation.

Thus the narrator, by means of multiple perspectives and direct and oblique commentary, distributes sympathy and judgment more or less impartially. The basic oppositions within the story and the narrator's more emphatic statements might lead the reader to the view that Balzac's preferences are clear, his sympathy restricted and his condemnation irrevocable. But initial impressions are modified as the characters become more fully known through being seen in changing situations and from different angles. The modes of existence represented are all granted a certain validity and are endowed with a reality which emerges even when a particular character seems close to a stereotype. . . . . In **"La Maison du chat-qui-pelote,"** as in many other works, Balzac's impartiality is not that of the mere observer, but rather that which comes from a deepening of perception and from a progressive revelation of value through knowledge of the characters' lives. It is in this context that it is appropriate to use the term realism to define not the faithfulness with which Balzac reproduces the exterior world but the fidelity with which he expresses the discovered reality of his characters. (pp. 59-65)

Undoubtedly Balzac is hypnotized by the momentum and 'poetry' of his most forceful and absorbing characters to such an extent that he appears incapable of judging them impartially. And yet there are throughout his work recurring moments when the narrator, as at the end of **"Facino Cane,"** disengages himself from even the most passionate, wilful and anarchical destinies, and creates an interlude of contemplative detachment. Such moments of transcendence occur either at a time of movement from life to death (Goriot, Véronique Graslin, Pons) or at a crucial transitional stage from one mode of existence to another. They may be experienced directly by the character, or expressed in hypothetical terms by the detached narrator. An example of the latter occurs in *Le Père Goriot* at the moment when Rastignac is about to isolate himself from his past idealism and fall in with the amorality of Parisian society. The narrator, heretofore almost unfailingly sympathetic toward his hero and closely involved in his actions, draws back and comments:

> Rastignac, semblable à la plupart des jeunes gens, qui, par avance, ont goûté les grandeurs, voulait se présenter tout armé dans la lice du monde; il en avait épousé la fièvre, et sentait peut-être la force de le dominer, mais sans connaître ni les moyens ni le but de cette ambition. A défaut d'un amour pur et sacré, qui remplit la vie, cette soif du pouvoir peut devenir une belle chose; il suffit de dépouiller tout intérêt personnel et de se proposer la grandeur d'un pays pour objet.

In making this analysis the narrator might seem, perhaps, to be playing with mere abstract notions if the reader were not aware of other figures in the *Comédie humaine* in whom these qualities are fully realized—d'Arthez, Michel Chrestien, Joseph Bridau, Bénassis, Bianchon. Such characters are as rare, no doubt, as the moments which call them to mind, but they do exist as a perpetual indication of the heights of Balzac's world. And the Protean narrator, as he regains his position of commentator and judge, demonstrates his awareness of these heights, and opens up a perspective which leads to the difficult discovery of value. (pp. 68-9)

> *Peter W. Lock, "Point of View in Balzac's Short Stories," in* Balzac and the Nineteenth Century, *D. G. Charlton, J. Gaudon, Anthony R. Pugh, eds., Leicester University Press, 1972, pp. 57-69.*

PETER BROOKS   (essay date 1976)

[Brooks is an American essayist, novelist, and academic. In the following excerpt from his The Melodramatic Imagination: Balzac, Henry James, Melodrama, and the Mode of Excess, *he describes Balzac's technique, vision, and ultimate goal in using melodrama in his short stories.]*

An ultimate demonstration of Balzac's engagement with the substance of melodrama might be found in a repeated structure of his short stories and novellas. It has never been much remarked how consistently Balzac's short fiction makes use of the traditional device of the framed tale. The first narrator may himself become the listener to a tale (the principal narrative) related by another, to reappear at the conclusion with the teller of the tale. Or the authorial voice may introduce a narrator and his circle of listeners, who at the end will comment on the tale told. Or there may be a succession of narrators and tales offered to one audience, which comments on their significance in the interstices. **"Gobseck," "Honorine," "L'Auberge rouge," "Z. Marcas," "Facino Cane," "Sarrasine," "Adieu," "Un Prince de la bohème," "Autre Etude de femme,"** are all examples of short fiction in which one of these methods of framing is of major importance. The list is no doubt incomplete, and among the full-length novels *Le Lys dans la vallée* and *Louis Lambert* employ a similar form. What is most significant in the use of the device is the final reflection on the tale or tales told by listeners and tellers, the registering of effect. In **"Facino Cane,"** for example, the story told by the blind musician who is convinced that he is the rightful doge of Venice leads to his extortion of a promise from his interlocutor to set out with him for Venice to recover the lost treasure from the depths of the Doges' Palace—a promise that results less from the interlocutor's conviction that Facino is telling the truth than from his magnetizing narrative presence. Facino dies soon after, leaving in suspense the question of the reality of his vision and the reality of his listener's promise. What we are left with is the force of Facino's tale itself, the haunting vision of treasures piled high in dark vaults, the strength of a belief. More complex and more remarkable still is **"Adieu."** General Philippe de Sucy rediscovers, in a retired country estate, Stéphanie, Comtesse de Vandières, whom he lost at the crossing of the Berezina, on the retreat from Moscow, and who lapsed into madness at that horrific moment, into amnesia and an aphasia from which she can pronounce only one word, her parting cry to Philippe, "Adieu!" Her uncle, the doctor who has been taking care of her, recounts the story of the crossing of the Berezina. This is then followed by another fiction, not recounted, but staged by Philippe, who has the idea that a perfect reconstruction of the moment of crippling trauma might lead to its reversal, to cure. He constructs in his park a reproduction of the banks of the Berezina, complete with its devastation, cannon, and carnage; hires peasants and costumes them as soldiers and cossacks; then, on a December day when snow has fallen, brings Stéphanie to the site. The fiction succeeds: Stéphanie recognizes Philippe, memory and consciousness return, she throws herself into his arms—but only to speak once again her word "Adieu!" and to die. The fiction has proved both curative and mortal, potent and dangerous. It devastates, bringing not only Stéphanie's death but Philippe's suicide as well.

There is in **"Adieu"** a striking dramatization of the potent effect of fiction making, of the stories we tell and enact. Fictions count; they act on life, they change it. As much as in the stage enterprise of a Pixerécourt, there is in Balzac's tale-telling a consciousness of action on a listener, of a life affected. With Balzac, this is not simplistic moralism, but rather a recognition that fictions are, or should be, engaged with the ethical substance of life and should take a moral toll on the reader. Another instance of this is represented in **"Sarrasine,"** which plays off fictions against their effect with considerable complexity. The narrator is asked by the Marquise de Rochefide, whom he is courting, to account both for the aged spectral person found at Mme de Lanty's soirée, and for the *Portrait of Adonis* by Joseph-Marie Vien they have found in Mme de Lanty's boudoir. His satisfaction of her desire implies her reciprocal satisfaction of his (erotic) desire when the tale has been told. His story recounts the sculptor Sarrasine's love for the Roman singer Zambinella, whom he takes for a woman but then discovers to be in fact a *castrato,* whereupon Sarrasine feels himself stricken by sterility, dead to both art and the erotic forever. He attempts to destroy the statue he has made of Zambinella and lifts his sword to punish the singer, but is instead himself struck down by the emissaries of Cardinal Cicognara, Zambinella's protector. The plaster statue is then executed in marble; the *Adonis* of Vien is subsequently copied from the statue (and this canvas in turn is imitated by Girodet for his *Endymion*), while Zambinella lives on, a neuter being who achieves great longevity, a kind of animated specter. Now that all is elucidated, the Marquise de Rochefide imposes silence on the narrator and tells him that he has created in her a disgust for life and love. Passion has been marked by castration in the narrator's tale; art has been discovered to originate, not in the plentitude of "ideal beauty," but in lack, in emptiness. This generalized mark of castration now transgresses the boundaries of the narrator's story to enter his life. As Roland Barthes well demonstrates, castration passes into the very relationship of narrator and interlocutor and renders their liaison impossible. "You know how to punish," the narrator says to the marquise, recognizing that he has been struck.

The last sentence of the novella—"And the Marquise remained pensive"—stands as an emblem of the expansion of the fiction into the lives that it touches. Fiction, in Balzac's conception, exists to make us "pensive," exists to make us reflect on the substance of life and its principles. Implicit here is a theory of reading and the nature of fictional referentiality. If the literary sign is interreferential, without transcendent referent—as the complex interlockings of **"Sarrasine,"** leading us back to an original emptiness, perfectly dramatize—it nonetheless ought, in the view of a writer concerned with the moral substance of life, to provoke this "pensiveness," this reactive reflection in the reader. Fiction is transmissible, and its transmission takes a toll. Through their structure, the tales reveal most clearly the function that Balzac assigns to storytelling. In the simplest and possibly the most pertinent terms, this has been designated by Walter Benjamin, in his essay "The Storyteller," as "Wisdom." Wisdom derives precisely from the carry-over of experience told—told as "counsel" in the living voice of the storyteller—into the experience of the listener; it depends on his remembrance of and reflection on the tale. Balzac is intuitively close to the traditional role and function of the storyteller described by Benjamin.

The analogue of the short fiction's tellers, listeners, commentators in the novels is of course nearly always the insistent narrative presence, with its constant intervention, explanation, emphasis. The narrator articulates both the meaning of his dramatized life and its intended effect. "Consider this: this drama is neither a fiction nor a novel. *All is true,* it is so true that anyone can recognize its elements close to home, in his own heart perhaps," This clarion call from the start of *Le Père Goriot* has many echoes throughout the texture of the narrator's speech. We should not be embarrassed by its excess but consider it as a necessary sign pointing to the melodramatic enterprise, engaging us in a melodramatic reading of the text to follow. Sainte-Beuve accused Balzac of conquering

his public through its secret infirmities, as though he brought (as Freud would announce arriving in America) a kind of irresistible plague. It is certain that this is a literature that wants to act on us, not in the predicative manner of Pixerécourt ("Pixerécourt, you write a drama and we believe in God!"), but through an active solicitation of the reader to enter into the highly colored drama played out behind the banalities of quotidian existence. We know that Balzac was haunted by a feeling that his excessive creation was almost a sacrilegious *imitatio dei,* a Promethean enterprise for which there would surely be a punishment. This could not have been the case had he not believed in the importance of fictions, and in their danger. Fiction making became itself a dangerous enterprise for him precisely because it meant working in the domain of discovery, revelation, laying bare. The motto of the utopian and pastoral *Médecin de campagne,* culled by Doctor Benassis from an inscription in a cell of the Grande Chartreuse—"*Fuge, late, tace*"—stands as a temptation to repose, silence, and the unmelodramatic existence. Yet the very hyperbole of the motto's form suggests the impossibility of its message for Balzac himself. The work had to go on: uncovering, unmasking, pressuring reality to reveal the terms of its drama, capturing the drama through large summary gestures, reorganizing the effects in terms of their causes, wresting meaning from chaos, proclaiming a world inhabited by significance. (pp. 149-52)

Peter Brooks, "Balzac: Representation and Signification," in his The Melodramatic Imagination: Balzac, Henry James, Melodrama, and the Mode of Excess, *Yale University Press, 1976, pp. 110-52.*

MARY SUSAN McCARTHY (essay date 1982)

[*In the following excerpt from* Balzac and His Reader: A Study of the Creation of Meaning in "La comédie humaine," *McCarthy uses "La grande bretèche" to exemplify "the function of structure as it relates to the reception of the text, its dynamics vis-à-vis the reader, and the author's use of a complex design."*]

Pierre Laubriet has claimed [in his *L'Intelligence de l'art chez Balzac*] that Balzac's artistry is most evident in his short stories, because the form demanded more from him than did others, because it concentrated within itself the major characteristics of the other forms, and because it obeyed the laws of the novel, adding a new and significant ingredient in its use of the marvelous. Within the context of my study, the short story serves as an excellent vehicle for examining the relationship between narrative structure and the reception of the text. The nature of the short story, with its many restrictions, makes the structure perhaps its most significant element in relation to the reader.

Through structure, an author can most assuredly position the reader in relation to the text, within or outside the narration, restricting our movement or directing it by dictating to us our interpretive possibilities. We find in structure the grand strategy for controlling reception of the text, the grand strategy that contains the others that I am considering. Structure provides authors with one means of reducing the distance between themselves and their readers and can minimize the difficulties posed by the absence of the reader.

In the short story, the primary restriction of length limits the functioning of all narrative elements. It is then logical to assume that great care must be taken in the development of each narrative element, in particular structure, the framework within which other textual strategies operate. Moreover, structure itself plays an important role in the dynamics of the narration. I maintain that the structure of a short story has more potential than any other narrative element for a complex and intricate manipulation of the reception of the text. Indeed, the carefully designed structure serves well the goals of clarity and simplicity that are of the essence in this form. Thus, using one of Balzac's well-known stories, we can examine the function of structure as it relates to the reception of the text, its dynamic vis-à-vis the reader, and the author's use of a complex design to guide us.

In **"La Grande Bretèche,"** the structure of the narration assigns to us a specific position within the audience represented in the narration itself, as well as a particular role in the fundamental dynamic of the text. Balzac has projected between himself and his reader several other readers who form links in a chain connecting the author to us through his text. The complicated structure of the tale constructs an axis, at the poles of which are narrator and narrataire, speaker and listener, performer and audience, and, by extension, Balzac and his reader. The fundamental association of sender and receiver is mirrored on several levels within the narration, creating a *mise en abîme,* representation within a representation, of transformed images of the relationship (storyteller to audience) that links us to the author himself. This multiplication of the axis, which is the essence of narrative dynamics, necessarily draws us into the story, linking the fictional and the nonfictional recipients of the tale, blending reality and fiction. The structure of the narration then reduces the distance between the actual and the projected reader, fostering our active participation in the coproduction of **"La Grande Bretèche."** It engages us in the narrative process itself and, in so doing, enhances the impact of the total narration upon us. Thus, the structure upon which this short story rests permitted Balzac to generate with his reader an *abîme* of relationships that parallel the essential relationship established upon our reception of the tale.

Diana Festa McCormick claimed that Balzac was "un très grand auteur de nouvelles, le plus varié et le plus original en francais" ("a very great short story writer, the most varied and the most original in French"). She stated that the goal of the short story writer was to work through the form's many restrictions in order to capture and fascinate the audience, to suggest rather than to say. **"La Grande Bretèche"** not only does what she has suggested but also represents the actual process of enchantment and engagement. The tale becomes both a successful short story and a commentary on its own effect, process, creation, and reception. Although **"La Grande Bretèche"** shares its fundamental structure (based on the manipulation of the framed tale and on the *mise en abîme*) with numerous other short stories, it is perhaps an extreme example, one more highly complicated than the others and clearer in its manipulation of the reader, especially as it indulges us in our search for literary pleasure. Inscribed in every level of the narration is the specific goal of audience entertainment, and it is that goal, pleasure, that directs the story toward its recipients and that focuses the narration upon its own reception. The pleasure that is ours is the pleasure of the charmed listener, the enchanted recipient of the tale. Thus, each of the three smaller narrations within the story, and the larger one of **"La Grande Bretèche"** itself, becomes an object of value. Indeed, the very process of narration, even more than the event being narrated, is the heart of the story.

The structure of **"La Grande Bretèche"** is rendered even more interesting by its placement as the final narration of four assembled under the title of **"Autre Etude de femme."** Nicole Mozet has called this collection a puzzle made of pieces of diverse origin. That it is tied to three other narrations within the context of **"Autre Etude de femme"** (after dinner storytelling) squarely places **"La Grande Bretèche"** in the milieu of entertainment, specifically, entertainment of an audience represented within the narration itself. Its placement in **"Autre Etude de femme"** makes **"La Grande Bretèche"** itself a puzzle, just one piece of a larger configuration. The most significant advantage to this positioning, however, is that it permits the actual representation of the audience, whose enthusiasm gives us a formal point of entry into the narration, an easily assumed position, and a clearly defined role. Furthermore, it puts us squarely in the presence of the narrator (one of the dinner guests), whose task it is to entertain us. By suggestion, at least, we will be as susceptible as the other members of the audience to the narrator's charm. Although we are initially outside **"La Grande Bretèche"** (its structure will reduce that distance), we are most clearly within the larger narration because we are fictionally represented there. As we take our place as members of the audience, we complete the axis narrator-narrataire; we are the audience for whom the narration is designed.

The context of the dinner party places us as well within an atmosphere of congeniality, relaxation, and enthusiasm. Not content simply to suggest that atmosphere, Balzac had his narrator stress it, explaining that it is the second and the better half of the evening, when only "quelques artistes, des gens gais, des amis" ("a few artists, high-spirited people, friends") remain: "la seconde, la véritable soirée . . . où l'on est forcé d'avoir de l'esprit et de contribuer à l'amusement public" ("the second, the true evening . . . where one is obliged to have wit and to contribute to the general amusement"). The narrator clearly announces what the structure will reveal: the audience is of extreme importance to this narration, to its completion and interpretation, and to the forces that will permit it to function. . . . To entice us even further into the narrations to come and into our role within their production, the narrator adds, "Jamais le phénomène oral qui, bien étudié, bien manié, fait la puissance de l'acteur et du conteur, ne m'avait si complètement ensorcelé" ("Never had oral performance, which when well studied and handled is the strength of the actor and the storyteller, so completely bewitched me"). As a final gesture of assurance, one that particularly emphasizes the goal of entertainment and the enthusiasm of the group, the narrator ends his preparatory remarks:

> Est-il besoin de dire qu'il n'y avait plus de domestiques, que les portes étaient closes et les portières tirées? Le silence fut si profond qu'on entendit dans la cour le murmure des cochers, les coups de pied et les bruits que font les chevaux en demandant à revenir à l'écurie.
>
> (It is necessary to say that there were no longer any servants present, that the doors had been closed and the curtains drawn? The silence was so complete that one could hear the sounds of the coachmen in the courtyard, the sounds of the horses' hooves and the noises that they make when they want to return to the stable.)

Thus, the narrator sets the stage for the four tales to come, encouraging us to see ourselves as part of the group of listeners, a group that he describes as consisting of the brightest personalities, the most sophisticated wits, and the best of friends.

The atmosphere created in the opening is maintained and enhanced throughout the recitation of the first three tales, which build up to the opening of **"La Grande Bretèche."** This last of the four narrations is introduced in a manner appropriate to the structure upon which it is built and to the dynamic that will propel it. It also introduces the singular element that serves as the catalyst for each internal narration within **"La Grande Bretèche"** as well as for the whole, that is, the desire of the recipient to hear another tale, the curiosity of the listener that entices the narrator to go on. The movement of **"La Grande Bretèche"** hinges upon the desire of the recipients represented in the text, and the structure depends on this element for its effectiveness. The transition then from the third narration in **"Autre Etude de femme"** to the fourth, **"La Grande Bretèche,"** is the expression of desire from the audience, and it establishes the axis between narrator and narrataire as well as the significance of audience approval and pleasure. (pp. 73-8)

One might well apply to **"La Grande Bretèche"** the description of structure that Nicole Mozet offered for **"Autre Etude de femme,"** "une vertigineuse construction en abîme" ("a dizzying and cavernous construction"). The structure of **"La Grande Bretèche"** creates the relationship that propels the entire narration, creates the very relationship that allows it to exist as structure. Not only does it establish the axis between storyteller and audience, but it multiplies and mirrors it at every level of the narration. Through this mirrorlike representation of the context and essence of narration, of the basic relationship between Balzac and his reader, every detail of the narration is placed within the framework that maintains contact with and entertains the active and subjective reader. The cause-and-effect relationship that functions along this axis is reciprocal: impact of the narration shapes audience response, which in turn shapes the form and the art of story-telling. The cause-and-effect relationship, so basic to all literature, is duplicated and transformed throughout **"La Grande Bretèche"** as the narrator, Bianchon, becomes the recipient of the tale and as former recipients step forward to narrate portions of it.

"La Grande Bretèche" contains three separate blocks of narration, each with its own narrator. Although each block relates to the central event of the story, each one pertains to a period different from the others (before, during, and after the central event). Because the individual blocks of narration give us new information to be integrated into the whole of our perception, we are moved closer to the central event. From another point of view, however, one could say that the block structure removes us by several degrees from the event itself. All three narrators have been recipients of their narrations and within **"La Grande Bretèche"** relate their tales to Bianchon, who, in turn, tells them at the dinner party. At least four receptions of the tale or bits of it precede ours, and the last two of those are represented within the narration itself. Thus, each block of narration revolves around an axis like the fundamental one of the text, linking narrator and narrataire, creating the *mise en abîme* upon which this structure rests and activating its dynamic cycle of desire and narration. Rather than the horrible story of Mme de Merret, the recitation and reception of the tale stand before us and compose, essentially, the theme of **"La Grande Bretèche"**: as each block engenders the next, using as sole transition the response

of the narrator-turned-narrataire, Bianchon, we become part of the dynamic in which the curiosity of the audience engenders a narration, which evokes a response from the audience, which leads to another narration, until the process is abruptly brought to an end. The focus of the tale thus falls squarely on the acts of narration and reception and on the transaction between audience and narrator. Thus, although we are separated by so many recipients from the event being narrated, we are not separated from the narration of **"La Grande Bretèche"** itself because our position and our function are so clearly framed within.

Bianchon's presentation of **"La Grande Bretèche"** opens with a description of the old house and the property that gives its name to the short story. The estate is portrayed mysteriously, its ruinous condition being the result of some unknown and probably awful event. Moreover, the opening description, mirroring the pattern of **"Autre Etude de femme,"** is put into a context of entertainment: Bianchon visited the abandoned property for the pleasureable effect it had upon him and upon his imagination. In fact, the pleasure kept him from wanting to know the truth about the old house, for fear that it would be less interesting than his own fabrications. But the very fact that the property arouses his curiosity or a desire for a narration (his own more than what he receives) is enough to engender the first block of narration, from which he and we find the first of the essential facts of the tale.

The opening description, however, is not merely a pretense to usher in the first of the supplementary narrators. It sets the tone for the narration to come. It combines realistic and abstract description as it alternately focuses our attention on the narration itself and on the narrator. The description is realistic enough in detail—"Quelques saules, nés dans le Loir, ont rapidement poussé comme la haie de clôture et cachent à demi la maison" ("Willows with their roots in the Loir have grown quickly, like the boundary hedge, and half conceal the house")—but the narrator interprets and transforms each detail to indicate its effect upon him and the questioning that it provoked, passing on to us a sense of the Gothic atmosphere that enshrouded the property: "D'énormes lézardes sillonnent les murs, dont les crêtes noircies sont enlacées par les mille festons de la pariétaire" ("Enormous cracks furrow the walls, whose blackened tops are festooned by a thousand garlands of pellitory"). Clearly, the description of milieu points to a grand cause and is designed to evoke in us the desire for search (to be fulfilled by the narration): "Une invisible main a partout écrit le mot: MYSTÈRE!" ("Everywhere an invisible hand has written the word MYSTERY"). The description focuses our attention not only upon the deserted property but also upon the narrator in the midst of all that he describes. Even as the house is represented as the effect of some terrible cause, it becomes the cause of a significant effect upon the narrator: "Quel feu tombé du ciel a passé par là? Quel tribunal a ordonné de semer du sel sur ce logis?—Y a-t-on insulté Dieu? Y a-t-on trahi la France? Voilà ce qu'on se demande" ("What fire from heaven has fallen this way? What court of law has given the order to scatter salt on this dwelling? Has God been insulted here? Has France been betrayed here? These are the questions you ask yourself"). The narrator concludes his impression of the property with the only interpretation possible: "Cette maison, vide et déserte, est une immense énigme dont le mot n'est connu de personne" ("The empty deserted house is an immense riddle to which no one knows the answer"). The key to the enigma will be contained only in the narration, which then becomes a necessity. Thus, the description represents the process by which we are to be drawn into the narration as well as our function within it. We must allow ourselves to be seized by the narration as Bianchon was by the sight of the property. We must question both cause and effect, allowing our curiosity and imagination to be aroused. (pp. 78-81)

The focus on the narrator in relation to the object described is significant for another reason as well. Bianchon's response to the sight is one of imagination and sensitivity, his description delicately drawn. Thus, the narrator is established as a talented one, a narrator from whom we can anticipate an entertaining and sensitive narration. Furthermore, he is represented here as a recipient (not yet of the narrations, but at least of the impact of the scene), and so our identification with him in that role begins.

We then move to the first block of narration and to a new narrator, M. Regnault. In general terms, the change of narrator focuses our attention once again on the narrative process, adding a certain intensity and vivacity to the storytelling. Moreover, it keeps us just the slightest bit off balance as Bianchon relinquishes in part his role as narrator to assume ours as narrataire. Bianchon retains the floor long enough, however, to offer us a caricature of the next narrator, a humorous portrayal of M. Regnault's appearance and dress that draws a sharp contrast to the seriousness of the opening description, its somber mood, and the excitement that its mystery stirred. . . . The caricature specifically draws our attention away from the deserted property and focuses it upon this character and even more directly upon the act of narration and the goal of entertainment. Even while it stalls the delivery of M. Regnault's narration, the caricature draws us into the text, enticing us with the curious question of what relationship could possibly exist between this character and the abandoned property. It arouses our curiosity, our desire for the next narration. Even as M. Regnault begins that narration, we are engaged in the appropriate search for clues about the truth of the old house, and we learn that many before us have sought these clues—"monsieur, je n'en finirais pas si je vous répétais tous les contes qui se sont débités à [l'égard de Mme de Merret]" ("Monsieur, I would never finish if I were to repeat to you all the stories which have been told about [Mme de Merret]).

The narration, however, offers only a few facts regarding the property: Mme de Merret, its owner, ordained in her last testament that the property not be entered or altered in any way until fifty years after her death; M. de Merret died alone in Paris, worn out by debauchery; Mme de Merret died a horrible death to which Regnault was a witness, after she had already abandoned the property in question. Bianchon's curiosity is aroused by the tale—despite a preference for his own romanticized versions of the story behind **"La Grande Bretèche."** "Il me fallait dire adieu à mes belles rêveries, à mes romans; je ne fus donc pas rebelle au plaisir d'apprendre la vérité d'une manière officielle" ("I had to bid farewell to my beautiful daydreams, to my romances. So I had no objection to the pleasure of learning the truth officially").

We witness then another scene in which Bianchon, the narrator-narrataire, is himself drawn into this narration. It is the narration itself, the "manière officielle," that pleases him more than the truth. Regnault's narration builds to a high point in the description of the death of Mme de Merret. Its intensity and its evocative language return us to the Gothic atmosphere alluded to at the opening of the short story. Re-

gnault himself, however, places the scene squarely in the context of storytelling: "Ah! mon cher monsieur, si vous aviez vu, comme je la vis alors, cette vaste chambre tendue en tapisseries brunes, vous vous seriez cru transporté dans une véritable scène de roman") ("Oh, my dear sir, if you had seen, as I did then, that enormous room draped with brown tapestries, you would have thought you had been transported into a veritable scene from a novel"). Indeed, storytelling is of the essence; when Regnault's narration becomes too confusing and boring or when it is delivered in a monotone, Bianchon steps in to take over again as narrator. Bianchon tells us Regnault's "observations étaient si contradictoires, si diffuses, que je faillis m'endormir, malgré l'intérêt que je prenais à cette histoire authentique" ("observations were so contradictory and so diffuse, that I almost fell asleep in spite of the interest which I took in this true story"). Only the well-told tale is worth the telling.

Even within this first block of narration, the internal cause-and-effect relationships are being altered, crossed, and transformed. The property is the effect of some terrible cause. It, in turn, causes Bianchon's curiosity to be aroused. That curiosity leads inevitably to M. Regnault's narration, spurring Bianchon to seek more information about the house and its story. But Regnault's narration is of the effect; he does not know the cause of Mme de Merret's actions, the terrible event behind the abandonment of the house. On the level of the short story itself, we are moving ever so slowly in the reverse direction of the mystery, from effect to cause. Structurally, however, the direction is clearly the contrary, from cause to effect, from desire to narration. At the time of Regnault's story, the relationship between the event narrated and its narration is singularly different from that established between the narration and its recipients. Nevertheless, as recipients we participate in both, which permits us to anticipate and to seek out the next block of narration, simultaneously questioning it in both a forward and a backward movement in an effort to relate cause and effect definitively.

The independent blocks of narration are joined by the observation, reactions, and reflections of Bianchon who reassumes his role as narrator. Each transition is tied to the opening of the story, reevoking the Gothic atmosphere of the property and focusing upon the imagination and sensitivity of Bianchon. The opening description, in conjunction with the transitions between blocks of narration, forms a context into which the facts of the tale are incorporated. It is a context that presents the act of reception, the search in progress, and the pleasure that they yield. Between the narration of M. Regnault and the one that follows, there is a short yet significant passage:

> je m'assis dans mon fauteuil, en mettant mes pieds sur les deux chenets de ma cheminée. Je m'enfonçais dans un roman à la Radcliffe, bâti sur les données juridiques de M. Regnault, quand ma porte, manoeuvrée par la main adroite d'une femme, tourna sur ses gonds.
>
> (I sat down in my armchair, putting my feet on the two firedogs in my fireplace. I became absorbed in a Radcliffe-like novel, based on the legal information given by Monsieur Regnault, when my door manipulated by a woman's light hand, turned on its hinges.)

We discover here the reaction of Bianchon to Regnault's tale, and the questioning to which that reaction leads offers to the

Portrait of Mme Hanska as a young woman.

reader an example of appropriate participation, as Bianchon ties together the Gothic atmosphere of the opening and the newly discovered facts. He still has insufficient evidence to begin serious detective work, however. What is essential, though, is the example he sets as narrataire and the attendant possibility for reader identification with that role. We are represented in the text not only in the form of the audience to whom Bianchon recounts his tale, but in the character of Bianchon himself as he dons the recipient's role and then, as narrator, comments upon it, accelerating our interest in the unfolding story with his own and further demonstrating the significance of Bianchon's alternating roles vis-à-vis the reader. The process permits, even encourages, identification with Bianchon. Built into the text, then, is the mechanism by which we are able to place ourselves within the narration at various levels, perceiving the relationship of recipient to narration mirrored throughout and perceiving as well the desire-and-narration cycle.

Bianchon's desire, the effect of the first narration, becomes the catalyst for the second, that of the hotel keeper, Mère Lepas. Because her block of information involves a leap to a temporal plane anterior to that of Regnault's narration, she is able to offer the first bits of information about the reasons behind Mme de Merret's testament. With this block, the story takes a new turn and requires of us a greater degree of association, questioning, and guessing. As Mère Lepas presents more questions to be answered, our desire for a specific narration increases, for the narration that will unlock the mystery of the abandoned property. Bianchon clearly indicates his desire as he coaxes the hotel keeper to give him more information, applying pressure when she resists. "Ma chère

dame Lepas! ajoutai-je en terminant, vous paraissez en savoir davantage. Hein? Autrement pourquoi seriez-vous montée chez moi? . . . vos yeux sont gros d'un secret. Vous avez connu M. de Merret. Quel homme était-ce?" (" 'Madame Lepas, my good woman,' I added as I finished. 'You seem to know more about it, don't you? Otherwise, why did you come up to my room? . . . Your eyes are laden with a secret. You knew Monsieur de Merret. What kind of a man was he?' "). We learn from Mère Lepas the story of the Spaniard whom she suspects of a liaison with Mme de Merret. He returned late each night to the hotel but was once found swimming across the river from La Grande Bretèche, and, finally, he mysteriously disappeared some time before Mme de Merret abandoned her property. The puzzle begins to take some shape, and our hypothesizing (mirrored within by the Gothic romanticizing and the specific questioning of Bianchon) is given some direction. Mère Lepas offers us information to tie her narration with that of Regnault, information that points equally to the narration to come. (A central object in **"La Grande Bretèche"** is a crucifix that Regnault says Mme de Merret kissed as a final gesture before her death. Mère Lepas tells us that the Spaniard possessed one identical to it but no longer had it when he disappeared.) As we leap from after to before the central event, from the effect to the cause, the narration assumes a form for us that is not presented in the text itself. The narration of Mère Lepas is filled with signs to guide us, not the least of which is the final one, pointing us directly to the next narrator. When Bianchon asks Mère Lepas if she has not questioned Rosalie, who works for her but who worked previously for Mme de Merret, Mère Lepas responds, "Cette fille-là, c'est un mur. Elle sait quel-que chose; mais il est impossible de la faire jaser." ("That girl, she's like a wall. She knows something but it's impossible to get her to spill the beans"). She thus closes her narration on a note of suspense but with a clear indication of the direction Bianchon is to take. On all levels of the narration, now, we are moving from cause to effect: one narrator points to another; one narration generates another; and we close in on the narration of the event at the heart of the tale.

The transition between this block of narration and the one to follow is more interesting and certainly more provocative than the first transition. Not content simply to recall the atmosphere of the opening description, Bianchon adds to it by creating new effects of mystery and the fantastic, enhancing the entertainment value of this block of narration by embellishing it. (pp. 82-7)

Within this atmosphere, then, the imagination and the curiosity of Bianchon are aroused to such a degree that inevitably he seeks out the third narration. We witness the process shown in this transition, however, through the attention he has fixed on the next narrator, following the lead of Mère Lepas. Bianchon describes in such detail his concentration upon the new narrator that we as well are forced to focus our attention upon Rosalie, the key to the narration we seek. Indeed, Rosalie takes on a symbolic value vis-à-vis the story being narrated, because she alone knows the most significant portion of the tale. But she also bears symbolic value in relation to the structural dynamic that is so important to our reading. Clearly, hers is the final block. Her narration will bring us as close to the center as we are able to get, as close to the actual event as is possible. Thus, the narrator concentrates upon her and upon his own reaction to her. Still, as narrator, he anticipates his role as recipient of her narration. The more he dwells upon her (and, therefore, as we do), the more

symbolic value she acquires as keeper of the narrative. . . .
All that has come before in **"La Grande Bretèche"** acts upon
Bianchon, once again narrative, now that he is so near to receiving the final narration, indeed, "the last chapter of [his]
novel," and to satisfying his desire. This is a high point of suspense in the narration for the narrator and audience alike.
Bianchon coaxes Rosalie to relinquish her narration, just as,
earlier, the audience had begged him to recount his tale.
Bianchon underscores the importance of his desire for the
narration and the way in which it serves as catalyst within
the narrative process. . . . Bianchon brings us to the edge of
the desired narration (after considerable stalling), but he
abruptly substitutes himself for Rosalie as narrator, emphasizing once again the goal of entertainment and the proposition that a tale is not worth telling unless it is well told. He
abbreviates what she has told him, explaining the event that
led to the abandonment of the property, the first two narrations, and, indirectly, his own search. On a structural level,
all that has come before has pointed us to this narration, prepared us for it, and made us await it with little patience. Rosalie's story is the effect of all that has preceded it in the text;
it is the structural completion or conclusion. On the narrative
level, however, it is the cause and not the effect of all that precedes it in the narration.

As Bianchon introduces the final block of narration, he signals to us yet another leap in time, reinforcing the concept
of countermovements of cause and effect within the structure
of the story. The opposite movements of the tale itself and of
its reading converge in the final narration, for which we have
been so fully prepared that only a few words need be spoken.

> Or, comme l'événement dont [Rosalie] me donna
> la confuse connaissance se trouve placé entre le ba-
> vardage du notaire et celui de Mme Lepas, aussi ex-
> actement que les moyens termes d'un proportion
> arithmétique le sont entre leurs deux extrèmes, je
> n'ai plus qu'à vous le dire en peu de mots. J'abrège
> donc.

> (Now, since the event of which [Rosalie] gave me
> a jumbled account is situated between the lawyer's
> and Madame Lepas' gossip as exactly as the middle
> terms of an arithmetical progression are between
> their two extremes, it only remains for me to tell it
> to you in a few words. So I abbreviate.)

In the third block of narration, then, Bianchon supplies only
the barest details, with neither interpretation nor association
with former passages. Nothing impedes the swift delivery of
the story. Speaking in a considerably accelerated rhythm,
Bianchon races to the climax of the tale with none of his former romanticizing. In this part of the short story, he is a pure
narrator, no longer a narrataire. We therefore learn quickly
the story at the heart of **"La Grande Bretèche"**: how M. de
Merret walled his wife's lover, the Spaniard, into a closet even
as he forced her to swear upon her crucifix that there was no
one inside and how he remained with her in the room for
twenty days as the Spaniard died. The end of the tale forces
us to reconsider each detail of the preceding narrations: her
terrible death, his in Paris, the state of the house, her last testament, the Spaniard in the river, the crucifix, and so on.
Once we have received the final narration, details fall into
their proper order, leaving us the task of rearranging all that
we have learned, a process that is not part of our actual reading but one that follows the reading once the narrator has
given us our leave.

The final passage of **"La Grande Bretèche"** (at which point
we are released) presents the reaction of the audience to
Bianchon's narration, thrusting us suddenly back to the outer
layer of the structure. That is, we return to the narrator-
audience axis exterior to the narration of **"La Grande Bretèche"** but interior to that of the collection, **"Autre Etude de
femme."** The conclusion completes the transaction that has,
by the mirroring of the narrator-narrataire axis and the block
structure, guided us to the center of the *abîme* and out again.

> Après ce récit, toutes les femmes se levèrent de
> table, et le charme sous lequel Bianchon les avait
> tenues fut dissipé par ce mouvement. Néanmoins
> quelques-unes d'entre elles avaient eu quasi froid en
> entendant le dernier mot.

> (After this story, all the women rose from the table,
> and the charm under which Bianchon had held
> them was dissipated by this movement. Neverthe-
> less, some among them had had something like a
> chill on hearing the last word.)

The dispersal of the group signals the end of its desire for further narration, and, thus, **"Autre Etude de femme"** comes to
a close. The cycle of desire-narration has been broken. The
concluding passage represents a second denouement to the
action that interrupts and therefore destroys the axis between
narrator and narrataire. The representation of the effect of
the narration at this level is certainly parallel to the frequent
representation of Bianchon's reaction to the various narrations within **"La Grande Bretèche."** It invites us to consider
our own reaction and the axis that exists between us as readers and Balzac as raconteur. The response of the audience is
important commentary on storytelling; even among
Bianchon's highly sophisticated audience, the well-told tale
has its magic power. So when we step back and rearrange the
pieces, we realize that the response of the recipient—
Bianchon, his audience, and ourselves—remains in large
measure the focus of the short story.

Clearly, a mystery story like **"La Grande Bretèche,"** a tale
for which the impact of the final scenes is of the greatest importance, relies on two facts: our reading follows a certain
order; through that ordered reading, information can be
withheld or given so as to maximize the impact of the ending
when all falls into place. The structure of **"La Grande Bretèche"** is the single most significant element in the control of
its reading and in the preparation of the reader for the impact
of the ending. It is largely because of the tale's complicated
structure that we are kept off balance, that the all-important
desire for narration is kept alive, that the tone is varied and
roles exchanged, and, finally, that we can function on various
temporal levels at once. More than simply controlling our interpretation, structure manipulates us into a position vis-à-vis
the narration itself so that all the other narrative elements
enjoy their fullest role in relation to the reader. In **"La Grande Bretèche,"** it is the structure that permits us to see ourselves reflected within the narration and that permits us to
become in part its subject. Furthermore, it is the structure
that induces us to contemplate the relationship between author and reader. The complexity of the structure and the
complicity that its dynamic requires of us, then, together
serve the text's stated goal, entertainment. (pp. 88-92)

Mary Susan McCarthy, in her Balzac and His
Reader: A Study of the Creation of Meaning in "La
comédie humaine," *University of Missouri Press,
1982, 155 p.*

DOROTHY J. KELLY (essay date 1985)

[*In the following excerpt, Kelly notes subtle differences between messages the narrator is asked to deliver in Balzac's "Le message" and the information he actually conveys.*]

In the very first sentence of Balzac's **"Le Message,"** the narrator describes his story as "une histoire simple et vraie." Yet very little, in fact, is at all simple in this complicated tale whose elements are woven together in intricate recurring patterns. We might begin, for example, by asking ourselves a "simple" question: what *is* the message in this story? The answer at first seems to be rather clear. While traveling, the narrator makes the acquaintance of a stranger who, like the narrator, loves an older, married woman. Unfortunately, during the voyage, the carriage overturns and crushes the stranger who, with his last breath, implores the narrator to do three things: first, to personally inform his mistress of his death; second, to take a key to his mother who would in turn give the narrator the love letters of his mistress; and third, to return these letters to "Juliette," his nickname for his mistress, the Countess of Montpersan. These three tasks constitute the "message" that the narrator must deliver. Thus from the outset, there is no simple, single message, but a complicated tripartite circuit of exchanges that have different destinations and purposes.

The bulk of the story recounts how the narrator goes about delivering his messages. He begins by taking the news to the stranger's family, and after picking up the letters there, he proceeds to the home of the Countess of Montpersan. When he first arrives at her home, he meets her as she is walking with her husband and child, and naturally finds himself in a very awkward situation, finally asking to speak to the *count* in private. He arranges then to speak with Juliette, and eventually conveys his message of death to her. The remainder of the story recounts the effects that the messages have on the various characters: the count dangerously gorges himself on dinner, to the delight of his daughter; and the countess disappears for the day, finally visiting the narrator in his room that night to learn all the details. The next day, the countess delicately helps the narrator with money and he returns to Paris.

If we now turn to the messages themselves, we find that most of them are curiously never directly transmitted. First of all, when the narrator arrives at the castle of Montpersan, he does not literally tell Juliette that her lover is dead, as we see in the dialogue between the two characters:

> —Cela est-il vrai? oh! dites-moi la vérité, je puis l'entendre. Dites! Toute douleur me sera moins poignante que ne l'est mon incertitude.
>
> Je répondis par deux larmes que m'arrachèrent les étranges accents par lesquels ces phrases furent accompagnées.

Death is *not* directly announced to her; the narrator brings instead a "non-dit," a non-message, so to speak. In fact, the narrator lies to her at first, for when she asks if her lover still lives, he replies, "Oui, Madame."

Hence, the message of death is never *literally* transmitted, but it is *symbolically* transmitted, because the tears of the narrator do reveal the truth. The tears represent his sadness in the face of Juliette's anguish and tragedy, and she correctly "reads" these symbols. The message of death is therefore communicated by a signifier (or a "symbol," here a metonymy), the tears, which stand for the signified, death. The truth

about death is not literally comunicated in this story, but it is either negated and suppressed totally in the narrator's lie, or indirectly expressed, displaced metonymically in a system of signifiers and signifieds.

But why must death be represented metonymically and not literally? What link exists between death and the signifier? We may find part of the answer in the second "failure" of the narrator to accomplish his mission. When he arrives at the stranger's home where he must give the key to the stranger's mother, he finds that she is absent. He contents himself, rather thankfully, with giving the key to a substitute for the stranger's mother, to an old servant woman who represents the mother metaphorically. Again, he inserts the message of death into a system of signifiers and substitutions. Here it is not a message destined to a lover, but to a mother. The fact that these two messages can only be transmitted indirectly establishes a parallel between the message to the mother and the message to the lover. As we can now see, the message in and of the text is anything but simple: death, substitution, mothers, lovers, signifiers combine in a system where it is impossible, or at least very difficult, to deliver a message. When the narrator says of this problem, "Il m'était alors assez difficile de m'acquitter de mon message," commenting upon the problem posed by the mere physical distance, his words become charged with a greater significance.

As we said earlier, there is a parallel between the message to the mother and the message to the lover, because they must be indirectly transmitted. In this story, one's message (signifier) to the mother cannot attain its real goal of the mother, and one's message to one's lover is replaced by a substitute for the real thing. This parallel between the message to the mother and the message to the lover does not remain a mere formal one, for the lovers in this story are of a very special kind. The fast friendship between the narrator and the stranger grows because they both share the same type of lover and love affair:

> Jeunes tous deux, nous n'en étions encore, l'un et l'autre, qu'à la *femme d'un certain âge,* c'est-à-dire à la femme qui se trouve entre trente-cinq et quarante ans.

Here the parallel between lover and mother becomes more apparent: the lovers of the two young men are almost old enough, or old enough, to be their *mothers.* The play of substitutions in messages to lovers and in addressees as mothers perhaps points to the need for substitution itself, and to the impossibility of representing the "real" Oedipal message of love to the mother. This message must always appear in a disguised form, signified by something else. It must always be displaced so that it never quite reaches its goal. Furthermore, this love-relation type shared by the two young men relates somehow to fear, to a vague and unnamed dread, as if they feel guilty for some reason. When they confess that they both love older women, they are "délivrés l'un et l'autre d'une espèce de crainte vague . . . ". Indeed, the filial relation disguised in the love for an older woman is reflected in the fraternal relation disguised in the alliance between the two young men who are "con*frères* en amour [emphasis added]."

We must approach this substitution of lovers for mothers very cautiously, for never in the text is this substitution made literally explicit. But it would be wrong to assume that because it is not made literally explicit, it does not exist or it is not important or it has no effect. The story itself shows us that messages which are not overtly expressed, but only symbolically alluded to, still communicate things, affect people, and have importance, such as in the case of the symbolic message of death sent to Juliette. The love relation with the mother is that which is in fact absent, just as the mother is absent, and can only play its role in our interpretation as an absent term. This structure resembles, in fact, that of the functioning of metaphor in Lacan's description: he states that the absent term creates meaning.

Indeed, it is extremely important that the message *not* be communicated literally, that it be transmitted as a euphemism. The stranger begs the narrator to deliver the message personally, because if he doesn't, Juliette will learn of it in too direct and blunt a manner. . . . We may perhaps interpret the deflection of this message as an allegory of the deflection involved in signifiers in general, especially since in almost every case of a message in this story, the message is not expressed directly by words but indirectly by a rather "physical" signifier. And we are, of course, invited to deduce something about messages or symbols since the very title of the story is **"Le Message."** We will discuss these "physical" signifiers at length after we investigate the "signified" of the narrator's message.

To return to the substitution of lovers for mothers, if we allow this Oedipal relation to play out its role veiled, we can perhaps clarify several other relations and structures in the text. As we noted before, there is a need for the veiling of the death of the stranger, a need for the repression of its brutality. In addition, the stranger brings about his own death; it is his *fault:* "—Encore y eut-il un peu de sa faute, me disait le conducteur." In relating this guilt and death to the Oedipal complex where castration (death) is the punishment for incest, we see that the stranger's fate parallels that of Oedipus. His story therefore may relay a certain hidden message about the Oedipal situation. (pp. 48-51)

For the narrator, this story of death carries a message whose primary function is to affect and form a love relation. It would accomplish this by a threat of loss, a threat of death that is again symbolically represented (never literally) by the serpent. Hence the story aims at putting lovers back on the right track, into each others arms, by showing them the menace of a threatening situation which they should avoid. This threatening situation, on a symbolic level, would be an incestuous love for the mother, symbolized by the love for an older woman, which interferes with the "normal" course of love, and which, of course, threatens one with death.

Now that we have perhaps described a hidden message, which can never be literalized in this text, we may return to our initial question, "What is the message?", in order to look not at the signifieds but at the signifiers that compose them. We have already seen that the message of death sent from the stranger to Juliette is sent in symbols (tears) that are never literalized. In the second part of the message, the stranger sends a key to his mother. The word "key" is, of course, always loaded with significance because it is an essential part of the unlocking of something hidden or protected (or repressed). It also has the more figural meaning of the essential part of a system. It is a privileged signifier. In the text, we first encounter this "key" in a rather gruesome way. . . . The narrator extracts the key from the stranger's body, as if it were a part of him, and the key leaves a wound in its absence. The relation here between this scene and a symbolic castration should be fairly evident, especially when the narrator

calls it a "fatale clef." This key, this key signifier, (the phallus in Lacan's terms) sent to the mother, links up with the desire of a dying man. It is interesting to note that tears, the key, and later a lock of hair, are in one way or another all "parts" of the body which have been detached from it. (This further links these signifiers with Lacan's concept of the phallus.)

But, because of deflection, the key can only arrive at a substitute for the mother, the old servant. Curiously, in the case of the message to the *other* mother substitute, Juliette, a very similar thing happens. The narrator actually gives Juliette a part of the stranger's body, just as he gives the servant the "key." . . . The key links up with the stranger's desire for the mother (it is the stranger's message directed to his mother) and the lock of hair links up with the substitute mother's desire for the stranger. Thus, these signifiers play an important role in defining and mapping out the desires of the various characters. The path of the communication of desire is a triangular one: from the stranger through the key to the mother, from the mother through the lock of hair to the stranger. The triangular structure shows the need for a third term in signification, of a third "space" that is the place of communication. This triangular pattern recurs in almost every relay of messages in the text. Let us investigate several of these to understand this structure a little better.

In one case, when the narrator arrives at the castle of Montpersan, he tries to find the best way to break the tragic news to Juliette. Feeling more and more desperate as Juliette and her husband approach him, he finally decides upon a method of attack:

> —Monsieur le comte, je voudrais vous parler en particulier, dis-je d'un air mystérieux et en faisant quelques pas en arrière.

Again we see that the message cannot arrive directly at its destination, but must first make a detour; here through Juliette's husband who occupies the symbolic place of the father in the Oedipal triangle. The message of desire and death goes not only to the symbolic mother but through and to the father also. The husbands in the story fulfill the specifications of this Oedipal "place" for they represent a *danger* for the couple lover/wife (child/mother). . . . (pp. 52-3)

Another indirect message, that more than adequately accomplishes its purpose, travels from Juliette to the narrator at the end of the story. As the narrator prepares to leave, the count of Montpersan approaches him and asks if he would oblige him by remitting a certain sum of money to an acquaintance in Paris. The narrator does so very willingly because, having spent all his money, he needs to use the sum to get back to Paris where he could replace it. . . . Here the actual signifier which circulates is money, the "universal signifier." Coming from Juliette, it represents the message of gratitude for, and a real return of, the favor accomplished by the narrator. But to get this message to the narrator, Juliette must go through a third term, her husband (again, the triangular structure, although more complicated here). This message is, in fact, so well disguised that the narrator does not understand it until the very end. Yet even though it is indirect, and not even understood by him, it *works.* It *must* in fact take a circuitous path so that the narrator will *not* literally understand the message. Juliette exercises "discrétion," tact in the face of "une pauvreté facile à deviner." She must disguise her message because a too literal enunciation would be embarrassing and insulting, and would perhaps be refused. Thus, again, indirect communication plays a very necessary role in a message.

The rhetoric of the text emphasizes this need for "tact" in the relay of messages by using a vocabulary that relates to diplomacy. The narrator describes his decision to speak first to the count of Montpersan as "une résolution diplomatique digne d'un vieil ambassadeur." This comparison shows that he exercises tact and "l'adresse des courtisans ou des gens du monde." The association of courtesans and ambassadors is an interesting one, for, as we have seen, the messages in the text consist for a large part in messages of *desire* expressed diplomatically or indirectly.

The message relates not only to diplomacy in the rhetoric of the text, but also to last wills and testaments. The message is composed of a chain of signifiers that continue to circulate after the death of the stranger. The message is a "reste" that communicates his wishes. The stranger "leaves" a task to the narrator. . . . This inheritance is the task of delivering a message to Juliette, a task that the narrator calls a "testament verbal."

In a sense, the messages of this text and the text itself have at their origin a death, a lack, an absence, an interruption (of life and love). The messages and the text itself are the remainder, the verbal testament, which endure after death, in the absence of the person who originated them. As traces of his death, they communicate it, are imbued with it. Yet death, absence, interruption, are not only the origins of the signifiers and the messages, but are an essential part of them, since this is what the messages communicate.

Hence any proper and literal conveyance of this message would not be "proper" because a certain lack, interval, or interruption is necessary for an accurate communication of the message. It is a message of loss, and cannot be a message of plentitude and properness. The messages in the text tell us that a message in general is a series of displacements, deflections, and substitutions that has at its origin an absence which is a necessary part of its functioning. This absence or deflection is not ended or brought home, but continues in a chain of messages and further deflections.

Curiously, death is not simply a *component* of the message. Messages *kill*. The message is performative in that when put into circulation, it brings about symbolic deaths. . . . "Autumn" and death have Juliette in their grasp, and the message has perhaps literally communicated death to her, almost as would a contagious disease.

The same thing happens to her husband. After he hears the news, and after Juliette disappears, he curiously stays at the dinner table in the following tragi-comic scene:

> . . . il avait mangé presque tout le dîner, au grand plaisir de sa fille qui souriait de voir son père en flagrante désobéissance aux ordres de la comtesse. La singulière insouciance de ce mari me fut expliquée par la légère altercation qui s'éleva soudain entre le chanoine et lui. Le comte était soumis à une diète sévère que les médecins lui avaient imposée pour le guérir d'une maladie grave dont le nom m'échappe . . .

Thus, through a suicidal desire for food, the count takes a chance on bringing death upon himself. Also, when the narrator tells the old servant the news of her employer's death,

she falls "demi-morte sur une chaise." The message is, indeed, a "fatal message."

Finally, in the case of the narrator, this communicated death is slightly more symbolic. First of all, the narrator emphasizes the similarity between the stranger and himself from the very outset of the story. . . . They identify with each other, especially because of their similar love affairs, so that, when the stranger dies, the narrator symbolically dies the death of his "double." We can see this identification clearly when the narrator takes the stranger's *place,* first of all very literally at the dinner table:

> Il y avait cinq couverts: ceux des deux époux et celui de la petite fille; le *mien,* qui devait être le *sien;* le dernier était celui d'un chanoine de Saint-Denis . . .

Not only does the narrator take the literal place of the dead man, he also symbolically puts himself (in a rather covert way) in the love relation with the countess of Montpersan. First of all, the desire of the narrator for Juliette is evident in the following quote:

> Elle portait une robe de mousseline blanche; elle avait sur la tête un joli bonnet à rubans roses, une ceinture rose, une guimpe remplie si délicieusement par ses épaules et par les plus beaux contours, qu'en les voyant il naissait au fond du coeur une irrésistible envie de les posséder.

In addition, Juliette comes to visit him in his room in the middle of the night, a very suggestive gesture indeed. Since the narrator takes the place of the stranger, he represents the stranger in his absence and death, he is *himself* a signifier, a substitute or symbol for the dead stranger, and thus he is himself linked with death (as we saw signifiers contain a certain absence or lack). In a sense, he disappears behind his role as messenger and as signifier, for he remains *unidentified* and *unnamed* throughout the story. We only know his function as a "messager de la mort," whose message is a message from, a signifier of, the dead and of death. He thus undergoes a certain death himself for he is not a subject in his own right, but a representative of another subject, of the Other, of Death. He is a signifier only.

We have now seen that the message is a circulation of signifiers with an absent origin, and that, as a message, it brings a certain death with it. If we look now at the actual *path* of circulation we discover a very interesting phenomenon. We have already seen the path often taken by messages is a triangular one. But in several cases, the messages eventually form a circle. The message that one sends comes back like a boomerang. These circular messages all relate to Juliette. First, we know that she has sent love letters to the stranger, love letters which express her desire for him, for the other. He receives these letters, but, before his death, he leaves them to the narrator who must return them to Juliette, who sent them in the first place. Her own message of desire for the other comes back to her.

In the second case, Juliette, at the end of the story, arranges for her husband to give money to the narrator who uses it, replaces it, gives it to a third party who (supposedly) returns it to Juliette and her husband. Her message of money is sent out only to return to her later.

Another more interesting case of the circuitous message or the recursive message involves the narrator. He initially sends out the story itself, **"Le Message,"** to the reader so that, as we saw before, the reader would pursue a love relation. But at the end of the story, this message comes back to act upon the narrator himself, for in the end he undergoes the effect of his own message:

> Quelles délices d'avoir pu raconter cette aventure
> à une femme qui, peureuse, vous a serré, vous a dit:
> "Oh! cher, ne meurs pas, toi?"

In the end, he himself is the reader who pursues a love relation. He finds that, in directing the story to another, he *is* that other. As Lacan says, "le langage humain constituerait donc une communication où l'émetteur reçoit du récepteur son propre message sous une forme inversée." Thus the message affects its own sender. The signifier defines and shapes the sender; language defines and shapes us after its articulation. This performance of language manifests the *performative* power of language which acts, and can act upon its own sender.

Since the story's title is **"Le Message,"** it invites the reader to interpret it as an allegory of message sending in general, something we have tended to do. Thus, as a message about messages, the text itself forms a circle: it is a metatext, a commentary on itself. It says: "I am a message about myself." This circle never ends, for, as in an infinite regress, the self-reflection leads to infinity: **"Le Message"** refers to messages that refer to **"Le Message"** and so on. As an allegory of signification, it tells us that meaning never ends. (pp. 53-8)

> Dorothy J. Kelly, "What Is the Message in Balzac's *'Le message'?"* in Nineteenth-Century French Studies, *Vol. 13, Nos. 2 & 3, Winter-Spring, 1985, pp. 48-58.*

JOAN DARGAN (essay date 1985)

[*In the following excerpt from* Balzac and the Drama of Perspective: The Narrator in Selected Works of "La comédie humaine," *Dargan offers an analysis of the characters the duchess, depicted as "La sœur Thérèse," and Montriveau in "La duchesse de Langeais."*]

In his book on Rodin, Rilke describes a great theme of the sculptor in words that apply also, appropriately, to Balzac: "There is something of the longing which makes great poets in all vice, in all lustful sins against nature, in all the desperate and vain attempts to find an eternal meaning for life. Here is humanity's hunger reaching out beyond itself; stretching out hands towards eternity." In *La Duchesse de Langeais* this pursuit of "eternal meaning" leads neither to mystical revelation, as, ambiguously, in *Louis Lambert,* nor to the fulfillment of sexual and emotional desire. Instead, the journey's destination is a poem: the poem in prose that is the narrative, and the conclusion pronounced by the hero Montriveau with reference to the eponymous heroine: "ce n'est plus qu'un poème." Shown as "la sœur Thérèse" at the opening and close of the novel, the Duchesse de Langeais represents more than a dubious tribute to Saint Teresa: she embodies the common longing for transcendence of the self experienced, in their different spheres, by mystic and lover—both truth-seekers ready to find meaning beyond need of language.

Neither Montriveau nor "la sœur Thérèse" can be called an aspiring mystic; unlike Louis Lambert, they contain their desire in the realm of poetical discourse prescribed by the narrator. Montriveau cannot tolerate ambiguity or compromise in

speech; like the cruelly deceived Colonel Chabert, he makes the error of confusing conventional language with literal representation of fact. As the Duchess professes love all the while refusing to express it physically, Montriveau plans retaliation: a crude, and aborted, attempt to brand her forehead with a convict's stigma, as if literally to render his judgment against her. Thus confronted, the Duchess in turn recognizes her obligation to relate words to action, thought to expression, if not in the simplistic sense understood by Montriveau. Each character introduces the other to the complexity of symbol, the Duchess discovering the necessity of common reference, Montriveau in the end embracing the non-literal, his "poème." The theme of the conflict between the sexes takes on the cosmic dimensions suggested by Rilke's words as the characters evolve a more comprehensive and tolerant understanding of symbolic expression. What Louis Lambert experiences as a conflict—sexual desire and the desire for "eternal meaning"—in *La Duchesse de Langeais* is one and the same yearning.

The use of flashback in the narration of the story frees the narrator from the restriction of adopting the uninformed perspective of a character, as in *Ferragus,* and allows him to engage in the active reconstruction of an episode presumably buried in Montriveau's memory. Thus, although there is a symbolic kinship between Montriveau and Louis Lambert, the narrator of *La Duchesse de Langeais* emphasizes a consciousness of art and not of genius: the later work is indeed the "œuvre plus ou moins poétique" shunned by Lambert's biographer. The narrator of *La Duchesse de Langeais* emphasizes thematically as well the importance of memory: as Montriveau holds the dead "sœur Thérèse" in his arms, he contemplates the same truth to which Chabert woke at Eylau: that reduction of Life to Death, resisted only by remembering fully who we are. Like Chabert, Ferragus and Louis Lambert, Montriveau must learn that possession of what one loves—knowledge, privilege, children, the beloved—is never absolute. Unlike them, he refrains from authorship, laying down his branding iron and seeking neither pen nor lawyer nor forged papers to establish his identity; and perhaps Balzac symbolically rewards him for this restraint by leaving his faculties intact at the novel's end.

Although the dramatic effect of *La Duchesse de Langeais* depends largely upon the unorthodox use of chronology, the reconstructed plot suggests its colorful mixture of Gothic horror and Human Comedy. (pp. 87-8)

Balzac originally gave *La Duchesse de Langeais* an epigraph taken from Saint Teresa of Avila's *Way of Perfection* which describes the vehemence and purity of spiritual friendship. Although the epigraph disappeared from the Furne edition of *La Comédie humaine,* the chapter heading "La sœur Thérèse" in itself alludes to the Spanish saint and, therefore, indirectly to the Christian mystical tradition and to the theme of the grandeur of Spain. Geographically and spiritually, we are a world removed from the sordid, materialistic Paris we found in **"Ferragus,"** but that is of no matter. We are literally a world removed from **"Ferragus:"** we have begun another novel.

The very first lines of *La Duchesse de Langeais* describe a Carmelite convent in which the reformed rule introduced by Saint Teresa is strictly observed, with the assurance to us worldly readers that this fidelity to tradition "est vrai, quelque extraordinaire qu'il puisse paraître." The convent is a relic of a former age, strangely intact, and its inhabitants are oblivious to the march of history. . . . (p. 89)

But this tribute to the enduring success of Saint Teresa's reform is qualified by the narrator's insinuation that the convent is remarkable precisely because it is an anachronism. This is an assessment he will make again in reference to the Faubourg Saint-Germain. The respectful, wondering tone with which he describes the color of the sea and the chapel's Gothic exterior is inspired not so much by an appreciation of their beauty as by a desire to magnify the mock-heroic dimensions of the hero's transgression of holy ground. In the typical pattern of Balzac's dramatic expositions, an unnamed character, "un général français," emerges from the setting, having found "sous ses murailles et dans ces chants [the liturgical music sung in the chapel] les légers indices qui justifièrent son frêle espoir." It is not that the passions of history and of the senses have been forcibly excluded from within the convent walls; it is rather that they have almost imperceptibly infiltrated an environment visibly opposed to them—geographically, architecturally, spiritually. And as in the narrator's self-conscious approach to the bedroom in **"Ferragus"**, the tone and the theme of insinuation warn us of the impending dramatic upheaval and flood of erotically charged language that will foreshadow the boudoir scenes of the second chapter.

It appears at first that Balzac calls upon the image of Saint Teresa only to turn it against her, but this is not entirely so. The narrator attributes certain aspects of mystical love—the singlemindedness of devotion, the all-consuming longing of the soul—to the Duchesse de Langeais and Montriveau's romance, and we cannot help but marvel with him: "L'amour arrive rarement à la solennité; mais l'amour encore fidèle au sein de Dieu, n'était-ce pas quelque chose de solennel, et plus qu'un homme n'avait le droit d'espérer au dix-neuvième siècle, par les mœurs qui courent?" He does not confuse the ardor of spiritual feeling and erotic passion; if he did, the humor and irony of the situation would be lost. But it is only much later in the novel that the narrator explicitly makes the distinction. . . . In the first chapter he is openly playing on the ambiguity of meaning his context gives the allusion to mysticism; he withholds the precise definition, in order that his readers may follow the narration "sans que la réflexion nuise à leurs plaisirs." The "daring" evocation of Saint Teresa is one of many incongruities: the shift of the setting to Spain, the convent as anachronism, the improbability of Montriveau's adventure and the discovery of a truly grand passion in such a jaded age and in such an unlikely setting. (pp. 89-90)

Like the narrative voice in the opening passage of **"Ferragus,"** the narrator in *La Duchesse de Langeais* intercepts signals from the setting and transmits them to the reader. He too refers to the poetic sensitivity that enables him to be a reliable and discriminating witness: "S'il faut un cœur de poète pour faire un musicien, ne faut-il pas de la poésie et de l'amour pour écouter, pour comprendre les grandes œuvres musicales?" Again like the narrator in **"Ferragus,"** he involves the reader in the scene by the use of forms of direct address: we are invited to visualize the scene, to draw upon our experience. . . .

However, the effects of the appeals to the reader's attention in the two novels are opposite. In **"Ferragus"** the reader is drawn into Maulincour's fundamental error by the obstructed vision of the narration; in *La Duchesse de Langeais* the reader is made accomplice to the flouting of convention performed both by the unrepentant characters and by the narrator. In **"Ferragus"** the issue is only the fall of a Platonic idol; here everything is at stake. . . . (p. 91)

It is in the interview that the protagonists actually confront that insurmountable barrier, a motif suggested as a theme of Sœur Thérèse's music and symbolized by the music itself, an incorporeal translation of physical passion. Thus, Montriveau, representing those forces restoring Roman Catholicism to political power in Spain, enters a room pervaded by the essence of spirituality, by a sense of the awful finitude of mortal existence: "Quelque chose de grand comme la tombe le saisit sous ces frais planchers. N'était-ce pas son silence éternel, sa paix profonde, ses idées d'infini?" Light pours in on one side, behind the grille, dimly reflecting upon the works of art on the other. . . . The grille divides the parlor into two symbolic zones: one of death, transparency and contemplation; the other of life, art and action. The male and female principles are divided: on one side the Carmelite without age or past and the mother superior who hovers at her side like the presence of death (reminding us of Madame Gruget in **"Ferragus"** and the duenna in **"La Fille aux yeux d'or"**), on the other the illustrious general intent this time on a personal victory. The simplicity of speech and humility of Sœur Thérèse, who twice reminds her visitor to call her by her adopted name, underscore the selfish motives of the general. Answering in Spanish to her superior, she admits her acquaintance with the "cavalier" and obediently turns to leave when ordered to do so. On Montriveau's side lies all the vanity of a self-interested pursuit, of French military glory and, interestingly, of the French language; on the side of Sœur Thérèse, all the virtues of renunciation, obedience and truthful speech. In true Romantic spirit, the encounter represents the clash of two nations: the glittering, artificial world of French culture, the stark and imposing splendor of Spain. For a moment the "burning symphonies" of the chapel scene are forgotten. (p. 92)

In the scene opening the novel, and especially in these final words, Balzac brings together the symbolic and mimetic dimensions of his story. Forces greater than mortal passion and will militate not against the lovers' reconciliation, but against their reunion. These forces are a double sign: thematically, of divine intervention; formally, of the narrator's. (The chapter title "Dieu fait les dénouements" is a friendly gesture from one sovereign to another.) Even the characters reflect this conjunction of image and form. Their subversion of traditional symbolism—the meaning of words and music, of the military uniform and the religious habit—represents the social necessity of clothing explosive feelings in conventional garb. But this necessity originates in both the impropriety and the inexpressibility of such emotions. The scene dramatizes the role of convention in society and in art; it introduces us to a vision in which irony, humor, fantasy and realism are all one.

The first chapter isolates the subject of the novel, the dramatic conflict of the protagonists—a statement of theme unencumbered by analysis and thrown into relief by its unusual context. The characters are identified simply by their first names and roles—general, nun, duchess, lover; their personal histories remain untold. The poetic effect precedes its prosaic cause. The opening scene is like a chord majestically struck on the organ, its vibrations felt and protracted in the succeeding pages of the novel. The "volcanic eruption" of emotions occurring there will be prolonged and qualified in the second and third chapters. Thematically, "La sœur Thérèse" reveals that the forces of history, in the persons of Montriveau and the Duchess, had somehow swerved from their anticipated course, and predicts that they will not easily, if at all, turn back again. But what is impossible for ordinary men is possible for the narrator: he will take us back in time. And thus, even though we are returned to the unmysterious world of manners and history, the spell of the novel remains unbroken. We are taken by surprise, not jolted, by the narrator's intervention: "Voici maintenant l'aventure qui avait déterminé la situation respective où se trouvaient alors les deux personnages de cette scène."

Immediately follows, in what is now the second chapter, a long "aperçu semi-politique" of the Restoration aristocracy of the Faubourg Saint-Germain—from "Ce que l'on nomme en France . . ." to ". . . du drame national appelé les Mœurs." The relationship of this passage to the first chapter does not become apparent until just after its close, when we are told that the Duchesse de Langeais is the personification of the Faubourg: "le type le plus complet de la nature à la fois supérieure et faible, grande et petite, de sa caste." The events leading up to her flight to the Spanish convent and Montriveau's meeting with her there are, therefore, only the logical extension of the contradictions and tensions inherent in her milieu and at a precise historical moment—and as formulated by Balzac. However, though the narrator uses certain rhetorical devices reminiscent of the beginning of **"Ferragus,"** the passage is not an example of the use of restricted perspective to set a dramatic tone. Instead, it is an historical interpretation of the forces of convention, now relocated in a Parisian setting. . . . (pp. 94-5)

[The] ordering of the narrative subtly dramatizes the theme of the Duchess' tragedy: that Montriveau's words and gestures "n'apportaient aucun souvenir et ne réveillaient aucune image" the sad heritage of a marriage of convenience. The reader, faced with an otherwise unintelligible passage, can reflect back upon the first chapter and the historical exposé to divine its meaning; the Duchess has no such privilege. Madame de Langeais is incapable of reflection, thematically and symbolically; upon viewing Montriveau for the first time, "elle prit son lorgnon et l'examina fort impertinemment, comme elle eût fait d'un portrait qui reçoit des regards et n'en rend pas." The irony of her adoption of the contemplative life is not lost on the reader. When, in the course of relating a conversation, the narrator says, "Ces paroles représentent imparfaitement celles que fredonna la duchesse avec la vive prolixité d'une serinette," he is only transposing on the formal level the theme associated with the character: the imperfect correspondence of words and their referents.

The narrator's use of euphemism in the second chapter also recalls "La Sœur Thérèse." The "admirable jésuitisme" which made the continuation of the interview possible recurs in the "secret et jésuitique oukase" which enables the Duchess to become intimate with Montriveau while remaining within the bounds of propriety. Like those sensations whose expression is "interdite à la parole," those inspired by the erotic overtones of the sacred music, the sexual relations of the characters are also associated with the theme of inexpressibility: "mais pour l'honneur du faubourg Saint-Germain, il est nécessaire de ne pas révéler les mystères de ses boudoirs, où l'on voulait tout de l'amour moins ce qui pouvait attester l'amour." The conflict between the literal-minded Montriveau and the insincere Duchess reappears in the second chapter, again associated with the theme of adopt-

ed names (Madame de Langeais was originally Antoinette de Navarreins) and the theme of physical disorientation:

> Eh! mon Dieu, que nous font la France, le trône. la légitimité, le monde entier? Ce sont des billevesées auprès de mon bonheur. Régnez, soyez renversés, peu m'importe. Où suis-je donc?
>
> —Mon ami, vous êtes dans le boudoir de Mme la duchesse de Langeais.
>
> —Non, non, plus de duchesse, plus de Langeais, je suis près de ma chère Antoinette!

The general once again finds himself in alien territory: "elle lui refit *Le Génie du Christianisme à l'usage des militaires.*"

In this light, it is significant that Madame de Langeais's involvement with Montriveau begins not with their formal introduction, but with a dream she had had the previous night: "S'être trouvée dans les sables brûlants du désert avec lui, l'avoir eu pour compagnon de cauchemar, n'était-ce pas chez une femme de cette nature un délicieux présage d'amusement?" The nightmare produces an uncanny effect in the way that "La Sœur Thérèse" prepares the reader's surprise at recognizing the protagonists in a different setting: "La duchesse, déjà frappée par l'aspect de ce poétique personnage, le fut encore bien plus en apprenant qu'elle voyait en lui le marquis de Montriveau, de qui elle avait rêvé pendant la nuit." The dream also anticipates the kidnapping scene of the third chapter, in which the Duchess at last connects her gestures to emotions, words to meaning, form to content.

This scene, the climax of the novel, is one of those grotesque moments in Balzac when the symbolic and mimetic levels of meaning cross each other. Occurring midway in **La Duchesse de Langeais,** it recalls the emotional violence of the opening scene, it parodies the boudoir scenes in the second chapter, and it is itself balanced later by the episode in which Madame de Langeais sends her carriage to Montriveau's door. The placement of the scene within the novel and within the **Treize** is stunningly effective. The branding iron is a throwback to **"Ferragus;"** the mystery surrounding the location of Montriveau's chamber foreshadows the even greater mystery of Paquita's boudoir.

However, the scene is above all remarkable for its symbolic violence. It is not simply that the Gothic parody of the novel is stretched to its limits or that Madame de Langeais's humiliation, carried to the point of her puffing on Montriveau's cigars, seems in its abruptness a rather crude form of poetic justice. It is the transformation of a metaphor into action, a substitution of the literal for the figural, that is disconcerting. (pp. 97-9)

A lesser writer than Balzac, caught in such dramatic straits, would stand open to the charge of sensationalism. In light of Balzac's fiction generally, however, we can detect the author's "but de profonde moralite" in this melodramatic incident. Montriveau's recourse to the branding iron immediately establishes a symbolic relation between the Duchess and Ferragus: the latter erases his stigma, only to lose himself, and the former welcomes the one intended for her, only to become, in Balzac's words, "la femme vraie." For the one brand represents a public marking in accordance with social convention, the legal system; for the other it represents a private verdict rendered, in Montriveau's eyes, on the level of simple, unmediated justice. Symbolically speaking, for society to mark a man physically—that is, superficially—is within its province, whether it commits error or not; but for a man to assume absolute moral authority and thus mark others is both a confusion of codes (imposing the personal or ideal upon the social) and a usurpation of power. Balzac consistently punishes those characters who fail to make vital distinctions when wielding powerful symbols: not only is Montriveau unable to carry out his intended act, but he also, in the end, loses the Duchess to an unforgiving God ("Dieu fait les dénouements"—a God made in the author's own image). Moreover, Ferragus, Chabert and Louis Lambert, all of whom receive similar treatment in this respect, find their inability to master distinctions in symbolic expression related to their corresponding inability to possess their beloved: Ferragus loses his daughter, Chabert is repudiated by his wife, Louis Lambert resorts to self-destruction rather than marry Pauline. It is as if Balzac's fictional mythology insists again and again on the need to integrate acceptance of the self and of one's sexuality in the individual search for meaning. Montriveau's branding iron, metaphorically illustrating his desire, enables him to demonstrate—and the Duchess to contemplate—this Balzacian precept. As for the Duchess, her acknowledgment of the significance implied by her actions saves her from physical disfigurement and transforms her into her "true" self. Even if her symbolic punishment has the same effect as that meted out to Lambert and Ferragus, she at least is allowed to bow out of her novel gracefully.

Appropriately, we find this most discordant of scenes integrated esthetically into the novel. The description of Montriveau's room recalls the convent parlor of the first chapter: like "la pensée fixe du cloître," "l'âme et la pensée de [Montriveau] . . . planaient." Next to the bed an open doorway, hidden by a curtain reminiscent of the grille, separates the lovers from the Treize, who are heating the branding iron in the next room. The blindfold with which Montriveau intends to cover the Duchess' eyes reminds us of the headband of the veil worn by Sœur Thérèse. The Duchess' words, "Mais je suis un peu curieuse," spoken as Montriveau goes to kiss her, echo the Spanish chaplain's remark in the first chapter: "Je leur [to the Carmelites] ai dit l'objet de la messe, elles sont toujours un peu curieuses." Madame de Langeais's flight to a foreign and inaccessible location seems to be involuntarily repeated here: "La frayeur de la duchesse fut si grande qu'elle ne put jamais s'expliquer par où ni comment elle fut transportée." Montriveau warns her of the kidnapping in words borrowed from the English—"Ne touchez pas à la hache"—and again in Italian; in the convent in Spain his native tongue, too, had been a foreign language.

Not only the chapter "La Sœur Thérèse," but also "L'Amour dans la paroisse de Saint-Thomas-d'Aquin" is evoked by the kidnapping scene. Montriveau relaxes in an armchair, wrapped in his robe, reversing the roles the characters played in the Duchess' boudoir: "Ne criez pas, madame la duchesse, dit-il en s'ôtant froidement son cigare de la bouche, j'ai la migraine." His exaggerated delicacy leads him to burn incense to clear the air, a gesture symbolically as evanescent and insubstantial as her previous shows of affection. Like Madame de Langeais in her natural setting, Montriveau is a virtuoso, adopting "l'air d'un maître de cérémonies." He delivers his words with an actor's flair for phrasing: "Ecoutez-moi bien, dit-il, en faisant une pause pour donner de la solennité à son discours"; and at one point he gives himself a silent cue: "il se dit à lui-même: 'Je suis perdu, si je me laisse prendre à des disputes de mots'." His dissertation on social justice echoes the long speeches on religion and marriage formerly given by

Madame de Langeais. For once, Montriveau is speaking her language and, like her, channeling sexual desire into a socially sanctioned form of expression, the branding iron. Moreover, the prophetic nightmare of the second chapter becomes an actual experience: "La terreur qu'Armand lui inspirait fut augmentée par une de ces sensations pétrifiantes, analogues aux agitations sans mouvement ressenties dans le cauchemar." These references to the other parts of the novel invite the reader to retaliate against the symbolic violence of the scene by perceiving its relationship to the whole, a splendid battle from which text, author and reader alike emerge victorious.

The convergence of themes in the kidnapping scene is further intensified by its central position in the *Histoire des Treize.* Montriveau's words explicitly refer to **"Ferragus"** and invoke its central theme—the irrevocability of social judgment: "Vous aurez enfin sur le front la marque infamante appliquée sur l'épaule de vos frères les forçats." The secrecy with which Madame de Langeais is conveyed to his apartment, as well as the slightly exotic touch of the incense, call to mind de Marsay's visits to Paquita in **"La Fille aux yeux d'or."** At the same time the three motifs of the *Histoire des Treize* appear with all their inherent ambiguity. The Treize wait behind the curtain, ready to avenge Montriveau, and yet they do not—a sign of their ultimate powerlessness. Two lovers confront each other, having finally reached a stage in which mutual understanding is possible, and yet, inexplicably, the barrier between them does not fall. The civilizing influence of Paris is reflected in themimicry of its manners and the analysis of its caste system; but the precise location of the room is unknown, and the event taking place there is ultimately the rejection of a conventional and particularized background.

After this moment of symbolic upheaval and suspension, prolonged by the state of confusion—"un état de stupeur morale"—in which the Duchess finds herself, the narrator signals that a turning point both in the story and in the narrative has been reached: "Quand une femme est en proie aux tyrannies furieuses sous lesquelles ployait Mme de Langeais, les résolutions définitives se succèdent si rapidement, qu'il est impossible d'en rendre compte. . . . Dès lors, les faits disent tout. Voici donc les faits." The familiar language of the narrative intervention puts us back on familiar territory, and we leave the kidnapping scene behind. The narrator provides comic relief to that episode by presenting the scene in which Madame de Langeais publicly declares her love for Montriveau by sending her carriage to his door.

The reunion of the Navarreins family inspires a series of satirical sketches of such supremely outlandish characters that the narrator feels obliged to remark on the general eccentricity of the upper classes "pour empêcher les critiques de taxer de puérilité le commencement de la scène suivante." (One can almost sense Proust waiting in the wings.) After leading Montriveau through an inferno of sorts, the narrator greets the reader with the wholly dispensable information that the general's uncle, the Comte de Montriveau, would eat twelve dozen oysters daily without the slightest ill effect. Comic, too, on the larger scale of human folly, is the misunderstanding between the Duchess and her family, whom she defies like a latter-day Antigone. Whereas her gesture to Montriveau comes nobly from the heart—and, not incidentally, from a clear-sighted recognition of her role as pawn to the family fortunes—her relatives are interested only in her violation of form: "Pour tout concilier, que venons-nous vous demander?

De tourner habilement la loi des convenances au lieu de la violer." Another source of humor in the scene is the contrast between the Princesse de Blamont-Chauvry's historical perspective on the evolution of courtly manners and the Duchess' immediate and exclusive grasp of the sole words of wisdom of practical interest to her: "—Chère tante, je puis donc aller chez lui déguisée?—Mais, oui, ça peut toujours se nier, dit la vieille."

This moment of revelation for the Duchess also shows us why she had been unable to meet Montriveau on common ground. After the abduction she had moved, symbolically speaking, from the level of conventional discourse—signs whose meaning derives primarily from context—to the level of the denotative or representational—language in whose field of direct reference lies meaning. The former requires interpretation as a response; the latter, corresponding action. Thus, in sending her carriage to her lover's door, Madame de Langeais commits the fatal (as we shall see) error of confusing codes—using a conventional sign (the carriage) to convey a message of a different order (her unconventionally profound love of Montriveau). When her aunt reminds her that in social parlance action need not correspond to language ("ça peut toujours se nier"), the Duchess glimpses a course of action that does not compromise her emotion. If her love is authentic, she need not fear appearances that suggest, falsely, the presence of ambiguity or hypocrisy at the source. This is the lesson learned with respect to his identity by Colonel Chabert, albeit much more painfully.

Thus, the family reunion in the wake of this scandal literally encircles the Duchess in her native symbolic territory, conventional language, and foils her attempted escape. It is by controlling memory, as the Navarreins know, that one resists extinction; and an aristocratic caste tenuously in power is not above expedient editing. Thus, the one intrinsically significant gesture the Duchess had made is ably denounced and erased from the public memory. This deliberate elimination of the sole visible proof of her love for Montriveau—proof that she had indeed crossed the "ligne droite et tranchée" between passion and love—repeats the failure of communication earlier symbolized in his failure to apply the branding iron to her forehead. Both characters had recourse to symbols to express their anguish to their unresponsive partner. Both bowed to the truth that the Duchess' social identity was inalterable and inescapable—and perhaps also to the truth that in contemporary society the heroic gesture or the noble emotion is no longer possible. When Montriveau's unpremeditated delay lets their last opportunity for reconciliation slip by, the Duchess leaves Paris for the convent in Spain—renouncing that identity and, therefore, life also. At this point the narrator intervenes once more, as if closing a parenthesis between the opening scene and the dénouement of the novel. . . . (pp. 99-103)

The second and third chapters of *La Duchesse de Langeais* comprise the nucleus of analysis around which the novel is structured, if we consider the novel as a study of manners, a form of social criticism. In these chapters we perceive the narrative's foundation in history and its role as a dramatic extension of that history, through the characters; at the same time two symbolic disturbances, the kidnapping scene and the carriage episode, reveal the cracks in that foundation and the frailty of those characters. This unfolding of events follows upon the great emotional convulsion of the first chapter and, in retrospect, establishes its necessity; and the theme of

the power of circumstances over effort, figured in the image of the Duchess fleeing from Paris, foreshadows the ending. But if the historical exposition and the analysis of the characters in their native setting are imbedded in the narrative, it is because Balzac clearly wished to give primacy to the poetic effect of the chapter "La Sœur Thérèse." Thus, the central chapters of the novel contain the internal logic of the story and are enhanced by their secondary position; but it is the poetic logic of the novel's form announced by "La Sœur Thérèse" that triumphs in the end—and in the ending, a return to the convent setting.

The dénouement of *La Duchesse de Langeais* is an acknowledgement of the supreme difficulties of expression and of the necessity of convention in speech and manners, of form in art. All the themes of the novel are gently drawn together. The light touches of Balzac's humor—de Marsay dressed as a Carmelite, a comic reference to **"La Fille aux yeux d'or";** the uncontrollable curiosity which leads the nun keeping vigil over the Duchess' body to search through the deceased's personal belongings—brighten the somber images of separation, death, powerlessness—and silence. Montriveau, after contemplating the Duchess' remains in his cabin, exchanges these words, the final words of the novel, with his friend Ronquerolles:

> Ah! ça dit Ronquerolles à Montriveau quand celui-ci reparut sur le tillac, c'était une femme, maintenant ce n'est rien. Attachons un boulet à chacun de ses pieds, jetons-la dans la mer, et n'y pense plus que comme nous pensons à un livre lu pendant notre enfance.
>
> —Oui, dit Montriveau, car ce n'est plus qu'un poème.
>
> —Te voilà sage. Désormais aie des passions; mais de l'amour, il faut savoir le bien placer, et il n'y a que le dernier amour d'une femme qui satisfasse le premier amour d'un homme.

This ending inscribes upon our memories an image preserving that necessary tension between theme and form, between those conflicting movements constantly streaming through the novel and shaping it: the forces of history and the forces of symbolism, the gravity of reference and the flight of poetry, the conventions of literary tradition and the autonomy of form. Ronquerolles speaks with the assurance and facility of the public man, the social creature; Montriveau, with the simplicity and concision of a mind returning from an immense and private emotion, an interior journey. Montriveau's words preserve the Duchess in an image, the poem; Ronquerolles's diminish the importance of her death and welcome its absorption into history. His words are a closure, bringing the reader back to the *Histoire des Treize* and returning Montriveau to the realm of familiar and reassuring experience.

But this final affirmation of realism is only a convention, not a distillation of the novel. *La Duchesse de Langeais* cannot be so easily simplified; too much has happened. The reader, in his own sphere, has experienced the Duchess' trauma and Montriveau's illumination. We have been compelled, by the fragmented chronology of the narrative and the symbolic violence of its scenes, to contemplate the ordering of images as a single experience of our own, as readers: to see the novel not as a story, but as a form.

But not all of the poetic effects of *La Duchesse de Langeais*, a novel Balzac dedicated to Liszt, are universal. One belongs to it alone. The unchronological presentation of the story creates the theme of a diminuendo, a theme struck like a chord by the "burning symphonies" of the opening scene, sustained by the melodies played by the Duchess on her piano in Paris, and concluded by the strains of Gregorian chant that captivate Montriveau just before he goes to retrieve his eternally silent lover. The last lines may remind us of the limitations of form, but it is the poetry that we will remember. (pp. 103-05)

> *Joan Dargan, in her* Balzac and the Drama of Perspective: The Narrator in Selected Works of "La comédie humaine," *French Forum, Publishers, 1985, 172 p.*

CHARLES ROSEN   (essay date 1987)

[*In the following excerpt, Rosen explicates the subject of revision as treated by Balzac in "The Unknown Masterpiece."*]

It is a convenient and pleasing Romantic myth that the true work of art springs full-blown from the unconscious mind. Revision comes from the conscious intellect or will, and this, as Wordsworth wrote, "is the very littleness of life, . . . relapses from the one interior life that lives in all things." Some years ago, a novelist—Muriel Spark, I believe—was asked how she was able to write so many books in such a short space of time. She replied, "I write very fast and I never correct." This is the ideal. Few writers are so fortunate. Most revise and, as they do so, create more problems than they resolve.

One of Balzac's most interesting tales, **"Le Chef d'oeuvre inconnu" ("The Unknown Masterpiece")**, deals imaginatively and succinctly with revision. It was a subject close to the author's heart: his books generally went through several versions before and after publication. However, no work of his was more completely or profoundly rewritten than **"Le Chef d'oeuvre inconnu."**

The scene is laid in Paris in 1612, and the central figure is an invention of Balzac's, a demonic personality who might have stepped out of the fantastic tales of E. T. A. Hoffmann: the old Frenhofer, the greatest painter of the age (all of Balzac's important characters possess their qualities in the superlative degree, and no moderately talented artist could play a significant role in his work—even Wenceslas Steinbock in *La Cousine Bette,* when he loses his talent, becomes obsessively and spectacularly incapable and the hopelessly mediocre, Pierre Grassou sees his work sold under the names of Rembrandt, Rubens, and Titian, becomes the favorite painter of the bourgeoisie, and enters the Academy). The two other painters in the tale are historical: the young Nicholas Poussin, just starting out as an artist, visits the atelier of the already established Franz Porbus, and meets Frenhofer there. For ten years Frenhofer has been working on one painting, a life-size portrait of a nude woman lying on a velvet couch—"but what are ten years," he says, "when it is a question of wrestling with Nature? We do not know how long it took Lord Pygmalion to make the only statue that walked."

Frenhofer will show no one the picture: to finish it, he says, he needs a model of absolutely perfect beauty. Poussin has such a mistress, the young and modest Gillette, who adores him. He persuades her with difficulty to pose in the nude for Frenhofer, who will in return allow him to view the unknown masterpiece. Alone in his studio with Gillette, Frenhofer compares his painting to the living form of the girl, and decides that it is finished, more beautiful than reality. . . .

Lost in admiration of his own work, Frenhofer does not comprehend that his ten years of revision have destroyed his painting, and Poussin loses his mistress, for Gillette cannot forgive his having sacrificed her deeply felt modesty simply to see a picture.

This moral tale of the terrifying effects of revision underwent wholesale revision after its 1831 printing in a periodical, *L'Artiste,* and its reappearance with some corrections in book form the same year. Six years later, in 1837, Balzac republished it, considerably enlarged and with a different ending as part of the seventeenth volume of his **Etudes philosophiques.** In this version, definitive except for some retouching in Balzac's own copy of **La Comédie humaine,** the old painter, observing the reaction of his fellow artists, realizes the disaster, and throws the two younger painters out in a blind rage. That night he burns all his pictures and dies mysteriously.

The additions of 1837 are largely discussions of the theory of painting, in which Balzac ascribes to his seventeenth-century artists the ideas current in the 1830s: the supremacy of the colorist over the draftsman, for example. The anachronism is compounded in the reader's mind by the development of art since Balzac's day, by the suspicion that Frenhofer's superposition of colors, his multitude of bizarre lines, his chaos of tones and indecisive nuances, might be found more sympathetic today than the banal life-size nude on a velvet couch. It is more significant, however, that the isolated foot that comes out of this chaos would have had a charm already in Balzac's time precisely because it is a fragment, and Balzac's description brings out this charm magnificently:

> This foot appeared there like the torso of some Venus in Parian marble risen from the debris of a city destroyed by fire.

Perhaps the most extraordinary textual change made in 1837 is an apparently small one. Frenhofer's refusal to display his picture to anyone else is a parallel to Gillette's reluctance to pose in the nude for anyone except her lover. Before yielding he expresses his resistance with passion:

> The work I keep under lock and key is an exception in our art; it is not a canvas, it's a woman! a woman with whom I weep, I laugh, I talk and think. Do you want me to abandon ten years' happiness as one takes off a coat? To cease in a single moment, being father, lover and God? This woman is not a creation, but a creature.

This is the version of 1831. In 1837 the final sentence was altered:

> This woman is not a creature, but a creation.

It is wonderful to be able to reverse the terms in this way, and the sentence still makes sense with no change of context. It is clear that for this to happen, the meaning of the words have shifted but then, as Lichtenberg once wrote, whoever decreed that a word must have a fixed meaning?

Placed so near to "creation" in both versions "creative" means not only a living being but one created, and Frenhofer's admission that he enjoyed playing God brings us to the first woman, Eve. A "creature" implies a living being, and "creation" only something made. What is imposed by the contrast is woman against portrait, the experience of life against the object. The two are fused ambiguously in both versions of this passage, but their opposition is the theme of **"The Unknown Masterpiece."** Poussin loses his mistress for the sake of the portrait; Frenhofer has made his portrait the substitute for a woman, and his ten years of happiness destroy his work.

The two versions can act only as a paradox—or different paradoxes. To make sense of both, the meaning of "this woman" must shift. In "not a creation, but a creature," we have "this portrait of a woman is alive"; in "not a creature, but a creation," it changes to "this woman is something I have made." What is disconcerting about the revision is the alteration of values. In the 1831 version, the living being takes precedence over the made object. (p. 22)

The change from 1831 to 1837 is, when you come to think of it, a parallel to the story. Both Frenhofer and Poussin allow the work of art to take precedence over the living being: Eve becomes not a creature, but a thing; the work becomes a fetish. The variant of 1837 reveals a moral deterioration of the author that reflects the tale, as if Balzac were corrupted by his subject (it is significant that the earlier version is not only more humane but more directly effective, the later version more subtly insidious).

Another variant reveals the same process. Poussin endeavors to persuade Gillette to pose nude for Frenhofer, and assures that her modesty will not be violated. In the periodical version, he says:

> *Il ne verra pas la femme en toi, il verra la beauté: tu es parfaite!*
>
> (He will not see the woman in you, he will see beauty: you are perfect.)

In the first edition in book form a month later, we find:

> *Il ne pourra voir que la femme en toi. Tu es si parfaite!*
>
> (He will only be able to see the woman in you. You are so perfect.)

In the first version "woman" is physical, sexual, and vulnerable: the woman in Gillette will be protected from the gaze of Frenhofer. In the second, woman has become a concept, abstract and general. This suggests the way revision in Romantic art moves away from direct experience to a mediated reflection.

In the case of **"The Unknown Masterpiece"**, however, there is no point in judging one version superior to the other. It is clear that a perception of the richness of meaning in these passages depends on a comparison of the different states of the text—the meanings may be implicit in each individual version, but they are more easily revealed when one version is superimposed over the other. In this sense, Frenhofer's "masterpiece" is less an allegory of the dangers of revision than an image of a critical edition with all the variant readings displayed to the reader—above all when we reflect that we would probably have preferred the magical appearance of Frenhofer's disaster to the more banal work he thought he had painted and that Porbus and Poussin all too reasonably expected to see.

Balzac's description of the picture does not correspond to the ordinary process of revision, in which the difficulties are smoothed away and the original awkwardness covered over. In the chaos of colors, tones, and decisive nuances we seem to see all of the different versions superimposed. The different variant states of **"The Unknown Masterpiece"** constitute a more profound and original work than any individually published text. (pp. 22, 24)

> *Charles Rosen, "Romantic Originals," in* The New York Review of Books, *Vol. XXXIV, No. 20, December 17, 1987, pp. 22, 24-31.*

FURTHER READING

Barthes, Roland. *S/Z.* Translated by Richard Miller. New York: Hill and Wang, 1974, 271 p.

>   Book-length study of Balzac's short work "Sarrasine" that inquires into the story's narrative structure. In his preface, Richard Howard claims that Barthes's analysis provides, "a convinced, euphoric, even a militant critique of what it is we do when we read."

Bellos, David. *Balzac Criticism in France, 1850-1900: The Making of a Reputation.* London: Oxford at the Clarendon Press, 1976, 278 p.

>   Describes in detail "the ways in which the critical reputation of Honoré de Balzac changed in the fifty years that followed his death in 1850."

Bertault, Philippe. *Balzac and "The Human Comedy."* Translated by Richard Monges. New York: New York University Press, 1963, 212 p.

>   Combines critical insight into Balzac's ideas with an analysis of his technique.

Brandes, George. "Balzac." In his *Main Currents in Nineteenth-Century Literature: The Romantic School in France, Vol. V,* pp. 158-204. New York: Macmillan Co., 1906.

>   Comprehensive survey of Balzac's life and career that includes stylistic and thematic evaluations of his ideas and stories.

Faguet, Émile. *Balzac.* Translated by Wilfrid Thorley. 1918. Reprint. New York: Haskell House Publishers, 1974, 264 p.

>   Critical study of Balzac's ideas, style, characters, technique, and world view. Includes a discussion of Balzac's reputation in late-nineteenth-century France.

James, Henry. "The Lesson of Balzac." In his *The Question of Our Speech. The Lesson of Balzac. Two Lectures,* pp. 55-116. Boston: Houghton, Mifflin and Co., 1905.

>   Astute and imaginative critical essay in which James acknowledges his debt to Balzac.

Marceau, Felicien. *Balzac and His World.* Translated by Derek Coltman. New York: Orion Press, 1966, 548 p.

>   Perceptive guide to the characters and themes of *La comédie humaine.*

Maurois, André. *Prometheus: The Life of Balzac.* Translated by Norman Denny. London: Bodley Head, 1965, 573 p.

>   Concise biography.

Mortimer, Armine Kotine. "Problems of Closure in Balzac's Stories." *French Forum* 10, No. 1 (January 1985): 20-39.

>   Examines denouements of several of Balzac's short stories to determine whether his closures enhance or detract from the tales.

O'Brien, Edward J. "Commentary upon 'An Episode under the Terror'." In his *The Short Story Case Book,* pp. 35-67. New York: Farrar & Rinehart, 1935.

Paragraph-by-paragraph analysis of Balzac's short story "An Episode under the Terror."

Parsons, George Frederic. "Honoré de Balzac." *The Atlantic Monthly* LVII, No. CCCXLIV (June 1886):   834-50.

Reviews Balzac's life and literary canon.

Pritchett, V. S. *Balzac.* New York: Alfred A. Knopf, 1973, 272 p.

Informative biography.

Proust, Marcel. "Sainte-Beuve and Balzac." In his *Marcel Proust on Art and Literature: 1896-1919,* translated by Sylvia Townsend Warner, pp. 157-89. New York: Carroll & Graf Publishers, 1954.

Disputes C. A. Sainte-Beuve's negative commentary on Balzac's works.

Pugh, Anthony R. *Balzac's Recurring Characters.* Toronto: University of Toronto Press, 1974, 510 p.

Comprehensive guide to Balzac's recurring characters that traces their development throughout his oeuvre.

Royce, William Hobart. *A Balzac Bibliography: Writings Relative to the Life and Works of Honoré de Balzac.* Chicago: University of Chicago Press, 1929, 464 p.

Exhaustive list of Balzac criticism through 1927.

Rudwin, Maximilian. "Balzac and the Fantastic." *The Sewanee Review* 33 (1925):   2-24.

Examines Balzac's portrayal of hell, the devil, and the supernatural in his stories and novels.

Sainte-Beuve, C. A. "Balzac." In his *Sainte-Beuve: Selected Essays,* translated and edited by Francis Steegmuller and Norbert Guterman, pp. 241-57. London: Methuen & Co., 1963.

Characterizes Balzac as a writer.

Sandars, Mary F. *Honoré de Balzac: His Life and Writings.* New York: John Lane Co., 1914, 312 p.

Biography of Balzac that is based on his correspondence with *L'Étrangère.* Sanders finds much of Balzac's life shrouded in mystery.

Zweig, Stefan. *Balzac.* Translated by William Rose and Dorothy Rose. New York: Viking Press, 1946, 404 p.

Biography that reveals Zweig's high esteem for Balzac.

Kay Boyle

1903-

American short story writer, novelist, poet, essayist, translator, editor, and author of children's books.

Boyle is an important figure of the American expatriate movement of the 1920s and 1930s. Like other writers of this era, she often employs terse understatement, interior monologue, stream-of-consciousness narrative, and flights of surrealist prose to reflect the atmosphere of alienation and disillusionment that permeated the years surrounding World Wars I and II. Deeply informed by her own experiences, Boyle's works are set chiefly in Europe and are characterized by intense psychological portraits of individuals searching for love and meaning in a disordered world. Although her writing is sometimes faulted for superficiality and stylishness, Boyle is admired for her accomplishments in many genres, and several of her stories and novellas, notably "The White Horses of Vienna," "The Crazy Hunter," and "The Bridegroom's Body," are hailed as among the finest short prose works of the twentieth century.

Boyle was born to affluent parents in St. Paul, Minnesota. As a child she traveled extensively in the United States and Europe and was tutored by her mother, who instilled in her an enduring appreciation of artistic and social values. Boyle's mother also greatly influenced her literary development, and as a teenager, Boyle wrote numerous short stories and poems. In 1922, she moved from her family home in Cincinnati to New York City, where she worked at *Broom* magazine as an assistant to Australian poet Lola Ridge, the publication's New York editor. Soon Boyle's own writing began appearing in *Broom,* as well as in Harriet Monroe's respected *Poetry: A Magazine of Verse.*

In June of 1922, Boyle married Robert Brault, a young French engineer she had met in Cincinnati. The following summer they traveled to northern France to visit his family. While there, Boyle hoped to begin work on a novel and secure a publisher's advance to finance their trip home. However, their stay with Brault's family went badly—Boyle was unable to write, and without enough money to return to the United States, the couple sought work in Paris. Boyle's association with *Broom* brought her into contact with many expatriates living in France. In 1925 Ernest Walsh, a young Irish-American poet and editor, asked Boyle to contribute to *This Quarter,* a new journal Walsh was editing, the first issue of which was dedicated to Ezra Pound and featured works by William Carlos Williams, Gertrude Stein, Ernest Hemingway, and James Joyce. Boyle moved to Grasse, a town in southeast France, without her husband to help Walsh edit the magazine. She also contributed several of her own short stories and poems, as well as an early version of her novel *Plagued by the Nightingale.* In 1927 Boyle's short story "Theme" appeared in the first issue of *transition,* an avant-garde magazine edited by Eugene Jolas. Until 1929 Boyle published almost exclusively in *transition;* fifteen of the first twenty issues contain her work. In the June 1929 issue, Jolas published his manifesto, "Revolution of the Word," which stated in part, "The writer expresses, he does not communicate" and "The plain reader be damned." His proclamation

was signed by Boyle and fellow expatriates Hart Crane, Caresse and Harry Crosby, Robert Sage, Laurence Vail, and others. Years later Boyle declared: "Our revolution . . . was against all literary pretentiousness, against weary, flowery rhetoric, against all the outworn literary conventions." This type of experimentation is evidenced particularly in Boyle's early short fiction collections, her initial novels, and in *Glad Day,* her first book of poems.

By the 1930s, Boyle's work was being published frequently in American magazines. "Kroy Wen," from *The First Lover, and Other Stories,* was the first of many Boyle stories to appear in the *New Yorker,* initiating a relationship that lasted several decades. During these years Boyle published many of her best-known novels, including *Plagued by the Nightingale, Gentlemen, I Address You Privately, My Next Bride,* and *Monday Night,* as well as translations, a children's book, and *365 Days* (1934), an anthology of short stories that Boyle edited with Laurence Vail and Nina Conarian, and to which she contributed nearly one hundred of her own stories. These years of prolific literary activity were characterized in Boyle's personal life by transient living conditions and fluctuating relationships. By 1943 she had divorced Brault, married and divorced Laurence Vail, and married Joseph von Franckenstein, an Austrian baron and classical language and culture scholar. Boyle lived in various places throughout Europe during this time, finally returning to the United States in 1941. Following World War II, Boyle journeyed back to Europe and served as a foreign correspondent for the *New Yorker* until 1953, living with Franckenstein in occupied Germany. Her experiences from these years are treated in many pieces from the collections *Thirty Stories* and *The Smoking Mountain: Stories of Postwar Germany*. Boyle taught at San Francisco State College from 1963 to 1979 and participated in many acts of protest in support of human rights. Her arrest during the early 1970s, following an anti-Vietnam demonstration, forms the foundation of her novel *The Underground Woman*. Since that time Boyle has continued to act publicly on her beliefs and to chronicle these experiences in her writings.

Boyle's work in all genres is closely related; similar themes and styles emerge throughout. Critics agree, however, that Boyle's most enduring writings are her short stories. *The Wedding Day, and Other Stories*, Boyle's first commercially published book in the United States, contains seven stories from her first book, *Short Stories*, and six additional pieces, most of which previously appeared in little magazines from 1927 to 1930. These stories derive from Boyle's own experiences in Europe during the 1920s and 1930s and explore many themes central to her later works, most notably the vagaries of love. Critics consider Boyle's early stories valuable as studies in the development of her artistry, and praise her command of language, adept metaphors, and passionate concern for her subjects. Such pieces as "Wedding Day" and "Keep Your Pity" exhibit the influence of the "*transition*-group" writers in Boyle's use of such stylistic techniques as startling imagery, fractured syntax, and variations on stream-of-consciousness prose, and are often listed as among her best works of this time.

A predominant theme that recurs in Boyle's short fiction is the moral and emotional impact on individuals of Europe's changing social and political climate during the 1930s. For example, in the story "The White Horses of Vienna," which won the O. Henry Award for best story of 1935, Boyle reveals the smoldering forces of prejudice and fear that precipitated the rise of nazism in Austria, while sympathetically portraying the allegiances and motivations of individuals, as well as their abiding compassion and humanity. "The White Horses of Vienna" focuses on the relationship between the resident doctor of an isolated Austrian Alpine village, who has injured his leg after lighting a swastika fire in the mountains to protest the current government, and a young Jewish student-doctor from Vienna, who arrives to assume the doctor's patients while he recovers. The friendship that develops between the two men, despite the student-doctor's Jewish lineage and the village doctor's political and ideological leanings, allows Boyle to explore the ironies and contradictions of humanity's spuriously constructed obstacles to understanding and acceptance. In one of the story's often discussed images, the village doctor, described as a "great, golden, wounded bird" in his longing for past glories, is characterized in an anecdote the student-doctor relates of the famous Lippizaner horses from Spain: "the royal, white horses in Vienna, still royal, . . . without any royalty left to bow their heads

to, . . . bending their knees in homage to the empty, canopied loge where royalty no longer sat."

Animal symbolism, which Boyle effectively employed in "The White Horses of Vienna," emerges as an integral element in "The Crazy Hunter" and "The Bridegroom's Body," two of Boyle's most critically acclaimed works. In these stories, which were originally published with "Big Fiddle" in *The Crazy Hunter: Three Short Novels* and later appeared with the story "Decision" in *Three Short Novels*, Boyle employs a blinded horse and a pair of nesting swans respectively to objectify her characters' fear of and need for love. In an essay on *The Crazy Hunter* and Boyle's novel *Monday Night*, Sandra Whipple Spanier stated: "Based neither on her own experiences in exile nor on her observations of the broad social scene, [these books] are unlike anything [Boyle] wrote before or has written since. The works are a perfectly balanced synthesis of her long-standing concerns for the personal struggle and for aesthetic experimentation and her emerging tendency to deal in her fiction with matters of the external world."

Throughout her career, Boyle has been admired for the range, depth, and technical brilliance of her prose. Although she also produced what has been labeled slick, commercial fiction, her more literary works are recognized for their conveyance of the evolution of individual sensibility amid historical experience. Commentators acknowledge her central role in the American expatriate movement of the 1920s and 1930s, and note her unceasing personal dedication to social and political activism. David Daiches concluded his introduction to Boyle's *Fifty Stories*: "Compassionate without being sentimental, moral without being didactic, contemporary without being ephemeral, *engagés* without being simply autobiographical or hortatory, these stories show one of the finest short-story writers of our time counterpointing imagination and experience in different ways as experience took on new forms and imagination shifted its role and scope to meet it."

(For further information on Boyle's life and career, see *Contemporary Literary Criticism*, Vols. 1, 5, 19, 58; *Contemporary Authors*, Vols. 13-16, rev. ed.; *Contemporary Authors Autobiography Series*, Vol. 1; and *Dictionary of Literary Biography*, Vols. 4, 9, 48.)

PRINCIPAL WORKS

SHORT FICTION

Short Stories   1929
Wedding Day, and Other Stories   1930
The First Lover, and Other Stories   1933
The White Horses of Vienna, and Other Stories   1936
The Crazy Hunter: Three Short Novels   1940
Thirty Stories   1946
The Smoking Mountain: Stories of Postwar Germany   1951
Three Short Novels   1958; reprinted, 1990
Nothing Ever Breaks except the Heart   1966
Fifty Stories   1980
Life Being the Best, and Other Stories   1988

OTHER MAJOR WORKS

Plagued by the Nightingale   (novel)   1931; reprinted, 1966
Year before Last   (novel)   1932; reprinted, 1969
Gentlemen, I Address You Privately   (novel)   1933

WILLIAM CARLOS WILLIAMS   (essay date 1929)

[*Williams was one of the most acclaimed American poets of the
twentieth century. Rejecting as overly academic the Modernist
poetic style established by T. S. Eliot, he sought a more natural
poetic expression and attempted to replicate the idiomatic cadences of American speech. Perhaps Williams's greatest ac-
complishement is* Paterson *(1948-1956), a cycle of poems depicting urban America. He is probably best known, however,
for such individual poems as "The Red Wheelbarrow," "To
Waken an Old Lady," and "Danse Russe." In the excerpt
below, which originally appeared in* transition, *November,
1929, Williams characterizes the American people as "som-
nambulists" and Kay Boyle as "anathema to United Statesers"
because she "has a comprehensive, if perhaps disturbing view
of what takes place in the human understanding at moments
of intense living, and puts it down in its proper shapes and
color."*]

There is, in a democracy, a limit beyond which thought is not
expected to leap. All men being presumed equal, it becomes
an offense if this dead limit be exceeded. But within the opacity which encloses them the American people are bright, active and efficient. They believe in science and philosophy and
work hard to control disease, to master the crime in their cities and to prevent the excessive drinking of alcohol. Alcohol
is the specific for their condition, thus they fear it; to drink
to excess breaks the shell of their lives so that momentarily,
when they drink, they waken. Or they drink, under subter-
fuge, as much as they may desire, but it is a public offense,
for all that, which the very drinkers themselves acknowledge.

When one wakes from that sleep, literature is among the
things which confront him, old literature to begin with and
finally the new. In the United States let us say first Emily
Dickinson and then Kay Boyle. To waken is terrifying.
Asleep, freedom lives. (p. 338)

Kay Boyle was quick to take up this realization. . . . [Her]
short stories assault our sleep. They are of a high degree of
excellence; for that reason they will not succeed in America,
they are lost, damned. Simply, the person who has a comprehensive, if perhaps disturbing view of what takes place in the
human understanding at moments of intense living, and puts
it down in its proper shapes and color, is anathema to United
Statesers and can have no standing with them. We are asleep.
(p. 339)

Kay Boyle's reception; the brilliant newspapers actively
trembling under a veil; the work of the poet H. D.; the young
wife that walked six blocks asleep in her husband's pajamas
one winter's night, the pants' bottoms trailing in the mud; the
boy that, thinking himself in an airplane, dived from a window in a dream head down upon the gravel path—this is
America accurately delineated. It is the School Board which,
to make a rule, made a rule that forbids themselves from
smoking at their evening meetings in the school building in
order that they might prevent the janitors from smoking in
the buildings while cleaning up the dirt after school. Fear to
vary from the average, fear to feel, to see, to know, to experience—save under the opacity of a mist of equality, a mist of
common mediocrity is our character.

The quality of Kay Boyle's stories has in it all of this strain.
They are simple, quite simple, but an aberrant American effect is there in the style. There is something to say and one
says it. That's writing. But to say it one must have it alive
with the overtones which give not a type of statement but an
actual statement that is alive, marked with a gait and appearance which show it to be the motion of an individual who has
suffered it and brought it into fact. This is style. Excellence
comes from overcoming difficulties. Kay Boyle has the difficulty of expression by Americans firmly in her mind and at
the same time the female difficulties to make them more difficult. And yet, showing all this, the work may be done simply
and directly; not with the horrible contortions, the agony of
emission, the twisting and groaning and deforming effort of
statement, seeking to disclose what it dare not acknowledge,
the style of the repugnant Jurgen, tortured without relief in
his quiet Richmond library—free from interruption. Kay
Boyle has succeeded in writing of difficult matters clearly and
well and with a distinction that is outspoken and feminine—
not resorting to that indirection and tortured deformity of
thought and language, that involved imagery which allows us
to lie and hide while we enjoy, the peep style of a coward.

Why do American artists go to France and continue to do so
and when there to drink, if they are wise, heavily? . . . In
France, they find themselves, they drink and they are awakened, shocked to realize what they are, amazed loosed—as,
in fact, they on their part shock and arouse the tenderest sentiments of astonishment and tolerance among the French.
They are, in fact, for the first time in their lives—and it is curious—with the sound frequently of slops emptied from a
bucket. Not always; however. Possibly, it will be enlightening, if something of spiritual worth is uncovered. But most
that appears is stale, mediocre, not equal to the continental.
The women, Americans, get to show their bodies—I don't
mean the contours only—and American women in Paris have
been anonymously very successful in latter years. At their
best they are perhaps always anonymous. They seem delightfully exotic with their natural faces, pretty legs and feet and
shoes.

Kay Boyle, in her stories, reveals herself, her body, as women must in any art and almost never do in writing, save when they are exceptionally distinguished. It is France again and she, partly from her own tragic history, more by France and alcohol, is awake. She has shown more than the exterior of her purely American female body. I don't know any other place where this has occurred. I speak of a work of art as a place where action has occurred as it occurs nowhere else. Kay Boyle has profited by her release to do a stroke of excellence which her country should honor her for. It never will. (pp. 340-42)

Few women have written like this before, work equal in vigor to anything done by a man but with a twist that brings a new light into the whole Sahara of romanticism, a twist that carries the mind completely over until the male is not the seeing agent but the focus of the eye. The dirty tradition of women's modesty and the cringing of women behind law and tradition gets an airing that certainly calls for a protest from the corrupt puritans. The usual reader will not be used to fairness from a woman, this straightforward respect for the writer's trade. Nearly all the noteworthy women writers of the past that I can think of, or nearly all, have been men, essentially. Perhaps I should have said, all the women writers acceptable to the public. (p. 343)

> *William Carlos Williams, "The Somnambulists," in his* Imaginations, *edited by Webster Schott, New Directions, 1970, pp. 338-43.*

KATHERINE ANNE PORTER (essay date 1931)

[*Porter was an American short story writer, novelist, essayist, and critic who is widely acknowledged as one of the finest modern authors of short fiction in English. She is perhaps most admired for the novellas* Noon Wine (*1937*) *and* Pale Horse, Pale Rider (*1939*), *which are viewed as outstanding examples of the genre. In the excerpt below from a review originally appearing in the* New Republic, *Porter provides a balanced assessment of Boyle's stories in* Wedding Day, and Other Stories.]

Miss Kay Boyle's way of thinking and writing stems from sources still new in the sense that they have not been supplanted. She is young enough to regard them as in the category of things past, a sign I suppose, that she is working in a tradition and not in a school. Gertrude Stein and James Joyce were and are the glories of their time and some very portentous talents have emerged from their shadows. Miss Boyle, one of the newest, I believe to be among the strongest. At present she is identified as one of the *transition* group, but these two books [*Plagued by the Nightingale* and **Wedding Day, and Other Stories**] just published should put an end to that. (p. 277)

She sums up the salient qualities of [the *transition* group]: a fighting spirit, freshness of feeling, curiosity, the courage of her own attitude and idiom, a violently dedicated search for the meanings and methods of art. In these short stories and this novel there are further positive virtues of the individual temperament: health of mind, wit and the sense of glory. All these are qualities in which the novel marks an advance over the stories, as it does, too, in command of method.

The stories have a range of motive and feeling as wide as the technical virtuosity employed to carry it. Not all of them are successful. In some of the shorter ones, a straining of the emotional situation leads to stridency and incoherence. In others, where this strain is employed as a deliberate device,

it is sometimes very successful—as notably in **"Vacation Time,"** an episode in which an obsessional grief distorts and makes tragic a present situation not tragic of itself; the reality is masked by drunkenness, evaded by hysteria, and it is all most beautifully done. (pp. 277-78)

In such stories as **"Episode in the Life of an Ancestor"** and **"Uncle Anne,"** there are the beginnings of objectiveness, a soberer, richer style; and the sense of comedy, which is like acid sometimes, is here gayer and more direct. In **"Portrait"** and **"Polar Bears and Others,"** Miss Boyle writes of love not as if it were a disease, or a menace, or a soothing syrup to vanity, or something to be peered at through a microscope, or the fruit of original sin, or a battle between the sexes, or a bawdy pastime. She writes as one who believes in love and romance—not the "faded flower in a buttonhole," but love so fresh and clear it comes to the reader almost as a rediscovery in literature. . . . **"Wedding Day,"** the title story, is the least satisfactory, displaying the weakness of Miss Boyle's strength in a lyricism that is not quite poetry. (pp. 278-79)

> *Katherine Anne Porter, "Kay Boyle: Example to the Young," in* The Critic as Artist: Essays on Books, 1920-1970, *edited by Gilbert A. Harrison, Liveright, 1972, pp. 277-81.*

RICHARD STRACHEY (essay date 1932)

[*In the following excerpt from a review of* Wedding Day, and Other Stories, *Strachey denigrates the influence of the writers surrounding* transition *magazine on Boyle's fiction.*]

transition was a brave venture and in that respect demanded and obtained one's sympathy—but it is a good thing for Miss Boyle and one or two other contributors that it is no longer able to confound their genius with (let us be kind) the high spirits of the mathematical sign writers. It was a cocktail with too much kick in it for most of us, and served only to hide from our muddled vision those works which deserved a more serious consideration. Miss Boyle's "stories" [in **Wedding Day, and Other Stories**] are very short: and it is, perhaps, only fair to warn the reader that they are not stories at all in the accepted sense of the word. Short prose exercises is the term by which I should refer to them, but I admit it is cumbersome. However, it may give some idea of what is to be expected. Her writing has the same economy of fuss as was shown in Miss Edwards' *Rhapsody:* each phrase and each word in the phrase are irreplaceable and made to carry their full weight of meaning—but here the likeness ends. (One would advise the reader of **Wedding Day** to look up *Rhapsody.* The comparison is most interesting.) Miss Boyle is much more compressed than Miss Edwards, more hurried, and her rhythm is not so delicately ordered; but her writing, if less subtle, gains in acuteness and virility. The following extract from **"Summer,"** one of Miss Boyle's stories, is a fair example of her prose:

> The girl listened to the lean shrivelled heart of the sound as it beat alone in the middle of his room with no grief fierce or great enough to come to it. And then it began to run in a frenzy in his room patting with quick hard paws on the glass of the windows. It was a trapped fox barking in frenzy to get out of the room, and flinging down with its soft gasping belly on the young man's belly, its worn thin bark snapping its teeth at his chest.

How vividly is the reader aware of the consumptive's dry

PROCLAMATION

TIRED OF THE SPECTACLE OF SHORT STORIES, NOVELS, POEMS AND PLAYS STILL UNDER THE HEGEMONY OF THE BANAL WORD, MONOTONOUS SYNTAX, STATIC PSYCHOLOGY, DESCRIPTIVE NATURALISM, AND DESIROUS OF CRYSTALLIZING A VIEWPOINT...

WE HEREBY DECLARE THAT :

1. THE REVOLUTION IN THE ENGLISH LANGUAGE IS AN ACCOMPLISHED FACT.

2. THE IMAGINATION IN SEARCH OF A FABULOUS WORLD IS AUTONOMOUS AND UNCONFINED.
 (*Prudence is a rich, ugly old maid courted by Incapacity...* Blake)

3. PURE POETRY IS A LYRICAL ABSOLUTE THAT SEEKS AN A PRIORI REALITY WITHIN OURSELVES ALONE.
 (*Bring out number, weight and measure in a year of dearth...* Blake)

4. NARRATIVE IS NOT MERE ANECDOTE, BUT THE PROJECTION OF A METAMORPHOSIS OF REALITY.
 (*Enough ! Or Too Much !...* Blake)

5. THE EXPRESSION OF THESE CONCEPTS CAN BE ACHIEVED ONLY THROUGH THE RHYTHMIC " HALLUCINATION OF THE WORD ". (Rimbaud).

6. THE LITERARY CREATOR HAS THE RIGHT TO DISINTEGRATE THE PRIMAL MATTER OF WORDS IMPOSED ON HIM BY TEXT-BOOKS AND DICTIONARIES.
 (*The road of excess leads to the palace of Wisdom...* Blake)

7. HE HAS THE RIGHT TO USE WORDS OF HIS OWN FASHIONING AND TO DISREGARD EXISTING GRAMMATICAL AND SYNTACTICAL LAWS.
 (*The tigers of wrath are wiser than the horses of instruction...* Blake)

8. THE " LITANY OF WORDS " IS ADMITTED AS AN INDEPENDENT UNIT.

9. WE ARE NOT CONCERNED WITH THE PROPAGATION OF SOCIOLOGICAL IDEAS, EXCEPT TO EMANCIPATE THE CREATIVE ELEMENTS FROM THE PRESENT IDEOLOGY.

10. TIME IS A TYRANNY TO BE ABOLISHED.

11. THE WRITER EXPRESSES. HE DOES NOT COMMUNICATE.

12. THE PLAIN READER BE DAMNED.
 (*Damn braces ! Bless relaxes !...* Blake)

Signed : KAY BOYLE, WHIT BURNETT, HART CRANE, CARESSE CROSBY, HARRY CROSBY, MARTHA FOLEY, STUART GILBERT, A. L. GILLESPIE, LEIGH HOFFMAN, EUGENE JOLAS, ELLIOT PAUL, DOUGLAS RIGBY, THEO RUTRA, ROBERT SAGE, HAROLD J. SALEMSON, LAURENCE VAIL.

Declaration of "The Revolution of the Word," published in transition, *June, 1929.*

cough, and (towards the end of this paragraph or paroxysm) the laboured and wheezy intake of his breathing! But Miss Boyle is not always so controlled and sure of her effect. Sometimes a howl of pain reveals (and writing in *transition* it must have been very difficult *not* to reveal) that she had been stung by the bee which Miss Stein was not able to keep in her bonnet—I mean the doctrine of the Continuous Present. This experiment, mildly embodied in *Three Lives,* was exciting and valuable; but its fanatical development seems doomed to obscurity or ridicule. And without pursuing that subject further one would like not to see Miss Boyle presently, and then continuously, running after a phantom.

> *Richard Strachey, in a review of "Wedding Day and Other Stories," in* The New Statesman & Nation, *n.s. Vol. IV, No. 83, September 24, 1932, p. 347.*

STRUTHERS BURT (essay date 1946)

[*Burt was an American man of letters whose short story collections include* John O'May, and Other Stories (*1918*) and The Scarlet Hunter (*1925*). *In the following excerpt, Burt favorably reviews* Thirty Stories, *recommending the European tales over those set in the United States.*]

Miss Boyle is a storyteller, a superb one; by and large, the best in this country, and one of the best now living. This somewhat belated point of view concerning her work emerges clearly, it seems to me, in [the tales collected in *Thirty Stories*], especially as they have been arranged chronologically and according to background; according, that is, to the country in which they are laid. Here is the grouping.

Early Group: 1927-1934. Austrian Group: 1933-1938. English Group: 1935-1936. French Group: 1939-1942. And then finally, three stories, all recent and well known, **"The Canals of Mars," "The Loneliest Man in the U. S. Army," "Winter Night,"** American Group: 1942-1946. These last were written after Miss Boyle's return to this country in 1941 from nineteen years of residence in Europe, principally in the three countries which engage her attention: France, England, and Austria. The background of the Early Group is mostly American, too, but that of an America not yet at war. Of the nine stories in this group, all but three, **"Wedding Day," "Rest Cure,"** and **"Keep Your Pity,"** have an American background. One, **"Kroy Wen,"** which happens to be "New York" spelled backwards, as you often see names on a lifepreserver, looked at from certain angles, takes place on a ship, to be sure, but it is an American ship bound for Italy, and the leading character is an American motion-picture director, with all the, by now, well-established rules as to what those abused characters must be. (Motion-picture directors as a whole are extremely sensitive, intelligent men, a beneficent leaven in Hollywood. It is not from them that the fantastic place derives its fantastic traditions.)

These early stories are mostly interesting as a study in the emergence of an artist; an artist with a beautiful command of language, a unique gift for striking metaphor, granted as a rule only to poets, and a passionate, impelling drive. An artist, original, rebellious, and bitterly observant. No wonder Miss Boyle was a sensation; at first, acclaimed only by the cognoscenti, later on received, but with reservations, by the general reading public. On the whole, these stories are not completely successful. That was the way they struck me when I first read them many years ago; and that is the way all but one, **"Friend of the Family,"** strikes me now. **"Friend of the Family"** is a beautiful story, delicate, straight-moving, and filled with implications, and is Miss Boyle at her best and in full control of her equipment. But the remainder of this group seem to me all implication, vague and confused, and not at all clear in the mind of the author.

There is no going deep down below the multitudinous impressions; swift, following upon each other, tumultuous like winds in a storm. But below any winds is the earth and people walking about on it. **"Keep Your Pity,"** for instance, is a splendidly told story, as are all Miss Boyle's stories, early or late, and the characters, on the surface, are as sharp as etchings, but they haven't the distance or depth that etchings should have. It seems to me that Miss Boyle has misplaced both her philosophy and psychology, and has substituted contempt and loathing for the pity the title implies.

It is when she goes to Europe, or, rather, when she begins to write with a European background, that she comes into her own. Like Henry James, like many American writers, something seems to have been released by the European scene, and European character, and the contrast between the latter and the American in Europe. These stories have a sure touch; the touch of a master craftsman. A sure direction. They go places, whether you do or do not always agree with them;

whether or not you find, at times, the faults, the reverse side, of Miss Boyle's virtues, too much metaphor; at moments, too much calorescence, too much heat. She has an eerie gift of bringing completely to life the European background; Austrian, English, French, and of bringing to life the people who live there. When she ascends mountains, she is superb. She has an affinity for snow, storm, glaciers, and high places, very moving to those who feel as she does. But once again, the more of a story she has to tell, the better she is. . . .

Struthers Burt, "The Mature Craft of Kay Boyle," in The Saturday Review of Literature, Vol. XXIX, No. 48, November 30, 1946, p. 11.

ROSEMARY PARIS (essay date 1947)

[*In the excerpted review below, Paris views the pieces in* Thirty Stories *as failed attempts by Boyle to deepen and expand her initial abilities, unfavorably comparing several stories to those of D. H. Lawrence and characterizing Boyle's work in this volume as undisciplined, superficial, and stylish.*]

The stories in **Thirty Stories** span a period of twenty years, but they give the impression that her initial very real ability has failed to broaden and deepen. Though she deals with the resounding materials of the contemporary world, the wars, the disruptions, racial discrimination and so forth, the generally static effect of her work results perhaps because her distracting stylistic mannerisms have been only slightly muted with time and her preoccupations have remained essentially the same. She has the acute sensibility of the romantic writer; she so indulges herself in descriptive detail that the result is sometimes nearer hysteria than intensity of mood; she uses indiscriminately, until their effectiveness is blunted or diffused, mesmeric words like sweet, golden and milky.

Love is the predominant theme of the stories, a tormenting, violent passion that sweeps in its path all earlier commitments and paler sentiments. Its setting is a wind-swept lost world of black mountain-sides or ashen sea; its women are tall and lean with bright painted mouths and its men are strong, remote and austere, but with wild kisses for the woman who at last kindles the flame of passion. There are curious echoes of Lawrence in these episodes. The guide of **"Maiden, Maiden"** is the familiar little dark man, and there are others as dark and as virile, Major Altshuster, Birdie, Dr. Heine. But unlike the lovers of Lawrence's novels, for whom sexual love is only a part of a very complex search for grace, Miss Boyle's seem to consider it an end in itself. The very echo of Lawrence condemns Miss Boyle most devastatingly; it points up the slickness and superficiality of the relationship between her men and women. Her lovers have no tragic stature; they simply posture, in all their leanness and beauty, like the stylish little figures in a Dali landscape.

Somewhere Miss Boyle has said that she would like to write for the magazines with large circulations. Her desire to reach a vast audience of—to put it politely—undiscriminating readers may have something to do with the fact that not only her love stories, D. H. Lawrence style, but a good many others as well sound as though she had picked up her material at cocktail parties. **"Let There Be Honour,"** for example, is a story set in France during the bitter days of German occupation, but Miss Boyle neglects all the really serious implications of the situation and tosses off a very neat and glittery boy-meets-girl tale, as palpitating as *The Scarlet Pimpernel,* eminently suited to slick paper and glamorous illustrations.

It is perhaps always too easy to generalize, and there are stories in this volume which come near the crystallization of substance and style which makes a good work of art. **"Black Boy,"** to name only one of them, is very delicate and moving, though even here Miss Boyle cannot resist the uncontrolled and unrelated imagery on which she relies for effect. At one point or another during the brief course of the story the boy's face is compared to tar, to a bat's wing, to a dark heavy flower and to marble. This is merely undisciplined.

And Miss Boyle's work as a whole is undisciplined. Reading straight through this book one gains the impression that it was written at fever pitch—oh, so intensely—and that the world it describes, vaguely familiar, sometimes disturbingly so, is nonetheless not seen clearly but through a rosy haze. Everyone, a little too beautiful, too glossy, moves in a dream-like trance. (pp. 81-2)

Rosemary Paris, in a review of "Thirty Stories," in Furioso, Vol. II, No. 4, Summer, 1947, pp. 81-2.

ROBERT ALTER (essay date 1964)

[*An American scholar, Alter has published highly respected studies of Maurice Stendhal, the picaresque novel, and American Jewish writers. In the following excerpt, he provides a brief study of narrative technique in* The Smoking Mountain, *noting how Boyle's style relates to and illuminates the central themes of her collection.*]

Many critics have commented on Miss Boyle's extraordinary ability to crystallize historical experience into unforgettable moments of revelation, but it may be profitable to ask how she manages to do this. The question is probably not altogether answerable, but the only partial answer that I can imagine must be approached first of all through as incorrigibly academic a consideration as the writer's handling of narrative technique.

It is tempting merely to quote Kay Boyle because her writing is so superbly selective that nothing is superfluous; every word, sentence, and situation is made to do its job with an incisiveness that defies paraphrase and tantalizes analysis. Miss Boyle's earliest stories tended to lyric luxuriance, with frequent use of incantatory repetition; it is clear that by the time she reached this mature peak of her work [in **The Smoking Mountain: Stories of Postwar Germany**], she had learned a great deal about the advantages of spareness and understatement. The first story in **The Smoking Mountain,** for example, describes a number of German hitchhikers consecutively picked up by an American woman driving alone on the Autobahn. One of the hitchhikers is a blond German girl talking slangy American, who has just parted from one G.I. boyfriend and is on the lookout for another. But she does have one reservation about future male companions:

> "I won't have nothin' to do with niggers," she said. "I don't know how a white girl can go out with a nigger. They're just like animals. They ain't like men. They sure ruin every place they go."
>
> "No, you're wrong," the American woman said. "They're like the rest of us—some good, some bad."
>
> The blond girl looked up from the sight of her face in the pocket mirror she held, and her eyes went blank. "Excuse me, but I don't understand your English very well."

Here the episode ends: a few lines of narrative and dialogue manage to say more about the persistence of Nazi mentality than volumes of documents on the role of Nazis in West German government. One notes in the passage touches reminiscent of Hemingway: the complete suppression of editorial comment; the "poker-face," deliberately non-specifying use of "and;" the flat directness of "her eyes went blank." And there is Kay Boyle's own gift of inventing perfect gesture: the blond girl's absorption in her pocket mirror is both dramatically appropriate and eloquently expressive of the way she relates to the world in general. If this sort of brilliantly imagined incident, frequent in these stories, reflects the presence of Hemingway, it is not merely Hemingway the innovator of a rhetoric, imitated by second-rate writers and derided by supercilious critics, but the truly great Hemingway of timeless short stories like "Old Man at the Bridge."

Miss Boyle's range, however, extends beyond this tautly understated kind of presentation. The early lyricism has not been discarded, only severely disciplined so that a choice of verb, a carefully placed adjective or prepositional phrase, can give a sentence the exact shade of emotional coloring that the writer wants. In one of the stories, she describes a Swiss watch given to a small boy by his father, to be kept in safety for him until he is old enough to wear such a precious possession.

> It had a delicate, copper-colored face, and a stop-watch gadget on its bevelled rim, and besides hours and minutes and seconds, the days of the month unfolded on it, and the mutations of the moon were marked on its disk, in accordance with the rising and waxing and waning and setting of the true moon in the sky.

The sentence is remarkable in the way it conveys the magical meaning the watch holds for the boy. The point of view, however, is not really the boy's, but that of an adult observer—who can precisely describe the "delicate, copper-colored face" and "bevelled rim"—and a skilled poet, interpreting the little boy's experience. The use of "gadget" and "besides" reminds us of the way the boy himself might talk about the watch, but the moon's "mutations" is clearly the wording of an adult, who has arranged an alliterative effect and selected a deliberately uncolloquial word to suggest the specialness, the wonder, of what the watch reveals. The choice of the verb "unfolded" (as for a hidden scroll or a treasure-map in a story), the marvelous breathless progress of "rising and waxing and waning and setting," the poet's addition on behalf of the boy of *true* moon *in the sky,*" all combine to complete this sense of child's wonder.

Each feeling, of course, requires its own verbal rhythm and image, but Miss Boyle is typically more succinct than this in scoring her emotional effects. A story called **"Home"** tells how a Negro soldier picks up a German waif and takes him into an army shopping center to buy him clothes. When the child takes off his ragged slippers to try on a pair of real American shoes, the soldier sees the "bleached, spongy flesh" of the boy's feet and realizes that they once must have been frozen. " 'Maybe when he was nothing but a baby lying in his crib,' he said, and he held the boy's feet cradled in his long, dark hands." The soldier's profound compassion for the little boy is effectively compressed into the participle "cradled," while the striking image of the black hands against the white flesh dramatizes the human bond of love that can unite ostensibly alien human beings, and, beyond that, reminds us of the kinship in suffering that exists between the Negro American man and the white German child.

One of the important ideas which I think these stories suggest is that such suffering is a very rare—and precious—thing. Displacement, mutilation, bereavement are ubiquitous in the stories (and in our unhappy world), but disaster merely brutalizes most people, desiccates the flesh and ossifies the heart. It is only the rare few who have the mortal fortitude to suffer—that is, to remain human in the face of disaster, to learn from it. (The vivid contrast between these two responses is made here in a story called **"The Lost,"** in which two teenage refugees are implicitly compared.) In general, however, the German landscape of these stories, like the portrait of German society in Hannah Arendt's *Eichmann in Jerusalem,* is chillingly devoid of genuinely human beings.

> It might have been a picture that Breughel had painted, all this which lay before him, the slate-blue houses of the town descending, roof by snow-traced roof, to the barren trees which bordered the dark waters of the river, with even the single crow set as trademark and signature in the leafless branches, except that the bright, myriad, scattered presence of the living, which was the speech of Breughel's heart, had been deleted from the scene.

The image of the solitary crow with no living people in sight expresses much of Kay Boyle's feeling for her post-war Germans: at a number of significant points, German characters are described as eagles, vultures, harsh-featured birds of prey. Or in some cases, the stories use recurrent images of skeletal thinness to suggest the same idea of a people that has died to its own humanity. The final story of the group climaxes this set of images with a description of a cabaret dance that metamorphoses into a grisly Dance of Death. "He could hear the girl's hand striking the tambourine with which she danced, and he could not bring himself to turn his head and see again the bony stalks of her white arms lifted, like the arms of those who have already perished, reaching from the grave." In an irony that is both gruesome and fraught with insight, we see the people that created Dachau and Auschwitz transformed into the pipe-stem horrors of its own death camps.

It should be clear that Kay Boyle does much more than "catch" the historical moment. Her control of description and dialogue, of gesture and symbol, forces us to see the historical moment in the context of ultimate questions about the nature and future of man. The massacre of European Jewry is not for her merely a question of anti-Semitism; as the very title of her story, **"Adam's Death,"** suggests, the destruction of Jews means the destruction of men—indeed, while Final Solutions continue to be thinkable and therefore possible, it may mean the destruction of man.

Partly because of this broad perspective, the occasional affirmations in these stories of human decency turn out to be unexpectedly poignant with promise. We feel not only that there are some individuals, whether German or not, still sensitive and compassionate, but what is more important, that the general possibility of sensitivity and compassion still exists, that the last particle of mankind's virtue did not go up in the crematoria chimneys. In all but two cases, the characters capable of compassion are those who have in one way or another been victims themselves. The connection between victimhood and the persistence of love is significant. Kay Boyle's fictional study of post-war Germany is unflinching in facing the ugly facts of man's self-brutalization, yet she does not allow what she has seen to sour her entirely on mankind. Her stories give believable expression to a faith that human goodness—at least some people's goodness—can survive even the terrible shocks we have experienced collectively and individually during the past three decades. (pp. 181-84)

Robert Alter, "Kay Boyle: 'The Smoking Mountain': Stories of Germany during the Occupation," in Critique: Studies in Modern Fiction, Vol. VI, No. 3, Winter, 1963-64, pp. 181-84.

RICHARD C. CARPENTER (essay date 1964-65)

[*Carpenter is an American critic and educator who has written books on Thomas Hardy and the Victorian novel. In the excerpt below, he examines style as a vehicle for central meaning in Boyle's fiction, focusing on "The Bridegroom's Body" and "The Crazy Hunter."*]

Put simply, Kay Boyle's theme is nearly always the perennial human need for love; her design is woven from the many forms the frustration and misdirection of love may take. Her style and the care with which she limns a setting are, as they inevitably must be with a creative artist, but vehicle and adjunct for her central meaning. Although on occasion she may have forgotten the artistic obligation in exchange for sheer virtuosity (always a danger for the virtuoso), using her style to bedazzle rather than to aid vision, or letting exotic setting obscure the human situation with which she is dealing, in her better fiction, style, setting, and theme form a seamless web in which all the threads are held under a precise tension.

In two of her best pieces, the novelle **"The Bridegroom's Body"** and **"The Crazy Hunter,"** she demonstrates this to perfection. A brilliant evocation of milieu is what strikes our attention at first—the rain-drenched coast of southern England where the Glouries live in their great, bare, stone manor and Lady Glourie preoccupies herself with the ancient art of swan-raising; the endless paddocks of **"The Crazy Hunter"** in which the Lombes' horses feed and run, the cold stream in which Nan and her mother swim, the lanes down which she walks with her father. But soon we come to recognize that setting, especially in **"The Bridegroom's Body,"** where background is more important, is only an objective correlative for the inner lives of the people in the story. Lady Glourie, ostensibly a ruggedly masculine woman, is in reality lost and isolated, drowning in her loneliness in this world of rain and animal life. She desperately feels the need of someone to talk with, another *woman* to whom she can speak of her children now separated from her, off at boarding-school. Lord Glourie is interested only in fishing and drinking, in his boon companions and getting away from his wife. It is a life for Lady Glourie as barren as the stones of the manor. "All day long, all year without a break" she suffers from the eternal ubiquity of men: "a man serving at the table, a man in the kitchen, as if it were not only the wild cold country-side that drew men to it but as if all life itself and right to life were man's."

In the midst of her daily routine as she goes about the estate, where the swans are significantly quarreling over their conjugal territories, especially the "old cob" swan who resents a young one newly mated (the bridegroom), and where the constant rain is causing foot-rot among the sheep, Lady Glourie dreams of the "woman-sort-of-thing" who has been engaged to act as nurse for the swanherd's pregnant wife and who will soon be down from London. As she smokes her Gold Flake cigarettes that she carries in her tweed jacket, like a man, and tramps about in "the heavy brogues a man might have worn," she converses mentally with the nurse, who will, of course, be an elderly woman or at least a middle-aged one knowledgeable in the ways of children and mothers: "Why, Mrs. Gilfooley, or Miss Williams it might be, or Mrs. Kennedy, Ferris used to walk as far as this when he was five . . . Or tell her Mary had never liked dolls for a minute, mind you, never once, never at any time." She would tell the nurse: "I never thought I'd be able to have them off to school like this and live, but then it happens, you can bear anything, anything, and there you are. . . ." But whether she can really bear it or not without withering away emotionally is a question, for her world is dying to everything she actually cares for: "succumbed to the sound of glasses, guns, to the smell of stone and fish dying with hooks through their gills."

Instead of a middle-aged woman, however, the nurse turns out to be a pretty Irish girl, quite unsuitable for a confidante, a girl at once childlike and self-possessed. Symbolically she wears "a green silk dress that buttoned up to her throat" when she dines at the manor with the Glouries. At first she is something of a puzzle to Lady Glourie with her combination of deference and covert amusement, but soon Lady Glourie realizes Miss Cafferty's own isolation, seeing her "suddenly and piteously clear, touchingly and bitterly in need not only of money but of the other things to which no name came voluntarily; those effects which were a family's and a life's accumulation and which Miss Cafferty had none of." In this wild land, this "whole restless malevolent estate abandoned to the willfulness of purely male desire," in "this domain of locked, welded mates . . . the Jo Luckys, the Panrandalls, the Glouries, the violently mated swans," Miss Cafferty is doubly isolated, both by her background and her singleness. Lady Glourie is filled with compassion as she comes to realize what she believes to be Miss Cafferty's life-problem.

But only briefly. Soon she begins to suspect Miss Cafferty of having found solace for *her* loneliness in Panrandall, the Glouries' farmer, a reputed Lothario. When she finds the print of Miss Cafferty's "narrow high-heeled shoe" close to Panrandall's house, she feels sure that her suspicions are justified, then discovers that the nurse walks out on the moor alone at night because she feels she must, because something happens to her, a "kind of desperation of the heart as well as of the flesh." Lord Glourie is not satisfied with this, persisting in thinking that Panrandall is having an affair with Miss Cafferty; his attitude, however, is only a projection of his own unconscious interest in the girl, as his wife clearly realizes.

Of course, they are both mistaken. When Lady Glourie is awakened one night by Jo Lucky, the swanherd, with the news that the swans have been fighting, she goes down to the lake in her dressing-gown, to find Miss Cafferty there. The nurse has seen the old cob murder the bridegroom but has been paralyzed by fear and a strange inability to call out Lady Glourie's name. On Lady Glourie's venturing out into the lake to rescue the bridegroom's body, Old Hitches, the vicious murderer, attacks her. Swans, as Miss Boyle has been at pains to remind us, are dangerous birds, their wings capable of inflicting serious injuries. Miss Cafferty is beside herself with fear for Lady Glourie; under the pressure of these circumstances the reason for the "desperation of her heart" comes out in a passionate, ambiguous but nonetheless intelligible declaration of her love, not for Panrandall nor any other man, but for Lady Glourie. Holding the bridegroom's body in her arms, after Lady Glourie has escaped from the water and Old Hitches, she speaks in "hot broken fury" of how she has come to worship Lady Glourie for her strength and peace and "the look in her eyes"; how she has walked the countryside night after night "talking out loud to you night and day . . . asking you to give me a little bit of it to take away with me when I have to leave you, asking you for just one drop of it, one hint of what it is you have that I haven't got, that nobody else has, just one weapon to fight the others—"

To Lady Glourie this is a shattering revelation, not so much because of the sexual inversion, "Platonic" though it may be, but because Miss Cafferty's words seem to her something she has heard before, long ago, given shape "at last in the moving and terrible statement of memory." That love should be directed toward her from this little Irish girl is the depth of chilling irony, the perverse response of life to her need for the kind of love that can bring warmth to her heart. As her husband and Jo Lucky approach through the darkness until their lights fall on the two women standing there, Lady Glourie becomes conscious of the "wet nightdress clinging to her own strange flesh." Suddenly she begins "shaking with the cold," not of the body only we may be sure, but also of the spirit quite as suddenly become aware of the icy abyss of her life.

It is this motif of cold combined with rain and water that infuses **"The Bridegroom's Body"** with its almost archetypally powerful effect. From the very outset we are constantly reminded of the rain and the cold, rain dripping from the brim of Lady Glourie's hat, rain falling and falling over the too-green land. Out of doors we can feel the chilling slant of it against our faces, indoors in the bleak stone vault of the manor the dampness seems to seep into our bones. Kay Boyle hardly misses an opportunity to remind us of the dismal cold, the need for fires in May, the feel of uncarpeted stone against the feet. Although the rains make nature green, there is no fertility imagery connected with them in this story; instead the effect is that of death and decay, from the trout Lord Glourie hooks to the rotting hoofs of the sheep on which Panrandall operates with his knife while we writhe in vicarious pain. Perhaps Miss Boyle learned from Faulkner, her acknowledged master, or perhaps from Dante or Coleridge, the effectiveness of cold and rain as a symbol of spiritual stasis or spiritual death; or perhaps she simply responded to the natural environment archetypally, as Maud Bodkin would put it, intuitively recognizing that in this image-cluster lies a universal human meaning. At any rate, **"The Bridegroom's Body"** becomes a living experience for the reader largely because of the "real presence" of these images.

In the climactic scene at the swannery, the rain has ceased but its imagistic function is taken over by the cold waters of the lake into which Lady Glourie wades to rescue the bridegroom's body. Here, however, there is an added significance. The rising of the deathly chill of the black water up Lady Glourie's legs, the clinging sedges and mud about her feet, the eerie calm and beauty of the moonlit lake constitute a symbolic situation of great intensity, although we naturally struggle in vain to express it in discursive language. It is in the truest sense a "crisis situation," in which Lady Glourie is facing not only physical danger but is approaching the uttermost verge of her life experience. She is, in effect, being baptized, but for death not for life: she is saving not the bridegroom, who symbolizes youth and life, but the bridegroom's corpse, only the empty shell of that vibrant dedication to love destroyed by the evil old swan.

Old Hitches is natural enough, with his incredibly pure plumage and his vicious disposition; yet in the context of the story he is clearly much more than this, too. The description of his approach is vaguely reminiscent of that of the White Whale, another god of nature combining unruffled purity with the power to wreak evil:

> Five minutes must have passed before she heard the ripple of the water breaking, and she lifted her eyes toward it and saw the great unmistakable bird issue from the rivulet at the lake's head and ride slowly and supremely forward, his immaculate breast kissing the surface and pressing the reeds aside as he advanced.

In a "profound, satiated languor" he rests on the other side of the little lake to begin his "ceremony of the bath," while Lady Glourie approaches him, her eyes drawn to him "as if it were his own luminosity that drew her like a sleepwalker to him . . ." As she comes closer she can see the "dark blotches on his pate and throat, staining the incredible purity as blood might have stained it, and she can see the feathers scattered like petals around on the metallic rings his ablutions flung quivering across the lake's perfect sheen." The swan is at once a picture of perfect beauty, bathing himself in the moonlight, and a murderer cleaning up after his crime. Although Lady Glourie does not think of him in these terms—she is too forthright, on the surface, for such high-flown notions—and later gives him a clout on the head when he attacks her, the impression is still created. Hitches *is* a swan (as Moby Dick is a whale), but he is also a living paradox, like the whiteness of the whale, a symbol of the mystic connection between beauty and evil, love and death. Appearance says he is the epitome of purity; "reality" says he is the epitome of destructive power; he is both, of course. Miss Boyle could hardly have chosen a more effective symbol of the simultaneous beauty and terror of love, at once something to cherish and something to fear.

Although **"The Crazy Hunter"** has no scene to match this climax of **"The Bridegroom's Body,"** animal nature is used in a similar way as catalyst and commentary on human nature. The core of the plot is the struggle between Nan Lombe and her mother over destroying the horse, Brigand, who has suddenly gone blind, with Nan insisting that his life can be made meaningful, and Mrs. Lombe insisting that a blind horse is useless and miserable, and should be put out of his misery. Like Lady Glourie, Mrs. Lombe is a strong-minded, masculine woman whose code of life is to be sensible and practical, especially where horses are concerned. For—once again like Lady Glourie—she is burdened with the responsibility of a large horse-breeding farm because her husband, completely ineffectual at practical affairs, drinks more than Lord Glourie and does not even go fishing. One might hazard a guess that Kay Boyle had set herself twice over the task of exploring the relationship of a strong woman and a comparatively weak man, except that **"The Crazy Hunter"** soon reveals itself as more complex and ambiguous than **"The Bridegroom's Body."** Instead of a love that has long ago died, we see here love that has been thwarted and shunted off into blind alleys but which still calls out strongly to the hearts of the Lombes. Mrs. Lombe loves Nan, and Nan loves her mother, but both are puzzled and frustrated by Nan's developing womanhood. Mrs. Lombe, trying to be close to her daughter, fears the sex that she sees burgeoning in Nan and wants to keep her close at home rather than letting her go to Europe to school. Nan yearns for her mother's love but is

Boyle and friends at Le Moulin, the country house of Harry and Caresse Crosby, Ermonville, France, 1929. From the left: Countess of Polignac, Laurence Vail, Kay Boyle, Hart Crane, and Caresse Crosby.

afraid of the indomitable spirit of the older woman. We first encounter them as they go swimming together (obliquely reminiscent of the "baptism" in **"The Bridegroom's Body"**), seeing how different they are, Nan ripping off her clothes and tossing them anywhere, her mother carefully folding hers and counseling Nan to do likewise, yet seeing in the mother the outlines of the daughter's "thinner, shyer, corporeity." And after their swim, as they walk home together, they find a thrush who has swallowed a fishhook, which Mrs. Lombe calmly removes while her daughter cannot bear to watch:

> She looked at the long pale cheek and the lips set and she said, Mother, not speaking aloud, you can touch these things, you can touch death and wipe it off in your handkerchief afterwards and touch pain without shrinking from it but you cannot take me in your arms any more and when I am with you I am afraid. Mother, she said in silence not looking at the bird, come out of your stone flesh and touch me too and see how tall I am, my eye almost up to your eye, and how big my feet and hands are, like a woman's.

The irony of it all is that Mrs. Lombe yearns just as much for her daughter's affection but no more understands how to convey her feeling than Nan does. The girl she once was, when she was newly married, was lost when she recovered from a long struggle with tuberculosis. (Hemingway's broken places that have healed.) Candy says that to all intents and purpose the woman he married and loved "died" to become his efficient and masculine breeder of horses who can only dimly remember what sentiment was once like and cannot reach out of herself to Nan and her husband.

The relationship is not, however, linear, but triangular, or perhaps rectangular, since Brigand becomes almost a character in his own right, as we shall see. Nan's father, fittingly nicknamed "Candy," is an abandoned soul who spends his day in pointless activity and inactivity—shaving, dressing in his country-gentlemen's tweeds, strolling about the farm, and drinking. To his wife he is a cross to be borne—in various attempts to assert his masculine position he has frittered away on defective or useless stock money she has earned through careful management: Brigand was one of his purchases. To Nan he is the father she would like to worship but must instead pity and pamper, although between them there is a strange, telepathic sympathy. To himself he is a vast emptiness decked out in appearances, an intolerable burden. Unlike his wife and daughter he fears and hates horses, both for their breeding and mating and because he thinks they are dangerous brutes, a notion effectively reinforced in the story by the death of the young veterinarian, Penson, who is kicked in the face by a skittish horse.

Despite his close relation to Nan, Candy is not taken into her confidence as to the event which occupies the center of the novella. In hope that she may be able to save the horse from death if he can be taught to run and jump, even though he is blind, she engages in a secret campaign with Apby, the groom, to give Brigand back to himself. Night after night she sneaks out of her room, first to lead, then to ride, and finally to take the hunter over the barrier again and again. Much of this we see through Apby, a small, tough man keenly aware of his inferior social position and at first not over-fond of Nan and her unconsciously callous snobbery. But as we watch with him Nan's devotion to her horse, even to the extent of risking death when she takes him over the barrier on a pitch-black night of rain, we come to admire, as he does, her courage and her love for the blind animal.

Without Apby, and later Candy, Nan would have been defeated by her mother, who has all the advantages of common sense when it is opposed to emotion. Mrs. Lombe, who does not know the secret of the horse's training and would not accept it as an argument if she did, seizes the opportunity of Nan's going to London for the day to get a vet in to "do what has to be done." She considers all this talk about giving the horse something to live for only weak sentiment, to which she will not be party. But her plan is frustrated by Candy who, after getting up considerable Dutch courage, slips into the horse's stall, directly behind those terrible hoofs, which he fears more than anything else in the world, the same kind of hoofs that killed Penson, and stays there despite threats and entreaties. When his wife and the vet approach to drag him out, he melodramatically takes a pistol from his pocket and fires it, sending the blind horse into a frenzy. Mrs. Lombe and the vet know that if he continues to shoot, the horse is liable to kick him to death; thus there is a stalemate, at which the novella ends. Candy is still in the stall when Nan returns from London, her mother "going forward to meet her, neither the thoughts nor the words ready yet, nor the emotion nameable that shook her heart."

Seemingly this shows the human need for love even more distorted and frustrated than in **"The Bridegroom's Body"**: father, mother, daughter, all three twisting and turning in a vain effort to understand and love one another. Actually, this is not the case; for, despite its ambiguities, **"The Crazy Hunter"** is more optimistic than the tale of Lady Glourie. The key to this more sanguine view lies in three elements of the story which complement and enrich the plot: a Freudian motif, a motif of sight and blindness, and an involutional technique that takes us into the minds and hearts of the characters.

Nan's inability to reach her mother is compensated for (at least in part) by her attachment to her father and to Brigand, who becomes a substitute both for Candy and for the young men in whom she should be interested. There is a deep current of sympathy running between father and daughter so that we have in effect a muted Electra situation where the mother is in opposition to daughter and husband, though certainly not hated by either of them. But Nan, unable to love her father completely because of his weaknesses of character, has turned most of her thwarted affection toward the horse, classic Freudian symbol of masculine energy. *This* love affair, because its nature is sufficiently submerged, can be passionate and unrestrained. Nan thinks of the horse as a lover; her caring for him is couched in terms (in her interior monologue)

of sexual experience seen as rite. A long paragraph early in the novella sums up her attitude, showing clearly its connection with her father, and as well typifying the lyrical style with which Kay Boyle has invested the story:

> She stood with her hand stopped under the black hairs of the mane still, her obsessed gaze moving from the ear's soft flick and the passive brow down the nasal bones to the nostril, her own dream-stupored, half-slumbering eye level with the horse's proud soft brilliant eye. So this is how they think of you, my horse, she said in silence to him. She lifted her other hand and touched the wide hard cheek-bone's blade. Not my first horse or my second or even the third, but this time my horse in protest, my hunter in defiance; not with race and nervousness flickering down your crest and loins, but my bony-legged monster to gentle, to murmur alone to in fortification of my father's errors; the substance of identity and revolt and love to hold to, until I can see you like the oriflamme of what is nothing more violent than Candy and me walking down a street arm in arm together in another country, she said, the gloved hand moving on his neck under the man's coarse glossy hair. With one finger she lifted the velvet of his lip and looked at the upper teeth laid bare in his mouth, breathing the warm hay-sweetened breath while the physical stab of love thrust in her. . . .

Although this sounds like imitation Faulkner, it is also significant in its intense emotion, and plainly shows that the horse is both a surrogate for the love Nan wants to have for Candy and an adored being in itself. Kay Boyle in this way emphasizes the fact that the need for love is so powerful and demanding that, denied its proper object, it will seek out another, finding in that other the qualities it desired in the normal relationship.

The irony of it all is that Brigand is a gelding. In this setting of a stud-farm, with its constant matings and breedings, its talk of sires and dams and blood-lines, sex is as much turned awry—at least symbolically—as is the spiritual and emotional side of love. (It can be noted in passing that similar symbolism is to be seen in **"The Bridegroom's Body"** where the foolishness of some of the swans, males who try to mate with males and females with females, is discussed by the Glouries, with Miss Cafferty vehemently denying that there is any "sensible" solution to such errors.) Mrs. Lombe objectively, though rather cruelly, reminds Nan that her lover is not a proper male: she speaks of "putting *it* down," that is, killing the horse, and Nan retorts that " 'Brigand's a He . . . He's a man. You might speak of him like that,' " but her mother replies, " 'It's a gelding . . . There's no need to flatter it with a sex.' " Nan's furious rejection of this evident fact is emotionally important, because in a sense she is indirectly defending her father who is spiritually gelded as surely as Brigand is physically. "A freak, a fool, a hack like me," Candy thinks to himself after protesting to Nan that the horse is not really human. To this she retorts that everyone jeers at her horse because he isn't to "sire or foal or isn't a colt or isn't to train, or hasn't a single action he's expected to perform." Such a description fits her father almost as accurately as it does Brigand: superfluous man and superfluous animal, for both of whom the sole reason for living is that they must be loved. Even the horse's blindness is parallel in its emptiness to the daily encounter with Nothing that is Candy's life, an encounter symbolized by his impotent desire to be a painter and especially by the blank canvas before which he has finally learned to "sit still in terror before nothing, learning, the way a convict learns by heart the words of his sentence, the emptiness of one's own indecision and the elusiveness of the idiom, the pronunciation, the sound even of one's own purposeless intention."

Complementing this sexual aspect of the novella is the more pervasive and insistent motif of blindness and sight with its archetypal overtones. The description of Nan's eyes as "obsessed," "dream-stupored, half slumbering" in the paragraph we have quoted above is typical of many such descriptions. Time after time, Miss Boyle reminds us that Nan's gaze is "seemingly drugged," "glazed," "dream-rapt," "oriental"—in short, she is living in her own inner world of emotion and fantasy much more than she is in the outer world of hard fact. Her father's eyes, on the other hand, are "swollen, aggrieved" in the few times they are mentioned. Whenever these two are together an intensely visual quality characterizes their relationship: their eyes constantly meet, their gazes sliding across each other, obliquely. Candy also looks out at the world from his own subjective feelings, in particular blaming it for the transformation of his life into meaninglessness. In contrast to both of them, Mrs. Lombe looks objectively at the facts—or thinks she does—but of course is unaware of those inner things which are so clear and important to Nan and Candy.

The animal corollary to this situation is Brigand's blindness, a mysterious malady that has come upon him like a stroke of lightning, and which, according to vets, is probably due to a faulty inheritance. The cure for this state in Mrs. Lombe's opinion, the opinion of "the world," is a bullet between his blind eyes. She is not really a hard woman, but repudiates the "false softness" of her daughter and husband, as she must, for only by clinging to the world of fact can she defend herself against Candy's inadequacy and Nan's adolescent emotion. She cannot and will not *see*, as the "dream-rapt" eyes of her daughter can see, the importance of love in defiance of all common sense. As Coleridge would say, she moves in the realm of the *understanding*, whereas Nan and Candy move in the world of the *imagination*. Nan is callous to the affairs of the real world: she insults Apby, and when she hears of Penson's injury, she thinks, her "strange, dream-stupored eyes profoundly and motionlessly drifting," only that he would not be able to put Brigand down. But she is aware of what it is like to be shut up inside a wall of darkness; fruitlessly she tries to remind her mother of this: " 'When you were ill and young sometime,' " she says in tears and desperation, " 'maybe you wouldn't have been ready, just because older people said you were incurable and it was better to shoot you, you wouldn't have wanted it just because people who didn't care any more said that it was the kindest—' ".

As the writers of the twenties and thirties realized, and as so many more recent writers have forgotten in an effort to emphasize the surface of things, an involutional technique is most effective in creating the feeling of inner life. Like Faulkner or Virginia Woolf or Joyce, Kay Boyle works largely with interior monologue, sometimes with stream of consciousness, thus setting the internal states of her characters in contrast to the outer world, or complementary to it. Technique functions in concert with symbolic motifs to reveal the relationship between appearance and reality. This is especially true, for example, of Nan's emotional intensity contrasted with her dreamy and drugged look, or Candy; the ostensibly spruce country gentleman who is in reality as damned a soul as any in the Inferno. Occasionally the involutional method be-comes structural, as in the passage where Nan conducts a Kafkaesque trial in the court of her mind, while her mother carries on a banal conversation that intrudes periodically, or the long interior flashback where Nan recalls her father maudlinly drunk but nonetheless pathetic, crying for the young wife he lost for this one who is at this time lecturing the hapless Penson on the efforts of *her* father to keep the stock of English horses "pure," and prevent the loss of "sound mares" to "foreign studs." To complicate the matter, this surface conversation refers by indirection both to Mrs. Lombe's worry over her daughter's lukewarm interest in a young Irishman and to her constant concern over sex and breeding, a displacement of her own emotive life into the lives of animals that parallels Nan's obsession with Brigand. Thus Miss Boyle presents us with coiling spirals of meaning, ironically juxtaposed, that define the complex relation between a harsh and heartless external world and a tender, but sentimental and impractical internal world.

What all this adds up to, nevertheless, is a more "optimistic" view (if so blunted a word can indeed be used at all to describe such nuances) of human relationships than we see in **"The Bridegroom's Body."** Candy's romantic and foolish gesture of placing himself behind the horse's murderous hoofs is his way of giving life to the horse who has become the vehicle of Nan's love, and at the same time of achieving some identity for himself. The superfluous man saves the life of the superfluous horse, and in so doing proves that love is in some ways stronger than common sense. In **"The Crazy Hunter"** the weak win, if not a victory at least a draw; the youthful, the silly, the useless prevail over the useful and mature. In turn, if we may judge from the final words of the story, where Mrs. Lombe says: " 'There's my daughter coming,' " and goes to meet her, "neither the thoughts nor the words ready yet, nor the emotion nameable that shook her heart,"—if we may judge from this, the blind have in a sense brought the sighted to really *see*. One cannot be too specific, the words themselves are as ambiguous as Mrs. Lombe's emotion; but the probability is that, in its own limited way, **"The Crazy Hunter"** has the *kind* of revelation we discover in *Oedipus* or *Lear:* only those who become blind come to have the insight necessary to see into the "life of things."

It would be destructively simple to maintain that in **"The Crazy Hunter"** Kay Boyle is showing a theme of "amor vincit"—the drift of her entire work in fiction is in the opposite direction. All that we can be sure of is that "amor" is at the very center of the human predicament, nine times out of ten bringing grief to those who love. Nevertheless, **"The Crazy Hunter"** allows us to feel that tenderness, devotion, self-sacrifice are not always doomed to frustration and despair. Some kind of a further comprehension of the meaning of love has been brought to each of the principal characters in this tale. Although we should be wary of taking Candy's drunken words at their face value, there is a good deal of truth in his saying that he and the horse are "the forces of good against the forces of destruction," because they are both "freaks" and "outcasts," because they are both "love" standing against the practical world. That Kay Boyle wants us to *half*-believe this at any rate is indicated by Candy's repeating his wife's words about Gandhi, ugly and thin, with his teeth out, being a "freak" too, and that she did not care about his beliefs because of his appearance. Mrs. Lombe *must*, we may feel, have been brought to some realization of the superficiality of such ideas by the desperate reality of Candy's willingness to sacrifice himself for this kind of love. Without preaching and al-

ways reminding us that Candy is a drunk and a sentimentalist, Miss Boyle still seems to be stressing the paramount value
of love for fallible and limited human beings, for whom nothing else is a proper substitute. **"The Crazy Hunter"** is an advance over **"The Bridegroom's Body"** not only in the relative
complexity of the "figure in the carpet," but also in the moral
significance which that design presents to us. Certainly there
is real meaning in this tale that goes far beyond its evocation
of a human situation in a lyrical and intense style, or its mastery of technique. Kay Boyle here shows that she is an artist
deeply involved with one of literature's most enduring and
significant concerns. (pp. 65-78)

> Richard C. Carpenter, "Kay Boyle: The Figure in
> the Carpet," in Critique: Studies in Modern Fic-
> tion, Vol. VII, No. 2, Winter, 1964-65, pp. 65-78.

W. J. STUCKEY (essay date 1967)

[*An American short story writer, poet, and critic, Stuckey has
published a book on American writer Caroline Gordon, as well
as a survey of the Pulitzer Prize-winning novels. In the following excerpt from a review of* Nothing Breaks except the Heart,
*Stuckey labels these stories "clearly the product of the commer-
cial side of Miss Boyle's talent."*]

The appearance of a new book by Kay Boyle is, paradoxically, an occasion that her admirers must look forward to with
a feeling that approaches trepidation. For, even as afficiana-
dos know, there are two distinct sides of her literary talent:
the serious side that has produced some first rate fiction, **"Effigy of War," "The White Horses of Vienna," "They Weren't
Going to Die,"** (to name only the best known and most widely admired of Miss Boyle's short stories), and the other side
that has turned out glamor fiction (like *Avalanche*) for the
slick magazines. Miss Boyle's first big collection, ***Thirty Stories,*** published in 1946, maintained a fairly stable equilibrium
between both kinds; admirers were pleased but also uneasy.
But in this new volume, ***Nothing Ever Breaks Except the
Heart*** uneasiness gives way to dismay. The book is very short
on quality and very long on slickness and glamor.

Of the twenty stories in this collection, which brings together
stories published over the past twenty or so years, only one
approaches the standards set by Kay Boyle's best work; of the
remaining nineteen, only six strike me as having any significant quality. The rest are clearly the product of the commercial side of Miss Boyle's talent.

The best of the twenty is undoubtedly **"Evening at Home"**
which was published in the *New Yorker* in 1948. It is interestingly complex, delicately written, and honest in its insights
and in the demands it makes upon the reader's emotions.
Partly for its own sake, partly because of the contrast it
makes with the other nineteen it deserves a rather full discussion. **"Evening at Home"** is told in retrospect by a woman
narrator. We gather that she is middle-aged; we learn that she
has rented an apartment in a brownstone house in New York
and that one July evening while watering her geraniums she
looked out of the window and saw on the steps of a church
across the street the inert body of a young woman. As the
narrator watches, a nurse emerges from the hospital next
door and moves to where the girl lies upon the stone steps.
From her post of observation behind the window, the narrator sees the nurse lean over the girl "not in gentleness . . .
but in distaste." After a gingerly inspection of the girl, the
nurse marches back into the hospital. The woman at the win-

dow waits for the nurse to reappear. When neither nurse nor
orderly comes to take the girl in, she telephones the hospital.

In a nicely handled scene we see her talking on the telephone
to the nurse, whom she can see through the open window and
whose actual voice she can hear above the mechanical voice
coming out of the telephone. What makes this scene so effective is that it renders dramatically the central concern of the
story, the old problem of human isolation. But the scene does
more than that; it not only objectifies this isolation in action;
it simultaneously, without insisting, makes us feel its wrongness, its absurdity.

The woman asks the nurse that something be done for the
girl. The nurse replies that the girl is "stinko" and that she
is a matter for the police to handle. The woman replies, "So
you're just going to let her lie out there all night?" The nurse
parries, "What's this woman got to do with you?" At this
point, the story might have turned sentimental—as many of
the stories in this book do—but Miss Boyle avoids that trap
by using a technique that though by now familiar enough is
nevertheless quite effective. She has the retrospective narrator
report that her memory of what she said to the nurse is vague.
What the reader sees is that the woman, who has a little more
self-knowledge than is comfortable, does not want to insist
too much on her own goodness:

> Maybe I did not actually say the things I am under
> the impression I said then. Maybe I did not tell her,
> with my voice shaking like a weak and foolish
> woman's, to telephone the police again and tell
> them that they needn't come, because her heart had
> just thawed out beneath the starch of the uniform,
> and human blood was running in her veins. For a
> long time, I believed that I had said a great many
> fine and noble things to the nurse, but I could not
> remember the words I had used to say them. It may
> be that I simply put the telephone down, without
> saying anything at all, but I don't like to believe
> this.

What this passage does, in addition to avoiding sentimentality, is to add complexity of feeling and motive to the narrator.
It also prepares for the rescue scene and makes the woman's
heroic struggle with the limp body of the drunken girl entirely convincing:

> I lifted her head, and I set the hat as well as I could
> on it, and then I put her head gently down again
> upon the stone. I stood two steps below her now,
> holding her feet between my feet, and I took her
> hands in mine to pull the reclining portion of her
> into the sitting position that her lower legs alone
> maintained. And when I leaned above her to gather
> her hands up, I saw there were no rings on her fin-
> gers, and I saw that weariness and perhaps some-
> thing like disappointment, only more moving, more
> profound, lay like a mask across her features, tak-
> ing the look of beauty away . . . I drew her up by
> her long, pliant, ringless hands, and her helpless,
> seemingly boneless arms followed after, and as her
> head lolled forward on her breast again, the white
> straw hat slipped from it and rolled down across
> the steps. . . .

By half-leading, half-dragging the girl, the narrator manages
to get her across the street and up the stairs into her own
apartment.

In some ways this is a typical *New Yorker* story: there is little
action, no deep philosophical commitment and the story

trails off with a wistful irony that turns gently back upon the narrator. And yet, as far as it goes, the story succeeds. Nothing is forced or stagey. The author does not try to get an emotional response not called for by the events of the story. And **"Evening at Home"** takes on significance, too. It may not be profound, but it is there, quietly waiting to be discovered.

There are other stories in this collection that have their good points. There is one, recently written (**"One Sunny Morning"**) about a white boy from the North who visits a Negro family somewhere in the South and without show or ostentation does a small act of kindness for the mother of the family. The situation is convincing, at least while the story is being read. But after putting it down, one begins to wonder how much of its effectiveness is due to Miss Boyle's art and how much to current sentiments about civil rights. In retrospect, one asks such questions as, does the story have to be set in the South? None of the characters, not even the Negroes speak in Southern idioms. Is the point, then, that only Southern whites are prejudiced against Negroes? Or is Miss Boyle merely manipulating stereotypes?

"A Christmas Carol for Harold Ross," though its conclusion is contrived, does manage to catch the sights and sounds of bombed-out Berlin. **"Army of Occupation"** and **"French Harvest"** both contain sensitively rendered accounts of life in France after the liberation, but they are little more than anecdotes. Two other stories, **"The Kill"** and **"A Disgrace to the Family,"** begin rather promisingly, but are then compromised by the author's refusal or inability to develop them seriously. The remaining stories are worth discussing mainly because of what they tell us about the commercial qualities of this book. (pp. 85-7)

It must be admitted that these stories (to borrow from the dust jacket blurb) consistently rise "above the level of the commercially acceptable well-told tale." Miss Boyle displays a remarkable aptitude for constructing slick plots, for creating suspense, and for camouflaging implausibilities beneath her glittering prose. Moreover, her attitude toward human relations is enlightened and she is to be found on the right side of every important conflict. Indeed, Miss Boyle is so consistently right minded about significant world events (the *anschluss*, World War II, the occupation of Germany, civil rights, Viet Nam, etc.) that about half way through the book one begins to suspect that she may have intended these stories to be taken seriously.

It would be uncharitable, of course, to blame an author for being on the right side of important historical events, but at the risk of being obvious it must be pointed out that admirable political views cannot make bad fiction good. What does make good fiction can hardly be discussed here, of course, but it is enough to say that in stories like **"Effigy of War"** and **"The White Horses of Vienna"** Miss Boyle has shown us what it is. (p. 88)

> W. J. Stuckey, "The Heart Is Not Enough," in Critique: Studies in Modern Fiction, *Vol. IX, No. 2, 1967, pp. 85-8.*

EARL ROVIT (essay date 1980)

[*Rovit is an American novelist and critic. In his novels, which include* The Player King *(1965),* A Far Cry *(1967), and* Crossings *(1973), Rovit creates intricate, complex thematic structures that often revolve around the lives of Jews, particu-*

larly those in the United States. His critical works include Herald to Chaos: The Novels of Elizabeth Madox Roberts *(1960),* Ernest Hemingway *(1963), and* Saul Bellow: A Collection of Critical Essays *(1975). In the following excerpt from a review of* Fifty Stories, *Rovit denotes "the unsentimental delineation of a solid, sometimes sullen momentum of traditional folk life" as "the strongest achievement in Boyle's work."*]

This selection of Kay Boyle's short fiction [in *Fifty Stories*] spans almost forty years of work and is itself only the sparest sampling of her total literary production. . . . (p. 286)

Most typically in her stories, [Boyle] presents herself as a vitally interested witness. The events that seize her sympathies tend to be those in which social determinations collide with human hopes, rendering the latter poignant in their twisted impotence. To some extent, the breadth of topicality which her stories reflect can be seen in the format of this collection: Early Group, 1927-34; Austrian Group, 1933-38; English Group, 1935-36; French Group, 1939-66; Military Occupation Group, 1945-50; American Group, 1942-66.

[As the headings suggest,] Boyle's fiction has an astounding variety of landscape, and especially in the rural countryside, whether French, Austrian or British, her stories seem to be comfortably at home. In general, although her European villagers receive a national or ethnic distinctiveness largely through commonplace details of language, custom and their attitudes toward their neighbors and enemies, the sense of a permanently rooted connection between them and the ageless life of the land (weather, topography, seasons, crops) is consistently and surely evoked. In fact, it seems to me that this aspect of her fiction—the unsentimental delineation of a solid, sometimes sullen momentum of traditional folk life—is the strongest achievement in Boyle's work. That twentieth-century technology has doomed what centuries labored to create—and this, with or without extraordinary political upheavals—provides a constant undercurrent of irony and pathos to the individual fate of Boyle's characters.

But what one misses in Boyle's fiction—and it may be her most salient deficiency as a writer—is a consistent recognizable *emotional* landscape, a steady personal viewing center which might impart a distinctive style or tone or perspective to her stories. . . . In Boyle's work, . . . the writer or the narrator/personal tends to take the role of impersonal reporter, and the stories, more frequently than not, become twisted into well-meaning but finally unpersuasive and melodramatic contortions.

A steady passionate concern for social justice and an equally unswerving compassion for the poignancies of human suffering are powerful and noble weapons in any artist's arsenal—and to these Kay Boyle can justly lay claim. Further, she has learned her craft and each story gives evidence of a concern for structure and an attempt to make language define with accuracy and resonate with feeling. And yet, too frequently, the passion and the compassion tend to become the predetermined goals of the stories. Without an emotional landscape in which the contrarieties of desire and revulsion can find resolution in the ambiguous responses of the human heart, the noblest of sentiments seem overly strident and mechanically forced. Thus, one ought to recognize the diligence, the persistent quality of caring and the integrity of a long lifetime of work as Boyle's distinguished achievement. And if she is finally a minor writer among her gifted contemporaries, she has never been self-serving or cheap. (p. 287)

A 1930 portrait of Boyle by Man Ray. Caresse Crosby described Boyle in Paris during this time: "Kay is built like a blade—to see her clearly you must look at her from one side and then from the other; both are exciting."

Earl Rovit, *"Distant Landscapes," in* The Nation, *New York, Vol. 231, No. 9, September 27, 1980, pp. 286-87.

VANCE BOURJAILY (essay date 1980)

[*Bourjaily is an American novelist, dramatist, journalist, and lecturer. He was an editor and co-founder of* Discovery *magazine and has also served as drama critic for the* Village Voice. *Critic John W. Aldridge has identified Bourjaily with the "after the lost generation" group, a cluster of writers, including Norman Mailer, Gore Vidal, Truman Capote, and James Jones, who matured and gained prominence after WW II, and who portrayed in their works the lives of those who lived through the war with ability and veracity. In the following excerpt, Bourjaily examines four stories from* Fifty Stories— *"Wedding Day," "Maiden, Maiden," "Defeat," and "The Ballet of Central Park"—to illustrate his contention that this collection chronicles the evolution of Boyle's literary techniques.*]

Kay Boyle remains a central character in that group legend that nourished us all, the literary Paris of the 20's. . . . [They] invented techniques we still practice, and introduced themes that still concern us.

Kay Boyle's *Fifty Stories* is a wonderful exhibit of these tech-

niques and themes in evolution. Among the techniques we have grammatical simplification, rhythmic repetition, the mixing in of vernacular, stream of consciousness, density of impressions, radical imagery and experiments with surrealism that may have originated with Gertrude Stein and James Joyce but became community property of the group.

These 50 stories are set as the author's life was set, and their themes and concerns follow her moving and maturing: There is the Midwest, Atlantic City, France, Austria, England, France again, occupied Germany and postwar New York. Changing as current history changed, the stories deal with childhood and parentage, sexuality, crass exploitation, prejudice, Fascism, war, American values and the disorientation of individuals. Looked at as a whole, they are notably free of a compulsion to romanticize. . . .

David Daiches, who contributes a thoughtful introduction to *Fifty Stories,* [states]: "The most remarkable thing about the best of these stories, . . . is that they combine accurate reporting of the 'feel' of an historical situation with all those overtones of meaning, those probings into the center of man's moral and emotional experience, which we demand of the true literary artist. . . . [They are] compassionate without being sentimental, moral without being didactic, contemporary without being ephemeral . . ." [see Further Reading list].

Let's look at four of the stories, each from a different decade.In the passages quoted there may be some evidence of the evolution of her style, from high-spirited language-play to a dark, straightforward sobriety as the European situation grew ominous, then to the bitterness felt by so many political activists of the 30's, and finally a return to the spirit of play in art—a play that reflects mature control and creative purpose.

There is a particular literary technique that recurs so often in *Fifty Stories* as to be a kind of Kay Boyle hallmark: the technique of surrealism. None of the stories collected here is avowedly surrealistic, but there are controlled and often magical flights of surrealism in most of them.

The story from the 20's is **"Wedding Day."** Sexuality declares itself in the chief characters, a brother and sister whose relationship is on the threshold of incest. It is the sister's wedding day. Their mother fears things will go terribly wrong. Things don't; so much for romanticization. Before the wedding, however, the siblings go for a walk in Paris, and for several paragraphs it is like a surrealist film: "Here then was April holding them up, stabbing their hearts with hawthorne, scalping them with a flexible blade of wind. Here went their yellow manes up in the air, turning them shaggy as lions." Inexplicably, they are in a little train together. "Here were their teeth alike in size as well as the arrogance that had put the proud arch in their noses. Wallop and wallop went the little train through the woods, cracking like castanets the knuckles their behinds." Then they are in a little boat, and swans come to stare at them. And then they're back at the wedding with guests arriving peacefully, and the old mother dancing.

"Maiden, Maiden," from the 30's, is admittedly more romantic. It involves a triangle: a couple, illicit lovers, mountain-climbing with a dark, appealing guide. The guide and the young woman have declared their mutual attraction; the guide is killed before it can develop. The surrealist personification of a flock of sheep mirrors what is being said perhaps of the mixture of persons: "There was a scattered flock making their way upward; strong mountain sheep as big as calves, their smooth ebony faces turned to the sight of the people. . . . A few whitish ones walked among the others, and under their eyes were shadows of disillusionment and the long potted cheeks of the old and evil and dissipated."

It's hard to imagine a story more counterromantic than "**Defeat,**" from the 1940's. In it an escaping French soldier is helped by a schoolteacher, and says to her gratefully that a country is not defeated so long as its women are not. The same evening, from a hiding place, he sees the French girls turn out to attend an outdoor picnic and dance which the conquering Germans are conducting. In this tale again, the surrealist flight is cinematic; it foreshadows the bitter young soldier's discovery of the appeal of the conquerors: ". . . the German ranks had advanced bareheaded, in short-sleeved, summer shirts—young, blond-haired men with their arms linked, row on row, and their trousers immaculately creased; having slept all night in hotel beds, and their stomachs full, advancing singing . . . the bright-haired, blond demigods would march on singing across their dead . . . then would follow the glittering display: the rustproof tanks and guns, the chromiumed electric kitchens, the crematoriums."

Finally, in the penultimate story—"**The Ballet of Central Park,**" a kind of fable—here is what complete ease with surrealism allows Kay Boyle to achieve: "It should be stated here that I am no relation to Hilary except inasmuch as all adults are related to all children. . . . I am perhaps that idle lady, twisted out of shape by the foundation undergarment she has chosen to trap the look of youth for a little longer, her feet crippled by the high-heeled sandals that grip her toes like a handful of cocktail sausages, who has strayed over from Fifth Avenue leading an evil-faced poodle, gray as a wasp's nest and as nervous . . . and I am equally the lady with the light orange hair and muscles knotted high on the calves of her shapely, still agile legs who taught Hilary ballet. . . . I am also, being adult, the police officer who apprehended Hilary except that Hilary could never be apprehended. She was beyond arrest or incarceration, for the walls of any prison would disappear if she laid the palm of her hand against the stone."

Kay Boyle's psychology is realistic and her situations credible, but surrealism is an authentic, unromanticized part of her vision of the world—a world of abrupt transformations from charm to anguish, anxiety to knowledge, delight to fear or—to borrow a phrase of her own from another source— "avidity for love . . . and . . . inexcusable despair." (pp. 9, 32)

> Vance Bourjaily, "Moving & Maturing," in The New York Times Book Review, September 28, 1980, pp. 9, 32.

SANDRA WHIPPLE SPANIER (essay date 1986)

[*Spanier is an American educator and critic who has written extensively on Boyle's life and career. In the following excerpt from her book* Kay Boyle: Artist and Activist, *Spanier provides a critical and biographical appreciation of Boyle's work, focusing on* The Crazy Hunter: Three Short Novels.]

In the summer of 1936, Kay Boyle and Laurence Vail left the political turmoil of Austria to spend a year in England. When they returned with their children to the continent it was to the village of Mégève in the French Alps, where the family lived in their chalet until war forced them back to America in 1941. For a while, thanks to Laurence's inheritance, Kay Boyle was free to write without regard for the marketability of her work. These were vintage years in which she produced two of her finest books, *Monday Night* (1938) and *The Crazy Hunter: Three Short Novels* (1940). Based neither on her own experiences in exile nor on her observations of the broad social scene, they are unlike anything she wrote before or has written since. The works are a perfectly balanced synthesis of her long-standing concerns for the personal struggle and for aesthetic experimentation and her emerging tendency to deal in her fiction with matters of the external world. As in many of her other works of the thirties, the author distances herself from the conflicts she explores, and her characters live in what she later would term a "functioning world." There are topical references to the postwar poverty of Germany and Austria, to the Spanish Civil War, and to the rise of Mussolini and Hitler. But unlike the contemporary events that motivate the conflict in *Death of a Man,* here they are simply stage props, lending the authenticity of a "real world" context to the human drama at hand. In *Monday Night* and *The Crazy Hunter* the author's primary focus is on the individual heart and psyche, and she probes them with an acuteness and intensity and in an experimental style reminiscent of her best work of the twenties. And in the works she produced in this brief interlude, she also makes some of her most eloquent and explicit statements of the human need for love. (p. 125)

"**The Crazy Hunter,**" "**The Bridegroom's Body,**" and "**Big Fiddle**" are stylistically sophisticated studies of complex characters in desperate need of connection. The author's focus is on the individual's search for a meaningful existence. But these works differ from her more personal fiction of the twenties in that the people and the conflicts she presents are products of her imagination rather than of her actual experience. By achieving a fine balance between emotional involvement with and intellectual detachment from her material, Kay Boyle has endowed the personal struggles of unique individuals with universal power and significance.

The protagonist of "**The Bridegroom's Body**" is a tough-seeming woman who grows into a painful new awareness of her loneliness in a world where women have no place. The one critic who has examined the story in depth remarks upon the "brilliant evocation of milieu." The setting—"the rain-drenched coast of southern England where the Glouries live in their great, bare, stone manor"—is "an objective correlative for the inner lives of the people in the story" [see Carpenter excerpt dated 1964-65]. Now that her two children have gone off to school, Lady Glourie lives alone with her husband on their country estate, where shooting and fishing, looking after the family swannery, and worrying about foot-rot among the sheep are the sum and substance of life. She is weary of this masculine world: "The sound of men, all day, all year without a break, the sound of men: a man serving at the table, a man in the kitchen, as if it were not only the wild cold countryside that drew men to it but as if all life itself and right to life were man's."

Yet, isolated in this environment, she has absorbed its values and become estranged from femininity. Lady Glourie has cropped hair and a "big pair of shoulders strong as a wood yoke set across her freckled neck," and she smokes Gold Flakes. She is proud that her daughter "had never liked dolls for a minute, mind you, never once, never at any time." When the swanherd's wife becomes ill in a difficult pregnancy, Lady Glourie sends reluctantly to London for a trained nurse, "a woman-sort-of-thing," although she fears they are "probably more trouble than they're worth." She writes "in a bold strong man-like hand," "I wouldn't be bother [sic] with women down here atall if it wasn't for this."

Yet the idea of a female companion gradually takes hold in her, and we begin to grasp the enormity of her loneliness. She walks the grounds engaged in imaginary conversations with the nurse she has never met, looking forward to the time she might speak to someone of the son and daughter who are gone. She imagines sharing with her new friend the poems she had written as a schoolgirl. Or, she thinks, "if you were not too old we might be able to laugh out loud, uproariously, senselessly, standing shouting with laughter at something the way men scream with laughter together." She confides, "Miss Smith, Miss Kennedy, Miss Forthright, there is nobody left, no one. . . . If I change the flowers every day and keep on talking to you, perhaps I can keep it from you for a little while that there is nothing left here, that everyone here has died."

But when the woman arrives she is not the middle-aged trained nurse Lady Glourie had pictured, with "parcels of pain tied up" in her legs "from having stood thirty years too long by bedsides." Miss Cafferty is a delicate Irish girl in a green silk dress and high-heeled shoes—a bitter dissapointment to the lady of the estate, herself given to tweeds and cardigans and "the heavy brogues a man might have worn." Lady Glourie gruffly warns her that the swanherd's baby must be a boy, for the swannery is passed on from father to son, and she snaps that Miss Cafferty ought to get better shoes for the country.

But a week later, as Lady Glourie passes the nests where the swans live in monogamous pairs, she experiences a shock of recognition. A "sudden and unforeseen vortex of compassion" for Miss Cafferty sweeps over her, and she thinks, "Even me, a woman, too hard, too defiant, so that she came into this domain of locked, welded mates an outcast, to be kicked up and down the hill from one wedded couple to another, the Jo Luckys, the Panrandalls, the Glouries, the violently mated swans, and nothing but suspicion offered her." Suddenly Lady Glourie sees her "gentle as a young lamb to be nursed in the heart." Her tenderness for the young woman grows as Miss Cafferty's spirit, intelligence, sensitivity, and social conscience emerge in her conversations with the Glouries. At the same time, Lord Glourie, seeing that his attentions to the girl are unreturned, grows bitter and suspicious. When Miss Cafferty tries to explain to them that sometimes in the night she feels a "desperation of the heart as well as of the flesh," that she then must get outdoors and walk no matter what the weather is, Lord Glourie becomes testy. His small mind, with its narrow concept of women, can fathom only one explanation: she must be seeing the young farmer of the estate.

In the climactic scene, Lady Glourie battles the vicious old patriarch of the swans to retrieve the body of a young cob he killed in a struggle over the younger one's right to establish a nest for himself and his mate on the older swan's territory. Miss Cafferty looks on, paralyzed with terror, as Lady Glourie wades into the freezing pond to retrieve the body of the young "bridegroom" who had died for the love and protection of his mate—her white nightgown billowing up and trailing behind her on the water so that she herself resembles the swans who had battled to the death. The scene illustrates the

skill and subtlety of Kay Boyle's craftsmanship at its best, the charged image woven into the narrative so that it seems at first a mere surface detail. Overcome with admiration for the other woman's strength and courage, Miss Cafferty bursts out in a sudden confession of passion that startles Lady Glourie and the reader: "Let me say it! I came out to think about you here alone where there might be something left of you somebody hadn't touched—some place you were in the daytime—some mark of you on the ground. . . . I couldn't sleep in the room. I couldn't bear closing the door after I'd left you, just one more door closed between what you are and what I am!" She had recognized Lady Glourie's loneliness and her entrapment in an existence devoid of women's tenderness. "Don't you think I see you living in this place alone," she cries, "alone the way you're alone in your bed at night, with butchers, murderers—men stalking every corner of the grounds by day and night? . . . don't you think I fought them all off because of you, because I knew that fighting them was taking your side against them?"

When the swanherd and Lord Glourie finally come upon them on the path, the women are staring at each other in the moonlight, transfixed. Then "Lady Glourie looked down at the nightdress clinging to her own strange flesh and suddenly she began shaking with the cold." The story ends there. Lady Glourie is shaken by the other woman's declaration of love and by this confrontation with the barrenness of her own existence. Yet in that charged moment we sense that the possibility of connection between these women will be their only hope for warmth and satisfaction in a cold, masculine world.

"Big Fiddle," another story of an isolated individual in desperate need of love, ends less "happily." The protagonist is an American musician—we know him only as "Big Fiddle"—leading a rootless existence in Europe, drifting from one job to the next. He is isolated even from the other players in his act, his own countrymen. . . . When this group breaks up after their London engagement, Big Fiddle heads south on the advice of a neurologist who has prescribed rest for the shakes and quivers that have plagued him for a year.

Boyle in a hotel room in Kitzbühel, Austria, working on 365 Days, *a book of 365 short stories, one for each day of 1934, that she edited with Laurence Vail and Nina Conarain.*

As in **"The Bridegroom's Body,"** the author uses setting to counterpoint the psychological state of her character. Big Fiddle awakens in "inexplicable alarm" in the strange boarding house of an English seaside town. Lying alone in a bed "as narrow and single as a hammock," he knows only by the "stamping of his heart" that "this wouldn't be the eternity box then . . . but just the dress rehearsal for it." As in some of Kay Boyle's works of the twenties, external reality takes on the configurations of the consciousness perceiving it: "The street light was still lit on the esplanade outside and in relief against its bright white ambiance the curtain's coarse lace rose, webbed, convoluted, and like a dying breath expired." In his mind Big Fiddle begins to compose "the nightly letter home," addressed to a Father O'Malley. He passes the sleepless night engaged in an hallucinatory dialogue with the priest of the orphanage where he had spent his childhood.

That afternoon he meets a young woman in a teahouse. Her manner and her readiness to abandon any plans and spend the rest of the day and night with him indicate that she is not unused to making the most of chance encounters with men, but after they make love in a field outside of town (in the shadow of a penitentiary), Big Fiddle believes he has finally found an object for the tenderness locked inside him. To him she has become "what still remained of pity's and salvation's corporeity," and he plans to make the rest of his life with her. Grateful to have found at last the one who would truly understand him, he begins to relax and confide to her his troubled past. He had been raised in a Catholic orphanage and bitterly betrayed by the only girl he had ever loved. The darling daughter of Mrs. Carrigan, who ran the institution, she had made overtures to him when he was in his teens, and he had succumbed to the seduction. But the girl was already "in trouble," and to save her own skin she accused him of rape. He spent a year and a half in prison. "Eighteen months for doing nothing, for being a sap, for letting a damned little whore—" he tells his new love.

She is repulsed. Instead of responding to the injustice with sympathetic outrage, she scrambles to her feet and runs off into the darkness, crying, "You, jail-bird, doing what you did to me, and calling nice girls what you did—". He hunts desperately all night for her but finally boards the boat to Capri, haunted by her memory. (pp. 133-37)

But **"Big Fiddle,"** like *Monday Night,* is also a detective story of sorts. Beginning in the second chapter, even before Big Fiddle meets the woman in the teahouse, the narrative is mysteriously interrupted by fragments of conversation between an unidentified "Superintendent" in London and various lawmen elsewhere. An Italian count whom Big Fiddle had met on the boat coming to Capri and who had treated him coolly on board begins to seek out the musician's companionship, and Big Fiddle is flattered to a pathetic degree. Tension mounts as the reader recognizes a suspicious undertone to the unlikely friendship. When the count invites him to dinner, Big Fiddle is overwhelmed that such a man would be "asking a jail-bird, a delinquent, home," and he eagerly accepts. An Englishman has also been invited. Over wine and hors d'oeuvres, Big Fiddle is lured into a conversation about his nerve problems, his interest in detective books, and his past relationships with women. The Englishman finally declares himself to be the Law. It seems the "little girl" Big Fiddle had picked up in the teahouse has been found dead and disfigured on the Downs near Brixton Beach. Big Fiddle is accused of her murder.

As the story ends, the voice of Father O'Malley, the orphanage priest, speaks the "pure, clear, exalted" words of the last rites as Big Fiddle, a victim once again, stands "swaying above the table at which the men still sat, holding to the chair's back for strength, and waiting, now that the voice had ceased praying, for the tears to gush, hot, childish, bitter from his eyes." Once more he has been made vulnerable by his desperate craving for love, and again fate has slapped him in the face for attempting to establish the human contact that would give meaning to his desolate existence.

"The Crazy Hunter" is another impressively crafted testament to the human need for love. Again, Kay Boyle explores what one critic calls "the complex relation between a harsh and heartless external world and a tender, but sentimental and impractical internal world." Nan Lombe, a seventeen-year-old girl, is back home in England on her family's horse-breeding farm after having spent the school year in Italy. She is restless within the confines of her childhood surroundings, aware now of a higher plane of existence, one peopled by students and artists. She longs to go back to that world in which "they are still on the adventure, looking for a thing nobody here wants or has heard of wanting: knowledge or the way to knowledge or else simply the way, because of what families and conventions want, of keeping curious and keeping free."

But she finds it impossible to communicate with her mother, to tell her how she has grown and changed. Mrs. Lombe is a strong woman, inaccessible behind her competence and confidence and common sense. On Nan's first day home, they go swimming together in a cold stream, and the silence hangs awkwardly between them. When Nan spots a bird dangling in a tree by a piece of fishing line it had swallowed, she is horrified, but her mother rescues it without fuss. The girl thinks:

> You can touch these things, you can touch death and wipe it off in your handkerchief afterwards and touch pain without shrinking from it but you cannot take me in your arms any more and when I am with you I am afraid. Mother, she said in silence not looking at the bird, come out of your stone flesh and touch me too and see how tall I am, my eye almost up to your eye, and how big my feet and hands are, like a woman's. But the cheek did not alter and did not color, and the girl made herself look down now at the bird.

Nan's father, Candy, is nothing like his wife. A bantam-like Canadian, he is a would-be artist who had married a frail consumptive girl with more money than he. After he had nursed her back to health in the high mountains of Europe, they had returned to her family home in England, where she gradually had become the strong, efficient horsewoman Nan has always known. Candy fills his days reading Woolworth paperback mysteries, meticulously grooming himself, and drinking. Long ago he had given up the pretense of sitting for hours paralyzed before a blank canvas.

As mother and daughter return from their swim, Mrs. Lombe confides to Nan her exasperation at Candy's latest foolishness. With strict instructions and some money, she had sent him to a horse fair, but, as usual, he had had a few too many drinks and had brought home a worthless gelding—a "crazy hunter" of a horse. But Nan will hear none of her mother's complaints about the man or the horse. As an act of defiance and a token of love for her father, she falls in love with the crazy hunter. Kay Boyle subtly but firmly makes a symbol of the horse and links it to Candy. . . .

The horse is "transformed to symbol for the separateness of two interpretations and two isolate despairs."

But suddenly the crazy hunter suffers a stroke that leaves him blind. The only sensible course is to destroy the animal. The local veterinarian, Penson, after examining the horse, says so, and the London doctor whom Mrs. Lombe brings in to satisfy her grief-stricken daughter concurs. But Nan and Candy square off against Mrs. Lombe and the veterinarians—irrational love versus common sense, the heart versus the head.

During the two-week reprieve Mrs. Lombe grants her daughter to come to her senses, Candy is torn between his loyalty to Nan and his own gut-terror of horses. He worries about her safety, and his fears are intensified when Penson is killed, kicked in the face by a horse he was treating. Nan clutches at any possibility to save her horse. She even writes for advice to an Irish student she had met at an afternoon tea in Italy. But like other inhabitants of Kay Boyle's world, she comes to a bitter realization: "She began seeing how it was now as a savage might have seen it and made a picture of it with berry stains, or some coloring as primitive, or stitched it toughly in beads or thread on cloth: the small helpless lone island of the self out of voice's call or swimmer's reach lying among the scattered inaccessible islands of those other selves." "She saw that unpeopled landscape and the vast waters washing forever unspanned between the separate islands, and she touched the bones in bed with her," realizing, "If there is any strength it is in these, it is here." In a world of isolated individuals, Nan can look only to herself for help.

In the course of the next two weeks, she steals into the stable every night, determined to make her horse understand that the world exists as it always had, even though he can no longer see it. She will teach him to walk, then be ridden, and finally to jump, in the conviction that with this evidence the standardbearers of common sense will be forced to recognize that his life has value. With hard work and love, she does begin to succeed in training the "worthless" animal. But the defenders of reason are not easily moved. When Nan receives an encouraging reply from her Irish friend saying he has heard of blind horses being successfully trained, Mrs. Lombe becomes bitter and exasperated. She tells the girl that she will not have her riding a blind horse and killing herself and the poor beast. "Thank God, there's a more humane way of putting it down," she says. Nan retorts: "Brigand's a He. . . . He's a man. You might speak of him like that." But her mother reminds her that the horse is a gelding: "There's no need to flatter it with a sex," she says. Again we are subtly reminded of the crazy hunter's resemblance to Candy, himself "useless" and emasculated.

When Nan goes away overnight to attend a wedding in London as a guest of the Irishman, Mrs. Lombe finally sees the opportunity for reason to prevail. As Candy pours himself his first drink of the morning, he looks out the window to see his wife walking down the driveway with a stranger in khaki riding breeches. He knows what is about to happen, and in a way he is relieved. In his soggy reverie, Kay Boyle again makes clear that the situation of the crazy hunter, who has outlived his usefulness, is Candy's, too: "Horse, it's your turn to die. This time it's not Penson or me but you, horse not man, you blank-eyed espial spying upon the secrets of eternity, you milky-eyed deserter. You're no good to anyone, he said, but he was looking at his own face in the sideboard mirror."

But after the fifth glass of whiskey, he thinks of Nan and he knows what he must do. The story concludes in a dramatic standoff between Mrs. Lombe, accompanied by the man who had come to mark the lines in chalk on the horse's forehead, and Candy, who plants himself, pistol in hand, in the stall with the beast he fears, determined to wait it out until his "little girl" returns. Kay Boyle makes it plain that she considers Candy's rescue attempt an act of heroic proportions and universal moment—representing nothing less than the power of love standing up to the forces of desiccated reason that would have the parched heart wither away. (pp. 137-41)

When the haulers come at eleven to remove the animal's body, Mrs. Lombe asks them to come back later. When they return in the afternoon, she requests their help in first removing her husband from the stall. Embarrassed and bewildered, but finally convinced the man is drunk, they begin to comply. Candy, confronted, shoots wildly into the air. The horse panics and rears, "while the little man lay pressed against the stall's side, his hands down, his head lifted, so far untouched and perhaps immuned by this passive, abeyant, this almost ludicrous posture of martyrdom." When at twenty past four Nan comes home, Mrs. Lombe quits the position she had taken outside the stable door and goes forward to meet her, "neither the thoughts or the words ready yet, nor the emotion nameable that shook her heart."

Candy, in his blind terror and blind love, pinned to the wood of the stable stall, is a ludicrous martyr, a freak—like the blind horse, like Gandhi, a bit like Christ. We are not allowed to forget that this is the act of a drunkard who must fortify himself in his heroic stand with draughts from his flask, who mortifies his wife throughout his sacred vigil by singing dirty jingles. His martyrdom is absurd—but truly noble. Once more, as she had in *Monday Night*, Kay Boyle allows love a small victory. In a work whose title coincidentally echoes that of another book published the same year by a woman who would come to be her close friend—Carson McCullers' *The Heart Is a Lonely Hunter*—she explores the insatiability of the human heart. Candy has performed an act of awesome selflessness, confronting head on his own deepest terror in the name of love, ready even to die for it. The story ends ambiguously, Nan's reaction and the horse's fate left to conjecture. But in the "unnameable emotion" that shakes the previously untouched heart of Mrs. Lombe there is the possibility of salvation. **"The Crazy Hunter"** is Kay Boyle's firmest and perhaps finest declaration of love's redeeming grace. (pp. 141-42)

> *Sandra Whipple Spanier, in her* Kay Boyle: Artist and Activist, *Southern Illinois University Press, 1986, 249 p.*

SUZANNE CLARK (essay date 1988)

[*In the following excerpt, Clark examines Boyle's relationship with the "revolution of the word," the tradition of women's writing, and the politics of feminism.*]

Modernist experiments with language have an especially problematic relationship to women's writing which is experimental. Kay Boyle's early work puts the old categories into motion and marks out a new literary space of intense descriptive prose. Yet her impact on literary history has not seemed so powerful as her writing would warrant. In 1929, Kay Boyle signed a manifesto for *transition* calling for "The Revolution of the Word." Other signers included Hart Crane, Harry and Caresse Crosby, and Eugene Jolas. The "Proclamation" asserted, among other things, that "The literary creator has the right to disintegrate the primal matter of words" and that "We are not concerned with the propagation of sociological ideas except to emancipate the creative elements from the present ideology."

Boyle's rewriting of the new word was a different matter from the poetics of someone like Hart Crane, a difference she in fact had signaled herself in a critique of his obsession with the primacy of words, in "Mr. Crane and His Grandmother." Nevertheless, though she prefers the American renewals of Williams and Moore, Boyle shows herself to be in the tradition of Baudelaire and Rimbaud as well. Her innovations in prose style qualify Kay Boyle as a revolutionary of lyric language. In her early works, such as **"Episode in the Life of an Ancestor," "Wedding Day,"** or **"On the Run,"** she swerves her narratives into a language of illumination and intensity that disorders story sequence and the familiar forms of remembering. She experiments in a way that recalls the hallucinatory surrealism of Rimbaud's prose and fulfills the aspiration of the poetic revolution for what the *transition* manifesto calls "the projection of a metamorphosis of reality."

But what does this powerful disintegration of conventional writing have to do with writing as a woman? The strong old forms of the sentimental novel were part of what modernist poetics rejected. And yet, for the modernists, the cultural image of women and writing was deeply involved with that past. A shattering of language seemed to be at odds with writing like a woman. Women writers, too, felt they had to separate themselves from that conventional past. Boyle herself has taken pains to disassociate her work from the older tradition of women's writing as well as from the politics of feminism. Nevertheless, Kay Boyle's reworking of the relationship between time and place, narration and description, may also make the connection between the time of poetic revolution and the place of the woman. (pp. 322-23)

Boyle's early work practices a resistance to extremism in the midst of a modernist extremism about gender. Modernism as it appeared in the 1920s featured an ideological either/or which would either deny the existence of gender difference in the name of equality or, in a move which Catharine Stimpson calls the "modern counterreformation in support of patriarchal law," claim gender difference, as D. H. Lawrence does, for example, to be the final truth.

If Boyle refuses to write polemically, in behalf of an alternative women's reality, she also refuses to omit gendered, female elements from her writing. Working within a culture of gendered extremism, she softly moves to put the contradictions into motion. The word "soft" has a certain significance; in an age which favored the tough over the tender, Boyle uses it so frequently it is almost a stylistic marker. A certain radical fluidity characterizes the forward movement of her narration. She makes visible the movement of what is left unspoken by the controlling enigmas of realism. So the luminous otherness of her work might well pass unremarked, since it is "soft," since it is neither an embrace nor a refusal of modernism's radical gendered Other. Boyle's work resists certain categories, traps of ideology, and this includes the categorical oppositions of male and female.

Kay Boyle's work might be thought of as revolutionary, then, not only because of the shattering of syntax which connects her experimental writing to the *avant-garde*. She makes the metaphorical connection between individuals, across differ-

ence. Her writing subverts the male plot, linear time, by a recursive, anaphoric temporality. And perceptions flow with the voice of the speaker across the boundaries of subject-object, rewriting the Romantic identifications with exterior images which Ruskin criticized as the "pathetic fallacy." Kay Boyle uses the fluidity of poetic forms to wash out the one-track temporality of male discourse and to undermine the singularity of gender ideology by a multiple sympathy. She unsettles the stabilities of identity. Time enters the problematic of space. Women's time enters into history, making it less singular, undoing its regularities.

Three of her early stories will serve as examples of how Kay Boyle's writing might participate in such a project. What kind of narrative time is operating, for example, in the story called **"Episode in the Life of an Ancestor"**? What kind of story is an "episode"? Is it singular or plural? A kind of turning point, or a repeated event?

In the story, a young woman defies her father's conventional desires for her to act like a submissive woman. The masterful way she treats their horses is like the mastery she exercises over her father and would-be suitor, the schoolmaster. But the conflict between the father and daughter is framed by the long view of history. This is the story of an ancestor, of a grandmother as a young woman. The whole shimmers ambiguously between the backward long vision of memory and the immediacy of a present moment: "But at a time when the Indian fires made a wall that blossomed and withered at night on three sides of the sky, this grandmother was known as one of the best horsewomen in Kansas."

The point of view also shifts to produce discontinuities in the linear structure of the plot. It is her father's egoistic will to

Boyle with her two youngest children, Faith and Ian Francken-stein, at Le Vesinè, France, 1947.

dominate which provides the conflict in the story: "Her father was proud of the feminine ways there were in her. . . . It was no pride to him to hear [her voice] turned hard and thin in her mouth to quiet a horse's ears when some fright had set them to fluttering on the beak of its head." The daughter/grandmother, however, is not drawn into the conflict. Her perceptions involve the repeated, habitual, physical world and her mode is exclamatory, even joyful: "What a feast of splatters when she would come out from a long time in the kitchen and walk in upon the beasts who were stamping and sick with impatience for her in the barn" (19). From the daughter's point of view, sympathy is a strong recognition of difference, and her "way with horses" is mastery without egotism. Her point of view flows into the animal sensations of the horse:

> This was tame idle sport, suited to ladies, this romping in the milkweed cotton across the miles of pie-crust. Suddenly he felt this anger in the grandmother's knees that caught and swung him about in the wind. Without any regard for him at all, so that he was in a quiver of admiration and love for her, she jerked him up and back, rearing his wild head high, his front hoofs left clawing at the space that yapped under them.

The wildness of the horse seems to represent some kind of primeval vigor and sexuality that might remind us of D. H. Lawrence. It is, however, an energy both shared and directed by the woman. Against this energy, the father's will appears as unreal imaginings: he longs for "the streams of gentleness and love that cooled the blood of true women." He doesn't know what is going on inside her or outside her. As he sees it, she goes off into the unknown for her ride into a night "black as a pocket." The ironic folds in the fabric of their relationship turn about the schoolmaster, a "quiet enough thought" by comparison to the woman and the horses until the father imagines him in the sexualized landscape of her midnight ride. Then his rage produces a paranoid close-up of the schoolmaster's face in his mind's eye—the detail of hairs and pores—in a failure of sympathy which wildly reverses itself again at the end with his unspoken cry: "What have you done with the schoolmaster?" The father's fantasies are chairbound and disconnected from life. In the end, he cannot even put them into words.

The grandmother has hot blood, a heat that spreads and permeates the vocabulary of the story in a membranous action. The women is woven into the fabric of the moment as she is into the words of the text, part of the whole cloth of experience. This displacement of human energy into the surrounding objects of perception makes the descriptions seem luminous, surreal—not imaginary, but strongly imagined. The grandmother's intensity spreads into the landscape with its contrasts of soft and hard, white and red, domestic flax and wild fire: "soft white flowering goldenrod," "Indian fires burning hard and bright as peonies." The deep valleys and gulfs and the blossoming prairies form a topology of pocketing and hollows. The father registers how the daughter is a very figure of thereness: "When she came into the room she was there in front of him in the same way that the roses on the floor were woven straight across the rug." He, on the other hand, is the very figure of absence, speechless, longing nostalgically for some one "of his own time to talk to." On the recommendation, apparently, of the schoolmaster, the woman has been reading the creation of Eve passage from *Paradise Lost*. Milton's lines expose Boyle's poetic figure, the

mutuality of flesh and landscape and the spousal emotion. But this revelation of poetic influence offends the father, perhaps as much as the sexuality implied in the passage.

Like Milton, her father takes an accusatory stance toward the woman's sexuality. However, the daughter's refusal to be feminine his way, "the cooking and the sewing ways that would be a comfort to him," undoes his ego-centered plot, an undoing which opens possibilities for the woman to be heroic in more multiple ways. Instead of a single hero dominating a single plot in time, Boyle produces the double figure of the daughter/grandmother and a narrative which circles through episode to a life time. Instead of a hero who would make the woman over in his own image, she produces a heroine who moves through mastery—of the horses, the schoolmaster, even her father—to a sympathy which is not identification with a male voice. The story is contained by long-distance temporality, as if written on a tapestry, a legendary mode which mimics the male heroic modes only to name them "episode." Female desire reshapes the forms of narrative as well as the forms of description: the woman is a hero who changes the forms of the heroic.

But in **"Wedding Day,"** Kay Boyle does not shrink from showing us female power of a less attractive kind, allied with the bourgeois projects of family and possessions, and the literary mode of "realistic" representation. In this story, it is the mother who works to dominate, through organizing the details of the wedding day which will initiate her all too energetic children, the too loving brother and sister, into the empty exchanges of proper social relations. The wedding will initiate them into culture—and separate them. It is the mother who makes the violent cut that institutes order—as if she were founding the very system of culture by preventing the incest of brother and sister—but the gesture is also absurd and grotesque. So it finds its image in the "roast of beef" that "made them kin again" as "she sliced the thin scarlet ribbons of it onto the platter." Not that the mother has, exactly, forced this marriage—she says it was not her idea, and her son defends his sister's choice—whose choice it was is confused. The issue is more primitive; the mother's negativity is on the side of the cut, the ceremonial structure, against any outbursts of trouble or love. She opposes her son with a prayer for "dignity," but, returning from a last excursion together, they find her on her knees tying "white satin bows under the chins of the potted plants."

She must maintain the objects of family life as intact mirrors—so it is that she counts the wedding "a real success, . . . a *real* success" when "no glass had yet been broken." Of course, it is the bride at the wedding who is "broken," but that happens beyond the precincts of the "real" which the mother so carefully maintains. Thus, from the point of view of the mother, the story has a happy ending; if she were the author of it, the incestuous energy of the brother and sister's love would be repressed.

Just as the brother and sister threaten the social order and its objects with their desire, the descriptive intensity of Boyle's style violates the decorum of the ceremony with a contradiction and violence that threatens to flood out the containing devices of concrete objects. What are these images doing at a wedding? The red carpet was to "spurt like a hemorrhage." "No one paid any attention" to the wedding cake, "with its beard lying white as hoar frost on its bosom." What is this negativity? There is the "thunderous NO" of the mother, who refuses to give the copper pans to her daughter as the spirit of a family inheritance might suggest. The mother must keep the pans orderly and unused, the "pride of the kitchen," "six bulls-eyes reflecting her thin face." She wishes, indeed, for the orderly household objects to serve as mirrors for the son and daughter as well, representations of the selves she would have them take on.

The young people challenge the civilizing project. These two are Nietzschean creatures, with "yellow manes," "shaggy as lions," "like another race." Like a refrain, the brother keeps repeating, "It isn't too late." But what else might they do except enter into the schemes laid out for them? Something, this story suggests, as it exceeds and overwhelms the bourgeois "real" of the mother: "in their young days they should have been saddled and strapped with necessity so that they could not have escaped. . . . With their yellow heads back they were stamping a new trail, but in such ignorance, for they had no idea of it."

The necessity of youth, of freedom, of a new race encounters the violence of April, like Eliot's April the "cruelest month," bringing the death, here, of childhood. "Here then was April holding them up, stabbing their hearts with hawthorne, scalping them with a flexible blade of wind." "Over them was the sky set like a tomb, the strange unearthly sky that might at any moment crack into spring." The brother and sister take a ride in a boat together. If the boat ride were solitary, it would be an easy allegory; the wedding would represent the shackling of the poetic spirit. However, they are two; what is between them we are less likely to see as a visitation of the romantic Imagination than as incestuous desire. Neither they nor we know if they should act on what they feel. "And who was there to tell them, for the trees they had come to in the woods gave them no sign."

The signs of the story produce not a judgment about how the plot should have gone, but a negativity that opens up the forms of the wedding and the story to something else, something which like the sister and brother does not wholly fit in the bourgeois "real," something full of energy, destructive and exuberant. At the end the daughter's "feet were fleeing in a hundred ways throughout the rooms, . . . like white butterflies escaping by a miracle the destructive feet of whatever partner held her in his arms." The wedding, far from locking her exclusively to one person, has propelled her into an anonymity of social exchange. The brother's antagonism scatters the calling cards around the rooms. An exotic, almost romantic energy inhabits the mother's performance as she dances, undermining her decorum, and destroying the very syntax of the sentence: "Over the Oriental prayer rugs, through the Persian forests of hemp, away and away."

In **"Wedding Day,"** Boyle reveals the hidden violence of the social contract and releases the energy of exposure to work on the forms of language itself. At the same time, she does not wholly cast the mother as executioner, the daughter as victim. Rather, she exposes the sacrificial violence of the wedding itself, and the relentless secularity of its bourgeois forms. Boyle resists a "women's writing" which would trap her in an oppositional category identified with the bourgeoisie; she neither endorses nor combats but rather eludes capture in the mother's forms.

Boyle's elusiveness produces an unsettling. She is always in favor of something which illuminates the landscape with significance—call it love—something which bends the narrative plot away from its resolutions, which turns the eye inescap-

ably to the detail, apparently decorative, but now repeating anaphorically the interestedness of the subject who writes. These are not stories about isolated selves, but about the mutual imbrications of relationships among people, and so they do not disguise the complexity of perspectives which our feelings for each other are likely to generate.

Even a story as purely focused as **"On the Run"** shows the contrary motions of resolution coming up against one another and that language of significance breaking closures, keeping the time itself open. The situation is close to biography: two lovers, like Kay Boyle herself with Ernest Walsh, are wandering across the south of Europe, unable to find a place for the sick man to rest—thrown out of hotels because he is dying. In **"On the Run,"** memory is left permeable—fragile, undecided, unpunctuated, determined only by the universal timelessness of death that thus seems everywhere. David Daiches says that Boyle's stories are like parables, with "a special kind of permanence" about them [see Further Reading list]. In our culture, this sense of permanence may be identified with women's time, appearing as a contrary narrative that works across the linear, historical plot. This is especially visible in **"On the Run,"** where the history is known, and the story exists nevertheless not in a past, but in a recurring present, like a parable.

The young couple must deal with a woman who orders them to leave rather than helping them. It is not just a person, but social convention itself which opposes them. The proprietress of the hotel is, in fact, in mourning. She seems to know all about the conventions of death. . . . She seems also to possess a kind of knowledge about religious conventions of sacrifice: there was her "rosary hanging like false teeth," and "the Christ bled with artistry" on her crucifix. But her knowledge has all been projected onto the objects, reduced and transformed to fetishes. So what she says is: "Your husband cannot die here, . . . we are not prepared for death." Here is the terrible irony, that the sick man must keep on going. Like the mother in **"Wedding Day,"** the proprietress does not seem to know what women are supposed to hold in custody: the value of relationship, the cycles of time, of the generations, of biological time. And like the mother, she has translated all of it into the social symbolic.

Thus women's time must return through the narrative of the

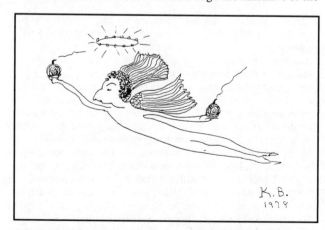

A 1978 self-portrait that Boyle captioned: "Since receiving several volumes of censored data through the Freedom of Information Act, I see myself as a dangerous 'radical' (they themselves put it in quotes) cleverly disguised as a perfect lady. So I herewith blow my cover."

story. Boyle's writing stops the forward pressing of historical time, like the train stopped at "Saint-André-les-Alpes," and sidetracks it into sensuous, loaded detail:

> As the train stopped a soft pink tide of pigs rose out of the station-yard and ran in under the wheels of the wagon. The crest of little alps was burning across the roofs of the town, with the dry crumbling finger of the church lifted and the sky gaping white and hot upon decay.

She strips the sick man's words of their history to let them fly out as if prophetic, repeated, stripping them even of punctuation:

> Get her out of here he said I am going to cough Christ is this where the death will get me take the cigaret and when I cough walk around the room and sing or something so they won't hear me

There is no period after his words.

The conflict with the proprietress does not appear as a single plot with a conclusion, but as the anaphoric structure of enduring betrayal. The message of betrayal is repeated three times, each introduced by the phrase "The bonne came back to say." It is a sacramental structure. At the end, too, the man's words are stripped of punctuation so that they seem to escape from the symbolic conventions of the story and sound in the mind like stream-of-consciousness, recurring. This is *anamnesis*, a resurrection of the past and not just memory: "Keep on keep on keep on he said maybe I'm going to bleed." Such a resurrection takes place in the process of a narrative dialectic between the linear time of history that is past and the personal time of remembrance, anamnesis. Anamnesis is the form of recollection which Plato associated with eros—and with access to eternal truth. It is the word for the "remembrance" of Christian communion. And it is the unforgetting of the past which Freud advocated, the healing reliving of pain which psychoanalysis could effect. This time which Boyle produces is associated, as well, with what Julia Kristeva calls "women's time."

This resurrection—and not just recollection—of a moment of pain and love inserts difference into the history. The position of difference which we may associate with women's time here is different from the polarized opposition which some of Boyle's characters, like the mother and the proprietress, seem to inhabit. This alternate version of narrative, with its descriptive intensity overwhelming the forward movement of plot, opens language up to the surreal, the hallucinatory. Narrative time gives way to descriptive space.

The energy is not in the story, or the forward movement of plot, but rather in the metaphorical connections among people and place—in relationship. Even though these connections shift and develop through time, so that it looks as though there is an elaboration of plot, the motive force of story is not erotic in the masculine mode. That is, the displacement of desire does not take the form of an adventure. The energy here is moral, even if the situations are unconventional.

And this is true not only for Boyle's early experimental stories, where condensation and stream of consciousness make the form private, intense, and lyrical. As the descriptive and metaphorical qualities of discourse appear in more and more public formulations, from the autobiographical novel, *Year*

Before Last, to a best-seller like *Avalanche,* they support more complex and yet more familiar forms of relationship.

Let us look a little closer at this descriptive language which so many of Kay Boyle's readers have noted—which Margaret Atwood cites as one of her most striking attributes. Sandra Whipple Spanier associates it on the one hand with a Joycean project and on the other with the romantic perspective in Boyle: she "depicts the external world as a reflection or projection of the perceiver's consciousness." Like Joyce, Boyle writes a "lyric" novel, which decenters the lyric subjectivity, the image of an ego. Boyle opens language to the pressure of the unspeakable; her words are saturated with the residues of what cannot be said, but can be mutually felt. In doing this, she changes the way we might think about the so-called "pathetic fallacy."

Boyle rewrites the romantic reflexivity, shattering the mirror relationship of self and nature under the pressure of a point of view that flows everywhere and comes from no single or stationary ego, or subjectivity. In this, she eludes the very categories of romantic, unified selfhood, of the "true and false appearances" with which Ruskin had thought through his influential critique of the "pathetic fallacy." Ruskin, let us recall, had argued that it is "only the second order of poets" who delight in the kind of description produced by violent feeling, a "falseness in all our impressions of external things" which "fancies a life" in foam or leaf instead of maintaining distinctions. Ruskin's "great poet" masters feeling:

> But it is still a grander condition when the intellect also rises, till it is strong enough to assert its rule against, or together with, the utmost efforts of the passions; and the whole man stands in an iron glow, white hot, perhaps, but still strong, and in no wise evaporating; even if he melts, losing none of his weight.

This nineteenth-century vision of the strong ego, the whole man, the rational individual has retained its heavy influence in twentieth-century criticism, visible in the work of critics like John Crowe Ransom and Yvor Winters, and visible in the great fear of the "sentimental" which permeates criticism.

Kay Boyle's practice, like Joyce's, breaks open this paranoid logic of the subject. In the place of individual heroic figures, she has the multiple connections of relationships; against the center of a linear plot she brings a counter narrative to bear. Words do not simply mirror subjects; the luminosity of her language tracks the energy of a freed desire to make connections. Hers is the logic of a poetic revolution which makes room for the woman, as for others. In this it is not simply experimental, and indeed, the chief characteristics I have observed here are to be found, in slightly different forms, in her later, apparently more conventional work.

Kay Boyle works to rewrite the extreme logic which erases woman from the place of the subject or installs her as the singular Other of male discourse. Hers is instead a lyric refiguring of the story which produces more multiple possibilities. It might simply be called the logic of sympathy.

Whether or not a writing which practices this kind of revolution may be powerful enough to work larger changes in literary culture remains, however, an open question. This is a writer who offers us the possibility of an artistic practice which exceeds the limits of gendered identity, which can say things that could not be said otherwise. As her readers, it is up to us now to find ways to speak about Kay Boyle's words and the revolution of the woman. (pp. 323-32)

Suzanne Clark, "Revolution, the Woman, and the Word: Kay Boyle," in Twentieth Century Literature, Vol. 34, No. 3, Fall, 1988, pp. 322-33.

EDWARD M. UEHLING (essay date 1988)

[*In the following excerpt, Uehling examines "Army of Occupation" and "The Lost" in terms of Boyle's "fascination with the possibilities and failures of language."*]

In his famous introduction to the anthology *Men at War,* Hemingway observes that in combat "learning to suspend your imagination and live completely in the very second of the present minute with no before and no after is the greatest gift a soldier can acquire." That statement has become, at least implicitly, the measure for all war fiction because the central figures in modern war novels have been revealed to us as they succeed and, more interestingly, fail to maintain such a perspective. . . . Yet there are many stories of war—Vietnam has reminded us of that—and Kay Boyle's short fiction of World War II makes equally compelling statements about war and its consequences.

Harold Krebs, the shell-shocked veteran of Hemingway's "Soldier's Home," longs for "a world without consequences"; in such a story as **"The Lost,"** Boyle captures what would terrify Krebs: a world of overwhelming consequences for "survivors" without homes to which they might return. It is Boyle's world of consequences that gives us the other side of the coin; however disquieting, it is one we must understand if we are to know the full cost of war. The social and political wisdom of Boyle's war fiction is all the more remarkable, though, for its skillful telling. Fiction written during or shortly after a war often struggles to find its moral and aesthetic center because the artist has not yet established sufficient distance (Vonnegut's *Slaughterhouse-Five* is more typical than Mailer's *The Naked and the Dead*). The relative speed with which Boyle could write about World War II and her control of difficult materials invite our closest critical attention.

But what, besides combat, is the proper material of war fiction? The nineteenth-century German historian Clausewitz understood "that war is simply a continuation of political intercourse"—an idea that helps us to consider the depth and complexity of its human components. Certainly his perception of war as "another form of speech or writing" expands our awareness of the tensions and consequences of war. It includes the before and after as well as Hemingway's "present minute": in short, the other side of the coin.

Such an interest in language forms the basis of the nearly overwhelming metaphor for war in the film *Apocalypse Now.* In *Heart of Darkness* (its source), when Marlow seeks Kurtz, he wants to hear the voice of the great man because he assumes a moral, reasonable order to the world is possible through communication. In fact, he thinks of Kurtz not as doing but discoursing. That faith dissolves when he discovers instead the atavistic figure who can only mutter "The horror! The horror!" The further dissolution of language is Marlow's, though, for when he returns to the presumed normalcy of society, he can offer only lies in explanation of what has happened.

Boyle exhibits a similar fascination with the possibilities and failures of language as she examines the people—soldiers and civilians; men, women, and children—of World War II Europe. I want to discuss two stories, **"Army of Occupation"** and **"The Lost,"** although there are many others (**"Hotel Behind the Lines,"** for instance) which similarly deal with this issue of language and are more overtly political, as well. But these two, both describing the aftermath of war, look from several angles at the gap between private thought and public utterance. In each story, as language fails, we see and hear more than the failure of moral courage: we discover a failure of human understanding and sympathy that suggests complete spiritual sterility.

"Army of Occupation" begins in Paris as a troop train prepares to return with American soldiers to occupied Germany "after a furlough spent . . . in pursuit of love." The presence of American GIs so dominates the scene that there is no other sense of time or place: we are told, "it was not a French train," and the MPs and GI ticket men stand, passing judgment on the French girls who have come to say goodbye. Whatever values emerge must come from the American soldiers on that train and the unnamed American correspondent who travels to meet her husband.

The intense drama of this brief story unfolds in a frightening counterpoint of voices and levels of meaning. As the woman boards the train, ignoring gapes from the men on the platform, we hear a chorus of voices from within. Drunken and terrible, it is described as a "sad, wild longing outcry—no longer recognizable as singing." " 'Roll me over / in the clover,' wailed the voices in grief from behind the closed compartment doors, and far ahead, in almost unbearable sorrow, other voices cried out 'Reminds me of / The one I love' in drunken, unmelodious complaint." We hear, but the woman is apart from this, perhaps by temperament: "the things that passed through her mind were different. She did not look toward the men, and she did not seem to hear them calling out." From the outset, Boyle underscores the difference in sensibilities between the woman, whose "look of modesty, of shyness and vulnerability" is reflected in the self-willed reality of her private thoughts, and the men, whose calls, whistles, and roaring are aggressively animalistic. The disparate voices of the story, motivated by fear, perverse longing, or disgust, are powerfully expressive but insular: no one hears or listens.

Stepping into one compartment of this soiled, discordant world, the woman faces three soldiers, each as distinctively ugly in speech as he is in physical presence and gesture. One, a sergeant, crudely waves and caresses a cognac bottle that hangs "between his spread knees." The second, a big red-haired man, is educated enough to refer to Lochinvar and Morpheus but joins the sergeant in trying to coax her to drink from their bottles. The third, described as a farm boy, isolates himself and only occasionally blurts out contemptuous remarks about French war brides being no ladies, "then turn[s] his face to the dark of the window again." From the moment she sets foot in the compartment, we witness a striking cluster of images that mock civilized, cultivated behavior. The sergeant's first "words" are not words at all but a baying wolf call. The big soldier apes polite conversation as he suggests that the woman is a commodity to be consumed: " 'Take a glance, gentlemen, at what they're passing around with coffee and leecures tonight.' " Indeed, throughout the confrontation of the story, he associates her with the bottle of cognac. Before the sergeant has grabbed the woman with encouragement from his big companion—" 'You take it first. I'll take what's left' "—she belies her assertion that she is not afraid.

As a signal of her growing fear, the narrator distinguishes what the woman does say from what she thinks by italicized passages that indicate her attempt to impose a sense of calm: for instance, *"in thirteen hours now, a little less than thirteen"*; or, *"They can't do anything, not a single thing. In a little while he'll walk down the platform, looking in every window for me."* Ironically, once inside the compartment, she does begin to hear the crude chorus, although it has grown less distinct, and even takes some comfort in the singing as she tries to think of her husband and not those with her.

At the same time, there are no instances of genuine communication as the two soldiers first attempt to seduce the terrified woman and then nearly succeed in forcing themselves on her. Their words, wholly artificial and perverse, distort the reality she internalizes and we would wish for. For instance, the sergeant attempts to evoke pity from the woman by showing her a certificate that verifies his attendance four days earlier at the funeral of his infant son by an English war bride. But as his comrade drunkenly observes, " 'Does it occur to you that the lady is bored with all this kind of talk? Does it occur to you that beauty incarnate doesn't give a snap of her dainty fingers for your relatives?' " By resorting to speaking about her as though she were not present, the two demonstrate their crude intention and the inadequacy of any response she might offer to halt its progress. At this moment, the third soldier, from whom one might hope for moral outrage, can muster only disgust for everyone unlike himself: "with the cap tipped low on his brows, [he] turned away from the rushing darkness of the night outside and looked at them bleakly, almost reproachfully, again." He issues another brief, unintentionally ironic condemnation of French war brides (and really all women); " 'I found out too much just in time. . . .' He looked at them in something like hesitation a moment, as if there were more to say and as if he were about to say it, and then turned back to the fleeting darkness. . . . 'Roll me over / In the clover,' came the faint, sad chorus of crying down the corridor."

Yet we have not experienced the utter failure of language until a blue-eyed corporal enters the compartment, ostensibly to offer his seat in another car to the woman, but really to make a childish bid for her favor. A brief sampling of his declarations reveals him as foolish, not gallant: " 'You're American. You're wonderful.' " Or, " 'You're beautiful. You're like all the girls at home who don't come over.' " And his last words: " 'My God, you're beautiful. I love you. I respect you.' " Although we are told "his ears [were] deaf to everything except what she might say," she says nothing to him until the increasing threat of physical violence drives her to attempt to accept the offer of his seat. Instead, the corporal literally takes the woman's place, is essentially raped with the ubiquitous bottle in her place.

While the "farm boy [sleeps] in peace against the cold, dark window glass," the sergeant knocks the corporal senseless with a bottle. As he lies "as if in sleep," the sergeant prepares for another blow, when the woman cries out: " 'Don't touch him! Don't you dare to hit him again!' " The story closes with an ironic juxtaposition of inadequate voices and silences. The woman's own private voice fairly races in an effort

to save from annihilation the actual flesh and bone of all that remained of decency. *"They're other peo-*

ple on this train, like people you know, like people you see in the street. . . . They're Wacs, and brothers, and sons, and husbands . . . they're people singing. . . . People who understand words, if I can get to them . . ."

But interspersed with these silent pleas are the voices of the chorus, "far, unheeding, calling out in nostalgia" and also the narrator's careful words which describe the woman's furious exit from the compartment. To the woman's final spoken words—"Get out of my way!"—the sergeant makes a noteworthy response: "And he did not speak, but, half smiling still as she flung by him, he lifted his hand and stroked her soft, dark hair." The story's final words suggest that what she runs from may be no worse than what she runs to—"toward the sound of the sad, sweet, distant voices in the rushing train." What is real? The loneliness of those voices, as well as the tenderness perversely evoked by their description? Or simply their message—"Roll me over / In the clover."

The paradox of Boyle relying on words for her art when developing this idea of failed language is perhaps even more pronounced in **"The Lost."** This is a story of children displaced by the war and the American woman who manages a Children's Center from which they may be officially relocated. As in **"Army of Occupation,"** setting reinforces a distorted pattern of historical connections. Once a massive baronial manor house in Bavaria, the Center conveys to the arriving America Relief Team "the chill of winter and silence and death that stood like a presence in its feudal halls." But that is only one past reality of the place: during the war, it served as a Selection Camp for genetic and racial losers who were dutifully recorded, photographed, and sent to labor or extermination. From their neatly alphabetized records, their pictures haunt us: "It was the eyes of these men and women, who were there no longer, which looked now at the Americans, and beyond them, upon some indescribable vista of hopelessness and pain." Against such a background, the American presence seems more orderly than useful—a source of food and playground equipment, but not of restored identity.

The story's most powerful representation of "hopelessness and pain" comes through its many voices. Three figures, called "boys" by the narrator, are addressed as "men" by the American woman. Orphans and mascots of various U.S. Infantry units, they are neither civilians nor children. How to name or understand them is more difficult still because of their speech and what it implies. The oldest, Janos, is fifteen, once was Czechoslovakian, calls himself Johnny Madden, and speaks with the accent of the black sergeant from Tennessee, Charlie Madden, by whom he hopes to be adopted. The other two are younger, perhaps fourteen and twelve, and remain unnamed. The fourteen-year-old, filled with cynicism, looks for an angle or a private deal and refuses to recross the threshold of the Center and the child's world it suggests. "His accent might have come straight from Brooklyn," we are told, "except that it had come from somewhere else before that, and, as he spoke, he folded his arms upon his breast, and spat casually." The youngest, whose grandfather is eventually located in Naples, is able at least superficially to rejoin the world of swings and sandboxes, but his voice parrots that of the GIs with whom he has lived.

During their initial interview, the woman discourages hope of adoption in the practiced litany of a middle-level bureaucrat:

"And probably when the G.I.s made you those promises they thought they would be able to keep them. . . . I've talked to some of these men, I've had letters from them, and I know they believed they would be able to keep the promises. But there were other kinds too. There were some kinds who didn't care what happened to you men afterward. . . . They wanted you to learn how to drink and smoke and gamble and shoot crap and use the kind of language they used—"

The twelve-year-old's reply betrays his misunderstanding: " 'I begin shooting crap in Naples,' the small boy said in his high, eager voice. 'I clean up seven bucks the first night there.' " For once her composure is punctured: " 'Look, kid . . . if Italy's your country, perhaps you ought to pack up and go back there.' " The play of language in this exchange is remarkable. Her irritation leads her to replace "men" with "kid," a term nearer to the truth but still without sympathy or even recognition of individuality. Moreover, both speakers' use of "crap" to describe the game of dice, "craps," suggests that neither the woman nor the child fits in this strange world of war; it further hints at the ineffectuality of such talk/"crap." The woman evokes a startling reply from the boy: " 'I ain't no Eyetie no more,' he said and he did not raise his eyes to look at her because of the tears that were standing in them. 'I'm American. I wanna go home where my outfit's gone.' "

Janos has watched the sunlight reflect blankly upon her glasses and has listened to her as "neither woman nor American, perhaps not human being even, but a voice—disembodied, quiet, direct—which might be coming now to the words they had been waiting to hear her say." The words will never

Boyle at her home in Oakland, California, June, 1988.

come; instead, this scene introduces a terrifying isolation as these characters continually fail to go beyond expressiveness toward communication.

In fact, throughout **"The Lost,"** people rarely look at or hear each other. That failure develops most obviously through numerous images of dark and lightness. For instance, the second hayloft scene, in which Janos brings table scraps to the second boy, contains many plays on light and dark that underscore shifts in language and its ultimate inadequacy. Janos crosses the stable door "in the darkness" and finds the boy framed by the window through which there are "stars shining clearly . . . and Janos could hear his [the other's] voice speaking out across the hay-sweet dark." The words are even harder and more defensive now: " 'My God-damned lighter's gone dry as a witch's tit,' the boy said. 'I've got to get me to a PX and get me some lighter fluid.' " Perhaps for him there is already no other possibility of light than that of the now empty Zippo. His sweater, we are told, "showed dark against the starry square of night." It might be argued that his language makes him darker than the night; certainly the contrast of his fierce despair with Janos' insistent hope for a future sense of place rings clearly in Boyle's representation of their voices. Offering a nearly empty bottle of schnapps to his older companion, the outsider says, " 'Have a swig, kid,' " echoing the woman's retort. Then there is more tough talk: " 'I've got to get me to a man's-size town where there's a PX quick,' the boy was saying in the darkness." To Janos' innocuous reply, the other begins laughing and Boyle writes, "He lay . . . beyond Janos in the darkness."

For the sixth time in this scene darkness is mentioned as Janos recalls Sergeant Madden's instruction on the naming and placing of stars. Two qualities of his declaration are noteworthy. First, the reference to stars and thus to light and hope is linked to the one trustworthy figure in Janos' world. Although we do not hear his buddy's words, they obviously have remained with Janos as proof of the order represented by Madden. Equally revealing, Janos conveys all of this as though he is speaking to himself or at least without expecting that his words can become part of a real communication in the darkened loft. We discover that such words, with their implicit faith in happy endings, can elicit only the briefest acknowledgment of pain before the facade of the Brooklyn accent resurfaces: " 'Oh, Christ' " the other boy mutters as he curses a system where rank has privilege, a system that will always exclude him. Another spasm of ironic laughter jerks from him and he dismisses Janos' hope: " 'You listen, kid, . . . The cards is stacked against us.' "

Hearing these American dialects apart from the sources that should accompany them makes us wince, particularly because the topics addressed would be painful even to adults. All three children speak of their parents' deaths matter-of-factly; their voices would be utterly detached except that they are eager to prove that they may go "home to America" because their parents have not survived. The unconscious mimicry of their voices echoes their empty lives.

Finally only Janos remains, writing every night to Madden, who has taught him to fix things, and practicing the mechanical skills that he hopes to use in Madden's garage. But the final image of darkness, Charlie Madden's race, catches him. It is, as the woman explains, "the color question."

Janos stood there listening to the words she said, and, as he listened, the woman again ceased being woman, ceased being human being even, and it was merely a voice in the shed that spoke quietly and bitterly of the separate lives that must be lived by people of different colors, as she had on that first day spoken of the hopes that might never come to anything at all.

Yet the final sorrow of this unresolved story is not that Janos cannot live with a black man in Tennessee. It is the manner in which he rejects even the compromise of living with another family in America. "Neatly and inaccurately" he composes the polite lie to Madden and disappears without a trace: "Yesstidy I talk to the US consil Charlie and what do ya think now? Seems my fammillys jus as good as they ever waz so Charlie I make up my mynd sudden to go back whar they waz waiting for me Im shure ya thinks its for the best Charlie so I says so long."

Earlier, Janos' writing every night might be regarded as a form of light in the darkness. But the effect of his final letter is quite different. Here its flawed form and substance underscore the displacement of meaningful language by an English that intends to protect both sender and recipient but does not connect; an English that is distorted, false, occupying yet lost. Either way, heads or tails, the world of Boyle's war stories is an unforgiving, lonely place. (pp. 375-82)

> *Edward M. Uehling, "Tails, You Lose: Kay Boyle's War Fiction," in* Twentieth Century Literature, *Vol. 34, No. 3, Fall, 1988, pp. 375-83.*

FURTHER READING

Carpenter, Richard C. "Kay Boyle." *The English Journal* XLII, No. 8 (November 1953): 425-30, 442.

    Biographical and critical discussion of Boyle's life and work, including novels and short stories.

Daiches, David. Introduction to *Fifty Stories,* by Kay Boyle, pp. 9-14. Garden City, New York: Doubleday & Co., 1980.

    Brief but illuminating introduction to Boyle's short stories.

Geismar, Maxwell. "Aristocrat of the Short Story." *The New York Times Book Review* (10 July 1966): 4, 16.

    Laudatory review of *Nothing Ever Breaks except the Heart* in which Geismar notes an increased maturity from Boyle's earlier works.

Graham, Gladys. "Artistic Fiction." *The Saturday Review of Literature* IX, No. 36 (25 March 1933): 501.

    Favorable review of *The First Lover, and Other Stories.*

Hardwick, Elizabeth. Review of *Thirty Stories,* by Kay Boyle. *Partisan Review* XIV, No. 2 (March/April 1947): 200.

    Brief review of *Thirty Stories.* Hardwick singles out Boyle's war fiction as unsuccessful.

Harter, Evelyn. "Kay Boyle: Experimenter." *The Bookman* LXXV, No. 3 (June/July 1932): 249-53.

    Early, mainly biographical portrait, including some critical remarks.

Hawthorne, Hazel. "Kay Boyle." *New Republic* LXXIV, No. 961 (3 May 1933): 342.

    Brief, lukewarm review of *The First Lover, and Other Stories.*

Hoyenga, Betty. "A Question of Fiction." *Prairie Schooner* XL, No. 4 (Winter 1966): 370-71.

    Brief review of *Nothing Ever Breaks except the Heart.* Hoyenga accuses Boyle of producing propaganda rather than literature in these stories.

MacLeish, Archibald. "The Lost Speakers." *The Saturday Review* (New York) XIII, No. 15 (8 February 1936): 6.

    Poem dedicated to Boyle.

Madden, Charles F., ed. "Kay Boyle." In *Talks with Authors,* pp. 215-36. Carbondale: Southern Illinois University Press, 1968.

    Transcription of an interview with Boyle that was conducted on May 11, 1964, as part of an interinstitutional course on English taught by Harry T. Moore, Research Professor of English at Southern Illinois University. Using "amplified telephone facilities," the course engaged students in person-to-person telephone conversations with literary figures. Here Boyle presents a brief lecture and fields questions from representatives of six universities, including Jackson State College, Tougaloo Southern Christian College, Langston University, and Morehouse College.

Rothman, N. L. "Kay Boyle's Stories." *The Saturday Review (New York)* XIII, No. 15 (8 February 1936): 6.

    Commendatory review of *The White Horses of Vienna, and Other Stories* in which Rothman designates the short story "the most perfect vehicle for those talents that are specially [Boyle's]."

West, Ray B., Jr. "Fiction and Reality: The Traditionalists." In his *The Short Story in America, 1900-50,* pp. 59-84. Chicago: Henry Regnery Co., 1952.

    Brief discussion of Boyle's story "The White Horses of Vienna," which West terms "a study in decadence" similar to works of Henry James and William Faulkner.

Ivan (Alexeyevich) Bunin

1870-1953

Russian short story writer, novelist, poet, journalist, translator, and memoirist.

An important transitional figure in the development of Russian literature, Bunin combined elements of traditional nineteenth-century realism with a modernist sensibility shaped by the effects of war and revolution. His works often incorporate precise descriptions and examine themes of death, dislocation, alienation, the loss of tradition, and the search for new, meaningful values. Best known for such short fiction as *Gospodin iz San-Frantsisko* (*The Gentleman from San Francisco, and Other Stories*), *Sukhodol* (*Dry Valley*), and *Tyomnyye allei* (*Dark Avenues, and Other Stories*), Bunin was the first Russian writer awarded the Nobel Prize in Literature, and he is considered one of the finest Russian short story writers of the twentieth century. Bunin's classical treatment of Russian society in his stories has prompted comparisons with the works of Leo Tolstoy, Mikhail Lermontov, Anton Chekhov, and Ivan Turgenev. His lyrical prose style and distinct narrative technique also have been highly praised. Gleb Struve extolled: "As an artist, as an individualist, as an original and distinguished exponent of a great aesthetic tradition in contemporary terms, and in the clarity and beauty of his vision, there are few who can stand beside him."

Born in the town of Voronezh, a provincial capital three hundred miles south of Moscow in central Russia, Bunin was the son of landed gentry and a descendent of the distinguished Russian poets Anna Bunina and Vasili Zhukovski. During his childhood Bunin witnessed the rapid decline of Russian nobility that followed the abolishment of serfdom in 1861, and his short stories, particularly his early tales, chronicle this changing social climate. Although he received only four years of formal schooling, Bunin was well educated. His first tutor taught him to read using Russian translations of *Don Quixote* and *The Odyssey,* and his elder brothers rigorously prepared him for university studies. Encouraged by his family to pursue a literary career, Bunin published his first short stories, "Nefedka" and "Dva strannika," in 1888 in the magazine *Rodina,* and from 1889 to 1892 worked for *Orlovskii vestnik,* a journal in which he published several essays and short stories. During this time Bunin became romantically involved with Varvara Pashchenko, his employer's niece. Their five-year romance ended in 1894 when Pashchenko left him to marry a mutual friend. Bunin was devastated and the failed affair greatly altered his impressions of love. During the winter of 1895, Bunin visited St. Petersburg and Moscow, where he became acquainted with many prominent literary figures of the period. He returned to the country in the summer of that year, having expanded his literary horizons, and in 1897 published *Na krai sveta,* his first collection of short fiction. In 1901 *Listopad* appeared, a collection of poetry for which Bunin was awarded a Pushkin Prize, the highest honor in Russian literature.

During the years prior to World War I, Bunin traveled extensively throughout Europe and the Middle East. These travels appreciably broadened his social perspective; several of his stories from this time are set in foreign lands and reflect his

increased social awareness. In 1909 Bunin's literary efforts earned him both a second Pushkin Prize and the title of Honorary Academician in the Russian Academy of Sciences. His popularity with the public was not secured until 1910, however, when he completed the novel *Derevnya* (*The Village*), a work that characterizes the collapse of early twentieth-century rural Russian society, a theme he would develop further in the novella *Dry Valley*. In 1916 Bunin published *The Gentleman from San Francisco*. His most popular work outside the Soviet Union, this volume of stories reflects a widening circle of thematic concerns and focuses on the materiality and moral degeneration of modern civilization. Opposing the Bolshevik Revolution, Bunin moved in 1918 from Moscow to Odessa, a city in the southern Ukraine, where he lived for two years. When the Red army threatened to invade Odessa in 1920, Bunin fled Russia, eventually settling permanently in France. His talents as a short fiction writer were soon recognized by the European literary community, and many critics considered Bunin the foremost Russian émigré writer of the period. Outstanding short story collections of his first decade of exile include *Solnechnyy udar* and *Grammatika lyubvi* (*Grammar of Love, and Other Stories*). In 1933 Bunin received worldwide recognition when he was awarded the Nobel Prize. In spite of this honor, his fame was short-lived. The atrocities of World War II devastated him both emotionally and financially, and his literary output was sporadic. Ironically, during the late 1940s while suspected in Europe and America of harboring Soviet sympathies, Bunin was simultaneously censured in the Soviet Union for writing anticommunist propaganda. Thereafter, though he continued to write, his popularity declined, and his works received significantly less public attention. Following years of illness and destitution, Bunin died of a heart attack in 1953.

Bunin's career as a short fiction writer spanned over five decades. Although his first short stories appeared during the late 1880s, his talents in the short fiction genre were not widely recognized until the publications of *Dry Valley* in 1912 and *The Gentleman from San Francisco* in 1916. Interested chiefly in creating atmosphere, Bunin often neglects plot and character development in favor of concise descriptive passages that evoke sensory images and capture a mood. This technique is perhaps best exemplified in *Dry Valley* and in *Dark Avenues,* a collection containing extremely brief sketches (frequently one page or less) that evoke powerful emotions. In his earliest fiction, Bunin dwelt almost exclusively upon social changes in Russia. His profound sorrow at witnessing the disintegration of traditional Russian society is chronicled in these works, particularly *Dry Valley,* a saga that serves as a microcosm of the deteriorating rural social order. Considered one of Russian literature's greatest hymns to the nation's vanished way of life, *Dry Valley* utilizes evocative language and portrays the physical and psychological decay of landowners and peasants on a provincial estate. In *The Gentleman from San Francisco,* Bunin extends his examination of society beyond Russia. The title piece revolves around the sudden death of a wealthy American gentleman vacationing aboard an oceanliner. A largely descriptive narrative, this tale criticizes contemporary attitudes toward what is valued in life and starkly contrasts the artificiality of the modern world with the individual's return to a natural state upon death. Julian Connolly wrote: "Throughout the tale Bunin exposes in relentless detail modern society's fatal preoccupation with the self and its profound indifference not only to other human beings but to nature and God as well."

Throughout his life, Bunin was obsessed with the concept of death and its relation to life and love. Unable to reconcile the joy of living with the inevitability of dying, he struggled to discover meaning in the transience of life. The majority of his fiction addresses the subject of death in some capacity and reflects the evolution of his perceptions and eventual resolution of his personal anxieties. Even in such later collections as *Grammar of Love* and *Dark Avenues,* in which Bunin appears to have resolved many of his anxieties and in each of which the dominant theme is love, he continues to examine death. While love is viewed as the penultimate experience in Bunin's works, it is actually encountered only briefly, as in "Ida," a story in which the characters acknowledge with a kiss love that will never be consummated. In other stories, including "Solnechnyy udar" ("Sunstroke") and "Legkoe dykhanie" ("Light Breathing"), mutual love ends in death as lovers are incapable of defying conditions that separate or destroy them. These stories are punctuated by tremendous heights of passion as well as by the futility of humanity's attempts to capture so fleeting an experience.

Bunin was an acknowledged master of the Russian language, and critics have noted that he modeled his prose after poetry, constructing passages with carefully chosen words that give his narratives a lyrical, understated quality. Although the es-

teem with which Bunin is held in the Soviet Union is evidenced by his tremendous critical popularity and wide readership, his works are not uniformly praised. Commentators have faulted the scarcity of plot and tendency toward understatement in many of his stories and have rejected his negative, fatalistic portrayals of society. More often, however, Bunin is hailed for his striking command of the Russian language, elegant style of literary expression, and unique narrative perspective.

(For further information on Bunin's life and career, see *Twentieth-Century Literary Criticism,* Vol. 6 and *Contemporary Authors,* Vol. 104.)

PRINCIPAL WORKS

SHORT FICTION

Na krai sveta 1897
Sukhodol 1912
  [*Dry Valley* published in *The Elaghin Affair, and Other Stories,* 1935]
Ioann Rydalets (short stories and poetry) 1913
Gospodin iz San-Frantsisko 1916
  [*The Gentleman from San Francisco, and Other Stories,* 1922; reprinted, 1963]
Sny Changa 1916
  [*The Dreams of Chang, and Other Stories,* 1923]
Roza Iyerikhona (short stories and poetry) 1924
Solnechnyy udar 1927
Grammatika lyubvi 1929
  [*Grammar of Love, and Other Stories,* 1934]
The Elaghin Affair, and Other Stories 1935
Tyomnyye allei 1943
  [*Dark Avenues, and Other Stories,* 1949]
Sobraniye sochineniy. 9 vols. (novels, short stories, memoirs, and poetry) 1965-67

OTHER MAJOR WORKS

Stikhotvoreniya (poetry) 1891
Listopad (poetry) 1901
Derevnya (novel) 1910
  [*The Village,* 1923]
Mitina lyubov' (novel) 1925
  [*Mitya's Love,* 1926]
Zhizn' arsen'yeva (novel) 1930
  [*The Well of Days,* 1933]
Vospominaniya (memoirs) 1950
Memoirs and Portraits (memoirs) 1951

J. MIDDLETON MURRY (essay date 1922)

[*Murry is recognized as one of the most significant English critics and editors of the twentieth century. Through his positions as founding editor of the* Adelphi, *and as a regular contributor to the* Times Literary Supplement, *among other periodicals, Murry was an early champion of the writings of Marcel Proust, James Joyce, Paul Valéry, D. H. Lawrence, and Thomas Hardy. Murry theorized that to evaluate fully a writer's achievement, the critic must search for the crucial passages which effectively "crystallize" the writer's innermost impressions and convictions. In the following excerpt, he assesses*

Bunin's short story "The Gentleman from San Francisco," assigning the author a place among the most important Russian writers of the twentieth century.]

When the admirable translation . . . of **"The Gentleman from San Francisco"** appeared last autumn in *The Dial,* our feeling was that a new planet had swum into our ken. The story was splendidly *written,* which is another way of saying that the author's imaginative realization of his subject had been not only complete but single. It seemed that he had had, as it were, an apocalyptic vision of his matter as a whole, and that he had transcribed it with a swift intensity which suggested a great reserve of power. Moreover, there was something new in the quality of the vision itself. The ruthlessness with which Bunin stripped the nakedness of modern civilization was comprehensive and synoptic, not petulantly and spasmodically cynical as are so many modern writers with the same theme. Bunin's story was at once swift and majestic, penetrating and powerful; not a scrap, but a finished and ordered work of art.

It is, indeed, a masterpiece, without a doubt one of the finest short stories—it is not so *very* short—of modern times. But the expectations which it aroused are not satisfied by the two volumes of Bunin's prose which have since been made accessible to the Western reader. They are interesting, and assuredly they were worth translating, but they are not on the same level. After Tchehov, Bunin's other short stories are disappointing. The comparison is inevitable. The subjects and the treatment suggest Tchehov, perhaps even derive from Tchehov, but we feel that Tchehov, simply because he was an almost infallible artist, would have handled them differently. If Tchehov had never existed they might have been good Bunin stories; coming after him, they are slightly inferior Tchehov stories. They are perceptibly mechanized; they lack the beautiful organic completeness, the rhythmic finality, of the master. They are works of his "school." . . .

[It is] perhaps not fanciful to trace a psychological connection between [Bunin's novel] *The Village* and **"The Gentleman from San Francisco."** On the evidence of *The Village,* and of certain short stories which appear in the French edition of his tales, we conceive Bunin as one convinced that Russia's only hope lay in "civilization." By 1905 the time of idealizing the peasant was over for the Russian; it was left to be the polite amusement of foreigners like Mr. Stephen Graham and the rest of the conscious or unconscious propagandists for the Tsardom. All the singleminded and honest spirits who came after the two great visionaries, Tolstoy and Dostoevsky, have cried like Goethe: "More light." Tchehov and Gorky are at one in this; and to me, like Bunin, whose depressing knowledge of the Russian reality is not lightened by a literary genius so powerful as theirs, we imagine the necessity of "civilization" was still more desperate. Then came the war, revealing the rottenness of the civilization on which his hopes had leaned, and by the very extremity of his despair Bunin was inspired.

That is, we admit, only a theory; but we need a theory to account for the striking difference between **"The Gentleman from San Francisco"** and Bunin's other writings, between work that is of the first order and work that is respectable. The masterly symbolism of the great liner *Atlantis,* which brings the millionaire and his family to the sham summer of a Naples winter and takes him back again, squeezed into a tarpaulin package at the bottom of the hold; the apocalyptic revelation of a "civilization" which cannot attain to life and

has no place for death; the narrative which sweeps, like one of the Atlantic billows amid which it passes, with a restrained and rhythmical fury from mockery to mockery—there is no visible parallel to these magnificent qualities in the rest of Bunin's prose-work which has been made known to us. Our expectations have been frustrated, but we are not disappointed. When a writer has given us one of the greatest short stories of our age, and perhaps the only great story which is truly modern in the sense that it gives a synthesis of existence under aspects which never existed before the end of the nineteenth century, we have no right to ask more. Bunin has earned a place in the literature of the world. Is there another Russian writer since Gorky of whom so much can be truly said?

J. Middleton Murry, "Ivan Bunin," in The Nation and the Athenaeum, *Vol. XXXI, No. 13, June 24, 1922, p. 444.*

THE NEW YORK TIMES BOOK REVIEW   (essay date 1923)

[*In the following review of* The Dreams of Chang, and Other Stories, *the anonymous critic comments upon "The Gentleman from San Francisco" and "The Dreams of Chang," noting in particular Bunin's artistry and realistic perspective.*]

Ivan Bunin's introduction to the English-reading public was made, felicitously enough, with **"The Gentleman From San Francisco,"** an astonishingly fine piece of objective description which yet contained a symbolism that was easily conveyed to the reader. This story is to be found in *The Dreams of Chang,* a volume in which the Russian has brought together fifteen of his shorter efforts, and it still stands out as the best thing that Bunin has done. The other tales, excepting a few which appeared in the little volume that originally introduced **"The Gentleman From San Francisco"** are offered in English guise for the first time, and from them a rather comprehensive understanding of Bunin's art is to be gained. Like most of these greater Russians who preceded him, he is a realist in the fullest sense of the word, a craftsman who fashions the incidents in his narratives with that adjusted ease that adds so much to the lifelike qualities of his characters. And, again like most Russian writers, a somewhat sombre symbolism threads his stories.

In spite of his realistic leanings, there is a deal of poetry and fine writing to be discovered in his work, and this side of his art is heightened by the subject matter of some of the tales in which the action is laid in the Far East. Ceylon, for instance, is a favorite country with him, and in **"Brethren,"** a study which, with **"The Dreams of Chang"** itself, comes perilously near **"The Gentleman From San Francisco"** in excellence, he has created a narrative that often swings into sheer poetry. It is but the tale of a riksha runner whose promised child-wife is taken from him and who eventually kills himself with a poisonous snake, but it takes on a symbolic quality through the juxtaposition of the primitive young Ceylon runner and a jaded white man who has traveled all over the world to escape the terror of life. The careful description of the day that these two men pass with one another as servant and silent white master displays to the fullest extent the undoubted artistry which Bunin carefully employs.

Bunin, it may be guessed, passed some time in the Far East, presumably on ship, for his descriptions of vessels and high seas (they occur frequently in his stories) are set down with an unmistakable touch of authenticity. In **"The Dreams of**

Chang," a story in which the visions of the starving dog of a starving master are set forth, we get this sense of the sea. Chang's master was originally a ship's Captain, and through Chang's fitful, broken visions the reader gets a glimpse of the domestic tragedy which has transformed the master from a dapper officer to an unshaven derelict. **"Brethren," "The Dreams of Chang"** and **"The Gentleman From Francis-co"** form a trio of stories which would make the reputation of any writer, but second only to them, in sustained excellence are such tales as **"The Son," "Light Breathing"** and **"A Compatriot,"** all tragic in their implications. It is, perhaps, the unforced quality in Bunin's stories which adds so much to their strength. The narrative runs along with a cold simplicity and rises almost imperceptibly to its climax. Indeed, the reader often reaches the climax and ends the tale before he is fully aware of how concentrated and inevitable it all is.

A review of "The Dreams of Chang," in The New York Times Book Review, *October 28, 1923, p. 9.*

PRINCE D. S. MIRSKY (essay date 1926)

[*Mirsky was a Russian prince who fled his country after the Bolshevik Revolution and settled in London. While in England, he wrote two important and comprehensive histories of Russian literature,* Contemporary Russian Literature: 1881-1925 (*1926*) *and* A History of Russian Literature from the Earliest Times to the Death of Dostoyevsky (*1927*). *These works were later combined and published in 1949 as* A History of Russian Literature. *In 1932, having reconciled himself to the Soviet regime, Mirsky returned to the U.S.S.R. He continued to write literary criticism, but his work eventually ran afoul of Soviet censors, and he was exiled to Siberia. He disappeared in 1937. In the following excerpt originally published in* Contemporary Russian Literature: 1881-1925, *Mirsky examines short stories written by Bunin between 1910 and 1920. Here he identifies a lyrical prose style in the tales set in Russia.*]

Much of Búnin's prose is more "poetical" and more subjective than his verse. Purely lyrical compositions in prose are to be found in every one of his books. This lyrical style was the first aspect of his prose that attracted general attention to his individuality. In his first volumes (1892-1902) they were certainly the most interesting item; the rest consisted of realistically sentimental stories of the conventional type, or of attempts to emulate Chékhov in the representation of the disintegrating "pinpricks" of life (*"The Schoolmaster"*). The lyrical stories went back to the tradition of Chékhov (*"The Steppe"*), of Turgénev (*"Forest and Steppe"*), and of Goncharóv (*"Oblómov's Dream"*), but Búnin accentuated still further the lyrical element, eliminated all narrative skeleton, and at the same time studiously avoided (except in certain attempts tainted with "modernism") the diction of lyrical prose. His lyrical effects were produced by the poetry of *things,* not of rhythms or words. The most notable of these lyrical poems in prose is **"Antónov Apples"** (1900), where the smell of a special kind of apples leads him from association to association to reconstruct a poetical picture of the dying life of his class, the middle gentry of central Russia. The tradition of Goncharóv, with his epical manner of painting stagnant life, is especially alive in the lyrical "stories" of Búnin (one of them even bears the title **"A Dream of Oblómov's Grandson"**). In later years the same lyrical manner was transferred to other subjects than dying central Russia, and, for instance, his impressions of Palestine (1908) were written in the same restrained, subdued, and lyrical "minor key." (p. 391)

[**"A Goodly Life"** (1915)] is the story told in the first person by a heartless (and naïvely self-righteous in her heartlessness) woman of peasant origin who succeeds in life after being the cause of the ruin of her son and the death of the rich young man who loved her. The story is remarkable, among other things, for its language—it is an exact reproduction of the dialect of a petty townswoman of Élets, with all the phonetic and grammatical peculiarities carefully reproduced. It is remarkable that even in reproducing dialect Búnin succeeds in remaining "classical," in keeping the words subordinate to the whole. This manner is the opposite of Leskóv's, who is always playing with his language and whose words always protrude to the point of beggaring the story. It is interesting to compare the two writers in the examples of **"A Goodly Life"** and Leskóv's sketch of a somewhat similar character, "The Amazon." It is like the difference of the same Jesuit style in the hands of a Frenchman and in those of a Mexican. **"A Goodly Life"** is Búnin's only story told in dialect from beginning to end, but the speech of the Élets peasants, reproduced with equal precision and equally "unprotruding," reappears in the dialogue of all his rural stories (especially in **"A Night Conversation"**). Apart from the use of dialect, Búnin's language is "classical," sober, concrete. Its only expressive means is the exact notation of things; it is objective because its effect depends entirely on the "objects" spoken of. Búnin is probably the only modern Russian writer whose language would have been admired by the "classics," by Turgénev and Goncharóv.

It is almost an inevitable consequence of this "dependence on object" that when Búnin leaves the familiar and domestic realities of the Élets district and sets his stories in Ceylon or in Palestine, or even in Odessa, his style loses much of its vigor and aptness. In his exotic stories he is often inadequate, and especially when he is poetical the beauty of his poetry is apt to become mere tinsel. To keep free from this inadequateness when dealing with a foreign (or even with a Russian urban) subject, Búnin must mercilessly keep down his lyrical proclivities. He must be bald and terse at the hazard of becoming cheap. He has achieved this baldness and terseness in a few stories, one of which is considered by most of his (especially foreign) readers his indubitable masterpiece—**"The Gentleman from San Francisco"** (1915).

This remarkable story is well known in English translations. It belongs to the progeny of *Iván Ilyích,* and its "message" is quite in keeping with the teaching of Tolstóy: the vanity of civilization and the presence of death the only reality. But no direct influence of Tolstóy can be traced in Búnin's story, as it can in the best of Andréyev's. It is not a work of analysis, for Búnin is no analyst and no psychologist. It is a "thing of beauty," a solid "object"; it has the consistency and hardness of a steel bar. It is a masterpiece of artistic economy and austere, "Doric" expression. Like the two rural "poems" *The Village* and *Sukhodól,* **"The Gentleman from San Francisco"** has also its accompanying constellation of foreign and urban stories told in bald outline and with austere matter-of-factness. Among the best are **"Kazimír Stanislávovich"** (1915) and **"Thieves' Ears"** (1916), a powerful study of criminal perversity.

Of the more lyrical exotic and urban stories, the most notable are **"The Dreams of Chang"** (1916) and **"Brothers"** (1914). In both of them Búnin's lyrical poetry, torn away from its native soil, loses much of its vitality, and is often unconvincing and conventional. His language also loses its color and becomes "international." Still, **"Brothers"** is a powerful work. It is the story of a Singhalese jinrikisha man of Colombo and his English fare. It avoids the pitfall of sentimentality in a masterly way.

In 1933 Búnin was awarded a Nobel Prize, and he has continued to produce and develop in emigration. In addition to several collections of short stories and verse, among which **Dark Alleys** (1943) has received particular praise, he has written a short novel of early love (*Mítya's Love*, 1924-5) and begun a longer work of autobiographical fiction (*The Life of Arséniev*). (pp. 392-94)

Prince D. S. Mirsky, "Prose Fiction after Chekhov," in his A History of Russian Literature Comprising "A History of Russian Literature" and "Contemporary Russian Literature," edited by Francis J. Whitfield, Alfred A. Knopf, 1949, pp. 374-406.

ALEXANDER NAZAROFF (essay date 1935)

[*Nazaroff is a Russian essayist, editor, historian, and translator. Here he assesses* The Elaghin Affair.]

These fifteen short stories by Ivan Bunin, [**The Elaghin Affair, and Other Stories**], are not the product of his most recent work. The Russian winner of the Nobel Prize for 1933 wrote them between 1911 and 1926. Some of them never were translated into English before. Others were. But even those of them which were attracted, at the time of their appearance, comparatively little attention in this country and are hardly obtainable now: in those days M. Bunin's name as yet did not mean much to American readers. It has been, therefore, a felicitous idea to rescue them from oblivion by bringing out the present volume, all the more so since there are among these fifteen stories masterpieces of the purest water exemplifying M. Bunin's noble art at its very best.

The stories gathered in the volume greatly differ in length, technique, subject-matter and style-few artists have a range of interests, a palette of colors and an arsenal of artistic methods as rich and variegated as M. Bunin. **"The Elaghin Affair"** (which is the title piece) and **Dry Valley** are rather novelettes than short stories—the former is fifty and the latter about one hundred pages long. And also one finds in the volume three or six page miniatures unforgetable in their effect.

Paintings of the old Russia with its peasantry and nobility, its countryside, cities and middle-class milieu (**Dry Valley,** **"Long, Long Ago,"** &c.); sex stories written with a concentrated, uncanny penetration into human psychology (**"The Elaghin Case," "The Mordvinian Sarafin"**); philosophic tales told in the form of Oriental parables and drawn against the background of the Near East or India (**"The Third Cockcrow"** and **"The Night of Denial"**); a fairy tale narrated with the inimitable accents and diction of a Russian peasant (**"Of Emelya, the Fool"**); and, finally, lyrically meditative pieces with no "short story substance" of any kind in them (**"Cicadas"**)—such, in a brief enumeration, are the contents, of this volume.

To choose among genuine works of art like those gathered between these covers always is an embarrassing task. Yet the reviewer will have much authoritative critical opinion to support him if he says that the most artistically significant, impressive and important item in this volume is not the title story, but **Dry Valley.** Indeed, this novelette, written in 1911

and so far little known in this country, is one of M. Bunin's greatest achievements. It stands at the same unusually high level of perfection as his **"Gentleman From San Francisco,"** *Mitya's Love* or *Well of Days*.

This novelette is the story of the ruin and decay of the noble Russian family of Khruschyovs. Both as children and as youths Khruschyov—the narrator—and his sister from time to time visited Dry Valley, which, in the days of their grandfather, was a comfortable and prosperous aristocratic estate and which now, with most of its land sold to peasants, with most of its once spacious manor house and outbuildings ruined by fire and with the remnants of its staircases and balconies overgrown with weeds, is but a sad shadow of the past.

From conversations with Natalia, his old nurse, who had been his grandfather's serf; from the contemplation of an ancient ikon in a heavy silver frame on the back of which the pedigree of the Khruschyovs is written, and from a few still surviving pieces of furniture and other objects which had witnessed the days of the family's prosperity; from a few casual remarks dropped by his old, half insane aunt Tonya, who, reduced by impoverishment to the style of life of almost a peasant woman, still lives on the estate, a pitiful ruin among ruins—the narrator, by piecing scraps of information together, reconstructs the panorama of his family's past.

Out of such evocation the novelette is built. M. Bunin handles this method with such unsurpassed mastery that the effect achieved by it is strikingly powerful, original and impressive. Fragment by fragment, the pictures of this past life, of the long since dead Khruschyovs and of the violent passions and emotions which animated them begin to emerge from the darkness. As one learns the story of Khruschyov, the grandfather, murdered by his illegitimate son, a serf; of Aunt Tonya's unfortunate romance which plunged her, formerly a proud, noble girl, into her present state of insane decrepitude, and of Peter Petrovich, her strong, brilliant brother, with whom Natalia (the narrator's nurse) had touchingly and desperately fallen in love; as, in a word, Dry Valley's silent ruins come back to life again and fill anew with the blood of reality which once flowed here, the reader experiences with unexpected and overpowering strength that feeling which he would experience if, while he were standing beside the shattered fragments of an ancient Greek temple, that temple were suddenly to resurrect itself from fragments, stand up in its former beauty and fill with a colorful crowd of worshipers dead for thousands of years.

Nor is it only the chronicle of the Khruschyov family that M. Bunin's pen summons back to life. "Socially" and "economically" minded critics see in **Dry Valley** above all the painting of that process of the impoverishment and ruin of the landed Russian nobility which began long before the revolution. Doubtless, the novelette may be viewed from that angle. But its implications are wider than that. Through the medium of the nobles and peasants figuring in the one hundred short pages of his novelette, M. Bunin has drawn so masterful a synthetic portrait of the Russian people, with its contradictions and untamed passions, with the almost biblical brutality and primitiveness of its native culture, with its cruelty and kindliness and with the "geological layers" of prehistorical medievalism and modernism coexisting but not mixing in it, that at moments one feels as though old Russia's very essence were captured.

M. Bunin's narrative is calm, reserved and strictly realistic.

Moreover, he speaks almost exclusively of solid, material things, be they the trees around Dry Valley, the sky over it, or its former inhabitants. And his gift to convey to the reader the appeal of these earthy sounds, odors, colors and shapes to human senses is unique. Yet the novelette is replete with potent poetry. There is a powerful call of life in it; there are in it, too, the measured, pitiless march of time engulfing human lives and the hopeless pathos of the human beings' struggle against this march. The masterful counterpoint of, so to speak, the weeds overgrowing Dry Valley's ruins and of the fullblooded life which formerly throbbed there—a counterpoint that runs all through the novelette—brings out this poetry with unusual power. Withal, as one finishes **Dry Valley** one feels like agreeing with those of the critics who assert that the day is near when the opinion of the civilized world will agree in placing Bunin's name above that of Turgenev.

"The Elaghin Affair" also is a remarkable piece of writing. It is the story of the youthful officer of a crack regiment who has agreed with his mistress, a Polish actress, hysterical, strange and fascinating, to kill her and to commit suicide. He, however, carries out only the first part of this program: seeing her dead body before him, he is seized with such indifference that he merely gives himself up to the authorities. The story is written in the form of the record of Elaghin's trial in a court of justice. Here also unfolding his narrative retrospectively, what gems of psychological insight and of almost mysterious penetration into the realm of sex M. Bunin uncovers. What, perhaps, is most remarkable, is that he captures human feelings in such a cross-section that the reader immediately recognizes them as a part of his own experience, but he knows that no one before M. Bunin has expressed them in words. That is the earmark of a great writer.

Of the shorter stories, the three-page **"The Third Cock-crow"** is perhaps the best one. It is almost an unbelievable tour de force. Perhaps no writer has so far written pages of such unusual "specific gravity": in its diminutive space, the story holds an unsurpassed amount of color, thought, feeling and atmosphere. There is no space to single out other items. Let it be merely noted that most of the other stories are excellent, too, each one in its own way.

> *Alexander Nazaroff, "Masterly Stories by Ivan Bunin," in* The New York Times Book Review, *February 3, 1935, p. 2.*

NIKANDER STRELSKY   (essay date 1936)

[*Strelsky was a Russian academic and essayist. In the following excerpt, he scrutinizes Bunin's literary contributions in light of the author's winning the Nobel Prize in literature.*]

The 1933 award of the Nobel prize for literature provoked a considerable storm among the critics. The name of the *émigré* writer was not well known to the public. Bunin's work had never had a popular vogue, as had the work of Gorki, Andreyev, and others of his contemporaries. News of the award was received with a mixture of surprise, satisfaction, and dismay. Those who knew his work immediately split into two camps: one applauded the choice as a fitting, if tardy, recognition of a great literature in the person of its leading representative; the other denounced him contemptuously as a morbid decadent with no social consciousness.

Recent reviews of Bunin's work, in this country and abroad,

have struck the sharpest contradictions and paradoxes. The rock on which the critics generally have split has been the old question as to whether art should function as social criticism. Since Bunin has never concerned himself with political or social doctrines, this has permitted certain people to dismiss him at once. This has naturally been the attitude of Fascists and Communists alike. Both friends and foes have credited him with being a virtuoso in style. Yet the widely divergent opinions as to the other qualities of his writing are simply proof that his work cannot be easily relegated to this or that category, and that a true estimate of him must transcend too facile comparisons and narrow political prejudice.

Bunin has been labelled "a miraculous anachronism." This is one of those half-truths which is no truth at all. It is a fact that Bunin is a logical continuation of the "classics," those great figures of Russian literature who ended with the turn of the century. In a narrow, literal sense, Bunin has concluded a tradition which can have no further continuity, since the conditions which created it have vanished. His is its last voice, and in certain technical aspects, its finest.

Yet Bunin is more than a mere link with the past, and the true significance and value of his work will not permit it to be contained within a period. What has been called his *uncontemporaneousness* is really his *timelessness.* The kind of people he writes about, the kind of life he pictures, will be as true in essence, and as living, decades from now, as they were before the Revolution.

Moreover, in his art and in his outlook, Bunin stands for the relation between the past and future more than any other Russian writer. There is considerable room for argument with the defenders of Gorki's claim to the Nobel prize, and it may be successfully debated that Bunin is not only less a figure of the past than Gorki, but is far more significantly a prophet of a new generation. This may be postulated, in spite of the fact that Bunin stands completely outside all Soviet writing, in spite of the fact that in his work there is an utter absence of any reflection of the Communist Revolution.

In a recent article on the newest trends in literature, a French critic, Jean Servière, says, "It seems to me that the most interesting young writers today seek to instill in their art a predominance of what Edmond Jaloux once called, 'magic realism', and which we prefer to name, 'transfigured realism'. This may be, strictly speaking, one of the pseudonyms of classicism. Thus, the post-war period may be able to serve us at least in this: to reveal in daily experience, the signs, the symbols, the poetry of life."

If he had been speaking specifically of Bunin, this French critic could not have been more apt. It is exactly this quality of "magic realism" which identifies Bunin. Thus, in his subject-matter, in his philosophy, Bunin is closely in tune with these newest voices in literature, and is indeed a forerunner of these new writers. (pp. 273-74)

It is in the field of the short story that Bunin has made his greatest and most perfect achievement. The Swedish Academy recognized this in awarding him the Nobel prize, for special commendation was given his best-known tale, **"The Gentleman from San Francisco."**

Bunin himself has defined his own subject-matter in the opening sentence of his marvelous short story, **"The Dreams of Chang"**: "What does it matter of whom we speak? Any that have lived and that live upon this earth deserve to be the subject of our discourse." Generally speaking, however, his work falls into three categories: studies of the Russian peasant and of the declining landowning class, studies of adolescents, and oriental tales.

There is little plot and sometimes none at all. The structure of his work is elemental, bare, and symmetrical. The number of characters is always small, often only one or two. Bunin frequently concentrates his attention on one figure, merely suggesting the others, or showing them only through the eyes of his central figure. This device is used in duplicate in his best-known novel, *The Village.* The book is a large diptich of peasant life, with two chief characters; in the first part, we see the story through the eyes of Tikhon, and only through his eyes do we know Kuzma; in the last half, we see Tikhon through Kuzma's eyes.

Throughout all Bunin's work runs an ever-recurrent theme: the mystery of life and death; and it is this mystery which chiefly occupies the writer. It is not the individual soul and mind and heart of the protagonist on which he focuses his attention, but on the relationship between this man or that woman to the eternal verities of love and death. Bunin has often been attacked as a pessimist with a morbid interest in destruction and finalities, because of this intense preoccupation with the manifestations of death. But nothing could be more untrue than to call it morbid. Instead, it is simply one other aspect of Bunin's intense love of life, and life and death are to him only two different manifestations of the same thing. In his last, semi-autobiographical work, *The Life of Arseniev, or The Well of Days,* he speaks of his own "former, immemorial lives," and declares that man is devoid of a sense of his beginning as well as his end. In this philosophy, we see another phase of his timelessness: life to him is a continuous stream of consciousness, like a mysterious effluvium in which we live and breathe and suffer and are enraptured; and it is in these exceptional acute moments of awareness in the presence of death, or in the anguish of love, that we most nearly approach a perception of the nameless secret of existence. It is an intense curiosity, an intuitive urge, which prompts him to return again and again to this theme, not in any sense a morbidity. For this reason, all the details in Bunin's descriptions, so marvelous in themselves, the actual events, and the implied underlying complexities in his characters, take secondary importance. One feels that one regards the scene a little obliquely, as if, with Bunin, one attended a larger moment, a more cosmic truth.

In this connection one observes another aspect of Bunin's relation to the vanguard of modern writers. His work contains within it an implication of that profound and elusive world of the subconscious, which is the chief object of study of many ultra-moderns. Occasionally he penetrates directly into that world. Yet he never attempts any sort of scientific analysis, as if he felt it too vast and mysterious for definition, and the reader is made aware of it only in brief, illuminating flashes.

In his marvelous evocation of atmosphere, we see the most striking quality of Bunin's talent. He accomplishes this by means of an extraordinarily acute sensory equipment, which renders him intensely alive to the shape and color and texture of the world about him. He has the keen perception of an animal, and a discrimination of the most fastidious refinement. In a few words, in a phrase or two, he can conjure up a whole scene. In **"The Dreams of Chang,"** he does not need to spend paragraphs to describe the heat of the Red Sea. He merely says, "The other men of the ship, whose faces were brick-red, with oily eyes, whereas their foreheads were white and perspiring"—and one immediately feels translated into that consuming, hot radiance.

Bunin says of himself that his early ambition was to become a painter, and he refers to his "peculiar sensitiveness to light and air." It is as a painter that Bunin has chosen to depict life. It is an intensity of being, rather than an intensity of doing, which marks all his work, and this intensity is wonderfully evinced in his descriptions. He has given us some indelible impressions of the Russian countryside, of the tropics, of the infinitely varied sea.

Yet the visual sense is not the only one expressed; this is so often the only one lesser writers seem to possess; but Bunin evokes a mood, a scene, through all five of his. One remembers the "reeking of coal and Jewish kitchens" in the house where he lived in Orel; the pungent smells in the printing shop, and the stench of the tanneries in Baturino; it is the "dry" quality of the rye lying ripe in the fields, which exactly conveys the quality of the autumn landscape; and how vividly one recognizes that smell of "cold sulphur breathed in the air coming from the inmost furrowed depths of the sea"!

But it is not merely an atmosphere of the world of the senses which Bunin so wondrously creates. Flaubert instructed the young De Maupassant always "to choose the exact word for the exact meaning." Bunin has profited by this precept, but he makes the exact word convey more than its literal meaning, as if through the prompting of an additional sixth sense. This gives his scenes a sort of fourth dimensional quality, and provides that pervasive suggestiveness, that haunting evocativeness, so characteristic of his work. Every word is chosen and placed for its specific shape and color and for its rhythmic and emotional relation to the rest of the sentence. This gives his language a perennial freshness and a quality of magic. Bunin inflicts despair upon the translator, for his effects are so often effects of style. There is never a superfluous word; everything is said with the utmost conciseness and subtlety, yet with transparent clarity.

It has been said that Bunin's true hero is the Russian language. Certainly he employs the rich and resourceful tongue of his native land to its fullest capacity in delicacy and point and meaning, reaching a refinement never before attained.

Even the harshest enemies of Bunin have praised this rare and magnificent talent. Prince Mirsky has said that Bunin is the only living Russian of whose language the old classic writers would have approved [see excerpt dated 1926]; and Renato Poggioli granted, that while he had no originality, he was nevertheless "one of those rarest of writers who have the divine right to be detached and uncontemporary."

It is useless to look to Bunin for profound expositions of philosophy, or for social criticism of life. He is not interested in the mechanics of our civilization. Nor is he interested in probing the individual, in the delicate dissection of personality, as was Chekov. There are no full-length creations of character in his work, as in Tolstoy. His men and women are usually types, and quite ordinary types. Only ocasionally are we allowed a penetrating flash of insight into individual souls. As Struve says, "the analytical methods of a Dostoyevsky are entirely alien to him."

This does not mean, however, that Bunin never sees people as individuals, as exceptional. The two remarkable beings in

"The Case of Lieutenant Yelaghin" are proof of the contrary. What, then, is the explanation for his apparent aversion to psychological exploration?

Bunin himself suggests the answer, when he says, "The most terrible thing in this world is man with his soul." Struve amplifies this idea further when he refers to Bunin's "characteristic conviction of the fundamental impenetrability and inconceivableness of another man's soul." It seems as if Bunin deliberately chose the average man or woman, or the immature youth, as a device of simplification, the better to express his marvelling sense of the wonderful and infinite contained within the commonplace.

It is his uncanny ability to communicate to the reader, directly and simply, this sense of marvel and mystery, which lifts Bunin above the status of a mere craftsman, however expert. It is not an act of definition, but rather a process of revelation. It is this faculty which makes Bunin unique and original in Russian literature. It is the faculty of a poet and a seer, and is the key to his whole purpose and method.

The definition of requirement for the Nobel prize specifies that a writer shall have produced "distinguished work of an idealistic tendency." Bunin is the perfect example of the pure artist, striving toward an ideal, the old ideal of truth, beauty and the wholeness of life. In his work we find it restated with new authority. Bunin stands for a sort of consummation of the past, but it is a past which has within it the germs of a new life. The "magic realism" which marks all his work, marks him also as the heir, not only of the past, before man doubted miracles, but of the more immediate past, the age of science and reason, the age of "realism." The newest voices of our decade speak again of a sense of the unknown and the unknowable in life. Ours is an age in which poetry and science, intuition and logic, find that they have more ground in common between them than they had suspected. Bunin stands in just this attitude toward life, and in the expression of this attitude in literature, he is an inaugurator of the new era.

As in the case of all truly great artists, it is not easy to place him in a pigeonhole. It is a truism that genius in any creative field becomes less easy to define within a narrow category the higher it aspires. One cannot say of Bunin that he is a classicist, a romanticist, or a realist. He is all three of these. He is a classicist in his perfection of form and style, in the symmetry and logic of his technical structure, in his objectivity and restraint. He is also a classicist in another sense. No one has written adequately of his poise, the poise of the relationship between himself and the sensuous world, between himself and the shadowy world of the psyche, between himself and the cosmos. This is the reason why Bunin, unlike most other *émigré* writers, has continued writing in exile, without sign of diminution or decline. His strength lies with himself, as if he felt an innate harmony and oneness of life, an infinite resource of spirit, and depended in no way upon environment to fertilize his creative power.

He is a realist in the so-called "clinical" detachment with which he observes and records. This has misled some people into calling him cold and metallic. Nothing could be farther from the truth. Even in his most subjective passages, such as his fictionized autobiography, *The Life of Arseniev,* he does not permit himself to abandon his cool impartiality; but underneath it lies deep and passionate feeling, by which he communicates to the reader "profound and troubled emotions," striking deep chords that echo in our minds long afterwards.

He is a realist also in the unflinching fidelity with which he examines the brutal and ugly side of life. Romantic, certainly, are his preoccupation with love and death, the sensuous beauty of his language, the exoticism of his oriental tales, and his poetic conception of existence.

Even in his studies of Russian peasant life, Bunin is the pure artist. He has been praised by some critics, otherwise hostile, for this section of his work, and the Soviet government selected many of these stories for reprinting. Bunin was the first important writer to reveal the reverse side of the prewar, fashionable worship of the simplicity of the Russian peasant. Yet even in his scathing indictment of the ugliness and degradation of the peasant's poverty, Bunin intended no social message. It was incidental that he was a Jeremiah of the future Revolution, and it was not his purpose to preach a warning or teach a lesson. He was simply painting a certain aspect of life.

Bunin is not without faults. He lacks the healthy, rugged vitality of a Pushkin. He has no sense of humor, and there is no high-spirited bravado in his fortitude. There is no robust laughter in him, no gusto, no red-bloodedness. This is the reason why his studies of the peasant are incomplete, and lack a full, rounded development. He can show no gallery of richly sculptured characters. It is not his purpose to expound wise philosophies of life. The melodic rhythms and cadences of his writing are that of chamber music, not the diapason of a full orchestra.

Yet as an artist, as an individualist, as an original and distinguished exponent of a great aesthetic tradition in contemporary terms, and in the clarity and beauty of his vision, there are few who can stand beside him. (pp. 277-83)

> *Nikander Strelsky, "Bunin: Eclectic of the Future," in* South Atlantic Quarterly, *Vol. XXXV, No. 3, July, 1936, pp. 273-83.*

CLEANTH BROOKS, JOHN THIBAUT PURSER, AND ROBERT PENN WARREN (essay date 1952)

[*Brooks and Warren are two of the most prominent figures of the school of New Criticism, an influential movement in American criticism that also included Allen Tate and R. P. Blackmur. Although the various New Critics did not subscribe to a single set of principles, all believed that a work of literature had to be examined as an object in itself through close textual analysis of symbol, image, and metaphor. In the following discussion, Brooks, Purser, and Warren interpret "The Gentleman from San Francisco."*]

[**"The Gentleman from San Francisco"**] seems merely to unfold a process, to give a simple chronicle, a chronicle with elaborate details and descriptive digressions but merely a simple chronicle after all. . . . [Behind] this simple chronicle there is a conflict, the conflict between those who rule the world and those who are ruled. The story, then, is about the oppressors and the oppressed, about justice. Having said this, let us . . . see how this theme is developed and to what it leads.

There is, first, the story of the Gentleman himself, the proud man who is struck down in the moment of his pride. He is the central character. But we know astonishingly little about him: he is proud, he is self-indulgent, he is contemptuous of others, especially those of inferior economic and social station, he is a complete materialist without even "a mustard seed of what is called mysticism in his heart." We do not even know his name—"neither at Naples nor on Capri could anyone recall his name." In other words, Bunin seems to imply, his individuality, his name, is not important. It is not important because the Gentleman as a person is not important; he is important only as a type, as a member of a class, the class who "taken together, now rule the world, as incomprehensibly and, essentially, as cruelly" as the Roman Emperor Tiberius did. This namelessness, then, points us beyond the individual to the real concern of the story, the development of an idea.

In support of this we find the method of the story. Bunin takes the tone of a historian, as it were, as if he were giving an account long afterwards of the way life had been at a certain period. He says, for example: "The class of people to which he belonged was in the habit . . ." Furthermore, observe the great detail devoted to the life of that class, the class upon which, Bunin ironically says, "depend all the blessings of civilization: the cut of dress suits, the stability of thrones, the declaration of wars, the prosperity of hotels."

Once we have accepted the development of a theme, an idea, as the main concern of this story, we understand, too, the significance of many digressions involving minor characters, the hired lovers on the ship, the Asiatic prince and the Gentleman's daughter, the valet Luigi, the boatman Lorenzo, the cab driver, the Emperor Tiberius, the Abruzzi pipers, the hotel proprietor on Capri. A few of these characters belong to the class that rules the world, but most of them belong to the class that, in one way or another, serves the Gentleman and his kind.

We may now notice what at first glance may appear a peculiar fact in a story which has an important element of protest against social injustice: the fact that we do not have a simple arrangement of the rulers as bad and the ruled as good. The daughter of the Gentleman, though she belongs to the class of the rulers and though her notion of love has been corrupted, is yet presented with a certain sympathy: she has some sensitivity, some awareness of her isolation, as we understand from her reaction when her father tells about his dream. On the other hand, most of the characters of the class of the ruled, for example, Lorenzo, the cabman, and the valet Luigi are presented as corrupted in one way or another. Lorenzo has been spoiled and turned into an idler and reveller by admiration for his picturesque good looks. The cabman is a drunkard and gambler. Luigi has been so embittered by his condition that his satiric humor appears even after the Gentleman's death. The general point here seems to be that the unjust system spreads corruption downward as well as upward, that the stain spreads in all directions, and that injustice has persisted from the ancient to the modern world.

Let us lay aside for the moment the theme of social justice. We can see that many of the elements in the story do not seem to be accommodated to it. For instance, the various references to love, the Gentleman's relations with prostitutes, the young couple who are hired to pose as lovers on the liner, the love of the daughter for the Asiatic prince, the figure of the Virgin on the road to Monte Solare. We have here a scale from a degraded form of human love up to Divine love. In between the two extremes there are the hired lovers and the daughter. They imply the same thing: even in the corrupted

world people want to believe in love, to have at least the illusion of love. The hired lovers provide a romantic atmosphere by their pretended devotion. The daughter, though she is drawn to the prince merely by social snobbery (personally he is described as very unattractive), must convert this into the emotion of love. Bunin says: "Beautiful were the tender, complex feelings which her meeting with the ungainly man aroused in her—the man in whose veins flowed unusual blood, for after all, it does not matter what in particular stirs up a maiden's soul: money, or fame, or nobility of birth." Bunin has put the matter ironically—"it does not matter." But it does matter, Bunin is implying, that the human being, even when the victim of his system, when accepting the false values of money, fame, and birth, must still try to maintain the illusion of love. That is, over against the injustice of the world there is the idea of love, culminating in Divine love.

A second set of elements that does not seem to be readily accounted for by the theme of injustice is the symbolism of the ship and the captain. It is true that the ship first appears as an easily interpreted symbol for society—the Gentleman and his kind take their ease in the dining room or bar, while the stokers sweat before the furnaces and the lookouts freeze in the crow's nest. But we begin to sense that more is meant. The darkness and the storm are outside the ship, but people ignore that terror for they "trust" the captain, who is presented as a "pagan idol." We can begin now to read the symbolism. The modern world worships its "pagan idol," the technician, the scientist, the administrator, the man who has apparently conquered nature and made irrelevant any concern with the mysteries of life and death. But we see that death does strike down the Gentleman—even though "men still wonder most at death and most absolutely refuse to believe in it." The mystery of death remains despite the skills of all the pagan idols. And even the pagan idol himself who reigns over the ship would be afraid of the darkness and mystery of the sea if he did not have the comfort of the wireless. But let us notice that the wireless is put down as a mystery, a thing "in the last account incomprehensible to him," and notice that the wireless shack is described as a kind of shrine or temple: " . . . the large armored cabin, which now and then filled with mysterious rumbling sounds and with the dry creaking of blue fires . . ." So in the end the idol, the man who is supposed to know the solution to all problems and who is supposed to bring all to safety, must trust a "mystery."

Before we try to relate this idea to the theme of justice, we may look at the last paragraph of the story, the scene where the Devil leans on Gibraltar and watches the great ship disappear in the dark and storm toward America. What is the Devil doing in this story? There are several details to be observed before we frame an answer. Gibraltar is defined as the "gateway of two worlds," the Old World and the New World, Europe and America. The ship is bigger than the Devil and leaves him behind, staring after it. The ship is a "giant created by the arrogance of the New Man with the old heart."

To put these details together into a pattern, we may begin by taking the Devil as the embodiment of Evil, a quite conventional and usual equation. Then we may say that the Devil is left behind in the Old World because the New World doesn't believe in Evil. The spirit of modernism, that is, takes it that all difficulties are merely difficulties of adjustment of one kind or another. If there is injustice in society, simply change the system. Moral problems, by such reasoning, are not really moral problems, they are problems in "conditioning." The chief concern is not with right and wrong, good and evil, but with what will work. To sum up this point, the modern spirit, which in the story is taken as characteristically American, ignores Evil; it thinks that it can solve all problems by the application of technical skills. Therefore the ship, the symbol of the achievement of the modern spirit, is "bigger" than the Devil.

Now for the second point. The ship is a "giant created by the arrogance of the New Man with the old heart." To interpret, we must say that the New Man, with all his skills has not solved the final problem, the problem of the heart. There can be no justice by merely changing systems, by tinkering machines, either literal machines or social machines. The problem is, in the end, a problem of a change of heart, a birth of moral awareness, a spiritual redemption. Systems must be changed, machines must be tinkered—but as a consequence of the "redemption." With this idea, which is the central and final theme of the story, we can now see how the elements concerning love and the elements concerning the captain as idol are related to the rest of the story. Love may be taken as the redeeming power, the beneficent mystery as opposed to the terrible mystery of death. Then the captain—*i.e.,* the technician, the scientist, the administrator, the being whom all men trust—must himself finally trust a mystery. There is always the mystery of nature and man's fate, for there are always love and death; there is the mystery of the human heart.

We must not conclude this interpretation without a word of caution. We must not be too ready to read the story as an attack on the achievements of the modern spirit. We might even go so far as to say that the story is not an attack at all, but a warning, rather, against a misinterpretation of the modern spirit, an oversimplification of it. The story provides, as it were, a perspective on a problem, and not an absolute and dogmatic solution for it. (pp. 174-77)

> *Cleanth Brooks, John Thibaut Purser, and Robert Penn Warren, in their discussion of "The Gentleman from San Francisco," in* An Approach to Literature, *Cleanth Brooks, John Thibaut Purser, Robert Penn Warren, eds., third edition, Appleton-Century-Crofts, Inc., 1952, pp. 162-77.*

JACQUES CROISÉ, PSEUDONYM OF ZINAIDA SCHAKOVSKOY (essay date 1954)

[*Croisé is a Russian novelist, journalist, essayist, and poet living in France. In the following excerpt, she presents the essence of Bunin's beliefs and perceptions as reflected in such short stories as "The Gentleman from San Francisco," "Brethren," and "The Elaghin Affair."*]

[Although] Bunin was Russian to the marrow of his bones, the universe was never foreign to him. Endowed with a prodigious memory which was the key to his creative power, Bunin, when he saw them for the first time, "recognized" the medieval castle of the West, or the sand-covered ruins of Baalbek. He was able to describe with the same understanding and the same love the dreary regions of his native land and the jungles of Colombo.

Love and women play an important part in Bunin's works. Woman is like the earth, full of unknown forces; she carries the eternal laws, like an amphora of love. This love has many facets; somber or radiant, it is never absent from Bunin's work. For love, a rickshaw boy dies in **"Brethren"**; in **"The Great Road,"** Parasha becomes insane because of it; Elaghin kills the beautiful Polish actress whose love was a joy and torment for him in **"The Elaghin Affair"**; the charming Nathalie dies just when her love finds fulfilment in **"Nathalie"**; and because love does not satisfy her, the beautiful girl of **"The Serpant of Fire"** becomes a nun. And if the end of **"The Gentleman from San Francisco"** is tragic it is because the protagonist spent his life being a business man without having the time to love either women or the world. Love is also memory; the soul is aware of its destiny. That which we have imagined, which we have dreamed about, which we have waited for, is but the memory of what we once knew. But memory is purer than reality. From disharmony, man seeks to escape into death. Bunin's most beautiful pages on love lead to death.

The key to Bunin's entire work is death. It is because of the reality of death that life is worth something. Without death, life would be boundless and incomplete. Death is the continuation of life, its justification, its release into the absolute. Unlike Tolstoy, whose religiosity was intellectual, Bunin, in spite of his own scepticism, had the gift of mysticism and metaphysics. "I knew for sure," he wrote, "that there exists something more ancient, even in comparison to the farthest terrestrial antiquity." That which is older than the oldest terrestrial antiquity, is death. With what "eagerness," so to speak, did Bunin study man's death. Death is the last examination that man takes, the only one where cheating is impossible, and where the judgment is final.

The old Russian peasant woman in **"Veselyi dvor"** comes back to die in the house of her son and does not find him there. "She made the sign of the cross, raising her hand with difficulty, kissed the ikon and put it on the little table, thought for a moment, remembered that she was dying and crossed herself once more, attempting to express by a sigh, and especially by slow, serious gestures of her hand, her complete submission to God, her complete adoration before His glory and His power, her hopes in His mercy."

The rickshaw man dies, worn out by running errands for his white brethren. "And the old rickshaw man, who for a long time had longed eagerly for the end of his sufferings, lay down in the stifling darkness of his shanty, under the roof of dry leaves rustling with small red snakes. He died in the evening from freezing cramps and diarrhea. The life of the rikshaw man was snuffed out with the sun which disappeared behind extensive mauve sheets of water stretching toward the West, in the purple of its ashes, and in the gold of the most beautiful clouds in the world. Night came, and in the forest near Colombo, there remained only a tiny shriveled corpse which had lost its number, its name, as the river Kalemi loses its name when it flows into the ocean. When the sun sets it becomes wind, but what becomes of a dead man?"

This simplicity in confronting death is the attribute of primitive beings. Other people, the civilized ones, through their terror of it, either run away from it—there are many murders and suicides among Bunin's characters—or are ignorant of it until the end, dying "despite themselves," missing therefore the most solemn human experience. This is true in the case of **"The Gentleman from San Francisco."**

It would be useless to look for a moral or logical synthesis in Bunin's work. Here we cannot agree with Zaitsev who speaks of one in his biography of the writer. If Bunin is a moralist, it is only because he does not know anything about falsehood, because no preconceived idea impels him to substitute, as did Tolstoy, his own truth for the truth of reality. . . . He does not construct a system, but leaves us free to recognize upon the tapestry that he presents the pattern of our own natural tendencies.

Bunin did not distinguish between the mystical disciplines and Oriental religions which inspired him to write beautiful pages. He comprehends God not through his will to understand Him, not through his intellect, but by being aware of His presence. "I live as a hermit, working from morning until evening. But I work easily, with that rare clarity of spiritual insight which brings incomparable happiness."

"To you my soul, the Lord has entrusted talent. Accept the gift with terror." He is in a way too intelligent to believe himself responsible for his gifts as a writer, therefore he is grateful to Him from whom they are derived.

In brief, the world for Bunin would not have been complete if he had not had someone to whom he could give praise. In the poetry of Bunin there is the gravity of the Psalms, and there is throughout his work the desire for an immense and coherent universe. He is against destruction. The Russian Revolution was abhorrent to him because it began with the destruction of all that which had been acquired by long generations of men.

"I passed the crowd composed of women, youths, and crippled old people, whose eyes were pale from time and the wind from the steppes, and I thought continually of old times, and of the strange power of the past. Where does this power come from? And what is its significance? Therein, perhaps, is hidden one of the greatest mysteries of life. And why does it rule man with such a miraculous power? In our religious feeling, in our homage to the past—of which we are not conscious sometimes—the relationship of our thoughts and actions with men who are no more, plays an immense part . . ." ("On the Donetz").

It is always memory, a pre-existential and prenatal memory, without which life would be nothing but a succession of insignificant and absurd facts, which is the center of Bunin's work. "The apex of each human life is the memory that remains of it. Is not this desire that we have to be remembered, our desire to react against death?" asks the author. For him there was no question. Memory is the prime evidence of immortality and because of this, literature is not a vain occupation, but one of the functions of life. (pp. 148-51)

> Jacques Croisé, "Ivan Bunin: 1870-1953," in The Russian Review, *Vol. 13, No. 2, April, 1954, pp. 146-51.*

ANDREW GUERSHOON COLIN (essay date 1955)

[In the essay excerpted below, Colin examines whether Bunin's strongest character portrayals are in his stories of Russians and Russia.]

There is no wonder that Bunin's renown in Russia turned into fame when his first important stories and novellas appeared in print. They had an incomparably greater number of readers than his poems could possibly have attracted. Apart from some minor stories, his first big piece was his most powerful novel *The Village*, which was published as a separate book in 1909.

Let me comment on his prose in general. There are those who

say that Bunin was particularly forceful, that his genius found its fullest expression when he wrote about people and localities of rural central Russia. Some of the critics go further and assert that when Bunin came to describe the two Russian capitals or places abroad he would weaken and tend to become artificial. I cannot share this view. A great many of his stories and the novellas **"The Brothers"** and **"The Gentleman from San Francisco"** are set outside Russia. The mastery is the same as if the figures were living and acting in his own province of Oryol. All his prose is typical of Ivan Bunin, without exception, and could be recognised as such from a few sentences taken at random. His descriptions of exotic places, in fact, are unique in Russian letters: he is the Russian Conrad or Somerset Maugham when it comes to scenes laid in the east. He is head and shoulders above Pierre Loti or Claude Farrère in this respect, and infinitely superior to those of his own compatriots who they wrote about overseas countries.

In one respect I will agree with these critics: Bunin obviously knew the districts around his own birthplace better than he knew other localities, and had therefore a greater assurance in writing about them. Another point may be conceded: in his novels and stories dealing with provincial life Bunin makes use of local dialects and ways of expression, varying them according to the speakers, and he does it admirably. Such renderings of particular human speech always make a lasting impression. This is perfectly true, but it does not follow that where no local peculiarities are reproduced the quality of his writing is on a lower level, for, in fact, it is not.

Speaking of his treatment of subjects in novels and stories, I must remark that he is merciless throughout. A Russian critic once said: 'Bunin possesses a cruel talent.' He showed the Russian muzhik on the eve of the revolution, and his rendering of life in the villages went far beyond Chekhov's pictures, for the average peasant received short shrift from Bunin on account of his blind ignorance, disloyalty and greed. The customary idealising of the peasant, started in literature by Grigorovich and Nekrasov, found no echo in Bunin's work.

The clergy, the merchants and the gentry do not fare any better. He knew them all very well, unlike Chekhov who, with all his deep understanding of the intelligentsia and of the merchant class, knew little of the peasantry or landed gentry.

Nevertheless, a genuine, even a hopeless, love of Russia permeates the whole of Bunin's work, including his poems, and a poignant compassion for his suffering and erring characters can be detected in his writings, although he was too great an artist to express his own feelings directly. In spite of this, the thought is inescapable that his sense of things evil was much stronger than his belief in the ultimate good.

His pessimism is however amply counter-balanced in his work by a very positive creative power. It may also be mentioned that Bunin does not attempt to teach or to attack anyone.

The Village was his first large work in prose. He stuns the reader, who is unfamiliar with his powerful style, by his bold frankness and his fearless unmasking of Russian provincial life at the beginning of the present century. It ought to be borne in mind that *The Village* was published before Rodionov's challenge *Our Crime*, a book not free from bias, but outstandingly independent. So much more astonishing and noteworthy was Bunin's boldness. At the very time when the intelligentsia was in love with the peasantry in general, he sounded an alarm that reverberated all over Russia. Only one conclusion could be drawn from his novel—that the peasants are no better than the rest, and possibly worse, that they are a lot of brutes, liars, good-for-nothings, and that many are simply hooligans and common felons.

It is true that representatives of other strata of the population appearing in *The Village* come off equally badly: every class depicted in the book merits the definition 'thoroughly bad', without a redeeming feature. In other words, the whole picture of pre-revolutionary provincial life is painted in the blackest possible tones. This is a pity; because, despite Bunin's artistry, the story does not ring quite true. (pp. 168-69)

The concluding chapter of *The Village* is written with such power and such unredeemed ruthlessness that the whole novel is unforgettable, even if single events and passing figures may become blurred with the passage of time.

Another remarkable novella is the **"Grammar of Love."** In Bunin's own family there was an example of a complete hermit, viz. one of his grandfathers who lost his wife. Bunin altered the facts, so that the man in the story is named Khvoshchinsky and, instead of his wife, the woman is a peasant girl, a serf, Lushka, who belonged to his household. The squire fell so deeply in love with this gentle and self-effacing girl that when she died he felt his own life was finished, although this happened when they were both very young. A boy had been born to them, but the squire took no interest in him after his mother's death. He literally barricaded himself in her room for the rest of his life, where he sat looking at her picture and reading an ancient little book called *The Grammar of Love*.

The writing in this book savours of the late 18th-century pastoral conception of life. There is the language of flowers, with naïve explanations and maxims such as this: 'A woman is never so strongly armed as when her weapon is weakness.'

The story is unfolded when a landowner visits the neglected estate and meets the now adult son of that union who is willing to sell his late father's library. In the ordinary way, a story like the **"Grammar of Love"** would tend to be sentimental, but not when Ivan Bunin's was the pen that wrote it.

A typical comment was made by Bunin upon the fate of the hermit: 'His life was one that was perhaps destined to be a most ordinary one, if it had not been for the advent of a girl, Lushka, mysterious in her charm.'

Yet another village-story is *Sukhodol*, as outstanding for its penetrating insight as *The Village*. Bunin was always fascinated by the fates of the ancestors of his own family. *Sukhodol* is a saga. It is permeated with the mysticism of family traditions which transcend a sequence of generations. These traditions compel the people to act not as they would themselves, but as the invisible powers of past generations force them to act. Bunin reminds us that in every family of the landed gentry there has been peasant admixture at various times, mainly through servant girls. He says that in the dim past the squire was only a peasant more wealthy than the rest. He adds: 'The life of the family, of the clan, is deep, knotty, mysterious, often frightening. But its very strength derives from its depth, also from its traditions and from its past.'

The greatest stir was produced among the Russian reading public when **"A Gentleman from San Francisco"** appeared in 1916. I remember the reception of this novella very well, although it coincided with momentous events on the Russian front during the first world war. Here was a story by a well-known poet and author which made him famous within a few weeks. The scene is laid on an ocean liner and in Italy, and there is nothing concerning Russia in it at all, except a fleeting sidelight on some professional revolutionaries living abroad. One of Bunin's masterly strokes is in the anonymity of the hero of the story, who is simply 'a gentleman'. I cannot think of any other narrative in which the central figure is not named, and I believe it was the author's intention to convey in this way that 'The Gentleman' is a typical, essentially American plutocrat whose 'name is legion'. Looking back over a lapse of forty years, one is inclined to think that there are naïve passages in the novella, and generalisations which suggest a certain bias. It is not the bias of the left-wing intellectual against wealth and exploitation, for this we cannot assign to Bunin at all, but there is the aversion of the thinking and deepfeeling Russian to comfort and idleness resulting from the mere possession of money, the aversion to a situation which makes it unnecessary for the 'chosen few' to think or to feel anything outside their very narrow family-circle. This attitude of Bunin's would be quite acceptable if he had not blotted his copybook by giving journalese twists to his otherwise invariably detached pen. These twists include some rather questionable descriptions of the way of life on a big Atlantic liner and in expensive hotels on the island of Capri, as if Bunin had never been on a long voyage himself or had not stayed in good-class hotels. Of course he had, which makes it worse, but ninety-five per cent of his Russian readers had not, and they must have been taken in, as I was myself, at the time of reading the story in 1916. However, this is only one negative feature of the story, as opposed to the many of a definitely positive kind.

In **"The Gentleman from San Francisco"** Bunin has revealed himself as an incomparable master of the Russian language. His choice of words and mode of writing are very impressive: for here we find a fascination which seizes the reader from the very start, and which seems to be brought about by purely verbal means. The adjectives and adverbs are often quite unexpected, yet completely adequate and acceptable in all their unusualness; the nouns offer a mixture of the conventional and the original, while verbs often hit the reader by their sheer force, though without any element of vulgarity. It is a pity that I cannot quote passages here, because even in translation, Bunin's power of expression would survive.

Another facet of Bunin's talent is in evidence in **"The Gentleman from San Francisco"**, an element which has been recognised by other students of his art. It lies in the atmosphere of the story. Not a word has been said which would make the reader think of a fatal ending, and yet he is from the outset haunted by the premonition of an unavoidable catastrophe, of an irreparable tragedy. Consummate art is required for this kind of writing.

The narrative in **"The Gentleman from San Francisco"** is concentrated and concise, and Bunin's personality is kept well in the background. The word-pictures are drawn outstandingly vividly and cannot fail to make a lasting impression on all who read them. I shall make bold to say that for **"The Gentleman from San Francisco"** alone Bunin would deserve the name of an outstanding writer. It is appropriate that this work has been translated into many languages.

While still in Russia, Bunin wrote a considerable number of short stories, but I have already suggested that his short stories and novels written in exile are possibly superior to those composed in Russia. In this respect he reminds us of Gogol', Herzen and Turgenev, some of whose best work was done abroad, away from their native Russia. Bunin's genius took a very long time to mature, but the results were such that his enforced separation from his homeland did not affect the quality of his work. It is possible that if he had not had to leave Russia his standard would have been higher still, but I cannot help thinking that there is little room for improvement in his *émigré* writing.

The most remarkable works written by Bunin in France are: *Mitya's Love,* one of the most disturbing and profound love-stories ever written anywhere; *Arsen'yev's Life,* already referred to in this article, an autobiography which reads like—and is indeed—an epoch-making novel; his *Reminiscences* and a series of short stories, a number of which are grouped in a volume called *Dark Avenues.* Here I must say that the erotic element, always present in Bunin's prose, very richly represented in *Arsen'yev's Life,* and particularly in the second part of 'Lika', has been the pivot round which revolve practically all of the short stories collected in *Dark Avenues.* Nevertheless, *Dark Avenues* clearly shows that Bunin, even at the advanced age at which he wrote these pieces, had still the youthful temperament necessary to give realistic and vivid colouring to his narrative. *Dark Avenues* reminds us once more that Bunin was a great psychologist, and in this fact lies the unquestionable merit of this collection of his late stories.

It is a pity however that one of the English literary critics who wrote immediately after Bunin's death in a well-known London quarterly review, seems to have derived his acquaintance with Bunin from *Dark Avenues* only. It is as if a Russian critic writing on Charles Dickens should base his judgment an *Great Expectations* and on nothing else.

All Bunin's verse and prose has to be taken into account, and from such a review of his achievement several considerations emerge.

Firstly, that Ivan Bunin was a man of truly outstanding intellect. There is more than penetrating judgment in his work, there is profound wisdom: his evaluations of life in general, whether Russian or foreign, strike the reader as intrinsically true and wise.

Secondly, Bunin's complete emancipation from all political and aesthetic taboos establishes him as a writer in the classical tradition, by making his work timeless and by securing for it a position of literary permanence.

On the other hand, his artistry is supreme: every word appears in its right place and in the right context, and his economy of verbal material only enhances the impression of aptness and force.

Bunin stands alone as the foremost Russian stylist of the first half of the 20th century, and whoever wishes to find contemporary Russian at its best and noblest should read him. He could not do better. (pp. 170-73)

> *Andrew Guershoon Colin, "Ivan Bunin in Retrospect," in* The Slavonic and East European Review, *Vol. XXXIV, No. 82, December, 1955, pp. 156-73.*

RENATO POGGIOLI (essay date 1957)

[*Poggioli was an Italian-born American essayist and translator whose critical writings are concerned chiefly with Russian literature. His critical text* The Poets of Russia, 1890-1930 (1960) *is considered one of the most important examinations of that literary era. In the following excerpt from an essay originally published in* Harvard Slavic Studies *in 1953 and revised in 1957, Poggioli compares Bunin's prose works with those of several Russian writers, including Ivan Turgenev, Leo Tolstoi, Anton Chekhov, and Maxim Gorki, to determine whether Bunin's short stories consistently demonstrate the traditions of Russian classical realism.*]

Besides his early volumes of verse and his early collections of stories, the literary heritage that Bunin will leave to posterity includes the novel *The Village* (1910), and four volumes of tales, which often contain at the end a few compositions in verse. The earliest of these volumes was *Dry Valley* (1912) which, like the others, opens with the title piece; it was followed by *Iounn the Weeper* (1913), *The Cup of Life* (1914), and, finally, by *The Gentleman from San Francisco* (1916). These works are the creation of Bunin's maturity, and contain all his masterpieces. The production of his years in exile is uneven, and in recent times all too often marred by writings full of a senile obsession with sex; yet it includes an outstanding novelette, *Mitya's Love* (1925); an excellent collection of tales, *A Sunstroke* (1927); and, finally, what is Bunin's most ambitious undertaking up to date, the long narrative cycle started in 1927 under the title of *The Life of Arsenyev.*

As any reader slightly acquainted with a few of these works can see, Bunin has written far more consistently and faithfully than Gorki in the straightforward tradition of Russian classical realism. His real masters are Goncharov, Turgenev, and Tolstoy; in the case of the last, Bunin was especially influenced by such pieces as "The Death of Ivan Ilich." It has been said that without the precedent of that Tolstoyan work Bunin would not have written his story **"The Gentleman from San Francisco,"** which is nonetheless a highly original creation, not only the masterpiece among his tales, but one of the greatest ever written in the Russian tongue. There is no doubt that Bunin's "Happiness" is reminiscent of Tolstoy's *Domestic Happiness,* as the very title implies. Bunin acknowledged in the same way his debt to Goncharov by writing **"The Dream of Oblomov's Grandson,"** and no Russian reader will fail to notice the attempt to reproduce the qualities of Turgenev's mood and style in such stories as **"Conversation at Night"** and **"The Grammar of Love."**

Yet very often Bunin follows less obvious models or less classical examples: for instance, the tale **"A Spring Evening"** (1913), where a peasant kills a beggar to rob him of a few cents, is clearly reminiscent of a strange and cruel true story which Dostoevski relates in *The Idiot,* the story of a merchant killed in a hotel by his roommate for the sake of a gold watch. It is equally evident that Bunin paid great attention to the "extravagant" writings of a peculiar master, Leskov, whom he imitated in structure, but not in the uniquely colorful texture of his style. Bunin's tale **"A Goodly Life"** (1910) is certainly modeled on Leskov's narrative "The Amazon"; while another story, **"The Cup of Life,"** is clearly related to one of the favorite subjects of Leskov, the provincial clergy, so keenly portrayed in Leskov's novel, *Cathedral Folk.*

It has been said that Bunin learned lessons also from Chekhov and Gorki, but their influence was more vague and less lasting. This is perhaps due to the fact that Bunin was predominantly interested in a social environment which, even in his youth, belonged to a past almost completely dead, but which had been a primary object of observation for Tolstoy and the other classical realists—Russian country life, as exemplified by both the landed gentry and the peasantry. Gorki, instead, paid far greater attention to the old class of provincial merchants and to the newly risen urban proletariat, while Chekhov devoted the best of all his creative energies to the portrayal of the intelligentsia and the petty bourgeoisie. This is why the atmosphere of *The Village* is so un-Gorkian and un-Chekhovian, despite the fact that the protagonists of that novel are a shopkeeper forever intent on amassing property and money and a plebeian intellectual, always intoxicated with ideas and words. Perhaps there are more traces of a Chekhovian than of a Gorkian influence in Bunin's writing. It can be located, however, only in his very early or his very late works. In his youth, Bunin often imitated the more lyrical side of Chekhov's genius, as expressed, almost uniquely, in "The Steppe." In his old age he was again attracted by the less typical Chekhov, by the unsentimental recorder of such pathetic cases as the one which is the theme of "The Lady with the Pet Dog," a tale which left its imprint on Bunin's story **"A Sunstroke."**

This absence of any significant Chekhovian or Gorkian influence may be explained also by the powerful attraction which Bunin felt no so much for the literary theories as for the stylistic practices of French realism, especially in its Flaubertian brand. Russian classical fiction had been strongly affected by the examples of such masters as Stendhal and Balzac, and from the end of the nineteenth century to the beginning of the twentieth, the late realists were bound to feel, although in their own way, the impact of Zola's work and of French naturalism. But the teachings of Flaubert and the Goncourts had never been received in Russia with great honor or favor, and we can safely assert that Bunin is the only Russian realist who was ever won over to the French method of the *écriture artiste* and to the Parnassian ideals of impersonality and impassibility.

This "esthetic" mood strongly differentiates Bunin on one side from his beloved masters, the great novelists and storytellers of the classical age, and on the other from the outstanding figures of his own generation—in other words, from Chekhov and Gorki, to whom he was otherwise bound by the strong ties of a common loyalty to the national tradition of literary realism. This particular attitude produced the paradoxical effect of making Bunin closer than Chekhov and Gorki, and far closer than he and his critics ever supposed, to the esthetic revival of the beginning of the century. In Bunin there is a decadent strain, which, however, as in the case of Flaubert, operates in harmony with the conventions of realism and within the rigid framework of a world clearly perceived with the mind and the senses. Yet this does not make that world intelligible and sensible; what is logical and meaningful is only the artificial order imposed by the artist on the chaos of nature and of human existence.

Within the macrocosm of the universe and within the microcosm of man's experience, Bunin contemplates, like Flaubert, only the workings of cruel and blind forces. His interest in the morbid and pathological in nature and life expresses itself with a kind of unimpassioned and objective detachment, which spurns the pathetic involvement so characteristic of the Russian decadents, and spurns even more the otherworldly longings of the Russian symbolists. Bunin's distaste for the esoteric and the occult, for the eclectic and the composite, for the mystical and the metaphysical: in brief, his artistic integrity and unswerving loyalty to the demands which his talent

makes on an artist's will, have transformed into an authentic master a writer who at first seemed fated to play merely an epigone's role. (pp. 133-35)

Despite the fact that his prose, even more than his verse, is frequently patterned after examples by other masters, Bunin is far from being a derivative artist—a truth that must be tested, since so far we have emphasized how much his creation is dependent upon previous models and sources. This reexamination of Bunin's fiction must thus begin with the task of showing the originality of his tales in contrast with their sources, and the genuine quality of an inspiration that relies on more than mere invention.

Let us start with the story **"Conversation at Night"** (1911), which characteristically betrays, as already remarked, traces of Turgenev's influence. As a matter of fact, it directly re-echoes "Bezhin Meadow," one of the most famous pieces in *A Sportsman's Sketches*. Both stories pretend to be the direct report of a conversation taking place among several people out-of-doors on a summer night. In both cases, the subject matter of the conversation is horror stories, terrible happenings which the speakers have experienced personally, either as actors or as witnesses. In their written versions, those horror stories are retold from the viewpoint of an outsider, one who overheard them by chance in Turgenev's tale, and one for whose benefit they were told for the first time in Bunin's.

In Turgenev the listener is an adult, a sportsman who regularly relates in the first person all the happenings he has witnessed in his hunting expeditions, and the storytellers are a group of youngsters who narrate a series of haunting visions of the supernatural, which their superstitious beliefs transform into real experiences. In Bunin, everything is reversed: the listener is a young nobleman keeping watch in the company of his peasants, while the storytellers are all mature, even aged, men. The happenings they relate are horror stories, not subjectively, but objectively true, and equally dominated by the sense of death. But death is now a human, not a supernatural agency: it is death by violence and murder, not menacing from above, but striking from below. Its presence is conjured up again by the matter-of-fact report that one of the narrators had once killed a fellow man in cold blood.

Turgenev's story, like practically everything he wrote, begins as an idyll and ends as an elegy. It is with a feeling of poetic sympathy that the writer relieves in his adult mind the fairy-tale quality of the children's imaginations and fears, and it is with poignant sorrow and awe that he compares in retrospect their superstitious forebodings with the early death, a short time later, of one of them. But the only sentiment mastering the soul of Bunin's listener and infecting the reader is, rather, the psychological agony aroused by the instinct of self-preservation, by the sudden discovery that one of the men so casually befriended is a murderer and that he may strike again.

The comparison of these two stories, so related and yet so unlike, reveals immediately all the differences between a realism based on a sense of sympathetic affinity between the heart of the artist and the object observed by him, and another kind of realism in which the artist alienates himself from the human content of the experience he contemplates in order to represent it better. Turgenev's is the realism of grace, and Bunin's the realism of necessity. For this reason, while Turgenev's vision remains in the reader's memory like the shadow of a dream, the echo of a song, the nightmare of Bunin preserves even in recollection the rigid and static impression of a bas-relief.

The same effect of plastic composition, the same sense of massive solidity, is produced by **"A Spring Evening,"** already described as the replica of a Dostoevskian "true story," as reported by one of the characters in *The Idiot.* In Dostoevski the story has the quality of a conversation piece or newspaper account, of a "slice of life" which the author finds meaningful despite its sordidness, or because of it. Thus it contains a "sign of contradiction," a redeeming trait, the mystical epiphany of something higher, and even more real than reality itself. This is to be seen in the emphasis laid on the fact that the murderer, as a good Christian, prays before committing his crime. In the same way, Bunin's murderer addresses his victim with the Christian epithet "brother" and begs him to yield his money peaceably, so that both may be relieved of the dreadful necessity of killing and being killed.

But in Bunin's story that act and that word play the role of strange details or curious traits, of peculiar and yet meaningless idiosyncrasies. The knife of Dostoevski's murderer, who mercifully slaughters his friend in his sleep, is here replaced by a flagstone which the killer, lowering his "bull head," tears away from the pavement with a "crash," and it is with that "cold" and "heavy" object that he crushes the skull of his victim through the face. The entire story seems to be engraved on that very stone, as if it were chiseled in granite.

A similar impression is produced by **"The Gentleman from San Francisco,"** which seems sculptured in a more polished and precious substance, like porphyry or basalt. It is the story of an American millionaire who has crossed the Atlantic with his family to enjoy a little fun and rest far from home, and who suddenly dies of a stroke, while dressing for dinner, in a Capri hotel. The management does both its best and its worst to hide the tragedy from the guests, and the corpse is snatched away in unseemly haste, without honor or respect. There is an obvious contrast between the plush glamor of the hotel, its luxury and comfort, and the cheapness and vulgarity of the millionaire's end; perhaps, also, there is the intent to relate significantly the prosperous materialism of the millionaire's life with the brutality of his death, which is not the death of a human being but of a brute slaughtered, like a bull, by a blow struck from nowhere. But what is far more important is the anonymity of that death, symbolized by the very fact that the hero, or rather the victim, remains nameless. He was the "gentleman from San Francisco," and nothing more.

This story differs basically from Tolstoy's "Death of Ivan Ilich," although there is some resemblance in several respects, especially in the emphasis on the callous indifference of the survivors at the spectacle of death. Ivan Ilich is an average man, a vulgar man, but one whom we know personally, almost intimately, as is shown by the use, even in the title, of his Christian name and patronymic, and with whom we get better acquainted during his illness, of which we know the causes and the progress. It is his malady, as a matter of fact, that makes even Ivan Ilich better acquainted with life and with himself, and humanizes and spiritualizes him. His death is as brutal as the death of the gentleman from San Francisco, but it is a gradual process; while the latter is struck by a sudden blow, Ivan Ilich is slowly sucked into the bottom of a sack, like a domestic animal which his master wants to get rid of. During his torture, Ivan Ilich utters human sounds, which only near the end become the meaningless whining of

a poor beast. But the gentleman from San Francisco has time to utter only an inarticulate gasp.

Finally, in spite of everything, the ordeal of Ivan Ilich ends with a sense of illumination and redemption: death transcends its ugliness and becomes a vision of grace, even though only for a passing moment. But the death of the gentleman from San Francisco is an "act of God" only in the natural sense of the phrase: a stroke of lightning, without mysticism or tragedy. The human drama of the mortality of the body reconciles itself in Tolstoy's tale with the hope of, if not the belief in, the immortality of the soul, while in Bunin's story there is only the triumph of nothingness, and there resounds only the bell of doom. Yet this story, conveying so powerfully the sense of the fragility of life and the certainty of the annihilation of all things, is an authentic masterpiece, ancient, mysterious, and perfect as a monolith.

Bunin's skill in changing alien material into a substance of his own is equally evident in **"A Goodly Life,"** which, as already stated, is derivative from Leskov's "The Amazon." In both pieces a cunning and scheming woman reviews, with complacency and self-indulgence, her own worldly career, and from her account we learn how, by using her wits and by exploiting her men, she has been able to feather her nest and to reach a position of prosperity and respectability. She is a self-righteous hypocrite, unscrupulous and unremorseful, who has sacrificed her friends for her profit, and even ruined her son. It is the old story of Moll Flanders, of the go-getter and the gold-digger, rewritten against the background of a provincial existence and the Russian way of life. Both Bunin and Leskov reproduce the idiomatic and personal peculiarities of her popular speech, but while Leskov, in doing so, aims at an effect of genial humor and amusing irony, the purpose of Bunin is more objective and functional. Leskov's piece is a vivid and grotesque caricature, as the title itself indicates, and it emphasizes the naïveté of the heroine rather than her duplicity, while Bunin's aim is to draw, without ethos or pathos, a lucid and merciless portrait.

As for **"The Cup of Life,"** it bears the same relationship to Leskov's *Cathedral Folk* as *Le Curé de Tours* does to the longer novels of *La Comédie Humaine.* Like Balzac's tale, Bunin's story is built around an ecclesiastical intrigue. While, in his great fresco of the life of the Russian clergy, Leskov aims both at producing the concrete and picturesque feeling of a unique milieu and at evoking the moral battle taking place within the walls of the church and within each individual soul, Bunin is interested only in the ironic contrast between the holy rituals of religious life and the mean passions of his frocked heroes. Balzac, with romantic exaggeration, raises the petty clerical plottings of *Le Curé de Tours* to the level of a military and diplomatic duel, to a high strategy so skillful and complex as to transcend the vulgar prizes of the victory, which are easy living and social prestige; the dry realism of Bunin lowers the rivalry between his characters to the plane of a struggle for life in the Darwinian sense.

The long warfare, without quarter or truce, between the two clergymen Iordanski and Selikhov, who are moved by identical ambitions and desires, by a reciprocal envy and by the same hatred, ends without conqueror or conquered, because the one dies while celebrating, almost triumphantly, the funeral rites of the other. The lady whom both had loved and whom one had succeeded in marrying is left a widow and dies without enjoying the house which she had long dreamed of owning. Everybody leaves the scene of the world without being able to drink fully from the "cup of life." Only Gorizontov, the giant, survives, by using his own energies sparingly and by exploiting even in life his future death, having already sold to the Medical School of the University of Moscow the skeleton which still supports his enormous body. The story closes in this way, with the unrelieved irony of bitter sarcasm.

Even exotic backgrounds and tropical settings are used by Bunin for the purpose of expressing with stern objectivity the cruelty of life and the absurdity of the world. Thus, in **"Brethren"** (1916) he describes the wretched existence of a Singhalese rickshaw-boy, pulling a tired and bored white man around the city of Colombo. During the tour, the boy discovers by chance that his girl friend has betrayed him, and he kills himself at the end of that day's work. In the second part of the story, Bunin reports the conversations of the same white man with the captain of the ship carrying him home, and from his words we learn that a different and yet equal burden of sorrow is oppressing the heart of the rich man, no less than it did the heart of the poor rickshaw-boy. Here Bunin aims at an effect of symmetrical parallelism and of symbolic contrast; the meaning of the story lies in the juxtaposition of two episodes which are related only by chance and by a common, but negative, trait: the mutual indifference of two sufferers.

The simple allegorical message which the narrative conveys lies in the composition itself, in the lucid arrangement of the artistic object, not in the human actors as such, or in any ethical judgment of the artist, who uses words for painting, not for preaching. The moral, if any, is contained in the title of the story, and in its epigraph, which is a quotation from the holy wisdom of India: "Look at these brothers who are killing each other; I do not want to utter words of grief." The artistic aim of Bunin is concisely and effectively stated in these very words; his intent as a writer is merely to point his finger in silence at the cruel wounds of life and at the cynical indifference of the material universe. If there is a lesson, it is taught to us by the things themselves. Such is the esthetic practice of a writer who is the master of what one might call a stoic realism.

Far less convincing is another famous exotic story, the one entitled **"The Dreams of Chang"** (1916). Here the past life of a retired sea captain who was once betrayed by his wife and who is now waiting only for death is evoked through the reminiscences of his old Chinese dog. This is not an "animal story" in the sense that Tolstoy's "Kholstomer" or Chekhov's "Kashtanka" are, because there is no attempt to understand or reconstruct animal psychology per se. Nor is it an "animal fable" in the traditional sense, like Cervantes' "Dialogue of the Dogs," where animals look at the human world with intellectual irony and philosophical wisdom. The weakness of Bunin's tale lies in the fact that it remains halfway between those two poles and that the perspective of the animal's reminiscences is essentially used as a dehumanizing and depersonalizing device, through which the various episodes of the captain's past life are deprived of their all too human content. The same device helps Bunin to adopt again his favorite method of a parallel juxtaposition of different scenes, which here, however, does not serve a higher artistic purpose. There are other exotic stories of Bunin, full of human insight, which recall the work of another storyteller of the sea, the Anglicized Slav Joseph Conrad.

Bunin's scorn for the pathetic does not prevent him from trying his hand at that kind of poetic and sentimental realism so frequently and lovingly practiced by the masters of the Russian classical age. One of the most charming stories of this kind is **"The Grammar of Love,"** which at first reminds us of Turgenev at his best. It is the description of a visit made by a young man to the empty house of a dead relative who had lived there for twenty years completely alone, with only the company of his memories and souvenirs—memories and souvenirs of a fiancée who died young. It is a pilgrimage to a sanctuary of faith and love, and we expect from the devout pilgrim not only piety and reverence but also some idolatry and fetishism.

The poet, however, destroys immediately this mystical mood by an ambivalent and almost decadent attitude toward the objects of that pious worship. The reader himself is infected by this half moved and half amused reaction toward the obsolete quaintness of the trifles left by a past only recently dead. Thus the author contributes toward preventing the revival of that religion of remembrance which the visitor tries to conjure within himself. When the latter discovers the necklace of the woman who was loved so much and so long, the view of that object arouses in him "the same indecipherable sentiment he had once experienced, in a small Italian town, at the sight of the relics of a woman saint." This allusion to a holy or sacred thing must not deceive us; the relics, no less than the necklace, are evoked only as unfamiliar, bizarre *objects d'art*. In this way, those outmoded, old-fashioned keepsakes are forever deprived of all traces of human life, of the joy or sorrow they once bespoke. Thus they become ancient and archaic, as distant in space and time as a meteorite or a fossil.

It was only in his later years that Bunin wrote his first real love stories, dominated, unlike the earlier ones, by the sexual impulse alone. Even here, however, love is seen as a sudden flame rather than a slow fire, as a "sunstroke," to use the title of one of the best tales of this kind. In **"A Sunstroke,"** an officer serving in a forgotten garrison on the Volga has a brief affair with a woman whom he meets by chance, never to meet again, but the ashes of that passion will remain forever in his soul, left as empty as the water stirred by the departing river boat. The situation is initially identical with the one in Chekhov's "Lady with a Pet Dog," where, however, the adventure started by chance is renewed by the will of the two partners, who bind themselves for the rest of their lives with the chains of affection and habit.

Completely un-Chekhovian is the atmosphere of another story, which, like the previous one, is among the best written by Bunin in exile: **"A Light Breath."** It is a "case history" reconstructed against the background of Russian "high life" before the revolution. A girl of the nobility, although in love with a young man, gives herself to a mature officer, who is also a distant relative of hers. The sordid adventure brings an aftermath of shame, and the girl kills herself. At this point the "case history" changes into a work of poetry and art: the image of the handful of dust, which is now suffocating even the memory of that lively breath which was the secret of her charm, symbolizes both the violence of fate and the sorrow of the soul for a creature of grace or a thing of beauty forever lost. Here there is a real feeling of pity for the "brief candle" of human life and feminine youth.

This sense of the fatality of Eros finds perhaps its highest expression in one of the best among Bunin's late works, the novelette *Mitya's Love,* where the protagonist is again a young person. It is an ordinary story: Mitya leaves the big city and his fiancée Katya for a brief stay on his country estate. For a long time he does not hear from his fiancée, and the first letter he receives is to be the last, for Katya writes merely to break the news to him of her decision to put an end to their tie, and Mitya shoots himself. The progress of passion and jealousy in a fresh, immature mind continually fed and tortured by love and desire, by trust and suspicion, by hope and despair, reminds us of the broodings of the Proustian protagonist over the shadow of his Albertine and over his own past. But in Bunin's narrative, as always, there is the candid and lucid vision of a mind which contemplates the human heart with compassion, but without illusion.

These last stories are more human and "softer" than the earlier ones, but not so solid and well constructed. They deal with more complex personalities and subtler feelings, while the earlier tales dealt with primitive psychologies and elemental passions. But even here we witness almost without exception the triumph of death, or at least the defeat of man. Life is still for Bunin a Pandora's box, even if now he does not look at it with the Gorgon's eye of his youth. He is no longer exclusively interested in crises and climaxes, in states of acute tension, in those moments when time seems to stand still. The catastrophes or cataclysms of our existence are now being replaced by more normal and human experiences, which Bunin contemplates as skeptically but not so cynically as before, with a touch of indulgent wisdom which is new in him.

Yet the stories of his maturity remain the best he ever wrote and constitute by themselves a high achievement and an imposing body of work, produced, like his novels, in the brief span of a few years, at the acme of his talent. Sometimes it may seem that they irradiate a light which is clear but too cold—that their colors are as bright and lifeless as the colors we see in the magic lantern or the kaleidoscope. But the best pieces are pure gold, and the skill of their maker is as perfect as the craft of the goldsmith. All too often, in regard to both his stories and his novel *The Village*, Bunin has been accused of treating the palpitating substance of life with the frigid efficiency of a surgeon. It has also been said that he pays excessive attention to the trifles of reality and the minutiae of physical experience by reproducing them with painstaking pedantry. The latter accusation is true, and this fault may be seen, even more than in the descriptive pages based on visual impressions, in those passages where he handles with exuberant detail the blind perceptions of the crudest senses. It is in such cases that we see Bunin at his worst, as shown by this almost ludicrous example taken from **"Brethren,"** and referring to the poor rickshaw-boy of that story: "The smell of his body had become worse; it was a scent of boiling tea, mixed with cocoanut oil and some sort of spirit: it was the smell of a handful of ants crushed between one's fingers and palm. . . ."

Yet the best of his production as a short story writer, that dozen tales which he wrote in his early maturity and which culminate in **"The Gentleman from San Francisco,"** will hold a place of their own in all anthologies, and their presence and permanence there will again attest to the singularity of Bunin's creation in his own nation and time. If there is anyone outside of Russia to whom we may compare the author of these stories, it is perhaps the Italian *verista* Giovanni Verga, and it is not a mere coincidence that the Sicilian and the Russian appealed equally, in the English world, to the keen and earnest mind of D. H. Lawrence. (pp. 136-44)

Renato Poggioli, "The Art of Ivan Bunin," in his

The Phoenix and the Spider: A Book of Essays about Some Russian Writers and Their View of the Self, *Cambridge, Mass.: Harvard University Press, 1957, pp. 131-57.*]

SEYMOUR L. GROSS (essay date 1960)

[*Gross is an American essayist, biographer, and editor. In the excerpt below, he illuminates the character of the Gentleman in "The Gentleman from San Francisco."*]

Ivan Bunin's masterpiece, **"The Gentleman from San Francisco"** (1915), has had a somewhat curious fate. Although such an eminent critic of Russian literature as Professor Renato Poggioli has called the story "one of the greatest ever written in the Russian tongue" [see excerpt dated 1957], and editors have anthologized it with striking regularity, there exists no analysis of the story consonant with such general approbation. All that exists are three textbook discussions of the story and some brief comments in larger studies of Bunin. Furthermore, the three discussions of the story which are in print, perhaps because they are limited by being textbook explications, create the impression that this remarkably rich and complex story is rather straightforward both in intention and execution. This is understandable because **"The Gentleman from San Francisco,"** like some of Hawthorne's finest tales, has a deceptively unambiguous surface. Superficially, it is the story of a middle-aged wealthy American businessman, who, after years of accumulating money (at the expense of overworked and underpaid Chinese laborers), goes off on a pleasure trip around the world as "a reward for years of toil." He is vain, proud and completely indifferent to the needs and demands of other human beings: he sees them only as mechanisms for the increase of his own comfort and well-being. Everywhere he goes he is treated with sham respect and deference; but when he is suddenly struck down with a heart attack, his cardboard world collapses: his family is unceremoniously shunted off by an irritated and offended hotel proprietor (death is bad for business), and his body is cynically dumped into an empty soda-water box and shipped back to America in the hold of the same ship which had so luxuriously transported him to the Old World.

This brief resumé of what "happens" in **"The Gentleman from San Francisco"** (and the simplistic moral which it invites) is, of course, absurd, for it totally ignores dozens of details: countless natural descriptions; the ubiquitous bells, gongs, and sirens; the hired lovers, the Asiatic prince, the "pagan" captain; the vignettes of Tiberius Caesar, Lorenzo, and the two pipers from Abruzzi. The commentators have not failed to recognize that these details—which actually constitute the bulk of the story—must be accounted for in any coherent explanation of the story. But they have had only partial success because they have tried to relate them to some baldly stated moral theme rather than to the story's overarching symbolic structure. That is, they have proceeded from the assumption that the story is an allegorical presentation of the *idea* that twentieth-century civilization has been corrupted by an unjust system, rather than from the assumption that it is a dramatization, full of sorrow and pity, of the *way* modern man has crippled his capacity for sentient response to this "evil and beautiful world." Moreover, **"The Gentleman from San Francisco"** should be seen in relation to Bunin's other work, especially **"The Brethren"** (1914), which, as Bunin tells us in his autobiographical note to the English translation of his novel, *The Village* (1923), was written at about the same time and out of the same dark apprehensions: " 'Woe unto thee, Babylon!'—those terrible words of the Apocalypse kept persistently ringing in my soul when I wrote **'The Brothers'** [i.e. **"The Brethren"**] and conceived **'The Gentleman from San Francisco,'** only a few months before the War, when I had a presentiment of . . . the abysses which have since been laid bare in our present-day civilization." **"The Brethren"** is particularly helpful in shedding light on **"The Gentleman from San Francisco"** because the disease in the world's soul, which in **"The Gentleman"** is handled in a distant and uninvolved manner, is in **"The Brethren"** finally focused in the psychology of a spiritually agonized British colonel who, haunted by the vanity and cruelty of life, ends up discoursing in a frenzied Dostoevskian manner to a group of ship's officers who think him mad. Because the colonel has come to understand and is able to articulate what the Gentleman dimly perceived in his painfully bewildered "It's terrible," **"The Brethren"** can be of help to us in understanding **"The Gentleman from San Francisco."**

We may best come at the meaning of **"The Gentleman from San Francisco"** by first concerning ourselves with the description of the two Abruzzi mountaineers who are making a pilgrimage to the statue of the Holy Virgin on Monte Solare. This passage, following as it does the degradation of the Gentleman and the vignettes of the "brutal and filthy" Tiberius and the "care-free reveller" Lorenzo, is not only the one ecstatic moment in a world of boredom, vanity, and cruelty, but is, I believe, the symbolic center of the story as well. Because practically every detail in the story leads to and away from this description, the passage must be quoted:

> Meanwhile, among the precipices of Monte Solare, down the ancient Phoenician road, cut in the rocks in the form of a gigantic staircase, two Abruzzi mountaineers were coming from Anacapri. One carried under his leather mantle a bagpipe, a large goat's skin with two pipes; the other, something in the nature of a wooden flute. They walked, and the entire country, joyous, beautiful, sunny, stretched below them; the rocky shoulders of the island, which lay at their feet, the fabulous blue in which it swam, the shining morning vapors over the sea westward, beneath the dazzling sun, and the wavering masses of Italy's mountains, both near and distant, whose beauty human word is powerless to render. . . . Midway they slowed up. Overshadowing the road stood, in a grotto of the rock wall of Monte Solare, the Holy Virgin, all radiant, bathed in the warmth and the splendor of the sun. The rust of her snow-white plaster-of-Paris vestures and queenly crown was touched into gold, and there were meekness and mercy in her eyes raised toward the heavens, toward the eternal and beatific abode of her thrice-blessed Son. They bared their heads, applied their pipes to their lips, and praises flowed on, candid and humbly-joyous, praises to the sun and the morning, to Her, the Immaculate Intercessor for all who suffer in this evil and beautiful world, and to Him who had been born of her womb in the cavern of Bethlehem, in
> ✳ a hut of lowly shepherds in distant Judea.

We must be careful not to take this passage merely as a contrast between peasant simplicity and urban corruption, such as is to be found in, say, [Ignazio] Silone's *Bread and Wine*. It is not a paean sung to the peasantry who shall inherit the earth from what Brooks, Purser, and Warren call the "arogant, rapacious, self-indulgent, and brutal capitalism" of the

Gentleman and the class he represents [see excerpt dated 1952]. To do so would be to give the story a "socialist" bias which it does not have. Bunin never subscribed to (or, as in the case of the modern Communist, gave lip service to) any sentimental disjunction of virtue according to class, as any reader of his bitter portrayal of peasant life, *The Village,* can attest to. Nor could he, as a matter of fact, see why men, such as his own brother, felt compelled to sacrifice themselves for unknown and perhaps debauched workers and peasants. As Willis Jacobs has commented, " **'The Gentleman from San Francisco'** is not a restricted story of socialist propaganda. It is an unrestricted revelation of rot infesting the whole world." The full and joyous response of the two Abruzzi pipers is potentially possible for all men—even the jaded colonel in **"The Brethren"**—if they can but sense their "pitiful Individuality" in the face of the mystery and majesty of the "All-Oneness" of the universe, and respond to it with "that ultimate, all-embracing thing which is called love, the yearning to encompass within one's heart all the universe, seen and unseen."

In this passage of the two pipers the force which triggers the release of this sentient vitality—love—is Christianity, and, indeed, the whole story takes its peculiar ironic tone as well as various details from the Revelation of St. John, especially Chapter 18, which, as Bunin has told us, was on his mind when he conceived **"The Gentleman from San Francisco"** and from which he chose "Alas, alas, that great city Babylon, that mighty city" as the epigraph for his story. This does not mean, however, that Bunin has excommunicated all beliefs save that which finds salvation in the Christian God. . . . The sin is not so exclusively Christian in Bunin's view, although, to be sure, it manifests itself in Christian terms in **"The Gentleman from San Francisco,"** probably because the story is set in Italy. (In **"The Brethren"** the epigraph is Hindu, and the religious background is oriental.) Bunin's religious convictions, as Professor Bedford has pointed out, were a composite of the many religions with which he was acquainted—Orthodoxy, Roman Catholicism, Hinduism, Mohammedism, Buddhism. And as Bunin makes explicit in **"The Brethren,"** man's self-imprisoning cruelty (such as Tiberius's) and his joyless vanity (such as Lorenzo's) are the perverted result of his having turned away from *all* "godhood," away from the mysterious "unseen" world, without which the "seen" world becomes no more than a deadening lump of clay on which men such as the Gentleman from San Francisco sting themselves into a living death with such futile and self-defeating gestures towards happiness as sumptuous dinners ("the crown of the day"), exquisite champagnes, and dreams of illicit lovemaking with "young Neopolitan girls." But the dinners become, "about eleven o'clock in the evening," dyspeptic nightmares; the champagnes hideously purple the face and accentuate the horrors of sea-sickness; and love, in any form, is as absent from this world as it was in the condemned Babylon where "the voice of the bridegroom and of the bride shall be heard no more."

In contrast, the two pipers of Abruzzi live the kind of full life which is described in **"The Brethren"** as being the "life of infantile immediacy, sentient with . . . all existence, and death, and the divine majesty of the universe." Unfettered by a worship of their own "self-hood," they are able to enter into a beatific communion with all of nature ("the sun and the morning"), man ("all who suffer in this evil and beautiful world"), and God (the "thrice-blessed Son"). For them, the world is, despite the presence of evil, dazzlingly gorgeous; life is hard but free; and death is preciously mysterious, for without it, as Bunin said on many occasions, life would become insipid and incomplete.

When the life of the Gentleman from San Francisco is seen against this vision of Grace, practically every detail in the story becomes ironically significant. For just as in *The Divine Comedy* (to which Bunin alludes in the story), where the vision of Paradise is intensified by memories of the infernal and purgatorial regions, so too in Bunin's story does the passage of the two pipers gain its intensity from its ironic juxtaposition with the lonely and imprisoned lives of all the other people in the story, whose existences are symbolized by "a lonely parrot babbl[ing] something in its expressionless manner, stirring in its cage, and trying to fall asleep with its paw clutching the upper perch in a most absurd manner."

The initial irony in the story is to be found in its title, not solely because, as has been pointed out, the Gentleman remains forever, like Chaucer's merchant, a nameless figure, but because Bunin has him come from San Francisco. I feel certain that Bunin chose that city as the origin of the Gentleman not only "because California represented, at the turn of the century, the raw, energetic materialism of the New World" [as M. B. McNamee has suggested in his *Reading for Understanding* (1952)], but also because it is the city of St. Francis. It is both terrible and sad, a rueful commentary on the modern world, that a life so esthetically and spiritually desiccated could originate in the city named for a man who had achieved, like the pipers, a perfect communion with nature, man, and God. And as free as this trilateral communion has made the pipers and St. Francis, so has the lack of it incarcerated the spirit of the Gentleman in a prison of its own devising.

The freedom which the Gentleman's wealth has given him is, in reality, an illusion. His life is a joyless round of activities (which somehow never quite come off) prescribed and proscribed by the segment of society to which he belongs: his "class of people . . . was in the habit of beginning its enjoyment of life with a trip to Europe, India, Egypt." He has thrown away his life working "unweariedly" only because he wanted to "come up to the level of those whom he had once taken as his model." And "the stream of life's pleasures" which he is about to enter into and for which he has worked so hard is, as it turns out, a narrowly restricting artificial canal, the passage down which is determined by the faceless forces of "itinerary," "day's program," and "set routine," which decide what man is "expected to relish," where he is "supposed to stroll," when it is "customary to take tea." Even the music in this world, in contrast to the flowing lyricism of the mountaineer's pipes, is the music of "the shrill voice of a bugle," the "commanding voice of the going," "the stentorian voice of the bell," "the furious screeching of the siren"—terrible voices summoning man to a living hell. It is significant that when the Gentleman, sitting alone in his hotel room looking at his gouty hands, dimly senses the futility of his life, it is the "voice of the second gong sounded throughout the house, as in a heathen temple," which shatters his meditation and sends him down to his lonely death in the library of a foreign hotel. The costume of this world is similarly binding, restricting, stifling: dancing shoes "encase" the feet, collars choke the throat, tight waistcoats squeeze the belly. But when the Gentleman is dying, the servants, in an intuitively symbolic gesture, tear off his tie, collar, waistcoat, "and even—for no visible reason—the dancing shoes from his black silk-covered feet." These artificial trappings of an artificial life are inappropriate for the most natural act of the Gentleman's life—death. Nothing becomes the Gentleman so well in life as his dying: "And slowly, slowly, in everybody's sight a pallor stole over the face of the dead man, and his features began to grow thinner and more luminous, beautiful with the beauty that he had long shunned and that became him well. . . ."

Bunin's strategy in weaving these images of imprisonment—the social regimen, the imperious gongs, the suffocating apparel—is to throw the lives of the Gentleman and his class into ironic perspective: they who think themselves so powerful and free are, in actuality, impotent and enslaved. Their lives are "a stage scene," in which they are condemned to act out the parts of a pointless play (replete with costumes, and bells to mark out the changes in act and scene) on a narrow, insulated stage. Like the couple hired by the ship company "to play at love," these people cannot live; they can only play at living—and the script is as cold as death. And all the while the two pipers of Abruzzi are rapturously alive with their yearning to encompass the whole universe, the seen and the unseen: nature, man, and God.

The natural world is for the Gentleman a hostile force, both because he can see it only in terms of itself and because he cannot ultimately control it. His only defence against the physical universe is in the "magic" of his own world, symbolized by the "many-stacked giant" *Atlantis,* the Elysium in the Western Ocean, "where," Homer tells us, "life is easiest for men: no snow is there, nor yet great storm, nor any rain; but always the ocean sendeth forth the breeze of the shrill West to blow cool on men" (*Odyssey,* IV). On the modern *Atlantis,* however, the forces of nature exist, but they are hidden: "an excellent string orchestra" covers the "hellish voice" of the pounding sea, "crystal lustres and gilt chandeliers" hold back the ominous darkness, and no one thinks of the "dreadful" ocean because "All had faith in the controlling power of the captain," who has faith in his armored cabin and wireless. In **"The Brethren,"** when the colonel overwhelmed by the frightful immensity of the sea asks the captain of the ship, "Is it a very eerie thing to be captain?," the captain nonchalantly answers, "It's a tiresome business, and responsible, but, in reality, not very complicated. . . . It is all a matter of habit." "Better say,—of our callousness," answers the colonel.

The world of **"The Gentleman from San Francisco"** is excitingly alive with the sights, sounds, and smells of the physical world, but the Gentleman himself is too calloused to respond to them. For him the world is made up only of endless rain, intolerable mud, and the foul smell of rotting fish—it is a world of seasickness, headaches, and irritation. It is a world from which he tries to insulate himself with "visits to lifelessly clean museums," with the sounds of rustling silks, and with the fragrant odors of perfumes and exquisitely prepared delicacies. And in doing so, he shuts himself out from the moist lemon-trees with their shimmering orange-colored fruit, the sweet smell of the earth after rain, and the "humbly-joyous" music of a wooden flute singing praises to the sun and the morning. Significantly, his first act upon entering his hotel room in Capri is to "shut the window which had banged when the maitre-d'hotel entered, and which let in the smell of the distant kitchen and wet flowers in the garden," and to insist that his dinner table "be placed farther away from the door in the depth [rear] of the hall. . . ." It is only when he is dead that he, at last, enters into the beautiful and evil rhythm of the universe: "A waiter opened the window in

Number 43—it faced a corner of the garden where a consumptive banana tree grew in the shadow of a high stone wall set with broken glass on the top—turned out the electric light, locked the door, and went away. The deceased remained alone in the darkness. Blue stars looked down at him from the black sky, the cricket in the wall started his melancholy, carefree song."

More crucial than his insulation from nature is the Gentleman's isolation from the rest of humanity, from all those who find joy and suffering in this evil and beautiful world. Like Tiberius, whose power made him fear all men, and Lorenzo, whose vanity condemns him to standing alone all day "wearing princely airs, showing off his rags," the Gentleman's life never intersects in any significant way with any other life. From the beginning until the end of his life (and even beyond when he lies alone in the hold of the ship), the Gentleman lives a lonely, detached, solitary existence. He remains contemptuously aloof from the urchins in the streets of the cities he visits, walks by servants (who now hug the walls but later, when he is dead, grotesquely parody their previous deference) "as if not noticing them," and "coldly eyes" his fellow tourists, hiding himself from them behind a newspaper. He and his wife live in separate rooms, and the only time he ever thinks of his daughter (who never spoke "about her feelings to her father") it is in a fractured, physical way—"of her wonderful hair, streaming on her shoulders."

Yet there is in this isolation, as Bunin makes clear, something pathetically ironic: This hard man of facts, this paragon of materialistic self-sufficiency, needs love and the feeling of being important to other human beings, but can find both only in the projections of his fantasies and in the illusions of his self-deception. Having lost the sun, be must believe in the warmth of the electric light. So it is that he convinces himself of "the complete sincerity and goodwill of those who so painstakingly fed him, served him day and night, anticipating his slightest desire, protected him from dirt and disturbance, hauled things for him, hailed carriers, and delivered his luggage to hotels." So it is that as he stands on the deck of the ship in Naples he believes that the band's "triumphant . . . ragtime march" thundered "for him alone," and "that him alone did the captain," with a wave of his hand, "congratulate on the safe arrival." But the saddest line in the story is the first: "The Gentleman from San Francisco—neither at Naples nor on Capri could anyone recall his name. . . ."

In such an ego-bound world love cannot exist, except in a distorted and artificial form. The famous beauty makes love to her "tiny bent peeled-off pet dog [a mangy pet dog]"; the hired lovers "painfully turn and twist" in a simulated dance of love, which is, in reality, a dance of death (he is described as resembling a leech), both "weary of torturing themselves with a feigned beatific torture"; the Gentleman's daughter experiences "love" (which has overtones of necrophilia) for an ugly Asiatic prince with a corpse-like appearance. "After all," Bunin comments ironically, "it does not matter what in particular stirs up a maiden's soul: money, fame or nobility of birth." And the Gentleman from San Francisco, an image of physical decay with his yellow face, bald head, fallen arches, false teeth, and gouty joints, dreams of sexual adventures with young Neopolitan girls and tawny Carmella of the fiery eyes—the dead longing for life.

The frozen prison of insulation and isolation which modern man has erected about himself is, in Bunin's view, the result of his having become insensitive to the mystery of the uni-

verse, of his having lost that religious sense of awe which pervades the lives of the pipers, and without which, communion with man and nature is impossible. In contrast to the piper's mystical response to the religious dimension of life, the Gentleman's life is completely devoid of any sense of something larger than himself: "there was not a mustard seed of what is called mysticism in his heart." For him, therefore, the mystery of the Crucifixion has been reduced to nothing more than "somebody's *Descent from the Cross,* infallibly [doubtlessly] famous," hanging lifelessly in a cold, wax-smelling church, and the Miserere at Easter to a spectacle to be taken in by tourists along with "bull-baiting [fighting] at Seville [and] bathing on the British Islands." In such a world-view, life flattens out: all things are somehow like all other things. Over and over in the story Bunin employs what might be called the ironic catalogue—a coordinate grouping of unequals to indicate how the purely naturalistic view is cursed with the inability to distinguish among the levels of reality: "it was warmer and sunnier there, the morals purer, and the wine less adulterated"; "the cut of dress suits, the stability of thrones, the declaration of wars, the prosperity of hotels." (pp. 153-62)

Even though the *sense* of mystery has evaporated from life, modern man, ultimately, has no defence against the mystery itself. Whirl as he will "amid the splendor of lights, silks, diamonds, and bare feminine shoulders," down below him, in the maw of the ship, in a tarred soda-water box, is the decaying flesh of the Gentleman from San Francisco. An intimate sense of death, such as the pipers have, makes life richer, more poignantly felt; but for the Gentleman and those who dance upon his grave, death, which they "most absolutely refuse to believe in," can come only as a meaningless, unreasonable blow from out of nowhere. For them it can only be a period put at the end of a sentence that has neither sound nor fury nor signifies anything.

For all the darkness of Bunin's portrait of modern civilization, it still does not seem to me to be accurate to say [as Renato Poggioli has stated], that "in Bunin's story there is only the triumph of nothingness, and there resounds only the bell of doom . . . conveying so powerfully the sense of the fragility of life and the certainty of the annihilation of all things . . ." Such an assertion ignores the promise of the two pipers of Abruzzi, the vision of Paradise on earth which is vouchsafed to us amidst our journey through Hell. In discussing his attitude toward modern life as it manifested itself in **"The Brethren"** and **"The Gentleman from San Francisco,"** Bunin asks [in *The Village*], "Does it mean that my soul is filled only with darkness and despair?" And answers: "Not at all. 'As the hart panteth after the water brooks, so panteth my soul after thee, O God!' " (p. 163)

> Seymour L. Gross, "Nature, Man, and God in Bunin's 'The Gentleman from San Francisco'," in Modern Fiction Studies, *Vol. VI, No. 2, Summer, 1960, pp. 153-63.*

THOMAS WINNER   (essay date 1968)

[*Winner is a Czechoslovakian academic and essayist living in the United States. In the following excerpt, he explores stylistic techniques employed by Bunin in his earliest short stories.*]

In this paper we shall discuss various stylistic characteristics of Bunin's early stories, written between 1892 and 1907. In discussions of the history of Russian literature, the prose of

Bunin is sometimes placed outside the mainstream of the development of Russian realistic prose, a view which is doubtless related to his departure from certain of the traditions of realism, particularly in the early years of his creative activity. Yet his relation to the masters of Russian prose of the last century cannot be denied, and his position in the development of modern Western prose is by no means insignificant. Bunin's debt to the masters of Russian realistic prose, Gogol', Turgenev, Gončarov, Tolstoj and Čexov, has not gone unrecognized [see excerpt dated 1926]. We find, in Bunin's works, Gogol's brightly colored landscapes and personified nature, and the musical use of the Russian language. Bunin's writings also show traces of Turgenev's lyrical nature settings and his characteristic musical and poetic prose style. Again, Bunin's use of evocative memories and recollections recalls Tolstoj and Gončarov; but in this respect, Bunin is, as we shall try to demonstrate, an important innovator. However, it is clearly to Čexov that Bunin is most directly indebted. The pervasive lyrical tone of Bunin's prose, its compactness and, above all, the very limited reliance in Bunin's works on external action, are all familiar to us from the art of Čexov, whose influence has been repeatedly noted, although it is later denied by Bunin himself. His relation to Čexov was not one of simple imitation. In certain respects, Bunin went far beyond Čexov. His early stories achieve greater compactness than Čexov's serious stories, and rely less on external action. In Čexov's "Step'" external action is relegated to the journey of the travellers through the steppe landscape, whereas in Bunin's early stories even such a slight external action is frequently absent. . . . The early stories may thus be characterized as prose poems, brief vignettes, or mood paintings which are centered around the development of a special atmosphere. Typically, they may be limited to a picture based on lyrical recollections evoked by sights, smells, sounds or taste.

While critics may agree that Bunin's connections with the Russian past are significant, the relation of Bunin's work to contemporary literary trends in Russia and in the West, and his contribution to developments in the literary art which followed him, have not been adequately defined. Thus few have noted Bunin's connection with the esthetic revival which flourished during the last decades of the nineteenth century and the first decade of the present one. Furthermore, some interesting stylistic affinities with his contemporary, Marcel Proust, which suggest Bunin's innovating abilities, have largely been ignored.

Although Bunin's relation to the literary reaction against realism and positivism, known in France and Russia variously as Modernism, Decadence and Symbolism, is somewhat obscure, an examination of his style leads us to conclude that he did share in some aspects of this movement. Other important factors bearing upon Bunin's relations to the Symbolists are his connections with the Symbolist publishing house Skorpion, which published, in 1900, the first edition of his verse, and his well-known friendship with Brjusov and Bal'mont. It is true that some have denied the importance of these relations to Bunin. Thus Mirsky maintains that, except in certain attempts "tainted with Modernism", Bunin avoided the diction of lyrical prose, characteristic of the Russian decadents. While Bunin did maintain close contact with the writers of the *Znanie* school, especially with Maksim Gorkij, it would seem that both relationships, in spite of their contradictions, were important formative influences. Thus Struve connects Bunin's verbal mastery to his kinship with the Symbolists and to the whole modern school of poetry, although

he reminds us that Bunin was, in substance, hostile to the Symbolists. Perhaps this problem has been best formulated by Wasiolek when he notes that Bunin's literary output at the turn of the century mirrors the contradictions inherent in his simultaneous friendship with Symbolist writers and with writers of the *Znanie* group. Later Bunin openly rejected the Symbolists; nevertheless, certain aspects of Bunin's early writings can be illuminated by their relations to the Symbolist school. We may first note certain differences between Bunin and the Symbolists. We find no evidence, in Bunin's works, of the verbal experimentation, the delight in obscurity, the pervasive mysticism and, above all, the striking imagery so characteristic of the Symbolists. Indeed, in Bunin's early prose imagery is sparse, metaphors are almost completely absent, and similes are conventional. We look in vain for the boisterous and emotional expressiveness of the Symbolists. Their ornamental prose is replaced by a style of almost classical simplicity; their involvement, by detachment. Hence we can appreciate Poggioli's observation concerning the presence of Parnassian ideals of *impersonalité* and *impassibilité* in Bunin's works [see excerpt dated 1957]. . . . What then are the evidences in Bunin's early stories of affinities with the Symbolists? There are first of all several stories which partake of the very essence of Symbolist poetics in theme as well as treatment, such as **"Pereval"** (1892), a general symbolic reflection on death and time; **"Velga"** (1895), a mythical allegory; **"Tuman"** (1901) in which Bunin draws in symbolic terms the contrast between the microcosm of man's life and the macrocosm of Life in general; and finally, **"Belaja lošad'"** (1907), a symbolic story about death. But there are also other early stories, not so directly linked to Symbolist poetics, characterized by the lyrical, evocative and suggestive moods and the absence of social coloration which suggest Symbolist writings. It has been said that Bunin's prose is more "poetic" than his poetry, and that its pure lyricism is accentuated by the virtual elimination of all narrative material which composed the traditional plot.

Secondly, and more specifically, we note various stylistic techniques which Bunin shared with the Symbolists. Thus the musical quality of his prose is striking, effected by a high concentration of systematic sound repetitions and the employment of certain sentence rhythms. Bunin did not share the Symbolists' view of an innate connection between sound and symbolic meaning, as expressed in Rimbaud's famous poem on vowels and elucidated in Bal'mont's study *Poèzija kak volšebstvo* (1922). Nevertheless, he did attribute great significance to the tonalities of the language. . . . Sound repetition is so characteristic of Bunin's early prose that only a few examples must suffice. In the story **"Na xutore"** (1892), a typical early prose poem in which the sound and smells of a summer night and the news of the death of the hero's former beloved cause the hero to reflect upon life and death, the initial paragraph is marked by vowel harmony. . . . In **"Pereval"**, one of Bunin's most symbolic works, written in the same year as **"Na xutore"**, the "I" of the story, alone with his horse and lost in nature, reflects in a generalized manner on life and death. Complicated chains of sound harmonies and repetitions contribute to the symbolic content, mystical mood and musical qualities. . . . Similar stylistic techniques can be found in other stories in which the poetic element predominates, such as **"Vesti iz rodiny"** (1893), **"Na kraj sveta"** (1895), **Svjatye gory"** (1895), **"Velga"** (1895), **"Antonovskie jabloki"** (1900), **"Sosny"** (1901), **"Tuman"** (1901), **"Tišina"** (1901), **"U istoka dnej"** (1906), **"Belaja lošad'"** and others. . . . A striking aspect of Bunin's prose is its rhythmic quality, effected by various techniques, among them the alternation of lyrical-sensuous material and the reflections evoked by it; occasional approximation of verse meter through relatively regular sequences of accented and unaccented syllables; and pure sentence rhythm accentuated by various syntactical parallelisms.

It is the latter technique which is probably the most frequent cause of rhythm in Bunin's early prose. We remember the intense concern of the Symbolists with various forms of parallelism, an interest derived in part from their concern with the repetitive forms and parallel constructions of folk poetry. In Bunin's prose, syntactical parallelism finds a variety of forms. It may be achieved by anaphora, epiphora or other repetitions of key words or phrases. . . . Another less frequent method of achieving rhythm is simple enumeration, reminding us of a stylistic peculiarity of Proust's. . . . Verse rhythms and approximation of verse meter through regular sequences of accented and unaccented syllables are also important, though less frequent, in Bunin's prose. In this respect, Bunin recalls Turgenev, some of whose prose scans like verse. Čexov also, though infrequently, employed a regular prose meter, as for instance in the opening of "Učitel' slovesnosti". . . . These, then, are a few examples of the stylistic traits of Bunin's early prose which depart from the realistic tradition. The lack of concern for external action, the interest in the musical qualities of language, and the occasionally exclamatory diction of his prose of these years, bear the imprint of the esthetic revival of Bunin's time.

As we have noted earlier, the literature on Bunin has remarked little upon certain interesting parallels between him and his contemporary, Marcel Proust. In a broad sense, the magic of the past charmed both writers, and, furthermore, for both men it was primarily sensory impressions which unleashed the nostalgia of recollection. Earlier, the Symbolist poet Baudelaire had voiced an esthetic view supporting a unity of inner and outer realities. In his poem "Les phares", which forms part of *Les fleurs du mal,* Baudelaire remarks upon such a fusion; and in many other poems, and essays, he comments upon the manner in which external data affect the inner recognition of the artist. To transmit a vision or an emotion, Baudelaire wrote, the poet must draw material from the outer, immediately apprehended, reality surrounding him. Yet this material must somehow reach beyond itself to suggest an inner world. Thus we understand Baudelaire's moments of enhanced lucidity, epiphanies catalyzed by a chance object on which the senses grasp, thereby setting off a chain of ideas. Proust's esthetics, which demonstrate Baudelaire's outlook, also rely on external, sensuous reality to provide a heightened sense of being; and thus colors, smells, tastes, and sensations may precipitate what Proust calls *souvenir involontaire.* There is the well-known opening of Proust's *Du coté de chez Swann,* in which the recollection of the taste of a piece of *madeleine* cake dipped in tea initiates a complex chain of memory associations. The focal role of sense data is also demonstrable in Bunin's early writings, in which impressions may stimulate a series of recollections, or even generalized reflections on philosophical themes, as is illustrated in **"Antonovskie jabloki"** (1900), **"U istoka dnej"** (1906), and **"Sosny"** (1901). In the first-named story, the smell of apples and the sounds accompanying the apple harvest, as well as the autumnal colors of nature which strike the narrator's eye as he watches the apples being gathered, combine to evoke in him intense memories of his youth, and a general poetization of the past. Like a *Leitmotif,* the smell of apples with its associated nostalgic recollections, pervades the story. In **"U istoka dnej"**, it is the sight of a room and its furniture which turns the inward eye toward lyrical childhood recollections. In **"Sosny"** sense impressions again bring with them past reflections. . . . Both Proust and Bunin rely on the use of first person singular narration in their evocations of *le temps perdu.* With the exception of *Un amour de Swann, A la recherche du temps perdu* is written in the first person, as is *Jean Santeuil.* And of the thirty-six stories written between 1892 and 1902 which Bunin included in the first edition of his *Collected Works,* twenty-two are first person narrations.

An important parallel in the works of Bunin and Proust is the conception that the transcendence of time can be overcome by reflections, initiated involuntarily through the unconscious association of sensory impressions and past experiences. Thereby a durational link is established between the past and the present. Thus it is not the intellect in Bunin's and Proust's works which recaptures the past, but intuition incited by the senses, an approach which anticipates the Joycean epiphanies so frequently based on memory intuitions. Here we again see Bunin the innovator, who in this early period makes the unconscious an important arbiter of time relations.

While Bunin and Proust shared common artistic predilections, we cannot demonstrate direct influences. Only *Plaisirs et regrets* (1896) had been published during the period under consideration. Nor is there any evidence to suggest that Proust was acquainted with Bunin's writings before he worked on *Du coté de chez Swann.* We do not know whether Bunin had read Henri Bergson, whose reflections concerning the preservation of memory and notions of the relations of time and memory influenced Proust. We can, however, assert some interesting stylistic and thematic parallels between Bunin and Proust, for the power and artistic potentials of memory fascinated both men and led them to employ some similar artistic techniques.

We cannot, however, overlook certain vast differences between these two writers, so similar in spirit. In addition to the divergence in scope between Bunin's short sketches and Proust's long novels, there are important divergences in style. Bunin did not employ the kind of imaginative imagery which Proust expressed in his typical metaphorical language. We recall Proust's words in an essay on Flaubert.

> Pour des raisons qui seraient trop longues a développer ici, je crois que la métaphore seule peut donner une sorte d'éternité au style . . .

An examination of the works of our period reveals that the thirty-six stories which Bunin included in his *Collected Works* are practically devoid of metaphor. We find only two or three metaphors per story, generally personifications of nature, not particularly striking or even fresh. The only story which may be an exception is **"Sosny"** (1901), which demonstrates an unusual richness in metaphors. While similes are more frequent in these works, with few exceptions they also present little that is striking. There is the comparison in **"Antonovskie jabloki"** of a pregnant woman to a *xolmogorskaja korova.* But such examples are rare.

We conclude that under the influence of the revival of estheticism at the turn of the century, Bunin began his career as a prose writer by creating an actionless story, a lyrical prose poem form which shares some of the characteristics of the Symbolists and shows affinities to the writings of Proust. In some respects, namely in the departure from traditional narrative structures, in the new use of time and in the treatment of the unconscious, Bunin anticipates the new prose of the twentieth century, though in his later years he returned to a more realistic tradition. (pp. 369-81)

Thomas Winner, "Some Remarks about the Style of Bunin's Early Prose," in American Contributions to the Sixth International Congress of Slavists: Literary Contributions, Vol. II, edited by William E. Harkins, Mouton, 1968, pp. 369-81.

SERGE KRYZYTSKI (essay date 1971)

[*Kryzytski is a Russian-born American academic and essayist. In the following excerpt from his critical study* The Works of Ivan Bunin, *he examines language, symbolism, and narrative direction in Bunin's* Dry Valley.]

For many reviewers **Dry Valley** is the supreme expression of Bunin's art, a perfect work, second only to *Mitja's Love* or *The Life of Arsen'ev*. Mirsky calls it "one of the greatest masterpieces of modern Russian prose", while the Soviet critic Kastorskij quotes Ivan Vol'nov's opinion of **Dry Valley** ("a jubilee cry of despair about the estate") and calls it "an apt expression", thus acquiescing in Vol'nov's view. **Dry Valley** is indeed a better work than *The Village* if only because it is shorter. . . . In our judgment Bunin is not at home with a long work: a true master of the short short-story, he does not have to write a long story in order to say all he means. As we have seen, he can encompass his meaning in the short form (*e.g.*, **"The Pines"**, **"Ignat"**) with a truly brilliant result.

Like *The Village*, **Dry Valley** has the subtitle *poem*. Actually it is a saga of the 'fall of the house of Xruščov', *i.e.*, of the ancestors of Bunin's own family. The subtitle suggests not only the mood of nostalgia, but it may also indicate to the reader that this story (or novelette, as Poggioli calls it) is a *prose poem*. There is no plot or action in **Dry Valley**. It is a colorful vignette of reminiscences of the times which seem to Bunin "now infinitely distant, now ever near". Bunin's attention is focused on his own class. The time span is wide; it shifts from contemporary Russia at the turn of this century to the period preceding the Crimean War. The structure of **Dry Valley** is most interesting and difficult to define. The chief story teller is a former serf girl Natal'ja; but at times the author takes the omniscient point of view; and then again he hands over the narration to a pair of young people who identify themselves by the first person plural 'we' or by 'my sister and I'. **Dry Valley**, preceded by the earlier sketches **"The Well of Days"** and **"Antonov Apples"** and followed by *The Life of Arsen'ev*, is central to a *family chronicle* resembling that of Sergej Aksakov in depicting the patriarchal mode of life among the landed gentry. However, at the time of Aksakov's chronicle the 'nests of gentlefolk' were still flourishing, while in Bunin's story they are in a state of decay, impoverishment (*oskudenie dvorjanstva*—a term coined by the now-forgotten Terpigorev), moral degradation, and even physical degeneration. Bunin himself characterizes Natal'ja's narrative:

There were in this narrative jests, reservations, evasions; there were animation, pensiveness, unusual simplicity. But along with all this, there were other elements: a mysterious air, a stern and canorous half-whisper. But the prevalent element was a certain sadness of long standing. And everything was permeated with the feeling of an ancient faith in predestination, with a feeling of never-voiced, vague, yet constant self suggestion that every one—every one!—of us must take one role or another upon himself, in accordance with one dispensation of fate or another.

This amounts to a resume of **Dry Valley** by the author himself.

L'vov-Rogačevskij's ironical remark that in **Dry Valley** Bunin "*ne vospel dvorjanskuju usad'bu, a otpel*" ('did not sing an eulogy to the gentlefolk's estate, but sang a dirge over it') is just a *bon mot* devoid of any deeper meaning. Bunin perfectly well realized (and we have shown it in the examples from his early works) that the old way of life had been gone from the start and that the only thing to be regretted was that even the remembrance of the past would soon be lost in history. Therefore, first of all, **Dry Valley** must be regarded as an attempt to recapture the *temps perdu* of Russian rural life. It is hard not to agree with R. Poggioli when he says:

This hopeless feeling that even the last memories will fade away forever, that no heart will survive where the religion of memory could be rekindled again, gives **Dry Valley** a sense of tragic pathos which no work of Bunin ever attained either before or after.

There is a symbolic image in **Dry Valley:** the peasants dredge ponds in the bed of an old rivulet. But these ponds dry out without fresh water supply. Similarly the Xruščovs' clan, with no fresh blood admixture, with only one male descendant of their family still alive, is doomed to extinction. "To us **Dry Valley** was only a poetical monument of the past. But what was it to Natal'ja?"

The half-crazy aunt Tonja and Natal'ja are the only true 'souls' of Dry Valley left. Natal'ja is the last living monument of the past, the last remaining link with 'times past'. But Natal'ja is just a servant, a former serf. What has she, a housemaid, to do with the noble Xruščovs "inscribed in the sixth Book of Heraldry"? In **Dry Valley** Bunin again underlines with a special force the kinship of the squires and peasants (he had previously done it in **"Antonov Apples"**, for example). "It's long, long since time for the Krushchevs to be reckoned as of kin to their domestics and their village!"

It is wrong, at least to our mind, to search for a 'Russian soul' in Dostoevskij's novels. But, a curious westerner can read **Dry Valley;** there he may find some clues to the mysterious *âme slave*, at least as it looked in Bunin's 'traditional Russia', that is, in pre-revolutionary Russia, from the time of her historical beginning until the end of the last century. In each of the character portraits as drawn by Natal'ja, one can find the contradictory traits of the 'truly Slavic soul': wisdom and want of sence, sluggishness and instability; individual sensitive brilliance and basic insipidity and coldness of feelings, and both quickness and poverty of imagination. And Natal'ja herself has been corrupted by this **Dry Valley** atmosphere because "there was all too little savour in the water she drank, drawn from those ponds which her grandsires had dug in the bed of the dried river".

The pre-revolutionary critic Derman wrote that "the last traits of the life dear to Bunin are fading away. This is a leitmotif of **Dry Valley**". That this 'motif' is very artfully presented is something Derman totally ignores. For "mastery is knowing how to communicate to the reader what the writer has in his heart; to do it in the most expressive, most emotional, most economical, and most euphonic way". This is not an easy requirement for a writer to fulfill, yet we believe Bunin has achieved it in **Dry Valley.** This story is written from beginning to end in a remarkably subtle language. Its realistic simplicity is permeated with spirituality and colored with symbolism. The concrete, visible, colorfully sketched **Dry Valley** is closely interwoven with the unreal, ethereal, symbolic **Dry Valley.** The seemingly disordered form of narration—the abundance of digressions and repetitions—is actually logical and justifiable: it is in accordance with Natal'ja's delirious memories. The suggestiveness of **Dry Valley** is based on intuition and insight, and its verbal art is often a matter of musical sonority. A cliché is used by most of those writing about Bunin; they say he is a 'magical' writer, and, indeed, there is a great deal of truth in this. **Dry Valley** is a magnificent example of Bunin's verbal mastery, of his marvelous facility in the selection of the right word which best conveys the given situation. And even if R. Poggioli is correct in deprecating nostalgia as "a characteristic aristocratic trait", there is nothing hackneyed in Bunin's masterful portrayal of it in **Dry Valley.** We rather inadvertently think of Majakovskij's two lines about the power of words:

> (I know the power of words, though they seem as
> small as petals ground under foot in the dance).

Indeed, 'the power of words' transfigures the nostalgia of **Dry Valley.** (pp. 99-102)

Serge Kryzytski, in his The Works of Ivan Bunin, *Mouton, 1971, 283 p.*

ALBERT J. WEHRLE   (essay date 1975)

[In the following excerpt, Wehrle traces themes and subthemes in Bunin's story "Petlistye ushi."]

Bunin's original plan called for a story larger than the twelve pages published under the hard-to-translate title of **"Petlistye ushi"** in 1917. This plan would indicate that he considered the theme of the story to be important and deserving of wider development, although this thesis does not imply the antithesis that the final size of the story indicates a lesser importance. For instance, it has been demonstrated [by James B. Woodward in his 1970 essay "Eros and Nirvana in the Art of Bunin"], that the most complete statement of Bunin's philosophy of life is found in **"Night,"** a story of the same dimension as **"Petlistye ushi"** [see Further Reading list]. It is worth noting that Bunin considered the latter important enough to be the title work in the selection of stories he arranged just before his death, **Petlistye ushi i drugie rasskazy,** New York, 1954. This title is interesting because the story seems untypical of Bunin, most notably in its big city setting and direct statement of social and philosophical ideas, and therefore would seem to be rather peripheral to his essential concerns. The purpose of this analysis is to correct this impression by showing that the central theme of **"Petlistye ushi"** illustrates a key point in Bunin's philosophical system. The place of the story in Bunin's stylistic development will be discussed in the second part of the essay.

"Petlistye ushi" encompasses about twenty-four hours in the life of Sokolovich, a nasty-looking "former sailor." After roaming the streets of Petrograd all day, Sokolovich drinks with two sailors in a cheap restaurant. He speaks little, but to the point, and what he says has, previous to the present analysis, been taken as the statement of the story's central theme. After leaving the restaurant, Sokolovich wastes some

Portrait of Bunin.

more time, and then goes to a hotel with Korolkova, a prostitute. He leaves early in the morning, and the last paragraph of the story describes the lifeless body he leaves behind.

According to the thesis of this article, the central theme is not to be discovered in Sokolovich's remarks in the restaurant. The most important thing in the story is not what Sokolovich says, but *how* he acts. This is not to deny the relevance of what Sokolovich says, but to assert that his statements reveal subthemes, which are subordinate to the central theme, and which will now be briefly examined. Three sub-themes can be differentiated: a psychological sub-theme, a "Dostoevsky sub-theme," and a social sub-theme.

The psychological sub-theme has been seen as developing from Sokolovich's statement that "The passion for murder and for all sorts of cruelty in general is found [. . .] in everyone." In his book on Bunin the Soviet scholar A. Volkov sees the story as an artistic development of the Freudian "aggression instinct." Naturally, he does not develop this observation. It is not really made clear whether he means that Bunin was purposely writing a story to illustrate a Freudian theory, or merely means that the story can be analyzed in these terms, although the former is strongly suggested. The distinction is important because, although Sokolovich can certainly be analyzed in Freudian terms, too much emphasis on this aspect of the story risks obscuring the place of its main theme in Bunin's philosophy of love and death.

The "Dostoevsky sub-theme" consists of a "false polemic" and a "real polemic." This sub-theme follows from Sokolovich's statement that the "passion for murder" is in everyone. "It is time," says Sokolovich, "to write about crime without any punishment." He contends that Raskolnikov's agonies of conscience are a myth, and voices a philosophy that amounts to "the law of the wolf." Volkov sees this philosophy as representing "a polemic with the ideas of F. Dostoevsky," at the same time admitting that the words of a character of fiction cannot be equated with the ideas of the author. He does not see that this principle practically forces one to make what, upon reflection, seems to be the one sound deduction, namely that this is a fictional polemic used as a method of characterization. If the purpose were a "real" serious philosophical polemic with Dostoevsky, it would seem that the author would hardly have chosen such an inhuman and lifeless figure as Sokolovich to be the exponent of the counter-argument. Indeed, the central theme of the story is Sokolovich's alienation from humanity, which makes him incapable of bearing any kind of universal philosophy. (pp. 443-45)

The "real polemic" with Dostoevsky is an esthetic one. As will be seen, Bunin does not "grab the reader by the lapels" in order to make his central point. He tries to influence the reader in a more objective, less personal manner. He avoids "fits," by which, we may assume, he meant the impassioned dialogues he so disliked in Dostoevsky, and the agonized soul-searching of Dostoevskian "nadryv," and makes the main idea of **"Petlistye ushi"** arise from how the central character acts, not from what he says. This is the "real polemic" with Dostoevsky. And finally, upon reflection, it should be clear that any real polemic based on the ideas of Sokolovich could not be confined to an attack on the ideas of Dostoevsky, but would be an attack on the ideas of Tolstoy as well.

V. Afanasiev's contrast between **"A Spring Evening"** (1914) and **"Petlistye ushi"** can serve as a transition to a discussion of the social sub-theme. In the former story, in which a peasant, frenzied with drink, murders a beggar for some money, Afanasiev finds "the darkness and savagery of [peasant] village life, in the second—the refined and cultivated cruelty of city civilization, [cruelty] intensified by the bloody influence of war." The basis of this statement—the difference between a crime of passion and a crime committed in cold blood—is, in fact, the key to the meaning of **"Petlistye ushi,"** as will be seen below. But, aside from this point, there is nothing "refined" or "cultivated" in the picture of city life presented in the story. The constant movement of traffic is elemental and savage: a man is run over in the street. Factories run all night, and their Moloch-like dehumanizing effect is hardly "refined": "Outside the window, beyond the black panes, voices hollowly rang out, the noise of some kind of a machine was heard and just like in hell the purple fire of a huge torch flamed." The prostitutes are hardly "refined" or elegant: "the faces of some of them strike you with such a nothingness of features that it becomes eerie, as if you had stumbled across some kind of creature other than human, one unknown to nature." And "refined" is hardly the word for the two sailors, or for Sokolovich, who describes himself as a "monster." He is a "monster" in keeping with what Volkov calls the "anti-military line" of the story, which is part of the social sub-theme. Sokolovich illustrates his theory of the "passion for murder" by presenting human history as a history of cruelty, culminating in what is now known as World War I, of which

he says "Soon all Europe will become a kingdom of murderers." Bunin's point is best expressed by a critic [E. Koltonovskaya] writing in 1917: " 'Petlistye ushi' represents Bunin's reply to those who were writing that war can bring out the best in men." Bunin argues that the philosophy of war is the philosophy of monsters.

In connection with the social sub-theme, it is noteworthy that in one draft Bunin sketches the background of Sokolovich, as an explanation of how his character was formed. Afanasiev writes:

> It is a pity that the author rejected the continuation of the story, which gave it greater social sharpness and concreteness, although in itself the author's rejection of it cannot be considered accidental. Not only Bunin's constant striving for laconism, but also the tendency, which was clearly emerging in those years, to reticence and "nedoskazannost'," leaving room for the reader's fantasy, [. . .] played its role here.

It is certain that Bunin did not leave out Sokolovich's background "by accident," but Afanasiev's remarks cannot be considered a serious attempt to account for the fact. A real explanation must be sought in considerations intrinsic to the text of this particular story. It would seem that Bunin's rejection of the family background material must reflect either (a) a change in what he wanted the central idea of the story to be, or (b) a realization that this idea would not be enhanced by the background material, or (c) a realization that the central idea would even be obscured by the background material. It is the thesis of this study that Bunin's was reason (c), which means that he felt the background material would enhance the psychological and social sub-themes, and thus obscure the central theme, which, as has been stated, is not as much concerned with why Sokolovich does what he does, as it is with how he does it, as the following analysis will show.

The act of murder is not described, but many details of the story make it plain that "the passion for murder" lacks "passion" for Sokolovich. He is dispassionate to the point of inertness in everything. Nothing arouses him. Nothing excites him. What he says about wine can be applied to his style of murder: "wine has little effect on me and does not afford me any particular pleasure. My taste is jaded. I am what they call a monster." This statement gets close to the central theme. Sokolovich is a "monster," not because he commits the act of murder, but because this act has no effect on him. Another variant of the story had to be dropped because it obscures this point. In this variant the police receive a letter in which Sokolovich names himself as the "perpetrator of this *disgusting* crime." (My italics here and below.) He describes his *"sensations"* after smothering the prostitute "with his paws." In this variant he then "senselessly" (that is, "without purpose") stabbed her with a dagger, having ripped her cheap dress "from top to bottom *in bestial fury*." This description had to be discarded because it is too vivid; even "bestial fury" is a sensation, and therefore too human for the "monster" Sokolovich. The peasant-murderer in **"A Spring Evening"** was drunk, to the point of "madness" and "fury." Sokolovich feels nothing, neither wine, nor passion in murder. The stripping of the body strikes a false note because Sokolovich is dead to sexual impulses. Note that it was Korolkova herself who "suddenly blocked the path of Sokolovich, who was striding along hunched over." They ride in a droshky; Sokolovich is silent, and does not respond when Korolkova presses her body against him.

This draft was unacceptable, not only because of the details of the letter, but also because the very fact that Sokolovich took the trouble to write it imparts an importance to the murder incommensurate with Sokolovich's obliviousness to sensations. Also incommensurate in this sense is the first-person confession which is part of the very first draft of the story, in which Sokolovich is captured, even though the following sentence throws his approach to murder into high relief. "Driving up to the hotel, I glanced at my watch—it was a quarter 'till two—and I thought: this creature has only forty-five minutes to live, and I carried out my thought precisely." In the published story the stress on accuracy becomes a property of the narrative after Sokolovich leaves the restaurant, which keeps the reader informed as to time, and establishes a mood that can be seen as a correlative of Sokolovich's inhuman lack of sensations, his mechanical deadness. Because the reader knows a murder will take place in the hotel, the stress on the measured movement of time becomes a dramatic device as well. Nianchuk, the desk clerk, "once again lay down in his place and fell soundly asleep under the even ticking of the clock at the end of the corridor of the semi-dark and silent hotel." Just before that, he had been awakened by a call for cigarettes, and had mistakenly taken them to the room occupied by Sokolovich and Korolkova. In response to his knock: "A coarse, low bass slowly asked from behind the door: 'What is it?' 'Your Miss asked for cigarettes,' said Nianchuk. 'My *Miss* did not ask for cigarettes and, what is more, would under no circumstances have been able to ask for cigarettes,' answered the bass authoritatively." This was at four a.m. Sokolovich remains with the dead body until seven, at which time he cooly pays the bill, "waits patiently" while Nianchuk unlocks the door, and calmly walks out of the hotel. Sokolovich's measured movements contrast to the abrupt and nervous actions of the clerk. " 'And how about [paying for] the grapes?' Nianchuk asked hurriedly and anxiously. [. . .] Sokolovich turned right and disappeared in the distance. Chilled, Nianchuk slammed the door and ran back upstairs." Besides being a dramatic device, this contrast of tempos accentuates Sokolovich's inertness.

Sokolovich's alienation from activity is emphasized throughout the story. He has no occupation. His life is a "bezdel'naya zhizn'." The story features a number of descriptions of bustling streets and crowds along Nevsky Prospect. Sokolovich spends all day among the crowds, but with no object or purpose. He is seen in front of a shop window: "Was it really that he was interested in all these neckties, watches, suitcases, and writing materials? It could be seen immediately that he was not." In the restaurant he takes no real part in the conversation of his two companions, whose talk, if crude, is at least animated by drink and imagination, as they recount the dirtiest deeds of their enemies, or brag about "giving it" to someone "in the snout," or throwing someone overboard, doubts being met by the repeated exclamation: "Wanna bet?" Sokolovich's infrequent talk is more intellectual, more abstract, as in his ironic remark that monsters can be recognized by their "petlistye ushi," ears shaped like a hangman's noose. One sailor objects: "Well, you know, anybody can kill if he flares up." Later the same sailor recalls that he had an uncle who killed his wife out of jealousy. These remarks prefigure the murder of the prostitute but, in doing so, contrast with it in that Sokolovich does not "flare up," nor does he have a reason for the murder. It is this lack of any kind of life that makes him a "monster." (pp. 445-49)

Death by murder or suicide is so often linked with love in Bunin's work because death can represent a finalization of the transcendence of one's personality. In **"The Son,"** written in 1916, the same year as **"Petlistye ushi,"** Madame Marot's love for a student half her age is consummated by her voluntary death at his hand, the same choice made by Sosnovskaya, the actress who dies in a suicide pact with Lieutenant Yelagin. Like Emile, the student, Yelagin does not kill himself: "For Yelagin suicide would be superfluous; in life he has attained the nirvana to which Sosnovskaya aspires through death." The preceding analysis of **"Petlistye ushi"** has shown that Sokolovich can neither delight in his physical existence, nor can he escape from himself, the latter evidenced, among other things, by his elaborate philosophy of self-justification. Thus he is a philosophical dead-end in Bunin's system, existing in a "no-man's land" between sensual self-awareness and self-forgetfulness. This is what it means to be a "monster."

"Petlistye ushi" can also be related to **"The Son"** and **"The Yelagin Affair"** (1925) in terms of composition and style. Both **"Petlistye ushi"** and **"The Yelagin Affair"** are based on actual criminal cases, the former on Petersburg's "Vadim Krovyanik Case" (1912), the latter on a sensational Warsaw case of 1890. In both stories the author makes use of actual details that came to light in the respective trials. It is interesting, in view of the "Dostoevsky sub-theme," that this practice seems to resemble Dostoevsky's "fantastic realism." Perhaps there is an element of parody in its use in **"Petlistye ushi."** But more general evidence suggests that this use of real events represents one solution tried by Bunin in his search for a method to organize his stories. In his article "The Evolution of Bunin's Narrative Technique," Woodward demonstrates that 1916 was a pivotal year in the development of Bunin's prose. Works of previous years had tended to be dominated by tone and atmosphere. In the extreme, Bunin had tried to do without organization, which meant the lack of plot and a randomness in the selection of details. It is indicative that "sound" was very important in Bunin's early prose. However, Woodward observes that as philosophical ideas began to gain importance for Bunin (about 1912), he began to search for a way of organizing them. To structure them around a plot is one solution, a solution made easier if the plot is already provided by real life. In this regard, **"Petlistye ushi"** and **"The Yelagin Affair"** can be viewed as experimental works. Indeed, in a margin of the manuscript of **"The Yelagin Affair"** Bunin jotted the words "probka pera," "a test of the pen." This experiment in organization was to bear its richest fruit in the interaction between biography and fiction of the novel *The Life of Arseniev.*

There is another type of organization, the basis of which can be compared to poetic imagery. This organization is sometimes called "eidolological," although it really does not have to be iconographic. This organization calls to mind Tolstoy's description of the "chains of metaphors" in his novels. It has been discovered, though, that this method is also used extensively by Dostoevsky. Thus, the presence of this type of organization in **"Petlistye ushi,"** like the presence of a crime plot a la Dostoevsky, can be viewed in two ways: a possible parody of Dostoevsky, as well as an experiment in the course of Bunin's search for methods of composition. The following analysis concentrates on the string of metaphors prefiguring the murder of Korolkova.

This chain consists of images leading to the final sentences of the story: "[. . .] and on the bed the short, naked legs of a woman lying on her back stuck out from under the covers. Her head was covered [pridavlena] by two pillows." The basic image anticipating the conclusion and therefore serving as a method of organization focuses on two details, the protruding legs, and the fact that Korolkova's face and head cannot be seen. The description of the restaurant includes mention of a billiard room three steps above floor level, which, in conjunction with the poor lighting, causes the players to be seen as "headless men: their heads were lost in the darkness." In his chronicle of murderers Sokolovich singles out a French executioner who cut off "exactly" five hundred heads in his career. Later, on the street, Sokolovich stares at a couple riding past; the woman's face is "hidden in an astrakhan muff." Kazan Cathedral is described as being "beheaded by the foggy darkness," while just before that window mannequins are described "in expensive coats, some of fur, with wooden feet lifelessly [mertvo] sticking out from under stylish, splendidly-pressed pantaloons." If the heads of the billiard players and Kazan Cathedral are hidden in darkness, Korolkova covers the lower part of her face with a muff of black fur, while her hat is of black velvet. These details lead up to the final scene in what might almost be described as an obsessive rhythm of images of murder.

There is also another, related set of images. Besides anticipating the murder, they may be related to the "Dostoevsky subtheme." In *Crime and Punishment* Dostoevsky draws a parallel between a mare that is beaten to death and the murder victims. Bunin may be playing on this parallel when he draws attention to the statue of Alexander III which the droshky passes on its way to the hotel. The tsar is a symbol of force, while the horse "bows [. . .] its large head," asking its rider, in vain, to slacken the reins. Note that, in the opening of the story, Sokolovich stares at this statue "with incomprehensible seriousness." In the description of the statue there is the same attention to the head as in the human images, while Korolkova's final position on the bed is prefigured in an accident Sokolovich witnesses upon leaving the restaurant: "[. . .] desperately beating and sliding its hooves on the slippery pavement, straining to right itself and scramble up, having fallen on its back, on the shaft, was a black stallion." This accident is explicitly connected with death; Sokolovich hears that some old man, "supposedly a famous writer," was "run over" (zadavlen). There is a sound echo between "zadavlen" and the participle describing how the pillows "press down" on Korolkova's head: "golova pridavlena." Finally, the fact that the old man was a writer might be seen as a pun (uncharacteristic of Bunin) on the "Dostoevsky sub-theme."

The poetic type of composition in **"Petlistye ushi"** can be compared to the organization of **"The Son."** On her honeymoon Madame Marot was hypnotized by a magician who "squatted before her" and put her to sleep with his "monotoned melodies" and the "slow motions of his hands." The position of the magician is paralleled by Émile, when he makes his feelings for Madame Marot explicit by falling on his knees before her. The melodies of the hypnotist are paralleled by Émile's "strange, but melodious poems," which he would read to Madame Marot with "some kind of somnambulistic expressiveness." The hypnotic motions of the magician's hands are paralleled by the swaying of the swing in the garden, which, indeed, seems to put Madame Marot into a trance. "When she suddenly regained consciousness, above her stood Émile." On that day she held the barrel of a gun to her temple and Émile pulled the trigger. The momentary spark that one might imagine occurred in her mind as the gun

went off can be seen as being prefigured by the direct impulse that causes Madame Marot to lose consciousness in the swing, "the brilliant silver spark with which a spoon in a glass of water burned in the sun." This is in keeping with the set of ideas discussed above: love as both self-realization and as a transcendence that can be compared to the hypnotic state as described in **"The Son:"** "that sweet fear and that blessed will-lessness as if in the minutes before death." The flash of the gun eternalizes the moment in which the spoon flashes, fusing "Eros" and "Nirvana." If **"Petlistye ushi"** were characterized in these terms, the story could be described as a study in stagnant and futile "Thanatos." (pp. 450-53)

Albert J. Wehrle, "Bunin's Story 'Petlistye Ushi' ('Loopy Ears')," in Russian Literature Triquarterly, *No. 11, 1975, pp. 443-54.*

JAMES B. WOODWARD (essay date 1980)

[*Woodward is an English editor, essayist, and academic. In the following excerpt from his critical biography of Bunin, he examines the "sudden 'flashes' of ecstasy and horror that briefly illuminate the splendor and tragedy of the human condition" in Bunin's love stories.*]

In the course of his conversation with Bunin in January 1894, Tolstoy remarked: "There is no happiness in life; there are only flashes of it. Value them, live them to the full." The point was taken up in one of Bunin's preparatory notes for *The Life of Arsen'yev:* "We are fully alive to everything that we experience only to the extent that we appreciate its value. Usually this value is very small. It rises only at moments of rapture— the rapture of happiness or unhappiness when we are clearly conscious of gain or loss." The term "flash" aptly defines the type of experience the fictional situations of Bunin's love stories are normally designed to generate—sudden "flashes" of ecstasy and horror that briefly illuminate the splendor and tragedy of the human condition. Since the intervals between such experiences were of little interest to him, his works are usually constructed around a single "flash." To this extent they may be viewed as typical short stories. But Bunin's love stories are distinguished by the customary absence of any connection between the "flash" and the purposeful or premeditated action of those who experience it. Motivated almost invariably by the susceptibility of the characters to influences that elude their conscious or rational control, it is usually experienced by them either as a complete surprise or as an act of inexplicable surrender. Occasionally, as in **"Light Breathing,"** the effects of these subconscious influences are examined without reference to any external source of stimulation, but more commonly, as we have seen, the victory of the irrational is the culmination of sustained interaction between the individual subconscious and the external forces of nature that are evoked in the descriptions of setting and landscape.

In none of Bunin's tales is interaction of this kind a more obviously significant element of the fiction than in the first two of the five major love stories that he wrote in the twenties— *Mitya's Love* and **"Sunstroke"** [**"Solnechnyy udar"**] (1925)— the latter of which seems to express the notion of the "flash" in its very title. Indeed, one's first impression of this seven-page story is that few works of comparable size combine so many typical features of Bunin's mature art. There is the usual pair of principal characters, in this case a married woman and a lieutenant in the czarist army, who are fellow travelers on a Volga steamer. The plot, which has been compared, to no useful purpose, to that of Chekhov's "The Lady with the Little Dog" ["Dama s sobachkoy"] (1899), is as skeletal as any he ever devised. It hinges on three events: the mutual infatuation of the characters, their decision to spend the night together at a stopping point on their journey, and their separation the following morning. Both are portrayed as completely average individuals, and "Everyman," as their anonymity suggests, is writ large on their brows. But their failure to disclose their names—even to one another—is felt to be less a mark of generalization than an attribute of their brief relationship. It is indicative of their momentary transformation into willess marionettes, of the sudden capitulation to depersonalizing sensuality that represents for both of them a completely new experience. "In all their lives," we read, "neither the one nor the other had ever experienced anything like it," and before her departure the woman declares: "I give you my word of honor that I am not at all the kind of woman you might think. I have never before experienced anything that even resembled what has happened, and it will not happen again. It was as though an eclipse came over me. . . . Or rather we both received a kind of sunstroke."

For the characters, of course, the term "sunstroke" is simply a metaphor of the willess state of mind from which they have emerged, but ironically the heroine unwittingly identifies in her remark the real cause of the experience. Again the sun enters Bunin's fiction as a potent influence on human behavior, as a force capable of usurping the authority of reason. Its dazzling light suffuses almost every scene, and even at night its presence is felt acutely. As the lieutenant, for example, kisses the woman's hand in the darkness before they disembark, he is struck by the smell of sunburn, and "in bliss and awe his heart sank at the thought of how strong and dark her whole body must be under the light gingham dress after lying for a whole month beneath the southern sun." When they enter the dark hotel room, the sun's power again assaults their senses: "They entered a large but terribly stifling room which the sun had filled during the day with its searing heat," and in this suffocating atmosphere the last vestiges of self-control are swiftly discarded.

No less typical than the plot of the work, the character types, and the motivation of the action are the expressive effects that Bunin obtains by varying the pace of the narrative. Disenchanted with his first two drafts, he noted in the margin of the final version the guiding principle: "Nothing superfluous," and promptly deleted much of what he had written. As usual, however, his application of this principle did not prevent him from introducing detailed descriptive passages, not only to evoke scene and atmosphere, but also to arrest the flow of the narrative as a means of offsetting the tensions experienced by the characters. A typical example is the passage that relates the events following their disembarkation:

> A minute later they passed through a small, sleepy office, stepped out onto the sand which was so deep that wheels sank into it up to their hubs, and silently sat down in a cab that was covered in dust. The uphill climb along a road that was soft from the dust and illuminated by a few crooked lamps seemed endless. But at last they reached the top and emerged onto the highway, and as they clattered along it they passed a square, some offices, and a watch tower and experienced the warmth and smells of a summer's night in a provincial town. . . . The cabby stopped at a brightly lit porch behind the open doors of which stretched an

old, steep, wooden staircase. Resentfully an old, unshaven lackey in a pink blouse and frock coat took their baggage and walked ahead of them on misshapen feet that had often been trampled on.

The slowing down of the narrative that results from the insertion of this highly detailed passage not only conveys a vivid impression of the arduousness of the journey with its initial climb from the jetty and the final climb up the steep staircase; it also forms an expressive counterpoint to the feelings of the hero, for whom every second is an excruciating eternity. His impatient desire for the contraction of time is offset by the expansion of narrative time, by the slowness of the journey mirrored in the fullness of its description.

At the same time, there is reason to assume that the meaning of some of the individual details included in this passage is as much symbolic as literal. Noteworthy in this connection is the imagined scene that, according to Galina Kuznetsova, served Bunin as his point of departure when writing the tale. She recalls: "The origins of 'Sunstroke' can be traced to a mental picture of coming out on deck after dinner—from the light into the darkness of a summer's night on the Volga." The scene is recreated in the opening sentence of the tale: "After dinner they left the hot, brightly lit dining room, and stepping on to the deck they stopped by the handrail." The setting on board a steamer is ideally suited, of course, to the theme of a "chance acquaintance," but the ensuing development of the story suggests that Bunin was equally attracted by the opportunities it offered for allusion. The transition from the light of the dining room to the darkness of the scene on deck introduces a contrast that is subsequently repeated on several occasions. Thus the third paragraph begins: "Ahead lay darkness and lights. A strong, mild wind blew from out of the dark and struck them in the face, while the lights sped by somewhere to the side." Shortly afterward the motif reappears in the contrast between the "summer's night" and the sprinkling of lights that illuminate the road to the hotel, and it is repeated on the protagonists' arrival. From the darkness of the night they pass through the "brightly lit porch" and up the staircase only to meet darkness once more on entering the room with its "white lowered curtains" and its "two unlit candles on the pier-glass table." and it is here, in this stifling darkness, that desire is finally gratified. The opening contrast, therefore, is echoed at each stage of the progression to the climax of the action, ultimately resolving itself in the triumph of darkness, and there can be little doubt that both the contrast and its resolution allude to the psychological experience of the characters. The alterations of light and darkness reflect the conflict between reason and the irrational that ends with the victory of the latter.

The externalization of psychological experience is yet another feature of Bunin's narrative technique in **"Sunstroke"** that is thoroughly familiar to us, but the same cannot be said of every aspect of the tale, for in one conspicuous respect it differs fundamentally from the love stories of the prerevolutionary period. The difference is immediately apparent in the much smaller proportion of the tale that is embraced by the external action, for by the end of the second page it is virtually complete. The remaining five pages are devoted entirely to the representation of the hero's reactions to the irreparable sense of loss that unexpectedly overwhelms him after the woman's departure. Once more Bunin portrays through the agonies of his hero the tragic implications of man's inherent degeneracy. The lieutenant, we note, now feels like an outcast from life. The sun no longer excites his senses. He is struck only by the "pointlessness" of its blinding light, by the vulgarity of the urban scenes that it illuminates, and by the incomprehensible contentment of the people performing in its heat their daily tasks. Like everything else, the light of the sun is eclipsed by the remembered "flash" of his own short-lived ecstasy and by the pain of its irrevocable passing, and his will to live is momentarily undermined. Whereas, however, in one of the early drafts of the story there is a reference to "the persistent thought of suicide," the nightmare in the final redaction is eventually survived. As the lieutenant boards his boat the following night, the symbolic sequence of the opening scenes is reversed. From the darkness of the irrational he passes once more into the comforting light of reason. "Because of the throng," we read, "the steamer, which was already lit up everywhere and smelling of the galley, seemed unusually welcoming and attractive." But although he is saved from self-destruction, it is clear that his life will never be quite the same again. The story ends with the simple statement: "The lieutenant sat under an awning on the deck feeling ten years older."

The most striking feature, however, of this second and longer section of the tale is neither the theme nor even its extended development, but rather the change of technique that is mainly responsible for this extension, for the psychological experience of the lieutenant is no longer conveyed here exclusively by allusion or externalization. It is represented with the aid of techniques that in Bunin's prerevolutionary stories make only the most fleeting appearance—the interior monologue and free indirect speech. In no prerevolutionary tale had he attempted to convey so directly or extensively the feelings of a character who was not patently a mouthpiece of his personal judgments, and this development marks a stage of some importance in the evolution of his art, for it is by no means confined to **"Sunstroke."** All his love stories of the mid-twenties display a similar inclination toward more direct methods of psychological portrayal which he had previously tended to shun. At the basis of all five stories, two of which, **"Ida"** (1925) and **"The Mordvinian Sarafan"** [**"Mordovskiy sarafan"**] (1925), are first-person narratives, we perceive a common pattern that centers on the directly expressed reactions of the hero to the heroine and to the feelings that she provokes in him.

This does not mean, of course, that every aspect of the hero's psychological drama is elevated to the surface and exposed to the light of day. As in the first section of **"Sunstroke,"** his subconscious receptivity to external influences continues to be represented by indirect methods. But his conscious reactions to the situations into which he is driven by these influences receive a totally unprecedented emphasis with the result that the tension between subconsciously or irrationally motivated action and conscious or rational response is significantly sharpened, and one of the most obvious effects of this development is the notably enhanced "presence" in the fiction of the heroes of these works compared with that of their predecessors. They enjoy a status that had previously been bestowed only on intermediaries like the colonel in **"The Brothers,"** Chang, and the Krasovs in their "reflective" role, and this status seems to suggest a degree of compassion on the author's part that is strikingly at variance with the consistently dispassionate attitude reflected in the narrative style of his prerevolutionary love stories. Perhaps the source of this compassion and of the sensitivity to pain that it implies was the pain of the émigré confronted at the age of fifty with new, horrifying evidence of the intrinsic cruelty of life. Neverthe-

less, it should be stressed that the fictional reality of his heroes is never compromised. The voice we hear is not that of the author; it is the voice of the hero expressing himself in a manner that accords with his personality and with the situation in which he is placed.

Despite, therefore, the familiarity of its theme, the impression produced by **"Sunstroke"** is quite distinctive. It is the first *short* tale in which Bunin combines the new element of direct psychological portrayal with the allusive style that characterizes such stories as **"By the Road," "The Grammar of Love,"** and **"The Son."** But the work that marks the transition to this synthesis is *Mitya's Love,* which had been written the previous year (1924). Not only is it the best known of all Bunin's love stories; it is also the longest, and its length is partly an indication of the unprecedented attention he devotes in it to the representation of mood and feeling. Never before had he subjected a mind other than his own to such intensive and sympathetic scrutiny.

In Bunin's prerevolutionary love stories the recurrent tension between conscious activity and subconscious, that is, "natural," impulse had only once expressed itself in conflicting notions of love—in **"By the Road,"** in which Parashka perishes because of her inability to reconcile with her ideal notion of love the initiation into the mystery of sexual love that she experiences with Nikanor. Bunin returns to this conflict in *Mitya's Love.* Like **"Sunstroke,"** the story is divisible into two unequal sections. In the first, which comprises only the first six of its twenty-nine short chapters, both hero and heroine are present, and the scene is Moscow. In the second, the setting is rural, and the heroine, like the lieutenant's "chance acquaintance," exists as memory alone. (pp. 181-88)

Although, however, everything in [*Mitya's Love*] is directly or obliquely related to the inner drama of the hero, this does not mean, as critics have tended to suggest, that everything is seen through the hero's eyes. The active role played by nature is not a role imparted to it by the hero's imagination. It is a subtly contrived representation of the *real* power of nature over the human psyche. Had it been otherwise, Bunin would presumably have adopted the form of a first-person narrative, and it may reasonably be supposed that it was precisely his wish to stress the reality and extent of nature's influence on human behavior that chiefly explains the relative rarity of this type of narrative in his major fiction. The most cogent evidence in support of this argument is the generally inactive role of nature in the first-person narratives he did write, including **"Ida"** and **"The Mordvinian Sarafan."**

"Ida" is arguably Bunin's finest—and certainly his most poignant—first-person narrative, though, to be precise, it is rather a first-person narrative within a first-person narrative. The technique is reminiscent of Turgenev. The setting is the restaurant of a Moscow hotel where the narrator is dining with three companions, one of whom, a composer, feels a sudden compulsion to relate an episode involving a friend of his that had occurred some three years ago. The main character of his story is a friend of the "hero's" wife, the beautiful Ida, who at one time, we are told, was a regular visitor to his house. He never failed, the composer continues, to marvel at her beauty and sometimes even imagined the "sweet torment" of an embrace, but on each occasion his dedication to "some nonsense called art" deterred him from succumbing to the temptation. Suddenly her visits stopped, and though he was dimly conscious of a sense of loss, her disappearance made little impression on him. Two years later, however, he met her again, now married to a handsome and wealthy student, in the restaurant of a railway station. Curtly dismissing her husband, she took him by the arm, and as they walked together along the platform, she confessed to him that for five years she had loved him passionately. The effect of her words was shattering. Momentarily paralyzed by the sudden realization that unconsciously he had always loved her and that a unique chance of happiness had slipped from his grasp, he was unable to utter a word in reply. Understanding his silence, she kissed him and walked away, and the composer ends his tale with the cry:

> Let us drink to all who have loved us, to all those whom we in our idiocy have not valued. Let us drink to all those with whom we have been happy and enjoyed bliss and with whom we have parted only to lose our way in life forever while still linked to them forever by the most awesome bond in the world!

The depth of feeling with which the story is told leaves little doubt that its hero is the composer himself. Even so, its tone is far from tragic, and in this respect **"Ida"** stands somewhat apart from the other love stories of 1924-25. No attempt is made here to probe the uncharted recesses of the human subconscious. The events are recounted with a kind of wistful humor, and tragedy is precluded from the start by the urbane *bonhomie* of the narrator, the interjections of his cheerful companions, and the general air of contentment in which the tale is told. Herein we perceive the importance of the frame of the work with its details of feasting and drinking and the raison d'être of the first narrator. The story of the composer is winnowed of its tragic implications by the frame in which it is set, and the work ends appropriately with the first narrator's salute to the rising sun as the revelers return to their homes in the early hours of the next morning. The reader, therefore, is left with the feeling that for all the sadness of missed opportunities, it is good to be alive in a world that offers such exquisite delights to the palate and the spectacle of such exquisite beauty as that of Ida. For the portrait of Ida, who seems almost an emanation of the sparkling winter background against which she is repeatedly projected, is itself a celebration of the feast with which life regales the senses of man, a feast which language is powerless to convey. Such is the import of the composer's description of her as she sits on the station platform:

> What can I say to you, apart from banalities, about that raised face lit by the paleness of that special snow which falls after blizzards and about her delicate, indescribable complexion which also resembled that snow? In general, what can I say to you about the face of a delightful young woman who, after walking along breathing in the snowy air, suddenly declares her love for you and waits for your answer? What did I say about her eyes? Violet? Quite wrong, of course. And the half-open lips? And the expression—the expression of all these features together, the face, the eyes, and the lips? And the long sable muff in which her hands were hidden, and the knees which were outlined beneath a Scottish material in blue-green check? Heavens, can words convey even the remotest idea of all this?

It is clear, therefore, from this summary that in **"Ida"** nature is simply an element in the portrait of the heroine that is suggestive of the beauty of life in general. The reader may be conscious of the irony that had the hero of the composer's tale grasped the beauty and happiness that were within his grasp,

the result, in accordance with Bunin's "grammar" of love, would almost certainly have been catastrophe. But the irony is absent from the story itself. Here there is no "flash" to blind the eye of reason, no submission to nature's seduction, and no anguish to distort the beauty of nature and woman as it is filtered through the haze of elegiac reminiscence. Very different is the situation in **"The Mordvinian Sarafan."**

Bunin's second first-person narrative of 1925 seems to have been conceived as an ironic contrast to his first. Creating in the person of the heroine a figure who contrasts with Ida in almost every conceivable respect, he asserts the power of even such a woman as this to exercise a no less irresistible attraction. His purpose is immediately apparent in the questions of the narrator that open the story: "Why am I going to see her, this strange and, moreover, pregnant woman? Why did I begin this unnecessary and even repugnant relationship and why do I keep it up?" The heroine is yet another of Bunin's nameless characters, and in this case anonymity seems again to be an indicator of spiritual vacuity. Her demeanor, the furniture in her apartment, and every sentiment that she utters proclaim a creature of mindless and pathetic vulgarity. Like the pedestrians on Gogol's Nevsky Prospect, she lacks all identity save that bestowed by the contours of her body and the idiosyncrasies of her dress—above all, by the grotesque sarafan of her own creation which she proudly displays to the horrified hero. He describes it as follows:

> There was something strange and dreadful in her hands: a long, shapeless garment made of the canvas used by peasants with stripes and embroidery in dark brown and indigo silk on the shoulders, the sleeves, the chest, and the hem of the skirt. . . . There was something somber, ancient, and seemingly deathly in this loose garment, and it aroused in me an eerie, unpleasant feeling connected with her pregnancy and unnatural gaiety. It occurred to me that she would probably die in childbirth.

Even the vulgar incongruity, however, of this bizarre imitation of peasant attire in the setting of an urban apartment fails to detract from the lure of her physical charms, and succumbing meekly to her pitiful coquetry, he draws her to him with the resigned air of a prisoner being led to the scaffold.

The voluptuous body of the heroine may be viewed as the counterpart in this short tale of the richly detailed landscapes in *Mitya's Love*. It is both the main object of sensuous description and the conqueror of the hero's will. But nature is not entirely absent from the work, and although it is confined exclusively to the frame—to the two brief portraits of a March night in Moscow inserted into the narrator's descriptions of his arrival at the apartment and his abrupt departure—its role is not only compositional. In a sense, it even contributes to the motivation of the hero's weakness, for the gloom and harsh wind of the opening scene evoke the image of an inhospitable universe from which even the apartment of the repugnant adulteress offers a welcome refuge. His relief, conversely, on reentering it at the end eloquently conveys his desire for escape from the force that holds him in thrall. In both landscapes nature is entirely inactive in the sense that it is not represented as an influence on the human subconscious, but they show that in the art of Bunin even an inactive nature cannot be dismissed as inconsequential.

Even so, its role in **"The Mordvinian Sarafan"** is plainly ancillary, and together with **"Ida"** the story presents additional evidence of Bunin's general reluctance to allocate to nature its customary role when entrusting his stories to fictional narrators. Nature becomes active in his fiction only when it is not seen through the prism of a clearly defined sensibility. Only thereby could he ensure that the activity of nature would not be mistaken for the activity of a narrator's imagination. Hence the inactivity of nature not only in his first-person narratives, but also in the stories with narrators who are simply chroniclers or observers of events in which they are personally not involved. One of his rare attempts at this type of work was written a month after the completion of **"The Mordvinian Sarafan"** (in August-September 1925)—the much longer **"The Cornet Yelagin Affair,"** which is devoid even of an inactive nature.

The exclusion not only makes this tale virtually unique among Bunin's works; it is also perhaps one of the reasons for its relative weakness, for it is certainly one of his least successful works. Its weakness is mainly attributable, however, not so much to the exclusion of nature as to the cause of its exclusion, that is, to the intrinsic limitations of its theme, for as in the dénouement of **"The Son,"** Bunin again attempts the impossible. Once more his attention is focused on the complexity of human nature as revealed in the experience of love, but now this complexity is related to the influence on man of his biological or genetic heritage. It is important to note that the story was written at the time when he was working on **"Night,"** and it may be regarded, in part, as an attempt to translate into a work of fiction one of its main philosophical propositions. But the difficulties were obviously immense, and the attempt ended in complete implausibility. Although Bunin made some minor adjustments to the work a few months before his death, it is clear that he considered it a failure.

"The Cornet Yelagin Affair" is the most conspicuous example in Bunin's fiction of a narrative constructed on the model of a court case, and the reason, of course, is self-evident: . . . it was actually based on a trial that had been widely publicized in the Russian press—the trial in Warsaw in February 1891 of a junior officer named Bartenev in a hussar regiment, who was charged with the murder of the Polish actress Maria Wisnowska. After confessing to the crime, Bartenev was sentenced to eight years' hard labor, but was released, partly through the intervention of influential relatives, before the sentence had hardly begun. It was a mystifying case in many respects, and its curious features have been summarized by L. Nikulin:

> Bartenev was an aristocrat from an old noble family. He did not kill Wisnowska out of jealousy. It seems that some agreement existed between them, for it was impossible for him, a hussar and an officer, to marry her in the conditions of that time. But after shooting his mistress, Bartenev did not kill himself. He presented himself to the court which examined the case without a jury. In his appearance and conduct both before the murder and after he showed himself to be a degenerate young man of limited ability, and his victim was also a woman of strange habits. The conditions in which the murder was committed, the behavior of Wisnowska before her death—everything indicated that Bartenev had killed his mistress at her insistence. In everything that happened there was a certain theatricality. A note left by the murdered woman stated: "In killing me this man is acting justly. He is justice."

Each of the points noted by Nikulin is reproduced in Bunin's

account of the enigmatic relationship between the cornet Yelagin and the actress Sosnovskaya, the fictional counterparts of Bartenev and Wisnowska, but his main object is to suggest an interpretation of the affair with the aid of one of his most cherished convictions. At the same time, he was obviously anxious to avoid any impression of forcing the facts into the straitjacket of his thesis—an impression to which the unusual and contentious nature of the thesis could easily have given rise. He wished merely to present the reader with the evidence and with the judgments expressed at the trial, to pinpoint the deficiencies of these judgments, and to order his presentation in such a way that the only valid judgment would suggest itself without being actually formulated. These would seem to be the considerations that prompted him to introduce as narrator and as a dispassionate commentator on the evidence submitted an inhabitant of the town in which Yelagin's trial took place. As an eyewitness of the trial, this worthy citizen is entrusted with the task of freeing the author from the charge of distorting the facts to suit his case. He simply reproduces the evidence as he heard it, exposes the flaws in the arguments of the prosecuting counsel, and replaces a chronological exposition of the events with an order that seems to him most conducive to a just verdict.

Thus, in effect, the story begins at the end with Yelagin's confession to his fellow officers and their discovery of Sosnovskaya's body in her apartment. These are the main events of the first three chapters. Thereafter, the narrator's method is basically the same throughout—to adduce statements made at the trial and then to subject them to his personal analysis. While chapter IV, for example, is wholly devoted to the arguments of the prosecutor, chapter V introduces the narrator's rejoinder, and in chapter VI he almost assumes the role of defending counsel, listing in response to the prosecutor's observations the points he would have stressed in his client's favor. In order to justify his doubts and reservations about the prosecutor's conclusions, he then passes, in chapter VII, to the evidence of Yelagin's character witnesses, subjecting it to the same painstaking scrutiny. The procedure, therefore, is essentially one of cross-examining both counsel and witnesses after the trial has actually taken place, and by the end of chapter VII the narrator's picture of Yelagin, as distinct from the picture of him presented at the trial as a calculating murderer and congenital criminal, is virtually complete. After employing the same methods, in chapters VIII and IX, in the characterization of Sosnovskaya, the narrator turns in the last five chapters to the last fatal meeting of the defendant and his victim and to the events that directly preceded it as described (in chapters X, XIII, and XIV) by Yelagin himself and (in chapter XII) by Sosnovskaya's maid, while in chapter XI he interpolates his remarks on Yelagin's evidence and his reflections on a number of points that at the trial had been completely ignored. His reexamination of the case is thus completed, and formulation of the final judgment is left to the reader.

Since the case of Bartenev seems to have fascinated Bunin from the time it was first publicized, one may reasonably ask why he allowed thirty-four years to elapse before attempting his imaginative reconstruction of it. The reason already suggested is that his memories of the case may well have been resuscitated by the issues that preoccupied him in **"Night."** But it is also conceivable that his interest in it had been indirectly rekindled by his work on *Mitya's Love,* specifically, by the question that could well have occurred to him in the course of its composition of the possible consequences of such an "unnatural" love as Mitya's if it were truly to be reciprocated. In other words, what might have been the outcome if the real Katya had proved to be the personification of her lover's ideal? It is certainly undeniable that Mitya's elevated conception of love is shared both by Yelagin and by Sosnovskaya—who, incidentally, like Katya, is an actress—and an approach to **"The Cornet Yelagin Affair"** from this angle seems to offer the most reliable insight into Bunin's intended meaning.

Like Mitya, Yelagin and Sosnovskaya are rebels against nature, but their rebellion takes the different form of an antipathy to their families and backgrounds—the form of an aspiration to "withdraw from the chain." The prosecutor's description of Yelagin as a "degenerate" is entirely apt, but in a sense of which the prosecutor himself is quite unaware. Again the term is invested here by Bunin with its primary etymological meaning of "one who departs from his race or kind," and herein we see the reason for the narrator's intriguing interest in Yelagin's parents and ancestry. He is the scion, we are informed, of a rich and noble family that could boast ten generations of army officers before him. His mother—"an extremely excitable woman"—had died when he was very young, and he had spent his entire childhood and youth in dread of his domineering father. In an attempt to blacken his character, the prosecutor cited this fact at the trial as evidence of his cowardice, but the narrator takes issue with him. He comments: "Yes, Yelagin grew up in fear and trembling before his father. But trembling is not cowardice, especially before one's parents and in a man endowed with a keen sense of the entire heritage that links him with all his fathers, grandfathers, and forefathers." The implication seems to be that Yelagin's "fear and trembling" were an expression of his instinctive rejection of his father and of the "entire heritage" his father seemed to him to represent—a heritage that had borne down on him with particular intensity after the premature removal of his mother's alleviating influence. In support of his point, the narrator introduces the subject of Yelagin's appearance. He states: "Yes, the appearance of Yelagin is not the classical appearance of a hussar, but I see in this one of the proofs of his exceptional nature. Look a little more attentively, I would say to the prosecutor, at his reddish hair, his round shoulders, and his thin legs, and you see almost with awe how far from insignificant this freckled face is with its small, greenish eyes (which avoid looking at you)." It is clear that for the narrator Yelagin's appearance, which differs so markedly from that of the typical hussar and, implicitly, from the bearing of his military ancestors, is a physical or biological expression of his rebellion. It is the visual emblem of his degeneracy. And in harmony with this physical contrast is the contrast of temperament between Yelagin and his fellow officers, his inability to rest content with the everyday pattern of a young officer's life in which they seem to find complete self-fulfillment. "He is a man of strong passions," one of them observes at the trial, "but he always seemed to be waiting for something real and unusual." When he met Sosnovskaya, his waiting evidently came to an end.

Although Sosnovskaya hails from a lower social class, her background displays significant affinities with that of her lover. She also, we are told, was brought up by a single parent, having lost her father at the age of three, and throughout her life she was schooled in strict observance of the bourgeois standards to which her mother was a living monument. From an early age, she sought refuge in books, and her rebellion expressed itself in the many extracts she copied down from

them. Among the examples quoted by the narrator are the statements: " 'Not to be born is the first happiness, while the second is to return with all speed to nonexistence.' 'The world is tedious, terribly tedious, but my soul aspires to something unusual'." Disregarding her mother's protests, she later attempted to realize this aspiration in the world of the theater, but disenchantment came rapidly. Her notes reveal her abhorrence of the lustful eyes that followed her movements on the stage. "They all demand my body," she laments, "not my soul." Repelled by this experience, she resolved to devote her life to the search for a love capable of satisfying the demands of body and soul alike, and to her astonishment she ultimately found it in her relationship with the unsightly hussar.

The two portraits, therefore, show obvious similarities of background, temperament, and aspiration. Both Yelagin and Sosnovskaya are rebels against their biological and social heritage with which their spiritual needs are as incompatible as those of Mitya with the love of Alenka, and in their love for one another they discover the answer to their needs for which Mitya looks in vain to Katya. But from what we know of the laws that govern the world of Bunin's fiction it is clear that they cannot but share his fate. Once more the truth is affirmed that rejection of nature is a rejection of life and that a love based on this rejection, like any other form of degeneracy, can end only in death. Such is the import of the suicide pact—of the decision of the two lovers to seek an eternal refuge and a state of blissful nirvana in a world that lies beyond nature's reach. Their estrangement from life and from all that is "natural" is conveyed by the room in which Sosnovskaya's body is later discovered: "In the right-hand wall of the corridor there was a small entrance leading into the next room which was also quite dark, lit by the sepulchral light of an opal lamp that hung from the ceiling beneath an enormous shade of black silk. All the walls of this completely sealed, windowless room were also covered from top to bottom in something black." The windowless room is the revealing symbol that links Yelagin and Sosnovskaya with the gentleman from San Francisco and the cloistered citizens of Streletsk in **"The Cup of Life."**

It is true that Yelagin, like Emile in **"The Son,"** omits to take the final step, but the similarity goes no further. Indeed, it is plain that in every other respect they are sharply contrasting figures. The murderer of Sosnovskaya experiences no temporary insanity after committing his crime. He fails to fulfill his promise, in his own words, because he "simply forgot about it." He concludes his statement: "I could not but keep the promise I gave her that after killing her I would kill myself, but I was overwhelmed by complete indifference. . . . And with the same indifference I now regard the fact that I am alive." Yelagin's crime is not intended to signify, like Emile's, a dramatic confrontation with an unsuspected reality. It is an expression of his conscious renunciation of life. It is entirely consistent, therefore, that having killed the one person in whom he found an escape from life he should remain totally indifferent to his continuing existence.

The differences between the two murderers are paralleled by equally salient differences between their victims, for although they meet death in an identical manner, the superficial similarity conceals a fundamental contrast. Mme Marot is no rebel against nature. On the contrary, her death is an allegory of her complete submission, of her victory over the final impediment to her reintegration with nature. Hence the contrast between the symbolic lightness of the death scene in

"The Son" and the oppressive gloom in which death comes to Sosnovskaya. Diametrically opposed attitudes to nature are symbolically represented by two identical forms of death, the first of which signifies surrender, and the second rejection. The only really significant feature the dénouements of the two works have in common is that neither can prevail on the reader to suspend his disbelief, and the evidence suggests that Bunin was aware of the fact. (pp. 195-206)

James B. Woodward, in his Ivan Bunin: A Study of His Fiction, *The University of North Carolina Press, 1980, 275 p.*

THOMAS GAITON MARULLO   (essay date 1981)

[*In the following excerpt, Marullo compares the character Sokolovich from Bunin's short story "Petlistye ushi," with Raskol'nikov in Fëdor Dostoevski's* Crime and Punishment, *postulating that Bunin intended to parody Dostoevski's novel.*]

Although Bunin often lashed out at many of the great artists of Russian literature, he was so disturbed by Dostoevskii and *Crime and Punishment* in particular that he attacked both the writer and his work in a short story entitled **"Loopy Ears"** (**"Petlistye ushi"**) written in 1917. Here, Bunin corrupts the image of Raskol'nikov in Adam Sokolovich who, as another "extraordinary man," also pursues nihilism as a life style, but, unlike Dostoevskii's hero, murders the prostitute, Korol'kova, without remorse.

Bunin's innovations in **"Loopy Ears"** are important for two reasons. First, they refute the traditional claim that Bunin's fiction concluded the classical tradition of Russian realism. Critics have maintained that Bunin's prose consummates a heritage in which the *prokliatye voprosy* or "damned questions of life" are treated with delicacy and restraint and that his aesthetic outlook is rooted in a world order which is clearly perceived by the mind. Moreover, these critics maintain that since Bunin repudiated modernism in art, he was the last *aristokrat*-practitioner of the aesthetic elitism of Pushkin, Goncharov, Aksakov, and Tolstoi and the only "Classicist" in Russian prose between the twilight of imperial Russia and the dawn of the Soviet state. Second, Bunin's experimentation in **"Loopy Ears"** bears out recent analyses of his fiction which hypothesize that, theoretically and artistically, Bunin was close to Russian writers of the Decadence and of the Silver Age and that, within these bounds, he was redirecting the focus of his fiction away from "realistic" portrayals of Russian life to the metaphysical problems of love, evil, and the psyche.

In **"Loopy Ears,"** Bunin looked to the content and method of Russian avant-garde culture to polemicize with Dostoevskii in *Crime and Punishment* and, in so doing, to dramatize the psychology and passions of a Raskol'nikov of the early twentieth century. Bunin liberated Sokolovich from the spiritual positivism of the past and showed him as indifferent to the moral dilemma which had tormented his prototypes in fiction. Much like Blok, Belyi, and Bal'mont, Bunin updated the backdrop of St. Petersburg, bypassing the traditional themes of urban injustice and insensitivity to focus upon a universe intrinsically hostile to mankind, embroiled in war, and devoid of morality and meaning. **"Loopy Ears"** can be seen as Bunin's conscious effort to experiment in the Modernist mode and to take his place among the literary innovators of the age. The work is indicative of the transition of the Rus-

sian short story from the "urban" realism of the nineteenth century to the avantgarde innovations of the twentieth.

Bunin ostensibly structures **"Loopy Ears"** on motifs associated with *Crime and Punishment* as well as those of the urban fiction of Gogol' and the writers of the Natural School: sordid taverns, seedy prostitutes, and the strident dissonance characteristic of Nevskii Prospekt. In reality, however, Bunin exaggerates select features of "Petersburg" literature, creating an essentially "Goya-esque" vision of his milieu. Events in *Crime and Punishment* often transpire in a setting that is the projection of a disoriented mind; the events of **"Loopy Ears"** take place in a world that is destined for catastrophe. In this, Bunin adheres to the dichotomy of *roi/stroi* or "chaos/order" advanced by the Modernists. This use of dichotomy is an appropriate choice of literary technique because the demise of "historic Russia" as Bunin had known it led him to believe that just beneath the surface of reality lurked dark forces that came to the fore in passion, revolution, war, the passage of time, and, ultimately, death. For Bunin, the past and its traditions were gone. Moral and social categories had become meaningless, and humankind, already deranged, hovered precariously at the edge of the abyss. Bunin sensed that Russia had passed from the "golden iconostasis of sunset" to the pagan chaos of night. As the Modernists were doing in their urban writings, Bunin presented St. Petersburg as a primordial inferno through which evil threatened to surge and engulf society. In a world in which reason had been replaced by madness, clarity by opaqueness, and substance by shadow, Bunin saw as anachronistic the carnival-like irreverence of Gogol''s urban tales or the Pauline mysticism of Dostoevskii's. Bunin was able to celebrate the city, as he had earlier extolled the Russian village, only by singing its requiem. Structurally, **"Loopy Ears"** can best be understood as a liturgy in which symbols do not represent life so much as they actually replace the tangible realities of man, his values, and his universe.

Adam Sokolovich initially conforms to the archetype of the gifted *raznochinets* or "déclassé" in Russian fiction. As Raskol'nikov had been, he is distant, indifferent to the fanfare of Nevskii Prospekt, and preoccupied with both personal and social concerns. Bunin, however, updates this "type" by paring away the copious details which have gathered about the *raznochinets* in fiction and by using the naked image as the key component of his characterization. These stark sketches resemble the manner of Belyi and Zamiatin with whom Bunin shares the belief that a few bold but suggestive features are sufficient. Whereas Dostoevskii's Raskol'nikov is a "strikingly handsome man with splendid dark eyes, brown hair, and a slender well-knit figure, taller than average," Bunin's Sokolovich is "unusually tall, thin and gangly, long-legged and with huge feet, with a freshly shaven mouth and a yellowish rather coarse trimming about his powerfully developed lower jaw."

Bunin brings Sokolovich into focus by using allusive detail and by positioning his hero strategically amidst the swirling chaos of Nevskii Prospekt. References to Sokolovich's height, stolidity, and gloomy countenance isolate him from the mob and induce fear and revulsion in onlookers. Sokolovich himself likens his "loopy ears" to a hangman's noose (*petlia*) and sports a tattoo depicting a Japanese dragon. Bunin thus precludes a Raskol'nikov-like resurrection for Sokolovich by marking his hero with a Scythian motif of darkness and destruction.

To underscore Sokolovich's estrangement from his world, Bunin exploits names and his hero's vocation as a sailor. Sokolovich refers to himself as *vyrodok;* he is, like Raskol'nikov, an individual who has "stepped apart" from his race and its values. Raskol'nikov's name and his position as a student imply that the human struggle between good and evil is alive and continuous; the tag of Bunin's hero casts him as a prototype of man locked outside of Eden. As Adam he recalls the sinful father of "mankind"; as Sokolovich, he evokes the image of a *sokol* or "falcon," intimating that he has striven for the ideal, but, like Icarus, has perished in the attempt. As a "former sailor," Sokolovich can be used by Bunin to affirm the complexities of human nature. In him, Bunin momentarily suppresses his own fascination for travel and exotic civilizations and, disgusted with a world at war, has Sokolovich express only his weariness with life and his anger at what he perceives to be the duplicity of human culture.

Further in keeping with Babel', Blok, and Belyi who looked to the Russian avant-garde theater for the aesthetic performance of their characters, Bunin defines his hero primarily through mime and gesture. Unlike Raskol'nikov who often unabashedly and carelessly pitted his theories and wits against Porfirii and others, Sokolovich calculates his every stance and projects a disconcerting finality about matters of life and death by his measured stride and speech, low, "thick" voice, slowly moving jaw, and quiet sucking of his pipe. Sokolovich's prolonged stares and concentrated facial expressions and the grim solemnity of his pronouncements reflect what critics have seen as problematic in Bunin himself: author and character perceived their world with vision which is clear but cold, candid but callous.

In addition to allusive detail and theatrical gestures, Bunin uses setting to highlight the plight of his hero. At the beginning of **"Loopy Ears"** the backdrop of a crowded, dingy tavern provides no more hope or inspiration for Sokolovich than such a setting initially did for Raskol'nikov. But Dostoevskii had the tavern serve as a battleground in which Raskil'nikov contested his "ideas" with Porfirii and ultimately came to terms with his wrongdoing. Bunin situates Sokolovich in a setting which suggests only apocalyptic motifs about the end of Russia: a flashing advertisement of fops with foaming mugs of beer suggests a decadent resignation to the chaos of life; the image of a "squat, roundheaded Tatar" reinforces the Scythian idea of the realignment of Russia with Asia; a billiard room in which men armed with cue sticks are made "headless" by rising cigarette smoke hints at the carnage of battle; gusts of icy, damp winds forebode the dissolution of all matter.

In **"Loopy Ears"** Sokolovich is given the role of a *raisonneur* or "spokesman" for Bunin's thoughts on life. In contrast to the *raisonneur* of classical drama, however, Sokolovich does not resolve dilemmas rationally. Instead, his rootlessness and anger at life cast him as a perverted prophet who, rather than working to reform mankind, only serves it with final warning. Sokolovich's pronouncements lack the seductive logic of Raskol'nikov's hopes for "extraordinary men" in that they do not deny human reason so much as they capitulate to a historical fatalism governed by surgings of primordial madness and cruelty. Sokolovich's conversation with "nonbelievers" lacks the moral force of a Socratic dialogue and seems ineffectual, like a "night conversation" of pagans awaiting the coming of dawn.

Momentarily expanding upon his polemic with Dostoevskii, Bunin has Sokolovich articulate his reflections beginning with an incident reminiscent of a scene from *The Idiot*. The meaningless banter of sailors is abruptly replaced by a collective unburdening of guilt and by a commentary upon the sinfulness of man. Warped by despair, Sokolovich's pronouncements recall the distorted thinking of Raskol'nikov and other of Dostoevskii's "demons." In Sokolovich's view, civilization has been built upon the bones of men. Man's callousness leaves him oblivious to the evil of war. Gorillas have evolved further than their human counterparts by abandoning pretenses to social justice and morality:

> Gorillas have long since left man; they have long ago lost their naïveté—since the time man built Babylon on the site of their so-called paradise. Gorillas have never had Assyrian kings, nor Caesars, nor inquisitors, nor the discovery of America, nor kings who signed death warrants with cigars in their mouths, nor the inventor of the submarine which sends to the bottom several thousand men at a time.

Sokolovich's nihilism implies three important elements of Bunin's world view. First, Sokolovich does not deny the past so much as the oral and written traditions which supposedly safeguard the memory of historical events. In a world crazed by war, the "golden letters" of myth, epic, and the Bible no longer engender in Bunin a love of life or creative impulses. They seem, rather, to belong in the same class as the garish advertising and police records which chronicle human savagery and sensuality. Second, having disavowed history, Sokolovich disclaims spatial, temporal, and religious referents. He functions in a timeless present, without heritage or dreams. Finally, Sokolovich rejects all recourse to higher moral authority. The story of Lazarus gave Raskol'nikov cause for hope; for Sokolovich the New Testament merely reaffirms the image of a vengeful God at odds with recalcitrant man. Sokolovich contends that the bombing of Nazareth cancels the hope for redemption and, echoing Bunin's views, that the healing love of Christ ill suits the "cheap" novels of Dostoevskii. Accordingly, Sokolovich fashions himself as a new "son of man" who, spurning the promises of salvation history, seeks to deepen the wedge between man and his creator.

As self-styled "extraordinary men," Sokolovich and Raskol'nikov are initially in accord in that they reject conventional forms of depravity. Unlike their comrades, they engage neither in drunkenness nor in boasting about misdemeanors. They disavow exclusively sociological explanations of crime, claiming that "murderers, wanderers, and generals are men who experience life metaphysically, who are burdened by a sense of death, and, who commit crimes which are premeditated and induced by atavism, accumulated hatred, or the need to test "ideas." Bunin repudiates Dostoevskii's belief that wrongdoing arises from twisted intellectuality, however, when he has Sokolovich assert that the "thirst for blood" is endemic to mankind and that depravity in fact affords cathartic "relief" for the pent-up passions of man. (pp. 614-20)

As Raskol'nikov had done, Sokolovich tests his nihilism by committing murder; but Dostoevskii used the prostitute Sonia to effect renewal in his hero, while Bunin uses the streetwalker Korol'kova to reenforce Sokolovich's theories. (p. 621)

In his portrait of Korol'kova, Bunin intentionally suggests parallels to Dostoevskii's Sonia. Korol'kova's frailty and slight stature bespeak a Sonia-like innocence abused by lust and life. Almost immediately, however, Bunin dissociates Korol'kova from Dostoevskii's heroine by emphasizing that, like Sokolovich, Korol'kova is crass and depraved. For instance, Korol'kova resembles a "bat" in her tiny face, wide cheekbones, and dark, piercing eyes. In contrast to Sonia, Korol'kova does not penetrate her lover's isolation. Her attempts at femininity are awkward and pathetic, confined to feigned shudders and attempts at snuggling. Her conversation with Sokolovich never rises above topics such as cigarettes and money. The details which surround Korol'kova similarly belie genuine equality. Sokolovich calls her a "lady." Her nickname is Korol'ka or "Queenie." Her artificiality is made further apparent by the glass cherries which trim her hat, the hard, unripe grapes which have been ordered for her, and the false silver piece with which she has been paid in advance.

In further contrast to Sonia, Korol'kova wants only to die. Bunin so manipulates this attitude that her liaison with Sokolovich is threatening and funereal. Thus, while Sonia's love for Raskol'nikov arises in part from her belief in an afterlife, Korol'kova's attraction for Sokolovich's *bezobrazie* is a thematic detail which allows Bunin to insinuate that his hero is like death, ugly and formless. Significantly, Bunin uses the setting to dramatize the dichotomous "loves" between the couples. Sonia confronts Raskol'nikov with his wrongdoing in a room which bespeaks the potential for reconciliation and healing: it is bright, airy, irregularly shaped, and overlooking a river. The scene of the liaison in **"Loopy Ears,"** however, carries a sensual impression of annihilation. The room is "warm, stuffy, and sweet-smelling." Its windows, however, are barricaded by roofs and construction, and the bright torches and confused sounds of men and machines involved in sewage disposal produce a Modernist's rendition of hell. In depicting the physical actions of Sokolovich and Korol'kova, Bunin forgoes even the slightest hints of intimacy, subordinating this potentially human act to the fact that the room "has been shrouded in mystery."

Lacking recourse to Dostoevskii's spirituality, Bunin resolves the dilemma of his characters in death. The portrayal of the murdered Korol'kova recalls the sinister requiem of Natal'ia Filipovna of *The Idiot*. Yet, Prince Myshkin and Rogozhin attend to Filipovna; only shadows dance about Korol'kova. Moreover, Bunin again uses images of headless torsos and protruding legs to comment upon the ultimate dehumanization of his heroine, Korol'kova. Bunin writes in the last scene of **"Loopy Ears":**

> The room was ominously quiet, not as if a sleeping person were there. The candles, nearly burnt out, crackled in the broken candle-rings. Shadows flitted in the gloom, but on the bed, a woman lay supine, her short naked legs protruding from under the blanket. She had been suffocated by two pillows.

Sokolovich experiences neither horror nor remorse at his wrongdoing. No details of the murder or of Sokolovich's immediate reactions are given, and Bunin uses a span of several hours to distance the criminal emotionally from the crime and the reader from them both. Far from parading the validity of his "ideas" as Raskol'nikov might have done, Bunin's hero, reversing Dostoevskii's motif, greets the dawn with cold neutrality, taking his place among the faceless, sleepy workers of the early-rising city. Unchallenged by the agape

of Sonia or the reaction of Porfirii, Sokolovich is unshackled by moral constraints and, in Bunin's view at least, is a genuine "hero of his time."

Bunin's vision of St. Petersburg is initially like that of *Crime and Punishment:* Sokolovich's journeys up and down Nevskii Prospekt bring to mind details and incidents of Raskol'nikov's adventures in the capital and project Bunin's own dissatisfaction with life onto the environment. Both Sokolovich and Raskol'nikov pursue a course logged with careful references to time and space. Sokolovich, as his predecessor had done, charts his own trail of death and destruction, passing by such landmarks as Nikolaevskii Station, Anichkov Bridge, and the City Duma. Bunin's St. Petersburg also perpetuates the insensitivity and suffering of the setting in Dostoevskii's novel. Sokolovich and Raskol'nikov are so preoccupied with their respective philosophies that they are oblivious to the jostling crowds which, ironically, have given rise to their "ideas." When Sokolovich sees a mistreated horse and an old man crushed by an onrushing carriage, the scenes recall Raskol'nikov's first dream and the death of Marmeladov. Significantly, the victim of the carriage accident in **"Loopy Ears"** is an aged writer, which may be Bunin's unflattering, if perverse, epitaph for both Dostoevskii and his world view.

Bunin's portrayal of St. Petersburg, however, departs radically from the setting in *Crime and Punishment* in two ways. First, Bunin does not follow Dostoevskii in mitigating urban misery with periodic human kindness and decency. In contrast to Raskol'nikov, Sokolovich neither carries the crushed man to his family, nor saves half-dressed waifs from lechers, nor throws money about wildly to help suffering mankind. Sokolovich prefers to leave the dirt at his feet, rather than kiss it at the crossroads. Second, Bunin's urban culture is revealingly devoid of the filth, noise, and smells which greeted Raskol'nikov in his travels and, more important, of the intense heat and suffocation which suggested his neurotic projection upon his milieu. Close inspection reveals that Bunin reduces St. Petersburg to a state of suspended animation, that is, to a terrifying intermediate phase in the passage of reality from the *stroi* or "order" of physical existence to the *roi* or "chaos" of internal life forces. The urban details of **"Loopy Ears"** become caught in a *potok* or "swirl" whose quickening vortex draws man and matter into its downward plunge. Motifs of movement, images of smog and smoke, and monochromatic colors obscure real life and vividly suggest that existence, racked by passion and war, responds more to Bunin's world view than to Dostoevskii's.

The portrayal of St. Petersburg thus frames and amplifies Sokolovich's pessimism. **"Loopy Ears"** opens with a scene in which circles and arcs inscribed by traffic blur the city's renowned angularity; a funeral procession with a starkly yellow coffin suggests the supremacy of death. Rendering the background formless and casting images of light and darkness against it, Bunin reduces St. Petersburg to a polar outpost, devoid of substance and life. Snow, ice, and artificial lighting contrast sharply with the darkness of night, intensifying it. A snowy barge stands adrift in murky waters. Frosty moustaches and beards, recalling Suzdalian icons, attract attention to otherwise dark and shadowy figures. The illumination of electric street lamps and lighted shop windows fail to penetrate the gloom. Harking back to Gogol's work, "The Nose," Bunin has the fog merge with steam from horses' nostrils and cigarette smoke to cloud further the clarity of urban realism.

To make matters worse, Bunin invests the polar metropolis with details intimating carnage and ruin. Accordingly, St. Petersburg in **"Loopy Ears"** no longer bears witness to the long-hailed geometry of its *stroi* or external plan, but capitulates to the encroaching *roi,* as a city gone mad with the corruption of the universe. Reinforcing the earlier thematic detail of "headless" billiard players, Bunin has the Cathedral of Our Lady of Kazan' appear "decapitated" in the fog and gloom. The tower of the City Duma, conceivably a symbol of reason, law, and order, seems monstrous with only the "red eye" of its clock piercing the night. Departing trains, in Bunin's fiction a motif of chaos and destruction, transport this corruption and inhumanity throughout the virginal depths of Russia. The familiar Nevskii Prospekt, no longer the center of Gogolian carnivality, infects Sokolovich with its sterile eeriness and portends ruin for the urban milieu. Bunin writes:

> Sokolovich slowed his steps and looked for a long time . . . there, where in the icy murk of the enormous flow which Nevskii seemed, an endless chain of wine-red tram lights disappeared into the distance and greenish summer lightning flashed forth. His large face grew savage in its concentration. . . . At night Nevskii is terrible in the fog. It is uninhabited, dead and the gloom which beclouds it seems part of the arctic gloom from which it has come. . . . The middle of this murky flow is lighted from above only by the whitish light of electric lamps.

Bunin in **"Loopy Ears"** thus exploited the world view of modernism to take issue with Dostoevskii in *Crime and Punishment* and to put forth an "extraordinary" man in keeping with the character and currents of Russia of the early twentieth century. Adam Sokolovich logically extends Raskol'nikov's misguided thinking: he, too, is a "metaphysical rebel," who, unlike his predecessor, experiences neither recrimination nor remorse for his crime. Within this framework, Bunin submits the "effects" of *Crime and Punishment* to radical scrutiny and change. Sokolovich rejoins society, neither better nor worse for his wrongdoing. Korol'kova, already condemned, falls victim more to her lover's philosophy than his passion. St. Petersburg reflects more graphically its coldness and cruelty. Absent from the setting in **"Loopy Ears"** are the caring friends and family or the crossroads, rivers, and large rooms which brought salvation to Raskol'nikov; without these, the city is judged by Bunin to be a polar outpost caught within the dichotomy of *roi/stroi* as advanced by the Modernists. Bunin's innovations in **"Loopy Ears"** belie those analyses which grouped him with the so-called "classical" tradition of Russian literature, and they link him to those writers who were redirecting the Russian short story from the urban realism of the nineteenth century to the modernistic probings of the twentieth. (pp. 621-24)

> *Thomas Gaiton Marullo, "Crime without Punishment: Ivan Bunin's 'Loopy Ears'," in Slavic Review, Vol. 40, No. 4, Winter, 1981, pp. 614-24.*

JULIAN W. CONNOLLY (essay date 1982)

[*Connolly is an American essayist and academic of slavic languages and literature. In the following excerpt from his critical biography of Bunin, he characterizes Bunin's short story collection* Dark Avenues.]

As one reads **Dark Avenues,** it seems that the entire order of human life conspires against the possibility of finding lasting joy in love. The Russian Revolution intervenes to keep two lovers apart in **"Tania"** [**"Tanya,"** 1940]; the possessiveness of an emotionally distraught woman drives her daughter's lover from the house in **"Rusia"** [**"Rusya,"** 1940]; and an avaricious father sends his son away from home to thwart his growing affection for a governess in **"Voron"** [**"The Raven,"** 1944]. Significantly, the lovers in these stories are unable or unwilling to combat the forces which oppose their happiness. In some respects, Bunin's heroes recall the weaker characters in Turgenev's works (the narrator of **"Natalie,"** for example, has been compared to Sanin in "Veshnie vody" ["Spring Torrents"]), but Bunin devotes so little attention to his characters' flaws that their failure to fight for their happiness seems less the result of a specific character weakness than a symptom of a general condition prevailing in the world at large. Life is ordered in such a way that struggle is simply unthinkable. Bunin evidently believes that intransigent forces rule human destiny, not the will of individuals themselves.

Some characters in **Dark Avenues** seem conscious of the impossibility of achieving permanent happiness. In **"Kacheli"** [**"The Swing,"** 1945], for example, Bunin describes a young couple spending an evening together in the country. As the boy remarks on the beauty of the moment, his companion makes a curious reply: "Yes, it seems to me that there won't be anything in my life happier than this evening . . ."; as the sketch ends, she declares once more, "There won't be anything better." No explanation is given for her somber view of the future; she simply senses intuitively that for her happiness comes but once in life, and for only a brief moment at that.

If brevity is a central characteristic of earthly love in Bunin's work, another key feature is the unexpectedness of its appearance. Indeed, the phrase "unexpected happiness" recurs as a refrain in **Dark Avenues. "Tanya,"** for example, vividly illustrates the enigmatic irruption of love into life. Tanya, a maid on a country estate, is seduced as she sleeps by a young visitor. Upon waking, she begins to cry, while he, "with a feeling not only of animal gratitude for that unexpected happiness which she had unconsciously given him, but also of ecstasy and love, began to kiss her on the neck and breast." Now she too feels a sudden rush of warmth: "Who he was, she still did not understand in her half-sleep, but it didn't matter—this was he, with whom she . . . was meant to be united for the first time in the most secret and blissfully mortal intimacy." Both individuals are so overwhelmed by this unexpected event that they become ardent lovers. Now, however, the stern law of love's inevitable termination comes into play, and their last separation, though ostensibly brief, becomes permanent. The final lines of the story explain why: "This occurred in February of that terrible year 1917. He was then in the country for the last time in his life." Frequently in the cycle, the final lines of the story unveil a sudden denouement that transforms one's perception of the preceding events and charges them with new meaning. Through such unpredictable shifts as this Bunin highlights the irrational nature of human existence itself.

As if to underscore the fact that romance, like life itself, follows unexpected paths, Bunin sometimes suggests how a relationship *might* develop, only to refute this projection with the actual event. In **"Antigona"** [**"Antigone,"** 1940], for example, he contrasts the fantasies of a student about a romance with his uncle's nurse with a very different reality. Upon first catching sight of the young woman, the hero begins to dream of their future relationship: "to stay here for a month, two months, enter into a friendship and intimacy with her . . . evoke her love, and then say—be my wife, I am forever yours." He anticipates the objections of his relatives: "persuasion, shouts, tears, curses, the loss of my inheritance—all of this will be nothing to me for your sake." This hackneyed melodrama, however, is not to be. The next day he meets the nurse in the study, they converse, and suddenly make love: his imagined months of courtship are telescoped here into a few minutes. Yet once again, just as quickly as happiness is found, it is lost. After a single night of love, their intimacy is discovered, and the nurse leaves the house. Despite his intention to renounce all for the sake of love, the youth instead watches her depart, overcome with despair. Again, Bunin does not indicate that the boy's inaction results from a particular weakness of character; he merely acquiesces to the implacable forces of fate.

For the most part the protagonists in **Dark Avenues** are ordinary, often nameless individuals, referred to merely as "he" or "she" or identified by such conventional designations as "student," "artist," and "officer," with little or no background history. This lack of background information derives from Bunin's tendency in the cycle to pare his work to a minimum of narrative detail, but it also underscores the magnitude of the impact produced by the onset of passion in his characters' lives. When passion strikes they leave their nondescript existences behind and become transformed into exceptional figures entirely galvanized by their emotions.

An example of this effect occurs in the story **"Vizitnye kartochki"** [**"Calling Cards,"** 1940], where, as in **"Sunstroke,"** a man and a woman meet on a steamer for a brief moment of passion. The prevailing perspective is also that of the male, here a noted writer, but the female character is developed much more fully than in the earlier work. Like the woman in the sketch **"In Autumn,"** she confesses to a loveless marriage, and expresses regret that life has passed her by: "I have experienced nothing, nothing in my life!" She seizes upon this chance encounter to experience the ecstasy of unsuppressed passion, "to utilize boldly to the limit all that unexpected happiness which had suddenly fallen to her lot." He, stirred initially by the thought of a casual tryst, finds in this relationship something more than physical gratification. As so often happens in Bunin's work, the flame of mutual passion burns away the dross of conventional feeling and forges a new, more extraordinary emotion. Thus, as he accompanies her to the gangway where she will disembark, he kisses her hand, not with ritual politeness, but "with that love which remains somewhere in the heart for a lifetime." Bunin does not condemn the two for their unrestrained desire; on the contrary, their mutual ardor has elevated them above the mundane routines of ordinary society.

Bunin was on occasion reproached for the open sensuality of certain works in **Dark Avenues,** but he offers a rebuttal to such criticism in the words of the male protagonist of **"Heinrich,"** himself a writer. Speaking of the "divine and demonic" web of sexual temptation, Bunin's character exclaims: "When I write about it, try to express it, they accuse me of shamelessness, of base motives. . . . Vulgar souls! It is stated well in one old book: 'An author has just as much right to be bold in his verbal depictions of love and its faces as has been granted . . . to painters and sculptors in all ages: only vulgar souls see something vulgar even in the beautiful or the horrible." Sensuality and eroticism are scarcely new to litera-

ture, and for the most part, Bunin utilizes these elements sensitively to suggest the powerful impulses that rule over human existence.

As **"Calling Cards"** indicates, these impulses affect women with as much strength as men in Bunin's work. Indeed, although frequently the reader perceives events through the eyes of male protagonists, the women are often the most energetic characters in a tale, and the men seem quite pale by comparison. Thus, the first-person narrator of **"Muza"** is startled one day by the title character who enters his Moscow room and announces her intention to make his acquaintance. They soon become lovers and move to his estate in the country where, several months later, she leaves his life as suddenly as she had entered it, taking up residence with a nondescript neighbor. The title figure of **"Galya Ganskaya"** is an equally impulsive girl, beautiful and lively, who commits suicide without warning when she discovers that her lover is apparently not as committed to their love as she.

Finally, of all the characters in **Dark Avenues,** perhaps the most complex and enigmatic is the female protagonist of **"Chistyi ponedel'nik"** [**"The First Monday in Lent,"** 1944]. At the outset of the tale her attention is divided between the enjoyment of material pleasures and the contemplation of such things as graveyards and religious rites. After her first night of sexual intimacy with the man who loves her, she ends the relationship and decides to take religious vows. In her contradictory actions one perceives a late reflection of that dichotomy explored by Bunin in **"Night."** Having enjoyed all the pleasures of the secular world, she decides to spurn life's empty distractions and enter upon a path of renunciation and peace. In such characters one senses the writer's admiration for the uncommon breadth of the human soul.

The immutable laws of love—its unexpected onset, its physical evanescence, its sudden disappearance—operate at all stages of human life, in middle age as well as in youth. In fact, in the story **"In Paris"** these fundamental rules take on a special poignancy as they affect the lives of middle-aged Russian émigrés, for, unlike the ardent youths of Bunin's work, they had long since ceased to expect any happiness in their lives. The two are drawn together by a lifetime of hardship and suffering, and their chance acquaintance in late autumn quickly blossoms into deep affection. After they spend a night together, she moves into his apartment, and their love seems to rejuvenate them: "I feel as though I were twenty years old" he says. In the very next paragraph, however, the reader learns that "on the third day of Easter he died in a subway car." Once more, a newfound joy is cruelly extinguished even before it has been fully savored. The anguish the woman feels is immense. As she returns from the cemetery, on "a charming spring day," "everything spoke of young life, eternal life—and of her life, finished." The autumn setting of their first meeting was perhaps a sign that they were in the autumn of their lives; now the spring landscape seems to bear this out—though nature is renewed, the couple's happiness is at an end.

"In Paris" lays bare the pathos of human existence. Filled with chance encounters, its allocation of happiness and sorrow defies rational understanding. Clearly, the basic contradiction expressed earlier in Bunin's work still obtains: although life offers great joy, the passage of time and the inevitability of death also undermine it. This sense of the inevitability of death leads some critics to regard Bunin's vision of love as nihilistic. Temira Pachmuss, summarizing Zinaida

Gippius's view of Bunin, has written: "For Bunin, love is a fleeting, evanescent feeling which cannot endure. Death, which takes away and obliterates everything, is the only true reality. Thus nothing is worth emotional involvement. Human life is devoid of meaning, for everything will eventually turn to dust."

While the first part of this statement has some validity, one may dispute the conclusion, at least as it applies to *Dark Avenues.* "Natalie," which depicts both the darkness and the radiance of human love, will illustrate this point. In the first part of the story, a narrator describes an unusual summer of romance at a relative's country estate. Searching for "love without romance," the narrator enters into a casual relationship with his cousin Sonya. Gradually, however, when he finds himself falling in love with Sonya's friend Natalie, he is torn between his physical passion for Sonya and the "pure ecstasy" of his love for Natalie. Unable to bear the strain, he decides to leave, but just at that moment Natalie unexpectedly avows her love for him. It appears, then, that all he need do is end his liaison with Sonya. In the climactic scene that follows, however, his vision of bliss collapses. As he returns to his room, a great thunderstorm breaks out, as if by its fury to discharge the powerful tensions built up over the course of the summer. Sonya is waiting for him in his room and passionately pulls him down onto the sofa at the moment Natalie appears in the doorway. She turns and flees, taking the narrator's dream of happiness with her.

The second part of the story describes a similar sequence of fleeting joy followed by pain. Natalie and the narrator are reunited after years of separation, and she declares that "you are again with me, and now forever." Yet this dream, too, is destroyed in the final lines of the story: "In December she died on Lake Geneva in premature childbirth."

It is not difficult to see here how one might conclude after reading **"Natalie"** that, because of death, "nothing is worth emotional involvement." Yet Bunin's own characters forcefully reject this idea. The same Natalie who suffered so much upon discovering the narrator's relationship with Sonya asks him rhetorically: "is there really such a thing as unhappy love? . . . Really, doesn't the most sorrowful music in the world give happiness?" and the narrator later asserts that "there is no unhappy love."

This statement might serve as the epigraph to the entire cycle. Despite the suffering that love may cause, it still illuminates and transforms one's life. Bunin has left behind the anxious formulations of **"Brothers"** and **"The Yelagin Affair,"** in which he showed that human desire inevitably leads to suffering and suggested that renunciation may provide a path to peace. In *Dark Avenues,* renunciation is a path chosen by only a few. The majority of the characters welcome love into their lives without reservation, and even though it may be destroyed by unforeseen forces, the experience of it remains a cherished memory.

Indeed, as the sketch **"Cold Autumn"** indicates, a brief moment of love may be the only bright spot in a cheerless life. The female narrator of this tale relates the story of her life, beginning with her romance with a young man destined to die in World War I. She recalls their last evening together, describing in lingering detail the crisp coolness of the autumn air and the ardor of their love. Then, in a long, dispassionate passage that contrasts vividly with the lyrical descriptions preceding it, the woman describes the difficult passage from

her country estate to a life in emigration, a tale filled with loss, deprivation, and suffering. Then she asks: "What was there in my life anyway? . . . Only that cold autumn evening. . . . The rest is a superfluous dream." As in *The Life of Arsenyev* Bunin suggests that the memory of love, no matter how shortlived that love was, can provide some consolation through years of separation, even hardship. This sketch, like numerous other stories in *Dark Avenues,* describes a love affair that occurred in the past. The frequency of works in which a romance is either recalled for the reader or recounted to others lends the cycle a certain poignancy. Still, through the device of recollection Bunin not only stresses the temporal brevity of love in one's life, he also demonstrates that such an experience has lasting meaning for the people involved.

This is the subject of the cycle's opening story, **"Dark Avenues,"** which depicts a chance meeting between a middle-aged officer and a peasant woman, Nadezhda, who had once been the officer's lover. Unnerved by their encounter at the carriage house she now runs, he minimizes the significance of the affair and his own guilt at having left her years ago: " 'Everything passes, my friend,' he mumbled, 'love, youth—everything, everything'." She, however, refutes him: "Youth passes in everyone, but love—that's a different matter." Again, when he maintains that "Everything passes. Everything is forgotten," she counters, "Everything passes, but not everything is forgotten." Finally he too acknowledges that the affair was an experience of unforgettable depth. Overcome by his memories, he kisses her hand and admits that "I lost in you the most valuable thing I had in life." Of course, the die is already cast, and as he drives away from the house and reflects on his early love, he realizes that its outcome could not have been otherwise because of his own social expectations. Nevertheless, the powerful impact of the reunion is undiminished. Such a love as he experienced in his youth leaves an indelible imprint on the soul.

Nadezhda's declaration that "youth passes in everyone, but love, that's a different matter" renews the affirmation which concludes *The Life of Arsenyev.* While the physical processes of time and death cannot be checked, the memory of love need not die. The very intensity of an emotion creates an indestructible bond that defies both the corrosive effects of time and the ravages of fate. These two elements of love—the transfiguring power of its fervent emotion and the tragic brevity of its realization—combine in *Dark Avenues* to create a subtle but truly impressive balance of moods: several of the stories in the cycle can be counted among the finest of Bunin's career.

Of course, it is not the intensity of human emotion alone that makes the stories in *Dark Avenues* so moving. Bunin compresses his already compact narrative style so far here that many of his stories become models of understatement and allusion. The very conciseness of these works underscores his concept of passion as a shortlived emotional experience. Among the techniques Bunin utilizes to animate his works are dramatic shifts in narrative tempo to convey sudden shifts in the fortunes of life, substandard or colloquial speech patterns in narration (*skaz*) to create special narrative effects (cf. **"Ballada"** [**"A Ballad"**]), and the manipulation of setting and detail to establish broad emotional or psychological moods.

To gain an idea of the way in which Bunin utilizes evocative detail in this cycle, one need only examine his first story, **"Dark Avenues."** The settings and descriptions in this work play an important role in creating atmosphere and conveying emotion. Bunin begins with a description of the "cold, nasty autumn weather" which envelops the officer as he approaches the carriage house. The autumn setting is a resonant image, and its connotations of age, passing time, and approaching death establish a palpable aura around the figure of the officer. Moreover, Bunin places a special emphasis on darkness and dirt in the first scene: "black ruts"; "a tarantass spattered with mud"; "a peasant . . . serious and dark-faced, with a sparse, pitch-black beard." The officer himself is described with dark, dull colors too: his coat is gray and his eyebrows black; only his moustache is white. This last detail serves to point up his age, as do certain others, such as the comment that he bore "a resemblance to Alexander II, which was so widespread among servicemen during his reign." Here Bunin hints not only at the officer's age, but also his aristocratic temperament, his concern with rank and status. Thus, already in the first paragraph the reader obtains a general idea of the protagonist's bearing and psychology, although the author has yet made no mention of his thoughts.

Bunin stresses the darkness and filth of the outside world to create a sharp distinction between it and Nadezhda's world, the character of which is evident in the very first descriptive line: "In the sitting-room it was *warm, dry,* and *tidy*—a *new golden* icon in the left corner, under it was a table covered with a *clean,* plain tablecloth" (emphasis added). When the officer steps into Nadezhda's room, he enters a realm of brightness and purity very different from the dark world in which he has been traveling. Nadezhda herself has something in common with the officer: she too has black eyebrows, and she wears a black skirt. Yet she is also in a red jacket and red slippers, which add a dash of color not found on the officer, and she is compared to an elderly gypsy, in an image that carries a connotation of liveliness not found in the officer's appearance. Significantly, when she addresses the officer by name, he opens his eyes and blushes (in Russian, *pokrasnel,* "reddened"). This sudden reddening is perhaps an external sign of the deeper emotional link established between Nadezhda and him. As the conversation continues, "his tiredness and distraction" disappear, and again he blushes, "reddening through his gray hair." Now it is clear that the emotional atmosphere of Nadezhda's world, in which the fires of love have not died out, has penetrated his cold and aging world. The subsequent conversation verifies this as his declaration, "Everything passes," gives way to his understanding of the true importance of his youthful love for Nadezhda.

Yet the patterns of life are long since set, and the officer must return to the cold world from which he came. Thus, the story's final scene shows him once more on the road. Again one notes the "black ruts," but there is now a new element as well. The sun is setting, and although this detail reinforces the atmosphere of age and approaching death established earlier, the low sun here "shone with a yellow light onto the empty fields." In this touch of subdued color one may detect a last echo of the passionate experience of the past: the faint rays of remembered love still shine in a heart that has grown dark and empty. Then, as if to shut out the troubling emotions roused when Nadezhda first spoke his name and he "opened his eyes," the officer closes his eyes as the story ends. Although one can identify still other evocative details in the story, this brief discussion should suggest the way in which Bunin employs descriptive detail. One critic who has studied this aspect of Bunin's work claims that "allegorical and sym-

bolic generalization turn out to be so important and weighty in Bunin's late work that in certain cases there is formed a distinctive code, without a knowledge of which the work remains unintelligible."

This tendency is evident too in Bunin's handling of geographical settings. Most of the tales in *Dark Avenues* are set in pre-Revolutionary Russia and feature young people in the first flush of romance. On the other hand, when Parisian settings occur, the characters involved are older émigrés. One may regard this as a simple projection of Bunin's own experience, but it also carries further import. When one reads Bunin's tales of young people discovering the joy of love amidst the beauty of a Russian country estate, one is conscious that the era described is itself drawing to an end. This awareness adds poignancy to the picture of actual loss that so often forms the denouement of the tale. Likewise, in Bunin's portraits of émigrés living in France, particularly those who recall the past, as in **"Cold Autumn,"** the tragedy of the loss of love is heightened by the tragedy of the loss of one's homeland; the two modes of loss reinforce each other.

On every level, *Dark Avenues* emerges as a triumphant culmination to an illustrious career. Although the cycle contains many images of loss, death, and shattered romance, the overall impression it produces is neither heavy nor depressing. Rather, the reader shares something of the writer's own feelings of wonder and appreciation at the intense experiences—both joyful and tragic—that illuminate human existence. Seldom in Bunin's work are the vagaries of life so dramatically portrayed, and yet seldom is his fervent love for life so expressively displayed. Among Bunin's readers there will be those who can agree with his own assessment that *Dark Avenues* is "the best and most original thing that I have written in my life." (pp. 125-34)

Julian W. Connolly, in his Ivan Bunin, Twayne
Publishers, 1982, 159 p.

CHARLES ISENBERG   (essay date 1987)

[*In the following excerpt, Isenberg explicates Bunin's short story "Ida."*]

Recent discussions of Ivan Bunin's short story **"Ida"** have centered on the author's use of that old chestnut, the frame-narrative, and on the story's place within the cycle of stories written during the mid-twenties, all of which treat the theme of passionate attraction and its vicissitudes. The present essay continues these concerns, chiefly by considering Pavel Nikolaevič, the intradiegetic frame-narrator, and other qualities in **"Ida"**—including the thematic and structural role of music and a certain ambiguity or instability of tone—which may advance an understanding of it.

The Shape of the Story. The narrative structure of **"Ida"** can be boiled down to the following. In a general exposition the frame-narrator sets the story in an indefinite "once during Christmas" and introduces a party of revelers, who are preparing to feast at the Grand Moscow Restaurant. The party consists of "three old friends" and "a certain Georgij Ivanovič Nikolaevič," who turns out to be a man whose sole occupation is being a friend of famous people in the arts. This evening he serves as the sidekick of Pavel Nikolaevič, a composer, the narrator of the inner text, which concerns a young woman named Ida and "a certain gentleman," who is unquestionably a mask for the composer himself. The composer opens his story with what amounts to a second exposition. Stylized after the opening of a *skazka,* the second exposition uses indefiniteness and reticence to create an ironic distance between the speaker and his tale. It also suggests that Ida's story will have overtones of universality: "Once upon a time, in a certain kingdom, a certain maiden used to visit the house of a certain gentleman. . . . She was waiting, as is the custom, for a bridegroom—and that's all. . . ." The complication of the narrative begins when Ida stops visiting the hero's household. Although he originally fails to notice her absence, he comes to feel it as a lack: "Once in a while he would remember her and would get a feeling that he was lacking something."

At this point the story moves from the gentleman's house to its second location, a well-appointed railway station in a western district, where the hero is detained on a journey by a blizzard. The story's culmination begins when he unexpectedly meets Ida there. She is now married to a wealthy and aristocratic youth, whose student uniform emphasized his subordination to Ida, who has become "unrecognizable," a beautiful grande dame. A further surprise follows. After peremptorily dismissing her boy-husband, she matter-of-factly declares her love for the hero; he himself realizes that he has been in love with her for several years. Recognizing that no words could adequately continue what has been said and understood, Ida answers his silence with a kiss of such intensity that it will be remembered "even in the grave."

After this culminating moment, the story shifts back to the outer text, as the composer abruptly concludes with a call for food and drink and a valedictory toast: "To all those who have loved us, to all those whom—idiots that we are—we didn't know how to appreciate; to those with whom we were blissfully happy and then parted, whom we've lost forever in life but to whom we are nonetheless bound by the most fearful tie in the world!" The story closes with a one-paragraph epilogue that gives the revelers' itinerary for the rest of the night, until the first peal of a monastery bell seems to engender the composer's tearful bellow: "Sun of my life! My love! Hurrah!"

The Appeal to Music. Does it make a difference that Pavel Nikolaevič is a composer, while Ida is from a family of musicians? To begin to answer this question, let us consider the significant role of music in Bunin's art. Bunin himself anticipated his critics by insisting upon the musical structure of his prose:

> The main thing is what I developed in **"The Gentleman from San Francisco"**—the symphonic quality that is inherent in the highest degree in any universal soul. I mean not so much a logical as a musical structuring of prose with changes of rhythm, variations, transitions from one key to another—in short, the kind of counterpoint that Leo Tolstoy, for example, made an attempt to apply in War and Peace: Bolkonsky's death and so on.

Indeed, it is not hard to find in **"Ida"** elements of that "suite construction" (*sjuitnoe postroenie*) that characterize the prose of Bunin, as it does so many of his poet-contemporaries. However, one of the curious features of **"Ida"** is the way in which music as a theme, particularly operatic music, coincides with music in its structuring function; as we shall see, the movement of the text is defined in part by the "musical" motifs that punctuate it. For the reader, these musical instrusions are emanations from the outer text, while for Pavel

Nikolaevič they are chance events which he, as a composer, cannot but turn to account.

Both as a composer and as the author of the Ida-story, Pavel Nikolaevič is also a surrogate for the implicit author of **"Ida,"** a writer influenced by musical composition. The pathetic Georgij Ivanovič, besides serving as a vulgar interlocutor for Pavel Nikolaevič, is also there to draw a tacit connection between creative artists of various kinds, the "*writers* [emphasis added], painters, and performers [Russ, *artisty,* a term which can refer to actors, singers, and musicians generally]" whose company he seeks.

Opera would seem to be an especially congenial reservoir of meaning for Bunin, because of its hybrid nature, combining the recursiveness of symphonic music with the linear movement of narrative. This makes it an appropriate analog for the theme of passion, because in Bunin's prose passion embodies the contradiction between ideal love, tending toward plotlessness and atemporality, and actual love, which, no matter how blissful its present, at least implies a future of change and decay.

Some of the story's operatic qualities are more obvious than others. Most obvious of all are those operatic selections, playing on a gramophone in the next room, that serve as a counterpoint to the story. The gramophone functions as one of Pavel Nikolaevič's interlocutors, prompting his story. This is evident in the machine's first intervention: "In the old room, the machine burst into song tenderly and sadly; it growled reproachfully." These notes of tenderness, sadness, and reproach just precede the beginning of the composer's story, serving as its overture.

The record player also prompts and accompanies Pavel Nikolaevič as he sings two snatches of aria that alternate with his recitativo to hint at what is at stake. The first example comes during the wind-up to Pavel Nikolaevič's story and forms part of his retort to Georgij Ivanovič's insinuation that the company is about to be regaled with an account of an amorous escapade:

> "An amorous story?" He said coldly and mockingly. "Ach, Georgij Ivanovič, Georgij Ivanovič, how will you answer for your sinfulness and your merciless intellect at the Last Judgment? Well, that is your problem. 'Je veux un trésor qui les contient tous, je veux la jeunesse!' " Arching his brows, he sang with the record player, which was playing *Faust,* and went on, addressing us.

This fragment from Gounod's *Faust* both anticipates the "freshness and healthiness of youth" associated with Ida and associates the composer with that Faustian appetite for life which is one register of Bunin's attitude. The aria also introduces the issue of youth and age, which is one of the story's hinges.

The composer's next aria, similarly accompanied, is "Laisse moi, Laisse moi contempler ton visage," also from *Faust.* It comes just at the point when he has surprised his audience with the first mention of Ida's unexpected declaration of love, but before he has told the concluding part of his story. Like the first aria, this musical phrase, no sooner intoned than broken off, has a significance for both the frame and inner narrative. In the outer narrative, it helps Pavel Nikolaevič to master his agitation. It resembles the *Faust* aria also in that it expresses a desire that cannot be fulfilled. In relation to the composer's story, however, both arias give voice to desires—

to possess Ida, to contemplate her face—which went unrecognized by the speaker at the time when their fulfillment, had he but known, *was* possible. In this connection, Ida's phrasing of her declaration as a question ("Did you know, and do you know now, that I loved you for a whole five years and that I still love you?") suggests that indeed he should have known, and that he is thus responsible for the missed opportunity. There is a similarly operatic quality to the interplay between this question and the musical climax that follows: "The machine, which had up to this moment been growling faintly and indistinctly in the distance, suddenly thundered forth heroically, solemnly, and loudly. The composer fell silent and gazed at us with eyes that seemed startled and amazed."

It is suggestive that the music is again described without reference to its text; in its lack of words it forms a counterpoint to the hero's wordless response to Ida's question and then to Pavel Nikolaevič's demand that his companions agree not to add a single further word to his story. The gramophone's final contribution also anticipates **"Ida's"** last wordless musical motif, an effect familiar from Romantic program music and opera (e.g., *Symphonie Fantastique, 1812 Overture, Boris Godunov*), the pealing of the monastery bell, which, answered by the composer's outcry, forms the work's final cadences. (pp. 490-93)

Pavel Nikolaevič. Attempts to come to grips with the ambiguous tone of **"Ida"** have sought to explain it as an effect of the frame-construction in conjunction with the composer's idiosyncrasies. The reader will be struck by the anachronistic quality of **"Ida,"** which is not only a product of the frame but of the pre-Revolutionary setting. The device of the frame is itself a metonymic evocation of classic Russian fiction, e.g., Tolstoj's "After the Ball" or Turgenev's *First Love*. However, the opening phrase, "Once during Christmas," may suggest a more specific allusion to the *svjatočnyj rasskaz* (Christmas tale), a subgenre whose best-known Russian practitioner is Leskov. Following the folk tradition, Leskov's Christmas stories are ghost stories, or at least they have overtones of the supernatural. From this perspective, **"Ida"** too can be thought of as a story of a haunting, if only by a memory that emblematizes an incomprehensible mystery. Moreover, while Pavel Nikolaevič hardly qualifies as a *skaz* narrator, he is apparently from a lower-class (peasant) background and his speech is a self-conscious fusion of high and low styles. To paraphrase Woodward, for example, the frame's good-natured interplay between the composer and his companions, along with "the general air of contentment," to which both Pavel Nikolaevič and the comfortable surroundings contribute, serves to winnow out the story's tragic implications [see excerpt dated 1980]. To this it might be added that the atmosphere of the Moscow restaurant is answered by the atmosphere of the comfortable train station, another instance of an effect of meaning that might by brought under the rubric of "musicality."

All this is persuasive enough, but somewhat general. In *S/Z* Roland Barthes has argued, concerning another frame-narrative, Balzac's "Sarrazine," that the narrator of an inner text is always involved in something like a contractual relationship with his listeners. If we look a bit more closely at Pavel Nikolaevič, perhaps we can discover what is at stake for him in this exchange with his audience and hence why Bunin's story has the shape it does. What I would like to do is first, to explore the consonance between the character of

Pavel Nikolaevič, the kind of story he tells, and the kind of story in which he and his story are embedded, and second, to situate Pavel Nikolaevič and **"Ida"** with respect to the story cycle to which **"Ida"** belongs.

One element of **"Ida's"** referential code that seems important for such a consideration is the significance of social class. The first description of Pavel Nikolaevič notes his "thickset frame" and his "broad peasant face with squinting little eyes"—strongly implying that, for all the "regal ways" he jokingly attributes to himself, Pavel Nikolaevič is from a peasant background. In the light of this physical description, his vitality and aggressiveness (conveyed by such gestures as his threat to assault with a champagne bottle anyone who dares to add a word to his story and his call for enough sherry "to plunge [his] mug into, horns and all" can be construed as peasant traits. As an artist, however, he belongs to Bunin's "aristocracy of talent," and so merits his air of entitlement. All this gains in significance, if we recall that in Bunin's model of the world, the Russian peasant (together with the provincial gentry, which in Bunin's view is scarcely to be distinguished from the peasantry) represents the "quintessential national type" (Woodward). Hence, Pavel Nikolaevič's status is ambiguous in ways that are strategic for Bunin's story, for he joins in one image the peasant and the gentleman as well as the composer and the writer. Interestingly, this duality is echoed in the very communicative status of the tale: the outermost (extradiegetic) narrator is really an undisclosed "I" speaking through a "we" (i.e., the story is presumably told by one of the three friends), and this blurring of agency corresponds to Pavel Nikolaevič's use of the nameless "gentleman" as a mask in the inner narrative.

As one who is both peasant and gentleman, Pavel Nikolaevič is ideally poised to experience and interpret the contradiction between nature and culture inherent in the course of the world for Bunin. This contradiction is figured in the composer's ways of thinking—or not thinking—about Ida. As long as desire is repressed, that is, as long as the gentleman in Pavel Nikolaevič's story is acting according to the dictates of propriety (Ida is his wife's friend) or his art (his habit of retreating to his study to work), his suppressed erotic perceptions of Ida gravitate towards nature: she is a fresh apple (presumably of the Antonovka variety). On the other hand, at the train station, where his wife and his work (the props to repression) are absent, his perception of who Ida has become is translated into language that clearly refers her to the realm of culture: "Ida had become entirely unrecognizable. Somehow she had completely blossomed, in a remarkable way; in the way that some magnificent flower might blossom in a crystal goblet in the most highly distilled water."

The note of extravagant refinement continues through the description of Ida's expensive clothes and culminates in the portrait of the husband who has given her the means to buy them. He is described down to the red moiré lining of his Prussian-style cap. His being not only wealthy but almost too refined, a blueblood bearing "one of the most illustrious Russian surnames," only makes Ida's declaration of love to the composer all the more operatic. Like Tat'jana [in Petr Čajkovskij's opera *Evgenij Onegin*], Ida now belongs to a very different world. But her husband's wealth and standing can only reinforce Pavel Nikolaevič's sense that there is nothing for him to add to Ida's question. The barriers between the world of desire (accessible to men and women as children of nature), and the quotidian world immediately re-establish themselves once the passion is acknowledged. Given his awareness of the aporia between these two realities, it is no wonder that Pavel Nikolaevič is ironic and self-ironic about the forces that keep him grounded in the quotidian. Thus his affectation of folk speech. His use of fairy-tale language is a form of ironic quotation, marking him not as a man of the people but as someone for whom the commonplaces of folklore are on a par with an archaic quasiclerical or quasi-courtly speech, to be used to mock-heroic effect. For example, "I vot, prostjas' s rabami i domočadcami, sel nas gospodin na borzogo konja i poexal" ("And so taking leave of his servants and his dependents, our gentleman mounted a swift steed and departed")—a rather too highfaluting way to signify the start of a train journey. Or consider the orotund "nevziraja na radost' utroby moej" ("regardless of the blissful state of my belly"), which associates a lexically and syntactically bookish coverb with a colloquial sense of the noun *utroba*. But what most condemns him to submit to the proprieties of the educated is his work. It is hardly surprising, then, that in a story about civilization and its discontents, the composer is ambivalent about his labors, which he dismisses as "some sort of nonsense called art [*tvorčestvo*], the devil take it altogether."

Yet art, though it belongs to civilization, is also the only way of redeeming the world of ideal passion. The composer is an artist and an author-surrogate. As such, he is driven to turn his experience into a story, a verbal artwork. A story needs an audience, and if it is in some way a commemorative story, it needs to be told on the right occasion, in this case three Christmases later. Beyond their participation in the feasting and drinking that becomes part of the commemorative ritual, the listeners' profit will be the usual profit of an oral narrative: an entertainment that proposes something about the way the world works.

As for Pavel Nikolaevič, to come to terms with the events he must ascribe a meaning to them, a meaning that will serve as a substitutive satisfaction for the story's significant nonevent: the sexual consummation of a shared passion. Distance is required if this substitution of an interpretative act for a sexual act is to succeed. Besides telling his story at a temporal remove from the experience, Pavel Nikolaevič disclaims his own role in his story by assigning it to another actor, and he adopts a language that makes for ironic distance. His irony is thus not only a response to the contradiction between desire and the decorum of everyday life, it is also a way of sustaining this distance, whose collapse would be as unbearable as its maintenance. Because his linguistic and psycholinguistic devices are just that—devices—the storyteller also needs to exhibit an unusual measure of control over interpretation; otherwise the distancing effects might be lost, and the significance with which he is obsessed would cease to be the obligatory significance. In fact there is an incipient challenge in Georgij Ivanovič's anticipation of what kind of story Pavel Nikolaevič will tell. Pavel Nikolaevič's retort can be variously interpreted. It involves a refusal, perhaps to see the sexual component which is obvious enough in the tale itself, and certainly a refusal to have his story received as a banal anecdote.

The Plot Against Plot. Pavel Nikolaevič's strategy seeks to limit interpretative ambiguity, yet it serves instead to heighten it. The composer's dilemma may serve as a point of departure for linking **"Ida"** with the cycle of explorations to which it belongs. For these five stories represent not only passion as enigmatic but also plot. In a letter of 1911 (quoted by Wood-

ward), Bunin expresses a wish which, on the surface, sounds remarkably like Flaubert's ambition to write a book about absolutely nothing at all: "I would like to write without any form, disregarding literary devices completely. . . . As a matter of fact, all literary devices should be sent to blazes." But in actuality Flaubert's aestheticism, that is, his desire to draw the sharpest distinction between the superior world of art and the degraded world of everyday reality, has little in common with the reasons behind Bunin's impatient utterance. On the contrary, Bunin's frequently expressed impatience with the requirements of plot is linked to a wish to bring art closer to life, or at least to what Slivickaja terms his "cosmic consciousness," his sense of life's boundlessness and inexhaustibility. As has already been mentioned, Bunin's ambivalence about plot is rooted in a contradiction that occupies a central place in his world view: the contradiction between understanding Nature and simply being in Nature. Understanding Nature means narrativizing it—seeing a plot in it—but it entails the suffering that traditionally attends consciousness, the sense of separation from any harmonious whole and a terrible epistemological anxiety in the face of time and death.

Bunin is thus at times in the difficult position of a storyteller who yearns to escape the prison of narrativity—and musical stucture may represent one alternative to the traditional constraints of plot. Indeed, the love stories of the mid-twenties can be viewed as attempted solutions to the problem of plot as Bunin seems to have understood it. The pretext for each story is a female character, who is represented as an enigma to be decoded by the story's hero, and in each case the solution of the enigma will yield some message to the hero about his own place in the world. This message is always conveyed through an experience of passion, which is linked, differently in different stories, to love and death. There is a suggestive symmetry in the arrangement, or grouping, of the stories as they first appear in book form. The first and last stories, *Mitja's Love* and **"The Elagin Affair,"** are by far the longest, giving, as it were, two versions of the full text of passion. As a result, they resemble each other far more than they do the remaining three stories, each of which focuses on a particular moment in the seasons of love. Nevertheless we can learn something about **"Ida"** by bracketing Pavel Nikolaevič with Mitja and Elagin. (pp. 495-99)

The narrator of *Mitja's Love* interprets the hero's behavior as explicable on the basis of natural laws. However, this is an interpretation that only deepens the mystery, since the laws themselves remain inexplicable. The rhetoric of **"The Elagin Affair"** produces a similar effect, only in this case the conflicting plots are represented by different voices. The narrative is modeled on a court report. The narrator/implicit author bases himself in the speeches of the defense attorney, but clearly goes beyond them, appealing to a different jury, the implicit readers. This narrative posture enables him to expose the limitations of plot, by showing that the (murder) "plot" constructed by the prosecutor is false, and that the tie between Sosnovskaja and Elagin cannot be encompassed by a plot. It can only be referred to the workings of mysterious natural forces, elective affinities.

In the two longer stories and in **"Sunstroke"** the youth of the heroes has an important bearing on their actions and understanding. Their love affairs turn out to be perilous rites of passage: Mitja kills himself, Elagin is shattered by his death compact with Sosnovskaja, even the nameless lieutenant of **"Sun-**

stroke" feels himself aged by ten years by his brief encounter. The theme of youth provides a way of situating **"Ida"** within the cycle. For the composer, it is not only Ida who represents youth but also her young husband. In this light, the encounter between the composer's surrogate and the student is an encounter between men in two seasons of love. Pavel Nikolaevič sings of youth as the treasure that contains all. But as one who has long since assimilated the lessons of youth, he immediately recognizes in the student-husband the fateful power of youthful passion. Unlike the young men in this and the other stories, Pavel Nikolaevič has learned to cut his losses. His passions are less urgent and more widely diffused. If he has passed the age of staking everything on a woman, the loss of intensity is at least offset by the pleasures of food, of luxurious comfort, of companionship—and of talking about his experience. Thus from the vantage point of **"Ida,"** it appears that in this group of stories Bunin is not only exploring the dynamics of passion but also of innocence and experience. It is the composer's experience of life, coupled with his mastery of artistic distance, that makes the tolling of the monastery bell not a death knell, but something which is at once both valediction and benediction: "Sun of my life! My love! Hurrah!" (pp. 499-500)

> *Charles Isenberg, "Variations on a Theme: Bunin's 'Ida'," in Slavic and East-European Journal, n.s. Vol. 31, No. 4, Winter, 1987, pp. 490-502.*

FURTHER READING

Connolly, Julian W. "Bunin's 'Petlistye ushi': The Deformation of a Byronic Rebel." *Canadian-American Slavic Studies* 14, No. 1 (Spring 1980): 52-61.

Explores rebel imagery in "Petlistye ushi."

————."Desire and Renunciation: Buddhist Elements in the Prose of Ivan Bunin." *Canadian Slavonic Papers* XXIII, No. 1 (March 1981): 11-20.

Gauges the potential influence of Buddhism on Bunin's writing.

Marullo, Thomas Gaiton. "Bunin's 'Dry Valley': The Russian Novel in Transition from Realism to Modernism." *Forum for Modern Language Studies* XIV, No. 3 (July 1978): 193-207.

Contemplates Bunin's modernist interpretation of traditional portrayals of Russian peasants.

————."Besmirching 'Bezhin Meadow': Ivan Bunin's 'Night Conversation'." *Studies in Twentieth-Century Literature* 9, No. 2 (Spring 1985): 301-21.

Cites Bunin's "Night Conversation" as an important transitional work in the portrayal of peasants in Russian literature.

Odoevtseva, Irina. "Days with Bunin." *Russian Review* 30, No. 2 (April 1971): 111-23 and "Days with Bunin: Part II." *Russian Review* 30, No. 3 (December 1971): 226-39.

Odoevtseva's chronicle of her friendship with Bunin during the late 1940s.

Porter, Richard N. "Bunin's 'A Sunstroke' and Chekhov's 'The Lady with the Dog'." *South Atlantic Bulletin* XLII, No. 4 (November 1977): 51-6.

Compares Bunin's "A Sunstroke" with Chekhov's "The Lady with the Dog," focusing on narrative and thematic elements.

Richards, D. J. "Memory and Time Past: A Theme in the Works of Ivan Bunin." *Forum for Modern Language Studies* VII, No. 2 (April 1971): 158-69.

Relates the importance of the past to Bunin's vision of life.

Struve, Gleb. "The Art of Ivan Bunin." *The Slavonic and East European Review* XI, No. 32 (January 1933): 423-36.

Characterizes ideas expressed in Bunin's prose.

Wehrle, Albert J. "Bunin's Story 'A Son' and the Chambige Case." *Slavic and East European Journal* 27, No. 4 (Winter 1983): 433-39.

Scrutinizes factual sources for Bunin's short story "Syn" ("A Son").

Woodward, James B. "Eros and Nirvana in the Art of Bunin." *The Modern Language Review* 65, No. 3 (July 1970): 576-86.

Interprets Bunin's portrayals and perceptions of love and death.

Zweers, A. F. "The Function of the Theme of Death in the Works of Ivan Bunin." *Russian Literature* VIII, No. 2 (March 1980): 151-65.

Considers the theme of death and its relation to the concept of love in Bunin's short stories.

Mavis Gallant

1922-

Canadian-born short story writer, novelist, nonfiction writer, and dramatist.

Considered an important contemporary fiction writer, Gallant is particularly admired for her finely crafted short stories, most of which have been published in the *New Yorker*. A Canadian who has lived most of her adult life in France, Gallant often depicts the plight of alienated people in unfamiliar and indifferent environments. Much of her writing focuses upon Canadian, American, and English expatriates whose romantic expectations of life in Europe have been upset. Her ability to vividly evoke surroundings and dramatize their effects on individuals is a central aspect of her work. Critics have compared Gallant's fiction to that of Anton Chekhov and Katherine Anne Porter for its detached tone, emotional balance, and profound insight into the human condition.

Gallant was born in Montreal, Quebec. She experienced a difficult childhood, and themes of alienation and loneliness surface frequently in her stories. Her father died early in her youth, and as a consequence, she was shuttled between various residences, eventually being sent to live with a guardian in the United States. Gallant attended numerous schools in both Canada and the United States, completing her high school education in New York. She subsequently returned to Montreal, where in 1944 she became a reporter for the *Montreal Standard*. In 1950, Gallant moved to Europe to write fiction, living in several cities before settling in Paris. The short stories in her first book, *The Other Paris,* explore the theme of dislocation, particularly as experienced by Americans in Europe, and emphasize the way in which society affects individuals. In the title story, for instance, a young American woman travels to Paris anticipating romance and adventure, but finds instead a somber postwar ennui engendered by the Occupation.

The novella *Green Water, Green Sky* examines the destructive relationship between a mother and her daughter, focusing on the latter's deterioration into madness. In this work, Gallant attempts to evoke a childlike view of the world through a disjunctive narrative style, implying that children create their own identities by reacting to the prevailing conditions of their parents' world. In *My Heart Is Broken: Eight Stories and a Short Novel,* Gallant further explores the themes of exile and despair that she developed in her early writing. The frequently analyzed story "Its Image on the Mirror," which is set in Montreal during World War II, explores the rivalrous relationship between sisters Jean and Isobel. The narrator, Jean, has always been envious of her younger, more attractive sibling, who seemed to live an exciting bohemian life. But Jean eventually learns that her impressions of her sister are illusory. When Isobel becomes pregnant and asks for help, Jean relinquishes her jealousy and complies. Gallant's travels in Germany during the early 1960s inspired her to compose several stories about German identity, many of which are included in *The Pegnitz Junction: A Novella and Five Stories.* In this volume, Gallant examines the impact of fascism and World War II on the German people and stresses

the importance of memory. The title piece, "The Pegnitz Junction," described by Gallant as her favorite story and regarded by critics as her most experimental work, centers on a disjointed, dreamlike train journey across Germany taken by a young woman, her lover, and his child. Several critics have interpreted the chaotic trip as symbolic of the uncertain direction of postwar Germany.

From the Fifteenth District: A Novella and Eight Short Stories again focuses upon deracinated characters and the unpredictable nature of memory, but the sense of hopelessness felt by many of Gallant's previous characters is not as prevalent here. In "The Moslem Wife," for example, the title character, a hitherto submissive woman who runs a hotel with her philandering husband, thrives when he abandons her at the outset of World War II. In *Home Truths: Selected Canadian Stories,* which won the 1981 Governor General's Award, Gallant investigates the essence of Canadian identity as it is developed and expressed both in Canada and in Europe. The stories in this collection are divided into three sections: "At Home," "Canadians Abroad," and "Linnet Muir." Critical commentary has often focused on the "Linnet Muir" sequence, which includes stories drawn from the events of Gallant's own life. Linnet Muir is an intelligent, independent young woman who goes to Montreal with little money and few prospects yet is determined to succeed. Like Gallant, Linnet becomes a newspaper reporter, but realizes that the men with whom she works are unwilling to accept her as an equal and that her position in the professional world is tenuous. The "Linnet Muir" sequence and the other stories in *Home Truths* have been widely praised for Gallant's perceptive portrayal of individuals adrift in confusing, rootless lives.

Gallant is an important contemporary writer whose international reputation developed after years of relative critical neglect, especially in her native Canada. Her significance derives largely from her short stories, which usually portray exiles vainly attempting to find happiness and freedom in unfamiliar settings. Although some critics have complained that Gallant's fiction is relentlessly pessimistic and emotionally cold, others have lauded her work for its understated irony, precise attention to detail, and penetrating insight into the human condition.

(For further information on Gallant's life and career, see *Contemporary Literary Criticism*, Vols. 7, 18, 38; *Contemporary Authors*, Vols. 69-72; and *Dictionary of Literary Biography*, Vol. 53.)

PRINCIPAL WORKS

SHORT FICTION

The Other Paris   1956
Green Water, Green Sky   1959; republished, 1983
My Heart Is Broken: Eight Stories and a Short Novel   1964;
    also published as *An Unmarried Man's Summer*, 1965
The Pegnitz Junction: A Novella and Five Short Stories   1973
The End of the World, and Other Stories   1974
From the Fifteenth District: A Novella and Eight Short Stories   1979
Home Truths: Selected Canadian Stories   1981
Overhead in a Balloon: Stories of Paris   1985
In Transit: Twenty Stories   1989

OTHER MAJOR WORKS

A Fairly Good Time   (novel)   1970
What Is to Be Done?   (drama)   1982
Paris Notebooks: Essays and Reviews   (essays)   1988

DAVID BOROFF   (essay date 1964)

[*In the review of* My Heart Is Broken *excerpted below, Boroff lauds Gallant's understanding of the nature of spiritual displacement.*]

All of the eight short stories in *My Heart Is Broken* (the volume also includes a novella) were published in [the *New Yorker*] and have in common meticulous craftsmanship and the play of an urbane and unimpassioned intelligence. The world inhabited by Mrs. Gallant's dramatis personae is precariously comfortable, psychologically cramped, permeated by a kind of ineffectual good will. Monstrous evil is foreign to this landscape; so are great unselfishness and nobility of character. Irony and gentle pity are the author's usual responses as she contemplates the shabby evasions, the stub-

born gentility and the inevitable humiliations of her characters.

Mrs. Gallant is a Canadian who has spent most of her adult life in Europe. Thus, as a highly civilized expatriate, doubly alienated from her native Montreal by virtue of her English background and from her native country by living in Europe, she has a keen insight into the condition of spiritual exile that provides the substance of so many *New Yorker* short stories.

Exile, in fact, is this author's preoccupation. Her stories deal with a variety of people leading exhausted lives far from home. There is Lily Littel, higher than a paid companion yet not quite a full-fledged boarder, living on an English pension on the Italian Riviera where "there was a whiff of informal nicety to be breathed, a suggestion of regularly aired decay." . . .

The most effective of the exile stories is **"An Unmarried Man's Summer,"** an utterly chilling, impeccably written account of a perennial "young" bachelor of 45, leading a vacuous existence in a borrowed house on the Riviera as the cossetted darling of old ladies to whom he is at once chaste lover and adored son. There is a poignant contrast between Walter Henderson's shrill and strained elegance and the dogged but almost despairing commitment to work and family of his equally exiled sister and brother-in-law who come to visit.

There are two stories in this volume which deal with Mrs. Gallant's native Montreal. The novella, **"Its Image on the Mirror,"** contains the raw material for full-length fiction: a shrewd sense of place, a family with a complicated interplay of personalities and an uncanny feeling for what life was like during World War II. However, the elements never quite coalesce, never seem more than preliminary notes for a novel which was never written. The short story **"Bernadette,"** however, is a jewel, virtually perfect. In a manner reminiscent of Katherine Mansfield, it deals with a sophisticated couple, Nora and Robbie Knight, the kind who chronically "talk things out" and "work things through" and are forever exiled from genuine emotion.

The focus of the story is their servant Bernadette, a simple French-Canadian girl who had been brought up to expect the worst in life and for whom "the mental leaps and guesses" of her employers were "as mysterious as those of saints or of ghosts." The clumsy, unfeeling efforts on the part of the couple to play the liberal lords of the manor with her—they ply her with highbrow French novels to read, totally beyond her ken—and their failure to reach her when she becomes pregnant are at once deeply moving and deftly ironic. **"Bernadette,"** a magical illumination, is one of the best short stories written in the last decade. And Mavis Gallant's collection exhibits a talent of uneven but substantial proportions.

David Boroff, "All Around Is a Kind of Ineffectual Good Will," in The New York Times Book Review, May 3, 1964, p. 4.

PETER STEVENS   (essay date 1973)

[*Stevens is an English-born Canadian poet, critic, and editor. In the following excerpt from an essay originally titled "Perils of Comprehension," he examines Gallant's treatment of sibling rivalry between her characters Jean and Isobel in "Its Image on the Mirror."*]

Those who know Mavis Gallant's stories will remember that

many of them revolve around one dominant theme: the stress of relationships within families, particularly the relation between parents and children, although she herself claims that this is not a conscious choice on her part. This recurrence seems to arise from her interest in people "trying to get out of a situation", because the family situation can be so inhibiting and confining and because people constantly want to break from the family while finding comfort within it as well. A family can paralyse and give false security; it can protect but shelter a person from the too insistent demands of an outside reality. It can lead to both domination and betrayal, withdrawal and smugness. All of these factors occur to a greater or lesser degree in Mavis Gallant's characters and their situations. (p. 61)

"Its Image on the Mirror," which appears in *My Heart is Broken* (1964), is a study of two sisters; Jean, the narrator, has lived in the shadow of Isobel, who is younger, more attractive and more lively. Jean has always regarded Isobel as living a bohemian life, full of romance and glamour; Isobel is the one who breaks away by an early marriage, who has an affair with a married man when her husband is away during the war.

But the usual Gallant irony operates; we discover that Isobel's life is not in fact at all glamorous. The married man is no dashing lover; he becomes an assistant headmaster with a "failed poet's face concave with discontent". Isobel herself marries a second time and is living in what sounds like a romantic ambiance—married to an Italian doctor in Venezuela. But when Isobel visits Jean with her family, the children are no different from Jean's, and Alfredo, her husband, turns out to be a finicky snob. Isobel, seen by Jean as the one who escaped from the narrow confines of the family, seems to have trapped herself within other situations just as confining.

The bulk of [**"Its Image on the Mirror"**] concerns Isobel during the war. Jean has been influenced by her, has married a man first interested in Isobel, and goes to live in Montreal while her husband has gone off to the war, trying to find there the imaginary life of romance. During the novel all the images of romantic life are broken down to a flat reality. Jean takes an apartment, "a bohemian, almost glamorous thing to do", but shares it with another girl and their life is the close, closeted life of two women living closely together. . . . Jean meets no romance, but only a furtive, fumbling Lesbian approach. The war produces no hero; only an epileptic veteran. Frank, her brother, goes to war and is killed, not in glorious action but in a freak accident. There are parties the sisters go to, peopled with what might be thought of as exotic foreigners; they turn out to be layabouts or pretentious artists without talent.

In all this ironic mélange, Jean still sees Isobel's affair with Alec Campbell as possessing the possibilities of a truly romantic world. In a kind of epiphany at the centre of the novel Jean sees Isobel and Alec walking out of the dark on a Montreal street. Before they see her, they are enclosed in a world in which romance and reality seem to meld, and for once Jean senses a romantic love existing, the love her mother has always rejected as being undesirable and "too fantastic to exist".

> They leaned inward as they walked, as if both had received an injury and were helping each other stand up. Isobel's face was a flower. Everything wary and closed, removed and mistrustful had disappeared. . . . He was an ordinary looking

man, but that made their love affair seem all the more extraordinary.

This picture of ideal love is broken when the lovers see Jean but the tableau of their union remains in Jean's mind. It presses upon her that all that she has thought about her sister's bohemian life was true, even though she herself has not experienced it, even though she is constantly though unconsciously resenting Isobel's illicit love-life, an attitude not unlike the confusion of love and resentment that Flor feels in *Green Water, Green Sky.*

At the end of the novel Jean is let into Isobel's life. Isobel calls on Jean to tell her she is pregnant and wants Jean to help her through the pregnancy. After Isobel's confession and her plea for complete attention, Jean reaches to Isobel, feeling sisterly, trying to take her hand. But Isobel sees this as too intimate or too sentimental a gesture and withdraws her hand from Jean's. There follows a very revealing paragraph which includes this comment by Jean: "She wanted my attention, and would pay for it." And so Jean seizes her opportunity. After being in Isobel's shadow for most of her life, she now is prepared to get the most out of her hold over Isobel.

But even this revelation of Jean's use of her sister's situation has already been undercut. Jean's power over her sister does not last and does not allow her to escape from her own position. Earlier in the novel there is an episode in which Isobel visits the family summer cottage with her children and her second husband. It is a disaster as a family gathering, and Jean narrates it with a kind of caustic humour. But, in spite of Jean's critical view of Isobel's later marriage, her distaste for Isobel's undisciplined life, her belief that her own married life has been more successful, there lingers the idea that in her own way Isobel has succeeded. Thus, in the end the power Isobel seemed to place in Jean's hands is empty, for when Isobel returns to the cottage several years later, Jean realizes that she has never had any control over Isobel. Isobel has retained her own individuality and broken through the barriers of the family relationship for good: "I was part of a wall of cordial family faces, and Isobel was not hurt by her failure, or impressed by my success, but thankful she had escaped". So the reversal at the end of the novel is doubly ironic.

Another way of looking at this novel is to see it, as Mavis Gallant herself sees it, as a study in domination. Isobel has dominated Jean for most of her life, and in a way Jean's telling of the story is a kind of exorcism of the dominance of her sister's spirit, though we have seen that, ironically, this has not really existed. There is also the domination of the mother over her two daughters, something that Isobel recognizes and breaks away from and Jean herself eventually comes to see.

Yet the author herself seems dissatisfied with it as a novel. She has complained that what is wrong with the novel is that Jean, as narrator, is "too lucid". Yet, for all Jean's lucidity, does she really know what is happening and, most particularly, does she know what is happening to herself? Her voice gives the impression of order and control, but scattered through the narrative are stray phrases which indicate that she is not as sure of events as the lucid tone suggests, so that one of the deepest ironies of the book may be the discrepancy between Jean's apparent comprehension of these events and her failure to see the reality as it exists. It is possible to see the story as a distortion: phrases such as "I suppose", "I must have dreamed", "I think", "I expect" occur at times. Jean even admits at the beginning (thus establishing that she is a deluded narrator) that the opening tableau of the empty house may be an invention on her part: "My mother says I saw nothing of the kind."

If there is this ambivalence in Jean's narrative voice, then the final paragraphs take on a more sinister tone. At the end Jean thinks she will write a letter to her husband Tom about Isobel's pregnancy in order to destroy any lingering idealism Tom may have about Isobel. But apparently she does not send the letter. In one sense it seems an act of kindness because "it would be Isobel delivered, Isobel destroyed." But there is something malicious about Jean's subsequent remarks: "The story could wait. It would always be there to tell." This implies that she will have it ready to use, even though she says "I might never tell it." Early in the story she has revealed the power she possesses. "It has often been in my power to destroy my sister—to destroy, that is, an idea people might have about her—but something has held back my hand. I think it is the instinct that tells me Isobel will betray herself." But the irony goes deeper still, because we have seen the later Isobel early in the story and she has not betrayed herself. She seems totally unaffected by the earlier experience and in fact by living in Caracas with her family she has removed herself from the sphere of influence of Jean's threatening knowledge.

One further thing should be mentioned about Jean. Although she holds up to herself as an idea Isobel's golden bohemian life, though she suggests she herself married in order to escape from the grip of her family, throughout the story she admits that she is really a re-incarnation of her mother. She sees that their gestures are alike, even their voices are similar. She remarks, "I am pleased to be like her. There is no one I admire more." Her lucidity, what she considers her real apprehension, is an inheritance from her mother: "I sounded like our mother: flat and calm and certain I was right." She repeats the notion a little later: "I am the only person who can tell the truth about anything now." (pp. 64-8)

Peter Stevens, "Perils of Compassion," in Canadian
Literature, No. 56, Spring, 1973, pp. 61-70.

WILLIAM H. PRITCHARD (essay date 1973)

[*An American critic and editor, Pritchard has written several literary biographies on major twentieth-century British and American authors, including Wyndham Lewis and Robert Frost. In the excerpt below, Pritchard favorably assesses the stories included in* The Pegnitz Junction.]

Readers familiar with Mavis Gallant's essay on the Gabrielle Russier affair—the persecution and prosecution of a French schoolmistress who fell in love with one of her pupils and after painful consequences committed suicide—know both the sympathetic intelligence and ironic penetration of her judgment. The grasp of a society, the refusal to treat it as freakishly unrelated to other societies and the rest of life, is admirable throughout. A similarly ironic intelligence presents itself on every page of her fiction, most recently embodied in the novella and short stories of her new collection [*The Pegnitz Junction*]. Yet, though all the stories are serious and crafted, with one distinguished exception they do not command full, responsive belief of the sort elicited by her essay.

"The Pegnitz Junction" is called a novella, a harmless term so long as we don't expect it to mean anything more than a

story that goes beyond 75 pages or so. As with Miss Gallant's other stories and her recent novel *A Fairly Good Time* the principal hero or villain is memory, and not only as it is expressed through the heroine Christine returning from a holiday in Paris with her lover and his formidable young son "Little Bert."

When an anonymous woman joins them in their compartment for the grotesque sequence of misadventures which passes for a railway journey back to Germany, the woman's supposed memories—italicized paragraphs evoking émigré life in Brooklyn during World War II—are juxtaposed with the heroine's consciousness of present and past, also with the elusive narrator's eagerness to enter any mind that appears on the scene, in fact or in memory. The reader is teased to make something of these juxtapositions, and no doubt they could be easily connected if one were willing to adduce themes like war and postwar deracination, the treacherous sentimentality of memory or the absurdity of men, who all (even down to Little Bert, who vomits up his lunch of plum cake) turn out to be a good deal less than fine figures of their sex.

That Mavis Gallant refuses to make such connections for us, refuses to speak as a thoughtful omniscience behind her characters, might be admired as indicative of her belief that life's oddities mustn't be ironed out into the orderly understandings of fiction. Yet by cultivating incongruities, juxtaposing voices and memories that fit together in only the craziest way the author might seem to evade responsibility for saying or caring very much about her characters and their situation. This is the Palace of Art, and Mavis Gallant is perilously close to residing there in a novella which in the long run feels too clever, too oblique, too arty for its own moral and human good.

Like **"The Pegnitz Junction,"** other stories in the collection are about the resources and treacheries of memory. . . .

Mavis Gallant's fund of skepticism about nostalgic memory is a very large one. Accordingly her heroines suffer, grim-lipped and unillusioned, as in **"The Old Friends"** and **"O Lasting Peace."** While not wanting to quarrel with the terms of these stories, one wishes the stories could be less unrelenting, more tolerant toward the possibility of their heroines' breathing free.

This happens in the book's final story, **"An Alien Flower."** A young refugee woman from Silesia named Bibby comes to live with the narrator of the story and the narrator's husband (a successful post-war German businessman), indeed becomes another in what the narrator eventually discovers to be her husband's series of lovers. It is the story's sad achievement to show the narrator (and us) how her life as an alien flower comes gradually to its wry fulfillment by moving into a painful freedom from the fatuous lies on which her husband has built his life.

By the end of the story the ghost has been laid; the secrets no longer are dreadful, and the wife summons up words which her non-listening husband can't understand. But the reader can, and at that moment enters most fully into Mavis Gallant's imagination, artful and moral in **"An Alien Flower"** to the extent that it bears comparison with a Chekhov's or a Katherine Anne Porter's.

William H. Pritchard, in a review of "The Pegnitz

Junction," in The New York Times Book Review, *June 24, 1973, p. 4.*

RONALD B. HATCH (essay date 1978)

[*In the following excerpt, Hatch traces the development of Gallant's short fiction from the beginning of her career to the 1970s, focusing on characterization.*]

[In Mavis Gallant's] early writing is a strong romantic influence whereby the outside world is portrayed as a product of her characters' perception. Yet Gallant's romanticism does not create strong, self-actuating people, as is normally the case with romantics; rather, her characters are troubled, somewhat beleaguered souls. A vision of a better, freer life is usually present, but inevitably this is circumscribed by a larger set of impulses towards censorship and control. One of the more noticeable features is the expatriates who people her pages. Generally English speaking, they attempt to eke out a life on the Riviera or some such place. With little money, they are forced to live frugally in material as well as spiritual ways. Even Canadian characters with modest wealth and liberal sentiments, such as the Knights in **"Bernadette,"** appear fenced round by conventions. It is almost as if these characters are unhappy until they have sought out their own prisons.

In looking closer at typical characters, one discovers Gallant is fascinated by individuals who desire to rebel against their circumstances. While Gallant writes from within the romantic tradition that sees the individual rebelling against society to attain dignity and freedom, she also places this rebellion within the larger perspective of liberal, middle-class norms. Although in the early stories, Gallant's characters may seem merely weak romantics caught in the debris of history, any sustained reading of Gallant soon reveals that her main interest is not the individual's problems in their own right, but the manner in which liberal ideology has spawned a nightmare of history. Taken as a whole, Gallant's fiction offers a devastating critique of liberal humanism, devastating, precisely because the account is also sympathetic. Indeed, this sympathy keeps Gallant's cutting edge sharp, revealing new insights, new involutions of liberal paradox. Moreover, as her work progresses—from the early stories of the fifties through the German material of the sixties and early seventies to her most recent Montreal stories in *The New Yorker*—her portrayal of man's entrapment in liberal, romantic ideals changes considerably, and may even hint at the escape route.

I regard Gallant's analysis of the problems besetting the individual conscience, alone in a public world, of the utmost importance. Since her own work reveals time and again the impossibility of divorcing content from perception, problem from form, I have chosen some representative short stories to show her developing portrayal of the individual's attempts to find freedom within society. Remember, however, all her writing works towards unification—the individual no longer seen as observer, standing alone, but as part of all he observes. As will be seen, questions of freedom, for Gallant, ultimately become questions of faith—faith, I might add, in process. Not faith as dogma.

Turning first to a number of Gallant's early stories to see her depiction of the romantic dilemma, one finds these to be delights of compression with the characters pressed into ever narrower spaces. One of the best stories to show this pattern is **"The Other Paris"** of 1953. Since Gallant left Canada for Europe in 1950 and only then began to publish her work (although she mentions to Geoff Hancock that she had been writing voluminously for many years earlier), **"The Other Paris"** almost certainly reflects her own first perceptions of Paris. Gallant has caught admirably the atmosphere of post-war triviality, and the dilemma of post-war Europe. People could sense the old forms of society closing in on them, could sense the sad retreat to a private life, where romantic love was the apex of excitement. Gallant's characters seem caught in this web, hearing the echo of a call to commitment, but restrained by hidden forces possessing inert strength.

In **"The Other Paris,"** we see Gallant, even at this early date, has full control of the classic short story structure: the initial scene contains the seeds of the action, with Carol, the North American, and Odile, the Parisian, at a dressmaker's rooms where Carol is being fitted for her wedding dress. The event should be a happy, companionable one, but Odile's single action, of picking "threads from her skirt fastidiously, as if to remove herself completely from Carol and her unoriginal plans" indicates the degree of separation between the two girls. . . . From Carol's point of view, life should just be beginning, but the wedding plans fail to transform any of the surrounding circumstances. Marriage is, of course, the perfect symbol for the coupling of both the private and the social. In this case, however, Gallant appears to show the inadequacy of marriage to transform for the individual, even for a time, the face of post-war Europe.

In many ways, **"The Other Paris"** is typical of Gallant's early work. The people are shabby, the weather is poor, and, in general, the setting appears a wasteland. Amidst narrowness and depression, however, is usually a character whose energy or perception belies, at least for a time, the wasteland. In this case it is Carol, and although Carol may be "unoriginal," she is genuinely searching for the other, romantic Paris. As so far described, the situation of the romantic youth in search of happiness amidst the depression of day-to-day factuality is reminiscent of many writers of the turn of the century. One thinks in particular of James Joyce's Dublin stories, such as "Araby," where the boy's imagination for a time outstrips the dull streets of Dublin.

Paradoxically, although Carol is in a long line of romantic heroines, she has within her attitudes that deny the fulfillment of those longings. For instance, Carol is not in love with her fiance, nor he in love with her:

> The fact that Carol was not in love with Howard Mitchell did not dismay her in the least. From a series of helpful college lectures on marriage she had learned that a common interest, such as a liking for Irish setters, was the true basis for happiness, and that the illusion of love was a blight imposed by the film industry, and almost entirely responsible for the high rate of divorce.

Notice that although the narrative tone is anything but humorous, Gallant's ability to capture indirect speech—the single example of the Irish setters—renders Carol's situation humorously. While never departing from her objective stance, Gallant introduces a delightfully acerbic humour that always threatens to tumble into pathos.

As a character, Carol embodies the superficial optimism of middle-class North American life. For instance, she believes if conditions are right in the outside world, and one is prudent with one's choices, then one's world must come right. More-over, since she has chosen Howard intelligently, "there was no reason for the engagement or the marriage to fail". One might agree, but add equally there was no reason for it to suc-ceed. The emphasis is taken off "making" and placed on "finding" the correct conditions:

> Given a good climate, enough money, and a pair of good-natured, *intelligent* (her college lectures had stressed this) people, one had only to sit back and watch it grow. All winter, then, she looked for these right conditions in Paris. When, at first, nothing happened, she blamed it on the weather. She was often convinced she would fall deeply in love with Howard if only it would stop raining. Undaunted, she waited for better times.

Since it never stops raining, the better times never arrive.

On a quick reading **"The Other Paris"** is simply a satire on Carol's "unoriginal" romanticism. Yet this would reduce a rich and complex story to a single dimension. As the story progresses we realize Carol is not altogether wrong in her dis-content with Paris, but when she sees the cause of her unease in something as trivial as the rain, the reader recognizes many reasons—economic and spiritual—for the drabness of post-war life in Paris. While Carol busies herself to find the right events, the right people, to complete her vision, the Parisians are equally busy attempting to return, as much as possible, to pre-war conditions. They do not participate in Carol's de-sire for a new style of life, but merely wish to restore middle-class affluence and security.

Gallant does not strongly criticize the French, although she is keenly aware of lost possibilities; she does, however, show that Carol's "unoriginal" aspiration to escape the cultural malaise is some how representative of the weak, ineffectual *zeitgeist* which feels the need to battle the old norms, but has neither the strength nor perspicacity. (pp. 93-5)

Europe has changed, but people refuse to admit it, and at-tempt to return to the old ways. Gallant, of course, is not writing a history, but in her depiction of Odile's family, with her sister Martine studying music, yet giving her recital in a sleazy hall, she shows that the old pretence to culture or "Kultur" as a way of life is no longer possible. (pp. 95-6)

Yet again, there is something more, for if Gallant were mere-ly reproducing the theme of the innocent North American in decaying Europe, then she would be rewriting Henry James. But the normal James situation is given an interesting reversal when Gallant depicts emerging in Europe an under-ground situation that promises something more. The new "underground" element is the character Felix, Odile's lover, who lives in a squalid part of Paris, and who seems to be a black marketeer. Carol denies the obvious attraction between Felix and herself, first, by ignoring him and then by pitying his poverty. Nevertheless, Felix, for all his squalor, is the only person who can respond to Carol's own needs. Unwittingly, Carol has found in Felix her ideal, for Felix truly is the "other" Paris. The romantic Paris of Carol's imagination has disappeared to be replaced by another Paris of Arabs and Al-gerians of which Felix, with no papers, or history, is a part. Although Odile's family spurn Felix, Odile, for all her preten-sions to the old norms, has changed sufficiently to develop a warm, if somewhat strained relationship with Felix. And Carol, to her great surprise, suddenly finds herself admitted. For a moment Carol recognizes this:

> Standing under the noisy trains on the dark, dusty boulevard, she felt that she had at last opened the right door, turned down the right street, glimpsed the vision toward which she had struggled on win-ter evenings when, standing on the staircase, she had wanted to be enchanted with Paris and to be in love with Howard.

Yet Carol draws back when she hears Felix. Her background will not permit acceptance, for when she compares the future open to Felix and Odile with that open to Howard and her-self, she decides, quite consciously, to remain with Howard. Does this mean that material comforts win out over emotion-al fulfillment? In some sense, yes. But that is not the point. It is not luxuries, not even material goods, that Carol desires; nor is it status, although all these are involved. With Howard, "no one could point to them, or criticize them, or humiliate them by offering to help". Ultimately what matters is inde-pendence. In other words, the old goal of the pioneers—to be self-sufficient—has led to a noble cul-de-sac in which Carol prefers the social dignity that comes from independence rath-er than the love that comes from dependence. So Carol de-cides to marry Howard. Marriage here is not seen as a social communion but an escape from a life of commitment; there is no outpouring of love.

How then is the conflict between desire for love and the desire for independence resolved? Not by a sudden confrontation. In Gallant's stories, characters cannot exist long in tension, but continually seek a state of repose. Once again it will be helpful to contrast Gallant's **"The Other Paris"** with Joyce's "Araby." With Joyce, there is a sudden blinding realization when the young boy at the fair finally realizes his self-deception. With Gallant, however, the individual erases the confrontation. As Gallant comments of Carol, hastening away from Felix, "After a while, happily married, mercifully removed in time, she would remember it and describe it and finally believe it as it has never been at all". The piling up of phrase upon phrase echoes time's effect on the mind, piling up new experiences on the memory of Paris, gradually easing the pain of lost potential. Carol in her memory will create "a coherent picture, accurate but untrue". As representative of the educated middle class, Carol closes her own circle of self-destruction, shutting out the possibilities of intimacy with Felix, the representative of a repressed class.

At first sight, Gallant's characters sometimes seem as if they ought not to deserve the reader's interest, since they are so ephemeral. Yet they are impossible to reject, partly because Gallant gives them enough self-knowledge to edge their games with irony; they play out their marginal existence with a flair that comes from a deep-seated knowledge of despair. But with Gallant, "dignity" itself becomes a pawn in the game; dignity is always a false dignity because it is won in miniature dramas of the characters' own making. Gallant's characters hasten away to find a stage, no matter how tawdry, for their puny games. Meanwhile, in the background, Gallant implies, the great battle of historical forces for the creation of a civilization goes on, and looks as though it will be lost— all for the sake of a few participants. (pp. 96-7)

In the years 1963 to 1972 Gallant published a series of short stories set in Germany, which, taken together, are clearly at-tempts to probe something of the German character in the post-war period. Mavis Gallant said in the Hancock inter-view she was attempting to explain the origins of Fascism. In 1973, some of these stories were collected, and along with the novella **"The Pegnitz Junction,"** were published in *The Pegnitz Junction: A Novella and Five Short Stories.* It is quite an extraordinary work, focusing always on individuals, but with the war never far away. What finally emerges is the sense of "atmosphere" surrounding middle-class Germany. For a reader coming to these stories after the earlier works, much is familiar. For instance, many of the characters are worn out, or shut in, or in some way dead to the forces of life. Similarly, the stories do not have much of a forward narrative line, the spaces between characters often being as important as the material itself. There is also something new: whereas the earlier stories seemed depictions of only one person's lifelessness, now there is a sinister feeling of an entire nation involved in a capitulation to a dead state of mind and yet at the same time alive with destructive forces. In one sense Gallant's theme is still middle-class enervation, but now the stories reveal how the enervation leads, not just to the destruction of an individual, but to the participation of an entire people in a monstrous "coloration." While the stories are not about the beginning of the war, but about post-war conditions, the patterns of behaviour suggest the same thing could happen again.

The best place to see this in operation is in **"The Pegnitz Junction,"** which Gallant considers as one of her best works. I was puzzled on first reading, not really understanding the increasing fragmentation, yet feeling strangely the sinister element behind even the most trivial event. On the surface, it is simply the description of a train journey from Paris to Strasbourg taken by Christine, her older lover Herbert, and his son, called Little Bert. They never reach their destination, but along the way we gradually become aware that nothing is right or normal in the journey or between the people. Moreover, by the end of the novella, so many stories have been introduced within stories that everything seems to be flying apart. Indeed, this work is bound to give many readers difficulty. . . . The storyline resembles the course of Germany itself with the young couple eventually on board a train continually rerouted all over the map. By itself, the metaphor of the train taking people on a journey over which they have no control works well to give a sense of political power, but Gallant is never content to present abstractions as abstractions, and thus introduces also the notion of authority breaking down in personal relationships, so that the political metaphor is rounded out with its psychic and even metaphysical dimensions. On the surface, Herbert, Christine and Little Bert are a family, but in fact all traditional bonds holding them together are gone. Herbert would like to be the *paterfamilias,* but Christine is not his wife; Little Bert is both spoiled and tyrannized. Christine would like to express her femininity, but feels she must guard herself lest Herbert dominate. The family situation is totally fragmented with no traditional bonds, and no acceptance of pattern in relationships. As the same sort of dislocation occurs with the political metaphor of the journey, one cannot tell where the psychic dimension leaves off and the political one begins.

The manner in which the private becomes social is shown at the start of the story in the Paris hotel, when Christine, Herbert and Little Bert are forced to rise early in the morning to catch a train back to Strasbourg; significantly, an airline strike has forced them to take the long train journey. When Christine begins to run her bath, she suddenly finds the hotel porter pounding violently on their door, because the old pipes in the hotel are banging. Obviously he is right to be annoyed, but his anger seems out of proportion, caused partly by their

being German. Certainly Christine did not realize that her bathwater would cause the old pipes to bang. Even more surprising is Herbert's passivity throughout the encounter, his only action being to correct a word in the porter's diatribe. As an engineer, Herbert prides himself on keeping control, but there is something disturbing about his behaviour when his only action is to write a letter of complaint. As the story proceeds, we learn that although writing letters of complaint is his forte, and although he is often highly critical, he takes care never to criticize anything that would throw disrepute on the governing powers.

Gallant draws back from any overt parallels, but clearly Herbert's lack of courage and humanity suggest the technocrats' cynical journey through fascism (along with the German governing classes) during the pre-war years when they acceded to the fanatics whom they despised, but were confident that they could eventually control. A similar example occurs when the train conductor, who seems at first a harmless, jovial person begins to terrorize the older people with his assumed power. A word from Christine is all it takes to subdue the conductor's wild antics, and for a moment essential humanity triumphs, but it is a small incident in an ongoing nightmare.

Although the notion of authority need not have its basis in the past or traditions, clearly in the West this association has often been made. And what we discover in **"The Pegnitz Junction"** is that none of the characters can use his knowledge of the past to enlighten the present or direct the future. An immensely funny, yet sinister example of this is the manner in which a tour guide first consoles his group for the erratic train schedule by mentioning "one hundred familiar names," like Bach, Brahms and Mozart, and then leads them back into acute anxiety by introducing "the Adolf time." Nowhere does there seem to be a resolution: the leader plays on the people's emotions and they follow into contradictions without end. The past is no longer a tradition or a synthesis of events, but a collection of names, each of which is capable of producing an emotional reaction. None of the characters is able to see the past as creating the present.

In some ways Christine is the exemplum of modern man, or rather, woman; while she is engaged to a theology student she is also the lover of Herbert, the engineer. She cannot make up her mind whether to embrace religion, with its metaphysical solace, or applied science, with its manipulation of present-day reality. She claims she enjoys Herbert because he is straightforward and does not analyze situations, but he also wants her to take on a domestic role and be a mother to Little Bert. As the journey goes on, seemingly without end, and there is less and less communication between the three, the atmosphere becomes thick with possibilities. Mysteriously, Christine suddenly begins to overhear the conversations that other people are having with themselves inside their heads. Clearly, she is ultra-sensitive, and in some ways, with her quick eye and her ability to sense or even hear what other people are thinking, she is like the artist. But the conversations she overhears of other people's lives do not clarify the situation; they lead to further fragmentation, suggesting that the only public reality is the externalized private thoughts of the individuals.

It is really impossible to do more than suggest the bare outlines of the novella here, but it is worth mentioning that Christine is reading a book by Bonhoeffer on which her fiance is about to write an exam. Bonhoeffer, of course, died for his beliefs, whereas these people seem incapable of enacting anything in their lives, at least with any sort of commitment. At the end, however, at the Pegnitz Junction, where they are changing trains, and when it looks as though the train for which they are waiting may have just arrived, Herbert becomes separated from Christine and Little Bert. Strangely enough, in the midst of everyone panicking, Christine calmly begins to tell the child a story—one that she had attempted to tell earlier—about a family with four sons, all named George. To tell them apart, the family pronounces each name differently. Clearly this suggests the brotherhood of man. For a moment, the reader wonders whether Christine is not reaching out to the child in a rare gesture of kindness. Then one realizes she does this at the very moment when action is needed to catch the train. From a liberal viewpoint, it might be seen as a positive gesture, but the story, I suggest, has radicalized us well beyond such liberal, utopian possibilities. Most readers will see Christine's action as a retreat to the abstract realm of the mind, of reason, when the requirement is a confrontation with the present moment. (pp. 101-03)

Before proceeding to the recent series of Montreal stories, it will be helpful to pause for a moment over **"Irina"** (Dec. 2, 1974), a story that in many ways marks a transition in Gallant's focus. Whereas many of the previous stories had only hinted at Gallant's unhappiness with the reigning outlook of liberal humanism—with its basically romantic notions of the natural goodness of man in an evolving providential universe—in **"Irina"** Gallant attacks the ideal outright. Irina is the wife of Richard Notte, who is portrayed as "the very archetype of a respected European novelist—prophet, dissuader, despairingly opposed to evil, crack-voiced after having made so many pronouncements." A little resembling Thomas Mann, Notte himself seems to embody the values of liberal humanism, an ideal whose virture have traditionally been the industrial and intellectual, with its creed of responsibility for the moral health of the individual in society. Above all, liberal humanism has stood for political and judicial equity. All fine virtues, one might say, and so they are. Gallant, however, begins the story soon after Irina has become a widow, and such terms as "crack-voiced" applied to her husband indicate she is beginning to question the value of her husband's life. His moral novels and ethical pronouncements have disappeared from the public memory and Irina is left feeling her husband had put all his energy into his public life. Leaving little for his wife and children.

Particularly interesting is Gallant's depiction of Irina, for she does not move immediately into Irina's mind and give her long soul-searching monologues in which she questions her husband's values. Giving her *ideas* opposed to those of her husband would leave her essentially the same kind of person as her husband, a rebel of ideas. And this is exactly what Gallant wishes to avoid: Irina is shown coming to terms with her life, rather than order it to meet a pre-conceived pattern. It is almost as if Gallant, despairing of using the romantic vision or man's critical faculties to change things, now begins to experiment with altering the individual's own positioning in the world. In this respect, she is delving down to primary changes in her characters' own mode of perceiving and thinking.

Since Irina has spent all her life in caring for the needs of her famous husband and in bringing up his children, fittingly our first view of Irina's changes is through the eyes of her grown-up children. This narrative device, moreover, allows Gallant to be suggestive and tentative about Irina's changes. As the

children only partially understand what is happening to their mother, we are left to infer much. In fact when their father dies the children expect their mother to die also, at least metaphorically. That is, they expect her to withdraw into a decent widowhood. And, indeed, she does lead a quiet life, performing the proper ritual, but she also becomes independent in her own quiet manner. A good example of this is the occasion when Notte's will is given its first reading. The will is gracefully written, and not a little rhetorical, but Irina cuts through all this: "In plain words . . . I am the heir." Notte had entrusted his favourite daughter with his unfinished manuscripts and journals; Irina simply refuses to give them up. Actions, for once, cut through rhetoric.

Irina's slow process of change is admirably captured by Gallant's prose in the way she piles up detail after detail, allowing the implications to speak for themselves. For instance, in the first years after Notte's death, the family take turns at visiting Irina at holidays; soon, however, she begins to visit them in turn. And finally she sends all her children the same letter. "This Christmas I don't want to go anywhere. I intend to stay here, in my own home." Ironically, her children see these changes in their mother as the expected changes any widow experiences after the death of her husband. And in part they are right, for what is happening to Irina is a break with her family. But the children are also wrong, for they universalize the change as one that all family members go through at one time or another, when quite clearly Irina's change is an independent one. Gallant, through her quiet, careful depiction of everyday events, gives us a fascinating picture of Irina turning away from a world conceived in terms of ideas, going through a change that alters the real shape and contour of her life. Gallant's point is not merely to give an accurate portrait of Irina, but to show a person altering in the seemingly inconsequential, but ultimately crucial trivia of day-to-day life. For instance, Irina has living with her, after a time, an older man who seems something of an alcoholic and who certainly lacks the sterling qualities of her previous husband. Yet he is welcome to share her life. No longer assimilating the absolutes to her own finite existence, Irina is beginning to value other finite existences as things in themselves, rather than as means to ends. (pp. 104-06)

While **"Irina"** obviously demanded a new direction for Gallant, I doubt whether many of her readers could have predicted the series of Montreal stories that followed. In part, what makes them new and exciting is the character of Linnet Muir. Unlike so many of Gallant's characters, Linnet is perceptive, strong and forthright. Moreover, her life in Montreal would appear at numerous points to parallel Gallant's own. Indeed, many readers will stumble with relief on Linnet Muir as the first character expressing something of Gallant's own strength as a writer. Surely one of the puzzles in Gallant's fiction is her interest in tired expatriates. Living in Paris, Gallant might be a kind of expatriate, but obviously anyone with nerve enough to leave a well-paying job in Canada for a life on the continent, supported by short story writing, could not be as lacking in vitality as her own characters. A further puzzle is that, while most writers begin writing about themselves, and only later achieve the larger perspective to develop characters different from themselves, Gallant appears to have achieved the larger perspective at once. Now, however, with **"In Youth is Pleasure"** (Nov. 24, 1975), Gallant begins to trace her own origins, coming to terms with the person she is—exactly Irina's undertaking in the preceding story.

No doubt part of the reader's delight with Linnet is that she appears to tell us something about Gallant's own early life in Montreal. But there is more to it. Gallant seems also to be clearing ground for the breakthrough hinted at in **"Irina"** by first discovering and revealing something of the patterning implicit in the growth of a person from youth to maturity, and, more precisely, in calculating the cost to a writer in the creation of highly analytical fictions. . . . Yet this series of Montreal stories is by no means a turn towards introspection; Gallant is as interested as ever in the interrelationships between individuals and society. But instead of portraying weak characters caught in history, she now has Linnet Muir, as a distanced commentator, offering a powerful critique of the Canadian society in which she grew up. While the initial assumption might be that Gallant is now speaking through Linnet so as to present overtly the social critique that had formerly been presented obliquely, a moment's reflection will reveal that such a view would completely undermine Gallant's perception of society and the individual being reflections of one another. The interesting feature of these new stories is precisely that Linnet *at first* believes she can stand aside and criticize the culture, behaving as if she were an eighteenth-century empiricist, who, skeptical about everything external, forgets to be skeptical about the observing "I." Gallant has also built into the story a narrative device which undermines this simplistic view: there is an older Linnet who is telling the story of her younger self. Only gradually does the reader become aware of this second complicating perspective, but slowly a dialectic is created that pushes towards a vision of individuals as a part of history and not as outside commentators.

Such comments are a little premature, however, so let us begin by turning to the first story **"In Youth is Pleasure."** Immediately we discover the land of Linnet's childhood is a place of repression where the child is imprisoned by the adult world. Indeed, there are many similarities to Gallant's depiction of post-war Germany. In both cases Gallant is describing the middle class with its ineffectual liberal ideals. An abstract moral code wreaks devastation on private lives, thereby creating the public disaster it was devised to avoid. For instance, when Linnet returns to Canada after living for several years in the United States, where she had gained a perspective from which to judge Canada, she notices immediately the poverty of people's private lives. As she says succinctly: "Their upbringing is intended for a crisis." Such an education, of course, has advantages, for in a crisis, "keeping a straight face makes life tolerable." But Linnet recognizes that it makes only "*public* life tolerable." For the greater part of life, "the dead of heart and spirit litter the landscape."

Clearly, Gallant uses Linnet's strength of perception and forceful character to expose Canadian hypocrisy, and to a large degree, Linnet's picture of Canada in the early years of World War II rings true, corroborating what other writers such as Alice Munro and Robertson Davies have shown about the stifling middle-class ethos. Against this background of restraint, which in Quebec also meant a large dose of Jansenist religion, Linnet's revolution must be seen. In returning to Montreal where she was born, Linnet sees herself assuming a new role, with older people no longer having power over her. As she says, "My life was my own revolution—the tyrants deposed, the constitution wrenched from unwilling hands." Yet the very tone of voice, the insistent demand that it is *her* revolution, soon begins to raise questions in the reader's mind as to the success of the young girl's revolution.

Moreover, if Linnet wants freedom, why then does she not remain in New York? At first sight, the answer seems a cliche: Linnet is searching for her ancestors, attempting to discover her parents behind their parental, public masks. As the search unfolds, however, we discover Gallant is actually edging the character of Linnet with irony, showing that she uses the past to support her own individual decision, and therefore unwittingly traps herself even as she asserts her freedom. This becomes particularly apparent when we learn that Linnet is searching only for the truth about her father, who has been dead for some years, and that she is uninterested in her mother who is still alive. She says of her parents: "Angus was a solemn man, not much of a smiler. My mother, on the other hand—I won't begin to describe her, it would never end—smiled, talked, charmed anyone she didn't happen to be related to, swam in scandal like a partisan among the people. She made herself the central figure in loud, spectacular dramas which she played with the houselights on; you could see the audience too. . . . You can imagine what she must have been in this world where everything was hushed, muffled, disguised; she must have seemed all they had by way of excitement, give or take a few elections and wars." Linnet's mother is obviously the individual counterpart of the freedom-loving expressionist culture that Linnet so much admires in the United States. Yet Linnet's denial of her mother, her failure to recognize that her mother embodies the very *elan vital* that Linnet says cannot be found in Canada, leads us to conclude that for all the young girl's perspicacity, she does not understand herself, does not understand that she is selectively using her own life and that of her family to support her own view of herself outside history.

The extent to which Linnet wins her freedom at the expense of engagement with history is seen when she pieces together her father's story and realizes that he probably committed suicide while extremely ill and attempting to return to England. At once, she decides that she must simply forget the entire matter: "Once I had made up my mind, the whole story somehow became none of my business." She recalls how she once looked in her father's drawer and found a loaded revolver, and had never looked into another person's drawer again. She says, "If I was to live my own life I had to let go. I wrote in my journal that 'they' had got him but would never get me, and after that there was scarcely ever a mention." In other words, she refused to involve herself with her father's private life—the aim of her original search. Just as the father committed suicide in order to extricate himself from a difficult and messy situation, so does the young Linnet commit a kind of suicide by refusing to live with the implications of her father's death. What began as a triumphant declaration of freedom has ended with the hollowness of the individual outside himself, outside the world as history, left in the present, where one is oneself, but the knowledge is cold. As she says, "Reality, as always, was narrow and dull."

Gallant's point, that the past enforces itself particularly strongly on those who would seek to forget it, is brilliantly evoked in the very timbre of Linnet's voice, which tells all, dispassionately, as matter-of-fact. As she says in the last line of the story, "Time had been on my side, faithfully, and unless you died you were always bound to escape." "Bound to escape"—a nice pun. Linnet has escaped, but having been bound to escape, merely lives out another version of the life from which there is no escape.

In one sense, then, this story is the prototype for all the earlier stories of frigid, restrained individuals coping with middle-class existence by the creation of an internal world that rejects the external. In the figure of the father who commits suicide leaving his daughter an "expatriate" in a strange land, we have the symbolic figure who, in the early stories, became the public world of male qualities. As we have seen, Gallant's characters refused to meet this world, always drawing back in alarm. While Gallant, manipulating her characters behind the scenes, was enormously successful in using this structure to present a social critique, she left her readers with little sense of how her own success as a writer correlated to the dismal life of her many misfits. Now, however, in the Montreal stories, she includes both the older and the younger person, thereby developing the process by which individual revolutions that are not centred in history will later be seen as pyrrhic victories, because they deny the public world. (pp. 107-10)

Ronald B. Hatch, "The Three Stages of Mavis Gallant's Short Fiction," in *The Canadian Fiction Magazine, No. 28, 1978, pp. 92-114.*

GEORGE WOODCOCK (essay date 1978)

[*Woodcock is a Canadian editor and critic best known for his biographies of George Orwell and Thomas Merton. He also founded* Canadian Literature, *one of Canada's most important literary journals. In the excerpt below, which was originally published in* Canadian Fiction Magazine *in 1978, Woodcock discusses common thematic and stylistic aspects of Gallant's short fiction from the 1960s and 1970s.*]

Absolute plausibility, though not mimesis as such, I take to be one of the principal goals of fiction. The vision, no matter how fantastic, must convince the reader through its self-consistency. And absolute plausibility demands absolute artifice, not faith to actuality, which is why Flaubert outshines Zola and Chekhov outlives Guy de Maupassant. It is also why Mavis Gallant, though little recognized in Canada, outwrites most other Canadians. If I had to define her short fictions—novellas and short stories—setting aside obvious matters of theme and narrative construction, I would—and shall—talk about the impeccable verbal texture and the marvellous painterly surface of the scene imagined through the translucent veil of words, the kind of surface that derives from a close and highly visual sense of the interrelationship of sharply observed detail. . . .

In this essay I have decided to restrict myself to sixteen stories, which fall into three rather clearly defined groups in terms of terrain and theme. They are all fairly late stories, the first of them dating from the early 1960s and most from the 1970s, at least in terms of publication. (p. 93)

These sixteen stories all concern people who in some way or another are alone, isolated, expatriated, even when they remain within their families or return to their fatherlands. One of the most significant features of Mavis Gallant's fiction is that, while she has never restricted herself to writing about Canada or about Canadians, and has written more than most creators of fiction on people of other cultures whose inner lives she could enter only imaginatively, she has never, during her period as a mature writer, written from immediate obser-

vation of people living in her here-and-now. Distance in time and place seem always necessary.

Almost all the stories I shall be discussing have been written in Paris, where Gallant has lived most of the time since she left Canada in 1950. By now she has so lived herself into the Gallic environment that most of her friends speak French, and the depth of her involvement in French affairs was shown very clearly in "The Events in May: A Paris Notebook" (*The New Yorker,* 14 September, 21 September 1968), which recounted her adventures and observations during the abortive revolutionary situation of 1968 in France.

The "Notebook" dealt almost exclusively with French people and their reactions to events around them, and it showed the same sharp observation of action, speech and setting that one finds in Gallant's stories. There were parts, one felt, that only needed to be taken out of the linear diary form and reshaped by the helical patterning of memory for them to become the nuclei of excellent stories. Perhaps one day they will, but up to now Mavis Gallant has rarely written in fiction about these Parisians among whom she lives. What happens when she infrequently does so is shown in **"The Cost of Living,"** where the two young French bohemians of the story (only one of them a Parisian) are less important than the two Australian sisters whom they exploit and whose education in "the cost of living"—to be interpreted emotionally as well as financially—provides the theme as well as the title of the story.

Similarly, though Mavis Gallant has written on occasion about Canadians in Europe, who usually find it hard to accept the lifestyles they encounter (or avoid encountering), it took her twenty years after her departure from Montreal to turn to the imaginative reconstruction of the vanished city of her childhood and youth, in the five interlinked Linnet Muir stories which have appeared in *The New Yorker* but are as yet uncollected. These examples of memory transmuted, which in intention at least bring Mavis Gallant very close to the Proust she has admired so greatly, form one group among the stories I shall be discussing.

It is virtually impossible to escape memory as a potent factor in Mavis Gallant's stories, and the next group of fictions, while they do not draw on the memory of personal experience, are imaginative constructions in which remembered observations and remembered history play a great part. They concern the Germans (a people Mavis Gallant does not know from experience as well as she knows the Canadians or the French or even the English), and specifically the post-Nazi-Germans. One novella and six stories are here involved. The novella and five of the stories comprise the volume entitled **The Pegnitz Junction;** one other German story, **"The Late-homecomer,"** appeared in *The New Yorker* (8 July 1974), but so far it has not been collected.

The last group are tales of people trapped as foreigners in the meretricious vacation worlds of continental Europe. The main characters in three of the stories—all set on the Riviera—are English, remnants of a decaying imperial order, at once predators and victims: these are **"An Unmarried Man's Summer"** (*My Heart is Broken,* 1964), **"In The Tunnel"** (*The End of the World and Other Stories,* 1974), and **"The Four Seasons"** (*The New Yorker,* 16 June 1975). The fourth, **"Irina"** (*The New Yorker,* 2 December 1974), is one of those rare stories in which Mavis Gallant touches on the literary life; its eponymous heroine is the widow—Russian by descent—of a famous Swiss novelist, but here too there is an English character who is not quite minor. (pp. 94-5)

To begin, there is no real generic division so far as Gallant is concerned between short stories, novellas and novels. She rarely writes the kind of story which Chekhov and de Maupassant so often produced, in which an episode is treated as if it were a detached fragment of life, and the psychological insight or the moving symbol or even the ironic quip at existence is regarded as sufficient justication for the telling.

Mavis Gallant never uses fiction with such aphoristic intent; she is neither an episodic writer nor an intentional symbolist, though in her own way she is certainly an ironist. Her stories are rarely bounded by time or place. Where the overt action is trapped in a brief encounter at one place, memory is always there to deepen and extend whatever action we have witnessed; sometimes the memory emerges in dialogue, sometimes in the thoughts of the participants, sometimes it is offered by the narrator, and this multiplicity of viewpoints is again typical of Mavis Gallant, and creates a kind of story never bounded by what "happens" within it, always extending in time beyond the overt present, and tending, no matter what way of evoking memory is used, to produce a kind of fictional "life," however condensed it may be.

This kind of biographical sweep is one of the special features of Gallant's fiction, making a story like **"An Unmarried Man's Summer"** the life portrait not only of an individual but also of a whole doomed caste of Englishmen. It means that her stories are never like fish hauled out of the flow of existence and left to gasp rapidly to their ends; they are, rather, left to swim in their element, which is the imagination that rejects the beginnings and ends necessary to linear fiction. Every one of the four stories I am now discussing is in this sense suspended in mid-flow; we are made aware of the past that has brought us to this particular eddy in time, and we even have an inkling of how the future might flow on out of the eddy. Gallant's novellas, and her novels, only differ from the short stories in their greater complexity and in the fact that more of a life is worked out within the observed present of the fiction.

I think the point I have made about Mavis Gallant's lack of an inclination towards intentional symbolism is really related to this aspect of her fiction. It is not a naturalistic fiction, but it is a fiction of enhanced reality, in which life is reshaped by artifice, but not distorted; part of the artifice is in fact to give this imaginative reshaping of existence a verisimilitude more self-consistent than that of existence itself. This means that what the story actually contains and not what it may suggest is of primary importance. The final effect of the story may be symbolic, but it is not written with symbolic intent in the same way as, say, plays like Ibsen's *Wild Duck* and Chekhov's *Seagull,* in which the named and central symbol becomes so important that the very action is shaped to fit it and in the end the ultimate goal of the whole work seems to have been no more than to give the symbol a manifestation in human life.

The difference can be seen if we look directly at **"In the Tunnel."** In this longish story a Canadian girl named Sarah, infatuated with a half-baked professor of sociology, is shipped off by her father to Grenoble, which she immediately leaves by the Route Napoleon, heading for the Mediterranean. Here she falls in with an Englishman, a former colonial civil servant named Roy Cooper, who charms her into going to live

with him in the Tunnel, which turns out to be "a long windowless room with an arched whitewashed ceiling," in the grounds of a bungalow in the hills away from the sea, belonging to a couple named Tim and Meg Reeve, who actually detest the Mediterranean and have come here as refugees from the enormities of labour governments in Britain.

Sarah falls hopelessly, masochistically, in love with Roy, who turns out to be appropriately sadistic, a typical English cad in whom the colonial years of witnessing hangings and inspecting prisons have encouraged a natural cruelty and a brutal conservatism. The Reeves are lower middle class "characters," speaking an absurd private language, feeding coarsely, despising everyone who is not English, and treating their impossible dogs (the "boys") to endless "chocky bits." They openly talk of Sarah as yet another in Roy's long succession of feminine appendages, and Sarah shows herself endlessly vulnerable. "In love she had to show her own face, and speak in a true voice, and she was visible from all directions."

Everything seems to go well until Sarah cracks her ankle and limps around with a grotesque swelling on her leg. Roy immediately turns away from her with distaste; his sadism is accompanied by an aesthete's repugnance for anything ugly or imperfect (he describes hangings as ways of ridding the world of flawed people), and Sarah's flaw, however accidentally produced, robs him even of desire, let alone the love he pretended to feel. He turns insultingly cold and, after a final monstrous incident in which they go on a picnic to visit a chapel housing a painting of the hanged Judas, and Sarah gets drunk on the liquor from a jar of plums in brandy, he refuses even to speak to her, and she trails away, swollen ankle and all, in despair. It is only at this moment, as Sarah goes on to her next failure in love, that the Reeves show themselves, under their coarse exteriors, as possessing the remnants of human kindness, covered over by layers of prejudice that clog their perceptions and allow them to reveal their good qualities only under stress and always too late.

The Tunnel is there in the solid centre of the story, the place where Sarah and Roy live, typical of the sluttier fringe of life on the Côte d'Azur. Victim and predator are trapped within this one room so that when the relationship becomes impossible, when the predator is sated, the only way out is for one—the victim—to go. Thus we first see the Tunnel as part of the actual area of living. It is the physical setting and in part the physical cause of what happens rather than—primarily—its symbol. But on another level it is a figure suggesting the tunnel of self-repetition in which each of the characters lives, the narrowness of insight and of view that limits their sense of life. Sarah at least can flee; for Roy and the Reeves the tunnels are unending, with darkness all the way. But the symbol is secondary and consequent; it is not contained within the story as the real Tunnel is. (pp. 96-8)

"Irina" takes us out of the moribund society of English expatriates on the Riviera to the between-world of Switzerland that is the frontier of the Germany of *The Pegnitz Junction.* Irina's own origins are not Germanic but Russian-Swiss, and there is a clue to them in the fact that two months before the story appeared in *The New Yorker* Mavis Gallant published in the *New York Times Book Review* (6 October 1974) an extensive review of *Daughter of a Revolutionary,* whose central figure is Natalie Herzen: after associating with those formidable revolutionaries, Michael Bakunin and Sergei Nechaev, Natalie lived out her long life as a Swiss lady of Russian birth and independent means. Irina's antecedents are deliberately left rather vague, to show how far, until widowed, she fell in the shadow of her husband, Richard Notte, one of those dynamically boring European literary men, rather like Romain Rolland, who were on the right side in every good cause, writing, speaking, signing manifestos, and behaving with profligate generosity to everyone but their own families, who were expected to exist in self-sacrificing austerity. (p. 101)

The early part of **"Irina"** is seen through the eyes of a third person narrator; it is a look at the literary life, and significantly it is an outside look. Gallant, as she remarked to Geoffrey Hancock in an interview published in the *Canadian Fiction Magazine* (No. 28, 1978), found after she had written the story that she identified not with her fellow writer, the formidable Notte, but with Irina, his patient wife. And this implicit rejection of the great man of letters prompts one to remark, in parenthesis, how little of the conventionally literary there is in Gallant's attitude or even her work. . . . There is perhaps a vestige of Gallant's past of left-wing enthusiasms in Notte, but that past she has abandoned completely, and this may be why she attaches it to a male writer made safely dead by the time the story begins. Her mature work is in no way male and ideological; it is feminine and intuitive, and the rightness of detail and surface which are so striking come not from intellectual deliberation but from a sense of rightness as irrational but as true as absolute pitch.

"In loving and unloving families alike," the narrator remarks, "the same problem arises after a death. What to do about the widow?" Irina in fact arranges matters quietly but very much to her own satisfaction, so that it is she whom we find in control of the posthumous fate of Notte's papers, and displaying a caustic and independent good sense in assessing their importance. Yet her children still feel obligated to carry out a kind of King-Lear-in-miniature act by entertaining her by turns at Christmas. Finally the Christmas comes when every son and daughter is abroad or engaged or in trouble, and there is nowhere for Irina to go. The solution is to send Riri, her grandson, to spend the season with her, and the boy sets off with great self-sufficiency, arriving to find that his grandmother already has a visitor, an old Englishman named Mr. Aiken. The rest of the story is seen a little through Irina's eyes, but mainly through Riri's, and what the child's eye reveals is the liberation which can come with someone else's death, for Irina now follows a vague and comfortable life that is very much her own, indulging without needing them, her children's anxieties about her, thinking a little of the great Notte—her recollections of whom bore Riri—but finding in her renewed friendship with Aiken the sweet pleasure of looking down a path her life might have taken but did not. Hers is the marvellous self-sufficiency which realizes that "anything can be settled for a few days a time, but not for longer."

In the stories I have been discussing, memory is important both as method and content, and the past, whose relationship to the present may seem as much spatial as chronological, is vitally there in our awareness. To an even greater extent this is true of the Linnet Muir stories, which are nothing less than deep immersions in memory, divings into a sunken world. A condition in which memory takes one constantly between past and present seems to Gallant a normal state of mind. And that gives a special significance to the group of stories about Germany, mostly included in *The Pegnitz Junction,* which are quite different from anything else she has written.

They are about people whose memories have become atro-phied; about people who have drawn blinds over the past. In writing such anti-Proustian stories Mavis Gallant was deliberately abandoning the very approach through reminiscence, with all its possibilities of suggestive indirection, which she had used so successfully in her earlier stories. She was entering into situations where the present had to be observed and recorded directly and starkly since memory had become so shrivelled and distorted that only what was before one's eye could give a clue to the past. Memory can play a part only in the limited sense of the author's remembered observations. Such a rigorous departure from an accustomed manner is a test, and Mavis Gallant passed it well; her German stories are some of her most impressive, and I think she is right when she says to Geoffrey Hancock that the novella **"The Pegnitz Junction"** is "the best thing I've ever written."

In the same interview, Gallant traces these stories to her interest in "the war and Fascism" and sees their origin in a set of photographs of concentration camp victims which she was given to write a newspaper story about before she left Montreal. Once she had got over the immediate horror, the deeper questions began occurring to her. "What we absolutely had to find out was what has happened in a civilized country, why the barriers of culture, of religion, hadn't held, what had broken down and why." The questions remained with her and she went to Germany "like a spy" to find out for herself. **"The Pegnitz Junction,"** she says, "is not a book about Fascism, but it's certainly a book about where it came from." (pp. 101-03)

I shall deal especially with **"The Pegnitz Junction"** itself, since this novella has a unique interest on a number of levels, but first I would say that what strikes me most about the other German stories is that they are almost all about people whose pasts have been mentally and even physically obliterated: people in other words who are exiled in the most dreaded way of all, by being banished from themselves. As the narrator says in **"An Alien Flower,"** when she talks about her daughter born since the war: "I saw then that Roma's myths might include misery and sadness, but my myths were bombed, vanished and whatever remained had to be cleaned and polished and kept bright."

The central character of **"An Alien Flower"** is a girl named Bibi, doomed to the suicide that eventually overtakes her, who comes to western Germany out of Silesia by way of refugee camps, having lost a past she may have forgotten deliberately, or involuntarily—we are never sure which.

> She never mentioned her family or said how they had died. I could only guess that they must have vanished in the normal way of a recent period—killed at the front, or lost without trace in the east, or burned alive in air raids. Who were the Brü-nings? Was she ashamed of them? Were they Socialists, radicals, troublemakers, black-marketeers, prostitutes, wife-beaters, informers, Witnesses of Jehovah? . . . Whoever the Brünings were, Bibi was their survivor, and she was as pure as the rest of us in the sense that she was alone, swept clean of friends and childhood myths and of childhood itself. But someone, at some time, must have existed and must have called her Bibi. A diminutive is not a thing you invent for yourself.

The use of the word "pure" in this context is significant, since it expresses the desire to see suffering as expiation, but it has a certain grim irony when one associates it with the narrator's remark that: "Anyone who had ever known me or loved me had been killed in one period of seven weeks." The idea of purification and the idea of forgetting or losing the past are closely linked in these stories. In **"The Old Friends,"** a police commissioner has a sentimental attachment to an actress, Helena, cherished in West Germany as a token Jewess, one who as a child inexplicably survived the death camps. "Her true dream is of purification, of the river never profaned, from which she wakes astonished—for the real error was not that she was sent away but that she is here, in a garden, alive." As for the commissioner, knowing "like any policeman . . . one meaning for every word," he cannot deny the horror of the experiences forced on his friend as a child, but he seeks desperately in his mind for a reason to think it all a mistake, something for which a single erring bureaucrat could be punished, rather than something for which his people as a whole might bear some responsibility. (pp. 104-05)

Then there is Ernst, the demobilized Foreign Legionary in **"Ernst in Civilian Clothes,"** whom we encounter in the Paris flat of his friend Willi; Ernst is about to return to the Germany he left as a teenage prisoner many years before. Ernst, we are told, knows more than Willi because he has been a soldier all his life. He knows there are no limits to folly and pain, except fatigue and the failing of imagination. He has always known more than Willi, but he can be of no help to him, because of his own life-saving powers of forgetfulness.

When Thomas Bestermann, in **"The Latehomecomer,"** returns from France, where he has stayed too long because the records of his past (and hence his official identity) were lost, he meets a man named Willy Wehler who with a certain peasant cunning ("All Willy had to do was sniff the air") has managed to slip through the Nazi age without becoming as scarred as most survivors. (p. 105)

In **"An Autobiography"** the narrator, a schoolmistress in Switzerland whose German professor father was shot by Russians in Hungary, had met in her poor refugee days a boy named Peter who as a child—like Helena in **"The Old Friends"**—miraculously escaped death by being arbitrarily taken out of one of the contingents of Jews headed for the gas chambers. Now when she is firmly settled in the womb-like refuge of Switzerland, she encounters Peter once again and realizes that he has become a mythomane, constantly changing his past to suit the company, but for that reason uneasy with someone who knew him in his actual past.

> But I had travelled nearly as much as Peter, and over some of the same frontiers. He could not impress me. . . . He knew it was no good talking about the past, because we were certain to remember it differently. He daren't be nostalgic about anything, because of his inventions. He would never be certain if the memory he was feeling tender about was true.

And even during that German past which everyone in Mavis Gallant's stories wants to avoid or to remember as it never was, those fared best who had the power of shedding their earlier pasts and hence their identities. An example is Uncle Theo, an amiable Schweikish nobody in the Bavarian story, **"O Lasting Peace."** Uncle Theo avoided involvement in the war almost literally by losing himself. When he went for his medical examination he found that all the physical defects he could rake up were insufficient to get him rejected.

> He put on his clothes, still arguing, and was told to take a file with his name on it to a room upstairs. It was on his way up that he had his revelation. Ev-

erything concerning his person was in that file. If the file disappeared, then Uncle Theo did, too. He turned and walked straight out of the front door. He did not destroy the file, in case they should come round asking; he intended to say he had not understood the instructions. No one came, and soon after this his workroom was bombed and the file became ashes. When Uncle Theo was arrested it was for quite another reason, having to do with black-market connections. He went first to prison, then, when the jail was bombed, to a camp. Here he wore on his striped jacked the black sleeve patch that meant "anti-social." It is generally thought that he wore the red patch, meaning "political." As things are now, it gives him status.

And so Uncle Theo lives on, a survivor by evasion who enjoys the repute and pension of a hero in a Germany that does not want to remember too precisely.

A striking feature of Gallant's German stories is the importance of childhood. There are those whose lives are shaped by ruined childhoods—Bibi and Helena, Thomas the late-homecomer who was bearing arms in his teens, and Ernst who was incorporated as a boy in the Werewolves. But children also seem to offer promise of a future in which there will be a memory of a real past, and it is significant that both the character Michael in **"An Alien Flower"** and Thomas in **"The Latehomecomer"** will marry girls who are mere children in the present of the stories. This is the generation that will again be able to think of "misery and sadness."

In **"The Pegnitz Junction"** we are on the verge of this world where renewal may be thought of. One of the important characters is the little boy Bert, four years old. And the central figure is Christine, eighteen years old and so too young to have any personal memory of the Nazi past. She comes indeed from a place where the re-creation of an older past has made it unnecessary to remember what went on more recently: "a small bombed baroque German city, where all that was worthwhile keeping had been rebuilt and which now looked as pink and golden as a pretty child and as new as morning." Yet she does not need to ignore the real past because she does not know much about it; she carries with her a volume of the writings of Dietrich Boenhoffer, one of the anti-Nazi martyrs.

It is through Christine that **"The Pegnitz Junction"** assumes its special quality. It is the most experimental of Gallant's works, in which she makes no attempt at that special Gallant realism where the web of memory provides the mental links that make for plausibility. Here she is trying to create, in a structure as much dramatic as fictional, a kind of psychic membrane in which recollection is replaced by telepathy.

Christine, it is obvious from the description which opens the story, is the kind of person who becomes a psychic medium or around whom poltergeist phenomena are likely to happen. (pp. 106-08)

Although Christine is engaged to a theological student, she is erotically involved with Herbert, and with him and his son, Little Bert, she makes a trip to Paris. The main part of the novella is devoted to a frustrating journey home which takes them to the Pegnitz Junction. There is an airport strike at Orly, so they return by train. When they change at the German border they find that railway movements have been diverted because of heath fires, and instead of going straight home they must travel in a great arc, changing at a station close up to the barbed wire and watchtowers of East Germany, and finally reaching Pegnitz Junction, where the train to Berlin should be awaiting them. It is not, and when the novella ends they are still at Pegnitz, waiting.

"The Pegnitz Junction" is a work of much complexity, and deserves an essay of its own. I will be content to dwell on three aspects that mark its distinctiveness among Mavis Gallant's stories. The first is the intrusion of what appears to be a much stronger element of intentional symbolism than one finds elsewhere in Mavis Gallant's writings. One cannot avoid seeing the train journey as an elaborate figure, representing the wanderings, without an as yet assured destination, of a Germany which has not recovered a sense of its role in history and, indeed, fears what that role might be if it were discovered.

Then there is the peculiar relationship between Christine and the other passengers. With Herbert it is mostly a simple matter of conversation and her inner thoughts about their relationship, and with Little Bert it is a question of exchanging fantasies. But with the other people encountered on the journey Christine falls into a state of psychic openness, so that messages are exchanged, and their flows of thought emerge to multiply the range of viewpoints.

Their immediate fellow passengers are a Norwegian professional singer with a mania for yogic breathing and an old woman who is constantly munching food from the large bags she has brought with her. The Norwegian, occupied with singing and breathing, has merely a few comments to offer, but from the mind of the old woman there emerges an extraordinary unspoken monologue. Surprisingly—in the context of these stories—it is a reminiscent one that reconstructs a past elsewhere; she lived through the dark years in America and came back to Germany to bury her husband and water his grave after the war ended. But there are remoter messages which trip the levers of Christine's telepathic sense. When the train stops at a level crossing, she suddenly enters the minds of the people waiting, and at the station on the East German border she catches a refugee's memories of the girl in his lost village. Then, at Pegnitz Junction, there is the pregnant country girl who pretends to be an American army wife, from whom Christine receives the strangest message of all: the contents of a letter about racketeering in PX stores from one GI to another that she is carrying in her bag. Not only does this technique give a dramatic quality to the novella, since it becomes so largely a pattern of voices heard in the mind's ear, but there is a cinematic element in the way the outer, visible and audible world cuts away from the inner world and back again; one is reminded of Mavis Gallant's days in a NFB cutting room.

Finally, there is the centrality of the child, Little Bert, who is present and intervening throughout the novella, occasionally making an Emperor's-clothes remark of penetrating aptness, but most of the time involved in his fantasy of the life of the sponge he calls Bruno, which he shares with Christine, but over which he seeks to maintain control, so that he rejects versions of Bruno's adventures that go beyond his ideas of plausibility. For Bruno after all—as Bert makes clear on occasion—is merely a sponge to which he has given a life. History—the irradiation of actuality by imagination—seems to be stirring in this infant mind.

The final group of stories I am discussing is the Linnet Muir cycle, set in Montreal between the 1920s and the 1940s. (pp. 108-09)

The Linnet Muir stories are no more autobiographical than Proust's great fictional quest, and no less so. Linnet Muir is about as near to Mavis Gallant as the linnet (a modest English songbird) is to the mavis, which is the Scottish name for the magnificent European song thrush. There are things in common between writer and character, and just as many dissimilarities. Gallant, like Linnet, spent her childhood in Montreal where she was born. Her father died when she was young, and at the age of eighteen one of the first things she did on returning to Montreal—this was 1940—was to try and find out how he died. A few people and a few incidents thus stepped from real life into the stories. But everything has been reshaped and transmuted in the imagination so that what emerges is a work of fiction on several levels. It is a portrait of Linnet Muir as a child isolated in her family, and later as a young woman between eighteen and twenty isolated in her fatherland. But it is even more, as Gallant herself has insisted, a reconstruction of a city and a way of life which have now been irrevocably engulfed in time past but which, as Gallant has said, were "unique in North America, if not the world" because the two Montreals, the French and the Anglo-Scottish, were so completely shut off from each other. And, since in this way these stories form a fiction about a collectivity rather than about individuals, one of their striking features is that the narrator, through whose consciousness everything is seen and who is the one continuing character, does not stand out more vividly in our minds than most of the other characters; all of them, down to the slightest, are portrayed with an almost pre-Raphaelite sharpness of vision. (p. 110)

In order of appearance in *The New Yorker,* which I assume is roughly the order of completion, the first story, **"In Youth is Pleasure,"** sets the theme by showing Linnet in search of the lost world of her childhood. A girl of eighteen, having suffered the contemptuous ignorance of Americans about the country above their borders, she returns to Montreal with a few dollars and immense self-confidence. Almost without thought, she seeks out the French-Canadian nurse of her childhood, and is given unquestioning hospitality. But when she moves into the other Montreal, that of her own people, and tries to find out about her father, she encounters reserve, distrust, even fear. The search for her father is significant in view of Gallant's own theory that perhaps the one distinctive Canadian theme is to be found in the role of the father, who in our literature seems always more important than the mother. Linnet remembers her mother in somewhat derogatory terms as a person who "smiled, talked, charmed anyone she didn't happen to be related to, swam in scandal like a partisan among the people." But the search for the father is, in a very real sense, the beginning of Linnet's search for truth. She never really does find out how he died; all she can assemble is a cluster of conflicting rumours and theories, so that she is never sure whether he actually died of the tuberculosis of the spine that attacked him in his early thirties or shot himself with a revolver she remembered seeing in a drawer in her childhood. In the end she shapes the past in her own mind: "I thought he had died of homesickness; sickness for England was the consumption, the gun, the everything." She realizes all at once that this is not her past. "I had looked into a drawer that did not belong to me." But what she finds in the process is that the world which saw him die with such indifference was a narrow provincial world where wealth and influence were the only virtues, the world of the Montreal tycoons.

"Between Zero and One" and **"Varieties of Exile"** are further stories about Linnet's experiences when she returns to Montreal, and they are dedicated to obsolescent kinds of people. In the first story Linnet works in a Montreal draughtsman's office (as Jean Price does in **"Its Image on the Mirror"**) and all the people around her, until a woman bitter from a failed marriage joins the staff, are either men too old to fight in World War II but full of recollections of an earlier conflict, or unfit men. It is an entirely English world—an office that does not contain a single francophone, a collection of men with the prejudices of their time who neither know nor wish to know the other nation that shares Quebec with them. Canada, for them, is English; its loyalties are imperial. And they have accepted limitations for themselves as well as for their world. It is a world to which Linnet does not belong, any more than does Frank Cairns, the remittance man in **"Varieties of Exile,"** with whom she strikes up the precarious relationship of two people out of their place and world when she encounters him on the train going from her summer lodgings into Montreal. Frank and his kind, the castoff young men of English families, were the nearest thing in Canada to the superfluous men of Russian literature, and as a species they vanished when World War II dried up the flow of cash from home and most of them went back to fight for a country that had thrown them out. Strangely enough, if the men in the office taught Linnet how narrow life can be made, Frank Cairns, who seems happy only when he is going home, helps to open her mind with his own restless questing, and when she hears of his death she is happy that "he would never need to return to the commuting train and the loneliness and be forced to relive his own past."

All these three stories display memory doubly at work. Linnet the narrator is looking back thirty years to another Linnet exploring a lost Montreal whose doom was sealed by the social changes World War II began in Canada. But the Linnet of thirty years ago in turn is remembering, seeing her own childhood again as she experiences aspects of the city of which she was unaware when she lived protected in the family which is the subject of the two stories that follow and that up to the present complete the published cycle: **"Voices Lost in the Snow"** and **"The Doctor."** They are stories of a family of the age between the wars: father and mother still young, but already separated by work ("I do not know where my father spent his working life; just elsewhere") and by relationships, for in **"Voices Lost in the Snow"** the father, who is already dying though nobody knows it, takes the child to see a woman, an estranged friend of her mother, with whom he still maintains contact.

In these stories, once again, we have the sharp visuality of Gallant's earlier work, and the gripping evocations of a Montreal that has long vanished beneath the blows of the wrecker's ball. (pp. 111-12)

As **"The Doctor"** shows, Linnet's family inhabits a shifting frontier territory where the two cultures of Montreal meet, as they rarely do elsewhere.

> This overlapping in one room of French and English, of Catholic and Protestant—my parents' way of being, and so to me life itself—was as unlikely, as unnatural to the Montreal climate as a school of tropical fish. Only later would I discover that most other people simply floated in mossy little ponds labelled "French and Catholic" or "English and Protestant," never wondering what it might be like to step ashore, or wondering, perhaps, but weighing

up the danger. To be out of a pond is to be in unmapped territory.

A frequent guest to her parents' house is Dr. Chauchard, who in another role is the pediatrician attending Linnet at the age of eight. The bicultural salons are dominated by a flamboyant Mrs. Erskine, who has been the wife of two unsuccessful diplomats and moves in Montreal society escorted by Chauchard (now transformed into genial Uncle Raoul) and various attendant young Québecois intellectuals. But even such encounters take place in a no-man's-land so insecure that the common language is always English, and Linnet does not know, until Dr. Chauchard dies, that he had another life in which he was a notable Québec poet, as she discovers on seeing his obituaries, one for the pious member of his family, one for the doctor, one for the writer.

> That third notice was an earthquake, the collapse of the cities we build over the past to cover seams and cracks we cannot account for. He must have been writing when my parents knew him. Why they neglected to speak of it is something too shameful to dwell on; he probably never mentioned it, knowing they would believe it impossible. French books were from France; English books from England or the United States. It would not have entered their minds that the languages they heard spoken around them could be written, too.

Vignettes of a dead time; of a lost world; of a vanished city. Yet it is easy to lay too much stress on the social-historical nature of the Linnet Muir stories. (Though Gallant herself gives some support to such emphasis when she talks of the "political" nature of her stories.) They are so successful as records of an age because they are inhabited by people so carefully drawn and individually realized that the past comes alive, in its superbly evoked setting, as experience even more than as history. And that is the true rediscovery of time. (pp. 113-14)

> *George Woodcock, "Memory, Imagination, Artifice: The Late Short Fictions of Mavis Gallant," in his* The World of Canadian Writing: Critiques & Recollections, *Douglas & McIntyre, 1980, pp. 93-114.*

ANNE TYLER   (essay date 1979)

[*An American novelist, short story writer, and critic, Tyler is acclaimed for her whimsical and revealing portrayals of eccentric families in such novels as* Dinner at the Homesick Restaurant (1982) *and* The Accidental Tourist (1985). *In the excerpt below, she offers a favorable review of* From the Fifteenth District.]

[**From the Fifteenth District**] is billed as "a novella and eight short stories," but it's not clear which is the novella. . . . Each is densely woven, wide-ranging, rich in people and plots—a miniature world, more satisfying than many full-scale novels.

In **"The Four Seasons,"** a young Italian servant girl watches an English family crumble and disintegrate as Mussolini comes to power. In **"The Moslem Wife,"** a fascinating marriage between two first cousins unravels against the background of wartime France. **"The Remission"** covers the downward spiral of a small family struggling through the father's slow death in a foreign village. **"His Mother"** is a study of life among the mothers of Hungarian émigrés—those women left at home in Budapest to compare one another's gift sweaters and birthday telephone calls, to decipher letters from English-speaking daughters-in-law, to puzzle over photos of their sons in distressingly tatty American blue jeans.

Nearly everyone in these stories is expatriated—figuratively if not literally. . . .

The hero of **"The Latehomecomer,"** returning to Berlin after serving time in France as a prisoner of war, remains an expatriate even in his mother's apartment. Everything about him, from his bleeding gums to his ragged clothing, "said 'war' when everyone wanted peace, 'captivity' when the word was 'freedom,' and 'dry bread' when everyone was thinking 'jam and butter.' " A Swiss grandmother is forced to ask her very French grandson what, exactly, he is called. A refugee, having discovered the nephew who is his only surviving relative, recalls with chilling dispassion the nephew's long-dead mother: "Her dress had short sleeves. She wore no stockings. She had a clockwork bear she kept winding up and sending round the table. She was hopelessly young."

Foreigners either in geographical terms, or in terms of time or slant of view, these people provide the sense of distance that makes Mavis Gallant's writing so coolly, dead-center accurate. They seem surprised to find themselves in their particular lives. They describe their surroundings with a clarity that appears to have been startled out of them. . . .

They are afflicted with bizarre handicaps that they treat as normal—a tendency to suspend one's breathing, for instance, or the audible, inner commands of a younger self requesting "a child's version of justice . . . an impossible world." In [**"From the Fifteenth District"**], the dead are haunted by the living. Their survivors are inquisitive, intrusive, anxious to impress upon the dead their own versions of the truth, while the dead (expatriates, too, of a sort) buck and chafe at the imposition. . . .

Most collections of short stories must be read in several sittings. Otherwise, the rise and fall of one writer's voice, repeated too often in too small a space, lessens the effect. But this book is not so fragile. There is a sense of limitlessness: each story is like a peephole opening out into a very wide landscape. The characters will go on with their lives, you feel, even when their slim allotment of pages has been exhausted. They have only briefly, graciously consented to allow us in, persuaded by the skill and tact of Mavis Gallant.

> *Anne Tyler, "European Plots and People," in* The New York Times Book Review, *September 16, 1979, p. 13.*

TED MORGAN (essay date 1979)

[*Morgan is an American critic, biographer, and autobiographer whose publications include* On Becoming American (*1978*) *and* Maugham (*1980*), *a biography of W. Somerset Maugham. In the following excerpt, he praises Gallant for the scope of her characterization in* From the Fifteenth District.]

Mavis Gallant is not a woman writer, she is one of our best writers of short fiction who happen to be a woman. In **"The Latehomecomer,"** the story [in *From the Fifteenth District*] written in the first person with a male narrator, she handles the subject of war from an undramatic, prosaic point of view: A German prisoner-of-war returns to Berlin five years after the war to find that his mother has remarried and that he has a stepfather.

The young man's name was not called when the repatriation order came, and he remained in France as a worker long after he should have. When he comes home, he finds a new name engraved on the brass plate next to the bellpull: "I put my hand over the name, leaving a perfect palm print. I said, 'I suppose there are no razor blades and no civilian shirts in Berlin. But some ass is already engraving nameplates.' "

Quietly, without engaging her characters in a confrontation, Gallant contrasts the young man's life in France with the situation he finds upon his return, and makes us feel that a certain kind of captivity is preferable to a certain kind of freedom. In France he was his own man, he fell in love, he traveled. Back home he is trapped between a stepfather who resents him and a mother who concentrates on housework. The young man asks himself: "Why am I in this place? Who sent me here? Is it a form of justice or injustice? How long does it last?"—precisely the questions a prisoner-of-war might ask about his place of confinement.

A common theme runs through the best of these stories, which have to do with people who are not living in their own country, people displaced by choice or circumstance—a Polish refugee in Paris, or the English who migrated to the south of France "with no other purpose than the hope of a merciful sky." Running parallel to the sense of geographical displacement is an emotional displacement caused by separation.

In **"The Moslem Wife,"** Jack and Netta Ross are cousins who have married and are running a hotel on the French Riviera: "They worked hard at an Englishness that was innocently inaccurate, rooted mostly in attitudes." Jack is gregarious and drawn to other women, recruited among the hotel guests, while Netta becomes known as "the Moslem wife" for her submissiveness and her unshakable love for her husband. During World War II, Jack is caught in America, where he attaches himself to another woman, returning five years later, "like the heir to great estates back home after a Grand Tour." For Netta, separation has been a slow death, and the burden of resuming their shared experience is entirely hers, since Jack shrugs off the past as if it did not matter. Jack's insensitive good humor disgusts Netta, but soon "the wave of revulsion receded, sucked back under another wave—a powerful adolescent craving for something simple, such as true love."

In **"The Remission,"** another story about the English in the south of France, Alec Webb is dying in a hospital while his wife Barbara takes care of their three children. Alec's absence has left a vacuum which is filled by another Englishman, Eric Wilkinson, but the children reject the newcomer. (pp. 77-8)

In **"Potter,"** the love affair between Piotr, a fortyish Polish refugee living in Paris, and a young Canadian girl, is almost a parable on the chasm between the new world and the old, except that Gallant has her characters so firmly rooted that they never become emblems. The Canadian girl "was spending a legacy of careless freedom with an abandon Piotr found thrilling to watch, for he had long considered himself to be bankrupt—of belief, of love, of license to choose." Her innocence, good nature, and optimism are set against his conviction that life always does one in. She leaves him for other lovers, making him miserable, but always returns. He is finally the one who leaves, when he is forced to return to Poland, and realizes that he is the stifled one, to whom passion is not permitted.

In Gallant's work, there is no obvious connection between the author and her material. One wonders how she knows so much about a young German soldier, a Polish refugee, a hotel owner, or other characters apparently outside the range of her experience. (p. 78)

Ted Morgan, "Writers Who Happen to Be Women," in Saturday Review, Vol. 6, No. 20, October 13, 1979, pp. 76-8.

GRAZIA MERLER (essay date 1980)

[*In the following excerpt, Merler favorably discusses the stories in* From the Fifteenth District *as astute studies of the unpredictable nature of memory.*]

The nine short stories in [*From the Fifteenth District*] have all appeared in *The New Yorker* between 1973 and 1979. The shortest story, [**"From the Fifteenth District"**], synthesizes with lapidary rapidity (7 pages) and understated humour the one major preoccupation running through the other eight stories: the quirky behaviour of memory.

In each story the reader is confronted with the filtering effect on events of time-duration. Events undergo various transformations according to the point of view and the emotional distance of the narration. Unlike any other of her short stories thus far (she has written about ninety between 1950 and 1980), **"From the Fifteenth District"** (1978) breaks the lifespan barrier of the characters presented. These characters are ghosts and they are being haunted by the living. Even though the two ladies (both loyal mothers and wives) and the one gentleman (a patriotic Major) have died at different times and in different circumstances, they all register a common complaint with the police department of the Fifteenth District: they are all kept from resting in peace by the unreliable and distorted memories of the living. In short, memory with all its variables is alive and well but it haunts both the living and the dead. Because the generating force of memory is complex and often contradictory, the clear delimitation of an event or detail is most arbitrary. In other words, the creation of the story, the artifact (the reconstruction of a situation by someone's recollections) generates in turn its own independent life. Unlike Pirandello's or Oscar Wilde's somber treatment of this observation, however, Mavis Gallant's is humorous, discreet and fanciful. Each dead character wishes to have his or her version of the events recorded so that the living will stop haunting him or her with their obtuse curiosity, their thirst for sensationalism, their guilt, their gratitude.

One is easily tempted to affirm that Mavis Gallant refuses to weave a linear plot in her stories. In fact, several possible plots are sketched simultaneously and infinite care is given to specific minute details relating to the events and the mannerisms of the characters. At times the reader feels that the pieces are more important than the entire fresco. What happens in the story is of little importance, what fascinates is the choreography of the narrative voice, and all the possible ramifications of a continually shifting focal point.

Only one story in the collection is told in the first person, **"The Latehomecomer"** (1974). The story begins in 1950 in Berlin. Thomas, at the age of twenty-one, is finally sent home from France where, by mistake, he was still held as a war prisoner. Although the main concern of all the characters in the story is to forget the past (because of guilt, of fear, of indolence) one's past is used and selected according to the material and emotional needs of the present in order to isolate and protect oneself from others. Towards the end of the story,

Thomas, still supposedly just arrived at his mother and stepfather's house, during his latehomecomer's dinner with neighbours, projects into the future (he will marry Gisela, still a child, asleep in her father's arms) either in a dream or a premonition or a simple piece of information. What matters is not the particular event or information, but how it is being filtered in the characters' minds. The first person narration in this case allows not only a closer insight into the personal alienation of the latehomecomer, but also a more "innocent" appraisal of the behaviour of the Germans during and after the war. Thomas is the outsider and he can thus cast a "naive" eye on what he perceives of post-war Germany.

The particular order of the nine short stories of this collection would suggest a moving-away from time and from chronology into a type of universalism. The last four stories of this collection: **"From the Fifteenth District"** (1978), **"Potter"** (1977), **"His Mother"** (1973). **"Irina"** (1974) are precisely situated in space, but not in time, although roughly because of specific details within the stories, one could think that they take place in the seventies. **"Potter"** and **"His Mother"** deal with the variables of memory and of imagination. In both stories the narrator interprets and comments on the point of view of the main character, his search for self-justification and purpose. Potter, the Polish poet and lecturer, tied to his visa and passport, is almost relieved when, after considerable filtering and manipulation of feelings and facts, he concludes that all he feels for Laurie is tenderness. He is in a sense relieved (even though disappointed) not to be burdened by love. In **"His Mother"**, it is only after the departure of the son that the mother acquires vitality, purpose, status. Left behind in Budapest, she has become an emigre's mother, she can create as she pleases the memories of her son as well as her own daily reality. In **"Irina"** the narrative voice focuses also on the main character, the grandmother, but, because of its emotional distance, it reveals the same determination of the character to isolate herself at one level in order to be able to live her own existence, but at another level to be able to manipulate reality as she pleases. Irina refuses to play the role of the famous writer's widow that her five grown children have cast for her. She affirms her consciousness of the shiftiness of reality: "Anything can be settled for a few days at a time, though not for longer." Both Irina and Riri, her grandson staying with her for the Christmas holidays, have their own way of "settling" things; what is essential, Irina affirms, is not to interfere.

The emotional and physical alienation of the characters gradually becomes the affirmation of self-survival by the creation of a perpetually-changing reality. By extension, this type of exile could be taken as the portrayal of the creative artist's isolation. The lack of a specific time-reference (apart from Christmas in **"Irina"**) in the last four stories in this collection emphasizes the isolation, the desire for self-determination and the creative forces of memory filtered and altered by the passing of time.

The first five stories of this collection, on the other hand, contain specific time references. **"The Four Seasons"** (1975) takes place on the Ligurian coast when Italy entered the Second World War. **"The Moslem Wife"** (1976) takes place again along the Ligurian coast in France before and after the war. **"The Remission"** (1979) takes place on the Riviera in the early fifties. **"Baum Gabriel, 1935-( )"** (1979) takes place in Paris, in Montparnasse mainly, between the early sixties and the late seventies. In spite of the fidelity to history and chronology, however, and in spite of the realistic portrayal of the Riviera in the fifties and forties as well as the vivid depiction of the changing face of Montparnasse since the Algerian crisis, realism, either social or psychological, is not at the heart of these stories.

The common theme of the three short stories taking place on the Ligurian coast before and after the war is the neutralizing effect of time in the course of exploitation and survival. In **"The Four Seasons"** the Unwins exploit the young maid, Carmela, and yet it is Carmela who in the long run will imperturbably affirm her dignity. In **"The Moslem Wife"**, soon after her marriage, Netta is tied to the business of running the hotel, she is alert and dull; it is only after Jack's departure, as she weathers the war by herself, that she acquires lucidity and light-heartedness, she acquires the capacity to evaluate, filter, transform, neutralize memories and reality. Jack, meanwhile, as he returns after the War and is taken back by his wife, seems to have lost the consciousness of the past. He has no guilt, no remorse, he has become dull, stolid, lifeless. He seems to have lost, with the memories of the past, the imagination to filter, evaluate and alter reality. In **"The Remission"** Alec comes to die on the Riviera. His wife, Barbara and their three children wait by him with some attention, no love, no hate, no impatience, occupied at first by the new situation and by the wait, but, as time passes, intent more and more on living, on creating their own present and yet another situation. With the passing of time, Mr. Wilkinson replaces Alec, and the rest of the colony of British expatriates joins in to form a new tapestry. As Alec's life is relinquished, Barbara's remission is assured. "He ceased to be, and it made absolutely no difference after that whether or not he was forgotten. In other words, Alec is no more part of the new situation, and the passing of time (the time it took Alec to die) assures the remission (the cancellation of life and the forgiveness) both of Alec and of Barbara. By the time Alec dies, his wife and his children have become another story.

"Baum Gabriel 1935-( )" similarly reflects on the disappearance of his uncle August. "He needed to add the dead to the living, or subtract the living from the dead—to come to some conclusion. . . . His uncle by dying had not diminished the total number of Baums but had somehow increased it." Unlike the three previous stories, whose tone is more serious, this is almost flippant, not unlike the ghost story that gives the book its title. Gabriel recalls, in some respects (his part-time occupation as an actor, his buoyancy), another character, Willi, appearing in other stories by Mavis Gallant: **"Willi"** (1963), **"Ernst in Civilian Clothes"** (1963), **"A Report"** (1966). Gabriel, like the Willi of these stories, becomes progressively more conscious and capable of assuming his foibles. As the narrative voice becomes more distant, it also becomes more sympathetic. Both Gabriel and Willi seem to be in a state of inertia, reliable, gratuitous, devoted to whatever role they assume from day to day.

As in the other stories of this collection, the reader is confronted with the neutralizing effect of time-duration and the revitalizing effect of the shifting of the roles played by the characters. As the story begins Gabriel is inconvenienced by two major complaints: "Sometimes, feeling strange and ill, he would realize that heart and lungs were suspended on a stopped held breath. . . . His second complaint was that he seemed to be haunted, or inhabited, by a child. . . . whose scores he had rashly promised to settle before realizing that debt and payment never interlock." As the story progresses, Gabriel assumes the precariousness and the injustice of life, he learns, like Irina, that "anything can be settled for a few

days at a time", providing he retains the capacity and the imagination to filter, rearrange, shuffle information and memories.

Gabriel is a part-time actor. Movies and television programs about the Resistance, the Occupation and the Liberation are being made. Dark and curly-haired young Gabriel plays the role of the victim, the haunted Jew, while the balding, chubbier, older Gabriel plays the role of the German surrendering officer. This time, even if he plays again the role of the loser, the helmet is light, comfortable, and the uniform is so impressive that German tourists still want to photograph it. Parallel to the roles that Gabriel assumes at the fictional level as an actor, are the roles Gabriel plays in the changing landscape of Montparnasse, in the cafe La Meduse, and the role Gabriel plays as a person: a nephew, a young man in love, an aging man keeping Dieter company. At all three levels the dominant trait of Gabriel is the capacity to transform, to sift facts and events. Gabriel is presented by a narrative voice that is incisive, ironical but tender, even though the emotional distance from the events narrated is great, or perhaps because of this distance, the narrator appears to be a sympathetic outsider. (pp. 35-7)

Grazia Merler, in a review of "From the Fifteenth District," in West Coast Review, *Vol. XV, No. 1, June, 1980, pp. 34-7.*

MICHAEL THORPE   (essay date 1982)

[*Thorpe is an English-born Canadian critic, editor, and poet whose critical studies include* Doris Lessing (*1973*) *and* John Fowles (*1982*). *In the following excerpt, Thorpe maintains that the pieces in* Home Truths *transcend stereotypical depictions of Canadian life and temperament.*]

[Gallant's introduction to *Home Truths*] reveals an unease with the category, "Canadian stories." She has never tried to "write Canadian," nor to claim the label of nationalist or even patriot. She embraces rather a "national sense of self," not questioning its identity, and rooted in that "deeper culture contained in memory . . . inseparable from language." "The writer . . . owes no more and no less to his compatriots than to people at large."

However dubious its principle of selection, this three-part sequence allows the reader to measure (though not chronologically) the emergence at varying intensities of that deep culture contained in memory and shaped by language. The opening story in the first, "At Home" section, **Thank You for the Lovely Tea** was written, she tells us, at eighteen. Its acerbic tone, bold character-placing and fluent manipulation of an action in which a schoolgirl strips her father's defencelessly "emotional" American mistress to the skin with a peeled, keen eye and then flays her with a sly tongue, are coldly precocious. One is reminded of the early Katherine Mansfield (to whom another piece pays implicit tribute) and discovers in later stories an evolution in depth and compassionate, yet detached, understanding, no less reminiscent of Mansfield's development. Beyond the cool precision of such shorter pieces as **"Tea," "Jorinda and Jorindel,"** with its ironic delineation of the hard gestures of caste and class, **"Orphan's Progress,"** a bitter tale of emancipation from love, and **"Prodigal Father,"** a bleak exposure of mere blood affinity, we are drawn into ampler explorations of family, class, the fortuitous relations of exile, that largely make up the second and third sections.

The unity may be hard to seek in the longer stories (as in Mansfield's *multi-cellular* pieces), but their power certainly stems from a fullness of rendering that enables a many-sided, complex understanding. In the second group of four stories, "Canadian Abroad," the condition of exile offers scope to explore conflicts of culture, dislocations of identity and occasions for acute self-questioning. The most impressive of these, **"The Ice Wagon Going Down the Street,"** takes the elaboration needed to develop a subtle, improbable yet convincing affinity between Peter Frazier, one of *the* "Ontario" Fraziers, pampered and purposeless, and Agnes Bursen, the mouse-like "Norwegian" girl who says, "I'm from Saskatchewan . . . I'm not from any other place." They meet in Geneva, expatriates adrift from the caste or creed that sustained and held them apart in their Canadian worlds. Each becomes enigmatically necessary (it is not sexual) to the other, incomplete without the other, yet in surface personality utterly contrasting. In its sibylline way **"Ice Wagon"** is the collection's most *Canadian* story. Almost as strong is **"Virus X,"** in which Lottie, Canadian academic student of minorities abroad, rejects the European inoculation, symbolizing otherness, offered her by Vera, the "Uke," a girl despatched by her family into French exile to bear an illegitimate child. In these stories the issue Canadian *versus* otherness employs nationality as a counter in the universal game of conformism *versus* individuality. In other pieces it is often the English, whether of the native or Canadian variety (unable to take seriously their new country) who are probed most deeply to expose their dependence upon a shallow, eroded national identity. . . .

The third group of (six) stories is linked through a character called Linnet Muir, who speaks in the first person. Published in the seventies, these stories are a richly matured evocation of the setting, atmosphere and manners of the Montreal where Gallant spent much of her youth. While she disclaims identity with Linnet, they share a tenacious independence, a hatred of conformity, of lying relationships and, not least, a horror—as she recently told a *Globe* interviewer—of ending up a "sensitive housewife." The stories read like an episodic memoir, braced with sceptical comment upon life—humorous, resilient, acute—exposing shams, self-delusion, false images, and with a keen political awareness (none of this markedly *Canadian*). Two stories, **"Voices Lost in Snow"** and **"The Doctor,"** stand out for their intense atmosphere, through which memories of childhood are thrown into shifting relief against an opaque adult world of mysterious gesture and verbal indirection.

Michael Thorpe, "A National Sense of Self," in The Canadian Forum, *Vol. LXI, No. 715, February, 1982, p. 40.*

DAVID O'ROURKE (essay date 1982)

[*In the following excerpt, O'Rourke explores the theme of exile in* My Heart Is Broken.]

Exile may well be Gallant's preoccupation, but it is not so much an exile of space as it is one of time. Her characters have typically taken a wrong turn in life and are unable to go back. In *My Heart Is Broken* (1964), Gallant fuses technique and theme in order to portray this universal dilemma. A careful analysis of each story reveals the unity of the collection and clarifies the Gallant "exile" as a person who is locked into a present situation, condition, stage of personal history, from which escape is difficult, and sometimes impossible.

"Acceptance of Their Ways" is set against the backdrop of winter, "the dead season," in an Italian Riviera pension distinguished by the smell of "decay." The story covers the span of one evening and the morning after. During Mrs. Garnett's "last meal" before her departure from the pension, an argument erupts between her and the owner, Mrs. Freeport. Watching the owner, water lily in hat, shouting at Mrs. Garnett reminds the only other guest, Lily Littel, of similar fights with her former husband. Mrs. Garnett finally, and literally, buckles under the verbal onslaught of Mrs. Freeport. After the rather orgasmic triumph, the victor becomes very loving toward the sobbing Mrs. Garnett. This tenderness is shown again the next day at Mrs. Garnett's farewell. It is when Mrs. Freeport is feeling her most wretched and, perhaps, most human, that Lily delivers the blow of her next-day departure for Nice. It should be remembered that "Mrs. Freeport couldn't live without Lily, not more than one day." Mrs. Freeport comes to the realization that eventually she will be abandoned completely. "Instead of answering," Lily adjusts Mrs. Freeport's water lily, "which was familiar of her." Not surprisingly, Lily becomes identified with the water lily. As Mrs. Freeport has cruelly triumphed over Mrs. Garnett, so Lily has won at the expense of her instructress, Mrs. Freeport. Lily has come to accept their antiseptic ways. She has become adept at stinging in a gentlewomanly, sophisticated fashion. (pp. 98-9)

In **"Bernadette,"** Robbie and Nora Knight, although considerably younger than Mrs. Freeport and Garnett, are also exiled from the vitality of their youth. They have come to live a façade: a picture of the liberal WASP, bourgeois lifestyle. Their maid, Bernadette, is everything that they are not—she stands for spontaneity and life, as opposed to analytical dissection. Bernadette is given books to read but, unlike Lily Littel, is not a very good student. She chooses not to accept the Knights' ways. Rather than trying to understand things to death, Bernadette stands in awe of the mysteries of life. She represents a youth that is ultimately compelling in attraction for Robbie, but a threat at the core for Nora. The reason is that Bernadette symbolizes something they might both have become. After college, Robbie and Nora sacrificed authentic feelings and desires in order to programme themselves for a materialistically rewarding existence. The route taken has left both discontented, resulting in a very precarious sort of marriage.

The time of the story is late December. The living-room has been set for a post-Christmas, discussion-group party. It is ironically described as being "like a room prepared for a colour photo in a magazine." As **"Acceptance of Their Ways"** builds to a climax in which a character loses all composure, so Nora loses control when the party gets out of hand. Throughout, Robbie's temperature rises. It is significant that his illness is a cold. . . . Winter is used to depict the decline of the Knight marriage; that it is the end of the year does not suggest a very optimistic future for Robbie and Nora as a couple. But winter is also employed to represent a stage in life into which Robbie, particularly, finds himself locked. It is not a coincidence that Robbie has a cold and feels frozen at the same time he is trying to get back to the warm centre of his school days. He has left behind an important vitality—"the only result of his reading was a sense of loss." By contrast, the younger Bernadette represents "an atmosphere of warmth and comfort": "She was the world they had missed sixteen years before, and they, stupidly, had been trying to make her read books."

Like **"Acceptance of Their Ways,"** the story covers a time-span of just under two days. On the second, Nora confronts Bernadette with the knowledge of the latter's pregnancy. She tries to dissect the situation in the same way that she dissects her relationship with Robbie. Not surprisingly, she is shaken by the prospect of Bernadette's harbouring new life. Her mistake comes in assuming that Robbie is the father. It leads Robbie and Nora to individually admit that their marriage is a sham—like their living-room, a picture lacking much substance.

Bernadette, like Lily Littel, flowers outside of a claustrophobic boarding house. She leads a secret, and double, life in which emotions are given full reign. She is also able to find refuge in fantasy. Sitting in a theatre, she identifies with the people in the film who are looking on, never expecting the "picture" to become true for herself. In this sense, she lives the authentic life compared to the Knights' rather empty existence. She feels nothing but warmth for the child, aware that it will become an "angel" awaiting death—very similar to her own situation, trapped in an environment and culture neither of which is conducive to life. (pp. 99-101)

"Its Image on the Mirror" is of novella length, yet the story line is relatively simple. The lives of two sisters—one vital and spontaneous, the other prim and predictable—are traced more for reasons of contrast than to arrive at any specific point in plot. This is not to say that **"Its Image on the Mirror"** is a simple story. Gallant orchestrates several levels of time and provides a well-intentioned but not totally reliable narrator in the person of the prudent sister, Jean Price.

Briefly stated, the chronology is all backwards. The story begins with a middle-aged Jean carefully trying to think back to the summer of 1955. She recalls helping her parents move from their Allenton home in July of that year, then remembers her sister's promise to join them at the cottage for the Labour Day weekend. The weekend is recounted in some detail before the reader is led even further back in time to a World War II Montreal. Still more light is shed on Jean and her Isadora Duncan-like sister, Isobel, before the reader is left "hanging" with a conclusion not unlike, in style, the ending of *The Great Gatsby*. Jean feels that, for the first time, Isobel needs her and, consequently, will never shut her out of her life again. Of course, this conclusion is quite ironic. The narrative has already shown that the sisters grow even further apart. Not only does Isobel end up moving to Venezuela, but Jean also becomes a perfect carbon copy of her mother.

"Its Image on the Mirror," being longer, magnifies the technique used in most of the short stories. References to the past are employed to inform the present. Middle-aged Jean, the picture of contentment, is revealed to be a very insecure person who is envious of her sister's rebellious spirit. Early in the story, Jean is seen to feel sorry for her father: "It seems hard to have your views shared by everyone around you all your life and then confounded in your old age." And yet there is a real danger of this happening to Jean. The narrative demonstrates that she clings to, and echoes, her mother's opinions like someone holding on to a lifeline. She has sacrificed spontaneity, vitality, in order to fulfill some preconceived notion of proper behaviour. Isobel is her opposite, and must be at-

tacked and criticized, or Jean's life will be revealed for the sham that it is. Isobel is the person Jean might have become.

There are a number of rather remarkable similarities between **"Its Image on the Mirror"** and **"The Cost of Living."** In the former story, there is a five-year age difference between Isobel and Jean. When they meet at the summer cottage after a separation of six years, Isobel is thirty-three and Jean thirty-eight. In **"The Cost of Living,"** Patricia and Louise also meet after a six-year separation; Patricia is thirty-three and Louise thirty-eight. Patricia describes herself as having been the "rebel" of her family: "I had inherited the vanity, the stubbornness, without the will; I was too proud to follow and too lame to command." In contrast, the older Louise is best described as "prudent." She has a predisposition towards proper behaviour, and frequently adopts not only her mother's stance but also her inflection. The echoes of **"Its Image on the Mirror"** are quite clear. Isobel and Jean are back with an important twist. Although Louise makes "a serious effort to know" Patricia, she eventually becomes more interested in Sylvie. The latter is described as "the coarse and grubby Degas dancer, the girl with the shoulder thrown back and the insolent chin": another Isadora Duncan. As the story unfolds, the differences from **"Its Image on the Mirror"** begin to multiply. In a sense, the other sides of an Isobel and a Jean are presented. Louise is prudent, but there can be little doubt about her warmth and love. Sylvie is energetic, but also selfish and immature. The most dramatic difference lies in the reaction of Louise to her own mother's death: "With every mouthful of biscuit and every swallow of tea, she celebrated our mother's death and her own release."

Louise's sudden liberation is like a springtime in winter. She meets Patrick on December 21st, falls in love, and begins to transfer the attention, previously paid to her invalid mother, to this new lover. It soon becomes apparent that Patrick represents to Louise more than simply his own person. After Patrick's departure, Louise says to Sylvie, "I've forgotten what he was like"; Patricia, the narrator, quickly notes, "But I knew it was Collie Louise had meant." Later, Patricia observes:

> Louise never mentioned him [Patrick]. Once she spoke of her lost young husband, but Collie would never reveal his face again. He had been more thoroughly forgotten than anyone deserves to be. Patrick and Collie merged into one occasion, where someone had failed. The failure was Louise's; the infidelity of memory, the easy defeat were hers.

In a theme typical of Gallant in *My Heart Is Broken,* one character employs another as a kind of double for a person who has been lost in the past. When Patrick rejects this love, Sylvie becomes the next emotional surrogate. In a sense, Louise's history has been one of displaced love—from Collie to her mother to two characters in Paris. It is significant that the narrator notes that Sylvie is young enough to be Louise's daughter: "Sylvie must have been born that year, the year Louise was married." The winter in Paris then becomes to Louise an opportunity to play out what might have been in her own life.

But Louise's attraction for Sylvie probably goes even deeper. If **"Its Image on the Mirror"** is considered an expansion of this situation, we may conclude that Sylvie represents to Louise a certain vitality or exuberance which she herself lacks. The interest in Sylvie then becomes a fascination with an aspect of herself which has never been developed. The difference is that by living a life that might have been, Louise is better able to adjust to her present situation instead of being left with a vague sense of loss. She comes to recognize by contrast with Sylvie's irresponsibility her own distinct merits. She even goes so far as to encourage Sylvie to adopt some of her own rather old-fashioned (for bohemian Paris) attitudes: initiative and prudence in monetary matters. By April, a genuine spring, the narrator observes of Louise, "the ripped fabric of her life had mended." It has been a painful process, hence the title of the story, but she has been able to accomplish in physical encounter what is usually only attempted on the psychiatrist's couch. Having come to terms with the past, Louise is able to leave the stage of the present for what appears to be an optimistic future in Australia.

The female characters in **"My Heart Is Broken"** and **"Sunday Afternoon"** are not so fortunate. They appear as helpless victims of lives that have "gone wrong." In **"My Heart Is Broken,"** Jeannie has been raped and beaten by an unidentified assailant. The assault is an implicit comment on the beating that Jeannie is taking at this stage of her life. She lies on the bed, pathetically still doing her nails. She is still trying to look pretty in an environment which steps on whim and penalizes any sign of sensuality. The stern and sexless Mrs. Thompson knowingly tolls "Winter soon," despite the fact that it is only August. She signals the reality that if Jeannie is to stay with her husband and adjust to the life presented in **"My Heart Is Broken,"** she will have to abandon her youthful instincts, her wonderful naiveté. But the story is as much Mrs. Thompson's as it is that of Jeannie. It is not unreasonable to assume that Mrs. Thompson may once have been as vitally alive as Jeannie, prior to accepting the grotesque sentence of pushing a doll carriage. In this sense, Jeannie is Mrs. Thompson's window on the past. It is therefore natural for Mrs. Thompson, when she looks at Jeannie, to end up "trying to remember how she'd felt about things when she was twenty." Mrs. Thompson's state is even more pathetic than Jeannie's. The younger Jeannie still has her humanity, still feels pain, whereas all Mrs. Thompson can do is sit "wondering if her heart had ever been broken, too."

The setting of **"Sunday Afternoon"** is a "married scene in a winter room." As in **"My Heart Is Broken,"** a brief sketch is offered of a young, and seemingly helpless, heroine trapped in a relationship—really a life situation—not older than five months. Veronica Baines clearly sees her forlorn position in the "black mirror" of the apartment window. Jim feels no more love for her than does the Algerian for the European girl being led from the Montparnasse café. Just as Jeannie wants to be liked, so would Veronica like to be loved. Unfortunately, she has to settle for "a ribbon or so, symbols of love" which she, herself, has to provide. The climax of the story arrives when Veronica discovers that not only has she not been sufficient reason for Jim to dip into his large cache of money, but in fact the money has been hidden for the express purpose of preventing her from spending it.

Veronica and Jeannie have much in common with the character of Sylvie in **"The Cost of Living."** All three are sensual women with child-like mentalities; they prefer to be taken care of as opposed to developing their own initiative. When something goes wrong, particularly in the case of Veronica and Jeannie, there is a tendency to stand bewildered rather than change course. They tragically lack the discipline of a Louise, and have not (yet) developed "double lives" to allow

for the protection of what is vital in environments hostile to emotional growth. (pp. 102-05)

Although the *New Yorker* stories collected in ***My Heart Is Broken*** range from the years 1957-63, they achieve a tight unity through a repetition of theme and technique which approaches pattern. Throughout, Gallant is shown to be primarily interested in problems of the status quo. The sterility of an old order, frequently manifested by a pseudo-aristocratic gentility and symbolized by the season of winter, is contrasted with a vitality traditionally assigned to the working-classes and youth. Characters suffer "revolutions" in which they come close to losing "control," or lead "double lives" in order to conform to societal expectations and, at the same time, retain what is essentially human and true. This is not to say that all of the younger characters in ***My Heart Is Broken*** are paradigms of desired behaviour. Many lack the very "control" without which independence is impossible. What is called for is a balance, a determination, a flexibility which allow for continued growth. (pp. 106-07)

> David O'Rourke, "Exiles in Time: Gallant's 'My Heart Is Broken'," in Canadian Literature, No. 93, Summer, 1982, pp. 98-107.

RONALD HATCH   (essay date 1982)

[*In the review excerpted below, Hatch describes the stories in* Home Truths *as insightful portrayals of the effects of Canada's puritanical past on its citizens.*]

Home Truths is divided into three sections: "At Home," "Canadians Abroad," and the recently written Linnet Muir stories. In the first two sections, the stories date from 1956, although many have never been reprinted since their initial appearance in *The New Yorker*. Gallant's collections have been so few that some of her most brilliant stories, for example **"Jorinda and Jorindel,"** appear here for the first time between book covers. (p. 125)

[With] the Linnet Muir stories as a core, there is good reason for [the publisher] to offer us a book about Canada and Canadians. Indeed, Gallant has remarked recently in a CBC interview in Vancouver that she would like to write more out of contemporary Canada, but to do this she would have to live here for a time, since "new civilizations" have appeared since she left in 1950. (p. 126)

On the Canadian question, however, Gallant herself is decidedly uneasy with the narrow limits that have sometimes been placed on what constitutes Canadian art, and finds herself puzzled that people should be in doubt about their nationality. As to what makes a Canadian, she comments that "the first years of schooling are indelible" in creating one's national base, and that "a deeper culture is contained in memory." Certainly one of Gallant's main concerns in fiction over the years has been the portrayal of children gaining social attitudes and the part that memory plays in the creation of the present.

Many of the stories contained in ***Home Truths*** are about children who are deprived of their own deepest personality, of their core, and the sorts of manoeuvres that their bodies and minds make to regain their lost centre. The story **"Saturday,"** Gallant comments, is about language, in that the main character, Gérard, has been deprived by his parents of his first language when, as French Canadians, they decided to leave behind the Roman Catholic Church to find freedom from darkest tyranny. Since the Church was tied to language (indeed, most things in Quebec are tied to language) it was necessary for them to make a complete break by speaking English. The irony is that the decision achieves anything but freedom for Gérard, who is spiritually hobbled without his own language—forced to speak English badly, and unable to feel his way back into French. The rest of the family have not really escaped the old patterns either: Gérard's mother, freedom-loving in theory, becomes another version of the self-sacrificing French-Canadian mother, with her abhorrence of sexuality; the daughters have happily married English Protestant husbands, but are going about their business of raising large families in the old style. Indeed, one of Gallant's points is that most people do not mind the restrictions of security. Satisfyingly comfortable, such roles provide tremendous security. The story depicts how each member of the family is trapped in his own particular labyrinth, with the exception of the youngest child, who appears to be altogether unusual in his single-minded pursuit of his own life. Having kept French for his personal, almost private language, Paul speaks spontaneously, thereby inhabiting a different world from the socially constructed people around him. The story ends in a blinding moment of illumination when Paul achieves a fragment of genuine communication with his father, choosing a French phrase which daringly echoes the words of God. A particular delight of these stories about Quebec is the way Gallant freely uses French phrases from time to time without feeling the need for a translation.

Although these stories are within the realist tradition, Gallant supplements realism with so many other techniques that one rarely finds a story that feels wholly realist. **"Jorinda and Jorindel,"** for example is about a young girl of eight, and her experiences at a summer cottage not far from Montreal. Nothing could be more familiar. But in fact the story begins late at night with a lonely woman shouting across the lake that she has finally learned to dance, a shout that wakens young Irmgard from a dream of a witch, a dream that will haunt the story to its end, and which will never be quite resolved. Gallant uses a virtually surreal frame "to place" the quite normal experience of children discovering that three is one too many. All summer long, Irmgard has played with Freddie, a French-Canadian boy, until Bradley arrives on the scene from New York and Irmgard discards Freddie for what she takes to be Bradley's superior virtues. But what I have called the "surreal frame" also intrudes at crucial moments, so that neither child remains simply himself. Freddie has some of the qualities of an intuitive *naïf*, and Bradley—with a sty in his eye, a poison ivy rash, and tennis elbow—is well on his way to developing all of the odious qualities of a self-serving individualist. Moreover, the scene where Irmgard chooses between Freddie and Bradley—two different ways of life—is enacted with extraordinary intensity, Gallant comparing it to the dizzying moment when, cycling down a steep hill, Irmgard loses control of her bicycle and is about to crash. Terrified, she closes her eyes, and chooses Bradley by default. The seemingly trivial act of throwing over Freddie becomes one of a series of crisis acts which tightens life into an irrevocable pattern, after which it will be impossible to return to Freddie and all he stands for. (pp. 126-27)

Although many writers have explored the ways in which Canada's puritanical past influenced children (one thinks immediately of Hugh MacLennan, Robertson Davies, and Margaret Laurence), Gallant is surely one of the more brilliant writers to show the dialectic which exists between the individual and this puritanism. Whereas many writers have simply criticized Canada's dour Scottish inheritance, Gallant seems far more aware that the social code is in large part maintained by the individual's need to sustain his sense of reality. Instead of attacking an abstraction, therefore, Gallant delights in portraying the various possible reactions to what has been called Canada's "curse." For example, in **"Thank You for the Lovely Tea,"** Gallant tells of three young girls being taken from a strict boarding school by a woman who hopes to marry the father of one of the girls. It soon becomes apparent that the school's sense of rigid decorum, where all emotionalism, all spontaneity, is discounted, has become the implicit model of reality for all the characters, even the adults. The reactions range from the conventional attempt to make oneself over into a life-time student, to a kind of schizophrenic obsession with private concerns, to a full scale rebellion which ironically turns the individual so far in the opposite direction that she becomes the perfect paradigm of the school's code: the policewoman figure, watching everyone else and judging them by her own austere standards. Interestingly enough, Gallant has prefixed to her Introduction to the volume as a whole a quotation from Boris Pasternak: "Only personal independence matters." As this story indicates, Gallant is only too aware of how difficult it is to escape from the reified sense of social reality into true freedom—if such a thing can be said to exist.

Indeed, one might even say that the concluding stories, those based on the character of Linnet Muir, are Gallant's most recent and subtle attempt to define and to *create* personal freedom, for it has become clear in her latest fiction that the very act of writing, of creation, is one of the ways to allow the imagination to develop freely with as few restrictions as possible. It is even possible to use Michel Butor's idea of fictional narrative as "research" in connection with these stories, for there is an ongoing sense of discovery that accompanies the narrative line. In other words, the emphasis is not so much on the well made plot as on the process of revelation made possible by the kind of circling narration that Gallant employs. For many readers, probably, this aspect of the stories may well be lost; the historical accounts of old Montreal are so graphically drawn that one is tempted to sit back and enjoy the evocation of a *genius loci* that has now practically vanished. (p. 128)

These Montreal stories also bear a certain resemblance to Margaret Laurence's *A Bird in the House* in that they are told by an older woman looking back over her earlier years. Like Vanessa MacLeod, Linnet Muir is very much a rebel, determined to live her own life from her own perceptions, to stand on her own feet. When she returns from New York to Montreal at the age of 18, she firmly believes that once the war is over a new world will be ushered in, a world where Truth with a capital T will reign. She has been reading Freud and Lenin, and believes these codes will unlock a new age. A new kind of character for Gallant, Linnet is a young woman with tremendous self-confidence and daring, who in her personal life believes it is time for the revolution to begin. When she applies for an office job with a Government department, she demands a position with the men and not the "coolies." Part of the interest is in watching how this young girl meets the challenge of the male establishment head-on, and then learns to her surprise that men create limits for themselves only slightly larger than women's. By jumping the fence to the men's side, she has only landed in another kind of compromise: there is no new truth, no new freedom, only different kinds of slavery. And so, as the stories progress, Linnet and the reader both discover that her revolutionary behaviour is as much a kind of *reaction* to the given sense of reality as the pusillanimous acceptance by the men and women around her.

Far more terrifying still is the knowledge that it is impossible to live forever in the space between zero and one—the undefined space before maturity. Eventually decisions must be taken that locate the individual firmly in the social world whether she likes it or not. And here is where Gallant's skill as a writer reveals itself, for she nowhere attempts to describe a solution; instead she allows the meaning to emerge from between the spaces of the narrative, leaving each reader to come to his own understanding of what Christopher Isherwood used to call a "dynamic portrait," one that changes the closer one looks. Indeed, the very balance of Gallant's prose style makes this apparent. In the closing sentence of **"In Youth is Pleasure"** Linnet says: ". . . time had been on my side, faithfully, and unless you died you were always bound to escape." In binding one to escape, we have a sentence that denies what it seems to be advancing—the very ambiguity that is central to Gallant's depiction of the real, which every individual both creates even as he is created by it. For Gallant, the problem is to bring this crucial relationship, which usually remains buried beneath and within perception, to the surface so that in critical moments the fissure between the individual and his world can be experienced. In this way, freedom itself may be achieved—if only for brief moments. For all their mimetic verisimilitude and seeming simplicity, then, the Montreal stories constitute a major challenge to the reader, a challenge that one could term, with some small hesitation, ontological. (p. 129)

Ronald Hatch, in a review of "Home Truths: Selected Canadian Stories," in The Canadian Fiction Magazine, *No. 43, 1982, pp. 125-29.*

MAUREEN HOWARD (essay date 1985)

[*An American novelist, short story writer, critic, and editor, Howard is known for works that focus on female characters whose striving for identity often conflicts with their career aspirations and their socially prescribed roles. In the review of* Home Truths *excerpted below, Howard classifies Gallant's best stories as those concerning displaced Canadians attempting to reconcile their histories.*]

[Mavis Gallant] is a very good writer indeed; so accomplished as a social critic of her country and of the European cities where she has chosen to live (Paris has been her home in recent years) that many of us who have admired her stories in *The New Yorker* over the years may not have given full credit to her range or to the strongly imagined shape of her work, the best of which is in [*Home Truths: Selected Canadian Stories*]. . . . Canada is not a setting, a backdrop; it is an adversary, a constraint, a comfort, the home that is almost understandable, if not understanding. It is at once deadly real and haunting, phantasmagoric: the Canadian presence varies from story to story.

In **"Jorinda and Jorindel,"** which sweeps together the fragmented myths of a summer and the commentary of a clever little girl into a fairy tale, Irmgard, who is not quite 8 years old, observes of her cousin: "Bradley is not required to think of answers; he is American, and that does. But in Canada you have to keep saying what you are." It is exactly this kind of

pressure that operates to good advantage in all the stories. (p. 1)

In *Home Truths* most of Mrs. Gallant's Canadians are either bound by convention or wasted by efforts to transcend a culture they perceive as imitative, provincial and second-rate. The struggle to wrench a personal identity out of a skewed national identity can lead her to create grotesques and buffoons: matrons, Red Queens, who wear pearl earrings like the Duchess of Kent's. Bertie Knox, clerk and mimic, can do any Canadian accent, but during World War II he keeps a photograph of himself over his desk "in full kilt, Highland Light Infantry, 1917: he had gone 'home,' to a completely unknown Old Country, and joined up there." . . .

With few exceptions, these stories are set in the late 1930's and 40's. Mrs. Gallant has a sharp sense of history. Incidents are carefully dated—Prohibition, Depression, treaties, the entrance of Canada into "Hitler's war." She writes of a Canada that was and makes good use of her Red Queens and clownish clerks to set up cultural pretensions and longings. She's funny and perceptive on houses, on dress—the customs of a country in which you could almost never be right.

Quick as she is with telling details—flat nasal accents, ugly reddish-brown streets—Mrs. Gallant never patronizes her country. There is no complicit wink at the reader, no easy put-down—the mere reference to shopping mall, beer brand, K Mart, the smart visual that asks for the conditioned response in too many American stories of recent years. Her Canadians are as particular and complex as Eudora Welty's Moodys and MacLains. When she uses types—the cold godmother, the remittance man—it is to redefine an attitude, correct a memory. . . .

In **"Varieties of Exile,"** the disreputable or younger son sent out from England—the remittance man—is played off against the real refugees who flood into Montreal. These "Belgians, French, Catholic German, Socialist German, Jewish German, Czech" come to Linnet Muir, she admits, "straight out of the twilit Socialist-literary landscape of my reading and my desires." The story is about Linnet's willful idea that people must behave according to the script in her head. The refugees are romantic. The remittance man she meets on a commuter train is not. Looking back, she can date her discovery that life does not adhere to literary models, nor can she peg people, get them all down. The refugees are busily assimilating, even taking out Canadian passports. The remittance man—vaguely intellectual, a woolly socialist—she has written off. But he appears heroically in casualty lists as "Maj. Francis Cairns, dead of wounds in Italy." . . .

Mrs. Gallant has a remarkable sense of place. Her snowy streets and stark row houses are as carefully drawn as Elizabeth Bowen's English cities in wartime. Her men and women do not live their exacting stories in a void. Where you are is as important as what you are. It's more than atmosphere—whether you find Paris, Geneva, the south of France liberating, therefore possible, or whether you live thinly in those cities as an outsider, but know that going home will never do. She is as sure of her Montreal as Joyce was of his Dublin—that it is the place from which the stories flow.

She has written well about France and Germany, though there is more dependence on reportage and a tendency to be anecdotal when she cuts free of her Canadians. **"The Pegnitz Junction"** was an arresting novel that strained for invention trying to get at the roots of Nazi culture and ended up mannered. (p. 26)

[In *Home Truths*] she is most likely to astonish when she buys her own wisdom and refuses to be orderly and neat, so that we hardly notice the plot within plot, or that the untidy asides, further reflections (she is always so bright) will not give a single or good answer. Many of these stories are quests—a search for answers that turn out to be conflicting or partial. At times it would seem to the young that the answers given them about the past are true and it is best to turn away.

In **"Bonaventure"** a musical prodigy is terrified of nature. Staying in Switzerland with the widow of a famous composer, a keeper of the flame, he is plagued by insects, plants, bird song. Water from a natural spring seems to him bilious, diseased. It is all too mysterious, too random. He does not want to learn the names of trees, or mountains. His parents have been overly explicit about the accident of his conception, which he has come to see as an unnatural act: "They kept feeding him answers when he hadn't asked for anything." Their love, the widow's primordial strength are abhorrent to him, and he makes a dash for civilization and its easier discontents. What pursues the prodigy is "the possibility of lapsed genius" and the possibility that he is sickly, ordinary like his father, a mild Canadian. The truth, which he runs from, seeps through in this story like a dark hereditary stain.

The same fears come to Linnet Muir, but there the dangerous debts to a moody, disconsolate mother and an attractive, bohemian father are acknowledged in a calm retrospective voice, though never completely set aside: "I began to ration my writing, for fear I would dream through life as my father had done. I was afraid I had inherited a poisoned gene from him, a vocation without a gift. He had spent his own short time like a priest in charge of a relic, forever expecting the blessed blood to liquefy." Mrs. Gallant cuts deep. It is not merely what you are that is problematic, there is also the terrifying proposal of what you may never be.

I have one quibble with *Home Truths* as a collection: aside from the amazing **"Jorinda and Jorindel,"** the opening pieces in "At Home" do not give the reader the full promise of what is to come. I recommend **"In the Tunnel"** and **"The Ice Wagon Going Down the Street"** from the next section, "Canadians Abroad," as particularly good examples of her success with more ambitious tales. I don't think this indicates that Montreal is better seen from Paris, but the ideas of exile and return, reclaiming and remembering do seem to up the ante in Mrs. Gallant's fiction. The Linnet Muir stories, written from the mid- to late 70's, are wonderful, actually full of a young woman's wonder at the past. They bear a thematic resemblance to Mary McCarthy's *Memories of a Catholic Girlhood* . . . in the search through family legends, hearsay, lies for a story that will approximate some version of the truth.

Like Miss McCarthy, Linnet Muir attempts, reasonably and unsentimentally, to discover what really happened, who people *were:* but that line of inquiry yields to and finally nourishes richer material—the more difficult stories that reveal herself. . . . Mrs. Gallant's reconstruction of Linnet's return home in the war years is closely informed by exact events, by place and authentic emotions, as good stories always are.

Linnet is 18 and already knows too much, then sets herself to finding out a good deal more. She has raced ahead and is engaged to be married. In **"Between Zero and One,"** we find her working in a wartime office among statisticians and engineers, faking a job she does not understand. "I spoke to Mr. Tracy: What occupied the space between Zero and One? It must be something arbitrary, not in the natural order of numbers. If One was solid ground, why not begin with One? Before One there was what? Thin air?" Mr. Tracy says, "Don't worry your head." Going back to that time, Linnet associates it with her belief that limits are different for women and men and with the terror that lay before her in a headstrong marriage, the warnings she did not heed. Many years later she can only repeat the same questions without answers: "How do you stand if you stand upon Zero? What will the passage be like between Zero and One? And what will happen at One? Yes, what will happen?" That "yes" still looks forward bravely, even if life does not prove out.

A Canadian friend of mine remembers going to a stadium to welcome the young Queen Elizabeth and her new husband—30,000 little boys yelling and waving the Union Jack. Canada has changed dramatically, irrevocably. Mavis Gallant has made it her business to look back. In the hard act of knowing her origins, she has written powerful stories. Her home truths tell us what we can (and cannot) do with what we have been assigned. (pp. 26-7)

Maureen Howard, "When the Identity Is the Crisis," in The New York Times Book Review, *May 5, 1985, pp. 1, 26-7.*

D. B. JEWISON   (essay date 1985)

[*In the following excerpt, Jewison analyzes imagery and narration in the novella* Green Water, Green Sky.]

Green Water, Green Sky, the short novel Mavis Gallant published in 1959 when she was thirty-five, contains the germ of much of her later writing: subtle, even enigmatic characterization; a plot which focuses upon a few significant moments of the lives of the characters and leaves the long stretches between to be dealt with by brief allusions or not at all; suggestive but unforced use of images that edge towards symbols but never become rigid or entirely predictable; themes of imprisonment and deracination, of people who frequently became mere ends to those whose weaknesses make them dangerous, of escape from, or entrapment in, time, and the related theme of memory. Above all, this story which portrays the destructive relationship between Bonnie McCarthy and her daughter, Florence, contains, as Desmond McCarthy once said of *Uncle Vanya,* real tragedy because it captures both the flatness and poignancy of life.

At fourteen, Flor is in Venice with her mother, her seven-year-old American cousin George Fairlie and his parents. She is thin, sunburned, haughty, and she despises her young cousin. From this time in his life George especially remembers one scene that seems in retrospect to be a prognostication of the disaster of Flor's life. Before Florence has the necklace which her mother just bought her around her neck, she has broken the string, intentionally George believes. She pointedly throws the beads away, embarrassing her mother with her wild gestures. George further displeases Flor by retrieving some of them, and holds onto one for more than a decade, regarding it as both a talisman and the symbol of that day when "someone once wished him dead." Flor's "mad" behaviour indicates her rejection of being appropriated by her mother and George into the clan of the Fairlies. It is the first indication of her symbolic rebellion and real capitulation which ends in madness. It is a scene that twelve years later George remembers as a "wild girl breaking a necklace, the circle of life closing in at fourteen, the family, the mother, the husband to come." By the time she is twenty-six, she suffers from vertigo and only pretends to read because by now the reading which was once her refuge from her uprooted state is impossible; she can no longer relate sentence to sentence. She sees a painting as exploding forms and, like a suicidal character from a novel by Virginia Woolf, believes that human ingenuity is concealing the ruin of Paris, a city in which, for her, there is no present. Her vision of a "ruined, abandoned city" eventually drives her to the darkness of her shuttered bedroom where she searches for the dreams that will allow her escape. A moment of ecstacy came at the age of twenty-four when, in the hotel room in Cannes with Bob Harris, she felt a "concrete sensation of happiness" that she believed was caused by "the passage of light." During this state of dark happiness she was "in a watery world of perception where impulses, doubts, intentions, detached from their roots, rise to the surface." The reader is thus prepared for her approaching madness in which her psyche achieves the rootlessness of her physical existence. The image of a "watery world" is again interesting in relation to Virginia Woolf. In *Mrs. Dalloway,* for instance, perceptions of the world as if it were under water suggest both ecstacy and madness. Water, used by Woolf extensively as a symbol of unity, often signifies reconciliation through death and is therefore dangerously ambiguous. Eventually, Flor, whose rejection of life extends, apparently, even to a psychosomatic avoidance of puberty, ("She never had her periods," her mother confides to Wishart), escapes into a world of water and dreams of green water and green sky.

Flor's image of "a watery world of perception" at her moment of happiness enriches the fox image through which she explains to herself her difficulty with reality. She attributes her vertigo, "The effort of lines to change their form," to "the triumph of the little fox," a torment that began when she first found herself uprooted and wandering across Europe with her mother. When she is inhabited by the fox, the ordinary power of language fails her. " 'Sometimes when I want to speak . . . something comes between my thoughts and words.' She loathed herself at this moment. She believed she gave off a rank smell. She was the sick redhead; the dying, quivering fox." She recovers in this instance and the fox departs. Later, when she reads in Doris's letter "All children eventually make their parents pay, and pay, and pay," she has no time or desire to say, "they have paid," but immediately senses her own triumph and sees the fox departing, its head breaking the water as it swims out to sea, while she leaves the sea behind and goes in the other direction into a memory of childhood where she is the perfect child welcomed into her father's arms. The irony is that it is Flor who is truly at sea, submerging as she does the pain of her rejection by her father when she was about to enter puberty in her own watery world of perception, just as she did earlier during the concrete sensation of happiness that she felt in the hotel room at Cannes. Her incompleted puberty shows how intensely she has clung to her "perfect" self. She is, in a sense, an extreme version of her mother who also would like to maintain her own self-image of innocence. Flor's vision of reconciliation with her father is the dream she has been searching for, although the reader might not at first be aware of this because of the way Gallant has interrupted chronology by reversing the order of events in Chapters II and III. The phrase "into her father's arms," while coming just a few pages past the exact middle of the book, is the last of Flor's thoughts ever recorded. It is indeed ironic that her mother once tried to establish the Flor-as-Venus version of her daughter; rather than being born out of the waves, she disappears into them, despite her vision that it is the fox who is vanishing.

Bonnie McCarthy, a "lost, sallow, frightened" woman who wanders "from city to city in Europe, clutching her daughter by the hand" after her husband divorced her for the silly affair with a man she had not in the least loved, retreats in her private moments into the role of a child. Or else, alternating between self-images of innocent young bride and wicked older woman with rolling violet blue eyes, she finds herself fragmented and unreconciled. Her self-contradictory comments about people reveal not her unfounded pride in her idea of what it is to be a Fairlie but her generally confused personality. He nephew George finds her insensitive to her son-in-law, Bob Harris, after Flor has been committed, and he is repulsed by her ability to say whatever is useful for the moment, as in "Florence loved the Paris night." "As a matter of fact [Florence] hardly ever went out at night." But George has the option of dismissing her. Her daughter cannot and pays a great price.

Flor and her mother are tied by a mutually destructive dependence. Flor's statement at the age of fourteen, "I'll always keep her with me," is a mixture of solemn promise and cry of despair; it is love and resentment so mingled "that even Flor couldn't tell them apart." Ten years later, George sees Flor's breaking of the necklace as a sign that his cousin knew she would spend the rest of her life with Bonnie. Flor's disillusionment comes slowly, and, although by the age of twenty-six she is able to reflect bitterly to herself that she "used to believe [Bonnie] was God," she remains unable to take charge of her own life and overcome her dependence. The effect of Bonnie's continued presence in her daughter's life is perhaps most poignantly stated when, at the moment Flor might have said something to her husband to alter the situation between them, Bonnie comes into the room and throws open the shutters, shattering the "delicate goblet" of past love. The narrator's suggestion that perhaps nothing would have happened anyway does not erase the irony of "terribly" in Bonnie's later boast to George, " 'I mattered terribly in their marriage, dear." No one sees the insidious nature of Bonnie's mother-love more clearly than George, who eventually realizes that Bonnie, impervious to seeing the results of her own actions, wants to use him to replace Flor and create "an unmarred Florence, and through her a spotless Bonnie." Bonnie's friend Wishart, a man with more than anyone's required share of inadequacies, sees in the Flor-Bonnie relationship merely a spoilt and demanding child of twenty-four and is disgusted by what he takes to be the world of women, "an area dimly lighted and faintly disgusting, like a kitchen in a slum. It was a world of migraines, miscarriage, disorder, and tears."

The images which most obviously tie together many elements of the novel, including Flor's and Bonnie's mutually ambivalent relationship, are those of mirrors. The first mirror image occurs in the novel's title and, throughout, Gallant uses them to explore the entrapment, relationships, narcissism and identity, as well as the reality and illusion in the situations she presents.

George relates the sky and the water to the time Flor broke

the string of beads in Venice. "Because of her, the twin pictures, love and resentment, were always there, one reflecting the other, water under sky."

Wishart, husbanding his limited resources, works at being ingratiating: "when he was doubtful, or simply at rest, he became a sort of mirror. Reflected in this mirror, Bonnie McCarthy saw that she was still pretty and smart." He also searches for his own image to confirm his position, and his relationship with Bonnie goes awry when, after an earlier successful sighting, he can no longer find himself in her sunglassed eyes. "The dark glasses that seemed to condense the long curve of the beach in a miniature image were averted now. Even a diminished penitent now Wishart could not find his own reflection." He knows that he has deluded himself and that Bonnie has never believed in him. "He had believed that the exact miniature he saw in her sunglasses was the Wishart she accepted, the gentleman he had glimpsed in the store window that first day."

Bonnie too searches for herself in the mirror but, significantly, has trouble focusing on a single image. She is looking for the lost Bonnie of her New York days, "pretty, pert, outrageously admired," but finds instead a triple reflection consisting of the innocent young woman and the middle-aged "Mrs. Hauksbee with rolling violet eyes," and somewhere between the two, something approaching the truth. At another time she sees a triptych of herself reflected in a three-part mirror and has a vision of a woman aging and dependent. Almost like a character in a Beckett play, she finds a focus for her dissatisfaction and says out loud, " 'This just isn't a normal hat.' " This gazing into mirrors suggests an inability to cope with reality. In Gallant's only full-length novel, *A Fairly Good Time,* Shirley prefers to deal with the image of Marie-Therese in the Mirror rather than the real person sitting with her in the room. In **Green Water, Green Sky,** the mirror-related image of the photograph foretells Atwood's later use of mirrors and photos. Flor thinks that, although human cunning keeps "the ruin of Paris concealed," the strangers invading the city are like busloads of tourists arriving in Pompeii who record with their cameras because they are trying "not to live the day but to fix a day not their own." Flor sees the tourist as she sees herself, one for whom "there was no present."

Flor has the most significant encounters with mirrors in the novel. She moves "out of range" of the looking glass in her mother's room to avoid being witnessed by Bonnie who is actually away at Deauville, but she also sees in the "long glass" an image of "a pale rose model in a fashion magazine, neat, sweet, a procelain figure, intended to suggest that it suffices to be desirable that the dream of love is preferable to love in life." That Flor's image in the glass is related to her movement into her world of dreams and madness is suggested by the addition to this scene of, "and still she hadn't achieved the dreams she desired." Her rejection of reality is pointed up when she tells her future husband in Cannes that the room they made love in was "like a place she had imagined. The only difference was that her imagined room was spangled, bright, perfectly silent, and full of mirrors." Two related passages help reveal the complexity of the image. Wishart sees Flor and Bob kiss on the beach and notices that Flor remains outside the kiss. At the same moment, Flor is wondering what it is like for a man to kiss her, and the narrator comments: "It was a narcissism so shameful that she opened her eyes and saw Wishart." This is the same egotism that led her

to say to her cousin George about Venice, " 'Do you remember how green it was all the time? . . . Everything was so clear and green, green water, even the sky looked green to me.' " Flor's description not only does emotional violence to how she actually felt at the time, but goes further and suggests that she has projected her fantasy world onto the past, for in the next sentence the narrator links Flor's apparently distorted memory to her general vision: "[George] had been staring, but now he looked inadvertently into her eyes, dark-lashed, green as the lagoon had been," thereby suggesting that the mirror world of the novel's title is Flor's essence.

In the end, the mirrors fail Flor and she seeks her dreams in madness, but this is only a further stage in her journey. Like the tourists, she has been trying to cope with a time and place not her own. She has, in fact, no place in the world. Bob Harris's imminent departure from Cannes throws at her the eternal question facing Gallant's protagonists: "Why did you come to this place?" The paragraph continues:

> Until now, she had known: she was somewhere or other with her mother because her mother could not settle down, because every rented flat and villa was a horrible parody of home, or the home she ought to have given Flor. When he had gone she would know without illusion that she was in Cannes in a rotting season, the rot was reality, and there was no hope in the mirrored room.

In her desperation, she decides a person can be a country, and so she marries Bob Harris. But when that attempt to define where is here fails, she dismounts from her girlhood pony and runs into the dream-arms of her father. Perhaps it is too harsh a judgement, certainly it is an incomplete view, to say that her association with water marks her as a female Narcissus rather than the Venus of her mother's hopes, but Flor is not born of the waves; she dies into the reflecting pool. Bonnie should have been able to see more of the truth and not distort the meaning of her dream of Flor as a mermaid with the ugly tail of a carp. Because of the distortions created by her own egotism, she saw the dream as meaning that "No one was good enough for Florence." The dream could have revealed to Bonnie her own destructive part in her daughter's life: " 'It was an ugly fish tail, like a carp's. It was just like a carp's and the whole thing was a great handicap. The girl simply couldn't walk." But Bonnie avoids the truth assiduously, and her daughter is too weak to avoid her except in dreams.

Flor finds in her diary the record of Father Doyle's advice: "If you look in the mirror too much you will see the devil." But rather than turn to face life, she flees into a permanent dream, finding in her own way the goal announced in Yeats's "The Shadowy Waters" which Gallant uses as the epigraph for **"Its Image on the Mirror"**:

> What is love itself
> Even though it be the lightest of love
> But dreams that hurry from beyond the world
> To make low laughter more than meat and drink,
> Though it but set us sighing? Fellow-wanderer,
> Could we but mix ourselves into a dream
> Not in its image on the mirror!

Yeats's poem suggests a Platonic world of true dreams in contrast to the mere emanation that is the image on the mirror. I do not believe that Gallant wants the reader to accept the existence of a metaphysical realm so that he may read her text, but the poem, with its reference to "Fellow-traveller" and its longing for a reality that is apparently forever beyond reach, operates as a telling epigraph not only for Flor and her mother, but for a host of Gallant's characters who wander in times not theirs and places unfamiliar, indeed much like the figures of the neo-Platonic vision exiled in this life from their starry home. (pp. 94-100)

> D. B. Jewison, "Speaking of Mirrors: Imagery and Narration in Two Novellas by Mavis Gallant," in Studies in Canadian Literature, Vol. 10, Nos. 1-2, 1985, pp. 94-109.

PETER BUITENHUIS (essay date 1986)

[*Buitenhuis is an English-born Canadian critic and editor who has written extensively on Henry James. In the excerpt below, he praises Gallant for her perceptive depictions of Parisians in the collection* Overhead in a Balloon: Stories of Paris.]

[With *Overhead in a Balloon: Stories of Paris*], Mavis Gallant returns to her familiar turf: the lives of various Parisian *petit-bourgeoisie*. It is difficult to imagine lives more petty. In her previous collection, *Home Truths: Selected Canadian Stories,* there seems to have been more magnanimity as well as more space; but Gallant, like Henry James, appears to find greater challenges to her talent in the more densely-layered—sometimes almost hermetic—society of Europe.

Overhead in a Balloon is a finely ironic title for a collection of stories closely tethered to a packed metropolis, in which the characters seldom lift their gaze beyond the dead level of the diurnal round. The title, however, may also apply to the position of the author herself, "invisible, refined out of existence, paring [her] nails." These stories, beautifully written, complex and spare, are bathed in the sharp, relentless, and knowing irony of the author's Olympian gaze.

Each story has a separate action, but many are linked by common characters and themes. Most of the stories fall into three groups, exploring respectively aspects of the art world, literary politics, and marital problems. Two stories lie outside the groups. The first of these, **"Luc and his Father,"** is about the tormented adolescence of an only son of a family with aristocratic pretentions. The boy is unintelligent and unenterprising and fails hopelessly in the highly competitive French school system. The second, **"The Assembly,"** concludes the volume. The opening story, **"Speck's Idea,"** is about the problems of the owner of a small art gallery who sees the solution to his economic woes in the idea of rediscovering a forgotten artist, Hubert Cruche. He finds the artist's widow, a thoroughly unpleasant woman, long ago uneasily transplanted from Saskatchewan to Paris, who possesses a large number of the artist's canvasses. Speck painstakingly cultivates her, in the hope that she will give him exclusive rights to show the canvasses in his gallery thus starting a Cruche boom. In sight of success, elaborate plans for a splendid opening and a fine catalogue all made, he is suddenly supplanted by a fast-moving Italian dealer, who, having charmed the old widow off her feet, gets prior rights to mount a travelling show. Speck's idea turns to ashes in his mouth. (p. 154)

The group of stories about literary politics is the most successful. They spring from the patronage of a wealthy American woman, Mary Margaret Pugh. Her arts foundation for a considerable time supported both a French writer named Grippes, and an English writer named Prism. After her death the foundation is dissolved, and Grippes and Prism become rivals for the residue of her estate and subsequently bitter literary rivals. In one of the stories in this group, **"A Flying Start,"** Grippes seizes a fine opportunity to triumph over his rival by writing a waspish account of him for a projected biographical dictionary of living authors. This entry, full of subtle denigration and ridicule, forms the substance of the story. The triumph is, however, frustrated by the withdrawal of support from the venture by the cultural ministry that originally backed it. Grippes is informed that his entry "is to be published in 2010, at the very latest." The last story in this group is **"Grippes and Poche,"** a wonderfully comic account of the relationship over many years between the writer and a tax inspector. It's at once a satire on the French bureaucracy and an ironic look at the petty dishonesties inevitably bred by the system.

The last group of stories is centred on the quixotic act of a young Frenchman who marries an older Jewish woman at the beginning of the Nazi occupation of Paris in order to save her from the deathcamps. Immediately afterwards, the man escapes from France and joins the Free French in London. There he meets the woman who eventually becomes his second wife. I say eventually because his first wife refuses to divorce him. Having turned Catholic she believes that the contract is irrevocable. As a consequence the second wife feels that she cannot have children since they would be illegitimate in the eyes of the law. By the time wife number one finally agrees to a divorce, it is too late for children. So the consequences of a disinterested action live on through the years to plague and partly spoil the second marriage.

As can be seen, there are few cheerful outcomes to Mavis Gallant's stories: rivalries, jealousies, obstinacies, stupidities, selfishness, and wilfulness blight human relationships and negate good intentions. The last brief story of the book, **"The Assembly,"** consists simply of the minutes of a meeting of the tenants of an apartment house who, in the wake of a sexual assault on one of their number, gather to discuss the possibility of installing an electronic code system for entering the building. It is a masterly summary of the irrelevancies, prejudices and petty rivalries that such a meeting inevitably produces. It concludes with nothing decided, since most present leave to watch the re-run of an early Fernandel movie on television.

This is an apt conclusion to this collection of stories which, in one way or another, have all touched on the problem of living in, or trying to find somewhere adequate to live in a chronically space-hungry city. Crowding, discomfort, and inconvenience all exacerbate the inherent potential for conflict and unpleasantness. Looming large as a consequence of such tensions is that ubiquitous anodyne and Polyphemus, television. Gallant subtly suggests that TV is both impoverishing and adulterating traditional French culture—particularly literature, art, and theatre. Hers is not a cheerful vision, but it is salutary and bracing. She seems to be saying: "Let me take you up in my balloon and show you the real Paris." It's not the one you find in the guidebooks. (pp. 155-56)

> Peter Buitenhuis, "From a Balloon," in Canadian Literature, No. 111, Winter, 1986, pp. 154-56.

NEIL BESNER (essay date 1986)

[*In the following excerpt, Besner examines the role of memory in* "The Other Paris" *and* "In Youth Is Pleasure."]

Mavis Gallant's stories retrace the past along the fault-lines between history and fiction, memory and imagination. Set in rundown pensions, or villas, or hotels, often on or near a border, often during a time of transition, her stories evoke an uncannily precise, local sense of postwar Italy, France, and Germany. The most important element in the texture and craft of Gallant's fiction—the element which seems at first to make her stories read so true to life—is her exacting use of detail; but the major effect of this fine web of detail is to confirm the abstracting powers of what Roland Barthes has called the "*indirect* language" of literature. Barthes suggests that in order for the language of literature *not* to name the "ultimate meaning" of things, it names things "in detail," because "the best way for a language to be indirect is to refer as constantly as possible to objects and not to their concepts." The workings of this paradox, writes Barthes, explain the "concrete vocation of literary writing." Barthes' comments should alert us to the dangers of assuming too little when we read realist fiction, and warn us away from reading stories like Gallant's as simple slices of life.

At one edge of Gallant's fiction—generally but not exclusively in her earlier work—it is tempting to say that her stories' strengths are reportorial, documentary. The issue is more obviously and more richly complicated in later stories, particularly in the Linnet Muir stories. Sometimes this documentary impulse seems so strong that editors and bibliographers vacillate between anthologizing or cataloguing a work as a story or as an essay, as fiction or as non-fiction, sometimes opting for one, sometimes the other, sometimes both. This is the case with **"When We Were Nearly Young,"** a first-person narrative published in 1960 in *The New Yorker* (and later collected in a book of Canadian essays). Is this work a report, an essay masquerading as a story? Or is it a story masquerading as a reflection, a memoir? Could it be both? How to distinguish; on what grounds? The presence or absence of documentary reference? The status of the narrator as reporter or storyteller? Which aspects of focus or style? These same difficulties that enrich a story like **"When We Were Nearly Young"** attend the whole issue of realism in Gallant's stories. To praise or dismiss, exalt or condemn her writing as realism—realism of whatever denomination, depending upon the reader's articles of faith—is to leave several important dimensions of her work unexamined, the first of which is the *uses* of these carefully realized settings.

The function of setting in Gallant's fiction can be clarified by drawing on two stories published over twenty years apart—**"The Other Paris"** (1953), the title story of Gallant's first book of stories (published in 1956) and **"In Youth Is Pleasure,"** the first of the Linnet Muir stories, published first in *The New Yorker* in 1975. These, like many Gallant stories, are shaped by what George Woodcock has called the "helical patterning of memory" as it encounters, evades, or reinvents setting. In both stories, the realization of setting is juxtaposed with setting remembered, providing readers with insight into the ways in which characters' memories play over the past to shape fictions which either remove them from history or replace them within it.

In **"The Other Paris,"** one invention of setting occurs through Carol Frazier's memory, which is the medium for Carol's story-making about Paris—both her dream Paris and the "other" historical Paris. In **"In Youth Is Pleasure,"** setting is realized through Linnet Muir's memory, through her recollections and her insights into her childhood inventions of a fabulous Montreal, inventions which she dissolves in the

course of telling her story. Carol Frazier is a young American innocent abroad who comes to work in the postwar Paris of the fifties and gets engaged to Howard, her American boss. She has a momentary, potentially revelatory encounter with Felix, a young Frenchman orphaned during the war, but she is left at story's end poised to retreat to North America and into marriage, in flight through the fictions of memory from the postwar Paris she has had an unsettling glimpse of—Felix's city, his girl-friend Odile's city. The narrator shows us Carol inventing, shaping her romantic memories of Paris into a story on the spot.

If we wanted to work towards the story's theme, we might begin by saying that it's a retreat from a glimpse of initiation; if we wanted to explore the story's antecedents, we might suggest that it's a sparer version of a Henry James story, a transatlantic, European-North American tale, told with sharp but delicate irony from outside the character, set in a closely observed postwar Paris. (Gallant remarks in a letter to Robert Weaver that the story "would simply be mystifying to a young foreigner in Paris today, but that *was* the city five years after the last war.") But if we ask what the narrator is doing with setting, memory, and history, then we need to consider **"The Other Paris"** for a moment more, because Carol's *inventions* of another Paris, in spite of what she sees, what she is forced to see over and again before her eyes, are the crucial events in the story's plot.

These inventions provide an insight for the reader—although not for Carol—which is anticipated in various other doubled presentations of setting or episode followed by their reinventions by a character. The story ends with a sentence which both frames and acts out Carol's retreat from history, from postwar Paris, from Felix, and into the comforting closure of memory as romance, as dream, as pure fiction, uncontaminated by experience artfully dodged—memory, perhaps, uncontaminated by imagination. The story closes with the narrator's reflection: "The memory of Felix and Odile and all their distasteful strangeness would slip away; for 'love' she would think, once more, 'Paris,' and, after a while, happily married, mercifully removed in time, she would remember it and describe it and finally believe it as it had never been at all." Carol's memory will be selectively creative; the agency of memory will impose form and so create meaning, but ironically, this meaning will deny experience. Carol's projected re-creation of her past is an art which loosely but ironically follows the sequence of a writer's re-creation of the past: first, as if she were going to write a story (and she is) Carol *remembers* something (call it subject, Paris, content, event, sensation); then she *describes* (she will shape, form, structure, pattern—turn these nouns into verbs, turn static content into signifying form) and finally *believes* (the end result, perhaps, of "sincerely imagining," something Carol does a lot of in this story). But when *Carol* remembers and describes and finally believes it as it has never been at all, she evades Paris and retreats from the history of her experience, and she is judged accordingly throughout the story.

"In Youth Is Pleasure" shows an opposed use of setting. In this story, depictions of setting chart a narrator's movement through memory, beyond memory, and into the present. Linnet returns to Montreal from New York at eighteen to strike out on her own and also to discover the "truth" (at least, in others' memories) about her father's death. Like many other Gallant stories, this one circles around what Gallant has called a "locked" situation (the uncertain outcome of Carol's engagement, Linnet's grappling with an unanswered, perhaps unanswerable question), and it weaves a course between setting encountered, as it merges with and emerges from setting remembered. Linnet had moved at ten from Montreal to a city in Ontario, where her memory of Montreal "took shape," as she puts it:

> I retained, I rebuilt a superior civilization. In that drowned world, Sherbrooke Street seemed to be glittering and white; the vision of a house upon that street was so painful that I was obliged to banish it from the memorial. . . . If I say that Cleopatra floated down the Chateauguay River, that the Winter Palace was stormed on Sherbrooke Street, that Trafalgar was fought on Lake St. Louis, I mean it naturally; they were the natural backgrounds of my exile and fidelity.

This is the voice of a character far more conscious and reflective than Carol, and clearly the meanings of memory are both more complex and ambiguous here. But there is also a radical difference between what *happens* through the agencies of Linnet's and Carol's memories, between what memory *does* in the two stories. As Linnet closes her inquiry into her father's death, she discovers that her dream past has "evaporated," and she finds herself standing on the street corner of a purely historical Montreal. But even this discovery, that the only real Montreal is the one she sees before her eyes, is one that she must balance against the insistent images of the Montreal she remembers, her memorialized Montreal. Linnet recalls: "One day, standing at a corner, waiting for the light to change, I understood that the Sherbrooke Street of my exile—my Mecca, my Jerusalem—was this. It had to be: there could not be two. It was *only* this." Montreal can no longer be a holy city because her pilgrimage, her return, has become time-bound, secular, historical, and she now escapes one of the pleasures of youth—making and believing in memorials—by realizing the nature of time. As she remarks in the story's tellingly ambiguous last sentence, childhood, which she now considers to have ended, is a condition from which she was "bound to escape."

The uses of settings in both stories engage readers in the directions and indirections taken by characters' (and sometimes narrators') "helical patterning of memory." In this context, documentary realism is a form serving a purpose; it is a means and not an end. It poses the prospect of meticulously realized settings *against* characters' "memorials," or inventions of setting. And whether we call these creations reflexive, or self-referential, or impressionist, or aspects of theme or form, one conclusion that we might draw is that realism in Gallant's fiction reflects as much as it refers, pointing to words and worlds with a particular emphasis on the ways in which the past is either called into being or banished into exile. By extension, we might infer that fiction that explores fiction is not atypical, or a "new" kind of fiction, somehow "beyond" or "after" or "post" modern, or in *reaction* to realist fiction, or written only by critic-writers or writer-critics possessed of or obsessed by special knowledge about the workings of imagination.

The significant ambiguities of setting in Gallant's fiction are inseparable from the functions of her characters. Analyses of Gallant's characters as autonomous wholes, as discrete, life-like individuals, are likely to bring the reader sharply up against what appears to be at once a sheer, impermeable surface and an impenetrable wall of character traits—as if *beneath* this surface there were a "deeper" layer of meaning, or

being, as if *behind* this wall there lay a garden more fertile with significance. Again, details concerning character may read like a gossamer-thin web, but a web connected at no center, radiating out and pointing precisely nowhere. But Gallant's characters might also be said to function as measures of the motions of time—as time is made manifest in different modes of perception and narration, particularly remembering, watching, seeing, and telling. (pp. 89-93)

> Neil Besner, *"A Broken Dialogue: History and Memory in Mavis Gallant's Short Fiction,"* in Essays on Canadian Writing, *No. 33, Fall, 1986, pp. 89-99.*

CONSTANCE ROOKE (essay date 1986)

[*Rooke is an American critic and short story writer as well as editor of* Malahat Review. *In the excerpt below, she explores the significance of the phrase "fear of the open heart" as it appears in "Its Image on the Mirror."*]

My intention in this essay is to apply the phrase 'fear of the open heart' to three Canadian women writers—Mavis Gallant, Margaret Laurence, and Alice Munro—and so to articulate the quite different kinds of satisfaction I have had in 'knowing' these writers through their work. . . . To begin, then, in a respectful mode, I will replace 'the fear of the open heart' in the novella [**"Its Image on the Mirror"**] from which I have so blithely extracted it.

Jean Duncan Price, the narrator of Gallant's **"Its Image on the Mirror,"** is talking about her Scots-Presbyterian heritage. She refers to her father's belief that 'Scottish blood was the best in the country, responsible for our national character traits of prudence, level-headedness, and self-denial. Jean's own understanding of this Protestant, Anglo-Scot inheritance is less complimentary: 'The seed of our characters came from another continent. Like the imported daisies and dandelions, it was larger than the parent plant. Flowering in us was the dark bloom of the Old Country—the mistrust of pity, the contempt for weakness, the fear of the open heart.' This is one explanation of a mind-set that has also been described without recourse to Scots-Presbyterianism. Possibly it was the vast space of Canada that scared us first of all; but, for whatever reason, we are often seen as a frightened or over-cautious people, concerned with external threats and drawing inward to the garrison of a narrowly defined social group, or the garrison of the self.

Jean Price is (somewhat atypically) capable of defining the problem, but not of overcoming it. She is one of a multitude of Gallant characters who imagine that life and happiness are happening elsewhere and that they have been unfairly shut out. Often these characters have a mean-minded and vindictive streak, as a result (or cause) of their exclusion from life, and often they congratulate themselves, smugly and blindly, upon the design of their garrison—so that our concern for their suffering is diminished. Often such characters are paired with another—perhaps another sister, as in the case of **"Its Image on the Mirror"** or **"The Cost of Living"**—who signifies a more reckless and romantic way of life. But it seems characteristic of Gallant that the focal character or narrator will be the more 'closed' of this pair, and that the happiness even of the more 'open' character will prove illusory.

The pairing of sisters interests me, especially in relation to the title of **"Its Image on the Mirror,"** which Gallant has taken from W. B. Yeats' 'The Shadowy Waters.' Jean's attraction to her sister Isobel is a desire for what Yeats (quoted in the epigraph) calls 'love itself.' The sister is a mirror image both of an idealized self and of the dream of love, which is always on the far side of the looking-glass and unobtainable for either. Jean wants to be united with that romantic image and so is encouraged to see Isobel in the climactic scene wearing '[t]he dressing gown [. . . that] belonged to both of us years before'; all along, she has 'wanted her to say, You and I are alike, and we are not like any other person in this room.'

Isobel is cast as a double who enjoys with men an intimacy that is impossible for Jean: 'I had an idea about love, and I thought my sister knew the truth. [. . .] They [Isobel and her lover] were the lighted window; I was the watcher on the street.' Thus, when Jean metaphorically stops 'being the stranger on the dark street' and enters 'the bright rooms of [her] sister's life'—in the mirror of fact, Isobel has entered *her* cold room—Jean believes that she will now learn 'what it [is] to be Isobel [. . . and] to be loved.' Ironically, Isobel has come to Jean because she is pregnant and needs ' "somebody's whole attention." ' Uninterested in reciprocity with her besotted sister, in the true intimacy that would return her gaze, Isobel knows exactly where to go to get the attention she wants. We may conclude, then, as Jean implicitly does, that 'to be Isobel' is to be selfish and 'to be loved' is to be in serious trouble.

Love is a risk—especially for woman, as the illicit pregnancy suggests—but paradoxically, at least as it exists on this side of the looking glass, it is also a condition into which we retreat to avoid risk. This is the 'secret' that Isobel calmly passes along to Jean, that love is 'someone between you and the others, blotting out the light.' Thus we learn that 'fear of the open heart' can take several forms. Isobel seems reckless, willing to journey into an adulterous affair and later to marry an Italian living in Venezuela; that witty double-dose of *machismo,* however, suggests accurately that if Isobel has escaped Jean's garrison, her propriety and dullness, she has nonetheless landed in a women's prison of her own. Out of fear—'She might have spent her life being a little weak, a little frightened, if it hadn't been for him'—Isobel has agreed to let a man blot out the light. And Jean, when she hears this, immediately thinks of the 'wall' that defines her own marriage. The two sisters therefore meet in the mirror after all.

What happens next is ambiguous. It may not involve incestuous feeling; it may not matter if it does. If Jean had imagined that through an identification with Isobel she might experience what it is to love and be loved by a man, she realizes now that this is a dead end. Man's claim to be all-sufficing is seen through, permitting Jean to make a claim of her own. The male wall yields to the female mirror and another image floats to the surface of the glass: woman alone, Isobel as the possible object of desire. Wanting to be beautiful for her sister, Jean removes the pins from her hair. Thinking that 'unless we could meet across that landscape we might as well die,' she drags herself forward—'against the swiftest current, in the fastest river in the world'—and takes Isobel's hand. Jean has left the garrison, risked everything—and is rejected absolutely. Isobel snaps at her, and Jean retreats. She returns at once to an adversarial relationship to Isobel, and will make her 'pay' with a counterfeit of intimacy for the attention she requires. 'It no longer mattered whether my hair was straight or curled.'

I do not know whether the love that is extinguished here is

sexual. I see a number of reasons for believing that it may be, but will not rehearse those here. What I am interested in is the fact that I have felt afraid to propose this, as if Gallant (in the role of Isobel, to my Jean) would make me feel a fool. But if I were silent, she might laugh at my cowardice. Perhaps I feel imprisoned in the mirror because she declines to take my hand, or to show hers. But somehow the fear of the open heart that begins as a national trait, and develops as a problem specifically for women, ends by determining my sense of the writer herself. A cold wind blows through this novella, and through nearly all the landscape of exile that is Gallant's fiction.

This chill is built into the imagery of Canada's winter climate and of course implies the yearning for something warmer, more 'out-going': 'a climate imagined, a journey never made.' But we see in the ambiguous location of that coldness—imaged sometimes as a condition of the world outside, sometimes as the world within—a problem that Gallant reveals also with her mirror-imaging of the two sisters. It would seem perhaps that Gallant's creation (in story after story) of people who suffer from the fear of the open heart, and plots that are determined by it, should cast her in the reader's mind as a champion of open-heartedness. The writer, by that reckoning, would be cast as the 'warm' sister of the 'cold' one caught in the mirror of her text. But it seems to me that Gallant 'is' both sisters—the reckless traveler and the cautious observer—and that the two images converge in the coldness that results from Isobel's denial of Jean.

I cannot properly engage here the vexed question of Gallant's relations to feminism, but I would suggest that the model of sisterhood is an interesting way to approach it. Gallant's female characters are variously imprisoned, and often in ways that are susceptible to a feminist analysis, yet one rarely feels that she is sorry for them, or cheering them on. She seems, therefore, to be denying the sisterly bond. Gallant is the 'exceptional woman,' aloof from, faintly contemptuous, and possibly fearful, of women who are left behind in her chilly texts. (pp. 258-60)

Constance Rooke, "Fear of the Open Heart," in A Mazing Space: Writing Canadian Women Writing, *edited by Shirley Neuman and Smaro Kamboureli, Longspoon Press, 1986, pp. 256-69.*

RONALD BRYDEN (essay date 1989)

[*In the following excerpt, Bryden comments on the strengths of Gallant's writing in the collection* In Transit.]

In Transit contains 20 stories published in the [*New Yorker*] during the 1950's and 1960's. Their backgrounds range from the resort country on the Vermont border where 40 years ago English-speaking Montrealers, believing they owned French Canada, behaved like characters in Racine, to the 1950's Paris of East European refugees and NATO staff; from the tourist-ravaged Malaga coast of the late 60's to the sullen, half-thawed Moscow of the Brezhnev years.

The story that gives the volume its title [**"In Transit"**] is characteristic in several ways. It deals with people traveling, removed from their habitual patterns and subject to emotional jumpiness. Out of a cloud of cacophonous detail—Japanese tourists, Finnish pottery, fried fish, temperance beer, loudspeaker announcements, signs reading "Oslo," "Copenhagen," "Amsterdam," the babel of a Helsinki airport lounge—

crystallizes a moment of heart-stopping finality. A young French couple, honeymooners, overhear a quarrel between an elderly American wife and husband. Something the wife says punctures their inattention, triggering private thoughts they cannot share. He remembers his first wife, an American woman he walked out on, taking his books and records. She imagines herself ending up like her predecessor. The moment, swarming and shapeless, suddenly elongates backward and forward in time to piercing images of love coming to its end.

Transit, noise and the symbiosis between them, one might argue, are Mavis Gallant's major themes—noise, that is, in the philosopher's definition of data that carry no meaning to the senses they fall on. During her decades there, Paris has been noisy, in every sense, with the assertions of linguists and semioticians hammering out their theories that we are prisoners of the languages and cultures whose sign-systems we inhabit. Mrs. Gallant, who shows no fondness for the assertive, spends much of her work demonstrating quietly how much of language, culture and their ideological designs on us is simply noise to most people, in this shifting world where fewer and fewer of us are at home, linguistically or otherwise. Eventually the inhabitants of Babel stop listening and become free.

The tyranny of language seems a particularly farfetched notion in Montreal, where everyone grows up between French and English. An older Montreal writer, Hugh MacLennan, once called Canada's two cultures "two solitudes," but in Mrs. Gallant's increasingly bilingual generation, the solitudes have come to feel more like Siamese twins, yoked reluctantly in an intimacy that forces them to see into each other's heads. This may account for the fact that a typical Gallant story deals with a solitude, usually Canadian, usually female, traveling abroad, buffeted by the noise of alien places and people she will never decipher. However she is framed, defined, linked in noisy symbiosis with them, like the young woman in Madrid.

The difference between her traveler's tales and those of Maugham and his epigones is that in hers the traveler not only sees but is seen. Mrs. Gallant's specialty is a sudden, breathtaking switch in perspective from one observing sensibility to the sensibility hitherto observed. Like late Picassos, her wandering protagonists have two faces, one looking out, one seen in profile. Her subject is both person and place, and the strange new harmonies and disharmonies they make together. . . .

The relationship between traveler and native is mostly hostile: in Mrs. Gallant's eschatology, the last battle of Armageddon will be between those who have made themselves at home on the earth and those who will not or cannot. In **"April Fish,"** a rich American expatriate considers bribing her maid to break the Venetian glass fish her adopted children, orphans from several European countries, have banded together to buy for her birthday. Their native vulgarity, she reflects sadly, is too innate ever to make them truly her own. In **"Careless Talk,"** a chic Irishwoman renting a house in Burgundy makes friends with the lonely English wife of the farmer next door, but betrays her trust by showing her off to French friends from Paris. "Look how peaceful we were without the men today," says a French hostess, with crushing casualness, to her daughter's American lover who, unwilling to hunt, has trailed with the women and children behind a Sunday shoot in Sologne, in **"The Hunter's Waking Thoughts."**

Usually Mrs. Gallant is on the side of the settled, but in spite of her decades in Paris, there is no background she describes as if it were home. It is clear that the world she knows best is that of the transient: pensions, rented villas, railway stations, restaurants and the expectation of dying in hospitals, alone. Still, there is a subtle development in her style that suggests she may have found, as actors say of their voices, her center. In the early stories, the moment of finality is usually achieved by a character innocently summing up a situation or a life. . . .

In later stories, she more often draws the bottom line herself. "In a moment of sexual insanity he had taken on a young, young wife." "They agreed that everything would be different once they had made a move. . . . Guy had been told it was sunny there all the year round." "Without another word, the Plummers climbed into the taxi and drove with Amabel back to the heart of their isolation, where there was no room for a third person." In sentences like these, Mavis Gallant calls to mind the great French *philosophes* of love: Madame de Lafayette, Pierre Marivaux, Benjamin Constant. It is among them, the masters of classical prose and the enigmas of the heart, that she has made herself at home.

        Ronald Bryden, "The Self in Strange Places," in
The New York Times Book Review, *May 28, 1989,*
p. 3.

FURTHER READING

Bonheim, Helmut. "The Aporias of Lily Littel: Mavis Gallant's 'Acceptance of Their Ways'." *Ariel* 18, No. 4 (October 1987): 69-78.
        Detailed analysis of Lily Littel in the story "Acceptance of Their Ways."

Canadian Fiction Magazine: A Special Issue on Mavis Gallant, No. 28 (1978).
        Issue devoted to Gallant. Articles include an interview with the author, as well as essays by many notable Canadian writers, including Robertson Davies and George Woodcock.

Fabre, Michel. " 'Orphans' Progress,' Reader's Progress: Voice and Understatement in Mavis Gallant's Stories." In *Gaining Ground: European Critics on Canadian Literature,* edited by Robert Kroetsch and Reingard M. Nischik. Western Canadian Literary Documents Series, Vol. VI, edited by Shirley Neuman, pp. 150-60. Edmonton: NeWest, 1985.
        Explication of "Orphans' Progress" focusing on Gallant's narrational techniques.

Hancock, Geoff. "Mavis Tries Harder." *Books In Canada* 7, No. 6 (July 1978): 4-8.
        Highly laudatory biographical and critical feature story.

Hatch, Ronald B. "Mavis Gallant: Returning Home." *Atlantis: A Women's Studies Journal* 4, No. 1 (Fall 1978): 95-102.
        Asserts that Gallant's fiction has moved from detached critiques of romantic individualism to a more personal approach that chronicles her own involvement in the fragmentation of society.

Keefer, Janice Kulyk. "Strange Fashions of Forsaking: Criticism and the Fiction of Mavis Gallant." *Dalhousie Review* 64, No. 4 (Winter 1984-1985): 721-35.

Survey of critical response to Gallant's work, maintaining that it has been largely misinterpreted and underappreciated.

———. "Mavis Gallant and the Angel of History." *The University of Toronto Quarterly* 55, No. 3 (Spring 1986): 282-301.
Examines "historical sense" in Gallant's fiction, which Keefer contends is underestimated by most critics.

McDonald, Marci. "Exile in Her Own Write." *Maclean's* 92, No. 47 (19 November 1979): 6-12.
Personal profile containing biographical information as well as critical observations on stories collected in *From the Fifteenth District.*

Ross, Robert. "Mavis Gallant and Thea Astley on Home Truths, Home Folk." *Ariel* 19, No. 1 (January 1988): 83-9.
Comparative study focusing upon the meaning of "home" in Gallant's *Home Truths* and Astley's *A Boat Load of Home Folk.*

Schrank, Bernice. "Celluloid Images and Social Control in Selected Short Stories by Mavis Gallant." In *Cross-Cultural Studies: American, Canadian and European Literatures: 1945-1985,* edited by Mirko Jurak, pp. 229-33. Ljubljana: Učne delavnice, 1988.
Investigates the significance of film references in "Its Image on the Mirror," "Bernadette," and "My Heart Is Broken."

Tyler, Anne. "Come to Canada." *The New Republic* 192, No. 3669 (13 May 1985): 40-2.
Favorable review of *Home Truths.*

O. Henry

1862-1910

(Pseudonym of William Sidney Porter) American short story writer, journalist, humorist, and poet.

O. Henry is perhaps the most popular and widely known American short story writer of the twentieth century. During the eight-year period that he lived and wrote in New York City, the short story form was at the height of its popularity, and dozens of periodicals featuring short fiction competed for the works of celebrated authors. It was against this background that O. Henry quickly rose to the position of the most sought-after and acclaimed American short story writer by virtue of his distinctive works: typically brief stories, characterized by familiar, conversational openings, circumlocutory dialogue, plots hinging on improbable coincidence, and variations on the surprise or twist ending. The highly ironic, sentimental, or unexpected story conclusion has been so closely identified with O. Henry that his name has become synonymous with fiction of this kind.

O. Henry was born William Sidney Porter, the second son of Dr. and Mrs. Algernon Sidney Porter of Greensboro, North Carolina. Following Mrs. Porter's death when O. Henry was three, Dr. Porter moved with his children into his mother's house, where the boys' grandmother and an aunt undertook their education and upbringing. As a teenager, O. Henry helped support his family by working as a pharmacist's assistant in an uncle's drugstore, and he obtained his pharmacist's license in 1881. Never in robust health, O. Henry worried particularly about contracting pneumonia, which had been the cause of his mother's early death. When at nineteen he developed a persistent cough, he sought the more beneficial climate of southwest Texas, where he worked on a cattle ranch owned by family friends. His health improved after several years, and at twenty-two he moved to Austin, where he met his first wife and found work as a bank teller. In 1894 he purchased a weekly humor paper, retitled it *The Rolling Stone,* and supplied virtually all of the paper's content. When the paper failed after a year's publication, he continued to submit humorous stories and articles to other newspapers. Also in 1894, O. Henry was dismissed from his bank post because of shortages in his accounts. When the case was reinvestigated in 1895, and embezzlement charges seemed imminent, he fled Austin for Houston and later New Orleans, sailing from there to Honduras. In 1897, after learning that his wife was seriously ill, he returned to Austin and surrendered to authorities. After his wife's death he was convicted of embezzlement and sentenced to five years in the Federal Penitentiary in Ohio, where he was assigned to the prison pharmacy's twelve-hour midnight shift. His duties included prescribing and administering medication and tending to injured prisoners. O. Henry had made his first professional story sale to a magazine shortly before his conviction, and he continued to submit short stories for publication, based on his experiences in the southwest, in Central America, and in prison, using his in-laws' Pittsburgh address as a screen for his actual circumstances.

O. Henry's criminal conviction and prison term was for some time the most uncertain and controversial aspect of his life.

One of his biographers, Al Jennings, who was in the penitentiary with O. Henry, recounts that the writer's greatest fear was that he would be recognized and greeted by a former inmate while in the company of others. Many of O. Henry's closest acquaintances never knew that he had spent time in prison, and he often juggled dates to account for the years spent in prison. As a result there was some initial uncertainty about several important dates in his life, but biographers now believe that they have established an accurate chronology. It was common for early biographical essays to hotly debate the question of his innocence or guilt. Most modern biographers conclude that while O. Henry may have been technically guilty of embezzlement, he was almost certainly following the extremely lax bookkeeping policies of the Austin bank.

Obtaining an early release after serving three years of his sentence, O. Henry lived for a short time with his wife's parents, but moved to New York City in the spring of 1902 at the urging of *Ainslee's Magazine* editors Gilman Hall and Richard Duffy, who had been printing his stories and were confident that he could make a successful career writing for New York magazines. O. Henry began publishing stories in numerous periodicals under pseudonyms that included variations of his real name. He quickly gained fame under his most often-used pen name, O. Henry. A contract with the New York *Sunday*

World for a weekly short story provided him with a steady income, while the *World's* circulation of nearly one-half million assured him a wide readership. O. Henry's remuneration from the *World*—one hundred dollars per story—was liberal for the time, and he also supplemented his income by selling stories to other magazines that were anxious to print his popular works. However, he was financially irresponsible and continually in debt. He loved to sit for hours in restaurants and bars, observing the other patrons and constructing instantaneous fictions about them, and then leave a tip that often exceeded his bill. He was also lavish in the handouts he dispensed to panhandlers and prostitutes who, he claimed, often provided him with the germ of a story whereby he more than recouped his initial investment. Increasingly, he turned out stories in haste to honor the generous advances he received from editors.

Biographer Richard O'Connor has written that "the year 1904 . . . was easily the busiest and most productive of [O. Henry's] career. As the price for his stories went up, he simply produced less. But that vintage year . . . saw him at the peak of his creative power." Since his arrival in New York two years earlier, O. Henry had been steadily gaining not only in popularity but also in critical regard as an important literary figure. In 1904, *McClure's Magazine* editor Witter Bynner suggested assembling O. Henry's stories with Central American settings as a novel under the title *Cabbages and Kings,* a work that most critics have regarded as a grouping of loosely connected short stories. His collection *The Four Million* followed two years later, and his works, rescued from the impermanence of periodical publication, became more widely known. Further compilations of his stories appeared yearly thereafter and for several years after his death, which was caused by a variety of health problems, including diabetes and cirrhosis of the liver exacerbated by alcoholism.

O. Henry's fame rests upon the type of short story he wrote and not upon the distinction of any individual work. The archetypal O. Henry story is described by his biographer and critic Eugene Current-García as possessing several unmistakable characteristics: "the chatty, shortcut opening; the catchy, piquant descriptive phrasing; the confidential, reminiscent narrator; the chance meeting of old pals; and half a dozen or more variations of the surprise ending." His stories are often divided into five distinct groups according to their settings: the American South, the West, Central America, prison, and New York. By far the best known and most often reprinted are the stories set in New York City. These one hundred and forty stories, making up nearly half of his total output, capture the essence of early twentieth-century city life, and include the frequently anthologized "Gift of the Magi," "The Furnished Room," "A Municipal Report," "The Skylight Room," and "An Unfinished Story." Commonly recurring themes in O. Henry's short stories are those of deception, mistaken identity, the effects of coincidence, the inexorable nature of fate, and the resolution of seemingly insurmountable difficulties separating two lovers. In the stories that revolve around deliberate deception, O. Henry often used a plot contrivance that he called "turning the tables on Haroun Al-Raschid," the caliph from *The Arabian Nights' Entertainments* who disguised himself to mingle with the common people. In O. Henry's stories it is the common people—the clerks, salespeople, factory and office workers—who save assiduously for the infrequent evenings when they can dress in their finest and mix with the rich and powerful. A favorite device of O. Henry was to depict a poor working man

or woman whose potentially romantic encounters come to nothing because of the ridiculous poses they feel obliged to adopt while pretending to be wealthy. Although plot resolutions of O. Henry stories often depend on improbable coincidence, some critics assert that the wealth of detail concerning characters and settings makes the stories appear naturalistic despite the sometimes fantastic plots.

During the last decade of his life and for about a decade following his death, O. Henry was the most popular and widely read American short story writer. He was commonly regarded as the modern American master of the short story form, ranked with Edgar Allan Poe, Nathaniel Hawthorne, and Bret Harte. His works were considered models of the genre and his short story techniques were taught in college writing courses. The growing tide of favorable assessments culminated in C. Alphonso Smith's *O. Henry Biography,* published in 1916. At about this time, however, O. Henry's critical reputation began to undergo reevaluation. Critics began to question the validity of the excessive praise that O. Henry had garnered in the previous two decades, and some—most notably Katharine Fullerton Gerould and Fred Lewis Pattee—dismissed his work as facile, anecdotal, journalistic, and of little lasting literary value. Gerould went so far as to denounce O. Henry's pervasive influence on the modern short story as "pernicious," while Pattee questioned the moral basis of the works, writing that O. Henry's nonjudgmental portrayals of criminals amounted to an endorsement of lawless behavior. Other critics noted how quickly O. Henry stories seemed to date, and his trademark surprise endings were called overly sentimental and predictable.

Concurrent with the growth of negative criticism in the United States came the first translations of O. Henry's stories and the beginning of his great renown abroad. He underwent a particular vogue in Russia, where he remains one of a very few American writers who is both popular with readers and sanctioned by the Soviet government. With the advent of experimental literary forms in American literature in the 1920s and 1930s, O. Henry's critical reputation reached its lowest point. The tendency of literary critics—when they mentioned O. Henry at all—was to relegate him to a minor place in American literary history. In the 1960s, however, another reevaluation began to take place, inspired largely by the fact that despite his decline in critical standing, O. Henry had always retained popularity with readers. Critics continue to reassess O. Henry's contribution to literature, with most maintaining that his characteristically brief, humorous, sometimes sentimental stories have earned him a permanent place as a skilled and inventive story writer who profoundly influenced the course of the American short story for half a century.

(For further information on O. Henry's life and career, see *Twentieth-Century Literary Criticism,* Vols. 1, 19; *Contemporary Authors,* Vol. 104; *Dictionary of Literary Biography,* Vols. 12, 78, 79; and *Concise Dictionary of American Literary Biography, 1865-1917.*)

PRINCIPAL WORKS

SHORT FICTION

Cabbages and Kings 1904
The Four Million 1906
Heart of the West 1907
The Trimmed Lamp 1907

The Gentle Grafter 1908
The Voice of the City 1908
Options 1909
Roads of Destiny 1909
Strictly Business 1910
Whirligigs 1910
Sixes and Sevens 1911
Rolling Stones (stories, sketches, letters, and poems) 1912
Waifs and Strays (stories and critical and biographical commentary) 1917
The Complete Works of O. Henry. 2 vols. 1953

OTHER MAJOR WORKS

O. Henryana (sketches and poetry) 1920
Letters to Lithopolis (letters) 1922
Postscripts (humor) 1923
O. Henry Encore (humor) 1939

HARRY PEYTON STEGER (essay date 1909)

[*In the following excerpt, Steger highlights aspects of O. Henry's writing and career.*]

For the last six or seven years O. Henry has been, perhaps, the most popular short-story writer in America. He has a large audience who look to him most of all for a satisfactory and entertaining interpretation of the life of "The Four Million," a title of his own that expresses his aloofness from a sympathy with the "four hundred." (p. 11724)

His wanderings have influenced his work. Texas gives the setting for the volume of short stories called *The Heart o' the West.* Central America is the scene of *Cabbages and Kings. The Four Million, The Voice of the City,* and *The Trimmed Lamp* are stories of New York City. *The Gentle Grafter,* naturally enough, has no home.

But this influence of place is insignificant. The qualities that mark his work are as universal as human nature and as free from the restrictions of locality. His New York stories are generally conceded to be his best, and to show the most level degree of excellence; but the reason for this lies in the stories themselves.

"People say I know New York well," O. Henry said to me. "Just change Twenty-Third Street in one of my New York stories to Main Street, rub out the Flatiron Building and put in the Town Hall. Then the story will fit just as truly elsewhere. At least I hope this is the case with what I write. So long as your story is true to life, the mere change of local color will set it in the East, West, South, or North. The characters in the "Arabian Nights" parade up and down Broadway at midday, or Main Street in Dallas, Tex."

His work commands the highest prices editors pay, and editors pay for breadth and depth of appeal. They reason that O. Henry gives them the cubic area they want. It is almost a fixed idea of publishers that volumes of short stories are bad risks; but a collection in book form of stories by O. Henry finds a waiting crowd. The crowd is large, like his titles—*The Four Million, The Voice of the City, Cabbages and Kings.* To him, those masses of people who figure in the census are neither abnormal nor subnormal. He accepts with sympathy,

wit, and occasional irony the unpleasant fact that a human being can be a drudge, the glorious fact that a drudge is a human being. There are wonder tales to be told of the lives of derelicts who sleep on benches in Madison Square, of people who dwell in narrow flats, of half-educated boys and girls in offices and behind counters. In O. Henry's telling, they lose no element of wonder; for he writes neither as reformer nor melodramatist, nor patronizing wit. In a flash here and a flash there, he sees and shows you what the succession of days and the recurring nights bring to the shop-girl, the clerk, the worker at this and that dull task for a wage that supplies little to the body and less to the soul. Usually each brief story—vivid, human, real—lays bare some cruel roughness of the social fabric at the same time that it gives a quaint, dear glimpse of good and happiness and fun. (p. 11725)

It is a common temptation to compare a recent arrival in literature with its veterans or its gods. O. Henry's indifference to the English language as he makes it do his bidding, is like the big indifference of Kipling. A likeness to Dickens is more obvious. There is the largeness of philosophy and sympathy, the gleam and flash of wit, humor grotesque and deep, and the half-intimate gaiety of manner that, after all, is not really gay and not really intimate.

His stories make a sort of "Comédie Humaine." He takes "rag-time" music and gives an effect that challenges the tragedy of grand opera. "Life," he says himself, "is made up of sobs, sniffles, and smiles, with sniffles predominating." The shop-girl who masquerades for a week as a great lady, the flat-dweller who has a glimpse of heaven through the skylight of her attic bedroom and of romance in an ambulance, the tawdry little actress whose faith is shattered, the young clubman who chooses between a fortune for himself and one for a homeless girl, are all people of his, portrayed with a quick, loving pencil, vigorous, apparently careless, in reality painstaking to the point of fineness. He has, too, an elusive way of interweaving the romantic and the ridiculous so that they are hard to distinguish. Take, for instance, a passage from a short story entitled **"Hearts and Crosses."**

> Santa was lyin' in bed pretty sick. But she gives out a kind of smile, and her hand and mine lock horns, and I sits down by the bed—mud and spurs and chaps and all. 'I've heard you ridin' across the grass for hours, Webb,' she says. 'I was sure you'd come. You saw the sign?' she whispers. 'The minute I hit camp,' says I. "'T was marked on the bag of potatoes and onions.' 'They're always together,' says she, soft-like—'always together in life.' 'They go well together,' I says, 'in a stew.' 'I mean hearts and crosses,' says Santa. 'Our sign—to love and to suffer—that's what they mean.'

O. Henry's methods of work, as he himself described them, are simple. "Rule 1 of story-writing is to write stories that please yourself. There is no Rule 2. In writing, forget the public. I get a story thoroughly in mind before I sit down at my table. Then I write it out quickly, and, without revising it, send it to my publishers. In this way, I am able to judge my work almost as the public judges it." (pp. 11725-26)

Harry Peyton Steger, "O. Henry: Who He Is and How He Works," in The World's Work, *Vol. XVIII, No. 2, June, 1909, pp. 11724-726.*

STEPHEN LEACOCK   (essay date 1916)

[*A Canadian humorist, essayist, and biographer as well as a professor of economics and political science, Leacock is best known as one of the leading humorists of the first half of the twentieth century. In his works, which include* Nonsense Novels *(1911) and* Sunshine Sketches of a Little Town *(1912), Leacock delights in parody and incongruity. In the following excerpt, he caustically describes the mechanisms of American publishing and singles out O. Henry as one of the few true artists to achieve commercial success, stating "that in matters of literature, indeed of all the arts, we must judge a man by his best, and never by his worst."*]

These, by the freak of circumstance that wills it so, are O. Henry days. With so much else that should absorb us—with Emperors dying almost unnoticed, with twenty million men struggling on a dozen "fronts," with the cost of living gripping at our vitals, and with the mad diversion of the New Luxury to hold us back from thinking of anything at all—by some odd chance we are all thinking and talking of the man who called himself O. Henry. Our neglected author is dead in his grave, with scarcely a publisher to walk behind his hearse, and lo! six years after his death he is bursting upon us afresh, as it were, with all the splendor of a rising genius. A "definitive edition" of his works is out, published—American slang and all—in war-stricken England. It is selling, so they tell us, by the hundred thousand. A professor of English is to the front with an "authoritative biography." Editors are calling eagerly for O. Henry articles, and the ponderous pundits of official criticism, with a full sense of their responsibility, are weighing the man in their scales as carefully as poor O. Henry himself might have measured out grains of morphine in the night silence of his prison dispensary.

Meantime the voice of the carping critic is lifted up, half doubtful even of O. Henry's best, and positively contemptuous of his worst. Most notable of all, the college professoriate has stepped in—that august fraternity who can only truly recognize literature a thousand years after the "plain people" have found it out, and who reserve their smiles for the so-called jokes of Aristophanes, and look to the writings of Plato for their horoscope of the Democratic party.

At the hands of these and their like, O. Henry is being tried and found wanting. We have it from one professor—a feminine one—that O. Henry could not write *stories* at all. Worse than that, he not only could not write the thing called the short story, but he actually degraded it. [see Kilmer in Further Reading list] That petted offspring of our hopes, the American Short Story, which is expected some day to bloom with such effulgence as to prove that we are after all a literary people—our peculiar product which is viewed even in the colleges with an indulgent eye—that, O. Henry would have strangled in its poor cradle. He would, they tell us, have choked it with his rough handling, poisoned its pure blood with the bacillus of his western slang, and marred its usefulness for the college textbook by his crude solecisms and his ignorance.

O. Henry's stories, we are informed by the adverse critics, are not stories at all, but for the most part mere "anecdotes" (such is the fatal word that has been found) dependent on some purely literary trick of surprise or enigma—some meretricious art of ending a story with a juggler's *coup de main*—the simplest thing in the world to do, for those who care to stoop to it. Alas! that the generation in which we live should need to be told again the story of Abraham Lincoln and Gen-

eral Grant's whiskey. Repeat it, at this late hour, one dare not. But if the tales of O. Henry are indeed "anecdotes," then, in the name of commonsense, let us have another barrelful.

The truth is that in matters of literature, indeed of all the arts, we must judge a man by his best, and never by his worst. When Homer nods we must turn our heads the other way, reading his Iliad aloud that we may not hear the raucous snoring of the bard that wrote it. It is by the highest reach of a man that we measure his stature. So it should be in art. So it always is, in fact, when with the lapse of years the grain is winnowed into the basket and the chaff has flown upon the wind. We think of Francis Bacon as the author of his immortal "Essays," not as the sneaking parasite that driveled of divine monarchy for the ear of his slobbering king. We think of Gray as the man who wrote the "Elegy in a Country Churchyard." In the twilight shadow of his ancient elms, we may forget the rest. When we talk of Washington Irving, let it be in the midsummer drowsiness of his Sleepy Hollow. Let us not hold it against Tennyson that he allowed himself to be washed from his anchorage by the flood tide of Victorian sentimentality; that he lived in a perpetual pose, a cloak draped about him, and a prepared look "registered"—as they call it in the moving pictures—upon his face. Let us forget that Carlyle had stomach-ache, and often put it down on paper; that Browning was as jealous as a débutante; that Dickens broke at times into sobs of literary hysteria; and that our good old Mark Twain himself—amid the financial ruin that he faced so bravely—inflicted upon an indulgent public such unspeakable trash as his "Double Barreled Detective Story" and his "Tom Sawyer Abroad." It is kinder to forget. And, in any case, such things go easily to their inevitable doom.

So it should be with O. Henry. There is no need to measure the master genius that penned **"The Furnished Room"** and **"The Municipal Report"** by the smaller standard of his lesser things. They need not count. They are but the careless product of genius fertile beyond our common ken, and great enough to be indifferent to fame itself.

More than all should such indulgence be exercised in these days when commerce and the money motive intrude their eager, selfish hands into the framework of literature and twist and mar it from the shape in which Heaven has tried to fashion it. For in these days of the Universal Press and the Syndicate and the Cable Service, it is not so much merit that counts as that last little increment of conspicuousness that lifts a man, let it be by ever so little, above the crowd—just for once—let it be but for five minutes—and thus certifies and hallmarks his every product with the sterling stamp of notoriety. The one thing needed above all others is an initial success. Grant this and the mechanism of modern commerce—the syndicate man and the moving-picture manager and the vociferous lecture bureau can multiply it by a thousand. With initial success to back him, a literary man, perhaps after years of unappreciated struggle and effort, finds the world about him changed. The Editor, who had seemed little better than a bandit, is wreathed in smiles—a jolly pleasant fellow he now appears—grossly misjudged in the days of adversity—who buys lunches and plans new tasks and clamors ever for more copy with a check-book ready under his obliging thumb. The Publisher—how could one ever have thought him rough?—is turned forthwith into a merry dog, hospitable, and appreciative even of stories that he never reads. For one soon learns that he reads nothing, but sits merely in his den waiting with a little golden crown to fit upon the brows of initial success. No worse is he, good soul, than other men. He knows his public, and what they want, they get. In the place of a real book he gives a name, instead of a drama a notoriety, and in place of art a public scandal, a divorce or suicide or whatever other thing can set the people talking of the author of the hour. Small wonder that as like as not, he often gives—in the real measure of things—for bread, a stone.

Smaller wonder still that in this forced draught of commercial successfulness masquerading as literary success, true art can scarcely live at all. Author after author flies like a moth into the money flame, and is there consumed, turning out mere jaded hackwork in place of literature, and yet in his very extinction kindling such a flashlight of advertised notoriety that all about him mistake it for the undying light of fame: till he snuffs out, and passes.

Yet of all those that live and have recently lived on the pinnacle of literary success, O. Henry better than any other resisted the temptation to multiply himself for money's sake. He lived for the most part a penurious life, with a sudden and transitory affluence at the close of it. It is not conceivable that he could altogether escape. He wrote, under a contract, so his biographer tells us, a story each week for over a year, to be fed into the greedy maw of the weekly press. Some sixty or seventy of his stories were poured forth in this fashion—with the prodigality of genius, unrevised and scantily considered and spun as it seems from the merest cobwebs. Is it strange, then, that sometimes his craft failed him, and that, great as his genius was, from time to time he handed to his employers a mere piece of task work—done with repugnance and forgotten?

For O. Henry in his real work could write only by the light within. There was no elaborate scheme of preparation to take the place of the inspired word. He read nothing, or next to it. He investigated nothing. He saw nobody. He had no propaganda, no views to expound, no lesson, in the meaner sense, to teach. His was not the dull industry that investigates, notebook in hand, the slum, the factory and the market place, and turns the mass of accumulated fact into the vast Contemporary Novel that pours its slow current of alluvial mud through the channel of a thousand pages.

Ignorant—undoubtedly, except of life itself—gloriously ignorant he was. No college, not even a theological school, could have matriculated him. Even of New York, so they now tell us, he knew practically nothing. But of little threads and patches, a vision of a haggard face seen for a moment in a crowd, a fallen word, the chance glance of an eye—of such as this interwoven with the cross thread of his marvelous imagination, he did his matchless work.

Let it so rest as his best monument. The little peckings of the critics about the base will but serve to keep clean the stone. (pp. 120-22)

Stephen Leacock, "O. Henry and His Critics," in The New Republic, Vol. IX, No. 109, December 2, 1916, pp. 120-22.

C. ALPHONSO SMITH (essay date 1916)

[*Smith was an American critic and the author of the earliest book-length biography of O. Henry, which contained the first published revelation of O. Henry's prison term and provoked severe criticism for making this detail known. In the following excerpt, Smith examines some of the predominant themes in O. Henry's fiction.*]

Every one who has heard O. Henry's stories talked about or has talked about them himself will recall or admit the frequent recurrence of some such expression as, "I can't remember the name of the story but the *point* is this." Then will follow the special bit of philosophy, the striking trait of human nature, the new aspect of an old truth, the novel revelation of character, the wider meaning given to a current saying, or whatever else it may be that constitutes the point or underlying theme of the story. Of no other stories is it said or could it be said so frequently, "The point is this," because no other writer of stories has, I think, touched upon such an array of interesting themes.

Most of those who have commented upon O. Henry's work have singled out his technique, especially his unexpected endings, as his distinctive contribution to the American short story. (p. 203)

The unexpected ending, however, is not, even technically, the main point in the structural excellence of a short story. Skill here marks only the convergence and culmination of structural excellencies that have stamped the story from the beginning. The crack of the whip at the end is a mechanical feat as compared with the skilful manipulation that made it possible. Walter Pater speaks somewhere—and O. Henry's best stories are perfect illustrations—of "that architectural conception of the work which perceives the end in the beginning and never loses sight of it, and in every part is conscious of all the rest, till the last sentence does but, with undiminished vigor, unfold and justify the first." In fact, it is not the surprise at the end that reveals the technical mastery of O. Henry or of Poe or of De Maupassant. It is rather the instantly succeeding second surprise that there should have been a first surprise: it is the clash of the unexpected but inevitable.

It is not technique, however, that has given O. Henry his wide and widening vogue. Technique starts no after-tones. It flashes and is gone. It makes no pathways for reflection. If a story leaves a residuum, it is a residuum of theme, bared and vivified by technique but not created by it. It is O. Henry's distinction that he has enlarged the area of the American short story by enriching and diversifying its social themes. In his hands the short story has become the organ of a social consciousness more varied and multiform than it had ever expressed before. . . . Whether in North Carolina or Texas or Latin America or New York an instant responsiveness to the humour or the pathos or the mere human interest of men and women playing their part in the drama of life was always his distinguishing characteristic. It was not merely that he observed closely. Beneath the power to observe and the skill to reproduce lay a passionate interest in social phenomena which with him no other interest ever equalled or ever threatened to replace.

Man in solitude made little appeal to O. Henry, though he had seen much of solitude himself. But man in society, his "humours" in the old sense, his whims and vagaries, his tragedies and comedies and tragi-comedies, his conflicts with individual and institutional forces, his complex motives, the good underlying the evil, the ideal lurking potent but unsuspected within—whatever entered as an essential factor into the social life of men and women wrought a sort of spell upon O. Henry and found increasing expression in his art. It was not startling plots that he sought: it was human nature

The Porter family drugstore in Greensboro, North Carolina, where O. Henry worked as an apprentice pharmacist.

themes, themes beckoning to him from the life about him but not yet wrought into short story form.

Take the theme that O. Henry calls "turning the tables on Haroun al Raschid." It emerges first in **"While the Auto Waits,"** published in May, 1903, a month after **"A Retrieved Reformation."** . . . O. Henry had discovered a little unexploited corner of human nature which he was further to develop and diversify in **"The Caliph and the Cad," "The Caliph, Cupid, and the Clock," "Lost on Dress Parade,"** and **"Transients in Arcadia."**

The psychology is sound. Shakespeare would have sanctioned it. . . . If Haroun al Raschid found it diverting to wander incognito among his poor subjects, why should not "the humble and poverty-stricken" of this more modern and self-expressive age play the ultra-rich once in a while? They do, but they had lacked a spokesman till O. Henry appeared for them. He, by the way, goes with them in spirit and they all return to their tasks happy and refreshed. They have given their imagination a surf bath.

Habit is another favourite theme. A man believes that he has conquered a certain deeply rooted habit, or hopes he has. By a decisive act or experience he puts a certain stage of his life, as he thinks, behind him. O. Henry is not greatly interested in how he does this: he may change from a drifting tramp to a daring desperado; he may marry; he may undergo an emotional reformation which seems to run a line of cleavage between the old life and the new; a woman may bid farewell to her position as cashier in a downtown restaurant and enter the ranks of the most exclusive society.

But, however the break with the past comes about, O. Henry is profoundly interested in the possibilities of relapse. Such stories, to mention them in the order of their writing, as **"The Passing of Black Eagle," "A Comedy in Rubber," "From the Cabby's Seat," "The Pendulum," "The Romance of a Busy Broker," "The Ferry of Unfulfilment," "The Girl and the Habit,"** and **"The Harbinger"** would form an interesting pendant to William James's epochal essay on habit. Indeed I have often wondered whether the great psychologist's fondness for O. Henry was not due, in part at least, to the freshness and variety of the story teller's illustrations of mental traits and mental whimsies. No one, at any rate, can read the stories mentioned without concluding that O. Henry had at least one conviction about habit. It is that when the old environment comes back the old habit is pretty sure to come with it.

Of these particular stories, **"The Pendulum"** makes unquestionably the deepest impression. O. Henry at first called it "Katy of Frogmore Flats" but reconsidered and gave it its present name, thus indicating that the story is a dramatization of the measured to-and-fro, the monotonous *tick-tock* of a life dominated by routine. **"The Pendulum"** should be read along with the story by De Maupassant called "An Artist." Each has habit as its central theme, and the two reveal the most characteristic differences of their authors. In the setting, the tone, the story proper, the conversations, the characters, the attitude of the author to his work, there is hardly an element of the modern short story that is not sharply contrasted in these two little masterpieces, neither of which numbers two thousand words. (pp. 204-09)

"What's around the corner" seems at first glance too vague or too inclusive to be labelled a distinctive theme. But it was distinctive with O. Henry, distinctive in his conduct, distinctive in his art. What was at first felt to be an innate impulse, potent but indefinable, came later to be resolutely probed for short story material. "At every corner," he writes [in **"The Green Door"**], "handkerchiefs drop, fingers beckon, eyes besiege, and the lost, the lonely, the rapturous, the mysterious, the perilous, changing clues of adventure are slipped into our fingers. But few of us are willing to hold and follow them. We are grown stiff with the ramrod of convention down our backs. We pass on; and some day we come, at the end of a very dull life, to reflect that our romance has been a pallid thing of a marriage or two, a satin rosette kept in a safe-deposit drawer, and a lifelong feud with a steam radiator."

From **"The Enchanted Kiss,"** written in prison, to **"The Venturers,"** written a year before his death, one may trace the footprints of characters who, in dream or vision, in sportive fancy or earnest resolve, traverse the far boundaries of life, couching their lances for routine in all of its shapes, seeking "a subject without a predicate, a road without an end, a question without an answer, a cause without an effect, a gulf stream in life's ocean." Fate, destiny, romance, adventure, the lure of divergent roads, the gleam of mysterious signals, the beckonings of the Big City—these are the signs to be followed. They may lead you astray but you will at least have had the zest of pursuit without the satiety of conquest. (pp. 209-10)

In **"The Complete Life of John Hopkins,"** fate and destiny give place to pure romance. . . .

John Hopkins experienced poverty, love, and war between the lighting and relighting of a five-cent cigar. But they were thrust upon him. He was no true adventurer. The first true adventurer is Rudolf Steiner of **"The Green Door."** (p. 213)

But the venturer is a finer fellow than the adventurer, and in **"The Venturers"** O. Henry tilts for the last time at a theme which, if health had not failed, says Mr. Gilman Hall, would have drawn from him many more stories. In a little backless notebook which O. Henry used in New York I find the jotting from which **"The Venturers"** grew. . . . **"The Venturers"** harks back to this entry, the last in the book: "Followers of chance—Two knights-errant—One leaves girl and other marries her for what may be 'around the corner.' " (pp. 214-15)

In fact, the central idea of **"The Venturers,"** the revolt against the calculable, seems at times to run away with the story itself. Ives marries Miss Marsden at last because he became convinced that marriage is the greatest "venture" of all. But what convinced him? The expository part of the narrative has put the emphasis elsewhere. The centre of the story seems not quite in the middle.

Another theme, one that O. Henry has almost pre-empted, is the shop-girl. (p. 216)

Certainly no other American writer has so identified himself with the life problems of the shop-girl in New York as has O. Henry. In his thinking she was an inseparable part of the larger life of the city. She belonged to the class that he thought of as under a strain and his interest in her welfare grew with his knowledge of the conditions surrounding her. . . . It has been said that O. Henry laughs with the shop-girl rather than at her, but the truth is that he does not laugh at all when she is his theme; he smiles here and there but the smile is at the humours of life itself rather than at the shop-girl in particular. (p. 217)

But the shop-girl is a part of a larger theme and that theme is the city. (p. 226)

A city was to O. Henry not merely a collective entity, not merely an individuality; certainly not a municipality: it was a personality. (p. 227)

His Latin American stories may serve as illustrations. They deal sparingly with native characters. O. Henry evidently felt some hesitation here, for in his rapid journey from Honduras around both coasts of South America the unit of progress was the coastal town. There was little time to study native character as he studied it on his own soil. The city, therefore, rather than the citizen, is made prominent. An American doctor, for example, who has travelled widely in Latin America, considers O. Henry's description of Espiritu unequalled in accuracy and vividness as a sketch of the typical Latin American coastal town. Certainly no one of his Latin American character portraits is as detailed or as intimate. (pp. 228-29)

But it is in his references to American cities that O. Henry's feeling for the city as a unit is best revealed. It has been said of George Eliot that her passion for individualizing was so great that a character is rarely introduced in her stories, even if he only says "Breakfast is served," without being separated in some way from the other characters. The same may be said of O. Henry's mention of American towns and cities. Sometimes the differentiation is diffused through the story from beginning to end. Sometimes it is summarized in a phrase or paragraph. (p. 229)

Nowhere does O. Henry's insight into human nature, his breadth and depth, his pervasive humour, or his essential Americanism show more clearly than in such stories as **"The Duplicity of Hargraves," "The Champion of the Weather," "New York by Campfire Light," "The Pride of the Cities," "From Each According to His Ability," "The Rose of Dixie," "The Discounters of Money," "Thimble, Thimble,"** and **"Best-Seller."** In each of these he stages a contrast between the North and the South or the North and the West.

The task was not an original one but he did it in an original way. Since 1870 American literature has abounded in short stories, novels, and plays that are geographical not only in *locale* but in spirit and content. (p. 238)

Before the advent of O. Henry, however, short story writers had fought shy of essaying such a contrast within the narrow limits of a single story, a contrast for which the drama and the novel seemed better fitted. Bret Harte and Hamlin Garland, Sarah Orne Jewett and Mrs. Wilkins-Freeman, Thomas Nelson Page and Joel Chandler Harris, and a score of others had proved that the short story could be made to represent as large a territory as the novel. But as an instructed delegate each short story preferred to speak for only one constituency. When it tried to represent two at the same time, there was apt to be a glorification of the one and a caricature of the other.

It is one of O. Henry's distinctions that he is fair to both. . . . O. Henry is "genial and equal-handed" not only in the characteristics selected but in the way he pits characteristic against characteristic, foible against foible, an excess against a defect, then again a defect against an excess. Art and heart are so blended in these contrasts, wide and liberal observation is so allied to shrewd but kindly insight, that the reader hardly realizes the breadth of the theme or the sureness of the author's footing.

O. Henry was not a propagandist, but one cannot re-read these stories without feeling that here as elsewhere the story teller is much more than a mere entertainer. He has suggested a nationalism in which North, West, and South are to play their necessary parts. It is not a question of surrender or abdication; it is a question rather of give and take. (pp. 240-41)

But each theme that has been mentioned is but an illustration of that larger quest in which all of O. Henry's stories find their common meeting-place—the search for those common traits and common impulses which together form a sort of common denominator of our common humanity. Many of his two hundred and fifty stories are impossible; none, rightly considered, are improbable. They are so rooted in the common soil of our common nature that even when dogs or monuments do the talking we do the thinking. The theme divisions that we have attempted to make are, after all, only subdivisions. The ultimate theme is your nature and mine.

It is too soon to attempt to assign O. Henry a comparative rank among his predecessors. We may attempt, however, to place him if not to weigh him. (p. 243)

A glance through O. Henry's pages shows that his familiarity with the different sections of the United States was greater than that of [Washington Irving, Edgar Allan Poe, Nathaniel Hawthorn, or Bret Harte]. He had lived in every part of the country that may be called distinctive except New England, but he has not pre-empted any locality. His stories take place in Latin America, in the South, in the West, and in the North. He always protested against having his stories interpreted as mere studies in localism. There was not one of his New York stories, he said, in which the place was essential to the underlying truth or to the human interest back of it. Nor was his technique distinctive. It is essentially the technique of Poe which became later the technique of De Maupassant but was modified by O. Henry to meet new needs and to subserve diverse purposes. O. Henry has humanized the short story. (p. 245)

C. Alphonso Smith, in his O. Henry Biography, *Doubleday, Page & Company, 1916, 258 p.*

FRED LEWIS PATTEE (essay date 1917)

[*Pattee was an American literary critic and historian who, in such works as* A History of American Literature, with a View to the Fundamental Principles Underlying its Development (1896) *and* The First Century of American Literature (1935), *called for the recognition of American literature as distinct from English literature. In the following excerpt, Pattee at-*

tacks popular American literature of his time as epitomized by the works of O. Henry.]

After thirty years of pretty continuous reading in American literature I can say that never has the published output been so clever, so sparkling, so arresting as at the present moment, and never has it been so shallow and inconsequential. Literature that has any excellencies save the mechanical ones connected with the modern art of "putting it over" seems to be disappearing. In place of the great still books of the earlier periods, more and more are we getting literary journalism,—clever and animated little scraps in the place of fiction, sparkling shallowness, ephemeral smartness for the pulp-paper magazine and the Sunday Supplement.

This is a terrible indictment of a generation, especially if one will admit—and who will not?—that the soul of an epoch is to be found in its written product. Is the indictment too strong? For an answer we can do no better than study what undoubtedly is the leading literary success of the generation, the author who in the last seven years, according to the statement of his publishers, has sold one million, eight hundred thousand copies of his stories,—O. Henry, already crowned, it would seem, as an American classic.

Never has there been in America a literary arrival more startling and more complete than his. He appeared with the suddenness of a comet. Hardly had we learned of his existence and his name before he seemed to be filling the whole east. He was one William Sydney Porter we were told, a southerner who had seen rough life in the south-west, in Honduras, in South America,—tramp, cow-boy, adventurer, crude realist, who was bringing exotic atmospheres and breezy sections of life in uncharted regions west and south of the Caribbean. Then suddenly we found him acclaimed—strange metamorphosis!—interpreter of New York City, Scheherazade of "little old Bagdad on the Hudson," first licensed revealer of the real heart of the modern Babylon of the west, and then, before we could rub our eyes, we were told that he was dead. From *Cabbages and Kings,* his first book, to the end in 1910, was six years,—six years and ten volumes. Two posthumous issues there were, then a set of twelve, advertised everywhere as by "the Yankee de Maupassant," and sold beyond belief.

But the mere selling of almost two million copies is not the remarkable thing about O. Henry: he has been given a place beside the masters. Editors of college texts are including his work among the classics. A recent book of selections from the work of the world's greatest short story writers includes only five Americans: Irving, Hawthorne, Poe, Bunner, O. Henry. (pp. 374-75)

Manifestly, to study the work of this modern crowned classic is to study the minds of those who crowned him. Through the works of O. Henry one may estimate O. Henry's period, for a people and a generation are to be judged by what they enjoy, by what they teach in their schools and crown in their academies. Success like his means imitators, a literary school, a standard of measurement.

The first approach to the man—the only approach until recently—must be through the twelve volumes of his writings. Read all of them if you would know him, but beware: they are intoxicating. One emerges from the twelfth book of the strange Harlequin epic completely upset, unable for a time rightly to evaluate, condemning, yet inclined by some strange wizardry to praise. Where else may one find such a melange,—stories bedeviled and poured into bomb-shells;

traversities and extravaganzas; rollicking farce often as vulgarly grotesque as the picture supplement of the Sunday edition; short stories violating every canon of the text-book, yet so brilliant as to tempt one to form a new decalogue of the art; sketches, philosophizings, burlesque hilarious? What spirits! what eager zest in life! what curiosity! what boyish delight in the human show! one must go back to Dickens to match it. Not a dull page, not a sentence that does not rebound upon you like a boy's laugh, or startle you, or challenge you, or prod you unawares. It is strong meat prepared for jaded palates: there are no delicate flavors, no subtle spiceries, no refined and exquisite essences of style. Its tones are loud, its humor is exaggerated, its situations and characters extremes. It is pitched for men, for healthy, elemental men: men of the bar-room and the frontier. . . . And yet, for all that, and notwithstanding the fact that the stories record life on isolated masculine ranches, in vice-reeking tropic towns, and the unspeakable areas of New York City, at every point that touches the feminine—paradox again!—the work is as clean as Emerson's. Not a page in the twelve volumes that may not be read aloud in the family circle.

Before one has spent an hour with the volumes, one is conscious of a strange duality in the work, one that must have had its origin in the man himself. It is as if a Hawthorne had sold his pen to Momus. There are paragraphs where the style attains a distinction rare anywhere in literature; one might cull extracts that would imply marvellous wholes. We realize that we are dealing with no uncouth ranchman who has literary aspirations, who writes in slang for want of legitimate vocabulary. We are in the hands of one who has read widely and well, one who has a vocabulary, not including his slang, which may be called unique, which may be compared indeed with that of a Pater or a James. His biographer records that for years the dictionary was his favorite reading, that he pored over it as one pores over a romance, and his reader may well believe it. (pp. 375-77)

[The] comic device most affected by O. Henry, one that may be called his most prominent mannerism, is a variety of euphemism, the translating of simple words and phrases into resounding and inflated circumlocutions. So completely did this take hold of him that one finds it in almost every paragraph; all his characters speak in it as a kind of dialect. A waiter becomes "a friendly devil in a cabbage-scented hell;" a tramp is "a knight on a restless tour of the cities;" a remark about the weather is "a pleasant reference to meteorological conditions." Instead of saying that Mr. Brunelli fell in love with Katy, he says: "Mr. Brunelli, being impressionable and a Latin, fell to conjugating the verb *amare* with Katy in the objective case." A little of this is laughable, but O. Henry wears it threadbare. The plain statement, The woman looked over at him hoping he would invite her to a champagne dinner, becomes, "She turned languishing eyes upon him as a hopeful source of lobsters and the delectable, ascendant globules of effervescence." It is too much.

His humor is more forced, more deliberately artificial, than that of Mark Twain. It is the humor of one who is *trying* to be humorous. He is brilliant rather than droll. He makes use constantly of incongruous mixtures for the last outrageous ingredient of which you feel he must have ransacked his whole experience. . . . Everywhere incongruous association: . . . "He had gout very bad in one foot, a house near Gramercy Park, half a million dollars, and a daughter." It is as if he had paraphrased Sterne's dictum into "If I knew my

reader could guess what is coming in the next sentence or even in the next phrase I would change it instantly."

But it is not with the literary comedians that O. Henry is being classed by the reading public who have crowned him: it is as a serious contributor to American fiction, as a short story writer *sui generis,* the creator of a new genre, a genius, an "American de Maupassant." Conservative criticism as always has been inclined to wait: a comet be it ever so brilliant fades if you give it time, but the hand of the critic of O. Henry has been forced. It becomes impossible to ignore the voices of the times that greet us everywhere,—in university and public library, in home and club and barber shop, in the work of even the critics themselves. What of O. Henry as the writer of American short stories? (pp. 382-83)

It seems that **"Whistling Dick's Christmas Stocking,"** which was published in *McClure's Magazine* in December, 1899, the story that first introduced him to northern readers, was the beginning of his work, and as we read we feel it was by no accident that it was accepted and published by the magazine which was among the earliest to popularize its subscription price and journalize its literary content.

The story was in the new field of fiction which had been opened by Kipling. Beginning with the closing years of the century had come the demand for the concrete, for exciting stories by writers who had been a part of what they wrote,—Jack London from Alaska, [Richard Harding] Davis from South America, and the like. A fiction writer to hold his readers must have had an unusual experience in a new and picturesque area. . . . The new tale with the strange name of O. Henry instantly gained a hearing because of the strangeness and freshness of its content. It seemed to deal realistically with the winter exodus of tramps to New Orleans, and it was told apparently by one who had himself been a tramp and who spoke with authority.

The story discloses much. It tells us for one thing that the transition from Sydney Porter, the Texas newspaper paragrapher, to O. Henry the short story writer, came through the medium of Bret Harte's California tales. Like Harte's work, it is a story of sentiment, theatric rather than realistic, theatric even to the point of falsehood. . . . Like Harte's work too, the tale is a dramatized paradox. . . . Even the style reveals the influence of Harte. (pp. 383-84)

This same attitude toward life and material we find in **"An Afternoon Miracle," "The Sphynx Apple," "Christmas by Injunction,"** indeed in all his stories of the south-west. All were molded by Harte as Harte was molded by Dickens. The West is used as startling and picturesque background; the characters are the conventional types of western melodrama: desperadoes, cowboys, train-robbers, sheep-men, miners,—all perfect in theatric make-up, and extreme always in word and action. Like Harte, the writer had no real love for the West, and he never worked with conviction and sympathy to show the soul of it. Here and there a glow of insight and sympathy may hover over the studies that he made of his native South, but one finds it rarely in others of the two hundred and fifty stories that make up his set of books; certainly one finds it not at all in the fifty-seven that deal with the south-west. By a change of some two hundred words any one of them could be transferred to the East, and lose nothing of its value. By the changing of half a dozen names, for instance, **"The Indian Summer of Dry Valley Johnson"** could be laid in Hoboken, New Jersey, and gain thereby. Johnson could just as well be a milkman from Geneva, New York.

The external manner of Harte he outgrew, but never did he free himself of the less obvious characteristic that renders the work of both men inferior when compared with absolute standards: neither had a philosophy of life and a moral standpoint. Of the two Harte is the greater, for Harte's work is single—never does he give us the serious mixed cheaply with buffoonery,—and once or twice does he make us feel an individual human soul, but even Harte must be classed with those who have debauched American literature, since he worked the surface of life with theatric intent and always without moral background.

In the second group of O. Henry's stories fall the South American studies and *The Gentle Grafter* series that fill two whole books and overflow into other volumes of his set. Despite much splendid description and here and there real skill in reproducing the atmosphere and the spirit of the tropics, *Cabbages and Kings* must be dismissed in its author's own terms as mere "tropic vaudeville," extravaganza of the newspaper comic-column type. In *The Gentle Grafter* series, moreover, we have what is undoubtedly literature at its very worst. It may be possible that the series rests on fact; a prototype for Jeff Peters undoubtedly there was,—a certain voluble convict in the Ohio prison who told the writer all these adventures; but for all that, the tales are false. They are not life: they are *opéra bouffe*. The characters are no more flesh and blood than are Punch and Judy. They talk a dialect unknown outside of the comic theater. Sophomores at dinner may occasionally use circumlocution for humorous effect, but here everybody is sophomoric and supersophomoric; they never speak save in words sesquipedalian. . . . An Irishman in the heart of the forest bids the first man he has seen for months to dismount from his mule in terms like these: "Segregate yourself from your pseudo-equine quadruped." This is not an occasional pleasantry for humorous effect: it is the everyday language of all the characters. It is not slang, for slang is the actual words of actual men, and since the world began no one ever talked like this. It is an argot deliberately manufactured for the burlesque stage.

Art is truth,—truth to facts and truth to the presumption fundamental, at least in civilized lands, that truth is superior to falsehood and right superior to wrong, and that crime is never to be condoned. Despite the freedom of his pages from salacious stain, O. Henry must be classed as immoral, not because he uses picaresque material, or because he records the success of villainy, but because he sympathizes with his lawbreakers, laughs at their impish tricks indulgently, and condones their schemes for duping the unwary. It does not excuse Jeff Peters to explain that he fleeces only those who have fleece to spare, or those rich ones who enjoy an occasional fleecing because it affords them a new sensation. *The Gentle Grafter* is cloth of the same loom that wove *Raffles* and all the others on that shelf of books that are the shame of American literature. The taint extends through all of O. Henry's work. He had no moral foundations. At heart he was with his bibulous rascals: train robbers, tramps, desperadoes, confidence men, sponges and all his other evaders and breakers of the law. He chuckled over their low ideals and their vulgar philosophy like one who sides naturally against law and order and soberness. (pp. 385-87)

The last period of O. Henry's life began in 1904 when he was engaged by the New York *World* to furnish a story each week for its Sunday Supplement. He had been in the city for two years, and had constantly written stories of life in the southwest and in Central America. He had studied the demands of the time. . . . He had gained in ease, in constructive art, in brilliancy of diction and of figure of speech. Now with the beginning of his contract with the *World* came the culmination of his later manner, that manner by many considered to be the real O. Henry. Seldom now did he attempt ambitious plot stories like **"A Black Jack Bargainer"** and **"Georgia's Ruling."** Often his weekly contribution to the *World* cannot be called a story at all. It was a sketch, an expanded "paragraph," an elaborated anecdote, a study, a "story" in the newspaper sense of the word. (pp. 387-88)

The requirements of the newspaper "story" are exacting. It must be vivid, unusual, unhackneyed, and it must have in it the modern quality of "go." It is an improvisation by one who through long practice has gained the mastery of his pen, and by one, moreover, who has been in living contact with that which he would portray. It is written in heat, excitedly, to be read with excitement and then thrown away. There must be no waste material in it, no "blue pencil stuff," and there must be "a punch in every line." The result is a brilliant *tour de force* called forth by the demand of the times for sensation, for newness, for fresh devices to gain, if only for an instant, the jaded attention of a public supersaturated with sensation.

Complaint has come that one does not remember the stories of O. Henry. Neither does one remember the newspaper "stories" he reads from morning to morning, brilliant though they may be. The trouble comes from the fact that the writer is concerned solely with his reader. Anything to catch the reader. It is a catering to the *blasé,* a mixing of condiments for palates gross with sensation. The essence of the art is the exploiting of the unexpected,—the startling comparison, manner, climax. Everywhere paradox, incongruity, electric flash-lights, "go"—New York City, ragtime, Coney Island, the Follies,—twentieth century America at full strain.

O. Henry lacks repose, and art is serene. He moves us tremendously, but never does he lift us. One cannot take seriously even his seriousness. How can one approach in the spirit of serious art a story with the title **"Psyche and the Pskyscraper,"** or one that opens like this:

> The Poet Longfellow—or was it Confucius, the inventor of Wisdom?—remarked:
>
> > Life is real, life is earnest;
> > And things are not what they seem.
>
> (pp. 388-89)

It is all fortissimo, all in capital letters. He slaps his reader on the back and laughs loudly as if he were in a bar-room. Never the finer subtleties of suggested effect, never the unsuspected though real and moving moral background, seldom the softer tones that touch the deeper life and move the soul, rare indeed the moments when the reader feels a sudden tightening of the throat and a quickening of the pulse. It is the humor of a comic journalist—an enormously clever and witty journalist we must admit—rather than the insight of a serious portrayer of human life; it is the day's work of a trained special reporter eager that his "stories" shall please his unpleasable chief and his capricious public long ago outwearied with being pleased.

On the mechanical side of short story construction O. Henry was skillful even to genius. He had the unusual power of gripping his reader's attention and compelling him to go on to the end. Moreover, he was possessed of originality, finesse, brilliancy of style and diction, and that sense of form which can turn every element of the seemingly careless narrative to one startling focus. It is this architectonic perfection that has endeared him to the makers of hand books and correspondence courses. He began at the end and worked backward. Skilfully in the earlier stages of the story he furnishes materials for a solution; the reader falls into the trap, sees through the whole plot, and is about to turn to the next tale when the last sentence comes like a blow. Study the mechanism of such tales as **"Girl," "The Pendulum," "The Marry Month of May"** and the like. One may detect instantly the germ of the story. (pp. 389-90)

Brilliant as this all may be, however, one must not forget that it concerns only the externals of art. His failures were at vital points. A short story must have characterization, and O. Henry's pen turned automatically to caricature. . . . A short story should be true: exaggeration is not truth. A short story should leave sharp cut and indelible the impress of a vital moment in the history of an individual soul. It should "take you by the throat like a quinsy" and not because of a situation, but because of a glimpse into a heart. O. Henry, however, deals not with souls but with types, symbols, stock figures of comedy. His point of view is that of the humorist who works with abstractions: the mother-in-law, the tramp, the fat man, the maiden lady. As a result he leaves no residuum. He amuses, he diverts, he startles, and we close his book and forget.

But his shop girls, are they not individuals? Are they not true? Do they not move us? Moved undoubtedly we are, but not because we enter the tragedy of any individual shop girl. His sermon like **"An Unfinished Story"** on the pernicious system that creates the type moves us even to anger, but we shed no tears over any individual. The atmosphere is too artificial for any real emotion. It is a tract, a sermon in motley, not a short story. One feels that the constructive art of a piece as brilliant as even **"A Lickpenny Lover"** overshadows all else within it. It is based upon an untruth: the form of the lover's proposal had to be carefully fabricated so as to make possible the final sentence which is the cause of the whole tale, and one knows that no rational man ever so worded a proposal, and that no lover as ardent could have failed to make clear his position. It smells of the footlights; it was deliberately manufactured not to interpret life, but to give a sensation.

In much of his later work he impresses us as a raconteur rather than as a weaver of that severe literary form, the short story. One feels almost the physical presence of the man as one opens a story like this: "Suppose you should be walking down Broadway after dinner, with ten minutes allotted to the consummation of your cigar while you are choosing between a diverting tragedy and something serious in the way of vaudeville. Suddenly a hand is laid on your arm." . . . One has the impression of a man blinking at ease over his cigar in the hotel lobby. His stories are brief—two thousand five hundred words the later ones average—and they follow each other breathlessly. He is familiar with his reader, asks his advice on points of diction and grammar, winks jovially, slaps him on the back and laughs aloud: "There now! it's over. Hardly had time to yawn, did you?" "Young lady, you would have liked that grocer's young man yourself." "It began way up in Sullivan County, where so many rivers and so much

trouble begins—or began; how would you say that?" He opens like a responder to a toast at a banquet, with a theory or an attitude toward a phase of life, then he illustrates it with a special case holding the point of the story skilfully to the end, to bring it out with dramatic suddenness as he takes his seat amid tumultuous applause. Many of his stories, even as Mrs. Gerould has declared [see Kilmer in Further Reading list], are mere anecdotes.

This then is O. Henry. Never a writer so whimsical. By his own confession *Cabbages and Kings* is "tropic vaudeville," and the book is not widely different from all that he wrote. He was contemporary with the ten-cent magazine; it made him and it ruined him. He drifted with the tide, writing always that which would be best paid for. A few times he tried to break away as in **"Roads of Destiny"** with its Hawthorne suggestions and **"The Church with an Overshot Wheel,"** but it was only fitfully that he even struggled to escape the vaudeville world. **"The Enchanted Kiss,"** an absinthe dream with parts as lurid and as brilliant as anything in DeQuincey, came at the very beginning of his work. The ephemeral press had laid its hands upon him and he gave it its full demands. (pp. 390-93)

We may explain him best, perhaps, in terms of his own story **"The Lost Blend"**: a flask of coarse western humor,—John Phoenix, Artemus Ward; a full measure of Bret Harte,—sentiment, theatric posing, melodrama; a dash of de Maupassant,—constructive art, finesse; a brimming beaker of journalistic flashiness, bubbles, tang, and then—insipid indeed all the blend without this—two bottles of the Apollinaris of O. Henry's peculiar individuality, and lo! the blend that is intoxicating a generation,—"elixir of battle, money, and high life."

Exhilarating surely, but a dangerous beverage for steady consumption. Sadly does it befuddle the head, the heart, the soul. It begets dislike of mental effort, and dependence solely upon thrill and picturesque movement. It is akin to the moving pictures, where thinking and imagination die. (pp. 393-94)

Are we not arriving at a period of ephemeral literary art, a shallow period without moral background and without philosophy of life, a period, dominated by the pulp-wood journal, a period, in short, in which an O. Henry is the crowned literary classic? (p. 394)

> *Fred Lewis Pattee, in an originally unsigned essay titled "The Journalization of American Literature," in* The Unpopular Review, *Vol. VII, No. 14, April-June, 1917, pp. 374-94.*

B. M. EJXENBAUM　(essay date 1925)

[*Ejxenbaum was a major Russian critic whose unwillingness to espouse the Party line in literary matters caused him to be ostracized by the Soviet literary establishment. A central figure in the Formalist literary movement from its inception until the Soviet condemnation of Formalism in the 1930s, Ejxenbaum was also a member of The Society for the Study of Poetic Language, a group which maintained that literary criticism should focus on the specific, intrinsic characteristics of verbal art, or "concrete poetics." During the purges of nonconformist factions in literature in Soviet Russia in the 1940s, the public "confessions of ideological error" that Ejxenbaum was constrained to make were so obviously ironical that he was denied "rehabilitated" status, and until the gradual loosening of strict governmental controls over literature in the late 1950s, he found it virtually impossible to publish. He was in the process*

O. Henry at age twenty-two when he was working for the State Land Office in Austin, Texas.

of reestablishing himself as a literary critic concerned with problems of concrete poetics when he died in 1959. In the following excerpt, originally published in the Russian periodical Zvezda in 1925, Ejxenbaum provides a formalistic analysis of the style and structure of O. Henry's short stories.]

For some reason [Russian readers] were completely unaware of O. Henry's name until 1923, although he had died back in 1910 and during the years preceding his death was one of the most popular and beloved authors in America. During the years O. Henry was publishing in his own country (1904-1910) his stories would hardly have attracted the Russian reader's attention. Their success in our day is all the more characteristic and significant: they obviously satisfy some literary need. Of course, for us O. Henry is only a foreign guest artist, but one who has appeared on call, by invitation, not accidentally. (pp. 1-2)

The short story generally has made its appearance in Russian literature only from time to time, as if by chance and solely for the purpose of providing a transition to the novel, which we here are accustomed to consider the higher or more dignified species of fiction. In American fiction the cultivation of the short story runs throughout the 19th century, not, of course, as an orderly, consecutive evolution, but as a process of incessantly elaborating the various possibilities of the genre. (p. 2)

It goes from Washington Irving, himself still tied to the traditions of manners-and-morals sketch writing in England, to Edgar Allan Poe, to Nathaniel Hawthorne; after them come Bret Harte, Henry James and, later, Mark Twain, Jack Lon-

don and, finally, O. Henry (I have listed, of course, only the most prominent names). O. Henry had good reason to begin one of his stories (**"The Girl and the Habit"**) with complaints against the critics' constant reproaches for his imitating this or that writer. . . . The short story is the one fundamental and self-contained genre in American prose fiction, and the stories of O. Henry certainly made their appearance in consequence of the prolonged and incessant cultivation of the genre.

On Russian soil O. Henry showed up minus those national and historical connections and we of course regard him as something else again than do the Americans. . . . Thus, literature coming from another country undergoes a curious and often far from invalid refraction when it passes through local national traditions. O. Henry in Russia is preeminently the author of "picaresque" stories and clever anecdotes with surprise endings—what for the American reader apparently seems a secondary or traditional feature. It is enough to compare Russian and American editions of O. Henry's "Selected Works." Of the 33 stories in a Russian edition and the 25 in an American one only five coincide. "Picaresque" stories and stories with humorous plots predominate in the Russian edition, while primarily sentimental "slice-of-life" stories are collected in the American one, with only those of the "picaresque" stories admitted which show the criminal repenting or on his way to reform. The stories about which American critics and readers rave pass unnoticed in Russia or cause disappointment. Tender stories about New York shopgirls have more appeal for the American reader. . . . American critics have been trying to "elevate" O. Henry (as the Russian critics have Cexov) to the level of classical traditions. They eloquently argue a resemblance between O. Henry and, for instance, Shakespeare on the basis of their common sympathies and frame of mind. (pp. 2-3)

The real O. Henry is found in an irony pervading all his stories, in a keen feeling for form and traditions. Americans cannot help wanting to prove a resemblance in outlook between O. Henry and Shakespeare—it is their way of expressing "national pride." As for the Russian reader, he, in this instance, does not care about comparisons. He reads O. Henry because it is entertaining to read him and he appreciates in O. Henry what is so lacking in our own literature—dexterity of construction, cleverness of plot situations and denouements, compactness and swiftness of action. Torn from their national traditions, the stories of O. Henry, as is true of the works of any writer on foreign soil, give us the feeling of being a finished, complete genre, and they contrast in our minds with that fluidity and vagueness now so evident in our literature. (pp. 3-4)

However consistent and homogeneous—and, in many people's opinion, even monotonous—O. Henry's work might appear, there are noticeable vacillations, transitions and a certain evolution to it. Sentimental stories—stories about New York shop girls or others of the type of **"Georgia's Ruling"**—predominate in the years immediately following his imprisonment (though they do also appear later). Generally speaking, the comic or satiric and the sentimental do very often go together in the poetics of one and the same writer in just their function of correlated contrasts; this is what we find in the work of Sterne, of Dickens and, to some extent, in the work of Gogol'. In O. Henry this combination stands out with particular relief owing to the fact that his basic orientation toward the anecdote with its unexpected and comically resolved ending is so extremely well-defined. His sentimental slice-of-life pieces, therefore, give the impression of experiments—so much the more because they are all of them, in terms of technique and language, much weaker than the others. Usually they are drawnout, wishy-washy, with endings which disappoint the reader and leave him feeling unsatisfied. The stories lack compactness, the language is without wit, the structure without dynamism. American critics, it is true, would seem ready to place these stories higher than all the others, but that is an evaluation with which we find it difficult to agree. An American, in his leisure time at home, readily gives himself over to sentimental and religious-moralistic reflections and likes to have appropriate reading. That is his custom, his tradition, a feature of national history conditioned by the peculiarities of his way of life and civilization. (pp. 10-11)

[The] construction of the story from beginning to end (rather, it would be better to say in this case—from end to beginning) had already formed in O. Henry's mind before he sat down to write, which is, of course, a very characteristic feature both for the short story . . . and for O. Henry. What he did at his desk was to work out the details of language and narration. What sort of work was that, what principles guided him, what procedures did he use? The basic principle was to get rid of stylistic clichés, to come to grips with "bookishness," with the slick "middle" style and to subject the "high" style to irony. This opened the way for his extensive use of slang in crime stories, his express avoidance of "artiness," his unfailingly down-grading images, their humor stemming from their oddity and unexpectedness, and so on. Frequently we find in O. Henry an attitude of outright irony toward one or another literary style, an irony which has the effect of bringing his own principles into the open. . . .

At those points in his stories where the need to advance the narrative or tradition would have made a special description requisite, O. Henry turns the occasion to literary irony. Where another story writer would have used the opportunity to wax eloquent or to transmit detailed information about his characters—their personalities, outward appearances, dress, past history,—O. Henry is either exceedingly terse or ironic: "Old Jacob Spraggins came home at 9:30 P.M., in his motor car. The make of it you will have to surmise sorrowfully; I am giving you unsubsidized fiction; had it been a street car I could have told you its voltage and the number of flat wheels it had." . . . There you have a typical O. Henry twist. (p. 14)

The parodic device of substituting the language of an official report for literary description . . . is systematically employed in the story **"A Municipal Report."** The story is, in the broad, a polemic—an answer to Frank Norris's assertion that only three cities in the United States were "story cities"—New York, New Orleans and San Francisco, whereas Chicago, Buffalo or Nashville held out nothing for a story writer. The story takes place, as a matter of fact, in Nashville, but instead of describing the city, O. Henry interpolates into the text quotations from a guidebook which clash with the style of the usual literary description. The very fact of inserting such quotations carries with it the character of parody. The narrator arrives in the city on a train: "All I could see through the streaming windows were two rows of dim houses. The city has an area of 10 square miles; 181 miles of streets, of which 137 miles are paved; a system of waterworks that cost $2,000,000, with 77 miles of mains." . . . Further on, in a conversation between the narrator and one of the characters: " 'Your town,' I said, as I began to make ready to depart (which is the time for smooth generalities), 'seems to be a quiet, sedate place. A home town, I should say, where few things out of the ordinary ever happen.' It carries on an extensive trade in stoves and hollow ware with the West and South, and its flouring mills have a daily capacity of more than 2,000 barrels." . . .

It is an interesting fact that this parodic or playful use of quotation—one of O. Henry's most constant stylistic devices—was noted long ago by American critics. O. Henry quotes Tennyson, Spenser and others, informing their words with new meaning, inventing puns, deliberately misquoting parts, and so on. Russian readers unfortunately miss all of this as they also do, for the most part, those instances of play on words in O. Henry's crime stories which are motivated by the speaker's illiteracy (for example, confusion of scientific words as in the case of "hypodermical" instead of "hypothetical"). (p. 15)

The general observation should be made that O. Henry's basic stylistic device (shown both in his dialogues and in the plot construction itself) is the confrontation of very remote, seemingly unrelated and, for that reason, surprising words, ideas, subjects or feelings. Surprise, as a device of parody, thus serves as the organizing principle of the sentence itself. It is no accident that he goes out of his way to avoid orderly and scrupulous descriptions and that his heroes sometimes speak in a completely erratic way; the verbiage in these instances is motivated by a special set of circumstances or causes.

O. Henry has provided us a sort of treatise on how characters should speak when undergoing emotional stress. This "treatise" is the story **"Proof of the Pudding,"** a story which brings us back to the old genre of "conversations" between the editor or journalist and the writer. O. Henry was altogether very apt to express himself ironically with regard to editors and editorial boards. . . . [In **"A Technical Error"**] we read: "Sam Durkee had a girl. (If it were an all-fiction magazine that I expected to sell this story to, I should say, "Mr. Durkee rejoiced in a fiancée')." In **"Proof of the Pudding"** the editor and the story writer meet in a city park. The editor has persistently rejected the writer's manuscripts because the latter followed the French and not the English manner in his stories. They join in a theoretical dispute. The editor reproaches the writer for spoiling his pieces at their very point of climax: "But you spoil every dénouement by those flat, drab, obliterating strokes of your brush that I have so often complained of. If you would rise to the literary pinnacle of your dramatic scenes, and paint them in the high colors that art requires, the postman would leave fewer bulky, self-addressed envelopes at your door." (pp. 15-16)

The editor is indignant because the heroine in one of the stories they are discussing, after having discovered from a letter that her husband had run off with a manicurist, says: " ' "Well, what do you think of that!": absurdly inappropriate words. . . . No human being ever uttered banal colloquialisms when confronted by sudden tragedy.' " . . . The writer argues to the contrary that " ' . . . no man or woman ever spouts "high-falutin" talk when they go up against a real climax. They talk naturally and a little worse.' " . . . The special humor of the story consists in the fact that, immediately after their conversation, both simultaneously find themselves in identical "dramatic predicaments." Having failed to resolve their argument, they go off to the writer's apartment where they find a letter from which they learn that their wives have left them. Their response "in practice" turns out to be the opposite of what each had expounded in theory. . . . The ironic meaning of the story is wholly directed against references to "real life," where things are always supposedly "not that way," the sort of references with which, one must suppose, editors had regaled O. Henry and brought him to a state of exasperation; in real life, it turns out, anything goes.

It is highly characteristic of O. Henry's general parodic bent that he frequently takes problems having to do with literary practice itself as themes for his stories, making theoretical and ironic comments on matters of style and now and again having his say about editors, publishers, reader demands and so on and so forth. Some of his stories remind one of the once very popular sonnet parodies where the subject matter was the process of composing a sonnet itself. These pieces disclose a very keen awareness on O. Henry's part of forms and traditions and confirm the view of his work as a sort of culmination point reached by the American short story of the nineteenth century. He was a writer of fiction no less than he was critic and theorist,—a feature very characteristic of our age which has completely dissociated itself from the naïve notion that writing is an "unconscious" process in which all depends on "inspiration" and "having it inside one." We haven't had a parodist with so subtle a knowledge of his craft, so inclined time and again to initiate the reader into its mysteries, probably since the time of Laurence Sterne.

However, first a few words more about O. Henry's style. His narration is invariably ironic or playful. His writing is studded with metaphors but only for the purpose of disconcerting or amusing the reader with the unexpectedness of the comparisons made—a surprise of a literary nature: their material is not traditional and usually runs counter to the "literary norm," downgrading the object of comparison and upsetting the stylistic inertia. This applies with particular frequency to descriptive passages about which, as we have seen above, O. Henry maintained an invariably ironic attitude. . . . Naturally enough, in the narrative and descriptive passages of his stories, O. Henry more often than not enters into conversation with his reader, making no point of arousing in him an illusion of direct contact or of reality but rather forever emphasizing his role as the writer and, therefore, conducting the story not from the standpoint of an impersonal commentator but from that of his own person. He brings in an outside narrator (as in his crime stories) in those cases where there is occasion for using slang, for playing on words, or the like.

Given such a system of narration, dialogue stands out with particular relief and takes on a substantial share of the effect of plot and style. The terseness of the narrative and descriptive commentary is naturally compensated for by the dynamism and concreteness of speech in the dialogues. The conversations of the characters in O. Henry stories always have a direct connection with the plot and with the role the character in question plays in it; they are rich in intonations, fast-moving and often devious or ambiguous in some special way. Sometimes a whole dialogue will be built on an incomplete utterance or on mutual misunderstanding with implications, in certain cases, not only for style but for the plot, as well. (pp. 16-17)

[In] O. Henry's hands the short story undergoes regeneration, becoming a unique composite of literary feuilleton and comedy or vaudeville dialogue. (p. 18)

Unexpectedness of ending is the most striking and consistently commented on feature of [O. Henry's] stories, the unexpectedness, moreover, being almost invariably of the "happy ending" variety. . . . [The] O. Henry story is parodic or ironic through and through—not only where the author himself interferes with the story in progress but also where nothing of the sort takes place. His stories are parodies on a certain, commonly accepted short story logic, on the usual plot syllogism. By itself, the surprise effect is a common feature of both the novel and the short story, and the American short story in particular. But for O. Henry this quality of the unexpected constitutes the very heart of the construction and bears a perfectly specific character. His endings are not merely a surprise or contrary to expectation, they appear in a sort of lateral way, as if popping out from around the corner; and it is only then that the reader realizes that certain details here and there had hinted at the possibility of such an ending. This is the surprise of parody, a trick surprise which plays on the reader's literary expectations, throwing him off center and very nearly mocking him. Frequently, the story is so constructed that it is not clear until the very end where the riddle actually lies or what, in general, all the events portend,—the ending not only serves as the dénouement but also discloses the true nature of the intrigue, the real meaning of all that has occurred. Therefore it often happens in O. Henry that not only the reader but also one of the characters in the story is fooled. 'It takes a thief to rob a thief '—that's the situation typical for O. Henry's system (*cf.*, **"The Ethics of Pig," "The Man Higher Up"**). He does not even set out "false tracks," as is commonly done in mystery stories, but operates with the help of ambiguities, half-statements or barely noticeable details which turn out at the end to have been highly significant. . . . (pp. 21-2)

No wonder "crime" material should have come in so handy for O. Henry. It was, of course, not so much a matter of the crooks in themselves but, rather, the fact that the "picaresque" story supplies excellent motivation for his plot devices. His crooks are not so much of American as of Arabian-Spanish-French origin, their tradition going back to the early "picaresque" stories and novels. What he had to have, for the most part, was motivation via some piece of trickery or cleverness or via a misunderstanding of the kind that supplied the basis for the well-known and truly typical O. Henry story, **"The Gift of the Magi"** (the husband sells his watch to buy his wife a set of combs while his wife sells her hair to buy him a watch chain). This amounts almost to a plot scheme in pure form, a kind of algebraic problem under the signs of which one could substitute any other facts one likes.

The principle of the surprise dénouement by itself makes it obligatory that the dénouement be a happy or even comic one. So it was in Puškin's *Belkin Tales* (parodies fundamentally) and so it is with O. Henry (compare Puškin's "Grobovščik" ["The Coffinmaker"] and O. Henry's **"The Head-Hunter"**). In the affairs of everyday life, we are very much accustomed to surprise of a tragic nature, but, at the same time, it brings in its wake an outcry against fate. In art, there is no one against whom to cry out. No one forces the writer to vie with fate, even if it be on paper. A tragic dénouement requires special motivation (guilt, nemesis and "character" are the usual ones in tragedy), and that is why it is more natural in a psychological novel than in a short story of action. The reader has first to come to terms with the tragic dénouement, to understand its logical necessity, and for that reason it must be carefully prepared so that the force of it does not strike on the *result* (in other words, does not come at the very ending) but on the *progression* toward the ending. Happy endings in O. Henry stories, as in *Belkin Tales,* are by no means a response to the pressure of the American reading public's "demands," as is customarily claimed, but the natural outcome of the principle of the surprise dénouement, a principle incompatible in a story of action with detailed motivation. And it is also for this reason that tragic endings are so rare and so paradoxical on the screen,—psychological motivation is altogether too foreign to the nature of the motion picture. In the O. Henry short story, with its parodic focus on the finale, a tragic outcome is possible only in the case of a *double* dénouement, as in **"The Caballero's Way,"** where Tonia is killed but, on the other hand, the Kid remains alive and celebrates his revenge. To put it more strongly, O. Henry's stories are so far from any psychology, any ambition to foster in the reader an illusion of reality and bring him into contact with his heroes as people, that the very categories of the tragic and the comic can be said to be inapplicable to his works.

O. Henry, as a general rule, does not address himself to his readers' emotions,—his stories are intellectual and literary through and through. Stories in which he tries to introduce an emotional tone, in the effort, perhaps, to attune himself to the tastes of his editors and the reading public, inevitably take on a sentimental character and simply fall out of his system. He has no "characters," no heroes; he works on the imagination of his readers by picking out and juxtaposing incisive and unexpected particulars which, by reason of their being very concrete, are striking. In this way, he compensates, as it were, for the schematic structuralism of his stories (a device connected with the art of parody: *cf.* details in Sterne). No wonder that the structures of his stories were habitually fully formed in his mind, as [his friend and biographer Al] Jennings bears witness, and no wonder that he could so easily change the facts,—he thought in schemes, in formulas, like an expert theoretician. The work went into details of language and delineation. That explains the impression of a certain monotony about which O. Henry's Russian readers often remark. Despite his popularity and his supposed lightness and readability, O. Henry is a very complex and subtle writer. He is so good at deceiving his reader that the latter more often than not even fails to notice where it is the author has led him to,—into what milieu of literary parody, irony and play on form he has turned up in O. Henry's company. (pp. 22-3)

> *B. M. Ejxenbaum, in his* O. Henry and the Theory of the Short Story, *translated by I. R. Titunik, University of Michigan, 1968, 41 p.*

CESARE PAVESE (essay date 1932)

[*A novelist, poet, translator, and critic, Pavese was one of the first modern Italian writers to break away from the academic tradition of literary Italian and create a vernacular style. A serious student of American literature, Pavese was well respected as a translator and literary critic, and his familiarity with American literature had a profound effect on his own creative writing. His diary,* Il mestiere di vivere (*1952;* The Burning Brand, *1961), with its clearsighted appraisal of Pavese's character, is considered a masterpiece of the literary journal. In the following excerpt from an essay that originally appeared in Italian in the journal* La nuova Italia *in 1932, Pavese discusses O. Henry's combination of popular and erudite elements in his stories, commenting on the author's characterization, use of colloquial speech, and pertinence as a chronicler of his times.*]

[This] excellent selection and translation . . . of O. Henry once more puts before us one of the most perplexing personalities in American civilization. Until now this capricious storyteller has been a little too much maltreated by us in illustrated magazines and the like, which every so often for want of news had recourse to his Thousand and One Nights. From there, translating by ear, cutting and reinforcing, they continued to dig out disconcerting and almost anonymous pages that for good or ill imported a little animation into the midst of the tired lucubrations of our storytellers. But this vulgarization of O. Henry has served a little too much to disseminate among us what in America, where at least they read O. Henry in whole volumes, is by now a widespread inclination: the suspicion that not all that dazzle of inexhaustible invention is of good quality, that O. Henry wrote too many brilliant stories. And at the twenty-first you shout "Stop!"

Still, who hasn't shouted "Stop!" at some point with any short-story writer? These things are like the collections, which were once the fashion, of epigrams and sonnets: they have to be read in small doses, on the installment plan. Except that on these terms O. Henry would be tiresome, not insofar as he was a short-story writer but insofar as he was a writer. His tales, we are now sure, end with a bang because they are *empty,* because they give us only the surface of reality, because in them puns and paradoxes are the trumpery of a barren inner life.

Let it lie—for the time being—the "inner life": I can personally declare that to read O. Henry is almost always entertaining and that you always have before you a most sympathetic kind of man who, as full of brio as one of his many heroes is full of whiskey, continues to recount little anecdotes and witticisms and adventures with a cordiality and a spirit quite exceptional. So that those who deplore the fact that O. Henry has created nothing, no *character,* are at least this one time wrong: a character there is, alive and speaking—even too much so—who at every moment has something of his own to say and (outrageously!) almost always says it well: O. Henry or, to his friends, William S. Porter. A writer even needs to be a little listened to, and if anyone had said to O. Henry's face that he wanted more aching humanity, or whatever, O. Henry surely would have told him to take it easier, because to insist on certain fixed ideas is to risk losing what little there is and to vex the soul over what little there is not.

For O. Henry is honest. He doesn't try to bluff, as so many of his most attractive characters do, but from the early pages of his best book there is revealed the trick, if trick it is and not rather the unconstraint of every artist worthy of the name:

> 'Tis contrary to art and philosophy to give you the information. . . . The art of narrative consists in concealing from your audience everything it wants to know until after you expose your favorite opinions on topics foreign to the subject. A good story is like a bitter pill with the sugar coating inside of it. I will begin, if you please, with a horoscope.
> (*Cabbages and Kings*)

Now such a confession, made where it is made, can clarify O. Henry's intentions and techniques. In the first place, he does not come from a cultivated society like that of a Maupassant or a Flaubert, and therefore he never dreamed of longing for an impersonal, realistic, or primitivistic literature. Not that one recipe is preferable to another, what is important is to say something with whatever recipe one uses; but it is useful in the present instance clearly to distinguish O. Henry from those others, because too many readers, not finding him another Maupassant, have rejected him. O. Henry clearly tells you that he conceives the short story as an oblique discourse, as a series of verbal and structural tricks that seem and are not, as a continuous comment and byplay of the narrator to the actions of his characters: so much so that, as I have already noticed, the character who leaps most conspicuously to the eye in his pages is the speaker himself.

Now this fact has deeper and more complicated roots than may appear. And if the reader of O. Henry's stories would think again about the cultural atmosphere from which these stories are drawn, many things might seem to him obvious that presently annoy him, since the singular nature of the writer was entirely conditioned by the intellectual moment into which he was born. He who thinks back to the only period of American letters at all well known in Europe, the period—naturally—of Poe and Emerson (1830-1850), will seem to find himself in absolutely another continent than the one of which O. Henry gives us an idea in his writings (1900-1910). The earlier writers had made a center of New England, nourishing themselves on European culture, while vitally transforming it, and ignoring all the great territory and the future variety of races in the nation. Then the polished speech of the best seventeenth-century English traditions prevailed, together with the writer shut in a tower to ruminate the almost invariably occult sciences, in short, the Puritan province of anti-Puritan rebels, aristocratic and isolated.

Consider instead the age of O. Henry. Roosevelt's administration has yielded its fruits: America is henceforth a single nation from the Atlantic to the Pacific, no more Puritan than necessary, with the business of the chosen people to excuse its conquests and its new riches, and it is so sure of itself, so much a "melting pot," that it dares to receive, in order to naturalize them, even the Armenians, the Negroes, and the Chinese. The cultural centers are henceforth spread through the whole huge country, with the consequence of a slight diffusion of forces, although a youthful simplicity—and not a poverty—of spirits just then sings its most frenetic hymns to the élan vital (Jack London). There no longer exists an Athens of the United States, New England. The new centers are as numerous as the free play of races, released from every traditional barrier, knows how to produce: California, with Norris and London; the Center (Chicago), with Sinclair and young Dreiser; New York, finally, with the first movies and O. Henry. One thing of immense significance and importance is the transfer of the movie studios from New York to California that occurs just at the end of this period, around 1912. The whole American territory is henceforward in this way crisscrossed by intellectual currents. Before, up to 1850, America was divided into two worlds: the New England which thought and wrote, and the West, broadly understood, from the Alleghenies to Wyoming and Texas, which conquered and broke ground. The former, slightly skeptical literary aristocrats, the latter, rough illiterate Puritans who chewed tobacco and fought with their fists.

This is not the place to tell the whole story. Suffice it to say that from Poe you get to O. Henry through a half century of revolutions: trappers, miners, new cities, new states, the War of Secession, contingents of Germans, Swedes, Italians, territorial conquests, industrialism, oil and coal, corn, the unrestrained love of life as life, no longer as mere thought or the printed page. The earlier New England dies because the English public forgets how to read, it no longer knows English well, much less the polished English of Boston or of Richmond, or it no longer has time to waste getting to the bottom of philosophies. The powerful body of the U.S.A. begins to look about restlessly, to search for writers who speak of its own life, who will tell it something more than the gambling parlor, or the racecourse, or the fever of work. But clearly: something more, not something different. The new short stories that triumph in all the American newspapers from 1870 to 1910 are essentially humorous or anyhow full of action and "suspense." It has been rightly said that the America of this period seeks in its short stories a duplicate of the emotions of Luna Park: distorting mirrors, chutes, thrills, clowns, sleight of hand, laughs, and noise. Elsewhere, mainly in the states of the Center (Illinois, Indiana, Wisconsin), there will be coming into vogue gloomy novels of which the whole interest consists in the attempt to give a grayly faithful reproduction of reality: from this vogue Dreiser will issue. Immediately after, from 1900 on, there enters the picture the tastes for the social question, these too more life than literature: the rally, the strike, the organization, the revolution (*The Iron Heel, Metropolis*)—tastes that persisted into the renaissance of 1912, which will be essentially a deepening of the new cultural centers on the basis of more vital problems. But this is another subject altogether.

Finally, this literature that culminates in the "prince" O. Henry has a new characteristic: it is a dialect literature. It is a curious kind of dialect, because we Italians imagine dialects to be local and we would have looked for a dialect literature rather from New England. But in America dialect is the colloquial speech spoken by everybody in contrast to the cultivated and upper-class English taught in the schools. Localisms (as they say over there) hardly exist in their language. Reasons: the youth of this language and the intricacy of communications which from one day to the next causes the New Yorker to live in California or the Great Laker in Florida. The dialect quality of the short stories from Mark Twain to O. Henry comes from the need to speak to a rather democratic public (miners, sometimes), and in any case always to speak to a bourgeoisie which tends toward solidity and wants to understand and to recognize itself in its newspapers. Because of course from Mark Twain to O. Henry all the literature that lives is journalistic.

It would certainly be sufficient, then, if it happened in poetry as in the cultivation of fruit, to define the O. Henry story as the final literary manifestation of that period which begins with the crude pages of anonymous miners where witticisms in dialect serve to cheer up a people rather trivial and rather tired of existence. But, I repeat, poetry is not a cultivation of fruit, and it has not yet been proved that a fine example of it arises from long seasons of selection and grafting; and so it happens that, having explained everything, it is just as well to begin again at the beginning and to ask yourself once more: Has O. Henry really "created something"? Or is he not rather the "light," "skin-deep," "fantastic" writer, and in the worst sense of these words?

Let us return to those previously mentioned *Cabbages and Kings.* This is a sequence of stories collected in a novel. The setting of the novel is already a proof of the new American cosmopolitanism and imperialism. A tiny Central American republic, Anchuria, easily turned upside down by factions, governed by Spanish types full of high-sounding words and essentially understood in terms of their own "price." O. Henry's hand begins to reveal itself in the way this material is treated: the events are seen from Coralio, a small town of many huts and a few residences on the shores of the Spanish Main, where American consuls and traders in bananas, rubber, and shoes assist the various local revolutions, helping them along, and attributing to them so much importance as is permitted a discreet citizen of the United States who doesn't too much believe in the politics even of his own country. The atmosphere of the tale is above all the blessed indolence of that sky and sea, where everything can happen and nothing does, or at least it leaves no trace and, as a president falls or a Christian dies, a hundred thousand of them could fall and die and the novel would always be the same. Therefore, its nature is excellent, clearly revealed in episodes, in varied stories.

O. Henry's notorious "insufficiencies," then, the mechanical quality of the action, the cerebral trickiness in the presentation of the adventures, must surely be quite plainly exemplified in this free and easy plot. Thus, for example, the fact that the two characters (President Miraflores and the actress Isabel, who have run off with government funds) imminent in and dominating the whole book, are not at all who they are thought to be, and that they have succeeded in escaping, and that their place is taken by two Americans, a father and daughter who have run off from their country with money from an insurance company, this fact appears to be only an oddity, a contrivance of the storyteller's, the final unexpected happening desired by the slightly gross and childish taste of the public. But after it has been said that the book is entirely constructed like the ordinary card castle, what has been revealed about O. Henry except what he himself has already too hastily confessed? The lecture can be repeated for each of the chapter-stories which comprise the book and for every other story that O. Henry ever wrote. We always find in him, in the structure of the action, these overturnings of values, these paradoxes, these bluffs.

And it is at this point that the critical labor ought to begin. What else should we expect from O. Henry but mechanical actions? And this (you observe) would be a defect as fatal as the other defect of even the most highly esteemed writers, in whom are found only fragments of observations, of "material," and the plot, the construction, is either nonexistent or virtually nonexistent. But reread, with that kind of goodwill indispensable to any enjoyment, the whole book of which I speak—for the moment the hundreds of other short stories aren't important—reflect upon it a bit, keeping in mind the historical bases that have been alluded to, and I am convinced that in the end you will begin to have doubts about the theory of the trick. Have we not before us instead a bizarre and delightful kind of writer who sees the entire universe as a bewildering stylization and who, far from inventing paradoxical adventures because he doesn't know what to say, feels these paradoxes as the very substance of life?

In sum, specific historical conditions suggested to O. Henry a certain taste, a certain manner; they imposed upon him, in short, certain themes. And why can't O. Henry have made of these themes poetry, a genuine creation, that is to say, a genuine *form* of a lively sensibility, of what can seem to be but is only at the beginning a trick (the aforementioned substitution of characters in *Cabbages and Kings*), which makes

an expression or a myth of the oddity and relativity and fundamental illogic of life?

The conclusion of the adventure of Miraflores and Isabel is characteristic; saved by a misunderstanding, they are constrained by it to live far away a fictitious and almost unbearable life. To conclude the various strands of the narrative, O. Henry has imagined a little cinematographic scene.

The Writing on the Sands

> SCENE—*The Beach at Nice*. A woman, beautiful, still young, exquisitely clothed, complacent, poised, reclines near the water, idly scrawling letters in the sand with the staff of her silken parasol. The beauty of her face is audacious; her languid pose is one that you feel to be impermanent—you wait, expectant, for her to spring or glide or crawl, like a panther that has unaccountably become stock-still. She idly scrawls in the sand; and the word that she always writes is "Isabel." A man sits a few yards away. You can see that they are companions, even if no longer comrades. His face is dark and smooth, and almost inscrutable—but not quite. The two speak little together. The man also scratches on the sand with his cane. And the word that he writes is "Anchuria." And then he looks out where the Mediterranean and the sky intermingle, with death in his gaze.

This would not seem to be cerebral. The account of the tricks in the action has naturally been exaggerated. Many times the O. Henry story presents only a humorous stylization of persons or events, or it is odd only in the way that a scene is perceived, an opinion expressed, or the "philosophy" of an event treated.

So we enter the real heart of the question about the "inner life" of O. Henry, a question that seems to me potentially answered already by the reply to the charges of trickery in the action—except that many people still, especially in America, boldly distinguish action from characters, characters from style, style from content. Returning therefore to the point of departure, imagine O. Henry as the American night owl who has lived by his wits in all the states of the Union and beyond, carefully saving up that little store of riches which enables him to rattle off stories in an unsophisticated manner, with his legs under the table, all his impressions of existence condensed in jokes, in demonstrations of good-humored paradoxes, and sometimes moved by a friendship, by a sorrow, by a distant sacrifice; only thus shall we have before us his "inner life."

All O. Henry's heroes, we notice, are from New York, or are provincials like himself who have made their apprenticeship through the whole nation and now end, experienced and tolerant, taking shelter in old Manhattan. These persons are naturally not monuments of psychology or pyres of passion: the language that describes them, the tone of the narrative, the good-natured intimacy of the recollection, everything conspires to reduce their proportions, everything casts over O. Henry's events a faint shade of jest and of "philosophy"— which permits no creative luxury, in the usual sense of the term. In the act of conversing, O. Henry describes his types; he gives a brush stroke and then he stops—looks at the listener—makes an observation on some related memory, winks with his eyes, gestures with his hands, changes the position of his cigar, gives another brush stroke. For it is not O. Henry's intention to describe such or such another character in the name of humanity; he tends simply to represent in the most direct and least pedantic way possible a memory of something incredible, curious, paradoxical. The principle that comprehends and unifies all his narrative art is just this, the knowing exposition of something intellectually unusual, bizarre, "queer."

In his characters no other law of unity can be found. There are vagabonds in his stories, genial burglars, melancholy gentlemen, drunks, naive young girls, déclassé nobles, politicians, prostitutes of strict morals, young wives desperate out of spite, assassins: all the scum and the flower of the American melting pot. But not even the appeal of the beatitude of liquor and indolence, the most common appeal in O. Henry's world, is sufficient to pull together all these characters. Their real affinity consists only in their strangeness, in the oddity of their cases, sometimes sad, almost always cheerful, more or less resigned. Here is an example. A decayed gentleman, reduced to sleeping on park benches and living by his wits, feels winter coming on in New York. What to do? Get himself arrested; three months on Staten Island; security and repose. How to get himself arrested? He tries to eat in a hotel, without money: they don't denounce him, they beat him. He tries to smash the window of a store, and accuses himself: they don't believe him. He tries to molest a lady: it's all right with her! Evening comes; the "never-wuzzer" walks desperately through the streets. He stops before a church. He hears an organ. Gentle thoughts begin to stir in his head, childhood, illusions, the abject present. He has made a decision: tomorrow he will go to work and reform his life. At that moment, a policeman, finding him without identification papers, arrests him. Three months of "repose" on Staten Island. A thousand such tales could be recounted. No need to be afraid of declaring that O. Henry exists precisely and only in the ironic and slightly saddened sense of these paradoxical contrasts.

Granted this conception of the short story—conversation at a bar about some chance happening—it follows that often it will be worth less as a unified story than in certain of its details: a mocking image, an exclamation, a scene. This, if anything, is somewhat the defect of O. Henry, not that other one of the "superficial action." You could make a whole list of expressions, of descriptive mannerisms, of crackling, well-turned, and quite fantastic epithets: their only defect is that they can be so easily detached and collected. But for every one of these slightly external expressions, how many there are of the utmost felicity! This can be verified on simply opening the book, and I don't at the moment want to go big-game hunting after flies. O. Henry's is a real "dialect" humor; no manufactured language would sustain so volcanic and continuous a shower of phrases and words. In this respect, O. Henry is truly the Rabelais of the United States. And also in the taste, half erudite and half popular, for letting things go, for living happily—la Devinière, the liquor store—the two resemble each other.

As Rabelais seems to be, more than an initiator, the necessary crown of a gauloise tradition that was essentially expressed in the fabliaux, so O. Henry concludes the carefree youth of the American novella or "short story." This genre (let us for once speak of genre), born with those early humorists of the miners' newspapers, carried to its first triumphs by punsters and dialect writers as notable as Artemus Ward, had already excelled in the hands of Mark Twain and Bret Harte, the self-conscious pioneers of the new literature no longer New En-

gland but national. At the time of O. Henry, everyone was writing short stories. The genre had enriched itself; no longer were there only stories half-humorous and half-sentimental, but Ambrose Bierce, for instance, was imitating, rather badly, in fact, Poe, and Jack London—everybody knows what Jack London was doing.

O. Henry found his tone with a rare security and timeliness. Of all the writers of his age, it was he who was also best suited to speak in a newspaper to the *whole* nation. The veins of the bizarre and of the cosmopolitan which he opened up were, even in their precise delimitations, the most comprehensive epitome of every short fictional effort up to then achieved in the new nation. And if although, like Rabelais, he concludes a period in such a manner that no one had to stop there any longer and other tendencies were developed, still, the language, the expressive American spirit, by him exemplified and justified in a thousand ways, could easily survive him. And indeed the generation that follows O. Henry—Dreiser, Lindsay, Lee Masters, Sandburg, Lewis, Anderson—doesn't forget the lesson, and in its work of interpretation and re-creation of the U.S.A. will carry to its termination the great linguistic revolution, and this will definitively become in new hands the conscious instrument for an exploration entirely intellectual. (pp. 79-90)

> *Cesare Pavese, "O. Henry; or, The Literary Trick," in his* American Literature: Essays and Opinions, *translated by Edwin Fussell, University of California Press, 1970, pp. 79-90.*

ARTHUR HOBSON QUINN (essay date 1936)

[*Quinn was an American educator, critic, and literary historian specializing in American drama. In the excerpt below, he assesses O. Henry's stature in American letters.*]

It is amazing, when we reread O. Henry's volumes now, to think how seriously he was taken at the time of his death in 1910. Even historians of literature who should have known better spoke of him as a great master of the art of fiction. But any study of O. Henry's stories becomes at once an exercise in discrimination. Neither the arrangement in volumes nor the date of serial appearance is very helpful, since some of the earliest stories appear in the later collections, and almost from the beginning O. Henry's method was established. That method he learned from Bret Harte. **"Whistling Dick's Christmas Stocking,"** which appeared in *McClure's Magazine* in December 1899, is a story of moral contrast in which a tramp nobly declines to help rob a house because a young girl has called out "Merry Christmas" to him. In another early story, probably written during his prison term, **"Georgia's Ruling,"** the influence of a dead child, another favorite theme of Bret Harte, sways a land-office decision. In **"A Blackjack Bargainer"** (1901) a drunken Southern lawyer, who sinks so low that he sells the rights to his feud, dons the coat and hat of his traditional enemy when he knows that if he does so, death is waiting for him at the turn of the road. When reading these stories the critic cannot help wishing he could have Bret Harte's opinion on the plot and the characters; it would be illuminating. The most definite impression is akin to that which is given by a melodrama on the stage. There is to be a "big scene" and everything else is built up to it. In **"A Retrieved Reformation"** (1903) a burglar, Jimmy Valentine, has reformed and, under another name, is about to marry the daughter of the president of the bank. When the new time vault is shown to them all, the president's little niece is shut in accidentally. Jimmy Valentine cuts his way into the vault with his burglar kit and walks calmly out to the spot where a detective is waiting for him. So far the thing is not badly done, although its inspiration in Jean Valjean's revelation of his identity to Javert, the detective, in *Les Misérables* is perhaps obvious. But O. Henry spoils the effect by having his detective refuse to recognize the convict! (pp. 546-47)

What lifts O. Henry at times above his general level was his deep sympathy for the under dog, for youth striving for a taste of joy before the humdrum of existence settles down, for the loyalty of true love, illumined by sacrifice. If his prison term had only made him acquainted with "gentle grafters" and noble-minded burglars, he would not be of any significance except as a humorist. But in the life of New York City he saw the pathos of the daily struggle of those whose margin is small, who live on the seacoast of insecurity, and he wrote in consequence of their few pleasures, magnified by their drab existence into great joys, of their temptations, sometimes overcome and sometimes submerging them, and finally but not often of the suicides which put an end to a struggle too bitter to be borne. Out of this sympathy came an instinctive art which respected the characters he had created, for however low they fall in fortune, in the really fine stories they are never futile.

What could be better of its kind than **"The Gift of the Magi"** (1905), a tender and compelling story of two young people who live on twenty dollars a week and who give their most cherished possessions—Della her hair and Jim his grandfather's watch—in order that they may buy a Christmas present for each other? Then when Jim buys the hair combs and Della the glorious watch fob, neither of which can be used, the story closes:

> The magi, as you know, were wise men—wonderfully wise men—who brought gifts to the Babe in the manger. They invented the art of giving Christmas presents. Being wise, their gifts were no doubt wise ones, possibly bearing the privilege of exchange in case of duplication. And here I have lamely related to you the uneventful chronicle of two foolish children in a flat who most unwisely sacrificed for each other the greatest treasures of their house. But in a last word to the wise of these days let it be said that of all who give gifts these two were the wisest. Of all who give and receive gifts, such as they are wisest. Everywhere they are wisest. They are the magi.

O. Henry called the volume in which **"The Gift of the Magi"** appeared *The Four Million,* in answer, according to the introduction, to Ward McAllister's remark that there were only four hundred people in New York City who were worth knowing. If there is any distinction to be made among his collections, *The Four Million* contains perhaps the best stories. There is to be found **"An Unfinished Story,"** in which Dulcie, a shop girl who has six dollars a week and lives in a hall bedroom, breaks the engagement she has made with a wealthy roué because of the look in the eyes of the portrait of General Kitchener, her idol. Here the best features of the story are the descriptions of her life. "Twice she has been to Coney Island. . . . 'Tis a weary thing to count your pleasures by summers instead of by hours." The story is saved from sentimentality by the implication that next time she may not resist. The natural longing of a girl who is not attractive for a little romance made two good stories, **"The Coming Out of Maggie"** and **"The Brief Début of Tildy."** O. Henry did not hesitate to repeat the motives of his stories, for **"A Service of Love"** strikes the same note of sacrifice with touching reality that sounded through **"The Gift of the Magi."** In **"The Furnished Room"** (1904) the interest of the story lies not in the fact that a lover takes unwittingly the same room to commit suicide as that in which the girl he has been seeking had also taken her life. This is sheer melodrama. But there is a sardonic power in the reproduction of the conversation of the landlady with her friend, which reveals how she has recognized the description of the girl that her new lodger had given, but had deliberately deceived him because she wished to conceal the suicide for business reasons. And all the time, unknown to her, he lies dead up in the room. This story illustrated another quality in the best of O. Henry's fiction—that which makes places and localities articulate. The cheerlessness of the room, its complete inhospitality and the pathetic impersonality of the relics of former feminine occupants are as real as can be. O. Henry had a remarkable knowledge of women, good and bad, and in **"The Trimmed Lamp,"** the title story of one collection, there is a vivid contrast of two types of working girl in the city. The shop girl is not always idealized by any means. In **"A Lickpenny Lover"** Maizie is incapable of knowing honest love from dishonest, and she is in consequence one of his least interesting women.

Next to his stories of New York City, those laid in the South are best. One of these, **"A Municipal Report"** in *Strictly Business* (1910), was prompted evidently by a remark of Frank Norris that there were only three "story cities" in the United States, New York, New Orleans, and San Francisco. So O. Henry drew a picture of Nashville, Tennessee, where "nothing happens after sundown," and then tells of the Negro cabman who supports his white mistress, who in turn is robbed by her worthless husband until in sudden revolt the Negro kills the wretched drunkard and boaster. The murder is not described, and the excellence of the story is due to the way in which the cab driver is never permitted to step out of his natural rôle, even to the narrator. His loyalty and devotion, his wrath and vengeance are only implied. When the narrator tries to find out something of the circumstances of "Miss Adair," the Negro simply says: "She ain't gwine to starve, suh; she has reso'ces, suh; she has reso'ces." It is the older and romantic South about which O. Henry writes, but the figures in **"The Duplicity of Hargraves"** or **"The Rose of Dixie"** are touched sympathetically and will be good fictional material for many years to come.

New York City attracted O. Henry because it is too multiform to be epitomized. In **"The Voice of the City"** he tries to show this, with only moderate success. But when he depends simply on humor and shows the weaknesses of humanity without any spiritual redeeming spark, he seems cheap and often dull. When he tries to imitate Frank Stockton in **"Thimble, Thimble"** he falls down completely. Perhaps the compelling necessity of turning out a story every week for the *World* accounts for the fact that the greater part of his fiction is second-rate. In the nine volumes of completed stories there are two hundred and six, out of which about a dozen are first-rate and another dozen creditable. Many more are entertaining, but the entertainment is of the quality furnished by the Sunday supplement. Facility, brevity, and economy of the reader's attention, some devices he had learned from past masters of the form like Harte, Maupassant and Kipling, and the human sympathy life had taught him—these were not enough to make an artist of the first rank. (pp. 547-49)

Arthur Hobson Quinn, "The Journalists," in his
American Fiction: An Historical and Critical Survey, *Appleton-Century-Crofts, Inc., 1936, pp. 521-49.*

CARL VAN DOREN AND MARK VAN DOREN (essay date 1939)

[*Carl and Mark Van Doren are considered two of the most perceptive men of letters of the first half of the twentieth century. Carl worked for many years as a professor of English at Columbia University and served as literary editor and critic of the* Nation *and the* Century *during the 1920s. A founder of the Literary Guild and author or editor of several American literary histories, Carl played an essential role in initiating an appreciation and respect for American fiction as a distinct and valuable body of works. Also an acclaimed historian and biographer, he was awarded the Pulitzer Prize for his biography* Benjamin Franklin *in 1938. Mark Van Doren, Carl's younger brother, was a prolific writer. His work includes poetry, novels, short stories, drama, criticism, and social commentary; his* Collected Poems, 1922-1938 *won the Pulitzer Prize in 1940. Mark has written accomplished studies of Shakespeare, John Dryden, Nathaniel Hawthorne, and Henry David Thoreau, and he served as literary editor and film critic for the* Nation *during the 1920s and 1930s. In the following excerpt from their critical compendium* American and British Literature since 1890, *the Van Dorens characterize O. Henry's short fiction.*]

Technically speaking, O. Henry is a raconteur. His stories are all short, his plots simple, his manner free and easy. He constantly interjects himself into his narratives, commenting upon them to his hearers. Seeming to have been everywhere, and to have seen everything, he reports his observations. What has interested him, however, is not himself but the persons he has encountered on his travels. He appears never to have overlooked any of them, and indeed appears to have got at all their secrets. Yet it is their customary hours which he has chiefly noted. He prefers not to probe too deep. As a raconteur, he avoids the somber, private emotions which cannot be discussed in a light tone. As a raconteur, too, he chooses episodes or situations which can be made to startle by the outcome. In this he was aided by the delight he took in such little accidents of fate as that which happens in his most familiar story, **"The Gifts of the Magi."** A husband and wife are each anxious to give the other a Christmas present, though they are very poor. The wife sells her hair, which is her greatest charm, to buy a chain for her husband's watch; the husband sells his watch, which is his proudest possession, to buy a set of combs for his wife's hair. The irony of the double sacrifice is of course far from tragic, since the husband and wife, whatever their disappointment, can promptly forget it in their joy over the affection which prompted their acts. Almost always O. Henry has what has been called the short memory of comedy. Instead of assembling evidences to prove that fortune is malign, as persons of a tragic disposition do, he looks at each prank of fortune separately, laughs, and passes on.

So much good humor might grow tiresome were it not for the wit and variety with which it is accompanied. As it is, O. Henry at times is undeniably sentimental. And yet he has a comic vigor which distinguishes him from the tribe of sentimentalists. His humor keeps his good humor from cloying or from turning sour. In what is probably his best story, **"A Municipal Report,"** he had a chance to be merely pathetic in his account of a woman hopelessly bullied by her worthless husband. But he was no more content to do that than he was con-

tent to exploit his materials for their own sake, without making anything of them. He rounds the action out with a robust deed, the murder of the husband by a faithful servant. Though the plot is romantic enough, it is complete, not a mere fragment of local color.

In two of his books, **Cabbages and Kings** and **The Gentle Grafter,** the same personages are repeated from story to story, but as a rule the volumes have no more unity than comes from their restriction to some special community as the scene, and this only in the case of the volumes devoted, like **The Four Million** (1906), to New York, or like **Heart of the West** (1907), to a wider region. The total effect of the body of O. Henry's work is that of a gigantic miscellany. He wrote in haste. He did not avoid the cultivation of certain mannerisms, such as the almost invariable surprise in his endings. Being extraordinarily full of his materials, he poured them out in a profuse stream. Being extraordinarily successful in pleasing his public, he made no particular effort to improve his art. Other writers imitated his methods without being able to capture his peculiar charm, and the art of the short story became as a consequence looser and more casual than it had been before him. In a sense, he cheapened the form, but he extended its scope and made it the most democratic form of literature in America. (pp. 67-8)

Carl Van Doren and Mark Van Doren, "Prose Fiction," in their American and British Literature Since 1890, *revised edition, D. Appleton-Century Company Incorporated, 1939, pp. 58-109.*

H. E. BATES (essay date 1941)

[*A master of the twentieth-century English short story, Bates was also a respected novelist and contributor of book reviews to the* Morning Post *and the* Spectator. *He is the author of* The Modern Short Story, *a highly regarded introduction to the history, development, and pioneering writers of the genre. In the following excerpt from that book, Bates illustrates O. Henry's attributes as both a literary "trickster" and a serious writer.*]

If Sarah Orne Jewett was the painter of a certain section of American life, O. Henry strikes one as being the itinerant photographer who buttonholes every passer-by in the street, wisecracks him, snaps the camera, raises his hat and hands him the inevitable card. O. Henry has just the natural buoyancy, cheek, good-humour, wit, canny knowledge of humanity and its demands, and above all the tireless flamboyant gift of the gab that characterizes any seller of carpets, cure-alls, gold watches, and something-for-nothing in the open market place. O. Henry is not, and I think never was, a writer. He is a great showman who can talk the hind leg off a donkey and then proceed to sell the public that same donkey as a pedigree race-horse.

All this can be simply deduced from the stories. A life of hard facts, of great adversity, confirms it. O. Henry had little schooling, began work in a drug-store, was forced by ill-health to try his luck on a ranch, worked later in a bank, bought and edited a weekly paper, saw it fail, worked on another paper, and finished up in the Ohio State Penitentiary on a charge of embezzling funds. Contrast that with the calm fortunes of the Miss Austens and Miss Jewetts of this world. The wonder is not that O. Henry could not write, but perhaps that he was ever able to put a consecutive sentence together at all. Such adversity would have crushed into complete oblivion a lesser man, just as it might have turned a greater man into that all-American genius of realism for which America still waits. It simply made O. Henry into a trickster—the supreme example in the history of the short story of the showman "wrapping it up so that the fools don't know it."

But it would be the greatest injustice to O. Henry to leave it at that. The body of his work alone, the achievement of his colossal industry, entitles him to something more. His manipulation and marketing of a new type of story (in reality borrowed from others), whose chief effect was that of the surprise packet, entitles him to more again. For however you talk round O. Henry he still emerges, by his huge achievement and the immense popularity of his particular method, as an astonishingly persistent influence on the short story of almost every decade since his day.

O. Henry had many of the qualities that make a greater writer. His eye was excellent, and he was able to focus it on an immense variety of objects, and always, thanks to an immense experience, realistically; he was tirelessly interested in people and could make people tirelessly interesting; he had a certain sense of tragedy, a deep if sentimental sympathy for the underdog, was at his best a sublime humorist, and was blessed with that peculiar faculty of being able to impress the flavour of himself on the page. These qualities, backed by a stronger attitude of mind, a certain relentlessness, might have made O. Henry really great. They were backed instead by a showman who was also a sentimentalist. As a journalist O. Henry knew how to spread it on and spread it out; he knew all about the human touch; he knew, as Bret Harte did, all about the laughter behind the tears. What his work never had was reticence or delicacy; his poetry was that of the journalist who, unable to conceive a lyrical image and knowing that it would be wasted anyway, reaches for the book of *Metaphors and Phrases.* On anything like a real test his work will fail because of a certain shallowness, the eternal touch of the cheapjack who palms you off with the imitation of the real thing.

Yet O. Henry, perhaps more than Maupassant, put the short story on the map. His brand of goods tapped a world market. And to-day you will still find him held in affection, as much as esteem, by a great many people who will not hear a word against his method and its results. For this reason I must not overlook a certain quality of lovableness about O. Henry—a quality well seen, I think, in such a story as **"The Cop and the Anthem."** But that quality alone could not, and does not, account for O. Henry's great popularity. That popularity sprang from a conjuring trick—the story with the surprise—or trick-ending.

This was nothing new. Some use of it may be seen in Poe and Bierce, and a good deal of use of it may be seen in Bret Harte, who apparently failed to grasp its greatest possibilities, as may be seen in the anti-climax of the last six lines of "The Iliad of Sandy Bar." But for some reason O. Henry's use of it captures the imagination not only of readers but also of writers, so that long after O. Henry's death writers like Maugham were still using it, though more perhaps on the Maupassant model than that of O. Henry. For to Maupassant, and not O. Henry, still belongs that supreme *tour de force* of surprise endings, "The Necklace," in which the excellence and the limitation of the method can be perfectly seen. Maupassant's story of the woman who borrows a diamond necklace from a friend, loses it, buys another to replace it, and is condemned to ten years' suffering and poverty by the task of paying off the money, only to make the awful discovery at

No. 55 Irving Place, an early New York residence of O. Henry.

last that the original necklace was not diamond but paste—this story, dependent though it is for effect on the shock of the last line, differs in one extremely important respect from anything O. Henry ever did. For here, in "The Necklace," trick and tragedy are one. By placing a certain strain on the credulity of the reader (why, one asks, was it not explained in the first place that the necklace was paste? or why, later, did not Madame Loisel make a clean breast of everything to a friend who had so much trusted her?), by the skilful elimination of probabilities, Maupassant is left holding a shocking and surprising card of which the reader is entirely ignorant. He is entirely ignorant, that is, *the first time.* Like a child who is frightened by the first sudden bo! from round the corner, but knows all about it next time, the reader of "The Necklace" can never be tricked again. For Maupassant is bound to play that card, which is his only by a process of cheating, and having played it can never again repeat its devasting effect. In story-telling, as in parlour games, you can never hope to hoodwink the same person twice. It is only because of Maupassant's skilful delineation of Madame Loisel's tragedy that "The Necklace" survives as a credible piece of realism. Maupassant, the artist, was well aware that the trick alone is its own limitation; O. Henry, the journalist, never was aware of it.

Yet by the use of the trick, by the telling of scores of stories solely for the point, the shock, or the witty surprise of the last line, O. Henry made himself famous and secured for himself a large body of readers. Apparently neither he nor they ever tired of this game of trick endings. Yet no one, so far as I know, has drawn attention to the technical excellence of O. Henry's trick beginnings. Mr. Ellery Sedgewick, following up his opinion that "a story is like a horse race, it is the start and finish that count most," goes on to say, "Of these two the beginning is the harder. I am not sure but it is the most difficult accomplishment in fiction."

O. Henry was well aware of that. In the marketplace the cheap-jack is confronted with precisely the same difficulty—the problem of making the public listen, even of making it listen, if necessary, against its will, since the nicely wrapped-up ending is entirely useless if the beginning has failed to attract the customer. And in reshaping the short story's beginning, in dispensing with its former leisureliness, its preliminary loquacity, and its well-balanced lead-up, O. Henry did a very considerable service to the short story. He recognized, as the following examples will show, the great value of an instant contact between reader and writer:

So I went to a doctor.

"How long has it been since you took alcohol into your system?" he asked.

Finch keeps a hats-cleaned-by-electricity-while-you-wait establishment, nine feet by twelve, in Third Avenue. Once a customer, you are always his. I do not know his secret process, but every four days your hat needs to be cleaned again.

The trouble began in Laredo. It was the Leano Kid's fault, for he should have confined his habit of manslaughter to Mexicans.

On his bench in Madison Square Soapy moved uneasily. When wild geese honk high of nights, and when women without sealskin coats grow kind to their husbands, and when Soapy moves uneasily on his bench in the park, you may know that winter is near at hand.

These are examples taken almost at random; there are many others. O. Henry rarely fumbles the beginning, and when he does so it is invariably by the two pieces of fancy irresistible to the journalist of his type: a desire to be moral, a desire to show that he knows all about poetry. Otherwise he can show a series of masterly lessons not only in how to begin a story but, perhaps more important, when to begin.

As a humorist O. Henry stands in the true line of what appears to be an essentially American tradition—the tradition in which Leacock, Thurber, and Runyon are true-blood descendants. That tradition appears to be largely the expression of the wider American revolt against the heavier values so held in esteem in the Old World: pomposity, class distinction, dignity, family tradition, and indeed almost anything liable to be taken over-seriously. By taking such things as pompous family tradition and treating them with levity (as in Leacock) or by taking trivialities and treating them with a language mixed into an affected combination of the academic and the vernacular (as in Runyon), American writers produce a high contrast that is, as in Wodehouse, very funny. In this method O. Henry, who excelled in the use of both vernacular and a certain pompous brand of journalese, was bound to be a success. (pp. 58-64)

H. E. Bates, "American Writers after Poe," in his The Modern Short Story: A Critical Survey, *1941. Reprint by The Writers, Inc., 1956, pp. 46-71.*

CLEANTH BROOKS, JR. AND ROBERT PENN WARREN (essay date 1943)

[*Brooks and Warren are considered two of the most prominent figures of the school of New Criticism, an influential movement in American criticism that also included Allen Tate and R. P. Blackmur. Although the various New Critics did not subscribe to a single set of principles, all believed that a work of literature had to be examined as an object in itself through a process of close analysis of symbol, image, and metaphor. For the New Critics, a literary work was not a manifestation of ethics, sociology, or psychology, and could not be evaluated in the general terms of any nonliterary discipline. In the following excerpt, Brooks and Warren closely examine the plot of the story "The Furnished Room."*]

[O. Henry's **"The Furnished Room"**] is obviously divided into two parts. The first part, which ends with the death of the lodger, concerns his failure in the search for his sweetheart and the motivation of his suicide; the second part concerns the revelation, by the landlady to her crony, that his sweetheart had, a week earlier, committed suicide in the same room. What accounts for the fact that O. Henry felt it necessary to treat the story in this fashion? What holds the two parts of the story together? To discover the answers to these two related questions, let us consider the story itself.

The most interesting question has to do with the young man's motivation. In one sense, O. Henry has deliberately made the problem of his motivation more difficult by withholding the information that the sweetheart is dead. The young man does not know that she is dead; indeed, in the room, he gets, with the scent of mignonette, a renewed hope. Why then, under these circumstances, does he commit suicide? Presumably, the explanation is this: he has been searching fruitlessly for five months; he is, we are told, tired—and, we assume, not only momentarily tired physically, but spiritually weary. Indeed, we are told: "He was sure that since her disappearance from home this great water-girt city held her somewhere, but it was like a monstrous quicksand, shifting its particles constantly, with no foundation, its upper granules of today buried tomorrow in ooze and slime." But we are not supposed to believe, even so, that he would have necessarily turned on the gas this particular evening, except as a despairing reaction from the hope which has been raised by the scent of mignonette. This is the author's account of the motivation of the suicide. But is the motivation, as presented, really convincing? That will depend on the character of the man. What sort of man is he? Actually, O. Henry has told us very little about him except that he is young, has searched for his sweetheart for five months, and is tired. Especially does the question of the man's character, and state of mind, come up in the incident in which he notices the odor of mignonette. Did he really smell it? Did he merely imagine that he smelled it? "And he breathed the breath of the house . . . a cold, musty effluvium . . . mingled with the reeking exhalations of linoleum and mildewed and rotten woodwork. . . . Then, suddenly, as he rested there, the room was filled with the strong, sweet odor of mignonette. It came as upon a single buffet of wind. . . . The rich odor clung to him and wrapped him around."

The suddenness with which he notices the odor, the power

of the odor, the fact that he can find no source for the odor, and finally the complete disappearance of the odor, all tend to imply that he merely imagines it. But over against this view, we have the testimony of the landlady that the sweetheart had actually occupied the room. This question is important, for it is crucial for the young man's lapse into acute despair. If the odor is real, the author must convince his reader that it exists; if it is imaginary, the author must convince his reader that the psychological condition of the young man will account for its apparent existence. These are the tests which the reader must apply to the situation. We have already pointed out that there is some evidence on both sides of the question. The reader must, of course, decide for himself which explanation must be taken, and more importantly, whether the explanation is convincing, and renders the action credible. The author, however, seems to weight the evidence toward the presence of the real odor. If this is the case, how are we to account for the fact that the search reveals no source of it, especially since the odor is so overpoweringly strong? Or, perhaps the author has in mind some idea that the odor provokes a mystical communion between the two lovers. But this does not relieve the fiction writer from the necessity for furnishing some sort of specific clue to his meaning. (Moreover, if we are to take the whole experience as an hallucination, the author is certainly not relieved from providing some clear motivation for the event.)

To sum up: it is obvious enough, from the detailed description of the room, that O. Henry is trying to suggest a ground for the man's experience in the nature of the room itself. That is, the room in its disorder, its squalor, its musty smell, its rubbish and debris of nameless lives, reflects the great city, or the world, in which his sweetheart has been lost, and in which all humanity seems to become degraded and brutalized. It is easy enough to see why O. Henry should want to suggest the contrast between what the sordid surroundings mean to the hero and what the odor of mignonette means to him. As the girl is lost somewhere in the great city, so the odor is lost somewhere in the room. After the young man is told that the girl has not been there, and after he has been unable to find the source of the odor, the room itself is supposed to become a sort of overwhelming symbol for the futility of his effort. This intention on the part of the author may be sound enough, but the fact that we see what the intention is does not mean that the intention has been carried out. The whole effect of the story depends on the incident of the odor, and we have seen that the handling of this detail is confused.

Assuming that this objection is valid, the basic remedy suggests itself at once. The author needed to go back and fill in the character of the young man much more fully. The reader might then have been able to follow the processes of his mind as he goes through his crucial experience, and the specific nature of his response to the odor would have been clarified. But O. Henry chooses an easier solution. Resting upon his rather thin and sketchy characterization of the young man, the author chooses to give a turn to the plot by a last-minute surprise. In the second part of the story the landlady tells her crony that she has lied to the young man about the girl.

What is the effect of this revelation? It is intended, obviously, to underline the "irony of fate," to illustrate the hardheartedness of the city in which the young man finds himself, to justify the young man's overwhelming sense that the girl has been in the room, and, all in all, to pull the story together. For the sympathetic reader this conclusion is supposed to suggest that the bonds of love stretch across the confusion and squalor of the great city, and that, in a sense, the young man has finally succeeded in his search, for the lovers are at last united in death. The young man finds, as it were, the proper room in the great city in which to die.

But is the story really pulled together? The end of the story depends on the lie. But are the lives of the lovers altered by the lie? Does the lie cause the death of the young man? It is conceivable that, had the landlady told the truth, the shock of the information might have saved the young man from suicide, but this is the merest speculation. The character, as given in the story, commits suicide in despair when the landlady tells him that the girl has not been there; the landlady's telling him that the girl is irretrievably lost, is dead, would presumably have had the same effect.

Actually, is there any point in the lie except to trick the reader—to provide the illusion of a meaningful ending? Whatever irony lies in the ending is based on a far-fetched coincidence, and does not depend on the fact that the woman said one thing rather than another. (Readers who are inclined to accept the conclusion of the story as meaningful might try reconstructing the story with the young man's calling at the door, finding with horror that his sweetheart has committed suicide there a week before, renting the room, and turning on the gas. We would then still have the ironical coincidence and a sort of union of the lovers, but the story would seem very tame and flat.) O. Henry, by withholding certain information and thus surprising us with it at the end, has simply tried to give the reader the illusion that the information was meaningful. The irony, in the story as we have it, simply resides in a trick played on the reader rather than in a trick which fate has played on the young man.

Readers who feel that the end of this story is a shabby trick will be able to point out other symptoms of cheapness: the general thinness of characterization, the cluttered and sometimes mawkish description, the wheedling tone taken by the author, and the obvious play for emotional sympathy in such writing as the following: "Oh, God! whence that odor, and since when have odors had a voice to call?" In other words, we can readily surmise that the trickery involved in the surprise ending may be an attempt to compensate for defects within the body of the story itself.

But a trick of plot does not make a story. A surprise ending may appear in a very good story, but only if the surprise has been prepared for so that, upon second thought, the reader realizes that it is, after all, a logical and meaningful development from what has gone before, and not merely a device employed by the author to give him an easy way out of his difficulties. The same principle applies to *coincidence . . .* in general. Coincidences do occur in real life, sometimes quite startling ones, and in one sense every story is based on a coincidence—namely, that the particular events happen to occur together, that such and such characters happen to meet, for example. But since fiction is concerned with a logic of character and action, coincidence, in so far as it is purely illogical, has little place in fiction. Truth can afford to be stranger than fiction, because truth is "true"—is acceptable on its own merits—but the happenings of fiction, as we have seen, must justify themselves in terms of logical connection with other elements in fiction and in terms of meaningfulness. (pp. 114-18)

Cleanth Brooks, Jr. and Robert Penn Warren, in an interpretation of "The Furnished Room," in Understanding Fiction, *edited by Cleanth Brooks and Robert Penn Warren, Appleton-Century-Crofts, Inc., 1943, pp. 114-18.*

DEMING BROWN   (essay date 1953)

[*In the following excerpt, Brown discusses reasons for O. Henry's popularity with Russian readers.*]

O. Henry's books first appeared in Russia in 1923. In the next four years over 750,000 copies of his works were published in the Soviet Union. During the period of the New Economic Policy, only two other Americans—Jack London and Upton Sinclair—exceeded him in popularity. Although his reputation has diminished considerably since then, he remains a minor classic in Russia, and new editions of his stories continue to come out.

The remarks of highly enthusiastic Soviet critics of the twenties indicate four reasons for O. Henry's unique appeal in those years. The first of these was his interest in the effects of urban life on little people. Anticipating the promised era of industrialization, in which Russia would have her own metropolises, Soviet readers sought a future image of themselves in O. Henry's elevator girls and stenographers. One critic found that the author had captured "the 'soul' of the big city," and another called him the "Rousseau of New York."

A second reason for his initial success was his exposition of American life itself. For decades the Russians had been extremely curious about the United States, but for most of them America remained an exotic land of wonders. In O. Henry the critics saw a poet of the common man, who would tell them the truth about the "average American." The brisk tempo of his stories, they felt, reflected the pace of American existence. He provided an antidote for the "spiritual boycott" of America which had been perpetrated by such writers as Gorky and Korolenko. For, as one critic put it, this writer "does not curse the 'kingdom of the dollar,' he meanders in it like a tadpole in a puddle. . . ."

The third cause of O. Henry's spontaneous acceptance by Soviet readers was the style and structure of his stories. Some critics were particularly impressed by his language, which Chukovsky called "laconic, rich in intonation, original, muscular and fresh." Even more attractive were his innovations in the form of the short story. In 1925, the prominent formalist critic Boris Eikhenbaum remarked that the Soviet reader "values in him that which is lacking in our own literature— adroitness of construction, a diversity of plot situations and denouements, compactness and swift action" [see excerpt dated 1925]. There were dissenting voices, it is true. Some complained that his stories were "prepared by machine methods" whose "monotony" was "almost tormenting." Likewise, he relied excessively on the surprise ending. Nevertheless, the critics repeatedly urged that Soviet writers try to emulate his devices, and there are indications that he did find imitators in the twenties.

The fourth, and probably the most important source of his appeal for Soviet Russians was his ability to divert and amuse. Several critics in the twenties were frank to point out his "escapist" value. As Sergei Obruchev remarked, ". . . it is so pleasant after a boring and unhappy life to drink in strange joys." There was some disagreement, however, concerning the Russian reader's motivation. Eikhenbaum stressed the intellectual charm of the stories, and suggested

that Russians read them chiefly for the sheer enjoyment of their convolutions of plot. Others, however, felt that while the author's narrative tricks were refreshing and entertaining, the basis of his appeal was mainly emotional, since his twists of plot served to convey a lightly ironic or sentimental message. All agreed, however, that O. Henry offered the Soviet reader a release, a temporary escape from his grim worldly cares.

But even in this period of greatest enthusiasm, the critics paid close attention to the social implications of the stories. And from the very first, he was found lacking both in breadth and depth of social understanding. As early as 1923, a critic regretted that O. Henry was "not one iota a contemplator." It was true that his stories frequently touched upon situations of social pathos, that he often concentrated on small tragedies in the lives of ordinary people, and that he showed a partiality for poor and obscure individuals caught in the web of adverse economic circumstances. It was easy to read a note of social protest into his writing, and many critics attempted to do so. But they were almost always disappointed. One critic wrote that while the author obviously perceived much that was "false and hypocritical" in America, "he does not have enough meanness to spit upon it. He speaks either with pain or with forgiveness." Another remarked: "He does not see that the country is split into two warring camps, that around him there is unfolding a very great social drama. If one is to believe his stories, all is well in the bosom of American democracy. There are no class contradictions, no exploitation. Under the shadow of the Star Spangled Banner social tranquillity reigns."

He was the slave of the bourgeois milieu about which he wrote; he accepted its standards and had no intention of objecting to them. The critics noted that millionaires fascinated him, and that he saw no particular social danger in them. The proletariat was entirely absent from his stories.

On the other hand, they felt, he was not altogether insensitive to the evils of bourgeois society. At times, almost unwittingly, he was possessed by a feeling of boredom in dealing with the "triviality" of life under capitalism. As an antidote to this boredom, he chose humor. But, according to the critic Friche, "this is the humor of a man of an intermediate class, for whom there is no other conclusion but just such a half-bitter smile with which to endure a life without perspective and horizons, a life in which there is neither content nor meaning."

Others felt that his humor was the traditional "laughter through tears," and indeed there were those who called him the "American Chekhov." But the majority agreed with the critic who wrote that his art was a "retreat in the face of the terrible problems of life, from which you can hide only in a sentimental story." He wrote only to please the dominant bourgeoisie, his sole desire was to entertain, and he had categorically refused to take part in the "struggle for a better life."

Practically everything that has been written about O. Henry in the Soviet Union since 1927 follows this same line. The *Great Soviet Encyclopedia* contends that "all of his technique was directed toward external, purely formal and therefore superficial effects," and that he "studiously avoids the contradictions of life. . . ." In some respects he was distinctly anti-social: "He has been correctly named . . . the 'great consoler.' Yes, he is a 'consoler,' since he sows illusions, he gives vain hopes, he deceives his readers into believing that every-thing will be all right, that the beautiful life can be built with-out the slightest effort or struggle. It is false, this art of O. Henry, it is dangerous like opium, since it diverts one from life and struggle."

In 1937, however, there were attempts to rehabilitate the au-thor as a social critic of sorts. It was suggested that under-neath his apparent sentimentality there was a deep sense of the tragedy of life in bourgeois society. The essential quality of an O. Henry plot was not its fortunate outcome, but the element of surprise. For the optimism of his happy endings was purely sham. Perceiving the shallowness of capitalist cul-ture, he had slyly developed his narrative innovations as a means of protesting against it: "Every story of O. Henry is a malicious mockery of trite notions about the ordinary American, a sharp polemic against the authors of bourgeois tales, against the editors of cheap newspapers and magazines, who cultivate banal language and trite plots. With his tricks of plot, O. Henry protested against the arithmetical-mean ap-proach to the ordinary American."

There were even more ambitious claims. He possessed a "firm belief in man, in the tremendous power of the human will," and his chief goal was the "exposure of bourgeois indi-vidualism." In contrast to most of bourgeois literature, his art was a "burning moral sermon," since he was "organically connected with the life of urban and rural poverty, of work-ing people crushed by need and sorrow."

A reply to claims such as these was not long in coming. The critic Startsev emphasized that O. Henry had been essentially a humorist, denied him any social value, and accused him of purposely distorting the facts of life. He had known the dark-est sides of America, but had refused to write about them. As a result, his stories, though fascinating to read, were "sugary and absurd."

Despite ideological strictures such as these, O. Henry is still published in the Soviet Union. In fact, the Russians probably think better of him than do his compatriots, for he obviously continues to answer some special need in the Soviet reader. Certainly, the factors of style and *genre* are important in this respect. Brevity, racy patter, the surprise ending with its lightly ironical or sentimental twist—O. Henry's stock-in-trade—are not common in Russia's own literary tradition. With the possible exceptions of Chekhov and Zoshchenko, no Russian has his flavor. This suggests that he continues to be popular because of the piquancy of his narrative method.

A more important source of his continuing attractiveness may be ideology itself. The stories of O. Henry, despite their evident sympathy for the underdog, their frequently satirical tone, and their preoccupation with life's disappointments, can all be classified as light entertainment. Soviet literature, on the other hand, does not often display a light touch. The obligation to instruct has been a guiding principle of the Sovi-et arts since the inception of the Five-Year Plans. Not only does Soviet Marxist literary theory condemn stories which are merely diverting; it also demands a didactic element in harmony with the principles which constitute the basis of So-viet culture. Soviet humor, for example, is expected to be based on social satire much stronger and sharper than that of O. Henry. Likewise, such devices as the fortuitous happy ending and the melancholy coincidence, which the author uses so frequently, are in fundamental conflict with the offi-cial Soviet literary doctrine which insists that man must not

be portrayed as a pawn of fortune. Finally, the sentimentality of which Soviet critics accuse the author is purported to spring from a false standard of values in which righteous so-cial indignation is displaced by pity.

But it is safe to assume that vast numbers of Russian readers fail to share the ideological prejudices of the critics. Constant strictures against the unreality of O. Henry's happy endings probably fail to impress the Soviet reader, for that reader is himself sentimental and enjoys short flights into a world of whimsy and gentle irony. The comments of the critics have frequently contained a note of caution, an implicit warning to the general reader lest he be seduced by the harmful moral and social values and the message of "consolation" which O. Henry's stories are purported to contain. Now the fact is that this writer *is* sentimental, glib and superficial, albeit clever. No doubt, most students of American literature would agree with the Soviet critic who characterized his stories as "mag-nificent railroad reading."

Russians, however, probably have as great a potential appe-tite for "railroad reading" as other people. Significantly, Sovi-et publishers under the NEP issued this type of literature in great quantities. O. Henry was the most prominent among the Americans represented, but there were dozens of others. In 1928 the importation of this kind of writing ceased. While American popular magazines still print thousands of stories whose style and quality is comparable to that of O. Henry, Soviet publishers have continued to shun them. The sole ex-ception is O. Henry himself. A huge stream of light fiction, the truly "mass" literature of twentieth-century America, is represented in the Soviet Union by this author alone. One may speculate on the motivation of the Communist Party in continuing to sanction his publication. But it is clear that, de-spite years of constant indoctrination, Russian readers still like to seek release in a good yarn. (pp. 253-58)

> *Deming Brown, "O. Henry in Russia," in* The Rus-sian Review, *Vol. 12, No. 4, October, 1953, pp. 253-58.*

GRANVILLE HICKS   (essay date 1953)

[*Hicks was an American literary critic whose famous study* The Great Tradition: An Interpretation of American Literature since the Civil War *(1933) established him as the foremost ad-vocate of Marxist critical thought in Depression-era America. During this period, Hicks believed it was the task of literature to confront sociopolitical issues. After 1939, Hicks denounced communist doctrine and adopted a less stringently ideological posture in his literary criticism. In the following excerpt, Hicks reminisces about his youthful enthusiasm for the stories of O. Henry and his later disillusionment with them.*]

Thirty-four years ago, when I was a freshman in college and was asked to write a theme on my favorite author, I unhe-sitatingly named O. Henry. During the preceding twelve months I had gone through every volume in the collected works, and it seemed to me that reading matter had never given me more pleasure. I wasn't prepared to argue that O. Henry was the greatest author who ever lived, but he was my favorite.

Less than a year later I was wondering what in the world I had seen in his stories, and the question has been bothering me ever since. In the intervening years I have read some of the stories now and then as I have run across them in antholo-gies, but there has never been a suggestion of the old spell.

Now, reading through all of them again, I have found no magic, but I think I have caught some hint of the way in which the magic operated thirty-five years ago.

I was reading O. Henry at the right time and place—in a small town and within a decade of his death—and, what is more important, at the right age, for I was still in my teens. To me the stories were full of the glamour of the big city, which I had never seen, and the strangeness of far-off places. They brought me a world of sophistication, populated with gentlemanly cynics and honorable rascals; and the slangy, hyperbolic, pun-strewn style seemed to me the acme of wit. Finally, they were romantic, and the fact that the romances took place not in Zenda or Graustark, regions of which I was growing tired, but in city boarding houses and Texas restaurants made me feel that life was worth living.

All these things counted heavily, but I am afraid, as I look back, that what counted most was the trick ending. I could not, of course, have read many O. Henry stories without learning that I was going to be tricked, but I still was all eagerness to see how, this time, it was going to be done. The magic, in short, was that of a first-rate prestidigitator—no more and no less—and I loved it. Then all of a sudden—I think it was when I discovered Sherwood Anderson's "Winesburg, Ohio"—I lost my taste for sleight-of-hand.

It was true in my time, and it continued to be true for some time thereafter, that most literate young people succumbed for a while to the O. Henry fever. And there must still be willing readers. . . . His work has survived, but his reputation and his influence have not. Many journalists have borrowed from his style, and through the decades countless derivative stories have been published, but the prestige of his kind of story has declined, and it must be years and years since an O. Henry Prize was given to an O. Henry story. The central tradition of the American short story has, fortunately, moved in a different direction.

O. Henry was a culmination rather than a source. His humor was basically the familiar humor of the tall tale; he had learned exaggeration from Davy Crockett and his descendants, the comic distortion of the language from Artemus Ward and Josh Billings and the art of the inverted axiom from Mark Twain. Mark Twain had also taught him something about the trick ending, and so had Bret Harte, Frank Stockton, Ambrose Bierce and many writers who have been forgotten.

Among his American contemporaries his chief instructor was Richard Harding Davis, whom he often satirized, and perhaps he was also acquainted with an author who, at close range, looked like Davis—Stephen Crane. Overseas there was the surpassing brilliance of Rudyard Kipling, sometimes acknowledged in the tales, and he knew Maupassant at what now appears to be his worst.

O. Henry was shaped in the age of Victoria, and a Victorian he remained to the end. Vagabond, embezzler, alcoholic and philanderer he might be, but, like the Pirates of Penzance, with all his faults he loved his Queen—or, at any rate, paid tribute to the standards associated with her name. He wrote more than 250 stories without a single situation that his contemporaries could call even remotely risqué.

In **"An Unfinished Story"** he admitted that underpaid shop girls might sometimes yield to temptation, but that was as far as he would go. Most of his rascals are perfect gentlemen in their relations with women, and if they are not, their indiscretions are veiled from the reader. . . .

Victorianism, however, was the least of his faults. If there had existed in his time, as there does now, a kind of unwritten law against the abuse of coincidence, O. Henry would have had to go out of business. Nor was it merely probability that was sacrificed for the sake of the trick ending; whatever understanding he had of human beings and the life they lead was thrust to one side whenever it threatened to interfere with the game he was playing with his readers. . . .

Yet the magic power of the stories, in the right circumstances, cannot be denied and has to be explained. Perhaps the explanation lies in the fact that they were strong magic for O. Henry himself. Despite his chatty style, he was one of the least personal of writers, and he never could have written the autobiographical novel that he often talked about. He was protecting, not revealing, himself in what he wrote.

He was creating a world for O. Henry, a world in which an unconventional way of life could be reconciled with great respect for convention, in which the golden hearts of ne'er-do-wells and rogues were exposed for all to see, in which romance was ever present but only in acceptable guises. The hand of fate—and it seems likely that at bottom he was gripped by a determinism as black as Mark Twain's—could be manipulated to achieve pleasant comedy and a miraculous succession of happy endings.

He wrote what he thought the public wanted, and his guesses were excellent, but he also wrote to please himself. Otherwise there would be no understanding the vitality that produced so many stories, and so many that are good by O. Henry standards, in not much more than ten years. . . .

He was, indeed, a master of make-believe and therefore in his own way a myth-maker. If he was, like his Jeff Peters, an adept at the shell game, he gave his readers the illusion that they were the ones who were bound to win, that they were the happy beneficiaries of fate. He knew a lot about illusions, including the fact that he needed them.

Granville Hicks, "A Sleight-of-Hand Master," in The New York Times Book Review, *December 27, 1953, p. 5.*

V. S. PRITCHETT (essay date 1957)

[*Pritchett is a highly esteemed English novelist, short story writer, and critic. Considered one of the modern masters of the short story, he is also considered one of the world's most respected and well-read literary critics. A twentieth-century successor to such early nineteenth-century essayist-critics as William Hazlitt and Charles Lamb, Pritchett employs much the same critical method: his own experience, judgment, and sense of literary art are emphasized, rather than a codified critical doctrine derived from a school of psychological or philosophical speculation. His criticism is often described as fair, reliable, and insightful. In the following excerpt, Pritchett discusses the relationship between O. Henry and his fiction.*]

O. Henry is one of the many casualties of American literature. Original, inventive and prolific in his short stories, he is one of those writers of whom the critics say: Could have done better if he had tried. In his life and in his work there is a failure of the sense of responsibility. Chekhov's beginnings were just as difficult and commonplace as the American's. Like O. Henry, he began by writing crude comic sketches for popular papers, and had to be fished out of vulgar employ by discerning editors; but whereas O. Henry perfected only his craft, Chekhov (like all great artists) strenuously perfected himself as a means of seeing and feeling his subjects. Chekhov grew; O. Henry copied himself. Chekhov was concerned to write less and better. O. Henry certainly worked hard, but rather in the Puritan way that finds in work of any kind a drugging or redemption in itself. The result is that behind the laughter of O. Henry's caricatures and the wit of his invention, there is a sensation of moral exhaustion and personal lassitude.

O. Henry was a modest, fastidious, impenetrable character. He was enclosed, furtive and evasive. The fact is he was shut in by an amiable and undisquieting alcoholism; his secret was that he had served a prison sentence of three years for embezzlement. These two matters were symptoms rather than causes of much earlier cooling-off from life. (p. 697)

Mr Gerald Langford's new biography *Alias O. Henry,* [see Further Reading list], goes thoroughly into [the confusing story of O. Henry's embezzlement conviction]. He finds it just as hard to make up his mind about O. Henry's guilt or innocence as others have done. O. Henry himself was evasive and self-contradictory; protesting his innocence, and yet clearly having no notion that what he was ready to admit displayed some kind of guilt. His attitude was ambiguous; and this ambiguity provides half the comedy of his tales of grafters and frauds. When the man becomes the artist, we see him converting what is a painful failure to face reality into low garrulous poetry of cunning and trickery. He becomes a fabulist. This is among the oldest delights of popular story-telling. O. Henry's enormous success with the great public does not depend on his shallowness and sentimentality, but on his sharing the common pleasure in watching people do each other down, in the out-smarting of the market. In his life, after he came out of gaol, O. Henry added incompetence to innocence. He shared Balzac's need of debt as a stimulus to work. He borrowed money incorrigibly and continuously, even when he was highly paid; he spent it or, rather, gave it away, absurdly. There are stories of him giving tips in restaurants many times larger than the bills. There is a drifting, indifferent quality in this carelessness. He was not the arrogant borrower; he was cringing, promising, sentimental, almost sobbing. We have the impression of a gentle, dandyish, pleasantly pickled man stuck in a dream and who soothed himself, when he woke up, by occasional fits of theatrical sentimentality.

O. Henry's earliest stories were written in prison. He emerged with a natural feeling for the lonely, the underdog and the rogue; also with a desire, not for security and affection, but for anonymity. For many writers the edge and freedom of the anonymous life have been indispensable. The security of his second marriage was intolerable to him. He was just the man to be lost with advantage in the streets of New York. He became domesticated to the backrooms of small hotels, the pavements, doorways, cheap bars, park seats of the city. He was a dedicated night wanderer—the habit was partly responsible for the breakdown of his second marriage. He hated literary society, preferring to talk with the shop girls, tarts, bar props and others who gave him his material. He was protected by his fastidiousness and by his work from the waste of literary Bohemianism. But, as Mr Langford says, when he attacked the sterility of literary company, he was not altogether sincere. Literary society is often sterile and too much

of it is fatal, above all to short-story writers who use up their material more quickly than any other kind of writer. O. Henry needed the streets and the bars. But literary society of the right kind might have given O. Henry the impetus to go beyond the commonplace limitations of his work, to resist the downhill tendency of his talent. Occasional stories, like **"An Unfinished Story"** or **"A Municipal Report"**, show how it was well within his powers to go deeper than contrivance and anecdotal trickery. Clearly he felt exposed without them, but he could have been given the courage.

The sudden extinction of O. Henry's fame after 1910 is saddening but natural. By the Twenties a major literary movement had begun in the United States, and O. Henry was lost in the journalistic and characterless period that preceded it. He belongs to the vernacular tradition, though H. L. Mencken thought he perverted it with false and ornate Broadwayese. Yet the hostile critics, I think, are merely copying each other when they damn O. Henry for his use of coincidence and for snap-endings that trick the reader. (The trick was, in any case, part of the gaiety.) The hostile forget that O. Henry's virtue is his speed of narrative; it moves forward freely; it jumps with confidence. He is economical and at home in his tale.

This technical proficiency of O. Henry's is in itself delightful because it has the attraction of daring and impudence. His gaudy phraseology, his colliding metaphors, his brilliant malapropisms are not always in excess. We can at once picture the woman in **"Telemachus, Friend"** who would have 'tempted an anchovy to forget his vows' and who had an air of welcome about her that 'seemed to mitigate her vicinity'; we see her, after supper, when her two lovers find her, 'with a fresh pink dress on and cool enough to handle'. The low comedy of courtship is a traditional subject, and in handling it O. Henry brought the American talent for using metaphors grotesquely wide of the mark. He had the important comic gift of capping a good joke with an even more powerful riposte to it. In **"Telemachus, Friend"**, for example, we are not only told the wrong method of seizing a lady's hand—'Some men grab it so much like they was going to set a dislocation of the shoulder'—but we are told the right method which begins with splendid sentences, straight out of the Mark Twain tradition:

> I'll tell you the right way. Did you ever see a man sneak out of the backyard and pick up a rock to throw at a tom-cat that was sitting on a fence looking at him. He pretends he hasn't got a thing in his hand, and that the cat don't see him and that he don't see the cat.

A great deal of O. Henry is hilarious, school-boy stuff on the surface. He has not the polish or the maturity of a writer like W. W. Jacobs, but he has a far greater range. He has the blessed American gifts of economy and boldness in comic writing; the gift also of bouncing the reader. When we object to his exaggeration and caricature, we should discriminate. The impulse is fundamental to American folk comedy and corresponds to the native and traditional sense of the tall and fabulous. Much of American comedy consists of bluffing and counter-bluffing fantasy: the duke and king episode in *Huckleberry Finn,* for example. This quality comes out very strongly in O. Henry's Texan stories which—after excepting his masterpiece **"The Municipal Report"**—seem to me his richest. . . .

Mr Langford makes much of O. Henry's statement (made in

New York street scene during the time of O. Henry.

his last year when he was planning to write a novel) that writers do not tell the truth. It is inferred that O. Henry was beginning to see through the haze in which he lived his stunned life and was about to face realities he had avoided. He was infantile about money, he was puritanical about sex: he disliked being compared with Maupassant who was a 'filthy writer'. We cannot imagine what O. Henry's 'truth' would have been, but we can guess that it would have been the end of him as a comic writer. It is fatal for the comics to resolve their problems; their only salvation lies in improving their jokes. Only serious writers seem to be able to get away, sometimes, with living above their moral means. It is unjust, but there it is. (p. 698)

> *V. S. Pritchett, "O. Henry," in* New Statesman, *Vol. LIV, No. 1393, November 23, 1957, pp. 697-98.*

DONALD F. PEEL (essay date 1961)

[*In the following excerpt, Peel examines and defends O. Henry's use of the surprise ending.*]

Probably the best known feature of O. Henry's writings is the "surprise ending." (p. 7)

Some writers seem to think that using the surprise ending is playing some kind of a trick on the reader. . . . This is surprising criticism. What kind of plot would one have if it were not premeditated? The surprise ending, after all, is only the

climax of the story placed at the end of the story. O. Henry used it to achieve the greatest possible climax, as will be shown later. If the reader is "tricked," it is usually because he tells the story himself and supplies a conventional ending.

One critic [H. C. Schweikert, in *Short Stories* (1913)] points out that O. Henry often uses coincidences that in a lesser writer would be "bunk." One of his most famous stories, **"The Furnished Room,"** rests on an almost incredible coincidence, yet most critics do not notice this. **"The Church with an Overshot Wheel"** and **"The Higher Abdication"** both rest on the coincidence of a child, lost from home at an early age, returning to that home by chance in later life, and being recognized by its remembrance of an object. . . . [Many] of his methods seem cheap or brassy today. However, O. Henry is not responsible for the change in tastes.

The surprise ending was not a new device in fiction when Porter began using it. Examples of it could probably be found in all the types of short fiction that preceded the American short story. (pp. 7-8)

Yet, in spite of its long history and the approval of the reading public, the critics have a tendency to look down on the "surprise ending." . . .

[Berg Esenwein, in *Writing the Short Story* (1908)], asserts that it is the easiest kind of plot from which to write a story.

One question is, does the surprise ending have a legitimate

place in the short story? Also, has O. Henry's use of the surprise ending done anything to change that status?

It should be kept in mind that the short story is fiction; it is not reporting a news event; it is not even a "human interest" news report; it is not a "column" in the newspaper sense of that word. The short story may be based on a news report, but it must be more than reporting. It must be an artistic presentation of the facts if it be based on facts, not a *sine qua non*. This assumption rests on the definition of the short story:

> A short story is a narrative presenting characters in a struggle or complication having a definite outcome. . . . Most critics insist that a short story shall have unity of action, unity of tone, and shall produce a single effect.
> [Blanche Colton Williams, *Short Stories for College Classes*].
> (pp. 8-9)

As the painter selects what he puts on canvas, so the fiction writer selects details to produce a single effect and a definite outcome. The reporter is not concerned with a single effect, or with a definite outcome, for life itself often does not provide a definite outcome to a struggle or complication. So the fiction writer must part company with the reporter. It might be argued that the photographer can affect the degree of reality which he records by use of equipment—filters, lens—or by darkroom technique, and that the reporter can vary his reporting by slanting. And so they may; but, as they do so, they move from the realm of fact into the realm of art.

The definite outcome is, or should be, the climax of the story. There is no universal rule as to where this climax should be placed. It could be at the beginning, in the middle, or at the end of the story. Generally it is towards the end of the story, and this climactic ending is what makes the story. As to the exact place—who could assign one? Some of the correspondence schools have tried to reduce writing to an exact science, but such it will never be. Art is more than mechanics. It is for the individual author to determine where the climax will be the most effective, not for the critic to set an arbitrary rule. If the artist, the author, finds that his most effective writing comes from placing the climax in a surprise ending or in a culminating sentence, he is guilty of no literary, no artistic, no ethical, no moral error. The surprise ending, after all, is no more than a climax to the story, placed at the end.

The surprise ending, however, should be distinguished from the culminating sentence. The surprise ending sums up and finishes the story, but details may follow. The culminating sentence is a "punch" line which ends the story immediately. In **"Gift of the Magi"** the surprise ending comes when Jim reveals that he has sold his watch to buy Della her present; then O. Henry goes on to add that of all who give gifts, these are the wisest. (This added moral is a favorite device of his.) In **"Romance of a Busy Broker,"** a culminating sentence sums up the whole story: "We were married last evening at 8 o'clock in the Little Church around the Corner." If there is anything of the vaudeville in O. Henry's stories as Pattee suggests [see excerpt dated 1917], it is more with the culminating sentence than in the surprise ending. Since the technique is similar for both, the term "surprise ending" will be used to include both, with the reservation that there is a distinction. (pp. 10-11)

A valid surprise ending . . . should be plausible. Though it may be unnatural, in the sense that it seldom occurs in real life, it must seem natural to the reader. It should depend on the shifts and twists of human agents. Changes in circumstances should be intrinsic to the story.

On the other hand, the ending should not depend on arbitrary arrangement of external circumstances. One of O. Henry's weaknesses is the use of coincidences that seem almost incredible. . . . **"The Furnished Room"** has already been cited as an example. It is almost incredible that in a city of four million people a young man should come by chance to the same room in which his lost love had committed suicide. **"The Higher Abdication"** has another coincidence: A bum climbs into a wagon and goes to sleep. While sleeping he is driven to a ranch. It turns out that he is the son of the owner of the ranch who was lost or stolen from home at the age of two. **"The Church with an Overshot Wheel"** depends upon a similar coincidence. A little girl is lost from home at the age of four. She returns at the age of twenty and is recognized because she recognizes an old song her father sang when she was a child. Another of his famous stories, **"The Third Ingredient,"** rests upon a far-fetched coincidence. A young man rescues a girl who has jumped off a ferry boat. Out of all the rooming houses in New York he comes by accident to the one in which she lives.

There are other reasons for the failure of the surprise ending. One of the devices of O. Henry to achieve the surprise ending is the story within the story. The surprise ending comes at the external story's ending and is too often an inconsequential or trivial statement. As in the **"Halberdier of the Little Rheinschloss,"** the story begins with the question of why a cigar case was broken; this leads to another story which has no connection with the first; the surprise ending comes in the explanation of the cigar case which is completely inconsequential. A surprise ending that leaves the basic conflict unsolved may be regarded a failure. **"Hearts and Crosses"** is such a story; the husband and wife are brought back together by the birth of their child, but the conflict between them is not thereby solved, only delayed to a future date.

The surprise ending must be nearly the same as the single effect. When a story becomes too involved for a single effect, a surprise ending is almost impossible. In **"An Afternoon Miracle,"** O. Henry uses two involved stories, and tries to bring them together in a "surprise ending." First, there is a story about the hero, Bob Buckley, and his pursuit of an outlaw; then there is an account of the heroine, snake charmer Alvarita, who is in pursuit of one of her snakes. When hero and heroine get together, the "surprise ending" is that she screams at the sight of a caterpillar. This climax is rather a letdown after Bob Buckley has a barefisted fight with a knife-wielding outlaw. (pp. 11-13)

The surprise ending was the method of writing that O. Henry found to be most effective. He sacrificed reality no more than any artist must sacrifice reality. That one form of writing—realism, naturalism, surrealism—is closer to reality than another is at best a matter of opinion. (pp. 16-17)

One outstanding characteristic of O. Henry's work of which critics have taken little note is his use of the technique of "after the thunder, the still, small voice." This is the adding of a moral after the punch line or surprise ending, which we have already noted. O. Henry's stories are often didactic in this fashion. Its use in **"Gift of the Magi"** has already been noted.

Another favorite technique of O. Henry is that of storyteller.

Someone has said that it is the old American game of "tell me another" or "I'll top that." Most of the stories in *The Gentle Grafter* are of this nature. He uses this method often to provide a surprise ending.

Besides these there are perhaps four main methods that O. Henry uses to bring about a surprise ending:

a. The withholding of information. An example of this is **"The Double Dyed Deceiver"** where we are not told the identity of the youth the Llano Kid murdered until the end of the story. The revealing of this information provides the surprise. There is a similar usage in **"A Municipal Report,"** and many other stories.

b. The angle of narration. This is not so much the withholding of information, as the telling of the story so that the information is not necessary until the denouement. This is the method used in **"Gift of the Magi," "The Love-Philtre of Ikey Schoenstein,"** and **"The Romance of a Busy Broker,"** among others.

c. Attempts to mislead. This is the old method of letting the reader tell the story. . . . If the surprise ending could ever be called a "trick plot" it is in this usage. Yet, the author does not mislead the reader so much as the reader misleads himself. In **"October and June"** O. Henry uses a conventional situation of a difference in age between a man and a woman. The reader assumes that the man is the older and is surprised (or should be) to learn that it is the other way around. In **"Girl"** a conventional situation is used: a wealthy man is pursuing a girl; the reader assumes that he wants to marry her; actually he wants to hire her to be his cook.

d. The misunderstanding. This is an old device in fiction. A typical O. Henry example is **"Hygeia at the Solito,"** in which a wealthy cattleman takes a sick man home to his ranch to recuperate; a doctor apparently examines the man and pronounces him well; the rancher puts him to work; the man does recover from his illness, and it turns out that the doctor examined the wrong man.

Possibly, there are other methods that could be mentioned, but most of O. Henry's stories could be classified under these headings. O. Henry found the surprise ending in use in fiction, made it his own, and passed it on to become one of the most popular short story devices.

The statement, in one form or another, has been made by critics that O. Henry was willing to sacrifice anything, even truth, for the sake of the surprise ending. The question of truth in fiction is one that has long vexed critics perhaps even before the Puritans charged that fiction was "lies." Porter was aware of the problem; he opens **"The World and the Door"** (*Whirligigs*) with the comment:

> As for the adage quoted above [truth is stranger than fiction], I take pleasure in puncturing it by affirming that I read in a purely fictional story the other day the line: "Be it so," said the policeman. "Nothing so strange has yet cropped out in Truth" [the capital T is Porter's].

This comment, of course, does not answer the question as to what is truth in fiction. Pattee's explanation as to O. Henry's failing is that he does not present "humanity as humanity actually is." This statement provides us with a guide that we can use in reaching a working definition. Pattee seems to suggest that there is a distinction between *fact, truth,* and *opin-*

ion. Fact can be defined in terms of its roots; that is, a *fact* is something that is done (a definition preserved in "an accessory after the fact"), a deed. A *truth,* on the other hand, is a generalization deduced from a fact or facts, and is to be distinguished from *true.* Thus, "God exists" is a truth but not a fact; "God created the heavens and the earth," is a *fact,* a *true* statement but not a *truth.*

According to these definitions, fiction may contain *truth* even though it is not *fact.* For example, in fiction, a writer may put a rocket ship in orbit around Mars. Since what he writes is admittedly fiction no demand should be made that he treat of *fact.* As to truth, having his rocket ship in orbit, the writer must then make his characters act in accordance with known laws of human nature. (pp. 17-19)

Does O. Henry make his characters act in accordance with known laws of human nature? In **"Gift of the Magi"** Della and Jim each sacrifice a prized personal possession to give a gift to the other; this surely is in accord with the known actions of people in love. In **"A Municipal Report"** a man conceals what might have been evidence of a murder; considering the character drawn of the murdered man, the *persona* might well act as O. Henry alleges. Then there is Dulcie of **"An Unfinished Story"**; she spends her last fifty cents for an imitation lace collar to wear on her first date. True to human nature? Instances of such observation of human nature might be multiplied. (p. 20)

O. Henry's stories possess truth and reality (not *realism* by the technical definitions of that term). The story **"The Third Ingredient"** rests on a highly improbable coincidence, but truth does not depend on probability. *Truth* rests on the question: Do the characters in the writer's universe, i.e. the story in question, act as people have acted in the universe which the reader knows? And for **"The Third Ingredient"** the answer must be yes.

Hetty, the lead, when fired from her job goes home and in a matter-of-fact way begins to prepare lunch. She finds a girl preparing potatoes and invites her to contribute them to the beef stew; later she meets a young man who has an onion to contribute and invites him to join. Surely nothing in this violates human conduct. The story revolves around a young artist (miniature painter, more accurately) who has been rescued from a suicide attempt. She and her rescuer have fallen in love at first sight; this is not unusual psychology. Now granted that in a city of four million people it is improbable that these two people should be brought back together, the question is: if they could be brought back together, would they still have this feeling of love? Records show that it is quite possible that the feeling would continue. The question of how long it would continue is not relevant since O. Henry does not attempt to answer that phase of the problem. O. Henry then does remain true to human nature. (p. 22)

William Sidney Porter was aware of his faults. He did protest the debasing of art and of literature. The artist, according to O. Henry's concept, has a responsibility to society and to his ideals.

The artist fulfills his responsibility to society by living up to his highest ideals. He has, according to Porter, no right to produce work simply because it will sell nor should he attempt to sell work for any reason other than its artistic excellence. Thus in *Heart of the West* he portrays a young cowpuncher as riding his horse through a picture he has painted rather than to allow the state legislature to purchase it for the deeds of his father (the cowpuncher's father).

An analysis of O. Henry's work will show that the writer did not always fulfill the critic's demands. Much of his work does not meet the highest standards of artistic excellence. Yet O. Henry should not be written off for this failure, anymore than Arnold and Wordsworth should be for their respective failures to live up to their respective written creeds. Much that O. Henry did write is of the highest quality.

Nor can O. Henry be summed up simply as a humorist. His best work is too profound for such a simple description; his best work has that mingling of comedy and tragedy that is the mark of great art.

Another reason for considering him as a great writer is that many of the objections to his work are not based on valid critical studies, but are rather expressions of the reaction against form and mechanics that began in the 'teens and which continues to a certain extent to the present time. Such transitory standards should not weigh heavily in judging an artist's work.

Therefore it seems likely that for his mastery of the surprise ending and for his insight into human nature William Sidney Porter will continue to rank as one of the masters of the short story. (pp. 23-4)

> Donald F. Peel, "A Critical Study of the Short Stories of O. Henry," in The Northwest Missouri State College Studies, *Vol. XXV, No. 4, November 1, 1961, pp. 3-24.*

EUGENE CURRENT-GARCIA (essay date 1965)

[*An American critic and educator, Current-Garcia is the author of* O. Henry (William Sidney Porter), *a thorough biographical and critical study that includes an examination of O. Henry's regional background and its influence on his works. In the excerpt below from that book, Current-Garcia scrutinizes many of O. Henry's New York stories, grouping them for discussion into four discrete categories.*]

Like a mosaic patiently assembled out of thousands of minute stone particles, the New York one meets in O. Henry's stories is both real and not real. Its essence is there, firmly and indelibly embedded in scores of passages which the casual reader seeking only transitory entertainment from a story plot may feel, yet fail to grasp intellectually—the changeless, turbulent, indestructible spirit of the place, as a recent New York writer has succinctly demonstrated. Speaking through one of his many masks, Raggles, the itinerant tramp who "came and laid siege to the heart of the great city of Manhattan," O. Henry struck the keynote of his love song to "the greatest of all cities." The special charms of other cities, though recognizable, "had been to him as long primer to read; as country maidens quickly to fathom; as send-price-of-subscription-with-answer rebuses to solve; as oyster cocktails to swallow; but here was one as cold, glittering, serene, impossible as a four-carat diamond in a window to a lover outside fingering damply in his pocket his ribbon-counter salary." This endless allure of New York with its thousands of beckoning contrarieties, inducements and denials, he was to celebrate in story after story—sometimes in maudlin outright praise, often in the subtler awareness revealed in a carelessly turned figure of speech, always with a profound understanding of the price

exacted by such a mistress from the poet who lays siege to her heart.

Fully aware of the difficulties involved, O. Henry's success in catching the essence of New York was due largely to the joyful eagerness with which he accepted the challenge, and brought into play all the blandishments his large stock of words and images could command. New York, he said, required that the outlander be either enemy or lover; and O. Henry chose to be a lover, though he never doubted that to possess the city's heart would be an unequal struggle. "Not only by blows does it seek to subdue you. It woos you to its heart with the subtlety of a siren. It is a combination of Delilah, green Chartreuse, Beethoven, chloral and John L. in his best days." To record its voice would demand "a mighty and far-reaching utterance," capable of mingling in one loud note "the chords of the day's traffic, the laughter and music of the night, . . . the rag-time, the weeping, the stealthy hum of cab-wheels, the shout of the press agent, the tinkle of fountains on the roof gardens, . . . the whispers of the lovers in the parks—all these sounds must go into your voice—not combined, but mixed, and of the mixture an essence made." To penetrate its mystery, one would have to turn bold adventurer, a prowler by night as well as a part of (yet apart from) "the dreary march of the hopeless Army of Mediocrity" during the rush hours of the day, so as not to overlook the myriad meaningful signs visible everywhere. For "at every corner handkerchiefs drop, fingers beckon, eyes besiege, and the lost, the lonely, the rapturous, the mysterious, the perilous, changing clues of adventure are slipped into our fingers." To appreciate its beauty would demand both perspective and understanding, the ability to comprehend that the city was "like a great river fed by a hundred alien streams. Each influx brings strange seeds on its flood, strange silt and weeds, and now and then a flower of rare promise. To construe this river requires a man who can build dykes against the overflow, who is a naturalist, a geologist, a humanitarian, a diver, and a strong swimmer." And to know its worth would take insight and imagination enough to see beneath its "ridiculous sham palaces of trumpery and tinsel pleasures," as Blinker suddenly perceived at Coney Island, that "counterfeit and false though the garish joys of these spangled temples were, . . . deep under the gilt surface they offered saving and apposite balm and satisfaction to the restless human heart." (pp. 96-7)

To find literary significance in O. Henry's treatment of this conglomerate mass of human activity, however, calls for classification of one sort or another, even though any attempt to classify his New York stories too rigidly must break down under the pressures of overlapping. One reason is that they do not conform so readily to the distinct patterns into which his Western and his Southern tales fall; moreover, no two stories are precisely alike in form and content, despite a general sameness of tone and atmosphere characterizing most of them. One basis for classifying them might be found in the kinds of activities their characters chiefly engage in; another, in the problems of adjustment these characters are obliged to face; still another, perhaps, in the several themes with which the stories deal.

But regardless of the pattern imposed, careful study of most of these stories under any legitimate criteria quickly discloses the basic unreality in the lives of O. Henry's New Yorkers. At least sixty of the stories center about the problems of men and women at work, but these problems seldom emerge from the nature or demands of their respective jobs. Another group of about thirty stories focuses on the problems of the unemployed and underprivileged, as against those of people who have more money than they know what to do with; and while a greater proportion of stories in this group do throw light on the pitiful consequences of economic disparity, they offer little if any more dramatic insight into the complex causes or possible alleviation of the social ailment. (Let the poor underpaid shopgirl meet a kind millionaire on the Coney Island steamer, or the park-bench beggar be given a generous handout by a lavish Caliph—it was the role O. Henry himself liked to play when he had the funds to spare.) Similarly, a third group, containing about twenty-five stories, deals chiefly with the living conditions and domestic affairs of representative members of the "four million"; but here again, the problems at issue tend oftener than not to arise from factitious causes rather than from normal family relationships, so that the solutions provided for them prove equally bizarre. There is, finally, a fourth group of stories in which the predominant activities of the characters are so diverse that no fully satisfactory catch-all term can be applied to them; the twenty-five stories (more or less) belonging in this miscellany, however, may be lumped under the loose heading of "Bagdad on parade," since the one trait common to most of them is the exhibition of typical, dyed-in-the-wool New Yorkers' behavior in public.

I   O. Henry's Toilers—Men and Women at Work

There are at least two contradictory ways of interpreting O. Henry's fictional representation of New York's toiling masses, and his Russian admirers, along with many others, seem to have adopted both at different times. On the one hand, his stories may be seen as an implied, if not an outright, criticism of the gross inequalities in the American capitalistic system, as indicated in this recent blast from the U.S.S.R. ["O. Henry—'A Really Remarkable Writer,'" by Roman Samarin, published in *The Soviet Review* (December, 1962)]: "He gave a general idea of the absurdity of the system under which dire poverty was the source of the amassing of fantastic wealth, and under which the rich became slaves of their millions and lost all human semblance. For O. Henry they were leeches who sucked their capital out of the poor, to whom they paid a pittance so that they might keep body and soul together and help the rich make their millions." On the other hand, the stories may be taken as offering a complacent, if sometimes cynical, approval of the *status quo,* and their author condemned for falseness, hypocrisy, sentimentality—for being "the great consoler," a slave of the bourgeoisie, sowing illusions, false hopes, another form of opium.

By depending on a picked assortment of stories, one could perhaps make out a plausible case for either view; but neither would stand up under scrutiny. One might argue, for example, that the well-known **"Gift of the Magi"** and **"The Furnished Room"** offer a bitter indictment of the inequities which cause intense suffering in America's materialistic society; or one might point to stories like **"The Shocks of Doom,"** **"One Thousand Dollars,"** **"A Night in New Arabia,"** and **"The Defeat of the City"** as evidence of O. Henry's full support of capitalism and the concentration of wealth in the right hands. But to assess his stories in these terms is to endow him with philosophical views he never possessed; for he is neither Realist nor Naturalist in outlook. Though sincerely humanitarian in his sympathies for the underdog, his view of the human predicament is consistently that of the Romanticist. "His half-dozen Jewish characters, for example, are superfi-

cial types, revealing no serious interest in the impact which New York had on the Jewish immigrant. Nor does he show an interest in one of the crucial issues of his day, the growing fight between capital and labor. Aside from his sentimental and somewhat ambivalent concern for the underpaid shopgirl, Porter's interest in New York was that of the perennial tourist."

O. Henry's portrayal of men and women at work accordingly reveals all the same Romantic postures and clichés visible in his Western and Southern stories, but his dexterity in sketching their harried existence produces the desired effect—a faint stirring of the emotions to laughter or tears, without disturbing unduly the reader's basic equanimity. Hence the widespread appeal of these stories; for, whatever the specific problem involved, the reader may remain comfortably detached, regardless of whether or not he finds that the characters and action, once his interest is aroused in them, touch his own personal concerns. Usually, the problem is pretty remote, but even if it is not, O. Henry's sleight-of-hand can quickly convert it into either a delightful farce, a touching little love story, or a shocking reversal of fortune. (pp. 99-102)

Always O. Henry's capacious bag of tricks yields up a new device or two with which he can spice up an otherwise empty or pointless plot. In **"A Midsummer Knight's Dream"** it is the contrast between Gaines's dream of his courtship days in a mountain resort and the letter he receives from his wife as he sits sweating in a hot office building. In **"The Diamond of Kali"** it is a rapidly diminishing supply of whiskey, which a newspaper reporter consumes while noting down the hair-raising details of General Marcellus B. Ludlow's pompously told story of his discovery and removal of a fabulous Indian jewel. A suite of adjoining cubicles in which a divorce lawyer places all three contestants in a suit provides for the comic fiasco of mistaken identity in **"The Hypothesis of Failure"**; and miscalculations based on an eccentric editor's method of having manuscripts evaluated by elevator operators and furnace tenders lead to the downfall of a writer's hopes for publication in **"A Sacrifice Hit."**

On the basis of these and numerous other stories like them, one is tempted to say that the more routine the occupation in real life, the more O. Henry may be counted on to embroider it in fiction. Marvey Maxwell, the broker, for instance, is so busy that when he gets to work accompanied by his stenographer, Miss Leslie, he has forgotten his previous day's instructions to his clerk to hire another stenographer and refuses to see any applicants for the job, saying that Miss Leslie can have it as long as she wants it. He has also forgotten—as he catches a glimpse of her and decides to propose to her during the one moment he can spare—that they "were married last evening at eight o'clock in the Little Church around the Corner." And again, in **"Witches Loaves"** poor Miss Martha Meacham's misjudgment of the reason why a shabby little German buys two loaves of stale bread from her bakeshop every day brings a shocking reversal of fortune to both of them. Mistaking him for a starving artist who might respond amorously to a friendly gesture, she one day surreptitiously puts butter inside the loaves but learns very shortly from the outraged Blumberger that she has "schpoilt" him: instead of eating the bread, he had been using handfuls of stale crumbs to erase the penciled lines on his finished architectural drawings; the buttered ones ruined in a moment the results of three months' labor on a prize competition.

Even in this far-fetched little tale, however, O. Henry's

amused sympathy for his puppets shines through the irony of their shattered hopes, and it infects the reader. His treatment of the pathetically futile lives of striving but untalented artists, writers, and show people, in fact, covers another fairly extensive group of the working population, and he usually presents them in a nicely balanced tone of mingled irony, pathos, and humor. Sometimes the predominant tone is lightly satiric, as in the story of Miss Medora Martin, headstrong Vermonter who comes to New York with easel and paints, determined to become a professional artist. Before long she is right at the center of Bohemia's "Vortex," gabbing and drinking with other artists, whose chatter of Henry James among the tables blends oddly with the popping corks and silvery laughter—"champagne flashed in the pail, wit flashed in the pan." And for a moment the reader fears that she may achieve her dream of becoming a conquering courtesan, until her old beau, Beriah Hoskins, comes to fetch her back home to Harmony. (pp. 102-04)

Sometimes the tone in these stories of artists and showmen strikes a deeper note, the laughter shading off into sighs of sadness and even despair; and in such instances the echo of O. Henry's own personal suffering may be felt. Two stories illustrating this shift of tone are **"A Service of Love"** and **"The Last Leaf,"** both of which rely on the sacrificial theme for their effect. Based on the same formula as the better known **"Gift of the Magi,"** **"A Service of Love"** tells of an earnest young pair of art students, Joe and Delia Larrabee, he a painter and she a musician, who bolster each other's courage when their funds run out by pretending to have a steady income from their professional skills; it turns out that she has been ironing shirts in a laundry while he has been firing the furnace in the same building. More touching yet, **"The Last Leaf "** has long been a universal favorite despite its glaring implausibility; for the story of kindly old Behrman, the artist *manqué* who gives up his life painting his one masterpiece—the last leaf on an outdoor vine—in order to restore a dying young girl's will to live, strikes a symbolic chord that transcends the sentimental gimcrackery of its plot.

More illuminating than either of these, however, is the story of Pettit, a hopeful young writer from Alabama whose stories are rejected by New York editors because they lack "living substance." When he falls in love and writes about that experience, his story is even worse—"sentimental drivel, full of whimpering soft-heartedness and gushing egoism. . . . A perusal of its buttery phrases would have made a cynic of a sighing chambermaid." Surviving the ending of his affair with the aid of whiskey and more writing, Pettit then finds another woman deeply in love with him, even to the point of attempted suicide over his unresponsiveness; and, when he converts this case into fiction, the editor whoops joyfully because now " 'Just as though it lay there, red and bleeding, a woman's heart was written into the lines.' " Pettit remains unimpressed, however, having discovered that " 'You can't write with ink, and you can't write with your own heart's blood, but you can write with the heart's blood of someone else. You have to be a cad before you can be an artist.' " Thoroughly disillusioned, he plans to return to Alabama to sell ploughs for his father.

Perhaps the bitterest of all in this group is **"The Memento,"** a story that embalms all the gaudy flavor of the early twentieth-century entertainment world, especially that of the cheap vaudeville circuits, as well as more than a touch of O. Henry's innate Puritanism. The story is built around the notorious vaudeville act of Rosalie Ray, whose *pièce de résistance* was swinging out from the proscenium high over "bald-head row" and kicking off one of her yellow garters, which all the men below scrambled to possess. After two years of this she had quit the stage, revolted by lascivious men pawing at her; and she had gone to a village on Long Island, where she became engaged to a young minister; but, before disclosing her own past, she learned that he owned a memento sent by a former " 'ideal love far above him in a roundabout way—yet rather direct.' " Instead of feeling flattered to discover that it was one of her own yellow garters, Rosalie returned to the playhouse in high dudgeon, convinced that all men were equally bad.

In its approach to the problem of the unattached girl obliged to earn her own living in the big city, **"The Memento"** is similar to many other stories O. Henry wrote on the same theme, most of them equally as dated and sentimental. There are at least twenty such stories in which the underpaid shopgirl, showgirl, model, clerk, waitress, or domestic servant presents a tearful spectacle of threatened innocence or unfulfilled hopes. Seldom does one find the aggressive young woman, capable of exploiting her physical resources successfully, and never the fallen woman triumphant, such as Dreiser's Sister Carrie; but there must have been a number of both types in O. Henry's extensive circle of acquaintances. For the mid-twentieth-century reader's taste, therefore, his generally cloying treatment of the agonized working girl is perhaps the least satisfactory of all his metropolitan vignettes. In **"The Trimmed Lamp,"** for example, two girl friends try to maintain a respectable appearance on meager wages, Lou as a laundry ironer at $18.50, Nancy as a department store clerk at only $8.00 a week. Besides her better-paying job, Lou also has Dan, a steady young electrician earning $30.00 a week and eager to marry her; she chides Nancy not only for being satisfied with a poorer job, even if it does enable her to mingle with "swell" people and to imitate in home-made clothes the "posh" styles of her rich customers, but also for turning down offers of marriage from wealthy men. But meanwhile Lou puts off marrying Dan, ditching him eventually to become a rich man's mistress; Nancy, of course, gets him. In the end Nancy adds to her trimmed lamp the unction of consolation for Lou, the foolish virgin, who on learning the outcome collapses, "crouching down against the iron fence of the park sobbing turbulently"—despite her "expensive fur coat and diamond-ringed hands." (pp. 104-06)

The archetype of . . . these suffering damsels, however, is Dulcie, heroine of what was "probably the most admired of all O. Henry's stories" during the decade following his death. What captured the public's heart especially in **"An Unfinished Story"** was the grim picture he drew of the joyless existence of the shopgirl who, on a $6.00 a week salary, had to provide for room rent, food, clothes, and all other needs. That Dulcie managed despite hunger and deprivation to preserve her chastity by turning down a dinner date with Piggy Wiggins, the rat (who "could look at a shopgirl and tell you to an hour how long it had been since she had eaten anything more nourishing than marsmallows and tea"), gave a lift to the spirit, even though the narrator observed ominously that on another day, while feeling lonelier than usual, she might not be so resolute.

Not all of O. Henry's working girls suffer from malnutrition or the menace of lost virginity. Some achieve comfort and security in the approved manner; others have these thrust upon them, though their inability to distinguish the real from the spurious article may deprive them of the offered prize. Such is nearly the fate of Miss Archer, crack model of Zizzbaum's wholesale clothing company, whose substandard intelligence (as compared with her hour-glass measurements, which were even better than "the required 38-25-42 standard") misinterprets a visiting executive's fumbling proposals of marriage as dishonorable advances. And such is the fate in store for both Claribel Colby in **"The Ferry of Unfulfillment"** and Maisie, the heroine of **"A Lickpenny Lover"**: for Claribel, exhausted from a previous night's dancing and a full day's work behind the counter, misses a golden opportunity when, half-asleep, she gives the wrong answer to the rich prospector who wants to marry her; while Maisie, even with her eyes open, rejects her wealthy suitor because she thinks that his promise to take her to faraway places only means that he " 'wanted me to marry him and go down to Coney Island for wedding tour.' "

The strong appeal of stories like these which dramatized so glaringly the contrast between the millionaire's world of values and the shopgirl's tells us much about the taste of a period just becoming fully aware of the hardening class structure which a burgeoning industrial era had imposed on America's democratic society. To break through class barriers by applying some variation of the Cinderella formula was still held as a valid romantic hope, even though in actuality it often proved a delusion. And O. Henry, shrewdly aware of his public's wavering between hopes and fears, played the game both ways in different stories. Meanwhile, however, his sympathet-

The Flatiron Building, Broadway and Fifth Avenue, a prominent skyscraper of O. Henry's era in New York.

ic portrayal of the working girl's hard lot was a new phenomenon which drew enthusiastic response chiefly because it was so accurate in minute details. . . . Moreover, as Smith long ago pointed out, the two kinds of New York society that interested O. Henry most were "those who were under a strain of some sort and those who were under a delusion. The first stirred his sympathy; the second furnished him unending entertainment. Both are abundantly represented in his stories." Since this dichotomy takes in most of us today, along with Manhattan's toiling millions of the 1900's, it is easy to see why O. Henry's stories about them still enjoy a widespread popularity. (pp. 107-08)

II THE RICH AND THE POOR

On the centennial anniversary of O. Henry's birth, the Soviets cannily issued a commemorative stamp in his honor, catching our own postal authorities flat-footed. And when the New York *Herald Tribune* took note of this event, observing that the Russians' tastes in American literature are curious because they have made favorites of writers like Jack London and O. Henry, "both of whom are rather out of fashion here nowadays," a dialectical riposte quickly followed in *Izvestia*. Many good American writers who criticized the "American way of life," said the writer, have gone out of fashion in the United States but will continue to be honored as classics in Russia. The implication that O. Henry—along with Steinbeck, Hemingway, Dreiser, and Mark Twain—deserves honor chiefly as a bitter critic of American capitalism can, of course be documented sufficiently to support the Communist propaganda line. But this image of O. Henry would come no closer to the truth than its exact opposite. For, although he was clearly a friend of the friendless and the poor, both in real life and in his fiction, he was certainly no publicly avowed enemy of the rich.

While portraying the horrors and pinched existence endured by his underpaid shopgirls, he does occasionally condemn in sweepingly Dickensian general terms the tight-fisted employers who keep them economically depressed. Occasionally too, he chides the idle rich, through irony and understatement, for having so much to waste while others have so little to live on. Yet, whenever he depicts the rich themselves in his stories, he generally presents them in tolerant, even affectionate terms. (p. 109)

In short, O. Henry romanticizes the rich as well as the poor; he gives the impression through those he selects to represent the wealthy that money is a good thing to have if only one knows how to enjoy spending it—that is, like a Caliph. The miserly and the greedy he condemns by indirection and in broad terms, but they are seldom given a name or a character role to play in the story. (p. 110)

Throughout these romantic tales of affluent caliphs, there is scarcely a hint either of the ascetic Christian view of the love of money as the root of all evil, or of the liberal sociological view that the rich owe a debt to society payable through graduated income taxes. Young or old, O. Henry's opulent heroes, however blinded their riches may have made them toward the suffering of the underprivileged, miraculously see the light at the touch of a magic wand and promptly set about trying, futilely of course, to rectify the balance. (p. 111)

[O. Henry] could turn a current muckraking topic to his own uses, producing an innocuously sentimental tale that evades the harsh realities, and yet makes its mass reading public feel warm and good inside. Repeatedly this is his tactic in dealing with the rich. Old Tom Crowley, the Caliph in **"What You Want"** (the very titles are a giveaway), who is worth $42,000,000 but bored with all his luxuries, goes on the prowl in search of something his money cannot buy. He finds it in the person of young Jack Turner, a scholarly hat-cleaner, who scornfully rejects the older man's offer to set him up in business and subsidize his education. When Crowley calls him an impudent pup, he retaliates; and presently their scuffling lands them both in jail on a disorderly charge, neither having the necessary bail in cash. Wondering whether the old man really was rich, Turner settles down contentedly on his cot to read; and his concluding response to the officer who announces shortly afterwards that Crowley has arranged to have him bailed out is: " 'Tell him I ain't in.' " The story is utterly ludicrous; yet in it O. Henry's suggestion of the New Yorker's bellicose independence, though exaggerated, is well taken.

A more fundamental implication, however, in this and most of his other stories dealing with both the rich and the poor, may be expressed by the romantic cliché: "money isn't everything." This theme receives a thorough working over in virtually every story in which money, as a symbol of desirability in life, is set forth in the scales against other less tangible values. . . . The underlying idea in all these stories is that love, freedom, pleasure—the attainment of the heart's desire—are all preferable to wealth and that sensible people will relinquish any amount of it to obtain them.

The other side of this coin is that poverty and deprivation have their compensations, so long as one accepts his hard lot gracefully and tries to live joyously and honestly within his limitations. O. Henry dramatizes this consoling, if unrealistic doctrine from a number of contrasting points of view, most of them tending to bring out the picturesqueness rather than the grimness inherent in the lives of the poor. Nothing could be grimmer or more depressing in real life than the dope-pushing derelicts that haunt the park benches and Salvation Army soup kitchens; yet in several stories O. Henry endows these characters with qualities of nobility, grandeur, tenderness, and wisdom—tales designed to evoke mingled tears and sympathetic laughter but not an urge to confront and grapple with a disturbing social evil. (pp. 112-13)

Common to these and other stories—**"The Higher Pragmatism," "The Cop and the Anthem,"** and **"Two Thanksgiving Day Gentlemen"**—is also the theme of appearance versus reality: things are not as they seem, nor do they turn out as expected, even under the most deceptively convincing manifestations. . . . Stuffy Pete, the Union Square bum, though already bursting from one Thanksgiving Day meal, must consume another so as not to disappoint an elderly benefactor who is himself suffering from malnutrition. Irony is here the tool enabling O. Henry to switch from pathos to humor and back again to pathos within a single story and throughout a series of such stories; and each is designed to entertain his Sunday morning readers with the oddities he found or could imagine to exist among the lowly.

Only occasionally in dealing with society's cast-offs did he allow a note of genuine bitterness to stiffen the harshness of his irony, and in these few stories there are hints of what he might have done with more of his material had he chosen to present these people as the individuals he had really seen, rather than as mere puppets. In **"Vanity and Some Sables,"** for instance, we meet "Kid" Brady, member of a tough gang of hoodlums and pickpockets from Hell's Kitchen. At his girl

Molly's urging, the "Kid" promises to go straight, works steadily for eight months, and then gives her an expensive set of furs, which he says were not stolen but bought with his own hard-earned money. When Molly and the "Kid" are picked up anyway on suspicion of a theft of furs from his employer, they escape arrest because her furs turn out to be cheap imitations costing only $21.50; but Brady angrily confesses that he would rather have spent six months in jail than admit he could afford so little for fake Russian sables. Though the plot is as obviously contrived as any, O. Henry did inject into the tale a shade of the realism he usually evaded. The same shade is deepened further in another story called **"The Assessor of Success,"** which tells of Hastings Beauchamp Morley, a fellow who lives entirely by his wits. Broke one day, flush the next from gambling, picking pockets, working a confidence game, and the like, Morley is yet kindly and prepossessing in appearance, charming and witty. The only important thing in life is gulling others without being gulled; he assures a beggar to whom he gives a dollar shortly after bilking another man out of $140: " 'The world is a rock to you, no doubt; but you must be an Aaron and smite it with your rod. Then things better than water will gush out of it for you.' " Nevertheless, as Morley goes jauntily on his way, he catches sight of a former schoolmate whom he can no longer face, and his last words are: " 'God! I wish I could die.' "

Stories like these, which end on a sour note, are rare in O. Henry's work, especially in his treatment of the dispossessed or the degraded. Had he chosen oftener to present life in the raw as he doubtless knew it, he would not have endeared himself to the public he was writing for. But neither would he have remained true to his own concept of life as an adventure to be confronted gaily. Whether rich or poor, one could scarcely avoid seeing life's drabness: for O. Henry the point was to transcend it.

III NEW YORKERS AT HOME

"I would like to live a lifetime in each street in New York. Every house has a drama in it," O. Henry is reported to have said on one occasion. To understand what he meant by "drama" in this context, one would have to consider carefully two of the stories which, by common consent, still stand at the head of O. Henry favorites: **"The Gift of the Magi"** and **"The Furnished Room."** These represent the polar opposites of joy and sadness with which his imagination clothed the domestic life of average New Yorkers; and, though both may seem somewhat dated now, they still possess a strong popular appeal based on a universal yearning for an unattainable ideal. It is not surprising that **"The Gift of the Magi"** still enjoys such widespread fame, for in this trite little tale of mutual self-sacrifice between husband and wife, O. Henry crystallized dramatically what the world in all its stored-up wisdom knows to be of fundamental value in ordinary family life. Unselfish love shared, regardless of the attendant difficulties or distractions—this is the idea repeatedly implied as a criterion in his fictional treatment of domestic affairs. If such love is present, life can be a great adventure transcending all drabness; if it is absent, nothing else can take its place. Conversely, because it is often absent—or when present, it exists only momentarily and in a fragile state—the world can recognize and take to heart the grim meaning of life without it. O. Henry wrote few stories of ordinary family life that approach in tenderness and universal appeal the qualities found in **"The Gift of the Magi"**; and fewer still of those that match the bleakness of **"The Furnished Room."** But among the two dozen or so in which he attempted to dramatize the family life of the four million, perhaps seven or eight deserve and can stand comparison with these.

One reason for such scarcity may be simply that O. Henry did not know very much about the home life of average New Yorkers and therefore had to rely chiefly on what he could see or hear of it from the outside. There are, for instance, almost no children involved in most of these stories, and only two of them deal specifically with the problems of childhood and child care. Except for single folk or young married couples living transiently like himself in furnished rooms, the lives he knew were largely public, they were observed externally rather than from within the family circle, and they moved predominantly on the lower economic levels. Hence the paucity of stories reflecting ordinary family problems at home, as against the many showing New Yorkers of all shades and levels in restaurants, shops, offices, and parks, on the streets, and at summer resorts. Another reason may be that O. Henry could not imagine a great variety of exciting situations taking place behind those private walls he seldom penetrated, despite his belief that every house has a drama in it. "There is a saying that no man has tasted the full flavour of life until he has known poverty, love and war. . . . The three conditions embrace about all there is in life worth knowing." Thus [in **"The Complete Life of John Hopkins"**] he begins one of his more amusing fantasies of ordinary family life in New York, and the three conditions he lays down as essential to the full life are indicative of the kinds of drama he sought. In order to find them, and also to elicit the adventuresome qualities inherent in even the dreariest existence, the domestic situations he conceived turn out to be pretty far-fetched, as well as somehow tied up with the outside world rather than self-contained. (pp. 114-17)

In **"The Pendulum"** the portrayal of both the dull flat-dweller's routine and its occasional disruption is more successfully carried off. "There are no surprises awaiting a man who has been married two years and lives in a flat." Thus, alighting from the elevated at 81st Street and approaching his apartment, John Perkins can gloomily foretell to the minute exactly what will occur at each stage of the evening's progress following his inevitable pot-roast dinner: his wife will show him her quilting; at 7:30 the plaster will start falling because of overhead thumping; then the drunken vaudeville team across the hall will begin its nightly carousal; and there will be other assorted neighboring noises. At 8:15 Perkins will reach for his hat and, facing Katy's ire, announce that he's going to McCloskey's to shoot a few games of pool with his friends. This time, however, things are different. Perkins finds the place in disarray, no Katy, and a hastily scrawled note revealing her sudden departure to care for a sick mother. As he begins to set the rooms in order and to prepare his lonely meal of cold mutton and coffee, Perkins gradually realizes how important his old routine has been to him. "The night was his. He might go forth unquestioned and thrum the strings of jollity as free as any gay bachelor there. He might carouse and wander and have his fling until dawn if he liked; and there would be no wrathful Katy waiting for him, bearing the chalice that held the dregs of his joy." But now there is no joy. With Katy gone, Perkins remorsefully thinks how lonely it must have been for her here during all his long evenings at McCloskey's, and he resolves, tearfully, to treat her more considerately when she returns. Then Katy opens the door and explains that the sick call was a false alarm, and the

household machinery silently shifts back into its accustomed order. At exactly 8:15, in response to Katy's querulous inquiry when John reaches for his hat, he says: "Thought I'd drop up to McCloskey's . . . and play a game or two of pool with the fellows."

Obviously, O. Henry could not play infinite variations on the theme of dull lives like the Hopkinses' and the Perkinses'. . . . [But he could achieve variety] by turning his attention to the more colorful lives of Irish laboring families, where his necessary ingredients of poverty, love, and war abounded. In six or seven stories, at any rate, that is what he did; and the results in several were fairly satisfactory. (pp. 117-19)

The best of these Irish dialect stories, accordingly, are the few that combine a more serious attitude toward family relationships with oddities of speech and mannerisms, which O. Henry always renders well. Instead of pure rackety farce, there is a certain winsomeness in the two stories entitled **"The Easter of the Soul"** and **"The Day Resurgent,"** both written as special Easter feature stories for his *Sunday World* readers. Young "Tiger" McQuirk, temporarily idle because the stone-cutters are on strike, cannot account for his restlessness at home; his little brother attributes it to a girl, Annie Maria; his mother, simply to spring in his bones. "Tiger" denies everything, saying there is no spring in sight; and then he goes searching for signs but finds no sure ones until he reaches Annie's house. When she assures him that spring is everywhere, he is convinced, happy, invigorated. The story, virtually plotless, is yet invested with charm and meaning through O. Henry's management of dialogue between McQuirk and the various others he meets fleetingly during his progress.

O. Henry again uses most of the same devices in **"The Day Resurgent"** with equal effectiveness. . . . (pp. 119-20)

Aside from these Irish dialect stories, there are very few others in O. Henry's gallery of Gothamite family portraits that deserve more than a passing glance. He showed his versatility at combining a variety of dialects, together with other tall-tale elements and satirical overtones, in **"The Gold That Glittered"** and in **"The City of Dreadful Night,"** both mildly amusing farces. (p. 120)

In most of the remaining stories of the domestic group, however, even the humor fails to redeem the artificiality and pointlessness of their plots. (p. 121)

The preponderance of light foolery and romance in nearly all these stories, most of them written under contract to fill the *Sunday World* page each week, offers fairly convincing proof that O. Henry not only gauged the taste of his mass reading public quite accurately but also knew how to satisfy it. That he was likewise more concerned with this problem of producing a weekly diet of light entertainment than with the more demanding problem of rendering artistically the manifold dramas inherent in Manhattan's domestic life also seems evident. If he could achieve now and then incidental criticism of greedy landlords, miserly employers, or crooked public officials along with his entertainment, well and good; but the entertainment took precedence over everything else. For the only other exception to his common practice (aside from **"The Gift of the Magi"** and **"The Furnished Room"**) is in **"The Guilty Party—An East Side Tragedy,"** a grim tale of parental neglect which "was made a full-page feature by the Sunday [*World*] Magazine editor, with a prize contest announced for the best letter regarding it." Somewhat reminiscent of Crane's *Maggie*, **"The Guilty Party"** tells of a twelve-year-old girl, Liz, who grows up to become a drunkard, murderess, and suicide because of her father's unwillingness to play with her as a child. Employing his typical "envelope" technique consisting of a brief opening scene and of a swift transition to the main scene couched in the form of a dream, O. Henry achieved in this story a meaningful domestic drama that suggests more truthfully than most of his others some of the festering social problems underlying the picturesque surface of metropolitan life. Like most of the others, it too suffers from an overdose of maudlin sentimentality in its conclusion; but it deserves nevertheless to be taken as seriously as **"The Furnished Room."** (pp. 121-22)

IV BAGDAD ON PARADE—NEW YORKERS IN PUBLIC

No characteristic of O. Henry's writing more clearly stamps his individuality than his unceasing fascination with the passing show, which he could observe at greater leisure and possibly with deeper insight while seated at a restaurant table, alone or with friends, than he could while ambling about the city's highroads and byways. The stories told of his fondness for dining out in all manner of eating places are, of course, numerous and colorful; but one would not need to know any of them to sense the excitement he must have felt in the presence of New York's constantly changing scene. Far more clearly than any recollections at second hand, his own stories convey both the impressions and their effect upon him—a sea of faces arriving and departing, the hum of lively talk, the flashing colors of women's clothes, the tinkle of silver and glassware, the popping of corks, and the savor of varied dishes served forth by hurrying waiters—as he presents the public image of New York in its scores of food and drink emporiums, from the most fashionable of dining halls to the obscurest of the Bohemian rathskellers. These stories show, even more convincingly than do his tales of family life, that the public spotlight was his special arena. The restaurant, not the furnished room, was where he found the real drama of New York life.

There is scarcely a story dealing with New York public life in which the restaurant does not somehow play a part, either as the central scene of action or as a point of reference against which life elsewhere in the city can be measured. The dispensing and consumption of food and drink in public are therefore major symbols—sometimes consciously, sometimes unwittingly employed—in O. Henry's portrayal of what he took to be the significant actions in the lives of his fellow New Yorkers. Indeed, the kinds of places they patronized, as well as their conduct in those places, were apparently the chief means he relied on for classifying and evaluating the patrons and would-be patrons who served as models for his fictional characterizations. For as C. A. Smith correctly pointed out many years ago, O. Henry divided these people into two broad classes: "those who knew and those who thought they knew, the real thing and those who would be considered the real thing." Viewed from the vantage point of the restaurant table, the passing throng of O. Henry's New York society accordingly receives its most picturesque treatment in this group of thirty or more stories, nearly all of which present a highly idealized version of romantic adventure framed in an illusorily realistic setting.

The basic themes dramatized in these stories, however, are fundamentally the same as those underlying his others; they are neither simpler nor more complex in their analysis of human motives, though perhaps oftener dressed in a more at-

tractive package. As a commentary on the follies and ambitions of human nature, they can hardly be called trenchant; yet their appearance in such a variety of forms exposes another illuminating facet of O. Henry's artistic skill. Four themes recur often enough to be singled out and examined separately: (a) pretense and reversal of fortune—"turning the tables on Haroun"; (b) discovery and initiation through adventure; (c) the city as spiritual playground for the imagination; and (d) the basic yearning of all human nature. One or more of these themes may be detected in virtually all his stories of New Yorkers on parade, but in some of them the theme may be coyly concealed beneath several layers of seemingly irrelevant chaff.

Without doubt the theme of pretense—the desire to pose for what one is not, if only for a few brief moments and regardless of the price exacted—is the most persistent one in O. Henry's writing; for it crops up again and again in nearly all his stories from the earliest to the last few he left unfinished at his death. It is the foundation of **"While the Auto Waits,"** one of the first tales that aroused the curiosity of editors and critics in the writing of an unknown author who called himself James L. Bliss. Still one of his best, the story dramatizes the pathos of false pretenses in the transparent claims to family grandeur with which a comely young woman seeks to impress a young man who stops to chat with her in a park. Taking his cue from her pretentiousness, he too masks his real identity by pretending to be a humble restaurant cashier, which is actually the position she fills; he is also the wealthy owner of the chauffeured car waiting for occupancy, which she has pointed to as hers. The loss to both individuals as a result of a natural human urge toward one-upmanship is pointedly driven home with an irony unmarred by either sentimentality or gratuitous moralizing.

O. Henry simply reversed the same situation in **"Lost on Dress Parade,"** this time portraying the man as victim of his own folly, but heightening the poignance of lost hopes with several additional touches of characterization. Towers Chandler, the hero in this instance, is a likable, generous young chap who scrimps along on a meager salary; he saves one dollar a week so that every tenth week he can blow himself to an expensive dinner at a fashionable Broadway restaurant. But on this icy evening he encounters a pretty girl, rather shabbily dressed, who has slipped on the sidewalk and sprained her ankle. Helping her up, he introduces himself and invites her to dine with him; she accepts reluctantly; and he brags throughout the meal about being an idle man about town, an habitué of clubs and fine restaurants, impressing the poor working girl. But, after thanking and bidding him good-bye, she returns to her wealthy home, saddened by the thought that although she could cheerfully marry a poor man so long as he had "some work to do in the world," she could never love a social butterfly, "even if his eyes were blue and he were so kind to poor girls whom he met in the street." Again, the double loss is what gives the story its special tang.

Sometimes, however, O. Henry could present situations similar to these in which profit rather than loss accrues to one or more of the persons involved without necessarily injuring others. The therapeutic effect of playing the poseur temporarily is quite amusingly set forth, for example, in **"Transients in Arcadia,"** which opens with a mouth-watering description of the elegant but unobtrusive Hotel Lotus on Broadway: "an oasis in the July desert of Manhattan" where one can get "brook trout better than the White Mountains ever served, sea food that would turn Old Point Comfort—'by Gad, sah!'—green with envy, and Maine venison that would melt the official heart of a game warden." Enter next the lovely, well-groomed Madame Heloise D'Arcy Beaumont, whose graciousness promptly charms bellboys and management alike; she stays a few days, seldom going out; and she soon meets handsome young Harold Farrington, also well groomed and obviously a leisured man of the world. They congratulate each other for having found this quiet retreat away from all the blatant foreign resorts, already overrun and cheapened by tourists. But after three days of such pleasant chit-chat, the lady confesses that she is actually Mamie Siviter, a hosiery clerk at Casey's Mammoth Store, who has but a dollar left from the fund she saved up for a year in order to enjoy this one week's glorious holiday; and that dollar must go to pay the installment due on her dress. Unperturbed, Farrington scribbles a receipt and takes her dollar, confessing on his part that he is actually Jimmy McManus, bill collector for O'Dowd and Levinsky; he too has saved up out of a paltry salary because, like her, he " 'always wanted to put up at a swell hotel.' " Both have got more than their money's worth with the *lagniappe* of blossoming romance to boot (for in parting at the elevator Jimmy and Mamie have made a date to go to Coney Island the following Saturday) in a brilliantly contrived idyll that combines all four of O. Henry's major themes within fewer than nine pages. (pp. 122-25)

Few others among O. Henry's remaining stories that develop the pretense theme can match these in either technical virtuosity or general appeal; yet the mere fact that he found numerous other ways of varying his treatment of the theme effectively is in itself remarkable. (pp. 126-27)

Though the two main themes of pretense and discovery through adventure often unfold concurrently in O. Henry's stories, they are not invariably yoked together or mutually dependent. The idea of eagerly confronting the unknown, with or without the protective coloration of a disguise, seems to have excited O. Henry throughout life, the more so during his last years when so little of it remained. And since he constantly saw life itself as an uncertain adventure at best, his eagerness to crowd in all possible chances spilled over into his stories like water flowing over a dam. Thus, the character he most admires is clearly a person like his hero Rudolph Steiner in **"The Green Door,"** to whom "the most interesting thing in life seemed . . . to be what might lie just around the next corner." Steiner, a true adventurer, is willing to pay the toll that will be charged for following up a lead, even though aware from past experience that the fee may come high. And there are many others like him in O. Henry's stories, most of them clearly projections of their author's own personality.

Nor are they necessarily always men. In an absurd yet charming tale called **"A Philistine in Bohemia,"** the adventurer is a winsome Irish lass, Katy Dempsey, who with her mother keeps one of the cheap rooming houses below Union Square. Ardently courted by one of their lodgers, the meticulous Mr. Brunelli, Katy is wary of him, first, because he is Italian and, second, because, in her mother's view, he seems a bit "too coolchured in his spache for a rale gintleman." Still, Katy accepts his invitation to dine at a real Bohemian restaurant in the Village, patronized by poor artists and sporty characters and managed by a fellow named Tonio. After escorting her to a table, Mr. Brunelli excuses himself; but presently one of the waiters brings her a truly Lucullian meal before he re-

turns. Fascinated by the gay atmosphere and overcome by the excellence of her food, Katy nevertheless begins to suspect Brunelli of being a titled patrician, "glorious of name but shy of rent money," and she wonders why he left her to dine alone. Meanwhile, all the other patrons are clamoring for Tonio, who treats them like a prince; and when the crowd thins out a little, Brunelli reappears at Katy's table, disclosing himself as "the great Tonio" and once more professing his "loaf" for her. Stuffed to the gills with fine food, she accepts him gratefully: " 'Sure I'll marry wid ye. But why didn't ye tell me ye was the cook? I was near turnin' ye down for bein' one of thim foreign counts!' "

Nor does the adventure and its consequent discovery have to be among the more sensational experiences that the big city provides. It can be the simplest departure from routine behavior and yet yield rich rewards. . . . (pp. 127-28)

The burden of his best stories that dwell on this theme is that both awareness and simplicity are as essential as courage in the pursuit of the adventurous life. (p. 129)

O. Henry's most ambitious effort on the theme of adventure and discovery, however, as well as one of his most interesting stories is the late one entitled **"The Venturers,"** published only a few months before his death. The story grew out of a brief seminal idea recorded as follows in his notebook: "Followers of chance—two 'Knights errant' one leaves girl and other marries her for what may be 'around-the-corner.' " On one level the story quite plainly expresses what Smith referred to as O. Henry's "revolt against the calculable," [see excerpt by Smith dated 1916] a problem that remained central with him from the beginning to the end of his career. But a deeper level, based on the immediate specific problem of his own second marriage can likewise be readily picked out; for in the two knights errant of the tale, Forster and Ives, are visible the unresolved halves of their creator himself: O. Henry, the adventurous literary artist, and Porter, the man who had taken a second wife in what was turning out to be a sadly mistaken venture for him. This element of the divided self accounts for both the story's depth of meaning and for what Smith notes as its seemingly misplaced center.

The story proper opens with John Reginald Forster's wondering where he can seek an exciting dinner as he leaves his exclusive Powhattan Club. He stops on the corner, fumbles through his pockets, and, though personally wealthy, discovers that they are all empty. Another well-groomed chap, Ives, noting his predicament, strikes up an acquaintance and, confessing that he too possesses only two pennies, proposes that they dine together in style at the swank restaurant across the way and then match coins to see which of them will have to deal with the proprietor's outraged wrath. Forster takes him up and the two men order a typical O. Henry meal, complete with fancy wines and exotic dishes, meanwhile entertaining each other with tales of their fondness for encountering unexpected but eagerly sought adventures in odd corners of the world. Ives has had more varied experiences than Forster, who has been largely confined to New York, though he too has always dreamed of doing things that would not lead to clearly predictable ends, such as their shared dinner.

At the dinner's end, however, both men have to confess that even this adventure was predictable, since it turns out that Forster, on losing the toss, has only to sign a credit chit and that Ives himself owns the place. But Forster, reluctant to break off their friendship, now discloses that he is engaged to be married to a lovely woman within a month and cannot decide whether to go through with the marriage or cut out for Alaska; for, although he loves the girl, it is the dead certainty of all their future that makes him doubtful. The two men agree to meet for another dinner on the following Thursday. Ives then goes to call on a beautiful girl, Mary Marsden, and the dialogue between them reveals that they've known each other since childhood and that he could have married her three years before if he had not decided to take off on another of his periodic jaunts around the world; but now it is too late—she is about to be married to another man. Seeing her in her unchanged, predictable surroundings, Ives thinks that she will always be the same there; the certainty of it was what had driven him away before. On Thursday Forster tells Ives that the dinner will have to be postponed, for he had decided to sail round the world and has explained this need to his fiancée in a letter. Ives, of course, tells him not to bother, for he has married the girl himself; he has discovered that this is the Venture, the one hazardous course that a man may follow all his life without ever knowing, even to his dying day, whether it is to end in the highest heaven or the blackest pit.

Whether or not **"The Venturers"** is actually a veiled commentary on the misgivings O. Henry felt toward his own marriage, the story does reveal his deep-seated conviction, the result of painful personal experience, that one cannot escape one's destiny regardless of the road taken, and that accordingly it is better to accept willingly the chances that come than to try to manipulate one's fate. Neither withdrawal nor escape will serve, for both lead to unsatisfactory ends. . . . (pp. 129-31)

That the great city is the inevitable spot for pursuing the adventurous life, simply because its store of chances is inexhaustible, marks another prominent thematic thread in O. Henry's work. Unlike the foregoing themes, however, the city as a spiritual reservoir for the imagination is a more pervasive one, appearing in many scattered passages, hints, and overtones, as in **"The Voice of the City"** and other tales already cited, rather than as the predominant motif of entire stories. Still, its prominence among the other themes can often be seen in the presentation of contrasting viewpoints or attitudes which O. Henry employs as a standard device in many stories. In **"A Little Local Color,"** for example, his main purpose is to satirize, spoofingly, himself and other feature-writing journalists in New York, all of whom are questing for the picturesque word, phrase, image, and metaphor with which to describe the city because their livelihood depends on giving the public what it wants. The writer-narrator accordingly badgers his friend, a "young-man-about-town and a New Yorker by birth, preference and incommutability," to show him around where he can note down the real local color in the people's polyglot speech, their mannerisms and idiosyncrasies. Wherever they go, however, the unexpected rather than the typical turns up—college professors talk Bowery slang, while a dyed-in-the-wool native Boweryite, using impeccable English, mercilessly ridicules the literary commercialization of alleged Bowery argot. In the end both are forced to admit that New York is too colorful and variegated to be easily stereotyped and classified. That the city does produce the unexpected where one is least prepared to find it is the real source of its charm, even though pulp feature writers thrive on their standardized but faked local-color portrayals.

This is a theme that O. Henry expresses continuously, even when poking fun at the city's manifest discomforts in mid-

summer heat. In the story **"Rus in Urbe"** he uses it as flavoring for an otherwise stale plot involving rich man versus poor man in pursuit of the same girl and manages to make both men's patently deceitful praise of the city's summer delights nevertheless sound quite authentic. Again, in **"The Call of the Tame"** he puts over the same theme by relating it to another of his favorite situations: the contrast between the confirmed Gothamite's viewpoint and that of the bluff, hearty man of the West, who becomes a convert as soon as he sees the light. Baffled and bored by all the metropolitan hubbub of Sixth Avenue, Greenbrier Nye can hardly wait to return to his native heath in Arizona, despite the luxury surrounding him in the exclusive café where his former partner, Longhorn Merritt, has taken him for luncheon. He scorns the effete drinks and dishes Merritt orders—dry Martinis, green Chartreuse, squab en casserole, etc.—and sticks to straight whiskey, saddened by the realization that city life has softened and feminized his old cowpunching pal of bygone days. Then his eye lights on the elegantly dressed woman in speckled silk at a table nearby, and before long the comforts of city life thus viewed in a new framework have cast their spell upon him.

Whether O. Henry found his symbol in a woman's stylish dress, an absinthe frappé, or a restaurant table's glittering array of silverware, his loyalty to the city's endless lure could be so fervently expressed that one need not wonder why New Yorkers loved him fifty years ago—and still do. But to appreciate his method of singing the city's praises one must often look beneath the insouciance and bravura of his approach. His most concentrated paean to the enchantment of New York occurs in the last few pages of **"The Duel,"** a story that resembles **"The Venturers"** in that again it offers two contrasting views, both of them his own, which are brilliantly synthesized in a concluding passage of poetic prose. The two young Westerners, William and Jack, who meet at luncheon after four years' residence in the city, are both projections of O. Henry's personality. William, the successful businessman, defends the city in rather crude, slangy terms, and for the wrong reasons—he is making his pile, meeting important people, seeing the plays he does not understand. Jack, the successful artist, condemns the city in more literate terms as "a monster to which the innocence, the genius, and the beauty of the land must pay tribute." He hates it because it is crude, base, materialistic—a city controlled by its lowest ingredients—and would return to the purer air of the West at once if he could, rather than sell his soul to it as his friend has done. Then at midnight Jack throws up his window and looks out over the city far below, catching his breath at the massive beauty of a sight he has seen and felt hundreds of times. As a Westerner, he sees its irregular background shapes in terms of canyons, cliffs, and gulches; but as an artist he responds to the implications of its myriads of glowing lights like a rapt devotee before an altar: ". . . out of the violet and purple depths ascended like the city's soul sounds and odors and thrills that make up the civic body. There arose the breath of gaiety unrestrained, of love, of hate, of all the passions that man can know. There below him lay all things, good or bad, that can be brought from the four corners of the earth to instruct, please, thrill, enrich, despoil, elevate, cast down, nurture, or kill. Thus the flavor of it came to him and went into his blood."

O. Henry leaves it up to the reader to decide which of the two men won the battle against the city; but, after such a purple passage as this, there is little doubt in the reader's mind concerning the effect of the city's "cup of mandragora" on O. Henry himself. It was the draught of vintage enabling him in imagination to escape all leaden-eyed despairs.

Though New York provided the stimulus for O. Henry's fertile imagination, the city as a microcosm in each of his 140 stories is, after all, simply the objective correlative that serves to pin down the broadest of his themes: namely, the idea of oneness at the heart of things in human society. A typically romantic approach to life, this notion that a strong common bond unites all people sweeps away or ignores as irrelevant superficialities the infinite gradations and distinctions existing between rich and poor, strong and weak, intelligent and stupid, good and evil, in order to focus attention on the centralizing principle or ideal for which all humanity strives. It is an approach abhorred by Realists who insist on the importance of those distinctions in the world as we know it and who urge the literary artist not to ignore them in his fictional portrayal of the world round about him. Whatever the tie between them may be, says the Realist, saints and sinners are not the same; and the differences between them are more significant than the Romanticist will admit.

Still, there is something indestructibly appealing in the Romanticist's creed which the world cherishes and clings to. And that is what explains O. Henry's hold on the world's reading public, despite the critic's scorn. The reader knows very well that things do not work out in the world as they do in O. Henry's stories; but in his heart he would like to believe they might. (pp. 131-34)

Eugene Current-Garcia, in his O. Henry (William Sydney Porter), *Twayne Publishers, Inc., 1965, 192 p.*

ARTHUR VOSS   (essay date 1973)

[*In the following excerpt from his* The American Short Story: A Critical Survey, *Voss briefly registers several of O. Henry's basic fictional devices and formulas.*]

By the end of the nineteenth century the carefully made, ingeniously plotted story had become a well-established tradition, but it was during the first decade of the twentieth century that the type was carried to its ultimate lengths in the stories of O. Henry. None of his predecessors exploited the contrived story with quite such deliberate calculation or with more facility, and none achieved anything like the phenomenal popularity of O. Henry, who produced his stories for mass-circulation magazines and newspapers with the intent, as he put it, of pleasing "Mr. Everybody." (p. 121)

O. Henry's stories have a variety of settings, but most of them are laid in either New York City or Texas. His characters include shopgirls and millionaires, policemen and burglars, cowboys and tramps, confidence men and southern gentlemen, and assorted other types. His manner is usually that of the garrulous taleteller, and his style is almost invariably breezy, flippant, and slangy, with puns, malapropisms, and big words being used for humorous effect. His stories are liberally sprinkled with asides in which he addresses the reader in a familiar and chatty tone. Literary allusions, often made facetiously, are common, and there are many references to other writers. Kipling, whom O. Henry greatly admired, is either mentioned or quoted frequently. In **"A Municipal Report,"** for example, besides a quotation from Kipling, both Frank Norris and Tennyson are cited, the latter being re-

ferred to as "My old friend, A. Tennyson," and there are in addition allusions to characters in two of Dickens' novels. Fond of referring also to *The Arabian Nights,* O. Henry often called New York City "Bagdad-on-the-Subway" and likened the wealthy New Yorkers in his stories to caliphs.

Although he usually used stock story formulas, O. Henry had an undoubted gift for devising ingenious variations on them. Coincidence figures largely in his stories, and they often have a surprise twist, or "snapper," as O. Henry called it. Unabashed sentiment and the broadest kind of comedy and burlesque are other conspicuous ingredients. In addition, O. Henry usually made his contrived stories illustrate some more or less serious theme. Most of his many stories of New York City, found mainly in *The Four Million* (1906), *The Trimmed Lamp* (1907), and *The Voice of the City* (1908), make the point that the humble, insignificant little people of New York are just as admirable and their lives as worthy of attention and interest as the members of the Four Hundred. Typical is **"The Gift of the Magi,"** O. Henry's famous story of the young married couple, each of whom sells a treasured possession to obtain money to buy a Christmas present for the other. Della sells her beautiful long hair to buy a platinum chain for Jim's watch, only to discover that he has sold it to buy jeweled tortoise-shell combs for her hair. O. Henry builds up to his surprise twist very artfully, and with deft touches he elicits the reader's admiration and sympathy for his young couple, whose love for each other more than compensates for Jim's meager salary, their shabbily furnished apartment, Della's old brown hat and jacket, and the fact that Jim needs a new overcoat and has no gloves. Artfully, too, O. Henry does not end on the note of irony and surprise but gives to what he calls his "uneventful chronicle of two foolish children" the appearance of a little parable with a significant meaning. The magi, he reminds the reader, were the wise men who brought gifts to the Christ child, and thus invented the giving of Christmas presents. As for Jim and Della, "in a last word to the wise of these days let it be said that of all who give gifts these two were the wisest. Of all who give and receive gifts, such as they are wisest. . . . They are the magi."

"A Municipal Report," another of O. Henry's best-known stories, provides an especially good illustration of virtually all his mannerisms and devices. The story takes its cue from a statement of the novelist Frank Norris, quoted at the beginning, to the effect that there are only three big cities in the United States that are "story cities," New York, New Orleans, and San Francisco. "Fancy," Norris had said, "a novel about Chicago or Buffalo, let us say, or Nashville, Tennessee!" This, suggests O. Henry, is a rash statement, and he proceeds to tell a tale refuting it. It is part of O. Henry's irony that he leads the reader to believe in the first part of the story that Nashville is a humdrum place, this being the initial impression of the first-person narrator, who gets off the train in Nashville one evening and after settling himself in his hotel can find nothing of interest to observe or do. But then comes a striking contrast when O. Henry manufactures a plot utilizing coincidence and surprise, which indicates that there can be excitement and romance aplenty in this apparently dull town. And, says O. Henry at the end, "I wonder's what's doing in Buffalo!"

O. Henry's stories of Texas and of Central and South America often have much vivid descriptive detail, and their backgrounds seem authentic enough, but they are like his other stories in that they have little realism in their characters and actions. In **"A Double-Dyed Deceiver,"** for example, a desperado known as the Llano Kid kills a man in Texas and flees to South America. There an unscrupulous American consul persuades him to pose as the lost son of a wealthy couple, with the idea that the consul and the Kid will rob them. But the Kid has a heart of gold under his hard exterior, and is so moved by the joy of the woman who believes him her son that he refuses to go through with the plot. Furthermore, it turns out that it was the lost son whom the Kid had killed back in Texas, and therefore the Kid, to make restitution, will take his place. None of O. Henry's grafters, burglars, and robbers are really bad men either. O. Henry is said to have got the ideas for some of his stories of these characters from his prison experience, but if he achieved any insight there into criminal mentality and psychology, he made no attempt to portray it in his fiction. Instead, he wrote stories like **"Babes in the Woods,"** in which a confidence man comes from the West to New York confident that he can find all kind of dupes on whom to practice his trade, but who is himself taken in. Some of these stories, however, like **"The Man Higher Up,"** which is one of several about a grafter named Jeff Peters, are among O. Henry's most cleverly done pieces. An especially artful con-man yarn, and quite possibly O. Henry's funniest story, is **"The Ransom of Red Chief,"** in which a kidnaping plot ludicrously boomerangs on its perpetrators. And there is the gentleman burglar who goes straight in **"A Retrieved Reformation,"** whose name became a household word when O. Henry's story was made into the highly popular play *Alias Jimmy Valentine.*

Besides his great popularity with readers, O. Henry also received much adulation from contemporary critics. He was often spoken of a "a Yankee Maupassant" and praised for his literary artistry and broad understanding of humanity. Although no one today would attribute these qualities to his stories, they have a special verve, freshness, and good humor which make for their continued readability, as witnessed by the fact that they are still frequently anthologized. . . . (pp. 122-26)

> *Arthur Voss, "The Rise of the Journalistic Short Story: O. Henry and His Predecessors," in his* The American Short Story: A Critical Survey, *University of Oklahoma Press, 1973, pp. 114-26.*

MARTIN B. OSTROFSKY (essay date 1981)

[*In the excerpt below, Ostrofsky documents O. Henry's use of stereotypes in his New York stories.*]

The short story was a prominent form of literature in the United States during the first couple decades of the twentieth century, and the most dominant influence upon short story writing during this period was O. Henry. . . . Although some of the stories for which he is most famous take place in other locations, O. Henry has always been closely associated with New York City, the location for the bulk of his work. One major contributing factor to O. Henry's success was that he employed a wide body of stereotypes of New York City and of New Yorkers in his stories, which aided him in producing his work and which helped insure his popularity. The use of stereotypes in O. Henry's New York City stories provides an excellent display of the application of folklore in literature. (p. 41)

Shortly after his arrival in New York City in 1902, O. Henry burst upon the scene of popular literature. O. Henry's short

stories soon appeared in syndicated magazines, in newspapers, and after a while, as collections in book form. During the short duration of his literary career in New York, O. Henry became a leading influence upon the state of the art of the short story, leaving behind many imitators in his wake.

The reasons for the quick acceptance and immense popularity of O. Henry's stories are many. O. Henry was expert at combining the proper proportions of humor, romance, sentimentality and sensation in his stories to keep the average reader interested week after week. Adding to his appeal as a popular writer, O. Henry's style of writing is light and chummy. O. Henry does not appear as a remote narrator, but almost as a physical presence in front of the reader, telling stories, trading jokes, familiar and intimate. At the same time, however, that O. Henry is playing the role of the convivial storyteller, often employing overly romanticized characters and situations, he is also adding just the right touch of realism. O. Henry makes abundant use of slang and dialect in his stories, giving his characters some illusion of reality. Moreover, one of O. Henry's most notable traits is his ability to concisely and accurately describe the locale of his stories, which gives them a flavor of authenticity.

The fusion of romantic sentimentality with the sense of realism in O. Henry's stories does much to endear them to the public. In effect, O. Henry creates an illusionary world of his own in which he presents a conflict between real life and life as we would wish it to be. In his make believe world, cloaked in the trappings of reality, O. Henry can manipulate the characters at will, creating denouements which satisfy our common desires. O. Henry resolves the conflict between real life and life as we would wish it, by creating a seemingly real situation, but then distorting, exaggerating, and often mocking it. In his stories, O. Henry plays the game of life by his own rules, and because of the intimate relationship he develops with his audience, his readers can play too. Not all of O. Henry's stories have happy endings. This adds to their appeal because the element of surprise keeps the readers continually alert and interested. The tension created by even the most tragic of O. Henry's stories, however, is relieved by some final comic remark, which allows the story social comment and impact without overly disconcerting the audience.

Equally as important as O. Henry's use of romanticism and realism is his profuse employment of humor. By a pervasive use of humor in his stories, O. Henry maintains a light and chatty atmosphere which makes them interesting and yet easy to read—traits which would have appealed especially to the newly literate masses at the turn of the century. O. Henry's use of humor also links his stories to a long tradition of humor as a characteristic element in American folklore and literature. The exaggerated, irreverent and sometimes selfmocking humor which O. Henry utilizes is typically American, and helps lend a peculiarly American spirit to his stories. O. Henry projects himself as the trickster; his audience must constantly be on the lookout for whatever he is going to pull next. O. Henry does not become malicious, however, and his humor is always mellowed by a sympathy for the human condition. By reflecting the overall spirit and values of his audience, O. Henry gives added impetus to his popularity.

In his short stories O. Henry combined the talents of the journalist, the humorist and the local-colorist. O. Henry had a superb command of vocabulary, which he could manipulate to achieve the effects he desired. With a few well-chosen words or sentences, O. Henry could effectively paint a locale, sketch a character, or describe a situation.

From a technical viewpoint, O. Henry's work has been described as mechanical. The mechanical nature of O. Henry's stories is attested to by the schools of imitators which arose in his stead. Although his imitators could never capture that unique spark of individual talent and spirit which was O. Henry's, they strived diligently at duplicating his manner of storywriting. O. Henry relied heavily upon the use of formulas when writing his short stories. All of O. Henry's stories may easily be dissected to show the use of such formulae as the seemingly irrelevant opening, the adoption of recurring themes, the continual use of various humorous devices, and the surprise ending.

The incessant use of formulas in O. Henry's stories served a necessary purpose. O. Henry spent his income freely and was in continual need of money. In order to provide for his financial needs, O. Henry tried to write and sell stories as frequently as he could to newspapers and syndicated magazines. The media which O. Henry wrote for catered to a mass audience, so O. Henry strived to produce stories which would have the greatest popular appeal. By continuously utilizing tried and true formulas for his structure, themes and idiom, O. Henry was able to quickly turn out stories in great numbers. Through his own ingenuity and prowess with language and humor, O. Henry was able to revitalize well accepted formulae and breathe new life into them. So adept was he at reworking his stock of formulas that O. Henry's works became not only immensely popular but were often acclaimed as brilliant and original creations.

Among the various kinds of formulas employed by O. Henry are his stereotypical depictions of characters and of setting. By using sterotypes of New York City and of New Yorkers in his stories, O. Henry is fulfilling the same functions as he does with the other formulas he utilizes. O. Henry's use of stereotypes helped him to write his stories quicker, so as to meet publication deadlines and financial needs. The stereotypes in O. Henry's stories also helped the stories gain mass appeal because they presented characters and situations which were readily accepted and popularly understood by the reading public. When the reader encounters an already accepted stereotype, he immediately perceives the situation O. Henry is projecting, and feels familiarly comfortable with it. At the same time that O. Henry gains the reader's understanding and familiarity by using stereotypes, he also economizes his storytelling and moves swiftly along with his narrative. Stereotypes play an indispensible role in the structure, characterization, development and success of O. Henry's short stories. (pp. 42-5)

The study of the process of stereotypes invites comment from several disciplines, including folklore. Scholars from various fields have recognized the utility of the application of folkloristic theory and methodology to stereotypical studies. One pioneer study conducted by Bayrd Still asserts that many cities are often defined by stereotypical "personalities" which are determined by such influences as architecture, odor and population. Still examines the personality of New York City, and cites four major attributes which have historically characterized the city: business-mindedness, conviviality, cosmopolitanism, and constant change. The attributes with which Still defines New York City are all to be found in O. Henry's stories. The trait of "notoriety," however, plays a significant role

in O. Henry's stories, and will therefore replace "constant change" as a category for this article.

O. Henry was aware of the reputed personalities of cities, and seized upon city stereotypes as subject matter for several of his stories. When describing the travels of the vagabond Raggles, O. Henry informs us:

> Through the ancient poets we have learned that the cities are feminine. So they were to poet Raggles; and his mind carried a concrete and clear conception of the figure that symbolized and typified each one that he had wooed.

O. Henry illustrates his observations on the personalities of cities with brief, personified descriptions of Chicago, Pittsburg, New Orleans, Boston, Louisville and St. Louis. New York City, however, poses an unprecedented challenge to Raggles, and his attempts to define New York provide the theme for **"The Making of a New Yorker."**

The search for a definitive formula with which to define New York City in O. Henry's stories does not rest with Raggles alone. The theme of **"The Voice of the City"** centers on the narrator's endeavors to isolate the essence of New York:

> Here are 4,000,000 people . . . compressed upon an island, which is mostly lamb surrounded by Wall Street water. The conjunction of so many units into so small a space must result in an identity-or, rather a homogeneity—that finds its oral expression through a common channel. It is, as you might say, a consensus of translation, concentrating in a crystallized, general idea which reveals itself in what may be termed the Voice of the City.

Once again O. Henry takes the opportunity to contrast New York with other major American cities. Contrast is a device which frequently appears in American folk humor, as in the "Arkansas Traveler" genre of anecdotes which pit the country rube against the city slicker. In stories such as **"The Pride of the Cities," "The Call of the Tame," "The Poet and the Peasant,"** and **"Elsie in New York,"** O. Henry contrasts New Yorkers with out-of-towners and in doing so, distinguishes between New York and other cities.

Business-mindedness is the trait which Still regards as the most prevalent characteristic of New York City. Beginning with its origin as the Dutch trading post of New Amsterdam, New York has had a vital interest in commerce and finance. New York's historic link with business resulted in a set of stereotypes which reduced the city's integral and complex commercial ties to simple and easily defined formulas.

One stereotype adapted by O. Henry, which reflects New York City's business-mindedness, is the preoccupation of New Yorkers with money and business. Occasional references appear in O. Henry's stories citing New Yorkers' mercenary interests, such as when he states that "there are many . . . who go their ways, making money, without turning to the right or the left. . . ." O. Henry even utilizes the stereotype of preoccupation with business so that it is essential to the plot and characterization of one story. In **"The Romance of a Busy Broker,"** Harvey Maxwell quickly enters his office and immediately throws himself into his work: "The machine sitting at that desk was no longer a man; it was a busy New York broker, moved by buzzing wheels and uncoiling springs." O. Henry's choice of language is significant. Mr. Maxwell is not described by O. Henry in terms which set him apart as a unique and complex character, but rather as a carbon copy of every other New York broker. The image that O. Henry conjures up of a New York broker is a businessman, in perpetual motion, totally devoted to his work and oblivious to all else. . . . By using unrestrained exaggeration as one of his stylistic devices, O. Henry plays upon the picture he has drawn of a typical New York broker, so as to achieve a surprise ending for his tale. Mr. Maxwell proposes to Miss Leslie, his stenographer, only to find out that in his preoccupation with business he had forgotten that they were already married the evening before!

Closely related to the stereotype which depicts New York City and its inhabitants as being preoccupied with business are those stereotypes which depict the continual hustle and bustle and pandemonium of the city. New Yorkers are addicted to business, and their ardent pursuit of business necessitates ceaseless rushing and crowding and clamor. The crowds of rush-hour workers being conveyed to and from their jobs, the incessant din of machinery in action, and the unending round-the-clock activity of a city which lives for business, are all aspects of New York City's business-mindedness.

O. Henry clearly reflects stereotypes of the hustle and bustle of New York City when he writes about the "rush-hour tide of humanity" and describes the elevated railroad where "a flock of citizen sheep scrambled out and another flock scrambled aboard" as "the cattle cars of the Manhattan Elevated rattled away." O. Henry meticulously depicts the discord of the city where "the elevated crashed raucously, surface cars hummed and clanged, cabmen swore, newsboys shrieked, wheels clattered ear piercingly," and from whose heights New Yorkers appear "like the irresponsible black waterbugs on summer ponds [where] they crawl and circle and hustle about idiotically without aim or purpose."

Even the outcome of one of O. Henry's romances hinges on the chaos and congestion of New York City's traffic. In **"Mammon and the Archer,"** a millionaire's son wishes to propose to the woman he loves before she embarks for a prolonged stay in Europe, but her busy schedule will not allow him ample time alone with her to pop the question. The millionaire, knowing his son's problem, engineers a traffic jam. . . . The traffic jam lasts for two hours, during which time the millionaire's son and his lady-love become engaged.

Another stereotype directly related to the business-mindedness of New York City is its cold indifference. New York is often pictured as a huge, crowded metropolis, populated by citizens who rush about concerned only with their personal business, and indifferent to all else. The lack of concern that New Yorkers are reputed to have for the affairs of others adds the element of anonymity to stereotypes of the city. The concept of being "lost in the crowd" develops, in which one may be surrounded by masses of people and yet remain unnoticed by any of them.

O. Henry delights in portraying scenes of newcomers first arriving in New York. A young man from upstate pays a visit to New York City, and

> knowingly, smilingly, the city crowds passed him by. They saw the raw stranger stand in the gutter and stretch his neck at the tall buildings. At this they ceased to smile, and even to look at him. It had been done so often. . . . Even the newsboys looked bored when he scampered like a circus clown out of the way of cabs and street cars.

In another of O. Henry's stories a Russian immigrant arrives, "pleased by the roar, and movement of the barbarous city" where "light as a cork, he was kept bobbing along by the human tide, the crudest atom in all the silt of the stream that emptied into the reservoir of Liberty." In yet another story by O. Henry, a Columbian general confronted by the noise and confusion of New York City exclaims: " 'Válgame Dios! What devil's city is this?' " Perhaps remembrances of his own arrival in New York prompted O. Henry to time and again depict such scenes.

O. Henry not only utilizes the stereotype of New York City's cold indifference in descriptive phrases and passages, but he occasionally incorporates the stereotype as a theme for his stories as well. Sometimes the theme of New York's indifference takes on a comical guise, as in the story of two Kentucky mountaineers who are caught up in a long and bloody feud. One of the mountaineers learns that the other is living in New York City, so he arms himself and travels to the city to kill his foe. Upon his arrival in New York the mountaineer is so disoriented and lonely, that when he does chance upon his enemy he is overjoyed at seeing a familiar face, and they clasp in friendship. Occasionally O. Henry ends a story in tragedy. In one story a young man and women succumb to poverty, overwork and frustrated hopes. Finding no source of comfort in the callous, impersonal city, they commit suicide— "transients in abode, transients in heart and mind."

Although O. Henry often depicts New York City as cold and indifferent, he also tends to reveal an underlying warmth and humanity which is not always apparent at first glance. In even the most squalid and dehumanizing surroundings, O. Henry's characters are generally possessed of a kindliness and human dignity which displays itself in self-sacrifice and concern for other people. New Yorkers may seem to be frozen in indifference, but in O. Henry's words:

> When a New Yorker does loosen up . . . it's like the spring decomposition of the jam in the Allegheny River. He'll swamp you with cracked ice and backwater if you don't get out of the way.

O. Henry's characters do not always demonstrate vehement outpourings of affection, but they usually do display at least a subtle gloss of benevolence. The good nature and nobility of some of O. Henry's characters may not seem realistic, but he is not striving for realism beyond the outward appearance of the story's setting. O. Henry is writing fanciful stories which will cater to the romantic sensibilities of the popular audience. The stereotype of the warmheartedness of New Yorkers, which is probably much more esoteric in nature, exists side by side with the stereotype of their cold indifference. By placing benevolent, self-sacrificing, noble characters in the midst of a seemingly callous and indifferent environment, O. Henry is creating a conflict which is usually resolved to the audience's satisfaction. (pp. 45-50)

One of the most popular pictures of O. Henry held by the public, which was fostered by his admirers, critics and biographers, was of an anonymous but gregarious stranger who scoured the streets of New York, visiting the haunts of both the high and the low with equal facility and impunity, in search of incidents and impressions which he would transform into stories. O. Henry's wanderings often led him to various establishments for food and drink throughout the city, such as those which lined Broadway, the Bowery and Greenwich Village. The profusion of saloons, bars, cafés, rathskellers, roof-gardens and restaurants in his stories testify to the significant role that such places played in O. Henry's view of New York City and the life he lived there.

Restaurants, cafés, and other related establishments appear regularly in O. Henry's stories, and range in variety from rough little saloons to fancy restaurants which provide orchestral entertainment. O. Henry frequently makes reference to various sorts of restaurants and cafés to provide the setting of a story or to advance the action of the plot. Food and drink establishments are often the scene, and sometimes the impetus, for business and social interaction in O. Henry's stories, and occasionally play a major role in the plot of a story. The plot of **"The Halberdier of the Little Rheinschloss,"** and the denouements of **"A Philistine in Bohemia"** and **"A Bird of Bagdad,"** for example, hinge on O. Henry's manipulation of restaurant life in those stories. Perhaps the final indictment of the intoxicating influence of New York City's stereotypical abundance of food and drink is Greenbriar Nye's conversion from a preference for the rugged life of the West, to the comforts of the city, when "he saw a New York restaurant crowd enjoying itself."

Resorts for drinking and dining are but one outlet for entertainment in O. Henry's New York. Theaters not only serve to attract young newcomers to New York in search of fame and fortune, but they are also a great source of diversion for the city's residents and tourists. O. Henry himself was known to have had a fondness for frequenting many of the less reputable, and more common, sources of public amusement such as saloons and vaudeville theaters. O. Henry's choice of theatrical settings seems to have been largely dictated by his own personal tastes in entertainment, for he concentrates primarily on musical comedy and vaudeville, while he tends to neglect the elite theater, opera, ballet, and symphony concerts.

The theater, whether mentioned in brief or at length by O. Henry, often exercises a profound, if not always evident, influence on its performers and their audience. The vaudeville team of Hart and Cherry, for instance, is the subject of one O. Henry yarn, and he describes them in considerable detail. Bob Hart had traveled the country for four years performing an act which included "a monologue, three lightning changes with songs, a couple of imitations of celebrated imitators, and a buck-and-wing dance that had drawn a glance of approval from the base-viol player in more than one house—than which no performer ever received more satisfactory evidence of good work." Winona Cherry is discovered by Bob while she is doing character songs and impersonations at a rival theater, and the two of them join together to perform a sketch written by Bob called "Mice Will Play." The sketch, of which O. Henry gives a lengthy description, is a big success for Hart and Cherry, and launches them on a successful career. Hart and Cherry are veteran troopers on the stage, but what of the audience they try so hard to entertain? Seeking an evening's enjoyment, and a little diversion from their everyday toil, Dan Owens suggests "a little vaudeville" to his companions Nancy and Lou. O. Henry shows insight into the importance of theater to the common working classes when Dan asks, "How about looking at stage diamonds since we can't shake hands with the real sparklers?"

The various saloons, restaurants and theaters which dot the pages of O. Henry's stories are the major sources of amusement and social interaction for his characters, but other diversions do occasionally appear. Miss Claribel Colby is drowsy following a night of frolic at the annual ball and oys-

ter fry of the West Side Wholesale Fish Dealers' Assistants' Social Club No. 2, while Kid Mullaly and Liz face their destinies at the bi-monthly dance of the Small Hours Social Club. Norah O'Donovan spends part of her wedding night riding a cab through Central Park and playing at a casino there, while Kid McGarry helps lead a police raid on an illicit gambling den. Even organ grinders, at one time a common fixture on New York City streets, provide inexpensive entertainment to the city's residents. (pp. 51-3)

Coney Island plays a prominent role in several of O. Henry's stories. The predictions of a fortune-teller plying her trade at Coney Island help Daniel Tobin find his lost sweetheart, Katie Mahorner, newly arrived from County Sligo, Ireland. Another colleen, Norah Flynn, and her boyfriend Dennis Carnaham, quarrel at the Dairymen and Street-Sprinkler Drivers' semi-annual ball. Against a background of the sights and wonders of Coney Island, which O. Henry describes in some detail, Dennis and Norah each wander to a secluded spot, where they meet and make up. The marriage plans of millionaire Irving Carter are, however, thwarted when the shopgirl he loves, Masie, mistakes his proposed honeymoon in Europe for a trip to Coney Island. The impact that Coney Island has upon another of O. Henry's millionaires is perhaps more dramatic. Blinker was spoiled, bored, thoughtless and class-conscious, until one day he ventures to Coney Island and meets a shopgirl named Florence. Blinker is at first contemptuous of the plebian multitude surrounding him, but his opinion is altered when he realizes that Florence sees him as the "holder of the keys to the enchanted city of fun." . . . Unfortunately, Blinker's awakening to the plight of his fellow man is too late, for he is separated from Florence, who lives in one of the slums he owns.

New York City's vast reservoir of amusements and entertainment, coupled with the sheer size and variety of its population, earned it the stereotype of a haven for excitement and adventure. O. Henry echoes the popular stereotype of New York City when he states that "in the big city the twin spirits Romance and Adventure are always abroad seeking worthy wooers." The abundance of places of interest in New York resulted in the development of a sightseeing industry to cater to the tourist trade, which included "rubber-neck wagons." O. Henry incorporates a sightseeing tour bus in a story, referring to it as "the Rubberneck Auto" and "the Glaring-at-Gotham car." So compelling is the tendency for diversion that "the sidewalk was blockaded with sightseers who had gathered to stare at sightseers, justifying the natural law that every creature on earth is preyed upon by some other creature." In his characteristic manner, O. Henry exaggerates the propensity of the curious to seek out events and objects of interest in "the Caoutchouc City." William Pry and Violet Seymour are such devoted rubber-neckers (as suggested by their surnames), that on the day of their wedding a search for the missing bride and groom reveals, that because of habit, they have joined the crowd of onlookers trying to see the ceremony.

The exotic and adventurous nature of New York City is epitomized by O. Henry's frequent comparisons of New York with the Bagdad of the monumental collection of Arabic folktales, *The Thousand and One Arabian Nights*. O. Henry takes great delight in drawing parallels between the legendary Bagdad and New York City:

> Night had fallen on that great and beautiful city
> known as Bagdad-on-the-Subway. And with the

night came the enchanted glamour that belongs not to Arabia alone. In different masquerade the streets, bazaars, and walled houses of the occidental city of romance were filled with the same kind of folk that so much interested our interesting old friend, the late Mr. H. A. Rashid. They wore clothes eleven hundred years nearer to the latest styles that H. A. saw in old Bagdad; but they were about the same people underneath. With the eye of faith, you could have seen the Little Hunchback, Sinbad the Sailor, Fitbad the Tailor, the Beautiful Persian, the one-eyed Calenders, Ali Baba and Forty Robbers on every block, and the Barber and his Six Brothers, and all the old Arabian gang easily.

By utilizing his familiarity with folktales, O. Henry was able to embellish stereotypes of New York City, and give them new vitality and appeal. (pp. 53-5)

Many of the characters in O. Henry's New York actually come from outside of the city. Artists, writers, shopgirls and other young people in O. Henry's stories, seeking independence and careers, come to the city from places such as Greenburg, New York or Harmony, Vermont. Businessmen who hail from cities such as Nome, Alaska and Cactus City, Texas arrive in New York to fulfill the obligations and duties of their respective businesses. Tourists and honeymoon couples visit New York in O. Henry's stories from such places as Cloverdale, Missouri and Topaz City, Nevada. (pp. 55-6)

The cosmopolitan stereotype of New York City implies much more than the city being a focal point for citizens from all over the United States; it implies that New York is heavily affected by influences from all over the world. One avenue for the international, particularly European, influence on New York City is the globe-trotting habits of the rich. O. Henry depicts several characters such as Honoria Clinton, who is preparing to embark for an overseas journey, and Mrs. Chalmers, who is on a European tour. One of O. Henry's better traveled characters is Ives, who returned to New York "from a three years' ramble around the globe."

The major source of international influence on New York City, and the city's primary claim to cosmopolitanism, is the diversity of its ethnic population. The period during which O. Henry lived in New York, 1902 to 1910, was a time when immigration to the United States reached unprecedented levels. New York was thronged with masses of immigrants from all the nations of the world, and the city's streets became a colorful tapestry of dress and sounds as varied ethnic communities grew and mingled. . . . O. Henry drew upon the unique experience of the mass turn-of-the-century immigration to New York, and used it to color his tales.

In **"The City of Dreadful Night"** O. Henry playfully depicts the residents of an apartment house named Beersheba Flats during a heat spell, refering to their different national origins:

> Now, 'twas a peaceful and happy home that all of us had in them same Beersheba Flats. The O'Dowds and the Steinowitzes and the Callahans and the Cohens and the Spizzinellis and the Joneses—all the nations of us, we lived like one big family together.

One trait of O. Henry's style, which may be noticed in the preceding quote, is that although he is actually describing the dreadful conditions of a crowded tenement, conditions which received vigorous condemnation from muckrakers and lead-

ing citizens at the time, he glosses over the full severity of the situation. O. Henry is not unaware of the true nature of tenement housing, but for the sake of effecting a light and humorous tale, he draws his picture of tenement life with tongue-in-cheek.

A second quirk of O. Henry's may be garnered from the language of the foregoing quote—the narrator is speaking with an Irish accent. The Irish were indeed the dominating immigrant force in New York during the nineteenth century, and the Celtic influence upon all facets of New York life was intense, but by the time that O. Henry came to New York, Central, East and Southern European immigrants were arriving in huge numbers. O. Henry does portray a few of the newer immigrants in his stories. For example, Demetre Svangvsk, in **"The Foreign Policy of Company 99,"** is Russian; Kenwitz, in **"The Unknown Quantity,"** is an East European Jew; and Tony Spinelli, in **"The Coming-Out of Maggie,"** is Italian. When using Italian characters, however, as in **"The Coming-Out of Maggie"** or **"The Transformation of Martin Burney,"** O. Henry tends to compare them unfavorably with the Irish, employing such epithets as "Dago" and "Guinea." The majority of O. Henry's working class characters are Irish, and he even has the Statue of Liberty adopt an Irish brogue:

> . . . I was made by a Dago and presented to the American people on behalf of the French Government for the purpose of welcomin' Irish immigrants into the Dutch city of New York.

Four reasons may account for O. Henry's disportionate representation of the Irish in his stories. For one thing, he may have found it easier to relate to Irish culture than to the more exotic, non-English speaking cultures of other immigrants. In the second place, by the turn-of-the-century the Irish had become well established in the journalistic field in New York, and O. Henry probably rubbed elbows with Irish colleagues. Thirdly, the greater part of O. Henry's audience were probably Irish (many of the newer immigrants could not yet read English), and he had to appeal to their tastes. Finally, the stereotype of New York City as an Irish city had developed during the last couple decades of the nineteenth century, and O. Henry was drawing upon already existent stereotypes to write his stories, even if the stereotypes did not correspond exactly with reality.

The surge of immigrants and migrant Americans who

Allegedly O. Henry's favorite photograph of himself.

flocked to New York City during the nineteenth century resulted in overcrowded, depressed neighborhoods where dirt, unemployment and crime became rampant. Prostitution, drinking, gambling and other sundry vices thrived in areas of New York City, and vagrants and street gypsies (homeless children) were prolific. Street gangs whose practices ranged from robbery to an occasional murder arose in some districts. Fueled by the incidence of such crimes, the stereotype of New York City's notoriety developed, which magnified the city's vices. New York's stereotypical notoriety was evidenced by scores of publications, popular during the nineteenth century, which warned prospective visitors of the dangers and sins of the city while creating an unsavory yet sensational lure. O. Henry utilized the stereotype of New York's notoriety to add a bit of spice and pseudo-realism to his stories.

The Five Points district of lower Manhattan was, during much of the nineteenth century, the city's most infamous slum, and a breeding place for dirt, poverty and crime. Towards the end of the nineteenth century, as the city expanded northwards, the slum districts extended to include the Lower East Side and Hell's Kitchen. The Lower East Side appears in several of O. Henry's stories, as in **"The Social Triangle."** . . . The Lower East Side also provides the setting for **"Past One at Rooney's,"** a tale precipitated by the rivalry of the Mulberry Hill Gang and the Dry Dock Gang. **"Past One at Rooney's"** leans heavily upon the stereotype of New York City's notoriety: it includes gang warfare, a knifing, crooked politicians, a disreputable bar, a reference to drugs, women smoking, illegal drinking, a police raid, and policemen on the take. The theme of **"Past One at Rooney's"** revolves around the romance of gang member Cork McManus and Fanny. Fanny is a prostitute, a rare character in an O. Henry story. Despite the scandalous and seemingly realistic trappings of the story, Cork and Fanny's courtship takes on an idealistic, romantic tone which results in a happy ending.

Much further to the north of the Lower East Side, on the west side of Manhattan, was Hell's Kitchen. In **"Vanity and Some Sables,"** O. Henry describes a few of the denizens of the area:

> The Stovepipe Gang borrowed its name from a subdistrict of the city called the 'Stovepipe,' which is a narrow and natural extension of the familiar district known as 'Hell's Kitchen.' The 'Stovepipe' strip of town runs along Eleventh and Twelfth avenues on the river, and bends a hard and sooty elbow around little, lost, homeless De Witt Clinton park. Consider that a stovepipe is an important factor in any kitchen and the situation is analyzed. The chefs in 'Hell's Kitchen' are many, and the 'Stovepipe' gang wears the cordon blue.

> The members of this unchartered but widely known brotherhood appeared to pass their time on street corners arrayed like the lilies of the conservatory and busy with nail files and penknives. Thus displayed as a guarantee of good faith, they carried on an innocuous conversation in a 200-word vocabularly, to the casual observer as innocent and immaterial as that heard in the clubs seven blocks to the east.

The members of the Stovepipe Gang, however, are far from innocent loiterers. O. Henry's description of their activities is colored with the sensational flair which characterizes the popular stereotype of Hell's Kitchen:

> . . . off exhibition the 'Stovepipes' were not mere street corner ornaments addicted to posing and manicuring. Their serious occupation was the separating of citizens from their coin and valuables. Preferably this was done by weird and singular tricks without noise or bloodshed; but whenever the citizen honored by their attentions refused to impoverish himself gracefully, his objections came to be spread finally upon some police station blotter or hospital register.

> The police held the 'Stovepipe' gang in perpetual suspicion and respect. As the nightingale's liquid note is heard in the deepest shadows, so along the 'Stovepipe's' dark and narrow confines the whistle for reserves punctures the dull ear of night. Whenever there was smoke in the 'Stovepipe' the tasselled men in blue knew there was a fire in 'Hell's Kitchen.'

Kid Brady, an ex-member of the Stovepipe Gang, and his fiancée, Molly McKeever, stumble into an awkward situation, but his sense of honor and her "stubborn true-heartedness" save the day. As ominous as the characters and locale of **"Vanity and Some Sables"** may have sounded, the story remains consistent with O. Henry's light, romanticized style.

Although O. Henry often made sly, sarcastic comments on society and its institutions, only occasionally did social comment actually become the theme of his stories. One of O. Henry's most powerful social commentaries is **"The Guilty Party."** **"The Guilty Party"** is a tragedy which takes place in the Lower East Side. . . . The protagonist of the story is Liz, the quiet daughter of a neglectful father, who is drawn to the ways of the street by her boyfriend, Kid Mullaly. The Kid decides to take someone else to the bi-monthly dance of the Small Hours Social Club, and a vengeful Liz searches for him. . . . Liz comes upon the Kid, and the encounter results in murder and suicide. O. Henry glosses over the full impact of the tragedy by adding a biting yet humorous ending to the story; nevertheless, **"The Guilty Party"** remains a shocking indictment of slum life in New York City. (pp. 56-61)

The focus of the article has been upon stereotypes of the city's personality, but O. Henry makes free and effective use of stereotypes of New York's citizens as well. Stereotypical character types are employed to represent members of various ethnic, social and occupational groups. . . . In **"The Trimmed Lamp"** O. Henry begins his introduction of Nancy by saying:

> Nancy you would call a shop-girl—because you have the habit. There is no type; but a perverse generation is always seeking a type; so this is what the type should be.

In his inimitable and forthright style, O. Henry has no qualms about coming straight out and telling his audience that he is employing stereotypes to gratify their expectations. (pp. 61-2)

Martin B. Ostrofsky, "O. Henry's Use of Stereotypes in His New York City Stories: An Example of the Utilization of Folklore in Literature," in New York Folklore, *Vol. 7, Nos. 1-2, Summer, 1981, pp. 41-64.*

KAREN CHARMAINE BLANSFIELD (essay date 1988)

[*In the essay excerpted below, Blansfield explores O. Henry's role as a popular artist, employing the* auteur *theory of criticism, which Blansfield describes as an approach that empha-*

sizes an artist's "entire body of material to discover and analyze structural characteristics and stylistic motifs."]

As a popular artist, Porter shares company with a host of literary luminaries: Homer, Shakespeare, Twain, Hugo, Dickens, Melville, and innumerable others. Like them, he stirred the mass imagination, drawing for material from the world about him, probing the foibles, dilemmas, comedies, and tragedies of human existence, speaking in a voice that could be understood by the multitudes.

This communal kinship lies at the heart of Porter's popularity, as it does for any popular artist. The public could identify with and respond to the people, places, and situations Porter wrote about. His stories offered the escape from daily drudgery so desperately needed by "the four million" and fulfilled the fantasies—if only vicariously—they so often longed for. [In his essay "Oh What A Man Was O. Henry," published in the *Kenyon Review* (November 1967), William Saroyan stated]: "The people of America loved O. Henry. . . . He was a nobody, but he was a nobody who was also a somebody, everybody's somebody."

Porter, of course, calculated this success to some degree; he knew his audience and gave them what they wanted. "We have got to respect the conventions and delusions of the public to a certain extent," he wrote to his prison comrade Al Jennings. "In order to please John Wanamaker, we will have to assume a virtue that we do not possess." Nevertheless, he perceived his subjects with a compassion and understanding that is unquestionably sincere. He specialized in humanity but did not exploit it. He accepted,

> with a mixture of irony, wit, and sympathy, the distressing fact that a human being can be a clerk, the remarkable fact that a clerk can be a human being. . . .
>
> To O. Henry, . . . the clerk is neither abnormal nor subnormal. He writes of him without patronizing him. He realizes the essential and stupendous truth that to himself the clerk is not pitiable.

Besides, Porter spins a good yarn, and he can turn a phrase as few authors ever have, rambling on in an easy, neighborly manner that slaps the reader on the shoulder, bandying an insouciant humor, and displaying a verbal range and precision that is astounding. He is a born raconteur; to listen to him is irresistible.

Above all, he is a master of technique. Even his severest critics acknowledge that as a designer of stories Porter "ranked supreme." His manipulation of elements into a tight literary structure . . . is effective, if mechanical, and were one aspect of Porter's art to be held up as the most important or memorable, it would surely be this one. (pp. 28-9)

All of these characteristics—his empathy for his fellow man, his sharp scrutiny of public demand, and his skill at the narrative craft—contribute to Porter's vast popularity. Furthermore, one other feature essential to popular art—wide-spread distribution—also accelerated Porter's rise to literary fame. . . . [The] superfluity of magazines and the tremendous need for material were propitious conditions for the fledgling author; joined with his talents and the public's desire, they propelled Porter into a position as a popular and widely read writer.

In the decades since, his stories have been anthologized, col-lected, and reprinted; they have been translated into numerous foreign languages; they have been performed as radio, stage, and television drama, with some also made into films. (p. 29)

Such broad appeal is the domain of the popular artist, be he author, musician, performer, painter, or other creative type. Although he manifests a style distinctly his own and is recognizable by his particular manner, the popular artist conforms to certain expectations, presenting his material in forms familiar to his audiences and mirroring the joys and frustrations, the excitement and ennui of their everyday lives. This direct, personal relationship is one which the popular artist strives for, aiming deliberately to reach and to please his readers or listeners. Unlike "elite" or "high" art, which springs from individual and aesthetic motives, or folk art, which tends to be anonymous and utilitarian, popular art purposely appeals to the masses, while displaying the unmistakable touch of a single creator. (p. 30)

The skills of Porter as popular performer fuse into a style as distinctive and memorable as Charlie Chaplin's or Alfred Hitchcock's, an indelible style which breathes "O. Henryism" into his tales. Two of the most predominant components of this style . . . are plot structures and character types. The most famous and easily recognized plot characteristic is, of course, the surprise ending, a trick which results from clever, careful strategy. Although Porter was certainly not the first writer to employ this device—de Maupassant being particularly inclined toward it—he popularized it and staked a peculiar claim upon it, so that it has come to be inextricably linked with him and dubbed "the O. Henry twist." In terms of characters, the most well-known is probably the shopgirl, a type which, again, is invariably associated with the writer.

Other idiosyncrasies also contribute to the "O. Henryism" that generated such enthusiastic response: the folksy narrative voice, confidential asides to the reader, intricate and sometimes outrageous language and dialogue, full-blown metaphors, hyperbole, and copious allusions.

Porter embroiders all these elements together to form a personal style that distinguishes his work from that of other popular writers, even though such writers may employ similar or identical devices. Less skillful popular artists may depend so heavily upon story formula or character stereotypes to accomplish their purposes that individual artistry is obliterated; indeed, a whole slew of nineteenth-century fiction manufacturers churned out material in such quantity and such anonymity that their work "was more or less comparable to the product of machines," and authors were easily interchangeable—names like Horatio Alger, Jr., Laura Jean Libbey, Edward Stratemeyer, and Edward Judson pertain. But a popular artist like Porter is an essential creative force behind his products; his shaping hand is always apparent, and his presence within his work helps to establish the rapport so important to the popular artist. As one critic points out, "To read him is at times almost to feel his physical presence."

This unique style, a compilation of several elements, defines Porter's work internally as well as externally. Besides setting him apart from other popular writers, Porter's style constitutes a kind of formula which recurs within and defines his own body of work. This evolution of a personal, recognizable formula is intrinsic to popular art: "the quality of stylization and convention" that is so important "becomes a kind of stereotyping, a processing of experience, a reliance upon formulae." In other words, the artist employs his selected materials—characters, settings, plots, etc.—over and over again, so that they become familiar aspects within his work, yet he also imbues them with a flavor distinctly his own. (pp. 30-1)

In a sense, because of the personal style that emerges through his recurrent use of specific literary elements, Porter can be considered an *auteur,* and the proposal to examine his body of work in terms of these elements is essentially the approach of *auteur* criticism. Originating in the 1950s as a mode of film criticism, the *auteur* theory offers a worthwhile model for analyzing and interpreting popular culture in general, as John Cawelti suggests in his seminal essay on the subject:

> The art of the *auteur* is that of turning a conventional and generally known and appreciated artistic formula into a medium of personal expression while at the same time giving us a version of the formula which is satisfying because it fulfills our basic expectations.
>
>   (p. 32)

For a popular artist like Porter, the *auteur* approach, with its emphasis on surveying an entire body of material to discover and analyze structural characteristics and stylistic motifs, seems particularly appropriate and useful. What is distinctive about *auteur* criticism is that it stresses "the whole *corpus*" of material rather than a single work, emphasizing recurring characteristics and themes; it "implies an operation of decipherment" and ultimately defines the *auteur*—the filmmaker, the author—in terms of these recurring elements, which come to be recognized as his particular style. "The strong director imposes his own personality on a film," [asserts Andrew Sarris in his *The American Cinema* (1968)], just as a writer can stamp his distinctive seal on his own creations. . . .

[Although not the *entire* body of Porter's work, the] New York stories form a singular portion of his literary output for several reasons: together, they comprise well over a third of his work; they are bound together by their urban characteristics; they were produced during the most significant period of his literary career; and they include most of the stories for which he is so well remembered. Furthermore, the recurring characteristics and themes which are discovered here through "an operation of decipherment" can then serve as models for examining Porter's other stories—of Texas, New Orleans, and South America—which display similar structural and character motifs though in different cultural contexts.

As a popular artist, Porter is similar to the type of filmmaker who emerges in *auteur* criticism, since the latter is essentially a cinematic popular artist. Both the *auteur* and the popular artist utilize formulaic elements of plot and character to create a personal, recognizable style, weaving new variations on old familiar themes. Both, in turn, develop this individual style into a kind of personal formula running through their work. Both are also confronted by similar restrictions—mainly, conventional limitations on characters, setting, and plots, and commercial demands in their given mediums. (p. 33)

So the identities of these two creative types are similar: like the popular artist, the *auteur* is neither absolutely original nor completely technical; rather, like the popular artist, he is, [as John C. Cawelti claims in *Popular Culture and the Expanding Consciousness* (1973)],

an individual creator who works within a framework of existing materials, conventional structures created by others, but he is more than a performer because he recreates those conventions to the point that they manifest at least in part the patterns of his own style and vision.

                                                          (pp. 33-4)

[The patterns] in the plots and characters of Porter's urban stories draw upon conventional situations, reinforce conventional values and expectations, and embody recognizable cultural types. By occurring repeatedly within the body of Porter's work, these plots and characters define it internally; by emulating more universal, archetypal patterns and characters, they achieve a broader recognition and a similarity to other artistic products, while remaining distinctive to Porter's art.

This continual recurrence of specific motifs, so central to Porter's art, to popular art, and to the theory of *auteur* criticism, constitutes the element of formula. For Porter, as for any popular artist, formula provides the fundamental structure for his art, and not surprisingly, it also contributes to his popular appeal. For as a constant and predictable pattern, formula is inherent to the cycle of human existence, and it also characterizes the earliest forms of literature most people learn—myths, fairy tales, songs, etc. Because it is so elemental, formula is familiar and comforting; it is an artistic expression of the subliminal human need for security and certainty in a life that promises just the opposite, and to some extent at least, the presence of formula in popular literature satisfies that need.

"High" or "elite" art, unlike popular or even folk art, lacks these elements of predictability and standardization, so that popular art is, by and large, the type most accessible to the ordinary individual, relating more closely to the experiences of everyday life and to the rhythms of existence. (p. 34)

In his important study *Adventure, Mystery and Romance: Formula Stories As Art and Popular Culture,* John Cawelti defines a literary formula as, in general, "a structure of narrative or dramatic conventions employed in a great number of individual works." This is a broad, encompassing definition, but in it Cawelti sets forth the two major elements of formulaic literature: convention and repetition.

The first major element is convention. As opposed to invention, which refers to original creations, convention denotes elements familiar to both the author and the reader. Conventions "consist of things like favorite plots, stereotyped characters, accepted ideas, commonly known metaphors and other linguistic devices, etc." While inventions, Cawelti says, confront us with new, previously unrecognized perceptions, "conventions represent familiar shared images and meanings and they assert an ongoing continuity of value." Conventions therefore may be cultural elements and thus be limited in their effect to a particular time, place, and people, or they may be universal and thus transcend such limitations. Or they may be fusions of these two aspects, with the universally held conventions being presented in terms of a specific cultural convention; thus, for example, Porter may present the familiar, universal character of the outcast in the cultural garb of the tramp, a figure who will, in turn, also be shaped by certain expectations. These two aspects of convention are equivalent to the more familiar terms "archetype" and "stereotype," the only difference between them being the range of their focus and the extent of their appeal.

Cawelti makes the same kind of distinction in defining formula, breaking the term down into two usages which, taken together, adequately define a literary formula. The first usage of the term, he says, "denotes a conventional way of treating some specific thing or person," such as Homer's epithets, standard similes and metaphors; and by extension, "any form of cultural stereotype commonly found in literature." What is important about this usage is its limited nature: "it refers to patterns of convention which are usually quite specific to a particular culture and period and do not mean the same outside this specific context." Porter's shopgirl, for example, who assumes specific characteristics as a type within the context of the stories, is a conventional embodiment of the innocent, vulnerable orphan, the same kind of role a young male Dickens character might play. But removed from Porter's stories or from the context of America's social and industrial conditions in the early twentieth century, the shopgirl would not convey the same meaning, while in the literature of another time or culture, the character of the shopgirl may assume different characteristics altogether from those she displays in Porter's stories. As Boris Ejxenbaum points out, "Tender stories about New York shopgirls have more appeal for the American reader" than for Russian readers [see excerpt dated 1925].

The second usage of the term "formula" encompasses larger plot types, which are not limited to specific cultures. Rather, these plot patterns "seem to represent story types that, if not universal in their appeal, have certainly been popular in many different cultures at many different times." They are, in other words, archetypal patterns: the adventure story, the romance, and the quest are three examples.

The fusion of these two usages—that is, the "synthesis of a number of specific cultural conventions with a more universal story form or archetype"—constitutes a formula. Put another way, formula can be defined as "a conventional system for structuring cultural products."

The other major element of formula, repetition, involves, like the term "convention," distinctions of degree. Within the context of one author's work—in this case Porter's urban short stories—repetition involves the frequency with which the author employs specific plot patterns and specific cultural elements. It is through such repetition that the works assume a formulaic nature. (pp. 35-6)

Secondly, repetition involves the frequency with which the plot patterns and cultural elements have been employed outside the context of the author's works. This is the universal aspect of repetition and the means by which plot patterns and specific elements become archetypal and serve as models of comparison for specific works. The existence of a universal story pattern, or of a general element such as a character type defined only by human traits, not bounded by cultural details, provides the standard of comparison for an author's works and the framework on which he can, with specific cultural elements, construct a story which will be relevant and meaningful to a certain group of people in a certain place and time.

Elements of repetition are quite apparent in Porter's urban short stories, for he draws recurringly upon a number of basic plot patterns and character types. Variations occur, of course, and not every single story can be neatly categorized according to plot and character; such extremism threatens to squeeze the life out of the literature. Still, in the nearly one hundred stories that deal with the city, recurrent plot pat-

terns and characters do emerge which can be identified and used as a means of classification.

The plots of these stories can be divided into four basic patterns, overlapping to some extent but nevertheless bearing distinguishing characteristics: they are the cross pattern, the habit pattern, the triangular pattern, and the quest pattern. All develop themes familiar to most readers: the cross pattern, for example, builds on the unexpected reunion; the habit pattern provides excitement by an unexpected change in routine; the triangular pattern inserts a new twist in the familiar love triangle, and the quest pattern is Porter's version of the adventure story. . . . Porter repeatedly uses these patterns, or some variation of them, in his stories.

The characters, too, can be divided into six basic types, although because they often play more than one role simultaneously, they are more difficult to classify definitively. These six types [are] the shopgirl, the habitual character, the lover, the aristocrat, the plebeian, and the tramp. . . . Each type is a composite of specific characteristics, such as appearance, lifestyle, and attitude—characteristics which identify the entire group, with little if any attention paid to individual tendencies. Furthermore, each character type responds to conventional expectations: the shopgirl is poor but brave; the habitual character sticks to the ordinary routine of domestic life; the lover places love above self-interest; the aristocrat places money below principle; the plebeian bears the standard marks of poverty; and the tramp sleeps on a park bench.

Thus, Porter draws upon a "conventional system" for structuring his stories. His plot patterns are formulaic within the context of his own works, for he uses a number of patterns repeatedly; they are also formulaic in their relationship to more standard universal models. His characters are formulaic because they appear repeatedly, as types, within the stories and also because they represent, underneath their garb of culture, more universal character types. This recurrence of character type and plot pattern, and the interweaving of specific cultural material with more universal standards, together form the basis of the formulaic art of Porter's urban short stories. (pp. 36-8)

> *Karen Charmaine Blansfield, in her* Cheap Rooms and Restless Hearts: A Study of Formula in the Urban Tales of William Sydney Porter, *Bowling Green State University Popular Press, 1988, 143 p.*

FURTHER READING

Abrams, Fred. "The Pseudonym 'O. Henry': A New Perspective." *Studies in Short Fiction* 15, No. 3 (Summer 1978): 327-29.
    Examines a number of theories about the origin of O. Henry's pen name.

Arnett, Ethel Stephens. *O. Henry from Polecat Creek.* Greensboro, N. C.: Piedmont Press, 1962, 240 p.
    Account of O. Henry's youth.

"Strange Opinions." *The Bookman* XLIV, No. 1 (September 1916): 31-3.
    Response to remarks made by Katharine Fullerton Gerould

concerning O. Henry during an interview with Joyce Kilmer (see Kilmer entry below).

Cannell, Margaret. "O. Henry's Linguistic Unconventionalities." *American Speech* XII, No. 4 (December 1937): 275-83.
Lively examination of O. Henry's unconventional, idiomatic use of language that, the critic maintains, is responsible for the widespread use of colloquialisms in modern fiction.

Clarkson, Paul S. "A Decomposition of *Cabbages and Kings.*" *American Literature* 7, No. 2 (May 1935): 195-202.
Traces the previous publications of the short stories that were gathered together as *Cabbages and Kings* and studies the ways in which O. Henry constructed a unifying plot.

Cooper, Frederic Taber. " 'O. Henry'." In his *Some American Story Tellers*, pp. 225-44. 1911. Reprint. Freeport, N. Y.: Books for Libraries Press, 1968.
Brief, sympathetic survey of O. Henry's life and career.

Courtney, Luther W. "O. Henry's Case Reconsidered." *American Literature* 14, No. 4 (January 1943): 361-71.
Reexamination of O. Henry's 1898 conviction on embezzlement charges, concluding that he was technically guilty.

Davis, Robert H., and Maurice, Arthur B. *The Caliph of Bagdad: Being Arabian Nights Flashes of the Life, Letters, and Work of O. Henry.* New York: D. Appleton and Co., 1931, 411 p.
Thorough biography quoting extensively from the letters and memoirs of friends, family members, and acquaintances of O. Henry as well as from his own letters.

Echols, Edward C. "O. Henry's 'Shaker of Attic Salt': Part I" and "O. Henry and the Classics: Part II." *The Classical Journal* 43, No. 8 (May 1948): 488-89: 44, No. 3 (December 1948): 209-10.
Demonstrates that O. Henry utilized an extensive background in classical literature for both serious and comic purposes in his stories.

Evans, Walter. " 'A Municipal Report': O. Henry and Postmodernism." *Tennessee Studies in Literature* XXVI (1981): 101-16.
Uses "A Municipal Report" to assert affinities between the fiction of O. Henry and that of such Postmodernist writers as Vladimir Nabokov, John Barth, Donald Barthelme, Robert Coover, and William Gass.

Fenton, James. "Set Form." *New Statesman* 88, No. 2259 (5 July 1974): 22.
Maintains that O. Henry produced awkwardly contrived stories and considers the famous surprise endings to be merely feeble devices.

Gallegly, Joseph. *From Alamo Plaza to Jack Harris's Saloon: O. Henry and the Southwest He Knew.* Paris: Mouton, 1970, 213 p.
Historical study of the social conditions prevailing in the areas of the American Southwest where O. Henry spent much of his early life. Gallegly presents some critical commentary on the stories that have Southwestern settings.

Gates, William Bran. "O. Henry and Shakspere." *The Shakespeare Bulletin* XIX, No. 1 (January 1944): 20-5.
Provides numerous examples of passages from O. Henry's stories that reflect or parody passages from Shakespeare's plays.

Green, Benny. "Oh, Henry!" *The Spectator* 232, No. 7617 (22 June 1974): 772.
Comments on the enduring popularity of O. Henry.

Harris, Richard C. *William Sydney Porter (O. Henry): A Reference Guide.* Boston: G. K. Hall, 1980, 229 p.
Comprehensive annotated bibliography of writings about O. Henry.

Henderson, Archibald. "O. Henry after a Decade." *The Southern Review* I, No. 4 (May 1920): 15-18.

A favorable reconsideration of O. Henry's place in literature ten years after his death.

Jennings, Al. *Through the Shadows with O. Henry.* New York: H. K. Fly Co., 1921, 320 p.
Autobiographical account by the former cowboy and train robber who claims to have known O. Henry while both were fugitives in Honduras, and who later was incarcerated in the Federal Penitentiary in Ohio with O. Henry. According to O. Henry biographer Gerald Langford, discrepencies of date and wildly improbable adventures that parallel O. Henry stories make Jennings's account somewhat suspect.

Kilmer, Joyce. "Is O. Henry a Pernicious Literary Influence?" *The New York Times Magazine* (23 July 1916): 12.
Interview with novelist, short story writer, and journalist Katharine Fullerton Gerould. Gerould's disparaging remarks about O. Henry stirred commentary in several publications of the day (see *The Bookman* entry above).

Knight, Jesse F. "O. Henry: Some Thoughts on the Urban Romantist." *The Romantist,* No. 3 (1979): 33-7.
Characterizes O. Henry as a Romantist whose stories re-create the innocence of the American spirit during the time of great hope and promise at the beginning of the twentieth century.

Langford, Gerald. *Alias O. Henry: A Biography of William Sidney Porter.* New York: Macmillan Co., 1957, 294 p.
Biography attempting to provide a complete and dispassionate examination of O. Henry's life by avoiding the romanticizing of many earlier biographical accounts that contributed to the "O. Henry legend" without shedding real light on O. Henry's elusive personality.

Larned, William Trowbridge. "Professor Leacock and the Other Professors." *The New Republic* IX, No. 115 (13 January 1917): 299.
Colorful rebuttal to the comments of Stephen Leacock on O. Henry (see excerpt dated 1916).

Lindsay, Nicholas Vachel. "The Knight in Disguise." In his *General William Booth Enters into Heaven, and Other Poems.* New York: Mitchell Kennerley, 1913, 119 p.
Poem in tribute to O. Henry.

Long, E. Hudson. *O. Henry: The Man and His Work.* Philadelphia: University of Pennsylvania Press, 1949, 158 p.
Biographical study.

————. *O. Henry: American Regionalist.* Austin: Steck-Vaughn Co., 1971, 43 p.
Brief biographical study, relating some incidents from O. Henry's life to aspects of his works.

Mais, S. P. B. "O. Henry." In his *From Shakespeare to O. Henry: Studies in Literature,* pp. 300-17. 1923. Reprint. Freeport, N. Y.: Books for Libraries Press, 1968.
Favorable overview of O. Henry's life and career.

McCreery, David J. "Imitating Life: O. Henry's 'The Shamrock and the Palm'." *Mississippi Quarterly* XXXIV, No. 2 (Spring 1981): 113-21.
Examines a historical incident of impressment into forced labor on a Guatemalan railroad from which O. Henry borrowed details for his story "The Shamrock and the Palm."

Mencken, H. L. "In Praise of a Poet." *The Smart Set* 31, No. 1 (May 1910): 153-60.
In an omnibus review, Mencken praises the "extraordinary and often painful vivacity" of the "amazingly ingenious" stories in *Strictly Business* and *Options,* but notes that O. Henry's stories all "suffer vastly from sameness."

Monteiro, George. "Hemingway, O. Henry, and the Surprise Ending." *Prairie Schooner* XLVII, No. 4 (Winter 1973/74): 296-302.
Compares Hemingway's "A Day's Wait" and O. Henry's "The

Last Leaf " to measure how Hemingway adapted O. Henry's characteristic surprise ending to his own purposes.

Munson, Gorham. "The Recapture of the Storyable: Some Notes on the American Short Story from O. Henry to Dorothy Parker." *The University Review* 10, No. 1 (Autumn 1943): 37-44.
  Briefly notes elements of O. Henry's fiction and assesses their effect on the development of the short story in the United States.

O'Connor, Richard. *O. Henry: The Legendary Life of William S. Porter.* Garden City, N.Y.: Doubleday & Co., 1970, 252 p.
  Thorough critical and biographical study.

O'Faolain, Sean. "On Subject." In his *The Short Story,* pp. 171-92. New York: Devin-Adair Co., 1951.
  Uses O. Henry's "The Gift of the Magi" as an example of a short story that, relying wholly on an anecdote, does not offer the exploration of human nature that is essential to good fiction.

Payne, L. W. "The Humor of O. Henry." *The Texas Review* IV, No. 1 (October 1918): 18-37.
  Analysis of the sources and devices of humor in the writings of O. Henry.

Rea, John A. "The Idea for O. Henry's 'Gift of the Magi'." *Southern Humanities Review* VII, No. 3 (Summer 1973): 311-14.
  Posits an impetus for O. Henry's best-known story.

Rollins, Hyder E. "O. Henry." *The Sewanee Review* XXII, No. 2 (Spring 1914): 213-32.
  Discusses some characteristics of O. Henry's short stories.

————. *The Texas Review* IV, No. 4 (July 1919): 295-307.
  Characterizes Texas and Texans as they appear in the stories of O. Henry.

Sinclair, Upton. *Bill Porter: A Drama of O. Henry in Prison.* Pasedena, Calif.: Privately printed, 1925, 58 p.
  A fictional exploration of O. Henry's mental state while imprisoned and an examination of the ways authors reshape their own experiences in literature.

Smith, C. Alphonso. " 'O. Henry'." *The Nation* (New York) CVI, No. 2758 (11 May 1918): 567.
  Theorizes on the origin of the pen name "O. Henry."

Van Doren, Carl. "O. Henry." *The Texas Review* II, No. 3 (January 1917): 248-59.
  Discusses essential traits in O. Henry's fiction.

Williams, Blanche Colton. "William Sidney Porter ('O. Henry')." In her *Our Short Story Writers,* pp. 200-22. New York: Dodd, Mead, and Co., 1941.
  Favorable overview of O. Henry's career.

Zamyatin, Yevgeny. "O. Henry." In his *A Soviet Heretic: Essays by Yevgeny Zamyatin,* pp. 291-95. Edited and translated by Mirra Ginsburg. Chicago: The University of Chicago Press, 1970.
  Introduction to a 1923 Soviet edition of O. Henry's short stories in which Zamyatin examines reasons for O. Henry's popularity with Russian readers.

Franz Kafka

1883-1924

Austro-Czech short story writer, novelist, and diarist.

Considered one of the most prominent and influential twentieth-century writers, Kafka is renowned for prophetic and profoundly enigmatic stories that often portray human degradation and cruelty. In his works, Kafka presents a grotesque vision of the world in which alienated, angst-ridden individuals vainly seek to transcend their tormented condition or pursue some unattainable goal. His fiction derives its power from his use of precise, dispassionate prose and realistic detail to relate bizarre, often absurd events and from his probing treatment of moral and spiritual problems. The oblique, allegorical quality of Kafka's stories has inspired myriad critical interpretations: his fiction has been variously described as autobiographical, psychoanalytic, Marxist, religious, Existentialist, Expressionist, and Naturalist. Most critics agree, however, that Kafka gave literary form to the disorder of the modern world, turning his private nightmares into universal myths.

Kafka was born to financially secure Jewish parents in Prague, a prominent provincial capital of the Austro-Hungarian Empire that incorporated Czech, German, and German-Jewish citizenry. His father had risen from poverty to success as a businessman, and the family was assimilated into Prague's Czech community by the time of Kafka's birth. Seeking acceptance into the German-speaking élite of the city, Kafka's father sent him to German rather than Czech schools. According to biographers, the dichotomy between the German and Czech communities led to Kafka's early feelings of alienation. As the eldest child and only surviving son, Kafka was expected to follow a planned course in life, but from his childhood he considered himself a disappointment to his father and felt inadequate when compared with him. Kafka's artistic motivation is revealed in this passage from an unsent letter to his domineering father: "My writing was all about you, all I did there, after all, was to complain about the things I couldn't complain about on your breast." Against his own wishes, Kafka studied law at the German University in Prague, earning his doctorate degree in 1906. Unhappy with the prospect of a legal career, he instead took a job in an insurance firm in Prague. He worked there from 1908 until 1922, when the debilitating effects of tuberculosis finally forced him to retire. Kafka spent his remaining years in various sanatoriums, writing fiction until his death in Kierling, Austria, in 1924. In his will, Kafka ordered nearly all of his manuscripts burned, but Max Brod, his friend and literary executor, disobeyed this decree and organized Kafka's writings into several posthumous publications.

Kafka was plagued by the discord between his vocation and his literary ambitions, as well as by his own ambivalence about marriage, which he believed offered the greatest happiness, but which he feared would stifle his creativity. Some biographers consider his relationship with Felice Bauer, to whom he was engaged twice but never married, the catalyst to a fertile period of literary production that began in 1912. During this time Kafka wrote "Die Verwandlung" ("The Metamorphosis"), "Das Urteil" ("The Judgment"), and the

first chapter of his novel *Amerika* (*America*). Many critics cite "The Judgment" as Kafka's "breakthrough" story, the one that established his central thematic preoccupation: the conflict between father and son that produces guilt in the younger character and is ultimately reconciled through suffering and expiation. Several commentators have noted the Oedipal rivalry between protagonist Georg Bendemann and his father and the illogical, dreamlike atmosphere of this piece. Georg's friend in Russia, who has exiled himself in order to write, represents Kafka's artistic side, while Georg symbolizes the Kafka who desires domesticity. After Georg announces his impending marriage, his father sentences him to death by drowning for defiling his mother's memory and challenging his father's status as head of the family. Acknowledging his guilt, Georg obeys the command and jumps into the river.

Kafka's next major work, "The Metamorphosis," is one of the most frequently analyzed stories in world literature. This elusive work, which portrays the transformation of Gregor Samsa from a man into an insect, has inspired diverse interpretations. The story has a threefold construction, demarcated by numerical headings and by Gregor's three emergences from his room after the transformation has occurred. Critics agree upon little regarding "The Metamorphosis" other than its three-part structure and its basic plot outline: Gregor Samsa works as a traveling salesman, a job he dislikes, to repay a debt incurred by his parents; he oversleeps one morning and awakens to find he has become a large insect; he and his family attempt to deal in various ways with the change, but gradually the situation becomes intolerable; Gregor ultimately dies, and his relieved family plans for a brighter future.

Three frequent critical interpretations of Gregor's transformation are that it serves either as retribution, as wish fulfillment, or as an extended metaphor. Those critics who see the metamorphosis as retribution for an unspecified crime committed by Gregor usually apply comparisons between Gregor and Josef K., the protagonist of Kafka's novel *Der Prozess* (*The Trial*), who never knows the offense for which he is arrested and executed. Critics who see the metamorphosis as a form of wish fulfillment on Gregor's part find in the text clues indicating that he deeply resented having to support his family. Desiring in turn to be nurtured by them, he literally becomes a parasite. The parasitical nature of Gregor's family and employer is then seen as an ironic foil to the reality of Gregor's parasitic being. Many critics who approach the story in this way believe the primary emphasis is not upon Gregor, but upon his family, as they abandon their dependence on him and learn to be self-sufficient. One interpretation of the story holds that the title applies more to Gregor's sister Grete than to Gregor: she passes from girlhood to young womanhood during the course of the story. A third interpretation is that Gregor's transformation is an extended metaphor, carried from abstract concept to concrete reality: Gregor is thought of as an insect, and thinks of himself as an insect, so he becomes one.

Kafka's next published work, "In der Strafkolonie" ("In the Penal Colony"), which he wrote in two weeks during a break from composing *The Trial,* is a characteristic fantasy of psychological and physical brutality that suggests a variety of readings due to the obscure nature of the events. In this story, a respected visitor is invited by the commandant of a penal colony to observe the execution of a soldier by means of an intricate torture apparatus. The machine, which uses needles to inscribe in words the criminal's punishable act upon his body, is intended to simultaneously induce beatific enlightenment. When the purpose of the device is described by its operator, a prison officer, the visitor is appalled. Attempting to assure his offended guest of the instrument's worth, the officer frees the condemned soldier and takes his place. During its operation, however, the machine malfunctions, and the officer is killed quickly and violently, without attaining the promised redemption. Many commentators have perceived "In the Penal Colony" as an allegory comparing the Old and New Testaments—the officer's willing sacrifice as an analogy to Jesus Christ's suffering and death. Others have viewed this story as prophetic of the Nazi concentration camps.

In 1916 and 1917 Kafka wrote a series of prose pieces known as the Country Doctor Cycle that reflects a sense of decaying order in Europe during World War I. These tales were later collected and published as *Ein Landarzt* (*A Country Doctor*).

In the title work (the most frequently discussed story of this volume), Kafka employs realistic prose to relate the surrealistic tale of a doctor's futile efforts to save a dying boy. The doctor initially pronounces his patient healthy, but the boy disagrees. Closer examination reveals a hole in the youth's abdomen in which worms writhe through clotted blood. After not-

ing this, the doctor is mysteriously stripped naked and left alone with the child, who says that his hole is his "sole endowment" in the world. The doctor reassures the boy that the wound is relatively harmless, and then flees the house without his clothes, riding home in a blizzard. Many critics have interpreted this story as symbolic of the impotence of modern science before the ruthless power of nature.

The stories in the last book published by Kafka during his lifetime, *Ein Hungerkünstler* (*A Hunger-Artist*), depict characters whose extreme isolation represents the status of the artist in a modern industrialized world. In "Erstes Leid" ("First Sorrow"), for example, a trapeze artist lives alone in the higher reaches of a circus arena, refusing to have contact with fellow workers, who nevertheless remain nearby. Uncomfortable in this situation but unable to perform without the aid of others, the trapeze artist remains paralyzed in his absurd position. In the title story, the protagonist, once celebrated by many for his ability to fast for days, is now viewed as a pathetic freak when public taste changes and circus spectators abandon him in favor of the animal exhibition. Denied public attention, the hunger-artist becomes disillusioned, weakens, and just before dying, confesses he stopped eating simply because he could not find food to his liking. He is replaced in his cage by a ravenous panther. Some critics see this story as symbolic of the plight of the misunderstood artist in modern times; when the hunger-artist's audience disappears, so does his faith in himself, and as a result, he expires. Other commentators perceive the protagonist as embodying humanity's spiritual nature and the panther as characterizing its bestial temperament. Still others view the hunger-artist as a holy man and describe the story as a parable about the impossibility of leading a completely metaphysical life. "A Hunger-Artist" is considered one of Kafka's most autobiographical works. Meno Spann cites a letter written by Kafka in 1912 that betokens the theme of this piece: "When it became clear in my organism that writing was the most productive direction for my being to take, everything rushed in that direction and left empty all those abilities which were directed toward the joys of sex, eating, drinking, philosophical reflection and above all music."

Kafka is ranked among the most important writers of the twentieth century for works that express modern humanity's loss of personal and collective order. His writing has inspired the term "Kafkaesque," which has come to describe situations of psychological, social, political, and metaphysical instability and confusion that defy logical explanation and typify Kafka's conception of humanity's absurd relationship with the universe. Although Kafka's work has elicited various critical interpretations, he himself characterized his fiction as symbolic manifestations of his "dreamlike inner life" in which he attempted to reconcile feelings of guilt and insecurity. For many critics, Kafka's greatness resides in his ability to transform his private torment into universal fables.

(For further information on Kafka's life and career, see *Twentieth-Century Literary Criticsim,* Vols. 2, 6, 13, 29; *Contemporary Authors,* Vols. 105, 126; and *Dictionary of Literary Biography,* Vol. 81.)

PRINCIPAL WORKS

SHORT FICTION

Betrachtung   1913

WYLIE SYPHER   (essay date 1946)

[*In the excerpt below, Sypher analyzes the nature of tragedy in the collection* The Great Wall of China: Stories and Reflections.]

If the usual Kafka narratives develop themselves within the "half-awake fantasies" in which, as Camus says, it would be wrong to interpret everything, these late, naked allegories [in **The Great Wall of China: Stories and Reflections**] with animals behaving as neurotically as men are a direct challenge to the intellect rather than the sensibility. We speculate on the symbolism of the dog that fasts or the creature that takes sanctuary in his complicated burrow, and we discover the relation of the giant mole to the faith of Kierkegaard, but at a sacrifice of the familiar "atmosphere" in Kafka's implausible, confused foregrounds. The themes are typical: the inscrutability of the will of God and its inescapable operation (**"Investigations of a Dog"** and **"The Great Wall of China"**), the involutions of anxiety far within the isolated self and the futility of either intellect or retreat before the Unknown (**"The Burrow"**), and the necessity of accepting the divine as absurd or even repulsive (**"The Giant Mole"**). At the last, evidently, Kafka was able to abbreviate the paradox of his living, his enormous fatigues, into a formal thesis instead of recording how incongruously it was revealed, perpetually astonishing as though to the eye of an amateur, within experience itself.

Yet if the tone is meditative, the defensive strategy, the ruses, the eventual frustrations of these animals are those of the Kafka tragedy. Kafka's humilities and revulsions at last expressed themselves in the perplexities of the beast.

Kafka suffers, but his pain does not assure his being in the right way. Thus his little maladjustments, his acceptance of life as an interrogation chamber, amount to a distinctive tragedy—or, perhaps, a comedy—of error. The comedy issues from his belief, affirmed by Kierkegaard, that living is a wisdom whose secret is foolishness and a hope whose form is madness. Unlike Kierkegaard, he is never able to make the "leap" of faith to God. Consequently his tragedy—or his comedy—is not ultimately religious; it remains secular and ethical, but without catharsis, without purgation of pity and fear, and thus either a parody of tragedy or a parody of religion.

In this drama the very laws of probability are in abeyance; tragedy occurs by whimsy. Kafka's intimation is that "inadequate, even childish, measures may serve to rescue one from peril," an intimation due to his incorrigible naivete, the impossibility of learning through suffering or any other way. His helplessness appears as wonder: he writes of himself, "All that he does seems to him, it is true, extraordinarily new." His heroes are all amateurs to whom each triviality is a crisis. He explains in **"My Neighbor"** how advantageous it is to exaggerate often "so as to make things clear in one's mind." The paradox of living is so utter that experience is leveled off to a continuous tension by exaggerating the insignificant, somewhat as in the distortions of Dostoevski. Karl in *Amerika* cannot get off the boat; K. in *The Castle* cannot manage to telephone; Joseph in *The Trial* cannot speak with his clients at the bank. Each, like the animal in **"The Burrow,"** is isolated by his own crises until he resembles Kierkegaard's individual without connections or pretensions, and with all the terrible responsibilities of solitude. The insecurity of the Kafka hero is desperate, for he is without benefit of either the resignation of faith or the retribution of tragedy. No propitiation can be made. "Our generation is lost," the dog considers, "but it is more blameless than those earlier ones." In *The Trial* before Joseph dies, bestially, under the knife, he explains, "My innocence doesn't make the matter any simpler." And by the Old Law the Enemy will demolish the burrow and, presumably, destroy its helpless recluse.

The paradox within the Kafka tragedy, the sustained pity and fear, its half-ethical, half-religious directions, are phrased with rich variations in the aphorisms and reflections: "Our relation to our fellow-men is that of prayer, our relation to ourselves, that of effort." In the notes on himself Kafka admits that "he has no conception of freedom" (the occupant of the burrow similarly confesses, "I have reached the stage where I no longer wish to have certainty"). His wishes are not wishes "but only a vindication of nothingness, a justification of non-entity, a touch of animation which he wanted to lend to non-entity." (pp. 731-32)

Then after we have read the allegories and all these subtle propositions we return to the handful of brief stories and fables printed here—**"The Married Couple," "My Neighbor," "The Knock at the Manor Gate"**—as we shall return to the novels, for the astonishing fantastic comi-tragedy of anxieties; in them we hasten, fatigued, "in almost guiltless silence towards death in a world darkened by others." Under a suspension of probability and the exaggeration that clarifies we revisit the psychological landscapes where a chance knock at the castle gate beneath the glare of noonday brings one, inexplicably, to the sudden and gross examinations of that perpetual court—a stone cell with bare walls and iron rings, and "in the middle something that looked half a pallet, half an operation table." When the exemption from probability is complete and the absurd is reduced to matter-of-fact, we have those vignettes of the paradox seen vividly by an amateur who is never ready for any contingency but who notwithstanding takes it for granted. In **"The Married Couple,"** for example, the implausible becomes dramatic and the comic becomes pathos: "Every now and then he would suddenly and quite unexpectedly clap his hat on his head; he had been holding it on his knee until then, slowly pushing it up and down there. True, he took it off again immediately, as if he had made a blunder, but he had had it on his head nevertheless for a second or two, and besides he repeated this performance again and again every few minutes." The crazy, intense drama of **"A Common Confusion"** cannot be played in the animal allegories, for in them Kafka capitulates to the answers that steal round the questions. His anguished "little investigations" must be followed through the strange vocations of K., of Joseph, of Gregor, of the nameless agents of these plain fables.

The Kafka malaise, it has been argued, is a symptom of the *galuth* mind, the mind of the Diaspora. In this collection Kafka's dread is not alone that of the Jew, or his trembling that of the Christian. An original sin has been committed upon man and, he concludes, "The state in which we find ourselves is sinful, quite independent of guilt." "A cage," goes another Kafka aphorism, "went in search of a bird." From this tragedy of gigantic anxiety there is no catharsis, no purification by the New Law. The expulsion from paradise is final, and the Furies still pursue.

Wylie Sypher, "The New Eumenides," in The Nation, New York, Vol. 163, No. 25, December 21, 1946, pp. 731-32.

R. W. STALLMAN   (essay date 1948)

[*An American critic, poet, and novelist, Stallman is a leading scholar of the life and work of Stephen Crane. In the following excerpt, he explores the multiple levels of meaning in "A Hunger-Artist," proclaiming that it is one of "the greatest short stories of our time."*]

"A Hunger-Artist" epitomizes Kafka's theme of the corruption of interhuman relationships, as one of his critics defines it. It is one of his perfections, if not his best story, and it belongs surely with the greatest short stories of our time. (p. 61)

The present essay attempts to open up the cage of Kafka's meaning in **"A Hunger-Artist,"** But first, as a starting point for our analysis, here is the story at its literal plane, a matter-of-fact account stripped of interpretation:

The story is about a once-popular spectacle staged for the entertainment of a pleasure-seeking public: the exhibition of a professional "hunger-artist" performing in a cage of straw his stunt of fasting. His cage's sole decoration is a clock. His spectators see him as a trickster and common circus-freak and therefore they expect him to cheat, to break fast on the sly. But fasting is his sole reason for existing, his life purpose; not even under compulsion would he partake of food. For him, to fast is the easiest thing he can do; and so he says, but no one believes in him. Because the public distrusts him, he is guarded—usually by three butchers—and prevented from fasting beyond a forty-day period, not for humane reasons, but only because patronage stops after that time. His guards tempt him with food and sometimes mistreat him; yet they breakfast on food supplied at his expense! A great public festival celebrates his achievement, and thus he is "honored by the world." But when he is removed from his cage he collapses in a rage, not from hunger, but from having been cheated of the honor of fasting on and on and on and of becoming thus "the greatest hunger-artist of all time." Though emaciated almost to the point of death, he quickly recovers and after brief intervals of recuperation performs again and again.

Nowadays, however, he has been abandoned for other spectacles. People visit his cage in the circus tent, but only because it is next to the menagerie. His spectators are fascinated by the animals. All's changed: there is, apparently, no clock, and the once beautiful signs to announce the purpose of his act have been torn down. Now no tally is kept of the number of fasting days achieved. There are no guards. "And so the hunger-artist fasted on without hindrance, as he had once dreamed of doing . . . just as he had once predicted, but no one counted the days; no one, not even the hunger-artist himself, knew how great his achievement was and his heart grew heavy." Thus the world robs him of his reward. Indifference replaces admiration and on this note he expires. He is buried with the straw of his cage and replaced by a panther, who devours fiercely the food he naturally craves. The people crowd about his cage.

We notice that the facts in this "matter-of-fact" account are not in themselves complete or sufficient, and that our attempt to take them at their matter-of-fact or literal level is quite impossible. They seem to compete with each other and to thrust us beyond their literal properties into the plane of their allegorical significance. That clock seems to be simply a clock; it does not apparently represent anything else. And yet no literal meaning can be ascribed to that bizarre clock. It strikes the hour just like a real clock, but (so to speak) it does not appear to tick. The life of this hunger-artist is unclocked. He exists outside time, and periodically he survives starvation sieges no ordinary man could endure. (Actually, a calendar would be the logical means for reckoning the artist's fasting days.) As for the other facts, these objects likewise suggest symbolic significance. It is impossible to reduce Kafka's facts to a single self-consistent system of meaning. The trouble is that his meanings emerge at several planes at once, and the planes are interconnected. No complete paraphrase is possible.

We cannot confine Kafka's meaning to a single circle of thought. The plight of the hunger-artist in his cage represents the plight of the artist in the modern world: his dissociation from the society in which he lives. By this reading of the story, **"A Hunger-Artist"** is a sociological allegory. But we can also interpret the hunger-artist to represent a mystic, a holy man, or a priest. By this reading the story allegorizes in historical perspective the plight of religion. A third possible interpretation projects us into a metaphysical allegory: the hunger-artist represents spirit, man as a spiritual being; the panther, in contrast, represents matter, the animal nature of man. If the story is translated into metaphysical terms, the division is between the spiritual and the physical; into religious terms, between the divine and the human, the soul and the body; into sociological terms, between the artist and his society. Kafka's blueprint—the groundplan of ideas upon which he has built this structure of parables—is toolmarked with these three different systems of thought.

Consider first the story as an allegory of the dilemma of the artist. He is set in contrast to the multitude. The people who attend his exhibitions of fasting cannot comprehend his art. "Just try to explain the art of fasting to someone! He who has no feeling for it simply cannot comprehend it." The artist starves himself for the sake of his vision. He has faith in his vision, faith in himself, and integrity of aesthetic conscience. As the initiated alone understood, "the hunger-artist would never under any circumstances, not even under compulsion, partake of any nourishment during the period of fasting. His honor as an artist forbade such a thing." It is his vision, solely this, which nourishes him. Of course the artist can "fast" as no one else can do. It's not everyone who is an artist. We concede, "in view of the peculiar nature of this art which showed no flagging with increasing age," the claim he makes of limitless capacity for creating works of art. But if his public is devoid of any sympathetic understanding of the artist and of his art, if his public has no faith in him, how then can he cling to this faith in himself? It is because his public is an unbeliever that the artist is in a cage (the cage symbolizes his isolation). Society and the artist—each disbelieves in the other. And so the artist comes to disbelieve, finally, in himself; he cannot survive in isolation.

The hunger-artist is emaciated because of the disunity within himself, which is the result of his disscciation of soul from body, and because of the disjunction between himself and his society. It is his denial of the world of materiality that is the source of his gnawing doubt and "constant state of depression." He repudiates half of life, and the multitude repudiate him. The public reject the emaciated body of the artist for the healthy body of the panther—they reject art for life itself. These two occupants of the cage, the purely spiritual and the purely bestial, represent, then, the dual nature of man. The people outside the cage, with whom he is also contrasted, crave the same food as the panther. For them, as for the beast, their joy in living issues from their throat—and from their belly. These human and bestial beings represent the sensuous physical realm of matter. They are all-flesh, whereas the hunger-artist is no-flesh. In the one we have pure matter; in the other, pure spirit. But the hunger-artist, as pure soul, is a failure. Though he is apparently free from those gnawing dissatisfactions which our purely physical appetites create in us again and again, nevertheless he is not entirely free from the claims of the body, from the claims of matter, from the claims of the world in which he lives. At the same time that he denies the evil natural social world he longs for some recognition of his fasting from the public; he wants the people to crowd around his cage. Finally, "though longing impatiently for these visits [of the people on their way to the eagerly awaited stalls], which he naturally saw as his reason for existence, [he] couldn't help feeling at the same time a certain apprehension." He apprehends the truth that he who is the faster cannot be "at the same time a completely satisfied spectator of his fasting." He sees that an existence of pure spirituality is impossible to man. He sees that this insatiable hunger with which he, as artist or as mystic, is possessed is at bottom only the sign of his maladjusted, and therefore imperfect, soul.

Complete detachment from physical reality is spiritual death. This statement sums up the meaning of **"A Hunger-Artist"**

insofar as the story is an allegory about the nature of man. What is man, matter or spirit? The story might be described as a kind of critique of this philosophical problem. Spirit and matter—each is needed to fulfill the other. At the moment of his death the hunger-artist recognizes his failure as an artist or creator. For this superannuated artist there is no possibility of resurrection because in our present-day world not spirit but matter is recognized. That matter has today triumphed over spirit is recognized by the dying hunger-artist as he confesses his secret. I had to fast, he admits, because I could find no food to my liking. Fasting, you see, was my destiny. But "'if I had found it [i.e., food to my liking], believe me, I should have caused no stir, I should have eaten my fill just as you do, and all the others.'" Those were his last words, but in his glazed eyes there remained the firm, though no longer proud, conviction that he was still fasting." Here, then, is the key to his enigma. Cut off from the multitude, the artist performing his creative act (his fasting) has to die daily and be daily reborn. This is a martyrdom, but for what purpose? The creative artist cannot also be his own public; he dies when no one cares that he and his art should live. Devotion to an aesthetic or spiritual vision cannot be an end in itself. Pure creativeness is impossible, even as absolute spirituality is impossible. The creative imagination must feed upon all reality. For art is but a vision of reality. The artist, no less than the mystic-faster, must live in the world of mundane life. Art requires the material conditions of life, and these conditions nourish it. Life is at once the subject of art and its wellspring.

It is the clock in the hunger-artist's cage that triumphs over the artist. It is time that triumphs over the very one who denies the flux of time, which is our present reality. The clock in his cage is a mockery of the artist's faith in the immortality of his creative act or vision, a mockery of his faith in his art as an artifice of eternity. The tragedy of Kafka's hunger-artist is not that he dies, but that he fails to die into life. As he dies he seeks recognition from those whom he has all his life repudiated: "'I always wanted you to admire my fasting,' said the hunger-artist." It is his confession that spirit has no absolute sovereignty over matter, soul has no absolute sovereignty over body, and art has no absolute sovereignty over life. . . . Kafka's hunger-artist represents Kafka's doctrine: "There is only a spiritual world; what we call the physical world is the *evil* in the spiritual one, and what we call *evil* is only a necessary moment in our endless development." **"A Hunger-Artist"** is a kind of critique of this doctrine. Matter here triumphs over Spirit.

Throughout the story the author laments the passing of our hunger-artists, their decline and extinction in our present-day civilization. But nonetheless throughout the story all the logic is weighted against this hunger-artist's efforts at autarchy. In his last words we are given his confession that the artist must come to terms with life, with the civilization in which he lives, the world of total reality. "Forgive me, all of you," he whispers to the circus manager, as though in a confessional before some priest. And they forgive him. They forgive him for his blasphemy against nature. The hunger-artist seeks Spirit absolutely; he denies the "*evil* natural social world" at the same time that he longs for it. And this is his dilemma, even as it is ours. It is not possible for man to achieve a condition of pure spirituality, nor again is it possible for him to achieve a synthesis of spirit and matter. As the agent of divine purity the hunger-artist is a failure. His failure is signified, for instance, on the occasion when he answers the person who has explained his emaciation as being caused by a lack of food: he answers "by flying into a rage and terrifying all those around him by shaking the bars of his cage like a wild animal." This reversion to the animal divests him momentarily of the divine, and it also betrays the split-soul conflict within him. His location next to the menagerie serves as reminder that the claims of the animal body are necessary claims upon the soul and cannot be denied. And this is true even though matter is wholly evil (i.e., "the evil odors from the stalls," etc.); complete separation from reality can never be obtained. (Compare the idea of "complete detachment from the earth" as it figures in **"The Burrow."**) Pure Spirit is as vacuous as Pure Matter.

In the same way that Kafka's sets of facts can be translated into allegorical terms at the philosophical and aesthetic levels of meaning, so too in terms of the religious allegory the multiple meanings of his facts overlap. Our post-Renaissance world has discarded the philosopher, the artist, and the mystic. The hunger-artist as mystic-faster is dead. Call him priest or artist, he has been rejected by the "pleasure-seeking multitude" and replaced by other amusements; for instance, by the exhibition of a live panther. It was different in times past. For example, in the Middle Ages and in the Renaissance he "lived in apparent glory, honored by the world." Then he had his patron. (The patron of the artist was the impresario.) He had his critics, the butchers who guarded him out of the public distrust of his creative act. And he had his historians, the attendants who recorded his creative act or kept count of his remarkable performances. In those times he was at least admired for his achievements as an imitator of life. . . . But what a poor imitation of real life he presented! In those times he was at least celebrated (albeit, not without hypocrisy), honored by rituals conscientiously enacted upon appointed fast days. Consider this hunger-artist as mystic-faster or priest. At one time, everyone attended his services daily. Regular subscribers sat, as in church pews, "before the small latticed cage for days on end." Everyone pretended to marvel at his holy fast. Actually, however, not one worshiper had faith. Nevertheless, despite this sham of faith in him, he submitted again and again to crucifixion by these pretenders to faith. He was a martyr for his divine cause. The multitude, because "it was the stylish thing to do," attended his "small latticed cage"—they attended it as they might a confessional box. But the multitude, since it does not understand what Faith is, has no sin to confess. The hunger-priest hears no confession. (Ironically it is he who, in dying, confesses.) In short, all mankind—apart from a few acolytes to his cult, disbelieves this Christ who many times died for man's sake. And when he dies, see how these disbelievers exploit the drama of his death. Here is Kafka's parody on the drama of the Virgin mourning the loss of her Son.

> But now there happened the thing which always happened at this point. The impresario would come, and silently—for the music rendered speech impossible—he would raise his arms over the hunger-artist as if inviting heaven to look down upon its work here upon the straw, this pitiful martyr—and martyr the hunger-artist was, to be sure, though in an entirely different sense. Then he would grasp the hunger-artist about his frail waist, trying as he did to make it obvious by his exaggerated caution with what a fragile object he was dealing, and after surreptitiously shaking him a little and causing his legs to wobble and his body to sway uncontrollably, would turn him over to the ladies, who had meanwhile turned as pale as death.

The ladies who so cruelly sentimentalize over his martyrdom represent sympathy without understanding; a sympathy which is devoid of understanding is mere self-sentiment. One of the ladies weeps—but not for him. She breaks into tears only in shame for having touched him. "And the entire weight of his body, light though it was, rested upon one of the ladies, who, breathless and looking imploringly for help (she had not pictured this post of honor thus), first tried to avoid contact with the hunger-artist by stretching her neck as far as possible, and then . . . she broke into tears to the accompaniment of delighted laughter from the audience. . . ." It is a mock lamentation that these two Marys perform. What a difference between the theme of the Virgin mourning the loss of her Son as treated in Kafka's parody and as depicted in the famous *Avignon Pièta* or in Giotto's *Lamentation*.

It is thus that the religious and the metaphysical and the aesthetic meanings of **"A Hunger-Artist"** coincide: (1) Christ is truly dead. Our post-Renaissance world has discarded the act of faith from its reality. (2) For the mystic, as for the artist, there is no resurrection because today not spirit but matter alone is recognized. And as we have seen, it is recognized, this triumph of matter over spirit, even by the dying mystic, who ends a skeptic and a defeatist (not unlike Kafka himself): I had to fast, because I could find no food to my liking. Fasting is my destiny. But " 'if I had found it, believe me, I should have caused no stir, I should have eaten my fill just as you do, and all the others.' Those were his last words, but in his glazed eyes there remained the firm, though no longer proud, conviction that he was still fasting." (pp. 63-70)

R. W. Stallman, "A Hunger-Artist," in Franz Kafka Today, *edited by Angel Flores and Homer Swander, The University of Wisconsin Press, 1958, pp. 61-70.*

CAROLINE GORDON AND ALLEN TATE   (essay date 1950)

[*Gordon was affiliated with the Southern Literary Renaissance, a movement composed of authors united by their belief in traditional agrarian values and their common practice of formalist literary techniques as defined by the New Critics. Tate was an important theorist and practitioner of the New Criticism, one of the most influential critical movements of the twentieth century. The New Criticism professed that a work of literature must be examined as an object in itself through close analysis of symbol, image, and metaphor. A conservative thinker and convert to Catholicism, Tate denounced Western philosophy for alienating individuals from themselves, one another, and nature by divorcing intellectual from natural functions. In the excerpt below, Gordon and Tate view the story "The Hunter Gracchus" as an allegory of a Christ figure who has been crucified yet is unable to enter Heaven.*]

Franz Kafka occupies somewhat the same position in the literary world of today that Ernest Hemingway occupied before the Second World War. The two writers have one thing in common: they are both masters of naturalism. But our age, as Edmund Wilson has shown in his *Axel's Castle,* has two trends, Naturalism and Symbolism, or Symbolism based upon Naturalism. . . . The symbolism which operates in Hemingway's stories refers to a narrow range of experience and seems inadequate today. The world appears to have shifted under our feet. We have seen whole countries ravaged, whole populations decimated. We can hardly believe any longer in the Divinity of Man. We are more concerned today with Man's relation to God. (p. 286)

Kafka presents a surface which is as strictly naturalistic as Hemingway's in details, but he is dealing with a problem more complicated than Hemingway's: the relation of Man to God.

There have been fiction writers before him who concerned themselves with the same problem, in this country, notably Hawthorne. Too often, with him, myth turns into allegory. Kafka's stories are more dramatic, consisting on the surface of action presented in convincing detail. His meaning, which constitutes another level of action, is cryptic, and must be sought for in his symbols.

"The Hunter Gracchus," which, though short, exhibits his fictional gifts in perfection, is the story of a Christ who has been crucified but has never been able to ascend into Heaven.

The viewpoint is that of the omniscient narrator. . . . The scenes are pictorial throughout. The opening scene shows the world of men at their various occupations. Boys are shooting dice, a man is reading a newspaper, a girl is filling her bucket at a fountain, two men are drinking wine in a café while the proprietor dozes at a table outside. The architecture of this setting reminds one of allegorical paintings of the fourteenth century. In such paintings a window or a vista often opens on what artists call "infinite space." In Kafka's scene spatial perspective is symbolic and also prepares for the Complication of the action . . .: the man is reading the newspaper in the shadow of a hero who is flourishing a sword on high, a fruit seller is lying beside his scales, staring out to sea, where a bark is "silently making for the little harbour as if drawn by invisible means over the water."

The Complication is the arrival of the dead hunter, Gracchus (Christ), in any harbour (any community). Kafka evidently thinks of Christ's passion as being continuously enacted. The boatman (the Church) transfers the bier to the shore. Doves light on the bier, as the Holy Spirit, in the form of a dove, once alighted on the head of Christ, but "nobody on the quay troubled about the newcomers . . . nobody asked them a question, nobody accorded them even an inquisitive glance."

The action proper begins when the burgomaster of the town, whose name is significantly "Salvatore," goes into the room where the body of the dead hunter lies on its bier, goes, that is, to church. He gives the boatman a glance and the boatman vanishes through a side door into another room. (Since the soul is seeking salvation in terms of a Protestant theology it dispenses with the Roman Catholic sacrament of Confession.)

Salvatore (the soul) then communes with the hunter (Christ), who deplores his condition: "It cannot be a pleasure to look at me," and then relates the story of his Incarnation and Crucifixion. Pursuing his calling (the saving of souls) he fell down a precipice (became Incarnate), bled to death in a ravine (was crucified), died, but did not ascend into Heaven; his death ship "lost its way."

Salvatore expresses his attitude towards the Doctrine of Original Sin when he asks whose was the guilt. The Hunter replies that it is the boatman's (the Church's) but he does not feel that the boatman has been guilty of anything more than "a wrong turn of the wheel," "a moment's absence of mind." The result of this mischance is the Resolution . . . of the ac-

tion: Christ has not been able to become Christ, but remains "forever on the great stair that leads to Heaven, sometimes up, sometimes down . . . always in motion." The Hunter (of souls) has been turned into a butterfly, an ancient symbol for the soul.

The artist, as such, does not defend or criticize the myth of his age, he merely portrays it. Kafka's subject-matter is the Scheme of Redemption, as set forth in Neo-Calvinist theology and the philosophy of "Crisis," and his allegorical symbolism is as exact, if not as full as Dante's, but his participation in the faith is not as complete. His skepticism shows itself occasionally in wry ambiguities. The dove which warns Salvatore of Gracchus's arrival is as big as a cock and it evokes the image of the cock which crowed to herald the betrayal of Christ. The pessimism of our age finds expression in the crowning sentence of this remarkable story: "My ship has no rudder, and it is driven by a wind that blows in the undermost regions of death." (pp. 287-89)

> *Caroline Gordon and Allen Tate, "Franz Kafka: Commentary," in their* The House of Fiction: An Anthology of the Short Story with Commentary, *Charles Scribner's Sons, 1950, pp. 286-89.*

WILLIAM A. MADDEN (essay date 1951)

[*Madden is an American critic and co-founder of the journal* Victorian Studies. *In the following excerpt, he discusses literary, psychological, and theological aspects of "The Metamorphosis."*]

I propose to approach Kafka's work here primarily through **"The Metamorphosis"** for the reason that this important piece has received far less attention than either *The Trial* or *The Castle,* and secondly, because it is one of the greatest things Kafka has left us. Everything that Kafka had to say is present here in embryonic form. It lies at the center of both his personal and his artistic life, and represents in its most finished form the method he finally selected to indoctrinate us into the harrowing lessons of life without hope, supported ultimately by a startling myth, which somehow gave it hope and which I shall finally call the myth of mediation. It is in **"The Metamorphosis,"** too, that we first receive the full benefits of Kafka's special insights, which open up a tremendous perspective leading deep into the human heart. His findings have significance not only for the literary critic, but for the psychologist and the theologian as well.

Kafka's handling of the problem of evil in **"The Metamorphosis"** has the same ambiguity and obscurity characteristic of everything he wrote. This abbreviated novel portrays what Kafka conceived to be the results of man's failure to escape the enormous guilt thrust upon him from the very outset of his life. In spite of its mysterious origin, this guilt has appalling consequences, and of these Kafka was continually and painfully aware. So profound and so horrible was the dislocation caused by this root affliction that he could find expression for it artistically only in his scrupulously detailed account of a man transformed into a cockroach. (p. 247)

The event simply occurs. In a particular room in an unidentified metropolitan city, a man who is a salesman by circumstance awakes one morning to find that he is no longer a man but has become an immense cockroach.

> What has happened to me? he thought. It was no dream. His room, a regular human bedroom, only

rather too small, lay quiet between the four familiar walls.

"Only rather too small." It is through such conscientious, touching, ironic details that Kafka disconcerts us. He mentions others—Gregor's cloth samples spread on the table, a picture he had recently cut out of a magazine, framed and hung on the wall, and even details about the picture—and confronted in this way the reader is not for a moment allowed to take the story as a mere "fantasy." His immediate concern is not with causes, though this interest is there and remains awaiting satisfaction; rather it is with the reactions which the transformation produces in the hero, in his family, and in others. Gregor's own attitude is one of unsurprised and total acceptance. . . . Gregor worries, entirely unrealistically and most pitiably, about "what was he to do now." Such preparations for a routine day strike the reader rather humorously at first, but the humor becomes more and more excruciating as the real proportions of the tragedy become clear. There is, in these tender details of Gregor's room, his past life, his family, the pathos of a joke told by a mutilated child. Though we laugh aloud, the tears ravage us within. As Austin Warren observed, "It is the chief horror of the story, perhaps, that no one within it sees what happens as 'impossible'." For eventually the reader finds that Gregor's family accepts the new situation just as easily as, if with greater horror than, Gregor himself. And Gregor himself says later, "this is no joke." It is this *impression* of realism that has earned for Kafka the label of a "realistic writer of myths."

Unquestionably the role of realism in Kafka is intimately connected with his "technique," and with an appreciation of what he was about. Sentimental titillation of the emotions for its own sake, similar to that produced by Gothic novels, is something we feel Kafka would never condone. The transformation of Gregor, therefore, must be accounted for by an explanation which will not do violence to Kafka's art. Nor will it do to suppose **"The Metamorphosis"** straight allegory. This work is at the heart of Kafka's matter; it is conceivably his most "finished" piece, as it was written when his powers were mature and not yet hampered by the distractions of physical distress. It will not suffice, then, to take the easy way out by appealing to sensationalism, or even to a more comprehensive psychological explanation. Psychology certainly is involved, but behind it lies a crucial metaphysical judgment dependent in its turn on something beyond the conceptual world altogether.

It is interesting that numerous rereadings of **"The Metamorphosis"** do not blunt its effect. Again and again Kafka takes us up into Gregor's sharply defined world; though the reader will invariably try to get at the "meaning" independent of the "story," he finds himself repeatedly involved with Gregor and the Samsas and the entire macrocosm in which they move. This alone disproves any attempt on Kafka's part at "allegory" in the strict sense. There is always this contingent, real world of Gregor and his family and friends, waiting to come alive once more, convincing, moving, disconcerting as ever. Why this is so has already been suggested in the mention of Kafka's generous provision of minute details, of quick, ironic comments that are based, as it seems, on a world which must exist and which, in fact, appears inevitable. The chief-clerk's ridiculous harangues, the intimate account of Gregor's animal diet and sensations, the tender family scenes, the incredible behavior of Gregor's father, all bear out this impression of a strange, horrifying, but very real world. Exam-

ples could be taken almost at random, but perhaps one connected with the distracted scene shortly before Gregor opens the door will serve. Hearing a strange twittering noise from Gregor's room in answer to the chief-clerk's peremptory demand, the Samsas sense that something has gone wrong, and Mr. Samsa sends out a maid and Gregor's sister for a locksmith and a doctor respectively. Sitting in his room, Gregor listens and conjectures.

> And the two girls were already running through the hall with a swish of skirts—how could his sister have got dressed so quickly?—and were tearing the front door open. There was no sound of its closing again; they had evidently left it open, as one does in houses where some great misfortune has happened.

Always the details precede the metaphysics. Or to state it more accurately, we must arrive at the meaning through the incidents that Kafka describes because these incidents contain the meaning. And when he allows himself to impose gently on the reader, as in the conclusion of the above quotation, something which he rarely does, Kafka does not distort or bend the incident, but as in this case, suggests a possible significance in the most tentative way, granting, so to speak, that this is only one possibility and perhaps not the best one.

It would seem then that Kafka goes out of his way to avoid fantasy. The last impression he wants to give is that of a fable, an entertaining flight of the imagination. He is presenting to the world not "facts" of course, as we ordinarily conceive such things, but a *real situation,* in this instance a real problem. Furthermore, the extravagant happenings in **"The Metamorphosis,"** as in *The Trial* and *The Castle,* serve as a kind of trap. If, on the one hand, Kafka wants to assure the reader that the story is not a fantasy, on the other hand, he does not want to alarm him by a brutal exposure of the hard truth; he invites him to look at the terrifying reality through the disarmingly simple tale. Combined with the realism, therefore, which prevents any misunderstanding about the realness of the experience described, there is a "fabulous" plot to prevent the reader from becoming frightened or belligerent as he would tend to be by the exposure of the raw truth. Intrigued at first by the magic of the other-worldly conjoined to the illusion of reality, the reader is scarcely conscious of what is getting said until, in a sense, it is too late. And it is the details which "take," which haunt the reader's imagination and demand some clarification, some answer, some meaning.

It is almost impossible to exaggerate the importance of the literal meaning of Kafka's work, first of all for its own sake as the sign of literary genius, and secondly as an instrument in Kafka's hands to destroy all doubt about what actually happens—it is "literally" a true account of man, life, and the cosmos. One can imagine Kafka, benumbed by his vision but desperately anxious to get it straight, to remove all possibility of its being mistaken for a dream, for a psychological study, for a literary exercise, writing with the greatest care, as indeed he did, and giving the most conscientious attention to the facts. While undoubtedly some men were aware of the same dilemma before him, and many more, guided by him, saw it afterwards, few have faced it as squarely, as inexorably, and, it can be said, as heroically as this Czech government clerk and writer. He saw it, consequently, all the clearer for that, and tried to give it in his writing the same force, the same reality, the same enervating fearsomeness which it had for him. And what Kafka had to say as a creative writer he said first and fully in **"The Metamorphosis."** All that followed is an elaboration of the same theme. **"The Metamorphosis"** has the least amount of that dream-substance, the gossamer veil of magic, which threatens to destroy his intelligibility at every moment. (pp. 248-51)

Kafka's realistic touches, as we have already suggested, serve to convince the reader that he is being presented with facts, not fancy. This necessity, as Kafka saw it, of preventing any misconception on the part of the reader is important. And the consideration of Kafka's realism is the really essential problem of criticism. The whole question of art comes into play, because we are dealing with the means used by the artist to express his conception. Stated as simply as possible, Kafka's man-turned-insect is Picasso's quarter-of-an-eye woman: it is one way of realizing a vision. Whether or not it is the only possible way makes no difference, since in the case of **"The Metamorphosis"** it is a way that Kafka approved. The term "vision" has been used advisedly in speaking of that which Kafka had to express, because it is something more than a group of "ideas," or even a system of metaphysics, although metaphysics is certainly involved. The immediate impact of Kafka's story is that of a metaphor, full of surprise and an unsuspected wealth of thought. It is by means of the metaphor, that is, by analogy, that he is able to realize his vision in such a way that we receive it as a whole, or nearly so, just as the author himself conceived it. When Kafka tells us that Gregor Samsa has been transformed into a cockroach, we understand not only that Gregor has become tainted by evil, but also something of the nature of that evil as Kafka understood it. Realism here is not simply a device, or a way of describing things, the jargon or appeal of a school, but an essential part of Kafka's art. And just as analogy is rooted in and leads back to supreme analogues, the metaphor is a limited way of understanding that aspires toward and is subsumed in the symbol. Kafka is attempting to provide an explanation of why man is in such and such a position, and of what it means; to do this, in art, he must resort to the symbol, which is always sunk deep in the world of reality. To communicate a unique conception of the world, Kafka resorts to a species of analogy which relies more on man's immanent intuitive capacity than on a vast and comprehensive system of reasoning. Now if the symbol is to be at all satisfactory, Kafka must be realistic; Gregor's change into "vermin" must be as real as possible, and even "vermin" is too vague; he changes into a cockroach which Kafka describes in some detail. In this way the personal experience of the writer is translated into terms which extend far beyond the level of the conceptual. (pp. 252-53)

All of Kafka's work rests ultimately on what might be called his myth of mediation, always understanding "myth" not in the pejorative sense of a pseudo-religion but as the world of unformulated truth, as a search process which "attests the fact that the suppositions are indeed somehow there before he 'discovers' or formulates them." The truth of myth in this sense can only be got at by indirection, using the "landmarks" of explicit concepts and judgments as guides.

"The Metamorphosis" once again provides a starting point for an inquiry into what is suggested by Kafka's myth of mediation. There is a reverse side to the coin of Gregor's suffering and of his family's involvement in his degeneration. This reverse side is shown us after Gregor's death in the immediate recovery of the family from what had seemed a hopeless state of affairs. It is largely a renewal of the spirit which bodes well

for their future fortunes. "Gregor" is disposed of, and on that same morning the family of the deceased, for the first time since the metamorphosis, decides to take the day off and enjoy a walk. Gregor's father and mother study their daughter, the "pretty" Grete, and decide that the time has come to find a husband for her.

> And it was like a confirmation of their new dreams and excellent intentions that at the end of their journey their daughter sprang to her feet first and stretched her young body.

This sudden change for the better had been adumbrated in the father's recovery earlier in the story. After a financial setback, Gregor's father had all but "retired," living a sedentary, one might say slothful and useless existence, when the change in Gregor revived his old interests and ambitions to the extent that he managed once again to take the family fortunes in hand. The budding beauty of Grete, the revitalization of the father, and the recovery of the mother appear as compensations in the order of time for a suffering which had been weighed in the scales of eternity. (p. 262)

If man is sinful, and if the community life is unattainable, and if further, as we would now suggest, Kafka conceives man as separated from his Creator by an unspannable gulf, then there is no solution to be proposed which will stand up against logic. These theological principles, in fact, would seem to lead to the conclusion that man is a pawn in the universal scheme, and the universe itself a practical joke of God's fashioning. Yet Kafka does not, as we have already inferred, accept this position.

At bottom Kafka's theology rests on the paradox of losing one's life in order to save it—expressed in a dark, non-rational, indirect vision which Kafka himself never fully brought into the light.

> How much more crushing than the most pitiless conviction of our present sinful state is even the feeblest conviction that there will be eternal justification for our temporal existence. Only our strength in supporting this second conviction, which in its purity completely subsumes the first, is the measure of faith.

This paradox, lacking a foundation in the Christian life, was for Kafka ever a "crushing" concept. "The most senseless seemed to me in this senseless world more probable than the sensible." So in spite of the strain and anguish it involved, Kafka clung to the "senseless" belief in self-expiation. In the darkest moments, and they were many and dark indeed, Kafka drew strength from his conviction, because his faith was not dependent upon the contingent but rather gave it meaning. "The fact that there is only a spiritual world robs us of hope and gives us certainty."

This will suggest, perhaps, the content of what I have called the "myth of mediation" which is the ultimate reference and world-picture of Franz Kafka's vision. And since Kafka's explicit principles are few, and those dark, the reader may be excused for speaking of them darkly. But let it be said again that "myth" here refers to a kind of truth rather than to a kind of falsehood.

Though it defies logic, there is a faith indispensable to man, a myth of mediation or of a bridge which exists, because it must exist, based on a logic superior to the logic of this world. We might add now that this logic took the form of faith in the Indestructible, a belief in man's destiny in spite of the "facts."

> Man cannot live without an enduring trust in something indestructible in himself. Yet while doing that he may all his life be unaware of that indestructible thing and of his trust in it.

This "mythological" statement is the total view of Kafka's art-work. While the intuition of a link between the man and the Absolute cannot be explicitly formulated and does not follow from the explicit judgment which Kafka was able to make, yet it is related to these areas of clear concepts as a dark sea to its lighthouses. The distinct, formulated statements are surrounded by and find their meaning in the vast and mysterious world of myth, of implicit truth, of which they are the "landmarks." In this world of the unconscious the explicit formulas undergo a sea-change which produces incalculable effects. An example of this in Kafka's dialectic between ultimate Being and nothingness might be the insistence, to borrow from St. John of the Cross, "where there is no hope, put hope, and you will find hope." Artistically, Kafka already expressed this "myth" in **"The Metamorphosis."** Gregor Samsa, Kafka tells us, surrounded by dust and hate, interiorly distraught, convinced of his own evil, on the point of dying a seemingly pointless death, "thought of his family with tenderness and love." The "realism" of Kafka's writing is ultimately bound up with the demands of this vision. He helped to evolve a technique which is the special contribution of modern man in the ever-changing course of art through history. (pp. 264-66)

> *William A. Madden, "A Myth of Mediation: Kafka's 'Metamorphosis'," in* THOUGHT, *Vol. XXVI, No. 101, Summer, 1951, pp. 246-66.*

STANLEY COOPERMAN (essay date 1957)

[*In the excerpt below, Cooperman examines Kafka's use of symbolism in the story "A Country Doctor."*]

An essential factor in successful symbolic art . . . is multi-level meaning which cannot be detached entirely from the work itself. The richer and greater the symbolism, the more complex will be the reader's response on several levels, each of which may be justified. The value of a sensitive eclecticism becomes especially apparent in discussing the work of Franz Kafka. Like other masters of the symbolic, Kafka may be approached from several directions; there is no one approach, and those who read Kafka (and comment on him) in order to grind a particular philosophical ax, run the risk of losing the work itself.

An examination of one of Kafka's shorter pieces—**"A Country Doctor"**—will demonstrate symbolic method in all its multiplicity. This story is only eight pages long, but it is rewarding from several standpoints. As a microcosm of Kafka's thematic basis and stylistic approach it is invaluable. It is immensely suggestive on the symbolic level, setting up repeated echoes in the mind. Psychologically the story is powerful and rich in possible interpretations. Finally, the technique is superb, showing Kafka at his best.

A familiar characteristic of modern fiction—the absence of traditional plot or story-telling development—is found in **"A Country Doctor."** There is no precise beginning, middle or end. The primary concern is with the significance of events rather than with the events themselves. Narration is interior and vertical rather than exterior and horizontal. The reader is plunged immediately into the situation, and must make his way out as best he can; there are, if anything, more unanswered questions at the finish than at the start. (pp. 75-6)

The unimportance of plotting is basic to **"A Country Doctor"**; we cannot "tell" the story and communicate more than a superficial orientation. Roughly, this is what occurs: a doctor, about to answer a call from the country, finds that his horse had died, and sends his servant girl to obtain another. She fails, but a groom and two great horses appear mysteriously from an old pigsty. The horses seem satisfactory, but the groom begins making sexual advances to the girl.

The groom ignores the doctor's objections, and the horses begin traveling with amazing speed, bringing him to his patient's house almost immediately. He finds his patient—a young country boy—suffering from a horrible wound which he cannot cure. This is resented by the family and friends, who undress the doctor and place him in bed with the boy, hoping for a cure. Preoccupied with the thought of the servant girl being assaulted by the groom, the doctor dresses and starts back home. The horses, however, travel with agonizing slowness, and the doctor fears his home and place have been usurped.

One must admit that in paraphrase, the story line of **"A Country Doctor"** is hardly impressive. Yet from this rather loose construction, Kafka gives us an art at once disturbing and subtle, meaningful and elusive—apparently simple yet technically sophisticated.

Like most of Kafka's work, the story unfolds within a single consciousness—a single point of view, which is, moreover, largely passive. The doctor . . ., is a logical little man bickering talmudically with the externals appearing to manipulate his fate. These externals are irrational, irreversible and fantastic, but despite his indignant posturing, the doctor is aware both of the inevitability of the process and his own role in creating it. (pp. 76-7)

"A Country Doctor" starts with a direct plunge into a situation of anxiety, and from the very first, introduces and confirms an impression of nightmare. The droning sentence structure, acceptance of the obviously impossible, distortions of time and space—in short, the entire nature as well as the contents of narration seem a description or reactivation of dream. "What was it about?" we may imagine a psychiatrist asking. The answer is, in part, given below:

> I was in great perplexity; I had to start an urgent journey; a seriously ill patient was waiting for me in a village ten miles off; a thick blizzard of snow filled all the wide spaces between him and me; I had a gig, a light gig with big wheels, exactly right for our country roads; muffled in furs, my bag of instruments in my hand, I was in the courtyard all ready for the journey; but there was no horse to be had, no horse . . .

Here is the combination which is to grow more striking as the story progresses: the monotone, the simple declarative clauses, the repetition. Then, from a "year-long uninhabited pigsty" come the man—a groom—and two magnificent horses, "their bodies steaming thickly." This is, certainly, fantastic; yet the sudden arrivals are accepted by the doctor-narrator and Rose, the servant-girl. When the groom turns abruptly to Rose, the doctor makes only feeble objection, for the girl has had a "justified presentiment that her fate was in-escapable." From this point, the dream-narrative intensifies:

> I could just hear the door of my house splitting and bursting as the groom charged at it, and then I was deafened and blinded by a storming rush that stead-ily buffeted all my senses. But this only for a mo-ment, since, as if my patient's farmyard had opened out before my courtyard gate, I was already there; the horses had come quietly to a standstill, the bliz-zard had stopped, and moonlight was all around.

The final effect, again, of realism and logic within sur-realism and illogic cannot be reproduced outside the story itself. (p. 77)

"A Country Doctor," like most dream literature, is rooted firmly in symbolism—so firmly, indeed, that any certain di-chotomy between the literal and the symbolic vanishes. It is necessary to accept a simple dream narrative as the literal level of **"A Country Doctor,"** since only a dream can give it any literal meaning whatsoever. On this basis, symbolic asso-ciations move within a psychological landscape and may be interpreted psychoanalytically. We are introduced to a situa-tion of anxiety and impotence—the demands of duty cannot be fulfilled by the doctor. Into this situation comes a potency figure—the groom—offering what seems to be a solution. No-tice the symbolism of birth permeating the entire "pigsty" se-quence (the darkness, the smell, the groom crawling out on all fours calling "Brother" and "Sister"). This culminates in the arrival of the horses, "their legs tucked close to their bo-dies, each well-shaped head lowered like a camel's, by sheer strength of buttocking squeezed out through the door hole which they filled entirely."

The groom, then, is an ambivalent figure; on the one hand, he aids the doctor by providing "Brother and Sister" and the means for fulfilling duty; on the other, he is a "brute" who subjects Rose to her "inescapable fate"—sexual violation. Rose, later called "the pretty girl who had lived in my home for years almost without my noticing her," is a mother figure, domesticity, the love-object, and "servant." In a sudden and terrible insight, the doctor becomes aware of the violation of this mother figure ("I could just hear the door of my house splitting and bursting as the groom charged at it").

At that moment time is destroyed, the doctor is plunged back into the timelessness of the unconscious, and he meets him-self as a youth—the boy with a wound. Here the atmosphere is one of disgust: "The air was almost unbreathable; I wanted to push open a window." This is a phase which appears in many of Kafka's works.

At first this aspect of himself—this youth—seems well, but the doctor is uncomfortable in his diagnosis. The family—especially the father—oppresses him. The situation finally be-comes one with obvious Oedipus overtones, as well as self-defense of potency: "In the narrow confines of the old man's mind I felt ill; that was my only reason for refusing the drink. The mother stood by the bedside and cajoled me toward it." On his second examination the doctor discovers the boy's wound, the Oedipus fixation ("a fine wound is all I brought into the world, that was my sole endowment"), and he suc-cumbs to an intense feeling of guilt and failure. He is guilty of the rape of Rose because he has left her to the groom's lust. And he is also guilty—a failure—because he is unable to ef-fect a cure.

The doctor feels completely isolated as the family and friends stare at him: "The family and the village elders stripped my clothes off me; a school choir with the teacher at the head of it stood before the house." Religion cannot help him, his sin is too great ("the parson sits at home and unravels his vest-ments"). He must get back to Rose and combat the groom; he must escape from the family and the nightmare of religious sanctions ("O be joyful, all you patients . . ."). The result, however, is impotence. He cannot return, or compete with the lustful tyranny of the groom: "Like old men we crawled through the snowy wastes . . . in my house the disgusting groom is raging; Rose is his victim; I do not want to think about it any more . . . I cannot reach it." The doctor's narra-tion ends on a note of complete impotence, and the dream stops.

This—a slice of dream life—is one of many possible psycho-logical interpretations. However, it by no means limits the meanings of **"A Country Doctor,"** since the story is rich in associations operating through, but beyond the literal dream level. From another standpoint, the story need not be consid-ered in terms of psychology, but rather as a poetic evocation of the individual buffeted by chaos in an age where all out-lines are blurred, and faith has turned to frost. The basic con-flict, as in *The Trial,* may be considered that of evil breaking suddenly into a rational, well-ordered life (perhaps a life which is over-regulated: "I was the district doctor and did my duty to the uttermost") and finally paralyzing it. The doctor is impotent when faced with the Sacred Wound—which, as Herbert Tauber points out, is the "awakened consciousness of the shattered condition of life."

Viewed in this light, the story becomes a symbolic restate-ment of the classic existential situation. On the one hand, we have a respectable and adjusted life; on the other, the swift insight, the crisis erupting within the placidly flowing se-quence of "duties" and prosaic tasks. "I could see no way out," the doctor cries, and his words are an echo of the phi-losophers of crisis from Kierkegaard to Sartre.

Suddenly, without warning, the dark, irrational and diabolic forces represented by the beast-groom and the great horses take command. They drive the doctor deeply and instanta-neously face to face with the insoluble—the "fear and trem-bling"—the moment when reasons fail, when "the center will not hold," when nothing is left but the scarlet wound—the beautiful wound—of awareness.

Rose's rape by the dark force of the groom represents the smashing of all that is near, protecting, feminine. But the guilt is strongly the doctor's in this violation; he has failed to realize the true value of Rose ("the pretty girl who had lived in my house for years without my noticing her"); everyday life has become formulistic, conventional, devoid of passion or awareness. As a result of this failure, the doctor is incapa-ble of coping with the crisis when it comes—again, like the other isolated heroes (or victims) of existential literature. His failure delivers him to the disgusting wound and the bitter cold.

Faced with the wound (which represents his own ruined state and so cannot be cured) the doctor is isolated, completely alone before a suddenly meaningless and hostile universe. The traditional answers are gone; they can no longer serve ("the parson sits at home and unravels his vestments"). Al-though the secular self must be relied upon ("the doctor is supposed to be omnipotent"), it provides neither meaning nor answer ("old country doctor that I am"), and, when the usual prosaic days and nights are shattered ("bereft of my servant girl"), there is nothing but sterility, the empty shell of what once were solutions ("strip his clothes off; then he'll heal us . . . O be joyful all you patients").

The nightmare ending is the doctor's chaotic spiritual state after meeting the wound: a wasteland of panicked effort and treadmill motion, a vain attempt to prevent the inevitable crisis. He is caught, now, between "neither—nor" in a ruined secularism ("earthly vehicle"), driven by a desperate necessity for something beyond himself ("unearthly horses"). But it is too late; he is incapable of making the choice made by those who meet the Wound but who arrive finally at acceptance through faith. And so he rides through the snowy wastes, the nightmare storm, an absurd and anguished figure ("I cannot reach it") in a shattered world ("It cannot be made good, not ever").

The two interpretations I have presented concern the same work, and in addition rely to a great extent on the same symbols. But they are not mutually exclusive; in the symbolic art of Kafka two methods of criticism may, and indeed must, occupy the same space at the same time. Kafka is ambiguous and difficult, but his material—the stuff of the human soul—would be violated if he presented a single dimension of meaning. The work has many truths, a weaving and reweaving of many themes, and it cannot be approached bluntly or singlemindedly. (pp. 78-80)

Stanley Cooperman, "Kafka's 'A Country Doctor': Microcosm of Symbolism," in The University of Kansas City Review, *Vol. XXIV, No. 1, October, 1957, pp. 75-80.*

WILLIAM C. RUBINSTEIN   (essay date 1958)

[*In the following excerpt, Rubinstein comments on the symbolic meaning of the ape character in the story "A Report to an Academy."*]

Kafka's story, **"A Report to an Academy,"** has never aroused much enthusiasm among his critics. To Charles Neider, " 'A Report to an Academy' . . . aside from its bright satirical tone and its empathy for the ape, is merely an exercise, whose function is to satirize the spiritual in man. The education of the ape, his transformation into a human being, depends upon a system of repression and destruction of memories. Kafka, like Swift, implies that man is a beast."

The comparison with Swift is implicit also in Brod's brief comment: "Or, what is still more horrible [than the degradation of **"The Metamorphosis"**], he lets the animal be raised to the level of a human being, but to what a level of humanity, to a masquerade at which mankind is unmasked." This interpretation, that the ape is in some way a satire of humanity, is approved of by Herbert Tauber, who writes that the ape "is really a picture of the everyday man who expands himself in the superficial, who cannot fulfill his being and realize it in freedom, but whose first commandment is to adapt himself."

Now there is no doubt that in general the story supports these explications, but this reader feels that there must be some more specific object of the satire than humanity. There seems to be a precision in the choice of the symbols which is not reflected in the analyses of the critics, possibly because they have not considered the story worthy of a full-length treat-

ment. Then too, the "bright satirical tone" reveals an underlying savage bitterness, an almost personal anger, which suggests that the story is more than "merely an exercise" in reversing **"The Metamorphosis."** (pp. 55-6)

Since many of the readers of the novels are not familiar with **"A Report to an Academy,"** a brief summary of it is given here.

> An ape is lecturing to an academy on his life before he transformed himself into a human being. Unfortunately he can tell the academy very little about it, for, since his transformation, he has forgotten the past. He was captured in Africa, and his first clear recollections are of the cage in which he was confined on the boat to Europe. Here he suffered numerous abuses. The members of the crew spit in his face, laughed at him, prodded him with sticks, and burned him with their pipes. He soon realized that the only way for him to get out of his cage was to become a human being. With great effort he succeeded in doing this. The climax of his efforts came the day he was able to drink "schnapps," a feat which repeatedly nauseated him, but one on which the members of the crew placed the greatest importance—the ape could not understand why. After that his progress was very rapid, although marred once by the fact that one of his teachers, as a result of his contact with him, almost became an ape himself. Today he has a smug satisfaction in the thought that he has reached the intellectual level of an average European. He is very tactful about mentioning the abuses he suffered as an ape and obsequiously goes out of his way to excuse human beings for having inflicted them. In the evenings, he goes home to his mistress, a half-human, partially crazed ape.

The key to the interpretation of the story is the symbolic significance of the ape. In order to determine precisely what he represents, it might be well to begin with the most trying experience in his transformation and the one to which the most space is devoted in the story.

"My worst trouble," the ape tells the academy, "came from the schnapps bottle. The smell of it revolted me; I forced myself to it as best I could; but it took weeks for me to master my repulsion. This inward conflict, strangely enough, was taken more seriously by the crew than anything else about me."

One of the crew members considers it his special duty to teach the ape to drink from the bottle. "He could not understand me, he wanted to solve the enigma of my being." Very patiently, this human being repeats before the cage the ceremony of drinking the schnapps. The ape describes himself as "enchanted with my gradual enlightenment," but this "theoretical exposition" exhausts him so that he hangs limply to the bars of his cage.

Of course there is obvious irony in describing the spectacle of a man drinking a bottle of whiskey as an enlightening or theoretical exposition, but the very obviousness of it should put the reader on his guard. Kafka does not usually work for such crude effects. It is, therefore, quite possible that some deeper meaning is intended, a double irony of some kind.

In spite of his "theoretical instruction," it is a long time before the ape can drink from the bottle. Each time he is about to do it, revulsion seizes him, and he throws the bottle from his lips. His teacher alternately tortures and cajoles him. The ape cannot understand his revulsion, and both he and the teacher try to conquer it, for "we were both fighting on the same side against the nature of apes."

Finally, "one evening before a large circle of spectators—perhaps there was a celebration of some kind, a gramophone was playing, an officer was circulating in front of the crew," the ape succeeds in drinking the schnapps. Instantly his transformation, in spite of a few subsequent lapses, is made. He breaks into human speech, "and with this outburst broke into the human community." He now feels the previously mocking and hostile faces of the crew "like a caress over my sweat-drenched body."

What is the significance of this strange episode at the climax of the story? Why does the crew place such great importance on the ape's drinking the schnapps—an emphasis which the ape is unable to understand? Why does drinking instantly make the ape a human being?

It may be that in accordance with the usual interpretation Kafka considers drinking the most characteristic symbol of human degradation, and, therefore, the ape is accepted as soon as he has learned to drink. But such an interpretation seems rather weak. The ape's teacher is not a drunkard, and intoxication does not seem to be the aim of his drinking. The drinking is rather a ritual, for the ape must learn not merely to drink, but to follow every movement and gesture of his teacher in doing it.

This ritual drinking on which such great emphasis is placed, which must be preceded by theoretical instruction, which is given during "a celebration of some kind," and which instantly transforms the ape into a human being accepted by the crew, is far more likely, it seems to this writer, to be a symbol for the sacrament of Communion, which is itself a symbolic act denoting the acceptance of Christ. By drinking the schnapps, the ape, or whatever he represents, becomes a Christian and is welcomed joyously by the assembled celebrants of the rite. If this interpretation is correct, the story is really about a conversion.

But who is the convert? Obviously his conversion is not a sincere one. He wants to be a human being only so that he will not be spit on, burned, or kept in a cage. Although the schnapps bottle revolts him to the last, he drinks in order to be accepted as human. His obsequiousness before the *real* human beings of the academy, even after his transformation, makes him a despicable figure. He is quite possibly a Jew who has allowed himself to be converted to Christianity in order to escape persecution. (pp. 56-8)

The ape comes from the Gold Coast, but he has no personal recollection at all of his life before his capture. "For the story of my capture I must depend on the evidence of others." His "own memories gradually begin—between decks in the Hagenbeck steamer, inside a cage." Here he must "stay motionless with raised arms, crushed against a wooden wall." Although it may seem extravagant, the early life of the ape is probably that portion of pre-European, Jewish history for which he must rely on the Old Testament, the evidence of others. All he can remember personally is his life in the cage (the ghetto, specifically, but more generally the whole situation of European Jews at this time).

Since life in the cage is unbearable, the ape must find some way to get out of it. Two courses are open to him: to attempt an escape to freedom (Zionism), or to become a human being

(assimilation and conversion). The dangers of the first course prevent the ape from ever considering it seriously. He is afraid he will drown in the ocean, and even if he does manage to get back to his home, what is there to prevent his recapture?

Actually he does not want freedom, but merely "a way out" of the cage. So he decides to become a human being "even though these men in themselves had no great attraction for me." After his conversion, he has several lapses, and, in order to avoid being put into the zoological gardens, on his arrival in Hamburg he embarks on a strenuous program of training. He engages teachers for himself and puts them into five communicating rooms. "By dint of leaping from one room to another" he takes lessons from all five at once. Who these five teachers are it is difficult to say. Possibly they are the four evangelists and Paul, but this is only a desperate guess.

At the end of his lecture, the ape again congratulates himself on his transformation. "In itself that might be nothing to speak of, but it is something insofar as it has helped me out of my cage. . . ." But in spite of his progress, he goes home in the evening to "a half-trained little chimpanzee . . . [with] the insane look of the bewildered, half-broken animal in her eyes," a look which the ape "cannot bear."

There is some interesting bibliographical evidence which may have a bearing on the interpretation of the story. According to Angel Flores, **"A Report to an Academy"** first appeared in the collection, *A Country Doctor.* Brod, however, without giving any details, mentions that there was an earlier publication in a magazine called *Der Jude.* (pp. 58-9)

Der Jude was conceived and published by Martin Buber, a leading Zionist. In the opening number (April, 1916), there was a declaration of purpose: to spread and promote knowledge of Judaism. Throughout the eight years of the magazine's history, it dealt exclusively with Jewish problems, usually from a Zionist viewpoint. While there is not the slightest reason to suppose that Buber would not have published a story by a friend of his friend Brod, unless it explicitly furthered the views of the magazine, the appearance of **"A Report to an Academy"** in *Der Jude* does add, however little, to the probability that the story dealt with the problems of European Jewry.

The Jew who, for some ulterior motive, allowed himself to be converted was a popular villain in the Yiddish literature of Europe. Kafka mentions in his diary (October 4, 6, 8, 1911), for example, seeing a play, *Der Meshumed* (*The Apostate*), in which Seidemann, a converted Jew, is also the murderer of his own wife and the would-be murderer of his daughter's fiancé. Bad as the play was, it made a profound impression on Kafka, for he devoted several pages of the diary to a summary and analysis of it. It probably furnished him with the first sketchy outlines for the two "assistants" in *The Castle,* and after being transmuted in his artistic consciousness might very well have emerged as **"A Report to an Academy."** (p. 60)

William C. Rubinstein, "A Report to an Academy," in Franz Kafka Today, *edited by Angel Flores and Homer Swander, The University of Wisconsin Press, 1958, pp. 55-60.*

RUDOLPH BINION (essay date 1961)

[In the essay on "The Metamorphosis" excerpted below, Binion argues that Gregor's transformation into an insect is not an actual physical occurrence but is instead a hallucination caused by mental illness.]

The first generation of Franz Kafka's critics has construed **"The Metamorphosis,"** like his other enigmatical tales, diversely as a fusion of naturalism and supernaturalism, or of realism and surrealism; or as an allegory, or as a mere psychotic projection. Gregor Samsa's metamorphosis into a bug serves, if supernatural, to magnify his natural anguish or despair; if surrealistic, to illumine the categories of the self, of the absurd, or of nonentity; if allegorical, to figure the reincarnation of Christ, the isolation of the artist, neurotic illness, or alienation at large. If, finally, it expresses literally Kafka's own view of the world, then its significance is autobiographical rather than artistic. (p. 214)

[The] tale does afford full *internal* evidence that Kafka meant Gregor's illness as mental and not physical.

For **"The Metamorphosis"** is simply a conventional account of a natural occurrence. It is the story of a man who thinks he has become a bug, told as if the content of his delusion were physical reality. The narrator's perspective is equivalent to that of the hero himself, who, like a typical victim of hallucinosis, sees the world accurately in all of its particulars save one. Thus what crawls out of Gregor Samsa's bedroom one morning, naked and drooling, to astound his parents and the chief clerk is not a man-sized bug but Gregor physically intact. Indeed, what other explanation is there for their instant-ly recognizing him?—or for the charwoman's mere playfulness with him later, or the lodgers' mere amusement?

The best way to grasp what Kafka has done is to imagine him having first invented his hero, then decided to tell his hero's story in accordance with his hero's own outlook. To devise a narrative idiom in accordance with the hero's perspective on reality is common literary practice in our century: Thomas Mann's narrators are as reflective as his heroes, Hemingway's as primitivistic, Camus' as absurd. And neurotic heroes too are common in our time. What is singular about **"The Metamorphosis"** is only Kafka's use of this narrative technique in the case of a *hallucinated* hero—though here of course the oddity of the effect far exceeds the singularity of the means employed. (p. 215)

[The] narrative respects the manner as well as the content of Gregor's delusion. Following his peculiarly psychotic pattern of awareness it tends to fix unnaturally on single elements of a whole physical complex, ones having special meaning for Gregor, which then becomes self-sustaining and quasi-absolute: the father's uniform of office, which dominates the father and through him the whole household, or the sound of the lodgers' teeth, which drowns out the other sounds of their eating "as if thereby to apprise Gregor that one needs teeth in order to eat." Also like Gregor's own mind the narrative notes sights and sounds by preference, it notes them in simple perceptive sequence, and it notes them indifferently as it were, in their bare externality, such that when quoted in bits and snatches it even appears naturalistic—especially the dialogue, which it records as if in stenographic transcript. Again like Gregor's own consciousness it prohibits direct evidence against his delusion, such as his being called a lunatic, and registers no contradiction when he sees only kindness in his mother's and sister's removing his furniture, or "foresight and thrift" in his father's having kept a nest egg on the sly.

His delusion is once extended, to include the lodging of an apple in his back—the hallucinatory conversion into a somatic trauma of a psychic one: his shock at his father's bombarding him with apples. The presentation of the scene according to Gregor's mode of perception brings out the affective basis for his shock. The rhythmic pursuit of Gregor by the father, agitated and erect in his uniform, followed by Gregor's slow passage through a double door back into his dark chamber, the father loading his pockets with apples and then discharging them while the mother, giddy, disrobed, "embracing him, in complete union with him—but here Gregor's vision was already failing—her hands behind the father's head, pleaded for Gregor's life"—the scene requires only an instant's elaboration by Gregor to become a fantasy of his own procreation, hostile and violent. Presumably it revives in him a like pseudomemory at the root of his illness. Schizophrenics have fantasies of the sort often enough without the benefit of provocation, so strong in them is the urge to undo their birth and conception. Obedient to this urge Gregor reverts to primary narcissism, simulates embryonic life in the sickroom, and finally curls up and dies. (pp. 217-18)

Kafka may well have been a prepsychotic who elaborated his fantasies into works of art as a defense against converting them into symptoms; but elaborate them he did, and into works of art as close to reality as any literary convention will permit.

Gregor's predicament is, like neurosis, common in our time. It deserves to be shocking; Gregor himself makes it so

Julie Löwy (1856-1934), Kafka's mother.

through his choice of illness, and the narrative follows suit. By dint of entering into his symptomatic perspective the narrative renders his choice of illness plausible at least, if not appealing. Then, by showing how weirdly well the family's treatment of him—not an unconventional treatment at the time—accords with such a perspective, it is able to make certain facts about families evident. This is doubly ironical: because the perspective is a false one, and because Gregor, whose perspective it is, does not himself see the evidence. The narrative technique is ironical also in a philosophical sense. In the end Gregor is, existentially, nothing if not a bug, since others deny him his old identity—"Indeed, how can it be Gregor?" asks the sister—and refuse to accept him under any other.

In sum, Kafka exposes an everyday social and domestic situation as psychologically destructive. Gregor's protest against his job is profoundly human. . . . So too is his revolt against not being loved save as son-provider—"the disgusting circumstances reigning in this house and family," as the chief lodger puts it—profoundly human. He is, however, no extraordinary young man. He lacks the intellectual and moral resources for his revolt to be anything but neurotic. As such it is as fatal to his personality as resignation would have been. It is, however, beneficient to his family—his decline revitalizes them—and so by way of his morbid choice, a free and deliberate one in the end, he acquires tragic dignity. His dilemma from start to finish is a specifically modern one, arising as it does out of conditions of financial insecurity and dehumanized social labor. Through it Kafka points to a vast historical problem, that of mankind's having generated social and domestic institutions destructive of its own humanity. (pp. 219-20)

> *Rudolph Binion, "What 'The Metamorphosis' Means," in* Symposium, *Vol. XV, No. 3, Fall, 1961, pp. 214-20.*

RALPH FREEDMAN (essay date 1962)

[*Freedman is an American critic and author of the acclaimed biography* Hermann Hesse: Pilgrim of Crisis *(1978). In the excerpt below, he contends that it is best to approach Kafka as a writer of realistic fiction.*]

In unraveling Kafka's obscurity, many critics have emphasized two modes of interpretation which, directly and indirectly, extend the notion of the romantic dream. The visionary's obscurity or the bright illuminations of the hallucinatory mind have become, in the twentieth century, symbolic torture gardens of the unconscious. Recognizing the precision of Kafka's thought, some of these critics have seen in his work exact allegorical correspondences or consistently applied metaphors whose symbolic meanings reveal an inner world. Others have sought to explain his worlds as compulsive dreams seen in orthodox Freudian terms. Yet Kafka is far less internal a writer than he is frequently assumed to be. In fact, neither approach does justice to the manifold nature of his vision.

Kafka uses symbolism, but shrinks from its consistent application. If, in **"The Metamorphosis,"** Gregor is hit by the apple thrown at him by his father, the conventional religious significance imparted by the choice of the fruit is no more than an allusion—almost jocular in its obviousness—suggesting one of several possibilities. If, in the story **"In the Penal Colony,"** the officer's martyrdom suggests Christ's sac-

rifice, one possibility is explored, and if the New Commandant's doctrine of mercy makes the officer's sacrifice necessary, another possibility and another (contrasting) Christ figure is alluded to. To seek consistent symbolic references in Kafka's prose may be interesting and often rewarding, but this course leads only to individual terms of multiple relations which Kafka plays against one another. Symbolism must be taken into account, but it is not the master key to Kafka's work.

Similarly, an exclusively psychological explanation leaves vast areas of Kafka's obscurity unexplained. We need not dwell on the obvious psychoanalytic motif which recurs in his fiction: the hero's relationship to an overwhelming authority, as in **"The Metamorphosis"** or *The Trial,* which can be diagnosed as an enactment of his relationship with his father and with the authoritarian society he found so intolerable. In fact, such an explanation sheds considerable light on Kafka's motives for choosing his themes and worlds. But to view his worlds as labyrinths of the *subconscious* would sharply limit the scope and depth of his work. For, as we shall see, the shadowy characters who appear to his heroes are independent entities, through which manifold relations are explored.

The most fruitful approach to Kafka's work would begin with a recreation of his world as he actually presents it to us, a world of concrete, albeit rearranged reality. This view presupposes that Kafka is essentially a realistic writer who does not seek to reduce the world to characteristic states of mind.

Experiencing the world as a self-contradictory manifold, Kafka envisions the constant and hopeless struggle of the discerning intelligence to come to terms with the objects by which it has been conditioned. Yet these objects and worlds are real; the demonic writer, seeking to demonstrate the full extent of the mind's entanglement with them, deliberately distorts them to reveal different ways in which a hero (carefully defined) would cope with a significantly rearranged world. Since it leads to a close scrutiny of the moral and spiritual problems involved in human existence, this approach may reflect Kafka's interest in Kierkegaard which he himself has recorded. His methods of execution, however, can also be explained through two literary traditions in which he developed: naturalism and expressionism.

Naturalism is an important base from which Kafka's method developed. (p. 63)

Nevertheless, it is clear that Kafka was not a naturalistic writer in the ordinary sense. Despite some faithful depictions of squalor in *The Trial, The Castle,* and elsewhere, his manner is nowhere reminiscent of Zola or Dreiser. His prevarications of reality did not seek to expose social evils or reflect ideals concerned with the improvement of mankind, but to reveal man's involvements in an apparently absurd world. But even such an expansion of the naturalistic premise does not fully explain Kafka's vision. Only in the imposition on his world of an expressionistic grotesque do we find a further clue to the nature of his distortions.

The importance of *expressionism* to Kafka has long been debated. Yet, quite apart from the merits of this debate, it remains clear that Kafka's work developed during that quarter century in which expressionism in literature and art had come into being and into maturity. It was a pervasive modern movement in which many of his friends were engaged. Its chief relevance to Kafka was its use of distortion and stylization to reveal the essential character, rather than the chang-

Hermann Kafka (1852-1931), Kafka's father.

ing appearances, of an object or world. In expressionistic novels like Alfred Döblin's *Berlin-Alexanderplatz* or Hermann Hesse's *Der Steppenwolf,* the writer sought to free his protagonist from the bondage of time, place, and milieu by dissolving the universe and reconstituting it in terms of a particular vision of reality held by the artist.

Kafka went his own way. He was neither a "naturalist" nor an "expressionist." No great artist can be caught in the categories set up by literary historians. Nevertheless, these two important ways of looking at reality shed some light on his manner and offer us points of departure for our unending efforts at exegesis. For Kafka does present reality as an external, not a psychological, dimension, and he distorts reality to reveal man's puzzling condition which his agonized and ironic mind envisaged. To cite Erich Heller's striking image: his world resembles that of Plato's cave which a malicious God has paneled with mirrors. The prisoner thirsting for true knowledge now perceives actual shapes, not shades, yet the concave walls of the cave reflect these forms in grotesque distortions in which the mind discerns its true relations. We therefore do not witness dreams and hallucinations as such, as we often view them in expressionistic stories and plays. It is made perfectly clear that Gregor's awakening in **"The Metamorphosis"** or K's search in *The Castle* are not dreams; we are soon convinced that the arrest in *The Trial* is not an internal event. (p. 64)

To allude once more to Kafka's affinity with naturalistic form, this method appears as an intensified version of Zola's prescriptions in *Le Roman expérimental.* The objective author-observer introduces his character into a carefully specified world. Keeping all elements constant, he then observes his character's adjustment to a particular change. Heller's God paneling the walls of the cave with mirrors is the writer himself, seeking to extract a particular meaning from his deliberately reconstructed encounter between protagonist and world.

"The Metamorphosis" illustrates this manner most clearly. The significant shift, of course, is Gregor's awakening in the shape of a stag-beetle. The story develops all consequent changes in both the hero and the world. As in *Gulliver's Travels,* once an initial change is accepted, all else follows with convincing logic.

The hero's transformation and the change in his relations to the world involve significant cognitive changes. Kafka's way of exploring the paradoxes Gregor confronts is therefore at first epistemological; that is, it is concerned with different ways of knowing reality, of exploring the shifting relations between self and world. From Gregor's point of view, the tragedy of **"The Metamorphosis"** consists in the self's gradual reduction to its most vital center—its self-consciousness. In two stages—a more superficial change in spatial relations and a more central change in the consciousness of time— Gregor is finally reduced to a mere speck of self-awareness which is ultimately extinguished. As in Swift's book, the story begins with shifts in cognitive relations and ends in a crucial change in the nature of the hero himself.

Immediately following the awakening, only physical appearances and perspectives seem to be changed while Gregor's essential self appears unchanged. With meticulous care and a great deal of fantastic realism, Kafka portrays shifts in spatial relations which suddenly circumscribe Gregor's movements and world. His bed is an immense obstacle. He can hardly reach the door-handle. His voice gradually transforms itself from a human voice to an animal squeak, while his memory and other mental faculties as a human being seem to remain essentially unimpaired. But more and more the trappings of humanity disappear, helped by the ill-concealed outrages of his employer and his family. Transformations now affect Gregor more substantially; his vision adjusts to his new perspectives. The room seems too big; the furniture oppresses him. He prefers closed windows and dirt. His sister perceives him sitting in an animal-like trance. But these changes are not wholly generated from within Gregor's transformed shell. They are also conditioned by the world's reactions to his condition.

The mortal wound inflicted by the father with the unfortunate apple provides a second shift in relations which affects the core of Gregor's self. The wound eats more and more deeply towards the center of his self, his human consciousness and memory. Before this event, appearances in self-perception and in perceptions of him by others undergo important shifts, but time continues to strike the hours with the alarm-clock's exactness. Gregor's sense of time is almost unchanged. But after his last foray into humanity, his fatal wound, his last response to his sister's music, self-consciousness begins to dim and, with it, his sense of time. In the end, the obliteration of time coincides with Gregor's obliteration.

Gregor's reduction to a "mere" self, and his consequent destruction, are conditioned by parallel changes in the external world. These changes occur in response to Gregor's mysterious *Verwandlung.* The father's assumption of "authority" by becoming a uniformed bank-messenger is the most obvious illustration, but equally important are changes which lead to the constriction of the household. The cleaning woman fully transforms Gregor's room into a garbage dump and becomes another mortal enemy. The entire home assumes an atmosphere of degradation as even the mother and sister "adjust" to the new condition. The three "lodgers"—whatever else they may be thought to signify—typify this oppressive shift in Gregor's former world. An unindividuated "chorus," introduced in a manner reminiscent of romantic and expressionistic fiction, they suggest the intrusion of an entire alien world. They push the family into the kitchen, usurp the dining-room and are treated by Gregor's parents with exaggerated deference. The world has been wrenched out of recognition. For the helplessly observing Gregor, its change has become irrevocable.

Shifts in both self and world condition and require one another. Gregor's own transformation had also been a function of his world. He had in fact been a vermin, crushed and circumscribed by authority and routine, before the actual transformation had taken place: Gregor recalls that when the manager had towered above him in the office he had already felt like an insect. Moreover, we noted that the most important changes had been evoked by others' reaction to his condition: his rejection by boss, father, even by his mother and sister. But it is crucial to this revelation of his condition—appearing more and more purely as he nears his end—that it had been an *aspired* condition. He had been imprisoned in his animal existence which had been implied by his human life, yet freed from intolerable burdens, including the tyranny of time. In his death likewise he is both extinguished and set free.

If Gregor's end is marked by a constriction of his physical universe and a paradoxical liberation from the bondage of himself (the true and final transformation of the hero), the family, we infer, had been similarly constricted and set free. In this way, relations constantly shift, unite, and contrast with one another. The self and the various figures representing the world are equally important, and the author focuses on them simultaneously. For this reason, the shift in point of view to the family is a perfectly defensible way of concluding the story. Gregor's extinction has, in the end, become the family's liberation. Since the self has been obliterated by the world, the emphasis must now be placed upon the world, for its figures have gained at last the liberation the hero had sought. Grete's yawn of freedom neatly ties the story to the transformation of the beginning. Yet this very conclusion has pushed us to the point of absurdity—reached by the simultaneous creation and dislocation of a particular world—in which contradictory solutions, like constriction and freedom, obliteration and awareness of existence, equally apply.

Gregor's role in the changing pattern of the world around him is deepened by our becoming aware of the significance of the form he assumes. Being reduced to a particularly repulsive specimen of animal life, he is made to enact part of his concealed nature, but he is also transformed into an effective, albeit passive, rebel against a world and values in which beetles have no place. Moreover, the very form of the insect mask deepens the moral implications of the changes in perception and point of view by which the story is ordinarily described. A good deal has been written about Kafka's use of animal figures as human masks and of human figures as animal masks. One reason for this practice is the same rationale which suggested Houyhnhnms and Yahoos to Swift. But for

Kafka there is also another reason; the animal widens human perception, because it frees it from moral necessity. Gregor as a human being with an animal mask therefore experiences peculiar conflicts between liberation from and subjection to moral choice, which are only gradually eliminated in his own obliteration. In this story the vermin carries with it the notion of disgust, but in other stories we encounter a similar effect without this element. In **"Report to the Academy,"** a monkey wears a human mask. In **"The Hunger Artist,"** the human "artist" kept as a caged animal is contrasted with the truly bestial spectators until in the significant inversion he is replaced by the actual beast—the panther.

These transformations finally suggest the intricate relations in man between a human and an animal nature. . . . As an expressionistic device getting at the essence of split humanity, as a point of transformation which reveals several layers of perception to be reflected against one another, and as a satiric mirror of man, the animal form becomes the logical counterpoint, the key to transformations through which a state of mind or awareness can be reflected against its cosmic or social antagonists. (pp. 65-8)

Ralph Freedman, "Kafka's Obscurity: The Illusion of Logic in Narrative," in Modern Fiction Studies, *Vol. VIII, No. 1, Spring, 1962, pp. 61-74.*

NORMAN FRIEDMAN (essay date 1963)

[*In the excerpt below, Friedman examines and rejects biographical interpretations of "The Metamorphosis" in favor of a strictly literal reading.*]

The problem that teases us in [**"The Metamorphosis"**] is how to explain Gregor Samsa's mysterious and disgusting change. Normally, we could attempt to solve such a problem by asking two questions: first, how and why did he become an insect in terms of the probabilities of the action? and second, what are Kafka's reasons for handling it in this way? The first question can usually be answered directly by examining the incidents in the story and their causes, while the second may be answered only indirectly by making inferences about what the author wanted to accomplish. (p. 26)

This transformation, then, must be accepted as a *fait accompli,* and so all avenues of explanation regarding the first question are closed. The story, however, deals exclusively with Gregor's and his family's reactions to this change, and it stands to reason that unless we understand the meaning of this change we will fail to understand the meaning of their reactions to it, and hence of the story as a whole. We must rely solely, therefore, on exploring the possible answers to the second question, and here at least two avenues of approach are open to us as we pursue Kafka's motives: the psychological and the artistic. Let us consider them in turn.

The search for psychological causes is the most common approach followed when dealing with this story, and it seeks to find in it an intelligible pattern by building on Kafka's biography, the Freudian hypothesis, and some scheme of literary or archetypal symbolism. Generally speaking, such an interpretation runs along the following lines: We know, to begin with, that Kafka felt inadequate in relation to his efficient and successful father, and therefore he was ambivalent about him, feeling ashamed at not measuring up while at the same time feeling resentful that he had to measure up, and admiring his father and wanting to please him to boot. Since Gregor's father plays a characteristic role in the story, wanting no nonsense from his bug-like son and even wounding him at the end, it seems plausible to attribute to the Samsa situation the factors involved in the Kafka situation (even the names are alike!). Thus Gregor has turned himself into a bug, however unconsciously, in order to spite his father and at the same time to punish himself for being an inadequate son. By becoming something non- or sub-human, he has symbolically allowed his hidden and suppressed self to emerge: his need to escape responsibility, his wish to hurt his father, his desire to express his guilt. (pp. 26-7)

A curious consequence of this kind of interpretation is that it ends by setting us against Gregor's family. Stodgy bourgeois *versus* sensitive artist becomes inevitably the story's formula, just as it is the formula of Kafka's life. Thus the ending, where the family is happily released of its dread burden and looks toward a better and healthier future with renewed hope and strength, has either to be wished away as an artistic mistake or to be read ironically as Kafka's final indictment of a sterile society returning once more to its superficial routines of marriage and work and respectability after an unlooked-for encounter with the profound forces of life and death in the unconscious. (p. 27)

And there are other details of the story which the psychological interpretation fails to explain or has to explain ironically. There is the crucial fact, for instance, that it is not the son who is inadequate, at least to begin with, but rather the father. Gregor has been supporting the family for the past four years, while his father has been lying around the house and growing fat ever since his business failed five years before. Now this could very easily be interpreted as a psychological displacement or inversion, so that inadequate Franz becomes adequate Gregor by way of wish fulfilment. . . . But why, then, does the story proceed to reinstate the father's power over the son by rendering that son incapable of meeting his responsibilities? Can we have it both ways—a Kafka who is symbolically placing himself over his father by means of a story which literally places the father over the son? or who is placing himself beneath his father by means of a story which begins by literally placing the son above the father?

Perhaps the question can be re-phrased in terms of whether we *need* to have it both ways, regardless of whether it is possible. What I want to suggest, in short, is that an answer may be sought within the story itself, regarded as an artistic whole. We can only speculate about the tangled inner forces which impelled Kafka to write such a story, and to write it in such a way, and this speculation can be interesting and valuable. But any answer it may produce regarding the story's meaning is perforce more broad and generic than is necessary, for the significance and function of any given element in that story are in the last analysis to be interpreted only in terms of that story. If such a literal approach fails to provide an answer, then it can only be concluded that there is none. Unless, that is, we are content to accept the story as a dream, and that I am not prepared to do. Certain psychological causes may be uniformly operative throughout an author's lifetime, and yet he may write many different sorts of stories. So we cannot, I believe, settle for a simple explanation of a complex thing: psychological principles are never suffi-

cient when one is asking artistic questions. At best they can point to certain things which the various stories may share in common, and thus are better suited to the study of an author's work as an expression of his personality than to the study of individual stories as works of art. But they cannot by their very nature explain the differences which may obtain among them. And in these differences lies the unique artistic quality of a work.

I do not mean to suggest, however, that we must blind ourselves to symbols when they appear in the story, or to hidden motives, or to our knowledge of family life; I mean only that we must interpret these things in terms of assumptions which are directly relevant to the story, and hypotheses whose ultimate justification lies within the story and its internal relationships. Psychological principles, after all, can and even should be used in the interpretation of the characters'—as distinct from the author's—motives within the framework of the story. Nor do I mean to say that such a literal reading will provide exhaustive and final answers: I mean only that such a reading may supply a sound basis for further inquiry. This is a powerful and mysterious and puzzling story, and it works on us in many ways. It is doubtful whether it can ever be fully explained, but in so far as it is a story it ought to be interpreted as such.

Just what is the story, then, and what is the function of Gregor's transformation in it? The basic problem Kafka set for himself, as I see it, was to show the family gradually freeing itself from its moral dependence upon Gregor, and the solution he hit upon was to turn Gregor into an insect in order to accomplish this. This will take some explaining.

The action is built on two changes: the first is Gregor's gradual deterioration and death, and the second is the family's gradual mobilization and recovery—the two together forming something of an hour-glass pattern. The inciting cause of both changes is, of course, Gregor's unexplained metamorphosis. Its immediate effect is to cut off Gregor from normal life and his family from their sole source of support. This creates in Gregor a pathetic but inevitably frustrated yearning to be recognized, to be understood, to be taken care of, and in his family an opposing disgust and revulsion. This in turn produces in Gregor a selfish unconcern for his family, and in them the need to support themselves combined with an ever-growing desperation as to how to get rid of this monster who was once their son and brother. (The family members, I realize, each react in different ways to his metamorphosis—the mother helplessly, the father tyrannically, and the sister charitably at the outset—but in the end they are united in their resolve to get rid of him.)

Now since we are told nothing about the probabilities of Gregor's change, and cannot therefore interpret it in terms of its causes, perhaps we can interpret it in terms of its effects. Why, to begin with, does his family react so negatively after he becomes a bug? The obvious answer is that he is repulsive. I still think with horror about the insect when I force myself to dwell upon its appearance and movements, although Kafka's manner of treatment softens this horror with pity. And I believe that indeed is part of the point, for the reader sees the story largely from within Gregor's point of view, while the family sees him entirely from without. This means that they are of necessity less sympathetic than we are toward the creature.

But is it not possible, a Freudian might ask, that their hostility toward this bug is in reality a symbolic disguise for their hitherto suppressed hostility toward the son? Surely there is loathing aplenty here, and it is certainly possible within the framework of the story to infer that they have been storing up against him a good deal of resentment for being his parasites. Similarly, it is quite possible to compound the symbol by having it stand for his disguised hatred of them for having to support them. (pp. 28-30)

This is possible, but again I ask whether it is necessary. The only reason for us to postulate a prior mutual resentment between them is our assumption that there must have been bad feeling in such a situation. But the only expressed hostility regarding the circumstances prior to Gregor's change we can find in the story is that which Gregor feels toward his boss, the manager, the other salesmen, and his job itself. He does not blame his family for his hard life as a salesman, nor do they blame him for their dependence on him.

Again, it is possible that Kafka was psychologically unable to confront such hostilities openly, and that this device was a means by which he could deal with them covertly, so that this story is a disguised incest-fantasy, with the bug symbolizing Kafka's suppressed desire to become a child again, and the sister standing cryptically for the mother whom he wishes to wrest from his father. But since such theories postulate a degree of control of the story over the author which I am unable to accept, I would prefer to continue my search for more literal causes. (p. 30)

I reject, on the same grounds, the possibility that the change represents Gregor's desire to escape from his responsibilities. It is true of course that he has been working for four years already and has five or six years to go before his father's debt is paid off; but, disagreeable as he has found his job, there are no expressed signs of any desire on his part to chuck the whole business. The only reason to think so is our assumption that he must want to get out of it. But why choose such a disagreeable way to escape? Is not being a bug even worse than being a travelling salesman? There is surely no pleasure in it for Gregor.

But, says the Freudian, he is also punishing himself: are you so simple-minded as to be unable to see how he can gratify himself and punish himself for this gratification at one and the same time? No one wants to be thought simple-minded, but I wonder whether such a heads-I-win-tails-you-lose assumption covers too many things, and hence fails to be sufficiently clear when applied to a particular case. And besides, why couldn't Gregor have merely developed some psychosomatic ailment and thereby have accomplished his purpose much more effectively? A convenient paralysis of the legs, for example, would have given him enough of an excuse for stopping work while at the same time providing him with enough pain for self-punishment. (pp. 30-1)

But this sort of solution would have hardly suited Kafka's purpose, for then the family would have had to care for him and pity him instead of rejecting him as they do. Robbing the family of their hostility would have robbed Kafka of his story. And that is just the point: not, however, because they have hated him for having been his parasites, but rather because *they* have fallen into a psychosomatic torpor as a result of their dependence on him, and because no other way could be found to bring them out of it.

I reason as follows: Gregor is changed into an insect through no evident fault of his own, nor through any fault of theirs

either. It seems to me that Kafka omitted any clues as to the how and why of Gregor's change precisely because he sensed the necessity of preventing the reader from assigning responsibilities in this matter. I believe he wanted us to sympathize with both Gregor and his family—with Gregor, because the story would lose the seriousness of its impact if we were made to feel simply disgust at his transformation; with the family, because without their anguished reaction we would never see for ourselves that Gregor was once human. A moral problem would become for us merely a housecleaning problem. (For the charwoman at the end, remember, it *is* merely a housecleaning problem.) Kafka wants us to sympathize with the family, because we must be prepared for the beneficial transformation they are to undergo: they are about to be released from a trap and we are to feel the force of their rescue as having some positive significance in their lives.

Indeed, if my analysis is correct, it may be that the title refers as much to their change as to his. Some readers have been so moved by Gregor's suffering, however, that they have lost sight of the family's anguish. But recall that Gregor's family do not see this bug as we do. As far as they are concerned, he is no longer their Gregor but a hideous monster with a claim on their affections. (pp. 31-2)

What they *are* accountable for, however, is the torpor into which they have fallen as a result of their dependence on his support. . . . And it is this torpor out of which the shock of Gregor's transformation wakes them, and with that awakening, it seems to me, we can only sympathize. (p. 32)

They have been, in effect, redeemed. The only trouble is that poor Gregor has been sacrificed in the process. Kafka mitigates the pathos of this necessity in two ways: first, he has Gregor get more callous and bug-like in his attitudes as the story progresses (although music retains its power to move him); and second, he has him die peacefully. (pp. 32-3)

Gregor was turned into a bug, then, because there was no other way to free his family from their moral degeneration, and he died because there was no other way to free them for the future. But granted they had to be freed by means of some external agency, it might be objected that Kafka showed poor artistic judgment in choosing so desperate and fantastic an expedient. Consider, however, the alternatives. Had Gregor continued working, they would have continued as his parasites. Had he simply quit his job and left them, they would have been able to blame him and feel sorry for themselves. Had he gotten sick or lame, they would have had to pity him. Had he simply died, they would have been able to feel sorry for themselves. My thesis is that, given the situation, they have to be made to *want* to be free, and the solution Kafka chose was to make Gregor repulsive to them, for only then could they reject him. All avenues of self-defeating escape from their decision are thus closed: blame, pity, remorse— any such emotion would have hindered their desire for freedom. Only by being made to reject him could they be made to want to be free.

It might be further objected that their having to be freed by means of some external agency places Kafka's conception of the situation in a rather poor light. Why were they not capable of rising to the challenge of their lives by drawing upon their own inner resources? Why were they not capable of undergoing an inner change? Why are they worth saving at all, and at so great a cost? The answer lies partly in the fact, I think, that the father and mother are both washed out. . . .

The parents simply have no internal resources left, and the sister, just on the threshold of maturity, is too young and inexperienced to expect great things from. They are ordinary people, the victim of a hard life and of a trap they do not know how to get out of. And this, I think, heightens the sympathy we are meant to feel toward them. I doubt, though, whether the parents are in themselves worth saving: it is rather the rescue of the sister which, if anything can justify the cost, explains the sacrifice of Gregor. And that is exactly the note on which Kafka ends. . . . (pp. 33-4)

It was a difficult artistic problem which Kafka set for himself, for he had to retain the reader's sympathy for both parties. Gregor was not to be blamed for turning into a bug, nor was the family to be blamed for rejecting him in this new shape. We were to be made to see both sides and to recognize the inevitable suffering involved in this family convulsion; neither side asked for trouble, but both were caught in a trap not of their own devising. But Gregor has to be destroyed to get them out of it, and the cruelty of this necessity, mitigated or not, cannot be put out of mind. Thus, when the family breathes freely once again at the end, our pleasure is crossed by our knowledge of the price of their redemption. A characteristic aura of Kafkan ambiguity remains as we look back over the whole, for the disagreeable shock of Grete's erotic health when seen in the light of her poor brother's miserable fate, coupled with our memory of the family's miserliness in having withheld some money from his hard-won earnings, of his mother's servile helplessness, and of his father's selfish vanity, prevents us finally from resting content with any simple attribution of sympathy.

The only thing which ultimately allows the story to produce its proper aesthetic satisfaction is our recognition of the fact that of the two possibilities—Gregor continuing on as the sole support of his family, or Gregor being transformed and dying so that they could be reborn—only the second could do any good to any of them. For Gregor was not really alive at all in his role as provider . . . and ironically his continued success in that very role could only have reduced his family further in their moral degradation. Even if he had paid off that impossible debt, they all would have lost in the end—he wasted by overwork and they wallowing in indolence. As it turns out, he paid off the debt after all. (p. 34)

> *Norman Friedman, "Kafka's 'Metamorphosis': A Literal Reading." in* Approach *No. 49, Fall, 1963, pp. 26-34.*

DOUGLAS ANGUS (essay date 1964)

[*In the following excerpt, Angus views the torturing device in "In the Penal Colony" as representative of the mechanistic universe that flourished during Kafka's lifetime.*]

Kafka's career illustrates a possible definition of artistic genius; namely, that genius is what emerges when an artist's personal experience peculiarly symbolizes, supports, or parallels the basic beliefs or metaphysical image of his time. The particular metaphysical image that analytical science had brought to Kafka's time was that of an astonishingly complex and orderly mechanical system that was meaningless since it produced pleasure and pain indiscriminately and rather more pain than pleasure. Equally paradoxical was the fact that the more complex and vast and self sustaining the system appeared to be, the more difficult it became to find, or even believe in, that warm and personal God so comforting to the

frightened and the lonely, or any other conceivable God. Kafka, like most existentialists, does not seem to have been particularly interested in natural science. He probably found its impersonality distasteful. His diaries show a remarkable lack of interest in the subject, considering how curious a mind he possessed. Nevertheless, the mechanistic, deterministic universe of analytical science was the basic source of the existentialist's religious problems.

This universe of meaningless order is paralleled in the bureaucratic society that Kafka grew up in, a society where order was a fetish elaborated to an excessiveness beyond utility or meaning, where contact with the central authority who ultimately controlled one's destiny was impossible. Kafka is the delineator *par excellence* of this cumbersome bureaucracy, but it is because his bureaucracies are symbols of the total system, the very orderly, cold, and mechanistic universe of analytical science, that they have stirred his readers so deeply.

Kafka's narratives are about bureaucratic systems in which human beings and their relationships tend to become mechanical and dehumanized rather than about machines, which after all, are not fruitful subjects for fiction. In **"In The Penal Colony,"** however, he has written a remarkable story about a diabolical machine. Austin Warren has shown how this machine represents the old scholastic theology that once existed for the meting out of justice upon all mankind condemned for sin in this world (the penal colony). Now the old system is disintegrating; the Old Commander (God) has died, although there is a legend that he will return again. With a sadistic logic, the machine kills its victims by carving with whirling needles the name of their sin ever deeper into their bodies. The law broken by the condemned man in the story is "Honor Thy Superior," a rule that had special overtones of bitterness for Kafka, but which also corresponds to the chief commandment of the old theology. There is no mistaking the religious references, such as the fact that the Old Commander was refused burial in the cemetery by the priests. There is little doubt that Kafka had consciously in mind these references to Christian theology.

However, there are elements in the diabolical machine that seem to go beyond mere reference to an old theological system. For one thing the suffering of the victim is too intense and too immediate to exactly represent spiritual problems of the past. Moreover, a machine isn't quite right as a symbol for a theological system. It is more appropriately analogous to a mechanistic universe, as Paley's watch was used to illustrate features of the diest's universe. Kafka's machine is a kind of combination of printing press and wood planing machine. There is the "draughtsman," a clockwork which determines the motions of the "harrow," which contains the whirling and vibrating needles that write out on the body of the victim the law he has broken. This body is placed upon the lower part of the machine called the "bed," which also vibrates and turns the body over like a log in the cradle of a saw mill or planing machine, and eventually tosses the body out of the machine.

That there were more immediate influences at work in the creation of this machine than thoughts of the old scholastic theology is revealed by its similarity to a machine described by Kafka in a report he made while working for The Workers' Accidental Insurance Institute. . . . (pp. 141-42)

It is difficult not to believe that the complicated machine

which tortures the condemned men in the penal colony is directly related to those dangerous factory machines which so mutilated the workers in Kafka's day and which his work with the Insurance Institute made him so conscious of. These machines were a part of that very real and monstrous world in which Kafka found himself; they were a part of, and a symbol of, that total mechanistic universe in which he lived. From this system too God had departed. If you sought Him for explanation, pity or recompense, you were likely to end up in the red tape of The Workers' Accidental Insurance Institute.

The machine in **"In The Penal Colony,"** like the mechanistic universe, is remarkably orderly, efficient, and logical. How logical to destroy you by carving into your body the words of the law you have broken! In the universe also when you break a law you are punished in a logically appropriate way. Only to the human heart the logic is the logic of madness. One does not have to consider the old scholastic theology to find this ruthless justice; every agonizing disease, every violent death reminds us that this is the justice we live by. The new synthesis of science by its presentation of the reciprocal interrelation of entropy and in order in the process of emergent evolution explains why, within the system, it must be so. "Death is the mother of beauty," enthusiastically cries the American poet Wallace Stevens, taking solace in the logic of the system. It is cruel and absurd that life should rest on pain and death, Kafka tells us. Stevens' view is that of one fortunately living on the positive upward stroke of life's cycle; Kafka's is that of one caught in the downward stroke. Stevens' view, accepting pain and death, seems to be the more rational and the more comprehensive, but the profundity of Kafka's view does not suffer by the comparison, for there is always the deeper mystery of why the system itself has to be based on such a harsh principle, of why pain and pleasure must evolve together. (pp. 142-43)

> *Douglas Angus, "The Existentialist and the Diabolical Machine," in* Criticism, *Vol. VI, No. 2, Spring, 1964, pp. 134-43.*

ALEXANDER TAYLOR (essay date 1965)

[*In his essay on "The Metamorphosis" excerpted below, Taylor finds Gregor's transformation an expression of his disenchantment with the structure of society. However, the transformation also represents the ambivalence of Gregor's position: he yearns to be free, yet is convinced that he is vile because he does not happily fit into the "dehumanizing world of order."*]

Perhaps the failing of some of the Kafka criticism is the attempt to clarify something that should remain a riddle. **"Metamorphosis"** has certainly had multiple interpretations, many of them prompted by the temptation to lay the corpus of Kafka's works neatly on the psychoanalyst's couch, thus viewing the story as an exercise in masochism or a session in therapy. However, it seems to me that if we look at the story from the viewpoint that it is not Gregor who is sick, but his environment, we will see the story as the reaction of a perceptive individual against a dehumanizing world of order, within which most people are enslaved. . . . [An] indication of the dehumanized world is the father's wearing his bank messenger's uniform at home, where it "began to look dirty despite all the loving care of the mother and sister to keep it clean." The world of order carried into the home destroys the possibility of true human love.

The riddle is Gregor's riddle—how to fulfill himself and simultaneously express his love and understanding among people who react unsympathetically, even violently, against his transformation, and who refuse to recognize his ability to understand them, because they can't understand him. Even more is the riddle Gregor's because he does not understand himself.

The story begins with Gregor's waking; it is a waking in more than one sense, and is therefore represented by his transformation to a giant beetle. Gregor's mind at first refuses to accept this condition even though he senses "it was no dream." He thinks, "What about sleeping a little longer and forgetting all this nonsense?" Then his thoughts turn to his job. It is obvious that he intensely dislikes his work as a travelling salesman . . . , but that on the other hand feels duty bound to continue working until he has saved enough money to pay back his parents' debt to the chief.

Other details of his thoughts, the spineless and stupid porter who checks on him and the insurance doctor who considers "all mankind as perfectly healthy malingerers" emphasize the distrust and suspicion surrounding Gregor and his disgust at this state of affairs.

This disgust stems from Gregor's desire to establish I-thou relationships in a world of I-it or I-she or I-he relationships. [The critic adds in a footnote: "I am using these terms (borrowed from Buber) in a limited sense. I-thou relationships are those of true human affection. I-it are those in which the I uses the person or object as a tool to reach his ends."] In general the people surrounding Gregor do not experience a warm love through a genuine communication, but see each other as objects that are useful or to be used. For instance, the chief clerk is sent to Gregor by the firm because Gregor is not functioning as an object or tool of the firm. (pp. 337-38)

Gregor's relationship to his family previous to his transformation had really become an I-it relationship (further emphasized by the fact that the father had money of his own salted away which he did not use to help pay back his own debt, a debt which kept Gregor in bondage to the firm). . . . Gregor desires desperately to achieve a relation with a "special uprush of warm feeling" but fails to do so in a dehumanized world. It is ironical that his unconscious desire to be his true self destroys his relationship to the two people with whom he most nearly achieved this warm feeling—his mother and his sister.

How do we interpret Gregor's transformation? First, we note that in the beginning Gregor does not consciously will the change, and in fact tries to deny it to himself. Second, Gregor is puzzled about his change, and is constantly questioning himself about it. . . . Third, Gregor yearns passionately for association with the family; he presses his body against the door to catch snatches of family conversation. Fourth, Gregor has always shown almost perverse consideration for the firm and for other members of his family at the expense of his own desires, and immediately after the transformation continues to do so. Fifth, that Gregor, upon waking, is "unusually hungry." And last, Gregor's transformation is a continuing process, initially a retrogression into the natural state of an insect, but later a gradual movement toward self-assertion at the expense of the comfort of others.

The riddle is Gregor's riddle because he is the only one in the story who acknowledges it. It is the riddle of man's existence in his yearning for freedom and self-fulfillment and in the knowledge of his enslavement to the established order.

Let us assume, then, the hypothesis that Gregor's transformation represents a cluster of feelings at the center of which is Gregor's ambivalence—a yearning for freedom from the established order which he does not understand and which he cannot trace back to its original causes, and the feeling that he is as vile as an insect because he does not want to belong to the established order, even though he desires I-thou relationships with individuals in that established order and feels that it is his duty to his family to work within that order. The beetle also represents Gregor's revolt and the established order's revulsion at such a revolt.

So we note that after Gregor's transformation he is "unusually hungry." This hunger theme is developed in much the same way as it is in **"The Hunger Artist"**—neither Gregor nor the hunger artist knows what food will satisfy his hunger, although Gregor gets a glimpse.

Gregor is repulsed by fresh food and eats the decayed foods which are natural to some insects. However, after Gregor defied his mother and sister and was bombarded with apples by his father, his feelings of hunger for love come to his mind and he thinks how they are neglecting him. (pp. 339-40)

So it was naturally not food at all that Gregor needed, but an unknown nourishment that he perceives but faintly when he hears his sister play the violin. . . .

His long day-dream that immediately follows deals with an I-thou relationship with his sister. . . .

It is important here to note that when Gregor saw and heard his sister play, he *followed his impulse* to enter the living room. . . . Thus, Gregor begins to follow his true impulse toward self-fulfillment in an existential reality which denies the world of mechanized and empty but functional public order.

However, the world of order cannot tolerate this monstrosity, and Gregor cannot live in an atmosphere of complete rejection. His sister pronounces sentence. "He must go." (p. 341)

It is interesting that Gregor on then returning to his room is astonished at the distance and wonders how he could have crawled so far into the living room without noticing it. The reader knows the reason—he had been receiving the unknown nourishment that he craved.

Just as **"The Hunger Artist"** ends with the image of the panther with its strong physical existence, unaware of the cage, so **"Metamorphosis"** concludes with the death of the spiritual and the triumph of the unquestioning physical existence in the established order. At the end of the family's journey into the country, Grete "sprang to her feet first and stretched her young body." (pp. 341-42)

> Alexander Taylor, "The Waking: The Theme of Kafka's 'Metamorphosis'," in Studies in Short Fiction, Vol. II, No. 4, Summer, 1965, pp. 337-42.

MARTIN GREENBERG (essay date 1965)

[*In the excerpt below, Greenberg asserts that "The Judgment" offers Kafka's most lucid fictional portrayal of his relationship with his father.*]

Kafka's imagination is a "psychoanalytic" one. Not because he studied Freud but because he grasped intuitively the split in the self and the struggle of the unacknowledged part against the public part. The single images unfolded in his dream narratives reveal the primitively literal at the heart of the abstract. Of all his stories **"The Judgment"** furnishes perhaps the clearest demonstration of his psychoanalytic vision—clearest because least complicated by other considerations. The true starting point of his work, it is primarily a psychological story; although even here, at the start, his utterly simple images seem to suggest an unlimited depth of significance and not only psychological depth.

The image that **"The Judgment"** unfolds is one of paternal condemnation and execution; it is the story of a father's sentencing his son to death. The essential metaphor of the story is contained in the title, **"Das Urteil."** "Urteil" (like the English "judgment") has both the literal ("primitive") legal-judicial meaning of "sentence" or "verdict," and the abstract meaning of "critical estimate; opinion." The literal death *sentence* reveals the murderous truth buried underneath the abstract surface of the father's *opinion* of the son. The destructive paternal judgment is laid bare symbolically in an actual condemnation to death. (p. 4)

[In] **"The Judgment"** it is just its own symbolism, and therefore its existence, which is at issue. What the story is about is just the question of whether it shall have a symbolical meaning, or whether its symbolical meaning shall be overthrown by the action of the story. Shall the father be a figure of godlike authority to his son, with the power to give life and take it away? Or shall he simply be one man like another, and a doddering old man at that? ("We are all simply men here, one as much as the other," K. says to the priest in *The Trial*.) Shall his father's judgment of Georg be a "sentence" of death on him, or one man's "opinion" of another? Is his father a god or a "comedian" playing god? The struggle in the story, which takes place entirely inside Georg's subjectivity, is between his "primitive," "childish," irrational conception of his father, the existence of which his confident behavior at the beginning of the story would deny, and the appreciation of his father as being just a man. What the story is about is Georg's struggle against his "neurotic" submission to his father's "comic" pretensions to absolute authority; it is a "psychoanalytic" story through and through.

Georg's life hangs on the question of whether or not his father shall prevail over him in his own soul as a symbol. In the upshot the symbolical (which is to say the "neurotic") triumphs within Georg and he executes himself at his father's command. But suppose Georg had triumphed over his "neurosis," i.e. had been able to reduce his father from a symbolically inflated figure to one that he is able to perceive in its literal dimensions? In that case the symbolical would have been overthrown by the—truth. The truth threatens to "expose" the lying symbolical and cancel the story. In Kafka's work, where everything tends toward the ultimate, there is an ultimate antagonism between literature and truth; by implication **"The Judgment"** raises the possibility of the "overcoming" of literature by truth. (pp. 6-7)

For all its brevity, **"The Judgment"** is a novella rather than a short story. The short story, being literary and prizing art, deals with what it can deal with and doesn't try to cram the whole story in. The *novella* on the other hand—the old Italian *novella* of the kind that Kleist and Stendhal wrote—is, literally, "news" and tries to tell the whole extraordinary story of some unheard of happening. For the old *novella* it isn't art that is extraordinary but what happens in life. The roughly carpentered impatient old *novella* form has been refined by Kafka's hand into the simple-subtle form of his dream narrative, but its aim remains life-truth rather than literary art. Here, on the ground of a literature of truth rather than of art, Kleist, Stendhal and Kafka are united.

"The Judgment" describes an "unheard of occurrence," in Goethe's words, but one so unheard of that it has passed beyond the limits of empirical reality into a dream world of poetic (metaphorical) reality. You can only call the reality of **"The Judgment"** metaphorical, however, by standing outside the story; it is an analytical statement. To *experience* the story you have to read it from inside, standing in Georg's shoes. Read from inside, the story's metaphor is felt as literally true. You have to stand inside the story and outside the story. This of course is what happens with dreams. Dreaming, you feel the dream as literally true; awake, you analyze it as a metaphor. Kafka's art unites feeling and analysis; it asks that you should respond to its reality directly and wholeheartedly without standing off at a distance, *and* that you should interpret it by analysis. It is an art that unites poetic vividness with intellectual subtlety.

The dream suggested to Kafka a narrative mode for expressing the absence that he felt of any ground but his own self to stand on. In his stories the narrator, like the dreamer, sees and hears only what is inside his own head. He knows the world only as it is reflected inside himself. The evolution of modern narrative shows a more or less steady surrender of the traditional godlike claim of the storyteller to omniscience. The distance between the narrator and his narration shrinks till in **"The Judgment"** it has disappeared completely; as Friedrich Beissner writes, the Kafka narrative does not "manipulate his characters like a puppeteer or . . . explain the external facts and the external course of events to the reader through some knowledge he possesses by virtue of his detachment—rather he has completely transformed himself into the lonely Georg. . . ." Georg is Kafka the narrator. Why then doesn't Kafka write "I" instead of "Georg"? Why doesn't he use first-person narrative rather than third-person narrative? Because in the dream "I" appears to the dreamer as "him"—the self looks at the self and judges itself. (pp. 8-9)

"The Judgment" turns upon the conflict between Georg's self as he thinks he is, would like to be and in part is, and his self as it really is, sleeping outside of his awareness but starting awake in the dream—between the apparently successful young businessman whose reverie opens the story and the helpless Georg for whom his father's word makes all things be or not be, the Georg who dies saying, "Dear parents, I have always loved you, all the same." There is the mystery of the friend in Russia, who is doubtless another side of the narrator's self—but more about him later.

The story opens on Georg looking out of the window of his room on a Sunday morning in spring, immersed in his own thoughts. A successful young merchant, he has just finished a letter to an old friend now settled in Russia belatedly announcing his engagement to a well-off girl. His lengthy reverie turns around his unsuccessful misanthropic friend whom he has hesitated to tell about his business successes and most recently about his personal success in becoming engaged. There is a touch of condescension in his thoughts and more than a touch of impatience; he would like to advise his difficult lonely friend to give up his unsuccessful Russian venture but cannot be sure that he would not be worse off at home. In the course of Georg's reverie we learn the main facts about his life: that he shares the household with his father, that his mother died two years before and that since then he has taken an active part in the family business, which his father used to run dictatorially, so that it has bloomed surprisingly.

When Georg crosses from his own room to his father's, which he hasn't visited for months, he is surprised how dark it is. The darkness is the interior darkness of his own self. As his father rises to meet him, his heavy dressing gown swinging open and the skirts fluttering, Georg thinks, with a touch of surprise: "My father is still a giant of a man." His surprise at his father's strength increases as they talk: "In business hours he's quite different, he was thinking, how solidly he sits here with his arms crossed." In the light of day, his father appeared elderly and enfeebled; at the level of dreams—at the symbolical level—he sits with solid strength.

Georg has come to tell his father that he has written the news of his engagement to his friend in St. Petersburg.

> "To St. Petersburg?" asked his father.
>
> "To my friend there," said Georg, trying to meet his father's eye. . . .
>
> "Oh yes. To your friend," said his father, with emphasis.

His father's interrogative echoes and emphases undermine Georg's words so that they begin to ring hollowly. Then finally his father speaks, "lengthening his toothless mouth"—there is a constant shuttling back and forth in Georg between seeing his father as a dodderer and seeing him as a giant. The latter's speech is a querulous complaint about things being done since the mother died "that aren't right," his not being "equal to things any longer," his failing memory, how "our dear mother's death" affected him more than it did Georg—ending in a sudden thrust at his son:

> "But since we're talking about it, about this letter, I beg you, Georg, don't deceive me. It's a trivial affair, it's hardly worth mentioning, so don't deceive me. Do you really have this friend in St. Petersburg?"

Georg's response to the elder Bendemann's questioning the existence of his friend in Russia is one of "embarrassment," in which fear of his father (who can simply wipe a friend out of existence with a question) and fear that his father has become senile—fear *of* the giant, fear *for* the dodderer—are mingled. Georg resolves to take better care of his father in the future, to see to it that he eats properly, to call in a doctor, to exchange rooms with him—he resolves to treat him as ailing and incapable and to put him into his (Georg's) bed at once. This satisfies his fear for himself, lest his father overthrow the successful, independent Georg who is about to cap his triumphs with marriage; but it is also a surrender of his bed to his father—and it is Georg's getting a partner for his bed that has incensed the old man most. His putting his father into his bed is both a counter-attack and a surrender.

When Georg undresses the old man and notices remorsefully his "not particularly clean" underwear, he decides to take him into his own future household. "It almost looked, on closer inspection, as if the care he meant to lavish there on his father might come too late." This is the high point of Georg's perception of his father's weakness (for the latter is indeed dangerously weak), but also the high point of his conceit about his own strength vis-à-vis the elder Bendemann's.

The father submits to being put to bed; the senile way he plays with his son's watch chain while being carried there and hangs onto it when he attempts to lay him down, gives Georg a "dreadful feeling." Bendemann Sr. draws the covers up and looks at Georg "with a not unfriendly eye." The comedy the father and the son are acting reaches its climax in the father's repeated question about whether he is "well covered up now." "Don't worry, you're well covered up," Georg replies soothingly.

At this point the *novella* explodes into a nightmare in whose lurid light the "primitive" truth about Georg Bendemann and his father is revealed.

> "No!" cried his father, cutting short the answer, threw the covers off with a strength that sent them all flying in a moment and sprang erect in bed. Only one hand lightly touched the ceiling to steady him.
>
> "You wanted to cover me up, I know, my young sprig, but I'm far from being covered up yet. And even if this is the last strength I have, it's enough for you, too much for you. Of course I know your friend. He would have been a son after my own heart. That's why you have been playing him false all these years. Why else? Do you think I haven't cried for him? And that's why you had to lock yourself in your office—the Chief is busy, mustn't be disturbed—just so that you could write your lying letters to Russia. But thank goodness a father doesn't need to be taught how to see through his son. And now that you thought you'd got him down, so far down that you could set your bottom on him and he wouldn't move, then my lordly son makes up his mind to get married!"

The father understands "covered up" as meaning "buried," the bed Georg wishes to confine him to as a grave, their relations as a death struggle. The covers that he flings off are all those trappings of civilization which conceal the primitive battle to the death between fathers and sons. Suddenly we are pitched out of history back into natural history, into a world a good deal like that of Freud's *Totem and Taboo*.

In the eyes of the father the son's succession as head of the family business is a usurpation, never mind his own failing strength. For the father, the son's life as a man is his own death; his life needs his son's defeat. Therefore he hits out cruelly (and comically—he is indeed a comedian, as Georg calls him) at Georg's engagement:

> "Because she lifted up her skirts," his father began to flute, "because she lifted her skirts like this, the nasty creature," and mimicking her he lifted his shirt so high that one could see the scar on his thigh from his war wound, "because she lifted her skirts like this and this you made up to her, and in order to make free with her undisturbed you have disgraced your mother's memory, betrayed your friend and struck your father into bed so that he can't move. But he can move, or can't he?"
>
> —And he stood up quite unsupported and kicked his legs out. His insight made him radiant.

The bellowing old man, cavorting in his son's bed, is transfigured by his insight into the truth of what is going on between him and his son; he hisses with self-gratulation over his own shrewdness. Bendemann Sr. takes Georg's engagement as a

blow at himself, just as if he were the leader of a horde and it was one of his own mates Georg was coveting. That is why he calls Georg a child and a devil in the same breath, just before he pronounces the death sentence:

> "An innocent child, yes, that you were, truly, but still more truly have you been a devilish human being!"

It is out of natural innocence, in the fulfillment of his most natural instincts, that Georg reaches for a wife; but in reaching for a wife he oversteps the "law" which gives all wives to the father and becomes a "devil." Child or devil is the alternative his father confronts him with—"childish" submission to sheerly arbitrary authority or "devilish" defiance of it. We are down to a level of the soul which reflects the earliest times, before there was a written law. (pp. 9-13)

Georg knew all along that a battle was going on between himself and his father! But he "forgot" it, and even as he recollects it now he forgets it again.

But the Georg who is wrestling for possession of his own soul and who tries to see his father as a man like any other, struggles desperately against the other Georg who bends hypnotically to the father's command. (pp. 13-14)

The elder Bendemann tells the "stupid boy" that he has been secretly communicating with his friend in Russia all along.

> " . . . he knows everything a hundred times better than you do yourself. . . ."
>
> In his enthusiasm he waved his arm over his head. "He knows everything a thousand times better!" he cried.
>
> "Ten thousand times!" said Georg, to make fun of his father, but in his very mouth the words turned into deadly earnest.

His own words turn against him, (for the father and the friend have indeed been in cahoots with one another), his attempt to reduce his father from a symbol to a human being is defeated; the time for his sentencing "to death by drowning" is at hand. As he rushes—or rather "feels himself driven"—from the room, down the stairs and to the river side, "the crash with which his father fell on the bed behind him was still in his ears"—the condemnation uses up the father's last-remaining strength. "Dear parents, I have always loved you, all the same," Georg whispers abjectly just before he drops into the river.

> At this moment an unending stream of traffic was just going over the bridge.

The powerful pulse of the life of the world that the son was unable to reach and make himself part of, the "human harmony" that he wished to join, beats in the story's last words. (Kafka likened the last sentence to an orgasm.) He dies pathetically, a tiny falling figure against the indifferent ceaseless streaming of human life.

The puzzle of the story is the friend in Russia. Is it possible to account for him in a way that is convincing rather than just ingenious? I think he can be accounted for, I don't think he can be justified; he is the one failure in a story of vivid, succinct art.

Kate Flores' suggestion that Georg's expatriated friend is a side of Kafka himself, the Kafka who was a writer and a bachelor, just as Georg is another side of Kafka, is surely right. Throughout Kafka's work Russia figures as an image of the most extreme solitude, which stands for his own solitude as a writer. (pp. 14-15)

In **"The Judgment"** the friend in Russia is described as a man who "was resigning himself to becoming a permanent bachelor"—Kafka had just met the woman to whom he later became engaged (twice over) but never married, and was carrying on a tortured debate with himself that lasted his entire life over the question of marriage, which he was painfully convinced was irreconcilable with his writing. The friend's unspecified business, which is doing so poorly, is (as Mrs. Flores points out) Kafka's own business of writing, in the doldrums too till he wrote this very story. The necessity for such biographical references indicates Kafka's failure to realize *in the story* the meaning he intended the friend to have.

Georg's friendship with the man in Russia, (i.e. Kafka's bent toward "Russian solitude" and literature) imperils his marriage; that is explicitly stated when his fiancée, "Fraülein Frieda Brandenfeld, " says: "Since your friends are like that Georg you shouldn't ever have got engaged at all." The two friends are in an uneasy relationship in which each refuses to accept the other as he is. Georg would like to persuade his friend, "who had obviously run off the rails," to give up and come home; the friend on his side has tried to persuade Georg to emigrate to Russia. Georg's writing the news of his engagement to St. Petersburg is a first step toward a rupture with his friend; his marriage would have completed the rupture (i.e. been the end of Kafka as a writer). But the father intervenes at this point and saves the friend (Kafka the writer-bachelor) from being "betrayed" by Georg:

> "But your friend hasn't been betrayed after all!" cried his father, emphasizing the point with stabs of his forefinger. "I've been representing him here on the spot."

The father, "representing" the interest of the friend, stops the marriage and condemns Georg (Kafka the man) to death.

The theme of **"The Judgment"** is "the opposition between fathers and sons," to quote a phrase from Kafka's little diary essay on the literature of small peoples (Dec. 25, 1911). But Kafka intended to represent the conflict between marriage and writing as an integral part of the father-son opposition (as I will try to show more clearly in a moment). Here he failed. The friend in Russia is unable to come alive in the story with the meaning that Kafka wished him to have. He remains a ghostly ineffectual presence, a mystery whose explanation must be sought in Kafka's life.

Kafka's failure can, I think, be traced to his inability, in these years of trying to marry, to see beyond the injuries his father had done him, recognize his bachelorhood as his own choice and embrace his fate as a writer—to a confusion in his understanding of his own responsibility for his life. This confusion shows up in the story in the puzzling, contradictory representation of the relations between the father and the friend in Russia. The father's attitude to the friend, we learn from Georg's words, was hostile at first: he "used not to like him very much. At least twice I [Georg] denied him before you (*vor dir verleugnete*), although he was actually sitting with me in my room. I could quite understand your dislike of him, my friend has his peculiarities." To placate his father, Georg has twice denied his peculiar friend before him (i.e. repudiated his connection with Kafka the writer). But when the father flings

the covers off and denounces Georg, he claims the friend as his own: "Of course I know your friend. He would have been a son after my own heart." He has been writing to him all along, he roars at his son some pages later; "in his left hand he crumples your letters unopened while in his right hand he holds up my letters to read through!" (That is, Kafka the writer-bachelor heeds only his father's "messages" and ignores all communications from Kafka the man.

Yet the father's sudden embrace of the friend menaces the latter's life. No sooner does the elder Bendemann trumpet his proprietorship in the friend than Georg sees him "lost in the vastness of Russia." . . . The better the father knows the friend the more the latter is "lost in Russia"—indeed he knows him "too well." And the contempt the father feels for the friend, in spite of his saying he would have been a son after his own heart, is unmistakable in his last words about him: he is only using him against the Georg who is fighting his father for his life:

> "How long a time you've taken to grow up! Your mother had to die, she couldn't see the happy day, your friend is going to pieces in that Russia of his [in seinem Russland], even three years ago he was yellow enough to throw away. . . ."

Bendemann Sr. is no friend of writing!

The contradictions in the father's relation to the friend in Russia can be explained only out of biographical sources. In the "Letter to his father" Kafka says that his father was the never-ending theme of his writing:

> My writing was all about you, all I did there, after all, was to complain about the things I couldn't complain about on your breast.

The friend is joined to the father in the story as Kafka the writer was joined to the obsessive theme of *his* father; the friend is in "league" with the father against Georg as Kafka the writer-bachelor was "leagued" with his father against Kafka the man who had recently met Felice Bauer and was thinking hard about marriage. In the sentence immediately following the one quoted above, Kafka betrays the perplexity in his own understanding of himself as a writer which is responsible for the failure in the story:

> It [his writing] was an intentionally long-drawn-out leave-taking from you, something, to be sure, which you were the cause of, but which took its course in a direction determined by me.

Kafka is saying that his father was the reason why he was a writer (although the kind of writer he became was his own doing), by having banished him from the world to the freezing inhuman solitude ("Russia") in which only writing was possible. (In the diary entry of January 28, 1922, two and a half years before he died, he wrote: " . . . why did I want to quit the world? Because 'he' [his father] would not let me live in it, in his world." In making the father the ally and support of the friend in Russia, Kafka is trying to give objective narrative expression to his sense of his father's responsibility for his being a writer. But this is to try and express a negative responsibility in positive terms and produces the absurdity that the closer father and friend in the story are allied, the nearer to perishing in Russia the latter is. The contempt the elder Bendemann shows for Georg's friend, who "is going to pieces in that Russia of his, even three years ago he was yellow enough to throw away," flagrantly contradicts his saying that the exile would have been a son after his own heart. It betrays the contempt Herrmann Kafka felt for his son's life of devotion to writing. Kafka's father's contempt for him is a negative fact that can't be accommodated within the positive metaphor of the alliance of Bendemann Sr. and the friend in Russia—just as Kafka's own writing is a positive thing that can't in the end be blamed on his father's shutting him out of the world.

The painful confusion in Kafka's understanding of himself lies in his feeling that his solitary existence as a writer was forced on him by his father; and in his feeling at the same time that writing was his own deepest choice, so that his lonely bachelor's life of exile from the world was something *he* was responsible for, an affirmation of his most authentic self. His affirmative sense of his writer's calling is obscurely indicated in the fact that the friend in Russia is also Georg's ally; they are both struggling against the father to affirm themselves and they both go down to defeat together, the one by direct condemnation and the other by exposure to Russian revolutions. But Georg (Kafka the man) has failed to protect the friend (Kafka the writer), has failed to draw him to him, away from the father.

Like so many writers of the modern age, like the modern age itself, Kafka starts out from a feeling of filial grievance. But to push his grievance to the point where he even blames his father for his writer's destiny, although his writing was everything to him, shows a baffled self-understanding. At this point the mythopoeic power of **"The Judgment"** declines into the obscure ingenuity one finds in the relationship between Bendemann Sr. and the friend in Russia.

Although **"The Judgment"** aims primarily at a psychological truth, it trembles on the point of saying all those other things which we find in Kafka's later works. In the subjective depths in which his stories swim, everything is spiritualized so that there is nothing, not even the most humble object or gesture, that does not become charged with ultimate meaning. Only consider the father's dirty underwear. As an "objective" fact it indicates the old man's fustiness and incapacity to take care of himself any longer; to Georg, who has been intent on marriage and independence, it is a reproach that works to draw him back into his father's orbit. But it also suggests something else. As Walter Benjamin notes, the element in which Kafka's bureaucrats live is dirt: the filth of the inhuman and the prehuman, the grime of the mechanical, the impersonal, the life-denying. That is also Bendemann Sr.'s element, who is about to swell out into the officialdom of *The Trial* and *The Castle;* he is pregnant with that meaning. With mythopoeic breadth he reaches from the prehistoric primitive past to the immediate present: the embodiment of a universal arbitrariness which opposes itself to life and freedom, the paternal idea on the point of being raised to a general principle of tyranny.

And yet if one reads the story as a tale of tyranny and victimization one has read only a part. Even in this early story, with its primarily psychological emphasis, his imagination strives to go beyond the ultimately futile reproaches and self-justifications which make up the argument between the generations and find a truth underlying the psychological one of oppressor-fathers and victim-sons. In the end—but only in the end—it does not matter where the "fault" goes back endlessly and forward endlessly through the generations. Somewhere inside the arbitrary inhuman authority of the father sticks the idea of something against which Georg Bendemann

has indeed offended. Somewhere within himself the father incorporates the "law"—the unreasonable law of life which Georg violates just by being defeated in his life. In truth Georg is innocent and his father robs him of his life. . . . "God," the supreme bureaucrat, hates life and denies it to man; man does not fall, "God" turns him out of the house of life. But in truth, too, Georg is sinful (*aside* from all questions of guilt and innocence), for he sins against his life by failing to live it. . . . Georg sins, but against himself, by failing to live, by failing to be human.

The atmosphere of surcharged significance peculiar to Kafka's stories most immediately expresses their character as dream narratives. Like dreams, their surface hides shadowy depths of meaning; inside their explicit content latent contents lurk. But another way to put this is to say that Kafka's words demand to be interpreted—significance in Kafka is a matter of the word and the interpretation thereof. Put thus, we can see how his stories are old as well as new and belong to a tradition of writing that goes back to the Bible. He describes this kind of writing himself in a passage already quoted from **"Investigations of a Dog,"** where the narrator speaks about the

> greater sense of possibility that moves us so deeply when we listen to those old and strangely simple stories. Here and there we catch a curiously significant phrase and we would almost like to leap to our feet, if we did not feel the weight of centuries upon us. . . . the true word . . . was there, was very near at least, on the tip of everybody's tongue, anyone might have hit upon it.

Kafka's work, too, has something of the quality of "those old and strangely simple stories" with their "curiously significant phrases" which "move us so deeply" because of the "greater possibility" of "the true word" coming to expression in them. (pp. 15-21)

Like Biblical narrative, Kafka's narratives reveal a perspective that, beginning with the few words on the surface of the page, extends downward or backward into an indefinite depth. They are literature trying to be revelation. The stark and homely details of **"The Judgment,"** glowing with the dark luminosity of things seen in a dream, portend revelation. It is as dream narrative that the story has something of a Biblical quality, which is the quality of any piece of writing that in aiming at truth tries to be more than literature. Of course only something of this quality, because **"The Judgment"** is literature after all. Nevertheless it tries to transcend art and "hit upon" the "true word." . . . I don't mean to say by this that the art that struggles to transcend art is better than art— not at all. But it is different. (p. 22)

> *Martin Greenberg, "The Literature of Truth: Kafka's 'Judgment',"* in Salmagundi, *Vol. 1, No. 1, Fall, 1965, pp. 4-22.*

J. D. THOMAS　(essay date 1966)

[*Thomas is an American nonfiction writer and literary critic who has published several studies of the Bible. In the excerpt below, he argues that the symbolism of "In the Penal Colony" is not Christian, as most critics interpret it, but Jewish.*]

To view as Christian allegory the tormented figures working their doom in the shadows of Franz Kafka's fictional tunnels is a temptation that has not always been resisted. . . . **"In** the Penal Colony" ("In der Strafkolonie") has yielded a fair crop of Christ images, though with some uncertainty as to which shoulders should bear the hydra's head. The old commandant, whose second coming is prophesied upon his hidden gravestone in the teahouse, is an obvious candidate, yet it is the living new commandant who represents the less ungracious dispensation of the present colony. (pp. 12-13)

Ambiguity is the keynote of Franz Kafka. What Heinz Politzer has termed the "ingrained *double entendre*" of Kafka's imagery is the hallmark of his work as a whole. Anyone who imagines himself to have discovered the one true significance should reserve judgment until he has read the stimulating essay on **"A Country Doctor" ("Ein Landarzt")** by Basil Busacca. Nevertheless, one need not despair of finding order and sense at last, particularly in the thin volume of stories, like **"In the Penal Colony,"** that Kafka completed and gave to the press. That they move on the familiar "several levels of meaning" does not foreclose all inference and statement of those meanings.

The prime fact about Franz Kafka, the one always to be remembered because not for an instant forgotten by him, is that he was a Jew. If he never openly used the word *Jew* in his creative writing, he made up for the omission a thousand times over in his correspondence, conversation, and journals, where *Juden* and *Judentum* are constantly in the foreground. The devil's island penal colony is a picture of hell, but specifically it is the Jewish community in Diaspora and still more particularly the colony at Prague. Long before Kafka's birth, to be sure, the ghetto as such had disappeared, and in Prague during his lifetime the old *Josefstadt* was largely razed and rebuilt. But memory of horrors "beyond the wire" (*hinter dem Draht*) never ceased to haunt the city, or to torment the spirit of Franz Kafka. (pp. 13-14)

The basic condition of Franz Kafka's neurasthenia was his sense of sin—generalized, pervasive, omnipresent, overwhelming. He had experienced in himself what the officer of the machine gives as the principle of administrative justice in the penal colony: "Die Schuld ist immer zweifellos" ("Guilt is always beyond doubt"). Upon him psychologically, nay even bodily, the machine had deeply inscribed its fatal marks of judgment.

The central image of **"In the Penal Colony"** is, self-evidently, precisely that machine—or, as it is first significantly called, apparatus. In a *locus classicus* for the religious interpretation of the allegory, Austin Warren senses the theological-scholastic nature of the apparatus, without recognizing that it is not Christian-ecclesiastical but Talmudic-synagogal:

> The earth is a penal colony, and we are all under sentence of judgment for sin. There was once a very elaborate machine, of scholastic theology, for the pronouncement of sentence, and an elaborate ecclesiastical system for its administration. Now it is in the process of disappearance: the Old Commander (God) has died, though there is a legend, which you can believe or not, that He will come again. Meanwhile the "machine" seems antiquated and inhuman to ladies, who are sentimental about criminals, and to the new governor, who is a humanitarian.

This interpretation requires Warren to argue, as a corollary:

> At the end of the story, the explorer has become converted to the doctrine of the machine: he excludes from his boat those who wish to escape from

the penal island. "Converted" is too strong: if really converted, he would stay on the island—at least if the machine still operated. But at least he makes no report to the new commander; and he takes the Prophecy of Return seriously: when the men about him ridicule the inscription, he does not join in their laughter: the Prophecy may be true. Like Pilate, he refuses to judge; he finds no fault in the just manipulators of the machine.

Well is it said that "conversion" would be too strong a term. If anything is certain, it is that the traveler (*Forschungsreisender*) is horrified by everything his research teaches him of the apparatus. The structural turning point of the story, when to the officer's final plea for aid against the new commandant he responds with a ringing "No. . . . I am an opponent of this procedure," follows an elaborate interweaving by the officer of what he imagines to be the traveler's approval of the proceeding, the commandant's conception (to the officer, misconception) of the traveler's opposition to the machine, and his own plan for duplicity by the traveler in the face of the commandant and his partisans. The reader is presumed to follow this intricate dialectic, sharing the traveler's growing sense of irony, and so the structural reversal (marked by the traveler's *Nein*) should surprise only the officer. Surprise or not, the denunciation by the traveler is complete and final: he rejects absolutely the officer and his devil's apparatus. The rejection leads directly to two subsidiary reversals that do constitute the surprises of the story for readers (the officer places himself upon the machine, and the machine destroys itself); and thence to the dénouement in which, after visiting the teahouse, the traveler takes his solitary departure from the island with a boatman.

The machine is the apparatus of rabbinism localized in the *(c)hul:* that is, the synagogue as the nucleus of Jewish life, education, religion, and law, the pledge of cultural and racial survival in exile and ghetto. As to its physical form, the machine is strongly reminiscent of the almemar, which focused the ritual and, along with the Ark, was one of the two most prominently Judaic areas of a synagogue building. One must not think of the *bimah* directly before the Ark in most American synagogues; but, rather, the great central, elevated platform for the reading of the scrolls, surrounded formerly by movable chairs, reached by steps (the "ladder" of the machine), and often surmounted by a baldachin supported on columns (the "rods") that could easily have become a canopied bed in Kafka's nightmares. (The repulsive physiological imagery of the story relates mainly to this secondary image of the bed.) In its action *qua* almemar, the machine's workings, ostensibly judicial, are also religious-educational. If, as seems likely, the twelve-hour period in which the Law of Moses is gradually incised and overlaid with Talmudic scrollwork is a typically Kafkan transform of the course of training toward *bar mitzvah* at puberty, the sixth "hour" would be an educational juncture followed by progressively deeper understanding of the Law, which is to say of being a Jew. When the process has been completed (Dann is das Gericht zu Ende), the learner is ready to be turned out. To Kafka, who had passed through formal Confirmation in the faith of his ancestors into a life of spiritual misery, it seemed a burial in the pit of hell.

The outward disappearance of the ghetto was by no means an unmixed blessing to the rabbinate. A menacing spirit of Reform, hovering over German Judaism since the eighteenth century, had reached Prague before the middle of the nineteenth century. If the old commandant of the penal colony is recognized as the tribal God of the Hebrews ("all in one . . . soldier, judge, mechanical engineer, chemist, and designer"), the new commandant is His image passed through the prism of Reform. The loyal officer still possesses the sacred scripts of the Law and the traditional apparatus for its execution; but the machine creaks, ersatz parts are growing scarce, the congregation has fallen away (*mangelnde Teilnahme an der Exekution*), and the machine is destined to fall apart. Only in humble synagogues of the deprived East Jews (the teahouse) does confidence remain strong that the old commandant will rise up again and make his face to shine upon the faithful; meanwhile a different era is symbolized by the new commandant, surrounded by his claque of ladies with their fine handkerchiefs and sweetmeats. To the traveler, "citizen neither of the penal colony nor of the mother state," but of the world—who, to the extent that he represents the author, would be the Europeanized, fully emancipated Jewish intellectual—the officer appeals vocally, and the black-bearded Hasidim of the teahouse equivocally, for support of the old regime. When the officer, who too after his fashion is an intellectual, sees that no such support will be forthcoming, he knows that all is lost and immolates himself. (On his dead face, however, is no transfiguration—no engraved realization of his own trespass of justice—even though he had been ready enough to assume guilt, which is *"immer zweifellos."*) The inmates of the lower depths in the teahouse, on the other hand, endure dumbly with their Messianic hope. The attitude of the traveler, shaking the sand of the penal colony from his feet and beating off those who would have entangled him further, is "A plague o' both our houses!" For such a departure into earthly and spiritual freedom Kafka always longed, but vainly—for "Prag lässt nicht los." If in one mood he wrote into his diary "What have I in common with Jews?" in another it was "Suicidal not to go to temple." Pathetically, during his last years he struggled toward Orthodoxy. "Dieses Mütterchen" (Prague), he had known as a youth, "hat Krallen"; of a victim of the machine on the devil's island, the final word was "wir . . . scharren ihn ein." In—as on—earth, Franz Kafka never could *loskommen:* he lies with his parents, under Hebrew inscriptions, in a Jewish cemetery of Prague. (pp. 14-17)

J. D. Thomas, "The Dark at the End of the Tunnel: Kafka's 'In the Penal Colony'," in Studies in Short Fiction, *Vol. IV, No. 1, Fall, 1966, pp. 12-18.*

HEINZ POLITZER   (essay date 1966)

[*In the study of "The Metamorphosis" excerpted below, Politzer examines in detail Gregor's relationship to his employers, his family, and himself.*]

The transformation of the commercial traveler Gregor Samsa into an enormous insect is completed in the first sentence of **"The Metamorphosis"** or, rather, before it. Like an analytic tragedy, the story shows but the last stages of the hero's ordeal; yet the crucial element of analytic dramaturgy—the posing of the guilt question and the gradual discovery of its answer—is neglected here. The reader finds himself in the unenviable position of a detective who is confronted by a culprit in safe custody but who is obliged to search for the culprit's guilt (a situation very similar to his attitude toward Joseph K. in *The Trial*).

To continue the metaphor, the last act of this play is confined to the interplay between the animal and its human opponents, the insect's inglorious end, and the final relief of the humans. This is the only act we see. At least on the surface Gregor's metamorphosis is taken for granted; the question why he was changed is never openly posed. When once drawn into the magic circle of the tale, the reader is forced to accept its premise as unquestionable, a process which is facilitated by the narrator, who continually shuttles back and forth between the world of the transformed and that of the ordinary figures, between suprarealism and realism.

"The Metamorphosis" is unique among Kafka's animal stories in that Gregor is a human in the form of an animal and not an animal who has been humanized. He does not mirror the world of the humans by way of a travesty—as does the ape in **"A Report to an Academy"** or the mouse in **"Josephine the Singer."** Moreover, if he was intended to serve as an allegory of Kafka's own existence, this intention is continuously disturbed by Kafka's insistence on the insect's *being* Gregor in addition to *representing* him. Even in the beginning the shock of the metamorphosis is increased by Gregor's rational reaction to it, and his death cannot fail to remind the reader of Georg Bendemann's submission to the verdict of his father.

The story stands out among Kafka's shorter narratives by being clearly divided into three parts. The first part shows Gregor in his relation to his profession, the second to his family, and the third to himself. This rather schematic structure is not aesthetically disturbing because the three parts are united by Gregor's fate, which is and remains an enigma. In spite of the symmetry and precision of its structure it is basically endless; the actual conclusion is a rather unconvincing addition.

The first part is as strictly limited in time as it is in space (Gregor's room). The alarm clock ticking on his bureau symbolizes the infinite and irrevocable circle of Gregor's professional life as a traveling salesman, to which he has sold himself. . . . The insect's attempt to leave his bed, that is, his gradual awareness of his transformation, is continually accompanied by statements of time. . . . The monstrosity of the scene—an insect preparing for a salesman's trip—is heightened and parodied by the cold mechanism of the passing of time. . . . The General Manager appears. The firm did not allow more than ten minutes before sending out after its missing employee. With uncanny and inhuman regularity, reflected in the incessant ticking of the clock, business moves in to reclaim the fugitive. To escape from the compulsion of his drab and strict job, Gregor may well have changed into an insect during his "agitated dreams" . . . of the past night. **"The Metamorphosis"** then, would be an escapist wish dream come true.

However, Gregor is more than a cog in a capitalistic machine. There is a very human side to his relationship with the firm. His parents once borrowed money from the boss and staked Gregor's services as a guarantee for the sum advanced to them. . . . Nobody can deny that he is a slave, but even slaves are men. If his animal shape were but a dream, then he would have paradoxically sacrificed his humanity in his attempt to escape slavery by his change into an insect.

"The Metamorphosis" is set at the end of one epoch in history and at the beginning of a new one. The boss's personal involvement with his salesman's family bespeaks the still patriarchal attitude of a liberal economic system when at the same time Gregor suffers from the uniformity of life inherent in the organization methods of later capitalism. The employer is both close to the employee and far removed from him. (pp. 65-7)

Obviously Gregor has some reason to complain about his job. At the same time we are given the incidental information that Gregor had been promoted a short while before. Now he is approaching the status of those elevated salesmen whom he envies. . . . Gregor craves success and runs from it at the same time. Thus he circles around in the treadmill of his job, strives forward toward his independence, then turns around to head in the opposite direction as soon as he comes closer to his aim. He is in perpetual motion and yet he does not move from the spot. His professional life is a self-imposed labyrinth. (p. 67)

The second part is characterized by a gradual dissolution of time. The first had lasted one hour, from half-past six to half-past seven in the morning. It was limited by Gregor's awakening at its start and the "deep sleep, more like a swoon than a sleep" . . . to which he succumbs at its end. With another awakening in the dusk of the same fatal day Gregor resumes the wanderings of his body and mind. But now we have left the sphere of everyday; the orderly march of time has been

Lithograph by Ottomar Starke that served as the cover illustration to Kafka's third book, "The Metamorphosis," which originally appeared as a two-number volume in the "Newest Day" series.

suspended; the alarm clock has vanished from the chest. Twilight fills the room, indefinite adverbs of time like "soon," "later," "daily," blot out the passing of days and nights. . . . [Gregor's] very life is now undergoing a metamorphosis: the distinct rhythm imposed on it by his professional activities has given way to a shapeless vagueness, such as is experienced by prisoners, the sick—and Kafka's bachelor. From now on the story will seem like a parody and refutation of the ideal of the bachelor.

Gregor is both diseased and caged. His sister enters his room "on tiptoe, as if she were visiting an invalid," . . . and he himself calls the time since his transformation an "imprisonment." . . . These phrases point to the interesting contrast that whereas time dissolves, space closes in on him. . . . He is now doubly encased, by his "hard, as it were armor-plated, back" . . . as well as by his room. Both images point back to a preordained solitude.

Nobody can change this solitude any more. The family can only adjust themselves to it and, by so doing, allow us to measure their own humanity. At the beginning of the story the individual members of the Samsa-household were introduced by the insect's reactions to their voices heard from behind his locked door. The mother's voice was "soft," . . . the sister's "low and plaintive," . . . but the father accompanied his summons by knocking with his fist against the door. The mother's softness is Gregor's comfort and the insect's despair. She is the first to catch sight of him after the metamorphosis, and she collapses. . . . For the rest of the story, however, she appears more and more as her husband's appendage; literally Gregor's mother becomes more and more a Mrs. Samsa (and is mentioned as such in the text).

Among all the figures in the breakthrough stories Mrs. Samsa is most closely modeled after life. Here Kafka has recaptured his own mother's selflessness and the superficiality of her understanding of him. But above all he seems to have suffered from the idea that his mother had surrendered to the father all her love. . . . That Georg Bendemann's mother had to die before **"The Judgment"** begins can now be seen in proper perspective: it was an act of grace as well as of shame.

Compared with Bendemann, Sr., Samsa, Sr., behaves very much like an ordinary being, conditioned and limited by his environment. Wisely Kafka used restraint here, for a realistic reproduction of the father was bound to heighten the contrast between man and animal. The father's aging during the heyday of Gregor's activity, his sudden recovery after the metamorphosis, when it falls upon him to resume his role of provider, and his display of relief after the fate of the insect has been decided are all realized on a thoroughly human plane. His mulishness, his self-assertiveness, and his brusqueness have little in common with old Bendemann's more-than-human stature; they are characteristics he shares with many a *petit bourgeois* father of his generation, which was, we must never forget, still a generation of pre-Freudian parents. There is a great distance between old Bendemann's archaic and unexplained wrath and old Samsa's thoroughly understandable reactions. This distance indicates how far Kafka has succeeded in traveling toward a solid mastery of his craft in a surprisingly short time.

If Samsa, Sr., is more acceptable logically than Bendemann, Sr., he is nevertheless of the same ilk—the family of Kafka fathers. (Even more than Bendemann's, his name resembles the name of Kafka.) Immediately after his metamorphosis

Gregor overhears his father explaining the state of the family's finances. . . . It turns out that the resources of the family have not been completely exhausted by old Samsa's bankruptcy; the self-abandonment with which Gregor had applied himself to salesmanship was, to say the least, overdone. Furthermore, the father has set aside certain small sums from Gregor's earnings which have never been fully used up. In other words, he has exploited Gregor's sense of duty, trusting that the son's ingrained submissiveness would prevent him from demanding a clear account. If Gregor's change into an insect was meant to dramatize certain parasitic traits in his character, we realize now that these traits are inherited. (pp. 68-70)

The most complex and decisive character in the Samsa household is the sister, Grete. The assonance between her name and Gregor's is indicative of a deep-rooted familiarity between them. While he was a human, she was the only member of the family with whom he had entertained human relations worthy of the name. After the metamorphosis she is at first the only one to interpret it as Gregor's, and not the family's, misfortune and the first to master her horror and enter the insect's room. Her humaneness seems to be in tune with her artistic talent; she "could play movingly on the violin." . . . Naturally her music is soon forgotten by everybody, including herself, since Gregor's transformation has forced her out into the world of commerce. Like the father, she supports the family now. Thus she serves as a provider to the animal in addition to being his nurse, messenger, interpreter, and an expert in all his dealings with the family. This has given her an undisputed authority in all matters concerning the welfare of her brother and determines her behavior in the first open family crisis.

It is she who has contrived the plan of removing the furniture from Gregor's room. The idea of this change seems to originate in her intuitive understanding of the insect's needs. . . . He clings to the room and its objects as to the last remnants of his identity. However, so great is Gregor's submissiveness and belief in Grete's wisdom that he soon comes to prefer her council to his own predilections and interests. And yet it is his very identity that he endangers by accommodating himself to Grete's design. Soon it turns out that even the mother wants to keep the room in its present state. . . . (p. 71)

In spite of his vacillations Gregor decides to fight for his identity. This struggle is carried out in a very strange way. In the second paragraph of the story we have learned that there hangs in Gregor's room a cheap print of a woman. . . . For the insect, the print becomes the one of his possessions to which he is determined to adhere both physically and metaphorically. He creeps up to the picture and covers it with his body when mother and sister threaten to remove it. (p. 72)

Gregor's defiance precipitates the crisis. We are not surprised to see the mother taking refuge in another of her swoons. The father joins the battle, plunging the insect into an unprecedented panic. He deserts the picture, the image of his love and his identity, and runs before his father, "stopping when he stopped and scuttling forward again when his father made any kind of move. In this way they circled the room several times." Again the image of the circle is chosen as a symbol of the inextricable self-involvement of Gregor's fate. With the consistency that characterizes Kafka's inspiration at its best, he now chooses a round object to put an end once and for all to Gregor's aimless circular wanderings: "It was an apple; a second apple followed immediately; Gregor came to a stop

in alarm; there was no point in running on, for his father was determined to bombard him. He had filled his pockets with fruit from the dish on the sideboard." . . . One of the missiles penetrates his armor-plated back and later causes his death by rotting in his body. The deadly bullet appears at first completely unexpected and unrelated to the actual setting of the scene. "It was an apple"; it comes shooting out of the blue, from nowhere or the armory of a whimsically unfathomable fate. Kafka takes his time to establish the provenance of these eerily flying projectiles: only after four main clauses and one dependent clause, running parallel to the victim's gradual recovery from his shock, are we told the origin of these apples in a dish on the sideboard. So cogent, however, is their choice that we never quite wake up to the scurrility of the drama performed before our eyes—the chase of an insect with apples. They seem quite naturally to belong in the imagery of this story; their roundness corresponds with the circles Gregor was running in when they stopped him.

As images these apples are also related to the Tree in the Garden of Eden, Paradise Lost, love, cognition, and sin. These are mere associations, to be sure; yet as such they are meant to turn our glances in the direction of a vague and veiled religious background. . . . (pp. 72-3)

The deathblow Gregor received during this battle was accompanied by another, more subtle, wound. Grete has become a turncoat. From a Good Samaritan, a "sister" in the Christian sense of the word, she has changed into the father's daughter. By taking over his gestures and glances, she has visibly joined forces with him. . . .

The title of the story might apply to Grete with greater justification than to Gregor, for it is her metamorphosis which is developed in the course of the narrative, whereas we have to accept Gregor's as an accomplished fact. More and more she plays herself into the foreground: the end will show her transformation completed, very much to the detriment of the story. (p. 74)

Without Grete's support Gregor succumbs completely to decay. He appears now as "an old dung beetle." . . . This name he is called by the charwoman, who in the meantime has emerged from one of Kafka's limbos, where the social underworld seems to have joined forces with his primal fears to generate a universal nightmare. This "dung beetle" also carries in its back the wound with the rotting apple, which is the symbol of guilt as well as of cognition. Gregor has never been closer to an understanding of his human failure than when he is in the shape of a hurt animal which perishes in its own filth. Deserted by his sister, released from the very last social contacts, he has now the chance to turn inward. Yet he misses even this last opportunity. Whatever attempt at introspection he might have undertaken is thoroughly blocked by his resentment of the others. (pp. 74-5)

We have arrived at the vertex of the story, which, thanks to Kafka's masterful counterpoint, is also the low point in the insect's development. We feel the icy breath of an existence fatally gone astray. The question of Gregor's guilt and the reason for his transformation face us once more. Does his guilt lie in himself, in his possessiveness, of which he remains unaware to his end? . . . Does his guilt consist in his inability to reach beyond himself, in his desire to grasp and digest the "unknown nourishment"? Is this nourishment identical with music? If so, has he been transformed because he had tried to dedicate himself to the unknown by proxy, by sending his sister to the Conservatory instead of attending it himself? Did he want to use her as his emissary to the high unknown? Should he have become a musician, thus partaking of the "unknown nourishment"? Could he have avoided the metamorphosis by renouncing his hated job and embarking on a profession he loved? Would he have found salvation in the pursuit of music? Is music here an image of art in general or of the "art of prayer" in particular, that is, of literature? Is the *ur*-bachelor's paradox repeated in the paradoxical image of a man turned insect? (pp. 77-8)

We have traced this circle through Gregor's human and animal stages. It ends in the state of inanimate matter.

> The rotting apple in his back and the inflamed area around it, all covered with soft dust, already hardly troubled him. He thought of his family with tenderness and love. The decision that he must disappear was one that he held to even more strongly than his sister, if that was possible. In this state of vacant and peaceful meditation he remained until the tower clock struck three in the morning. . . .

Gregor's mediations are not only "peaceful" but "vacant." He agrees to his own demise as he once had submitted to the yoke of his job and, again, to the father's concealment of his savings. (pp. 78-9)

He has not really lived; existence, physical and metaphysical, has moved past him and left no trace. The metamorphosis has failed to change him. He dies, as he lived, a thing. The salesman has been dealing in things; the insect has clung to things; love and music he has craved as if they were things. Resigning himself in his last words to an animal existence, this human being reduces himself to impersonal matter. He does not die, he is put out. The charwoman sweeps "it" away.

Kafka succeeded in creating so complex and inexplicable an image that not even Gregor's "thingness" can be construed as his ultimate guilt. We would moralize unduly if we assumed that his preoccupation with the material side of life has caused his metamorphosis and eventually transformed him into a heap of useless matter. The content of the story contradicts any such moralizing: Gregor is never offered an alternative to his fate. He is given neither a choice between good and evil nor a genuine opportunity to repent or atone for his absorption in the superficial realities of his existence. He is condemned without accusation and judgment, and ultimately he remains in the dark about the reasons of his punishment. He and his readers are forced to accept it unconditionally.

Kafka's story describes the invasion of the material world by a power which resides beyond empirical experience. Empirical experience can only register this invasion and, as the Samsa family tries to do, come to terms with it. . . . [In] Kafka's world only the empirical has limits; the "unusual," the unempirical, is at liberty to transcend these limits wherever and whenever it pleases. It chooses its victims, but the criteria for the choice remain obscure; the selection is grotesquely cruel in its arbitrariness. Why was Gregor Samsa chosen and not one of the three lodgers whom he resembles so closely? No answer is given. Yet in this arbitrariness there is a hidden element of universality. Precisely because Gregor Samsa is an average man, his incredible fate could befall any average man among the readers of this tale. So far does Kafka's skill as a narrator extend that the extraordinary begins to look commonplace.

Because of Gregor Samsa's commonplace character it is difficult to agree to the description of **"The Metamorphosis"** as a fairy tale in reverse, i.e., an "anti-fairy-tale," which shows "the world as it ought not to be." Gregor's craving for his sister, Grete, has not been taken from the old legend of Beauty and the Beast and reprinted here, so to speak, in reflected face. Gregor is no enchanted prince, languishing in the shape of an animal for his redemption. Nor is he the opposite, the legendary pauper, whose sufferings are rewarded by a happy end. The concept of the fairy tale does not apply to him. He is a modest and mediocre salesman who had the misfortune to awake, one morning, in the shape of an insect. There is no tragic plunge from the noble and unique in this transformation. Quite the contrary, the metamorphosis appears consistent and strangely appropriate to Gregor's thoroughly unheroic character. The beast into which this nonhero has been changed remains as nondescript as Gregor was when he still functioned as a human salesman.

Moreover, even if Kafka intended **"The Metamorphosis"** to be an anti-fairy-tale, he would have had to suggest the power which transformed Gregor. Witch or magician, fairy or fate, this power would have had to appear in order to indicate the means by which it could be either placated or exorcised. Furthermore, the outlines of the desired order in the world would have had to become visible if the tale was to be considered an image of "the world as it ought not to be." Such an outline appears indeed in the very last pages of the story, after the insect's death, but it left Kafka, and leaves the attentive reader, dissatisfied. The epilogue of **"The Metamorphosis"** shows the Samsa family on their way to recovering their physical health. But the power which transformed Gregor Samsa is infinitely more than an image of bodily disease. Nowhere does Kafka encourage us to interpret Gregor's insect shape as an expression of his physical or even mental disorder. The principal law of the force which caused his metamorphosis is its incomprehensibility. It can only be described by not being depicted at all. Its image is a blank space yawning amidst the everyday reality of the Samsa household.

The thoroughly negative quality of the transforming power seems to have been imparted to the animal itself. In the first sentence of the original, Gregor is introduced by two negatives as *ungeheures Ungeziefer* ("enormous vermin" . . .). Apart from the repeated negative prefix *un-*, the German word *Ungeziefer*, like its English equivalent, "vermin," is a generic term, a collective noun denoting all sorts of undesirable insects. Kafka never divulges the kind of insect into which Gregor has been transformed, nor does he specify its form and size. In the beginning he is flat like a bedbug, so thin that he can find accommodation under the couch, and yet long enough to reach the door key with his teeth. It would stand to reason that he was changed into precisely that animal which he—and other European salesmen—dreaded most when they entered the dirty and cheap hotels open to them on their route. . . . Whatever vague contours the animal possesses are blurred in the course of the story by the "dust, fluff and hair and remnants of food" . . . which have assembled on its back. When the charwoman finally calls him "an old dung beetle," . . . she does not, as one critic maintains, pronounce an entomological classification, but simply adds an insult to Gregor's fatal injury. By his metamorphosis Gregor Samsa has been turned into an untouchable in the most literal sense of the word.

What Kafka could not describe by words he likewise wished

to keep unexplained by pictorial representation. When Kurt Wolff, the publisher, submitted to him a sketch of the title page which showed Gregor as a beetle, Kafka remonstrated: "The insect proper cannot be designed. Not even from far away is it possible to disclose its shape." . . . The *un-,* the dark, the void, are the only designations Kafka could find for the mystery at the center of the tale. Gregor's metamorphosis is the image of his own negative possibilities as well as of the incomprehensibility of the power that changed him into an insect.

The epilogue shows the Samsa family on an excursion into the open country. The insect has been removed, the char-woman dismissed, the triad of lodgers given notice. Nature itself seems to conspire with the rejuvenated Samsas. The trolley in which the family travels alone "was filled with warm sunshine." Sinister past has given way to a future of freedom and light. Now it appears that the prospects of the family are "on closer inspection . . . not at all bad." The tale that had begun with Gregor's "agitated dreams" is ended by "new dreams," in which the parents anticipate a life of petty-bourgeois comfort in an apartment better than the old one, "which Gregor has still selected." Most obvious, however, is Grete's change. The parents are struck by a sudden outburst of vitality, which seems to have changed her into a complete-ly different girl. "In spite of all the sorrow of recent times . . . she had bloomed into a pretty girl with a good figure." . . . Now she is joining the regenerative forces of nature and thereby completes *her* metamorphosis. Precisely because Kafka has devised this end as a counterpoint to Gregor's transformation and precisely because this counterpoint con-cludes harmoniously, it appears as a somewhat forced adap-tation of the now hackneyed antithesis of "art" and "life" to the paradoxical nature of Kafka's new style. But Gregor can-not be accepted as an artist, however frustrated. His meta-morphosis is not counterbalanced by Grete's awakening to normalcy, however trivial. Neither the warm sunshine of an early spring day nor the social rehabilitation of a middle-class family nor the successful passing of a young girl's puberty can make us forget the unknown which reached through Gregor into life as it is known to us. So persuasively has Kafka im-pressed the image of the insect upon reality that the ordinary world itself seems to have changed. After Gregor's metamor-phosis Kafka's reality will never be the same. (pp. 79-82)

> *Heinz Politzer, in his* Franz Kafka: Parable and Paradox, *revised edition, Cornell University Press, 1966, 398 p.*

DALE KRAMER (essay date 1968)

[*Kramer is an American critic and editor of the* Journal of En-glish and German Philology. *In the essay on "In the Penal Colony" excerpted below, he maintains that Kafka advocates tolerance in questions of relative morality.*]

A close reading of what is nearly the paradigmatic Kafka ut-terance, **"In the Penal Colony,"** reveals a sophisticated and functional artistry. We usually read the story as an allegory of the fate in a changing, unsympathetic world of an old sys-tem of belief, either religious or political. This reading is not inaccurate in its broad outlines; indeed, it is hard to conceive of another reading that so well accounts for the variety of al-lusions in the story. Still, an observation of the progress of events, that is, of the structure, affords considerable clarifica-tion of the point regarding the death of the old system that

Kafka makes through his tale. Put simply, Kafka urges the desirability of tolerance and suspended judgment in matters of relative morality.

The point is best got at by first noting the end of the story. The New Commandant of the penal colony has asked the for-eign explorer, who serves as the focus of narration, to observe an ingenious machine executing a brute of a soldier who had neglected a trifling duty. The officer in charge of the machine attempts to convince the explorer of the value and beauty of the machine, which had been invented by the now-dead Old Commandant. Upon being told that the explorer would not defend the machine to a conference board convening on the morrow, and knowing that his method of punishing guilty persons is therefore doomed, the officer places himself in the machine and dies violently. The explorer visits the burial-place of the Old Commandant, which is below the floor of the colony's teahouse because the priest would not let him be buried in the churchyard; he then leaves the island without paying the expected visit to the New Commandant to give his opinion of the machine. Through this unplanned departure, the explorer expresses some sort of sympathy for the self-immolated officer. That the sympathy has some bearing upon his final response to the ideology of the officer—that is, to the old system of belief—is suggested through his refusal, just be-fore he leaves the colony, to mock the prophecy that the Old Commandant will rise from his grave to "lead his adherents . . . to recover the colony." Of course, the [explor-er's] sympathy is far from total. His refusal to defend the ma-chine is not rescinded, even though he knows the officer is about to kill himself because of his refusal. There is, likewise, no indication that the explorer's distaste for the Old Com-mandant's methods of justice ever lessens. But that there is sympathy for the officer as there is antipathy for his methods Kafka is careful to point out: "If the judicial procedure which the officer cherished were really so near its end, possibly as a result of his [the explorer's] own intervention, as to which he felt himself pledged—then the officer was doing the right thing: in his place the explorer would not have acted other-wise." Just what in the narrative explains the explorer's sud-denly leaving the island has never been clearly established. Most critics have overlooked the techniques of fiction as a basis for resolving the issue. Yet, such obvious matters as characterization and comparison of details provide a direct apprehension of Kafka's resolution of the conflict between so-cietal beliefs.

The most direct explanation of the explorer's sympathy for the officer is the similarity of their personalities, so close that the explorer becomes the psychological double of the officer. Although they oppose each other in the "matter" of the story, an attitude toward justice, in all other features they are quite alike. First of all, the two men approach the "matter" of the story with similar dedication. Neither is corruptible, the officer by the opprobrium into which his machine has fall-en, the explorer by thought of anyone's agreement or dis-agreement with his ideas. Both are concerned with the honor of their behavior. The officer scrupulously heeds his concept of justice, even towards himself ("Guilt is never to be doubt-ed"); the explorer initially hesitates to express his opinion of the machine for fear of offending either of his hosts, the New Commandant or the officer. Both the explorer and the officer are convinced of the rightness of their stands toward the ma-chine, so much so that each may be thought of as an absolut-ist personality. The ultimate development in the similarity of the two men has already been noted: the explorer's feeling that if he were in the officer's situation he would also have placed himself in the machine. After the officer is in the machine, and it has begun its aborted performance and is discharging its cogwheels, the explorer feels he should stand by the officer since the officer can "no longer look after himself." After the machine has finished butchering the officer, the explorer alone of the three witnesses feels any compulsion to remove the body from the self-destroyed machine.

This similarity between the two central characters is one of the reasons we come to accept the explorer as the interpreter of the action. In addition, he is not merely a simplistic outsider who judges a social custom on surface qualities. Eclectic and tolerant of national modes, he brings far-reaching sympathies to the evaluation of human behavior that allow him to give more than a limited conventional response to an inhumane procedure. Indeed, he had come into the situation in the penal colony with "no intention at all of altering other people's methods of administering justice"; but his shock upon learning about the harshness of punishment for the smallest offense leads eventually to his determination to condemn the machine to the New Commandant. His climactic fleeing the island as he does marks a return to the detachedness he had displayed when ignorant of the nature of the officer's machine. A basic difference, of course, is that his refusal to become involved initially reflects only professional principle, while at the end it highlights his "learning" Kafka's point.

The sometimes subtle but always consistent parallels between the explorer and the officer reinforce the inevitability of the explorer's final act, which hinges upon the manner of the death of the officer. Immediately before the machine begins to operate on the officer, the explorer is still determined to make clear to the New Commandant his unfavorable opinion of the method of execution that the officer's impassioned explanation has brought him to. He is "resolved to stay till the end" of the self-execution out of respect for the officer's sincerity, but he has not altered his opposition to employment of the machine on unwilling victims. He remains "pledged" to the "intervention" that has led the officer to release the condemned prisoner and to place himself in the machine. Of necessity, then, the explorer's abrupt departure from the island stems at least in part from his response to the officer's death. Kafka does not state directly why the explorer acts as he does, but the details of the machine's handling of the officer as self-sacrificial victim clearly point to the cause.

Upon learning the hopeless prospects for his system of belief, the officer releases the prisoner he had been about to execute, strips himself, and prepares the machine for his own execution. The machine tattoos into its victims' bodies the law they have disobeyed. The released prisoner would have had "HONOR THY SUPERIORS" punched into his body; the officer sets the machine to write "BE JUST" into his own body. The implication is obvious: having executed untold numbers according to his ideal of harsh justice (he is the jury and judge *and* executioner), he is now prepared to die in the machine himself. A goal other than justice is suggested by his envy of the other victims' look of beatitude when they discover (after six hours in the machine) the message that the machine has been writing into their bodies; but this goal does not clearly play a determining role in the officer's suicide.

But rather than execute the officer with slow and exquisite torture, as was customary, the machine begins to operate as if with intentions of its own, spews forth its cogwheels even

though working silently, and kills the officer within a very short time. Such an outcome of a conscious effort to achieve a particular kind of death might seem to represent a repudiation of the officer by the system he worshipped, as if to suggest he had perverted the justice he administered. Many considerations, in addition to the explorer's continued sympathy with the officer's action, nullify this possibility, and make the officer's death a vindication, if not of the system he served, at least of his own personal role in that system.

There is no reason to believe that the machine has executed the officer inappropriately. Rather, the variation in the machine's pattern is inevitable, given the conditions of the machine's normal successful operations. In the first place, the officer, unlike the other victims, has not committed a crime against the society supporting the machine; in fact, he is the last self-proclaimed member of that society. Similarly, unlike the other victims, the officer knows what the machine will write on him, thereby obviating the moment of the excruciating illumination for which he had envied those who had previously suffered in the machine. Because he is already an initiate, the "calm and convinced look" that the explorer sees on the face of his corpse is all that the officer could expect to attain to. A third unorthodoxy in the officer's planned self-execution is that the motto "BE JUST" does not signify the law the officer has broken. The officer lacks not justice—he is the walking manifestation of absolute and unflinching justice—but compassion, moderation in guilt-finding, and fellow-feeling. In other words, in his case the machine was asked to perform, ironically, an unjust lettering. The very process of its rebellion suggests the integrity of the system it stands for.

The manner in which the machine varies its pattern of operation is significant. As I have already recounted, in killing the officer the machine starts by itself, runs in defiance of the programmed instructions the officer gave it before he lay in the Bed, and continues to operate even though its internal workings are being discarded. Obviously, Kafka marks out the officer in some way—either as unworthy of the machine, which is hardly likely, or as being beyond the usual educative and punitive function of the machine, which as I point out above is more probable. Through the abnormal action of the machine, which cannot be fully explained by noting inadequate maintenance and the shortage of spare parts, the officer becomes not a victim, not a martyr, but a hero. The special treatment given the officer by the Old Commandant's invention is, in a genuine sense, similar to the special treatment given to Christ at death by the forces of nature that His Father had created. This general echo of an established religion is, of course, in full accordance with the usual reading of **"In the Penal Colony."** (pp. 362-66)

It does not follow, however, that by having the explorer behave as he does at the end of the story, Kafka supports totalitarian "justice." Judgment upon the system of justice itself is essentially incidental to Kafka's allegory of the decay of a social practice. Most allegories are more conventionally and clearly in support of a specific moral belief, but Kafka's highly individualistic employment of imagistic patterns prevents an interpretation obviously applicable to group morality. . . . In **"In the Penal Colony,"** Kafka is making a case for basic understanding and tolerance. The personality of the explorer implies an amenable morality that survives the decadence of the old system; but it survives without rancor, refusing to placate the New Commandant by attacking the

Old at the same time that it refuses to reinstitute the Old. To do either would be to play false to a new insight into the permanent virtues of loyalty and principle in the human personality. (p. 367)

> Dale Kramer, "The Aesthetics of Theme: Kafka's 'In the Penal Colony'." in Studies in Short Fiction, Vol. V, No. 4, Summer, 1968, pp. 362-67.

PAUL NEUMARKT   (essay date 1970)

[*In the following excerpt, Neumarkt analyzes the stories collected in* A Hunger-Artist *from a psychoanalytic perspective.*]

Kafka's collection of short stories which has come down to us under the heading of *Ein Hungerkünstler* represents the author's last creative production. In each of these stories the ego finds itself largely isolated; yet, there are varying degrees of relatedness by means of which the ego gauges its isolation. In **"A Hunger Artist,"** Kafka has carried this predicament to its most plausible conclusion. The aim of this paper is to explore a psyche exposed to the vicissitudes of a border-line existence. By dwelling on the potential of this unique phenomenon in terms of individuation, I will try to elucidate its concomitant triumphs and pitfalls within the wider framework of the collective setting as it affected Kafka's personality.

"A Hunger Artist" may be divided into two parts. The first is dominated by the "contract" between the hero and his impresario while the second deals with the period between the dismissal of the impresario and the death of the Hunger Artist. This division is not arbitrary but closely follows the course of the particular neurosis in this story in which the pathological background remains paramount. (p. 109)

The psychic dilemma of the Hunger Artist lies in his inability to transcend his pathological setting towards new goals, or as we would say in colloquial terms, to come to grips with his neurosis by putting it in its proper place. This pathological streak in his psyche pervades the entire story like a *basso ostinato* that reverberates mightily throughout the composition.

We are dealing here with the Leitmotif of a "Liebestod," that is, flirtation with the finality of death. If "the instinct to eat . . . is one of the most elementary of man's psychic instincts," [as Erich Neumann maintains], we must *ipso facto* assume that the hero's abstinence from food is his own, mainly unconscious choice in his preparation for death, even as he has consciously chosen the profession of Hunger Artist. His protracted exercises in going hungry constitute, in fact, a process of self-dissolution which bears the distinctive mark of nostalgic regression. The longing to consummate "marriage" with death is, however, constantly thwarted by the letter of the "contract" which forbids the fast to go beyond its forty-day limit. This is an indication that defensive, that is, positive forces within the psyche are still active and strong enough to frustrate any sudden surprise move by the ever present destructive elements. The Tristan and Isolde syndrome we are dealing with in this context has a Wagnerian tone. The chromatic, tension-evoking technique of the musical scale appears in Kafka as a literary device. Each time the fast is interrupted by the impresario, it is as if the Hunger Artist has been cheated out of his natural propensity to complete the cadence on a note of final rest. The "contract" is the lease of life, the *modus operandi,* that remains in effect as long as the association between the artist and impresario is not questioned. Thus

the show will go on, for the "impresario . . . is present in every man, the essence of the forces that inevitably and without question cling on to life, [according to Herbert Tauber]. The setting is existential. Being means being with others, and as such is a sort of contractual assurance that the performance will continue. The possibility of upheaval, that is, of a severe disturbance of the delicate psychic balance with a sudden swing to the dialectical alternative is, as I have pointed out elsewhere, an ever present challenge. Kafka is only too aware of this psychological insight, for no sooner has the Hunger Artist taken leave of the impresario—termination of contract is implicit within each such formal agreement—than the show is fatefully interrupted, and the final marriage with death is about to be consummated. Herbert Tauber alludes to the negative forces as the "falsity of the forces deriving from the negative." However, the term 'falsity' in its contextual association with the negative, is a psychological misnomer. The negative contents of the psyche are just as formidable as reality itself and can never be discounted, as anyone dealing with matters of the unconscious must be aware of.

The trauma of the Hunger Artist furthermore harbors a synchronistic element which is not causally related to his very being: the refusal of the collective to let him continue the fast to his heart's desire. His yearning is "to set the world agape," to fulfil himself in this world which, however, is utterly disinterested in his private desires. "Kafka realized," states Harry Slochower, "that the laceration of individuality could be circumvented only by communal attachment." The trauma of this realization, however, lies in the very essence of "this hopeless Kafkaesque world of blind necessity . . . this absurd world," [according to Max Bense]. The human stage and its background which is the *sine qua non* of the genuine artist, is suddenly transmogrified into a circus setting with the cage of the Hunger Artist being hardly discernible among the animal stables that hold the attraction of the audience during the intermission. While he is actually begging for a pittance of attention, he has the bitter experience that his cage is "strictly speaking only an obstacle in the path of the stables" around which the people throng. In this synchronistic juxtaposition of artist and world, the latter is completely unrelated to his efforts. The dilemma of the Kafkaesque personality is that "he finds no reliable witness" for his despair. This is reminiscent of the world of Camus' *The Stranger* from which the dialectical struggle has vanished. "Each event of this absurd world is simultaneously real and unreal, possible and impossible," asserts Bense]. The meaningful causal relationship between the artist and his world has irrevocably been supplanted by a non-causal, hence, indifferently syncronistic coexistence between actor and stage, or as Slochower states: "Kafka reaffirms the paradox of co-existing opposites."

The phenomenon of a "Liebestod" or a nostalgic regression in its encounter with the "contractual," that is, life-affirming postulates leads us further to the assumption that there may be a latent homosexual tendency within Kafka's personality. The contract with the impresario, the father-figure, who makes decisions for the Hunger Artist, is terminated as soon as the absurdity of his circus-existence has dawned upon him. Hand in hand with the collapse of the meaningful outside world goes the unconscious rejection of the father image and its substitution by contents indigenous to the maternal, pleromatic sphere. It is at this particular juncture that the latent homosexual tendency within Kafka can be discerned. (pp. 110-12)

While I do not infer that Franz Kafka was actively homosexual, there remains the suggestion of such latent propensity in his psychic disposition. This is manifested by his frequent need to rationalize the merits and demerits of marriage as a solution for himself. . . . In all this rationalization he is, however, not unaware that there is some imbalance in his psychic makeup that thwarts all his attempts to consummate marriage. Thus, with reference to the daydream in which he, now a man of twenty-eight, saw himself as a rescuer of the beautiful maiden, there is the dawning realization that his daydreams, "this silly make-believe . . . probably fed only on an already unhealthy sexuality." If Kafka's dilemma is seen within the context of the "Liebestod" syndrome, activated by nostalgic regression and characteristic of the uroboric incest motive, the assumption of the latent homosexuality is adequately substantiated. Kafka's border-line psyche is the tightrope walk of an ego in isolation. However, the tightrope walker must never permit himself—on a conscious level—to trip into the path of no return, because he is ever bound to cross the dangerous path anew in his never ending game of brinkmanship. . . . Kafka's awareness of his "unhealthy sexuality" may be considered a safety valve which prevented him from crossing the border-line into the sphere of psychosis. Within the depth of the psyche, there are no clear cut borders and the analyst is forever in a quandry because he can never be [in C. G. Jung's words] "quite certain that a neurosis never steps beyond the danger-line." Kafka's awareness at times reached dimensions that might leave even the trained observer awestruck, as in the quasi casual conversation between the Inspector and the Hunger Artist:

I.	"You are still fasting? . . . Will you ever stop?
H. A.	"I have always wanted you to admire my going hungry."
I.	"Well we admire it."
H. A.	"But you shouldn't admire it."
I.	"All right, then we don't admire it . . . but why shouldn't we admire it?
H. A.	"Because I have to go hungry, I can't help it."
I.	"And why can't you help it?"
H. A.	"Because I . . . have never found the right food to suit my taste. If I had . . . I would have made no fuss and gorged myself as you and the rest of your kind."

The absurdity of this situation lies in the utterly uncoordinated synchronicity of artist and world. Since it cannot be visualized within a dialectical frame of reference, it forces the creative personality into a state of uncontested awareness of desolate, moribund isolation. It lies furthermore in what Max Bense defines as simultaneity of the "real and unreal, possible and impossible," in the dilemma of craving for admiration, yet simultaneously rejecting it as soon as it is expressed. Even on this level of border-line existence, however, the psyche puts up as much of a defensive counter-force as it can muster under the circumstances. If the process of harnessing the archaic, negative forces is to serve the life affirming mechanism of defence, it must relate meaningfully to the individual in question.

If fasting is reflective of the ego in a state of unqualified isolation, then it is, in its widest possible application, simultaneously an expression of the author's relatedness to the world around him, a relatedness which evidently bears no longer the mark of collective standards but of a baroque, silhouetted reflection of the ego, cut loose from the common roots of life. In other words: the concept "meaning" has ejected its inherently collective content and, in terms of moral standards, is reduced to a thoroughly subjective, questionable abstract. Kafka is well aware of this psychic condition. In his story **"Investigations of a Dog"** the author states: "For today I still hold fasting to be the final, and most potent weapon of research. The way goes through fasting; the highest if it is attainable, is attainabe only by the highest effort, and the effort among us is voluntary fasting. . . . My whole life as an adult lies between me and that fast, and I have not recovered yet." Kafka's confession may appear as if he were postulating fasting as a "most potent weapon of research." This is, no doubt, a neat bit of rationalization by means of which the conscious ego would justify its existence. The quoted exchange between the Inspector and the Hunger Artist stresses that the isolation depicted in this story is a finality, lacking an alternative. Van Gogh expresses himself in a similar vein in a letter to his brother Theo: "either fast or work less, and add to this the torture of loneliness." Thus fasting becomes a means of breaking away from the path of loneliness. In fact, it is within the process of creativity that the artist may go hungry without being aware of it. In this state of transcendence of the material stratum, in this state of weakened physical existence the artist, quite paradoxically, may reach the maximum in terms of productivity. Loneliness as used by Van Gogh and in an implied manner by Kafka, is the exact antonym of isolation, because the latter, within the context of fasting, is the conscious expression of the individual in terms of conative experience, while the former fundamentally reflects a state of deficiency within the individual's collective psyche. Isolation in this reference is the very existential setting of the artist. It is, as I have tried to demonstrate, a synchronistic datum that leaves the personality in a state of uncontested awareness of irreconcilable alienation. (pp. 113-16)

That Kafka envisaged the possibility of a fateful crossing of the border-line without the alternative of return is suggested in the last part of **"A Hunger Artist."** Theoretically, at least, that is, within the framework of the story, the author made the possibility of no return a viable alternative. The dismissal of the impresario is the first danger signal in so far as it spells the end of the period associated with the "contract," the symbolical guaranty that the ego defences are fit to ward off any intrusion from the subliminal strata. With the removal of this last safety measure, the existential setting of the Hunger Artist is no longer dominated by the ego complex since it has been divested of its supremacy. In terms of expenditure, the hero of the story has paid in full for his unbridled desire to continue the fast. His death constitutes the final atonement of the artist in relation to the community whose tenets he has violated. This is the literary device by means of which the *dramatis persona* can bow out of his performance. The real hero, however, the author behind the uncompromising figure of the Hunger Artist, the man of flesh and blood, is not quite so negative as his literary figure. He is aware of the possibility of returning to his previous *modus operandi*. This is indicated by the receding water that "must turn back between its banks again."

A thorough perusal of Kafka's work will furthermore confirm my suspicion that Kafka was fully aware of the danger inherent in his border-line existence.

In his story **"A Little Woman,"** in which the process of alienation touches on the very psychic balance of the author himself, the synchronicity no longer reflects the artist as an island of psychic manifestations. But unlike the Hunger Artist who crosses over into the sphere of oblivion, the hero in **"A Little Woman"** establishes a *modus operandi* this side of the danger-line. He is, of course, aware of his predicament he must live with day in and day out, but has come to understand that one cannot stray off the beaten track or flaunt the capricious whims of society with the hope of going unnoticed for any length of time. Thus the author states with plausible confidence: "From whatever standpoint I may look at it my opinion remains unshaken. If I keep this matter [the questionable relationship with his feminine counterpart] under cover, I will be able to continue living in this world." A similar, strong desire not to carry the dissociation of his psychic makeup to an extreme is depicted in **"First Sorrow,"** a short story in which the trapeze artist maintains his existence by physical isolation. He makes his abode high up in the dome structure of the circus and refuses to come down or to have any truck with his fellow workers. The flight of the trapeze artist into his self-chosen "splendid isolation" is, however, not to be looked at as a psychic finality, because the world below—his co-workers and audience—are at all times visible and within earshot, hence at the lowest perimeter of his conscious awareness. This ambivalent situation is part of the Kafkaesque absurdity as well. He can't live with the community, and can't perform without it. The flood-lit vaulted roof above, representative of the sphere of ego consciousness, does not provide for repressive tendencies as such. Thus his "overburdened memory," or in psychological terms, his dissociated existential setting has forced him to live in constant awareness of his absurd state of affairs. The border-line is ever dangerously near, but so are cast and audience to whom he is obligated under "contract." As a result, his delicate psychic condition is kept in a precarious balance.

In sum: The study of the literary masterpiece **"A Hunger Artist"** has revealed a number of danger zones to which the ego in isolation is prone. There is the particularly grave threat implicit in the "Liebestod" syndrome which initiates the process of nostalgic regression. There is furthermore the Kafkaesque absurdity, a setting which is thoroughly a causal, hence to be grasped in terms of synchronicity only. The implication of latent homosexuality which is intimately tied up with the regressive propensity of Kafka's psyche, and his constant need to rationalize his dilemma are additional phases in this never ending game of brinkmanship. Added to this is the threat to the psyche from utter dissociation due to modern man's "overburdened memory," a gentle reminder to our present day world that the breaking asunder of the ego sphere may engulf humanity in the psychotic darkness of chaos. This legacy of doom transmitted by the artist, due to his exposed station in life, is countered by the life-affirming, psychic contents, represented symbolically by the "contract," the concrete expression of public approval that checks excessive, individual appetites. Thus, the individual can never completely escape the scrutiny of the society that sets his limits. In fact, the process of individuation is only possible because of the *a priori* existence of the undifferentiated state of the sphere of collective consciousness. With this realization, Kafka creates a *modus vivendi* for himself that enables him to skirt the dangerous border-line, the vicissitudes of which the ego in isolation is constantly exposed to. (pp. 118-20)

Paul Neumarkt, "Kafka's 'A Hunger Artist': The Ego in Isolation," in American Imago, Vol. 27, No. 2, Summer, 1970, pp. 109-21.

RONALD GRAY (essay date 1973)

[*In the following excerpt, Gray contends that "The Metamorphosis" was not intended to be a general allegory on human nature and society but rather an examination of several dilemmas in Kafka's life*].

Kafka was usually reluctant to have anything he had written published, and this remained true of **"The Metamorphosis"**: he declined [the publisher] Kurt Wolff's invitation to send it to him in April 1913, perhaps because Kafka intended it for a book planned long before, to be entitled 'Sons'. He did, however, send it in 1914 to the novelist Robert Musil, who accepted it for the *Neue Rundschau*, where it would have appeared but for opposition from the conservative management. And in the following year he came as near as he ever did come to urging a publisher to print a work of his, saying he was 'particularly concerned' to see publication. Considering Kafka's normal hesitancy, this suggests a strong feeling that the story came up to his expectations.

The formal excellence is striking enough in itself. Whereas very many of the stories are incomplete (including a large number of fragmentary beginnings in the diary, not normally printed in collections of the stories as such), or rambling and repetitive, **"The Metamorphosis"** shows all the signs that Kafka was able both to portray his own situation and to achieve artistic mastery over it. That this is Kafka's situation, as he saw it, need not be doubted. He himself comments on the similarity between the name Samsa and his own, noting that this time he has come closer than he did in the case of Bendemann. The parents and the sister correspond closely to his view of his family. . . . It remains, of course, a projection from his own circumstances as much as any autobiographical subject in a novel does. The distinctive feature is the device by which Kafka omits all the repetitive doubts, the neurotic self-circlings, packing them all into the one image of the transformation, and viewing that as though from the outside. The transformation is at first sight incomprehensible, without some experience of it through Kafka's diaries. Yet it remains the obvious and most compelling image for his condition, as he saw it, and there is no symbolism about it, or rather the metaphorical element seems so slight, so ordinary, so much a matter of everyday speech that one scarcely wants to translate when Gregor discovers himself to be 'ein Ungeziefer' (a word which means 'vermin', rather than 'insect'). Gregor is, as one says, a louse. Nor does Kafka allow the comfort which might come from the expectation that the whole affair is a dream from which there will be an awakening. Exceptionally, there is no quality of dreams in this nightmare. Kafka insists on what the reader knows to be a physical impossibility, even though the general idea is common enough, because that is the only way that the full weight of his meaning can be conveyed, without overloading the story with the minutiae of self-recrimination. The conviction of being verminous is given full statement, once and for all, on the first page, and the rest becomes a matter of working out the practical details so that the truth comes home in concrete form.

This conviction is not the conviction of humanity at large,

nor does the story ever make it out to be so; the implications exist for Gregor alone, and the rest of the characters are far from thinking themselves or being vermin. (pp. 83-5)

The whole story is worked out in terms of Gregor being an insect, and at no point does the reader have the sense of being slyly invited to see more than meets the eye. There are no enigmas in the dialogue, to be resolved (as in **"The Judgment"**) only by reference to Kafka's own life; though his life is latently present throughout, it is independent of the story and allows it to proceed without hindrance. At times in Kafka's writing he suggests compassion through some artificial device, as he does in **"A Hunger-Artist"**. In **"The Metamorphosis"** there are no devices, and the compassion is felt in the writing. (p. 86)

[A] paradoxical mood characterises the moment of Gregor's death; not in itself, for the description here has nothing ironical or melodramatic, but in its context, in the events which follow immediately on it. Left alone in his room with the apple festering on him, he feels his strength ebb. . . .

> He thought again of his family with affection and love. His feeling that he had to vanish from the face of the earth was, if possible, stronger than his sister's. In this state of vacant, peaceful contemplation he remained, until the tower clock struck three in the morning. . . .

There is no such moment as this anywhere else in Kafka, no such calm recognition of what was a reality of his own condition. He is convinced here that Gregor must disappear from the face of the earth, and the conviction has no resentment in it, nor has it any expectation of Gregor's being rewarded by some dialectical reversal of fortunes. . . . Considering the savagery with which **"In the Penal Colony"** describes a death without prospect of benefit, the calm of **"The Metamorphosis"** is surprising. On the other hand, it is not a passage to which one can do more than assent. There is no other way out for Gregor, it is true, so far as one can see from the story. Yet 'vacant, peaceful contemplation' is not particularly admirable, and the general sense is of a feeble rather than a serene calm.

It is not a calm proudly presented for inspection. As soon as Gregor's death has passed, Kafka allows the charwoman, one of his best comic creations, to burst in. The reaction she shows is inhuman if one still regards Gregor as a human being. But that is the point: for the charwoman Gregor is not a human being; he is an insect and always has been. In allowing her to show such indifference Kafka does, it is true, indicate that the attempt of the sister at bridging the gap between herself and Gregor is vain. The story has this utterly pessimistic note, so far as Gregor is concerned, but the reader who finds this assertion of a human being's unloveableness unbearable may have to see that it is also ineluctable. Gregor must vanish, and the charwoman is chosen to say so. . . . (pp. 87-9)

This is still not the end of Kafka's comment. . . . There remains the final scene when, Gregor being dead, the family is at last free of him and decides, since it is springtime, to take a tram-ride for an excursion into the country. The last sentences have some of Kafka's best cadences as well as his fullest vision. . . . This is Kafka most fully in possession of himself as a writer. The verminous self must go: it has no hold on life, and no destiny but extinction. On the other hand, the brave new world now emerges, not unsatirised: the parents

are still slightly uniform and symmetrical, and such good intentions as they may have are coloured by the half-conscious, and presumably calculating glances they exchange, their minds half-fixed on what advantages a suitor may bring. But the story does end with that glimpse of a woman ready for love and marriage; there are subtleties and simplicities here of a human order. (pp. 90-1)

In **"The Metamorphosis"** [Kafka] had seen his own existence as though from outside, in its relation with other lives, and though there was always another self which watched this self, he had recognised the need for this self to die. It was a personal affair, and he made no more of it than that, in this story. Had he realised the implications, he might never have written in the same vein again.

Within a short while, however, the conviction that his own state could represent a universal fact of existence entered his consciousness, and the stories he wrote after this are given a more general symbolic value. (pp. 91-2)

Ronald Gray, in his Franz Kafka Today, Cambridge at the University Press, 1973, 220 p.

EMIL E. SATTLER (essay date 1977)

[*In the following excerpt, Sattler examines the narrative viewpoint of "Josephine the Singer, or the Mouse Folk," concluding that the story offers a detailed study of the artistic condition.*]

Many of the difficulties of Kafka scholarship seem to stem from an inability to agree on how to interpret his metaphors, a problem often further complicated by the nature of his fictional point of view. Nowhere do these problems seem more acute than in the story **"Josephine the Singer or the Mouse Folk."** Almost all of the relatively few studies devoted to this work see it as representing a significant, if not *the* definitive statement on the role of the artist in society, a topic with which Kafka dealt in one form or another in most of his works. Yet no one has undertaken a close investigation of the narrator figure in **"Josephine."** I propose to interpret the story through an examination of the shifting perspective of the narrator. The story represents, I believe, a thorough analysis of the status of the artist—not a condemnation, not a defense, but merely a statement of the condition.

From what we know, or are able to deduce, of Kafka's creative process, it is clear that the narrator always plays a significant role in his stories. In **"Josephine"** too he assigned the narrator a special role, that of mediator between the artist and her public, the society of mice within which she must function. The narrator is obviously one of the mouse folk, therefore basically opposed to Josephine's contentions. At the same time, he is clearly sympathetic to her situation, although he admits he does not know why. He even goes so far as to comment on his own equivocation, attributing it to an inability to comprehend Josephine's view of her position. A close examination of the narrator's position reveals that his is a dual role, also involving his participation in the story, so that his involvement becomes rather complex. His role, however, is quite well defined, as I shall demonstrate.

We note that the different perspectives which the narrator assumes while telling the story are remarkably consistent with the type of statement he makes. A look at the text will establish the similarity between his manner of presentation and the viewpoint he is representing. The opening sentence, indeed

Max Brod, Kafka's lifelong friend and literary executor, who dis-obeyed Kafka's order to burn his manuscripts when he died.

the entire first paragraph, is devoted to providing background information to establish the uniqueness of Josephine's position. Already in the second paragraph he begins to equivocate by raising the question of Josephine's importance. How can they be moved by her singing if they don't understand music? He first states the obvious answer, "The beauty of her singing is so great that even the most insensitive cannot be deaf to it." Then he proceeds to refute this statement by posing a counter argument and concludes that her singing is nothing out of the ordinary, being very careful to qualify it as his opinion, supported by what others have confided to him.

He moves on then, in the following paragraph, to the next question, "Is it in fact singing at all?" Here he cites legends which testify to the fact that their people did once have a musical tradition, from which he concludes that, in spite of the inability of anyone to remember the singing, or indeed to sing the few songs which have survived, they do have an inkling of what singing is. He decides, therefore, that whatever Josephine does, it is definitely not singing. Continuing then in an effort to find out what it is, he poses still another question: "Is it not perhaps just a piping?" After an explanation of the characteristic nature of piping for the mice, he launches into another hypothetical proposition. If it were true that she only piped, then one could prove that she does not sing. The subjunctive formulation makes it clear that it cannot be proved. Yet he makes the observation, qualified as merely his opinion, that her piping hardly rises above the level of the casual piping of the people. He even neutralizes his premise by stating that it does not really matter whether one could disprove Jo-

sephine's vocal skill, for that would merely clear the way for the major question, that of her influence. And in spite of the unsuccessful progress of his reasoning, he concludes in the opening line of paragraph four that it is after all only a kind of piping that she produces.

In the next paragraph he proposes a test which will prove that Josephine only pipes. "If you post yourself quite far away from her and listen, or, still better, put your judgment to the test, whenever she happens to be singing along with the others, by trying to identify her voice, you will undoubtedly distinguish nothing but a quite ordinary piping tone. He counters immediately with the condition, "Yet if you sit down before her, it is not merely a piping." Thus in the first four paragraphs, scarcely three pages into the story, our narrator has presented quite distinctly an outline of the points at issue. We have learned that there are two major questions which need answering. Rather, these are simply two facets of the same question: does she sing? and how does one account for her influence?

Most of the story in these opening paragraphs has been taken up depicting the narrator's role as a participant in the story, that is, as one of the people. In the material which follows he seems to concentrate on his role as narrator, limiting his commentary essentially to matter necessary for the reader's understanding of the situation. Although one finds very little interpretation of the facts in this portion of the narrative, one cannot avoid the impression that our narrator has become somewhat omniscient. The equivocation so noticeable in his presentation of the people's position was necessary to preserve the fact, or myth, if you will, of his impartiality. For if he participated in the story in any role other than that of impartial mediator, the reliability of his statements would be subject to doubt by the reader, and we would see merely a restatement of the same old arguments on the topic of art and society with no analysis of the question.

In his report to the reader, however, it becomes quickly obvious that our narrator's perspective is limited, despite his posture of omniscience. The references to mice and frequent plays on words provide ample indication of this. The necessity of pointing out these limitations is consistent with Kafka's style in other stories where he used animal figures, most notably **"Investigations of a Dog"** *and* **"The Burrow."** (pp. 410-12)

If one is familiar with Kafka's mode of writing and with his frequent use of animal figures, it becomes quite clear that the story is told by a mouse, about mice, but—and this is significant—it is told to humans and in human language. Otherwise there would be no need for the lengthy discourses on the history, traditions, and characteristics of the mouse people. Between the main figure and the reader Kafka has placed a narrator, and all events are seen through his eyes. Thus the story has much in common with traditional animal fables, and many of the same advantages. It achieves the effect of distance and perspective for the writer as well as for the reader. The animals also attain the same characteristic simplicity for the reader as in a fable. Human complexity thus becomes veiled. (p. 413)

The continual appearance of images and figures such as horses, dogs, moles, and mice in Kafka's stories is, to my thinking, an indication of his creative state of mind. Entries in his diaries, letters, and notebooks, for example, lead us to believe that phenomena appeared to him already in the form of literary figures. These figures were then retained, used experimentally, almost observed, as it were, and allowed to develop in a literary, fictional milieu. The comment of the supplicant is also an example of such a process: "You see, I have only such a fugitive awareness of things around me that I always feel they were once real and are now fleeting away. I have a constant longing, my dear sir, to catch a glimpse of things as they may have been before they show themselves to me." It would appear that Kafka did not manipulate his figures into situations in an ordinary creative sense, but merely brought them into contact with a situation and observed, much as a reader would, how they reacted and developed. Into these figures he then projected various segments of his "self" and allowed them to compete with each other in a given fictional setting which may or may not have a configuration of reality. In the case of the former, it is usually to observe a conflict of his artist self with the world. In the latter case, it serves the function of dividing various spiritual powers and levels of his existence into independent figures. . . . In his stories and fragments, Kafka often rehearses various situations, potential or real, from his inner being. The foregoing would tend to account for the lack of formal plot and structure in most of Kafka's writing. The "plot" of a story represents the exposition of such a situation; hence we see no psychological development of a hero figure, but rather a transcript of a thought process which develops according to fictional, artistic laws, rather than logical ones. The fragmentary nature of his work results from the recognition of a resolution (not necessarily a solution) of such a problem. Kafka was obviously more interested in the narrative process than in the form of the finished work in any traditional sense. His aim was to merge himself with his figures, but at the same time to remain apart from the experience in order to gain perspective. (pp. 414-15)

Scholarship has long agreed that Kafka's writing represents the depiction of his inner life. It seems to me that my interpretation of **"Josephine"** is not inconsistent with this view. However, in relating the foregoing to my analysis of the role of the narrator, we must be careful not to make any too-sweeping pronouncements regarding specific identities of any of the figures involved either in the creation of this story or in the playing of it. It is noteworthy in this connection that the biographical first person as it appears in Kafka's letters and diaries is probably just as literary as are his fictional figures. The so-called "inner Kafka" as revealed in his biographical sketches is also a part of his art. It is safe to say that Kafka the person is kept separate from Kafka the artist. It is virtually impossible, however, to distinguish one from the other.

So it is with our narrator. One can readily identify the various roles he assumes in the course of the story. One cannot, however, say with any certainty which is the most reliable role, or which facet of Kafka's existence any of them represents. Beginning with the passage where he relates the differences between Josephine and the people on the issue of protection, the narrator is suddenly no longer a reporter but an interpreter. He has progressed from an impartial reporter, as he was relating the attitude of the people, to authoritative reporter, when he was stating Josephine's position, to his present stance. He is now apparently attempting to explain to the reader the exact effect of Josephine's art on the people. In the course of his commentary on the relationship between the artist and society, he has begun to deal with the nature of art itself. He launches into a discourse on the effects of Jose-

phine's singing which is as eloquent a description of art as one is likely to find:

> There is yet something—it cannot be denied—that irresistably makes its way into Josephine's piping. This piping, which rises up where everyone else is pledged to silence, comes almost like a message from the whole people to each individual; Josephine's thin piping amidst grave decisions is almost like our people's precarious existence amidst the tumult of a hostile world.

And then as if to point up the significance of this passage, Kafka has his narrator comment, "One would do well to ponder that." This justifies, I believe, seeing the passage as a definitive statement on the nature of art. In a subsequent passage he continues his descriptive interpretation:

> Here in the brief intervals between their struggles our people dream. . . . And into these dreams Josephine's piping drops note by note; . . . here it is in its right place, as nowhere else, finding the moment wait for it as music scarcely ever does. Something of our poor brief childhood is in it, something of lost happiness that can never be found again, but also something of active daily life, its small gaieties, unaccountable and yet springing up and not to be obliterated. . . . Of course it is a kind of piping. Why not? Piping is our people's daily speech, only many a one pipes his whole life long and does not know it, where here piping is set free from the fetters of daily life and sets us free too for a little while.

This statement, more precise than the previous one, could well represent Kafka's own definition of art. It says in effect: Art is not the imitation of the pure and the beautiful, nor even an imitation of life. It is rather the very expression of life itself. This is what attracts us to it and this is why we cannot recognize it out of its context. It is too much a part of ourselves, just as the thin piping of Josephine is indiscernible among the everyday piping of the mice.

In the preceding are presented some standard, accepted precepts about the effects of art—among other things, a release from the trammels of everyday life. Similarly, we might conclude that poetry or writing must be a freeing of language from its daily function of communication. In one of his reflections, Kafka comes close to this same conclusion. "For all things outside the physical world language can be employed only as a sort of adumbration, but never with even approximate exactitude, since in accordance with the physical world it treats only of possession and its connotations." Art becomes a revelation of that feature of language which normal speech conceals. Josephine's piping is in every respect, then, a consistent metaphor for the art of language. This correspondence between art and the ordinary is, however, denied by Josephine, as by most artists.

Through his narrator Kafka has investigated every aspect of this claim of art. In the course of his description of the relationship between Josephine and her people, and his attempts to explain it, the narrator concludes, as he had earlier, that the people are devoted to Josephine and are willing to give in to her whims and demands for the sake of her art. But only up to a point. This brings him to the issue of Josephine's demand to be relieved of daily work, in order to devote all her strength to her singing. The response to this is absolute denial, or even stronger, simply a refusal to consider the arguments. On this point the people present an immovable front. Here Kafka is dealing with perhaps the most universal claim of the artist, one which he felt strongly himself. And, although this story can be viewed as a catalog of all the claims and pretenses of artists, this one receives the most detailed examination. But far from being the blanket condemnation of the artist's viewpoint, as Professor Emrich would have us believe, it appears to me to be a simple description of the situation. The claims of the artist are not denied; rather they are put into perspective. The fact that the point is not debated among the people would indicate that Kafka was assuming here an attitude of acceptance, perhaps even resignation. What point is there in arguing the matter? These claims of the artist are valid and logical and cannot be refuted. Nevertheless, society will not change. The story then presents a reconciliation of the problem without demeaning the claims of the artist.

The figure of Josephine symbolizes not Kafka himself, but the artist in general. Josephine's situation is one which Kafka saw prevailing for all artists everywhere. The narrator figure functions as an objective spokesman for Josephine's point of view, as well as an authoritative source for the nature and attitudes of the people. In this narrative duality, however, he ends the story in the same confusion so evident in his initial equivocations. The story itself represents a thorough investigation of the status of art in society. Of course no interpretation can be exclusive. The very use of the animal setting elevates the treatment into the realm of generalization, thereby transcending the possibility of direct application to Kafka's personal situation. Josephine's fate nonetheless, is probably what Kafka expected would happen to him. The heightened redemption that the narrator predicted for her serves as an ironic afterglance, so typical in Kafka's writing, of life going on beyond the end of the hero. Josephine has her victory, but hers is no greater than, nor any different from, that of every other Kafka figure who perishes from his inability to deal with the world. (pp. 415-18)

> *Emil E. Sattler, "Narrative Stance in Kafka's 'Josephine'," in* Journal of Modern Literature, *Vol. 6, No. 3, September, 1977, pp. 410-18.*

KURT J. FICKERT (essay date 1977)

[*Fickert, a German-born American critic and translator, is the author of* Kafka's Double *(1979) and* Franz Kafka: Life, Work, and Criticism *(1984). In the excerpt below, Fickert explores Kafka's use of the "double" motif in the story "Blumfeld, an Elderly Bachelor" and its relationship to his own life.*]

Because it is a story replete with images of twin identities, **"Blumfeld, an Elderly Bachelor"** lends itself particularly well to an investigation of Kafka's use of the *Doppelgänger* motif. Written in February 1913, but first published, because of its fragmentary nature, in 1936, its autobiographical purport is heightened by the fact that it refers at least to some extent to Kafka's elderly bachelor uncle, Rudolf Löwy. Kafka's closeness to this uncle, his seeing in Rudolf Löwy a double of himself, is attested to in a revealing comment in his journal: "He was in (many) particulars a caricature of me—essentially, however, I am a caricature of him." The strongest link between the two was obviously their bachelorhood, which Kafka many times castigated as an aberration. In a summary statement about his life, written in a letter to Max Brod at the end of July 1922, he reiterated the pointlessness of his single state: "a son incapable of marriage, of contributing to the perpetuation of the (family) name; solely concerned with writing, (itself) eccentric, relevant only to my own salvation or damnation. . . ."

When Blumfeld first appears in the story, he is content in his bachelor but extremely regimented existence. Lienhard Bergel, one of the few commentators who deals at length with **"Blumfeld,"** makes Blumfeld "an exception among Kafka's characters in that he has a good conscience and feels secure and satisfied." It is this complacency which is attacked by the first event in the story: Blumfeld's discovery of the two celluloid balls which have disrupted with their presence the orderliness of his bachelor quarters. As is the case with the celluloid balls, Kafka's symbols function in a way peculiar to his work. The literalness of their existence, which Kafka portrays carefully and convincingly, has no particular point. It is rather the meaning of the symbol—vastly ambiguous—which prevails. Thus, in **"The Judgment,"** which Kafka had written shortly before **"Blumfeld"** and which he considered a true achievement, the motif of the hero's absent friend (another *Doppelgänger*), upon whose existence the plot turns, is introduced mainly to indicate a relationship between the hero and his father, leaving aside the reality of the person cruelly contended for between them. . . . The advent of the bouncing balls, in itself amusing, almost ludicrous, gives the story its tragic import.

The fact that there are two balls has significance. Their identical nature, which nevertheless represents two selves—one defends the other when it is attacked by Blumfeld; one hides under the bed, the other explores the top of the bed—graphically elucidates the meaning of the *Doppelgänger* motif, the posing of the supposition that the personality is not a whole, but fragmented, and that the parts are aware of each other and of their own insufficiency, their inability to function independently. For Kafka himself the dichotomy which is evoked in almost all of his (overwhelmingly autobiographical) work relates to the two halves of the artist's personality, the hermetic creative self and the outreaching familial self. His journal is rife with descriptions of the conflict caused by his attempt to meet the demands of the artist in him and of the dutiful son and jobholder in him. . . . (pp. 419-21)

In **"Blumfeld,"** the intrusion of the celluloid balls signifies Kafka's awareness of his inability to live the life of the office-worker exclusively. His bachelorhood is in itself, he realizes, a sign of his inadequacy in the bourgeois role he has foisted on his dichotomous self. What is for Blumfeld the inexplicability of his being haunted by two bouncing balls is for Kafka an expression of the relationship between Kafka the bureaucrat and Kafka the writer. The peculiar activity which occurs in his room after the day's work is his writing. (p. 421)

Having established the basic premise, that of the writer's dilemma, his leading both a bourgeois and a secret life, Kafka proceeds in his usual fashion to retell the introductory episode of **"Blumfeld"** by varying the symbolism. Blumfeld brings the first adventure of the bouncing balls to an end by locking them up, concealing them, in a cabinet. With the intent of resuming his "normal" activities, he leaves for work. On impulse, however, he decides to make a second attempt to deal with his problem: he will dispose of the troublesome balls by giving them away. He returns to the downstairs hallway of his apartment house, having observed there his housekeeper's dimwitted and misshapen son, who is to have the balls for a plaything. Blumfeld's peculiarity, or Kafka's need to write, is now to be reduced to the status of a harmless, if infantile, activity. . . . In order to put the balls in the hands of the uncomprehending child, Blumfeld finds he must rely on the assistance of the landlord's two young daughters, who promise to execute the feat with suspicious eagerness. Under these inauspicious circumstances, Blumfeld turns his back on his difficulties.

In this scene, the artist's double nature once again has its representation: the symbol of the defective child, to whom the gift is given, stands for Blumfeld's other self, the author. Counterbalancing this pairing, the landlord's two daughters serve, as women generally do in Kafka's work, as an aid in helping the distraught protagonist overcome his problems, specifically by reducing them to foibles, by putting an end to his hectic activities and restoring normalness. But Blumfeld's flight from the apartment house emphasizes his irresoluteness, the lack of conviction on his part that anything has been resolved. Kafka, so the second episode in **"Blumfeld"** suggests, is unable to adjust to the dichotomy resulting from his wanting to write and his wanting to be a son and husband.

In the third part of the story, which depicts Blumfeld in his office in the course of a normal day, the man victimized previously by the extraordinary, the strange, falls prey to the disruption of the ordinary, the habitual. Blumfeld, the officeworker, cannot fulfill his obligations . . . because he is plagued by the two apprentices assigned to him in their awkwardness. Thus duality figures in the final instance of symbolism in **"Blumfeld."** The *Doppelgänger* motif appears again, as in the depiction of the celluloid balls, in that the identicality of the apprentices is stressed and yet dissipated by their acting individually on occasion. . . . (pp. 421-23)

In their mirroring one another, the apprentices, who in the inappropriateness of their activities undermine Blumfeld's efforts to maintain order, have represented to critics opposing forces to Blumfeld: for Martin Walser they turn the protagonist aside in his pursuit of selfhood, for Lienhard Bergel they are "those who have not yielded to routine (and) struggle against its encroachments." However, since they are more than twin images and the mass of detail describing them is considerable, their significance would seem to be greater and the possibilities of interpretation they present more subtle. In keeping with the theme of the story, the dichotomy in the artist's personality, the two apprentices reflect the division which exists in the man who sees himself as two people, existing side by side. At the same time they are Blumfeld's second self, the artist-self, suppressed because of its sinfulness, its strangeness. They are his "fault"; Blumfeld burdens them with his own inadequacies, just as Kafka makes the writer shoulder the function of being "the scapegoat of mankind (who) permits mankind to enjoy sinning without (a sense of) guilt, or almost without a sense of guilt." . . . Kafka's writing, symbolized by Blumfeld's bachelorhood, by the celluloid balls, by his apprentices, is his "sin" against his bourgeois self, the orderly and efficient bureaucrat who leads a circumspect life, insulated against irrationality. The story of Blumfeld ends or, rather, is broken off at the moment when he despairs of making the apprentices' behavior tractable. Ultimately **"Blumfeld"** in its very incompleteness expresses Kafka's inability to expunge that part of him which is the *Dichter*—either by shutting it away in a locked compartment or by making it a toy, a hobby, or by becoming the complete bourgeois in spite of it. It is the agony of the dichotomous personality, frequently depicted by the *Doppelgänger* figure, which characterizes much of Kafka's work. (p. 423)

Kurt J. Fickert, "The 'Doppelgänger' Motif in Kafka's 'Blumfeld'," in *Journal of Modern Literature, Vol. 6, No. 3, September, 1977, pp. 419-23.*

ROBERT T. LEVINE (essay date 1977)

[*In the excerpt below, Levine provides a Freudian analysis of the story "The Judgment."*]

Kafka, in one diary entry, refers to "my talent for portraying my dreamlike inner life." Indeed, he had the energy and the courage to hold on to thoughts from the unconscious so that he might memorably depict what we others allow to recede into the comfortable darkness of oblivion. His comments about writing **"The Judgment"** [**"Das Urteil"**] imply that it contains much dreamlike inner life: he records that the story emerged from him "like a real birth, covered with filth and slime," and that as he composed it he had "thoughts about Freud." But most significant, of course, is the texture of the story itself. Upon close reading, we find the sort of irrationality customarily found in dreams, an irrationality that is imposed on verboten unconscious thoughts by the censorship of the preconscious to make them less threatening to the ego. (p. 164)

From the story's first paragraph, we learn that Georg and his father reside in a "ramshackle" house. . . . But as the story unfolds, we learn that the family business is unbelievably successful. Georg thinks to himself that his father "is still a giant of a man." . . . But he treats his father like an infant, undressing the father and carrying the father to bed in his arms. . . . And then there is the matter of the friend in St. Petersburg. At first, the father denies that such a friend exists: "You have no friend in St. Petersburg." . . . But later on, the father claims that not only does he know the friend well . . . but he has maintained a steady correspondence with the friend. . . . (pp. 164-65)

As startling as the story's contradictions are its non sequiturs. For example, in the exchange between Georg and his fiancée concerning Georg's friend, Georg explains to her that he has not told the friend of their engagement. She asks: "But may he not hear about our wedding in some other fashion!" Georg answers: "I can't prevent that, of course, but it's unlikely considering the way he lives." And then comes Frieda's illogical retort: "Since your friends are like that, Georg, you shouldn't ever have got engaged at all." . . . (p. 165)

I wish to focus on other absurdities in **"The Judgment."** We are told that, because he doesn't want to make his friend feel like a failure, Georg "could not send him any real news." . . . Now this extreme statement—"*any* real news"—is typical of the hyperbolic, hysterical, paranoic aspect of the story. Another ridiculously extreme statement is that Georg "had not entered for months" . . . his father's room. The explanation for Georg's absence is pathetic in its attempted reasonableness: "There was in fact no need for him to enter it, since he saw his father daily at business and they took their midday meal together at an eating house." . . . We must be alert to *superficial* rationality. Freud has discussed the process in which unconscious material, having been distorted by the censoring preconscious, undergoes a second censorship because the material is still too threatening to the ego. In this second censoring process, which Freud terms "secondary revision," the unconscious material acquires a superficial logic that tames heretofore threatening elements: the secondary revision makes these elements less conspicuous by minimizing their absurdity. Thus the secondary revision, in Freud's words, "fills up the gaps in the dream-structure with shreds and patches." . . . [When] we carefully examine **"The Judgment,"** when we apprehend its dreamlike structure, then the feeble logic of secondary revision quickly breaks down. (p. 166)

Undeniably, **"The Judgment"** is riddled with illogic. Whatever veneer of logic may be present in the opening scene as Georg contemplates his situation, dissipates once Georg enters his father's room. We might even contend that the story shows an awareness of its irrationality. In the first paragraph, we are told that Georg is behaving "in a slow and *dreamy* [or languorous] fashion" . . .; while near the end of the story, the father says to Georg, "I suppose you wanted to say that sooner. *Now it does not fit* any more." . . . And, in fact, the whole story proceeds like a dream, where thoughts, speeches, and actions do not quite fit. Let us then apply to **"The Judgment"** a critical method that can deal with the story's irrational, dreamlike structure. Such a method is Freud's dream-analysis.

Freud has emphasized that dreams contain the disguised thoughts of the unconscious mind. The concept of disguise is crucial to understanding dreams. The unconscious cannot express itself undisguised because its thoughts, unacceptable to the ego, will be rejected unless they can pass into the dream-world unnoticed. In **"The Judgment,"** the principal disguise involves the friend, who really represents Georg. Whereas numerous critics have argued that the friend represents some part of Georg's personality, I suggest a complete identification of the friend with Georg. Here, I am following Freud's belief in the egoistic nature of dreams: "All of them [dreams] are completely egoistic: the beloved ego appears in all of them, even though it may be disguised." (pp. 166-67)

By being able to represent Georg in the guise of his friend, the dream/story can express certain ideas that otherwise might be rejected by the censoring ego. Georg appears to be succeeding *in propria persona.* He is doing well in business. He is doing well in relationships with women. But actually, I would suggest, he is not doing well in either endeavor. His failures, unacceptable to the ego, are assigned to the friend. In contrast to the successful Georg, the friend has a business that is "going downhill," . . . and "he was resigning himself to becoming a permanent bachelor." . . . That the friend represents Georg explains the intensity of Georg's remark to Frieda about the friend: "He'd have to go away again alone. Alone—do you know what that means?" . . .

But despite these failures economically and socially, the friend has achieved something that Georg hasn't: he has escaped from the home environment that a dominant father makes stifling. The dream/story disguises the wish to escape from home by giving the impression that to leave home is undesirable. In truth, however, Georg longs to escape to "a foreign country" from the overshadowing father who "had hindered him from developing any real activity of his own." . . . (p. 168)

As critics have perceived, a major part of the story deals with the Oedipal competition between father and son. Sometimes, the father is ascendant, demonstrating that he remains "a giant of a man." At other times, Georg asserts his power by treating his father as a child: undressing the father, carrying him to bed, and tucking him under the sheets. The story ends with a disguised parricide. The father crashes, but Georg—

thanks to the distorting process imposed by the ego censor on unacceptable material—is not to blame. As Georg is mysteriously "urged from the room," . . . he seems dissociated from his father's fall. Yet, truly, it is the act of parricide rather than the preoccupation with himself that makes Georg "a devilish human being" . . . and merits the judgment of death by drowning.

Having sketched the conflict between Georg and his father, we must now complete our account of the Oedipal situation by focusing on the mother, for whose love the father and son are rivals. One recent critic has suggested that the "rivalry for the mother" is *not* an important element in **"The Judgment"** and has characterized the rivalry as "a Freudian idea which seems to have made little impression on Kafka." But I would maintain that, consciously or unconsciously, Kafka has expressed this rivalry in his writing. Consider **"The Metamorphosis"** [**"Die Verwandlung"**] which, like **"The Judgment"** and so much of his work, has a distinct Oedipal content. (p. 169)

If we are to understand the mother's role in **"The Judgment,"** we must again be alert to disguise. In the dream/story, as we have earlier observed, both Georg and his friend have not shown a proper attachment for the mother, have indeed exhibited toward her a certain coldness: the friend has "expressed his sympathy . . . dryly" over her death . . . ; the father reminds Georg, "The death of our dear mother hit me harder than it did you"; . . . and the father avers to Georg, "You have disgraced your mother's memory." . . . But the actual situation is just the reverse. Georg, as part of his sexual predicament, is *too much* attached to his mother. One hint of this attachment is the father's reference to the mother as "*our* dear mother." . . . As she is *our* dear mother, so by displacement is she *our* dear wife—wife to both husband and son who compete for her love. A second hint is Georg's offer to the father, "You can lie down in my bed for the present." . . . If the father sleeps in Georg's bed, Georg can be free to sleep with the mother in the father's bed.

The "latent disease" . . . afflicting the friend may be interpreted as Georg's Oedipal fixation. Georg needs to be cleansed of his Oedipal love for his mother and hate for his father. . . .

In my opinion, the Freudian approach yields valuable insights about the story that are not otherwise to be obtained. But I do not want to deny the legitimacy of other approaches. For example, while in the cluster of meaning I have been exploring the friend represents Georg, the friend may well have other significations; and the friend's escape to Russia may signify many other things besides the breaking away from the father. A dreamlike structure such as **"The Judgment"** can bring together significations almost as unending as the stream of traffic just going over the bridge. (p. 170)

Robert T. Levine, "The Familiar Friend: A Freudian Approach to Kafka's 'The Judgment' ('Das Urteil')." in Literature and Psychology, *Vol. XXVII, No. 4, 1977, pp. 164-73.*

KATHERINE STOCKHOLDER (essay date 1978)

[*Stockholder, a Canadian critic and educator, is the author of* Dream Works: Lovers and Families in Shakespeare's Plays *(1987). In the following excerpt, she analyzes "A Country Doctor" as a dream of the title character.*]

I am going to comment on Kafka's **"A Country Doctor"** as though the narrator of the story were a dreamer inside his dream. All aspects of plot, that is, the events that occur, and of character, the dreamer's and other persons in the story, will be considered as dream occurrences—that is, their significance will be seen in relation to the dreamer. This means that the dreamer's reaction to another person or to an event cannot be explained only in themselves, but the existence of the person or event must be seen as emanating from and revealing aspects of the dreamer. (p. 331)

In this paper, taking the story as a dream, I analyze the experiences of the dreamer in order to pursue the psychological drama that it depicts. The person whose dream it is need not be a doctor; the dreamer's identity as a doctor in the dream is part of what must be analyzed in the dream, rather than a donnee. The story is not one about a doctor, but one about a man dreaming he is a doctor. (p. 333)

"A Country Doctor" begins with a challenge to the protagonist, or the dreamer, and indicates his incapacity to meet that challenge. The dreamer is a doctor called on a journey to heal a wounded boy. He is unable to make the journey because his horse has died, and he himself is in the snow "more and more unable to move." The boy whom he is to heal we find out later is wounded in the hip, is also unable to move. The identity between the doctor and his patient is suggested by this similarity and this identity is borne out by other details of the story. Both express a wish to die, the boy whispering in the doctor's ear "Doctor, let me die," and the doctor, after reviewing what appears to him the martyred circumstances of his life and responsibilities, connects the boy to his own life circumstances in saying, "and then the boy might have his way and I wanted to die too." The terms of that identification can be extended if one considers the boy's wound further. As I said, the wound in the hip identifies the boy with the doctor in so far as they are both unable to move. The doctor's lack of power to move toward his patient is associated with his having "hardly noticed" his servant girl, later called Rose, was around until the groom took her away. In this way his incapacity to move becomes associated first with his lack of sexual response, and with his lack of power to keep Rose. Both aspects of his incapacity can be expressed as a state of castration. This state in turn becomes associated with the boy's wound because the wound is likened to a "rose red" flower, and the servant girl is first called Rose by the groom who takes her away from the dreamer. Therefore we can consider that the boy's wound in the hip represents a castration wound, and the displacement of it to the hip associates the sexually inadequate feelings with a more generalized inability to move, or be potent, in the world. Therefore the dreamer, in evoking the wounded boy expresses his feelings of impotence on both levels, and these feelings derive, for him, not so much from a fear of castration, but from a feeling that he has already been castrated—that he has become like a girl. The action of the story confirms this association between the wound and Rose, for the closer the doctor moves toward the boy, the more is his mind preoccupied by Rose and the groom. The castration wound then functions doubly. On the one hand it represents the feeling of not having or not having the use of male genitals. On the other hand it expresses the desire to have, or the feeling that he does have, female genitals.

If we consider the identification of the boy with the dreamer to be established, then the story renders the dreamer's unsuc-

cessful attempt to heal himself. The call to the journey marks the onset of the challenge, and his inability to travel to the place of healing derives from the same illness that he is called upon to cure. His illness is powerlessness, and, naturally, he is powerless to cure it. The existential ennui expressed in the thought or 'conscious' attitudes within the dream, or story, reflects the emotional contradiction within which he is caught.

He dreams himself an impotent doctor who functions only mechanically. He says, "to write prescriptions is easy, but to come to an understanding with people is hard." In so far as he dreams himself a doctor, he expresses a desire to heal, presumably the vision of himself healing others conceals his desire to heal himself. That he dreams himself an impotent and unloving doctor expresses the illness of which he needs to be healed, but also expresses his unwillingness to be cured. This unwillingness to be cured finds expression in the reiterated assertions of restlessness, despair and passivity in the face of circumstances, as well as in the thought of himself as unloving in his professional capacity.

His failure to love in that general or social way expresses his sexual impotence. This connection can be seen in the doctor's declining sense of urgency as the story progresses. We encounter the doctor eager to go to the boy's bedside, acting like a conscientious doctor moved by the welfare of his patient, and restrained by what appear to him to be external circumstances, the cold, the snow, the lack of a horse. As the apparently external hinderences are overcome, the doctor's impetus to cure the boy diminishes. It is as though his approach to the reality of healing involved in his confrontation with the boy reveals the shallowness of the professional stance, and the internal rather than external nature of the hinderances he first encounters, whereby the cold and snow express his repression of all emotion, and his lack of a horse expresses his reluctance, his fear, of taking the journey toward the restoration of feeling. His incapacity to love sexually, his castration, and his incapacity to love socially are both expressed when he refuses the hot rum and family warmth proffered him when he arrives at the boy's house.

Instead of loving feelings the most pervasive feelings of the dreamer are those deriving from his sense of himself as sacrificial victim. He expresses pride in that role, resentment, and self-pity. He expresses this sense of himself as a long-suffering victim of an unworthy population for the first time after he looks at the boy and decides that the boy is not ill and ought to be thrown out of bed. The sense of himself as martyr increases in intensity as he comes closer to joining the boy in the bed. His passivity is so intense that he is stripped by the family and townspeople, and carried naked to the boy's bed, but his defense against knowing the sexual nature of that passivity is to think about himself as exemplifying a metaphysic, replacing the parson who "sits at home and unravels his vestments, one after another," and functioning as a kind of Christ figure, or sacrificial priest victim—"if they misuse me for sacred ends, I let that happen to me too." This passive martyr vision of himself functions both to defend against and to express his libidinous desire to be associated with the boy—to know himself as having a castration wound which can be penetrated.

The boy's wound has two aspects. On the negative side it represents the doctor's castrated state of feeling—his inability to love sexually or socially. On the positive side it represents the female genitals. To "cure" it, to recover male potency, would involve giving up the feared, disguised, but desired sexual passivity. The positive energy associated with the feeling of being castrated is articulated through the figure of Rose. As I said before, her name associates her with the "rose red" wound, but more than that, his concern with her increases as he approaches the wounded boy, and fuses with his passive sense of himself, since he sees himself as having sacrificed her to his calling as a doctor. He experiences the latent sexual excitation that increases as he approaches the boy as longing for and concern for Rose, and as rage and anguish at the vision he conjures of the groom upon her. Again, this both expresses and conceals from himself his desire to be one with the boy. The self-defeating irony of desire and defense is poignant here, for he uses the vision of health—of full heterosexual potency in which he can contend with the groom and desire and reclaim Rose, as a phantasy with which to defend against accepting his own perverse sexuality (his desire to be penetrated) which alone could return to him his vitality.

All of these lines of feeling come together most intensely in relation to the boy's family. The doctor underscores the significance of his irritability with them by himself judging it to be irrational. He reminds himself that they are not to blame, yet continues to blame them for the loss of Rose—"I had somehow to get it reasoned out in my head with the help of what craft I could muster, in order not to let fly at this family, which with the best will in the world could not restore Rose to me." This is the only place in the story where the dreamer experiences doubt and confusion over his own reaction to the events he experiences. The significance of that confusion emerges if we consider that since the doctor and the boy are identified, then the boy's family must function in the story as representatives of the dreamer's family. Therefore, analysis of the details of the family takes us into oedipal situation expressed in the emotional and sexual dynamic of the dreamer.

When the doctor approaches the house, the storm stops, moonlight emerges, and in the moonlight he encounters the parents, followed by the sister. The moonlight suggests that this encounter is emotionally charged, his feelings and sexuality no longer frozen. But the dreamer cannot fully engage in the confrontation—he cannot understand their "confused ejaculations." Dismissing the parents in this way, he finds the boy "Gaunt, without any fever, not cold, not warm, with vacant eyes." The only sign of energy, when the boy throws his arms around the doctor's neck, is accompanied by the boy's wish to die. After that, and as though as a consequence, the horses rear, he thinks of Rose, and there comes a closer engagement with the family. He permits the sister to take from him his fur coat, signifying that his relationship to the sister has the power to evoke the gesture that announces his intention to stay.

The fur coat is prominent in the story, and represents the dreamer's relationship to the perverse, though not enough detail is given—we don't know what animal the fur comes from—to say specifically how it functions. But the doctor is wrapped in it at the beginning of the story to protect him from the cold. If the cold—which pervades the beginning and the end of the story—represents the state of repression in which he lives, then the fur coat represents those ideas about himself and the world that he uses to comfort himself for the lack of warmth in his life. That he evokes the sister, and allows her to take the coat from him indicates that he gets from her sufficient warmth to part with the coat, and that the coat is given to her means that she can provide that warmth for

the doctor because she represents a more sexualized version of the ideas and values that function as sublimated substitutions for the repressed. Since the repressed has earlier in the story been associated with the bestial—the pig-sty, the animal-like quality of the groom when he first appears, and the horses, the fur coat becomes associated with that cluster of images. Therefore, that he allows the sister to take the coat from him indicates an oedipal structure in which the figure of the sister has the potentiality of making the perverse available to him in a sexual rather than a defensive way. The passive anal quality of that sexuality is suggested by the detail at the end of the story in which the fur coat catches on a hook by its sleeve and hangs from the back of the gig, probably expressing the dreamer's body, unavailable to the rider.

Then "a glass of rum was poured out for me, the old man clapped me on the shoulder, a familiarity justified by this offer of his treasure. I shook my head; in the narrow confines of the old man's thoughts I felt ill; that was my only reason for refusing the drink." The physical affection and warmth, and perhaps the sexual identification suggested by the word "treasure," offered by the father is rejected; presumably if the doctor accepted the drink, then he would be loved "within the narrow confines of the old man's thought" and that possibility makes him sick or fills him with revulsion. If we consider this revulsion as a reaction formation, and remember that it is the dreamer who evokes the image of the father offering warmth, love, and potency, what emerges is a highly ambivalent and charged relation in which the dreamer wants and fears physical contact with the father, as well as identification with him—"the narrow confines of the old man's thought." He interrupts that approach to the complex of feelings around the father by evoking the mother who "stood by the bedside and cajoled me towards it." He "yields" to her, thereby escaping the difficult feelings surrounding the father, and permits himself the slight sensuousness involved in putting his head to the boy's breast. But that physical contact, as though connected to guilt at yielding to his mother's cajoling, produces an instant recoil into defensive moral indignation; the boy had "best be turned out of bed with one shove." He sees the boy, and consequently himself, as malingering trying to get attention and love he hasn't a right to. But his guilty desire is now sufficiently strong to prevent him from throwing the boy out of bed, or exposing him, and to resolve the conflict between guilt and desire he resorts once again to his role of passive martyr, "I am no world reformer." He is caught between the oedipal desire and the rejection of it, and can go in neither direction energetically. In so far as he is identified with the boy on the bed he can neither permit the mother to approach him, nor get out of bed and move away from the oedipal conflict. His oedipal desire is expressed through the mother who cajoles him to bed, but since he is castrated, turned into a girl, it isn't his mother, or the female, who sexually arouses him. Therefore he must disappoint her, and, since presumably what he wants is to be penetrated, he must also disappoint the father who expects him to act like a man. He expresses his anger at the parents who first castrate him, then expect him to perform, by, irrationally, wanting to "let fly at this family" because of his loss of Rose. His loss of Rose expresses at another level his loss of his male sexuality, and on that level his anger at the family is not irrational, but he doesn't understand it.

This first approach to accepting his identification with the boy has been accomplished through his yielding to the mother's cajoling. It's an abortive attempt, and leaves in its wake a sense of the parent's disappointment, the father sniffing the rejected rum. Their power to move him by their expectations remains, but as the associations with the fur coat would lead one to expect, the more potent figure in moving him toward a second approach is the sister, "fluttering a blood-soaked towel." The blood-soaked towel emerges suddenly, as it were, from behind the unresolved oedipal feeling involved in the preceding details, as though symbolizing those feelings in a newly charged way. The blood-soaked towel carries two associations. First it is associated with the sister, presumably with her menstrual blood, and thereby with her sexuality, or her 'wound,' and second, with the boy's wound to the discovery of which the towel leads him. And since the towel is associated with both, then the boy's wound and the sister's sexuality must be associated for the dreamer, leading to the conclusion that the dreamer has identified himself with the sister in the process of becoming castrated. And it is this identification that has the power to move him back towards the boy to discover the wound. This association of the sister with potency is also suggested earlier in the story when the groom addresses the horses as "Brother" and "Sister," the same horses who whinny excitedly as he discovers the wound. The centrality of the wound to the configurations that lead up to its discovery is indicated by the vividness with which it is described—many shades of reds, irregular clots of blood, and finally the white worms, disgusting in context, but suggestive of life. This life now pervades everything; the house comes to life with the family whispering to each other and guests coming in, and the boy, who previously expressed a wish to die, now sobs, "Will you save me?" and is "blinded by the life within his wound." All this vitality extending from the wound to the activity in the household preceeds the doctor's most fully indulged passivity. He becomes immersed in his sense of himself as sacrificial victim and moral commentator while he allows himself to be undressed and laid beside the boy and his wound. Because of the guilt he feels, he must experience himself as passive in order to permit himself to approach the sources of his own vitality, and must further defend against experiencing the reality of his sexual desires by interpreting the source of his vitality, the castration wound, as an illness he must, as a doctor, cure rather than suffer.

This suggests that the doctor's bitter-sweet self-sacrificing ennui both disguises and expresses a perverse sexual form in which he wishes to be penetrated, like a girl, but since he is male, presumably anally. If this is the case, then his uneasiness at being within the confines of the father's thought can be seen to suggest some sexual uneasiness, and his inner vision of the groom pursuing and on top of Rose contains the possibility of a double identification. On the one hand the figure of the groom represents his own active male sexuality, but that is very remote. On the other hand the figure of Rose, being identified through the name with the wounded boy, is consequently also identified with the dreamer. Therefore for him to accept his identification with the boy would signify that he accepted and experienced his desire to be penetrated. The closest approach he makes toward such a resolution is to allow himself to be "misused" "for sacred ends," accepting for the moment that he is "bereft of his servant girl." However, the moment he finds himself beside the boy on the bed, there comes an abrupt end to the progress of the dream toward actualization of the repressed. This abrupt repression is signaled by the sharp decline in vitality. The moon, which has been shning from the moment the doctor arrived at the house, is now covered with clouds, the sounds of singing and the movement of people cease, the horse's heads "wavered

like shadows," and the boy, whom the doctor had previously experienced as eager for his aid, now becomes hostile and distrusting. The energy of the surroundings subsides because the doctor, confronted with the possibility of fulfilling his desire to become one with the boy, and of actualizing his passive homosexuality, is overtaken with self-loathing and hatred, which are expressed through the actions of the boy. The boy first says, "Why, you were only blown in here, you didn't come on your feet." This casts doubt upon the source of energy that brought the doctor this far toward realizing the repressed. The loving and sexuality suggested by lying together in bed is turned into its opposite; "you're cramping me on my deathbed," and finally the sexuality is expressed only as rage; "What I'd like best is to scratch your eyes out." That the doctor envisages the boy (a version of himself) inflicting upon him the punishment of Oedipus confirms that for the dreamer, lying with the boy represents the fulfillment of a reversed oedipal wish.

All the emotions of the situation are expressed through the boy and the surroundings. The emotional neutrality of the dreamer reflects the repression, as does his resort to ennui and a sense of martyrdom, and it is only in this, ironically, that the boy and the doctor for a moment merge, as the boy expresses the jaded despair so characteristic of the doctor. He says "Am I supposed to be content with this apology? Oh, I must be, I can't help it. I always have to put up with things, a fine wound is all I brought into the world; that was my sole endowment." The doctor takes up the boy's tone as he placates him, asserting that his condition is usual; "many a one proffered his side and can hardly hear the ax in the forest, far less that it is coming nearer to him." In effect, he turns a symptom into a philosophy, a state of castration into a comment on the nature of reality, and so comforts his adolescent self, represented by the boy, for being castrated, and himself for having failed to accomplish his mission of healing.

The failure of his mission is related, as the boy's words suggest, to the means by which it was made possible. We find him at the beginning of the story "muffled in furs," all equipped for the journey except that he lacks power, for his horse has died, and he rejects as futile "the servant girl's" attempt to find one for him. His frustrated impotence seems the other side of the coin from the jadedness that pervades the rest of the story. In the midst of this impotence, he kicks "at the dilapidated door of the year-long uninhabited pigsty." The kick functions like the touch of Aladdin on the magic lamp, for there emerges from the pigsty a groom, crouching, then crawling in a way that suggests an identification with animals, before emerging fully a man, along with two magically powerful horses. A strong birth image is suggested by the way in which the horses fill the opening of the sty before emerging and this birth image adds to the mythic association of the pig with female sexuality. The magical quality of the episode suggests that in his frustrated impotence he has touched upon the energies of a repressed perversion, but in a way that is sudden and out of control. The anally passive desire manifests itself, as has been discussed, in the later developments of the story, but a potentially active, aggressive but more deeply buried sexuality is suggested by the details here. The groom bites Rose's cheek (suggesting anal sadism), the doctor expresses a desire to whip the groom. These details are echoed, though in a much more remote form, later in the story when the doctor evokes the image of axes coming in the forest, and in the boy's desire to scratch out the doctor's eyes.

The fullest expression of the active possibility is in his vision of the groom raging after Rose in the house.

In kicking the pig-sty the dreamer has touched upon and released the power of the perverse form, but he has done so without knowledge or capacity to integrate that power into his life. Therefore he experiences the horses as out of his control and magically swift. In conjunction with the appearance of the horse and the groom he, for the first time, experiences Rose as a sexual creature, but again he experiences that sexuality as unavailable to him because controlled by another. That uncontrolled power energizes two sexual drives in the dreamer, but the dreamer by experiencing them in conflict, uses the conflict itself to re-press them both. The first drive is active and heterosexual and is manifested primarily in the groom's behavior. He bites Rose's cheek, asserts his intention to stay with Rose, and is envisioned by the dreamer as pursuing and mastering her. Some of that active energy spills over to the dreamer when he yells "do you want a whipping" and when he experiences Rose running toward him, her cheek showing "in red the marks of two rows of teeth." But he retreats quickiy into the passive mode, reflecting that he needs the groom's assistance, as though, in so far as the groom represents a father image, he fears to engage the oedipal struggle with the father which he would have to do once he accepted identification with his maleness. As a consequence of his denial of engagement, the father figure is not internalized—the groom remains separate, threatening, a stranger. The groom's active energy functions to set the horses off, and to carry the doctor toward the encounter with his own passive sexuality as represented by the boy. Each time later in the story that he approaches closer to the boy, the horses heads appear at the window, noisy and energetic. This indicates the rise in his sexual excitation in that situation, but he reacts to that excitement by pulling back rather than going forward. He rationalizes his fear by associating the horses with Rose and the groom. He withdraws from the encounter with the boy, using as an excuse his desire to rescue and retrieve Rose, but the painful irony is that he can do so only by drawing closer to the boy. The connection between the two drives is supported by the fact that when he finally withdraws from the boy's bed, deciding that he won't bother dressing since the horses are so fast, he reflects, "I should only be springing, as it were, out of this bed into my own," and doesn't at the moment of withdrawal from the boy think of Rose in his house or bed. The discharge of energy toward the boy has also discharged the energy toward Rose.

The end of the story, though it indicates the dreamer's failure to fulfill his mission of healing, can be seen in one way as positive. The doctor can no longer return to his former life—he is naked and will not return to his house, he will no longer be a false doctor who can dispense prescriptions but cannot understand people, who congratulates himself on his irritable self-sacrifice. Some of his pretense is gone—not all, since when he envisions someone else taking over his practice he comforts himself by thinking that the successor "cannot take my place." But all energy has been drained away. He finds himself an old man in an "earthly vehicle"—his body, drawn by "unearthly horses"—his own perverse powers now discharged and repressed. Through seemingly unending ice and snow the fur coat trails behind him out of his reach and use, and he is lost in the cold, caught between the life that once was his, and the life that might have been his had he met the challenge. But he denies that there was a challenge, since naked in the gig he thinks about the night-bell, which must repre-

sent a peak of frustration, that called him to the boy as a "false alarm," cancelling out his previous recognition that there was an illness to be cured. He has been, as he says, "betrayed," but not by the townspeople whom he so often blames. He has been betrayed by his own repressed desires which were sufficiently evoked to ensure that he cannot go back to his previous defenses, and sufficiently denied to prevent him from going forward. The last line shows him congealing his self-deception into a general comment on the nature of life—into a philosophy, "A false alarm on the night bell once answered—it cannot be made good, not ever." (pp. 334-46)

Katherine Stockholder, "Franz Kafka, 'A Country Doctor': The Narrator as Dreamer," in American Imago, *Vol. 35, No. 4, Winter, 1978, pp. 331-46.*

DOREEN F. FOWLER   (essay date 1979)

[In the following excerpt, Fowler discusses similarities between the Bible and "In the Penal Colony."]

During the past decades of Kafka literary criticism, critics have discarded the possibility of an integrated synthesis of the Biblical symbols that pervade Kafka's **"In the Penal Colony."** The reason for such a critical rejection seems clear. A coherent interpretation of the Biblical symbols in the story, in which all the parallels function meaningfully, presents an unorthodox and uniquely personal vision of traditional theology.

In order to uncover the Biblical analogues implicit in Kafka's **"In the Penal Colony"** it is necessary to reconstruct briefly the major narrative developments of the work:

An explorer visiting a penal colony is introduced to two orders—the old and the new. The old order instituted a harsh, merciless system of justice; the new order favors a milder doctrine. At the time of the present action of **"In the Penal Colony"** the new order is gradually replacing the old. The old Commandant, who founded and promulgated the old order, is dead, and the officer is the last ardent champion of the old tradition.

As the story opens, the explorer is about to witness an execution which typifies the old order's stern judicial procedure. The explorer becomes concerned when he learns that the condemned man has had no opportunity to defend himself and is in almost total ignorance of his crime and his sentence. Even more disturbing to the explorer is the nature of the condemned man's offense. He has failed to perform a meaningless and nearly impossible observance: "It is his duty, you see, to get up every time the hour strikes and salute the captain's door." Finally, the explorer is told the officer's guiding principle in all matters related to justice: "Guilt is never to be doubted."

Having explained the central tenet of the old order's judicial process, the officer describes how the piercing writing of a deadly machine inexorably metes out justice on the body of the condemned man:

> "And then the execution began! No discordant noise spoilt the working of the machine. Many did not care to watch it but lay with closed eyes in the sand; they all knew: Now Justice is being done. . . . Well, and then came the sixth hour! It was impossible to grant all the requests to be al-

lowed to watch it from near by. The Commandant in his wisdom ordained that the children should have the preference; I, of course, because of my office had the privilege of always being at hand; often enough I would be squatting there with a small child in either arm. How we all absorbed the look of transfiguration on the face of the sufferer, how we bathed our cheeks in the radiance of that justice, achieved at last and fading so quickly! What times these were, my comrade!"

Even at this early stage in the unfolding narrative, it is possible to discern the essence of the old order: human existence is essentially characterized by guilt, and justice demands the terrible agony of the machine.

In the course of describing the old order's judicial procedure the officer beseeches the explorer to assist him in preserving the old tradition. The explorer, after a moment's hesitation, refuses this request. Faced with this rejection, the officer announces, "Then the time has come"; he frees the condemned man and takes his place on the torturing device. The execution then proceeds with this substitution of the officer for the condemned man. The officer is clearly a willing sacrifice to the apparatus: "Everything was ready, only the straps hung down at the sides, yet they were obviously unnecessary, the officer did not need to be fastened down." The machine, however, fails to function properly, and the anticipated moment of transfiguring justice is not experienced: "And here, almost against his will, he had to look at the face of the corpse. It was as it had been in life; no sign was visible of the promised redemption; what the others had found in the machine the officer had not found."

"In the Penal Colony" concludes with the explorer's departure from the colony. Before leaving, the explorer visits the grave of the old Commandant, which is located under a table in a teahouse. The explorer is told that the officer had attempted "several times to dig the old man up by night, but he was always chased away." The inscription on the grave of the old Commandant reads:

> "Here rests the old Commandant. His adherents, who now must be nameless, have dug this grave and set up this stone. There is a prophecy that after a certain number of years the Commandant will rise again and lead his adherents from this house to recover the colony. Have faith and wait!"

Immediately after this visit to the old Commandant's grave, the explorer leaves the penal colony, driving away the soldier and the condemned man who seek to depart with him.

Implicit in this summary of the narrative developments of **"In the Penal Colony"** are a number of striking analogues to Biblical events and religious doctrines. The old order, which is the central subject of **"In the Penal Colony,"** immediately evokes a comparison to the old tradition of the Old Testament—the "Old Law." The similarity between the old tradition in Kafka's story and the Hebraic tradition is, however, more than merely nominal. In order to point out that substantive similarities do exist between the penal colony's old order and the Hebraic tradition, as it is commonly understood, it will be helpful to turn to Matthew Arnold's description of Hebraism in his essay, "Hebraism and Hellenism."

Arnold states that both Hebraism and Hellenism have for their ends the same goal—"reason and the will of God, the feeling after the universal order." However, after noting this

Kafka and Felice Bauer, the woman to whom he was twice engaged but never married, Budapest, July, 1917.

similarity of purpose, Arnold stresses the fundamental methodological dissimilarities between the two traditions. This divergence, according to Arnold, is largely to be attributed to the large role that sin plays in the Hebraic conception of man as opposed to the Hellenistic conception. . . . The Hebraic conception of man, as described by Arnold, bears a close resemblance to the view of man asserted by the adherents of the old order in Kafka's **"In the Penal Colony."** "The body of this death" that Arnold refers to is human guilt and sinfulness, from which, according to Arnold's interpretation of Hebraism, release is secured only by "groaning that cannot be uttered." Similarly, in **"In the Penal Colony"** the adherents of the old order maintain that human existence is characterized by guilt and sinfulness (the officer's guiding principle is: "Guilt is never to be doubted.") Deliverance from this inherent guilt is attained only by suffering the agony of the machine. Thus, the Hebrew tradition's emphasis on guilt and suffering is fundamentally analogous to the old order's conception of man and subsequent prescription for punishment.

Once an analogy between the old order and the Hebraic tradition is recognized, it is immediately clear that the old Commandant represents God-the-Father, the Creator of the Genesis account. Like the God of Genesis, who created the earth, the old Commandant invented the torture machine and is responsible for the entire structure of the penal colony. . . . By means of this analogy between the old Commandant and the God of Genesis, Kafka clearly implies that our world is like a penal colony, and even more specifically (because the torture machine represents a microcosm of the penal colony), like the torture machine. This parallel suggests that the world, like the torture machine, was created to induce the suffering necessary for the expiation of human guilt.

The belief that guilt is inherent in existence and that men live to expiate this guilt by suffering is clearly evident in other works of Kafka—*The Trial* and **"The Judgment."** The appearance of identical ideas in these works substantiates the assertion that an analogy between the torture machine and the earth is suggested in **"In the Penal Colony."**

Just as the penal colony's old order evokes a Biblical parallel, so also does the new order. At first glance, the new regime might seem to resemble the Hellenistic tradition which Matthew Arnold describes as both opposing and alternating with the Hebraic tradition in the course of history. Like the Hellenistic tradition, the new order is mild, is opposed to torture as a means to human salvation, and does not stress human guilt and sinfulness. However, the terminology that Kafka employs to describe the new order clearly points to an analogy with the New Testament tradition or the "New Law." The new tradition is described as "our new, mild doctrine," and it is the order approved of by "the ladies," suggesting an association with love and gentleness. Clearly such descriptions are meant to evoke Christ's new law of love, which contrasts with the sterner law of the Old Testament. Finally, just as the new law of the Christian tradition follows the harsher, old law of the Hebraic tradition, so also in **"In the Penal Colony"** the new order follows a harsher former order.

Once this connection is understood, it becomes apparent that the Christ-figure in Kafka's Biblical analogy is the officer. Like God-the-Son who existed from time immemorial with God-the-Father and who aided in the creation of the world, the officer contributed to the institution of the penal colony from its inception: "I assisted at the very earliest experiments and had a share in all the work until its completion." Like Christ, son of God-the-Father, the officer pays filial-like devotion and allegiance to the old Commandant. The officer's youth further reinforces this resemblance to God-the-Son. Finally, the officer's willing sacrifice of himself in the place of the condemned man clearly suggests an analogy to Christ's suffering and death, which, according to Christian theology, were accomplished in order to redeem condemned humanity from the effects of original sin.

With the suggestion of this last correspondence, Kafka's divergent interpretation of New Testament theology becomes fully apparent. The New Testament affirms that Christ died in order to free humanity from bondage to original sin. According to Kafka's construction of Biblical events, as suggested in **"In the Penal Colony,"** Christ died for an opposite reason—in affirmation of man's guilt and the necessity of suffering for that guilt. The Christ-figure of Kafka's analogy, the officer, sacrifices himself in order to bear witness to the old order that identifies guilt with human existence and justice with punishment. *Thus, in Kafka's inversion of traditional Christian theology, Christ is not the originator of a new law of love and forgiveness. Rather, Kafka's Christ-figure is the last proponent of the old, stern law which decrees that atonement for human guilt is won only by suffering.* Implicit in **"In the Penal Colony,"** then, is Kafka's own personal construction

of Biblical events. Christian theology teaches that Christ willingly submitted to torture and crucifixion in order to expiate man's burden of sin and guilt. The Christ-figure of Kafka's analogy suffers and dies in order to affirm that only by such suffering and death is human sinfulness to be overcome.

Kafka's frequently reiterated feelings of guilt and inferiority may provide an explanation for this unique interpretation of Biblical events. It is widely acknowledged that Kafka was overawed by his father, and that he also magnified and deplored his own limitations. . . . To Kafka, who was overwhelmed by a sense of guilt, the Christian doctrine that Christ's crucifixion freed man from the effects of original sin might very possibly have seemed remote and unreal, and, because Kafka was filled with dread and fear of authority figures, the Christian vision of God as a loving redeemer might also have seemed untenable. Thus the meanings attached to Biblical events by Kafka's skillful manipulation of analogies in **"In the Penal Colony"** might represent an interpretation of Sacred Scripture uniquely suited to a man of Franz Kafka's temperament.

One final Biblical parallel in **"In the Penal Colony"** remains to be interpreted—the inscription on the grave of the old Commandant which prophesies his resurrection, return, and resumption of power. This prophecy clearly recalls the resurrection of the New Testament and the Biblical prophecy of Christ's second coming. Here, as elsewhere, however, these Biblical parallels are infused with unorthodox meanings. The New Testament describes the resurrection as Christ's triumphant victory over sin and death . . . and the second coming as the return of a loving redeemer. In **"In the Penal Colony"** the resurrection and the second coming both refer to the return of the old order espoused by both Kafka's God-the-Father-figure, the old Commandant, and Kafka's Christ-figure, the officer. Thus, the inscription's words, "the Commandant will rise again and lead his adherents from this house to recover the colony," clearly indicate that the resurrection and second coming in **"In the Penal Colony"** will herald the return of the old, stern system of life-long punishment for intrinsic human sinfulness. By this manipulation of Biblical analogues, Kafka suggests his own personal interpretation of Biblical events. For Kafka, the second coming will not bring the return of a resurrected, loving redeemer, but the return of a harsh and unforgiving system of justice.

The meanings that I have inferred from Kafka's use of Biblical symbols in **"In the Penal Colony"** are so clearly implied that it seems odd these meanings have remained so long unstated. It should be noted that the Biblical symbols have been recognized by scholars of Kafka's works. However, these symbols have not been seriously analyzed by critics. A case in point is Heinz Politzer's treatment of the Biblical analogies in **"In the Penal Colony."** Politzer writes:

> Following this trend of thought to its conclusion, we may compare the teahouse with another old inn from which another old belief, Judaism, proceeded into the world, rejuvenated, as Christianity. The execution machine may be likened to the Cross, the suicide of the officer to a sacrificial death. The words on the tombstone, "Have faith and wait!" acquire an almost evangelical ring. The imagery of the story as a whole suddenly seems to carry definite overtones of Christian symbolism.
>
> But as soon as we take the inscription on the old Commandant's grave seriously, a strictly religious

interpretation of "In the Penal Colony" becomes untenable. The faith that the old Commandant's followers are admonished to preserve cannot be anything but belief in their master's rigorous martial law. This law is no more to be identified with Judaism than Christian hope is to be derived from the old martinet's return to the Colony.

In this passage Politzer identifies several of the major Biblical analogies in Kafka's story. However, he does not attempt to discern the end to which these symbols are employed. Instead, he states that it is impossible to view the proceedings of **"In the Penal Colony"** as in any way analogous to the events of the Bible: "But as soon as we take the inscription on the old Commandant's grave seriously, a strictly religious interpretation of **"In the Penal Colony'** becomes untenable." Politzer's reason for this assertion is not clearly stated; however it is implied in these words: "This law [the old order] is no more to be identified with Judaism than Christian hope is to be derived from the old martinet's return to the Colony." Implicit in this statement is refusal to impute to these Biblical events highly personal meanings. Politzer implies that the second coming can be interpreted only as a source of "Christian hope." Similarly, an analogue to Judaism must conform to traditional, established definitions of Judaism. Politzer's words suggest that it is impossible that Kafka might, by means of an analogy, suggest an unorthodox interpretation of Biblical events.

And yet numerous precedents for such unorthodox interpretations of Biblical episodes exist in literature. Yeats' poem, "The Second Coming," for example, clearly ascribes to a traditional Biblical phenomenon a meaning incompatible with the definitions promulgated by Christian doctrine. Surely, any student of literature could supply many such examples in refutation of Politzer's implicit premise that art must conform to orthodox theology.

Politzer is not the only critic of Kafka's writings who has rejected analogues which impute to Biblical events original interpretations. Anthony Thorlby, in *Kafka: A Study*, writes:

> Let critics beware, who have been struck by phrases like "rise again," "redemption," and even mingling of "blood and water" in this story, and jump to the simple-minded conclusion that Kafka is prophesying the return of Christ. Doubtless the old order he has described was religious in origin, but he has discredited it thoroughly.

Thorlby notes only two of the major religious symbols in **"In the Penal Colony"**—the references to the Biblical redemption and resurrection. Because he has not examined the whole pattern of Biblical imagery, it is impossible for him to discern the new meanings that Kafka is attributing to the resurrection and redemption in **"In the Penal Colony"** by narrative manipulation of Biblical symbols. Thus, Thorlby finds that a parallel between the return of the old order and the return of Christ (which is clearly implied in **"In the Penal Colony"**) is "simple-minded" because the old order is "thoroughly discredited." Underlying Thorlby's statement is the premise that an analogy between a "discredited" order and a Biblical referent could not be made. It is questionable that the old order is "discredited . . . thoroughly" in Kafka's **"In the Penal Colony"**; however, whether or not the old order is discredited does not eliminate the possibility that Kafka is suggesting an analogy between the return of the old order and the return of Christ. The essential point is that correspon-

dences should not be dismissed because of dissimilarities between the analogue and the Biblical event as it is traditionally defined. Like Politzer, Thorlby is rejecting the Biblical parallels in **"In the Penal Colony"** on the grounds that differences exist between Kafka's analogue and the Christian interpretation of the Biblical occurrence. But by imputing to the events of the Old and New Testament personal interpretations Kafka is communicating to us his unique vision of human existence. (pp. 113-19)

Doreen F. Fowler, " 'In the Penal Colony': Kafka's Unorthodox Theology," in College Literature, *Vol. VI, No. 2, Spring, 1979, pp. 113-20.*

ROY PASCAL (essay date 1982)

[*Pascal was an English critic who wrote extensively on German history and literature. In the following excerpt taken from his* Kafka's Narrators: A Study of His Stories and Sketches *(1982), he assesses the significance of the dual narrative perspective in "The Judgment."*]

It is clear that [the narrative perspective of **"The Judgment"**] has much similarity to that of the novels since the objective voice that tells the story normally chooses the chief character's angle of vision and, while communicating to us the latter's thoughts, wishes, feelings, and intentions, can in the main describe the other characters and the physical settings only in so far as the chief character knows them. Most readers feel the last sentence of **"The Judgment"**, referring to the stream of traffic crossing the bridge as Georg falls into the river, and the last pages of **"The Metamorphosis"**, describing the recovery of the Samsa family after the death of Gregor, as a dislocation of style, since elsewhere throughout both stories we are so tightly held within the orbit of the chief character. But this feeling is not fully justified, and the objective narrator, the objective viewpoint immanent in these endings, appears at many moments of the story. If I now proceed to disentangle the stylistic evidence for the narrator's objective viewpoint, as distinct from that of the character, I do this only in order to assess the effect upon the meaning of the story that this double perspective produces. (p. 21)

The first paragraph of **"The Judgment"**, in which Georg Bendemann and his home are described from outside, might seem to be a conventional introduction to the story. It creates a mood of uneventful idyllic innocence on a Sunday morning in spring, a row of inconspicuous houses, a lovely outlook, and a young man putting his letter into an envelope 'with playful slowness'. With the second paragraph we enter into the troubles and questions of the story and at the same time into the perspective of Georg, for it is through his thoughts that we are introduced to the friend in St Petersburg and then, in a long passage of free indirect speech, to his internal debate about what he should tell the friend. So the narratorial opening is not without thematic function, even if it is only a means to make the coming gloom more striking by contrast. But there are also narratorial intrusions later. As Georg goes to see his father about the letter, we are told about their habits since the mother died. This also must be narratorial, and the brief description of their daily routine, a close association at work and home lacking all intimacy, is more than a sort of stage direction, for it creates in us a feeling of inert cohabitation that bears an objective judgment on them both. It is consonant with this that the description of Georg's final flight to the river also is an objective, not subjective account, even more emphatically so through the two striking similes—Georg hurtles 'as over a tilting surface' and he clutches the railing of the bridge 'as a hungry man clutches at food.'

There is the same double perspective in the presentation of the characters. We see and hear them only in so far as they appear to Georg, we know their thoughts only as their behaviour and speech indicates them to Georg, through our repeated identification with his angle of vision. But here too the narrator may add something, an observation from outside the character. (pp. 21-2)

Usually the two perspectives are not clearly separate but more subtly interwoven; in many cases we are not able to be sure in what perspective a particular statement stands. The reason for this is the extensive use of free indirect speech and, more particularly, the modern form that Kafka's free indirect speech takes.

The thoughts, inner reactions of most characters are given directly, as they themselves express them in speech, and indirectly as inferences from their behaviour. The narrator has immediate access only to Georg's thoughts, and only in his case can he use introductory verbs like 'he thought, imagined' etc. followed by reported speech. If the thought or intention of the other characters is detected, it is legitimised as an inference from their expressions and behaviour. Free indirect speech is therefore almost completely reserved for the main character, and for him it is indeed abundantly used.

Just as Kafka follows an old convention in the reproduction of thoughts by putting them in direct speech enclosed in inverted commas, as if they were spoken, so he also often uses the conventional indices that betray free indirect speech and leave no doubt in the reader's mind as to the source of the statements concerned. Thus he can open a passage with exclamatory questions that transfer the reader to the consciousness of the character. Or statements can be accompanied by an explicit 'he thought', 'he believed', 'he remembered', 'he felt' (*er dachte, er glaubte, er erinnerte sich, er fühlte*), which clearly define from whose mind they emanate. Sometimes we may be misled on first reading, though closer attention reveals the subjective nature of a statement. (pp. 22-3)

In all these respects Kafka's use of free indirect speech is essentially the same as that which we meet in nineteenth-century novels and rests likewise on a clear distinction of an objective narrator from the subjective character. It shares some of the uncertainties that dog this form, especially those arising from the fact that its syntax is identical with that of a narratorial report, its tenses are normally the same and the characters referred to in the third person, while it lacks the verb and conjunction ('he said, thought that') that identify normal reported speech. Thus Georg may, in the thoughts ascribed to him, seem to think of himself not only as 'he' but even as 'Georg', not as an infantile self-address but simply as a stylistic device, needed because 'he' might apply to someone else. Thus, 'quite contrary to Georg's intention' is not a narratorial intrusion but Georg's own thought. At the same time it is a marked feature of free indirect speech that it can alternate very freely, from sentence to sentence, with objective narrative, so we cannot always be sure which is intended. . . . [At one point] we read a reference to the death of Georg's mother, and the addition of 'which had occurred some two years previously' must be a bit of information the narrator conveys to his reader rather than a thought in Georg's head; while . . . [later] the explanation that his fi-

ancée was 'from a well-to-do family', that at first sight seems also to be a narratorial explanation for our benefit, turns out to be the phrase that Georg has used in his letter to his friend, so we recognise that here his thought is quoting the smug phrase intended to excite his friend's envy or silence his disapproval.

But this paragraph shows problems of perspective that are not traditional, and needs closer examination. After the first sentence that tells us that Georg had hitherto not been able to bring himself to write to his friend about his betrothal, it continues: . . .

> He often spoke to his fiancée about this friend and the special relationship that he had with him because of their correspondence. 'So there is no question of his coming to our wedding', she said, 'but after all I have the right to get to know all your friends.' 'I don't wish to upset him', Georg replied, 'don't misunderstand, he would probably come, at least I think so, but he would feel awkward and inferior, perhaps even envious of me: certainly he would be discontented and have no way of shedding his discontent, and then he would have to go back on his own. Do you know what that means—to be on one's own?' 'Yes, but could he not learn of our marriage in some other way?' 'I cannot prevent that, but, given his way of life, it is unlikely.' 'If you have such friends, Georg, you ought not to have got engaged at all.' 'Yes, that's a guilt we both share, but I wouldn't have it any other way now.' And when she, breathing faster under his kisses, still managed to interject 'but even so it does actually offend me', he thought that there could be no real harm in writing everything to his friend. 'That's the way I am and he'll have to accept me on those terms', he said to himself.

The passage is stylistically surprising. It represents Georg's memory of several discussions with his fiancée that have led to his finally telling his friend about the betrothal. But these 'frequent' discussions are boiled down to one, and this is given in direct speech, i.e. a form that belongs to an objective narrator. It has been taken as a single conclusive conversation, but this is a mistake. The memory of the character reduces the conversations to their salient points and the narrator reproduces these in the form that best communicates the experience involved, for this purpose subjecting his separate identity to that of the character. The passage lays bare the transition from the traditional narrative situation of the nineteenth-century novel to that of the modern novel. The narrator relinquishes his separate view or identity in the interest of expressing the experience of the character, but does not thereby disappear. He re-asserts himself in his function as the arranger, the composer of the story whose presence, as we have just seen, can be detected even in those passages where he seems only to be the instrument of the character. This double function of the Kafka narrator, that of giving the experience of the character and that of narrating events, has been accurately and extensively analysed by Hartmut Binder in relation to **"The Judgment"** and other tales.

What help towards the understanding of Kafka's story does this more precise recognition of the narrative perspective give? We cannot expect that it alone will cleanse the Augean stable of conflicting interpretations; but it may to some extent explain why there is such diversity in these and even rebuff some, especially those which result from the imposition of a preconceived stereotype upon a narrative structure that is the reverse of typical—I think of interpretations that see the tale as a religious or a sexual allegory. The clearest gains from our analysis can be summed up as follows:

1.   Since Beissner first defined the narrator of Kafka's novels as 'dwelling in the soul of the character' even saying of that of **"The Judgment"** that he has 'completely transformed himself into the lonely Georg', critics have been able to grasp the subjective quality of this impersonal narrator and have been chiefly concerned to define more precisely the relationship between narrator and character. Thus Ellis, one of the most observant of readers, properly insists that though the narrator of **"The Judgment"** usually adopts the standpoint of the main character, his identity is not absorbed into that of Georg. But Ellis, no more than Sokel, comments on the significance of the occasional, truly objective intrusions of the impersonal narrator, if indeed he notices them. For instance, like Sokel he interprets the first paragraph of the story as a communication of Georg's thoughts as he sits in his comfortable study. Ellis makes indeed the valuable observation that the description of the setting is not the harmless bit of realism it has usually been assumed to be but betrays a strange confusion of mind, since the row of houses is said to be differentiated 'almost only' in height and colour, whereas such a difference would mean a marked variety. As a consequence Ellis must explain this oddity, like the 'playful deliberateness' of Georg's gesture, as a sign of Georg's misrelationship with reality. These and other difficulties fade if we recognise that the spatial and psychological focus of this first paragraph lies outside Georg's consciousness, that this paragraph is a comment from outside the events to be related and indeed, with its confusion and oddities of expression, is an amusingly misleading parody of a conventional story. In general, the mistake that even good critics make is not to recognise the mobility of Kafka's narratorial standpoint, which among other things allows for the frequent intrusion of humour.

2.   Ellis's grasp of the prevailing subjectivity of the narrative provides the insight for the best analysis of Georg's character that exists, for he sees that ostensibly narratorial statements about his generosity, friendliness, love, consideration for his friend and his father are only Georg's own self-justifications and his means to disguise his real envy and furtive hatred of these two and to depreciate, triumph over, his rivals. But again Ellis does not differentiate clearly enough. The subjectivity of the statements does not mean that everything is false, only that every statement is suspect. Thus, we can well accept the deep falsehood in Georg's professed kindness and generosity, but we have no reason to doubt his claim that the friend's business is not doing so well as his own, or that the father is ill and incapable of leading the business. Ellis considers that Georg is a failure and a parasite on his father, the stay-at-home son of the parable of the Prodigal Son, while the Petersburg friend is the favoured prodigal. But the only basis for this interpretation is the claim of the father in his violent battle with Georg, and Ellis seems indeed to accept as true everything the father throws at the son. Quite apart from the fact that there is no external, objective corroboration of the father's charges (that he is in league with the Petersburg friend, that he has Georg's customers 'in his pocket', that Georg is thoroughly incompetent in business etc.), there is such spiteful malevolence in his behaviour that we have no right to believe either the truth of his accusations or the justice of his sentence. It is strange that the acumen that detects the inner falsity of Georg should not recognise that of the father. But, it may be argued, the abject failure of Georg in

their contest and his consent to the death-sentence prove the truth of the father's assertions. I would suggest that Georg's ludicrous evasiveness in the argument and his acceptance of the sentence are due, not to the truth or falsehood of arguments, but to the terrible conflicts of love and hate, in both father and son, that is nakedly revealed through the father's reckless malevolence, the culmination of which is the father's collapse and the son's suicide. Such an interpretation is consistent with what the narrative perspective permits.

3.   It is the absence of an authoritative voice in **"The Judgment"** (as in many other Kafka stories and in all the novels), both in respect to facts and to judgments and meaning, that has provoked so great a variety of interpretations. The puzzle of the meaning and even connexion of events invites a search for symbolic and allegorical structures, and since there is little authoritative control in the text, these are often based on very frail and arbitrary associations. Ellis's discussion of them, though sympathetic, shows how slight and contradictory is the 'network of Christian imagery', into which the figure of Georg as a sacrificial Christ can be fitted only on the philological principle of *lucus a non lucendo*. But there is a more general and serious error that Kafka's narrative structure invites.

Its source is not simply in the narrative perspective, for it arises also from the opacity of meaning. Most readers, like most critics, approach Kafka with the expectations that traditional works of fiction arouse, in which apparent incongruities of behaviour and puzzling contingencies are ultimately cleared up in an ending that brings understanding and order (often in a moral as well as logical sense) into the events and relationships recounted. It cannot be too emphatically asserted that in the case of Kafka's stories such expectations are totally misleading. A glance at his fables or parables like **"Kleine Fabel"** ("Little Fable"), **"Vor dem Gesetz"** ("Before the Law")** and **"Heimkehr"** ("Homecoming"),** can warn us, for these, inviting us by their form to expect an unambiguous moral, in fact present us with an abstract model of reality that baffles our efforts to find in it a lesson. The stories, more realistic in their form and seeming in their structure more like normal relationships and situations, also seem to promise a meaning, but as they proceed our hopes are deceived and ultimately we are left before a baffling and painful puzzle.

It is painful merely to accept this fact; even more, the influence of traditional narrative literature leads us to believe there must be a meaning, and even a palatable meaning. Even Ellis, whom I quote because of the intelligence of his examination of **"The Judgment"** succumbs to this habit and provides a moral explanation of the catastrophe in terms of guilt and punishment. Georg's self-centredness and destructive hostility to others, Ellis believes, has woven him into a cocoon of falsity, of unreality, that is broken apart by his father; the sentence of death pronounced by the latter expresses symbolically the meaning of the story. This analysis of Georg's character seems to me, as I have already said, to be true; but are we satisfied with his punishment? Do we feel this to be a moral tale? Politzer was surely right when he wrote that there is no guilt in Georg's life that would justify a sentence of such severity, but when he calls this misrelationship 'a technical flaw' he also, it seems to me, is judging the story by a wrong stereotype. All such critical judgments supply that objective observer, that trustworthy narrator, that is not there in this and other stories of Kafka. But his absence is not a mere technicality, nor a mere attempt to bring immediacy into the narration; it means that an objective and authoritative moral understanding of the events is not accessible as well. There is guilt in the world, in Georg, there is consciousness of guilt, there is punishment, but though we can experience and recognise suffering and the evasive tricks men devise to deaden their consciousness of pain and guilt, yet we cannot understand why men should suffer so, nor can we see a necessary relationship between guilt and punishment. The story does not demonstrate a moral, it sets before us a moral riddle; and the title. The judgment, that is appropriate for the father and the son, to the reader must seem deeply ironic.

4.   Ellis rightly says that the terms 'nightmarish' or 'dreamlike' so frequently used in respect to Kafka's stories do not by themselves 'carry understanding further'. His own explanation of the irruption of grotesque elements as products of the unreality that Georg's self-centredness requires goes some way towards the understanding of this nightmarish quality. But here again, I believe, the lack of an intrusive narrator and objective perspective plays a large part. For, immersed in the subjective perspective of Georg, the reader lacks any objective reference, any norm against which he can judge the reality of the forms that emerge. Except at odd moments, when another perspective may be suggested or when a touch of humour intervenes, the reader is held spellbound, lacking those pauses for reflexion which the more traditional narrative forms, even those with a first-person narrator, provide. This spell extends to areas of Kafka's narrative that in themselves contain no fantastic or grotesque elements, like for instance the opening passages of **"The Judgment"** that describe Georg's thoughts about his friend; it is the fact that we are so deeply immersed in his consciousness that makes the fantastic elements in his great contest with his father so readily assimilable. It is real nightmare country, swarming with potent significances which we feel, though we lack the keys for their interpretation.

For all this, however, we are not utterly lost; indeed if we were, the spell would be broken, for spells must have a binding quality. At moments, as we have observed, a narrator is evident, not as an interpreter or judge but as a guide who spins the thread of the story. The opening belongs to a mind that knows the outcome, that carries on the story by unobtrusive means, sets the changing scenes, describes its close. The structure of a story is that aspect of which the reader is, as a rule, least conscious and perhaps especially so with Kafka, where the narrator who guides the story's destinies refuses to appear as an authority over against the characters. Yet this itself perhaps greatly contributes to the spellbinding character of the text since it is carried so swiftly from the opening to the dénouement and has so self-confident a structure, even though we are rarely aware of the agency that brings this about. (pp. 24-32)

> *Roy Pascal, in his* Kafka's Narrators: A Study of His Stories and Sketches, *Cambridge University Press, 1982, 251 p.*

FURTHER READING

Barnes, Hazel E. "Myth and Human Experience." *The Classical Journal* 51, No. 2 (December 1955): 121-27.
    Interprets "The Metamorphosis" in terms of classic Greek mythology.

Beck, Evelyn Torton. "Kafka's Traffic in Women: Gender, Power, and Sexuality." *The Literary Review* 26, No. 4 (Summer 1983): 565-76.
    Feminist interpretation of Kafka's principal works and characters.

Brancato, John J. "Kafka's 'A Country Doctor': A Tale for Our Time." *Studies in Short Fiction* 15, No. 2 (Spring 1978): 173-76.
    Views "A Country Doctor" as a surreal story about the helplessness of "scientific man" before the ruthless power of nature.

Brod, Max. *Franz Kafka: A Biography,* translated by G. Humphreys Roberts and Richard Winston. New York: Schocken Books, 1960, 252 p.
    Loving appreciation of Kafka's life and work by his friend and literary executor.

Corngold, Stanley. "Kafka's *Die Verwandlung:* Metamorphosis of the Metaphor." *Mosaic* 3, No. 4 (Summer 1970): 91-106.
    Examines Kafka's use of metaphor in "The Metamorphosis."

Emrich, Wilhelm. *Franz Kafka: A Critical Study of His Writings.* New York: Frederick Ungar Publishing Co., 1968, 561 p.
    One of the most comprehensive studies of Kafka's work.

Flores, Angel, and Swander, Homer, eds. *Franz Kafka Today.* Madison: The University of Wisconsin Press, 1958, 289 p.
    Critical essays divided into sections on the short stories, novels, diaries, and letters, including studies by Heinz Politzer, Carl R. Woodring, and Clement Greenberg.

Hatfield, Henry. "Life as Nightmare: Franz Kafka's 'A Country Doctor'." In his *Crisis and Continuity in Modern German Fiction: Ten Essays,* pp. 49-62. Ithaca and London: Cornell University Press, 1969.
    Interprets the story "A Country Doctor" as a surrealistic parable that employs the structure of a nightmare to signify humanity's predicament in a bleak age.

Holland, Norman N. "Realism and Unrealism in Kafka's *Metamorphosis.*" *Modern Fiction Studies* 4, No. 2 (Summer 1958): 143-50.
    Advocates reading "The Metamorphosis" with a focus upon the realistic and naturalistic plot elements in order to reduce the danger of viewing Gregor's transformation as a symbolic representation of Kafka's feelings about his relationship with his father.

Ingram, Forest L. *Representative Short Story Cycles of the Twentieth Century: Studies in a Literary Genre.* The Hague: Mouton & Co., 1971, 234 p.
    Contains a thematic and structural analysis of the story cycle collected in *A Hunger-Artist.*

The Literary Review, Kafka: Centenary Essays 26, No. 4 (Summer 1983).
    Special issue devoted to Kafka studies in the year of his centenary.

Mahlendorf, Ursula R. "Kafka's *Josephine the Singer or the Mouse Folk:* Art at the Edge of Nothingness." *Modern Austrian Literature* 11, Nos. 3-4 (1978): 199-242.

> States that "Josephine the Singer, or the Mouse Folk" both represents Kafka's attempt to assess his life and art and details the division in his psyche that determined the nature of his work.

Rolleston, James. *Kafka's Narrative Theatre.* University Park: Pennsylvania State University Press, 1974, 165 p.

> Emphasizes the importance of the narrator in Kafka's fiction.

Spilka, Mark. "Kafka's Sources for *The Metamorphosis.*" *Comparative Literature* XI, No. 4 (Fall 1959): 289-307.

> Cites Leo Tolstoy, Charles Dickens, and Nikolai Gogol as significant influences upon Kafka's writing of "The Metamorphosis."

Steinberg, Erwin R. "The Judgment in Kafka's 'In the Penal Colony'." *Journal of Modern Literature* 5, No. 3 (September 1976): 492-514.

> Views "In the Penal Colony" as representing Kafka's repudiation of the God of the Old Testament.

Stine, Peter. "Franz Kafka and Animals." *Contemporary Literature* 22, No. 1 (Winter 1981): 58-80.

> Discusses the significance of animals in Kafka's fiction, contending that of all his characters, the animals most poignantly symbolize humankind's fallen condition.

Tauber, Herbert. "The Metamorphosis." In his *Franz Kafka: An Interpretation of His Works,* pp. 18-26, 1948. Reprint. Port Washington, N.Y.: Kennikat Press, 1968.

> Considers Gregor's metamorphosis as an expression of his "feeling of alienation from the world around him."

Thiher, Allen. "Kafka's Legacy." *Modern Fiction Studies* 26, No. 4 (Winter 1980-1981): 543-61.

> Explicates several stories, including "The Judgment," "The Metamorphosis," and "In the Penal Colony," and discusses Kafka's influence on twentieth-century literature.

Tiefenbrun, Ruth. *Moment of Torment: An Interpretation of Franz Kafka's Short Stories.* Carbondale and Edwardsville: Southern Illinois University Press, 1973, 160 p.

> Psychoanalytical study of Kafka's fiction, maintaining that his latent homosexuality influenced the thematic nature of his work.

Weigand, Hermann J. "Franz Kafka's 'The Burrow' ('Der Bau'): An Analytical Essay." *PMLA* 87, No. 2 (March 1972): 152-66.

> Exegesis of the story "The Burrow."

Weinstein, Arnold. "Kafka's Writing Machine: Metamorphosis in the Penal Colony." *Studies in 20th Century Literature* 7, No. 1 (Fall 1982): 21-33.

> Analyzes the importance of language and communication in "In the Penal Colony," revealing "the disturbing, echoing analogies between the narrative frame, the nature of the Machine, and the purposes of art."

Wiley, Marion E. "Kafka's Piping Mice as Spokesmen for Communication." *Modern Fiction Studies* 25, No. 2 (Summer 1979): 253-58.

> Investigates the relationship between artists and the public in the story "Josephine the Singer, or the Mouse Folk."

Wolkenfeld, Suzanne. "Christian Symbolism in Kafka's 'The Metamorphosis'." *Studies in Short Fiction* X, No. 2 (Spring 1973): 205-07.

> Finds in the first part of "The Metamorphosis" "certain parallels between Gregor and Christ that are later developed as an ironic parody."

——. "Psychological Disintegration in Kafka's 'A Fratricide' and 'An Old Manuscript'." *Studies in Short Fiction* XII, No. 1 (Winter 1976): 25-9.

> Views "A Fratricide" and "An Old Manuscript" as Kafka's most enlightening depictions of mental dissolution.

(Joseph) Rudyard Kipling

1865-1936

English short story writer, poet, novelist, essayist, and autobiographer.

Creator of many of the world's best-loved short stories, Kipling is considered one of the finest writers of short fiction in world literature. Credited with popularizing the short fiction genre in England, Kipling is perhaps most famous for his insightful stories of Indian culture and Anglo-Indian society and for his masterful, widely read stories for children, which are collected in *Just So Stories for Little Children,* the two *Jungle Books, Puck of Pook's Hill,* and *Rewards and Fairies.* Many commentators consider Mowgli, the central figure in the *Jungle Books,* one of the most memorable characters in children's literature. Somerset Maugham concluded of Kipling: "He is our [England's] greatest story writer. I can't believe he will ever be equalled. I am sure he can never be excelled."

Kipling was born in Bombay, India, of English parents. At the age of six he was sent to school in southern England, an unhappy experience that he wrote about in his story "Baa Baa Black Sheep." For five years he lived with unsympathetic guardians in a foster home he called the "House of Desolation," and at the age of twelve he was sent to boarding school at the United Service College in Westward Ho!, Devon. Despite being bullied and ostracized by his schoolmates during his first years there, Kipling wrote fondly of his public school experiences in the collection *Stalky & Co.* Just before his seventeenth birthday, Kipling returned to India to work as a journalist on the Lahore *Civil and Military Gazette* and the Allahabad *Pioneer.* The stories he wrote for these two newspapers, published in 1888 as the collection *Plain Tales from the Hills,* earned him widespread recognition in India.

Kipling returned to England in 1889 to pursue a literary career. Soon after arriving in London, he began collaborating with Wolcott Balestier, an American literary agent. The two men co-authored the novel *Naulahka,* and Balestier was responsible for publishing Kipling's works in America. In 1892 Kipling married Balestier's sister Caroline, and the couple lived on her family's estate in Vermont for four years. During this time Kipling produced the two *Jungle Books* and began writing *Kim,* considered by many his finest novel. Disenchanted with American society in general and devastated by the death of his daughter Josephine in 1899, Kipling returned to Europe, eventually settling in Sussex, England, a locale that figures prominently in the stories from *Puck of Pook's Hill* and *Rewards and Fairies.* In 1907 Kipling received the Nobel Prize in Literature for both his short fiction and novels, the first English author to be so honored. The tragedies of World War I and the loss of his only son, John, in 1915 greatly altered Kipling's personal and literary perspectives. Such stories as "Mary Postgate" and "Sea Constables" reflect the bitter anger and desire for revenge he felt at having witnessed so much destruction. Kipling never completely recovered from the loss of his two children. He died in 1936 after several years of illness and was buried in the Poet's Corner of Westminster Abbey.

Kipling's fame as a short fiction writer is based predominantly on three types of stories: his exotic tales of India, his narratives about the military, and his children's books. As a journalist in India, Kipling had the opportunity to explore many facets of Anglo-Indian culture, and the East provided the setting for much of his early fiction. His portrayal of India and its culture occupies many dimensions; he wrote stories about virtually every sector of society. These tales are imitative of the French *conte* and are considered remarkable for their innovative plots and deceptively simple structures. In general, critics concur that Kipling's best stories of India are those in which he reveals an underlying chaos and lack of control amidst a seemingly well-ordered society. "The Bridge Builders," for instance, dwells on the exotic appearances of Indian laborers, the arcane Indian pantheon, and the catastrophic flooding of the Ganges to show, in contrast, the pathetically limited imagination of British architecture and its ineptitude in controlling nature.

Kipling was fascinated by the military—the lives of British soldiers in India, the far East, and during World War I inspired many of his stories. His early portraits of British soldiers during peacetime are light-hearted and diverting, but also realistic and without illusions. Kipling's best known military tales are those that focus on three British soldiers: Mulvaney, Ortheris, and Learoyd. The "soldiers three" are jauntily portrayed in their manic lives of romancing, drinking, mischief-making, and occasional fighting in such stories as "The Madness of Private Ortheris" and "Private Learoyd's Story." The personalities of the trio are developed further in stories from the collections *Plain Tales from the Hills, Soldiers Three,* and *Life's Handicap.* Kipling's later military tales depict the horrors of World War I with tragic insight and exactitude. His grim yet lyrical delineation of agony and irrecoverable loss is starkly revealed in "Mary Postgate" and "The Gardener," two stories that reflect both the hate and undying love inspired by the war.

Kipling achieved perhaps his greatest literary success with the stories he wrote for children, most of which contain elements of humor intended for adults as well. Kipling fashioned these tales to be read aloud, and critics agree that the oral beauty of his writing makes these stories particularly memorable. The *Just So Stories,* written in a nonsensical secretive language, are intended for very young children and comically consider such timeless mysteries as why camels have humps or how writing was developed. Kipling's most famous collections, the two *Jungle Books,* chronicle the life of Mowgli, a boy who is abandoned by his parents and raised by wolves to become the master of the jungle. Commentators often note Kipling's gift for anthropomorphism in his fiction, and the animal characters in the *Jungle Books* are presented with simplicity, humor, and dignity. Kipling's final collections for children, *Puck of Pook's Hill* and *Rewards and Fairies,* feature the fairy Puck, who entertains two children with a series of stories about the successive generations—from Roman times to the French Revolution—that have inhabited the land where the children now blithely play. In these tales, Puck shows the children examples of both vice and virtue in the history of England, taking them on adventures that simultaneously entertain and teach moral lessons.

Kipling began writing short stories in the mid-1880s; by the turn of the century he was one of the most widely read authors in England. Prestigious newspapers including the *Times* of London and the *Scots Observer* published his stories regularly, and by 1896, his works had been collected in a uniform edition—a rare honor for so young a writer. Such powerful contemporary men of letters as Edmund Gosse, Thomas Hardy, Andrew Lang, and George Saintsbury praised his stories, and Henry James called him "the most complete man of genius that I've ever known." Kipling was not without detractors, however, and such commentators as Robert Buchanan rejected his stories as imperialist, vulgar, simpleminded, and unnecessarily brutal. Critics concur that Kipling's early success stemmed, in part, from his ability to inspire deep emotions in his audiences. Few readers reacted with indifference to his writing. The imperialist views Kipling expressed in his Indian stories also contributed to his initial success; however, later in his career after political tides in England had shifted, his stories were considered outdated and his popularity waned. Critical attention concentrated upon the jingoist and racist aspects of Kipling's writing almost to the exclusion of his literary accomplishments. Following Kipling's death, a major reassessment of his talents led to his recognition as an astute storyteller who possessed profound insights and a rare gift for entertaining. Although his stories are not uniformly praised, he is nonetheless regarded as one of the masters of the short story form. His exotic tales of India and entertaining children's stories are enjoyed by readers of all ages. Indeed, at the time of his death in 1936, Kip-

ling's collected stories—roughly 250 of them—had sold over fifteen million volumes. James Harrison has remarked: "To have reached, as no English author since Dickens had done, a world-wide readership of immense size and the widest possible intellectual and social range, and to be quoted scores of times a day by people who have no idea of whom they are quoting, is to be honored in a way many authors of the front rank might envy."

(For further information on Kipling's life and career, see *Twentieth-Century Literary Criticism,* Vols. 8, 17; *Contemporary Authors,* Vols. 105, 120; and *Dictionary of Literary Biography,* Vols. 19, 34.)

PRINCIPAL WORKS

SHORT FICTION

In Black and White   1888
The Phantom 'Rickshaw, and Other Tales   1888
Plain Tales from the Hills   1888
Soldiers Three   1888
The Story of the Gadsbys   1888
Under the Deodars   1888
Wee Willie Winkie, and Other Child Stories   1888
The Courting of Dinah Shadd, and Other Stories   1890
Life's Handicap   1891
Many Inventions   1893
The Jungle Book   (short stories and poetry)   1894
The Second Jungle Book   (short stories and poetry)   1895
The Day's Work   1898
Stalky & Co.   1899
Just So Stories for Little Children   (short stories and poetry)   1902
Traffics and Discoveries   (short stories and poetry)   1904
Puck of Pook's Hill   (short stories and poetry)   1906
Abaft the Funnel   1909
Actions and Reactions   (short stories and poetry)   1909
Rewards and Fairies   (short stories and poetry)   1910
A Diversity of Creatures   1917
Land and Sea Tales for Boys and Girls   (short stories and poetry)   1923
Debits and Credits   (short stories and poetry)   1926
Thy Servant a Dog   1930
Limits and Renewals   (short stories and poetry)   1932
Complete Works in Prose and Verse.   35 vols.   (short stories, poetry, novels, essays, sketches, speeches, and unfinished autobiography)   1937-39

OTHER MAJOR WORKS

Schoolboy Lyrics   (poetry)   1881
Departmental Ditties, and Other Verses   (poetry)   1886
The Light That Failed   (novel)   1890
Barrack-Room Ballads, and Other Verses   (poetry)   1892
The Naulahka: A Story of West and East [with Wolcott Balestier]   (novel)   1892
The Seven Seas   (poetry)   1896
Captains Courageous   (novel)   1897
From Sea to Sea. Letters of Travel.   2 vols.   (sketches)   1899
Kim   (novel)   1901
The Five Nations   (poetry)   1903
Songs from Books   (poetry)   1912
The Years Between   (poetry)   1919
Letters of Travel, 1892-1913   (sketches)   1920

A Book of Words (speeches) 1928
Souvenirs of France (essays) 1933
Something of Myself for My Friends Known and Unknown
    (unfinished autobiography) 1937

EDMUND GOSSE (essay date 1891)

[*A distinguished English literary historian, critic, and biographer, Gosse wrote extensively on seventeenth- and eighteenth-century English literature. His commentary in such works as* Seventeenth-Century Studies *(1883),* A History of Eighteenth-Century Literature *(1889), and* Questions at Issue *(1893), is regarded as sound and suggestive. Among his other works are studies of John Donne, Thomas Gray, and several French authors of the late nineteenth century. In the following excerpt, Gosse assesses Kipling's portrayal of British soldiers in India and his treatment of Anglo-Indian society.*]

I cannot pretend to be indifferent to the charm of what Mr. Kipling writes. From the first moment of my acquaintance with it it has held me fast. It excites, disturbs, and attracts me; I cannot throw off its disquieting influence. I admit all that is to be said in its disfavor. I force myself to see that its occasional cynicism is irritating and strikes a false note. I acknowledge the broken and jagged style, the noisy newspaper bustle of the little peremptory sentences, the cheap irony of the satires on society. Often—but this is chiefly in the earlier stories—I am aware that there is a good deal too much of the rattle of the piano at some café concert. But when all this is said, what does it amount to? What but an acknowledgment of the crudity of a strong and rapidly developing young nature? You cannot expect a creamy smoothness while the act of vinous fermentation is proceeding. (p. 901)

In the following pages I shall try to explain why the sense of these shortcomings is altogether buried for me in delighted sympathy and breathless curiosity. Mr. Kipling does not provoke a critical suspension of judgment. He is vehement, and sweeps us away with him; he plays upon a strange and seductive pipe, and we follow him like children. As I write these sentences, I feel how futile is this attempt to analyze his gifts, and how greatly I should prefer to throw this paper to the winds, and listen to the magician himself. I want more and more, like Oliver Twist. I want all those "other stories"; I wish to wander down all those by-paths that we have seen disappear in the brushwood. If one lay very still and low by the watch-fire, in the hollow of Ortheris's greatcoat, one might learn more and more of the inextinguishable sorrows of Mulvaney. One might be told more of what happened, out of the moonlight, in the blackness of Amir Nath's Gully. I want to know how the palanquin came into Dearsley's possession, and what became of Kheni Singh, and whether the sealcutter did really die in the House of Suddhoo. I want to know who it is who dances the *Hálli Hukk,* and how, and why, and where. I want to know what happened at Jagadhri, when the Death Bull was painted. I want to know all the things that Mr. Kipling does not like to tell—to see the devils of the East "rioting as the stallions riot in spring." It is the strength of this new story-teller that he re-awakens in us the primitive emotions of curiosity, mystery, and romance in action. He is the master of a new kind of terrible and enchanting peepshow, and we crowd around him begging for "just one more look." When a writer excites and tantalizes us in this way, it

seems a little idle to discuss his style. Let pedants, then, if they will, say that Mr. Kipling has no style; yet if so, how shall we designate such passages as this, frequent enough among his more exotic stories?

> Come back with me to the north and be among men once more. Come back when this matter is accomplished and I call for thee. The bloom of the peach orchards is upon all the valley, and *here* is only dust and a great stink. There is a pleasant wind among the mulberry trees, and the streams are bright with snow-water, and the caravans go up and the caravans go down, and a hundred fires sparkle in the gut of the pass, and tent-peg answers hammer-nose, and pony squeals to pony across the drift-smoke of the evening. It is good in the north now. Come back with me. Let us return to our own people. Come!
>
> (p. 902)

There can be no question that the side upon which Mr. Kipling's talent has most delicately tickled British curiosity, and British patriotism too, is his revelation of the soldier in India. A great mass of our countrymen are constantly being drafted out to the East on Indian service. They serve their time, are recalled, and merge in the mass of our population; their strange temporary isolation between the civilian and the native and their practical inability to find public expression for their feelings make these men—to whom, though we so often forget it, we owe the maintenance of the English Empire in the East—an absolutely silent section of the community. Of their officers we may know something, although **"A Conference of the Powers"** may perhaps have awakened us to the fact that we know very little. Still, people like Tick Boileau and Captain Mafflin of the Duke of Derry's Pink Hussars are of ourselves; we meet them before they go out and when they come back; they marry our sisters and our daughters; and they lay down the law about India after dinner. Of the private soldier, on the other hand, of his loves and hates, sorrows and pleasures, of the way in which the vast, hot, wearisome country and its mysterious inhabitants strike him, of his attitude towards India, and of the way in which India treats him, we know, or knew until Mr. Kipling enlightened us, absolutely nothing. It is not surprising, then, if the novelty of this portion of his writings has struck ordinary English readers more than that of any other.

This section of Mr. Kipling's work occupies the seven tales called *Soldiers Three,* and a variety of stories scattered through his other books. In order to make his point of view that of the men themselves, not spoiled by the presence of superior officers or by social restraint of any sort, the author takes upon himself the character of an almost silent young civilian who has gained the warm friendship of three soldiers, whose intimate companion and chum he becomes. Most of the military stories, though not all, are told by one of these three, or else recount their adventures or caprices. Before opening the book called *Soldiers Three,* however, the reader will do well to make himself familiar with the opening pages of a comparatively late story, **"The Incarnation of Krishna Mulvaney,"** in which the characteristics of the famous three are more clearly defined than elsewhere. Mulvaney, the Irish giant, who has been the "grizzled, tender, and very wise Ulysses" to successive generations of young and foolish recruits, is a great creation. He is the father of the craft of arms to his associates; he has served with various regiments from Bermuda to Halifax; he is "old in war, scarred, reckless, resourceful, and in his pious hours an unequaled soldier." Learoyd, the second of these friends, is "six and a half feet of slow-moving, heavy-footed Yorkshireman, born on the wolds, bred in the dales, and educated chiefly among the carriers' carts at the back of York railway-station." The third is Ortheris, a little man as sharp as a needle, "a fox-terrier of a cockney," an inveterate poacher and dog-stealer.

Of these three strongly contrasted types the first and the third live in Mr. Kipling's pages with absolute reality. I must confess that Learoyd is to me a little shadowy, and even in a late story, **"On Greenhow Hill,"** which has apparently been written in order to emphasize the outline of the Yorkshireman, I find myself chiefly interested in the incidental part, the sharp-shooting of Ortheris. It seems as though Mr. Kipling required, for the artistic balance of his cycle of stories, a third figure, and had evolved Learoyd while he observed and created Mulvaney and Ortheris, nor am I sure that places could not be pointed out where Learoyd, save for the dialect, melts undistinguishably into an incarnation of Mulvaney. The others are studied from the life, and by an observer who goes deep below the surface of conduct. How penetrating the study is, and how clear the diagnosis, may be seen in one or two stories which lie somewhat outside the popular group. It is no superficial idler among men who has taken down the strange notes on military hysteria which inspire **"The Madness of Ortheris"** and **"In the Matter of a Private,"** while the skill with which the battered giant Mulvaney, who has been a corporal and then has been reduced for misconduct, who to the ordinary view and in the eyes of all but the wisest of his officers is a dissipated blackguard, is made to display the rapidity, wit, resource, and high moral feeling which he really possesses, is extraordinary.

We have hitherto had in English literature no portraits of private soldiers like these, and yet the soldier is an object of interest and of very real, if vague and inefficient, admiration to his fellow-citizens. Mr. Thomas Hardy has painted a few excellent soldiers, but in a more romantic light and a far more pastoral setting. Other studies of this kind in fiction have either been slight and unsubstantial, or else they have been, as in the baby-writings of a certain novelist who has enjoyed popularity for a moment, odious in their sentimental unreality. There seems to be something essentially volatile about the soldier's memory. His life is so monotonous, so hedged in by routine, that he forgets the details of it as soon as the restraint is removed, or else he looks back upon it to see it bathed in a fictitious haze of sentiment. The absence of sentimentality in Mr. Kipling's version of the soldier's life in India is one of its great merits. What romance it assumes under his treatment is due to the curious contrasts it encourages. We see the ignorant and raw English youth transplanted, at the very moment when his instincts begin to develop, into a country where he is divided from everything which can remind him of his home, where by noon and night, in the bazar, in barracks, in the glowing scrub jungle, in the ferny defiles of the hills, everything he sees and hears and smells and feels produces on him an unfamiliar and an unwelcome impression. How he behaves himself under these new circumstances, what code of laws still binds his conscience, what are his relaxations and what his observations, these are the questions which we ask and which Mr. Kipling essays for the first time to answer.

Among the short stories which Mr. Kipling has dedicated to the British soldier in India there are a few which excel all the rest as works of art. I do not think that any one will deny that of this inner selection none exceeds in skill or originality **"The Taking of Lungtungpen."** Those who have not read this little masterpiece have yet before them the pleasure of becoming acquainted with one of the best short stories not merely in English but in any language. I do not know how to praise adequately the technical merit of this little narrative. It possesses to the full that masculine buoyancy, that power of sustaining an extremely spirited narrative in a tone appropriate to the action, which is one of Mr. Kipling's rare gifts. Its concentration, which never descends into obscurity, its absolute novelty, its direct and irresistible appeal to what is young and daring and absurdly splendid, are unsurpassed. To read it, at all events to admire and enjoy it, is to recover for a moment a little of that dare-devil quality that lurks somewhere in the softest and the baldest of us. Only a very young man could have written it, perhaps, but still more certainly only a young man of genius.

A little less interesting, in a totally different way, is **"The Daughter of the Regiment,"** with its extraordinarily vivid account of the breaking-out of cholera in a troop-train. Of **"The Madness of Ortheris"** I have already spoken; as a work of art this again seems to me somewhat less remarkable, because carried out with less completeness. But it would be hard to find a parallel, of its own class, to **"The Rout of the White Hussars,"** with its study of the effects of what is believed to be supernatural on a gathering of young fellows who are absolutely without fear of any phenomenon of which they comprehend the nature. In a very late story, **"The Courting of Dinah Shadd,"** Mr. Kipling has shown that he is able to deal with the humors and matrimonial amours of India barrack-life just as rapidly, fully, and spiritedly as with the more serious episodes of a soldier's career. The scene between Judy Sheehy and Dinah, as told by Mulvaney in that story, is pure comedy, without a touch of farce.

On the whole, however, the impression left by Mr. Kipling's military stories is one of melancholy. Tommy Atkins, whom the author knows so well and sympathizes with so truly, is a solitary being in India. In all these tales I am conscious of the barracks as of an island in a desolate ocean of sand. All around is the infinite waste of India, obscure, monotonous, immense, inhabited by black men and pariah dogs, Pathans and green parrots, kites and crocodiles, and long solitudes of high grass. The island in this sea is a little collection of young men, sent out from the remoteness of England to serve "the Widder," and to help to preserve for her the rich and barbarous empire of the East. This microcosm of the barracks has its own laws, its own morals, its own range of emotional sentiment. What these are the new writer has (not told us, for that would be a long story) but shown us that he himself has divined. He has held the door open for a moment, and has revealed to us a set of very human creations. One thing, at least, the biographer of Mulvaney and Ortheris has no difficulty in persuading us, namely, that "God in his wisdom has made the heart of the British soldier, who is very often an unlicked ruffian, as soft as the heart of a little child, in order that he may believe in and follow his officers into tight and nasty places."

The Anglo-Indians with whom Mr. Kipling deals are of two kinds. I must confess that there is no section of his work which appears to me so insignificant as that which deals with Indian "society." The eight tales which are bound together as *The Story of the Gadsbys* are doubtless very early productions. I have been told, but I know not whether on good authority, that they were published before the author was twenty-one. Judged as the observation of Anglo-Indian life by so young a boy, they are, it is needless to say, astonishingly clever. Some pages in them can never, I suppose, come to seem unworthy of his later fame. The conversation in **"The Tents of Kedar,"** where Captain Gadsby breaks to Mrs. Herriott that he is engaged to be married, and absolutely darkens her world to her during "a Naini Tal dinner for thirty-five," is of consummate adroitness. What a "Naini Tal dinner" is I have not the slightest conception, but it is evidently something very sumptuous and public, and if any practised hand of the old social school could have contrived the thrust and parry under the fire of seventy critical eyes better than young Mr. Kipling has done, I know not who that writer is. In quite another way the pathos of the little bride's delirium in **"The Valley of the Shadow"** is of a very high, almost of the highest, order.

But, as a rule, Mr. Kipling's "society" Anglo-Indians are not drawn better than those which other Indian novelists have created for our diversion. There is a sameness in the type of devouring female, and though Mr. Kipling devises several names for it, and would fain persuade us that Mrs. Herriott, and Mrs. Reiver, and Mrs. Hauksbee possess subtle differences which distinguish them, yet I confess I am not persuaded. They all—and the Venus Annodomini as well—appear to me to be the same high-colored, rather ill-bred, not wholly spoiled professional coquette. Mr. Kipling seems to be too impatient of what he calls "the shiny toy-scum stuff people call civilization" to paint these ladies very carefully. **"The Phantom 'Rickshaw,"** in which a hideously selfish man is made to tell the story of his own cruelty and of his mechanical remorse, is indeed highly original, but here it is the man, not the woman, in whom we are interested. The proposal of marriage in the dust-storm in **"False Dawn,"** a theatrical, lurid scene, though scarcely natural, is highly effective. The archery contest in **"Cupid's Arrows"** needs only to be compared with a similar scene in *Daniel Deronda* to show how much more closely Mr. Kipling keeps his eye on detail than George Eliot did. But these things are rare in this class of his stories, and too often the Anglo-Indian social episodes are choppy, unconvincing, and not very refined.

All is changed when the central figure is a man. Mr. Kipling's officials and civilians are admirably vivid and of an amazing variety. If any one wishes to know why this new author has been received with joy and thankfulness by the Anglo-Saxon world, it is really not necessary for him to go further for a reason than to the moral tale of **"The Conversion of Aurelian McGoggin."** (pp. 903-05)

Now Mr. Kipling, in his warm way, hates many things, but he hates the prig for preference. Aurelian McGoggin, better known as the Blastoderm, is a prig of the over-educated type, and upon him falls the awful calamity of sudden and complete nerve-collapse. Lieutenant Golightly, in the story which bears his name, is a prig who values himself for spotless attire and clockwork precision of manner; he therefore is mauled and muddied up to his eyes, and then arrested under painfully derogatory conditions. In **"Lispeth"** we get the missionary prig, who thinks that the Indian instincts can be effaced by a veneer of Christianity. Mr. Kipling hates "the sheltered life." The men he likes are those who have been thrown out of their depth at an early age, and taught to swim off a boat. The very remarkable story of **"Thrown Away"** shows the effect of preparing for India by a life "unspotted from the

world" in England; it is as hopelessly tragic as any in Mr. Kipling's somewhat grim repertory.

Against the régime of the prig Mr. Kipling sets the régime of Strickland. Over and over again he introduces this mysterious figure, always with a phrase of extreme approval. Strickland is in the police, and his power consists in his determination to know the East as the natives know it. He can pass through the whole of Upper India, dressed up as a fakir, without attracting the least attention. Sometimes, as in **"Beyond the Pale,"** he may know too much. But this is an exception, and personal to himself. Mr. Kipling's conviction is that this is the sort of man to pervade India for us, and that one Strickland is worth a thousand self-conceited civilians. But even below the Indian prig, because he has at least known India, is the final object of Mr. Kipling's loathing, "Pagett, M. P.," the radical English politician who comes out for four months to set everybody right. His chastisement is always severe and often comic. But in one very valuable paper, which Mr. Kipling must not be permitted to leave unreprinted, **"The Enlightenments of Pagett, M. P.,"** he has dealt elaborately and quite seriously with this noxious creature. Whether Mr. Kipling is right or wrong, far be it from me in my ignorance to pretend to know. But his way of putting these things is persuasive.

Since Mr. Kipling has come back from India he has written about society "of sorts" in England. Is there not perhaps in him something of Pagett, M. P., turned inside out? As a delineator of English life, at all events, he is not yet thoroughly master of his craft. Everything he writes has vigor and picturesqueness. But **"The Lamentable Comedy of Willow Wood"** is the sort of thing that any extremely brilliant Burman, whose English, if slightly odd, was nevertheless unimpeachable, might write of English ladies and gentlemen, having never been in England. **"The Record of Badalia Herodsfoot"** was in every way better, more truly observed, more credible, more artistic, but yet a little too cynical and brutal to come straight from life. (pp. 905-06)

The conception of Strickland would be very tantalizing and incomplete if we were not permitted to profit from his wisdom and experience. But, happily, Mr. Kipling is perfectly willing to take us below the surface, and to show us glimpses of the secret life of India. In so doing he puts forth his powers to their fullest extent, and I think it cannot be doubted that the tales which deal with native manners are not merely the most curious and interesting which Mr. Kipling has written, but are also the most fortunately constructed. Every one who has thought over this writer's mode of execution will have been struck with the skill with which his best work is restrained within certain limits. When inspiration flags with him, indeed, his stories may grow too long, or fail, as if from languor, before they reach their culmination. But his best short stories—and among his best we include the majority of his native Indian tales—are cast at once, as if in a mold; nothing can be detached from them without injury. In this consists his great technical advantage over almost all his English rivals; we must look to France or to America for stories fashioned in this way. In several of his tales of Indian manners this skill reaches its highest because most complicated expression. It may be comparatively easy to hold within artistic bonds a gentle episode of European amorosity. To deal, in the same form, but with infinitely greater audacity, with the muffled passions and mysterious instincts of India, to slur over nothing, to emphasize nothing, to give in some twenty pages the very spicy odor of the East, this is marvelous.

Not less than this Mr. Kipling has done in a little group of stories which I cannot but hold to be the culminating point of his genius so far. If the remainder of his writings were swept away, posterity would be able to reconstruct its Rudyard Kipling from **"Without Benefit of Clergy," "The Man who Would be King," "The Strange Ride of Morrowbie Jukes,"** and **"Beyond the Pale."** More than that, if all record of Indian habits had been destroyed, much might be conjectured from them of the pathos, the splendor, the cruelty, and the mystery of India. From **"The Gate of the Hundred Sorrows"** more is to be gleaned of the real action of opium-smoking, and the causes of that indulgence, than from many sapient debates in the British House of Commons. We come very close to the confines of the moonlight-colored world of magic in **"The Bisara of Pooree."** For pure horror and for the hopeless impenetrability of the native conscience there is **"The Recrudescence of Imray."** In a revel of color and shadow, at the close of the audacious and Lucianic story of **"The Incarnation of Krishna Mulvaney,"** we peep for a moment into the mystery of "a big queen's praying at Benares."

Admirable, too, are the stories which deal with the results of attempts made to melt the Asiatic and the European into one. The red-headed Irish-Thibetan who makes the king's life a burden to him in the fantastic story of **"Namgay Doola"** represents one extremity of this chain of grotesque Eurasians; Michele D'Cruze, the wretched little black police inspector, with a drop of white blood in his body, who wakes up to energetic action at one supreme moment of his life, is at the other. The relapse of the converted Indian is a favorite theme with this cynical observer of human nature. It is depicted in **"The Judgment of Dungara,"** with a rattling humor worthy of Lever, where the whole mission, clad in white garments woven of the scorpion nettle, go mad with fire and plunge into the river, while the trumpet of the god bellows triumphantly from the hills. In **"Lispeth"** we have a study—much less skilfully worked out, however—of the Indian woman carefully Christianized from childhood reverting at once to heathenism when her passions reach maturity.

The lover of good literature, however, is likely to come back to the four stories which we named first in this section. They are the very flower of Mr. Kipling's work up to the present moment, and on these we base our highest expectations for his future. **"Without Benefit of Clergy"** is a study of the Indian woman as wife and mother, uncovenanted wife of the English civilian and mother of his son. The tremulous passion of Ameera, her hopes, her fears, and her agonies of disappointment, combine to form by far the most tender page which Mr. Kipling has written. (pp. 906-07)

What tragedy was in store for the gentle astrologer, or in what darkness of waters the story ends, it is needless to repeat here.

In **"The Strange Ride of Morrowbie Jukes"** a civil engineer stumbles by chance on a ghastly city of the dead who do not die, trapped into it, down walls of shifting sand, on the same principle as the ant-lion secures its prey, the parallel being so close that one half suspects Mr. Kipling of having invented a human analogy to the myrmeleon. The abominable settlement of living dead men is so vividly described, and the wonders of it are so calmly, and, as it were, so temperately discussed, that no one who possesses the happy gift of believing

can fail to be persuaded of the truth of the tale. The character of Gunga Dass, a Deccanee Brahmin whom Jukes finds in this reeking village, and who, reduced to the bare elements of life, preserves a little, though exceedingly little, of his old traditional obsequiousness, is an admirable study. But all such considerations are lost, as we read the story first, in the overwhelming and Poe-like horror of the situation and the extreme novelty of the conception.

A still higher place, however, I am inclined to claim for the daring invention of **"The Man who Would be King."** This is a longer story than is usual with Mr. Kipling, and it depends for its effect, not upon any epigrammatic surprise or extravagant dénouement of the intrigue, but on an imaginative effort brilliantly sustained through a detailed succession of events. Two ignorant and disreputable Englishmen, exiles from social life, determine to have done with the sordid struggle, and to close with a try for nothing less than empire. They are seen by the journalist who narrates the story to disappear northward from the Kumharsan Serai disguised as a mad priest and his servant starting to sell whirligigs to the Ameer of Kabul. Two years later there stumbles into the newspaper office a human creature bent into a circle, and moving his feet one over the other like a bear. This is the surviving adventurer, who, half dead and half dazed, is roused by doses of raw whisky into a condition which permits him to unravel the squalid and splendid chronicle of adventures beyond the utmost rim of mountains, adventures on the veritable throne of Kafiristan. The tale is recounted with great skill as from the lips of the dying king. At first, to give the needful impression of his faint, bewildered state, he mixes up his narrative, whimpers, forgets, and repeats his phrases; but by the time the curiosity of the reader is fully arrested, the tale has become limpid and straightforward enough. When it has to be drawn to a close, the symptoms of aphasia and brain-lesion are repeated. This story is conceived and conducted in the finest spirit of an artist. It is strange to the verge of being incredible, but it never outrages possibility, and the severe moderation of the author preserves our credence throughout.

It is in these Indian stories that Mr. Kipling displays more than anywhere else the accuracy of his eye and the retentiveness of his memory. No detail escapes him, and, without seeming to emphasize the fact, he is always giving an exact feature where those who are in possession of fewer facts or who see less vividly are satisfied with a shrewd generality. (pp. 907-08)

Edmund Gosse, "Rudyard Kipling," in The Century, *Vol. XLII, No. 6, October, 1891, pp. 901-10.*

HENRY JAMES   (essay date 1891)

[James was an American-born English novelist, short story writer, and essayist of the late nineteenth and early twentieth centuries. He is regarded as one of the greatest novelists of the English language, valued for his psychological acuity and complex artistry. He is admired also as an insightful literary critic whose criticism reveals a thorough understanding of European culture, particularly English and French literature of the late nineteenth century. In the following excerpt from his introduction to an 1891 edition of Soldiers Three, *James extols Kipling's short stories.]*

[Kipling's] bloom lasts, from month to month, almost surprisingly—by which I mean that he has not worn out even by active exercise the particular property that made us all, more than a year ago, so precipitately drop everything else to attend to him. He has many others which he will doubtless always keep; but a part of the potency attaching to his freshness, what makes it as exciting as a drawing of lots, is our instinctive conviction that he cannot, in the nature of things, keep that; so that our enjoyment of him, so long as the miracle is still wrought, has both the charm of confidence and the charm of suspense. And then there is the further charm, with Mr. Kipling, that this same freshness is such a very strange affair of its kind—so mixed and various and cynical, and, in certain lights, so contradictory of itself. The extreme recentness of his inspiration is as enviable as the tale is startling that his productions tell of his being at home, domesticated and initiated, in this wicked and weary world. At times he strikes us as shockingly precocious, at others as serenely wise. On the whole, he presents himself as a strangely clever youth who has stolen the formidable mask of maturity and rushes about, making people jump with the deep sounds, and sportive exaggerations of tone, that issue from its painted lips. He has this mark of a real vocation, that different spectators may like him—must like him, I should almost say—for different things; and this refinement of attraction, that to those who reflect even upon their pleasures he has as much to say as to those who never reflect upon anything. Indeed there is a certain amount of room for surprise in the fact that, being so much the sort of figure that the hardened critic likes to meet, he should also be the sort of figure that inspires the multitude with confidence—for a complicated air is, in general, the last thing that does this. (pp. 226-27)

Mr. Kipling, then, has the character that furnishes plenty of play and of vicarious experience—that makes any perceptive reader foresee a rare luxury. He has the great merit of being a compact and convenient illustration of the surest source of interest in any painter of life—that of having an identity as marked as a window-frame. He is one of the illustrations, taken near at hand, that help to clear up the vexed question in the novel or the tale, of kinds, camps, schools, distinctions, the right way and the wrong way; so very positively does he contribute to the showing that there are just as many kinds, as many ways, as many forms and degrees of the "right," as there are personal points in view. It is the blessing of the art he practises that it is made up of experience conditioned, infinitely, in this personal way—the sum of the feeling of life as reproduced by innumerable natures; natures that feel through all their differences, testify through their diversities. These differences, which make the identity, are of the individual; they form the channel by which life flows through him, and how much he is able to give us of life—in other words, how much he appeals to us—depends on whether they form it solidly. (pp. 228-29)

It is a part of the satisfaction the author gives us that he can make us speculate as to whether he will be able to complete his picture altogether (this is as far as we presume to go in meddling with the question of his future) without bringing in the complicated soul. On the day he does so, if he handles it with anything like the cleverness he has already shown, the expectation of his friends will take a great bound. Meanwhile, at any rate, we have Mulvaney, and Mulvaney is after all tolerably complicated. He is only a six-foot saturated Irish private, but he is a considerable pledge of more to come. Hasn't he, for that matter, the tongue of a hoarse siren, and hasn't he also mysteries and infinitudes almost Carlylese? Since I am speaking of him I may as well say that, as an evocation, he has probably led captive those of Mr. Kipling's readers who

have most given up resistance. He is a piece of portraiture of the largest, vividest kind, growing and growing on the painter's hands without ever outgrowing them. I can't help regarding him, in a certain sense, as Mr. Kipling's tutelary deity—a landmark in the direction in which it is open to him to look furthest. If the author will only go as far in this direction as Mulvaney is capable of taking him (and the inimitable Irishman is like Voltaire's Habakkuk, *capable de tout*) he may still discover a treasure and find a reward for the services he has rendered the winner of Dinah Shadd. I hasten to add that the truly appreciative reader should surely have no quarrel with the primitive element in Mr. Kipling's subject-matter, or with what, for want of a better name, I may call his love of low life. What is that but essentially a part of his freshness? And for what part of his freshness are we exactly more thankful than for just this smart jostle that he gives the old stupid superstition that the amiability of a story-teller is the amiability of the people he represents—that their vulgarity, or depravity, or gentility, or fatuity are tantamount to the same qualities in the painter itself? A blow from which, apparently, it will not easily recover is dealt this infantine philosophy by Mr. Howells when, with the most distinguished dexterity and all the detachment of a master, he handles some of the clumsiest, crudest, most human things in life—answering surely thereby the playgoers in the sixpenny gallery who howl at the representative of the villain when he comes before the curtain.

Nothing is more refreshing than this active, disinterested sense of the real; it is doubtless the quality for the want of more of which our English and American fiction has turned so wofully stale. We are ridden by the old conventionalities of type and small proprieties of observance—by the foolish baby-formula (to put it sketchily) of the picture and the subject. Mr. Kipling has all the air of being disposed to lift the whole business off the nursery carpet, and of being perhaps even more able than he is disposed. . . . We are thankful for any boldness and any sharp curiosity, and that is why we are thankful for Mr. Kipling's general spirit and for most of his excursions.

Many of these, certainly, are into a region not to be designated as superficially dim, though indeed the author always reminds us that India is above all the land of mystery. A large part of his high spirits, and of ours, comes doubtless from the amusement of such vivid, heterogeneous material, from the irresistible magic of scorching suns, subject empires, uncanny religions, uneasy garrisons and smothered-up women—from heat and colour and danger and dust. India is a portentous image, and we are duly awed by the familiarities it undergoes at Mr. Kipling's hand and by the fine impunity, the sort of fortune that favours the brave, of *his* want of awe. An abject humility is not his strong point, but he gives us something instead of it—vividness and drollery, the vision and the thrill of many things, the misery and strangeness of most, the personal sense of a hundred queer contacts and risks. And then in the absence of respect he has plenty of knowledge, and if knowledge should fail him he would have plenty of invention. Moreover, if invention should ever fail him, he would still have the lyric string and the patriotic chord, on which he plays admirably; so that it may be said he is a man of resources. What he gives us, above all, is the feeling of the English manner and the English blood in conditions they have made at once so much and so little their own; with manifestations grotesque enough in some of his satiric sketches and deeply impressive in some of his anecdotes of individual responsibility.

His Indian impressions divide themselves into three groups, one of which, I think, very much outshines the others. First to be mentioned are the tales of native life, curious glimpses of custom and superstition, dusky matters not beholden of the many, for which the author has a remarkable *flair*. Then comes the social, the Anglo-Indian episode, the study of administrative and military types, and of the wonderful rattling, riding ladies who, at Simla and more desperate stations, look out for husbands and lovers; often, it would seem, and husbands and lovers of others. The most brilliant group is devoted wholly to the common soldier, and of this series it appears to me that too much good is hardly to be said. Here Mr. Kipling, with all his off-handedness, is a master; for we are held not so much by the greater or less oddity of the particular yarn—sometimes it is scarcely a yarn at all, but something much less artificial—as by the robust attitude of the narrator, who never arranges or glosses or falsifies, but makes straight for the common and the characteristic. I have mentioned the great esteem in which I hold Mulvaney—surely a charming man and one qualified to adorn a higher sphere. Mulvaney is a creation to be proud of, and his two comrades stand as firm on their legs. In spite of Mulvaney's social possibilities, they are all three finished brutes; but it is precisely in the finish that we delight. Whatever Mr. Kipling may relate about them forever will encounter readers equally fascinated and unable fully to justify their faith.

Are not those literary pleasures after all the most intense which are the most perverse and whimsical, and even indefensible? There is a logic in them somewhere, but it often lies below the plummet of criticism. The spell may be weak in a writer who has every reasonable and regular claim, and it may be irresistible in one who presents himself with a style corresponding to a bad hat. A good hat is better than a bad one, but a conjuror may wear either. Many a reader will never be able to say what secret human force lays its hand upon him when Private Ortheris, having sworn "quietly into the blue sky," goes mad with homesickness by the yellow river and raves for the basest sights and sounds of London. I can scarcely tell why I think **"The Courting of Dinah Shadd"** a masterpiece (though, indeed, I can make a shrewd guess at one of the reasons), nor would it be worth while perhaps to attempt to defend the same pretension in regard to **"On Greenhow Hill"**—much less to trouble the tolerant reader of these remarks with a statement of how many more performances in the nature of **"The End of the Passage"** (quite admitting even that they might not represent Mr. Kipling at his best) I am conscious of a latent relish for. One might as well admit while one is about it that one has wept profusely over **"The Drums of the Fore and Aft,"** the history of the **"Dutch Courage"** of two dreadful dirty little boys, who, in the face of Afghans scarcely more dreadful, saved the reputation of their regiment and perished, the least mawkishly in the world, in a squalor of battle incomparably expressed. People who know how peaceful they are themselves and have no bloodshed to reproach themselves with needn't scruple to mention the glamour that Mr. Kipling's intense militarism has for them, and how astonishing and contagious they find it, in spite of the unromantic complexion of it—the way it bristles with all sorts of ugliness and technicalities. Perhaps that is why I go all the way even with *The Gadsbys*—the Gadsbys were so connected (uncomfortably, it is true) with the army. There is fearful fighting—or a fearful danger of it—in **"The Man Who Would be King"**; is that the reason we are deeply affected by this extraordinary tale? It is one of

them, doubtless, for Mr. Kipling has many reasons, after all, on his side, though they don't equally call aloud to be uttered.

One more of them, at any rate, I must add to these unsystematised remarks—it is the one I spoke of a shrewd guess at in alluding to **"The Courting of Dinah Shadd."** The talent that produces such a tale is a talent eminently in harmony with the short story, and the short story is, on our side of the Channel and of the Atlantic, a mine which will take a great deal of working. Admirable is the clearness with which Mr. Kipling perceives this—perceives what innumerable chances it gives, chances of touching life in a thousand different places, taking it up in innumerable pieces, each a specimen and an illustration. In a word, he appreciates the episode, and there are signs to show that this shrewdness will, in general, have long innings. It will find the detachable, compressible "case" an admirable, flexible form; the cultivation of which may well add to the mistrust already entertained by Mr. Kipling, if his manner does not betray him, for what is clumsy and tasteless in the time-honoured practice of the "plot." It will fortify him in the conviction that the vivid picture has a greater communicative value than the Chinese puzzle. There is little enough "plot" in such a perfect little piece of hard representation as **"The End of the Passage,"** to cite again only the most salient of twenty examples.

But I am speaking of our author's future, which is the luxury that I meant to forbid myself—precisely because the subject is so tempting. There is nothing in the world (for the prophet) so charming as to prophesy, and as there is nothing so inconclusive the tendency should be repressed in proportion as the opportunity is good. There is a certain want of courtesy to a peculiarly contemporaneous present even in speculating, with a dozen differential precautions, on the question of what will become in the later hours of the day of a talent that has got up so early. Mr. Kipling's actual performance is like a tremendous walk before breakfast, making one welcome the idea of the meal, but consider with some alarm the hours still to be traversed. Yet if his breakfast is all to come, the indications are that he will be more active than ever after he has had it. Among these indications are the unflagging character of his pace and the excellent form, as they say in athletic circles, in which he gets over the ground. We don't detect him stumbling; on the contrary, he steps out quite as briskly as at first, and still more firmly. There is something zealous and craftsman-like in him which shows that he feels both joy and responsibility. A whimsical, wanton reader, haunted by a recollection of all the good things he has seen spoiled; by a sense of the miserable, or, at any rate, the inferior, in so many continuations and endings, is almost capable of perverting poetic justice to the idea that it would be even positively well for so surprising a producer to remain simply the fortunate, suggestive, unconfirmed and unqualified representative of what he has actually done. We can always refer to that. (pp. 232-41)

Henry James, "Mr. Kipling's Early Stories," in his Views and Reviews, *1908. Reprint by Books for Libraries Press, 1968, pp. 225-41.*

ANDREW LANG (essay date 1891)

[*One of England's most influential men of letters during the closing decades of the nineteenth century, Lang was a translator, poet, folklorist, and revisionist historian. Among the chief proponents of Romanticism, he espoused a strong romantic vision throughout his literary criticism, finding little to commend from among the works of Realists or Naturalists. In the following excerpt, which was originally published in* Essays in Little *in 1891, Lang briefly considers Kipling's character portrayals in short stories from* Plain Tales from the Hills, Soldiers Three, *and* Wee Willie Winkie.]

Mr. Kipling's work, like all good work, is both real and romantic. It is real because he sees and feels very swiftly and keenly; it is romantic, again, because he has a sharp eye for the reality of romance, for the attraction and possibility of adventure, and because he is young. If a reader wants to see petty characters displayed in all their meannesses, if this be realism, surely certain of Mr. Kipling's painted and frisky matrons are realistic enough. The seamy side of Anglo-Indian life: the intrigues, amorous or semi-political—the slang of the people who describe dining as "mangling garbage"—the "games of tennis with the seventh commandment"—he has not neglected any of these. Probably the sketches are true enough, and pity 'tis 'tis true; for example, the sketches in **Under the Deodars** and in **The Gadsbys.** That worthy pair, with their friends, are to myself as unsympathetic, almost, as the characters in "La Conquête de Plassans." But Mr. Kipling is too much a true realist to make their selfishness and pettiness unbroken, unceasing. We know that "Gaddy" is a brave, modest, and hard-working soldier; and, when his little silly bride (who prefers being kissed by a man with waxed moustaches) lies near to death, certainly I am nearer to tears than when I am obliged to attend the bed of Little Dombey or of Little Nell. Probably there is a great deal of slangy and unrefined Anglo-Indian society; and, no doubt, to sketch it in its true colours is not beyond the province of art. At worst it is redeemed, in part, by its constancy in the presence of various perils—from disease, and from "the bullet flying down the pass." Mr. Kipling may not be, and very probably is not, a reader of "Gyp"; but **The Gadsbys,** especially, reads like the work of an Anglo-Indian disciple, trammelled by certain English conventions. The more Pharisaic realists—those of the strictest sect—would probably welcome Mr. Kipling as a younger brother, so far as **Under the Deodars** and **The Gadsbys** are concerned, if he were not occasionally witty and even flippant, as well as realistic. But, very fortunately, he has not confined his observation to the leisures and pleasures of Simla; he has looked out also on war and on sport, on the life of all native tribes and castes; and has even glanced across the borders of "The Undiscovered Country."

Among Mr. Kipling's discoveries of new kinds of characters, probably the most popular is his invention of the British soldier in India. He avers that he "loves that very strong man, Thomas Atkins"; but his affection has not blinded him to the faults of the beloved. Mr. Atkins drinks too much, is too careless a gallant in love, has been educated either too much or too little, and has other faults, partly due, apparently, to recent military organisation, partly to the feverish and unsettled state of the civilised world. But he is still brave, when he is well led; still loyal, above all, to his "trusty chum." Every Englishman must hope that, if Terence Mulvaney did not take the city of Lungtung Pen as described, yet he is all ready and willing so to take it. Mr. Mulvaney is as humorous as Micky Free, but more melancholy and more truculent. He has, perhaps, "won his way to the mythical" already, and is not so much a soldier, as an incarnation, not of Krishna, but of many soldierly qualities. On the other hand, Private Ortheris, especially in his frenzy, seems to shew all the truth, and much more than the life of, a photograph. Such, we presume, is the soldier, and such are his experiences and temptations and repentance. But nobody ever dreamed of telling us all this, till Mr. Kipling came. As for the soldier in action, the **"Taking of Lungtung Pen,"** and the **"Drums of the Fore and Aft,"** and that other tale of the battle with the Pathans in the gorge, are among the good fights of fiction. They stir the spirit, and they should be distributed (in addition, of course, to the "Soldier's Pocket Book") in the ranks of the British army. Mr. Kipling is as well informed about the soldier's women-kind as about the soldier: about Dinah Shadd as about Terence Mulvaney. Leaver never instructed us on these matters: Micky Free, if he loves, rides away; but Terence Mulvaney is true to his old woman. Gallant, loyal, reckless, vain, swaggering, and tender-hearted, Terence Mulvaney, if there were enough of him, "would take St. Petersburg in his drawers." Can we be too grateful to an author who has extended, as Mr. Kipling in his military sketches has extended, the frontiers of our knowledge and sympathy?

It is a mere question of individual taste; but, for my own part, had I to make a small selection from Mr. Kipling's tales, I would include more of his studies in Black than in White, and many of his excursions beyond the probable and natural. It is difficult to have one special favourite in this kind; but perhaps the story of the two English adventurers among the freemasons of unknown Kafiristan (in the **"Phantom Rickshaw"**) would take a very high place. The gas-heated air of the Indian newspaper office is so real, and into it comes a wanderer who has seen new faces of death, and who carries with him a head that has worn a royal crown. The contrasts are of brutal force; the legend is among the best of such strange fancies. Then there is, in the same volume, **"The Strange Ride of Morrowbie Jukes,"** the most dreadful nightmare of the most awful Bunker in the realms of fancy. This is a very early work; if nothing else of Mr. Kipling's existed, his memory might live by it, as does the memory of the American Irishman by the "Diamond Lens." The sham magic of **"In the House of Suddhu"** is as terrible as true necromancy could be, and I have a *faiblesse* for the **"Bisara of Pooree."** **"The Gate of the Hundred Sorrows"** is a realistic version of "The English Opium Eater," and more powerful by dint of less rhetoric. As for the sketches of native life—for example, **"On the City Wall"**—to English readers they are no less than revelations. They testify, more even than the military stories, to the author's swift and certain vision, his certainty in his effects. In brief, Mr. Kipling has conquered worlds, of which, as it were, we knew not the existence.

His faults are so conspicuous, so much on the surface, that they hardly need to be named. They are curiously visible to some readers who are blind to his merits. There is a false air of hardness (quite in contradiction to the sentiment in his tales of childish life); there is a knowing air; there are mannerisms, such as "But that is another story"; there is a display of slang; there is the too obtrusive knocking of the nail on the head. Everybody can mark these errors; a few cannot overcome their antipathy, and so lose a great deal of pleasure. (pp. 3-6)

Andrew Lang, "Mr. Kipling's Stories," in Kipling and the Critics, *edited by Elliot L. Gilbert, New York University Press, 1965, pp. 1-6.*

HARRY THURSTON PECK (essay date 1904)

[*Peck was an American historian, literary critic, and editor who is recognized for his contributions to American cultural history. In articles regularly published in such journals as the* Bookman *and* Munsey's Magazine, *he discussed at length themes of the Naturalist and Realist movements in American literature. In the following excerpt, Peck reviews* Traffics and Discoveries.]

Rudyard Kipling's books are unlike those of most authors in this respect, that each one of them reveals in some measure the whole range of his extraordinary powers and also his casual defects. Take almost any volume which bears his name upon the title-page and you will find in it alike the vigour and the delicacy, the tenderness and the cynicism, the coarseness and the fineness, the artistic sense and the love of the bizarre—all of which from the very beginning of his brilliant career have entranced the public and made the stall-fed critics gasp. He gives you his best and his worst with equal readiness and with the same indifference to what you think of it and him. And each book illustrates his coincidental fondness for the materialistic and the mystical. Thus in *Many Inventions* there is the first glimpse of the strange, glimmery secrets of the green *rukh,* side by side with his Zolaesque portrayal of a reeking London slum, when the old hag robs the dying prostitute, her daughter, and when Badalia Herodsfoot is "bashed" in the face by her drink-crazed man, until he hears her blood and hair squelch under his boot-heel. And together with these two quite antithetical yet equally marvellous stories and the unforgetable **"Love o' Women"** there is the almost fatuous tale of **"Brugglesmith,"** whose stodgy British humour is so very stodgy and so very British as to seem like a rancous echo of Ally Sloper. And so in *The Day's Work* there is the strange superstition of **"The Tomb of His Ancestors"** and the dreamy fancy of **"The Brushwood Boy"** set beside the mechanical dreariness of **".007."** It is all Kipling, a creature of infinite variety and violent contrasts.

In *Traffics and Discoveries* the eleven stories have the same representative character, and would suffice to show the range of Kipling's genius even though nothing here can be confidently classified with the best of his past work. Several of the tales relate to the Boer War—one of these being told by a Sikh trooper and one by a Kiplingized American, Mr. Laughton O. Zigler, of Akron, O., who is described pleasantly as "a ginger-coloured man with the hunger of a press-ridden people in his close-set iron-grey eyes." Certain other stories are of the British Navy, and one is specifically an automobilist's yarn. Three of them—**"Wireless," "They,"** and **"Mrs. Bathurst"**—touch the borderland of the occult, and of the last two we shall presently have something to say.

Taken as a whole, these eleven stories show Mr. Kipling's deftness of technique; but (with one exception) they likewise show a loss of freshness, a diminished vitality, a slightly impoverished invention. The talk, of which there is much, is not good talk. It lacks pregnancy and picturesqueness. It is just talk, when it is not actually gabble. Furthermore, it does not make the story move. It serves only to mark time and fill space. Now and then a vulgar phrase, a gross brutality of speech, is introduced, by way of giving a fillip to the reader's attention. But somehow or other these things do not seem to come in naturally. One feels that the author saved them up and inserted them at the proper moment to produce a definite effect; and the result is by no means happy. One is conscious of a certain embarrassment and of being a little sorry for Mr. Kipling. Indeed, you keep thinking all the time about the author and seldom lose yourself in his narrative,—a fact which sufficiently reveals the presence of conscious effort. In many of the stories there appears a Mr. Pyecroft, to whose sayings

and doings a large amount of space is given. Pyecroft is a naval machinist, and it is evident that Mr. Kipling intended to make him a permanent addition to the world's fictitious heroes,—a companion to the three immortals, Mulvaney, Ortheris, and Learoyd. But no one will ever accept Pyecroft. His talk has neither the raciness and Irish wit of Mulvaney, nor the quaint Cockney humour of Ortheris, nor the magnificent stolidity of Learoyd. Pyecroft is not a success. Pyecroft, in fact, is a good deal of a bore. He neither interests nor amuses. We hope never again to encounter Mr. Pyecroft.

Two stories—**"They"** and **"Mrs. Bathurst"**—deserve especial notice. In manner and substance they are mutually antipodal. Yet they have this much in common that they have puzzled multitudes of readers and evoked a great amount of controversy and discussion. Their appearance in two popular magazines is so recent an event that it seems unnecessary to relate them and we shall assume an acquaintance with their text on the part of everyone who reads this review. What we intend is simply to consider their alleged obscurity and the puzzle of their meanings; for they have undoubtedly proved too much for many of their expositors in the press. **"They"** is in many respects one of the loveliest and most exquisite of Kipling's imaginative creations. Technically it is absolutely flawless. Nothing more delicately fanciful, more wonderfully elusive, could be conceived; and we have here a triumph of literary art in the projection of an atmosphere of old-world mysticism in close contact with the realities of intensely modern life. Indeed, this contrast only heightens the effect; and when the motor-car puffs across the sun-bathed lawn before the house where "they" have made their home, no incongruity is felt; but rather do the natural and the supernatural blend into one harmonious and unchallenged verity. Yet the way of illusion is artfully prepared for us. The beautiful old manor-house is isolated from the world of every day. It is approached through "the confusing veil of the woods"—green cuttings full of liquid sunshine, dark glades where the dead leaves of other years whispered under the tires, until at last the narrator emerges through a tangle of shimmering leaves.

> As the light beat across my face my forewheels took the turf of a great still lawn from which sprang horsemen ten feet high with levelled lances, monstrous peacocks, and sleek round-headed maids of honour—blue, black, and glistening—all of clipped yew. Across the lawn—the marshalled woods besieged it on three sides—stood an ancient house of lichened and weather-worn stone, with mullioned windows and roofs of rose-red tile. It was flanked by semi-circular walls, also rose-red, that closed the lawn on the fourth side, and at their feet a box hedge grew man-high. There were doves on the roof about the slim brick chimneys, and I caught a glimpse of an octagonal dove-house behind the screening wall. . . . The doves on the roof cooed to the cooing water.

Could anything be more subtly perfect than this beautiful transition from the realm of prosaic fact to that of poetical fantasy? And the pity of it is that all readers can not just steep themselves in the mood which writing such as this induces, receiving as much or as little of the revelation as their own natures are attuned to understand, and letting the rest of it go unquestioned. Yet since so many have chosen to dissect a dream and analyse a vision, it is perhaps permissible to say that even this rude process has not given them a knowledge of the secret. **"They"** has this meaning: that infinite desire can at last create its own sufficient satisfaction. "Miss Florence," the blind woman, was born with the maternal instinct as her master passion. She has never wedded and never been a mother; but the intensity of her yearning has at last called about her the spirits of happy children, whose whisperings and merry laughter comfort and soothe her with a sense of their perpetual presence. One may have lost children by never having borne them as well as through the agency of death; and to exceptional natures the sense of loss—profound, unspeakable—may summon back the gentle spirits that have vanished from the sight of those whose mourning is but for a time. The compelling power of the blind woman in Kipling's story is shown by the fact that even in her blindness she can see the Egg, the Brahminical symbol of generation and creativeness. For here Kipling reverts, as is most natural in him, to the lore of India, whose Sacred Books thus tell the story of creation. In the beginning all was void and darkness; but the Divine Being created water and into the water he cast a seed, and the seed became an Egg. Then was the Egg divided, the upper half becoming the heavens and the lower half the earth, and between them were fashioned those things which now fill the heavens and the earth. This Egg—*das Welt-Ei*—is, therefore, the sign of reproduction; and to those in whom child-love is supreme it is given to behold the symbol. But most readers of "**They**" have overlooked or else misunderstood one phase of the story. Although it is told in the first person, we need not suppose that the narrator is Mr. Kipling himself, or that, when the visitor's hand is brushed by unseen lips, the lips are those of his own lost child. There is nothing in the story to justify this thought and there is something toward the end which makes it seem impossible. For the man says that for him to come again to the home of childish souls would be wrong.

"For me it would be wrong. For me only. . ."

Because only those who had lost and mourned could come there.

"**Mrs. Bathurst**" is for the most part just an ordinary story, full of the maunderings of Pyecroft and the vulgar speech of British marines, their talk indeed being so long drawn out and utterly inept as to discourage many readers from finishing the tale. Yet few stories have been more talked over, because when you have read the last word you are left in a state of bewilderment as to what on earth it is all about. One critic, who confesses that he can make neither head nor tail of it, compares the later Kipling with the later James, and makes them literary partners in obscurity. But the mystery or nebulosity of a typical James story is wholly different from the opacity of "**Mrs. Bathurst.**" In James you plunge into a fog. In "**Mrs. Bathurst**" you run up against a blank wall. In James there are many ways out, only you don't quite know which one to take. In "**Mrs. Bathurst**" you can't get out at all, for you are led into a *cul de sac,* a veritable *impasse.* And on the whole you resent it, for the mystery has to do with something that can not possibly be worth while. However, having read the story half a dozen times we offer the following solution for the benefit of the exasperated. Vickery, the warrant officer, had a wife in England, when in the course of his voyage he met Mrs. Bathurst in Auckland. He fell in love with her and his love developed into an infatuation; but he was not free to marry her and she did not let him know that she, in turn, loved him unreservedly. So he went away, eating his heart out and becoming morbid through perpetual brooding. Later, when in Cape Town, he visits a cheap show where there is a cinematograph. In one of its pictures he sees the arrival of

a train at the Paddington Station in London, and among the figures emerging from the train, he recognizes the face and form of Mrs. Bathurst. Evidently then she had loved him all the time. More than that, she had even returned to England—for him. And it is only now that he learns it, as he has also learned that his own wife has died and that he is free. His brain, already unbalanced, is completely crazed, and he goes to the captain of his ship who recognizes that the man is for the time insane, and sends him on an expedition up the country so that he may pull himself together. But he is killed by lightning and does not return, so that he is officially recorded as a deserter.

This is the key to the story of Mrs. Bathurst. As we said, it is not worth while, even when explained. Yet nothing could so much prove the hold which Mr. Kipling has upon his readers as the fact that this halting, half finished, discrepant bit of writing has led thousands of persons to waste hours in speculating upon its possible implications and that the magazine in which it originally appeared became practically unattainable within ten days after its publication. (pp. 155-57)

Harry Thurston Peck, "Mr. Kipling's 'Traffics and Discoveries'," in The Bookman, *New York, Vol. XX, October, 1904, pp. 155-57.*

JOHN PALMER   (essay date 1915)

[Palmer was an English novelist, essayist, and theater critic. In the following excerpt from his 1915 critical biography of Kipling, he examines Kipling's perceptions of machinery in stories from The Day's Work.]

When we come to **The Day's Work** we are getting very near to Mr Kipling at his best. We should notice at this point that in all the stories we have so far surveyed the men have mattered less than the work they do. The great majority of Mr Kipling's tales are a song in praise of good work. Almost it seems as if, in the year 1897, their author had himself realised the significance of this; for it was in that year he published the volume entitled **The Day's Work;** and it was the best volume, taking it from cover to cover, that had as yet appeared.

The first and best story in **The Day's Work** at once introduces the theme which threads all the best work of Mr Kipling. "**The Bridge-Builders**" is the story of a Bridge and incidentally of the men who built it. The crown has yet to be set upon a long agony of toil and disappointment. The master builder of the Bridge has put the prime of his energy and will into its building. Now it stands all but complete, with the Ganges gathering in her upper reaches for a mighty effort to throw off her strange fetters. The Bridge before the night of the flood has passed away becomes the symbol of a wrestle between the most ancient gods and the young will of man. Mr Kipling has put the Bridge into the foreground of his picture, has made of it the really sentient figure of the tale. Here definitely he writes the first chapter of his book of steam and steel; and we begin to be aware of an enthusiasm which is lacking in many of the highly finished proofs which preceded it that Mr Kipling could write almost anything as well as almost anybody else. In **The Day's Work** he passes into a province which he was insistently urged to occupy by right of inspiration.

The Day's Work brings us directly into touch with one of the most distinctive features of Mr Kipling's method. He has never been able to resist the lure of things technical. If he writes of a horse he must write as though he had bred and sold horses all his life. If he writes of a steam-engine he must write as though he had spent his life among pistons and cylinders. He writes of ships and the sea, of fox-hunting, of the punishing of Pathans, of drilling by companies and of agriculture; and he writes as one from whom no craft could hide its mysteries. This fascination of mere craft, this delight in the technicalities and dialect of the world's work, is not a mannerism. It is not a parade of omniscience or the madness of a note-book worm. It is fundamental in Mr Kipling. It is wrong to think of **"Between the Devil and the Deep Sea"** or of **".007"** as the unfortunate rioting of an amateur machinist. To those who object that Mr Kipling has spoiled these stories with an absurd enthusiasm for bolts and bars it has at once to be answered that but for this very enthusiasm for bolts and bars, which the undiscerning have found so tedious, the great majority of Mr Kipling's stories would never have been written at all. A powerful turbine excites in Mr Kipling precisely the same quality of emotion which a comely landscape excited in Wordsworth; and this emotion is stamped upon all that he has written in this kind. . . . This is the method of Homer as applied to the shield of Achilles, the method of Milton in enumerating the superior fiends, the method of Walter Scott confronted with a mountain pass, the method of the sonneteer to his mistress' eyebrow. Mr Kipling's enthusiasm for these broken engines would be intolerable if it were not obviously genuine. Unless we shut our ears and admit no songs that sing of things as yet unfamiliar to the poets of blue sky and violets dim as Cytherea's eyes, we cannot possibly mistake the lyrical ecstasy of the above passage. When Mr Kipling tells how a released piston-rod drove up fiercely and started the nuts of the cylinder-cover, it is an incantation. His machines are more alive than his men and women. It is more important to know about the cast-iron supporting-column of Mr Kipling's forward engine than to know that Maisie had long hair and grey eyes, or to know what happened to any of the people whom it concerned. **".007,"** which is the story of a shining and ambitious young locomotive, is ten times more vital—it calls for ten times more fellow-feeling—than the heart affairs of Private Learoyd or the distresses of the Copleigh girls at Simla. The pain that shoots through .007 when he first becomes acquainted with a hot-box is a more human and recognisable bit of consciousness than anything to be shared with the Head of the District or the Man Who Was. The psychology of the Mill Wheel in **"Below the Mill Dam"** is quite obviously accurate. That Mill Wheel, unlike scores of Mr Kipling's men and women, is a creature we have met, who refuses to be forgotten. When he is dealing with men Mr Kipling celebrates not so much mankind as the skill and competency of mankind as severely applied to a given and necessary task. It follows that Mr Kipling's men at their best are most excellent machines. It follows, again, that when Mr Kipling drops the pretence that he is deeply concerned with man as man, and begins to celebrate with all his might the machine as the machine, we realise that his machine is the better man of the two.

The inspiration which Mr Kipling first indulged to its full bent in **The Day's Work** lives on through all the ensuing books. It reaches a climax in **"With the Night Mail,"** a post-dated vision of the air. It is one of the most remarkable stories he has written—a story produced at full pressure of the imagination which, but for its fatal prophesying, would keep his memory green for generations. The detail with which the theme is worked out is extravagant; but it is the extravagance of an inspired lover. To quarrel with its technical exuberance

on the ground that Mr Kipling should have made it less like the vision of an engineer is simply to miss almost the main impulse of Mr Kipling's progress. It is true that unless we share Mr Kipling's enthusiasm for The Night Mail as a beautiful machine, for the men who governed it as skilled mechanicians, and for all the minutiæ of the control and distribution of traffic by air, we are not likely to be greatly held by the story. But this is simply to say that unless we catch the passion of an author we may as well shut the author's book.

This does not imply that we must love machinery in order to love Mr Kipling's enthusiasm for machinery. We have to share the author's passion; but not necessarily to dote upon its object. It is not essential to an admiration of Shakespeare's sonnets that the admirer should have been a suitor of the Dark Lady. It matters hardly at all what is the inspiration of an imaginative author. So long as he succeeds in getting into a highly fervent condition, which prompts him to write, with entire forgetfulness of himself and the reader, of things whose beauty he was born to see, it is of little moment how he happens to be kindled. . . . The exact source of Mr Kipling's inspiration matters not a straw. We simply know that his machinery is alive and lovely in his eyes. He communicates his passion to his reader though his readers are unable to distinguish between a piston-rod and a cylinder-cover.

The Day's Work throws back a clear and searching light upon some of the tales, Indian and political, which we have already passed in review. As we look back upon these stories of men and women we realise, in the light of **The Day's Work,** that machinery—the machinery of Army and Empire—enters repeatedly as a leading motive. Far from regarding Mr

Six-year-old Kipling after his removal to the House of Desolation.

Kipling's passion for technical engineering as something which gets in the way of his natural genius for telling human tales, we are brought finally to realise that many of these human tales are no more than an excuse for the indulging of a passion that helplessly spins them. (pp. 77-86)

John Palmer, in his Rudyard Kipling, Nisbet & Co. Ltd., 1915, 127 p.

WINSTON CHURCHILL   (speech date 1937)

[*An English statesman, historian, memoirist, and journalist, Churchill was prime minister of Great Britain from 1940 to 1945 and from 1951 to 1955. His writings on British history were extremely popular; prior to his death, his works* The Second World War (1945), and History of the English-speaking Peoples *(written during the 1930s but not published until 1956), were outsold only by the Bible in Great Britain. In the following excerpt from a speech delivered on 17 November 1937 at a Kipling memorial dinner, Churchill applauds Kipling's contribution to British literature.*]

Rudyard Kipling holds one of the foremost places in the last century of English letters. During the long noonday of his activity his literary output, though always distinguished by a sense of rarity, reached impressive dimensions. Behind it lay a volume of knowledge always penetrating, often profound, which was vast and majestic. This knowledge was gathered by increasing study, observation and reflection, and constituted the most wonderful mental equipment that can be imagined.

To place these treasures at the service of his country and his age, there was needed the magic gift of genius. This supreme reagent he enjoyed in a glorious intensity. The pith, the force, the terse and syncopated vivacity of his style immediately arrested and commanded attention. The immense variety of subjects to which he seemed to hold the master key is a source of unending amazement to his innumerable readers and admirers throughout the King's Dominions and far beyond them.

There seemed to be no gallery of human achievement which Kipling could not enter easily and unchallenged, and which, having entered, he could not illuminate with a light unexpected, piercing, enchanting, and all his own. All sorts and conditions of men, all classes and professions, every part of the Empire, the souls of children, the lives of animals, became in turn visible, intelligible, fascinating, to that ever-increasing company by whom he was attended in his journey through life. He created a whole series of new values for his fellow-countrymen, and made them participate in an unbroken succession of novel experiences and adventures.

There have been in our own time greater poets and sages, more vehement and sentient interpreters of pathos and passion, more fertile imaginations, and certainly more orthodox stylists, than Rudyard Kipling. But in the glittering rank which he took by Right Divine there never has been anyone like him. No one has ever written like Kipling before, and his work, with all its characteristics and idiosyncrasies, while it charmed and inspired so many, has been successfully imitated by none. He was unique and irreplaceable.

The light of genius expressed in literature does not fail with the death of the author. His galleries are still displayed for our instruction and enjoyment. But the magic key which could have opened new ones to our eager desire has gone for ever. Let us, then, guard the treasures which he has bequeathed.

The structure and pageant of British rule in India gave him his first and main inspiration. To read with faithful eye Kipling's Indian stories, short or long, is to gain a truer knowledge of that great episode, the British contact with India, than will be found in many ponderous blue-books, or in much of the glib, smooth patter which is now in fashion.

We serve the Queen with **"Soldiers Three"**. We see the life of the young officer, of the lonely Collector. We satirise the bureaucracy and viceregal society. We share the domestic troubles of the Anglo-Indian official; we shed bitter tears with **"Wee Willie Winkie"**. On the hard Frontier we follow **"The Drums of the Fore and Aft"**. We play polo with the Maltese Cat. We fight for dear life in the skin of the mongoose Rikki, against the poison cobra. We roam the jungles with Mowgli, and we walk with Kim among the vast multitudes of Hindustan. Even should the British Empire in India pass from life into history, the works of Rudyard Kipling will remain to prove that while we were there we did our best for all.

But from India he travelled far afield. The whole Empire which had sprung from the will and stamina of our ancestors in this small island excited his lively interest. Those were the days when what was proudly called Imperialism, or 'Greater Britain', was the dominating idea in British life. Kipling set himself to portray in vivid outline and gleaming colour every part of that spacious panorama. (pp. 8-10)

Winston Churchill, "Churchill on Kipling," in The Kipling Journal, *Vol. 60, No. 237, March, 1986, pp. 8-10.*

EDWARD SHANKS   (essay date 1940)

[*An English poet, novelist, and critic, Shanks won honors for the poem* Queen of China (1919). *Editor of the* London Mercury *from 1919 to 1922, he wrote notable critical essays on such authors as Bernard Shaw, Edgar Allan Poe, and Rudyard Kipling. In the following excerpt from his critical work,* Rudyard Kipling: A Study in Literature and Political Ideas, *Shanks explores in Kipling's later stories the idea of consolation for the "evils of pain, death and loss" brought about chiefly by World War I.*]

In 1913 Kipling published a story called **"The Edge of the Evening"**. It is not one of his best but there is a reason for mentioning it in a survey from which so many better pieces have to be omitted. It describes how a German aeroplane, after taking illicit photographs, came down in the park of a country-house in the south of England, and how its occupants, foolish enough to shoot at the members of the house-party who found them, were accidentally killed—one of them by a blow from a golf-club, the other in a Rugger tackle. Their bodies were replaced in the aeroplane and an American, who happened to be present and who happened also to have designed the engine, managed to get them into the air again with the hope that they would fall into the Channel. One character in the story says:

> It'll make an infernal international stink. What did I tell you in the smoking-room after lunch? The tension's at breaking-point already. This 'ud snap it.

Thus, a year before the Great War broke out, Kipling was ready for it and the warning which this story conveys is, in retrospect, all the more impressive for its twilight setting. He had indeed dreaded it for a long time. He knew that it would be horribly unlike the wars of which he had dreamt in earlier days—the wars in which Stalky, with a handful of Sikhs, was to work miracles. (pp. 232-33)

Kipling had made for himself images of two worlds. In the first the White Man carried his Burden towards the millennium. In the second, England blossomed and regenerated the world by her example. And now he was faced, as he had feared that he would be, by "steel and fire and stone". (pp. 233-34)

There was in Kipling a cruelty towards the enemy during the Great War which he had never shown before. Mary Postgate, a gentle-natured woman, carries on steadily with her work in hand, knowing that a crashed German airman is dying slowly a little distance from her. Maddingham in **"Sea Constables"** relentlessly chivvies a "neutral" vessel, carrying oil for German submarines, up and down the Irish Channel until her owner falls desperately ill and puts into a small Irish port. There he begs for mercy, to be taken to where he can get medical help:

> "I said: 'Look here! I'm a middle-aged man, and I don't suppose my conscience is any clearer than yours in many respects, but this is business. I can do nothing for you.'"

> "You got that a bit mixed, I think," said Tegg critically.

> "*He* saw what I was driving at," Maddingham replied, "and he was the only one that mattered for the moment. 'Then I'm a dead man, Mr. Maddingham,' he said. 'That's *your* business,' I said. 'Good afternoon.' And I went out."

> "And?" said Winchmore, after some silence.

> "He died. I saw his flag half-masted next morning."

In these tales there is a grim relish indicative of strong passion.

It was the destruction of good, useful and innocent lives which above all tormented him—even before he had lost his only son. (pp. 234-35)

As had happened to him before, the experience of the War helped to ripen in him changes that had already begun. And now we reach Kipling's final, most difficult, least understood period, in which, as usual, it will be necessary to include things that were written before the War. It hardly needs to be added that frequently among the post-War pieces we find recapitulations, returns to earlier themes and moods, such as are to be expected in the last work of an old man.

We are all rather mealy-mouthed nowadays about the application of the word "old" to individuals, just as we are hopefully vague about the use of the word "middle-aged". Absurd as it may seem, I cannot help feeling that the phrase "the last work of an old man" suits ill with the fact that Kipling was only seventy when he died and that much of the work of which I am speaking was done when he was in his fifties and sixties and some of it even earlier. But there is one thing that makes it easier for us to see why in his last period he showed many of the characteristics which, when fortune is kind, distinguish the artist who has grown not merely old but very old in the practice of his art. His precocity followed him to the

end. He had full fifty years as a practising artist of high achievement. Problems of technique yielded to him very early. In the first of his middle years he found himself able to deal very handsomely and fruitfully with problems of temperament and character. He advanced rapidly to that stage in the growth of the mind which is what we mean when we talk about the very old artist—a stage in which all that is possible has been done and the impossible beckons with an enticing finger. (pp. 237-39)

[It is] possible to say what were the themes which most interested Kipling at the end of his life. He was concerned with the immortal problems of pain and death, of ill-doing and punishment, of the other world, and of religion. No doubt the War must in any case have quickened the sensitiveness of every mind towards these problems. But there is no mistaking the fact that Kipling chose a particular approach to them, an approach to which he would eventually have come even if there had never been any War. This particular approach takes the form of a preoccupation with the accidents to which the human machine is liable—both in the flesh and in the mind.

One of the stories in his last collection appears to be on the surface, as indeed he incidentally proclaims it to be, his sole attempt at the detective-story. A girl is found killed beside a country road, with a hole neatly punched in the back of her head, and two men set out in search of the murderer. Her death is at last found to be due to a queer but quite convincing accident. In earlier days Kipling would have been quite content with such a story to tell. If we consider it purely as a competently told story, it would probably have been safer in his hands then. But here the emphasis is laid on a man who is wrongly suspected of being the criminal, and it is so laid because Kipling is interested in a complicated mental condition resulting from shell-shock.

This is, to be sure, a fault in artistry. Each part of the story is beautifully done, but each wastefully distracts interest from the other. Can one, however, say that this is a fault in the artist? No—because there are now matters which concern him more than perfection in story-telling. His simple mechanical problem in detection has led him to the problem of the bedevilment of a human mind. Impatiently engrossed by this he cares little what effect is produced on the reader. He is the old artist, hurrying on through the mists. Let his companion follow as best he can. And even if the companion does find it a rather difficult task, that will perhaps the more impress on him the truth that life's ultimate puzzles are difficult indeed.

In this story, at the end, Kipling shows full mercy to the victim. In **"Dayspring Mishandled"** he does nothing of the sort: he shows no mercy to anyone concerned, not even to the narrator. Of all the compositions of his final years, there is none providing a better example of his deliberate subtlety and obscurity. (pp. 241-43)

Judging by ordinary technical canons, we might easily dismiss **"Dayspring Mishandled"** as a bad piece of story-telling. And we might as easily condemn it as a story about morbid people conceived by a mind with more than a streak of morbidity in it. But to do either of these things would be to miss the point. The story is effective to this degree that the reader, having begun it, must go through it to the end and, having finished it, cannot help remembering it, just as he remembers the most sinister incidents in a nightmare. This is because, whatever demerits it may have, it is full of the sincerity of the old questioning artist. Kipling appears throughout to be asking: But what does it all mean? And perhaps he thinks he has caught a glimpse of an answer, of which, however, he can give us no more than a bafflingly cloudier glimpse. It is no valid condemnation of him to say that he writes of people in morbid states of body and mind. For most people the whole interesting business of life ends in a morbid state of body or mind and sometimes of both. Kipling asked: Why? What does it all mean?

There is no need here to labour by repeated examples the fascination exercised on him by malignant disease. In an earlier story he had written: "Human nature seldom walks up to the word 'cancer' ". Now he did walk up to it again and again. "Auntie Armine", in **"A Madonna of the Trenches"**, sends by her nephew a message to her secret lover at the front, who is the boy's sergeant. . . . The sergeant is due to go on leave on the twenty-first. He begins his journey but does not go far. He is found poisoned by charcoal-fumes in a dugout. But before that he repeats mysteriously to the boy, "If after the manner of men, I have fought with beasts at Ephesus, what advantageth it me, if the dead rise not?" And this text might almost be the motto for the work of Kipling's last years. He had seen a glorious pageant of life, men and women and countries. But what—the question dwelt with him—was it all for?

Like all writers of the short-story he had dealt in the supernatural from his earliest years. **"The Phantom Rickshaw"** was one of his first tales. **"At the End of the Passage"** and **"The Mark of the Beast"** came not much later. But these were, in the sense in which that word was used about Kipling then, only "anecdotes". They showed considerable powers of invention and the technical ability to produce a shudder. But they offered no evidence of any spiritual disturbance in the mind of the writer and they left none in that of the reader. They were "thrillers", meant for entertainment only, postulating, as is necessary, when the supernatural is used for purposes of entertainment, "the willing suspension of disbelief ".

Perhaps **"The Brushwood Boy"** should be classified with these. Yet it is written to a richer and subtler music. It is the story of a young man and a young woman who, but for a casual encounter as children which neither of them remembers, have no knowledge of one another, yet have for years shared the same dreams. Fate brings them together. Recognition is established. There is neither explanation nor any hint of a search for one. Probably this piece should be considered chiefly important as one of Kipling's earliest handlings of English life and landscape as a background. But, looking back, we can hardly help thinking of it also as having been written by the man who was going to write **"They"**.

"They" is a beautifully wrought story. Its maker loved it so much that he lavished on it all the decoration it could carry. . . . Let us here remember what Kipling said about the *Puck* stories: "I worked the material in three or four overlaid tints and textures, which might or might not reveal themselves according to the shifting light of sex, youth and experience". There are, clearly, at least three elements in **"They"**, if not more. One of these is its lovely decoration. Another is the story of a woman blind since a few months after birth, who lived in a beautiful house and kept it for the ghosts of children untimely dead. This was a story certain to draw tears from all sorts of eyes. But there is much more than that beyond. The only question is: What is it?

There is undoubtedly an element of the sinister. A child is ill and the narrator uses his car to fetch a doctor, then waits for the result:

> A woman, wiping the suds off her arms, came out of the cottage next the sweetmeat shop.
>
> "I've be'n listenin' in de back-yard," she said cheerily. "He says Arthur's unaccountable bad. Did ye hear him shruck just now? Unaccountable bad. I reckon 'twill come Jenny's turn to walk in de wood nex' week along, Mr. Madden."
>
> "Excuse me, Sir, but your lap-robe is slipping," said Madden deferentially. The woman started, dropped a curtsey, and hurried away.
>
> "What does she mean by 'walking in the wood'?" I asked.
>
> "It must be some saying they use hereabouts," said Madden. "They're an independent lot in this country. She took you for a chauffeur, Sir."

Jenny is the (unmarried) mother of the child that is believed to be dying. The wood is that which belongs to the blind woman who keeps open house for children whom neither she nor anyone else can see.

In a final scene the blind woman brings matters to a head by crying, "Oh, you *must* bear or lose. There is no other way—and yet they love me. They must! Don't they?" . . . At the end this story reveals itself as the expression, all the more poignant because of its elaborate reticence, of a personal grief. That is only one aspect of it, however. If we look at it from another point of view, we can see how the author has preserved himself from growing too egotistic by working "the material in three or four overlaid tints and textures, which might or might not reveal themselves according to the shifting light of sex, youth and experience." Looking at it from yet another point, we can see how early Kipling began to be preoccupied with those problems of pain, death and loss—problems which led direct to the main theme of his last years.

And the main theme of his last years is the possibility of there being a consolation somewhere for the evils of pain, death and loss. He explored in various directions. His explorations into the region of the supernatural may be regarded chiefly as symbolism. On an even more symbolistic plane he made up a mythology of his own, a Heaven of his own, a Universe in which justice was dealt out in accordance with the fundamental ideas from which he never in the whole of his life departed. **"On the Gate"**, written in 1916, shows the Angel of Death and St. Peter discussing the new responsibilities which have been thrust on their departments by the War. Death shows St. Peter his expanded staff and St. Peter takes Death to see how the new arrivals are handled at the Gate. In **"Uncovenanted Mercies"** Satan exhibits with pride to Azrael and Gabriel one of his ingenious contrivances—a replica of a railway terminus. . . . In these stories we have set another remarkable example of Kipling's trick of painting his pictures with one tint laid over another. An idea of conduct and reward of suffering and redemption is projected by means of a mocking machinery, with yet an insistent note of pity in the sound of the machine.

This light-hearted mythology shows but one side of the Kipling of the later years. There is another in the stories which definitely show him as a man who sought for a Church. He was always a man to whom co-operation was the essence of religion or, perhaps better, the soil out of which religion springs. The sense of brotherhood was strong in him when he founded the alliance which united Beetle, Stalky and Turkey. It needs little imagination to see that, whatever else may be said, the alliance was a real thing and that Beetle found the cement for it. Without him the other two would have drifted into, and out of, all manner of other friendships, as schoolboys commonly do. Throughout his life he displayed a particular sensitiveness for any sort of freemasonry. His feeling can be summarised in Mowgli's call: "We be of one blood, thou and I!" It is significant that Mowgli had been taught to utter this call to all manner of created beings. During most of his life, Kipling showed a desire to be accepted by almost every freemasonry that he encountered. Towards the end of it he sought quite plainly for one in which he could find fulfilment and peace, the answer to the questions which old age put inexorably before him. A glimpse of this seeking occurs in the stories in which we are introduced into "the Lodge of Instruction" . . . , where soldiers on leave from the front are received as Visiting Brothers. The narrator is asked to help in the work of proving these applicants. . . .

He does not seem to have looked with any confidence to Christianity for the consolation and assurance that he needed. There are signs that he was attracted by another religion, one which had already disappeared from the earth when our civilisation was only just beginning to take shape. Valens, in **"The Church that Was at Antioch"** (has anyone ever noticed by the way that this story is virtually an austerer repetition of **"Only a Subaltern"?**) follows Mithras because he "wants more" than the official Roman religion. But Mithraism makes a much earlier appearance in Kipling's work than this. Parnesius, in **"Puck of Pook's Hill"**, first came to know his friend Pertinax "at a ceremony in our Temple—in the dark. It was the Bull Killing. . . . In the Cave we first met, and we were both raised to the Degree of Gryphons together". . . . No doubt the fact that Mithraism was essentially a military religion and was widespread through the armies of the Empire goes some way to explain the attraction it held for Kipling. But there was another reason, which is betrayed in the words of Parnesius. It had also something of the character of a semi-secret society, with initiations, and degrees of advancement and ceremonies which were guarded from all but the initiates of the proper degree. This appealed to something very deep in Kipling's nature. It engendered, he felt, an intimacy of strength and co-operation which satisfied a craving in him. And it was in fact a mature version of the mysteries and catchwords by means of which Beetle, Stalky and Turkey distinguished themselves from the alien, uninitiated world outside Study Five. (pp. 246-57)

Edward Shanks, in his Rudyard Kipling: A Study in Literature and Political Ideas, *Doubleday, Doran & Co., Inc., 1940, 267 p.*

PETER PENZOLDT (essay date 1952)

[*In the following excerpt form his* The Supernatural in Fiction, *Penzoldt discusses supernatural elements in Kipling's short stories, focusing in particular on "The Phantom 'Rickshaw."*]

Most of Kipling's ghost stories owe their fame less to their intrinsic merit than to the name of their author. Kipling is not one of the great ghost-story writers. There are only about a dozen true tales of the supernatural to be found amongst the enormous quantity of short stories he has written, and

only one of these, **"They"**, ranks with his other masterpieces. It is true that Kipling often writes of the marvelous, the region that lies on the borderline between the natural and the preternatural, but true tales of the supernatural are rare. Of these tales, six belong to Kipling's Indian period. These are **"The Phantom 'Rickshaw"** and **"My Own True Ghost-Story"** from *The Phantom 'Rickshaw* (1888); **"The Return of Imray"**, **"At the End of the Passage"**, and **"The Mark of the Beast"** from *Life's Handicap* (1891) and **"The Lost Legion"**, from *Many Inventions* (1893). These six stories are very different in theme and quality. **"The Return of Imray"** and **"The Lost Legion"** are orthodox ghost stories. The first is about a murdered man, who haunts a bungalow, until his body is discovered. The second deals with the reappearance of a dead regiment. **"The Mark of the Beast"** is a werewolf story, a straightforward tale of horror and the supernatural, with the horror predominant. It describes the misfortunes of a man, who, on New Year's Eve, was drunk enough to grind the ashes of his cigar butt into the red stone image of Hanuman, the monkey-god. In revenge, a leper priest embraces him, and endows him with the nature of a wolf. A transformation takes place, which first affects the victim's character, and finally even his appearance. The description of the green light behind the man's eyes, and his inhuman howls, leads up to the final horrible scene, in which the leper priest is compelled by torture to undo his work.

"The Phantom 'Rickshaw" and **"At the End of the Passage"** belong to the domain of fictional psychiatry. In **"The Phantom 'Rickshaw"**, Dr. Heatherlegh maintains to the last that the hero was killed by overwork, and that bad digestion and optical illusions were responsible for Pansay's visions of the ghostly rickshaw and the dead mistress he had betrayed. There are other important elements in this story, which will later be discussed in detail. **"At the End of the Passage"** is also a story about a man who went mad, but the ghost, if there really is one, is certainly not a revenge ghost. While both these tales may be regarded as stories, or case-histories of insanity, their moral themes are totally different. In the first an unfaithful lover is haunted by the ghost of his mistress, while in the second a man who is driven by his sense of duty to refuse leave goes mad through loneliness. Finally, in **"My Own True Ghost-story"**, there is no spectre at all. The noise of the billiard players in the next room proves to be nothing more than the intermittent clicks of a loose window and the rats scuffling behind the walls.

Thus the six important ghost stories of Kipling's Indian period diverge widely in style, subject matter and treatment. The only link between them is the bare fact that they all deal with some aspect of the supernatural. As will be shown later, **"The Lost Legion"** and **"The Phantom 'Rickshaw"** are more closely related to some of Kipling's other tales, which do not deal with the supernatural, than they are to each other.

The same lack of unity is noticeable among the ghost stories of Kipling's second period, the English period. A straightforward, orthodox ghost story, such as **"The House Surgeon"** (*Actions and Reactions*), has little in common with a lyrical poem in prose, such as **"They"** (*Traffics and Discoveries*), which springs from deep personal experience. Nor, as the survey of the Indian period shows, is there any particular development in this sideline of Kipling's work. Orthodox ghost stories, fictional psychiatry, and stories with a natural ending, follow each other haphazardly, and there is no trace of the usual historical change from one type of main theme to another. Nor has Kipling noticeable idiosyncrasies as a ghost-story writer. He has neither a marked preference for one particular theme, as have H. G. Wells and Algernon Blackwood, nor a style or structure that is peculiar to his ghost stories. Indeed, most of his tales of the supernatural were not primarily written as such. Kipling often uses the supernatural simply as a means of developing his favourite themes more effectively.

For these reasons Kipling's ghost stories cannot be treated as a group, nor be studied apart from the rest of his work. Their significance can only be understood if they are regarded as springing from tendencies that can be traced in his other short stories and novels.

Although Kipling introduces the supernatural element into stories with very different themes and settings, yet in nearly every case his *use* of it arises from the same combination of interests. It is therefore unnecessary to analyse every one of his ghost stories. I propose to take two only, and study them in detail. The first, **"The Phantom 'Rickshaw"** from Kipling's Indian period, shows traces of nearly all the different interests that led him to write ghost stories. The second, **"They"**, belongs to the English period. Like the tales in *Puck of Pook's Hill* and *Rewards and Fairies*, it was written after, and as a result of, Kipling's loss of his first-born child. But it is not a fairy tale. It is the best tale of the supernatural ever written by Kipling, and is the only successful attempt in the history of the ghost story to depict child-ghosts, without either sentimentalising, or shocking the reader's feelings. This tale must therefore be discussed, not only in relation to Kipling's other work, but also in relation to the historical development of the ghost story as a genre.

In order to understand why Kipling, the reputed realist, and matter-of-fact thinker, wrote a genuine ghost story like **"The Phantom 'Rickshaw"**, we must consider more closely three important tendencies in his work, none of which leads necessarily to the ghost story in general, or **"The Phantom 'Rickshaw"** in particular, but which may conceivably have induced him to write of the supernatural.

The first tendency to be noticed is Kipling's preoccupation with nervous and mental diseases. It is difficult to discover the reason for this particular interest, but it seems probable that there is a connection between his preoccupation with violence and cruelty, and the diseases which lead men towards violent and cruel acts. Curiously enough, the author of *Just So Stories* filled his work with accounts of sadism. The description of the galley slaves in **"The Finest Story in the World"** (*Many Inventions*), and the scene in **"Beyond the Pale"** (*Plain Tales from the Hills*), in which a jealous husband cuts off his wife's hands, and she greets her lover by lifting up the stumps against the moonlight, are only two examples out of many that may be found in his tales.

Nevertheless, one cannot maintain that Kipling's interest in mental disease is solely due to his taste for cruelty. The stories, in which mental disease is described, with the single exception of **"The Mark of the Beast"**, do not stress the scenes of violence more than tales by other authors on the same theme. But they do show an incredibly accurate intuitive knowledge of the working of the human mind, and more especially of the unbalanced mind, which indicates that Kipling must have had a genuine interest in mental disease quite apart from the violence connected with it. It is uncanny how, without the slightest medical knowledge of the disease, he divines

a madman's reactions. Considering that **"The Phantom 'Rickshaw"** was written more than ten years before the turn of the century, we might even think of Kipling as one of the forerunners of the psychological ghost story, or rather fictional psychiatry with a touch of the supernatural. The latter term seems more appropriate, because there is really very little psychology in his work. Baker said that in his tales psychology was 'telescoped or taken for granted', and indeed, even in the kind of story now under discussion, Kipling never traces back to a psychological cause. Heat, overwork, optical illusions, and liver trouble have to account for everything. Yet if the explanations he offers are rather unconvincing, the symptoms he describes are very near to truth. (pp. 118-21)

[Kipling's] ghost stories cannot be considered simply as the result of his interest in mental disease. Such stories on the supernatural as **"The Brushwood Boy"** (*The Day's Work*), and **"The Finest Story in the World"** (*Many Inventions*), from Kipling's English period arise clearly from a strong liking for the marvellous. This taste may be regarded as the second of the three tendencies we have mentioned.

With an Indian childhood, English schooling, followed by a journalistic career in India, Kipling was marked by two cultures. Baker says that he had 'two racial souls'. (pp. 122-23)

Kipling's mind was also formed under the influence of two cultures: that of the visionary East, and that of England, where Celtic and Germanic traditions have made the incredible one of the basic elements in literature. (p. 123)

[The] fact that Kipling's taste for the marvellous is partly responsible for his writing short stories of the supernatural is beyond doubt. The best proof for this is his own words, quoted from the short preface with which he introduces the volume entitled *The Phantom 'Rickshaw*. This volume contains one genuine ghost story, **"The Phantom 'Rickshaw"**, one ghost story with a natural ending, **"My Own True Ghost-story"**, and two tales of the marvellous, **"The Strange Ride of Marrowbie Jukes"**, and **"The Man who would be King"**.

> This is not exactly a book of downright ghost stories, as the cover makes belief. It is rather a collection of facts that never quite explained themselves. All that the collector is certain of is that one man insisted upon dying because he believed himself to be haunted; another man either made up a wonderful lie and stuck to it, or visited a very strange place; while the third man was indubitably crucified by some person or persons unknown, and gave an extraordinary account of himself.

Kipling's interest in mental disease and his taste for the marvellous may account for his interest in ghosts as ghosts, but in some of his tales of the supernatural it is clear that he is regarding them primarily as a means of producing certain effects, to aid in the development of his main theme. **"The Lost Legion"** is an example of this. It is one of the tales Kipling has written in praise of the Anglo-Indian army, a stanza in his long epos of the Empire, and the men who keep it alive. It must be understood and read as such. The supernatural element is only added to heighten the effect.

The particular motif chosen for this story is that of the dead soldier or hero. If we disregard the preternatural element, the story is the exact pendant of **"The Drums of the Fore and Aft"** (*Wee Willie Winkie*). Both are tales about regiments that failed in their duty, and made good for this failure afterwards. In the **"Drums of the Fore and Aft"** the heroism of two children adds a special touch to the theme. In **"The Lost Legion"** it is the ghostly element. But in both cases these romantic additions must not be mistaken for the real theme of the story.

"The Phantom 'Rickshaw", too, belongs to a certain group of Kipling's stories. Their common theme is love, and more particularly love and intrigue, among the Anglo-Indian society, and there seems no real reason why a ghost story should appear among them. *The Story of the Gadsbys,* which is wholly devoted to the ups and downs and small annoyances and frictions of married life in the officers' quarters, appeared in the same year as **"The Phantom 'Rickshaw"**. Other examples are **"The Courting of Dinah Shadd"** (*Life's Handicap*), **"Kidnapped"**, and **"The Other Man"** (*Plain Tales from the Hills*), but these are by no means the only ones.

It would be going too far to say that **"The Phantom 'Rickshaw"** is merely another story of this group. It is not as close to the rest of Kipling's love stories as **"The Lost Legion"** is to the rest of the stories celebrating the Empire. In it the supernatural is not used only to illustrate the main theme. Indeed, I think it is true to say that in **"The Phantom 'Rickshaw"** the supernatural is at least as important as the love theme. In this respect **"The Phantom 'Rickshaw"** stands between **"The Lost Legion,"** where the supernatural is subsidiary, and **"The Mark of the Beast"** or **"The Return of Imray"** in which it is dominant.

It is not at all surprising that in at least one of Kipling's stories the love theme should appear in conjunction with the supernatural. (pp. 124-25)

The theme of love and insanity often appear together in Kipling's tales, as in **"The Other Man"**, **"In the Pride of his Youth"**, and **"Bertram and Bini"**. Insanity and the supernatural, similarly, are often found linked, as in **"The Conversion of Aurelian McGoggin"** and **"At the End of the Passage"**, but in **"The Phantom 'Rickshaw"**, the three themes love, insanity and the supernatural are combined in one story.

The connection between the love theme and the supernatural through Kipling's interest in the marvellous can be demonstrated in a similar fashion. **"The Brushwood Boy"** (*The Day's Work*) is the most famous example. The connection between the marvellous and the supernatural in Kipling's work has already been discussed. Kipling was by no means the only writer to bring together the marvellous and the love theme. Similar examples may be found in literature throughout the ages. The connection is important here as providing a link between those interests which, in combination with others, led to the creation of **"The Phantom 'Rickshaw"**. (p. 126)

The question that immediately arises in the mind of the reader of this tale is, what was the real nature of this haunting? Does Kipling's story belong to the domain of fictional psychiatry, or is it a tale about an unfaithful lover's guilty conscience, or again, is it nothing but a straightforward ghost story? The story has all three elements. Kipling's interest in pathological psychology induced him to consider the nature of a madman's illusions, and his strong taste for the marvellous led him to the discovery that these illusions may take on the appearance of a supernatural visitation, where a pure realist would have never gone beyond the medical facts. Thus a true ghost story was born, which may be considered as one of the earlier examples of the psychological ghost story. But **"The Phantom 'Rickshaw"** is also one of the tales in which Kipling has painted love and intrigue in Anglo-Indian soci-

ety, and from this point of view it may be regarded as a moral tale, in which the villain is also the victim, and the task of retribution, usually assigned by Kipling to society, is performed either by the forces of the other world, or by his own conscience. (p. 127)

Although **"The Phantom 'Rickshaw"** is a combination of analysis of a mental case history with the ghost story, and the plain love story, the structure of the story is clearly that of fictional psychiatry. It is a rather uncommon and remarkable structure. There is no definite climax, nor can one speak of a series of climaxes. It is true that Mrs. Wessington's ghost appears again and again, and at least twice (the first time, and when the hero believes himself cured of what he hoped was a physical disease), comes unexpectedly, so that the appearance could be mistaken for a climax. Yet the ghost comes so frequently, that the reader has the impression less of separate visitations than of a continuous presence. The story is told by a man obsessed by these visitations, so that the actual appearance of the ghosts is not a climax, as it is when the supernatural breaks into reality. Indeed, one experiences neither terror nor surprise, for the atmosphere of the tale is already that of the other world.

A story such as **"The Phantom 'Rickshaw"** must necessarily be read with a certain detachment rather than lived through by means of identification as most ghost stories are. The reader is not expected to watch the tragedy breathlessly, and feel as if it all happened to him as much as to the hero. The effect of the story is depressing rather than exciting. The reason for this can be understood more easily if one considers Pansay's history as a 'drame intérieur', showing the inevitability of the hero's slow mental and spiritual decay. The reader, who is called upon to witness this process, will not experience the thrill that an 'objective' ghost is likely to convey. The feeling of terror that increases till it culminates in the climax is of necessity absent from fictional psychiatry, for there is no such climax, unless the victim's increasing obsession is directed against some other person. In **"The Phantom 'Rickshaw"** there is never the suggestion of a threat to any other person. (p. 128)

Though it has no single climax, **"The Phantom 'Rickshaw"** has something in the nature of an inverted double climax. The story begins with a few introductory words from the author, and an account of the doctor's opinion on the case. We know from the beginning that the hero will die, and that the author learned about the story through the manuscript left by the dead man. We are also informed on the first page that the manuscript was written by a man who 'was in high fever while he was writing', and that, in the opinion of the doctor, at least, Pansay was mentally deranged. Similarly, we become acquainted with the author's theory of the case—'that there was a crack in Pansay's head, and a little bit of the Dark World came through and pressed him to death'. We are thus at the very beginning informed of the two possible explanations for the strange events connected with the death of the hero. In the ordinary form of the double climax, such solutions are found at the end of the story. Placing them at the beginning naturally takes away a good deal of the suspense, but it has already been shown that in absence of a single, or a true double, climax, this is a matter of no importance.

The character of the apparition itself in **"The Phantom 'Rickshaw"** deserves closer analysis. The reader is presented with the ghost, not of one person or being only, but with that of five: Mrs. Wessington, and her four coolies. Moreover, that is not all, there is a ghost of the 'rickshaw as well.

The presence of the 'rickshaw has nothing astonishing or particularly original about it. Folklore knows headless horsemen to appear with their horses, and some ghosts will appear only with their entire surroundings, houses, castles, gardens, ships, etc. M. R. James's "A View from a Hill", E. A. Poe's "MS. Found in a Bottle". Richard Middleton's "The Ghost Ship", and Daphne du Maurier's "The Escort", are only a few well-known examples.

The ghosts of the four coolies strike one as far more remarkable. It seems difficult to believe that coolies must needs be coolies in the next world also, and even there exist only for the use of the all-superior mem'sahib. Kipling himself confesses his astonishment at the appearance of these ghostly servants.

> So there *were* ghosts of 'rickshaws after all, and ghostly employments in the other world? How much did Mrs. Wessington give her men? What were their hours? Where did they go?

Kipling was not the first, and not the only, author who has made his ghosts appear with a staff of attendants. Sheridan Le Fanu in "The Spectre Lovers" marches a whole battalion into the town where its Colonel is going to appear. Yet I cannot help thinking that with his ghostly coolies carrying the 'rickshaw of a ghostly mem'sahib, Kipling oversteps the line which should decently contain his rather naïve admiration for the white master race.

Another rather extraordinary point about **"The Phantom 'Rickshaw"** is that it only appears in broad daylight and out-of-doors. At night Pansay is left in peace. This peculiarity has already been mentioned in "The Main Motif", sub-chapter "The Ghost", where similar instances have been quoted. The main reason for such an unorthodox time of appearance is probably the fact that the hero is going out of his mind. At least, it could be said that it stresses this aspect of the story. It is a universally admitted convention in literature that at midnight almost any normal person can meet a ghost, but even in the short story of the supernatural, day-time visions seem to indicate madness. The exactness with which the spectre is described may be a similar indication.

> She was wearing the dress in which I had last seen her alive: carried the same tiny handkerchief in her right hand; and the same card-case in her left (A woman eight months dead with a card-case!).

This description occurs in the last quarter of the story. At first Mrs. Wessington remains hidden in the 'rickshaw, but as the hero slowly descends the path into darkness, the spectre becomes more and more real. The culmination of this development is reached when the apparition begins to speak. (pp. 129-31)

The conversation between the ghost and the hero must be considered as the last stage of insanity. If one cannot consider it in this light, one is led to subscribe to Mr. Hart's criticism, that Kipling 'was unaware of Scott's warning against the "chatty" ghost' and that 'ghosts that talk too much, indeed lack dignity.' As a rule, any ghost that appears too often, or is too clearly defined, becomes subject to intellectual analysis, and in consequence fails to make an impression. But **"The Phantom 'Rickshaw"** is an exception to the rule. Here we have to do less with an apparition than with an obsession.

The ghost must therefore be constantly present, and as the obsession becomes stronger, it naturally becomes more clearly defined. (p. 131)

Kipling's **"They"** is not a typical ghost story, yet it is certainly the finest tale of the supernatural he has written. It is not a tale of terror, but one full of deep emotion. It could be called what Alexander Laing called A. E. Coppard's "Adam and Eve and Pinch Me,"—'a true adventure of mind and spirit'. (pp. 141-42)

If we should ask what is the nature of the vision, we can be answered by T. S. Eliot's words which he wrote of Kipling's **"The Wish House"**, and **"Friendly Brook"**,

> It is not a Christian vision, but it is at least a pagan vision—a contradiction of the materialistic view: it is the insight into harmony with nature which must be re-established if the truly Christian imagination is to be recovered by Christians.

The ghost stories of Kipling's second period resemble those of the first period, in that they too are the product of tendencies observable in his other work rather than the result of the development of themes and technique inside the genre of the ghost story. In **"They"** and **"Swept and Garnished"**, as in **"The Lost Legion"**, the supernatural is simply employed as an effective means of treating the main theme. **"The House Surgeon"** can be related most closely to **"The Return of Imray"** in the first period, and Kipling appears to have been led to write the story by the same interests in mental disease and the marvellous that I have remarked in his first period.

Although Kipling's ghost stories are few, and not many rank with his best work, they are important, in that they reveal most clearly what T. S. Eliot called Kipling's

> queer gift of second sight, of transmitting messages from elsewhere, a gift so disconcerting when we are made aware of it, that thenceforth we are never sure when it is *not* present.

In his ghost stories this curious quality of Kipling's work comes to the surface. The unseen world that we sense behind such tales as **"The Dog Hervey"** (*A Diversity of Creatures*), **"Wireless"** (*Traffics and Discoveries*) and **"The Wish House"** (*Debits and Credits*) becomes clearer, and open to our comprehension. It is the understanding of the invisible world that pervades much of Kipling's work, which can alone lead us to a true appreciation of his tales. His ghost stories provide us with the key to this other world. (p. 142)

> *Peter Penzoldt, "Rudyard Kipling," in his* The Supernatural in Fiction, *P. Nevill, 1952, pp. 118-45.*

FRANK O'CONNOR (essay date 1962)

[*O'Connor was an Irish short story writer and man of letters. His fiction is hailed for its realistic portrayal of life in Ireland and its detached yet sympathetic humor regarding the human condition. O'Connor's critical commentary is distinguished by an insistent probing into the connections between society and the individual as well as by an attempt to analyze the creative process. In the following excerpt from his* The Lonely Voice: A Study of the Short Story, *originally published in 1962, O'Connor relates deficiencies in Kipling's short stories to the author's upbringing and subsequent perceptions of society.*]

When it comes to the short story I always feel a certain embarrassment in discussing the work of Rudyard Kipling beside that of storytellers like Chekhov and Maupassant, an embarrassment I find it hard to explain. If I disliked it, it would all be much easier, but I don't. I have read and reread it with genuine admiration, but at the same time I cannot help thinking that if they are real writers then Kipling is not; if, on the other hand, Kipling is a real writer there is something obviously wrong with them. (p. 99)

[If] I cannot define I can perhaps illustrate by discussing one of his stories which is famous—and deservedly so, for it is clearly a masterpiece. I mean **"The Gardener."** This story describes the relationship of an aunt and nephew, Helen and Michael Turrell. Michael is the illegitimate son of Helen's dead brother and of the daughter of a retired non-commissioned officer—hardly the sort of a woman a brother of hers could be expected to marry. (p. 100)

Now, **"The Gardener"** is a great piece of writing, a most moving piece of writing, and I have never read it without wanting to weep, and yet there *is* something about it that makes me uncomfortable. Naturally, not being entirely unfamiliar with the devices of the storyteller, I have wondered whether this was not caused by the Celestial Gardener—the literary equivalent of a Celestial Choir—a gimmick deliberately introduced at a point when the reader is so deeply moved—or should be so deeply moved—that any comment of the author's is a breach of good taste. Undoubtedly, the story would be immensely improved by the Celestial Gentleman's removal, but I can't help thinking that He Himself is not a cause but a symptom of something false in the story and that the gimmick in a short story is no more than the consequence of all the false steps the author has already taken.

As a writer I can put up a very good case for the form of the story as Kipling wrote it. I can say that this is a story of hypocrisy that has blasted the life of an innocent child and that it is proper that the form of the story should be the external representation of all the hypocrisy up to the supreme moment when it is confronted by God and collapses. But really, I don't believe a word of it. Instead I have found myself rewriting the story as it might have been written by Chekhov or Maupassant, just to see what would happen: if instead of beginning, as Kipling does, with "Everyone in the village knew that Helen Turrell did her duty by all her world, and by none more honorably than by her only brother's unfortunate child" I wrote, "Helen Turrell was about to have an illegitimate baby"; and, instead of the fine irony of "She most nobly took charge, although she was, at the time, under threat of lung trouble which had driven her to the South of France" I wrote, "So as to have the baby she had to pretend that she was suffering from lung trouble and had been ordered by her doctor to go to the South of France."

It does not seem to me that the theme—the essential part of the story—suffers much in the transposition, but what happens in the actual treatment is very interesting. One moves out of the world of Celestial Gardeners and Celestial Choirs in which everyone looms twelve feet tall into a real world in which people are five-feet-ten, and having an illegitimate baby is not an inspired act of motherhood but a terrifying and humiliating experience, and one realizes that in bringing the child home with her Helen Turrell shows herself a woman of heroic stature—at least six feet. In fact, the whole center of the story changes, and the mother rather than the son becomes the subject. One can see that it is not only that the son is being deprived of his mother's love but that the mother is being deprived of her son's love, which might mean more to

her than hers to him. But whether the process is right or wrong artistically, the falsehood drops away, so that the reader, instead of having his brains battered in by Celestial Gardeners is persuaded into sharing a real human experience, that of having an illegitimate baby in a world in which babies can be seriously described as "illegitimate."

Now if I could say straight out what is wrong with Kipling's treatment of **"The Gardener,"** I could put my finger on what is wrong with Kipling as a writer, but it is not enough merely to point out how somebody else could have done it better. What does emerge from the rewriting is that Kipling does not keep his eye on the object. He is not really thinking at all of that mother and son but of an audience and the effect he can create on an audience. That is to say, he is not thinking of me in my private capacity as a solitary reader, sitting at home by my own fire with my book; detached, critical, and inclined to resent any assault on my emotions as an invasion of privacy, but in my public capacity as a member of the Young Conservatives' League who can be appealed to on such general issues as "Should a Mother Tell?" As an individual reader I don't give a damn whether she tells or not. I want to know at once which mother, and what she has to tell, and to whom, and what the consequences are likely to be, and I am quite ready to be persuaded either way, according to the facts and the ability of the man who states them. In other words, if Kipling had written this story as an example of a mother's self-sacrifice it would be all the same to me.

This oratorical approach, this consciousness of the individual reader as an audience who, at whatever cost to the artistic properties, must be reduced to tears or laughter or rage is characteristic of Kipling. There is another coarser example in a well-known story of his called **"Love-O'-Women."** The occasion is the trial of a sergeant named Raines who has murdered the seducer of his wife. Mulvaney reminisces about another seducer and the sticky end to which he came. Mulvaney, on loan to the Black Tyrones, notices that the man he calls Love-O'-Women is trying to get himself killed in action. Love-O'-Women is enduring torments of conscience from the memory of the woman whose love he has thrown away, hereinafter known as "Diamonds an' Pearls." Mulvaney also realizes that Love-O'-Women is suffering from the consequences of venereal disease and has not long to live. When the dying man is being carried into Peshawar after the campaign, whom does he see entering a brothel but Diamonds an' Pearls herself, and with furious strength he hurls himself out of the cart and follows her.

> "Fwhat do you do here?" asks Diamonds an' Pearls, "that have taken away my joy in my man this five years gone—that have broken my rest and killed my body an' damned my soul for the sake av seein' how 'twas done. Did your expayrience afterwards bring you acrost any woman that give you more than I did? Wud I not ha' died for you, an' wid you, Ellis? Ye know that, man. If iver your lyin' sowl saw truth in uts life ye know that."

"I'm dyin', Aigypt,—dyin' " says Love-O'-Women, remembering his expensive education, and "Die here!" retorts Diamonds an' Pearls, offering him the loan of her breast, which he hastens to accept, and then, like the true Cleopatra she is, Diamonds an' Pearls produces a gun and "dies for him an' wid him." Thanks to a kindly doctor they are buried together in the one grave with full benefit of clergy—Church of England, of course.

Now, everything in this preposterous story comes straight out of Victorian melodrama. It is not enough to reply that there are scenes in Dickens and Hardy which are almost as embarrassing, because that is merely to emphasize what we know already—that the novel and the short story are two different art forms and that the novel can take handicaps which the short story cannot take. The novel is the more primitive of the two forms; it is closer to the children's tale in which one can prepare for a fantastic event by a single sentence—"And *whom* do you think Little Brown Bear saw when he was walking down the road?" In a novel such a scene as the final episode in Kipling's story could be prepared for through chapter after chapter until the reader was almost led to demand a scene of hysterical emotionalism, but the short story does not permit of such preparation. In fact the reader of the short story cannot be induced to expect anything. The short story represents a struggle with Time—the novelist's Time; it is an attempt to reach some point of vantage from which past and future are equally visible. The crisis of the short story *is* the short story and not as in a novel the mere logical inescapable result of what has preceded it. One might go further and say that in the story what precedes the crisis becomes a consequence of the crisis—*this* being what actually happened, *that* must necessarily be what preceded it. Chekhov was the greatest storyteller who has ever lived, but I am certain he would have reduced any intelligent small child to hysterics. When my responsibility as a parent compelled me to entertain small children, I always read them Kipling's *Jungle Book.*

In a curious way this awareness of an audience seems in Kipling's comic stories to be represented by a mania for practical joking. The practical joke requires an audience; it must not only be perpetrated but be seen to be perpetrated; and the larger the audience that rolls on the floor when the victim is trapped the more effective the joke. (pp. 101-06)

That brings me to another weakness in these stories and perhaps a more serious one. Not only is Kipling not speaking to me in my private capacity as an individual reader, he is not speaking to me in his own private capacity as an individual author. All the other great storytellers speak to us with a lonely human voice, almost as though we were strangers and they were apologizing for their intrusion, but Kipling always speaks as though he himself were one of a gang—the Upper Fourth or the Eleventh Hussars (**"The Slashers"**) which is opposed to another gang—council school boys, niggers, Jews, or Russkys—and expects me to belong to it as well. In fact, he flatters me by implying that, being the intelligent man I am, I couldn't possibly *not* belong to it. But I don't, and his flattering assumption that I am really one of the boys merely irritates me.

Now, Kipling had a real obsession with secret societies, and almost certainly it is connected with the hurt he experienced in childhood when his parents sent him home to England to stay with a family that persecuted him. Edmund Wilson was the first critic to point out the significance of that painful little story, **"Baa, Baa, Black Sheep,"** in which two children, Punch and Judy, are brought home from India and left with a family of three—Uncle Harry, Auntie Rosa, and their son Harry. Judy is petted, but Auntie Rosa and Harry conspire to make little Punch's life a misery, and, after the death of Uncle Harry, he is beaten and humiliated in every possible way. He is even sent to school with Jews and Negroes, a fate which he apparently considers worse than death. He is de-

prived of the books which are his only escape from a brutal reality, and when he starts to go blind and knocks over objects he cannot see, the two sadists have a fresh excuse for beating him. Finally, when his mother comes back, little Punch shrinks away from her and puts up his arm to counter an expected blow. This is precisely the incident Kipling recounts in his autobiography. The story ends in Kipling's usual Celestial Choir manner with "When young lips have drunk deep of the bitter waters of Hate, Suspicion and Despair, all the Love in the World will not wholly take away that knowledge; though it may turn darkened eyes for a while to the light, and teach Faith where no Faith was."

That is hysteria, too, and it is pointless to argue about it, pointless to reply that when he says of his acquaintances at school that "some of them were unclean, some of them talked in dialect, many dropped their h's, and there were two Jews and a Negro" that things might have been worse and that if he had made friends with the Negro or the Jewish kids he might really have learned what it meant "to drink deep of the bitter waters of Hate, Suspicion and Despair"; or even suggest the obvious, that his weakness as a human being might be traced back beyond the incidents he recounts and that he may have been an exceedingly unpleasant small boy. Hysteria is not to be argued with, and a hurt child is always a hurt child.

But to understand Kipling, it is worth while to read **"Baa, Baa, Black Sheep"** and then read one or two of the stories in *Stalky and Co.* In terms of autobiography these continue the story of little Punch. The particular school he writes of would seem to most people atrocious and the circumstances as bad as those in **"Baa, Baa, Black Sheep,"** but it is plain that Kipling never thought of that and was perfectly happy in the memories of his schooldays.

Why? I would suggest because at school he was not alone, and being alone was the one thing in the world he could not face. Beetle, unlike Punch, is one of a gang, the gang that includes Stalky and MacTurk. Like the newspaperman, showman, and Member of Parliament in **"The Village That Voted the Earth Was Flat,"** they could practice elaborate practical jokes on their enemies. They could kill a stray cat and stick it under the floor of a rival dormitory; they could persecute boys who were smaller than themselves. Kipling seems to have desired no more, and he recounts it all, not only without shame but with pride and glee. Man and boy he loved to "gloat."

Obviously, this satisfied something very deep in him—something that went far deeper than the small boy's ordinary longing to be accepted. I suspect that it was an utter inability to face crises alone, and that this was something he had acquired from his upbringing as a little member of a colonial group, the impression that one was never alone or at least never should be alone. If one were left alone, nightmare succeeded.

And this seems to me Kipling's real dilemma. It was the instinct of the short-story teller that made him choose India as the scene of his best work; and it was proper that his submerged population, the British colonials—always lonely, frequently industrious, sometimes idealistic and self-sacrificing—should have their spokesman. But, in fact, they never really were a submerged population, always an ascendancy, or so at least their spokesman chose to think them, because that weakness in his own character made it impossible for him to describe people who were alone. Besides, their circumstances do not permit them to be alone, for they live in the middle of hostile alien groups that will destroy them if ever they are left alone. Their schools, regiments, classes, races, always rise up to protect them from their essential loneliness. Sometimes in Kipling a man may be left alone just long enough to permit him to commit suicide or he may be captured and tortured to imbecility by Russkys or black men, but this is always a horrible accident, and sooner or later his friends will gather round to provide a thrilling military funeral and a Burial Service according to the rites of the Church of England—anything else would be unthinkable. Punch in **"Baa, Baa, Black Sheep"** is abandoned, just as little Vanka in Chekhov's beautiful story is abandoned, but whereas Vanka, having written that despairing letter to his grandfather, addresses it to "Grandfather in the Village," so that we know there is no hope for him, Punch is rescued in what his creator would call "the nick of time" by a military personage known as Inverarity Sahib, who cries in horror, "Good God, the little chap's nearly blind!" Chekhov, the doctor, can face the fact that little chaps go blind, and mad, and desperate. Kipling can't.

That sense of the group makes it almost impossible for Kipling or his readers to believe in individual loneliness, and when it does appear it is always in some monstrous disguise, such as the pit of the living dead in **"The Strange Ride of Morrowbie Jukes"** or the horror that kills Hummil in **"At the End of the Passage."** When Kipling should be moving in the direction of Chekhov he always moves in the direction of Poe. When an officer is unjustly accused of having sexual relations with the wife of a brute called Bronckhurst, the whole machinery of a secret society is put into operation to prevent the Indian servants from perjuring themselves, and when an unpleasant young man from the Lower Classes who has been sent as assistant to a bank where, in his arrogance, he makes a mess of everything, falls ill, his tough superior not only covers up for him but forges testimonials from the bank which has long ago dismissed the wretched boy, and even pays his salary out of his own pocket. Kipling is not only President of the Society for Persuading Unmarried Mothers To Tell, he is also Secretary of a thousand other groups from the Freemasons and Janeites to the Deceased Syphilitics Friendly Burial Fund and the Society for Defending Innocent Co-Respondents. Everyone is covering up, everyone is rushing to the rescue, and all the time one seems to hear the thud of the hoofs of the Eleventh Hussars **("The Slashers")** coming to save the hero from a fate worse than death at the hands of niggers, Jews, and Russkys. As a weak man I like to believe that not only is God watching over me but the Eleventh Hussars are keeping an eye on me as well. As a mature one I know that Kipling is a damned liar.

Perhaps this was inevitable in a colonial society such as that of India in the nineteenth century, but it involves a contradiction which at once distinguishes Kipling from every other great writer of stories. He cannot write about the one subject a storyteller must write about—human loneliness. He has never said with Pascal, "The eternal silence of those infinite spaces terrifies me." (pp. 107-12)

Frank O'Connor, "You and Who Else?," in his The Lonely Voice: A Study of the Short Story, *The World Publishing Company, 1963, pp. 99-112.*

W. W. ROBSON (essay date 1964)

[*In the following excerpt, Robson offers a close analysis of several of Kipling's later stories, noting a lack of artistic development in Kipling's short fiction over the course of his career.*]

[One] of the peculiarities of Kipling's art in his short stories is that, while showing obvious variety and range, it does not in any obvious sense show *development.* Of no author is it more true than for him "in my end is my beginning." This can readily be illustrated from what every reader of Kipling must have noticed, the characteristic unevenness of his work; unevenness, that is, not within a particular story, but in any of his collections of stories considered as a whole. It is not only that the stories are not all equally good; in a prolific author that might well be expected. The case is odder than that. Masterpieces as assured as anything he ever wrote can be found, at any period of his work, side by side with very inferior things; and yet on these inferior things the same minuteness of care and skill seems to have been expended. So in his work of the eighteen-eighties we find the poignant and noble tale of **"The Man who would be King"** inhabiting the same collection as **"The Strange Ride of Morrowbie Jukes"**; and at the very end of his career, in the collection called *Limits and Renewals,* which contains work as subtle and complex as he ever wrote, such as **"Dayspring Mishandled,"** we find so unpleasant and negligible a piece as **"The Tie."** In any book of Kipling's stories ostensibly written for adults we must be prepared to find the ethos of *Stalky & Co.* cropping up in places where it is inappropriate. Beetle represents a self that he never outgrew.

But of course the statement that Kipling did not develop needs both qualification and explanation. Like most writers, he made some false starts before he found his real bent. And, as in most writers, a certain balance of loss and gain can be seen in comparing his later with his earlier work. The fresh vividness of the early work, registering the impact of India on a boy journalist of genius, he never perhaps quite recovered. On the other hand, some irritating immaturities, typified by the recurrent "But that is another story" of *Plain Tales,* vanished from his style; his technical ingenuity increased; his skill took more complex and intellectualised forms; and he brought to its strange perfection that narrative manner of implication, abstention, and obliquity of which the first considerable example is **"Mrs Bathurst"** (1904). He turned to new subject-matter, the Sussex countryside, the historic past of England, the Navy, and, in his last phase, the work of mental and spiritual healing of war-sufferers. But all this seems extension rather than growth; what insights Kipling had, he seems to have had from the beginning; we do not get from his later work the sense of a profound and radical change of outlook, the discovery of a new spiritual dimension, issuing from the author's changing response to his changing experience: the sort of change we can detect in the life-work of a Melville or a Dostoevsky. Quite apart from any question of relative value, Kipling does not seem to be that *kind* of artist at all. Even his best work shows this curious undeveloping poise: a formal self-sufficiency which suggests a fixity. We may contrast Joyce's *Dubliners:* in reading these stories we feel that the author could and must broaden his form and develop his insights by going on to something quite different. But in reading Kipling's stories in chronological succession, we come to feel that our knowledge of the sense of life transmitted by this writer is only being quantitatively increased; there is no perceptible modification of its quality. He seems to have worked out his distinctive technical formu-

1892 cartoon of Kipling with "India on the brain."

las, themselves reflecting a narrow range of fixed sympathies and antipathies and set attitudes, and applied them to a variety of subject-matter which, while giving the stories their sensationally contrasting surfaces and colourings, leaves these formulas essentially unchanged.

This art, however, produced remarkable triumphs; there are compensations for the reader in Kipling's invariable realisation of his particular intention, even if at times we mistrust the intention and dislike what is done. The unceasing craftsmanship, the rigorous subduing of the matter in hand to an artistic discipline, itself becomes a moral quality and an important, if always implicit, part of the author's "message." Henry James, as is well known, complained that the pursuit of this particular kind of perfection necessitated a descent "from the less simple in subject to the more simple—from the Anglo-Indians to the natives, from the natives to the Tommies, from the Tommies to the quadrupeds, from the quadrupeds to the fish, from the fish to the engines and screws." This of course is not an accurate description of the progress of Kipling's work; the bent which produced such *tours de force* as **"The Ship that Found Herself"** and **"The Maltese Cat"** and **".007,"** or the various kinds of beast-fable ranging from *Just So Stories* and *The Jungle Books,* where didactic allegory can be far or near as the author chooses, to such relentless fables as **"The Mother Hive"** or **"A Walking Delegate"** or

"Below the Mill Dam," where the message is continuous and insistent—this bent was not just a middle-period preoccupation of Kipling's, but was something he reverted to at every stage of his literary career. Nor can James's account be extended to Kipling's later work, which was yet to come, and which cannot be said to be "simple" in subject-matter. Nevertheless, James's remark points at something fundamentally true about the frequent results of Kipling's intent desire to have the completest possible *control* of his form and his medium. This desire can lead to impressive achievements in the realm of allegory, satiric fantasy, and fable—sometimes to the attainment of the higher reaches of symbol and myth. But it can also lead to a simplification and distortion of human character and human behaviour which, in an author with so recurrent and emphatic a didactic purpose as Kipling, can become irritatingly tendentious. The danger of a strongly symbolic art, when it deals directly with human beings, is that it makes the reader feel he is being illicitly "got at"; he is receiving, in the place of the really seen and the strongly imagined, nothing but the author's theory of life. Kipling's supreme achievements in prose fiction seem to be those in which his genius as a fabulist and myth-maker is felt to be shaping the story without detriment to the author's true and sensitive perceptions of actual human beings, **"They"** and **"Mrs Bathurst"** and **"The Wish House," "Mary Postgate"** and **"The Gardener"** exemplify this power of the short story to suggest the *distillation* of a human life, the rendering of its essence as latent within a momentary situation, or an anecdote, or an episode. Without the artistic economy, in which every detail is significant, these stories would not have their power; but the power of this selectiveness depends upon our conviction that behind the selection there is a latent reserve of fuller knowledge. They have what Kipling calls in **"The Bull that Thought"** (*Debits and Credits*) "a breadth of technique that comes of reasoned art, and, above all, the passion that arrives after experience."

This "reasoned art," the conscious craftsmanship of Kipling, is the most obvious and distinctive feature of everything he wrote, and it is the only aspect of his work about which he permitted himself to depart from his usual reticence. His emphasis in these remarks—strange as it must seem to those who still equate Kipling with the Jelly-bellied Flag-Flapper—is less on a "message" or a "self" to be expressed, than on a medium to be manipulated. (pp. 258-61)

It would be easy to find openings of stories, like the famous first paragraph of **"Love o' Women,"** that proclaim Kipling's authorship more flamboyantly than [the opening of **"Friendly Brook"**], but none more essentially typical of him. Here, unmistakably, is this personal style, which, without ostentatious economy, establishes at once the brook itself, the animistic "hero" of the tale; the November weather; the two hedgers, with their pride in their ancient craft, their knowledgeableness, their ceremonious etiquette of "artists and equals"; the real if modest triumph of human endeavour ("By noon a length of unclean jungle had turned itself into a cattle-proof barrier"), and the final touch, that hint of "inside" knowledge which in its blatant manifestations can be so tiresome in Kipling's stories, but is here perfectly right in its tone of respectful approval (". . . little plumes of the sacred holly which no woodman touches without orders"). Kipling had implicitly criticised much in his own early work when he complained, in **"Wressley of the Foreign Office,"** that "one of the many curses of our life in India is the want of atmosphere in the painter's sense. There are no half-tints worth noticing. Men stand out all crude and raw, with nothing to tone them down, and nothing to scale them against." This chastened later style is the opposite of "crude and raw"; it is full of "half-tints"; and much in these later stories which the reader vaguely recognises as "background" and "atmosphere" is there precisely to "tone down" and to "scale against."

One of the first stories in the distinctively "late" manner is **"They"** (1904), and it is convenient to open discussion of the later Kipling with a work so totally different from the conventional account of him. Even that account allows Kipling an interest in the eerie and the occult (in one mode **"Wireless"** or **"The Finest Story in the World,"** in another **"The Mark of the Beast"** or **"At the End of the Passage"**). But the first thing to be noticed about **"They"** is that the part played by the ghostly children and the blind childless woman whose love draws them to the beautiful house she has made for them, has nothing to do with a ghost-story strumming on the nerves. The mode of the tale is nearer to "Burnt Norton" than to "The Turn of the Screw." The appeal of the fantasy is to poetic feeling and imagination. Not that we are to take the ghosts as simply the projection of the blind woman's longing or the narrator's bereavement (he, it is finally made known to us, has lost a child, whom he is to find again, once, at the end of the tale). They exist for other people in the tale, the butler, his wife, and the village mother. But their "reality" is equivocal:

> When I paused in my work I listened, but the wood was so full of the noises of summer (though the birds had mated) that I could not at first distinguish these from the tread of small cautious feet stealing across the dead leaves.

One effect of this potently evocative use of the sound of the children's footsteps, whispering, and laughter is to assimilate the narrator's and our perception of them to the blind woman's; an effect echoed in the final fading-out of the story, after the blind woman has told the narrator he must never come again:

> She left me to sit a little longer by the screen, and I heard the sound of her feet die out along the gallery above.

The reason for the equivocal status of the earth-bound spirits is plain when the significance of the story as a parable is taken; the fancied glimpse of the world of the dead is there to confirm that it *is* another world, and the living must go back to the world of the living.

All this is part of the manifest meaning of the tale. But there is another theme in **"They"** interwoven with the theme of the children, and its presence has puzzled some readers, who may not have been conscious of its distinct existence, but who have noticed certain elements in **"They"** which do not seem relevant. What, for instance, is the point of the incident of the dishonest tenant-farmer (who is terrified by the ghosts) at the end? We may approach this more hidden theme by asking another question: why is there so much about the narrator's motor-car? This car is one of those somewhat comic early models which frequently appear in Kipling's work, usually (as in **"They"**) breaking down at some point in the story. It introduces a note of stridency into the dreamland of the beautiful house with its lawn and yew trees: "It was sacrilege to wake that dreaming house-front with the clatter of machinery." The narrator's references to it tend to have a *gaucherie*

and a blatancy which contrast with his generally quiet and sympathetic tone: "In two minutes I was blowing all the horns of Jericho in front of the House Beautiful, and Madden, from the pantry, rose to the crisis like a butler and a man." This sentence by itself could be used to exemplify Kipling's bad style. But in the context this manner of referring to the car seems to be part of a social or sociological observation. The narrator is very conscious of not being one of what the fat village woman calls "carriage folk." This comes out in what he says to the blind woman, who *is* one: "If you had done your duty as a pillar of the State and a landed proprietress you ought to have summoned me for trespass when I barged through your woods the other day." And it is twice repeated in the story, with significant emphasis, that he comes "from the other side of the country." Of course this last touch refers also to the mystical theme. But this way of contrasting the old England and the new, the motor-car and modern people with the House Beautiful and the villagers, "deep-rooted trees of that soil," runs right through the story. The imaginative bias of the writing is *against* the modern world; the least sympathetic character is the dishonest tenant-farmer, who is represented as a characteristically modern product. And the narrator feels it "sacrilege" to "wake that dreaming house-front with the clatter of machinery." On the other hand, it is the car which takes the narrator to the House Beautiful—the second time he feels that "my car took the road of her own volition." And it is thanks to the car that the sick child is saved. "Useful things, cars," says Madden the butler. "If I'd had one when mine took sick she wouldn't have died . . . Croup. No one knew what to do . . . I drove eight miles in a tax-cart for the doctor. She was choked when we came back. This car'd ha' saved her. She'd have been close on ten now." One function of this incident of the sick child is to safeguard against idealisation of the past.

We may wonder whether Kipling showed artistic tact in interweaving these two themes. Other stories in which the motor car plays a prominent role can show him in a more defiantly philistine mood; and hostility to the "county" undoubtedly occurs in stories like **"The Village that Voted"** and **"Beauty Spots,"** in such a way as to suggest that the author is working off some personal resentment. But in **"They"** the narrator, with his sensitive humanity and quiet grief, is an entirely sympathetic figure, and, with his poise between wistfulness and renunciation, the best possible spokesman for the present in relation to a past which it knows is irrecoverable. The two themes join delicately in the symbolic moment early in the tale, which foreshadows the end: "Here, then, I stayed; a horseman's green spear laid at my breast; held by the exceeding beauty of that jewel in that setting."

This wrenching-apart of the thematic materials of **"They"** must give a false impression of the tale itself, where the fabric is continuous and delicate. But for close working and subtlety of means it is far surpassed by the later story **"The Wish House"** (1924), which has claims to be regarded as the most remarkable story Kipling ever wrote. Certainly it is difficult to think of any other short story in the language which is richer in content, and yet gives no suggestion of overcrowding. When it is brought together with **"They"** we see at once a parallel, in the skill with which in both tales the element of the supernatural (or non-natural) is introduced into the tale without disturbing the reader's sense of the human centrality of the story; and another in the importance in both of the mysterious powers of a woman. But **"The Wish House"** represents a far rarer order of achievement. The setting and atmosphere of **"They,"** with its beautiful old house set in an idealised English countryside, gives a licence for a daydream indulgence of fancy; in **"The Wish House"** we are never for a moment allowed to forget the hard realism of the poor suburban villa, the two aging women in the little room shaken by charabancs, one of them going blind, the other dying of cancer. The story cannot be summarised; everything is done by means of touches, implications, details. Through the ordinary, realistic talk of the old countrywomen (this is one of the tales in which the suggestion of dialect is not overdone, as it sometimes is in Kipling, and is essential to the effect) there emerges the wholly credible picture of their two interconnected lives; by way of the secondary story of Liz Fettley, in response to her confidence and her sympathetic questions, we learn from Grace Ashcroft the story of the Wish House, which for her represents the sacrifice of her health and life she believes herself to have made for the man she loves. The story of the Wish House, reduced to the bare bones of anecdote, is fantastic. (pp. 264-68)

[Judgment of human significance in **"The Wish House"**] must partly depend on how we are to regard Grace Ashcroft's sacrifice. Clearly the business of the Token is literally incredible, and Grace is a superstitious woman. The distinction of the story is that she is none the less convincingly established for us as a tragic figure. The Wish House comes to stand for those forces in human life which are not under the control of man, but which the stoic confronts and accepts. That we do not find Grace's behaviour incredible, or a neurotic vagary, is due to the completeness with which we are made to believe in her as an ordinary person—ordinary in so far as we admit that we ourselves are ordinary people. She is seen as real and immediate, with her early amorous waywardness (so well brought out in the account of her relationship with her husband), and her later proud resignation and pathos, all conveyed amid the crisp brevities of her speech. But she is also a figure of history; for through the tale, as in **"They,"** but quite differently and more subtly, there runs the sense of the changing English life, both local and national, which changes her individual life and the lives of her friends; the moves from country to town, and from town to country, the displacement of horse-drawn traffic by motorbuses and everything that that implies—all are brought in, not as mere background, but as a means to establishing her reality as a living reminiscence of older ways and older habits of thinking and feeling. In front of us is the little house in the modern village, a heavy tea laid out (Grace was a cook who never "owed me belly much"), and geraniums on the window-sill; in the nearer distance is London, with that other horrible little house of the walled garden and the basement kitchen; further back still the Sussex countryside of the women's youth. The richness of this treatment might lead us to suppose that the story required development at fuller length; but on reflexion we see that something corresponding to the laconic stoicism of Grace Ashcroft is artistically appropriate; without this economy there could not be that sense, at once sympathetic and ironic, of the distillation of a whole life, of the universal tragedy of possessive love, in one bizarre encounter with the powers of darkness.

There is much in **"The Wish House"** that would repay analysis; T. S. Eliot, while praising it, has called it "hard and obscure," and in a fuller treatment of the story due consideration should certainly be given to the use of the symbolism of cancer which recurs, some would say obsessively, in Kipling's later work; we notice its association, though perhaps this is non-significant in **"The Wish House,"** with blindness, another recurring symbol. (We remember the terrible image of "a blind face that cries and can't wipe its eyes" in **"At the End of the Passage."**) No doubt these symbols meant something intensely personal to Kipling. But in our impulse to psychological investigation of the author we should not forget the actual force these symbols have in the stories, and the insight (as shown in **"The Wish House"**) which leads us, not back to the author, but to ourselves and the world. (And if Kipling *was* obsessed with cancer, is it not the characteristic obsession of modern man?)

These questions about the degree of insight and the general human significance of Kipling's more "unusual" stories are posed in a sharper form by **"Mrs Bathurst,"** which has always been one of the *cruces* in the criticism of his work. Here the obsession of the sailor Vickery with the kind and pleasant and motherly Mrs Bathurst is powerfully done—her "blindish look" as she walks forward in the news-reel picture (the "biograph") is unforgettable, as is the grotesque business of "Click" Vickery's four false teeth, by which he is identified as a charred corpse at the baffling end of the story. But what exactly happened, and what is the significance of what happened, many readers have puzzled over. Some have thought that Kipling in this story has overdone his passion for "cutting." **"Mrs Bathurst"** (1904) is one of the earliest of Kipling's experiments in indirect or suppressed narrative, and its experimental character might make that explanation plausible. But it may well be that the point of the story lies in this obscurity. Pyecroft, the observer of the story, does not claim to understand Vickery and his doings. He knows, and his friends can confirm, the power of love (" 'it takes 'em at all ages' "), and its destructiveness. This is what the story is "about." **"The Wish House"** also testifies to this destructiveness in love. But the effect is totally different, because we have heard Grace Ashcroft's own story, seen the pattern of her life as she sees it, and seen her "close to" through the eyes of Liz Fettley. In **"Mrs Bathurst"** we see only glimpses of a stranger through the eyes of a boon-companion who, despite his assurance to the contrary, has very little essential idea of "what transpired." The emotion generated in us, as in Pyecroft and his friends, is a sort of impersonal awe or terror. We feel no incongruity when the incongruous Vickery can say "The rest is silence." Any one of us, in his relationship with his mother, may have lived through the experience of a childish Hamlet; and the rest—indeed, most—of Vickery's story *can* be silence. That the woman whom Vickery is found dead with in the teak-forest is never identified in the story is psychologically right; the sense of a pattern of life (and death) from which certain things have been dropped or repressed is essential to its human significance. Kipling makes a shell-shocked soldier say in "Epitaphs of the War":

> My name, my speech, my self I had forgot.
> My wife and children came—I knew them not.
> I died. My Mother followed. At her call
> And on her bosom I remembered all.

Vickery, as we hear of him, was in something like that condition of shock.

"Mrs Bathurst," with its cryptic quality, might be dismissed as a mere oddity. When we turn to **"Mary Postgate,"** however, the challenge to our human and moral judgment cannot be evaded. Here nothing is hidden; we are looking at Mary Postgate from beginning to end of the story, and everything relevant to understanding and judging her is supplied. **"Mary**

Postgate" has been more attacked than anything else Kipling wrote. No one denies that his full powers are engaged in this story, and some have regarded this as clinching their condemnation of him as a cruel writer who is here vicariously indulging a morbid passion of hatred and revenge. Now undeniably Kipling's writings during the First World War do show bitterness. There were poignant personal reasons for that. And he did not make the critical defence of **"Mary Postgate"** easier by appending to it a poem about how "the English began to hate," nor by including in the same volume, *A Diversity of Creatures,* the queer fantasy called **"Swept and Garnished,"** a sort of parody of **"They"** in a Berlin setting, which does show some signs of a desire for reprisal. But I believe that **"Mary Postgate,"** horrible as it is, can be shown to have the intelligence and insight which those who hate it wish to deny. It is certainly a tale of horror. The middle-aged English spinster gloating over the dying German airman—it is not a tableau that the reader will want to revert to very often. No one will deny that, in the circumstances of the story, Mary Postgate's indulgence is understandable, if still terrible. What is at issue is the author's attitude towards it. (pp. 269-72)

It will be clear that the diagnosis of Mary Postgate's contradictory state of mind, due to her emotional upheaval, is fully given; we have only to reflect on the contrast between her words on hearing of Wynn's death, and her self-justification for hating the German airman. What those who condemn Kipling would say is that the author is quite aware of the moral incoherence of Mary, but exploits her as a vent for the release of emotions which a sahib himself cannot admit that he feels; women, as contradictory and inferior beings, can be allowed the indulgence which the author himself desires. But this amounts to attributing to Kipling—the Kipling of this story—the outlook of young Wynn. It ignores the careful art of the story in avoiding any sentimentalisation of Mary or Wynn or the relationship between them. Above all, it ignores the essential identity—symbolic, of course, not literal—between the dying airman and Wynn. (He too, like Wynn, has fallen from his aeroplane.) The tale perhaps could not have been written by someone who had not experienced the agony of the bereaved civilian in war-time. But what it gives us is not a self-indulgence, but art: the imaginative understanding of what has happened to a Mary Postgate, and the moral intelligence to direct our horror to what *is* horrible, the stripping of a human soul, war and the cruelty of war.

It is natural to contrast the compassion of the later tale, **"The Gardener,"** with the cruelty of **"Mary Postgate."** But this contrast need not be used to emphasise a change of heart in Kipling. No doubt the dates are significant; **"Mary Postgate"** belongs to 1915, **"The Gardener"** to 1926. But the dramatic self-sufficiency of each tale is complete. **"The Gardener"** is a piece of grave irony; the ironic tone is sustained to the very end. What is remarkable is that this irony does not preclude—indeed, is the medium for—compassion. (pp. 273-74)

[It] may be said that, though **"The Gardener"** is one of Kipling's best stories, it is hardly typical of him. And, indeed, it may well be that Kipling's best stories are not his most representative. We do not find, in the stories I have discussed, the typical Kipling "world-picture," the emphasis on the tribal and the arcane, the passion for being an initiate, "one of the brotherhood," in the know, and above all, the overriding insistence on the Law. Certainly this "world-picture" never disappears from Kipling's work, and it is one of the things that

makes it hard to describe his art as showing development. To bring out the essential line of continuity in Kipling's work we may look finally at one of his latest stories, **"Dayspring Mishandled"** (1928). This tale is so sombre and bitter in feeling, as well as so complex and elliptical in style, that it is not at first easy to recognise the closeness of its relationship to one of Kipling's most characteristic and frequently exploited *genres:* the story of a hoax. The place of these stories in Kipling's work, and his sense of the ludicrous in general, is not always understood. Often the *ethos* of his comedies seems to contradict what we all tend to regard as the most fundamental of Kipling's beliefs—the necessity of obedience to the Law. It need not be stressed how often this is reiterated, in different keys, all over Kipling's work. It is the message of the *Jungle Books.* Purun Bhagat, in his withdrawal to the contemplative life, is "looking for a law of his own." St Paul in another story tells the neurotic sea-captain to serve Caesar: then, at least, he will be following some sort of law. Yet, in the farces, law and order is constantly being flouted with the author's evident approval. This comes out oddly in *Stalky & Co.* The message of the book is ostensibly the breaking-in of the young colts by the benevolent Chirons. But most of the action in fact consists of a series of rags and practical jokes in which the school authorities are constantly being disobeyed and outwitted. How is this contradition reconciled in Kipling's world-picture?

The answer seems to be that Kipling's emotional interest in hoaxes is closely connected with his feeling about imaginative creation. All his practical jokers are artists, but artists in the manipulation of men and circumstances rather than the usual media of art. There is no mistaking the creative joy of the impresario Bat Masquerier in his organising of the vast hoax of **"The Village that Voted."** It may be, as indeed is indicated in the story, morally irresponsible. But by itself it represents a triumph of imagination, as much as the scheme of conquest in **"The Man who would be King."** In imaginative creation man seems to be a free agent, no longer the powerless victim of circumstances and forces outside his control. So Kipling's delight in the farcical hoax is not really in contradiction with that sense of the impotence of the lonely individual which makes him insist so strongly on the necessity of subordination to the law or the tribe. The hoax, as work of art, supplies an emotional holiday, in allowing man the illusion of freedom.

What is remarkable about **"Dayspring Mishandled"** is that, uniquely in Kipling, it is both the story of a hoax and a tragedy. And the tragedy resides precisely in the eventual demonstration, in the story, that human freedom *is* an illusion and that man is powerless. **"Dayspring Mishandled"** is a tale of revenge; or rather, of a plan for revenge to which a man devotes his whole life without ever carrying it out. The scheme of revenge thus remains a pure imaginative creation, but one in the elaboration of which the essence of a man's life has been drained away. (pp. 275-76)

Many readers have found **"Dayspring Mishandled"** difficult. In its elliptical mode of narrative, significant turns and developments are played down. The point at which Manallace's "real life-work" began is indicated cryptically. It is never quite clear just what Castorley's original offence was—the offence that has poisoned two lives. And the business of Lady Castorley and the doctor, Gleeag, remains somewhat obscure. But these obscurities are appropriate in a tale which deals so much in the hidden springs of action. Manallace himself cannot have been clear about the motive which led him first to delay and then to abandon the consummation of his life's work. We must not overlook the element of compassion. But it would seem that the main reason was that he was an artist, a worker in the imagination. The plot against Castorley became an end in itself. He could not bear to see his art transposed into the world of action, because in that art, although the impulse to create it sprang from hatred and revenge, he could feel the creator's delight. **"Dayspring Mishandled"** can thus be seen to occupy a similar place in Kipling's work to that of "Bartleby the Scrivener" in Melville's. Both are bitter parables of the artist and his illusory "freedom." It seems appropriate that a discussion of some of Kipling's later tales should close with so poignant an example of his general sense—which is here a tragic sense—of the ultimate powerlessness of man. (pp. 277-78)

W. W. Robson, "Kipling's Later Stories," in Kipling's Mind and Art: Selected Critical Essays, edited by Andrew Rutherford, Stanford University Press, 1964, pp. 255-78.

J. M. S. TOMPKINS (essay date 1965)

[*Tompkins was an English essayist and academic. In the following excerpt from her The Art of Rudyard Kipling, she traces psychological, physical, and supernatural themes of healing in Kipling's short stories.*]

The theme of healing is not, like that of revenge, one of Kipling's original themes. It emerges strongly in what I have called the halcyon period of his art, the tales that were collected in *Actions and Reactions* and *Rewards and Fairies,* and continues to act as a powerful focus of his imagination until in *Limits and Renewals* half the tales are, in one way or another, concerned with it. It is not, therefore, a development due to the War, though the War gave it a special colouring and stimulated its growth. In so far as it appears at all in his earlier work, it is incidental or consequential. The famine in **"William the Conqueror"** is the test of Scott's quality and the setting of his love for a girl who shares his work and his allegiance. When she sees him in the sunset, 'a young man, beautiful as Paris, a god in a halo of golden dust, walking slowly at the head of his flocks, while at his knee ran small naked cupids'—the children he has saved by his 'absurd' performances with goats—Kipling can use the simile of the god, not only because of the pastoral grouping, but because Scott has been indeed the preserver of life and restorer of hope. The stress of the tale, however, lies on work and service and the kind of woman who understands their claims, not specifically on healing. Elsewhere the string is slightly touched now and again. Thus Kim, 'overborne by strain, fatigue, and the weight beyond his years', is drenched, massaged and fed back into life by the Sahiba, in a packed page in which the sense of wonder, so strong all through the book, sweeps in the ancient curative methods of the East; while, when the little boy of **"Baa Baa, Black Sheep"** returns from the House of Desolation to the security of his mother's love, we see a sample of her dealings with him.

It is significant that *Actions and Reactions* begins and ends with a tale of healing. It is the new theme. In the collections of his middle and later life, Kipling seems to have intended the first and last tales to serve as the pillars of an archway, corresponding to each other in some part of their meaning, and framing the section of life we see between them. This refinement in arrangement begins with *Many Inventions,* but

it is not apparent unless we take the 'tides' that overset poor Dowse's mind in **"The Disturber of Traffic"** in the sense that they bear in the introductory poem, as 'the wheel and drift of things', the terrible 'toil' of the Lord, which must be veiled from man lest he should see too clearly for his sanity. If we do this, the connection with **"The Children of the Zodiac"** is sufficiently clear, though the modes of the two tales are entirely different. In the allegory we have the 'trampling stars'—the Heavenly Houses that destroy men at the appointed time—and the 'veil' of daily life and necessary labour that hangs between men and the mystery of their fate and enables them to support it. In *The Day's Work* the two visionary tales, **"The Bridge Builders"** and **"The Brushwood Boy"**, frame the concrete, busy, limited world between them and give it another dimension. I should not care to make too much of the correspondences between **"The Captive"** and **"Below the Mill Dam"** in *Traffics and Discoveries,* but Zigler's half-amused, half disconcerted experience of British phlegm in South Africa is confronted by a demand that Britain shall be brought up to date. There is substance in Zigler's criticism, and the lessons of the Boer War have not all been well learnt. *A Diversity of Creatures* has an ironic opposition of first and last tales. The far view of the world of the future, when war is unthinkable and few men see death, is answered by **"Mary Postgate"** In *Debits and Credits* there are no substantial links between **"The Enemies to Each Other"** and **"The Gardener"**. *Limits and Renewals,* however, beginning with the reduction to nullity of Manallace's life—a limit that cannot be passed—ends with the ultimate renewals of **"Uncovenanted Mercies"**.

In the first tale of *Actions and Reactions,* **"An Habitation Enforced"**, the healing is already at all levels, physical, intellectual and spiritual. George Chapin, broken by the pace and strain of the American financial world, and his wife Sophie find health and satisfaction in the ancient, composed, fruitful life of the English countryside. When Kipling made his first acquaintance with country life in Vermont, ten years before, he wrote in "From Tideway to Tideway" that there the visitor 'is set down to listen to the normal beat of his own heart—a sound that very few men have ever heard'. This was in the New England winter, and the conditions and his own sensitiveness exaggerated the rarity of the discovery. **"An Habitation Enforced"** is soaked in summer air, and the heartbeat that steadies the Chapins is the pulse of nature, of rural society and, to quote Mr Eliot, of the past in the present. Sophie, delighted and growing daily into closer comradeship with her husband, thrusts her roots at once into the good soil; George, more uncertain of himself and suspicious of his surroundings, takes longer to yield to acclimatization, but the birth of his son and the restoration of the derelict estate he buys in the Weald combine to fix him. These agencies are the magical elements of **"A Charm"**, with which Kipling introduced *Rewards and Fairies.* . . . Often Kipling takes pains to relate or juxtapose the healing of the flesh and of the soul, as he does in **"The Eye of Allah"**. It is when the Abbot of St Illod's, himself a physician, is storing the opium from Spain in the cell behind the hospital kitchen-chimney, that he speaks to the young artist, whose mistress is dead, of the pain of the soul for which 'there is, outside God's Grace, but one drug; and that is a man's craft, learning, or other helpful motion of his own mind'. The tales that turn on the ills of the soul sometimes employ fantasy; for the healing of an aching imagination Kipling in **"On the Gate"** and **"Uncovenanted Mercies"** uses the salves the imagination itself can provide. It is the comprehensiveness of the theme, at many levels and in many connections, that makes the classification of these tales as tales of disease or of neurosis inadequate. It is as if we called Shakespeare's Romances plays of error and loss. They are so; but the description is insufficient. It is against the pervasiveness of the conception of healing in the later books that we see, in strong relief, the tragedies of those who are not healed, Manallace's mistakes in diagnosis and Helen's erroneous treatment of her hurt. Even within the tales of restoration there are marginal figures who are not so lucky. In **"Fairy-Kist"** Wollin is saved, and the interest of the tale is focused on his saving, but Jimmy Tigner, standing unsteadily in the surf, is casually washed back to sea. 'He'd been tried too high—too high', says Keede. 'I had to sign his certificate a few weeks later. No! he won't get better.' (pp. 158-61)

"The House Surgeon", the last tale in *Actions and Reactions,* leads us into shadows and uncertainties. The house of the title, open and sunny like Friar's Pardon in **"An Habitation Enforced"**, is not, like that, a healing presence but requires to have its own evil excised. This is a bodiless oppression of despair and horror, directed on it at times 'like a burning glass', and followed, when it is shut off, by a 'live grief beyond words', as if it were a dumb thing's helpless desire to explain. The evil is diagnosed when 'I' traces the former owner, a rigid, elderly, unlovely Evangelical spinster, who is convinced that her younger sister's fall from a window was suicide and consigned her to damnation. The house and its innocent inmates are filled with the reflection of her obsessed brooding. When, after a narrow escape from a similar fall herself, Miss Moultrie is persuaded to revisit the house and examine the window, the house is cleansed. We do not enter the room with her or know what intimations she received, but the burden of the double anguish is lifted.

This tale is closely related in subject and treatment to two in Kipling's next book [*A Diversity of Creatures*], **"In the Same Boat"** and **"The Dog Hervey"**. The first of these is straightforward; it is also the only one of the three in which the mysterious and painful manifestations are completely rationalized, leaving no residue of the preternatural. The horrific recurrent dreams that afflict Conroy and Miss Henschil, hanging between them and natural life, are ascribed in the end to pre-natal shock; the images in them—the accident at sea, the encounter with lepers on the sandy, windy island—derive from the experiences of their mothers before they were born. **"The Dog Hervey"** is to me Kipling's most difficult tale, but it is the details that are difficult, not the theme. This can be defined without misgiving. The desolate longing of a woman makes a vehicle for itself out of the little sickly dog she cherishes, and projects its wraith into the hallucinations of the drunkard who, years before, was kind to her. This, then, is a tale of sorcery, of such a 'sending' as we might read of in a northern folk-tale or find paralleled in the beliefs of a savage people. The scene, however, is contemporary, and the unhappy plight of the young 'witch' is carefully accounted for. It is not unlike that of Conrad's Flora de Barral, though Moira Sichliffe has no comeliness and no romantic love to cloak her, but is everyway ungainly and embarrassing, though courageous. The 'mid-Victorian mansion of peculiar villainy', where she lives, was the home where her father, a retired doctor, received 'stormy' young men, patched them up, insured them heavily, and 'let them out into the world again—with an appetite!' One man, Shend, saved her from the insults to which she was exposed, but he has effaced himself, for honourable reasons. Moira is not aware of her power, and is troubled by the behaviour of the dog on whom she discharges her anguished love and deprivation. Harvey's sickliness, like Shend's drunken illusions, is a state penetrable by the psychic force. The dog is bewildered and suffers; he sits outside one particular door in the corridor where the young men used to be kept, and he fixes the narrator with 'an intense, lop-sided stare', as if trying to attain some object through him. The function of 'I' in this tale is much what it was in **"The House Surgeon"**; he does not here deliberately explore the strange currents that flow past him, but he is sensitive to them; perhaps in some measure they work through him, too, but this is to me the obscurest part of the story, and I am not sure how Kipling conceived the psychic mechanism that made the shadow perceptible beside the closed door and convinced Shend that the squinting dog in his delusions knew his fellow-traveller, or whether, indeed, we are to understand that the dog's appearances began, or grew more frequent, after he met the narrator. At all events, 'I' acts as liaison, bridges the separation of the loveers, and removes the obstructions to the healing exercise of love. In so doing he also returns Harvey, 'cowering beneath some unfair burden', to natural doghood, and the joyous flurry of a normal dog-fight brings the tale momentarily into full daylight. At the end, 'I' declining to attempt an explanation, calls the strange sequence of events 'all woman-work', and says it scared him horribly.

It is hard to find direct evidence in Kipling's work for what is sometimes said, that his attitude to women retained something of primitive awe, yet it carries conviction; it provides the counterweight to his belief that she should not attempt to play a man's part in a man's world. In **"The Pleasure-Cruise"** one of the returned dead of the Great War, disquieted to find that 'the Island now stands again with shut eyes on the brink of fate', and that this is largely the responsibility of the women, wonders why they seek political power, since 'the power of women in themselves is dreadfully sufficient'. This is the power of Mrs Bathurst and of the frivolous little girl who destroyed Wressley of the Foreign Office. But beyond this, it seems, the unassuaged anguish or desire of a woman, not mitigated by the daily practical compromises of a man's life, can generate a psychic force like that exerted by Miss Moultrie or Moira Sichliffe, and this fits her to make contact, more readily than a man, with powers or existences outside human life. In Western civilization these powers are overlaid and forgotten. Miss Moultrie and Moira Sichliffe are ignorant of what they have done; they are unconscious 'witches'. When Kipling, therefore, deals with these borderlands of consciousness, setting his tales in a concrete, substantial modern world, with tennis-parties, hydropathic establishments, and the 10.8 train from Waterloo rolling out milkcans at every stop, he creates extreme types to enable the intrusion of the preternatural into it, the fanatic Miss Moultrie, the blind, craving woman in **"They"**, the lonely, contorted Moira Sichliffe and the archetypal peasant-woman, Grace Ashcroft. Like so many of his deep convictions, this leaves its traces, under carefully controlled conditions, in the children's books. There are Priestesses in **"The Knife and the Naked Chalk"**, who make prayers to the Old Dead in the Barrows, ask questions of the Gods and answer on their behalf, and hold in their hands the spiritual life of their tribes; nor does the woman in **"The Cat that Walked by Himself"**, even earlier in the history of man, require any instruction before she lets down her hair beside the fire and makes a Magic. She is a mother, and so is the Priestess of the Flint Men, and perhaps the figure of the Mother in Kipling, obscured as it often is with period draperies, holds some remnant of this ancient awe.

These three tales, then, are built with folk-lore material, a haunting, a sending and—to stretch the point a little—a curse. Since these influences are not willed but imposed in ignorance, all three tales illustrate the lines in "The Rabbi's Song", that follows **"The House Surgeon"** and closes *Actions and Reactions:*

> The arrows of our anguish
> Fly farther than we guess.

The victims who are stuck by the arrows are innocent and, in two tales, entirely ignorant of their source. Their world fills with a mysterious pain and darkness as the 'shadow of [the] past' moves over them, and the imaginative diversity and infectious force with which these sufferings are conveyed should of themselves suggest that we have to do with more than particular queer cases. When Nurse Blaber in **"In the Same Boat"** is able to confirm her patient's recovery by telling her how her dream originated, she says: 'You never imagined the thing. It was laid on you.' These tales are about the burdens that are laid on men, without any fault of theirs and sometimes because they have been doing their best. The hauntings in themselves constitute an upper layer of meaning; below that there is the ultimate mystery of the general condition of man, of which they are examples or symbols. Kipling had a profound sense of this strange and, to human judgment, unjust dispensation, as he had of the capacity of the human being for suffering and his loneliness in it. It is here that we find the likeness between these earlier tales and those of war injuries, which I consider later in this chapter.

If this is so, then any improbabilities that may appear in the medical parts of the tales, exceeding what might be expected as the result of the inevitable foreshortening of the form when its content is so complex, are only superficial flaws. They cannot split the heart of the tale. In these three stories, however, professional healers play a very small part. They appear only in **"In the Same Boat",** and there they are concerned not with their patients' dreams, but with their addiction to a drug to which their misery has driven them. One of the specialists disbelieves in the dreams; the other has the imagination and boldness to attempt to break Conroy's self-centredness by putting his fellow-sufferer, Miss Henschil, in his charge on a night journey. Here, as in the other tales, it is love, of some kind, at some level, that is the true healer. The doctors, like 'I' in the other stories, place their patients in such a position that it can do its work. Their fellowship in misfortune, their efforts to help each other, have already saved and renewed their smothered souls, before Nurse Blaber, less sceptical and specialized than the doctors, is able to remove their last apprehensions. There is no need to comment on the lovers of **"The Dog Hervey".** In **"The House Surgeon"** it is Miss Moultrie's distorted and despairing love for her sister that has haunted the house; when the despair is abolished, the unburdened love can do its work of renewal, and even the unhealthy, ageing body moves youthfully again.

There is not, then, in these three tales, anything that directly illustrates the new principles and techniques in psychiatry of the twentieth century. These may, however, have been in Kipling's mind. The interest in them provided a climate of thought in which traditional material, that had a deep symbolic meaning for him, could be related to the reality of daily life and explored for its human content. There is a great difference between the early supernatural tales, **"The Return of Imray",** and **"The Lost Legion",** on one hand, where the traditional material is accepted and the writer devotes himself to evoking an atmosphere that will engender faith, and **"The House Surgeon", "In the Same Boat"** and **"The Dog Hervey"** on the other, which are moved by a positive moral force and by a far-reaching imagination, speculating on the unknown potentialities of human nature and the ways in which they may work. The likeness between the three later tales, however, does not permit us to assume that Kipling had a programme in writing them. The publication of them covers five years, and they are full of observations and interests and briefly seen sections of people's lives and occupations, as Kipling's later stories always are. (pp. 161-66)

Kipling's later tales hook into each other in all directions; if one is lifted up for inspection, several others come up attached to it; but the closest links are not always those that are at first apparent. Thus **"Unprofessional"** has been related to **"A Doctor of Medicine"** because both of them have to do with astrology, but the closer link is with **"Marklake Witches".** The two stories from *Rewards and Fairies* are companion pictures of medicine old and new, presented to the children, and no imaginative act of faith in astrology is required of them. Nicholas Culpeper's successful handling of the plague-stricken village is not, as he thinks, due to his reading of the stars, but to common-sense, devotion and a lucky chance. Puck takes his astrological expositions very lightly and puts down the victory to 'a high courage tempered with sound and stubborn conceit'; and the concluding verses, dismissing with amusement the world-picture of the introductory 'Astrologer's Song' as one of the 'enormous and manifold errors' of our fathers, praises their 'excellent heart', that wrought so well with such faulty tools. In **"Unprofessional",** however, the influence of the stars is taken seriously, and the 'tides' they cause in human cells are traced and logged with the latest scientific devices. Like **"Marklake Witches"** the tale deals with an advance in science, and with these two we may associate **"The Eye of Allah". "Marklake Witches"** is simplest, as befits one of the tales that children were to read 'before people realized that they were meant for grown-ups'. René Laennec, French prisoner on parole, discusses his invention, the stethoscope, with the shrewd local wise-man, and meets the hostility of superstitious fear in the village folk and of conservative professional jealousy in Dr Break. It will not deter him, but his science will not save the high-spirited girl who tells the tale, in ignorance of its meaning and of her own disease, nor the outer ring of the momentarily seen sick—old Gaffer Macklin and young Copper—not yet himself. This is a straightforward tale; **"The Eye of Allah"** is complex. It tells of the possibility of a great scientific advance that looms for an hour and is declined, because it is untimely. Abbot Stephen destroys in the presence of Roger Bacon the microscope that John the artist has brought from the Moorish parts of Spain. But though the problem of scientific advance in a world not ready for it is central, the tale, like many of Kipling's, is doing several things at once. The scientist is contrasted not only with Abbot Stephen, the administrator, but with John of Burgos, the artist, 'to whom men were but matter for drawings'. John makes no protest against the breaking of the Eye of Allah; he has used it to get 'patterns' for the devils he has limned in his Great Luke, and has finished with it; his trade, he says, is with the outside shapes of things. Abbot Stephen, however, is a physician, like Roger of Salerno and Thomas the Infirmarian who, with Roger Bacon, plead against the destruction; he knows well what he does and why. The image of birth knits the themes together. John's Jewish mistress dies in childbed. He himself brings his stored conceptions triumphantly to birth. But when Abbot Stephen destroys the microscope under the hungry eyes of the men of science, a birth is aborted. 'The choice lies between two sins. To deny the world a Light which is under our hand, or to enlighten the world before her time.' When the little group of monks, ruler, artist, scientist and working physicians, walk on the leads to get foul water to put under the Eye of Allah, they see, in one of Kipling's marvellous compressed sentences of landscape, atmosphere, period and symbol

> three English counties laid out in evening sunshine around them; church upon church, monastery upon monastery, cell after cell, and the bulk of a vast cathedral moored on the edge of the banked shoals of sunset.

The moored cathedral is a ship of war, not yet wrecked on shoals in the blindness between one day and the next. The whole principle of order of their world lies in beauty and visible menace round them. It is not only that the audacious scientist would face the fire, but that in the struggle what order there is would be shaken and debased. The Eye of Allah would but bring 'more division and greater darkness in this dark age'. Western man is not yet ready to see with it. The claws of the *immedicabile cancer* that has gripped Anne of Norton are not yet to be blunted. (pp. 167-69)

In **"The Children of the Zodiac"**, the earliest tale in which cancer occurs, it is certainly symbolic, but certainly not of rejected love. The whole fable is an arrangement of symbols. It is a statement of the conditions of human life and of the spirit in which these can be supported, and the characters are drawn from the ancient Signs of the Zodiac. Half of these are the mysterious slayers of men from their heavenly Houses; the others (but Kipling counts the Twins as two and omits the Goat) wander on earth and, conforming in time to the modes of human life, are able, as half-gods, to strengthen and comfort men, though at the cost of sharing their experience. Given this scheme, it was obvious that the Archer and the Crab must be slayers, the lords of the quick and the slow doom. The procedure of the Crab is wholly appropriate; it touches the Girl on her woman's breast, and she goes on loving, and Leo, the singer, on the apple of his throat, and he sings his song to the end. But this gigantic Crab is much more than a specific disease; it is all the sorrow and evil of the world that tries to stifle the singer's voice and fastens on the heart of his wife. The arbitrary division of the Signs, not merely into the benevolent and the malevolent, but into beings of two different orders, confuses the allegory. (pp. 171-72)

It was natural that Kipling should be drawn to write of . . . obscure and tragic injuries. He had already explored the shadow-world, trodden in loneliness and fear by the mind that feels its sanity giving way under strain. He had also explored the mysterious borderlines of consciousness and haunted places and people. These hauntings are sometimes merely recorded, sometimes tentatively explained, but it is not until his later work that they are exorcized and the wounds of consciousness healed. With this change of interest, as I have already indicated, the tales take up a new element, that of detection. There enters them a character, often serving as narrator, who gropes for a clue and aims at a solution. He may be a professional healer or an amateur cast by chance for the part. The cases are often intricate, and there is more commentary and explanation than Kipling usually conceded. There is also in two of the pre-war tales, as has been seen, an irreducible element of the preternatural. With the appearance of the war cases, this preternatural element drops out. There

was no need to look for strange and exceptional cases; too many were present in the accepted order of things. The thought that we are fearfully and wonderfully made had always been much in Kipling's mind. He had dealt in types, but he had been far from over-simplifying human nature. Now he shows himself more and more aware of the frailty of man's body and brain, his liability to manifold injury, his capacity for suffering and his fortitude in it. We have these treasures in earthen vessels. (pp. 174-75)

There remain other expressions of the theme of healing of a quite different kind. These are the indulgences of the imagination, the oases, or mirages, of the wilderness. Like *Cymbeline* or *Winter's Tale,* they reveal a permitted play of the compassionate fancy, restoring, healing, renewing, 'making up' in terms of the imagination for the uncomforted miseries, the irretrievable mistakes, that lie outside the charmed circle. Sometimes Kipling draws the circle on common earth, enclosing common miseries, and, once it is drawn, not only are the miseries and the aching imagination that recorded them assuaged, but even the daily chattels within the circle are refined to an unmatched perfection. Thus he joyously elaborates the perfect equipment of a tobacconist's shop, a research laboratory, and a Masonic Lodge. Even in a tale that is not in the least concerned with healing, he will allow himself some unexpected salvage. In **"The Bull that Thought"**, Apis, the brilliant and brutal artist among bulls, comes alive out of a Spanish bull-ring, and Chisto, the inferior matador, 'a laborious, middle-aged professional who had never risen above a certain dull competence', retrieves and achieves for one miraculous hour 'the desire, the grace, and the beauty of his early dreams'. The French stock-breeder, who tells the tale, ascribes to Apis, the unique bull that thought, 'the detachment of the true artist who knows he is but the vessel of an emotion whence others, not he, must drink'. There is something less than such complete detachment in some of these tales of Kipling's old age, and the artist moistens his lip at the fountain of his own fantasy. Sometimes the charm detaches him from earth, and in a mood of mercy, veined with mischief, he designs, 'with brushes of comets' hair', the landscapes of Heaven and Hell, the impressive Department of Normal Civil Death, with the temporary extension of the war-sheds clustering round its knees, or the vast organization where the damned souls are 'reconditioned for re-issue'. Not all the products of this mood are his best work, but it is difficult to grudge them to an old artist who knows so well what he is doing. Nor does he ever carry us quite out of sound of the sea of human misery; indeed, it is a condition of the charm that it should not be forgotten. (pp. 182-83)

> *J. M. S. Tompkins, in her* The Art of Rudyard Kipling, *second edition, University of Nebraska Press, 1965, 277 p.*

J. I. M. STEWART   (essay date 1966)

[*An English novelist and literary scholar, Stewart has written and edited numerous works in a variety of genres. Among his scholarly texts are studies of William Shakespeare and biographies of Rudyard Kipling, Thomas Hardy, and Joseph Conrad. Under the pseudonym of Michael Innes, Stewart has also been a prolific writer of crime novels centering on academic and aristocratic characters. In the following excerpt from his critical biography of Kipling, Stewart assesses Kipling's ability as a children's writer.*]

The **Jungle Books** (1894-1895) were written in Vermont, and initiate a phase of Kipling's career in which he can be considered as having become a writer for children. On a superficial view, one might regard this development as being the consequence of some failure of confidence in himself as a "serious" author. He certainly did not so estimate the situation. Writing retrospectively in *Something of Myself,* he has more to say about the group of children's books than about any other—and indeed it is his main point that only in a limited sense ought they to be regarded as children's books at all. Most mature readers who like Kipling will be found to agree with him in this. And the books are most keenly appreciated by those who read them first in childhood (or listened to them being read) and have then come back to them in later life. This is the road to finding those layers of significance which Kipling, in fact, claimed to have put into them.

A child's natural start is with *Just So Stories* (1902), which is above everything else a nursery book. Nothing in English is more unchallengeably the work of one who possessed the art of telling stories to children, and who enjoyed exercising it. The narrative style, seemingly so naïve and spontaneous, represents in fact one of the most notable triumphs of Kipling's craft. And here he had to overcome a bad or unreflecting habit which he had caught from the taste of the age: that of introducing into writing for or about children a sentimental convention of baby talk. In the *Just So Stories* the element of misapplied, invented and oddly transformed words renders a wholly different effect. It is felt from the start as part of the ritual of a special or secret language which the narrator shares with his hearers, and it is associated with infancy only in the sense of wonderfully suggesting the infancy of the world, when all creatures and things were pristine and plastic still. The style is, moreover, and in a degree varying from story to story and from place to place within a story, incantatory and therefore full of a strong magic; and it is capable (as in **"The Sing-Song of Old Man Kangaroo"**) of compassing rhythmical effects which are totally new.

The *Just So Stories* are often compared with Lewis Carroll's *Alice's Adventures in Wonderland* and *Through the Looking-Glass* as the greatest English achievements in writing for young children. Carroll shares with Kipling the faculty of appealing to children and adults alike. With each there is a certain hit-or-miss element to be observed, since there are some children and adults upon whom the magic of one, or both, fails to work. Each inhabits what must be called a real world, although it is certainly not an actual world. Carroll's is the world of dream, although of dream at once drastically censored and cunningly intellectualized in the interest of a rather egg-headed Victorian nursery. Kipling's is the world of myth.

Most of the *Just So Stories,* indeed, are myths of one particular kind: the kind technically known as aetiological. An aetiological myth is one evolved—generally in a more or less "primitive" society—to explain and render intelligible some existing state of affairs which in itself perplexes and challenges the human spirit. The most famous of all aetiological myths is that of the Creation and Fall of Man as it is recounted in the Book of Genesis. In this, answers to nearly all the great riddles are bound together within a single narrative satisfying to the imagination—and satisfying, too, to the intellect working within the limits of a "pre-scientific" cultural context. The *Just So Stories* are little myths solving little riddles: how the camel got anything so strange as a hump, and the elephant anything so strange as a trunk. It is true that, to be quite accurate, we must qualify the description of these stories as myths. They have been invented for the satisfaction not of a primitive people but of modern children, who are "primitive" only in the metaphorical sense that their intellectual development does, to some extent, recapitulate the course of human evolution. This is why the stories are made to hover—and, again, it is a miracle of craft—between a level of fantasy and a level of simple conviction. So in one aspect they are like make-believe games, such as children love. In another, they are an introduction to one of the great literary kinds—a kind reflecting something radical in the development of the human imagination. To appreciate *Just So Stories* is to establish a basis for appreciating *Paradise Lost* or *Moby Dick.*

The fame of *The Jungle Book* and *The Second Jungle Book*—the most widely popular of all Kipling's writings—is owing to their central figure, Mowgli, the child nurtured by wolves, who survives and grows to manhood as Master of the Jungle. Mowgli's origin (as a literary creation, that is) is attended by some obscurity, and it is best to begin with the last that we hear about him. This is in **"In the Rukh"** (*Many Inventions*), a story designed to be entirely realistic, and quite certainly not written for young readers. (pp. 136-39)

What is interesting about **"In the Rukh"** is the entire absence of the magic which the *Jungle Books* were going to create. Kipling has not yet glimpsed what material he has under his hand; this Mowgli is an implausible mixture of Noble Savage, Indian native properly respectful of the raj, and a godling strayed out of Greek mythology in a manner rather reminiscent of some of the more whimsical short stories of Mr. E. M. Forster. Mowgli plays a flute, "as it might have been the song of some wandering wood-god." This last association is emphasized; "the hint of the wood-god was not to be mistaken," we are told a few pages later.

"In the Rukh" was almost certainly written before Kipling had conceived the Mowgli stories proper, but in its published form it may embody revisions designed to make it fit in with the evolving series. As it is, Mowgli's story seems to have been developed without much planning. Taking the two *Jungle Books* together, he appears in eight out of fifteen stories—including the first, which begins with his being adopted by wolf parents, and the last, which tells of his final departure from the world of the beasts. That there is true imaginative coherence between the Mowgli stories proper appears as soon as we try to set this last of them, **"The Spring Running,"** in any relationship with **"In the Rukh."** The Mowgli of **"In the Rukh"** walks into the story with nothing much behind him except (with an obvious effect of paradox) certain unusual educational advantages. "Hard exercise, the best of good eating, and baths whenever he felt in the least hot or dusty, had given him strength and growth far beyond his age." He is a cross between a Wordsworthian child of nature and a boy scout. He walks out of the story at the other end in the company of a nice girl and with the intention of settling down. He knows all the answers—just as the uninspired Kipling always did. The Mowgli of **"The Spring Running,"** on the contrary, knows neither his world nor himself with any certainty, because he is a human spirit in the throes of some painful and mysterious process of growth. It is Spring. "The year turns," Bagheera the Black Panther tells him. "The Jungle goes forward. The Time of New Talk is near." Mowgli must have heard this before. But now he is on the verge of manhood, and there faces him a hard truth, obscurely seen. A boy may run with the Jungle People, but "Man goes to Man." His old companions do not reject him, but—this Spring, he notices it—they come tardily at his summons, having concerns which can be none of his. Yet all this, and the mere surface solution of his problem in the last pages of the story, make too finite and identifiable the occasion of the unhappiness that has come to Mowgli. Something else is elusively present.

This is a characteristic of all the Mowgli stories. All are moral fables—even to the extent of sometimes making us feel that Mowgli is over-lavishly provided with tutors, and is rather constantly having to put up with what the hymn calls Instruction's warning Voice. But this is not, in fact, oppressive—perhaps because there is always some hinted further significance which we have to strain to catch. Take, for example, the monkey-folk, the *Bandar-log.* They stand for something outside themselves, answer to something in our own experience which we are not proud of. But just what? Here, and in some other places, the fable beckons us to territory where we must think for ourselves. And there is one puzzle bigger than all the others. It is what the books mean when they talk about "the Law." (pp. 140-42)

If we wish to criticize the whole conception we shall probably say that, here in the context of the *Jungle Books,* Kipling is casting the impressive disguise of authentic moral law over certain aspects of animal behaviour instinctively evolved to secure the survival of a species. To test the validity of this criticism we should have to enter deeply into Kipling's theory of society. He certainly believed that moral ideas can be derived only from experience, but that as there is much that is common and universal in all human experience so is there a common and universal law lying beneath all the variations of racial and national cultures. It is a law codified in custom, and its recognition and preservation is the distinguishing principle of civilization. Peoples or societies or individuals ignoring "the Law" thereby diminish themselves—becoming (in the famous and unfortunately ambiguous phrase in "Recessional") "lesser breeds." To show a wolf pack as within "the Law," and a chatter of monkeys as outside it, is simply to use the method of fable to enforce the depth and reach of the idea. But to account for the appeal of the *Jungle Books* we have to go back to Kipling's almost unexampled command of the sense of wonder; his power to bring, as from very far away, reports which validate themselves in the telling, so that our disbelief is suspended in the face of whole new ranges of experience. (pp. 143-44)

> *J. I. M. Stewart, in his* Rudyard Kipling, *Dodd, Mead & Company, 1966, 245 p.*

ELLIOT L. GILBERT (essay date 1971)

[*In the following excerpt from his* The Good Kipling: Studies in the Short Story, *Gilbert discusses Kipling's technique in "The Arrest of Lt. Golightly," disputing critics who consider Kipling's early short fiction "simple-minded journalism."*]

In the early eighteen-nineties, when [Kipling] was just beginning to make his literary reputation, much criticism of his works centered on what were then regarded as inadequacies in his style. By some readers the young author was taken to task for what was considered the insufferably knowing tone of some of his stories, for his complacent, almost vulgar clubbiness, for his transparent attempts to seem a blasé insider, privy to every sort of official secret. To others, his pieces, especially those in *Plain Tales from the Hills,* seemed too journalistic, too breezy in presentation, too slap-dash and chatty.

"The style," C. E. Carrington writes, "is that of the gossip-column" [see Further Reading list]. The charge could safely be made, since much of Kipling's work, up to the time of his first appearance in London, had been done in his capacity as newspaper reporter and editor and since most of the pieces in *Plain Tales* had originally been written to order as filler for *The Civil and Military Gazette.*

Still, the criticism is a reasonable one, for Kipling often appeared to be taking the easy way out in his narratives, intruding himself baldly into his tales in order to save time, addressing his readers directly, explaining instead of dramatizing. Indeed, this habit of including himself in the cast of characters of his own stories earned him some of his harshest rebukes. The nine-days wonder of the literary world seemed to many critics to be, in the words of Francis Adams, "full of sickening egotism and vanity," no more, in short, than "a little-brained second-rate journalist," a phrase which strikingly anticipates the judgment of a large percentage—perhaps even a majority—of sophisticated readers today. It may be worth while, however, considering with care one or two of Kipling's more apparently trivial and "second-rate" journalistic endeavors, for while the negative view of much of this work predominates among intellectuals, as sensitive a reader as James Joyce is known to have felt that the "little-brained" and gossipy-seeming *Plain Tales from the Hills* showed "more promise than any other contemporary writer's youthful work."

Any one of the pieces from *Plain Tales,* chosen at random, would serve our purpose, but ideally, we ought to consider a tale which Adams himself might have selected as a good example of the sort of simple-minded journalism which Kipling supposedly produced during his apprentice years. **"The Arrest of Lt. Golightly"** is such a story. It is hardly a profound tale and is certainly not the most memorable of the forty vignettes in the collection. It has never had any critical consideration, as some of the other stories in the book have, nor is there anything particularly surprising about this neglect. The episode in which Lieutenant Golightly figures seems little more than a "slight anecdote," as Professor Carrington has called it, a farcical interlude, a joke. (pp. 51-2)

Yet for all its slightness, **"The Arrest of Lieutenant Golightly"** is a wonderfully artful piece of work. Analysis of it shows that Kipling had this early found not only the subject matter of his later fiction, but also the major themes; and that even at the beginning of his career he was already a quite conscious artist, skillful at embodying an idea in action without sacrificing any of that action's ability to entertain. For example, what is important about Lieutenant Golightly is that he is a young man whose special nature it is to see and deal with the world superficially. His ticket name suggests as much, and we are not surprised to learn that the young officer is proud of his ability to get through life in "light marching-order." His preoccupation with clothes is the most immediate indication of his character. Traditionally in literature, an obsession with personal appearance and especially with clothing is the mark of a superficial man, usually of a man who must be taught a lesson. Kipling is obviously writing in this tradition, and he reinforces our impression of Golightly by introducing him at once as a man who is proud—that word appears often in the story—of "looking like 'an officer and a gentleman.'" Of *looking* like an officer and a gentleman. Appearances would seem to be quite enough for Golightly, at least at first. By the end of the story we will find him, foolish and unaware as ever, taking exactly the opposite stand without at all knowing what he is doing.

This superficiality of Golightly's, symbolized by his passion for clothes, is further dramatized by the trip from Dalhousie to the railway station at Pathankote. Golightly's notions about how the universe works seem to be as lightheaded as his ideas about clothes making the man. The lieutenant prides himself on his "faculty of organization," but the plans he makes require for their success a sweetly reasonable and orderly world, more than anxious to be subdued. And such a world, Kipling would have us understand, does not exist; anyone, he says repeatedly in his best stories, who fails to see that the universe is a chaotic, irrational place, hostile to man, and who fails to come to terms with that universe, is certain to suffer. And no one more certain than Lieutenant Golightly, whose whole style of life, like the helmet that he wears, is made for sunny days and collapses grotesquely in the rain.

Golightly, ready to start on his trip, makes plans for the superficial world of his own invention, plans designed to save him trouble and to help him travel in light marching-order. But no sooner has he set out on his journey than the-world-as-it-really-is begins to encroach on these plans. Almost at once, and quite unreasonably, clouds appear and begin to produce a "good, tepid, monsoonish downpour." Golightly

Title page from an early British edition of Wee Willie Winkie, and Other Stories.

has not, of course, included an umbrella in his plans, but he consoles himself with the thought of the fresh clothes and the supply of money he has cleverly sent on ahead with his servant. Unfortunately, the delightful perversity of that servant is also no part of Golightly's plan. "He did not know . . . that his *khitmatgar* would stop by the roadside to get drunk, and would come on the next day saying that he had sprained his ankle." Thus the universe is quick to punish Golightly for his presumption, and to punish him in a most appropriate way. Item by item it destroys the clothes of which he is so inordinately and foolishly fond and in the act of destroying them reveals their shoddiness.

The thematic use that Kipling makes of this episode may help to explain why he lavished such care on his description of Golightly's undoing, why every detail of the disintegration is so lovingly presented. The plot of the story requires a complete alteration in Golightly's appearance, and so Kipling must do his best to make the later confusion of identities plausible by describing elaborately the effects of the monsoon on the lieutenant's clothes. But more important, it is the gross inadequacy of Golightly's style of life, and certainly not any sadistic penchant on Kipling's part for making people uncomfortable, that produces the young officer's very special and picturesque disaster. The author obviously relishes the scene, but the description throughout is good-natured and the final phrase quite charming. "The effect," Kipling writes of the mingling of purple and green dyes on the lieutenant's face and neck, "was amazing."

The transformation of the proud, handsome young officer of Dalhousie into the filthy, nearly naked apparition who struggles on foot into Pathankote is only the first of many ironic reversals that Kipling presents in the course of his story. Golightly has not been in town long, for example, when he is mistaken for a runaway army private, is arrested in the act of arranging for a railway ticket by the Station-Master and four constables, and begins to receive some unpleasant instruction in the old adage about what happens to men who live by the sword. For the Station-Master and the constables are, like the young officer, also men who believe in the importance of appearances, and the one thing they are absolutely certain of is "that no lieutenant could look such a ruffian as did Golightly." Golightly begins to shout at his captors but only succeeds in confirming their suspicions. " 'Without doubt this is the soldier-Englishman we require,' " says the Station-Master. " 'Listen to the abuse!' "

The lieutenant is ignominiously bundled off and placed in the custody of a military search party whose members have been out looking for one Private John Binkel, deserter, and who now imagine that they have found him. And here the story takes an even more amusing turn. For as long as Golightly tries to maintain the artificial dignity of the officer he really is, the corporal and the two privates are disgusted. "This is a very absurd mistake, my men," Golightly begins priggishly, but his explanation is quickly interrupted. "*You* a orficer," says the corporal. "It's the like o' *you* as brings disgrace on the likes of *us*. Bloomin' fine orficer you are!" Which, in its convoluted way, is a not wholly unreasonable thing to say about the young lieutenant.

The moment, however, that Golightly, in his frustration, begins to shout and swear "like a trooper," he wins his captors over completely, all the while, of course, convincing them even further that he is the runaway private they have been looking for.

"I've heard a few beggars in the clink blind, stiff and crack on a bit; but I've never 'eard anyone to touch this 'ere orficer,' " [says one of the men.] They were not angry with him. They rather admired him. They had some beer at the refreshment room, and offered Golightly some too, because he had 'swore wonderful.'

The irony of all this, clearly, is that at last, and quite by chance, the reader has gotten down to something in Golightly that is real, that isn't a matter of illusion or appearance. For at bottom, it seems, Golightly is neither an officer nor a gentlemen, despite his elaborate efforts to look the part. What he really is becomes plain in this small crisis, and instantly the reality is recognized and the young lieutenant is gathered into the honest fellowship of the privates and the corporal. It is at this point that the mistaken identity is most outrageous, but, paradoxically, it is also at this point that Golightly is most truly and most appealingly himself.

Not that he knows it. Golightly is extraordinarily ignorant of the reasons for his own behavior. We have seen that when he acts, it is never on any sort of intelligent principle but only out of a concern for personal convenience. Thus his travel plans have nothing whatever to do with the realities of life on the road, but are designed solely to permit him to hurry along beautifully dressed and in unburdened comfort. Nor is his dandyism based on any strong conviction about the importance of appearances in life. Even worldliness can be elevated to the level of principle, but Golightly is a dandy only because dressing well is the most pleasant and least uncomfortable way he has found of demonstrating that he is an officer and a gentleman. This fact is plain from the way he handles himself in his crisis. Anyone powerfully committed to dandyism would, in Golightly's disreputable condition, have crept into town in an agony of self-consciousness, imagining, no doubt, that natives of the lowest caste were cutting him dead in the street.

Not so Golightly. No sooner does he arrive in Pathankote than he begins to go about his business as if nothing had happened to him. He looks for his servant, he orders a drink, he negotiates with the Station-Master for a ticket to Khasa, and a first-class ticket at that. This dandy, for whom, only a few hours before, appearances had been everything, now behaves as if he were wholly unaware of his own villainous appearance and, what's more, as if everyone else were unaware of it too. This is the cream of Kipling's jest. Golightly, under the pressure of circumstances, has shifted his ground. He has conveniently forgotten about the importance of *looking* like an officer and a gentleman and now takes the position that there is such a thing as a pure essence of gentlemanliness, which he clearly possesses and which ought to be asserting itself in spite of his unpromising appearance. So firmly does he maintain this position that in the end he passes the greater part of the summer "trying to get the corporal and the two soldiers tried by court-martial for arresting an 'officer and a gentleman.' "

Superbly unconscious throughout his adventure, Golightly is funny because he so determinedly fails to learn the truth either about himself or about the way the world works. The truth about Golightly we have already seen. The truth about the world is, even in this slight anecdote, extremely complex, but Kipling gives us a clue to his vision of it in the story itself. When Golightly first arrives in Pathankote, he buys a drink and pays eight annas for it. "This revealed to him that he had

only six annas more in his pocket—*or in the world as he stood at that hour*" (italics mine). The phrase is a significant one. **"The Arrest of Lieutenant Golightly"** is crowded with accidents and mistakes, with illustrations, as it were, of the randomness and irrationality of the universe, and in such a universe it is axiomatic that any sort of elaborate planning will be useless. True, Golightly's plans are foolish because they are irresponsible, but we might easily imagine, under the same circumstances, a man on horseback loaded down with monsoon equipment and changes of clothing looking quite as foolish. When we see people carrying umbrellas on sunny days, our first thought is not that they are wise and provident planners but rather that they look ridiculous. Yet their only mistake has been to guess wrong about the weather, and they might just as easily have guessed right.

Kipling is obviously not opposed to planning in itself, though in such stories as **"A Germ Destroyer"** he humorously warns against a mere proliferation of policy which may make a man inflexible in the face of new challenges. His real point, however, is that the universe, in its fortuitousness, is always able to come up with some unexpected challenge for which no amount of planning could have prepared, and that in such an hour, all a man has in the world is what, figuratively speaking, he has in his pockets. And what he ought to have in his pockets for such a time is precisely what Lieutenant Golightly does not have and for the lack of which he is "arrested" in mid-career, a consciousness of the truth about himself—the only universally useful tool in an uncertain world.

A shock is in store for readers who turn from this explication of **"The Arrest of Lieutenant Golightly"** to the story itself. The tale or anecdote is so light-weight that the solemnity of the analysis seems out of all proportion to the slenderness of the subject. Yet there need be no correlation between a narrative's solemnity (or lack of it) and its structural complexity, and indeed, it is precisely because **"The Arrest of Lieutenant Golightly"** is so innocent of conscious "serious" intentions that I picked it for consideration here. For what its constructional sophistication reveals is that Kipling, young as he was when he wrote his tale, and pressured as he was by a newspaper deadline, was nevertheless able to handle even such admittedly slight material as this like an artist, to give even these stock elements of farce a single center and a serious theme. Thus, though some of his work may have been journalistic in style and subject, the author ought not, in the light of a story such as this, to be dismissed as a mere journalist. (pp. 53-60)

> *Elliot L. Gilbert, in his* The Good Kipling: Studies in the Short Story, *Ohio University Press, 1971, 215 p.*

JEFFREY MEYERS   (essay date 1971)

[*Meyers is an American critic, literary biographer, and professor of English. Among his many books are biographies of Wyndham Lewis, Katherine Mansfield, D. H. Lawrence, and Ernest Hemingway; bibliographies of George Orwell and T. E. Lawrence; and critical studies of several contemporary authors. In the following excerpt originally published in the* Kipling Journal *in 1971, Meyers investigates heroism and destruction in Kipling's short story "At the End of the Passage."*]

Kipling's early stories show his heroes' conflict with the power of India. In **"At the End of the Passage"** the traditional idea of heroism is too rigid and too constrained, and the would-be hero becomes a victim when his standard of conduct fails to sustain him during a crisis. The protagonists of **"The Man Who Would Be King"** and **"Without Benefit of Clergy"** attempt to transcend the traditional code of the white man in India, but are unable to replace it with an alternative moral system of their own. The "kings" fail because they do not possess the moral authority requisite for enlightened imperial rule. In **"Without Benefit of Clergy"** even powerful love is insufficient to transcend racial differences and the lovers are doomed for breaking the Sahib's code. The hero who is able to cope with the power of India and embrace both cultures does not emerge until Kim, who understands and sympathizes with the Indians, and embodies the best elements of both the Indian and English worlds.

The fascinating thing about Kipling's stories is the difference between their intended and actual effect. He wrote for an audience who accepted his values and agreed with his beliefs, but when we test our ideas against Kipling's we see that his art is sometimes in conflict with his thought. In **"At the End of the Passage"** he attempts to glorify a code but actually shows how unsatisfactory it is. The theme of **"The Man Who Would Be King"** is seriously undermined by his glorification of the men he intends to criticize. In **"Without Benefit of Clergy"** he begins to write a lyrical Indian *Romeo and Juliet* about a love that transcends social differences and ends by punishing the lovers for their racial transgression. And the racial tolerance in *Kim* is undercut by the theme of white superiority. The effect of Kipling's stories is like that of a revolving lighthouse which radiates momentary gleams of revealing light far out into the surrounding gloom, and then suddenly lapses into complete darkness. W. H. Auden writes that, unlike most writers, Kipling is obsessed by a sense of external, rather than internal dangers threatening civilization. "For him civilization (and consciousness) is a little citadel of light surrounded by a great darkness full of malignant forces and only maintained through the centuries by everlasting vigilance, will-power and self-sacrifice". **"At the End of the Passage"** (*Life's Handicap,* 1891), portrays a man whose vigilance and will-power are broken down and destroyed by these external malignant forces, and who is so tortured by the powers of darkness that only death can release him from his hellish existence. Kipling ably describes the destructive power of India, but is less successful when he writes of the little citadel of light that opposes it. Kipling's English standards of civilized behaviour, especially his idea of self-sacrifice, are unsatisfactory and unreliable in India, and his code of conduct and idea of heroism too rigidly constrained.

Kipling describes this destructive setting in the opening paragraph:

> Four men, each entitled to 'life, liberty, and the pursuit of happiness', sat at a table playing whist. The thermometer marked—for them—one hundred and one degrees of heat. The room was darkened till it was only just possible to distinguish the pips of the cards and the very white faces of the players. A tattered, rotten punkah of white-washed calico was puddling the hot air and whining dolefully at each stroke. Outside lay gloom of a November day in London. There was neither sky, sun, nor horizon,—nothing but a brown purple haze of heat. It was as though the earth were dying of apoplexy.

This paragraph states the major motifs and dominant images of the story, evokes the setting and mood with startling vividness and intensity, and carefully defines what the civilized

European must endure. The physical facts are the most striking. The heavy heat is terrible, and causes the outside world to become undifferentiated and unfamiliar when the normal bearings—sun, sky and horizon—are lost. The image of the apoplectic earth suggests the mode of death: the loss of sensation and consciousness from brain damage. The unhealthy pallid faces in the darkened prison, the doleful whine and the gloom outside, evoke a mood of desolation and deep despair. The tattered rotten punkah, like the battered little camp-piano and the miserable goat chops and curried eggs, is a symbol of their disintegrating and chaotic world. The mention of London recalls as a frame of reference the civilized and familiar world that the men unsuccessfully and poignantly strive for. Finally, instead of 'life, liberty and the pursuit of happiness', Hummil achieves only bondage, despair and death.

Kipling has rendered the artful *progression d'effet* by revealing how pitiless and inexorable nature causes physical decay in Hummil, and how the nervous strain of boredom, anxiety and isolation leads to spectres and delirium, and causes a fatal relaxation of his moral fibre. This saps his vitality, enfeebles his will, and forces Hummil to succumb to panic, terror and madness. (pp. 1-3)

Each of the four men in **"At the End of the Passage"** who eagerly and irritably meet every week is subject to . . . extraordinary destructive and disintegrating forces, and is thrust into a struggle for existence in which the weakest succumbs first. Hummil's ghastly death suggests the fate of the other men just as Jevins' death foreshadows and hastens Hummil's: for Hummil must add the burden of Jevins' work to his already strenuous duties. Though one of the ideas in the story seems to be "judge no man this weather", suicide is condemned not on theological but on occupational grounds: it "is shirking your work". The hazards and hardships of this work are almost as unendurable as the heat itself. Lowndes, a political advisor to an Indian Native State, is in constant danger of being poisoned; Spurstow, a doctor, is threatened by an epidemic of black cholera; Mottram, the surveyor, suffers from opthalmia as well as isolation and loneliness. But it is Hummil who suffers most and, threatened by madness, clings to morphia, the last appeal of civilization.

Kipling makes clear that these men are living in an earthly Hell, and as they attempt to sleep in the house of torment they suffer the cruelties inflicted upon the damned. They endured the foul smell of kerosene lamps combined with the stench of native tobacco, baked brick, and dried earth; the punkah flagged, almost ceased, and then fell apart; a tomtom beat with the steady throb of a brain-fevered skull; the sweat poured out of the sleepless men; and Hummil, already half dead, was as rigid as a corpse. After Hummil dies, his servant explains that his master has descended into the dark places and has been frightened to death by an unearthly fear.

When Spurstow, who stays with Hummil after the others leave, realizes Hummil's condition, he urges him to forget his work and wire to headquarters for leave. But Hummil refuses because he knows his replacement is physically weak and has a wife and child who would surely die if they left the cool hills. The camp-piano, the wreckage of a couple who had once lived in the bungalow, is a warning of the fate that overtakes families in the Indian heat. Kipling's dedicated men maintain the tradition of sacrifice to duty, and reveal the terrible irony in his stories: that the rulers of India often become its victims.

Kipling wisely spares the reader the horrors of the final week of the victim's life and when Hummil's friends return the following Sunday they find him dead. The tireless punkah-wallah, who is unaware that anything unusual has occured and continues to pull the cord of his punkah, suggests the lack of connection between the Englishman and the mass of hostile or indifferent natives whom he attempts to rule.

Hummil's hands are clenched, and the spur that he rested on to keep him from sleep and tortuous nightmares falls to the ground, a vivid symbol of how he urged himself, beast-like, to work and to duty. His friends faithfully return to the work that keeps their wits together; all that remains is the indignity of hasty disposal, mandatory in the Indian heat.

The story should have ended here, a powerful tale of terror, hopeless despair and spiritual disintegration. But Kipling, not satisfied to rest with this achievement, pushes on to the realm of the supernatural, and nearly destroys the total effect of the story. The very real horrors—physical, spiritual and mental—were certainly sufficient to destroy Hummil without the introduction of supernatural elements (and further unnecessary explanations). The fact that the horrors which killed Hummil remain on his eyes after death and are recorded by a camera adds nothing to the story and is irrelevant to Kipling's intention of showing the self-sacrifice and devotion to duty of these shattered men of imperial fibre.

Kipling fails to recognize that there is something self-defeating about this gladiatorial heroism. He habitually assumes that in such a situation a typical colonial character can behave in one way only, so that Hummil never has a choice to make. There is no possibility in the story of another system of values, no doubt of the inflexible standard of conduct. Kipling believes that Hummil contains within himself all that is needed to survive, and that there is only one kind of manliness and heroism, which is self-dependent and based entirely on will-power. Hummil is intended to be a brave hero and the story is meant to be a tragic defeat of a strong man by a dark colonial fate. The story allows us to imagine an unending succession of martyrs sacrificing themselves to the cause of empire, and shows how completely Kipling believes in the colonial mission.

For these reasons, there is no conflict in Spurstow's mind about his responsibility to Hummil, for the interests of the empire always override those of the individual. Kipling always demands the suppression of the individual, who is important only for his organic value—as a link in the chain or a part of the team.

It is precisely Kipling's assumptions about the nature of civilization, which Auden has observed, that do not allow Hummil to learn from the unhappy example of Jevins, and reveal a fundamental weakness in this and other stories, for the threat to civilization *is* internal. Because Hummil lacks the imagination to see the possibility of acting differently, his rigidity destroys him. What Kipling sees as something external really comes from the rigidity itself. When Hummil must face the power of India, his inner resources and moral strength, his narrow code, his little citadel of light, fail to sustain him, and he succumbs to the doom that waits for "civilized" men at the end of the passage. (pp. 3-5)

Jeffrey Meyers, "Rudyard Kipling: Codes of Heroism," in his Fiction & the Colonial Experience, *Rowman and Littlefield, 1973, pp. 1-28.*

GILLIAN AVERY (essay date 1972)

[*Avery is an English novelist, essayist, and editor. In the following excerpt, she assesses which of Kipling's short stories continue to appeal to children.*]

Perhaps [Kipling] has never really been popular with the common run of children, perhaps we delude ourselves in assuming that he was from the qualities that we recognize in the stories as adults; from the enthusiasm of a few specially perceptive readers, and from the tributes by writers who remember the intensity with which they read him in childhood. J. M. S. Tompkins, in *The Art of Rudyard Kipling,* prefaces her chapter on the children's tales with a recollection of what they meant to her fifty years before. Rosemary Sutcliff was brought up on them too, and the spell has never left her. 'Good hunting!' her Roman legionaries call to each other, and salute another affectionately as 'cubling', echoing the greetings of the *Jungle Books.* Her novels of Roman Britain take up the story at the point where Kipling laid it down: the disintegration of the Empire, the withdrawal of the legions from Britain. Her account of the last galley leaving Rutupiae Harbour and the extinction of Rutupiae Light must have sprung from the sadness of **"On the Great Wall"**, the second of the Roman stories in *Puck of Pook's Hill,* when the young centurion, proud of the greatness of Rome, sees the humiliating word 'finish' on the bricked-up arch over the Great North Road. And admirers of E. Nesbit's Bastable family will remember how they acted the *Jungle Book* with such vigour—borrowing the odd tiger-skin rug—that a timid visitor turned a dreadful green colour and fainted.

But the ordinary child—what is it that defeats him? The trouble may partly lie in the way that Kipling tells his historical tales. Children love reading about going back in time, of present-day children being magicked into the past. But Kipling brings his historical characters forward, and somehow the magic vanishes. There they sit in Edwardian Sussex—Sir Richard Dalyngridge the Norman knight, with a horse real enough to break away clods from the bank where it crosses the stream, Parnesius the centurian fingering Dan's catapult—and tell the children their adventures. Where these are difficult Puck, who is the convenor of the proceedings, supplies a gloss, and Dan and Una ask questions. They are not ghosts, there is no nimbus of mystery about them, and they seemed to me as a child like dressed-up figures from a pageant. I felt too that the history was all too grown-up, and that it lacked the delicious magic of E. Nesbit. Like many other children, I was also prejudiced against stories told in the first person. I still feel that too many people get in the way of the narrative, and that the interruptions do it no good.

This was *Puck of Pook's Hill.* It is rare to hear of anybody who made much of its sequel, *Rewards and Fairies,* as a child. Technically the stories are superb, but Kipling's virtuosity is almost oppressive here. With immense élan he identifies himself with the various narrators, at one moment a seventeenth-century astrologer talking like a character out of *The Alchemist,* neolithic man at the next. He whirls his readers round the centuries. The effort of adjustment is considerable, and many of the stories are too compressed, too subtle for a young reader. In **"The Knife and the Naked Chalk"** he considers how a stone-age man from the chalk downs might dread the unknown, fever-infested forest lands below, and their inhabitants. . . . The finest is the last story, **"The Tree of Justice"**, incomprehensible to children, yet neglected by the adult enthusiast because it falls in what is assumed to be a children's book. It is, in fact, a development of **"The Man Who Was"**. (p. 114-15)

It is more difficult to understand why the *Jungle Books* are not more widely enjoyed. Perhaps the official hand of the Scout movement has helped to deaden them. All the ritual of the Wolf Cubs is derived from the first *Jungle Book,* and a drab re-telling of **"Mowgli's Brothers"** appears in the Wolf Cub Handbook. Cubs weekly stalk and kill Shere Khan the Tiger and Tabaqui the Jackal, so that for many the jungle is overlaid by the thought of a dusty church hall and little boys in green caps chanting 'Akela, we'll do our best'. (p. 115)

The Mowgli stories make up only a proportion of the two *Jungle Books;* there are three of them in the first, and five in the second. The remainder are all stories about animals, but they have not that savage enchantment which held the imagination of people who remember loving Mowgli as children. The Bastable family indeed despised their timid visitor long before she fainted, because she skipped the Mowgli stories and read **"Rikki-Tikki-Tavi"** and **"The White Sea"** instead, the very ones that children of today are said to prefer.

Considered as an animal story, **"Rikki-Tikki-Tavi"** is a better one than any about the jungle. It really does convey the character of the mongoose and the cobras without a touch of the anthropomorphism that lies so heavily over the other. So does the macabre **"Undertakers"**, a conversation between a crocodile, a jackal, and an adjutant bird concerning various sorts of carrion flesh, with the crocodile wistfully recalling his satiation in the Mutiny days. But the Mowgli stories possess what the others do not, a fantasy and a wonder and a sadness. 'The grip of the stories was extraordinary', recalls Miss Tompkins, 'and a sense of something wild and deep and old infected me as I listened'. As a child I myself could never understand Mowgli's tactics when he trapped Shere Khan, I was bored by his visits to the Human Pack, and missed most of the point of the superb **"King's Ankus"**. But my imagination was seized by the description of the monkey-folk carrying Mowgli between them in their headlong flight through the tree-tops: 'the terrible check and jerk at the end of the swing over nothing but empty air brought his heart between his teeth' (a marvellously convincing detail that). And I went back time and again to the description of Cold Lairs, the lost city in the jungle where the monkeys hold court and where they fight and lose the battle with Kaa the python. (p. 116)

It is often asserted that the best children's books come from authors who are not writing deliberately with children in mind, but for themselves. It is also said that the best children's authors are those who have their own childhood in mind, or who still retain in some respects a child-like outlook. But when the point is made it is usually assumed that the childhood was a happy one. Kipling's was not. In **"Baa Baa, Black Sheep"** the tormented and lonely Punch, alias ten-year-old Rudyard, 'brooded in the shadow that fell about him and cut him off from the world, inventing horrible punishments for "dear Harry", or plotting another line of the tangled web of deception that he wrapped round Aunty Rosa'. The story concludes: 'When young lips have drunk deep of the bitter waters of Hate, Suspicion, and Despair, all the Love in the world will not wholly take away that knowledge; though it may turn darkened eyes for a while to the light, and teach faith where no Faith was'.

This experience left its mark on *Stalky,* and on the *Jungle Books.* The Puck stories escaped, but these were written with his own children in mind. So were the *Just So Stories,* and it is undoubtedly these which nowadays have the greatest success with children. He had always loved the company of small children, and telling them stories. The *Just So Stories* began some time during the 1890s when the Kiplings were at their Vermont home. Their first daughter Josephine had been born in 1892, and to her and her little cousin Kipling used to tell tales about camels and whales and the cat that walked in the wet, wild woods up the road. By 1898 Kipling was telling them to two small daughters, and Angela Mackail, another cousin, remembered the joy of hearing them in the study at Rottingdean:

> The *Just So Stories* are a poor thing in print compared with the fun of hearing them told in Cousin Ruddy's deep unhesitating voice. There was a ritual about them, each phrase having its special intonation which had to be exactly the same each time and without which the stories are dried husks. There was an inimitable cadence, an emphasis of certain words, an exaggeration of certain phrases, a kind of intoning here and there which made his telling unforgettable.

They were not written down, it seems, until a late stage, and were not published until 1902. They are, thus, like *Alice,* one of the very few children's books which actually have been told to children first. It is probably because of the questions of Josephine, Elsie and their small cousins that we get explanations such as, what the Rhinoceros's skin was like when he took it off ('it buttoned underneath with three buttons and looked like a waterproof'), and their delighted horror at other people's naughtiness that was responsible for the Elephant's Child going home and spanking all his relations. And it is certain that the eldest Kipling child would have heard the sonorous chant 'Change here for Winchester, Ashuelot, Nashua, Keene, and stations on the *Fitch*burg Road', for these are all stations near Brattleboro, the old Vermont home.

The *Just So Stories* are far more than a family joke, though; they have the universal touch which his other children's books lack in some measure, however good by adult literary standards. You do not have to be specially perceptive to love them, you do not have to skip bits. They are wonderful to read aloud, of course. But if you read them to yourself you have the pictures. Kipling drew them himself, two to a story, the best illustrations any of his books had, and embellished them with illustrations that answer every question any one could want to ask. 'This is the Parsee Pestonjee Bomonjee sitting in his palm tree . . . he has a knife in his hand to cut his name on palm trees. The black things on the islands out at sea are bits of ships that got wrecked going down the Red Sea but all the passengers were saved and went home'.

There is humour and a smacking good moral to each story (it is always pleasant to feel smug when the naughtiness is not your own), there is cumulative repetition and a wild logic, and long words that sound good and are only put there for their sound. But it is their humour that is so endearing. Small children's humour is crude; a joke that pleases them usually makes adults wince. It is Kipling's triumph that in *Just So Stories* he found a vein of humour that captivates both the old and the young. (pp. 117-18)

Gillian Avery, "The Children's Writer," in Rudyard Kipling: The Man, His Work and His World, ed-

ited by John Gross, Weidenfeld & Nicolson, 1972, pp. 113-18.

VASANT A. SHAHANE   (essay date 1973)

[*Shahane is an Indian short story writer, editor, and essayist. In the following excerpt from his* Rudyard Kipling: Activist and Artist, *he studies Kipling's portrayals of Indians and Indian culture, recognizing a progression toward verisimilitude in character delineation in his later short stories.*]

Realism and creation of atmosphere are considered to be Kipling's great assets as a short-story writer. But he is equally a great artist in the fields of fantasy and fable. His short stories are an extraordinary synthesis of realism and lyricism. Chesterton's comment on the nature of Kipling's talents, that he is a "most extraordinary and bewildering genius," is particularly true of his short stories. Modern critics such as J. M. S. Tompkins and C. A. Bodelsen have offered very sensitive, profound, and intelligent insights into many of the short stories, yet the task is by no means complete.

A distinctive quality of Kipling as a short-story writer is the very wide range of his subject matter and the extraordinary sweep of his imagination. His stories, like those on Simla Hills, range from actuality of life, elements of experience of everyday life in India, England, the barrack-room, the high seas, to exploration of the animal world and also the world of fantasy exemplified in his immortal *Jungle Books.* The range of his subject matter is shown in the many themes of cruelty, violence, suffering, joys of masculine companionship, camaraderie, and feeling for a cause. Kipling is primarily concerned with the real world, the world here and now in all its beauty and beastliness, but he is also concerned with the romantic and fabulous world, the world of the hereafter. His stories revolving around ghosts or the idea of reincarnation conjure up a fantastic universe which cannot be described as real. The sweep of his imagination is so wide that it extends over not only varieties of men but also lands as far apart as England, Europe, Asia, and Africa, which become the living organisms of his art. The sweep is not merely wide, it is also deep, and balanced by exploration in detail. Kipling's stories reflect his insight into various layers of the unconscious and the dimensions of the psyche which rise in the structures of his tales. He is a genuine artist in exploring the wide variety of life in the form of his short stories. It is of course true that the creative genius of Kipling has to be considered a single, indivisible whole, and that his roles as poet, novelist, short-story writer are only facets of that one imaginative mind. Yet it must be said that it is in the area of the short story that the best aspects of his creative talent are vividly reflected. (pp. 82-3)

Verisimilitude is one of the outstanding qualities of Kipling's short stories and it has been acknowledged by new as well as old critics. He was the first short-story writer to create faithfully the scenes and atmosphere of the barrack-room and to make his soldiers seem real. His keen observation, his unflinching fidelity to the facts of life, and his innate power to create living, breathing, real people account for the deep impression of verisimilitude that he produces on the sensibility of his reader. Kipling is a professional of professionals, as is shown in his continuous search for finding the ways and methods of professionals. Examples of his interest in the work of professional artisans have been cited. On his walks Rudyard talked at length with builders, masons, carpenters,

and craftsmen to know their skills, their lingo, their selective phraseology, their attitudes, and his comprehensive grasp of the day-to-day life of workmen is reflected in **"The Bridge-Builders."**

"Kipling," writes Randall Jarrell, "like it or not, admit it or not, was a great genius. . . . one of the most skillful writers who ever existed," who made the reader exclaim: "Well, I've got to admit it really is *written.*" This feeling, in my view, is the heart of the matter of Kipling's created world. Kipling cannot be described as a lord of language, a new Victorian Virgil, nor can he be considered one of the masters of English prose style. Yet it must be said that he used English with great skill and with telling effect. His use of Indian words or cockney speech gives a new vitality to his style. And, ultimately, the reader's response is beautifully summed up in these words: "Yes, it really is *written.* Really, it is, my word!"

"The Bridge-Builders" is one of Kipling's most fascinating stories not merely because its theme is so central to his philosophy of life but also because it attempts to bridge the gap between this world and the other, between reality and imagination, between prose and poetry. As the first story in *The Day's Work,* **"The Bridge-Builders"** sings the gospel of work, the doctrine of activism which is the cardinal element of Kipling's credo. The story is told on two levels—those of the physical and the spiritual—and the events in the story are passages to these. It is also a bridge between the human and the divine, this world and the other. The story is about the giant bridge over the Ganges "one mile and three-quarters in length, a lattice-girder" construction of great proportion supervised by Findlayson, the Chief Engineer of the Public Works Department. Kipling presents all the details of the physical reality with great accuracy and professional knowledgeability. (pp. 84-5)

The physical reality of the bridge is closely linked with Findlayson's belief in activism as a value of living. He and his assistant Hitchcock had worked very hard for years through official red tape, the delays caused by the War, the cholera, the small-pox and other handicaps. Behind everything "rose the black frame of the Kashi Bridge—plate by plate, girder by girder, span by span—and each pier of it recalled Hitchcock." The bridge arose out of the initiative, calculations, and dedicated hard work of the two engineers.

Kipling swings to the human plane from the physical and we get a glimpse of bevies of workmen with their firepots and hammers working round the clock on the bridge. Then, there is Peroo, a skillful *Lascar* from Bulsar, who had traveled all over the world and gained wide experience, and who spoke wonderful English mixed with his lingo of Portugese origin. He was a genuine Hindu, deeply involved in the mysterious workings of the Hindu divinities. He asked Findlayson: "Our bridge is all but done. What think you Mother Gunga will say when the road runs over?" Peroo had performed *poojah* in the big temple by the river for the God within, and he was the trusted lieutenant of Findlayson and Hitchcock.

Peroo's apparently casual remark about what Mother Gunga will think of the bridge being built across her sets into motion the bewildering forces of her swift currents. Telegrams are received warning the engineers of the rising floods of the Ganges and heavy rains, and Findlayson has only fifteen hours to save as much material as possible from the rising fury of the river. The night gongs and conches were sounded, and the naked, devoted workmen set to work in pale darkness clearing the riverbed and saving machinery and materials of all kinds. (pp. 85-6)

Kipling presents the second level—the spiritual—in this assembly on the island. In Hindu mythos animals are closely associated with gods. The stumps of the indigo plants crackled and a huge Brahminee bull made his appearance under a tree. Findlayson and Peroo both saw this vision before the shrine—the bull, the parrot, the blackbuck, a tigress—all came into their ken. Then the blunt-nosed Mugger (crocodile) of the Ganges draggled herself before the assembly. The crocodile complained that the waters of the Ganges were polluted and she was defiled. But the elephant answered the Gunga's charge that the bridge defiled her waters: "It is but the shifting of a little dirt. Let the dirt dig in the dirt if it pleases the dirt." It is the vision of the eternal as against the temporal, the infinite against the finite, the immortal against the mortal. As Miss Tompkins, in her extremely perceptive analysis of **"The Bridge-Builders"** has pointed out, the "enormous bridge and its swarming life" is reduced to an atom and the infinitesimal is displaced by the immeasurable.

The dimensions of the elements of the spirit in **"The Bridge-Builders"** are revealed through the Hindu Pantheon, or the assembly of gods, who discuss and give judgment on the complaints of the crocodile, which is the animalistic image of the Ganges. Shiv, Ganesh, Hanuman, and Krishna participate in the proceedings, and the final judgment is pronounced by Indra, the supreme god: "Ye know the Riddle of the Gods, when Brahm ceases to dream, the Heaven and Hell and Earth disappear. Be content. Brahm dreams still. The dreams come and go, and the nature of the dream changes, but still Brahm dreams." Brahma created the universe in ecstasy and it rose out of his divine imagination. Indra says the divine dream continues and regeneration will follow decay and that the complaint of the Ganges regarding the bridge is like making disproportionate fuss over a little, transitory, dirt in a vast expanse. The mutable is silhouetted against the immutable, the transitory against the eternal. The material vastness of the bridge is thus reduced to infinitesimal smallness and the Hindu Pantheon is shown indirectly setting its seal on the project of the great bridge over the Gunga.

Kipling's vision connects the past with the present, and Hanuman, the Hindu god, as the leader of the "builders of the bridges as of old," is linked with the modern bridge-builders in British India. The continuity of human endeavor is suggested in this tradition from the past to the present, and this is similar to men's devotion to the gods. Shiv will be worshipped in schools, Ganesh shall have his worshippers, and people "will do no more than change the names" of the deities. The devotion will show the continuity of man's response. This continuity also marks the task of bridge-building by the ancients and the moderns, Hanuman and Findlayson. Kipling's visionary quality is revealed in the delicate poise which he creates between change and immutability, the temporal and the timeless. The poise points up the unity that he visualizes between past and present, between ancient and modern bridge-builders which is central to the theme of the story. "Yes, Findlayson's bridge was safe and serene," there's not a stone shifted anywhere, partly because it is a symbol of unity between the human and divine, past and present, temporal and eternal.

"The Miracle of Purun Bhagat," the first tale in *The Second Jungle Book,* is one of the most extraordinary stories of Rudyard Kipling. It is so superbly designed, tightly written, and

dexterously controlled that the apparently sprawling flux of its material falls into shape, the shape of its vision. It seems to me a masterpiece of Kipling's art, partly because it demonstrates the basic process of his creativity. I have propounded, elsewhere in this book, the argument that Rudyard Kipling is essentially an activist in the late-Victorian tradition and that his activism is transformed into art in his fiction and poetry. **"The Miracle of Purun Bhagat"** demonstrates, in my view, this fundamental process operative in Kipling's creative mind of the transformation of the activist into artist. The story is, therefore, not merely Kipling's portrayal of Purun Bhagat, but also the creative writer's way of looking at his art. (pp. 86-8)

Purun Dass was an activist and Purun Bhagat a man of contemplation and devotion. In his character this growth shows a transformation from an activist into a man of god. He achieves a new dimension of the awareness of the divine through renunciation of the world and becomes a real savior of men. Within the structure of the story, the swift movement in the earlier part of the story is changed into a slow motion of divine intensity in the latter part of the story. Words seem to wade through the still waters of Purun Bhagat's existence.

The meaning of Purun Bhagat's miracle lies in realizing the significance of this transformation and relating it to the mode of Kipling's art. "'The Miracle of Purun Bhagat' was beyond me," wrote J. M. S. Tompkins. "I did not understand what was happening." What exactly is happening in **"Purun Bhagat"** is described by Kipling as a miracle, and the miracle is not so much that Purun Dass has become Purun Bhagat overnight but that he commenced his search with love for all men and animals. The great man of action has become a greater man of contemplation and aimed at synthesizing the concretions and abstractions of life. Purun Bhagat, writes K. R. Srinivasa Iyengar, "was a St. Francis re-enacting the drama of common friendliness and fellowship with man, beast and all nature." In the character and personality of Purun Bhagat the Christian values are subtly synthesized with those of the Hindu way of life.

The miracle of Purun Bhagat is also, in part, the miracle of the growth of Kipling's art. Kipling too, like Purun, was a great lover of animals and visualized their communion with men. He believed, as the early Purun did, in the concretion of activism, from which his art sprang. Thus the concrete and the abstract, the real and the ideal, body and soul are harmonized in the unity of Kipling's vision.

In **"Without Benefit of Clergy"** the artist in Kipling emerges as a writer of dream and reality. This aspect of Kipling as an artist is woven into the fabric of the story which is marked by two worlds—the house of Ameera overlooking the city, with a courtyard full of marigolds, and Holden's bachelor bungalow with its "unlovely" life-style. In the lovely rooms of the first house Holden was king of all he surveyed, and Ameera the queen. Holden was leading a "double life" as he passed from one world to the other. Ameera was wild with delight as she was expecting a baby, and even her money-minded mother was pleased at the prospect of this new arrival. Holden came to Ameera to break the unhappy news that the government "with singular care, had ordered him out of the station for a fortnight on special duty." (pp. 90-2)

Kipling, it appears, is slowly building up the tragic passages in the narrative structure through scene and image. Holden fills out a telegram for Pir Khan, the gatekeeper, and then returns to his headquarters with "the sensations of a man who has attended his own funeral." After the birth of the child Holden acted out the ritual of killing the two goats, as sacrifice to safeguard the life of his son. But, in the process the raw blood spurted over his riding boots. The club secretary saw it and exclaimed, "Great goodness, man, it's blood!" On the auspicious Friday, Ameera settles herself in John's arms and the atmosphere is warm and stuffy. "The dry earth is lowing like a cow for the rain." She asks him to count the stars, but the sky is overcast. Then she tried to play the *sitar* and sing a song of Rajah Rasalu but instead sings a rhyme of the crow.

Kipling shows that the ecstasy of fulfillment, of the love of Ameera and Holden, was short-lived. Tota died and Ameera wept bemoaning her fate. On Tota's death Ameera "at the end of each weary day" led Holden "through the hell of self-questioning reproach," which is the fate of those who lose their children. Ameera, too, became a victim of cholera.

The image of the stars is central to the narrative content since Ameera, John, and their son are all involved in a compelling, ruthless, unkind circle of destiny. The tragic world in **"Without Benefit of Clergy"** is a lyrical presentation of man's unequal confrontation with an indifferent and unkind universe. As Elliot L. Gilbert has perceptively pointed out, the story "is not just a sentimental idyll," but its theme is "nothing less than the enormous hostility of the universe," which is "blundering, directionless and very nearly incapable of supporting human life."

"Without Benefit of Clergy" is almost Shakespearean in its tone and temper, and the world of John and Ameera is a minor variation, in the context of nineteenth-century India, of the world of Romeo and Juliet. Love triumphs only after the body, the perishable clay, is consumed in the fires lit by fate. **"Without Benefit of Clergy"** is also an indirect reflection on the futility of ritual, and Ameera's love for Holden transcends all narrow ritualistic limitations and reaches the reality of the human spirit. The story also shows, indirectly, the process of the emergence of Kipling's art. The world of Ameera is a dreamworld of love and romance, whereas the world of Holden is a world of hard work and unlovely surroundings. These two worlds come together by sheer chance and are separated by the cruelty of Fate. The prosaic world of facts is transformed into a poetical world of love and lyricism and this progression in **"Without Benefit of Clergy"** is also the progression of Kipling as an artist.

The Indian's innate love for, and involvement with, children is portrayed with greater tenderness and pity in **"The Story of Muhammad Din"** than in **"Without Benefit of Clergy."** Kipling shows great economy in expression in portraying Imam Din's love for Muhammad Din and the Anglo-Indian master's attachment for the "tiny, plump figure in a ridiculously inadequate shirt." Whereas Ameera's love for Tota, her child, finds intense lyrical expression in language, Imam Din's affection for his son is shown in phrases which are terse and concentric. Even the exchanges between the Anglo-Indian Sahib and the little boy are limited to briefest expressions, *"Talaam Tahib,"* and *"Salaam, Muhammad Din."* Yet the tenderness and delicacy of human relationships is beautifully portrayed in this very brief story. The boy was punished by his father for having entered the Sahib's room. The boy sobbed and said, "It is true my name is Muhammad Did, *Tahib,* but I am not a *budmash,* I am a *man!"* The child busied himself in the garden with broken pieces of bricks and china. His act of half burying the Sahib's old polo-ball in dust

is a piece of dramatic irony as it is a premonition of his own burial by his father. The accidental trampling by the Sahib of the little boy's handiwork in the garden is also an event which casts its shadows on Muhammad Din's small world. He was always alone and always crooning to himself. He was told the Sahib was not really angry and that he was free to rebuild his palace. He designed it on a grand scale, but suddenly the fever claimed him. And the last scene is an accentuation of the tragic suffering of the father, Imam Din. The Sahib "met on the road to the Mussulman burying-ground Imam Din, accompanied by one other friend, carrying in his arms, wrapped in a white cloth, all that was left of little Muhammed Din."

This is one of the most terse descriptions of death in Kipling's fiction in which is concentrated great and deep passion for an offspring. The words, like those of Hamlet spoken to the queen, become daggers and administer stabs to human consciousness and create a powerful effect on human sensibility. The inscrutable ways of destiny are thus worked out into the small, sad and still world of Muhammad Din. (pp. 92-5)

The delicacy of emotional response between father and son, Imam Din and Muhammad Din, is also extended to the relationship between the Sahib and the boy, because it is through the Sahib's consciousness that we get a glimpse of the love between father and son. To interpret the Sahib's loving response to the Indian boy as an attitude of "condescension," as K. Bhaskar Rao has done, seems to me a case of oversimplification, since these relationships transcend the narrow racial or political barriers and become truly human. **"The Story of Muhammad Din"** is the finest example of Kipling's art in miniature. It is a delicate and sensitive painting of the dreamy, lovely boy confronted with his tragic destiny.

The synthesis of dream and reality is nowhere so pervasively reflected in Kipling's creative cosmos as in the beautifully designed story, **"The Brushwood Boy."** It depicts the pure dreams of George Cottar, of his childhood, adulthood, and of his stay in subaltern's quarters in India. (p. 95)

"The Brushwood Boy" is an extraordinary, almost unique, story of Kipling's, not merely because it portrays a series of George's dreams but also the growth of Kipling as an artist. Kipling's art grows out of the tension between two opposites—the world of facts and the world of spirit. These two opposites are also reflected in the divided self of George Cotter. **"The Gardener,"** the last story in **Debits and Credits,** written in 1925, is one of the most intricately designed and effectively rendered stories of Kipling. Its genesis could be traced to an intensely emotional phase of Kipling's life, the loss of his son, John, in the war and the painful uncertainty that surrounded his son's death. Kipling's visits to Ronen Cemetery provided the immediate setting and substance to the story which is marked by his overwhelming feeling of compassion.

That art lies in concealing art may be a half-truth but no story of Kipling demonstrates this view more powerfully than **"The Gardener."** It is a story of intense and moving passion, but the words hardly express it. The silences in **"The Gardener"** are more eloquent than speech and the gaps more expressive than complete sentences. Some of the details of Helen Turrell's life were public property, but not all. The village knew that Helen stood heroically by her brother's son and brought him to a happy home from France. But her actions in France are shrouded in mystery. We are told that she paid the passage of the child and the nurse from Bombay, nursed the baby through an attack of dysentery at Marseilles, dismissed the unsatisfactory nurse, and at last returned home "thin and worn but triumphant." There is a tinge of irony to these adjectives as they probably suggest her state of pregnancy and the birth of an illegitimate son.

It is Helen Turrell's confrontation with her own self that is central to the theme of **"The Gardener."** She is consciously wearing a mask that she unconsciously is trying to remove. Michael had "the Turrell forehead, broad, low, and well shaped," and his mouth "was somewhat better cut than the family type," but Helen, "who would concede nothing good to his mother's side, vowed he was a Turrell all over." Helen's refusal to concede anything good to Michael's mother is a confrontation with her own self, strengthened by the feeling that there is no one "to contradict" her. The irony of the situation is sharply focused on the scene in which Michael wishes to call her Mummy and she explained that "she was only his auntie." She agreed to being called Mummy only at bedtime, which was a dent in the mask, but the dominant note is one of secrecy and suppression of self. Helen's contention that "it's always best to tell the truth" is ironical since she herself is consciously trying to suppress it. Michael's childlike anger expressed in "And when I'm dead I'll hurt you worse!" is a foreboding of the future and breaks through Helen's "stammered defences." Michael was to have gone up to Oxford, but he went to the war theater in France instead. A shell-splinter killed him on the spot and another shell destroyed a wall the ruins of which were all spread over his body making identification difficult. The thread of this loss of physical identity is woven into the fabric of the story. Michael was reported missing, and a long correspondence resulted in utter frustration. Later the news of the death came and Helen's "world had stood still." His body was re-interred in Hagenzeele Third Military Cemetery and Helen decided to visit the grave. Helen's meeting with Mrs. Scarsworth is significant because she realized the other lady's identical problem of breaking the fences of falsehood: "Because I'm *so* tired of lying." But Helen could not confess because she could not really rid herself of her mask.

The last scene in **"The Gardener"** is indeed very touching, partly because of its subdued tone. Helen Turrell is a twentieth-century Mary Magdalene in search of the stone of the sepulcher, and the lost identity of her son. This scene is obviously related to the story of Magdalene in the Gospel of St. John (20:15). Jesus appeared before her and said, " 'Woman, why weepest thou?' . . . She, supposing him to be the gardener, saith unto him, 'Sir, if thou hast borne him hence, tell me where thou hast laid him, and I will take him away.' " The biblical parallel is obvious, and clearly implied in the title, but Helen Turrell's predicament is different from the problem of Magdalene and is expressed in her question to the gardener at the cemetery. Helen saw that a man "knelt behind a line of headstones—evidently a gardener, for he was firming a young plant in the soft earth." He asked her, "Who are you looking for?"

> "Lieutenant Michael Turrell—my nephew," said Helen slowly and word for word, as she had many thousands of times in her life.
>
> The man lifted his eyes and looked at her with infinite compassion before he turned from the fresh-sown grass toward the naked black crosses.

> "Come with me," he said, "and I will show you where your son lies."
>
> When Helen left the cemetery she turned for a last look. In the distance she saw the man bending over his young plants, and she went away, supposing him to be the gardener.

The gardener by substituting the word "son" for "nephew" at last confirmed the pent-up truth in Helen's heart. It was the first voice of the world without, that Helen heard, which echoed the world within. (pp. 96-9)

In conclusion, the question should be raised briefly about Kipling's rank as a short-story writer. A short story must create a single effect upon the sensibility of the reader, of the intensity of an incident or a character. The stages in its structure include the rising action culminating in a climax or crisis followed by a denouement. The theme of the short story implies its total meaning. Character delineation and creation of atmosphere are the other important elements of its structure. These are some of the essentials of the short story as a form.

Does Kipling achieve this objective of creating one, single, unified impression? The answer is that Kipling does not always achieve this objective, yet he is a great craftsman. This primary objective of the art of the short story is sometimes vitiated in his work by Kipling's habit of allowing surplusage in the content of his stories. Yet, he succeeds as a great writer because his stories present his conception of life and also because they offer such excellent character-delineation and achieve verisimilitude. As a craftsman Kipling is great, but as an artist he is even greater. (p. 107)

> *Vasant A. Shahane, in his* Rudyard Kipling: Activist and Artist, *Southern Illinois University Press, 1973, 157 p.*

WILLIAM J. SCHEICK (essay date 1986)

[*Scheick is an American educator, author, and editor of* Texas Studies in Language and Literature. *Scheick's critical works include* The Will and the Word: The Poetry of Edward Taylor (*1974*) *and* The Slender Human Word: Emerson's Artistry in Prose (*1978*). *In the following excerpt, he utilizes Tzvetan Todorov's structuralist concept to explore "The Phantom 'Rickshaw."*]

To appreciate **"The Phantom 'Rickshaw"** we need a critical perspective as appropriate as is Gilbert's focus on ritual behavior in **"Without Benefit of Clergy."** For this purpose, then, we might turn to Tzvetan Todorov's idea of the fantastic [discussed in *The Fantastic: A Structural Approach to a Literary Genre* (1973)], as a place to begin. I stress *as a place to begin* because I do not wish merely to demonstrate how Kipling's story conforms to Todorov's theory. Rather, I want to use Todorov's structuralist concept as a point of entry in my exploration of the complexity of Kipling's art in **"The Phantom 'Rickshaw."**

In order to qualify for the genre Todorov classifies as the fantastic, **"The Phantom 'Rickshaw"** must make the reader hesitate between a natural or a supernatural explanation of the events narrated, a hesitation which the reader usually shares with the protagonist of the story. Todorov explains, "The fantastic occupies the duration of this uncertainty. Once we choose one answer or the other, we leave the fantastic for a neighboring genre, the uncanny or the marvelous. The fantastic is that hesitation experienced by a person who knows only the laws of nature, confronting an apparently supernatural event." Kipling's story of how Theobald Jack Pansay rejects his lover, who dies in grief and who *apparently* haunts him to his own death, satisfies Todorov's criterion for the fantastic. As readers of **"The Phantom 'Rickshaw,"** we remain uncertain whether Pansay's experiences with the apparent ghost of Agnes Keith-Wessington are real encounters or hallucinations deriving from guilt over his callous treatment of her.

On the one side, there is Dr. Heatherlegh, who relentlessly insists that Pansay suffers from "too much conceited Brain, too little Stomach, and thoroughly unhealthy Eyes," that he suffers from "a Stomach-*cum*-Brain-*cum*-Eye illusion," which is medically treatable. Pansay tries to accept this natural explanation, but everything he does in accordance with his doctor's instructions fails to result in a remission of these so-called "persistent 'delusions'." Through much of the experience Pansay hesitates between a natural and a supernatural explanation of events: "Either that I was mad or drunk, or that Simla was haunted with devils." Just prior to his demise Pansay tends to believe that he is being punished as a "condemned criminal" for having caused Agnes' death.

"But you shall judge for yourselves," Pansay writes, and this important remark directs our attention to the readers of Pansay's narrative, which comprises most of the short story. Pansay's prospective readers include Kitty Mannering, to whom he was engaged until she broke off the relationship and coldly rebuffed him (much in the same manner as he had rejected Agnes) when she learned about his treatment of his previous lover; his readers include the narrator, who "suggested that he should write out the whole affair from beginning to end, knowing that ink might assist him to ease his mind"; and his readers include us. We identify with the narrator, whose framing introductory remarks Kipling insightfully added in a revision of the story; with the narrator we hesitate as we struggle to judge for ourselves whether Pansay's experiences are real or imaginary. Like the narrator we are unable to accept Dr. Hetherlegh's natural explanation (which would make the tale uncanny—that is, according to Todorov, its strangeness is explained by physical or mental causes) because Pansay enjoys "perfect health" and "a well-balanced mind," because none of the doctor's cures succeed, and because even full confession fails to remedy the problem. Like the narrator, we are also unable to accept Pansay's final supernatural explanation (which would make the tale marvelous—that is, according to Todorov, its strangeness is explained by spiritual causes) because neither we nor anyone other than Pansay in the story have seen the ghosts. As Todorov observes, "Either total faith or total incredulity would lead us beyond the fantastic: it is hesitation which sustains its life." As readers of **"The Phantom 'Rickshaw"** we are like the narrator Kipling eventually included, someone with whose uncertainty we could identify; we continue to hesitate between a natural and supernatural explanation of events. Todorov's structuralist paradigm takes us this far in appreciating Kipling's artful management of the revised version of **"The Phantom 'Rickshaw."** However, Kipling's artistry in focusing on the reader's hesitation extends beyond Todorov's notion of the fantastic, for as readers we hesitate not only between a natural or a supernatural explanation of events, but also over the rightness or wrongness of Pansay's eventual sense of guilt in the story. This latter mode of hesitation is important to remark because our inability to judge for ourselves and resolve this issue of guilt profoundly reinforces our incertitude over whether the

apparitions seen by Pansay are real or imaginary. The framing narrator clearly urges the reader toward a continued hesitation over the matter of Pansay's guilt when he says in his introductory comments that Pansay "may or he may not have behaved like a blackguard to Mrs. Keith-Wessington." The narrator, deliberately added to the story by Kipling, explicitly indicates his reluctance or his inability to judge Pansay, whom he knew well and whom he certainly knew better than we, the readers, who ought to be at least as hesitatingly cautious as the narrator in this matter of judging Pansay.

Consider Pansay's position. When he first met Agnes, he and she became "desperately and unreasonably in love with one another." He never planned to seduce and then abandon her; he had become infatuated—a human, natural occurrence. After the love affair progressed for a while Pansay discovered that he really did not love Agnes, that he had been only infatuated with her: "my fire of straw burnt itself out to a pitiful end with the closing year." He had no early inkling of this outcome; but it has happened, and he finds himself in an embarrassing situation. He tells Agnes the truth and tries to end the affair. Agnes, however, insists over and over that "it's all a mistake" and asks Pansay to forgive her (the reason why is never clear). Nothing will convince her that the affair is over, and consequently Pansay's feelings evolve from "passive endurance" to "blind hate" in combatting her resistance

Title page from an early British edition of The Phantom 'Rickshaw, & Other Eerie Tales.

to the truth of the situation. His rebuffs, never gentle even from the first, become still more curt and cruel; and although he realizes Agnes is the victim of his change of heart, he cannot help but note that in the matter of his increasingly angry treatment of her "she was much to blame." He later thinks that he "might have been a little kinder to her," but he knows this "really *is* a 'delusion' "; for what was he to do in the face of the reality of his dislike: "I could not have continued pretending to love her when I didn't, could I?"

The reasonable answer to Pansay's query is, of course, no, he could not continue with such a pretense. To have done so would have been a crime against himself and against Agnes. He did not "honestly, heartily" love her the way he came to feel about Kitty Mannering. So Pansay finds himself between a rock and a hard place: either he must live a lie and be miserable (and perhaps make Agnes miserable too) or he must tell the truth and make her so miserable that she "haunts" him to a miserable end. Herein is the hub of the narrator's and our hesitation over Pansay's guilt, whether "he may or he may not have behaved like a blackguard to Mrs. Keith-Wessington."

At this level of the story we are well beyond Todorov's structuralist paradigm of the reader's hesitation between a natural or a supernatural explanation of events; at a deeper level of the text this uncertainty is reinforced by our hesitation over the rightness or wrongness of Pansay's guilt. From the vantage point of this deeper mode of uncertainty we can penetrate Kipling's artistry still further in the tale if we realize that the very act of hesitation we are experiencing at two levels of the text informs the central meaning of the narrative. Although Pansay might or might not see ghosts and although he might or might not be guilty, he is at fault for having failed to pause—that is, he did not hesitate before beginning his desperate and unreasoned affair with Agnes, and he did not hesitate before hastily and curtly breaking off this affair.

His failure in the latter instance is mirrored in Kitty's curtness and lack of hesitation in breaking off her engagement to Pansay. He now finds himself feeling what Agnes must have felt; indeed, Pansay even repeats Agnes' refrain, "there *is* a mistake somewhere," and, as did Agnes with him, he begs Kitty to forgive him. The "mistake" to which he, Agnes, and Kitty obliquely refer, the mistake that requires forgiveness, is that Pansay had never hesitated to consider how Agnes would feel; as a result of an insensitivity that is certainly a flaw in his character he could only at first feel a "pity . . . [of] passive endurance" towards her. It is no accident that the final words of his narrative focus on compassion: "Pity me"; "in justice, too, pity her." Had he felt real pity for Agnes earlier, he would have paused before acting and through reflection, found a better way to handle the problem, rather than direct curtness. The most he had been able to manage by way of such reflection was a "feeling, *but only for a moment or two,* that [he] had been an unutterably mean hound" (emphasis mine). Not until the "haunting" by Agnes or his dismissal by Kitty has Pansay been a reflective man, or hesitated.

For, finally, in **"The Phantom 'Rickshaw,"** to hesitate means to reflect. The story suggests that before we act, before we judge, we should hesitate—that is, enter a liminal space when time is arrested, where we can reflect before reentering and acting in the world of time. The pity Pansay asks for himself and Agnes derives from this liminal space of reflection to which he has been driven; and compassion is what we and the narrator should feel for Pansay in spite of his initial insensi-

tivity (a character flaw which might or might not deserve such guilt that he dies from it). Like the narrator, we hesitate, and in reflection find compassion or pity in judging Pansay's guilt for ourselves. As readers we ideally enact the very hesitation, with its implication of compassion, that Pansay lacked at first and is driven to at last, if too late. In pausing before passing judgment on Pansay, we hesitate to pass judgment on ourselves; for the point of Kipling's story is that just as Pansay should have pitied Agnes, and Kitty should have pitied Pansay, we and the narrator should pity Agnes and Pansay. We are all in need of compassion in the wake of life's events.

This sense of the propriety of universal compassion lies at the heart of the function of hesitation in **"The Phantom 'Rickshaw."** As readers of the tale we pause over natural or supernatural explanations of events and between the rightness or wrongness of Pansay's guilt, finally to hesitate over ourselves hesitating; that is, we ideally enter into the liminal space of reflection as we (with the narrator) glimpse our own share in Pansay's and Agnes' human plight. These deepening layers of hesitation constitute the keen artistry of **"The Phantom 'Rickshaw."** Just as patterns of ritual behavior convey a depth of meaning in **"Without Benefit of Clergy,"** patterns of hesitation convey a depth of meaning in **"The Phantom 'Rickshaw"**; and this artistry in both stories should make us hesitate and be reflective when reading even Kipling's early stories—tales such as **"The Strange Ride of Morrowbie Jukes"** (1885, 1888), **"The Man Who Would Be King"** (1888), and **"The Mark of the Beast"** (1891)—which can be far more subtle artistically than their "simple" narrative surface at first encounter seems to suggest. (pp. 48-52)

William J. Scheick, "Hesitation in Kipling's 'The Phantom 'Rickshaw'," in English Literature in Transition: 1880-1920, *Vol. 29, No. 1, 1986, pp. 48-53.*

TERRY CAESAR   (essay date 1986)

[*In the following excerpt, Caesar considers Kipling's short story "Dayspring Mishandled" distinctive for its "chill insistence upon origins—textual and emotional," and powerful for its silences.*]

"Dayspring Mishandled" is not simply compelling but difficult, and perhaps it fairly offers itself to be misunderstood because of its peculiarly dislocating energies. I believe the central omission is at least its most puzzling feature, and that Kipling's text is generated because of a certain kind of silence about itself, a silence which is continually reinscribed since there is nothing to sponsor it—save an act of revenge upon the very notion of some sponsoring presence. (p. 54)

I assume here a fundamental distinction for the analysis of narrative between story and discourse. In an admirable treatment of this distinction, Johnathan Culler concludes that the sequence of actions or events and the discursive presentation of this sequence must each be taken to participate in the other. The sequences are presentations of events and the events "in principle have features not reported by the discourse," for "without that assumption, which makes the discourse a selection and even a suppression of possible information, texts would lack their intriguing and dislocatory power." As with many texts, the question of **"Dayspring Mishandled"** is one of what its discourse suppresses. A significant event, Castorley's words about Val's mother to Manallace, is equally a part of the discourse, and even more apparently a part of what this discourse chooses not to disclose. **"Dayspring Mishandled"** is the story of, and the discourse about, a conflict between two narrative logics: what happens, and what is reported to have happened. Castorley *speaks*. But what he actually says only Manallace is permitted to know.

There is no easy answer to this question. It is, first of all, part of a whole structure of suppressed and inferred information in the text. We initially read, for example, of Manallace receiving a small sum from the syndicate head, "at which Castorley was angry and would have said something unpleasant but was suppressed." Even earlier certain plagiarized "masterpieces" in the beginning days of the syndicate are, we are told, "now never mentioned for fear of blackmail." Still later, in concluding pages of muffled obliquities which are almost Jamesian in their reticence, Manallace declares to the narrator that he wishes some banal reassurances the physician, Gleeag, has given about Castorley's health were not capable of being understood as "common form," and therefore suspicious. Or again, Manallace broods to the narrator that the "sacred hours" which Lady Castorley has agreed to give over to her husband and his friend in order that they may complete the book may now in fact characterize the time she is free to spend with her lover. "She saw exactly how I had set my traps," Manallace continues, "I know it! She's been trying to make me admit it." But Manallace never does admit it. The problem of what is either not said or deviously said in the story is reproduced by what is suppressed or elided in the discourse of the story. "The tale is written with such drastic and sober economy," notes J. M. S. Tompkins in the most searching discussion of it, "that the reader is sometimes put to it to trace a strong impression to its source."

The matter of source, in fact, is crucial to **"Dayspring Mishandled,"** because it is implicit in the pervasive accounts of various kinds of textuality that the text itself presents. What these texts have in common is that they are all fraudulent. In part, Kipling's own text is, perhaps to some, of an almost too irresistibly fashionable kind today: a text about other texts. What makes it nevertheless most distinctive is its chill insistence upon origins—textual and emotional, for the two are entangled with each other in ways impossible to separate or even to represent. There is something very close to the source of **"Dayspring Mishandled"** which needs to be suppressed, or at least not fully disclosed. I have centered upon the fact that we are not told specifically what Castorley said to Manallace about Val's mother in order to create a space in which to investigate the logic by which Kipling's text evacuates itself as a condition of its own discourse. In **"Dayspring Mishandled"** there are sources about which it is necessary to be silent, even though they are everywhere represented, and, indeed, can only be because of this silence. Of nothing is this more true than textuality itself, which assumes an authority so fraudulent and yet so encompassing and powerful that it disables any emotion from knowing itself and confounds any other fact of life which would have its own being.

The most significant tissue of textuality in **"Dayspring Mishandled"** is of course the Chaucer fragment that Manallace concocts; one of two lines quoted from it provides Kipling's own text with its title. This could be taken as a way of disclosing the implication of the one in the other, or even of marking its very source. The quoted lines, as Castorley reads them, speak of "a girl praying against an undesired marriage." We might read his reading with a sense of irony when we consider the position of his own wife, as Manallace understands her,

by the time of Castorley's death; "plangent as doom," the critic celebrates the very title words to the narrator, "plangent as doom." We may also want to consider the possible ways in which the larger narrative which encloses it bear upon the Chaucer narrative Castorley goes on to summarize. This narrative of thwarted young love and betrayed ideals certainly appears to stand in some relation to the larger narrative, or else perhaps to distill the larger narrative in more attenuated, fragmented form; the theme of knighthood, for example, is prominent in each—disingenuously renounced in Chaucer, openly desired in Kipling, and apparently the source of blocking young love in both.

However the Chaucer narrative does not stand in a purely analogical relation to Kipling's, nor does the analogical relation it provokes have quite a logically intelligible force which can be decisively clarified. Instead, the undecidable relation remains merely teasing and its force something that is all the more compelling because it is broken off. Of the Dutch copyist Castorley cries that he "spoils his page and chucks it." Unlike him, we know of course that the copyist is in fact Manallace and that his forgery is authenticated by being so "spoiled." The Chaucer narrative is the clearest example of something everywhere in Kipling's: what is not disclosed appears everywhere under the sign of what is. Moreover, what is disclosed merely leads, in turn, to further indisclosures: in this case, the "Statement" Castorley mentions wherein he has written the rest of Chaucer's narrative is something we are never given in Kipling's. In all three cases—Manallace's, Kipling's, and Castorley's—we are given evidence of narratives which are partial or suppressed, implicated in each other, and fraudulent. Each one gets represented in the other two but never gets completed. There is a ceaseless textualizing in **"Dayspring Mishandled"** hopelessly entangled with itself.

This leads to a decisive question: can Manallace's revenge upon Castorley be fully represented by his own fraudulent text? The answer of course is that it cannot. Not only does Manallace's revenge need to be represented elsewhere; his plan nearly to the end is to expose the pseudo-Chaucer text as such in "the popular press." The revenge needs to be completed by Castorley himself, in the form of the magisterial edition of Chaucer he plans after the discovery of the fraudulent fragment. What Manallace discovers is that his very revenge, like his text, is divided against itself. Ultimately, it becomes impossible for him to determine his own authority. "He taught me," Manallace tells the narrator, speaking of the formula for the birdlime used in the preparation of his Chaucer that Castorley once told him about. Does Castorley's acceptance of this Chaucer as genuine testify more to the genius of Castorley or Manallace? What vantagepoint outside the necessary authority of each of them can be used to answer this question? At another point Lady Castorley reminds Manallace if it is a question of completing her husband's text before he dies, "you know ever so much better how his book should be arranged than he does himself." In a sense, the object of Manallace's revenge is finally inadequate to its reception and so Manallace must fully enact it himself, as if repossessing its original power. In another sense, the representation of the revenge is so exquisitely achieved that neither Manallace nor Castorley can be humanly adequate to it, neither quite able to recreate himself in its terms, terms which abide in the consummate fragment and not in life at all.

By the end of **"Dayspring Mishandled"** two kinds of textual energy, sponsored respectively by the creative and the critical, have become coterminous. So have two very different kinds of emotions, for Manallace's devotion to Castorley is yoked inseparably with his original desire for his destruction. Manallace's creative aims exist to be made good in Castorley's critical industry, just as he needs to attend to the life of the man in order that there be something upon which to shatter his reputation. What makes these symmetrical equations possible is the same thing which disturbs them: Lady Castorley's ostensible scheming, and then Manallace's horrified realization that his own revenge has become embedded in what he takes to be her lustful, cold wish for her husband's death. It needs to be emphasized that there is no discourse apart from the events of **"Dayspring Mishandled"** that renders any judgment about Manallace's gradually certain intuition concerning Lady Castorley and Gleeag. This intuition originates when Manallace senses something suspicious in a phrasing of Lady Castorley's to the effect that even her husband does not realize the full extent of his obligation of Manallace. It is another example of what I have been emphasizing as the trope of undisclosed significance—still another instance of how the energies of the fraudulent *spread* in Kipling's text, and finally perhaps the best indication of how this text emplots its basic oppositions. Love and hate, true and false literature, life and art, revelation and suppression: all these get entangled with one another, caught up in larger designs, and dispersed. Oppositions are not binary. Or rather, though predicated as binary, they get worked out according to another logic entirely.

By the end of **"Dayspring Mishandled"** it is impossible to establish difference. The jaunty, sardonic, confident discourse expressed in the first paragraph has long been diffused among sudden veerings of tone, quick imbrications of events, extended patches of reported dialogue, and the appearance of an unnamed narrator whose indistinct voice has gradually merged with the breathless suppositions of Manallace. What a drowsy Castorley said about what his wife said turns out to be something that Dr. Johnson said—and neither the narrator nor Manallace is sure what else the wife said, which is something almost exactly like what Castorley had said, although neither of them seems to be aware of this and there is no longer any authority in Kipling's text to indicate whether or not a reader should be. "Oh God!" we read, "Life had always been one long innuendo!" Insofar as it is a question of Lady Castorley's behavior, it is as if there is something in Kipling's text more than half-willing to concede the hapless fatuity of its own designs, even as, from Manallace's point of view, an appalled fascination over her behavior, thoroughly squalid, persists to the last sentence. We may remember or we may not that the motive force for the narrative resides in something Castorley once said to Manallace about Val's mother that was not an innuendo. And yet, since we were not told precisely what it was, it has retained the character of an innuendo. It transformed life quite literally into text. By the end this text appears to have become transformed again into life—with the addition now that "life" is inscribed with textuality. This is literally the case with Manallace, who learns to his consternation that Castorley wants to inscribe the book to him as his "most valued assistant." It is figuratively the case with Castorley, whose face "came to look like old vellum." We recall that from the outset of the narrative the very will to live of both these men has been defined by their capacity to produce texts, and we can conclude, I think, that it is simply undecidable whether Manallace's interpretation of Lady Castorley's behavior is correct or whether his interpretation is instead a product of what might be called his own "textual" energies.

Another problem with Manallace's interpretation of Lady Castorley is that his desire to protect Castorley for the purposes of his own revenge is inseparable from his continuing need to preserve the possibility of defaming him by having him alive. There is in fact a strange relation in **"Dayspring Mishandled"** between protection and defamation, and by examining it we may understand more sharply the logic according to which oppositions, just as Manallace and Castorley, get entangled with each other.

Once again, the oppositions appear to be as distinct as Val's mother from Lady Castorley. The one woman, old, abides as so revered that she does not have to be spoken about. The other woman, young, emerges to be vilified. "She's the devil," cries Manallace at one point, as if voicing the curse upon Lady Castorley that Castorley had made so fatefully upon Val's mother. Furthermore, it is in defense of Val's mother that Manallace began what we are told was to be "his life's work." Lady Castorley, on the other hand, emerges under the sign of Castorley's death's work. To each man (though more explicitly with Manallace) each woman functions in the role of muse. The difference is that Val's mother is a true muse and Lady Castorley a false one. Yet the very fact that Val's mother dies of paralysis suggests that she is an inadequate, if not tainted, muse herself. The two women seem to be opposites—one so desexualized she is known only as a mother, the other sexualized as the type of the adulterous wife. Neither, however, inspires her respective devotee to fulfill his potential genius. Whether sexless or destructively sexual, the figure of the muse evokes either glib mediocrity or spurious pedantry. "The Colonel's lady and Judy O'Grady are sisters under the skin," runs a line from one of the *Barrack-Room Ballads*. Much of Manallace's response to Lady Castorley can be explained as a ferocious recognition of her sheer fraudulence, and possibly a suppressed intimation of her kinship with Val's mother.

The starkness of these ostensible differences between the two principal women of the text is even more dissolved by the presence of a third woman. She may not be named, and her presence conforms to the structure by which **"Dayspring Mishandled"** produces a certain kind of silence about itself by disclosures not given or information suppressed. At the beginning of the narrative Manallace gets drunk one night, recites some poetry, and eventually "after words, by the way, with a negress in yellow satin—was steered to his rooms." Years later, during a conversation with the narrator in which Manallace tells him what Castorley said about Vidal's mother, the narrator recalls to Manallace that "you told Kentucky Kate outside the old Empire that you had been faithful, Cynera, in your fashion." We perhaps may assume that "Kentucky Kate" is the same "negress" mentioned earlier—except that this does not explain the curious (if seemingly trivial) puzzle of why she was not named then, and this does not dispel the possibility that it is she, not Val's mother, whom Castorley begs to see at the end.

The latter incident reads: "*Please* would we let him out, just to speak to—he named her; he named her by her 'little' name out of the old Neminaka days?" Again, a strange refusal to name, or to be explicit, on the part of the discourse of the story constitutes an event in the story, and I do not think Tompkins is entirely satisfactory in glossing "Castorley's confused mind" which expresses "from very deep down the hidden, denied sense of guilt and remorse about the woman who rejected him." Val's mother did, true, once reject Castorley's proposal of marriage. But it is simply not clear that this is the woman to whom he would speak before his death, and, far from clarifying this point, the discourse of the story acts to suppress it, although, by repeating the matter of naming, it only exacerbates the reference. Why should this be so? It seems that the very question of a man's fidelity to a woman—as well as by extension the identity of the kind of woman to whom he would be faithful—cannot be disentangled from the negress who may be called Kentucky Kate. What are we to make of the fidelity that the narrator reminds Manallace he once pledged to her? What is its relation to the devotion he has for Val's mother? What, for that matter, was his relationship with this woman—and could it have been one which the delirious Castorley at the end wants somehow bitterly to appropriate for himself, as once he did Val's mother, whom Manallace adored from the beginning? These questions are undecidable, and they are only enabled, again, by the presence this time of a character who is only partially represented, who disturbs difference rather than mediates it, and who is disclosed only to be entangled with what is not disclosed.

There is at the source of **"Dayspring Mishandled"** something which would not know itself, and yet which knows itself only too well, and so participates in a structure of displaced signification as a condition of deferring the knowledge that it both does and does not have. This knowledge has been traced under the figure of entanglement, as when at one point the narrator comes upon Manallace in his toolshed-schullery "boiling a brew of slimy barks, which were, if mixed with oak-galls, vitrol and wine, to become an ink powder. We boiled it to the Monday, and it turned into an adhesive stronger than birdlime, and entangled us both." Out of this material Manallace eventually constructs the Chaucer manuscript, which seals the entanglement he already has with Castorley, as here its very existence so immediately entangles the narrator with him. Entanglement is what draws us into an elaborately wrought network of oppositions, as if to suppress the fact that the text is already divided against itself. **"Dayspring Mishandled"** occasions an example of the kind of deconstructive reading so lucidly set down by Barbara Johnson: "The difference *between* entities (prose and poetry, man and woman, literature and theory, guilt and innocence) are shown to be based on a repression of differences *within* entities, ways in which an entity differs from itself."

The distinctive quality about **"Dayspring Mishandled"** is the way it consistently marks its repression by a pattern of incomplete disclosures or overt suppression. There is one time when a repression does erupt. The time, noted earlier, when Castorley "would have said something unpleasant but was suppressed," returns at the very end when Castorley, "like a beast in agony," raves: "I was going to tell you fellows that it would be a dam' long time before Graydon advanced *me* two quid." But by then such a voiced resentment seems too trivial to be mentioned, and it has no climactic force. Castorley's words burst out with a revelation virtually irrelevant to the revenge logic of the whole chain of events, and therefore seem yet another way of displacing the violence of this logic, revealing its lack of coherence with itself, and disclosing a knowledge hardly disentangled from ignorance. There is imposture and there is authority everywhere—of utterance, action, and knowledge—yet each is so wholly inscribed, quite literally, in the other that what we have is a series of substitu-

tions of one for the other. Nothing grounds these substitutions. Textuality only entangles them further. There is nothing in the text we can substitute for what is not said, and yet what *is* said appears to be said because of an intimacy with what is not being said.

One of the more provocative statements of the story's discourse occurs when it is said of Castorley that, in his early days as a critic after he had left the Fictional Supply Syndicate, he "went out of his way to review one of Manallace's books with an intimacy of unclean deduction (this was before the days of Freud) which long stood as a record." Such a statement can only be confidently made with some certainty about what a "clean" deduction would be—and yet this is precisely what **"Dayspring Mishandled,"** presumably with post-Freudian deliberation, does not provide. Finally, if literature is fraudulent (or fatally complicitous with fraud), what is the purpose of the fraud? We are offered no suggestions about the idea of purpose except something Castorley once avers: "If you save people thinking, you can do anything with' em." It would be tempting to privilege this avowal. The brisk, cerebral economy of the narrative is conducted along something very like such lines, and the ironic, cynical mechanics of revenge are saturated with such spirit. What this principle does not contain, however, is an idea of motive.

Tompkins makes the casually inspired suggestion that **"Dayspring Mishandled"** "might—had the feminine element been stronger—have provided a theme for Henry James." I have tried to show that even this element is divided against itself in the text, where it is not simply muffled at the source. If the text is ultimately sponsored by hollow manipulation (or at least insufficiently disentangled from it, like a clean deduction from an unclean one), we are left with something rather knowingly groundless, which needs to produce justification in order to make revenge meaningful, but withholds the precise justification that is the basis for revenge in the first place. Without this justification—so strangely *marked,* as I have argued the refusal to disclose what Castorley says about Val's mother does—a gap between life and art is opened up that can only be bridged by a series of displacements and substitutions which reveal that the gap was already there. John Bayley has made this brilliantly offhanded reading: "'**Dayspring Mishandled**' resembles James's story ['The Beast in the Jungle'] in its bleak and subtle portrayal of the inability to be other than oneself: Manallace refrains from consummating his triumph, not through a free and virtuous moral choice—such things do not exist in Kipling's world—but because as an artist he cannot bear to see his work collapsed into the triviality of life." With Bayley's point in mind, we might say that there is nothing in **"Dayspring Mishandled"** to make any "deduction" from text to life "clean." Or vice versa, which is why the "feminine element"—that might sponsor such a movement in a transcendent sense, as it ostensibly does for Manallance himself—is so weak.

Precisely what Castorley said about Val's mother to Manallace, then, is not disclosed because disclosure would have been both too powerful and too irrelevant, or at least so the signification of the text would have it. Instead, **"Dayspring Mishandled"** gains the sign of what is not said, of what is suppressed, or what is *refused.* Just as it is in the nature of revenge to be more capable of representation in its designs rather than its cause, it is in the nature of the text to be more authoritative in its effects rather than its source. It may have mattered to have known what Castorly said, although the effect is more a detached curiosity about it rather than an in-flamed outrage. It matters more to see that his words produce effects that are limited to being textual. (Manallace's horror at Lady Castorley by the end is that of an artist's who has seen his work vulgarized.) It matters most crucially of all to become aware of a text whose authority is so entangled with its own dispossession that it turns inward as if out of an act of vengeance upon itself. The sign of refusal is the sign of dis-possession, which is, in turn, the sign of textuality itself, be-cause what makes **"Dayspring Mishandled"** so rich and strange is what it does not say, and how this is implicated in what is said.

"Dayspring Mishandled" is prefaced by four lines of verse from a French fairy story. Rather like the lines from the Chaucer fragment quoted and the narrative summarized, both these lines and the story itself have a certain applicabili-ty to what follows them. The most telling line, however, is one that is not given. Upon being told that the mandragora cannot speak, the young man who has just repeated the "song of the mandragora" that constitutes the prefaced lines drops the plant to the ground, saying, "Then this is not yet the one." If we can assume that prefatory material is usually the place where textual mastery is being decided, already the text inscribes its own renunciation. There is a song and there is a singer. But the singer is not the right one, and so whatever status the song has it is absented from its source. This may be because the source is poisoned; the text, we can hardly fail to forget, is utterly absorbed in producing revenge, which uses up both its object and its subject with the force of its own destructive logic. Or the song may be absented from its source because there is no source there; we may recall Castor-ley's dictum about manipulation for its own sake, however heedless of how the manipulation can then proceed to get en-tangled in its own designs. The "song of the mandragora," in any case, is recited over an authenticated origin which is not there.

In Kipling's late fiction, Bayley writes, "the daemonic pro-cess came thus almost to parody itself: uncertainties, divi-sions and queries were increased not by intelligent brooding but by a kind of arbitrary operation of the unconscious." I have not of course tried to discuss **"Dayspring Mishandled"** by reference to Kipling's own authority, nor have I tried to situate it among other late fictions. It can be discussed solely as a text because there are sufficient representative moments in it to indicate how peculiar, silent, and entangled its own energies are. As a text, it extracts a very real measure of re-venge upon its energies by marking them as fraudulent while failing to be disturbed about the matter; it is, so to speak, at ease with its own divisions, and withholding precisely what Castorley said about Val's mother to Manallace is an expres-sion of this ease. The fact that such things are done is not without a certain admixture of parody, though this is as it should be. The text does not release its own energies as other than textual ones because there are no other energies than textual ones. But the "process" is not "arbitrary." It is the logical result of a lack of justification within itself that emp-ties itself out in the manipulation while the words continually fold back into silence, as if there were nothing remaining and nothing else to be said. (pp. 55-62)

> Terry Caesar, "Suppression, Textuality, Entangle-ment, and Revenge in Kipling's 'Dayspring Mishan-dled'," in English Literature in Transition: 1880-1920, Vol. 29, No. 1, 1986, pp. 54-63.

FURTHER READING

Amis, Kingsley. *Rudyard Kipling and His World*. New York: Charles Scribner's Sons, 1975, 128 p.
      Concise biography and critical study that contains numerous il-lustrations.

Beachcroft, T. O. "Kipling." In his *The Modest Art: A Survey of the Short Story in English*, pp. 130-48. London: Oxford University Press, 1968.
      Surveys Kipling's career, suggesting reasons for Kipling's early success as a short story writer.

Bennett, Arnold. "Rudyard Kipling." In his *Books and Persons: Being Comments on a Past Epoch, 1908-1911*, pp. 160-66. New York: George H. Doran Co., 1917.
      Discusses *Actions and Reactions* and ways in which Kipling's social and political opinions affected the quality of his work.

Brooks, Cleanth, and Warren, Robert Penn. "Interpretation of 'The Man Who Would Be King'." In their *Understanding Fiction*, pp. 28-57. New York: Appleton-Century-Crofts, 1971.
      Provides an interpretation of Kipling's short story "The Man Who Would Be King" as well as suggestions for class discus-sion.

Carrington, Charles. *Rudyard Kipling: His Life and Work*. London: Macmillan & Co., 1955, 549 p.
      Seminal biography of Kipling that links his life with his writ-ings.

Coates, John. "Thor and Tyr: Sacrifice, Necessary Suffering and the Battle against Disorder in 'Rewards and Fairies'." *English Litera-ture in Transition: 1880-1920* 29, No. 1 (1986): 64-75.
      Examines patterns of theme and imagery as well as Kipling's use of Scandinavian legends in *Rewards and Fairies*.

Dobrée, Bonamy. *Rudyard Kipling: Realist and Fabulist*. London: Oxford University Press, 1967, 244 p.
      Biographical and critical work in which Dobrée presents Kip-ling "as he appears to me, as he has affected me, spoken directly to me."

Duffy, Dennis. "Justified by Implication: The Imperial Theme in Three Stories by Kipling." *Dalhousie Review* 48, No. 4 (Winter, 1968-1969): 472-87.
      Scrutinizes "The Conversion of Aurelian McGoggin," "The Bridge-Builders," and "The Church That Was at Antioch" to determine whether Kipling supported imperialism.

Fussell, Paul, Jr. "Irony, Freemasonry, and Humane Ethics in Kip-ling's 'The Man Who Would Be King'." *ELH* 25, No. 3 (September 1958): 216-33.
      Labels "The Man Who Would Be King" an ironic Christian-Masonic tale of high ethical import.

Green, Roger Lancelyn. *Kipling and the Children*. London: Elek Books, 1965, 240 p.
      Examines fiction Kipling wrote for and about children, paying particular attention to events in Kipling's own childhood that are recast in his stories.

Harrison, James. "Kipling's Jungle Eden." *Mosaic* VII, No. 2 (Win-ter 1974): 151-64.
      Studies Eden mythology and imagery in Kipling's *Jungle Books*.

Hart, Walter Morris. *Kipling the Story-Writer*. Berkeley: University of California Press, 1918, 225 p.

Examines Kipling's fiction technique in a format designed for classroom use.

Hopkins, R. Thurston. *Rudyard Kipling: A Literary Appreciation.* New York: Frederick A. Stokes Co., 1915, 356 p.
Critical biography that includes commentary by various scholars.

Lewis, Lisa A. F. "Some Links between the Stories in Kipling's 'Debits and Credits'." *English Literature in Transition: 1880-1920* 25, No. 2 (1982): 74-85.
Traces thematic and metaphoric connections between the stories in *Debits and Credits* and concludes that the tales are more enjoyable when read together.

Logan, A. M. "Kipling's Tales." *The Nation* LI, No. 1328 (11 December 1890): 465-66.
An originally unsigned essay that characterizes Kipling as a young writer, assessing *Plain Tales from the Hills, Indian Tales,* and *The Courting of Dinah Shadd.*

Mason, Philip. *Kipling: The Glass, the Shadow and the Fire.* London: Jonathan Cape, 1975, 334 p.
Critical study in which Mason seeks to "re-awaken a lost interest" and to demonstrate that stories from the last phase of Kipling's career reveal "a deeper and more consistent body of belief than most people have recognized."

McClure, John A. *Kipling and Conrad: The Colonial Fiction.* Cambridge, Mass: Harvard University Press, 1981, 182 p.
Defines Kipling's vision of the British empire and its inhabitants, examining in depth Kipling's use of colonial themes in stories written during the 1880s and 1890s.

Meyer, Rosalind. "But Is It Art?: An Appreciation of 'Just So Stories'." *The Kipling Journal* 58, No. 232 (December 1984): 10-33.
Asserts that Kipling's *Just So Stories* are a reflection of "the matured perfection of his craft."

Meyers, Jeffrey. "The Idea of Moral Authority in 'The Man Who Would Be King'." *Studies in English Literature, 1500-1900* VIII, No. 4 (Autumn 1968): 711-23.
Examines the thematic development of "The Man Who Would Be King," concluding that Kipling "fails to maintain a consistent moral perspective in the story."

Moss, Robert F. *Rudyard Kipling and the Fiction of Adolescence.* New York: St. Martin's Press, 1982, 165 p.
Reveals Kipling's treatment of adolescent experience in his short stories published between 1888 and 1901.

Pritchett, V. S. "Kipling's Short Stories." In his *The Living Novel and Later Appreciations,* pp. 175-82. New York: Random House, 1964.
Characterizes Kipling as "the only considerable English writer of fiction to have been popular in the most popular sense and to excite the claim to genius."

Rao, K. Bhaskara. *Rudyard Kipling's India.* Norman: University of Oklahoma Press, 1967, 190 p.
Reevaluation of Kipling's stature as a writer about India. Rao concludes, "Kipling managed successfully to create the illusion that he knew and understood India."

Raskin, Jonah. "Kipling's Contrasts." In his *The Mythology of Imperialism,* pp. 37-45. New York: Random House, 1971.
View of Kipling as a writer of distinctions and separations.

Schaub, Danielle. "Kipling's Craftmanship in 'The Bull That Thought'." *Studies in Short Fiction* 22, No. 3 (Summer 1985): 309-16.
Claims that "The Bull That Thought" "displays Kipling's mastery of the art of short-story telling both on a superficial and on a more profound level."

Sharma, S. T. "Kipling's India: A Study of Some Short Stories." *The Literary Criterion* XXII, No. 4 (1987): 54-61.
Suggests that four short stories, "The Maltese Cat," "William the Conqueror," "The Tomb of the Ancestors," and "The Bridge-Builders," reflect Kipling's identification with and understanding of India.

Stewart, J. I. M. "Kipling." In his *Eight Modern Readers,* pp. 223-93. Oxford: Oxford at the Clarendon Press, 1963.
Biographical essay in which Stewart offers a balanced appraisal of Kipling's short story canon.

Stinton, T. C. W. "What Really Happened in 'Mrs. Bathurst'?" *Essays in Criticism* XXXVIII, No. 1 (January 1988): 55-74.
Uses Kipling's short stories "A Madonna of the Trenches" and "By Word of Mouth" to illuminate "Mrs. Bathurst."

Tarinayya, M. "Kipling's 'Sea Constables' and Conrad's 'The Tale'." *The Literary Criterion* XVI, No. 3 (1981): 32-46.
Examines conclusions reached by Bonamy Dobrée concerning Kipling's "Sea Constables" and compares Kipling's story with Conrad's "The Tale," emphasizing differences in the artists' "tone and attitude to what happens in the tales and to life in general."

Tompkins, J. M. S. "Kipling's Later Tales: The Theme of Healing." *The Modern Language Review* XLV, No. 1 (January 1950): 18-32.
Inquires into Kipling's concept of healing as presented in *Debits and Credits, Rewards and Fairies,* and *Limits and Renewals.*

Wallis, Bruce E. "The Resurrection Motif in Kipling's 'The Gardener'." *Studies in Short Fiction* X, No. 1 (Winter 1973): 99-100.
Christian interpretation of the role of the gardener in "The Gardener."

Weygandt, Ann M. "A Study of Kipling's Use of Historical Material in 'Brother Square-Toes' and 'A Priest in Spite of Himself'." *Delaware Notes* 27th series (1954): 83-106.
Explicates Kipling's recasting of historical events in two short stories.

Thomas Mann

1875-1955

German novelist, short story writer, essayist, and critic.

Mann was a prominent twentieth-century writer whose international renown extends to both the novel and short fiction genres. In such works as *Buddenbrooks,* "Tonio Kröger," "Der Tod in Venedig" ("Death in Venice"), and *Der Zauberberg* (*The Magic Mountain*), Mann presents a synthesis of aesthetic, philosophical, and social concerns, while combining elements of literary Realism and Symbolism with an ironic sensibility. Though his fiction typically reveals a somber and cerebral fascination with death and decay, most critics agree that beneath this complex surface Mann expresses a deep, often humorous sympathy for humanity and a desire to resolve what he sees as the dualities of life. Critics have frequently observed a thematic unity in Mann's work and often refer to his use of leitmotiv in this regard. His many recurring themes include the isolation of the artist in society, the relation of life and art, the nature of time, and the seduction of the individual by disease and death.

Born in Lübeck, Germany, Mann was the son of a successful grain merchant. His mother, an accomplished musician, was born and raised in Brazil, and his older brother, Heinrich, was a noted writer. Mann's bourgeois background and the contrasting natures of his parents—his father was austere, his mother passionate—figured prominently in much of his fiction. Mann's first story, "Gefallen," was published in the prestigious journal *Die Gesellschaft* when he was nineteen years old. While this story displayed a marked Romantic influence, Mann abandoned the tenets of Romanticism in his later works and developed an ironic sensibility that became the signature of his art. Although health problems prevented him from serving in World War I, Mann remained involved in the conflict through his nationalistic political essays. Following the war he cultivated interests in the writings of Goethe, Freud, Nietzsche, and Schopenhauer, and published his novel *The Magic Mountain,* for which he was awarded the Nobel Prize in Literature in 1929. Despite his nationalism during World War I, Mann fervently opposed the growth of national socialism and fascism in the 1930s. In 1933, he left Germany and went into self-imposed exile, eventually settling in the United States. In 1952, Mann left the United States and migrated to Switzerland where he spent the remaining years of his life.

In his first collection of stories, *Der kleine Herr Friedemann,* Mann contrasts the motivations and sensibilities of characters who look for comfort and success through conventional life—those Mann calls the *"banale Bürger,"* or commonplace citizens—and individuals who seek fulfillment outside mainstream society. The title story, for example, centers on Johannes Friedemann, a cripple who attempts to find happiness in nature, literature, music, and especially the theater. Through his use of deception and imagination he constructs a disciplined existence characterized by self-limitation and austere intelligence. At the age of thirty, however, Friedemann meets a woman whose beauty becomes his obsession and whose scorn propels him to take his own life. Frequently viewed as a prototype of the character Gustave von Aschenbach in

"Death in Venice," Friedemann personifies the clash of elemental impulses with the prohibitions of society, intellect, and physical disability. Critics have attributed the thematic and structural unity of *Der kleine Herr Friedemann* largely to Mann's use of the leitmotiv, a literary technique—perhaps his most characteristic device—by which individual stories are linked through common elements.

Mann's second volume, *Tristan,* contains many of his most successful stories, particularly "Tonio Kröger" and "Mario und der Zauberer" ("Mario and the Magician"). The character Tonio Kröger has been viewed as an embodiment of Mann's own cultural heritage. An outsider as a youth, Tonio struggles with inner conflicts later in life and considers completely removing himself from society. He realizes, however, that this choice would deny a fundamental aspect of his heritage. In accepting his status as an outsider while remaining within society, Tonio allows himself a chance to find love and happiness. Critics have stated that "Tonio Kröger" documents Mann's path away from the disillusioned romanticism of his first collection of stories and toward a new artistic intellectualism. "Mario and the Magician" is an allegorical piece that is based on experiences Mann and his family had as vacationers during the 1930s in Mussolini's Italy. Generally considered an attack on fascism, this story involves the psychological power of an evil hypnotist and the emotional passivity of his audience. Like other works in which Mann treats the issue of fascism, "Mario and the Magician" contains both an implicit denunciation and a subtly expressed condonation of its subject that represents the contradictory perspectives of many of Mann's German contemporaries.

Mann's most famous story, "Death in Venice," is considered a masterpiece of short fiction. Poignantly reflecting the artist's struggle to reconcile discipline with impulse, this story depicts the decline and ultimate collapse of Gustave von Aschenbach, a renowned German author who, after years of living a morally and artistically ascetic life, surrenders to the sensual side of his nature during a sojourn in Venice. The sultry Venetian setting incites Aschenbach's homoerotic passion for Tadzio, a beautiful, godlike youth. As Aschenbach succumbs to long-repressed spiritual and physical desires, he loses control of his will. His resulting degradation leads to his death. In this work, Mann skillfully combines psychological realism and mythological symbolism to create a multidimensional story that explores the moral transformation of an artist in quest for perfect beauty.

Another often-discussed tale, "Die vertauschten köpfe" ("The Transposed Heads"), is Mann's adaptation of a Hindu legend that parables the striving for harmony between the inner and outer self. This story of two inseparable youths whose friendship rests upon their dissimilarity depicts how each admires the other and seeks an exchange and union of their contrasting natures. Through a restrained, exotic narrative style, Mann satirizes humanity's tendency to divide existence into two separate parts: the actual world and a realm of ideal, unattainable values. Mann posits that when the mind and body become rivals, they eventually destroy one another and thus, all beauty is sacrificed. "Die Betrogene" ("The Black Swan"), one of Mann's later works, focuses on the paradox of a failing body and a youthful spirit in an aging German widow who falls in love with the young American tutor of her son. Here Mann juxtaposes the central character's belief in the forces of nature with the antipathy of her daughter, an artist whose absorption in the powers of the spirit is symbolized by a physical disability, and whose alienation from life is represented by her art. Often considered a companion piece to "Death in Venice," "The Black Swan" explores the dialectic between nature and spirit and presents an expansion and verification of the moral philosophy that Mann presented in his earlier story.

Critical opinion of Mann's work has been consistently favorable. While some critics have suggested that Mann's writings suffer from pretentiousness and verbose rhetoric and that his characters are often cold and distant, most praise him for the depth of his vision and the vastness of his intellect. In spite of great personal and societal adversity, Mann maintained his artistic composure, and his literary development steadily continued until his death. He has been called a master of style, and his compositions, realistic yet deeply symbolic, have rarely failed to reach a large audience.

(For further information on Mann's life and career, see *Twentieth Century Literary Criticism*, Vols. 2, 8, 14, 21, 35; *Contemporary Authors*, Vols. 104, 128; and *Dictionary of Literary Biography*, Vol. 66.)

PRINCIPAL WORKS

SHORT FICTION

"Gefallen" 1894; published in journal *Die Gesellschaft*
Der kleine Herr Friedemann 1898
Tristan 1903
  [*Tristan*, 1960]
Der Tod in Venedig 1912
  [*Death in Venice*, 1925]
Children and Fools 1928
Mario und der Zauberer 1930
  [*Mario and the Magician*, 1931]
Stories of Three Decades 1936
Die vertauschten Köpfe 1940
  [*The Transposed Heads*, 1941]
Die Betrogene 1953
  [*The Black Swan*, 1954]

OTHER MAJOR WORKS

Buddenbrooks (novel) 1901
  [*Buddenbrooks*, 1924]
Königliche Hoheit (novel) 1909
  [*Royal Highness*, 1916]
Betrachtungen eines Unpolitischen (essays) 1918
  [*Reflections of a Nonpolitical Man*, 1983]
Der Zauberberg (novel) 1924
  [*The Magic Mountain*, 1927]
Die Geschichten Jaakobs (novel) 1933
  [*The Tales of Jacob*, 1934]
Der junge Joseph (novel) 1934
  [*Young Joseph*, 1935]
Joseph in Ägypten (novel) 1936
  [*Joseph in Egypt*, 1938]
Lotte in Weimar (novel) 1939
  [*The Beloved Returns*, 1940]
Joseph der Ernahrer (novel) 1943
  [*Joseph the Provider*, 1944]
Doktor Faustus (novel) 1947
  [*Doctor Faustus*, 1948]
Joseph and His Brothers (novel cycle) 1948; includes *The Tales of Jacob, Young Joseph, Joseph in Egypt,* and *Joseph the Provider*
Der Erwahlte (novel) 1951
  [*The Holy Sinner*, 1951]
Bekenntnisse des Hochstaplers Felix Krull (novel) 1954
  [*Confessions of Felix Krull, Confidence Man*, 1955]

D. H. LAWRENCE (essay date 1913)

[*Lawrence was an English novelist, poet, and essayist noted for introducing themes of modern psychology to English fiction. In his lifetime he was a controversial figure, both for the explicit sexuality he portrayed in his novels and for his unconventional personal life. His novel* Lady Chatterley's Lover *(1928) was the subject of a landmark obscenity trial in Great Britain in 1960 that turned largely on the legitimacy of Lawrence's inclusion of hitherto forbidden sexual terms. In the following excerpt from an essay originally published in the* Blue Review, *Lawrence comments on "Death in Venice," acknowledging Mann's technical skill, but stating that he finds Mann's work "somewhat banal."*]

Thomas Mann is perhaps the most famous of German novelists now writing. He, and his elder brother, Heinrich Mann, with Jakob Wassermann, are acclaimed the three artists in fiction of present-day Germany.

But Germany is now undergoing that craving for form in fiction, that passionate desire for the mastery of the medium of narrative, that will of the writer to be greater than and undisputed lord over the stuff he writes, which is figured to the world in Gustave Flaubert. (p. 260)

It is as an artist rather than as a story-teller that Germany worships Thomas Mann. And yet it seems to me, this craving for form is the outcome, not of artistic conscience, but of a certain attitude to life. For form is not a personal thing like style. It is impersonal like logic. And just as the school of Alexander Pope was logical in its expressions, so it seems the school of Flaubert is, as it were, logical in its æsthetic form. "Nothing outside the definite line of the book," is a maxim. But can the human mind fix absolutely the definite line of a book, any more than it can fix absolutely any definite line of action for a living being?

Thomas Mann, however, is personal, almost painfully so, in his subject-matter. In **"Tonio Kröger"**, the long *Novelle* at the end of the *Tristan* volume, he paints a detailed portrait of himself as a youth and younger man, a careful analysis. And he expresses at some length the misery of being an artist. "Literature is not a calling, it is a curse." Then he says to the Russian painter girl: "There is no artist anywhere but longs again, my love, for the common life." But any young artist might say that. It is because the stress of life in a young man, but particularly in an artist, is very strong, and has as yet found no outlet, so that it rages inside him in *Sturm und Drang*. But the condition is the same, only more tragic, in the Thomas Mann of fifty-three [Mann was actually just 38 when this article was first published.] He has never found any outlet for himself, save his art. He has never given himself to anything but his art. This is all well and good, if his art absorbs and satisfies him, as it has done some great men, like Corot. But then there are the other artists, the more human, like Shakespeare and Goethe, who must give themselves to life as well as to art. And if these were afraid, or despised life, then with their surplus they would ferment and become rotten. Which is what ails Thomas Mann. He is physically ailing, no doubt. But his complaint is deeper: it is of the soul. (pp. 260-61)

He is a disciple, in method, of the Flaubert who wrote: "I worked sixteen hours yesterday, to-day the whole day, and have at last finished one page." In writing of the *Leitmotiv* and its influence, he says:

> Now this method alone is sufficient to explain my slowness. It is the result neither of anxiety nor indigence, but of an overpowering sense of responsibility for the choice of every word, the coining of every phrase . . . a responsibility that longs for perfect freshness, and which, after two hours' work, prefers not to undertake an important sentence. For which sentence is important, and which not? Can one know beforehand whether a sentence, or part of a sentence may not be called upon to appear again as *Motiv*, peg, symbol, citation or connexion? And a sentence which must be heard twice must be fashioned accordingly. It must—I do not speak of beauty—possess a certain high level, and symbolic suggestion, which will make it worthy to sound again in any epic future. So every point becomes a

standing ground, every adjective a decision, and it is clear that such work is not to be produced offhand.

This, then, is the method. The man himself was always delicate in constitution. "The doctors said he was too weak to go to school, and must work at home." I quote from Aschenbach, in **"Der Tod in Venedig."** "When he fell, at the age of fifty-three, one of his closest observers said of him: 'Aschenbach has always lived like this'—and he gripped his fist hard clenched; 'never like this'—and he let his open hand lie easily on the arm of the chair." (pp. 261-62)

And then comes the final revelation, difficult to translate. He is speaking of life as it is written into his books:

> For endurance of one's fate, grace in suffering, does not only mean passivity, but is an active work, a positive triumph, and the Sebastian figure is the most beautiful symbol, if not of all art, yet of the art in question. If one looked into this portrayed world and saw the elegant self-control that hides from the eyes of the world to the last moment the inner undermining, the biological decay; saw the yellow ugliness which, sensuously at a disadvantage, could blow its choking heat of desire to a pure flame, and even rise to sovereignty in the kingdom of beauty; saw the pale impotence which draws out of the glowing depths of its intellect sufficient strength to subdue a whole vigorous people, bring them to the foot of the Cross, to the feet of impotence; saw the amiable bearing in the empty and severe service of Form; saw the quickly enervating longing and art of the born swindler: if one saw such a fate as this, and all the rest it implied, then one would be forced to doubt whether there were in reality any other heroism than that of weakness. Which heroism, in any case, is more of our time than this?

Perhaps it is better to give the story of **"Der Tod in Venedig,"** from which the above is taken, and to whose hero it applies.

Gustav von Aschenbach, a fine, famous author, over fifty years of age, coming to the end of a long walk one afternoon, sees as he is approaching a burying-place, near Munich, a man standing between the chimeric figures of the gateway. This man in the gate of the cemetery is almost the *Motiv* of the story. By him, Aschenbach is infected with a desire to travel. He examines himself minutely, in a way almost painful in its frankness, and one sees the whole soul of this author of fifty-three. And it seems, the artist has absorbed the man, and yet the man is there, like an exhausted organism on which a parasite has fed itself strong. Then begins a kind of Holbein *Totentanz*. The story is quite natural in appearance, and yet there is the gruesome sense of symbolism throughout. The man near the burying-ground has suggested travel—but whither? Aschenbach sets off to a watering-place on the Austrian coast of the Adriatic, seeking some adventure, some passionate adventure, to which his sick soul and unhealthy body have been kindled. But finding himself on the Adriatic, he knows it is not thither that his desire draws him, and he takes ship for Venice. It is all real, and yet with a curious sinister unreality, like decay, the "biological decay". On board there is a man who reminds one of the man in the gateway, though there is no connexion. And then, among a crowd of young Poles who are crossing, is a ghastly fellow, whom Aschenbach sees is an old man dressed up as young, who capers unsuspected among the youths, drinks hilariously with them, and falls hideously drunk at last on the deck, reaching to the author, and slobbering about *"dem allerliebsten, dem schönsten Liebchen"*. Suddenly the upper plate of his false teeth falls on his underlip.

Aschenbach takes a gondola to the Lido, and again the gondolier reminds one of the man in the cemetery gateway. He is, moreover, one who will make no concession, and, in spite of Aschenbach's demand to be taken back to St. Mark's, rows him in his black craft to the Lido, talking to himself softly all the while. Then he goes without payment.

The author stays in a fashionable hotel on the Lido. The adventure is coming, there by the pallid sea. As Aschenbach comes down into the hall of the hotel, he sees a beautiful Polish boy of about fourteen, with honey-coloured curls clustering round his pale face, standing with his sisters and their governess.

Aschenbach loves the boy—but almost as a symbol. In him he loves life and youth and beauty, as Hyacinth in the Greek myth. This, I suppose, is blowing the choking heat to pure flame, and raising it to the kingdom of beauty. He follows the boy, watches him all day long on the beach, fascinated by beauty concrete before him. It is still the *Künstler* and his abstraction: but there is also the "yellow ugliness, sensuously at a disadvantage", of the elderly man below it all. But the picture of the writer watching the folk on the beach gleams and lives with a curious, gold-phosphorescent light, touched with the brightness of Greek myth, and yet a modern seashore with folks on the sands, and a half-threatening, diseased sky.

Aschenbach, watching the boy in the hotel lift, finds him delicate, almost ill, and the thought that he may not live long fills the elderly writer with a sense of peace. It eases him to think the boy should die.

Then the writer suffers from the effect of the *sirocco*, and intends to depart immediately from Venice. But at the station he finds with joy that his luggage has gone wrong, and he goes straight back to the hotel. There, when he sees Tadzio again, he knows why he could not leave Venice.

There is a month of hot weather, when Aschenbach follows Tadzio about, and begins to receive a look, loving, from over the lad's shoulder. It is wonderful, the heat, the unwholesomeness, the passion in Venice. One evening comes a street singer, smelling of carbolic acid, and sings beneath the veranda of the hotel. And this time, in gruesome symbolism, it is the man from the burying-ground distinctly.

The rumour is, that the black cholera is in Venice. An atmosphere of secret plague hangs over the city of canals and palaces. Aschenbach verifies the report at the English bureau, but cannot bring himself to go away from Tadzio, nor yet to warn the Polish family. The secretly pest-smitten days go by. Aschenbach follows the boy through the stinking streets of the town and loses him. And on the day of the departure of the Polish family, the famous author dies of the plague.

It is absolutely, almost intentionally, unwholesome. The man is sick, body and soul. He portrays himself as he is, with wonderful skill and art, portrays his sickness. And since any genuine portrait is valuable, this book has its place. It portrays one man, one atmosphere, one sick vision. It claims to do no more. And we have to allow it. But we know it is unwholesome—it does not strike me as being morbid for all that, it is too well done—and we give it its place as such.

Thomas Mann seems to me the last sick sufferer from the complaint of Flaubert. The latter stood away from life as from a leprosy. And Thomas Mann, like Flaubert, feels vaguely that he has in him something finer than ever physical life revealed. Physical life is a disordered corruption, against which he can fight with only one weapon, his fine æsthetic sense, his feeling for beauty, for perfection, for a certain fitness which soothes him, and gives him an inner pleasure, however corrupt the stuff of life may be. There he is, after all these years, full of disgusts and loathing of himself as Flaubert was, and Germany is being voiced, or partly so, by him. And so, with real suicidal intention, like Flaubert's, he sits, a last too-sick disciple, reducing himself grain by grain to the statement of his own disgust, patiently, self-destructively, so that his statement at least may be perfect in a world of corruption. But he is so late.

Already I find Thomas Mann, who, as he says, fights so hard against the banal in his work, somewhat banal. His expression may be very fine. But by now what he expresses is stale. I think we have learned our lesson, to be sufficiently aware of the fulsomeness of life. And even while he has a rhythm in style, yet his work has none of the rhythm of a living thing, the rise of a poppy, then the after uplift of the bud, the shedding of the calyx and the spreading wide of the petals, the falling of the flower and the pride of the seed-head. There is an unexpectedness in this such as does not come from their carefully plotted and arranged developments. Even *Madame Bovary* seems to me dead in respect to the living rhythm of the whole work. While it is there in *Macbeth* like life itself.

But Thomas Mann is old—and we are young. Germany does not feel very young to me. (pp. 262-65)

> *D. H. Lawrence, "Thomas Mann," in his* Selected Literary Criticism, *edited by Anthony Beal, Heinemann Educational Books Ltd, 1956, pp. 260-65.*

WILSON FOLLETT (essay date 1936)

[*In the following excerpted review, Follett discusses Mann's focus on the dilemma of artists in repressive environments and suggests that* Stories of Three Decades *presents a definitive summary of Mann's career.*]

In these two dozen stories [in **Stories of Three Decades**], ranging in length from less than five pages to nearly eighty and in the times of publication from 1897 to 1929, the reader of *Buddenbrooks* and *The Magic Mountain* is provided with a new conspectus of Thomas Mann. The volume, a substantial one containing over a quarter of a million words in 570 pages of text, has from beginning to end a singular continuity and unity. A comparable net effect is sometimes produced by an arrangement of tales expressly chosen for implicit mutual harmony: but these tales are neither chosen nor arranged. The collection is complete and in a sense definitive: it is all of Thomas Mann's fiction in the shorter forms, arbitrarily presented in the order of first appearances in print. What we should normally expect is a miscellany exhibiting not only growth, but also change. But, as it happens, there is simply nothing miscellaneous about Thomas Mann. . . . The twenty-four stories show their author with a steadfast singleness and simplicity which even the wayfaring reader cannot miss, an integration astounding to all but those intensive students of Mann's work who, having long followed it in the original language, have in effect already brought the present collection together in their own minds.

The continuum in *Stories of Three Decades* is the author as character, an identity unseen but still unalteringly present from tale to tale. This observation does not mean that the stories, taken singly, are to be read as autobiography. Certainly Thomas Mann is not among those authors who make a career of writing what they have done (a posture of which the natural corollary is doing all manner of things in order to write about them). It is clear that he has never had the weakness of treating a story as a mere catchall for whatever he felt himself to be at the time of composition. Tonio Kröger is not Thomas Mann; Aschenbach, in **"Death in Venice,"** is not Thomas Mann; Cipolla the magician is not he; but each of these is a careful transmutation of something central in Thomas Mann—the same something always. It is that common element which, emerging from piece after piece over a span of nearly a third of a century, gives the volume its revelatory significance as a personal record. And this significance is as far as possible from being one of those beguiling subtleties which criticism is prone to invent out of its own need for reducing complications to simplicity or illuminating a darkness. The author himself not only sanctions this construction of his work: he anticipates it. In a preface written with the urbanity of which he is never a more distinguished master than when speaking of himself, he expressly calls his *Stories of Three Decades* "an autobiography in the guise of fable."

In *Buddenbrooks,* in *The Magic Mountain,* and currently in *Joseph and His Brothers,* we have a very great modern mind so refracted through the prism of reality that it reaches us in the form of a spectrum of the utmost richness and variety. In the tales, on the other hand, this same mind is passed through the lens of a single idea, a single interest, and its component colors are bent together into white light and focused on one point as if by a burning glass. The method of dispersion is replaced by the method of concentration. Where the great novels mean a search for one meaning in all things, the stories mean a search for all meanings in but one thing.

That one thing is the inveterate dilemma of the creative artist in this world.

To Thomas Mann the artist is chiefly interesting as the congenital outcast from life—the man with a supreme and splendid affliction. Between him and his normal fellows is a barrier which neither he nor they can overlook and which they know to be impenetrable; and on his side of it he lives his lonely life in a sort of spiritual quarantine. The true artist is marked out from the beginning for unique privileges, for unique compensations unintelligible to other folk, but most of all for unique sufferings. He suffers simply for what he is—a being able to comprehend the life of common humanity, able to analyze it and illuminate it and shine in the reflection of the radiance he has himself cast upon it, but forever unable to participate in it; one locked up in his own duality and condemned to make the best of a situation as irremediably tragic as if he were Siamese twins.

Tonio Kröger, who is of all his creator's spokesmen the most fully articulate on this subject, says among many utterances to the same purport:

> We who are set apart do not conceive it [life] as, like us, unusual; it is the normal, respectable, and admirable that is the kingdom of our longing: life, in all its seductive banality! That man is very far from being an artist . . . whose last and deepest enthusiasm is the *raffiné,* the eccentric and satanic; who does not know longing for the innocent, the sim-

ple, and the living, for a little friendship, devotion, familiar human happiness—the gnawing, surreptitious hankering . . . for the bliss of the commonplace. . . .

> A genuine human friend. Believe me, I should be proud and happy to possess a friend among men. But up to now all the friends I have had have been dæmons, kobolds, impious monsters, and spectres dumb with excess of knowledge—that is to say, literary men. . . .

> It is against all sense to love life and yet bend all the powers you have to draw it over to your own side, to the side of finesse and melancholy and the whole sickly aristocracy of letters.

And then comes this sentence, as true as it is terrible:

> The kingdom of art increases and that of health and innocence declines on this earth.

Not that all of the protagonists in these twenty-four stories are practising artists. They do not have to be: for the outcast of whatever degree will serve well enough as a prototype of the artist, a dramatization of his problem. The meaning throughout is Conrad's meaning in the place where he refers to his "pages in which so many lives come and go at the cost of one which slips insensibly away"—slips away unlived, is the implication. Conrad, too, was a portrait painter of the outcast, though of the outcast in any guise except Mann's favorite one of the artist. It is a fact not without its suggestiveness that these two great men of racial origins so dissimilar, authors of work thematically so unlike and yet animated by basic perceptions so closely akin, should both have come to show the harassed eyes and the ravaged faces of all the self-conscious ones who are too wise in that they should not know—the Hamlet look. Thomas Mann's last decade has added more than its share to that expression, if there is anything in published likenesses; and that for reasons not confined to whatever disillusionments he has undergone as a good man and a good German. Too deeply read in the soul to be blithe, too experienced in the pleasures of expression to be morose, he is probably the saddest happy man alive today.

Wilson Follett, "The Saddest Happy Man Alive," in The Saturday Review of Literature, *Vol. XIV, No. 6, June 6, 1936, p. 5.*

LOUIS KRONENBERGER   (essay date 1936)

[*A drama critic for* Time *magazine from 1938 to 1961, Kronenberger was a distinguished historian, literary critic, and author highly regarded for his expertise in eighteenth-century English history and literature. His critical works* The Thread of Laughter: Chapters on English Stage Comedy from Jonson to Maugham *(1952) and* The Republic of Letters *(1955) contain some of his best literary commentaries. In the following excerpted review of* Stories of Three Decades, *Kronenberger suggests that Mann often allows his philosophical and thematic concerns to overshadow his aesthetic intentions.*]

Bringing together all of Thomas Mann's shorter fiction in one volume is an event of some importance. In this age of so many omnibuses, it might well have been done earlier. At any rate, here [in *Stories of Three Decades*] is more than a sound tribute to one of the most distinguished of living writers; here also is our first opportunity to encounter in English a half dozen of Mann's fictional writings. Two of these, the dialectical piece in the form of a play called *Fiorenza,* and the first section of an unfinished novel called "Felix Krull," have been much talked about. I am afraid that *Fiorenza* will be found disappointing; the subtle and lively "Felix Krull," on the other hand, will only be found disappointing because it was never finished.

Thirty-three years of work are represented in this collection, extending all the way from the early stories which engaged Mann's attention before he began writing *Buddenbrooks* through a middle period which begins with **"Tonio Kroger"** and ends with **"Death in Venice"** on to the two famous novelettes of recent years, **"Disorder and Early Sorrow"** and **"Mario and the Magician."** Such a collection—though as Mann points out in his foreword it is a very uneven one— would be enough of itself to keep his reputation green though he had never written a *Buddenbrooks,* a *Magic Mountain* or a *Joseph.* **"Tonio"** will long remain the classic document of a very recurrent adventure, the bourgeois turned artist; **"Death in Venice"** speaks for itself as perhaps the finest novelette of our time; and the two later novelettes, particularly **"Early Sorrow,"** occupy a high place that would be higher if **"Death in Venice"** did not overshadow them.

Mann in his foreword presents us with some brief notes telling how and why most of these tales were written, indicating the artistic problems they presented and the particular significance they had for him at the time he wrote them. One cannot fail to find a certain value in these personal comments, yet I must remark that I know of no other important writer who speaks in the first person less ingratiatingly than Mann does. The shockingly complacent tone he adopted throughout his *Sketch of My Life* is modulated here to a sort of grave discussion of his artistic self, yet even here there is a lack of modesty and a total lack of charm. Nor, to be frank, has he said here anything very revealing about his work.

Fortunately most of the work demands no marginalia, but can stand alone. The body of it is not only in the long tradition of humanism and culture which has produced much great fiction, but is even a kind of explicit expression of that tradition. It is no accident or misapprehension that so often leads us to think of Thomas Mann less as a novelist and story teller than as a man of letters, for the final effect of his work is a literary effect—if by literary one may be allowed to include cultural and philosophical. Life in the raw, even life in the mass, does not exist for him. He is constantly preoccupied by the special problems of the artist, the philosopher, the moralist; by such matters as discipline, tradition, knowledge, beauty, spirit; by the old German sensibility to inner promptings and dilemmas. The world he inhabits is large, but it is on a highly intellectual plane, and the least of his stories is akin to the greatest in the sense, at any rate, that it addresses itself more to our minds than our emotions.

This is partly a racial characteristic, and nobody can go all through this book without perceiving how often Mann suffers as an artist because of a certain heaviness and lack of creative yeast. Even where one part of his mind is controlled by irony, another part is in the clutches of didacticism—not to speak of the occasions when he altogether forgets he is telling a story and launches forth on the favorite German pastime of dialectics. At such times he is by no means uninteresting and sometimes is even brilliant; but it is only the force of his mind that engages us, not the force of his art or the interest of his story. Thus it seems to me that some of the things in this book are not only of inferior quality, but of inferior unity. They are

mere lumps in which we dig for the particles of gold they conceal.

Yet Mann, one need hardly say, can also be a very distinguished artist: **"Death in Venice"** is much else also, but it is formally perfect above everything else. **"Mario"** is perhaps not so much else, but it too is formally perfect. And I think that if Mann had persevered with "Felix Krull" he might have brought off another nearly perfect work, though already here and there one detects heavy and not quite correctly proportioned passages. But what exists of "Felix Krull" fascinates us, perhaps because it obviously fascinated Mann. The story, told with great skill in the first person, concerns the youth of a criminal with a highly, doubtless an excessively, artistic temperament. Felix Krull is a sort of Wildean, to whom things are not good or bad, but beautiful and ugly. He is squeamish, unconventionally moral, self-conscious, self-dedicated. Though it is not the world's, he has a very severe code of his own. Mann cunningly allows Krull to betray and reveal himself down to the last susceptibility and pose. It is a great pity he did not carry the story through, for it might have provided us with a thorough individual who is also a complete but neglected type. . . .

Of four other stories now for the first time put into English, two very early ones are no more than pleasing, while the two others, though more mature in presentation, hardly add anything to Mann's stature. One, **"Gladius Dei,"** simply tells in a sort of comic vein about a modern Savonarola; the other, **"The Blood of the Walsungs,"** contrasts the doomed and barbaric Siegmund and Sieglinde of **"Die Walkuere"** with a free-willed and sophisticated twin brother and sister who repeat the pattern in modern Berlin. Simply as a story, however, **"The Blood of the Walsungs"** is very effective.

> *Louis Kronenberger, "Thomas Mann's Briefer Fiction," in* The New York Times Book Review, *June 7, 1936, p. 1.*

MALCOLM COWLEY   (essay date 1936)

[*Cowley has made several valuable contributions to contemporary letters, including his editions of works by such American authors as Ernest Hemingway, William Faulkner, and F. Scott Fitzgerald; his writings for the* New Republic; *and above all, his chronicles and criticism of modern American literature. The critical approach Cowley follows is undogmatic, characterized by a willingness to view a work from whatever perspective—social, historical, aesthetic—that the work itself seems to demand for its illumination. In the following excerpt from a review originally published in the* New Republic, *Cowley suggests that* Stories of Three Decades *presents Mann's development from a symbolist to a socialist artist.*]

The line that divides Symbolist or "art" novels from social novels is probably not so straight or definite as people seemed to think a few years ago, when the subject was being vehemently argued. It is a border without guards or customs officials, and doubtful travelers are privileged to stand with one foot in either country. They can even become leading citizens of both, as witness the example of Thomas Mann, who is probably more respected than any other living writer. During the last twenty-five years, Mann has gradually become a social novelist, in an admirable sense of the word, yet he has not abandoned the technique or the emotional color of the Symbolists. He has never made the gesture of violently deserting an ivory tower.

His career can be traced in *Stories of Three Decades,* an omnibus volume containing everything he has written for publication except his essays and his four big novels. The book includes two long stories, **"Death in Venice"** and **"Tonio Kröger,"** which Mann says in his introduction that he is inclined to reckon "not with my slighter but with my more important works." It includes two other long stories which, with much hesitation, I should be willing to place above Mann's favorites: these two are **"Tristan"** and **"Mario and the Magician."** **"Blood of the Walsungs,"** describing a family of rich, hateful, pitiable Jews, is a shorter story almost as good; so too is **"Disorder and Early Sorrow,"** in which all the hysteria of the German inflation is distilled into the tears of a six-year-old girl. There are stories still shorter than these last; there are episodes, sketches and a long, beautifully accurate biography of Mann's dog, recommended as corrective reading to people who believe that dog stories are childish. There is the first chapter of a novel, "Felix Krull," that Mann did not continue; and there is *Fiorenza,* a historico-philosophical drama that had some success on the stage, but not enough to make its author a professional playwright. In all there are twenty-four pieces, written at every stage of his life—from the year 1896, when he was twenty-one, to the year 1929, when he won the Nobel Prize. In their chronological order they give a fairly clear picture of his development.

His early work was centered round the familiar Symbolist theme of the artist's solitude. "There are two worlds," Mann always seemed to be saying. "There is the world of happy, normal people, to be envied even for their stupidity, and there is the lonely world in which the artist tries to bridle his nightmares, but often lets them run away with him." Almost all his stories dealt either with artists or else with moral or physical cripples (and he tended to place all these people in the same category, little Herr Friedemann the hunchback, Detlev Spinell the dilettante and Felix Krull the swindler).

His nearest approach to a hero is Tonio Kröger, the young, successful, hard-working novelist; yet this autobiographical character is the one who says most forcibly that art is a product of decay and that artists by their calling are barred out of ordinary society. "Literature is not a calling, it's a curse," Tonio tells his good friend Lisabeta Ivanovna. "It begins by your feeling yourself set apart, in a curious sort of opposition to the nice, regular people; there is a gulf of ironic sensibility, of knowledge, skepticism, disagreement, between you and the others; it grows deeper and deeper, you realize that you are alone." Both the artists and their audience are "always and only the poor and suffering, never any of the others, the blue-eyed ones. . . . The kingdom of art increases and that of health and innocence declines on this earth." It is curious to find that Tonio does not feel in the least angry or contemptuous toward the world that half rejects him; in this respect he is unlike Joyce's Stephen Dedalus and Huysmans' des Esseintes and almost all the other Symbolist heroes. He really loves and envies the ordinary people, "the blue-eyed ones" who have no need of art. His good friend tells him, "You are really a bourgeois on the wrong path, a bourgeois *manqué.*"

"Tonio Kröger" is an unusual story, warm and open-hearted in mood, skillful in craftsmanship, the first work in which Mann learned to interweave his themes like a composer writing a symphony. Yet with the passage of years it is losing part of its effectiveness: the ideas behind it are beginning to seem localized in time and space. In writing it Mann did not foresee that the conflict between artist and bourgeois would not

be an eternal subject, nor that it would soon become impossible to use the upper middle class as a symbol of health. He would soon be forced to go into his material more deeply.

That is exactly what he did in writing **"Death in Venice,"** which was finished eight years later. Ostensibly it is another story of the relation between life and art, between art and self-discipline. Gustav von Aschenbach, the hero, is a distinguished novelist who has sustained himself through fifty years by obeying his Prussian sense of duty. Then, in the late afternoon of his life, he yields to the dissipation that is, for Mann, both a symbol of art and a symbol of death. He finds that Venice is a plague-stricken city, but he has fallen in love with a beautiful Polish boy and refuses to go northward until it is too late for him to escape. The story is extraordinary for its musical structure and for the complicated suggestions it evokes. But among these suggestions is one of a historical nature. **"Death in Venice"** was published two years before the War, and Mann is inclined to believe that its popularity was due to its "intense timeliness"—the delirium in which Aschenbach foundered belonged to the mood of the day and was a prophecy of the general delirium in which Europe would shortly founder. Aschenbach was not merely a picture of the artist yielding to his vices: he came to represent a moment of the European mind.

I am trying to describe the process by which a Symbolist novelist developed into a social novelist without greatly changing his aims or his methods, but chiefly by broadening his human sympathies. In another story—it is the last in the volume and appeared in 1929—the point becomes much clearer. **"Mario and the Magician"** relates the misadventures of a German family at a little Italian watering place. They do not like Torre di Venere; the chip-on-the-shoulder nationalism of the Italian tourists makes their lives mildly but persistently disagreeable. Nevertheless they remain, by inertia, and get themselves involved in the dangerous affair of the Cavaliere Cipolla. This magician, as he advertises himself—this hypnotist, as he is in reality—proves to be crippled and hateful and compelling. At his one performance he overawes and insults the audience, forcing one man after another to obey him, and the audience likes it; even the German children laugh and clap without quite knowing what is taking place. But Cipolla goes too far and one of his victims shoots him down, thus clearing the air of hysteria and constraint.

"Mario and the Magician" is not on the face of it a political story, in spite of occasional references to Mussolini and Italian pride. It deals with one episode witnessed by an ordinary German family. Yet it conveys, more strongly than anything else I have read, the atmosphere of Europe in these days of dictatorship and mass insanity: it suggests in miniature the great meetings at the Sport Palace in Berlin where Hitler sways the crowd like wind-bowed aspens; it gives us the essence of the Blood Purge, the Saar Plebiscite, the Ethopian war—everything is there, if only in the germ, and it was there six years before most of it was printed in the morning papers. We should not demand that poets be prophets; this is not part of their trade. But sometimes it happens that a writer, by going into his subject deeply, finds in it the spiritual tendencies that grew out of yesterday's events and will become the political tendencies of tomorrow. Thomas Mann, like Tolstoy, has done this more than once, and not for his country alone. In this age of crazy nationalisms, he is almost the last great European. (pp. 291-94)

Malcolm Cowley, "The Last Great European:

Thomas Mann," *in his* Think Back on Us: A Contemporary Chronicle of the 1930's, *edited by Henry Dan Piper, Southern Illinois University Press, 1967, pp. 291-94.*

AGNES E. MEYER (essay date 1941)

[*Meyer was an American journalist, humanitarian, translator, and writer on social issues. In the following excerpt, she discusses the theme and philosophical outlook of Mann's story "The Transposed Heads."*]

Between his great epic works, Thomas Mann likes to do "little finger-exercises," as he calls them, shorter pieces which constitute a restful interlude and at the same time prepare his mind for the mood and theme of the next major composition. In these periods of relaxation he has written stories of impeccable beauty, such as **"A Man and His Dog," "Disorder and Early Sorrow," "Mario and the Magician"**; and now, as a transition from the humanistic world of Goethe to the mythical sphere of Joseph, he tells us the curious Hindu legend of **"The Transposed Heads,"** in a narrative style as restrained in its exoticism as the form is architecturally perfect.

Research into the psychology of the myth, the journey backward into remote periods of time and equally remote recesses of the mind, is not a new adventure for Thomas Mann, nor is it surprising that the sensual-ascetic dualism of India should interest this erstwhile disciple of Schopenhauer; but even the most gifted Occidental writer tempts the gods when he challenges comparison, as Mann does here, with the masterful and poetical productions of Sanskrit literature. Yet, strange as that cultural atmosphere must have been to him, he has made himself at home there through a sensitiveness to tone and rhythm, which enables him to capture the secret harmonies of a foreign style and through his gift for sympathetic penetration of a novel environment which teaches him to create in its spirit and idiom. Nevertheless, the foundation of the story remains European. Though the author has dipped his pen in Indian colorings, he transforms the Hindu scene through the magic of an Occidental perspective. The supernatural elements are given a rational and psychological basis; the mysticism of the Orient is wedded to the order, sobriety and humor of our highest classical tradition.

The fantastic superstructure of this long short-story is borrowed from an old legend in honor of Kali, the dark mother-goddess, giver of life and death, of bondage and freedom.

In some remote period when folk-memory arose in the souls of men as mysteriously as if a sacrificial vessel should fill itself from beneath, there existed two inseparable youths, Shridaman and Nanda by name, whose close friendship rested upon a dissimilarity, which caused each to admire the other and seek for an exchange and union of their contrasting natures. Shridaman, the elder of the two, was a thoughtful young merchant of Brahmin caste, light of color, delicate of feature, his nose thin as a knife blade, his eyes soft-lidded and gentle, his chin covered by a soft fan-shaped beard. Soft, too, were his limbs, as a body should be when it carries a wise and noble head.

Nanda's head, on the other hand, was by no means his outstanding feature but merely the suitable accompaniment of his charming body. Nanda's Karma had never led him to occupy his mind with spiritual problems. He was a joyous, simple son of the people, dark of skin and hair, strong-armed and

beautiful, slightly goat-faced with full lips and black eyes that were prone to laughter. Nanda's joyous disposition was epitomized in the curl of happiness upon his breast. The friends are the two personifications of Shiva, one the ascetic, the other a blooming youth. (p. 1)

Through the mysterious power of poetical suggestion, more penetrating and persuasive than the strongest argument, Mann satirizes in this legend the atavistic tendency of mankind to divide the universe into two widely separate parts, the actual world and a realm of ideal values unattainable on earth. Desires and illusions surge up from the aeons of dualistic thinking that lie submerged in the unconscious, tempting men back toward established habits of making imaginary choices between mind and matter; but the final arbiter of behavior is the world of reality, whose moral values and spiritual discipline are the true source of knowledge and growth.

When mind and body become rivals, they eventually destroy each other, and all beauty is sacrificed. The scene in which Shridaman, Nanda and Sita visit the hermits in the rain-green Dunkaka forest is one of the most brilliant that Mann has ever written, for even Nietzsche has never submitted asceticism to a more devastating and hilarious analysis. But it is made equally clear that if selfishness leads mankind to grasp for bodily satisfactions, the pride and honor of the higher self cannot be forgotten amid all the weakness and confusions of the flesh. The inner voice will not be silenced and those who seek happiness beyond the limits of moral responsibility can only meet with suffering and the heavy punishment ordained for sacrilege.

Why should Mann write a story on so abstruse a subject as the body-mind relationship? Why warn us that vacillation between thought and action leads to destruction? Because it is the central problem of his thinking, just as it is the crux of our Christian-democratic civilization. If we listen carefully to this artful tale, we hear overtones that say: "Let us live what we think; let us die if necessary to maintain the dignity of man, for if we are caught in an unresolved conflict between the ideal and the real we shall die anyway of weakness, futility and shame."

Such wisdom comes with all the more force from Thomas Mann because it is the product of a life-long and heroic determination to understand and accept the meaning of experience. His earlier work expressed the typical view of romantic idealism that body as the source of appetites is simply a hindrance to the free development of spirit and art. To the youthful Tonio Kröger, feeling is always banal and futile in comparison with the icy ecstasies of mind; and ten years later the beauty-loving Aschenbach is still condemned to death in Venice because he could not resist the humiliating lures of a forbidden Eros. Throughout this period life and art were always in competition. Life was, on the whole, a rather contemptible business; and even when it was victorious, as in Tristan, it won the day only because its brutality was insensitive to all the fineness and beauty of human nature. After the first World War had shattered Mann's firm belief that spirit and intellect are too pure to be contaminated by the dust of the marketplace, Hans Kastorp brought back from the Magic Mountain a new wisdom, which taught Joseph to revitalize his spiritual heritage through service to his fellow-beings; and the Goethe novel, "Lotte in Weimar," is but a humanistic prelude to the mystical generalization of **"The Transposed Heads"** that art and life, spirit and body, thought and action, are forever joined in a close and fruitful embrace.

"The world is not so constituted," declares the narrator of this legend,

> that spirit is fated to love only spirit, and beauty only beauty. The contrast between the two indicates with a clarity as spiritual as it is beautiful, that the world goal is the union of spirit and beauty, in other words, the revelation of perfection and of a salvation that is no longer divided: and this story is only an example of the disappointments and errors, under which mankind strives toward this goal.

That this goal, this striving for harmony between the inner and outer self, is invigorating and salutary can be gathered from a review of its effect upon Thomas Mann. While most writers whose roots go back as far as his have been silenced by death or despair, or have become repetitious and ineffectual, he has had the organic tenacity to survive two world upheavals, banishment from his native land, from Europe, from all the sources that are the mainspring of his creative genius; and yet in the face of such overwhelming outward difficulties his growth has steadily continued, both as a human being and as an artist. Beginning with *The Magic Mountain,* which is the story of his reorientation to life, his work has constantly gained in significance and beauty, and his style has kept pace with the expansion of his social and imaginative insight. The more Thomas Mann progressed in the conquest of his romantic nineteenth-century isolation, and the more he felt himself a member of an infinite brotherhood, the more clearly was the maturing of his personality reflected in his subject-matter and in an ever greater mastery of form and craftsmanship. The structure of his latest work is as firm as the struggle he experienced was intense.

In this story, for example, the author's art attains the high goal of which he speaks, the fusion of spirit and matter. The chief personages in **"The Transposed Heads"** are purely abstract, much more so than any other characters that Thomas Mann has ever created. Shridaman is obviously Spirit, Mind and Reason; Nanda, Life, Body and Intuition, whereas the girl is Beauty; and yet they are not phantoms, mere walking allegories, but living and lovable human beings who capture our whole sympathy and attention as such. They are both more unreal and more real than their famous predecessors in Thomas Mann's earlier work, and the beautiful settings in which they are placed have a tactile quality so compelling that we remember the whole story as a vivid moving picture.

If we compare Thomas Mann's style of the pre-war period with that of **"The Transposed Heads"** we find that it formerly had a pellucid but less vital quality. Then he was dominated by the Platonic concept that beauty does not live in things but is made visible through them; charm and attraction are not in bodies but in the immortal idea that shines through them. Now that he has arrived at a point where the world of sense and the world of spirit meet and are mingled, he beholds the universe with a new and brilliant clarity under a light that warms what it illuminates. The author's perception never loses its hold upon reality even when his imagination looks far beyond it to that ultimate realm of psychological and poetical divination which we call insight. But only a magician of the word who can conjure up the lure of earth in all its seductive power could persuade us that there is no inevitable conflict between sensuality and purity, and that the ultimate salvation of man lies in the reconciliation of his animal and his divine heritage.

Through concentration upon these lofty human principles, Thomas Mann has raised a citadel within himself in which he can take refuge and resist the superficial, confusing and dishonest philosophies of our tempestuous era. Such a man is never above the battle. Strife is his daily portion and his writings are, so to speak, reports from a spiritual front where perpetual war is being waged with the whole force of instinct and reason for the survival of goodness and truth. **"The Transposed Heads"** is another of the author's contributions to the vision of a new humanity, which will surmount the disastrous effects that have grown out of the enfeebling divorce of religion and morals from the art of conduct, a free humanity which will emerge from its present trials to build a new society wherein all of its emotional and rational powers can be integrated and rejuvenated.

This is literature, not of passing interest, but of deep, enduring value, a miraculous union of criticism and creation, which awakens understanding, dissolves prejudice and tends to clarify and elevate human aspirations. It also helps us to appreciate the intimate and inspiring role which art will assume in a genuinely democratic world. For if the struggle of both art and democracy lies in the ultimate reconciliation of spirit and body, of thought and action, of reason and will, then the poet, like Thomas Mann, who achieves that unity, who combines exegesis and ecstasy in permanent form, may be considered the high priest and prophet, the truly religious guide to the future, for his genius is a mediator between the moment and eternity, between the detailed fragmentary aspect of life and universality. (pp. 15-16)

> Agnes E. Meyer, "Thomas Mann's Fable for Today," in The New York Times Book Review, June 8, 1941, pp. 1, 15-16.

PHILIP RAHV   (essay date 1954)

[*Rahv was a Russian-born American critic who served for thirty-five years as co-editor of the journal* Partisan Review. *Focusing on the intellectual, social, and cultural milieu influencing a work of art, his critical writings are intellectually eclectic and non-idealogical. According to Richard Chase, "What one admires most about Rahv's critical method is his abundant ability to use such techniques as Marxism, Freudian psychology, anthropology, and existentialism toward his critical ends without shackling himself to any of them." In the following review, Rahv comments negatively on "The Black Swan." Calling the piece "a feeble parody" of "Death in Venice," he purports that Mann's attention to elaborate symbolic detail detracts from the authenticity of the work.*]

[**"The Black Swan"**] will scarcely add anything substantial to its author's fame. Its theme of the fatal attraction of age to youth reminds us, though far from irresistibly, of **"Death in Venice."** Actually it reads like a feeble parody of that early work of genius, with Frau Rosalie von Tümmler, a middle-aged Düsseldorf widow, put in as a ringer for the truly formidable Aschenbach, and with Ken Keaton, the young American, who has nothing in common with Tadzio but sheer youthfulness, somewhat casually enacting the role of that splendid and richly meaningful figure. Missing are the ardors and rigors of the Venetian tale: the closed form and classical discipline of style and craft triumphantly containing a thoroughly modern fiction of ambiguous desire, dissolution of personality, and death conceived of both as the secretly longed for consummation and inevitable issue of the collapse into guilty love—the *Liebestod,* in other words, fully brought up to date.

Moreover, in **"The Black Swan"** the dazzling dialectic of life and art, providing **"Death in Venice"** with its ruling idea, is replaced by the more restricted polarization of psyche and soma. These the author, in his typically dualistic fashion, assimilates to the traditional idea of a struggle between "Nature" and the soul. So conceived, these antagonists turn out to be metaphysical essences, all the more ferocious because of their abstract dynamism, and between them they make short shrift of Rosalie's love for young Keaton. In the end the antagonist that goes by the name of Nature wins the battle by playing a peculiarly malignant trick on the poor deluded cheated woman (**"Die Betrogene"** in the German title) even as she proclaims her victory over her aging flesh in speeches at once passionate and magisterial. Fulsome are her praises of "great beneficent Nature" for the miracle it had wrought in her in arresting the dreaded menopause and restoring her to the status of a "functioning female." But it is exactly this dubious physiological "miracle" that marks her doom. At the point, virtually, of surrendering to her lover she has a hemmorhage and a few weeks later dies of cancer of the womb.

Thus Rosalie, like so many of Mann's protagonists, suffers a kind of *Liebestod;* and where her version of it differs from the others is that it is rendered almost entirely in psychosomatic terms. Now what must be kept in mind is that for Mann, with his penchant for irony at all costs, the psychosomatic is merely another correlate of the ambiguous, that is to say, it is emptied of all definable empirical content and invested with those sinister qualities which his dialectic of disease and disorder calls for. No wonder, then, that one cannot really say whether the rejuvenescence and sexual revitalization that Rosalie finds so gratifying as she is swamped by erotic feeling is in some mysterious way induced by the cancerous growth in her body, or whether, on the contrary, it is this revitalization which lays her open to illness, inciting the cancerous cells to do their worst. It is not Mann's intention that we learn the answer to this question. It is true, of course, that in her deathbed speech Rosalie, pious to the end, absolves Nature of all blame for her fate. These last words, however, may well be taken as spoken "in character"; it is unlikely that her understanding of what has happened coincides with that of the author. For one must allow here for his all-pervasive irony and unending delight in the problematic and equivocal.

Mann has always been a very deliberate artist. Temperamentally incapable of spontaneity, if not actually hostile to it, he succeeded in turning this very deliberateness into an imaginative resource of a high order. But in some of his recent works, and particularly in such shorter ones as this latest novella, he seems to overreach himself in deliberateness, taxing our patience with effects not so much subtle as cunning, effects ultimately discountable as the products of a contriving will. Thus one comes, in this grisly tale, upon a species of symbolism so obviously and neatly pre-designed for its purpose that it generates resistance rather than assent on the part of the conscious reader. What is one to make, for instance, of a piece of symbolism such as that of the dank and mouldy passageway in the castle where Rosalie, confessing her love, embraces Keaton for the first time? "Ugh, it smells of death. . . . I will be yours, but not in this mould. . . . In your room . . . tonight." In the context it becomes altogether plain that this scene of passionate avowal has been rigged up with a décor of decay simply as a convenient means of prefig-

uring symbolically the disaster to come. Similarly, in an earlier chapter there is a great to-do made about Rosalie's "sensual fervor" in absorbing "whatever Nature offers to gratify our sense of smell—sweetness, aromatic bitterness, even heady and oppressive scents"; and in the very next page we are brought up short by a repellent scene, that of Rosalie and her daughter walking in the woods and coming upon a teeming little mound of putrid stuff the smell of which makes the women run. This again strikes me as artificial and arbitrary. The symbolic detail of the teeming little mound is much too starkly antithetical to the exposition of Rosalie's "sensual fervor" preceding it; it has been maneuvered rather than integrated into the narrative.

More impressive is the long interior monologue in which Rosalie discloses her state of complete abandon; and equally good are some of the dialogues she conducts with her daughter Anna. It is especially the mother's speeches that at times achieve a very fine effect, suggesting those "tirades" of classic tragedy in which analytic finesse is unaccountably though brilliantly combined with the unrestrained expression of feeling. To secure this effect Mann disregards the modern conventions of realistic dialogue. Rosalie's language has nothing in common with the breaks, pauses, falterings, and ellipses of "real" speech. It is an utterance formal yet impassioned, oratorical yet at the same time emotionally fluent. One might characterize it as a kind of "educated" rant of a smitten middle-aged woman of culture who, with true Germanic earnestness, cannot help enlisting higher ideas in the service of her libidinal strivings.

But virtuosity of this sort cannot undo the general impression that the story is at bottom lacking in significance. It means too little for the frightfulness it contains. One would be hard put to it to say what the author had in mind in constructing his insidious plot. Are we to take it as a satire on the nature-worship to which his countrymen are known to yield so readily? If so, the means are peculiarly ill adjusted to the end. Then there is the fact of Keaton's Americanism, which appears to be gratuitous in the sense of being essentially unrelated to the scene and the action. Keaton is an expatriate who runs down his own country in favor of Europe's historical opulence, but what he says and thinks is entirely unconnected with Rosalie's situation. In the last analysis what catches one's interest is not the story in its own right but that fact that it was produced by a writer close to eighty years of age; and at this point the literary concern gives way to an interest in the writer's personal psychology. I have heard Mann praised for his audacity in composing at his age the plot of this book. I prefer to describe the plot as insidious. It suggests not so much the boldness of a poet like Yeats who in late life found in "lust and rage" the spur to song but rather a sensibility seeking to discover in meaningless enormities a cure for ennui. (pp. 82-4)

Philip Rahv, "The Triumph of Decay," in Commentary, *Vol. XVIII, July, 1954, pp. 82-4.]*

JOSEPH FRANK (essay date 1954)

[*In the following review, Frank describes "The Black Swan" as an unsuccessful attempt to re-examine themes that Mann had previously explored in "The Transposed Heads."*]

Thomas Mann is now in his seventy-sixth year, and it is only natural that his latest work—a brief novella called in German

"Die Betrogene" ("The Deceived")—should turn to a typical crisis of old age for its central symbol. In contemporary English literature, this crisis has also preoccupied the later poetry of W. B. Yeats, another great writer whose genius has waxed rather than waned with advancing age. And no better description can be found of the dilemma of Mann's heroine in **"The Black Swan"** than these lines from Yeats:

> What shall I do with this absurdity—
> O heart, O troubled heart—this caricature,
> Decrepit age that has been tied to me
> As to a dog's tail?
>   Never had I more
> Excited, passionate, fantastical
> Imagination, nor an ear and eye
> That more expected the impossible. . . .

It is this paradox of the failing body and the youthful spirit that Mann portrays in the history of Rosalie von Tummler, and which he transposes into his familiar symbolism of the dialectic between Nature and Spirit. Unlike Yeats, however, Mann does not wish to flee to a timeless Byzantium where nature is totally transformed into "monuments of unageing intellect"; nor does he desire to be gathered "into the artifice of eternity." This would be to sacrifice Nature to Spirit, and, for Thomas Mann, it is man's tragedy as well as his blessing that he stands midway between the two. For man is nothing if not "master of contradictories," as Mann wrote in the great snow-vision scene of *The Magic Mountain.* And even though, in **"The Black Swan,"** this reconciliation of Nature and Spirit is based on a terrible illusion, perhaps, Thomas Mann implies, this illusion is finally the only human reality.

Mann's heroine in **"The Black Swan"** is an ageing German woman past her female prime, who falls in love with the young American tutor of her son. The freshness of her emotion, however, is in painful contrast with her physical debility, although externally she is still attractive enough to a young lover. Her daughter Anna advises her to reconcile this dilemma by adjusting her soul to her body, turning her love for the young man into a maternal affection that takes cognizance of her years. But Rosalie accepts her disequilibrium with agonizing joy, and refuses to strike Nature in the face "by stifling the spring of pain with which she has miraculously blest my soul."

For one moment, indeed, it seems as if Rosalie's faith in Nature's omnipotence were to be rewarded. The forces of her soul apparently exercise a miraculous effect on her body and her womanly functions are restored. But nature's miracle turns out to have been the presage of a deadly cancer; and she dies shortly thereafter. Yet she tells her daughter Anna at the end:

> Never say that Nature deceived me, that she is sardonic and cruel. Do not rail at her, as I do not. I am loth to go away—from you all, from life and its spring. But how should there be spring without death? Indeed, death is a great instrument of life, and if for me it borrowed the guise of resurrection, of the joy of life, that was not a lie, but goodness and mercy.

Besides Rosalie, the only other figures in the book of any consequence are the daughter Anna and Ken Keaton, the young American. Rosalie's intuitive trust in the organic forces of life, her refusal to reconcile herself willingly to sedate sterility, are juxtaposed against Anna's antipathy to Nature and to the organic. Anna is a character familiar to all readers of

Mann's early work—the artist whose absorption in the realm of the Spirit is symbolized by a physical disability. For Anna, born a clubfoot, is also an abstract artist, the one being a function of the other; both represent her alienation from life, which she transforms into intellectualized patterns on the canvas. Ken Keaton, the young American with a passion for local Rhineland history, is an amiable nonentity whom Mann good-naturedly caricatures.

None of the characters is developed with enough amplitude to make them very interesting, and Mann lavishes all his attention on the invention of symbolic detail. What determines the pattern of symbolism, of course, is the special quality of Rosalie's experience—the deceptive flowering of life and joy from death and corruption. Rosalie and Anna, in the course of a woodland walk, come upon a decaying piece of excitement and the rotting corpse of a disintegrating animal. But this disgusting pile exhales the distinct scent of a musk-like perfume; and so too is Rosalie's late blossoming, as she will learn all too soon, the effect of organic decay. Similarly, the scene in which Rosalie declares her love for Ken takes place in the abandoned rococo alcove of an old castle, once a pleasure-chamber for aristocrats but now mouldering with damp and presided over by a decrepit Cupid.

Given the nature of Mann's symbolic purpose, it is quite understandable that **"The Black Swan"** should abound in slightly scabrous and repellant physical detail. This is not the first time that Mann has employed such material; and the critical question is whether he succeeds here, as he has in the past, in making the symbolic value of such material outweigh its ugliness. So far as **"The Black Swan"** is concerned, the answer must be that he does not.

Far too much of the brief novella is taken up with elaborate dialogues between Rosalie and Anna on intimate problems of female physiology; and Rosalie's experience never rises above the biological level. The human dimension of her metamorphosis is hardly developed at all, and the result is that her dying speech carries little conviction in terms of her character. Mann's intention in **"The Black Swan"** is movingly clear, and it is impossible not to respond to his mastery in certain descriptive passages; but his execution seems far too summary and perfunctory for so difficult an artistic task.

Thematically, **"The Black Swan"** is most clearly related to **"The Transposed Heads,"** a work that Mann himself called "a metaphysical farce." There too Nature played her tricks on man, and body and soul could never quite get into the proper relation to each other; but the earlier work was conceived in a far more light-hearted spirit. The exotic Indian coloring of **"The Transposed Heads"** gave it the air of a fable or a fairy-tale; its delicious irony arose precisely from its remoteness and incredibility. **"The Black Swan,"** however, is set in twentieth-century Germany, and there is a macabre cruelty about the situation which, combined with the lack of fantasy, creates a distressing uncertainty of tone. The situation is too tragic to be taken as a joke, yet it is difficult to know whether Mann is being consciously or unconsciously grotesque when Rosalie says fondly of Ken Keaton: "In any case, he sacrificed one of his kidneys on the altar of his fatherland!"

Thomas Mann's work has a tendency to run in cycles, and it may well be that **"The Black Swan"** is the first imperfect approximation to the serious treatment of the theme handled comically in **"The Transposed Heads."** Between this Indian *jeu d'espirt* and **"The Black Swan,"** Mann has interposed two major works of a different cycle. Both *Dr. Faustus* (whose towering greatness has not yet been fully appreciated in this country) and *The Holy Sinner* dealt with sin and grace rather than with the body and the soul—the first book with apocalyptic seriousness, the second in a vein of affectionate parody and a mood of reconciliation. Perhaps Mann is now going back to the body-soul entanglement, and, reversing the order of his sin-grace cycle, converting his metaphysical farce into a metaphysical morality. If so, **"The Black Swan"** shows that he has not yet found the proper means to make this transition successfully. (pp. 18-19)

Joseph Frank, *"Mann—Death and Transfiguration,"* in The New Republic, *Vol. 131, No. 1, July 5, 1954, pp. 18-19.*

KENNETH G. WILSON　(essay date 1954)

[*Wilson is an American critic, essayist and editor who is known chiefly for his studies of English linguistics. In the following essay, he examines Mann's use of dance as a leitmotiv in "Tonio Kröger."*]

The old, honored metaphor of life as dance is a basis of both structure and theme in Thomas Mann's **"Tonio Kröger."** The dance often serves literature as a figure in little of man's social existence; man and woman are partners as they express their feelings through a pouring-out of physical and emotional energies according to a rhythmic pattern. Mann is a civilized author and is writing of Tonio, a civilized poet; he uses as symbol the quadrille, a civilized dance of couples, a "society" square dance. The quadrille, with its five parts, is a particularly sophisticated dance form; the patterns are highly complex, rigidly conventional, and extremely formal, although the pace and the level of emotional and physical expression are often enthusiastic and sometimes even boisterous. In essence the dance is a seeking of partners; in the quadrille, the social patterns are strictly ordered: boy meets girl, loses and finds her again and again in the intricate patterns, and finally recovers her just as the dance ends. All physical and emotional expression, however spirited, is rigorously controlled. The dancers may not proceed according to will or caprice or inspiration, but must be skilled in following the maze of the pattern. They must train their bodies to perform a series of mechanical reflexes, and they must have an instinctive awareness of their relationship to the pattern, because there are so many dancers that one misstep by an awkward individual will destroy the whole ordered pattern of the dance. The implications of the dance as metaphor are both personal and social, and the thread of the dance can be broken both by those who cannot master the skills and so fall down in the dance, and by those who cannot close their minds to everything but their part in the dance, and so fail to concentrate themselves into a simple state of emotional and physical expression.

In **"Tonio Kröger"** the dance as symbolic act is employed structurally only in the first, second, and last episodes; thematically, its use is more widespread, but suggestive rather than rigid. Once it has been thoroughly established as a metaphor it often serves simply as a kind of leitmotiv, several of which Mann employs profusely throughout the story. There are many such formulas which serve as figures for ideas or complexes of feeling, but only the dance and the dancer are symbols in the full sense of the term, if one considers change and development and structural integration necessary to the symbol. The leitmotiv in **"Tonio Kröger,"** as distinct from the fully developed symbol, is a constant which, while it may symbolize roughly, stands for an unarticulated and undifferentiated complex of idea and feeling. It serves exactly as does a Wagnerian leitmotiv, as an announcement or reminder of matters which cannot be stated fully. For example: Tonio's mother is dark, southern, fiery, and somehow irresponsible; his father is tall, fastidious, silent, and somehow northern. But the *matter* behind these phrases and words is never made more explicit; the diction remains the only concretion, and merely suggests idea. The story is not a study of heredity, except in the broadest sense. Tonio is like both his parents, but they are so deliberately oversimplified in their respective southernness and northernness that even the compass qualities are merely suggestive and relative. They recur several times in the story, but without development or change; they are leitmotivs, consciously formulated and petrified references, which are then repeated to evoke in the reader a constant recognition whenever they occur. Unquestionably, all these leitmotivs invite predominantly emotional rather than intellectual grasp by the reader. The dance and the dancer are often thematically employed like leitmotivs, but structurally they serve as symbols, for they involve change and development, and they invite both intellectual and emotional understanding in the reader. The structural use of the dance is simple: the dancers seek love, and the final position is a claiming of partners. Tonio as would-be dancer begins with Hans Hansen, fails to win him, turns to Ingeborg, fails again, and then seeks Lisabeta, though not as a partner in the usual sense of the dance; with Lisabeta and throughout the remainder of the story he is simply trying to find a way into the dance; the dance goes on without him. After his failure to gain recognition in his home town, he goes back to the blue-eyed, blond-haired dancers, only to withdraw in the end while the dance continues without him. He can hear the music and laughter and excitement of the dance, but he must remain apart. He can only watch, or stare at himself in shuttered windows, or stand outside the hall; in the end he goes away to dance alone to another rhythm, "the cruel and perilous sword-dance of art." He can never dance the quadrille. All his attempts are unfinished.

That the dancer is the key to the symbolic meaning of the story becomes clear almost at once with the literal image of the second episode, the dancing school. Literally, Tonio discovers that he cannot concentrate on the dance: he loves Ingeborg, but only the Hans Hansens can dance with the Ingeborg Holms; only the blue-eyed, blond-haired, handsome ones can concentrate their existence into the single level the dance requires. In Magdalena Vermehren, Tonio sees one of those pitiful, injured souls who fall in the dance. She understands him, she would love him, but her incapacity as dancer is different from his. He cannot accept her, for he can love only the true dancers. After his blunder in the *moulinet des dames* Tonio retires to the shuttered window, a kind of mirror, an opening through which only he with his special perceptivity can see, there to observe himself and the dancers and to realize that he must always be apart. He vows to love Ingeborg forever unrequited, but his love for her, like his love for Hans, inevitably fades. He lives on the sensitive recognition of his own inability to participate. He is happier apart, viewing his unhappiness, contrasting it with the animal happiness of the blue-eyed, blond-haired dancers. The repetition of this scene at the dancing school in the final episode at the Danish resort many years later makes explicit the symbolic significance of dance and dancers: "What was coming? They

Dust jacket for Tristan, *1903, in which "Tonio Kröger" first appeared.*

Immerthal departs and Hans returns to Tonio, the wooing begins again. There is a brisk, interrupted end to the dance along the wall, an abrupt and somehow unsatisfactory parting at the gate, and Tonio walks home alone. Here is the dance in little. At the very outset Tonio is clearly different from the blue-eyed race of dancers. When the two boys set off on their walk that is a dance: "Tonio's walk was idle and uneven, whereas the other's slim legs in their black stockings moved with an elastic, rhythmic tread." Immerthal is not of the blue-eyed race, but he moves to the same rhythm: when he left them, "he jumped upon a bench that stood by the way, ran along it with his crooked legs, jumped down, and trotted off."

The symbolic use of dance and dancer in the structure of the story is not completely systematic. The quadrille here is only a sophisticated patterned dance of couples; its five-part structure and the particular styles of its parts are only briefly, fragmentarily reflected in the literal structure of the story. The episode in which Tonio returns home is an illustration of the discussion in Lisabeta's studio. He still walks slowly, according to his own rhythm, which is not the rhythm of the dancers; he still cannot lose himself in the dance, but views it from a distance, always thinking, watching, weighing. His experiences are not the same as the dancers' experiences. There are echoes suggestive of the dance-life metaphor in the episode, particularly in the walks through the streets, but the reference to symbolic levels is only suggestive. Nor is there a systematic use of the symbolic dance in the episode of the voyage to the Danish resort. Here the rhythm is of the sea: the sea dances. At this point Tonio meets the reddish-blond young man who for a moment stands apart with Tonio, watching the dance of stars and ocean. But the difference between the two men is clearly marked: the young man rejoins the dancers next morning, while Tonio remains apart.

Another fragmentary application of the symbolic act of dancing the quadrille is the *moulinet des dames* mentioned above. This is the only *movement* of the dance singled out for special attention in the story. Tonio, abstracted by his musings, blunders into the *moulinet,* a figure intended only for the girls. One is tempted here to see Tonio's pursuit of love, his desire for acceptance by the blue-eyed blond girls, acting as a force—to see a Freudian slip. In a way, of course, in his brief relationships with Hans, Ingeborg, Magdalena, and Lisabeta, one can see the whole of Tonio's life from his school days to his letter to Lisabeta at the end, as a kind of *moulinet des dames,* a figure of the dance into which Tonio blunders seeking love. But, as in the *moulinet* at the dancing school, he is rejected and the dance cannot be finished until he withdraws. But the most of this explication is fairly tenuous: this use of metaphor is suggestive, but not explicit. Further exploration of the Freudian possibilities in the *moulinet* figure shows a more important and a more positive significance for the symbolic level. Tonio does not belong with the boys—not with fair-haired Hans or even with dark-haired Irwin Immerthal; he doesn't fit with their life of riding lessons and dancing, their physical and emotional expressions of themselves. His reading of *Don Carlos,* his poetry-writing, his dreaming, and his different rhythm deny him entry to their world. Later, on shipboard, Tonio sees clearly demonstrated the *articulation* of feeling, the *control* of emotion which sets him apart from the reddish-blond young man. On the trip to his childhood home, he meets rejection at the hands of still another group. He has already returned home really, for his books are on the shelf of the library his townsmen have made of his father's

formed squares of four couples each. . . . A frightful memory brought the colour to Tonio Kröger's cheeks. They were forming for a quadrille." "The music struck up, the couples bowed and crossed over. The leader called off; he called off—Heaven save us—in French! And pronounced the nasals with great distinction. Ingeborg Holm danced close by, in the set nearest the glass door." At Aalsgard even the dancers are the same: an Ingeborg and a Hans are there, together now, young, healthy, breathless, and handsome. The caller is just like Herr Knaak of the dancing class. And there is a Magdalena too, who falls down in the dance. Now Tonio understands her, pities her because she would use him as a salve for her rejection by the dancers; when she falls, Tonio helps her up and gently says, "You should not dance any more, Fräulein." Then he goes away to write, while the dance continues and the sound of the music floats urgently up to him.

Structurally, then, the dance is more than leitmotiv. Once it has been made explicit in the second and final episodes, its symbolic force can be felt in others. The boy Tonio slips his arm into Hans Hansen's, and the after-school walk is a troubled dance. Tonio woos Hans into taking the walk, and for a time things go well and the pattern seems outwardly correct, though Tonio feels some gnawing doubts. Then Irwin Immerthal interrupts, and Tonio is outside once more. When house, but, ironically, Tonio the man is unrecognized and un-welcomed. He is viewed with suspicion at every point. He carries no passport, and the only papers he has are proof sheets. He is not like other men, and so he is misunderstood: the room clerk at the hotel does not know how to type him, and later he is mistaken for a criminal. Finally, even after he is excused, he remains unrecognized, rejected. And with the realization that he can never belong, he stands again at a window, finally ready to accept his fate. The blunder into the *moulinet des dames* in the dancing-school episode, then, is a literal sounding of what will henceforth be a figurative note in the story, a leitmotiv. Herr Knaak jeers at "Fräulein Kröger," but everyone knows it is a jest; Tonio is different and does not belong with the boys, but neither does he belong with the girls, nor with any other part of the society from which he comes. He is simply not a dancer.

The literal meaning of the story is stated directly in the long conversation in Lisabeta's studio, when Tonio describes at length the terrible separation he feels. Here is a full exploration of the literal side of the dance-life metaphor. Tonio is an artist, his reason must control his feelings, and he is therefore a man apart. He cannot enter the simple world of feeling his fellows occupy. This scene is devoid of direct reference to the dance; the artist is only by implication the dancer, for preceding Tonio's literal expression of his tormented thoughts, the dance-life metaphor has been made explicit in two episodes.

As *structural* symbol, therefore, the dance is used in a limited way—in approximately two-fifths of the story. Elsewhere it functions as leitmotiv. I submit that any case for a detailed equivalence between individual parts of the quadrille and parts of the story must be forced and arbitrary. The clearest evidence of this is the fact that Tonio withdraws from the dance and the dance goes on without him; in the story, the dance is unfinished. The major function of the dance as symbolic act therefore is thematic, not structural.

"Tonio Kröger" has a real existence at the literal level; Tonio speaks directly of the position of the artist in society. He is explicit on the personal fate of the artist who denies himself—or rather who *is* denied—real participation in ordinary human relationships. Lisabeta is calm about the unique separateness of her role as artist, but Tonio cannot cease to want what he cannot have. Yet it is in terms of emotion—of love and sensation and feeling—that he writes to Lisabeta from his room at Aalsgard, while the dancers whirl in the rooms below. (Note the echoes of the dance image, as well as the other uses of leitmotiv): "I am looking into a world unborn and formless, that needs to be ordered and shaped; I see into a whirl of shadows of human figures who beckon to me to weave spells to redeem them: tragic and laughable figures and some that are both together—and to these I am drawn. But my deepest and secretest love belongs to the blond and blue-eyed, the fair and living, the happy, lovely, and commonplace." "Do not chide this love, Lisabeta; it is good and fruitful. There is longing in it, and a gentle envy; a touch of contempt and no little innocent bliss." Earlier, in the studio, Lisabeta has told Tonio that he is a bourgeois who has gone astray, and that he wants somehow to go back to being an ordinary man. Tonio then returned to his childhood home to search again for an entry to the dance, for a chance to become again a *Bürger* who could love without a constant perception of irony and the fleeting qualities of love. But it could not be. At the end of the story he is still essentially the boy Tonio leaving Hans Hansen at the gate. (The language is nearly

identical.) His feelings are "longing . . . and a gentle envy; a touch of contempt and no little innocent bliss." Whatever the rational qualities may be, the whole is dominated by feeling.

The degree to which symbol is employed structurally is thus significant in an appraisal of Mann's early story technique. The artist cannot be a dancer in the *Bürger*-quadrille. The emotional limitations of this kind of artist are suggestively explored as Tonio tests these restrictions, as he tries to overcome them. The metaphor of the dance of life is explicitly symbolic in the structure of the story in a few episodes; for the rest, Mann relies on the suggestive echoes of the metaphor and the techniques of the leitmotiv, together with the overt literal statement (in the studio) wherein there is no reference to the key metaphor. What the story might gain through a fuller exploitation of the structural symbol of the quadrille—down to its last step and figure—Mann has rejected in favor of the hazier, vaguer sense-and-feeling-effects of leitmotiv. In the end, for the artist as intellectual, with his emotional privations caused by the perceptions the artistic soul is heir to, Thomas Mann has supplied in **"Tonio Kröger"** a romantic aura rather than an intellectual justification. (pp. 282-87)

Kenneth G. Wilson, "The Dance as Symbol and Leitmotiv in Thomas Mann's 'Tonio Kröger'," in The Germanic Review, *Vol. XXIX, No. 4, December, 1954, pp. 282-87.*

FRANK DONALD HIRSCHBACH (essay date 1955)

[*In the following excerpt, Hirschbach comments on the tragic characteristics of love in Thomas Mann's short stories.*]

"*Is* there really much love in Thomas Mann's works, and is it really important?" The posing of this question is the direct result of three decades of criticism which has represented Mann mainly as a serious and sober novelist, and frequently also as a prosy and prolix author who "clutters up" his works with superfluous bits of erudition. His *Magic Mountain* bids fair to join the list of immortal works of world literature which people bring back from their summer vacations—unread. Mann is, of course, serious and sober and very North German in most of his works, and the charge of occasional verbosity and divagation can well be substantiated. Nevertheless, Mann has, in my opinion, tried to be fundamentally a humorist throughout his life and career, not in the conventional sense of the word in which Fritz Reuter, P. G. Wodehouse or Ring Lardner qualify, but as a man who at an astonishingly early age saw through his fellow humans, analyzed and defined their basic conflicts and decided to be a mediator, a prophet of the realm of the middle. The humor in Mann's works derives from his manner of looking at the human comedy, and our amusement is in direct proportion to our ability to discern a comic element in life, even in tragedy.

Certainly there is nothing humorous about the majority of the actual love stories which Mann tells: too many of them begin and end in tragedy. But there is something essentially and delightfully humorous about the warm light of interest and sympathy which Mann sheds on the denizens of the shady side of life's street, about the friendly irony with which he treats their brethren from across the street, and about the hope which he holds out for an eventual narrowing of the street which might bring the two groups closer together.

Love has a place in almost every one of his works, and the more important works contain the element of love in prominent position. To define the concept of love is a most difficult task, however, and I am not sure that I have been able to include all its various facets. Love to me means any type of erotic relationship between human beings which includes any one or all of the following elements: friendship, respect, esteem, veneration, adoration, sympathy, kinship, passion, sexual desire, and lust, all of which generally have in common a desire for greater intensity of the relationship with the beloved. I have also given some consideration to the subject of self-love although not as much as it deserves in connection with Mann's works.

Thomas Mann, never a mere narrator of stories, constructs his novels and stories carefully and loads them with the cargo of his thoughts. It remains to us, his public, therefore, to discover the role which certain persons or affections in his fiction are meant to play. Thus, love is the king-pin in a carefully thoughtout system which might be called Mann's philosophy of life. . . . (pp. vii-viii)

As we look at the *Novellen* of Thomas Mann, we see that a large variety of turning points exists in them. The story **"Fallen"** supplies us with a very definite and conspicuous turning point when the ardent love of the student for the actress is suddenly and vehemently punctured by his discovery of her past and present. A somewhat more subtle approach is taken in **"Little Herr Friedemann"** when Gerda von Rinnlingen's arrival in town, more specifically the moment at which Friedemann first catches sight of her, represents the turning point in the cripple's hitherto halcyon existence. In this story Friedemann is only dimly aware of the change that the event may wreak in his life. In the story **"Death in Venice"** we may perhaps speak of two turning points. In terms of Gustav von Aschenbach's life and career the turning point comes when he meets the first stranger at the streetcar stop, and his thoughts are sent off to dreams about travel and relaxation. In terms of the story itself the first glimpse of Tadzio sets off the chain of reactions which finally lead to catastrophe and death. Both events are apparently of no importance to the hero, and he is totally unaware of their future import.

Thus, if we assume that the turning point is of supreme importance to the author and his audience, it becomes doubly significant that a large number of the stories' turning points revolve around love. Some of the stories deal chiefly, or even exclusively, with an erotic relationship, but in many of them love assumes an important role only through its connection with the turning point.

The story [**"Fallen"**], told by a Dr. Selten, to three intimate friends with whom he is having supper, concerns a student who falls in love with an actress and spends a few weeks in great happiness with her before he finds out that she has been selling her love to others. The theme of the story is the shattering of the hero's illusion that love is an ideal romantic relationship between two persons.

One after the other, the student's youthful illusions regarding love fall like veils concealing a human body. And as in the case of veils, it is not until the last one falls that the nature of the object stands revealed in all its nakedness. Before he meets Irma Weltner she stands on a pedestal where she is inaccessible to him. The very fact that four walls must enclose her and that these walls must have an address and be listed in a directory has never occurred to him. After he has met

her and received assurance of a further meeting he feels that his happiness is now complete. His friend's insinuations that he should now carry the matter further are brushed aside disdainfully. Then, however, his ardor awakens anew, and again he is dissatisfied until he possesses her fully. When he first embraces her, another illusion falls.

> It was a strange and almost painful sensation for him to see how she began to stagger under his kisses, she who had been a towering goddess to his shy love and before whom he had always felt weak, awkward, and small . . .

This is followed by another "high" period during which he composes a little poem which with all its clichés and imitations is as pathetic as it is sincere.

But all of these disillusionments are normal disillusionments, common to a youthful idealist who finds himself in love for the first time. It is the final disillusionment which is unique to this story, unveils the nature of reality to the youth (or so, at least, it seems to him at the time) and provides the turning point of the story. At the moment when he discovers that Irma's love is purchasable his ideal statue has not only been toppled from its pedestal, but he also begins to have a foreboding that the pedestal may remain forever empty. As he kisses her for the last time, he has gained a new insight:

> Perhaps he learned from these kisses that henceforth he would find love in hatred and lust in wild revenge; but perhaps it was only later that all this made sense to him. He does not know himself.

Even if the bitterness of the first experience ever wears off (and from Selten's manner of telling the story it is manifest that ten years have failed to soften the memory) the realization will remain that love has not only a bright and happy side but also one that is dark and painful.

The plot of this story could be that of the tritest moving picture of today. Its remarkable feature is the fatigue, the somewhat superior amusement with which a nineteen-year old here tells a love story. Love is not, of course, a prerogative of the young, but it is a young man's privilege to be reckless and foolish in his love, predatory, unsparing and unreasonable. The student in love exhibits all these characteristics, but Dr. Selten, his *alter ego,* who is at the same time Thomas Mann's narrator, smiles and, on occasion, sneers at so much foolishness. Expressing it differently: the nineteen-year old author dons the mask of a thirty-year old narrator to reflect ironically on the confusion of a twenty-year old. He is not interested in and perhaps incapable of writing a pure love story at this time. The anguished cry of Detlef in **"The Hungry,"** "Oh, not to be an artist for one night like this, to be human," his sigh for the pleasures of banality are rooted in this inability. But Mann knows at the same time that a realistic description of "being human" or of "behaving banally" would be dull and unartistic. Irony is his chief weapon against this danger, and there is a peculiar effectiveness to this first experiment in irony on the part of the young Mann. (pp. 2-4)

There are two basic experiences which influence and shape the life of Johannes Friedemann [in **"Little Herr Friedemann"**]. One occurs when the nurse, given to excessive drinking, drops the month-old baby and thus causes an injury to his body which is visible to all and frustrates his chances for normal relations with the other sex, although otherwise it permits him to live completely like other human beings The other experience comes at the age of sixteen when, unwittingly, he becomes an eyewitness of a romantic scene between a robust, red-headed boy and a gay, blond girl with whom Friedemann is in love.

It is significant that in both cases Friedemann has been injured by a woman. While he cannot be expected to have been conscious of the sex of his nurse at the age of one month, it is possible that a realization of it lives in his subconscious mind, and besides he knows, of course, the circumstances of his injury. In the case of the second experience Friedemann swallows his pain, and there is no indication that he begins to hate this girl. He relegates this bitter experience to the depths of his soul, and finds other outlets for his drives in aesthetic enjoyment, such as reading and playing the violin.

But a deep hatred lingers on, a subconscious aversion to life, as represented by those who live a more extroverted life than he does, to his fate, to human beings, but above all, to women. For many years Friedemann remains totally ignorant of this. He finds reasons why he should be grateful to life. He sees certain intrinsically positive qualities in living itself, regardless of the relative happiness of the individual. He lulls himself into believing that he really loves life, and that he, a cultured gentleman, possesses a greater capacity for enjoying it than his denser fellow citizens. He builds a whole new life out of his situation where happy and unhappy experiences lie on the same level and an unstilled yearning is deemed more enjoyable than its fulfillment.

This is not a "ripe situation" which was bound to erupt sooner or later. It is entirely conceivable that Friedemann might have lived out his life in the relative peace and stability which he had so ingeniously constructed. But he comes to a distinct turning point in his life at the moment when he espies Gerda von Rinnlingen for the first time, and his failure to answer a remark by his walking companion is an indication that Friedemann is dimly aware of the significance of this moment.

His hatred of women erupts and concentrates on an object when he personally meets Gerda von Rinnlingen with whom he now fancies himself in love. It is on the evening of the "Lohengrin" performance when his hatred flares up for the first time. During the second act their eyes meet, and Gerda von Rinnlingen looks at him with a steady gaze until he finally feels compelled to avert his eyes. "He turned a shade paler and felt a strange, sweet pang of anger and scorn." From then on this rage is a constant element in his relation to her. He hates her both as a woman as such and as an individual woman who has shown him with a single look that she does not believe the lie upon which he has founded his life. As he reflects on the incident in the theater during the long night that follows, a powerless, sensuous hatred rises within him.

Friedemann's hate-love for Gerda is mentioned several more times. He wants to conquer and subdue her, and in her he wants to conquer and subdue all women and punish them for what they have done to him. It is logical and tragic that he falls in love with Gerda von Rinnlingen, a cold and sexless woman whom Mann might have borrowed from one of Strindberg's dramas or novels. Having married a man twenty years her senior in order to escape boredom and insecurity, she now sees a potential companion, a fellow sufferer, in Friedemann, a confidant to whom she can tell her strange fantasies. But he refuses to act the part, destroys her hope, and thrusts his physical self upon her, an act for which she would probably condemn any man (the Rinnlingens are, after

all, childless after four years of marriage). Gerda sits shocked and numbed for a few moments and then rejects him—not because he is a cripple but because he has dared trespass the zone of coolness and isolation which she has created around herself.

Friedemann, whose experience with women is exceedingly limited, already imagines when he first calls on her that she wants to torment and ridicule him. When toward the end of the interview she directs a look at him which he imagines to be full of scorn,

> . . . there shot through him once more that strangely sweet and torturing sense of impotent rage.

We had seen before that Friedemann is a master builder of thought systems, that he likes to develop and then stoutly maintains certain *idées fixes* regarding his relationship to the world and other people. Now that he is certain that Gerda wishes to make him suffer, he enjoys the pain and finds it "strangely sweet and torturing," a feeling which later occurs with a slight variation as "anguishingly sweet." Friedemann is a masochist, and thus we can explain his self-destruction at the garden party. Totally frustrated in his desire to subjugate Gerda and unmistakably rebuked, he jumps up, runs a few steps and falls at the water's edge.

> What were his sensations at this moment? Perhaps he was feeling that same luxury of hate which he had felt before when she had humiliated him with her glance, degenerated now, when he lay before her on the ground and she had treated him like a dog, into an insane rage which must at all costs find expression even against himself—a disgust, perhaps of himself, which filled him with a thirst to destroy himself, to tear himself to pieces, to blot out himself utterly.

The same theme—the test of a life lie in the fire of an erotic experience, followed by catastrophe—is treated in the story **"The Dilettante"** with slight variations. Unlike Friedemann, the dilettante has no physical defects which exclude him from the pursuit of normal pleasures. His defect is rather an early realization—inspired by a conversation which he overheard when he was eighteen—that he has an artistic penchant without being talented or energetic enough to become an artist. He likes to see himself suspended between two worlds, the world of art and artists on one side and on the other side the world in which "the favorites of the gods" live,

> children of light who move easily through life with the reflection and image of the sun in their eyes; charming, amiable, while all the world surrounds them with praise, admiration, envy, and love.

Like Friedemann, he has built a precarious structure of aesthetic enjoyments which carefully shields him from the strong rays of actual experience and within which he feels he is as happy as he can ever be.

Having devoted more than half of the story to a highly introspective analysis of his personality and early life, the dilettante then proceeds to relate his encounter with Anna Rainer who by her mere existence manages to destroy his peace. The affair itself is almost ridiculously insignificant. He only sees the object of his affections on three very impersonal occasions and only speaks to her once when at a public bazaar he asks her to sell him a glass of wine. Nevertheless the realization that Anna Rainer can never belong to him, convinces him so completely of his own insufficiency that it begins a "furious process of disintegration" within him. He has suffered a disastrous and fundamental defeat at the hands of life, as personified by Anna's beau, Witznagel, whose spotless and elegant shirt-front becomes a symbol of his inner composure. The dilettante does not have Friedemann's intensity and does not commit suicide; disgusted with himself and the way in which life has treated him, he will merely vegetate henceforth.

The third of the aesthetes is Siegmund Aarenhold whose incestuous union with his sister, Sieglinde, is the culmination of the story, **"The Blood of the Walsungs."** He is the decadent aesthete whom we had encountered in the previous two stories or in the figure of the stranger in **"Disillusionment,"** carried to a near-ridiculous extreme. For Siegmund, being wealthier than his predecessors, can surround himself with more luxuries, but he has little of the good taste and engages in few of the intellectual pursuits which had once made life enjoyable for Friedemann and the dilettante. To Siegmund life has become a series of conventional motions through which he feels obliged to go. He lives in a household which is marked by an excessive and empty formality (lunch is announced at exactly 11:53 A.M., and the family attends it in very formal attire), and in which everybody employs a peculiar, unnatural, parodistic speech. To behave naturally would mean to show sentiment and sincerity which they consider indigenous to the lower classes.

Siegmund has no passions, either positive or negative, and he enjoys only the exotic pleasures which are available rarely and to the few. The company of others repels him, and if his twin sister is excepted from this, it is only because she has always been a part of himself. Since in art and literature he only accepts that which is perfect, he is totally lacking in enthusiasm for anything and finds everything that comes to his attention "pitiably weak."

And yet, there are moments when Siegmund, like the stranger and like the dilettante, feels that he fails to penetrate to the core of life. Under the intoxicating influence of Wagner's music, these fleeting moments lengthen into an hour, and "the actual" crystallizes in his mind and becomes "creation." After years of passivity he thirsts for a deed, but never having made a decision or committed a deed, it remains an uncertain feeling.

> Creation? How did one create? Pain gnawed and burned in Siegmund's breast, a searing anguish, which was yet somehow sweet, a yearning— whither, for what? It was all so dark, so shamefully useless! He had two thoughts, two words: Creation, passion.

Finally and still with Wagner in his ears, Siegmund decides that in order to attain creativity, one must have had the experience of passion, and thus his course is charted. Owing to the manner in which he has grown up, he cannot possibly seek this experience with anyone but his sister, but the act is also characteristic of the sterility and the mysteriously stagnant atmosphere of which the reader has been conscious from the beginning of the story.

It is difficult to locate the turning point in our story. Possibly it comes at some indeterminable moment during Siegmund's afternoon when his vague feeling of dissatisfaction concentrates on the necessity for action. But the afternoon's resolve focuses on a goal only during the evening's performance of

Wagner's *Die Walküre* which Siegmund and Sieglinde attend, and it is here that we find the true turning point.

"The Blood of the Walsungs" is a subtle parody on the first act of Wagner's opera. The latter-day Siegmund, an overfastidious, overbred, contemptuous youth is nothing but a caricature of the noble father of Siegfried whom Wagner intended to portray. Nor does Sieglinde Aarenhold, who sneers at her fiancé because "only beasts wear tuxedos in the afternoon," compare favorably with the Sieglinde of the opera. And the comparison becomes perhaps most humorous when we place Beckenrath, the pale, officious clerk who is so anxious to improve his manners, next to the gigantic and primordial Hunding. It is as if Mann meant to say to his audience: "There you have your beloved Wagner in modern dress; how do you like him now?"

Siegmund Aarenhold's search for life and reality ends in a dim failure. We feel that the experience has been an intoxicating step to self-annihilation for him. Neither one of the two partners has found happiness in the relationship, and it is not destined to last long. The comfort and inspiration of "being human" has been denied to them who in a brief moment of passion wished to be alive.

The reader of Thomas Mann's story **"Tristan"** might very well feel reminded of one of Ibsen's finest dramas, *The Wild Duck*. In the latter, the peaceful and mutually satisfying, if somewhat hum-drum marriage of Hjalmar and Gina Eckdal and their family life are violently disrupted by a self-appointed reformer, Gregers Werle. This sincere but troublesome do-gooder is obsessed with something which he calls "the claim of the ideal," a notion that everybody must be totally conscious of the real foundations of his existence in order to develop his own personality and talents to the greatest, i.e. the ideal degree. Seeing a man of rare talents and vision in his friend Hjalmar (who is in reality a very mediocre person), Gregers arrogates to himself the role of the retriever whose task it is to rescue this particular "wild duck" from the miasmic swamp of lies and illusions into which he has fallen through the weight of circumstances. Alas, the rescued refuses to stay rescued for very long, and as the curtain falls, a slightly lacerated wild duck is about to relapse into the warm and homey swamp of the "life lie."

Whether or not Detlev Spinell, who "awakens" Gabriele Klöterjahn, is quite as sincere as Gregers Werle is a matter of conjecture. He is not an artist but a man of artistic sensibilities who has studied the artist type well enough to act it. His style is pompous and presumptuous, his manner unmanly and effusive. Exceedingly proud of his own well-turned phrases which he quotes occasionally or of his one great achievement, his book, he is the only worshipper at his own altar, the only participant in a Spinell cult.

When Spinell begins to "enlighten" Gabriele Klöterjahn about herself, he is greatly helped by her personality. Untouched by the responsibilities of marriage and motherhood she has essentially remained a teen-ager ("ein Backfisch"). She is given to introspection and deliberation about life and happiness, mainly *her* life and *her* happiness, but at the same time she has a bad conscience about such "selfishness." In such a moment of a disturbed conscience when she saw a need for greater practicality and attention to life she accepted a proposal of marriage from the intensely practical, hard-headed, businesslike Mr. Klöterjahn. But now, weakened by years of "practical living," undermined physically by the birth of the baby and by tuberculosis, she welcomes the opportunity of being able once more to lose herself in thoughts of the "would-have-been" and the "could-have-been."

Spinell encourages her in talking about herself, he subtly suggests to her ways of looking at her past life, her marriage, and her offspring; he flatters her by raising her on a pedestal and by endowing her with a stature which she really does not have. For Gabriele's soulfulness, her receptivity for the finer things in life, her "Innerlichkeit" are largely illusions, created by Spinell for his and her satisfaction. Her edified virginity, the song on her lips and the shimmering crown on her head as she sat with her six girl friends (shall we assume it as significant that Thomas Mann brings his fascination with the number seven into play in this early story?), all these are Spinell's embroidery, and we are far more inclined to believe the realistic Klöterjahn who tells us that the seven girls were knitting and that potato pancakes were the subject of their deliberations. Gabriele's husband is a well-meaning and totally a-poetical bourgeois, a harmless and insignificant man whose tears at his wife's relapse betray his warm and simple sentiment. He becomes hateful only in the picture which Spinell induces in Gabriele: a barbarian in hob-nailed boots, crushing the tender flower of her soul. Little wonder that this is a comforting and flattering picture to Gabriele.

In his letter to Klöterjahn Spinell writes:

> . . . it is my inescapable task on this earth to call things by their right names, to make them speak, to illuminate the unconscious. The world is full of what I call the unconscious type, and I cannot endure it; I cannot endure all these unconscious types.

He hates life, he says in another place, "this dull, uncomprehending, unperceiving living and believing," and eye-opening is his noblest task. And in a very similar mood Gregers Werle had shouted to his father: "I can rescue Hjalmar from all the falsehood and deception that are bringing him to ruin." When his father asks him: "Do you think that will be doing him a kindness?" he answers with resolution: "I have not the least doubt of it." There is nothing satanical about Spinell; rather we feel inclined to agree with Klöterjahn when he calls him "a tomfool . . . a cowardly sneak . . . a contemptible cur . . . a lazy lout . . ." and similar epithets just as we feel somewhat on the side of Relling in Ibsen's drama when he offers to throw Gregers down the stairs.

Thus, through many conversations the process of "making Gabriele look at her foundations" proceeds satisfactorily for Spinell until the climactic afternoon of the sleigh ride. Gabriele and Spinell both absent themselves from this community activity, the latter undoubtedly with a clearer motive in mind than the former. It is hardly too bold to assume that the score of Wagner's *Tristan* has intentionally been placed on top of the piano to play its part in what now has become a design. With an almost childish eagerness Spinell coaxes Gabriele into sitting down at the piano, into playing some Chopin nocturnes, and finally into playing the Wagner music which on another occasion Mann has called ". . . sublime and dangerous . . . with its sensuous, supersensuous ardor, its voluptuous desire for sleep just the thing for young people, for the age when the erotic rules supreme."

The choice of the *Tristan* music on Spinell's part for the crucial stage of Gabriele's education is significant. Love, or rather an unsatisfied desire for it, was the source of her introspection and daydreaming. Her marriage to Klöterjahn was an ef-

fort to suppress her desires or rather to make Klöterjahn the object of her romantic drive, an effort which suffered shipwreck on the rock of Klöterjahn's general lack of romantic feeling. It would be a mistake to assume that Spinell becomes at any time the object of Gabriele's affection. The "dissipated baby," as the other patients call him, is not the lovable type nor does he particularly encourage any such notions on her part. Having deprived Gabriele's love of the only object which it has had (her husband and her baby) Spinell acerbates the aimlessness of her affection by making her play the most erotic of European music. But here he has overplayed his cards; Gabriele is not ready to assume the reins of her emotions which run away unchecked and carry her to a complete breakdown and the abyss.

Love in the hands of a clever manipulator has once again been used to destroy a life lie, to test an illusion. But the love in this story is a romantic and very uncertain love, a love which turns away from an object and in its concentration on the self comes close to being sterile narcissism. It is important to remember that the Klöterjahns—father and son—emerge as the victors in this story. Gabriele Klöterjahn dies, and Detlev is defeated by a baby, the fat little product of the Klöterjahn union who merrily shakes his rattle and chews on his teething ring and through his very health makes the writer turn tail. (pp. 5-14)

Of the . . . stories by Thomas Mann which have not been discussed, many contain the element of love in varying degrees of importance. **"The Will to Happiness"** is the story of the artist Paolo Hofmann who remains alive in spite of a critical heart condition in order to see the fulfillment of his love for Ada Stein. When finally all obstacles are overcome and his iron will to happiness has been satisfied, he dies during the wedding night. In contrast to this amazing manifestation of the will to live, we have an even more astounding demonstration of the will to die in the story **"Death"** where a count "decides" to die on October 12th and does so, of course. Among the reasons for his death wish is a feeling of guilt about the death of a young woman after she had given birth to their child. In **"Little Lizzy,"** the lawyer Jacoby, an excessively fat and evidently apopleptic man, dies at the very moment when he recognizes that Amra, his wife, whom he adores, is deceiving him.

"Tobias Mindernickel" is a sketch of a melancholy and lonely man who bestows all his love upon the dog Esau but murders the dog with a bread knife because the animal has shown signs of strength and joy of living. A very similar struggle takes place between Lobgott Piepsam and the cyclist in **"The Way to the Churchyard."** Here, too, the cyclist represents life and joy to Piepsam who has been maltreated by life and is faced with years of loneliness and misery. Loneliness is again the theme of **"The Hungry,"** a story in which Detlef, an artist, finds it impossible to join a throng of carefree dancers (among whom is Anna, a girl he loves) because he feels that he does not belong to them.

If we analyze the four main characters in **"A Gleam,"** we find that Baron Harry, an army officer with a zest for activity, and Emmy, the dancer, represent life whereas Harry's wife Anna and the young officer's candidate personify a more introverted, sentimental type. The two women love the two men who are their opposite types, and it is interesting that here, for the first time in the stories, a member of the "life" group is represented as having an erotic interest in a member of the opposite group.

In **"Gladius Dei"** and **"At the Prophet's"** we have two highly sarcastic pictures of would-be saints and self-styled reformers. Hieronymus is bent on destroying the image of a naked madonna which adorns the window of an art shop because he regards art as something profoundly suspicious which awakens the animal in man. To the fettering of this animal the young iconoclast has dedicated his life. The narrator of the second story leaves a meeting, at which the eccentric prophet has harangued his followers, with the feeling that something was lacking, "perhaps the human element, a little feeling, a little yearning, a little love?" (pp. 26-7)

The outstanding and common feature of all the stories is that in every case the romantic element is one of unhappiness and tragedy. Not a single one of the love affairs ends happily, and in many cases it is a one-sided love which finds no response from the beloved object. In **"The Will to Happiness," "Little Herr Friedemann," "Little Lizzy," "Tristan," "Death in Venice"** and **"The Transposed Heads"** one or several of the lovers die at the end of the story. In **"The Dilettante"** we have the feeling that his fatigue of life will undoubtedly soon get the better of him. **"The Hungry," "A Gleam,"** and **"Blood of the Walsungs"** end on a note of hopelessness and sadness. Tonio Kröger evolves an essentially positive attitude at the end, but his attitude towards happiness in love is one of quiet resignation. Only in **"Disorder and Early Sorrow"** and **"Fallen"** does the youth of the two lovers give us a right to believe that their bitter experiences were temporary and not necessarily characteristic. (pp. 27-8)

When we disregard the nature of the protagonists and consider the matter of love as such, we find that love in Mann's stories is always a bittersweet thing with the bitter taste prevailing at the end. Only the student in **"Fallen,"** Lorchen in **"Disorder and Early Sorrow"** and Schridaman and Nanda [in **"The Transposed Heads"**] have moments or periods of undisturbed happiness, though the tragic ending is foreshadowed in all three stories. Tonio Kröger is happy in his love for Hans Hansen and Ingeborg Holm ("for his heart was alive") even though he is fully conscious of the hopelessness of his love. All the others have either loved happily in the past, i.e. before the story opens, or they have never loved happily at all. (p. 29)

In the stories as well as in the novels there are a few fortunate people who rise above the sea of their troubles and manage to find a solution by renunciation. Their death sentence has been commuted to life—a life of yearning for the love and affection of a member of that group to which they cannot belong. Later stories, such as **"A Gleam"** and **"The Transposed Heads"** show a realization that in the relationship between intellect and life it may sometimes be the latter that woos the former, and Mann himself has called this realization the first step in the revision of his views on Nietzsche.

But the magnitude of the catastrophe that love may represent is such that many of Mann's heros never have the choice between renunciation or surrender. To them love is but a part of life, and life may roll over them as cruelly and inexorably as a thundering wave. (pp. 31-2)

Frank Donald Hirschbach, in his The Arrow and the Lyre: A Study of the Role of Love in the Works of Thomas Mann, *Martinus Nijhoff, 1955, 195 p.*

SEYMOUR LAINOFF (essay date 1956)

[*In the following essay, Lainoff comments on the role of the narrator in "The Railway Accident."*]

In Mark Schorer's excellent anthology *The Story* (1950), the first tale is Thomas Mann's **"Railway Accident."** Set in Germany before the first World War, it centers around a train collision that causes the narrator to revise his earlier estimates of some fellow passengers and himself. Before the accident, the narrator—an author of bourgeois background—envies these passengers (especially a patrician with a handsome dog) as embodiments of state authority and aristocracy. After the accident, he sees them as hollow symbols, since they acted ineffectually in the crisis. In contrast, the writer seems to find new inner strength in himself: he feels that if his manuscripts, stored in the baggage car, were destroyed, he would patiently begin them all over again.

Mr. Schorer, commenting on the story, accepts the narrator's newly gained knowledge as *bona fide*. Accordingly, the story has what Forster in *Aspects of the Novel* calls an hour-glass plot, one in which the chief characters exchange values or perspectives, and the theme would be the ancient one of appearance contradicting reality. Schorer writes: " 'Railway Accident' is a story of contrasts, of oppositions between two kinds of men and between the inside and outside of several individuals." More specifically, the story would imply that the artist has greater moral stamina than the authoritarian.

The validity of this comment depends on our accepting the narrator's account of events as objective. However, many details, both before and after the accident, refute the idea that he tells an unvarnished tale. Instead, he seems to interpret events in a way that appeases his vanity, that rationalizes his position as a writer and a bourgeois in an authority-loving society. His account has only subjective validity at best. The narrator may believe his theory, or he may be trying to convince us that his theory is true; but he is deluding himself or deceiving us. The irony of the story, therefore, is not directed primarily against the aristocrats whom the narrator deplores; it is ambiguous, directed against both aristocrat and artist. The accident seems to unsettle appearances, but the moral victory belongs to no one. The story has been interpreted to declare the narrator the moral victor; with equal justice the narrator can be shown to be a humbug.

If we adopt this second view, what evidence can we muster to support it? We are struck first by the character of the narrator. His dominant trait is vanity, almost narcissism, born of ease and self-indulgence. This weakness reveals itself at the beginning: "Tell you a story?" (Teasing opening.) "But I don't know any." (Tempt me.) "Well, yes, after all, here is something I might tell." (Attention granted, he gives in.) He reveals his love of banquets and ceremonies—"not for nothing is one a subject of William II." (The irony of the remark reflects on the speaker.) He has a feminine regard for the storing of his manuscripts: "To this end I had put my manuscript at the bottom of my trunk, together with my notes—a good stout bundle done up in brown paper and tied with string in the Bavarian colours." The string image appears again at the end, when he finds the manuscripts unharmed: "All the things that lay strewn about came out of the freight train: among the rest a quantity of balls of string—a perfect sea of string covering the ground far and wide." The sea of string seems to deprive his manuscripts, his writings, of purpose:

they make up an enormous spider web, the product of pure self-gratification.

Second, his attitude toward aristocracy does not really undergo a change. His initial servility toward the patrician and his dog is mixed with contempt, expressed in derisive metaphor: the dog is compared to a circus performer, and its master, with his monocle and defiant moustache, can pass for a circus swell. The writer's servility and animus toward authority remain intact after the accident, but whereas earlier his servility predominated, now his animus explodes to the fore. He is ready to condemn without evidence an official, the stationmaster, for causing the accident. At the same time, the station-master's cap, the badge of authority, can still invoke his respect: his fund of hero-worship has not been exhausted. Mingling with the crowd, he is as ready as they to bestow praise upon an engineer for rumor-enhanced deeds of glory. He agrees that the mysterious chap has saved their lives.

Thus, throughout, the narrator renders the accident convenient to his vanity and his need to justify himself; it does not penetrate to either his senses or understanding. In the last paragraph, the writer states that the accident was somehow decisive: "I feel that I now have every chance of escaping another." What this may indicate is that the writer failed his first and perhaps last opportunity to see beyond his vanity. Other impressions to come will only hit a blank wall.

So interpreted, **"Railway Accident"** raises important questions about story-telling and the story-teller. It throws light upon the ambiguity of his motive and upon his equivocal place in society. And so it can be related to Mann's other early stories, among them **"Tristan," "The Infant Prodigy,"** and notably **"Tonio Kröger,"** where the claims of art and society are balanced against each other, with neither declared the victor. (pp. 104-05)

> Seymour Lainoff, "A Note on Mann's 'Railway Accident'," in College English, Vol. 18, No. 2, November, 1956, pp. 104-05.

JOSEPH MILECK (essay date 1957)

[*Mileck is a Romanian critic who has written several critical studies of German literature. In the following excerpted essay, he examines the moral dilemmas of the protagonists in "Death in Venice" and "The Black Swan," suggesting that "The Black Swan" presents an expansion of the moral philosophy developed in "Death in Venice."*]

When Thomas Mann first began to lose interest in the adventures of Felix Krull, he turned his attention to the fortunes of Gustav von Aschenbach. In 1952 Mann's interest in Krull again lagged and, just as in 1911, he turned to a more serious subject. The result was **"Die Betrogene"** [**"The Black Swan"**], a companion piece to **"Der Tod in Venedig"** [**"Death in Venice"**].

"Die Betrogene" is a shocking story of a woman who is caught in the physiological and psychological problems of menopause. She experiences an unexpected rejuvenation which is occasioned by the rapid growth of cancer and then dies abruptly before the consummation of her love affair with a twenty-four year old American expatriate. Rosalie von Tümmler's ordeal is essentially that of Gustav von Aschenbach. At the critical age of fifty and after a lifetime of propriety, both widow and widower succumb weakly and pathetically to a wayward passion. In each instance attention is fo-

cussed almost exclusively upon this deviation and the accompanying moral and physical dissolution. Coincidence alone can hardly account for the many striking similarities in these aberrations.

Rosalie's attachment to Ken Keaton is just as immediate and just as physical as Aschenbach's affection for Tadzio. Aschenbach lingers over Tadzio's godlike features and promptly thinks of Eros. Rosalie feasts her eyes upon Keaton's handsome physique and at once wonders about his success with women. Warm attachment becomes a passion within less than four weeks. Encountering Tadzio accidentally one evening and overwhelmed by his unexpected enticing smile, Aschenbach rushes off into a dark corner of a park and, throwing himself upon a bench, feverishly stammers out his confession of love. When Rosalie is suddenly confronted by Keaton's strong bare arms and magnificent chest, she, too, loses all composure, retreats hastily to her room and there falls upon a couch and feverishly confesses her love.

Both Aschenbach and Rosalie stand intimidated by youth. Ashamed of their aging bodies and anxious to please their youthful idols, they resort to artifice. Aschenbach is easily persuaded by his coiffeur that he should never have allowed his hair to become grey. Rosalie is soon convinced that she should have begun to dye her greying hair long ago. Both hopefully seek rejuvenation in massages and cosmetics.

Each is very anxious to rationalize his dubious attachment and to lend respectability to his conduct. Both find comfort in recalling analagous situations: Aschenbach placates his conscience by dwelling upon Socrates and Phaedrus; Rosalie lingers over the rejuvenation of Sarah and Abraham. Assuming a liberal attitude, Aschenbach attempts to find some justification for his passion by alluding to ancient Greece where love such as his was not only condoned but acclaimed. Rosalie simulates broad-mindedness and tries just as futilely to justify her behavior by reminding her daughter Anna that this freer type of conduct is quite in accord with the mores of their enlightened postwar society.

The desire that possesses both Aschenbach and Rosalie is accompanied by a confusion of joy, pain, guilt, and shame. Rosalie's coquettishness is just as pathetic as Aschenbach's scandalous pursuit. Each of them becomes humiliatingly servile. Both fear exposure and ridicule, but the prodigious sweetness they anticipate proves to be irresistible. Each has three real opportunities to extricate himself from his plight. Sickened by the sweltering heat and foul odors, Aschenbach realizes that he should leave Venice. His desire to remain, however, is greater than his will to leave; the trivial suitcase episode affords a welcome pretext to return to his hotel. Acting upon her son's willingness to forgo further tutoring, Rosalie could have dismissed Keaton, but she prefers to resort to every ruse and pretext to keep her lover in the family circle. Had Aschenbach followed up his impulse to make Tadzio's acquaintance, their relationship could have become a normal and wholesome one. If Rosalie had acted upon her daughter's admonitions, she could either have put Keaton out of her life or have let her interest in him become a normal maternal attachment. Each has one last chance to redeem himself, but neither is strong enough to take advantage of it. Aschenbach can only flirt briefly with his laudable desire to warn Tadzio's family to leave plague-ridden Venice, from which he himself would then flee. Rosalie realizes that there is much truth in her daughter's argument about debauchery and the necessary harmony between one's life and one's moral convictions; but, like Aschenbach, she can only trifle with the notion that happiness may also be found in renunciation. It is immediately after this last hesitation that both Aschenbach and Rosalie resort to cosmetics. Reason and prudence now cease to have any appeal, and practical consequences are meaningless.

The intermingling of life and death is the most persistent background theme in both **"Der Tod in Venedig"** and **"Die Betrogene."** In each *Novelle* the motif is introduced early and continues until the very end, and in both instances it is couched in such subtle symbolism that it almost passes unnoticed. In **"Der Tod in Venedig"** life and death are first presented in four separate symbols: the first stranger, brash life itself, stands silhouetted against the façade of a mortuary; the old fop, who suggests decay and death, revels among his youthful companions; the brutal boatman wields the oar of his coffin-like gondola with great vigor; and the mendicant singer performs lewdly in the very midst of death. Yet each stranger connotes *both* life and death: the first suggests strength and assertiveness and at the same time recalls a death's head; the old fop looks youthful from a distance; the vigorous gondolier is reminiscent of Charon; and the animated singer reeks of disinfectant. This same duality of life and death is evident in Aschenbach; in his ideal, St. Sebastian; and in Tadzio, his ideal incarnate. It is also from the jungles teeming with life that the plague spreads, and the fertility dance of Aschenbach's ominous dream is a carousal of death.

Mann in 1900.

Although the life-death theme in **"Die Betrogene"** is not woven in such a complicated pattern, Mann's manner of juxtaposing these opposites is reminiscent of the technique he used in **"Der Tod in Venedig."** A moist, heavily scented warmth wells up from Rosalie's favorite hollow overgrown with jasmine bushes and *Faulbaumgesträuch*. Here everything suggests life except the *Faulbaumgesträuch* which leaves a faint impression of decay. The little mound of excrement, putrid vegetation, and rotting flesh, which Rosalie and Anna come upon unexpectedly, teems with blowflies. Rosalie's old oak tree is virtually dead, but each spring the tips of a few branches come back to life. The crocus of spring and the autumn colchicum are so alike that Rosalie can hardly distinguish one from the other. Either can therefore suggest both the beginning and the end of the year, life as well as death. Rosalie's black swans gliding sadly and majestically about in their most recall Aschenbach's black coffin-like gondola. Their bills, however, are blood-red, and it is bread, the staff of life, that Rosalie throws to them. The pleasure chamber in which Rosalie and Keaton embrace smells like a moldy grave. Rosalie herself represents Mann's most startling juxtaposition of life and death: Her rejuvenation is actually a physical deterioration, and death is caused by a malignant growth which spreads rapidly from the very source of life, the ovaries.

In **"Der Tod in Venedig"** this life-death complex is highlighted by Mann's calculated use of two colors. Red and yellow, or some color approaching yellow, almost always appear side by side. Red obviously connotes life, and yellow is suggestive of decay and death. The first stranger has red hair and red eyelashes and is wearing a yellowish suit. The second has a yellow suit and yellow false teeth; his tie is red and his cheeks are rouged. The third, whose eyebrows are red, has a pallid complexion. Sickly Tadzio's red tie contrasts sharply with his yellowish skin. Significantly, red is not associated with Aschenbach until he is hopelessly enamored and vibrant with new life. It is from a glass of ruby-red pomegranate juice that he sips as he listens to the mendicant singer's sentimental songs and casts sly glances at Tadzio. Lingering over his drink, he recalls the family hourglass and sees the last few grains of rust-red sand swirling into the lower half of the instrument. Deep within himself Aschenbach knows that his own life is ebbing just as rapidly. He now has his pale lips painted raspberry-red, his brown, leather-like cheeks are made youthfully crimson; putting on his new red tie, he begins the last and most frantic stage of his courtship.

In **"Die Betrogene"** Mann's use of colors is somewhat less calculated. The juxtaposition of red and yellow again suggests life and death, but it occurs only once: The rouge which Rosalie puts on her cheeks to celebrate her rejuvenation does not create an effective illusion against the yellowish pallor of her complexion. Red and white are frequently used side by side (e.g., the red and white hawthorne and the red and white "candles" of the chestnut trees), but the combination does not have any consistent significance and has no bearing upon the life-death motif. Red, however, appears again as the color Mann refers to most often. It is the color most closely associated with the protagonist, and again it connotes life and has the same erotic undertones as in **"Der Tod in Venedig."** Both Rosalie's virile husband and her very masculine son have red hair. Red roses are her favorite flowers, and their fragrance is associated with Psyche and Amor. The very thought of Keaton is enough to cause Rosalie's nose to redden. Her passion persuades her to resort to rouge. Rosalie's red-checked coat, which reminds us of Aschenbach's red tie, harmonizes with her restored youthfulness. Even Rosalie's name seems to have been more than a casual choice.

The conclusion of **"Die Betrogene"** is deceivingly simple. Before Rosalie can pay her promised visit to Keaton's room she has a severe hemorrhage. Cancer is discovered, and death follows a few weeks later. Rosalie's calm acceptance of her fate, her final lofty sentiments, and the gentle manner in which she dies rouse our deepest sympathy. She appears to have regained her lost dignity and to have grown in stature, to have redeemed herself and to have become a heroic figure. In short, Mann appears to be much more sympathetically inclined toward Rosalie than toward Aschenbach. It is as though he no longer feels that the consequences of a moral aberration need be as severe or as inevitable as they are in **"Der Tod in Venedig."** The conciliatory spirit of *Der Erwählte* seems to have been carried over into **"Die Betrogene."**

As Rosalie lies dying she sustains herself and tries to comfort Anna by becoming philosophical. . . . Almost overnight Rosalie seems to have attained to a philosophical notion which Hans Castorp is able to arrive at only after more than two years of pondering. Has Rosalie actually experienced the inner transformation implied by her words? Has not that which is convincingly expounded by Castorp become little more than parody when uttered by Rosalie? Does her remark not recall Aschenbach's dream-like distortion of Plato, and does it not ring just as hollow as this final effort of his to extenuate moral dissolution and to achieve philosophical acceptance of the abyss confronting him? Following Rosalie's prolonged and feverish defense of Keaton, Anna notes that her mother is no longer her old self but has begun to speak like a writer. Now as death approaches, she begins to hold forth like a philosopher. Yet Rosalie herself has not changed. She continues to rationalize her predicaments and to move from illusion to illusion.

Rosalie clings to her nature-myth to the very end. She is convinced that nature has always been kindly disposed toward her and is thankful that death has come in the guise of new life and love. Assuring Anna that nature has not deceived her, Rosalie dies firm in the belief that nature has taken a personal interest in her welfare. The title, **"Die Betrogene,"** refers not to nature and Rosalie's death but to Rosalie herself.

Rosalie is possessed by a sweet passion and, like Aschenbach, has absolutely no intention of extricating herself. She convinces herself that insipid Keaton is a person of noble simplicity, a heroic figure, and nature's means of rejuvenating her. Not to respond to nature's beckoning would be an unforgivable breaking of faith. She refuses to consider practical consequences and closes her mind to all admonitions. So fervently does she argue her cause that she gradually ceases to be aware of any real transgression or to feel any sense of responsibility. Rosalie is most certainly her own deceiver. One is prompted to recall the three "betrogene Betrüger" of Lessing's *Nathan der Weise*.

Rosalie is therefore quite right when she insists that nature has not deceived her. What she does not realize is that she herself, and not nature, is ultimately responsible for her death. In his diagnosis Professor Muthesius concludes that Rosalie's cancer can be traced to unused ovarian cells which tend to develop malignantly during menopause if subjected to some unknown process of agitation. What was this "Reizvorgang" but Rosalie's refusal to accept her change of life to-

gether with her obsessive desire for Keaton? Rosalie is just as much to blame for her death as Aschenbach is for his, and in each case death is a natural consequence and not a moral retribution.

Although Mann makes no deliberate attempt to moralize in either **"Der Tod in Venedig"** or **"Die Betrogene,"** there is a decidedly Schillerian moral inherent in each *Novelle*. . . . Neither Aschenbach nor Rosalie hesitates very long in this dilemma. Each prefers indulgence to renunciation; and moral retribution is just as severe and inevitable for the one as for the other. Both lose their dignity, and, except for a timely death, each would eventually have lost all self-respect and the respect of society.

In view of Mann's extremely close attachment to Schiller in the closing years of his life, it is inconceivable that he should approve a person such as Rosalie. If anyone emerges a heroic figure in **"Die Betrogene,"** it is surely Anna. Anna's ordeal is remarkably similar to her mother's. She, too, succumbs to a purely physical desire for a handsome man unworthy of her respect. Rosalie is saved from complete ignominy by illness. Anna retains her dignity and self-respect only because she is jilted by her opportunistic suitor. At this point their paths diverge sharply. Rosalie dies refusing even to recognize any moral transgression. Anna, on the other hand, is torn by remorse and determines to redeem herself. In renunciation she manages to achieve that harmony between conduct and moral convictions, which Rosalie spurns, and without which self-respect and inner peace are impossible.

It was probably this very Schillerian moral issue which was foremost in Mann's mind when he acknowledged that **"Die Betrogene"** did mark a return to his earlier *Novellen*: "But then, it is not unnatural for a man of my age to cite himself, as long as he is trying to verify or expand his conclusions and to broaden his outlook." **"Die Betrogene"** does indeed present both an expansion and a verification of the moral philosophy which Mann presented in **"Der Tod in Venedig."** (pp. 124-29)

> *Joseph Mileck, "A Comparative Study of 'Die Betrogene' and 'Der Tod in Venedig',"* in Modern Language Forum, *Vol. XLII, No. 2, December, 1957, pp. 124-29.*

HOWARD NEMEROV   (essay date 1961)

[*Nemerov is an American poet, critic, essayist, and novelist. In the following excerpt, he proposes that "love is the crucial dilemma of experience" for the hero figures of Mann's early stories.*]

Rapidly and very generally resuming Thomas Mann's career in fiction, from the somber naturalism of *Buddenbrooks* through the symbolic and allegorical fabrics of *The Magic Mountain* and *Doctor Faustus*, the triumphant "God-invention" of *Joseph and His Brothers*, the miracle-tales of **"The Transposed Heads"** and *The Holy Sinner*, to the satyr-play of *Felix Krull* which crowns and in a sense redeems the entire *oeuvre*, we are struck not only by the immense reach of this author's development, but also by the great constancy at all times dominant over it. Beginning, as it were, with original sin in the shape of the artist's expulsion from a Nineteenth Century bourgeois Eden, the fatally corrupting flaw of knowledge, the reflexive splitting-off of consciousness from self, becomes the dialectical instrument for re-creating history, gradually expanding to take in the furthest realms of power, politics and the practical life. To say something of the beginnings of all this, of how much of it, to hindsight at any rate, is already present at the start, is the object of this essay.

Disappointed lovers of life and the world, those whose love has turned to hatred or to cynicism, those whose love is an abject and constantly tormenting surrender in the face of scorn, those whose love masquerades as indifference and superiority which a chance encounter will destroy—such are the protagonists of Mann's early stories.

Perhaps the simplest expression of the type occurs in **"Little Herr Friedemann"** (1897). Deformed by an accident in infancy, Friedemann learns by the age of sixteen that love is not for him. Very well, he will settle for what remains when that is subtracted: the innocent pleasure one takes in nature; the almost equally innocent pleasures afforded by books, music, and especially the theater. And so he lives quietly until he is thirty, when he meets a woman whose beauty becomes his obsession, and whose scorn for his hump-backed, pigeon-breasted self causes him to take his own life. But her scorn can gain this final power only after her kindness has broken through his carefully constructed defenses:

> "Thirty years old," she repeated. "And those thirty
> years were not happy ones?"
>
> Little Herr Friedemann shook his head, his lips
> quivered.
>
> "No," he said, "that was all lies and my imagina-
> tion."

With the help of "lies and imagination" he has composed for all these years a disciplined, critical life not without elegance, a life based precisely upon his infirmity and what it has forbidden him. In this life, love is characterized as "an attack," and associated with physical symptoms of fever and fatigue. It is not so much the woman Gerda who destroys Herr Friedemann, as it is what she evokes from within him in the way of the forbidden, the long-buried will-to-live which is for him a mortal sickness. There is in this figure, with his masochistic stoicism, his deliberate self-limitation, his rigid intelligence, already much of Aschenbach, whose more elaborate destiny in **"Death in Venice"** is similarly grounded on the clash of archaic impulses with the prohibitions of civilization, art, and intellect, to say nothing of a certain physical debility.

The same revelation, the same knowledge of scornful betrayal on the part of the beloved, destroys the hero of **"Little Lizzy"** (1897), the lawyer Jacoby, whose disability in life it is to be enormously, grotesquely, painfully fat, and to despise himself on this account. His life is an endless apology, a will to humiliation . . . , and he is most abject in his love for his wife, who betrays him with a musician, Alfred Läutner. It is the sudden knowledge of this betrayal which brings about Jacoby's death, as his wife and her lover compel him to participate in some amateur theatricals as "Little Lizzy," "a *chanteuse* in a red satin baby frock."

It is worth dwelling in some detail on the crisis of this story, because it brings together a number of characteristic elements and makes of them a curious, riddling compound obscurely but centrally significant for Mann's work.

The wife, Amra, and her lover are both savagely portrayed, she as incarnate sensuality, "voluptuous" and "indolent," possibly "a mischief maker," with "a kind of luxurious cun-

ning" to set against her apparent simplicity, her "birdlike brain." Läutner, for his part, "belonged to the present-day race of small artists, who do not demand the utmost of themselves," and the bitter description of the type includes such epithets as "wretched little poseurs," the devastating indictment "they do not know how to be wretched decently and in order," and the somewhat extreme prophecy, so far not fulfilled: "They will be destroyed."

The trick these two play upon Jacoby reveals their want not simply of decency but of imagination as well. His appearance as Lizzy evokes not amusement but horror in the audience; it is a spectacle absolutely painful, an epiphany of the suffering flesh unredeemed by spirit, untouched by any spirit other than abasement and humiliation. At the same time the multiple transvestitism involved—the fat man as girl and as baby, as coquette pretending to be a baby—touches for a moment horrifyingly upon the secret sources of a life like Jacoby's, upon the sinister dreams which form the sources of any human life.

The music which Läutner has composed for this episode is for the most part "rather pretty and perfectly banal." But it is characteristic of him, we are told, "his little artifice," to be able to introduce "into a fairly vulgar and humorous piece of hackwork a sudden phrase of genuine creative art." And this occurs now, at the refrain of Jacoby's song—at the point, in fact, of the name "Lizzy"—; a modulation described as "almost a stroke of genius." "A miracle, a revelation, it was like a curtain suddenly torn away to reveal something nude." It is this modulation which reveals to Jacoby his own frightful abjection and, simultaneously, his wife's infidelity. By the same means he perceives this fact as having communicated itself to the audience; he collapses, and dies.

In the work of every artist, I suppose, there may be found one or more moments which strike the student as absolutely decisive, ultimately emblematic of what it is all about; not less strikingly so for being mysterious, as though some deeply hidden constatation of thoughts were enciphered in a single image, a single moment. So here. The horrifying humor, the specifically sexual embarrassment of the joke gone wrong, the monstrous image of the fat man dressed up as a whore dressing up as a baby; the epiphany of that quivering flesh; the bringing together around it of the secret liaison between indolent, mindless sensuality and sharp, shrewd talent, cleverness with an occasional touch of genius (which, however, does not know "how to attack the problem of suffering"); the miraculous way in which music, revelation and death are associated in a single instant—all this seems a triumph of art, a rather desperate art, in itself; beyond itself, also, it evokes numerous and distant resonances from the entire body of Mann's work. (pp. 4-7)

Love is the crucial dilemma of experience for Mann's heroes. The dramatic construction of his stories characteristically turns on a situation in which someone is simultaneously compelled and forbidden to love. The release, the freedom, involved in loving another is either terribly difficult or else absolutely impossible; and the motion toward it brings disaster.

This prohibition on love has an especially poignant relation to art; it is particularly the artist (Tonio Kröger, Aschenbach, Leverkühn) who suffers from it. The specific analogy to the dilemma of love is the problem of the "breakthrough" in the realm of art.

Again, the sufferings and disasters produced by any transgression against the commandment not to love are almost invariably associated in one way or another with childhood, with the figure of a child.

Finally, the theatrical (and perversely erotic) notions of dressing up, cosmetics, disguise, and especially change of costume (or singularity of costume, as with Cipolla), are characteristically associated with the catastrophes of Mann's stories.

We shall return to these statements and deal with them more fully as the evidence for them accumulates. For the present it is enough to note that in the grotesque figure of Jacoby, at the moment of his collapse, all these elements come together in prophetic parody. Professionally a lawyer, that is to say associated with dignity, reserve, discipline, with much that is essentially middle-class, he is compelled by an impossible love to exhibit himself dressed up, disguised—that is, paradoxically, revealed—as a child, and, worse, as a whore masquerading as a child. That this abandonment takes place on a stage, during an 'artistic' performance, is enough to associate Jacoby with art, and to bring down upon him the punishment for art; that is, he is suspect, guilty, punishable, as is anyone in Mann's stories who produces *illusion,* and this is true even though the constant elements of the artist-nature, technique, magic, guilt and suffering, are divided in this story between Jacoby and Läutner.

It appears that the dominant tendency of Mann's early tales, however pictorial or even picturesque the surface, is already toward the symbolic, the emblematic, the expressionistic. In a certain perfectly definite way, the method and the theme of his stories are one and the same.

Something of this can be learned from **"The Way to the Churchyard"** (1901), an anecdote about an old failure whose fit of anger at a passing cyclist causes him to die of a stroke or seizure. There is no more "plot" than that; only slightly more, perhaps, than a newspaper account of such an incident would give. The artistic interest, then, lies in what the encounter may be made to represent, in the power of some central significance to draw the details into relevance and meaningfulness.

The first sentence, with its platitudinous irony, announces an emblematic intent: "The way to the churchyard ran along beside the highroad, ran beside it all the way to the end; that is to say, to the churchyard." And the action is consistently presented with regard for this distinction. The highroad, one might say at first, belongs to life, while the way to the churchyard belongs to death. But that is too simple, and won't hold up. As the first sentence suggests, both roads belong to death in the end. But the highroad, according to the description of its traffic, belongs to life as it is lived in unawareness of death, while the way to the churchyard belongs to some other sort of life: a suffering form, an existence wholly comprised in the awareness of death. Thus, on the highroad, a troop of soldiers "marched in their own dust and sang", while on the footpath one man walks alone.

This man's isolation is not merely momentary, it is permanent. He is a widower, his three children are dead, he has no one left on earth; also he is a drunk, and has lost his job on that account. His name is Praisegod Piepsam, and he is rather fully described as to his clothing and physiognomy in a way which relates him to a sinister type in the author's repertory—he is a forerunner of those enigmatic strangers in **"Death in Venice"**, for example, who represent some combination of cadaver, exotic, and psychopomp.

This strange person quarrels with a cyclist because the latter is using the path rather than the highroad. The cyclist, a sufficiently commonplace young fellow, is not named but identified simply as "Life"—that and a license number, which Piepsam uses in addressing him. "Life" points out that "everybody uses this path", and starts to ride on. Piepsam tries to stop him by force, receives a push in the chest from "Life", and is left standing in impotent and growing rage, while a crowd begins to gather. His rage assumes a religious form; that is, on the basis of his own sinfulness and abject wretchedness, Piepsam becomes a prophet who in his ecstasy and in the name of God imprecates doom on Life—not only the cyclist now, but the audience, the world, as well: "all you lightheaded breed". This passion brings on a fit which proves fatal. Then an ambulance comes along, and they drive Praisegod Piepsam away.

This is simple enough, but several more points of interest may be mentioned as relevant. The season, between spring and summer, belongs to life in its carefree aspect. Piepsam's fatal rage arises not only because *he* cannot stop the cyclist, but also because God will not stop him; as Piepsam says to the crowd in his last moments: "His justice is not of this world".

Life is further characterized, in antithesis to Piepsam, as animal: the image of a dog, which appears at several places, is first given as the criterion of amiable, irrelevant interest aroused by life considered simply as a spectacle: a dog in a wagon is "admirable", "a pleasure to contemplate"; another wagon has no dog, and therefore is "devoid of interest". Piepsam calls the cyclist "cur" and "puppy" among other things, and at the crisis of his fit a little fox-terrier stands before him and howls into his face. The ambulance is drawn by two "charming" little horses.

Piepsam is not, certainly, religious in any conventional sense. His religiousness is intimately, or dialectically, connected with his sinfulness; the two may in fact be identical. His unsuccessful strivings to give up drink are represented as religious strivings; he keeps a bottle in a wardrobe at home, and "before this wardrobe Praisegod Piepsam had before now gone literally on his knees, and in his wrestlings had bitten his tongue—and still in the end capitulated".

The cyclist, by contrast, blond and blue-eyed, is simply unreflective, unproblematic Life, "blithe and carefree". "He made no claims to belong to the great and mighty of this earth."

Piepsam is grotesque, a disturbing parody; his end is ridiculous and trivial. He is "a man raving mad on the way to the churchyard". But he is more interesting than the others, the ones who come from the highroad to watch him, more interesting than Life considered as a cyclist. And if I have gone into so much detail about so small a work, that is because it is also so typical a work, representing the germinal form of a conflict which remains essential in Mann's writing: the crude sketch of Piepsam contains, in its critical, destructive and self-destructive tendencies, much that is enlarged and illuminated in the figures of, for instance, Naphta and Leverkühn.

In method as well as in theme this little anecdote, with its details selected as much for expressiveness and allegory as for "realism", anticipates a kind of musical composition, as well as a kind of fictional composition, in which, as Leverkühn says, "there shall be nothing unthematic." It resembles, too, pictures such as Dürer and Bruegel did, in which all that looks at first to be solely pictorial proves on inspection to be also literary, the representation of a proverb, for example, or a deadly sin.

"Gladius Dei" (1902) resembles **"The Way to the Churchyard"** in its representation of a conflict between light and dark, between "Life" and a spirit of criticism, negation, melancholy, but it goes considerably further in characterizing the elements of this conflict.

The monk Savonarola, brought over from the Renaissance and placed against the background of Munich at the turn of the century, protests against the luxurious works displayed in the art-shop of M. Bluthenzweig; in particular against a Madonna portrayed in a voluptuous style and modeled, according to gossip, upon the painter's mistress. Hieronymus, like Piepsam, makes his protest quite in vain, and his rejection, though not fatal, is ridiculous and humiliating; he is simply thrown out of the shop by the porter. On the street outside, Hieronymus envisions a holocaust of the vanities of this world, such a burning of artistic and erotic productions as his namesake actually brought to pass in Florence, and prophetically he issues his curse: *Gladius Dei super terram cito et velociter.*"

Hieronymus, like Piepsam, is alone, withdrawn, a failure, ugly, dressed in black; a representative of spirit in the sense that one manifestation of spirit is pure negation based on the conviction of one's own and the world's utter sinfulness. He is like a shadow on "radiant" Munich—again it is early summer, the time belongs to Life—with its elegance, unconventionality, loose morals, its emphatically Renaissance and Italianate ambition of viewing life altogether as "art". On this scene he cannot fail to appear graceless, awkward, depressing; nor can any remark of his, in this context, be other than ridiculous. To a salesman he says that the painting of the Madonna "is vice itself . . . naked sensuality", and that he has overheard how it affected two simple young people and "led them astray on the doctrine of the Immaculate Conception"; to which the salesman replies: "Oh, permit me—that is not the point," and goes on to "explain" that "the picture is a work of art".

This parable is similar to that of **"The Way to the Churchyard"** in posing against the brilliant, careless commonplace of the world a rebellious figure who insists with all his being that all around him is a vicious sham, and that the truth of life consists in suffering, misery, failure. But in the figure of the monk this attitude is much enriched, complicated, and, accordingly, compromised.

Like Friedemann's life, and Jacoby's, that of Hieronymus is based with Freudian piety on what is forbidden, on denial; and his catastrophe amounts to a return of the repressed. The painting of the Madonna, which he objects to as blasphemous and tending to the corruption of morality, has become his erotic obsession: always with him, even in church, "it stood before his outraged soul." "And no prayer availed to exercise it." (Compare the treatment of the theme in *Fiorenza,* where Savonarola's religious hatred of Lorenzo's mistress is depicted as the consequence of his unrequited lust). The ambiguous reference of beauty, to the ideal on one side, to the flesh on the other, to the spiritual and the sexual equally, is the stumbling-block for many of Mann's characters: "Beauty alone . . . is lovely and visible at once . . . it is the sole aspect of the spiritual which we can perceive through the senses, or bear so to perceive." Thus Aschenbach, in **"Death in Venice"**, feverishly recollecting Socrates in the *Phaedrus* and characteristically stressing the implication that the spiritual, in becoming visible, also becomes compromised and corrupted.

Hence the problem of art, with its double allegiance to the spirit and the senses inextricably and at once. Hieronymus' rage is not inchoate like Piepsam's; at first, anyhow, it is orderly, eloquent, as well intellectual as impassioned, and directed especially against the affinity of art for elegance, decoration, illusion, laxness and luxury; he would reject that art in favor of an art bent on spiritual knowledge, "in which the passions of our loathsome flesh die away and are quenched." For him, "art is no conscienceless delusion, lending itself to reinforce the allurements of the fleshly. Art is the holy torch which turns its light upon all the frightful depths . . ." One notes that this definition equably accepts it that art is in the service of knowledge, and that knowledge in turn is in the service of negation and utter annihilation: illuminate to destroy. The agon upon this question continues to be played out, in varying forms, with varying results, through all Mann's works.

An element of composition, of method, also of enduring significance, makes its first appearance here. The central figure is as it were not an "individual" at all, but is based on a prototype from history; he is Savonarola, somewhat clumsily taken over in all his features and attitudes from fifteenth century Florence; and this identity is accented: "Seen in profile his face was strikingly like an old painting preserved at Florence in a narrow cloister cell whence once a frightful and shattering protest issued against life and her triumphs." This circumstance raises some odd questions about the relation between character and deed, will and fate, the actor and his part; it introduces for the first time that further question, so poignant for Mann's art, whether and in what sense the work has to do with life, how the one is fitted, if it is, to interpret the other; how far the idea of destiny, for example, is nothing more than a law of literary composition, having no more status in reality than the device of a magician. For the moment, it is enough to note the early presence of this question, deferring the discussion of it until we shall have collected other examples, in which this "taking over" of the historical, legendary, or literary extends beyond the persons to the action of the drama itself.

The examples we have so far considered share one dominant trait, and that is the doomed impotence of the lonely protagonist against a world which is cruel, mocking, or indifferent; a world in which the inevitable end of his attempt either to live more fully or to overcome life is defeat: his humiliation, followed three times out of four by his death. Whether this death be literally suicide, as with Friedemann, or the result of a stroke of some sort, as with Piepsam and Jacoby, it comes from within; it is a product of self-knowledge, and somehow suggestive of a fulfillment of a wish; one might say that the suppressed erotic nature in these persons reaches out and forces the world to destroy them. For the solitude in which they live is an absolute one; their efforts to break the charmed circle of their isolation appear as impulses to self-destruction.

There is another, and somewhat more fruitful, sort of isolation exhibited in these works, and the examination of some instances of this sort may serve to conclude our discussion of the early stories and sketches.

This is the isolation of the artist, the being who has some not altogether satisfactory yet not necessarily fatal way of responding to the world. Like the other kind, that of Piepsam, Friedemann, etc., it is an enforced loneliness often associated with disease and death; it ends not in violence, however, but rather as a dream, distancing itself and losing itself in the distances; its tonality is different from that of the other. The suffering protagonist may be viewed with some mockery, may even view himself with contempt (**"Disillusionment"**, **"The Dilettante"**), but upon the whole he is regarded with sympathy by the author, perhaps because he has some insight into his own sufferings (**"The Hungry"**, **"A Weary Hour"**).

In **"The Wardrobe"** (1899) Albrecht van der Qualen, though still a young man, is mortally ill; doctors have given him only a few more months to live; we scarcely need his name to relate him with agonies and torments. Traveling on the Berlin-Rome express, he yields to impulse and gets off at a way-station, a town whose name he does not know. Here, he reflects, he is free; he experiences what Hans Castorp will later know as "the advantages of shame": "Honest unhappiness without charity," thinks Van der Qualen, "is a good thing; a man can say to himself: I owe God nothing."

In this nameless town he rents a room; in the room is a wardrobe; from the wardrobe appears to him at night a girl who tells him sad, ballad-like stories, and also, in a fevered phantasy somewhere between dream and reality, sweetness and shame, becomes his mistress . . . and that is all, there is no more "story" than that. But that any of it ever "really" happened is a matter of doubt to the author. "Would any of us care to take the responsibility of giving a definite answer?"

This lonely traveler, diseased, bemused, on a journey without beginning or end (he never gets to Rome and we are specifically told that Berlin had not been the beginning of his trip), is the embryonic form of the artist hero; more exactly, the bourgeois artist hero. One observes that Van der Qualen has a first-class compartment, just as his fellow artists and fellow sufferers do: the writer-narrator of **"Railway Accident"**, Tonio Kröger, Gustave Aschenbach. Tonio Kröger supplies the reason, which is that "anyone who suffered inwardly more than other people had a right to a little outward ease." While Tonio Kröger goes North "to the polar bear" and Aschenbach South "to the tiger", Van der Qualen gets off somewhere in between, where nothing has a name . . . and he vanishes, is without issue. His muse of eros, pathos, pathology, tells him stories, but he doesn't write the stories down; and his status in reality is that of a dream, a Nineteenth Century dream reminding us of lonely streets in the lost cities of Balzac and Stendhal.

Though Van der Qualen's isolation, like that of the others, is associated with melancholy, illness, boredom, disgust, and though it is once again primarily the inwardness of the character which is stressed, the idea of art, however ineffectual, unreal, fevered, is represented as an alleviation of his condition; it is identified with erotic fulfillment, though also with guilt (his mistress-muse, after yielding to him, tells no more stories for some time); and by the sweet remoteness of its melancholy this little sketch seems to hint that art, a kind of ideal equivalent or substitute for sexuality (perhaps at once the equivalent and the antithesis of masturbation?), is the possibility of escape from the world, a transcendence of it if not its redemption.

Together with and over against this portrait of the artist as sufferer there must be placed the antithetical figure of the artist as illusionist, cynic, or even charlatan; the artist as virtuoso and actor. While we see such persons as Van der Qualen, Spinel, Detlev, Kröger, Aschenbach, and the anonymous protagonists of **"The Dilettante"**, **"Disillusion"**, **"Railway Accident"**, as almost invariably alone, or at most engaged in private conversation, the Greek boy, Bibi, of **"The Infant Prodigy"** (1903), is depicted in the fullest glare of publicity, giving a concert. He is of course not less alone than the others; but his loneliness is public, aggressive, confident and assured of mastery.

This most interesting piece is scarcely a story in any usual sense; instead of plot we have a kind of rudimentary musical organization of anecdote. Several themes are introduced and dismissed, only to return in variations. The major contrast of the work is between Bibi's thoughts about his own performance and the thoughts evoked by this performance in the minds of selected members of the audience. These latter take the form of variations on the theme which connects the idea of art simultaneously with the secret-erotic and the composition of society: Bibi's virtuosity arouses in his hearers sexual and forbidden thoughts, while his innocence, or the innocence which they presume in the fact that he is a little boy, makes these thoughts permissible and even rather religious.

Just at the finish a decisive point is made in the confrontation, after the concert, of an elegant young lady accompanied by her officer-brothers, and a bohemian, or early beatnik, couple, a gloomy-looking youth and "a girl with untidy hair". This girl has just said, "We are all infant prodigies, we artists", causing an old gentleman who overhears her to think that "she sounds very oracular"; now, however, she looks after the beautiful and aristocratic girl ("steel-blue eyes", "clean-cut, well-bred face") and her brothers: "she rather despised them, but she looked after them until they turned the corner."

This compound of eros, art, delicate envy, and social climbing is not arbitrarily introduced at all, but forms the climax to a number of preparatory references. Bibi's performance, which he himself regards with a cold pleasure from the technical point of view, in terms of cleverness, calculation, intelligence, virtuosity, arouses warmer sentiments in his hearers, from the old gentleman who compares Bibi to the Christ child, thinking that one could kneel before a child without being ashamed, to the young girl who thinks of kissing the little musician because what he is playing "is expressive of passion, yet he is a child." And she asks herself, "Is there such a thing as passion all by itself, without any earthly object, a sort of child's play of passion?"

The meaning of such reflections is brought out when the impresario climbs on the stage and, "as though overcome", kisses the little boy, "a resounding kiss, square on the mouth." "That kiss ran through the room like an electric shock, it went direct to people's marrow and made them shiver down their backs. They were carried away by a helpless compulsion of sheer noise." A music critic thinks: "Of course that kiss had to come—it's a good old gag. Yes, good Lord, if only one did not see through everything so clearly—". And when Bibi finishes with a piece incorporating the Greek national anthem this critic goes on: "I think I'll criticize that as inartistic. But perhaps I am wrong, perhaps that is the most artistic thing of all. What is the artist? A jack-in-the-box. Criticism is on a higher plane. But I can't say that."

This remarkable composition plays with great though quiet effect on subjects which remain central to the author's work throughout his career. **"The Infant Prodigy"** is Mann's first representation of some sinister qualities belonging to the underside of the artist nature. A figure like Van der Qualen, with his fever, near to death, and with his sexual muse, might be thought quite sinister enough, but in comparison with Bibi and his like he looks innocent and sympathetic. Here for the first time art is explicitly related to childhood, to perverse sexuality, to a kind of cynical innocence, and to power. Also to criminality, fraud, and imposition. For though Bibi is not a fake, he really can play the piano, we have only to compare his concert to the fake violin concert given by the child Felix Krull on a fiddle with greased strings, to see that the latter is but an intensification of meanings already present in the former: Krull's parents, for instance, profit socially by their son's "little joke". And the "realism" of Krull's performance does depend, we are told, on his being truly inspired, "enchanted" by music. Thus the fraudulent is not completely so, but rooted in real feelings; and the artistic performance, however real, is to a degree fraudulent, depending on illusion; people applauded, we are told, before Bibi played a note, "for a mighty publicity organization had heralded the prodigy and people were already hypnotized, whether they knew it or not." Art, then, takes place in a mysterious realm where nothing is either true or false; the realm of Van de Qualen's dreamy, nameless town, the realm of the theater where in some sense only the child is at home, while the adult must suspect in himself those real feelings which are evoked by means of illusion, and subject these to criticism, that is, to the reservations of shame and guilt.

This relation of art to the theatrical goes very deep in Mann's work, and develops very far. We may observe, about the stories we have been considering up to this point, that the theater is in some way always present. Some of them, like **"The Infant Prodigy"** and **"Little Lizzy"**, have theatrical performances for their subject. But the ambulance men take Piepsam away smoothly and efficiently, "as in a theater"; Friedemann "loved the theater most of all", and he falls in love at a performance of *Lohengrin;* **"Gladius Dei"**, though chiefly concerned with painting, contains several references to the theater, and Hieronymus' vision of doom has for a background Theatinerstrasse, Theater Street.

Anticipating, it is possible to see the relation of Bibi to the development of those artist figures most involved with evil, with "the questionable" and the powers of darkness: Cipolla, artist and illusionist of the political-erotic; Leverkühn, the artist as Faust, compacted for his powers to the devil; Krull, the artist as criminal, working directly on life. Many minor episodes and vignettes deal with the same compound of beauty and its dubious beginnings: for instance, Tonio Kröger's anecdote about the banker whose talent for short stories emerged only when he served a prison sentence; Felix Krull's horrifying sketch contrasting the actor Muller-Rose's appearance on stage and off; the ambiguous characterization of art in *The Magic Mountain* and in *Doctor Faustus* as "alchemical", as inorganic imitation of the organic; as bound up with the *illusory* (or *spiritual:* the doubt is everpresent) transmutation of lower into higher: of nothing into matter; matter into life; life into thought; those successive quantum jumps of creation which are characterized also as intensifications of shame and guilt.

There are thus already revealed two views of the artist. In one

he is the lonely sufferer of the dark horror of the world; in the other he is the cynical magician whose illusionistic powers enable him somewhat coldly to exploit his own suffering and that of others, for ends which may possibly be redemptive but which are always regarded by the author with much misgiving, at the least because they are remote from the ends of practical life. . . . (pp. 7-19)

Over against both views of the artist there is the commonplace view of "the beautiful", relating it to amusement, entertainment, health; as with the lieutenant in **"Tonio Kröger"** who "asks the company's permission to read some verses of his own composition". The disaster, says Kröger, was the lieutenant's own fault: "There he stood, suffering embarrassment for the mistake of thinking that one may pluck a single leaf from the laurel tree of art without paying for it with his life." (p. 20)

Howard Nemerov, "Themes & Methods: The Early Stories of Thomas Mann," in The Carleton Miscellany, *Vol. II, No. 1, Winter, 1961, pp. 3-20.*

EUGENE McNAMARA　(essay date 1962)

[McNamara is a Canadian poet, fiction writer, and critic. In the following excerpt, he suggests that Mann's use of ambiguous imagery in "Death in Venice" conveys the dual nature of the story's protagonist, Gustav von Aschenbach.]

Through an ambiguous structuring of the imagery in the story, **"Death in Venice,"** Thomas Mann made an observation about a problem common to all men: living in harmony with a diverse nature.

Hence, **"Death in Venice,"** often regarded as an "artist-fable," like Kafka's "Hunger Artist" or James's "The Figure in the Carpet," can be read as a parable of the unexamined life and its dangers. Mann seems to say that no one can live a splintered existence. A human being is not an angel; neither is he completely an animal. Being both spirit and matter, he must somehow reconcile these two diverse natures and live in harmony with them. Failure to do so ends in destruction of the self.

Gustave Aschenbach had lived for too long as an austere stoic. His submerged animal nature, long repressed, struggled for expression. But it was not only the atmosphere of Venice ("Southern," artistic, and corrupt) and the presence of Tadzio that brought the hidden self into full eruption—an eruption that not only gave expression to the buried self but destroyed the unity of the human being. A hint could be seen in Aschenbach's "new type of hero" that appeared in his latest works. This "new type of hero" might be a disguised expression of the artist's hidden nature: It is an image taken from Botticelli's painting of St. Sebastian ("an intellectual and virginal manliness, which clinches its teeth and stands in modest defiance of the swords and spears that pierce its side.") This could either indicate a sublimated masochism or give rise to a new prototype: the suffering homosexual as hero. (p. 233)

A close look at Mann's image patterns in the story gives ample indication of this more generalized theme. It is more a matter of inference, of mood generated by atmosphere, than it is one of direct reference. The time of the story gives added impetus to this universal meaning. It is immediately before World War I, which Mann has elsewhere seen as the great watershed of modern times, separating the old corrupt world from the new, healing a sick civilization through amputation.

Aschenbach's ruminations before the deserted graveyard are interrupted by the apparition of the foreign traveller. The word "apparition" is used quite literally here. "Whether he had come out of the hall through the bronze doors or mounted unnoticed from outside, it was impossible to tell." Immediately before the manifestation of this bizarre figure from the house of death, Aschenbach had been reading the Byzantine texts carved on the tomb: "They are entering the House of the Lord." Then the sight of the stranger sets off a chain of feelings in Aschenbach: "He felt the most surprising consciousness of a widening of inward barriers, a kind of vaulting unrest, a youthfully ardent thirst for distant scenes."

This is certainly in keeping with the connotations of the traveller's garb, but is surprising in the context of death and the future life suggested by the graveyard and tomb. And the malevolent quality of the stranger's gaze is hardly an incentive to feelings of youthful unrest. Surely the stranger, in the context of the scene, suggests more a Summoner for Everyman, an emissary of death, than merely a fortuitous image of travel. The lines, "True, what he felt was no more than a longing to travel; yet coming upon him with such suddenness and passion as to resemble a seizure, almost a hallucination" reinforce the notion of a vision, giving the entire scene outside the graveyard the quality of the supernatural. In light of this, Aschenbach's whole adventure can be seen as a dream-journey, as a parable.

It is in this scene too that the image of the jungle with its rank vegetation and a "crouching tiger" looms up. This landscape vision fades, never to recur in the story. The land Aschenbach visits is no jungle, but a civilized city. Yet the tiger appears again. When Aschenbach first learns of the plague from the English travel clerk, he thinks of the breeding place of cholera, "that primeval island-jungle, among whose bamboo thickets the tiger crouches."

In light of the close and careful structure of the story, the tiger does not appear again by chance. In the initial vision, outside the graveyard, he not only brings up thoughts of the far-off and exotic, but occasions a set of ambiguous feelings in Aschenbach: "He felt his heart throb with terror, yet with a longing inexplicable." Even so does he regard the plague. It is dangerous and horrible; yet it keeps him near Tadzio and seems, moreover, to represent his own hidden corruption. The crouching tiger might represent Aschenbach's destiny, lying off in the future, as the crouching beast waited for John Marcher in James's *The Beast in the Jungle*. It might also represent Aschenbach's long-repressed animal nature, coiling for its spring.

The image of the malevolent foreign traveller who summons Aschenbach to the journey recurs in the same ambiguous manner. As the elderly artist lies on the beach, just before his death, it seems to him that the far-off figure of Tadzio moves and changes. "It seemed to him the pale and lovely Summoner out there smiled at him and beckoned; as though, with the hand lifted from his hip, he pointed outward as he hovered on before into an immensity of richest expectation." If the traveller before the tomb was an ambiguous messenger, calling him either to death and judgment or simply to far places, there is no question here. The "pale and lovely Summoner" beckons him to death.

This ambiguous shift in context occurs in the use of sun imag-

ery throughout the story too. From a light of pagan joy it becomes a source of corruption. Aschenbach's approach to his relationship with Tadzio undergoes the same ambiguous treatment. He begins, naturally enough, in literary allusion. With a host of mythological and literary rationales (Socrates and Phaedrus, Apollo and Hyacinthus, Narcissus, Oceanus, Eros) he tries to "poetize" his feelings for the boy. But the Platonized structure soon breaks down into the physical, the sentimental, and the erotic. This double-leveled imagery lends itself to the central ironies of the story; the divided self, the hidden forces suppressed within, the coming downfall of intellectual pride. As much as Aschenbach invokes Apollo and Hyacinthus or tries to sublimate his interest in "a page and a half of perfect prose" the tiger lies in wait within the bamboo thickets of the secret self.

This same element of ambiguity is seen in the theme of disguise that pervades the imagery. The mysterious traveller may be a disguised Summoner for Death. Aschenbach is alone and incognito in Venice. The terrible old man on the boat who is imperfectly disguised as a youth becomes Aschenbach disguised to himself in the final stages of his disintegration. Tadzio, the beckoning fair one on the beach, is really a Summoner for Death. And Venice itself disguises its hidden sickness under a fog of lies, official silence, sweet-smelling disinfectants. The imagery creates a mood in which the disintegration of Aschenbach the artist can be seen as an example of what Robert Penn Warren called "the tragic division of our age." Man lives a splintered, truncated existence. Either he lives in an impossibly idealistic intellectuality or he lives as the most bestial of beasts. To live as either, and not as both, is to invite destruction. The "opening of inward barriers" left Aschenbach without human balance. His moral rigidity, a weapon of his intellectual creativity, left him vulnerable and open to invasion from the world of the senses. (pp. 233-34)

Eugene McNamara, " 'Death in Venice': The Disguised Self," in College English, *Vol. 24, No. 3, December, 1962, pp. 233-34.*

WILLIAM V. GLEBE (essay date 1965)

[*In the following essay, Glebe discusses Mann's development of the artist-hero in his early short stories.*]

Calderón de la Barca, the Spanish poet, wrote in his *La vida es sueño*: "Pues el delito mayor / Del hombre es haber nacido (For man's greatest fault is that he was born)." These words might well sound the keynote for Thomas Mann's earliest literary period. The protagonists of these tales appear to have come into the world accursed and guilt-ridden; at their worst, ugly and misshapen; at their mildest, ill-fitting creatures—all doomed to suffer at the hands of life. Isolation, hopelessness, suffering and unhappiness are the dominant notes sounded here.

Unlike the case of many another poet whose hesitant beginnings are lost sight of and are overshadowed by later more mature and more famous works, Thomas Mann's **"Little Herr Friedemann,"** as one of the first of his tales to appear in print, is of the utmost importance in any evaluation of his creative output, setting the tone for all his subsequent stories. It establishes his basic style with its lucid prose and its brilliant irony, and it introduces the important themes of "disease" and suffering of the artist-type of character together with the motif of art and artist versus life. The dropping of the infant Johannes Friedemann on the floor by his inebriated nurse may be likened to the dropping of a stone into a lake: from him as central point, Mann's writings emanated outward like waves renewing themselves in ever widening circles always born of little Johannes's pitiful wails.

Johannes Friedemann's accident, which left him crippled for the span of his short life, was, in effect, a carefully engineered "literary" accident designed to give the youthful Thomas Mann an opportunity to put into the spotlight of artistic scrutiny the freakishness of his own nature, personality, and life—as they appeared to him at that time. Mann's earliest opinions about the artist and his profession are all symbolized in this hump-backed, pigeon-breasted, aesthetically-minded little dwarf who, although a comical figure, arouses the sympathy and pity of the reader.

Thomas Mann, aware early in life of his artistic leanings, came to look upon himself as an oddity. He brooded upon what he considered his fate as a bourgeois who had gone astray in art. His awareness of his isolation from the normal world caused him much suffering and agony. In such a state he turned the more ardently to his art, using it as a means of striking out at a world which, as he felt, had cut him out of its existence because of what he was. In this process art became a cathartic which enabled him to cleanse himself of some of his nebulous "humors" and a therapeutic which gave him the strength and courage to go on living. Wishing to solve the enigma of the artist, Mann determined to write about him; that is, he would actually be writing about himself and, perhaps, by objectifying himself through the characters in his tales, he would be able to gain an insight into his own nature and problems.

It was out of the question to begin writing about the artist as if he were a perfectly average person; the evidence against this was far too strong. He saw it first of all in himself and found it substantiated, furthermore, by others, especially by Nietzsche, Schopenhauer, and Wagner. He had been shown that of all human beings the artist was doomed to suffer most. He had come to understand that the artist is never normal in the mundane sense—he is, so to speak, deformed, "diseased," his very calling is a disease. Yet he must continue to live or, at least, human nature demanded that he make an attempt to go on living in spite of his divergence from the normal and healthy. Accordingly, little Herr Friedemann's "accident" became the symbol of the "accident" of Thomas Mann's own birth and of the perversity which nature had imposed upon him in the form of aesthetic and artistic leanings foreign to his social heritage by all the standards he knew.

Johannes Friedemann, too, was born a bourgeois, refined and delicate. Now, there is nothing to indicate that Johannes would not have had the same aesthetic impulses which he displayed as a cripple even if he had not had the unfortunate accident and had remained physically normal throughout his life. However, fated to be crippled and thus set apart from the norm, incapable of joining children of his own age in their rowdy games and usual physical activities, he does what follows of itself in human nature—he seeks instinctively to compensate for his physical deficiencies by turning almost wholly to the things of the mind.

At sixteen, when he sees a girl with whom he had fallen in love being clandestinely kissed by a physically attractive youth, he renounces the last of his "normal" impulses and resolves to put his whole soul into a search for happiness out-

Dust jacket for Mann's short story collection Der kleine Herr Friedemann, *1898, his first published book.*

side of the one realm which brings to man the greatest happiness of all—outside of the realm of love.

Without closing the door to life altogether—for at thirty he had gone through an apprenticeship and was established in a business of his own—he sought his pleasures in the beauties of nature, in the world of music and literature. To all appearances he put into successful practice the principles of the mind-escape from the harsh and crude realities of life, while yet not divorcing himself entirely from that sphere. Johannes Friedemann believed that he had built up within himself a quiet and peaceful happiness. But in the end this turned out to be an illusion, a delusion after all; for one day "life," in the person of Frau von Rinnlingen, created dreadful havoc in the carefully laid-out and controlled sanctuary of his mind.

The world of mind, of art, and the world of life stood facing each other in the lists, and one or the other had to emerge victorious. Cruel, unfeeling, lusty life found the artist not yet strong enough, not yet sufficiently schooled to ward off its unerring thrusts. Little Herr Friedemann knew that he had to succumb.

Having conceived a mad passion for Gerda von Rinnlingen, Johannes now follows a rapidly downhill course to disintegration. The climax is reached when, grovelling on his knees before her, blubbering out the words meant to convey his desire for her flesh, he is heartlessly and disdainfully flung aside, irrevocably rejected. There is no alternative left for him but annihilation. Not even in dying is he spared indignity and humiliation: dragging himself along on his belly like a stricken animal, he drops his head into the stream and ceases his unequal struggle with life. Only in unsatisfied yearning can there be any salvation for the artist. If he is not strong enough to remain alone in an isolated world of his own making, if he attempts to become an integral part of that other world which despises him and excludes him, he meets tragedy. There is no middle way as yet: the choice is either suffering in isolation and loneliness or a return to nothingness—death. Little Herr Friedemann had known all along that he had been deluding himself; to Frau von Rinnlingen's mocking question as to whether or not his thirty years had been happy ones, he is forced to reply: "No, that was all lies and my imagination."

To be sure, there had been in Johannes Friedemann evidence of the will to live. He had tried to make a life for himself largely apart from normal "life." Then, in desperation, he attempted what the natural instincts of man bade him attempt, namely, to make his way back into the realm of life through the flesh. But in doing so he overstepped the mark, he attempted the unallowed, the impossible, and retribution had been swift and merciless. He met failure on both counts.

Vigorous, robust life had no time nor place for a refined and gentle cripple any more than for the bourgeois who had betrayed his heritage for the world of art and spirit. To the genuine bourgeois such a misfit was as much out of place in his world as little Herr Friedemann's ludicrous figure was out of place on the athletic field or on the lover's bench.

For Thomas Mann, the artist and the cripple were one insofar as their position in society was concerned. If they ceased to breathe, the crickets might, perhaps, stop chirping for a moment, but the boisterous forward march of life ceased not at all. The crowning blow to the artist's ego, the final thrust implying the futility of the existence of the world's Friedemanns, lies in the last clause of the tale: ". . . and down the long alley came the faint sound of laughter." With this brilliant stroke of irony Thomas Mann appears to have "polished off" his first artist-type character. Who cares that little Herr Friedemann has literally crawled to his ignominious death? No one! Life goes merrily on its way, laughing!

"Little Herr Friedemann" is, among other things, Mann's first call for understanding and tolerance of the artist, subtly concealed behind a façade constructed of a combination of ruthless cruelty and apparent light-heartedness and unconcern. Beyond this façade, however, lies the shadow of Thomas Mann's own sufferings and doubts, the specter of his ardent longing for a "place in the sun" and for justification of his existence. Johannes Friedemann is Mann's first "diseased" artist: Friedemann's physical deformities, his refined and cultured nature, his dualistic attempt to find happiness both in the realm of spirit and in the realm of life, his isolation, his mental suffering, his eventual resignation to the fate which awaited him—all these constitute his "disease," and from this disease he must die. It is Thomas Mann's disease, too: what Johannes Friedemann *is* in actuality in this tale, Thomas Mann *feels*—crippled, constricted, restricted, dwarfed in the face of life.

The tales **"Tobias Mindernickel," "Little Lizzy"** and **"The Way to the Churchyard"** perform essentially the same func-

tion in Mann's first period as does **"Little Herr Friedemann."** The treatment accorded the protagonists is, however, considerably harsher, more bitter and cruel than in the latter work. Life, too, except in **"The Way to the Churchyard"** where it is presented affectionately, is cruder and more sordid. Again there are bourgeois characters who have fallen from grace, this time individuals who are diseased in the true medical sense.

With Tobias Mindernickel it is not a case of a deformed body as it was with Johannes Friedemann, but rather of a sick psyche. Mindernickel is mentally ill. Desperately unhappy, though he may not be aware of it in his deranged state, he is a combination of masochist and sadistic psychopath who cannot bear the sight of anyone—not even an animal—being happy. This pathetic specimen of humanity has reached the stage where he can find perverted satisfaction only in the suffering and unhappiness of others. Rejected, despised, jeered at by all healthy children and laughed at by all adults, he satisfies his Nietzschean will to power by purchasing a dog so that he may have something living over which he can "lord it" and to which he can feel superior. When the dog asserts its canine independence and refuses to cater to the dictatorial whims of its maniacal master, it is cruelly beaten until it lies cringing, suffering and imploring at Tobias's feet. Reduced to the same state as Tobias himself, it can now be pitied and comforted. The animal is, then, also something which Mindernickel can love and protect, something which makes him feel wanted and necessary and important. The dog needs its master for sustenance; when it is accidentally wounded, it needs Tobias to nurse it back to health. But as soon as it is well enough to frolic about and be its merry self again, Mindernickel instinctively senses the danger to the position which he has established over it. In a frenzied burst of pent-up, sadistic rage he slashes at the poor creature with his knife, and only when the dog lies bleeding and dying before him can he revert once more to his role of protector and comforter.

What quirk of fate, one asks, caused Mindernickel to become what he is? It is essentially what Thomas Mann might have been asking himself: "What made *me* what I am?" For want of an answer Mann launches into what on the surface appears to be a cruel and unmitigated attack upon one of life's excrescences, upon one of bourgeois society's misfits. He flays Mindernickel unmercifully, he holds him up to ridicule and scorn, he lays bare the repellant workings of his sick and distorted mind by presenting him in his cringing demeanor before other human beings and in his incredible, diabolic treatment of the one living creature whom he has made dependent upon himself. Mann shows him no quarter from beginning to end. In the stark cruelty of its presentation, **"Tobias Mindernickel"** is, perhaps, one of the most openly revolting stories in the annals of German literature.

Tobias Mindernickel embodies a contemptible and pitiful aspect of the spurned individual's attempt to make a place for himself in the natural order of things. He displays a much stronger innate will to self-assertion than Johannes Friedemann though, unfortunately, in a perverted form. Mindernickel is another outcast from bourgeois society—we are told that he once enjoyed better circumstances. He possesses such a powerful urge "to belong" that his repressed and sublimated natural instincts assert themselves in a variety of mental aberrations and acts of viciousness which only the trained psychiatrist would be fully qualified to explain. Clearly, it is his mental disease which drives him to the extremes witnessed in the course of the tale, for no one in his right mind would commit such acts. Here lies the key to the interpretation of the tale and the explanation as to why Thomas Mann wrote it at all—we know that he did not use the pathological for its own sake. Tobias Mindernickel must be understood to symbolize the frustrations and repressions of the rejected artist, of that deviate from the normal bourgeois pattern, who is looked upon by his contemporaries as mad, queer, useless, superfluous, as a blot on their social escutcheon, as an object to be jeered at and laughed at by healthy society, as something veritably *un*-human.

Lawyer Jacoby in **"Little Lizzy"** is as revolting as Tobias Mindernickel but in a different way. Here is a freak of another hue, sick in both body and mind. The hardness of Thomas Mann's language in portraying the elephantine obesity of Jacoby and the repulsive and crawling aspects of his character, to say nothing of the depravity of his wife, Amra, who stands for "life," is unequalled anywhere else in Mann's works.

Johannes Friedemann had quietly and for the most part withdrawn from life until his natural sex-instincts forced him to make a weak and unsuccessful attempt to return to it; Tobias Mindernickel had crept into his room where, in love-hate acts of sadistic cruelty, he wreaked his repressed urges upon a helpless dog; Lawyer Jacoby clung desperately to his adulterous wife, hoping in that way to retain a toe-hold upon life. Somewhere in the depths of his ludicrous corpulence there was buried a fantastic ego which led him to believe that his beautiful, sensuous, evil-minded spouse could overlook the monstrosity he was and love him in return for the abject love he felt for her. So strong was the desire of this mountain of diseased fat "to belong," that he submitted knowingly and voluntarily to the sordid whims of his wife in order to maintain his place in society. The only difference between the treatment accorded Esau, the dog, by Mindernickel, and that apportioned by Amra to her husband, was that she did not maltreat him physically and did not kill him with a kitchen knife. For the rest, she treated him "like a dog"; we read that when Jacoby crept to his wife's bedside at night to fawn there on his knees for her love, she would stroke the bristles which were his hair and exclaim: "Yes, yes, good doggy, good doggy!"

On the night of the party, then, Jacoby stood upon the stage in his ghastly costume, singing the idiotic song "Little Lizzy," pawn of the perverse mind of his wife. Suddenly, in one blinding flash he understood everything, understood his delusion, understood that his wife had long been unfaithful under his very nose with the dilettante musician, Alfred Läutner, while he alone had not detected it, realized the utter hopelessness and sordidness of his existence; and then the colossal sponge which was his body crumbled under the weight of the naked truth, and he collapsed and died, Johannes Friedemann had willed his death and committed suicide; Lawyer Jacoby may have died of a heart attack. Then again, he may have willed his end and simply stopped breathing. Or is it more to the point to say that he was murdered, figuratively, by his wife who personifies "life"? Thomas Mann leaves us to draw our own conclusions.

Neither Friedemann nor Mindernickel nor Jacoby had stood up to, and fought back at, life. Very different is the situation in **"The Way to the Churchyard"** where Praisegod Piepsam, a physically and mentally degenerated alcoholic, does so. He challenges Life in the person of a youthful bicyclist who dares to use the path reserved for strollers, on which Praisegod is making his way to the churchyard to visit the grave of his deceased wife—the only thing left for him to do in his debauched state. But his efforts to remove the lad from the path are in vain; for Life, having tugged its maddening, merry little cap firmly back on its head and having given Praisegod to understand in no uncertain terms that he is wasting his breath, speeds onward unconcerned in the firm and just conviction that nothing so insignificant as a Piepsam shall impede its way. Then the futility of his struggle with the world penetrates even the besotted brain of Praisegod Piepsam; passing over into maniacal rantings against the crowd which has been attracted by the altercation and against life in general, he, too, in an armwaving paroxysm of unintelligible screams, falls to the ground in an apparent apoplectic fit and breathes his last.

We feel sorry, of course, that anyone should reach the stage which Piepsam has reached, but we cannot help laughing and being vastly amused. Thomas Mann has apparently written the tale in such a joyful vein, the scene has been so much like a "Punch and Judy" show for our amusement, that we feel instinctively how good life is, after all, and how brightly the sun can shine once the defunct body of Herr Praisegod Piepsam has been packed in to an ambulance and blithely trundled off stage. Piepsam, we read, stood there and looked at Life—unbudgeably," yet it availed him nothing. It is all such a ridiculously and pathetically funny little farce that it is almost impossible not to feel that it is quite right and as it ought to be.

It is, however, just in the very fact that the reader can feel this way that the real tragedy lies. No more than when he wrote **"Little Lizzy"** was Thomas Mann writing for amusement or only for his art's sake when he produced **"The Way to the Churchyard."** Decadence and life have clashed tragically once more, and life has emerged the victor. However carefully Mann has concealed the fact under cover of his polished prose and ironical turns, Jacoby and Piepsam are meant to portray the position of the "diseased" artist vis-à-vis healthy bourgeois life; they constitute objectifications of the suffering and frustrations of Thomas Mann himself. Mann's true intentions are not obvious, because he actually spares neither the misfits nor their mortal enemy, life, in these tales. All appearances to the contrary, the boy on the bicycle in **"The Way to the Churchyard"** is but a preview in miniature of what may be expected of adult life.

Of the protagonists examined thus far, only little Herr Friedemann, by virtue of his refined nature and cultural inclinations, is an actual artist-type himself. Certainly Tobias Mindernickel, Lawyer Jacoby, or Praisegod Piepsam do not stand per se for the artist. It is the ramifications of their lives and the cruel, unfeeling, heedless treatment meted out to them by the world into which fate has thrown them, which parallel the life of the rejected, isolated, unhappy, "diseased" artist. Yet they do exist, they "happen" just as the artist "happens." Why has nature produced them? Where do they fit in? Where does the artist fit in and of what use can he be to the society in which he is forced to live?

The question of "usefulness" and of "fitting in" is pursued with still greater intensity in the story **"The Dilettante."** The nameless protagonist in **"The Dilettante"** has a constitutional make-up approximating even more closely than that of Johannes Friedemann the qualities of the genuine artist-genius who was destined to become the object of Thomas Mann's chief concern in later works. That the tale is heavily autobiographical is evidenced by the details of Mann's early life as these are known to us today. Many of the Dilettante's traits become characteristic features of all Mann's artists. One outstanding example is the dualism in the character of the artist, a kind of split personality which is inherited in every case from parents who are vastly different in nature.

Like his creator, the Dilettante is "a bourgeois gone astray." He displays early in life a variety of artistic leanings, none of which are ever fully developed or show much potentiality. In addition to these, he possesses a certain affability and certain social graces which win him the approbation of his social companions—a somewhat hesitant approbation at times, containing undercurrents of doubt on the part of those who extend it. In short, the boy-and-youth displays character traits and personal proclivities which are not reconcilable to those prevalent in the society to which he belongs. His artistic talents are clearly only half-talents—of the "dilettante" variety, according to his father—and he lacks any of the practical virtues commonly attributed to the genuine bourgeois.

The Dilettante is the first of Thomas Mann's artist-types to be struck down by the artist's "disease." It is not symbolized this time in distorted limbs or in biological malfunctions; the Dilettante's disease is that "something," that part of the constitution which makes the artist what he is. The progress of this disease is already heralded by a warning bell sounded by the bourgeois core of the Dilettante's being at the very outset of his voluntary withdrawal from life. No sooner has he set up his quarters than he senses a vague fear that something is not quite in order about his decision to devote his life to quiet contemplation and the pursuit of selfish pleasure in isolation. It is the same guilt which Thomas Mann felt early in life, it is the beginning of a case of "bad conscience." The Dilettante is to find himself trapped in a vacuum between two worlds, torn by the desire to belong to both at the same time. The more he ponders his philosophic isolation, the more he questions whether he had done right to shut himself off from "people," to deny the honorable pursuits of his fellow burghers. Yet such lines of thought are invariably countered by those from his artistic side. In painful awareness of his own semi-talents, he imagines what it would be like to be an artist in fact, to be able to express himself in music or word or sculpture, perhaps even in all three, winning thereby applause and approbation. Thomas Mann's own occasional feelings of uselessness at this stage of his career are, perhaps, best summed up in the words used by the Dilettante to describe his reactions at the sight of a self-possessed young man paying court at the opera to a young girl for whom the Dilettante had taken a fancy. From the darkness of the orchestra he watches the pair:

> I sat . . . sulkily observing that priceless and unobtainable young creature as she laughed and prattled happily with this unworthy male. Shut out, unregarded, disqualified, unknown, *hors ligne—déclassé*, pariah, a pitiable object even to myself.

"The Dilettante" is not yet the story of a genuine artist-genius; but the symptoms of his "diseases" are to appear with greater force, for evil and for good, in subsequent real artists in Thomas Mann's work. Our Dilettante symbolizes the man doomed by the dualism in his nature, half bourgeois, half artist, to a life of misery and disappointment in an in-between world of futility, emptiness, and uselessness. The Dilettante is Thomas Mann's first "middle-man," standing for the bourgeois artist, for Mann himself. The Dilettante needs direc-

tion, and the tragedy is that he lacks it both from external forces as well as in himself. His artistic talents, semi-talents that they are, are entirely worthless; the fact that he has them at all makes him suspect in the eyes of the bourgeois world and results in his being forced, eventually, out of that world into isolation; the fact that he has them, but not in sufficient measure, precludes him from joining the ranks of those who can practice their art in disciplined fashion and thus win acclaim from their own kind if from no one else.

The Dilettante's life is eminently tragic. Unlike Friedemann, Jacoby, Piepsam, he cannot end his misery in death nor, indeed, find escape in the world of mental derangement, one which had been granted Tobias Mindernickel. Nor can he find salvation through projection into the sphere of art as Mann and other artists later created by Mann were able to do. The Dilettante is completely sterile. His story serves as a warning to the "artist" with only half-talents to find a place for himself in other spheres before it is too late. Mann sounds this warning equally clearly in **"Little Lizzy"** where he strikes out at Alfred Läutner, Frau Amra's paramour. What Mann says further in that tale in connection with Läutner is that the artist, the *genuine* artist, will not tolerate any attempt by the "healthy" bourgeois dilettante to establish a foothold in the world of art with his wretched little talents, any more than the genuine bourgeois will tolerate the artist's trifling in his affairs. Let those untainted by *Weltschmerz* beware—there is no place for them in the world of genuine art. Thomas Mann has found no solution, no escape for such a "middleman" as the Dilettante—if, indeed, there is one to be found at all. For the moment, at least, it does not lie in death nor in the Nirvana of the kind of "mind-escape" which was permitted Tobias Mindernickel.

In two ways Thomas Mann has portrayed the formula "art is disease" or "disease is art" in these early tales: (1) by using actual physical malformations and/or pathological disease or psychical abnormalities as symbols; (2) through the lives and actual persons of the protagonists who may themselves be symbols and in whom the deficiencies in (1), whatever their form may be, are to be found. The Dilettante must be considered separately. He has neither actual physical deformities nor specific pathological or psychical malfunctions which may be interpreted as visible concrete symbols of the artist and his "disease." Unlike his counterparts in this group of tales, his life, therefore, is not conditioned by the presence of any such abnormalities in his make-up. It was suggested above that Johannes Friedemann's fate was partially due to an innate refinement in his nature, which became intensified by physical drawbacks. In the Dilettante's case, although he is not yet a true artist-genius, it is entirely in the nature of the man, in a nature which conditions the events of his life, that we find the symptoms of the artist's "disease." In the Dilettante we have, already, a preview of the more subtle and insidious facets of the artist's make-up, which are characteristic of his disease and consequently condition his art. In **"The Dilettante"** Thomas Mann made a much bolder attempt to write about himself and about the peculiarities and deviations from the average bourgeois pattern in his own nature than he did in **"Little Herr Friedmann," "Little Lizzy," "Tobias Mindernickel"** or **"The Way to the Churchyard"**; in these tales he was as much concerned with portraying "life" as he was with the symbolization of the artist and his peculiar "disease." **"The Dilettante"** is almost exclusively a study in the psychology of the hero, a probing into the mental processes which result in the inner dissolution and degeneration of an apparently physiologically healthy character.

"Disease" in the stories with which we have dealt here is still a negative quantity; its consequences for the artist are suffering and unhappiness, it devitalizes and destroys him. He is still desperately uncertain about his position. He does not yet know whether he dare forsake his natural heritage to devote himself completely to the priesthood of art, for he is uncertain whether he possesses sufficient talent and strength to maintain his position in that sphere. For the moment, then, he belongs neither to the one world nor to the other and is forced into an empty twilight zone between the two, plagued by his desire for a place in both at the same time. That this is impossible in Thomas Mann's view at this point can be seen from **"The Dilettante"**: Mann's experiment with this dilettante shows what the results would be in such a case. In short, when Mann completed **"The Way to the Churchyard"** (it was written last of our group, in 1901) he still saw the artist as a misfit, useless to his fellow man, a victim of his dualistic nature, a middleman without a fixed abode or a definite goal—a man who inevitably succumbed to a "disease" at the root of which lay art. Many years were to pass before the Lübeck-born burgher who became lost in the realm of art was to see the "disease" of the artist as something which could be *beneficial* to the artist and his art and, thereby, conducive to the greater "health" of humanity at large. (pp. 261-68)

William V. Glebe, "The Artist's 'Disease' in Some of Thomas Mann's Earliest Tales," in Books Abroad, *Vol. 39, No. 3, Summer, 1965, pp. 261-68.*

RONALD GRAY (essay date 1965)

[*Gray is an English educator and critic specializing in German literature. In the following excerpted essay, he analyzes "Mario and the Magician" from a political perspective, commenting on the narrator's oscillation between a conservative and liberal point of view.*]

Mann's opposition to the Nazis was made not only from the public platform but also in the cycle of four novels treating of the biblical Joseph, which occupied him for over a decade, and then in the novel *Doktor Faustus,* the epitome of all he had said and thought on German matters for nearly half a century. He had also, however, declared himself in a short story which, since it is so clearly an allegory of fascism, demands special attention here. It contains, as one might expect, both an implicit denunciation and a subtly expressed condonation, neither of which can be clearly disentangled from the other. And consequently, it is particularly useful in getting to understand the frame of mind in so many of Mann's contemporaries, who disapproved and yet approved the events of 1933 at one and the same time.

[**"Mario und der Zauberer"** [**"Mario and the Magician"**] (1929) is an account, related in the first person, of a German's encounter with a travelling hypnotist in a performance at a small Italian seaside resort. The narrator is presented to us as a man of urbanity, tolerant and thoughtful, who witnesses with some misgivings the uncanny fascination exercised over his audience by the hypnotist, Cipolla, in whom the resemblance to Mussolini is unmistakable. It is fair to say, then, that while the story has many features of a general nature, it also presents Mann's forebodings at the movement already afoot on the Continent which might yet spread to his native land. The narrow-mindedness of the small town's population, its prudishness and its distrust of foreigners are first revealed in a series of incidents which might well have taken place a few years later in Germany itself. At the evening entertainment provided by Cipolla this rigidity and principled rectitude are seen to be the soil in which the hypnotist's powers can most readily take root. One after another of the inhabitants comes under his influence and is both literally and metaphorically made to dance to his tune, until at length a certain young man, Mario, driven beyond endurance, turns on his tormentor and shoots him dead.

> Somehow or other [says the narrator] the atmosphere was lacking in innocence and unconstrainedness; this public 'thought well of itself'— one could not tell at first in what sense and in what spirit—it set out to be dignified, presented itself and the stranger with a show of seriousness and reserve, of an alert love of honour—but how? One soon realised that politics were in the air, that the idea of the nation was playing a part. In fact the beach was swarming with patriotic children—an unnatural and depressing sight.

In other words, there was a self-consciousness in these people, which, while it had something in common with the self-regard which Mann commonly admired in his other stories, was rather akin to that of Thomas Buddenbrook than that of his grandfather Johann—it was in this sense and in this spirit that the public's good opinion of itself was later to be revealed. In such an atmosphere Cipolla is best able to display his powers, for such subjects, neither integral in the innocent enjoyment of their will nor aware of the ambiguous nature of their desires, readily fall victims to him. The tricks he performs are a demonstration of the evil which underlies such attempts at virtue: all have in common the feature that a man or a woman who appears to will one thing is made to will its opposite.

Thus the young man Giovanotto, who makes a polite reminder to the magician that he has bored the audience by his tardy beginning, is swiftly brought under the hypnotic influence and compelled to stick out his tongue at the entire audience. Similarly, when the same young man returns to the attack a few minutes later with what looks like bold defiance, he is soon writhing on the ground with the physical manifestations of extreme fear, apparently doubled up with colic. Later still, the gentleman from Rome who is noted for his moral rigidity and his determination to expose Cipolla's trickery is defeated in much the same way. His rigidity is seen to be the obverse of his concealed desire for abandonment: he is, it is suggested, one of the 'Neinsager' whose affirmation is all in terms of 'Thou shalt not', and Cipolla's power over him derives from his fuller awareness of the double aspect of the human will. Cipolla is aware, as his subjects are not, of the relationship between the opposites known as politeness and contempt, defiance and fear, virtue and licentiousness, and he has the means to transform one into the other.

In this knowledge of human nature, however, Cipolla resembles Mann's 'artist' figures more closely than he does any dictator, and in fact he is frequently referred to in the story as an 'entertainment-artist', a 'magic-artist', and as 'the artist' pure and simple. Mann's use of this last term was always broad: men like Hans Castorp, who never engage in any strictly artistic work, are as likely to be called artists as those who are really poets, novelists, musicians or painters. In this generalized sense, Cipolla has much in common with, for example, Gustav von Aschenbach [of **"Death in Venice"**] or even Mann himself. His ability to read the thoughts of others is presented by the narrator as a result of secret sympathy with them, which is also the reason given for the success of Aschenbach. Where Mann spoke of himself as a seismograph, faithfully recording the trends of his times, Cipolla 'lives himself into' the situation of his audience, and in guessing the nature of a hidden object is led to success by just this sympathy: 'He groped about like a visionary, guided and borne along by the public, secret will.' He is successful just as Aschenbach is successful, because he fulfils the requirements made on him by 'mass-confidence': he can make Giovanotto seem to experience the pains of colic because he is, in imagination, experiencing them himself. There is even something of the martyr about him in his own estimation, which recalls the description of Aschenbach as the Saint Sebastian of his times. When the audience calls out in pity for one of his subjects Cipolla claims that pity for himself: 'Poveretto!', he mocks bitterly, 'That is addressed to the wrong man, gentlemen! Sono io, il poveretto! I am the one who is bearing all that.' Just as remarkable is his profession of love for Mario, whom he calls his Ganymede as Aschenbach does Tadzio, and the way in which he is brought to his death through his homosexual attachment. The title of 'cavaliere' which he claims recalls the patent of nobility which Aschenbach acquired, on doubtful merits. His display of patriotism, which looks assumed, his affinity with Aschenbach's seemingly hypocritical love for Germany, and with Mann's own incredible moment of jingoism during the First World War. More important, his style of speech, if not of writing, is one of the things which most endear him to the audience at the outset. He is in his own way a master of language, so far as rhetorical influence is concerned, as much as Aschenbach was. In all these ways Mann suggests that he expected the appellation 'artist' to be taken with some seriousness, for all that he is much more obviously detached from his fictional creation than he had been in **"Der Tod in Venedig" [Death in Venice"]**. He is still drawing an aspect of himself, a possible development of his own personality, although another self, the narrator, is now more decisively set over against the first.

All this is little more than one would expect from any writer obliged to draw a good deal on his knowledge of himself in order to create characters of fiction. It is only the implicit suggestion that Cipolla is in some way typical of 'the artist' that is likely, so far, to cause us any hesitation. Looking more closely, however, it grows clear that Mann is not so much divided between the hypnotist and the narrator, seeing the one aspect of himself through the other, as he is actually sharing himself out between them, so that features of the one appear in the other. In the light of the first few pages of the story the reader is inclined to sympathize with and to put a considerable trust in the narrator, who is after all his only means of knowing what went on. The civilized tolerance of this man is highly attractive, and may even dispose us to accept all he says as true. Yet there are times when he seems concerned not merely to provide an account of the evening's happenings, but also to confuse the reader in such a way that he too is lulled into acknowledging a mysterious omnipotence in Cipolla.

There is the incident in which the gentleman from Rome goes up to the platform resolved not to yield to the hypnotic influence, and yet succumbs after a brief resistance. This the narrator explains as being due to the gentleman's lack of any positive will of his own: 'If I understood the event correctly', he observes, 'it was the negative character of the young man's

fighting position that was his undoing.' The Roman, by simply 'not-willing', was doing the very thing that Cipolla required of him, providing the blank sheet on which the hypnotist could write: we are reminded of Cipolla's claim that he could enforce subdual 'even if you do not will'—words which, the narrator says, have rung in his ears ever since. Yet only in the preceding paragraph the narrator has offered a precisely opposite explanation. 'This fine fellow', he said of the same gentleman from Rome, 'wanted to rescue the honour of the human race'; there was, then, after all an effort of will and the man was not simply 'not-willing'. Yet the narrator offers his contradictory explanations as though both were equally valid, creating thus the impression that there is no possibility of evasion, and that whether the subject does or does not exert his will-power, he is lost.

Taken alone, this incident has little significance. We might well write it off as a momentary slip on the narrator's part, were it not that such contradictoriness is a feature of all Mann's writing and that it occurs again within this same story. A similar instance occurs in the episode of the colonel who, under the hypnotic influence, was unable to raise his arm. Rather earlier than this, Cipolla had put forward a subtle philosophical theory justifying or explaining the basis of his power. 'Freedom exists', he had said, 'and the will also exists; but freedom of the will does not exist, for a will that is directed towards its own freedom thrusts into emptiness.' The point had not seemed particularly clear to the reader at the time: it certainly did not seem to disprove the existence of free will, and even the hesitations of the most scrupulous would have been dispelled by the narrator's immediate disclaimer. 'One had to admit', he observed on this occasion, 'that [Cipolla] could not have chosen his words better, in order to obscure the issue and institute intellectual confusion'. At this, we naturally pass on, assuming that the argument is not to be understood except as part of the hypnotist's usual duplicity. Yet when the story reaches the episode of the Italian colonel, the narrator himself reverts to the idea in surprising fashion:

> I can still see the face of that stately, moustachioed colonel, smiling and clenching his teeth as he struggled to regain his lost freedom of action. What confusion! He seemed to be exerting his will, and in vain; the trouble, however, was probably simply that he could not will, and that freedom-crippling entanglement of the will in itself, which our conqueror had scornfully prophesied earlier on to the gentleman from Rome, was in full operation.

This can only refer to Cipolla's theory, or to its summary restatement in the phrase 'Even if you do not will'. The earlier dismissal of that theory has now been forgotten; the narrator accepts and uses it himself, despite his avowal that it creates intellectual confusion. And this is done so nonchalantly that in the course of a normally attentive reading one inclines to let it pass unnoticed. In short, the narrator is apparently concerned to persuade his reader that freedom to resist Cipolla is non-existent, and is either confused in his own mind or prepared himself to use duplicity for the purpose.

It is hard to say which of these two possibilities is the more likely. In view of the actual preference for ambiguity and contradictoriness in so much of Mann's work, it seems probable that the narrator's oscillation between two points of view is the product of his philosophy rather than of deliberate dishonesty. On the other hand, it does bear a resemblance to the dishonesty of the hypnotist which is explicitly criticized in the story. At all events, there can be no question of confusion in the narrator's mind in one other episode, that of Cipolla's mind-reading act, in which he guesses with seemingly miraculous intuition that a member of the audience was formerly very much attached to the famous actress Eleonora Duse. The point about this particular instance of Cipolla's powers is that the person in question, Signora Angiolieri, runs a boarding-house in the town, known as the Casa Eleonora. It is thus perfectly possible that Cipolla has made discreet inquiries before his performance, and that his amazing knowledge is just extremely astute guesswork. This the narrator acknowledges, in fact he draws our attention to the idea. 'There was only the question', he remarks, 'how much he knew of all this himself, how much he might have heard in his first professional eavesdropping after his arrival in Torre.' Having raised this doubt, however, he breaks off, inserts three dots, and continues with remarkable disingenuousness: 'But I have no reason whatsoever to render rationally suspect faculties which brought about his downfall before our very eyes.' At first sight, this seems highly cryptic. Why should not faculties which brought about Cipolla's downfall be rationally suspect as well? Why is the narrator reluctant to press the point he has just made? The answer to these questions is probably to be found in the opening paragraph of the whole story. Cipolla is not merely a hypnotist, nor yet a dictator, or an artist, or a reflection of one aspect of the author: his story is meant to convey also a metaphysical significance. Thinking over the events before unfolding them, the narrator observes in parenthesis that their terrifying ending was one which 'resided in the essence of things'. This remark is never expounded, nor is it ever referred to again, but in view of the frequent talk of 'the Will' throughout the story we may guess that Cipolla is meant to stand in an unusually close relationship to the Will as we hear it spoken of in such works as *Buddenbrooks* and **"Der Tod in Venedig"**: the brutal, ruthless, relentless Will whose ultimate goal is both self-affirmation and self-destruction. It is to this close relationship, if not identification with the Will that Cipolla owes his uncanny mastery over the crowd, for in a sense he is the Will of which they remain always unconscious, and his assertions thus correspond to their own Will, whether they acknowledge it or not. To cast rational doubts on his powers, to suggest that he is, even in a single instance, an ordinary trickster, would thus be to detract from the suggestion that his downfall is the outcome of an essential process in the very heart of things. The narrator must, therefore, suppress such doubts, although at the same time he is frank enough to admit their possibility. He must induce the reader to believe that Cipolla is invincible, that neither willing nor 'not-willing' is of any avail, that his powers are super-rational and, as we shall see, liable to destruction only at his own, the hypnotist's volition. Hence the disingenuousness, the cryptic allusiveness, the plain statement of Cipolla's weakness in argument and the subsequent adoption of the same argument. The reader himself must be lulled into acceptance by the apparent recognition of his possible objections.

This aim once achieved, the implications of the story become more convincing. They are, briefly, that Cipolla and the Will which he represents or embodies are both evil and irresistible, and yet doomed to destruction by their essential negativity. In the final long episode, which culminates in the shooting of Cipolla by the youthful Mario, it becomes apparent that, while the hypnotist still holds the whip-hand, it is a hand which he uses almost deliberately for encompassing his own downfall. We see him first taunting the young man with the realization that his sweetheart Silvestra is deceiving him with another man, then with his memories of her as an 'angel of paradise'. Having awakened in Mario, who remains in a hypnotic trance, this ambiguous feeling towards Silvestra, a feeling normally suppressed, Cipolla offers him his gruesome cheek for a kiss, suggesting at the same time that the cheek is Silvestra's. Mario accepts the substitution, being perhaps in that frame of mind where distinctions are no longer possible: seeing that the angel can be a deceiver, it is surely possible that the deceiver Cipolla may represent an angel. Yet the physical expression of love for his tormentor suddenly takes a surprising turn. Awakening from the trance, Mario turns on Cipolla and shoots him dead.

In the context of the other incidents in the evening's entertainment it seems probable that we should also see this awakening in terms of the ambivalence of emotions. Just as earlier politeness was transformed by Cipolla into rudeness, courage into fear, resistance into compliance, so here love is turned into hatred. Yet to make this interpretation is difficult, since it might imply that Cipolla had for once made a fatal error, and one he was not likely to make. This difficulty can, however, be met, at least in reasonable measure. For from the very first moment of Cipolla's encounter with Mario, when he silently beckons him to come out of the audience and mount the steps of the platform, the hypnotist seems to have foreknowledge of his end. His words to Mario, though not out of keeping with the situation, have overtones of almost symbolical import.

> Well, ragazzo mio? [he said]. How comes it we make acquaintance so late in the day? But believe me, I made yours long ago. . . . Yes, yes, I've looked you in the eyes a long while now, and assured myself of your excellent qualities. How could I forget you again? . . .

There is a strange impressiveness about these words, something that is not quite called for by an ordinary conversational remark preluding a display of hypnotism. If Cipolla has met Mario before, and has actually looked into his eyes for a long while, it is strange that Mario should have no recollection of it. Indeed, Cipolla's initial failure to remember, his suggestion that they are meeting for the first time now, indicates that he only afterwards realizes in what sense he has made Mario's acquaintance. The 'excellent qualities' in the young man are not qualities of character but, surely, those of the death which he symbolizes in Cipolla's eyes, and which the hypnotist now sets out to encompass in the manner we have seen. He encourages Mario to love him in the knowledge that the feeling experienced in the state of trance will, as in the other cases, be the opposite of that experienced in full consciousness. Or so we may reasonably conclude from the structure and symbolism of the story.

Mario, for his part, is not so much the agent as the tool of the Will: it is not because of any determination on his part that Cipolla dies, but rather by an instinctive revulsion, on the certainty of which Cipolla has calculated. It is not even Mario who is thought of as the destroyer, but rather 'the small, squat, metal, scarcely pistol-shaped piece of machinery dangling from his hand, whose almost non-existent barrel had steered Destiny in so unexpected and strange a direction'. And the pistol itself is evidently described in such periphrastic fashion in order to suggest a further level of meaning, a symbolical agent. That the barrel should be not merely short, but 'almost non-existent' is a reminder that the Will is often equated in Mann's writing with 'the Naught'—Mann goes as near as he may within the limits of realism to suggesting that Cipolla's death was due to an agent as null as his own Will, while the genital overtones in the description recall the fleeting associations of phallus and Will in the final climax of *Buddenbrooks*. The pistol is deliberately made to look as little like a pistol as possible, in order to bring out the idea that conscious human agency and even material objects had only an ancillary part to play in the defeat of the Will by itself.

"Mario und der Zauberer" is a work of great subtlety whose ramifications of meaning could lead to reams of exposition. All that is possible here is to indicate certain essential features. In the context of Mann's development, it is clear that he no longer emphasizes the value of self-assertiveness as he had done, however ironically, in pre-war days, but is alarmed at the consequences of such an attitude as they now loom on the horizon of real life. Yet he still holds to the essential framework of his earlier thought: there is for him the same ambiguity at the heart of things, with the difference that stress is now laid on the self-destructiveness inherent in it. In many ways, the change of attitude is hard to perceive. As in the earlier stories and novels, Mann remains curiously aloof from all that happens, despite his tendency to identify himself also with both sides. He is, in fact, still represented in much the same way as ever by the narrator in this story who is present at the entertainment, who expresses horror, disgust, and admiration at what he sees, yet remains throughout unattached, calmly setting down the catastrophe as one might record an earth tremor. There is little sign here of the 'wholly unequivocal "No"' which Mann was impelled to utter as a human being against the dictatorship in his own country; the writer who saw some justification on all sides is much more in evidence. But the result of this continuing attachment to Mann's earlier modes of thought and feeling is not that just appraisal and balance which we could properly expect from a story of this kind. Without demanding that Mann should have composed a moral tract on the subject of hypnotists or dictators, we have a right to insist as readers that the sympathy of a writer with his own creations should not turn into a spurious defence of them. The disturbing element of the story is the way in which the narrator, wittingly or unwittingly, tends to delude the reader into acknowledging the invincibility of Cipolla, and the way in which this delusiveness serves the underlying 'Weltanschauung'. It may well be, after all, that the metaphysical implications of the story are true: that the evil which Cipolla represents is inherently bound to destroy itself. A story which made the reader feel the truth of that might well be gratifying. But a story which arouses such a feeling by hoodwinking the reader to some extent, loses impact. The narrator has to persuade us that Cipolla is possessed of supernatural powers, or powers that are often thought of as supernatural, and he has to persuade us that nothing can resist these powers, in order to make the ending the more impressive. To the extent that he fails in this attempt he fails to round off the narrative satisfyingly.

So, at least, we should judge according to traditional standards. In reading a story by Mann, however, we must be constantly aware that for him these standards do not apply. He does not regard truth as a matter of fidelity to facts or logic, but rather as a life-giving myth, a fiction in which it is better to believe than to disbelieve—better, that is, because it enables men to live more intensely and with greater enjoyment both of their suffering and their happiness, and better because it is more in keeping with the irrational and even delusory

ways of the Will, or Providence, or God. There has been plenty of evidence so far of Mann's disregard of logic, the tricks which he seems to play on the reader, the inconsistency of his attitudes to various moral and religious issues. The question that remains before us now is the one that ought to be in any critic's mind all the time: the question whether he may not after all be wrong. For what Mann set out to do throughout the whole period of Nazi rule in Germany was to construct a myth which would stand over against their myth, a series of memorable stories in which a view opposed to theirs, yet taking full cognizance of it, should be embodied. (pp. 173-84)

Ronald Gray, "Mario and the Magician," in his The German Tradition in Literature, 1871-1945, *Cambridge at the University Press, 1965, pp. 173-84.*

JAMES R. McWILLIAMS   (essay date 1966)

[*In the following excerpt, McWilliams examines thematic parallels between "Death in Venice" and "The Black Swan," noting specifically the incongruous coupling of emotional spontaneity and sexual desire with spritual decay and death.*]

Thomas Mann, who has not always proved a reliable critic of his own creations, maintains that his tale **"Die Betrogene"** [**"The Black Swan"**] is by no means connected to **"Der Tod in Venedig"** [**"Death in Venice"**]. . . . Joseph Mileck's detailed comparison, however, reveals that there are striking similarities between the two works which cannot be accidental and show that **"Die Betrogene"** is a companion piece to the earlier work [see excerpt dated 1957]. Surveying Mileck's findings, we find that Rosalie von Tümmler, the widowed heroine of **"Die Betrogene,"** succumbs pathetically, like Gustav Aschenbach, to a wayward passion for a person much younger than she, the American Ken Keaton. In each instance the accompanying moral and physical dissolution is emphasized. The desire of each turns to passion in a relatively short time. Both are overwhelmed by the physical qualities of the beloved, stammer out a feverish confession of love while alone, seek rejuvenation in massages and cosmetics, and attempt to still the hunger within, no matter what the cost in propriety and self-respect. The mood of **"Die Betrogene"** is also similar in that signs or symbols of death go hand in hand with an atmosphere of life in a state of ferment: the black swans, putrifying matter, the castle in decay are set off against the heavy and overpowering scent of spring and the unbridled luxuriousness of the castle, which is the destination of the "exotic" excursion. As in **"Der Tod in Venedig"** where the jungle vision of life in all its fertility is contrasted with the Stygian world of Venice, ambivalence is the distinguishing feature of the later novella.

Rosalie has an overwhelming passion for nature. She invests it with her own feelings, which are sexually conditioned. Born in the spring, a child of May, she becomes ecstatic about nature's phenomena. . . . Roses remind her of Psyche and Cupid; she favors red roses over white, the symbol of purity. The sweet scents of nature, almost stupefying, and the heated days of June transport her into raptures. By contrast, her daugther Anna, whose entire emotional life is repressed, is against nature and is even physically discomfited by nature's odors and vapors. Rosalie accuses her of being against nature and of transposing her sense perceptions into frigidity. Rosalie associates an old oak tree with herself, with her ebbing sexual life and the rejuvenation she later feels. Rosalie finds in nature a preoccupation with sex that haunts her mind. Her words and thougths continually turn about the sexual. She envies men because their sex life is less restricted than women's and less subject to repression than hers. Originally her interest in Ken Keaton is partly due to her having heard that he was very successful with women. In her emphasis on sex Rosalie is again close to Aschenbach, who at one point can no longer disregard the ebullient urges within. As will be seen in our discussion, Mann's characterization of mother and daughter in this story brings out vividly the guilt associations and repressions connected with Rosalie's over-interest in sex.

Of more crucial significance is the fact that once again emotional spontaneity is paired off with disaster. Death in the form of a merciless and consuming disease is the final price paid by the two protagonists for transgressing the command of their conscience. As in the case of Gustav Aschenbach, death follows soon after the heroine allows her feelings to run rampant. A further parallel is seen in the fate of Hanno Buddenbrook, who was also doomed by a ravaging malady. The death of Rosalie von Tümmler represents the final retribution; her conscience demands that she atone through death for her permissiveness of feeling. What was a symbolic punishment to Hanno Buddenbrook, and a deliberate self-sacrifice on the part of Gustav Aschenbach, is in Rosalie's case an automatic physical penalty for being wayward in her feelings, for we learn from the physician Muthesius that her emotional license was directly responsible for her fatal cancer. (pp. 56-8)

The association of doom with the sexual is directly pointed up by the mouldy air of the castle's secret passageway in which there is a satyr-like and licentious statue. The same connection seems to be made in the scene in which Rosalie, on a walk with her daughter, encounters a pile of putrifying animal and vegetable matter. . . . The scent of musk, which is a secretion of the sex glands of certain animals, and consequently linked to procreation, is thus identified with the last stages of decomposition.

The proximity of death with emotional involvement is also reflected in the nature of Rosalie's passion for Ken Keaton. Although she calls it love, her desire is, like that of Aschenbach, based on a need to find an outlet, a flight from inhibitions. She is consistent with previous Mannian heroes in that tender love is beyond the reach of her mental structure. What is represented in both Rosalie and Aschenbach is an inexorable quest for gratification. It is a questionable and forbidden love in which lust plays the major role. Rosalie is exceedingly jealous of Ken Keaton's other affairs and her thoughts dwell constantly on his physical charms. The primacy of the instinctual is in fact enhanced by her occasional references to lust and craving. . . . The drive to experience has been slumbering in her for a long time. The need to alter the unbearable and deadening effect of repression becomes irresistible and gnaws away at the demands of propriety. Indeed, Rosalie seems to provoke fate and the ensuing punishment: she plans the excursion to the castle as if to force a showdown and almost in defiance steals the bread from the mouths of the black swans, symbols of death.

The object of Rosalie's passion, Ken Keaton, is depicted as mediocre and commonplace. It is probably no accident, as W. H. Rey notes, that this blond-haired broad-shouldered, and narrow-hipped representative of "das Leben" possesses a name which alliterates like Hans Hansen. As an American expatriate who has rejected his own society and leads an ir-regular life, he appears to deviate at first glance from Mann's conception of the middle class. Yet in his enthusiasm for Europe and knowledge of its history and traditions he is in a very real sense less American, and the dichotomy between the Bürger and the one standing apart is thus reinforced to some extent.

It is Rosalie, even more than Ken Keaton, who seems to fall out of character as a typical Mannian protagonist. Simple and cheerful, she is sociable by nature and her attitude towards art is naive; her daughter finds fault with her taste in painting. Rey finds her to be essentially a bourgeois type and as such sufficient to make **"Die Betrogene"** unique among Mann's works. Yet on the other hand she is invested with certain features and traits which, besides those uncovered by Mileck, are consistent and familiar. There are bluish shadows around her brown eyes and before her excursion a yellow pallor to her complexion. Despite her fall through her shameless and, in some measure, exhibitionistic passion, she is a model of propriety, as we note, when Ken Keaton attempts to hurry their affair. (pp. 58-9)

Rosalie's position as the Mannian chief figure is apparently weakened by contrast to her daughter Anna, who possesses all the characteristics as well as the temperament of the artist. Crippled, and thereby "gezeichnet," by a club-foot, Anna is alienated from dancing and sports and from all participation in the activities of people her own age. Endowed with unusual intelligence, she found no challenges in school and then ceased to pursue the academic. Instead she turned to the creative and became a painter of the most extreme intellectualism, going over. . . . Like Adrian Leverkühn (*Doktor Faustus*) with his parody, and Tonio Kröger with his "frigid art," she purges every element of feeling from her works. And again like this earlier figure she was unsuccessful in love. Her bitter resentment of Ken Keaton's "primitive guilelessness" reminds us of Cipolla's **"Mario und der Zauberer"** antagonism based on sexual renunciation.

This inconsistency in characterization can presumably be overcome if we make the assumption that mother and daughter complement each other, that we are dealing here with a montage effect, and that, as with Serenus Zeitblom (*Doktor Faustus*) and Clemens der Ire (*Der Erwählte*), the two poles of the author's personality, the desire for sexual indulgence and the inner necessity for repressive propriety, are split apart into two separate characters in order to gain a measure of distance.

The use of montage may perhaps explain in part why Rosalie is entrusted with more than the usual amount of basic emotions and is permitted, as opposed to the passive Aschenbach, to be actively involved in a love affair. In the secret passageway at the castle she embraces Ken Keaton and pours forth a confession of love highly charged with feeling and sensuality. This exceptional behavior can however be ascribed, like that in *Der Erwählte,* to the place of this work among the creations of Thomas Mann. The mellowing effect of extreme old age probably played a large role in the portrayal of the chief figure. In this work Mann yielded slightly and permitted himself a greater margin in expressing feelings laden with guilty connotations. (pp. 60-1)

An even fifty years after Tonio Kröger's pronouncement, "Ich liebe das Leben" ["I love life"], the Mannian protagonist comes to the same conclusion. And Rosalie's view that death is the great instrument of life recapitulates the remark by Hans Castorp more than a quarter of a century before. We discover essentially nothing new in the dénouement of **"Die Betrogene"**. That it is, further, a question of the hero's defensive reaction to an inner misgiving concerning the value of life emerges from these pages if we look behind the facade of words. It is in Rosalie's yearning for the aristocratic black swans, which Rey calls the most striking death symbol in the story, that we discern the most convincing confirmation of this view. . . . (p. 61)

The heroine's spontaneity contrasts strangely to her repeated avowals of love for nature. Justifying her claim of love becomes in fact a central leitmotif in the work. Perhaps this is why several critics have found the language to be "false" and "stilted." Rosalie, and Anna, who takes the opposite view from her mother, literally endow nature with human qualities. But the feelings which they ascribe to this abstraction hardly seem appropriate in a human relationship. If we consider seriously the unnaturalness of the topic we see that there is here an urgency to dispel a fundamental doubt. Idris Parry states the problem as follows: "Nature is a non-collaborator in human morality. To attribute benevolence or antagonism to Nature is a fallacy: it is Rosalie herself who wills the end, and Nature, as we see from Rosalie's final collapse, is working indifferently in quite another direction."

One must set Rosalie's love for life next to her implacable fate to feel the intended mood of this tale. The title itself lends stress to the basic scepticism underlying the supposed reconciliation at the end. And again Thomas Mann is utterly ruthless in describing the course of the fatal disease. He seems to take delight in the clinical precision with which he destroys his leading figure, in the same manner as he did Hanno Buddenbrook and Nepomuk Schneidewein (*Doktor Faustus*).

In the end it is Anna's viewpoint which prevails. . . . Her deeply ingrained distrust and suspicion of the world and the value of love, the morbid common denominator of all Mannian heroes, is confirmed by the final pitiless mood. The ending of **"Die Betrogene"** re-echoes the beginning of *Doktor Faustus,* in which Jonathan Leverkühn by means of his biological experiments, demonstrates the belief that life is a fraud. Here are seen weird phenomena of nature in which animate and inanimate forms can scarcely be distinguished, e.g. insects and snails which survive by trickery and deceit or which are death-dealing in their beauty. The guilt-ridden Adrian Leverkühn, unable to stop denying the world and to find a hold through love, is affected deeply by the illusions of nature—hence his morbid laughter. So too we find in **"Die Betrogene"** that there is an ambivalence in Nature and that its phenomena of life, love and beauty are presented incongruously in images of death, which seem to devaluate man's natural sense impressions and typical reactions: the crocus and the colchicum, the stench and the scent of musk, and, of course, Rosalie's rejuvenation and its basis of decay. (pp. 62-3)

> James R. McWilliams, "Thomas Mann's 'Die Betrogene'—A Study in Ambivalence," in CLA Journal, Vol. X, No. 1, September, 1966, pp. 56-63.

ALBERT BRAVERMAN AND LARRY DAVID NACHMAN (essay date 1970)

[*In the following essay, Braverman and Nachman examine the conflict between spiritual and physical love in "Death in Ven-*

ice," suggesting that this story represents the fullest expression of Mann's early views of the artist.]

"Death in Venice" marks the end of the beginning of Thomas Mann's literary career. In the twelve years between *Buddenbrooks* and **"Death in Venice"** Mann's many short novels and tales dealt with fundamentally similar themes; in the following twelve years he published almost no fiction at all. True, it was at the outset of this relatively silent period that he began work of *The Magic Mountain,* which was originally intended to be "a humorous companion-piece to **'Death in Venice.'**" But he left off working on this novel and when it was finally completed and published at the end of this period (1924), the problems of his youth appeared in a radically altered context.

"Death in Venice" was thus the last place in which Mann's primary dilemmas were presented in the same basic terms in which he originally understood them: the dialectic of the decadence of culture in the context of bourgeois society—the familiar theme of *Buddenbrooks,* **"Tonio Kröger,"** and *Fiorenza.* What progress of development there was in Mann's first period amounted to the ability to state these problems as consummately and explicitly as he did in **"Death in Venice."** The profound tragedy of the story lay in the fact that it was, like Venice, a *cul-de-sac;* the complete articulation of the problem led to the inevitable conclusion that there was, after all, no solution.

For Thomas Mann, Gustave von Aschenbach was the ultimate development of the ideal of pure and fulfilled individuality. His rich and fastidious self-consciousness, unlike that of the neurotic heros of the earlier period, the Hannos and the Detlev Spinnels, was free to realize itself, and was finally consummated in his work. His initial successes were ascribed to something besides pure talent:

> For an intellectual product of any value to exert an immediate influence which shall also be deep and lasting, it must rest on an inner harmony, yes an affinity, between the personal destiny of its author and that of his contemporaries in general. Men do not know why they award fame to one work of art, rather than another. Without being in the faintest connoisseurs, they think to justify the warmth of their commendations by discovering in it a hundred virtues, whereas the real ground of their applause is inexplicable—it is sympathy.

In his first works, Aschenbach's sympathy was for "the heroism born of weakness." His heros, of course, bear a striking resemblance to many characters in Mann's own works, particularly to Lorenzo and Savonarola in *Fiorenza.* Aschenbach was concerned with the warrior whose battle was internal and whose victory was over himself; he was thus a psychological writer.

But later Aschenbach was to renounce this sympathy and frame a

> rebuke to the excesses of a psychology-ridden age . . . Explicitly he renounces sympathy with the abyss, explicitly he refutes the flabby humanitarianism of the phrase: *"Tout comprendre, c'est tout pardoner!"*

Sympathy with weakness and degradation was, for Aschenbach, as for many another realist, the substance of his relation to life. In his maturity as a man and writer he "regained detachment." His new content was the perfected and entirely aristocratic personality; his new form a classical style from which every common word is abolished.

As his art became aristocratic, so also did his personality. He no longer required any contact at all with that vulgar and ordinary life for which Tonio Kröger (for example) never ceased to long. Tonio's fear of isolation and coldness would have struck Aschenbach as an evocation of his own callow youth. His complete self-sufficiency was based upon the strength and richness of his own inner life and the power of his creativity. The pathetic heros of Mann's earlier works were solitary because of a self-centeredness and sensitivity which led to nothing but their own destruction. Aschenbach's solitude arose from a triumphant perfection of inwardness which was objectified in his works.

At this point we must recall the context of this development in Mann's thought. He began, as it were, with the problem of Thomas Buddenbrook, a sensitive and able man who sought complete personal fulfillment in the worldly activities of bourgeois society. *Buddenbrooks* makes it clear that that society, at its best, made fulfillment for such a man impossible. From **"Tonio Kröger"** to **"Death in Venice,"** Mann was concerned with the alternatives: a series of artists or charismatic figures whose work was outside the world and whose satisfaction was in themselves. Georg Lukács pointed out that during this period "Mann takes artistic activity as a symbol for any kind of genuine culture, for any profession or career that comes from within." Aschenbach represents the highest development of this kind of career.

Now that perfect, self-subsisting individuality had, at long last, been realized, now that the ideal of personal development had found embodiment in a specific human form, Mann was ready to deal with a broader, more world-encompassing subject matter: the status of the free human spirit in the context of the life of the body, whose end is death. For it is the imminence of death which may drive the strongest and most autonomous personality to unite itself with a life outside itself. Aschenbach was not aware that his sudden thirst for life was evoked by his advancing age, but his vision of the jungle and the swamp at the beginning of the tale, as he stood before the mausoleum with its exquisite inscriptions must be understood as an old man's yearning for that sensual life which was rapidly passing from him.

It is clear that Aschenbach's sudden desire for life was not equivalent to Tonio Kröger's love for the healthy and the ordinary. Though his impulse to flee from his routine activities clearly arose from his decreasing capacity to meet their physical demands, the idea of flight came to Aschenbach as he watched a vagabond standing in the portal of the mausoleum.

The vagabond, with his satyr features and slightly criminal air, repelled the fastidious old artist by his rootlessness. Whatever appeal the traveler's freedom and youthful strength may have had for Aschenbach was masked by a kind of terror. This vision of insolent and irresponsible life only suggested the loss of discipline and the abandonment of obligation. There was no hint of renewal.

The juxtaposition of such a figure and the mausoleum was no coincidence. The death of the body is the end of all sensuality. But the prospect of death may lead to the decision to kill the ego in order to free the body for its final fling. Hence, Aschenbach's vision of the tiger and the swamp and his sudden decision to travel to refresh his creative powers.

But what was the refreshment he sought? Certainly, he did not undertake this journey to relieve his loneliness, though he clearly needed some change in his isolated, contemplative and intensely disciplined life. His vitality was consecrated to the creation of sublime forms. This consecration had long ago relieved him of any need for contact with other men, and he did not need them now. Yet, as Mann makes clear, this solitary state was to account for the radical and unexpected consequences of his trip:

> A solitary, unused to speaking of what he sees and feels, has mental experiences which are at once more intense and less articulate than those of a gregarious man. They are sluggish, yet more wayward, and never without a melancholy tinge. Sights and impression which others brush aside with a glance, a light comment, a smile, occupy him more than their due; they sink silently in, they take on meaning, they become experience, emotion, adventure. Solitude gives birth to the original in us, to beauty unfamiliar and perilous, to poetry. But, also, it gives birth to the opposite: to the preverse, the illicit, the absurd.

But if Aschenbach was somehow searching for the perilous jungle of sensuality, what he found, at least initially, was something quite different—a stimulus to his emotions which satisfied that refined appreciation of the beautiful which was the enterprise of his later life.

From the moment he first saw the boy Tadzio, at the Venetian resort to which his restlessness ultimately led him, Aschenbach expressed his thoughts in a curious classical imagery. His was the appreciation of the connoiseur, surprised and delighted to find the embodiment of the ideal form close at hand. This was, of course, consistent with the "classical style" of his later works, and with his status as a truly detached artist.

But there is a whole world of specific allusion here. The tense, sensual, yet cool word pictures of the boy clearly refer to Nietzsche's Apollonian mode—the mode of the plastic artist, smilingly contemplating the glorious surface of things. Aschenbach was particularly taken with the state of his own feelings. He could admire the boy, and yet retain his detachment to such a degree that he wrote an essay while watching him. The essay was not about Tadzio, but its structure was inspired by the boy's perfect proportions.

In fact, there were allusions in Aschenbach's thoughts to the boy's likeness to a statue; he inwardly transformed the living flesh into marble forms as he had transformed the painful knowledge of his youth into an epic and classical style. And this detached admiration was profoundly consistent with the pride of his individuality; like Schopenhauer's vision of the artist as pure, will-less subject of knowing, individuation for Aschenbach meant freedom from attachment and desire.

One day Aschenbach, being close enough to Tadzio to notice his frailty and his bad teeth, remarked to himself, "He is delicate, he is sickly—he will most likely not live to grow old." Of course, this was Aschenbach's projection and an early example of Mann's use of illness to stand for the reality of the flesh. The statue had become a body, to Pygmalion's mingled delight and horror. Aschenbach's sudden awareness of Tadzio's body transformed his connoisseur's appreciation of the boy's classic beauty into an overwhelming passion. Of course, the passion had always been there, though masked by the Apollonian illusion; hence, Mann uses the image of the Dionysian orgy to represent Aschenbach's sudden consciousness of his state.

And Nietzsche's category was, once more, appropriate, appropriate just because it had been developed in the context of an aesthetic theory. There is great poignancy in knowing that the beloved is a body, functioning as an animal, liable to change and death, a poignancy which is the source of the deepest tenderness. But Aschenbach did not now become noticeably closer or more tender to Tadzio. He did not approach him personally, nor did he make use of the obvious opportunity to warn the boy's mother of the danger of the plague.

Aschenbach's lust was as impersonal as his detached Appollonian contemplation had been. It could not be consummated physically; it led to no worldly intercourse. In other words, for all its intensity his love affair, like the crush of a tongue-tied boy, was completely internalized.

Aschenbach's regained detachment from all mankind was permanent; he could not overcome his distance. Nor could he hope for the actual pleasure of the flesh—not, at least in this world. If he abandoned himself, if he gave up all order and even laid his life on the line, he might somehow join the orgy. But he never, in his most fevered dream, imagined the one other alternative to detached individuality or orgiastic immersion in the sensual: to lose himself in the real and independent existence of another human being.

Throughout Thomas Mann's works there is a recurrent association between sexuality and perversion or psychopathology. Tonio Kröger "fell into the adventures of the flesh, descended into the depth of lust and searing sin, and suffered unspeakably thereby." **"The Blood of the Walsungs"** ended with incest between an overbread and highly cultured sister and brother, and **"Death in Venice"** with the senile homosexuality of a world famous writer. Although this association was greatest in the period culminating in **"Death in Venice,"** *Dr. Faustus* probably provides us with its most remarkable example. The stern and self-sufficient Adrian Leverkühn, a great composer, could consummate physical love only with a prostitute he knew to be diseased. He courted a woman but once, and in such a way to make failure inevitable, consoling himself afterwards with a short-lived homosexual affair.

In *Dr. Faustus,* and in **"Tonio Kröger,"** Mann provided an obvious contrast to perverse love, in the characters of Serenus Zeitblom and Hans Hansen. Both were rather ordinary men, bourgeois and successful at relatively modest endeavors. Both found that living in accordance with the forms society imposed on human life was a natural and spontaneous expression of their characters. Love came easily to them, because they developed no intense involvement with any particular object. They may have been passionate, but they were not selective. Serenus chose the daughter of a colleague, not because he felt the force of convention, but because he had no reason to do otherwise. Moreover, her name, Helen, appealed to him because of its classical associations, and may have been the deciding factor. To a man who makes few distinctions between one woman and another even so whimsical a consideration may be decisive. Aberrant sexuality is associated with the richest and most refined personality, in particular with the artist. Creativity, a profound and serious sense of self, seems somehow involved with this tragic kind of loving.

Human love may be resolved into two elements: pure libido or physical sexuality, and selection. Selection, in its simplest terms, merely means that the lover chooses one human being rather than another. For a Serenus Zeitblom or Hans Hansen the field of choice is rather broad, but we expect the passions of the highly developed personality to fix themselves on a particular individual. Since the grounds for this selection are entirely personal and purely subjective, the choice may easily be inappropriate from any number of worldly perspectives. Thus this kind of love frequently has a tragic character.

But for Mann, as we have seen, selective love is depicted as not merely impractical and difficult, but decadent and perverse. Why is this so? We should note that perverse sexuality performs an important literary function in Mann's works. By describing such sexual relationships, Mann underscores the fact that what he is examining is wanton love, pure and simple. All other elements, e.g. procreation and the family, have been excluded.

But why does Mann see such relationships as decadent and unhealthy? What absorbs the gifted man, the highly developed individual, is himself. In his early period, Mann could find no worldly context for gifted personality. Society, bourgeois society, was demonstrated in *Buddenbrooks* and **"Tonio Kröger"** to be inimical to self-development. Developed personality could be achieved only over and against the world; its only context was the inner life. A figure such as Aschenbach could then look upon the body only in one of two ways: either it was beautiful (its form was aesthetically pleasing) or it was common and base (every man's body was *substantially* the same as every one else's). Aschenbach's body, particularly now that it was old, weak, and vulnerable, was not an adequate representation of his uniqueness as a human being. But this is the general case for mankind. The body is the vessel of the soul, not its mirror. (For all his refinement, little Herr Friedmann was a hunchback.) What, then, can be the object of selectivity? Not the body, for "in the dark of night all cats are grey." But if the personality itself, then what personality is worthy of being loved? Only that which is unique and highly developed. But insofar as we see other people *as* bodies, our feelings towards them must be at least in part conditioned by our reactions to their bodies. When one man sees another man, he looks at a body. But when he considers himself, he sees only that which is within. The conclusion is clear and need not be labored. The highly developed individual is extremely susceptible to narcisstic love. His own complex personality, which alone makes it possible for him to be selective, becomes the standard by which he judges the value of other human beings. And the same pride and heightened self-consciousness which were the basis of his drive to develop himself force him to reject all others as unworthy. (pp. 289-95)

Selective love, then, depends upon highly developed personality which in turn tends to be inward, worldless and exclusive. But love cannot remain entirely subjective for long, at least not without disastrous consequences for the lover. In the first place, the lover's passions are directed outward; they demand a consummation that is not mere fantasy. And, secondly, the beloved has a reality, or perhaps more precisely, is part of the real external world from which the lover has thus far isolated himself.

Selective love, therefore, has its origin and end in the human personality. It involves the assertion of a distinction between the personality and the body. The body, as we have seen, is regarded as base, common and totally unsanctified. But human love demands a physical consummation. We see now the ultimate reason why the love of highly developed individuals must, in Mann's terms, be unhealthy and depraved. The reason is immanent in the whole nature of such personality. *For them,* physical love must be illicit because insofar as the body is involved, love must necessarily demean. The sensitive and developed man comes to regard his bodily needs as contemptible and unworthy of himself. When he does yield to them, he does so with the full conviction that he is degrading himself. Such a man has completely failed to come to grips with his body, to integrate his spirit and his flesh. On account of this failure, he is uniquely vulnerable to the vicissitudes of the flesh: age, disease, death, and the violence of sexual passion.

Just in this way, Aschenbach's passion for Tadzio led to the most all-encompassing degradation of his personality. The obscene attempts at preserving youth which so disgusted him in the old fop he saw on the boat to Venice now became his own obsession. It was for this self-mummification that he sacrificed his fastidiousness, a more worthless goal than the most perverse of sexual contacts. His choices were so rigidly fixed that when he relaxed his extraordinary discipline for a short rest, he became the fool of his impulses. And of course, his final degradation involved the destruction of the ultimate classic form, life itself, which he loosely abandoned in order to remain in the plague-stricken city with Tadzio.

"Death in Venice" presents the dialectical working-out of the perils of any personal development which is estranged from the world and the body. The exaltation of the personal and the immersion in the spiritual have been shown to be potentially the reverse of humanistic. Thus, the tone of the work is despair. (pp. 296-97)

> *Albert Braverman and Larry David Nachman, "The Dialectic of Decadence: An Analysis of Thomas Mann's 'Death in Venice'," in* The Germanic Review, *Vol. XLV, No. 4, November, 1970, pp. 289-98.*

GRAHAM GOOD   (essay date 1972)

[*In the following excerpted essay, Good examines the thematic role of language in "Death in Venice."*]

George Steiner, in his recent essay "The Language Animal," states that "there occurred in the first quarter of this century a crisis of language and a reexamination of language in the light of that crisis." (p. 43)

This crisis, which Steiner takes as the concentration of a wider "malady of civilisation," may be stated as the opposition between a societal language felt as untrustworthy or meaningless, and various attempts at founding a "pure" language, whether purely logical, purely self-referring, or pure in the sense of "original, uncorrupted." These attempts may end in the ultimate purity of silence. (A second answer is the critique of impure language; in literature this often takes the form of parody, the attempt to raise a structure of implied meaning through the arrangement of outdated or corrupted styles.) But this kind of linguistic purism is very precarious; by retreating, by refining itself so drastically, it comes to lack the cultural vitality it needs to affect the general use of language. Although all artistic and philosophical language is in some degree a heightened or purified version of ordinary language, the distance between the two is now felt as almost unbridgeable. On one hand the "pure" languages develop into

closed, autonomous systems demanding initiates rather than common readers, while societal language is rejected or parodied on the other.

Thomas Mann's **"Death in Venice"** (1912) fits squarely into Steiner's framework (Central Europe, 1900-1925), and may usefully be read in terms of the "crisis of language." Although both the themes (most obviously the conflict between 'art' and 'life') and the language of the story have been thoroughly analysed, the thematic role of language *within* the story has been relatively neglected. The conflict between Aschenbach and Venice is not only a battle between art and life, but also an opposition of two modes of language: the "pure" writing style of Aschenbach and the "impure," vague, and suggestive speech patterns of Venice.

Of course Aschenbach cannot be taken as a representative of all the different linguistic "purists," yet the austere and fastidious character of his art clearly associates him with this trend. Among the qualities central to his mature work are "A discriminating purity, simplicity and evenness of attack," "mastery and classicism." But at the point where the story opens, Aschenbach's language is showing signs of *rigor mortis:* "He inclined toward the fixed and standardized, the conventionally elegant, the conservative, the formal, the formulated, nearly . . ." His straining for a cold purity of language is starving his art to death. Yet instead of dying in the solitude of the study, it dies in Venice. Aschenbach abandons the solitary work of refining language into written art and becomes captivated by language as sound, echoing and fading in the open. The active writer, exhausted, becomes the passive listener, seduced by the disintegration of language in the public spaces of Venice (the canals and squares, the hotel and beach) into a multilingual buzz, into repeated lies and echoed servilities, into whispers and mutterings and mumbled confessions, into music and meaningless sound.

This linguistic and aesthetic transition is linked to an ethical one. Aschenbach's classicistic style defies his period's predominant use of language to suggest, vaguely and impressionistically, more than it states, and this is linked to his moral sternness in defying that period's apparent sympathy and intellectual complicity with ethical weakness. In Venice he comes to welcome both of these tendencies that he had previously defied. Steiner speaks of "Kraus' maniacal conviction that clarity and purity of syntax are the ultimate test of a society," and Mann's Venice fails on both counts: its moral degradation is expressed in its degradation of language. Thus between isolated purity and public corruption, whether linguistic or ethical, there is no longer any continuity, no longer any middle possibility of honest and straightforward relationships. The most striking thing about Aschenbach is that he is unsociable, a writer who cannot or will not speak. His love affair is predicated on the absence of normal social relations, in fact, on the absence of speech altogether. Between the solitary perfection of literary art and the corruption of social speech, the sane and vital middle ground of language has disappeared. In the gap which it leaves, Aschenbach's quite normal fatherly admiration for Tadzio—Mann hints, "He had never had a son"—is left *unspoken,* and because of this it slowly becomes *unspeakable* in the sense of tabu.

Aschenbach does not plan his holiday with a view to making friends. The spoken word, the vehicle of normal social life, does not attract him. Resting from writing, he does not want to talk, but to enjoy in his accustomed solitude a release from the bonds of words. He wants to hear languages that he cannot understand, and he is attracted to the Adriatic island partly by the prospect of its "natives who . . . made strange sounds when they spoke," but the relief is baulked by what he finds in the hotel: "a provincial and exclusively Austrian patronage at the hotel." The last thing he wants is a linguistically closed circle, particularly a German-speaking one. The island is far from the "popular resort" which he initially planned for himself, and which he finds in Venice.

Here, like the elements of sea, land and sky, the languages of the world erode their dividing lines and flow into one another. In the Lido hotel Aschenbach finds, instead of German alone, a mixture of many tongues: "Sounds of all the principal languages formed a subdued murmur." The Babel of the hotel is echoed on the beach by Tadzio's friends, who chatter in Polish, French and several Balkan languages. On Aschenbach's first evening, dinner is announced in English, while Tadzio's mother speaks to the governess in French. After Aschenbach's abortive departure the Swiss liftboy says to the German writer, "Pas de chance, monsieur." The latter's arrival in Venice is accompanied by the jeering French phrases of the old dandy. French, as Joel A. Hunt has noted, is often used by Mann in contexts of charlatanry or eroticism; it appears as the specious "*lingua franca* of the international set," the language into which the Russian Clavdia Chauchat lures the German Hans Castorp, and in which the swindler Felix Krull is so fluent. It is the linguistic medium of the international hotel and sanatorium, both melting pots of the separate identities of nations and individuals.

The situation of the two protagonists, a German writer and a Polish boy in a cosmopolitan Italian resort, is almost maximally polyglot. Indeed, one of the contributory factors of Aschenbach's infatuation is Tadzio's linguistic remoteness. A comparable affair with a German boy in Munich is unthinkable. For the writer, the incomprehensibility of the boy's "soft vague tongue" gives it the musical seductiveness of sound without sense: "Aschenbach did not understand a word of what he said, and though it might have been the most ordinary thing in the world, it was a vague harmony in his ear. So the foreignness of the boy's speech turned it into music. . . ."

The counterpoint to this seduction of Aschenbach by the music of uncomprehended language is the falling silent of his own tongue. As Venice breeds lies to conceal the plague, German is the first language to be hushed. German is the voice of truth for Aschenbach, the voice of his past literary life, but now he is left alone among the exotic sounds which he had originally sought merely for refreshment. Suddenly it seems to him "German . . . seemed to be dropping away, so that finally he heard nothing but foreign sounds at table and on the beach." Searching for the truth about the epidemic in the newspapers, he found nothing in the foreign-language ones; only those in his own language, owing to the death of an Austrian tourist shortly after returning from Venice, are at all aware of the gravity of the situation; and printed German, like spoken German, soon vanishes from his hotel. This language thus becomes the symbol of the order that Aschenbach has abandoned.

The few conversations Aschenbach has in Venice are all with social inferiors, with those in a position to serve him in some capacity. From the beginning these dialogues are absurd, pointless or perfunctory, and they are the only verbal contacts he makes. Their governing characteristic is repetition. He often receives a fawning echo of his own words instead of a real reply. The ticket clerk on the steamer faces Aschenbach like a grotesque double, mocking the art of writing with his unnecessarily elaborate script and his mannered manipulations of paper, ink and sand. His spoken words too are a mere unctuous echo: " 'To Venice!' He repeated Aschenbach's request . . . 'To Venice, first class!' " This servile manner is parodied by the drunken old dandy, who endlessly reiterates his compliments to Aschenbach's "Liebchen."

Communication also breaks down with the unlicensed gondolier who rows Aschenbach to the Lido, and whose rhythmic and incomprehensible muttering to himself is a leitmotif of the encounter. Aschenbach repeats his orders ineffectually: " 'But it's to the steamer dock,' he said . . . 'To the steamer dock!' he repeated." The gondolier's words "I am rowing you well" are echoed twice in the mind of the now submissive Aschenbach, along with the words of his admission of their truth: "That is so . . ." Mostly, however, Aschenbach meets subservience; more typical of those who serve him is the obsequious gondolier whom he employs to follow the Polish family's boat, and who takes up his customer's tone with lewd complicity and repetitious flatteries, assuring Aschenbach "In the same tone that his wishes would be carried out, carried out faithfully."

Now Aschenbach's tone in this case is "a hurried undertone," just as later he speaks to the street singer "in an undertone, almost mechanically." In imprecision and repetitiveness he begins to imitate the corrupted Venetian speech patterns that surround him, and on both sides this corruption spreads with the plague. Even when he is privately sure of the truth, Aschenbach takes a perverse delight in hearing repetitions of the same false answer to the same false question, desiring to be

Mann in 1950.

soothed again and again by the Venetians' musical lies. He enquires about the disinfectant successively of the shopkeeper, the hotel manager and the street singer. The replies he gets constitute between them a desperately false-sounding series of variations on the same themes and words, and a mocking use of the leitmotif technique: "a matter of precaution . . . a police regulation . . . a precautionary measure . . . a police regulation . . . a regulation of the police." One of the most frequently recurring words ironically picks up Aschenbach's original idea of his holiday as "a hygienic precaution"; both of these measures end in failure. Repetition approaches hysteria when he utters to the singer the fatal word "Ubel" and gets this as a reply: "A plague? What kind of plague? Is the Sirocco a plague? Perhaps our police are a plague? You like to joke! A plague!" Speech here degenerates into a cheap and hollow quasi-musicality.

Even the English travel clerk at first takes up familiar phrases about preventive measures, but then he tells Aschenbach the truth "in his forthright, easy-going English," English forming a sufficient contrast to the sounds of the "tricky, nimble-witted South" to be a vehicle of the truth without shocking Aschenbach by a revival of his own silent and forsaken language. This conversation with the Englishman is the only exchange of important true information in the story, and yet even this is ineffectual since its aim is to get Aschenbach to leave at once. Not only does he ignore this advice himself, he also fails to communicate it to others, even though he actually phrases his warning to Tadzio's mother. Thus the truth fails to break through the predominating use of language to deceive, flatter and reassure, to produce acquiescence rather than action. Words are uttered and then evaporate without effect; heedless of words the gondolier goes on rowing to the Lido, the plague goes on spreading, Aschenbach stays on in Venice.

Besides the mixture of languages and the ineffectuality of the dialogues he is involved in personally, Aschenbach is surrounded by many instances of actual physical erosion of speech, where the words go beyond uselessness to imperceptibility. If his own conversations dissolve into quasi-musical repetition and variation, it is a pattern he hears all around him. Speech and its close counterpoint of gesture becomes indistinct and incomprehensible. This process is already prefigured on the steamer to Venice as Aschenbach, reclining half asleep on the deck, is troubled by shadowy figures who pass him "with vague gestures, muddled dream words." When the gondoliers gather round to pick up the ship's passengers, their dialect is even further removed from understanding by the very atmosphere of the city: "The rowers were wrangling, harshly, incomprehensibly, with threatening gestures. But the strange silence of this canal city seemed to soften their voices, to disembody them, and dissipate them over the water." The very acoustics of Venice thus seem to exert a disembodying and destructive effect on words while giving them a haunting, almost Wagnerian beauty.

On the beach, too, words float unheeded in the air: the Russian parents are always calling the names of their heedlessly playing children and soon the ritual calling of Tadzio's name, whether by his friends or by his all-female family party, becomes a leitmotif. Charmed by it, Aschenbach manages to ascertain "that it must be 'Tadzio,' the shortened form of 'Tadeusz,' and sounding in the vocative like 'Tadziu.' " This orderly piece of deduction costs him a considerable exertion because he is already beginning to accept speech as pure non-

referential sound or music; he is already "diverted by the childish voices." Even when he has worked out the boy's name, his only use for it is a private relishing of its music: "He was pleased with the resonance of this; he found it adequate to the subject. He repeated it silently . . ." Aschenbach makes no audible contribution to Tadzio's aureole of sound, but only listens with closed eyes to "this song ringing within him."

Just as speech tends to disintegrate into music, so music itself is an important accompaniment to the disintegration of order. Except for Tadzio's friends, each of those noisy, gesticulating groups which prefigure the Bacchic rout of Aschenbach's final dream has an actual musical accompaniment. The sound of military horns excites the gang of clerks and draws them up on to the deck of the steamer as it lies in the lagoon. The singers who entertain Aschenbach on his way to the Lido have mandolins and guitars. In the Mass at San Marco, he stands among the murmuring congregation listening to the singing of the priest. To Aschenbach himself, Venice is historically a city [that] "suggested to composers seductive notes which cradle and lull."

The scenes of the street singing and of Aschenbach's dream bring to a climax the dissolving of rational speech into chaotic sound. The leader of the singers is "with not much of a voice," his song is "stupid enough so far as the words went," and the final encore is "a 'big number' in incomprehensible dialect." Even these worthless words, even the musical accompaniment, vanish in the laughing chorus, and the mouth is abandoned to pure noise. This development culminates soon afterwards in the orgiastic sounds of the dream: "Clanking, blaring, and a dull thunder, with shrill shouts and a definite whine in a long-drawn-out u-sound—all this was sweetly, ominously interspersed with and dominated by the deep cooing of wickedly persistent flutes which charmed the bowels in a shamelessly intrusive manner." All that remains of words is an isolated phrase, not linked to other words to make sense, but left to gain a terrible obscurity through its detachment from discourse: "But he knew one phrase; it was veiled, and yet would name what was approaching: 'The strange god!' "

The converse of the disintegration of outward communication is the increase of introspection. Feeling, undisciplined by clear expression, grows beyond bounds. Words which would be unutterable to another are turned inwards and privately savoured. Tadzio, that name he dare not call out, he repeats instead to himself on the beach, and as he falls asleep alone by the open window in the dawn, his lips slowly form a name. It is made clear that talking to himself is not one of Aschenbach's previous habits, but something that overtakes him in Venice. About to leave for the station, he thinks he is seeing Tadzio for the last time, "He did what was unusual with him, really formed the words on his lips and spoke them to himself; then he added: 'God bless you!' " Normally, Aschenbach keeps speech, thought and writing apart and orderly; but here he succumbs to half-utterance, his lips forming the words but no ear catching them. Near the end we see the famous writer sitting in the deserted square: "His loose lips, set off by the cosmetics, formed isolated words of the strange dream logic created by his half-slumbering brain." The words which he has refused to utter have rotted inside him and lost all order and sense. They are neither wholly suppressed nor properly uttered, but merely bubble to the surface and agitate the lips to no purpose.

In the midst of all this corruption of the spoken word, the love of Aschenbach and Tadzio is eloquent by its very silence. Aschenbach's verbal declarations of affection and love are made unheard and in solitude. It is to himself, alone in the darkness of the park, that Aschenbach whispers the universal formula of longing, "Ich liebe dich!" Tadzio knows his secret and guards it by silence. "He saw him, and did not betray him." Theirs is the language of looks, the adoration of the "man who lives alone and in silence" for one who epitomizes "the divinely arbitrary." Fritz Martini's formula for this affair is a just one: "a wordless love out of pure feeling." There is a strong correlation between the wordlessness and the love: feeling, released from the restraints of communication, is intensified beyond all reason, beyond all limits.

Silence is the ultimate fate of language on either side of the gap which has opened up within it. It must die either of its own aloofness from social life or of its own degradation by that life. The story of Aschenbach demonstrates this. The moral and artistic purity of his writing makes it more and more arid and lifeless; as a silenced writer, he falls silent as a social, moral and emotional being. He displays successive and interrelated failures to speak: first, he does not open normal friendly relations with Tadzio and his family; second, he does not warn them about the plague; and third, he does not declare his love to Tadzio. Instead of speaking to others he either talks to himself or listens to others, and this listening passes from an aesthetic music-appreciation into an immoral acquiescence in the face of lies. Aptly enough, Aschenbach's avowal of support to the Venetians' effort to "hush up" the plague is itself yet another of those repetitive whispers that go unheard. " 'It must be kept quiet!' he whispered fiercely. And: 'I will keep quiet.' " The moral impurity of this silence makes it the opposite of Wittgenstein's "Whereof one cannot speak, thereof one must be silent." Aschenbach refuses to tell the truth, Wittgenstein refuses to tell untruths. And yet, after all, silences sound very much alike. How is one to tell the pure silence of the artist or philosopher who refuses to risk flattery and lies from the impure silence of those who fail to speak out against flattery and lies of others?

At the beginning of the story the plight of Aschenbach's writing is its loss of emotional persuasiveness: "It seemed to him that his work lacked those marks of fiery, sportive emotionalism which, themselves the fruits of joy, and more direct in their appeal than any depth of content, set the conditions for the delight of an appreciative public." Language as austere truth-content will earn respect, but will seem impoverished without the excitement of sensuality and feeling. Aschenbach abandons the one only to be swamped by the other. This is his language crisis: that veracity and persuasiveness, the sense and the music of language, have parted company, leaving a choice between lifeless truth, flattering lies, and silence.

There is, however, one example in the story of how language can regain its wholeness and reunite its estranged capabilities. It is, of course, the essay that Aschenbach writes as he sits on the beach watching Tadzio, "listening to the music of his voice." From this inspiration come the qualities of "clarity, . . . poise, and . . . vibrant emotional tension" which distinguish the piece from the stiff correctness of his recent work. It is not, as one might have imagined, some last frenzied and poetic outpouring, but a very social piece of writing, a "little tract" composed in response to a topical cultural controversy. The striking incongruity between this intellectual product and its erotic and musical inspiration

shows how far their respective qualities have drawn apart. Yet, despite its tantalizing slightness, the essay hints at a possible reunion between meaning and music, clarity and feeling, truth and persuasion. By this time it is too late for Aschenbach to realise this possibility in any substantial work. But Mann, in **"Death in Venice"** as a whole, makes good Aschenbach's failure in his triumphant description of it, a description whose intellectual reach and musical-emotional richness makes it a major step in overcoming the crisis of language. (pp. 44-52)

> *Graham Good, "The Death of Language in 'Death in Venice',"* in Mosaic: A Journal for the Comparative Study of Literature, *Vol. V, No. 3, Spring, 1972, pp. 43-52.*

JOHN HERMANN   (essay date 1973)

[*Hermann was an American author and critic whose affiliation with several well-known and controversial expatriates, including James Joyce, Ezra Pound, and Ernest Hemingway, caused American censors to ban publication of his autobiographical novel,* What Happens *(1925), though it was an inoffensive tale of adolescence in the Midwest. Among Hermann's other works,* Summer Is Ended *(1932) signaled his conversion to communism and* The Salesman *(1939) describes the character of a man who has lost himself among the great masses of society. In the following excerpt, Hermann discusses the narrator's shifting perspective in "The Railway Accident."*]

To relegate Thomas Mann's **"Railway Accident"** to an example of anecdotal story-telling "too slight to support a heavier structure" [according to Mark Schorer] or to assume from its conclusion that the narrator of the story "failed his first and last opportunity to see beyond his vanity" [see Lainoff excerpt dated 1956] seems to shunt that literary journey onto a siding where it had no intention of stopping. Even though the tone is familiar and the story brief, those are not minor "clearing operations" that are to be undertaken on manuscripts put together like spiderwebs and peopled with characters who at a glance have been labeled with epithets that supposedly define them forever—whether they be railway guards, old ladies in threadbare capes, sleeping-car attendants, or monocled nobs.

The casual beginning of the story, as if it scarcely merits the name of a story, as if it were indeed but an anecdote such as one might tell after a journey, indicates what the narrator himself has learned about art concealing art. "Tell you a story? But I don't know any. Well, yes, after all, here is something I might tell." *Might* tell? What dissembling under the guise of truth. He has realized from the events of the railway accident that little old ladies who seem to belong only in third-class carriages suddenly at the conclusion of the story crowd into first-class seats to warn him of how superficial, if easy, stereotypes are. It is this new awareness that the writer, stowed higgledy-piggledy on another train, carries with him when he reaches Dresden three hours late—that the clearing operations on his spiderweb manuscript will be to avoid the temptation of facile epithets, will be to cloak the mathematical inevitabilities of fiction in the semblance of actuality. (p. 343)

The problem was not new even then (1907) to Mann—of how to keep his characters from becoming abstractions too easily, of creating not people but uncompromising types to fit into the architectonics of fictional form. The **"Railway Accident"** is, in effect, an exemplum not only for Mann but for all other writers as well: take care of the well-ordered compartments of fiction that invite ease, comfort, and a second cigar, because just when the folded-down sheets of accustomed generalities seem the most comforting, the accidents of experience will scatter those illusions helter-skelter into the night.

As the narrator says at the end of the story: "I suppose it had to happen once [before an author learns his lesson] but whatever mathematicians say, I feel that I now have every chance of escaping another." The anecdotal tone of the **"Railway Accident,"** the make-believe of a true story, is evidence that the narrator at least has learned the difference between spiderwebs and art. This is neither a slight theme nor a failure to see beyond his vanity; it is fiction under the guise of truth.

The story, in two parts, separated by the accident, is a "literary and artistic pilgrimage" such as from time to time the narrator undertakes not unwillingly. With him he brings a manuscript on which he plans to work. The two parts of the story—before and after the accident—give contrasting looks at a set of characters, at places, and finally at modes of fiction, at the differences between honeycombs and anecdotes.

Before the accident, the world is a catalogue of logic and order that the narrator observes "beyond the expanse of window-pane," where trains run on time, social classes are kept in their proper compartments, and his manuscript, his precious package "tied with string in the Bavarian colors," is in the secure hands of authority, the State.

After the accident, the world is "a perfect sea of string," where the superficial categorizing of characters is sent "higgledy-piggledy" into deepening complexities, where the admirable, comfortable train finds itself canted precariously in the night, having "run onto the wrong line;" where "clearing operations" are to be started on his manuscript. It is upon the last, on what clearing operations one is to make on the honeycombs of fiction that the emphasis of the story finally rests.

The narrator before the accident is surrounded with an air of complacency and self-satisfaction. He is going on one of his literary and artistic journeys. The train from Dresden to Munich is a model of efficiency, his compartment a "real little bedroom" with leather wall-hangings and a nickel-plated washbasin. The lower berth is "snowily prepared." He smokes. He observes. If he is slightly pompous, expansive, we can forgive him. He is a writer; he likes to travel; he is full of "joyful anticipations."

On the platform of the station, there are everywhere those assurances that he likes, that make him feel secure. A guard with a sergeant-major's mustache and a leather cartridge belt ("he is authority, he is our parent, he is the State") keeps old ladies in threadbare capes from entering the second-class. "Two stout fellows" pull the handcart piled with luggage. His trunk, his manuscript, is in good hands. A nob, in spats, rains down lordly epithets and assumes for himself all the prerogatives of his monocle-wearing, of absolute authority in his world. The narrator, the writer, cannot withhold his envy. To take one's dog into the sleeping compartment! To throw one's ticket into the attendant's eye! "it did my heart good," the narrator confesses (to see a nob act like a nob). His manuscript in such a world "reposes as if in the bosom of Abraham."

The details of this world that he selects to observe represent what he likes—the predictabilities of a spiderweb, the term

he himself applies to his manuscript, that "honeycomb" into which he stores "his ingenuities and industry." He, his manuscript, his concept of reality ride along unperturbed. Then the accident.

The second part of the story shows the order he likes reduced to chaos. Once pushed from an observer's role to that of a participant by a jerk that seems at the time "of deliberately foul intent," the narrator witnesses one after another of his character judgments and assurances disappear.

The guard, that symbol of the State with the "inhospitable eye," comes limping down the track saying, "Oh, dear, oh dear, me." The sleeping-car attendant, who was the grimy-handed "swine" with the ticket thrown in his eye, now suddenly takes on another dimension: he is the husband of a wife to whom that very morning he said, "Somethin's goin' to happen today." The nob, his voice "distorted by fear," bursts from his compartment crying for help, no longer his own absolute authority, exclaiming, "Great God. *Dear* God." Even the station-master, who is supposedly in charge of that part of the track, "had no cap and no self-control."

The train itself, that little bedroom away from home, is a waste of wreckage. Women's shoes are strewn up and down the track. The cars of the train that leaves regularly every evening from Munich and every morning deposits its passengers safely in Dresden lie aslant in the flickering lights of the lanterns. "The great express engine . . . lay smashed up and done for. Price seventy-thousand marks." Ladies, hastily covering up their nakedness, jump to the ground from the canted platforms of the sleeping-cars. The baggage car is reported to be demolished.

Everything from which the narrator had taken assurance has been overturned—both his concept of characters and the comfortable world from which he has observed them.

But it is the manuscript that now becomes his principal concern. "Clearing operations were to be undertaken with my manuscripts." His spiderweb? His honeycomb? His squirrel's hoard? Those ordered arrangements that gave him so much assurance in the first half of the story? Clearing operations on such a manuscript, on such beliefs? Of course. He has the courage to recognize in the events of the railway accident how precarious, if facile, stereotypes are, how easy but incomplete such observations from behind window panes can be, what dangers might lie in trains that run on time and in fiction with the geometry of spiderwebs. The courage to start again if his manuscript has indeed been lost is based on this added knowledge which the railway accident has given him—that the honeycombs of fiction need versimilitude as well. One of these versimilitudes, one of these movements to bring fiction away from being programmed, is to tell a story as if it were an anecdote, as if it were true. It is for that reason that the **"Railway Accident,"** the story of a writer and what clearing operations have to be done on his manuscript, is in anecdotal form: "Tell you a story? But I don't know any." He not only knows a story; he knows how to tell it.

At the end, it is the tiny, old grandmother in the threadbare cape who confirms this new knowledge. Out of breath, she is helped into the carriage where they have all been crowded. "Is this the first-class?" she keeps repeating, as if only on those plush cushions did she properly belong. The narrator moves aside for her, makes room, not only there but in his stories as well, thinking twice now before he assigns her, at a glance, to third-class generalities.

It is on this track, in the **"Railway Accident,"** on how to camouflage the spiderwebs of fiction with the anecdotes of truth, that Thomas Mann has set his story as well as those other literary and artistic pilgrimages that he undertook "not unwillingly from time to time." (pp. 343-46)

John Hermann, "Thomas Mann: What Track for the 'Railway Accident'?" in Studies in Short Fiction, Vol. X, No. 4, Fall, 1973, pp. 343-46.

FRANKLIN E. COURT   (essay date 1975)

[In the following excerpt, Court examines deception and irony in Mann's "Disorder and Early Sorrow."]

Professor Cornelius's loss of his young daughter, Ellie, and Ellie's loss of Max Hergesell, the "fairy prince" who captures her tiny heart at the "big folks' " party in Mann's **"Disorder and Early Sorrow,"** are but the final movements in a narrative that suggests fraud and hopelessness from beginning to end. The opening paragraph, for example, quite appropriately begins with a reference to one of the most deceptive of all foods—croquettes—deceptive because the ingredients are disguised. The Corneliuses, a very "proper" middle class family, living in an illusory house outwardly appearing elegant but actually badly in need of repair, a house in which "they themselves look odd . . . with their worn and turned clothing and altered way of life," sit to eat a dinner of "croquettes made of turnip greens" followed by a trifle that is "concocted out of those dessert powders" that the reader learns really taste like something else—soap.

Here we have a small example at the outset of how Mann uses a stylistic device called "parody of externals" to create irony, a subject that John G. Root discusses in an enlightening article on Mann's style [see Further Reading list], but one which has never been successfully applied to an analysis of **"Disorder and Early Sorrow."** This brief study will attempt to explain how the *leitmotiv* of deception in this unusual tale is reinforced through the description of physical externals. We will find that in each character considered, except one, outer traits complement inner peculiarities. The one exception is the servant, Xaver, who has the ironic last name of Kleinsgutl, ironic because he is without doubt the only character in the story who is "his own man."

In contrast to Xaver, the other characters are poseurs, bearing more resemblance to puppets or mannequins than to real beings. The "big folks" (Bert and Ingrid), for instance, seem to lack integrity. They are much like the telephone that plays such a prominent part in their lives: expressionless, capable only of audible contact, an artificial sound device. Bert, the Professor's seventeen year old son, having succumbed to Ivor Herzl's influence, "blackens the lower rim of his eyelids" and assumes the unnatural pose of a performer. Like Oscar Wilde's Dorian Gray, who is a creation of the artistic imagination of Lord Henry Wotton, Bert is Herzl's creation. From a distance, Bert is said to resemble Xaver, but there the resemblance ends; the doubles are inconsonant—Xaver is not a puppet. He toys with the idea of being engaged by a cinema director, but he is, as the Professor envisions, too much of a "good-for-nothing . . . with quite distinct traits of character of his own" ever to take the cinema dream seriously. He must be taken "as he is." Xaver does what he has the urge to do (he smokes thirty cigarettes a day, for instance); Bert, because he lacks "the means to compete with Xaver," or, for that

matter, with anyone else, is forced to mimic others. Bert's deficiency manifests itself by the paternal envy his father experiences when comparing Bert's failures with the accomplishments of a number of male guests at the party. Bert's fraudulent, showy outward behavior mirrors his inner failure: " 'poor Bert, who knows nothing and can do nothing . . . except playing the clown'." His external appearance parodies his hollow, self-deception.

Ingrid, the Professor's older daughter, is also a markedly deceptive character whose entire life appears to have been comprised of sham and impersonation. She is said to know how to "wind masters, and even headmasters, round her finger," and she is in school working for a certificate that she never plans to use. The performance that she and Bert put on in the bus, at the expense of the unhappy old gentleman sitting opposite them, and the delight she takes in ridiculing Max Hergesell's nasal drawl reflect a bizarre and sadistic inner quality. Both she and Bert foreshadow through their outward behavior the pose and affectation which will later distinguish the many painted figures who turn up for the party.

What the Professor observes of Herzl the actor seems to encompass the entire guest list: " 'Queer,' thinks the Professor, 'You would think a man would be one thing or the other—not melancholic and use face paint at the same time. . . . But here we have a perfect illustration of the abnormality of the artist soul-form'." "The artist soul-form"—shades of Aschenbach, Cipolla, and Tonio Kröger are conjured up by the professor's comment; no doubt the painted, artificial host of guests at the party share with them the soul-form of the artist. The artist-figures who attend the party emphasize by contrast the commonplace, rather mediocre nature of the professor's entire family; the extent of their mediocrity is emphasized finally by the professor himself—who is as self-deceived as his children.

The Professor sees something abnormal in the artist's soul. Unlike the "big folks," he does nothing or wears nothing that gives one the impression that he is self-deceived. Ironically, however, the professor appears less and less attractive as the party progresses. The revelers are artist-figures living devoid of class awareness; the same cannot be said for the "big folks" and the Professor. The artists seem to find their identity in artifice, in a self-created world. They must, because the generation of the "old folks" has given them nothing with which they can identify. And whatever else these art seekers might be, they are not hypocrites. Like the "madmen" and the "immortals" in Hesse's *Steppenwolf,* whom they resemble, their strange outward behavior does not conceal inner deformities. They are surrealistic externalizations of a total acceptance of life's absurdity, and they do not take themselves seriously. The same, however, cannot be said for the "big folks" or for the Professor himself.

The one external feature associated with the Professor, his glasses, suggests the essential weakness in his character. They are bifocals with lenses "divided for reading and distance" and are symbolic of his divided personality which adjusts his view according to the circumstances. Mann explains that being a history professor, Professor Cornelius's heart belongs "to the coherent, disciplined, historic past." We are also told that inwardly the Professor dislikes the pose and artificiality of the artists and resents the party "with its power to intoxicate and estrange his darling child." Yet all of his inward resentment and opinions are hidden by an exterior far more deceitful than the rouged cheeks of Herzl the actor. The Professor laughs at the sick humor of the "big folks," not because he really wants to, but because "in these times when something funny happens people have to laugh." Although he attacks the changing times in his lectures, he, nevertheless, has shaved his beard, the symbol of his once academic individuality, and now smooth-faced—his "concession to the changing times"—he outwardly embraces the society and world view he detests. He seems to associate the "big folks' " party with the tone of the new society that he attacks in his lectures, yet his mind wanders during the very process of formulating his argument to a pleasurable anticipation of the coming festivities. And when the time does arrive, we see him polishing his glasses (it is time to readjust his perspective to suit the circumstances) and practicing "appropriate" phrases to impress the guests whom he will flatter with undue approval and unnecessary praise. The Professor is a hypocrite.

The devastating irony that Mann achieves mainly through the parody of externals in this story reaches its culmination in the characterization of the Professor. The *leitmotiv* of deception, that pervades the story, ends with the lie that appears at the end of the narrative—the lie that the professor forces himself to believe: that tomorrow the glittering Hergesell will be, for Ellie, "a pale shadow." The story, however, suggests otherwise. His prayers to heaven that Ellie will forget Hergesell and the festive world he symbolizes is the professor's final act of self-deception. She will not forget.

The title of the story is appropriate: the world out of joint, the "disordered" world, is viewed in microcosm in the lives of the Cornelius family; the revelers, at least, seem to have come to terms with the "disorder"—they ignore it or find happiness in spite of it. Ellie's "early sorrow" is destined to intensify as long as she believes so firmly in "swan knights" and "fairy princes" like Hergesell. As Hergesell uncannily seems to know, " 'she's beginning young'." (pp. 186-89)

> *Franklin E. Court, "Deception and the 'Parody of Externals' in Thomas Mann's 'Disorder and Early Sorrow'," in Studies in Short Fiction, Vol. XII, No. 2, Spring, 1975, pp. 186-89.*

J. M. LINDSAY (essay date 1975)

[Lindsay is a Scottish educator and critic who has written several studies on German literature, including a critical volume on Thomas Mann. In the following excerpt, he discusses the theme and style of Mann's first short story, "Gefallen."]

Thomas Mann wrote **"Gefallen"** in 1894 and published it for the first time in the journal *Die Gesellschaft* (Leipzig, 1894). After that it did not appear again until it was included in a volume of *Erzählungen* in the *Stockholmer Gesamtausgabe* (published posthumously at Frankfurt in 1958). No doubt the gap of 64 years between the first and second publications of the work suggests that he had a rather low opinion of it. However, it seems to me that this first completed work by Thomas Mann is well worth looking at more closely, both for its own sake and because of his subsequent achievements. It did after all attract the favourable attention of the poet and critic Richard Dehmel in the year of its first publication when Dehmel had no reason to suppose that this new young author was going to attain a world reputation within a very few years. In the following pages I shall begin by attempting to look at the work as if it had just appeared for the first time.

The tale is told by one of a group of four young men, obvious-ly all well known to one another, in an atelier in Munich towards the end of the nineteenth century. The narrator is a doctor, a few years older than the others and regarded by them as having more experience than they and having above all enjoyed the dissipations which make them describe him as 'wüscht'. For this reason they are prepared to give him a hearing when he offers to tell them a story. The doctor is prompted to tell the story by the rather silly talk of Laube, who has an obsession about the unfavourable position of women in society and will not stop talking about it. Laube has just made a passionate speech concerning the responsibility of both partners when a woman is said to have 'fallen'; then Selten says he would like to tell a story since they have come to talk about such matters. The young men all make themselves comfortable in a corner of the room and Selten tells his story.

In summary this concerns a love affair between a medical student of nineteen or twenty and a young actress. The boy sees the girl by chance on the stage at the local Goethe theatre. He visits her and introduces himself, having first rendered himself acceptable by a gift of flowers. Soon the young people become lovers and meet regularly. As far as the youth is concerned the whole affair has an almost sacramental quality. Its intensity is matched by the heavy and delicious scent of lilac from a bush in the garden of the girl's house. There is evidence quite early on that the girl is less unequivocally committed than her lover, but to all appearances both young people are very much in love.

After a few weeks of this almost rhapsodic state the student goes to the girl's house and there finds a middle-aged man drinking coffee with her at 9 a.m. He and the man at first eye one another sullenly, then exchange insults; the student orders the older man out of the flat—and then he finds banknotes on Irma's bedside-table. He can scarcely take in the fact of her manifest infidelity, and when she explains it by references to the cost of living, the expense of dressing properly and the general custom of theatrical people he is absolutely confounded. He weeps from pure sorrow at his painful disillusionment.

The student is never named though he is often referred to as 'der gute Junge'. He is in fact not very individualized; he shows the characteristics of the amiable but rather feeble undergraduate. He is easily manipulated by Irma, who has the superior poise and control of the young woman over a man of her own age. The revelation of the student's identity at the end scarcely comes as a surprise; nor can we be too shocked by his evident growth in worldly wisdom in the course of the decade or so that has passed since the time of the story. At the age of nineteen the student went naively through life, accepting all the gifts it offered him, including Irma's love, as though they were absolutely his, without cost and without limitation. Now, eleven years later, he has become a Mr. Worldly Wiseman, expecting but little from life and that little at its appropriate price. He looks back wryly on his early naïveté, regards his behaviour as immature and uncritical, even sees Irma's betrayal of him as something which might have been expected and hardly reflected very adversely on her. It was really unreasonable to expect her to behave differently, although the student's optimistic innocence did him credit.

Irma's older lover clearly expects the student to take in the situation as it affects the two of them and the girl more quickly than he does in fact take it in. He immediately realizes that a young rival has appeared and loses no time at all in addressing him rudely as 'Bube'. This term can only be explained in terms of sexual jealousy, for young Selten has offered him no provocation. Selten then becomes rather stiff and not quite polite, although his behaviour always remains restrained and certainly does not suggest at any point that he is uncivilized, or 'ungebildet' as he put it.

The girl really behaves in a somewhat mercenary, discreditable and inexplicable way. It is not surprising to learn that she is prepared to have an affair with Selten, who is portrayed as a not unattractive youth and evidently very much in love with her. Her willingness to change lovers casually only a few weeks after her first affair with Selten hardly rings true. To have fallen for young Selten seems perfectly natural and does not reflect on her character; to be selling herself to a man who could easily be her father destroys the carefully built up atmosphere. Her excuses for her infidelity make her seem cheap and shallow, and it is quite clear that Selten has taken the affair too seriously. If he had not been lacking in worldly wisdom he would scarcely have expected more from a casual young female acquaintance from a third-rate provincial stage, but he obviously regarded the whole affair in a very idealistic light. One must admit, however, that for a time it really looks as though the medical student's affair is going very well and as though our fears on his account of a coming let-down are quite unfounded. Of course, everything that Irma says about the economic stresses of her life is perfectly true, but it does not accord with the *sublime* image of his mistress which young Selten has created within his own mind. Perhaps the young Thomas Mann is being more harsh and sceptical about women and about life than the cruel real world itself; perhaps he is simply putting on a hard-boiled front so that he shall not seem as vulnerable as he really is.

The other figures in the story are sketched in well enough. Dr. Selten is mature and ironical, having after all been through such experiences in his youth as the love for Irma Weltner. He does not emerge as such a fully drawn, rounded character as Serenus Zeitblom or the monk Clemens in *Der Erwählte*, but he fulfils approximately the same function. We may well wonder at first how he has come by the very full and intimate knowledge of the events of the story which he evidently possesses. Of course when it emerges that he was himself the principal participant in the action everything is explained. For most of the duration of the piece, however, we are simply surprised at the extent of his information concerning the lives of people who at first must be regarded as strangers to him. In a sense Dr. Selten is the same man as the former medical student and knows all about his own earlier life; in another sense he has grown away from the naive attitudes and instinctive behaviour patterns of his own youth. He evidently sees his younger friends as going through the tormented, unbalanced, simple-minded phase of life from which by virtue of his greater age he believes he has now escaped to greater clarity of mind and more balanced judgment. Since he has lived somewhat longer and gained wider experience he is perhaps entitled to be regarded with respect by his young friends; yet his rather complacent assumption of ironical superiority over them does somewhat jar.—The old lover plays his tiny, undignified role more or less as one would expect; it is strange that he should expect to enjoy permanent proprietorial rights over Irma just because he has paid her for a night. He cannot really suppose that he is entitled to more than the favours he has already enjoyed, nor, since he evidently knows that she has a lover should he be surprised that the lover should appear. His payment for favours received cannot really be ex-

pected to conceal the truth about Irma's character indefinitely.—Rölling, the lightly sketched, older medical student with his robustly cynical view of life, his obvious function as leader of the young male pack and his low opinion of female invulnerability, is an amusing minor figure. So, too, are little Meysenberg, who plays host to the party and Laube, with his advanced social views and his 'Dessertbonbons'. The fourth member of the party is the one whose character somehow fails to emerge properly. Almost the only thing we learn about him is that he was present at the party and heard Selten tell the story 'fix und fertig in Novellenform'. It is Selten who is said to have some experience of writing 'Novellen', not the first person narrator at all.

Perhaps this is as appropriate a point as any to ask ourselves what was the author's intention in writing "Gefallen." Is Thomas Mann really suggesting that Irma Weltner's first 'irregularity' is bound to lead to others? Does he imply that Irma is 'soiled goods' as soon as she begins the affair with young Selten and does he think that the greater depravity of her association with the old gentleman is a natural or inevitable consequence of her first lapse? Certainly Dr. Selten does say so, and this is undoubtedly the drift of the story. The young man in "Gefallen" remains a pure if disappointed idealist at the end. Irma, on the other hand, takes a casual, pragmatic attitude to the whole question of sexual morals. Girls like her in the theatre cannot afford to be pure or strait-laced, they are bound to 'fall" sooner or later, and having done so they may well sell themselves to the best advantage. This is certainly Dr. Selten's assessment of the situation and it was probably also that of the young Thomas Mann. And certainly Selten's representation of the respective rôles of man and woman in his story does not confirm Laube's view that in such matters men and women are equally 'fallen' creatures. His story suggests very strongly that while Irma has certainly 'fallen' the medical student was very far from being in the same position, in fact till her infidelity he felt himself only improved and uplifted by the whole affair.

Through his narrator Dr. Selten it becomes clear that the feelings of 'der gute Junge' were wholly comprehensible and readily accessible to Thomas Mann. Whereas Irma soon tired of playing the rôle of 'die Heilige' and regarded her affair with the student Selten as the beginning of a justifiable career of self-abandonment, Selten easily persuades himself that this affair with Irma represented a stage on the way of self-sanctification. In fact Selten's self-indulgence seems positively divinely ordained to him—he has a moment's doubt just after losing his virtue when he wonders if he has been a cad, but he rather easily persuades himself of the rightness of his behaviour. One senses that Thomas Mann considers it to be rather odd of Selten to feel purified and chastened the morning after his first experience of sex. In a way the fact that Selten is made to analyse his feelings and decide that he has behaved correctly is even stranger than if he had simply not given the matter any thought at all.

The blatant difference between Irma's casual view of her infidelity and the student's feelings of total betrayal is a notable feature of the work. She resents his anger and disappointment and tells him that he is making an unreasonable fuss about nothing; he feels quite crushed and infinitely resentful; she has destroyed his whole world, and almost the worst part of it is that she has done so without malicious intent.

This story recalls those works of Kleist in which infinite, pure aspiration is confronted by pedestrian callousness (e.g. Eva and Ruprecht or Eva and Marthe in *Der zerbrochene Krug*), the absolute intensity of the young Selten's love with the calculating matter-of-factness of Irma's attitude. What spoils the world completely for him is cheerfully and almost without perceiving it accepted by her. Laube, the feminist, pleads for equal judgment of man and woman in matters of sexual morality. The burden of Selten's story is that Irma is quite unworthy of her student's generous feelings. He forgets that in these matters the girl faces the risk of pregnancy, economic stress and social ostracism and that she cannot afford to seek divine sanction for her self-indulgences like the young man. Anyway, there is a certain irony about the divergent attitudes of the two young people to the recent events in their emotional lives. They are not united by their love but manifestly and clearly divided by it. Or perhaps one could merely say that the love affair is used as a means of demonstrating clearly their very different characters.

We shall consider the person of the narrator for a moment here. Selten cynical, sceptical, realistic and ironical. He faces fact about life although this is evidently something he has learned to do only through bitter experience. He is at least ten years older than his creator, who perhaps enjoys vicariously assuming attitudes of disillusionment and maturity which he does not really yet possess in his own right. We may regard him as in more ways than one a projection of how Thomas Mann at eighteen felt he would like to be in a few more years—established in a profession, poised, superior, experienced, to an extent at least a master of the 'Novelle' form, viewing the behaviour of his younger contemporaries with an ironical, almost Olympian detachment. (pp. 297-302)

["Gefallen"] concerns a real moral issue, even if the point of view adopted by Dr. Selten/Thomas Mann may be quite untenable. Each of the persons represented in the story stands out as a distinct individual, and the interplay of personalities is well represented. Even the total lack of contact and understanding between the two young lovers is well communicated. They are absolutely different in their approach to life and they fail to discover it till that fateful morning when he finds the banknotes on her bedside table. Even after the event, the student has learned only that the girl has betrayed him for money; he has no understanding of her difficulties as a single girl alone in the world and he does not begin to think that if he enjoys her favours he ought in all good conscience to spare a thought for her economic survival. As far as he is concerned she has simply and wantonly destroyed their idyllic love. From the girl's point of view, at least the old man was prepared to pay for his pleasures. The attitudes of the two young people to this question are as far apart as they possibly could be. The student is a perfect specimen of the sentimental poetic idealist with no sense of reality; Irma Weltner, as her name suggests a young worldling, has her feet firmly planted on the ground and is above all interested in survival in a cruel world. The whole affair is turned into a neat little narrative (personal distress, recollected in tranquillity after the lapse of a decade and given substance and form by an artist who, even then, as soon as his tale is told, again feels with full acuteness the hurt of that old wound and reacts savagely against the lilac blossom, symbol of his false sweetheart). The 'Novelle' is full of promise, raising as it does an interesting moral problem, relating past events with taste and clinically cruel detachment; it deals with that same world of affairs of the heart and the enchantment and disillusionment of love as many of Thomas Mann's later stories. The author has at his command an unusually rich vocabulary, a love of exotic terms and the effec-

tive contrast, a very keen eye for pictorial quality, a wholly unusual awareness for a boy of eighteen or nineteen not only that the world will look quite different in another few years but also in what ways it will differ from the world he knows. One might just mention the first tentative use of 'Leitmotive'—the lilac bush and the hat pushed back off the young student's brow. Later on Thomas Mann would be using this device with far more skill and variety. The narrator Selten with his modest narrative prefigures other narrators with their more ambitious narratives. **"Gefallen"** may indeed be but a first step on the road of authorship, but it is the first step of a young giant and the quality of the new, young author is apparent on every one of those few pages. (pp. 306-07)

J. M. Lindsay, "Thomas Mann's First Story, 'Gefallen'," in German Life & Letters, *n.s. Vol. XXVIII, No. 3, April, 1975, pp. 297-307.*

JEFFREY MEYERS (essay date 1986)

[*Meyers is an American educator, bibliographer, and critic who has written and compiled several studies and bibliographies on George Orwell. He has commented: "I take an interdisciplinary, comparative, and biographical approach to modern English and European literature, and believe criticism should be based on fact, not theory." In the essay from which the following excerpt is taken, Meyers compares the sociopolitical themes of "Mario and the Magician" and Robert Wiene's film* The Cabinet of Dr. Caligari.]

In "On the Film" (1928), published the same year that he wrote one of his greatest stories, **"Mario and the Magician,"** Mann expressed enthusiasm for the cinema and acknowledged the possibility of its fruitful influence on fiction: "lately I have come to entertain feelings for this phenomenon of our time that amount to a lively interest, even almost to a passion. . . . The film possesses a technique of recollection, of psychological suggestion, a mastery of detail in men and in things, from which the novelist, though scarcely the dramatist, might learn much." Robert Wiene's *The Cabinet of Dr. Caligari* (1919), the most widely discussed film of its time, had a direct influence on the atmosphere, plot, characters, and political theme of Mann's story.

The film portrays a contemporary incarnation of an eighteenth-century hypnotist who had traveled through northern Italy and forced his medium, Cesare, to commit numerous murders. Imitating his Italian alter-ego, the modern Dr. Caligari reenacts his crimes in Germany. In Mann's story the sinister Italian hypnotist also wreaks havoc on the Germans on holiday in northern Italy. And the narrator of the story remarks: "Perhaps more than anywhere else the eighteenth century is still alive in Italy, and with it the charlatan and mountebank type so characteristic of the period." Dr. Caligari—whose name is an anagram of the Sardinian capital, Cagliari, and suggests the emperor Caligula—becomes Cavaliere Cipolla; Cesare becomes Mario; and the innocent beloved, Jane, becomes Silvestra.

The film begins with the young hero Francis exclaiming: "Everywhere there are spirits. . . . They are all around us. . . . They have driven me from hearth and home, from my wife and my children." The atmosphere of the expressionist film is menacing and macabre—nothing is real, nothing is natural—and filled with sinister omens, acts of terror, and moments of panic. In Mann's story, the atmosphere remained "unpleasant in the memory. From the first moment the air of the place made us uneasy, we felt irritable, on edge." The threatening nationalism in Italy, far from the narrator's hearth and home, causes constant friction and discord. As he enters the unfamiliar and unreal world of the magician's public hall ("where during the season there had been a *cinema* with a weekly programme," he is increasingly apprehensive about the welfare of his children. He wants to protect them and to leave the theater, as he had wished to leave the oppressive holiday resort, but he is much more absorbed in the necromantic spectacle than he is willing to admit.

When Caligari seeks a permit to perform at the fair, he is treated rudely by an arrogant bureaucrat perched on a clerk's high stool. Caligari bitterly resents the oppression by official authority and feels compelled to revenge himself against society. The entire first part of **"Mario and the Magician"** catalogues, with increasing frustration and rage, the series of personal humiliations that the German family suffers at the hands of the chauvinistic foreigners. They are forced to give up their table on the restaurant veranda; they are evicted from the hotel when the Princess complains of their child's harmless cough; and they become an offense to public morals when their small daughter, playing on the beach, innocently removes and rinses her bathing suit. These incidents help to create the hostile atmosphere that leads directly to "the shocking business of Cipolla, that dreadful being who seemed to incorporate, in so fateful and so humanly impressive a way, all the peculiar evilness of the situation as a whole."

Both the film and the story reflect the precarious democracy of the Weimar Republic, which swayed between tyranny and chaos in the fifteen years between Germany's defeat in the Great War and the Nazi takeover in January, 1933. Both works warned about the dangers of the traditional German belief in obedience to authority. As S. S. Prawer observes of *Caligari:* "The [origins of the] questions it leads us to ask about . . . social legitimation, about the protection of society from disrupting and destructive influences, and about the shifting points of view that convert enemies into friends and friends into enemies . . . may well be sought in the German situation after the First World War." Similarly, the walk the German family takes from the hotel to the theater places ["**Mario and the Magician**"] in its political context and symbolizes the decline of Italy that culminated in the dictatorship of Mussolini in October, 1922: "You reached it by following the main street under the wall of the '*palazzo*,' a ruin with a 'For Sale' sign, that suggested a castle had obviously been built in lordlier days. In the same street were the chemist, the hairdresser, and all the better shops; it led, so to speak, from the feudal past the bourgeois into the proletarian."

Dr. Caligari is a grotesque though confident cripple whose physical movements and jerky shuffle are exaggerated and warped. His sensitivity and animosity, his sadism and urge for destruction, "his lust for power and desire for revenge . . . [are attempts] to compensate for physical inferiority." The screenwriters Mayer and Janowitz mentioned that Caligari's external appearance was suggested by a photograph in old age of the philosopher Arthur Schopenhauer, whose concept of the will had a profound impact on Mann's work. Like Caligari, Cipolla—who wears the same outmoded clothing: frock coat, white gloves, cloak and top hat—is a deformed, demonic artist. Instead of ignoring his hunchback, he defensively calls attention to it and asks sympathy for his physical defect: "the malformation of the back did not sit between the shoulders, it took the form of a sort of hips or but-

tocks hump, which did not indeed hinder his movements but gave him a grotesque and dipping stride at every step he took." Cipolla is particularly resentful and sadistic toward the handsome Italian youths who have been spoiled by the favors of their girlfriends.

Dr. Caligari makes his first public appearance by demonstrating his occult powers at a fair. His strange costume and theatrical gestures attract the audience and encourage them to attend the exciting spectacle in his tent. He advertises a somnambulist, acts as a puppet-master, awakens Cesare on command, and substitutes a dummy when Cesare is out on his homicidal missions. By subversively subjecting Cesare to his will, he proves that "a somnambulist can be compelled to do things of which he knows nothing, things he would never do himself and would abhor doing . . . that one in a trance can be driven to murder." Cipolla, another cruel and uncanny traveling virtuoso—"*forzatore, illusionista, prestidgatore*"— promises "to display extraordinary phenomena of a mysterious and staggering kind." Cipolla makes an exhibition of Mario as Caligari does of Cesare. He also imposes his overpowering will on his victims. He forces one man to stick out his tongue, makes another screw himself up with imaginary cramps, bewitches and enslaves the sympathetic Signora Angiolieri. The hunchback's minatory attacks on the will power of his "puppets" illustrate the dark theme of the story. Remembering perhaps Mussolini's proclamation ("La parola Italia deve dominare sulla parola Libertà," Mann states: "Between not willing a certain thing and not willing at all—in other words, yielding to another person's will—there may lie too small a space for the idea of freedom to squeeze into."

Caligari compels Cesare to murder the Town Clerk and Francis' friend, Alan. But Cesare is a mere instrument of Caligari's will. His inability to kill Jane, whom he abducts and abandons in the great chase scene of the film, reveals that he is more an innocent victim than a guilty murderer. Both Cesare and Mario are dominated and doomed by the malevolent power of the hypnotists. Cipolla deliberately perverts Mario's sexual feelings and publicly exposes his timid and deluded passion for Sylvestra, who has made him suffer the pangs of love. By substituting himself for the beloved, the hunchback compels Mario to kiss him on the cheek, and his lust for domination ruthlessly violates Mario's rights and values. By forcing Mario to act out of his own dark desires and by pushing human dignity beyond endurance, Cipolla transforms the gentle Mario into a murderer—with Cipolla himself as the victim. Cipolla thus proves that in a tyrannical regime, the will may exist, but freedom cannot. As D. H. Lawrence perceptively observed of Italy in the 1920s: "All bloody revolutions are the result of the long, slow, accumulated insult to the quick of pride in the mass of men. . . ." (pp. 235-38)

In his allegory of fascism and portrait of a dictator, Mann employs a theatrical metaphor and subtly fuses Gabriele D'Annunzio's ritual, artistry, and oratory with Benito Mussolini's ideology, brutality, and lust for power in the deformed figure of the nationalistic Cipolla, whose person and performance suggest that fascism is a disease of the social body. Cipolla's hypnotic powers, his whip and cognac (symbols of force and fraud), and his dominating will extract the last vestiges of individual and collective freedom from the blindly enthusiastic crowd, who (like the narrator) do not realize the extent of their submission. The murder of Cipolla, which shatters the hypnotism and liberates the captive audience, is, paradoxically, an assertion of human dignity. (p. 238)

Both Cesare and the Magician and **"Mario and the Magician"** have ironic and ambiguous endings, "singularly devoid of comfort or reassurance." Francis, who narrates the story to another lunatic in a madhouse, may or may not be insane. The Director of the asylum, who appears to have a split personality, may or may not be Dr. Caligari. His final, disturbing words are: "At last I understand the nature of his madness. [Francis] thinks I am that mystic Caligari. Now I see how he can be brought back to sanity again." But it is also possible that good and evil have been reversed, that Francis is perfectly sane, that his "fantasy" is in fact reality, that the Director is the one who is actually crazy.

Cipolla's fatal end is called a "liberation." For the waiter Mario, whose very profession demands obedience, stands for all the Italians who have been hypnotized by Mussolini. His involuntary murder of Cipolla breaks the magic spell and extinguishes the source of evil. Yet Mario will have to pay the penalty for Cipolla's power and his own crime of passion. And it is unclear whether Mann believed that only the naive and emotional Italians would succumb to the rabid nationalism that allowed Mussolini to seize power or if he was warning his countrymen that the same tragedy could also occur in Germany.

Wiene's film, which sprang from the same cultural milieu as Mann's story, provides a classic example of how one medium can nourish another. The contrast of Italians and Germans, the sinister atmosphere, the desire for revenge against society, the precarious existence of the Weimar Republic, the crippled villain, the hypnotic performance, the dominant will, the incitement to murder, the innocent instrument of evil, the warning against political tyranny, the ambiguous ending, and the reversal of good and evil in **"Mario and the Magician"** were influenced—as Mann hinted in his essay "On the Film"—by the vivid detail, the innovative technique, and the psychological power of *The Cabinet of Dr. Caligari.* (pp. 238-39)

> *Jeffrey Meyers, "Caligari and Cipolla: Mann's 'Mario and the Magician','" in* Modern Fiction Studies, *Vol. 32, No. 2, Summer, 1986, pp. 235-39.*

A. F. BANCE   (essay date 1987)

[*Bance is an English editor, translator, and critic. In the following excerpt, he discusses the dual role of the narrator as artist and member of the bourgeois in "Mario and the Magician."*]

One reason why the narrator of **"Mario und der Zauberer"** [**"Mario and the Magician"**] (1930) has escaped close scrutiny is the overwhelming presence of the demonic magician Cipolla. So powerful is this creation of Thomas Mann's that the effect upon critics has been comparable to the effect of Hitler's personality upon historians of National Socialism. In **"Mario und der Zauberer,"** to concentrate upon the Magician at the expense of the narrator's function is to distort the poetic economy of the Novelle.

However, the question of the role played by the narrator is a complex one. It is easy to see why some readers, encouraged by the recognizable similarities between the narrator's circumstances in the Novelle and Thomas Mann's own, have

preferred to make certain autobiographical assumptions about the text. The family holiday at Torre de Venere and what happens there correspond to the events that befell the Mann family at Forte dei Marmi in the summer of 1926, and the narrator's children to the two younger Mann offspring, Elisabeth and Michael. The author has included no significant detail (such as naming his narrator's profession) that would rule out the identification of the narrator with himself. The narrator's persona is close to what we know to be Thomas Mann's own, so that the former can be perceived as the vehicle of a truth that the author wishes to convey (notwithstanding widespread critical doubts, not originating with or confined to the post-structuralists, about the very concept of narratorial *or* authorial authority, 'the subject/author as originating consciousness, authority for meaning and truth').

One recent critic has gone so far in the direction of granting the text this confessional or autobiographical status as to regard the story—as have some of its Italian readers—as a 'flawed performance' because of its *author*'s supposed 'German bias' or nationalism: 'Why, then, is it [*Mario*] a little less than perfect? This has to do with Mann's attitude towards the Italian populace at Torre di Venere. . . . He inveighs against what are nothing more than dialectical and folk idiosyncracies in the same way as he does against obviously Fascist inspired behaviour.' Strangely, though, critics who pursue this autobiographical line do not at the same time treat the narrator-figure as cautiously as they would the artist who is the author of works like **"Tonio Kröger"** or **"Der Tod in Venedig"** [**"Death in Venice"**], with all their ambiguities and doubts about the phenomenon of the artist. Yet the narrator of **"Mario und der Zauberer,"** like his creator, is obviously an accomplished, if not a professional storyteller, carefully marshalling and arranging his effects and manipulating his reader's response. While I do not intend to fall back into a different kind of autobiographical fallacy by suggesting that we accord the narrator in **"Mario und der Zauberer"** the status of one of those fully-fledged artist-figures who are in some ways projections of Thomas Mann himself, I should say that since all of an author's works are part of his spiritual or intellectual autobiography, the only admissible autobiographical approach is one that lies in tracing the continuity of Thomas Mann's earlier themes into a story often thought to be (in the widest as well as the narrowest sense of the term) purely political. Trying to understand the nature of this addition to the spiritual autobiography is a complex task which precisely precludes simple one-to-one equations of textual and referential circumstances.

For example, if the anti-Italian bias is taken at face value, as it was by the Italian readers mentioned above, there is no possibility of accommodating another recent interpretation which uncompromisingly views the Novelle as an analysis of Hitlerism: 'One should not be misled by the story's Italian setting into believing that it relates to Mussolini's Italy, and not to German Nazism.' If this critic [Anthony Grenville] is right, and one of Thomas Mann's main objects in **"Mario und der Zauberer"** is the analysis of a virulent *German* form of nationalism, then some way must be found to approach the undeniable nationalistic bias of a narrator who cannot be identified with the author. If author and narrator are equated, on the other hand, one has to assume that the *author* has fallen victim to the malaise that Thomas Mann is analysing in his story; this produces a rather strange reading of the Novelle. In my view, the *narrator*'s (relatively mild) nationalism is clearly presented by the author as the loss of a sense of proportion, a weakness on his part which is a symptom of that very malaise.

But that is only a part of what Thomas Mann is conveying through his narrator-figure. This anonymous creation has two aspects: that of depicting a world-citizen, who is also a German, caught in the menacing atmosphere of the 1920s; and that of fictionalizing and problematizing some facets of Mann's personal experience as an artist. These two aspects are brought together and subtly related at a juncture in European history when, through the notorious 'aestheticizing of politics', the aesthetic was impinging upon the life of the ordinary citizen in a novel and sinister way, and one not at all welcome to the artist, despite (or because of) his recognition of his own affinity to the phenomenon. Neither of the aspects I have mentioned justifies the *identification* of the author and the hero/narrator, any more than such an identification is justified in Goethe's *Werther* or Thomas Mann's own **"Der Tod in Venedig."** In all these cases, the narrator or hero has an oblique but revealing relationship to the author, as representing a path that he might have taken himself but that he prefers to explore vicariously by means of his fictional character.

Another reason why attention has not been focused on the narrator is that he seems to prefer a secondary, almost invisible role. Reasonable, plausible, and self-effacing as it mostly is, his stance of painstaking objectivity displaces attention almost entirely from his own person to that of Cipolla and, towards the end, to Mario. Yet, perhaps because of this stance, an intriguing aura of evasiveness and defensiveness surrounds the narrator. The occasional direct addresses to the reader, whether on the subject of the unbearable, brazen weather of an Italian August or on his state of mind as a parent anxious to protect his young children from harm . . ., do not merely serve the purpose of establishing a directness and vividness in the text: they also contribute to an elaborate apparatus of apology for the narrator's part, however passive, in the disturbing events he is recounting.

Why should the narrator feel guilty? On the face of it, because of his failure to play the responsible role of parent and protect his unsuspecting children from an evil experience. The representative 'parent' role of the narrator, rather than his other role of mere aesthetic observer, is constantly stressed, by the use of the pronoun 'wir' (presumably referring to the complicity of the children's mother, who otherwise remains a completely shadowy figure), by the frequent references to the children's reactions and putative state of mind, and the narrator's reaction to their reactions, and above all by the stress on the 'alibi' provided by the children. The narrator is presented as the would-be relaxed mentor, all of whose problems are produced by some factor involving a holiday-mood wish to indulge his children. Their thwarted attraction to the red-shaped lamps on the veranda of the Grand Hotel leads to the family's being ignominiously obliged to decamp to the nearby and more homely Pensione Eleonora. The young daughter's nudity on the beach, caused by her wish to rinse the sand out of her costume before leaving at the end of the day, results in a further defeat at the hands of local xenophobia. Finally, the children's excitement about the prospect of an evening of 'magic' disarms parental opposition and produces ultimately the most sinister result of all: the exposure of the narrator's own lack of will to resist the Magician's power. It is clear that this is a long-term outcome of the evening, one which is perhaps even more significant than Mario's assassination of

Cipolla (an outcome missing from the Mann family's prototype experience in Forte dei Marmi) and with which the narrator is still trying to come to terms as he writes the story. The desire to come to terms with the experience is in fact a kind of hidden agenda, the implied but never explicitly-stated reason for the narrator's writing of the story. The absence of the kind of deictic indicators that might have been offered at one time in a 'morality' tale such as this ('dear reader, I write only to exorcize the memory of that dreadful night, and yet I do not delude myself that it can ever be expunged . . .') reflects a change in the conventions of fiction, but more significantly it reflects a greater complexity in the subject-matter, involving the open question of *why* the narrator is presenting his tale.

For it is clear at least, from his very language, that the narrator's 'failure of will' on the fatal evening, expressed in his failure to remove his children after the interval—if not earlier—is not due only to the children's insistence on staying to the end of the performance; it is also a surrender on his own part to the Cavaliere's hypnotic influence. . . . In the context of such an evening, where the concept of the Will is a central concern, to stress that one *wanted* to carry out such and such an action and then to repeat the statement with even more emphasis is to confess a failure to assert one's will which is equivalent to the failed attempt by the Roman gentleman or by the 'Giovanotto' to pit their will against Cipolla's.

Looking back upon this humiliation, the narrator suffers from a bad conscience; so much is clear. But the ostensible reasons for his feelings of irresponsibility, genuine though they are, are only a part of the story. They are the kind of feelings which it would be appropriate to explain to the reader in rather old-fashioned, pre-Nietzschean terms: 'You see, dear reader, how even so concerned a parent was drawn against his will down into the power of that awful other Will. . . .' Certainly, what we are seeing is a recollection, not in tranquillity but in continuing anguish, of 'the [European] liberal mind in the grip of the demagogue's will', and hence of the European liberal exposing his infant charges to the ultimate horror of the Enlightenment, the betrayal of a sacred pedagogic trust. But are there not suggestions that the narrator's guilt lies deeper? For all we know, he alone in Cipolla's audience is fully initiated into the mysteries of the Magician's uncanny art. . . . (pp. 382-85)

'Mind-reading' (or the appearance of it), along with hypnotism, is a central manœuvre in Cipolla's performance, and it is unlikely to be an accident that a writer as supremely self-aware as Thomas Mann allows his narrator to draw attention to the same gift in its more conventional artistic guise: the insight of the artist. Even without this overt reference to the artist's penetration of the reader's mind, however, the cleverly-built-up effects and intensification of the story's atmosphere betray the superior artistic will at work to draw the reader into the narrator's (ultimately, of course, Thomas Mann's) power. There is no art disguised as artlessness here. In other words, if it is a commonplace to classify the Magician (Cipolla) as a kind of demonic artist, it is not much less apparent that the artist-narrator is a kind of magician in his own right. The secret affinity between artiste and artist is no doubt all the more embarrassing for this particular narrator, in view of his bourgeois claims to a superior educated culture and morality. (pp. 385-86)

Rather as in the case of Aschenbach in **"Der Tod in Venedig,"** the narrator of **"Mario und der Zauberer"** is placed in the schizophrenic position of being set up as a model, and yet undermining this role by his own privileged and subversive insight into the illicit. In the case of **"Mario und der Zauberer,"** the narrator's schizophrenia is manifest in the paradox of what amounts to a warning against himself . . . , while he is also warning against the likes of Cipolla. At the same time, a related complexity is that the Novelle cannot help being a demonstration of the 'aesthetic opportunist' at work 'to whom the aesthetic success of his sentences is bound to matter more than the success of the moral or political opinions those sentences may advocate'. The civic virtues claimed by the narrator in his parental role and his stance of Guardian (in a wider metaphorical sense) are at odds with his neutral, not to say irresponsible, aesthetic drive to produce a 'performance' of his own that does justice to the fascinating performance of his fellow-artist, Cipolla. (p. 386)

If as an *artist*—or a representative of the artist in Thomas Mann—the narrator is undependable because of his ability to defer moral judgements beyond normal tolerance, it must be noted that as a *citizen* he is also undermined, by the prevailing deterioration in political attitudes: that is, by nationalism.

The stifling and oppressive (in both the political and the meteorological senses) atmosphere begins at an early stage to loosen the narrator's self-control. The Cipolla evening brings to a head the process of deterioration visible in his mood. Like the Lord of Misrule of the Roman Saturnalia, the Magician (referred to as 'der Herr des Abends') helps the audience to discard its normal inhibitions, a process begun by the regressive influence of chauvinism. The climax of the evening sees almost the whole assembly tirelessly dancing to Cipolla's command, in blissful unconsciousness. As George Orwell said, one of the aims of totalitarianism is not merely to make sure that people will think the right thoughts but actually to make them less *conscious;* this is exactly the course taken by Cipolla's gradually-increasing power over his audience. The preordained fate of the original Roman Lord of Misrule, in his earliest, primitive incarnation, is that he is put to death after the festivities. The nightmare of the modern version encountered in **"Mario und der Zauberer"** is that barring accidents, only the tyrant himself seems in a position to bring the spell to an end. The 'guardian' role of the narrator thus becomes irrelevant. Having been caught up from the beginning in the atmosphere which produces the climax of Cipolla's performance, the narrator emerges as one of the symptoms of the malaise represented by Cipolla instead of as a possible protector against it. It is no wonder that he displays ambiguous feelings about the outcome, the very much *un*preordained shooting of Cipolla. He does not have the clear conscience that would allow him to ally himself with this apparently liberating act.

The earliest infectious symptoms revealed in the story have to do with the nationalism of an international holiday resort, and are summed up in the near-oxymoron of 'patriotic children'. A *Flaggenzwist* among the children on the beach reflects the regression and infantilism of competing European nationalisms while at the same time making a point about the adult world's dereliction of moral duty (prefiguring the same dereliction on the part of the narrator as a parent later), nowhere more evident than in the ideological corruption it has passed on to youth. Despite his air of urbane liberalism, the narrator is not immune to the prevailing nationalist infection:

as witness his attitude to Italy and the Italians, which can at best only be called patronizing.

The first impression created by the narrator, however, is that he places the barrier of his educated culture between himself and the world, in a manner both condescending and ironic (an impression frequently created by Thomas Mann himself). He addresses and reasons with an implied reader who shares his values, and he employs the impersonal form 'man' in *ancien régime* style with the unconscious assumption of superiority befitting a member of the tone-setting leisured class. . . . In itself, this tone of one who discerningly selects for himself and his the best pickings of the earth has a hubristic ring about it, which gives the story's development an edge of poetic justice by demonstrating that the privileged tourist is not wearing some kind of *Tarnhelm* that protects him against the reality of local events. (The story is, in fact, an early recognition of the existence of a 'global village'. We are all reluctant cosmopolitans now.) The narrator mistakes his command of irony for command of the situation he finds himself in (or retrospectively tries to impose his command by irony). The manoeuvre is evident as early as the incident where the Roman princess displaces the narrator's family from the Grand Hotel, a setback he masters, retrospectively at least, by means of an irony as patrician as the aristocrats themselves. (pp. 390-91)

Nationalism is not a source or an indicator of strength but a revelation of weakness. To go further, nationalism is indeed a *compensation* for weakness. The key to the readiness of the audience at Cipolla's show to identify with this unappealing character lies, it has been suggested, in the fact that 'whereas the audience is made up of individuals whose bravado conceals weakness and uncertainty about their identity, Cipolla appears to be a personification of weakness transformed into strength'. Here is a connexion between the artist's psychological make-up and contemporary psycho-political phenomena which helps to explain Thomas Mann's/the narrator's involvement in and sensitivity to the atmosphere of nationalism. It is disturbing for the artist to see in operation around him the mechanism which is at work in himself to *make* him an artist: 'weakness transformed into strength'. Cipolla is a grotesque, caricature version of the process commonly observed in Mann's artist-figures. His apparent self-confidence is a front which hides resentments, and the imposition of his will on others obviously a compensation for his misbegotten physical shape. . . . The crippled artist's envy of ordinary, healthy life (one notes the healthy teeth of the Torre fishermen) recalls a milder version, Tonio Kröger's 'sanfte Rache' through art as a critical reply to life. Cipolla's physical deformity is only an extreme formulation of the link between art and disease, of intellectual or artistic powers both bred by and compensating for physical or psychological deficiencies. Like a positive mirror-image of Cipolla, Tonio Kröger had productively rather than destructively sublimated his failure to gain the affection of Hans Hansen or Ingeborg Holm by developing and living from his love for 'normal' people collectively, a curious but working blend of concrete and abstract. . . . In a negative reflection of Tonio's symbiotic relationship to the ordinary reader he cannot do without, Cipolla woos, seduces, and dominates a whole audience, where he cannot relate in human terms to any one individual. Cipolla is a projection of his audience: he feeds on (and feeds—note the ingenious ways he finds to introduce nationalistic elements into his act) their prejudices and reflects their comic pride and their *machismo:* the latter in spite of the fact that like other Mann artists, Cipolla shows androgynous or homosexual tendencies, as in the last few minutes of his life when he illicitly harvests a kiss from Mario by 'disguising' himself, through hypnotism, as the loved one he can never be in his own right.

Morally, the worst effect achieved by his act is the display of his utter contempt for, and attempt to destroy, the very basis of individuality, of the ego itself. His own *Selbstgefühl* is a façade, supported by props like the cigarettes and strong spirits he continually indulges in, and he will not rest content until he has exposed to ridicule the flimsy egos of his audience. . . . Lurking behind Cipolla's outright assault upon the very foundations of individual identity there is a hint of the most insidious 'thoughtcrime' to which Thomas Mann's patrician artist-figures are prone: the condescending assumption that the ordinary citizen, lacking the artist's powers of self-reflection, also lacks anything worthy to be called an 'identity' or selfhood and is merely the raw material upon which the creative spirit works to fulfil his urge to form. This is the temptation to which Tonio Kröger almost gives way, and the reason for his renewed pledge of attachment to 'ordinary' humanity at the end of the Novelle. Why else would he need to make such a pledge? The artist is symbiotically dependent on his raw material, and the reverse of his latent arrogance towards it, the punishment that fits the 'thoughtcrime', is that *without* love for ordinary mortals the artist is left in a narcissistic, even solipsistic world in which he too forfeits his identity for lack of any authentic and concrete 'other', an object to which he as subject can relate. (pp. 393-95)

The revenge of the material out of which Cipolla has shaped his evening comes through the action of Mario, as though in direct repudiation both of Cipolla's and of the narrator's underestimation of ordinary people, particularly 'die Stillen im Lande'. Mario, whom the narrator has previously regarded as just one among the collection of colourful ethnics who form the audience, most surprisingly lives up to his heroic name after all. Cipolla and the narrator have in common an antipathy to ignorance which is both nationalistic and cultural. At that late point in the story when attention finally turns to Mario, the narrator questions the degree of comprehension the waiter is capable of bringing to the evening's events. . . . If his understanding is limited, this may be a positive advantage, for the narrator's own knowledgeable ability to locate the display of hypnotism within a context is clearly not what Mario needs to precipitate his effective revolt against Cipolla. His role as a waiter, a 'Ganymede', appears to give him more protection. There is something in the description of him that recalls the biblical spirit of 'in [His] service is perfect freedom'. He has learned a kind of inner freedom and detachment because of, and not despite, his habit of obeying commands: something which is concealed, untouched by his menial public role. Unlike the intellectual narrator, whose situation of vulnerability is almost the opposite of his own, he has a citadel, a well-prepared position to fall back on. Not, of course, that one could rely on all waiters to react in the same way. But there is in Mario a combination of characteristic sensitivity and a particular emotional state: unrequited love and deadly rivalry. There is a positive contrast between his reserve and the self-assertion of such as the Roman gentleman or the Giovanotto which serves only to reveal their underlying weakness and sense of threat. . . . His decent self-respect is far removed from his contemporaries' arrogance, and he is clearly well able to draw the line between what is

due to his customers and what he has a right to reserve to himself. Like Frau Angolieri, whose *idée fixe* about the splendours of her past, when she was a close companion of Eleonora Duse, provides Cipolla with an easy handle to her psyche, Mario is perhaps rendered vulnerable by being despairingly in love; but this state of mind also gives him an area of private and personal integrity to protect, metaphorically a 'Torre di Venere'. Love, even if unrequited, appears to be (unlike Frau Angolieri's self-love, contained in her nostalgia) a creative principle to oppose to Cipolla's sickly destructive one.

It is true, of course, that Mario's mind also harbours *destructive* thoughts: a fixation upon revenge against his apparently successful rival, the Giovanotto, which explains why he is carrying the fateful pistol on this particular evening, when he can be quite certain of encountering his opponent. But when he turns the weapon not upon the latter but upon Cipolla, it appears that he is wittingly or unwittingly striking a blow on behalf of something more than simply hurt pride. It is a matter of the restoration of order: not the 'law and order' for which the Fascist state is famous (but which has nothing to do with morality, for it has allowed Cipolla's performance to take place unhindered) but the redressing of a moral balance. It is as though Mario has realized, or has instinctively grasped, that Cipolla embodies a far more significant enemy ranged against him—in his role as a representative of the ordinary, average, and human—than the rival suitor who is merely the embodiment of his *personal* disappointment. Mario's action has the enviable quality of being simple, human, and un-Hamlet-like. Vicariously, the narrator, too, is enabled by this action to cut through all the complications of this evening and his recounting of it and to give an apparently unambiguous answer to the children's question. . . . It is a highly ambiguous ending, suggesting at least two levels of interpretation: the reluctance of the liberal humanist to sanction the murder even of one who does not respect human life, and the guilty conscience of the intellectual/artist who has explored what his liberal politics tells him is forbidden territory and will never truly be 'befreit' from an experience which spoke to the dark places of his own mind. What *is* unambiguously demonstrated is that in the hands of the artist the relationship between insight and political responsibility is sufficiently complex to make him an unreliable guide when it comes to a political crisis. Yet it was as such a guide that Thomas Mann bravely set up shop after his progress from the position of the 'unpolitical' artist. It was by the *force majeure* of a German defeat that he became 'political' after 1918, and by another superior force that his politics became marginalized. . . . In **"Mario und der Zauberer"** there seems to be an implicit idealistic hope that if humanity is shown an unbearable disrespect there will be an equal and opposite reaction to defend the citadel of humanity from alien encroachments. Yet the hope which raises Mario out of his anonymity to become the moral agent of Nemesis is the exact opposite of our knowledge, in this second half of the century, of how easy it is to be plunged into anonymity. The photograph albums of surviving relatives all over the world are full of commonplace snapshots of uncles, aunts, children, and parents who are impossible (in every sense) to identify with those lemures, the indistinguishable denizens of Auschwitz and Treblinka.

But the optimistic and idealistic message, if such there is, is in any case subordinate to the Novelle's other focus: the equally implicit statement that the moral and the aesthetic domains are no longer one, if they ever were. Cipolla's performance is clearly an image of the Fascist leader's aestheticizing of politics. He who is at home in the world of aesthetic *Schein* is not well able to hold a moral position in the face of the aestheticizing of the world around him. Thomas Mann's perception of the ironies which bedevil the relationship between literature and social responsibility contrives to show him up still for what by instinct he always was, but by conviction latterly was not: an unpolitical man. The shift of convictions enabled and obliged him to tackle political subjects, nowhere more evidently than in **"Mario und der Zauberer,"** but he does so indirectly, in the only way that was natural to him.

"Mario und der Zauberer" certainly has a great deal to offer as an analysis of the psychological factors underlying historical developments. Anthony Grenville's recent comparison of this story with Brecht's play *Der aufhaltsame Aufstieg des Arturo Ui* (1941), which enjoyed the benefit of an extra ten years of hindsight and a Marxist model of interpretation claiming total explanatory power, concludes that Mann's more indirect and limited treatment of the phenomenon of the dictator-figure has more to offer the historian than Brecht's monocausal materialist approach. Yet at the same time, as I have attempted to indicate, Thomas Mann's interests are further from the historian's than those of an ideological writer like Brecht. . . . The colossal egoism of the artist is still in evidence in **"Mario und der Zauberer,"** as it must be if Thomas Mann is to remain true to his chief and abiding concerns. The problems of the artist—according to this egoistic view—happen to have been writ large in the demonic figure of the Magician (or Hitler), and therefore Thomas Mann has some special insights to offer into this phenomenon. But he cannot do so except through his own literary—artistic medium, thus working once more the magic whose demonic and extreme version he is at pains to analyse in Cipolla's performance: neither can he do so without revealing through the narrator the natural limits imposed, by his dubious existence as an artist, upon him in his other, enforced role as moral guardian. Moreover, the narrator as citizen, for all his breadth of culture and his reasoning power, reveals himself to be as helplessly drawn into the sphere of Cipolla's magic as the others around him are. When the day is saved by the hero, Mario, it is an outcome which can do little at a deeper level to comfort the intellectual or the artist. That is the brutally honest and historically very pertinent thought with which Thomas Mann leaves us. His narrator is a part of the malaise which he deplores. (pp. 395-98)

> *A. F. Bance, "The Narrator in Thomas Mann's 'Mario und der Zauberer'," in* The Modern Language Review, *Vol. 82, No. 2, April, 1987, pp. 382-98.*

FURTHER READING

Auden, W. H. "Lame Shadows." In *Forewords and Afterwords by W. H. Auden,* edited by Edward Mendelson, pp. 404-10. New York: Random House, 1973.

Discusses H. T. Lowe-Porter's translations of Thomas Mann's works.

Basilius, H. A. "Thomas Mann's Use of Musical Structure and Techniques in 'Tonio Kröger'." *The Germanic Review* XIX, No. 4 (December 1944): 284-308.

Suggests that "Tonio Kröger" is an example of Mann's habitual "literarization" of music.

Beharriell, Frederick J. "Psychology in the Early Works of Thomas Mann." *PMLA* LXXVII, No. 1 (March 1962): 149-55.

Comments on the influence of Freudian psychoanalytic theory in Mann's early stories.

Benet, Stephen Vincent and Rosemary. "Thomas Mann: Honored by the Free World." *New York Herald Tribune Books* 17, No. 44 (29 June 1941): 6, 12.

Overview of Mann's life and work.

Bolkosky, Sidney. "Thomas Mann's 'Disorder and Early Sorrow': The Writer as Social Critic." *Contemporary Literature* 22, No. 2 (Spring 1981): 218-33.

Discusses the relationship between Mann's political views and his fiction.

Brown, Calvin S. "Fiction and the Leitmotiv." In his *Music and Literature: A Comparison of the Arts,* pp. 208-18. Athens, Ga.: University of Georgia Press, 1948.

Discusses the reciprocal interaction between literature and music, commenting on Mann's use of the leitmotiv in "Tonio Kröger."

Diller, Edward. "The Grotesque Animal-Heroes of Thomas Mann's Early Works." *German Life & Letters* XX (April 1967): 225-33.

Examines the significance of physical deformities among the artist figures in Mann's early short stories.

Ezergailis, Inta. "Spinell's Letter: An Approach to Thomas Mann's 'Tristan'." *German Life & Letters* XXV, No. 4 (July 1972): 377-82.

Analysis of the story "Tristan" as a self-contained work, focusing on a letter written by the character Detlev Spinell to his opponent Klöterjahn.

Fleissner, R. F. "The Balking Staircase and the Transparent Door: Prufrock and Kröger." *The Comparatist* VIII (May 1984): 21-32.

Compares themes and characterization in T. S. Eliot's "The Waste Land" and Thomas Mann's "Tonio Kröger."

Hannum, Hunter G. "Archetypal Echoes in Mann's 'Death in Venice'." *Psychological Perspectives* 5, No. 1 (Spring 1974): 48-59.

Discusses the patterns of Jungian theory in the works of Goethe, Hesse, and Mann.

Hatfield, Henry. "Thomas Mann and America." *Salmagundi,* Nos. 10-11 (Fall 1969-Winter 1970): 174-85.

Comments on the significance of Thomas Mann's emigration to the United States.

Heller, Erich. *Thomas Mann: The Ironic German.* Cleveland: World Publishing Co., 1961, 303 p.

Comprehensive critical study of Mann's literary techniques.

Hoffmann, Ernst Fedor. "Thomas Mann's 'Gladius Dei'." *PMLA* 83, No. 5 (October 1968): 1353-61.

Analysis of the structure and themes of "Gladius Dei."

Mertens, Gerard M. "Hemingway's 'Old Man and the Sea' and Mann's 'The Black Swan'." *Literature and Psychology* VI, No. 3 (August 1956): 96-9.

Discusses similarities of symbol and theme in these stories.

Oliver, Clinton F. "Hemingway's 'The Killers' and Mann's 'Disorder and Early Sorrow'." In *Thirty-Eight Short Stories: An Introductory Anthology,* edited by Michael Timko and Clinton F. Oliver, pp. 69-86. New York: Alfred A. Knopf, 1968.

Focuses on the similar disenchantment and psychological frustration experienced by the protagonists in these two stories.

Rey, W. H. "Tragic Aspects of the Artist in Thomas Mann's Work." *Modern Language Quarterly* 19, No. 3 (September 1958): 195-203.
    Examines the development of Mann's concept of the artist in his fiction.

Root, John G. "Stylistic Irony in Thomas Mann." *The Germanic Review* XXXV, No. 2 (April 1960): 93-103.
    Discusses Mann's subtle use of irony throughout his fiction.

Schwarz, Egon. "Fascism and Society: Remarks on Thomas Mann's Novella 'Mario and the Magician'." *Michigan Germanic Studies* II, No. 1 (Spring 1976): 47-67.
    Examines "Mario and the Magician" from a sociological perspective.

Traschen, Isadore. "The Uses of Myth in 'Death in Venice'." *Modern Fiction Studies* XI, No. 2 (Summer 1965): 165-79.
    Suggests that "Death in Venice" is structured on the Appollonian-Dionysian myth.

Woodward, Anthony. "The Figure of the Artist in Thomas Mann's 'Tonio Kröger' and 'Death in Venice'." *English Studies in Africa* 9, No. 2 (September 1966): 158-67.
    Examines the origins and development of Mann's artist characters.

Yourcenar, Marguerite. "Humanism in Thomas Mann." Translated by Grace Frick. *Partisan Review* XXIII, No. 2 (Spring 1956): 153-70.
    Discusses the style and major themes of Mann's fiction.

Frank O'Connor

1903-1966

(Pseudonym of Michael O'Donovan) Irish short story writer, critic, novelist, autobiographer, poet, and editor.

Credited with bringing international attention to the modern Irish short story, O'Connor is renowned for his realistic portrayals of Irish provincial life and his detached yet sympathetic humor. O'Connor believed that the short story should be "the literature of submerged population groups" and should "stimulate the moral imagination." Consequently, he focuses in his works on characters who have been ostracized by society and dramatizes their attempts to overcome loneliness and attain individuality. O'Connor's stories usually pivot on conflicts these characters experience as they try to escape the restrictions of family, church, and country. Drawing on the Irish oral storytelling tradition of the *shanachie,* O'Connor captures in his writing the essence of Irish character and speech without sacrificing universality. The result is an engaging and highly readable style of fiction that has earned a large, devoted following.

O'Connor grew up in extreme poverty in Cork, Ireland, the only son of Michael and Minnie O'Donovan. His father was a laborer whose alcoholism wreaked emotional and financial havoc on his family. As a result, O'Connor formed an intimate relationship with his mother, who encouraged him to read and protected him from his father's drunken rage. O'Connor's deep love for his mother and his jealousy of the love and understanding she showed toward his father became the subject of many of his stories. O'Connor's lonely childhood, stemming from his unathletic, bookish nature in an environment hostile toward education, led him to recognize loneliness as a pervasive condition of existence, a theme that appears throughout his work. Although forced to leave school at age 14 due to his family's penury, O'Connor continued his studies on his own, haphazardly immersing himself in literature, politics, and Gaelic language and culture. The influence of Daniel Corkery, an Irish author, nationalist, and former teacher of O'Connor's, was crucial in shaping his political sympathies and sparking his interest in nineteenth-century Russian literature. In 1918 under Corkery's guidance, O'Connor joined the Irish Republican Army, where he met noted writer Sean O'Faolain and fought in the civil war. Although a treaty ending the war was signed in 1921, O'Connor and the Republicans continued fighting to include the province of Ulster in the new Irish Free State. O'Connor was subsequently arrested and imprisoned for nearly a year by the Free State government for his part in the struggles.

During the 1930s, O'Connor became involved in the Irish Literary Renaissance that was striving to produce a distinctly Irish literature. The writers of this nationalistic movement endeavored to revive in their fellow citizens an awareness of Ireland's rich history and colorful mythology. During this time, O'Connor began contributing stories to the *Irish Statesman,* a magazine that served as the focal point of literature in Ireland. The *Statesman* was edited by George Russell, also known as AE, who was one of O'Connor's strongest advocates and best friends. Russell introduced O'Connor to many leading figures of the Irish literary society and Abbey Theatre

Company in Dublin, including W. B. Yeats, Sean O'Casey, and Lady Gregory. With Yeats, O'Connor served as director of the Abbey Theatre from 1935 until 1939, when he left because of a dispute over censorship. During the 1940s, a number of O'Connor's books were officially banned by the Irish government. He left Ireland in 1951 to lecture and teach at several American universities, although he returned frequently to his homeland until his death in 1966.

O'Connor's early stories, collected in *Guests of the Nation,* center on his experiences in the Anglo-Irish War and the Irish Civil War, also known as The Troubles. Unlike Sean O'Faolain and Liam O'Flaherty, fellow Irish authors who also wrote about The Troubles, O'Connor employs detachment and humor in his war tales. In most of these pieces, he portrays the alienating effect the conflicts have had on ordinary people. The title story, considered a classic of Irish literature and one of O'Connor's best-known works, concerns the fates of two British soldiers who are captured by Irish rebels. In spite of their political differences, the rebels develop a camaraderie with the soldiers, and O'Connor poignantly dramatizes the dilemma that arises when circumstances provoke the rebels to execute their British captives. Several other stories in *Guests of the Nation* veer between romantic idealism and disillusionment about war, while demonstrating the importance of love and humor in relieving the loneliness and estrangement that war engenders.

In *Bones of Contention, and Other Stories,* O'Connor focuses on the Irish peasantry, while experimenting with various narrative techniques. Several pieces in this collection, including "Michael's Wife" and "The Majesty of the Law," center on the common O'Connor theme of loneliness. In such stories as "Peasants," "In the Train," and "The Man That Stopped," O'Connor champions the unruliness of common folk in confrontation with authority. O'Connor's next volume of short stories, *Crab Apple Jelly,* is generally considered his most accomplished. In this work, he continues his exploration of loneliness as the essential condition of humanity, while expanding his range of "submerged population groups" to include priests, teachers, and businessmen. In "Uprooted," O'Connor contrasts the lives of two brothers, a teacher, and a priest, to show the misery caused by choosing a career that contradicts one's natural instincts. In addition, some pieces condemn what O'Connor views as the widespread sexual repression of Irish society. "The Bridal Night," for instance, concerns the attempts of a schoolmistress to calm the fits of a mentally disturbed boy who has fallen in love with her by sleeping with him. When one night the teacher tries to pacify the boy with words rather than sex, he reacts uncontrollably and is committed to an asylum the next morning.

In *The Common Chord,* O'Connor focuses upon the nature of romance among the Irish, chastising their puritanical notions of love and sex. The ignorance and hypocrisy that riddle the relationships in these stories leave their romantic and idealist characters disenchanted. In "The Holy Door," for example, a young man enamored of Shakespeare's *Romeo and Juliet* desires to infuse his own life with passion. He marries an excessively priggish woman, however, and his love life becomes a ludicrous failure. Another story, "Judas," details the conflicts a teenage boy experiences when his love for a young woman endangers his emotional fidelity to his mother. Other stories in this volume examine emotional hardships that afflict priests.

With *Traveller's Samples* and *Domestic Relations,* O'Connor begins to explore more thoroughly childhood and youth, frequently employing as his alter ego the character Larry Delaney to portray difficulties of growing up in Ireland. In several of these stories, O'Connor depicts characters who exhibit an increasing awareness of the drawbacks of championing recklessness and who begin to realize the advantages of prudence. These tales are narrated from the perspective of adults reminiscing about their youth. In "My First Confession," a seven-year-old boy, frightened at the prospect of disclosing his sins, is surprised when the priest shows compassion and assigns him to pray only three Hail Mary's as penance. "My Oedipus Complex" details a boy's fierce competition with his father for his mother's affection. After a second child is born, however, the boy and his father become allies as the mother devotes most of her attention to the infant. *A Set of Variations,* which consists of stories mainly written in the 1960s, features several pieces that document troubled marriages, while others concern the plight of priests contending with loneliness and death.

Generally regarded as one of Ireland's most important short story writers, O'Connor is celebrated for his illuminating depictions of Irish provincial life and his revitalization of the oral storytelling tradition. While some critics have faulted O'Connor's stories for superficiality and a tendency toward sentimentality, most agree that they skillfully blend humor and pathos to delineate the experiences of people living on the fringes of society. Eschewing symbolism and artifice, O'Connor wrote in a fluid, clear, realistic style, which he believed was the best way to communicate with "the individual, solitary, critical reader," who he felt was his ideal audience. Although the scope of O'Connor's work is primarily local, many critics maintain that it is universal in its understanding and portrayal of human nature.

(For further information on O'Connor's life and career, see *Contemporary Literary Criticism,* Vols. 14, 23 and *Contemporary Authors,* Vols. 93-96.)

PRINCIPAL WORKS

SHORT FICTION

Guests of the Nation 1931
Bones of Contention, and Other Stories 1936
Crab Apple Jelly 1944
Selected Stories 1946
The Common Chord 1947
Traveller's Samples 1951
The Stories of Frank O'Connor 1952
More Stories by Frank O'Connor 1954
Domestic Relations: Short Stories 1957
My Oedipus Complex, and Other Stories 1963
A Set of Variations 1969
Collected Stories 1981
The Cornet Player Who Betrayed Ireland 1981

OTHER MAJOR WORKS

The Saint and Mary Kate (novel) 1932
Three Old Brothers, and Other Poems (poetry) 1936
Dutch Interior (novel) 1940
Towards an Appreciation of Literature (criticism) 1945
The Mirror in the Roadway: A Study of the Modern Novel (criticism) 1956
An Only Child (autobiography) 1961
The Lonely Voice: A Study of the Short Story (criticism) 1963
The Backward Look: A Survey of Irish Literature (criticism) 1967
My Father's Son (autobiography) 1968

THE TIMES LITERARY SUPPLEMENT (essay date 1944)

[*In the following excerpt from a generally favorable review of* Crab Apple Jelly, *the anonymous critic praises O'Connor's evocative portraits of Irish life.*]

The twelve Irish stories in Mr. Frank O'Connor's *Crab Apple Jelly* are very Irish indeed, and the rash thought occurs to an un-Celtic mind to try to explain how and why. W. B. Yeats, we are told, said that "O'Connor is doing for Ireland what Chekhov did for Russia." That may be so; there is a likeness, at all events, in that in writing as he does for the most part about the way of life of the Irish peasantry Mr. O'Connor keeps closely to an observant realism while seeking to distil the poetic essentials of their experience. Take **"The Long Road to Ummera,"** which is about an old, decrepit woman, most of whose life has been spent in the town, who is all but half-wittedly intent on going back to die and be buried in the tiny village in the Cork mountains where she was born. . . .

To her son, a prosperous shopkeeper in the town, Ummera stands for the hunger and misery they came from; her sudden threat to haunt him if he will not take her back there when her time comes belongs to the foolishness of fairies and spells. But the mumbling old woman is implacable in her demand that she shall not leave her bones among strangers:—

> I brought you from it, boy, and you must bring me back. If 'twas the last shilling you had, and you and your children to go to the poorhouse after, you must bring me back to Ummera. And not by the short road either! Mind what I say now! The long road! The long road to Ummera round the lake, the way I brought you from it. I lay a heavy curse on you this night if you bring me the short road over the hill. And ye must stop by the ash tree at the foot of the boreen where ye can see my little house and say a prayer for all that were ever old in it and all that played on the floor.

The tale is beautifully told, accurately, humorously and with delicate economy of words. Its poetic realism, if that is what it should be called, is not, of course, specifically Irish or specifically anything else; it might be said, indeed, above all with Chekhov in mind, that the modern short story always aspires to the condition of poetry. But there is, nevertheless, a quality of sentiment or style in this story of **"The Long Road to Ummera,"** as in almost every other in the volume, that may be described as peculiarly Irish. This is the flow of imaginative temperament which belongs to the Irish story-teller, which indeed seems to belong to Irish life.

Almost every one of Mr. O'Connor's twelve stories brings into view a way of peasant or small-town life rooted in seclusion, poverty, religion, drink, a sense of Irish locality—and a truly inimitable gift of narration. His is a tang of warm and vivid life because so often his characters, so to speak, do the imaginative work for him; they themselves, since they are Irish, are born story-tellers. And it is the expressiveness of their fantasy, a fantasy that is quickened by a historic sense of community and is always very near the bone, which gives an Irish realistic writer like Mr. O'Connor his poetic appeal. At one end of the Irish imaginative scale is Synge; at the other is mere literary blarney, all too often with the misty shapes and shadows of the Celtic twilight upon it. In between lies the danger for the faithful observer of the Irish scene of finding charm and poetry in nothing more than a native instability of temperament.

Mr. O'Connor, in some of the later stories, notably the last of all, **"The Mad Lomasneys,"** does not wholly avoid the danger. And in one or two of them, such as **"The House that Johnny Built,"** he is content to rely for his effect upon a superficially lively trick of Irish dialogue. But elsewhere he is remarkably sure and alert in observation, by turns touching and wickedly comic. In the first and legend-haunted story in the volume, **"The Bridal Night,"** in which an old woman in a lonely place by the sea tells how her son went out of his mind through love of a stranger, Mr. O'Connor makes it plainer perhaps than anywhere else why only an Irish Nationalist writer could write as he does.

> *"Irish Road," in* The Times Literary Supplement, *No. 2205, May 6, 1944, p. 221.*

PATRICK KAVANAGH   (essay date 1947)

[*Kavanagh was an Irish poet, novelist, and critic, noted for his bitter depictions of Irish peasant life and his irascible attitude toward the English-speaking literary establishment. In the following excerpt from a controversial essay originally published in 1947, he assesses O'Connor's short fiction and concludes that it is finely crafted entertainment, but lacks the substantial content necessary for enduring art.*]

As I pursue [O'Connor] I am continually losing the trail. Has he a direction? His feet are too seldom on the earth for me to follow. Is he merely a high-flying entertainer? Does his work hold the mirror up to life? Does he mean anything?

All these questions can only be answered by an examination of O'Connor's work. He began as a poet and his first book, published in 1931 by the Cuala Press, was comprised of translations from the Gaelic. This very fact that he began as a translator is somewhat of a key to his work—that his technical and imaginative machinery is greater than his material. For, like a great actor who is useless without a theme, O'Connor is inclined to be futile when left with only his own experience. (p. 42)

O'Connor has written two novels but his reputation is rightly founded on his short stories. The first collection of his short stories to be published was *Guests of the Nation* based on his experiences in the Civil War. These stories touch the earth at more points than any of his other work, and yet for all that they lack a very vivid detail. Granted that O'Connor is right in his protest against Corkery's claim that writing should be merely representative, is there enough poetic excitement and vitality in these stories to compensate for the dimness of the representation? He seems to me to fall between two stools. He is neither on the safe earth nor among the stars. What makes his work deceptive is the fact that he is very nearly on the earth. He is—as it were—about an inch from the top of the grass. . . . *Guests Of The Nation* has in lieu of real blood a good deal of the treacle of sentimentality. . . . (pp. 43-4)

The title story in *Guests Of The Nation* reveals the O'Connor to come. The main characters, two English soldiers held as hostages by the I.R.A. to be executed, are a pair of cliché sentimental characters—the dumb good-natured Englishmen. They evoke our maudlin pity. What is worse, they evoke the author's pity; he himself weeps over their deaths and in this he lacks the courage and integrity of the great artist.

> I alone of the crowd saw Donovan raise his Webley to the back of 'Awkin' neck, and as he did so I shut my eyes and tried to say a prayer. 'Awkins had begun to say something when Donovan let fly, and as I opened my eyes at the bang, I saw him stagger at the knees and lie out flat at Noble's feet, slowly and as quiet as a child, with the lantern light falling sadly upon his lean legs and bright farmer's boots. We all stood still for a while watching him settle out in his last agony.

The fact that the story is told through a third party, a participant in the affair, does not excuse the author making him take sides in the tragedy. The whole thing makes us sick and unbelieving. Neither is the vivid detail which lights up the whole scene present. There are too many words, too much "literature," and the final effect is enervation.

The house among the mountains where the hostages are being held and where they all sit around playing cards is seen only vaguely. The story gives the impression that the author had only got one look at the place and wasn't deeply impressed. The authentic note is seldom struck. Everything is partly believable in and there is its danger. (p. 44)

In some of these stories there is a charming poetic atmosphere, but even it is always half and half. You cannot damn it without being wrong and you cannot praise without being equally wrong. (p. 45)

[O'Connor] has hardly ever written a story that is not entertaining. He has hardly ever written a story that does not bear some resemblance to reality. But as in his novels and other work there is a "kitchening" of the material, a tentativeness. He is a showman, getting the laughs where he can, but from the more serious point of view purposeless. His second collection of short stories called *Bones of Contention* has a number of very enjoyable pieces. **"The Majesty of The Law"** is a burlesque as brilliant as O'Kelly's "Weaver's Grave." An old man who has cracked a neighbour's skull is waiting to go to jail to spite a neighbour whose "wake, wandering, watery eyes" are looking down on the scene. This is the best of comedy, and like the majority of comic writing it is detached—from Life. The main character is a lie, the sort of good-natured myth which makes good-natured fools, open-mouthed, uncritical, say: "Aren't these Irish charming?" The author is in that particular mood which most of us have experienced to our spiritual cost in which we are being corrupted by our audience. On such occasions a mob's collective lie is in our mouths.

I have heard O'Connor compared to Chekov. No two writers could be more unlike. Chekov's genius is the cutting edge of sincerity ruthlessly piercing through the crust of the ordinary. His courageous poetic mind is never the slave of his audience. (pp. 46-7)

One of the best stories in *Bones of Contention* is **"In The Train."** This is about a group of people who are returning from a court trial:

> "Ah, Delancey is a poor slob," said the sergeant affectionately.
>
> "Oh, yes, but that's not enough, Jonathan. Slob or no slob he should make an attempt. He's a young man; he should have a dinner-jacket at least. What sort of wife will he get if he won't even wear a dinner-jacket?"
>
> "He's easy, I'd say. He's after a farm in Waterford."
>
> "Oh, a farm! A farm! The wife is only an incidental, I suppose?"

There you have O'Connor "on the cod" with his characters. I feel as I read that he has never allowed himself to be involved in the lives of these people. He is an outsider even more than Synge was in this thing. It is the prudent mind carefully spreading the material thin. This is pure fiction, an invention. Relating it to life what would the crude unliterary self in us say? We would say that it was great fun but meant nothing as a revelation of life.

"First Confession" is a popular story, but sentimental. I would say that O'Faolain even when he appears anti-clerical is much nearer to the Catholic mind. Throughout all O'Connor's stories I am being continually mesmerised by the easy hum-hum of the narrative. Sometimes he says things which may shock, but they are artificial shocks as when he

takes pleasure in the weakness of human beings. The creative shock of truth revealed is a different thing. His next collection of stories is *Crab Apple Jelly,* and it is a very jelly-like book.

One of the stories is called **"Bridal Night"** and is about a girl who went to bed with a madman to cure him:

> "And wasn't it a strange and wonderful thing? From that day to the day she left us there did no one speak a bad word about what she did, and the people couldn't do enough for her. Isn't it a strange thing and the world as wicked as it is that no one would say the bad word about her?"

I agree that the action of the girl does throw some light on human nature, but the reactions of the people to her, as O'Connor presents them, are just nonsense. It is too abnormal, a "special" case. Dostoieffsky's supposed abnormalities are merely intensities of the normal, but here we are dealing with the aberrations of disease. This story seems phoney and in keeping with the Synge-like style. The principal story in this book is the **"Long Road to Ummera,"** a frightfully sentimental account of an old woman's wish to be buried in her native place.

> Always in the evenings you saw her shuffle up the road to Miss O's for her little jug of porter, a shapeless lump of an old woman in a plaid shawl faded to the colour of snuff that dragged her head down on to her bosom. . . .

That is really the limit of treacly sentimentality. She just sickens me. As sticky as Marie Corelli.

Another story is about a pious old fraud and what the New Teacher thought about him:

> "Extraordinary man," said Sam. "Extraordinary blooming man making a will like that."
>
> "He was," agreed Johnnie, a bit doubtfully. "Of course he was always very religious."
>
> "He was," said Sam airily, "particularly with Children of Mary."
>
> "That so?" said Johnnie, as if he had never heard of a Child of Mary before.

I am afraid I find an implied sneer, an insincerity, in this. A great poet never sneers. He may show people sneering but he does not take part in it as the author of this seems to take part. You cannot satirise fraudulent piety unless you stand on some dogmatic centre of truth. This is necessary even as a hypothesis. In so far as O'Connor has a centre it is in his unholy laughter which is fairly constant.

It would be hard to overpraise the skill with which the stories in O'Connor's latest book, *The Common Chord,* are composed. Yet, these sexy stories are utterly unreal. How often as I read did I wish that the author could have thrown in a few spadefuls of the earth's healthy reality—roots, stones, worms, dung. In this patch intelligence could grow. It will be observed that the greatest writers never take themselves seriously—only their work. O'Connor takes himself seriously but his characters lightly. A Calvinistic leer grins from every page. O'Connor's Nora Lalor's, Tim O'Regan's, etc., are not people but silly "attitudes" which are to be found less in Ireland than in a war-hysterical England, and their intellectual level is that of the gossip columns of the *Daily Mirror.*

Passing an interim judgment on O'Connor I find that he is

a purveyor of emotional entertainment, and that he has surrendered to this minor rôle. There is tension in his mind but most of this tension is expended on the construction of the container so that there is little left for the contents. He is like a powerful engine drawing a light load. The same is true of many writers who have achieved great contemporary fame—Joyce is a good example. Every generation produces fine technicians, designers, entertainers. But time destroys the tension of the wrapping paper, which their contemporaries mistook for inner excitement, leaving the dusty contents to be blown by the wind. (pp. 47-9)

> Patrick Kavanagh, "Coloured Balloons: A Study of Frank O'Connor," in The Journal of Irish Literature, Vol. VI, No. 1, January, 1977, pp. 40-9.

JAMES STERN (essay date 1948)

[*Stern is an Irish critic, short story writer, editor, and translator. In the review of* The Common Chord *excerpted below, he lauds O'Connor for his insightful delineations of sexual relationships among small-town Irish people.*]

It takes some courage to travel the road O'Connor has chosen in **The Common Chord.** The signpost above it says Sex. Giving that word a broad wink, he rubs his hands with expectation, takes you by the arm, and way with you to the road's most important house, the pub, its most important man, the priest. The men you meet with him in the pub are described in vivid flashes, characteristic of O'Connor. Many are like Ned Lynch, "a decent slob of a man with a fat purple face," whose brother, during "some disagreement about politics . . . had opened up Ned with a poker." Typical of the women you hear consult the priests in the confessional is Nora Lalor, who, "like many of her race . . . combined a strong grasp of the truths of religion with a hazy notion of the facts of life."

The Irish facts of life would probably not interest Mr. Alfred S. Kinsey. What interests O'Connor is not the Sexual Behavior of his Males and Females but the ignorance, the hypocrisy, the intrigues that surround and swamp their grim married lives. Of great importance to his wedded couples is whether or not they have a gossoon or gligeen of a girl to inherit their property. In **"A Thing for Nothing,"** Katty and Ned have a shop, but no child. If Ned (who has a nephew) dies, will he leave Katty the shop? He will not.

> "Why not?" she said, stamping.

> "Because, 'tis an old custom. The property goes with the name."

In **"The Holy Door,"** a complicated story ninety pages long, childless Charlie and Polly travel all the way to Rome. There, listening to the natives "bawling away about love" in cafes, Charlie is reminded of the story of Romeo and Juliet. "It was all damn well for Romeo," he thinks, "but Romeo hadn't to live in an Irish country town." The pilgrimage to Rome is a failure. When, back home, Polly hears of a married woman for whom "everything went smack smooth" after "she imagined her husband was Rudolph Valentino," Polly asks the priest "would it ever be right" for a woman to imagine such a thing?

> "Ah, I don't know that there would be anything wrong about it," said Father Ring. "Provided, of course, that she didn't get any pleasure out of it."

Here is the common chord struck by O'Connor in his latest stories. Some . . . are so tenuously told that a single reading will not reveal all the subtleties of their plots and people, particularly of the important roles played by O'Connor's priests. And of all his large gallery of characters it is Fathers Ring and Foley who are the most human, humane and lovable. O'Connor's compassion for and understanding of their predicament in the face of personal emotion and the strict code of their religion are qualities that in an author call for extraordinary objectivity, a rare sense of justice, and, above all, love for his fellow-men. Such qualities O'Connor possesses to a degree shared, I believe, by no other writer of short stories alive today. (pp. 5, 25)

> James Stern, "More Crab Apple Jelly," in The New York Times Book Review, February 15, 1948, pp. 5, 25.

HORACE REYNOLDS (essay date 1952)

[*In the following excerpt, Reynolds extols* The Stories of Frank O'Connor *for its humorous, affirmative portrayals of Irish life.*]

To understand Mr. O'Connor's skill and power, one must realize something of his difficulties as a writer in Ireland. Ireland is far from the land many American readers of Irish romantic fiction dream it to be. It is a small, poor country with no gangsters, on the one hand, and no Bostonians or Charlestonians, on the other. It is not polyglot and polygenous like America. It is largely a one-class nation. Its puritanical, pietistic clergy has a decisive if unofficial voice in its government, a government which censors the books of all its most distinguished writers, so that its *index expurgatorius* is an unofficial roll of honor, an informal Irish Academy.

Ireland manifests its growing pains, its struggle to become a stratified, integrated nation, in what one Irish writer described to me as "monstrous defenses, loony complexes, and head-in-the-air assurances." All of which makes its life a wild, mad, churning, surge into God alone knows what. The smallness of its reading public is an insidious disadvantage to the Irish writer; it means he is ultimately dependent for his livelihood upon sales to British and American readers. In short, it is a difficult country for a writer to work and live in.

Some of these limitations have their adjunct advantages. They have sent the Irish writer into nunneries and monasteries, places neglected by American writers, whence Mr. O'Connor has come back with the delicate, St. Francis-of-Assisi mood of **"Song Without Words,"** a story of two monks that might have been written by a humorous Browning. . . .

Frank O'Connor probably writes most individually about the lanes of his native Cork. But surely at least three of his most powerful stories [in **The Stories of Frank O'Connor**] are of peasant Ireland. Anyone who has read **"The Long Road to Ummera"** is unlikely to forget its thrust of old age's claw-like tenacity of will into the face of death, with humorous side glances at the fondness of the old for talking of death and the hereafter, because "there are so many more of us there than here."

He has the art of being gleeful and serious in the same moment without either mood destroying the other. Surely **"The Majesty of the Law"** is a masterful presentation of the Irish love of the oblique approach. No story more humorously reveals the curious, history-bred attitude toward law which one finds in Ireland, and with which every individualist is secretly in sympathy.

Mr. O'Connor is most himself in his quiet, richly plaited studies of town life, such pieces as **"Old Fellows," "First Confession"** and **"Don Juan's Temptation,"** with its subtle echo of Joyce's "The Dead." These stories, with here and there a hint of Gaelic oral story-telling in them, demand an attentive reader. Only such can see what the author is about in a story like **"The Masculine Principle."** Here he presents a quietly independent man, a motor mechanic, who thinks things out for himself and acts from his own center of being, a man beholden to nobody, neither to lover, mother, employer, priest or neighbor.

Control is not a conspicuous Irish virtue, but Frank O'Connor has it, and it individualizes his work. It is manifest both in his concentrated, measured dialogue, which frequently, as in **"The Majesty of the Law,"** has the grave balance of the dance, and in the clear, spaced veer of mood to mood in such a story as **"The Masculine Principle."** It is especially manifest in the author's humor. O'Casey comes down front and lets loose grandly with everything he has, letting the laughs fall where they will. O'Connor's humor, in contrast, is usually not only quiet but guided and directed. O'Connor had this control early. It is this restraint which has kept him off the words, a temptation that has spoiled many Irish writers.

In his short stories, Joyce wrote out of contempt for Irish life; O'Connor writes out of love for it. This does not mean that O'Connor is not critical of the lunacies he weaves into artful fantasies. It does mean, however, that he respects his characters. His life has not been an easy one. He has known struggle with poverty; he is self-educated. But there is not a stime of real bitterness in him. His compassion is equal to any provocation. His ironies are never savage. To read him is a major experience, one that can influence the reader's way of life.

The wise and sane stories lift and hold up the heart, because they discover and affirm in terms in which we can believe that life—no matter how thick its complexities and injustices, how harsh its anguish—is fundamentally a gay and worthwhile experience. By adding the glint and twist of Irish humor to Chekhovian insight, Frank O'Connor has given a new voice to the short story in English and made perdurable contributions to its literature.

> Horace Reynolds, "Told Out of a Love for Irish Life," in The New York Times Book Review, August 17, 1952, p. 1.

HELMUT E. GERBER (essay date 1955)

[*Gerber was a German-born American critic and editor who specialized in Anglo-Irish literature. In the excerpt below, he explores the relationship between structure and theme in the story "Uprooted."*]

Frank O'Connor's apparently simple and loosely constructed story on close examination appears complex and tightly organized. First, O'Connor joins the five sections of his story by the common device of the geographical journey. But the journey is also a psychological one that takes the two brothers from sophistication and disillusionment to a brief contact with naturalness, childish wonder, innocence.

Their revelation (V) is painful and, because externalized, also a relief. Both men maturely recognize their problem, and Tom resigns himself to the ways of life. But Ned does not stop at fatalistic resignation.

> There was a magical light on everything. A boy on a horse rose suddenly against the sky, a startling picture. Through the applegreen light over Carriganassa ran long streaks of crimson, so still they might have been enamelled. Magic, magic, magic! He saw it as in a children's picture-book with its colors intolerably bright . . .

Ned, then, accepts his limitations and sublimates the frustrating knowledge to the realm of myth ("magic") and aesthetics ("a startling picture," "apple-green light . . . streaks of crimson . . . enamelled," "a children's picturebook").

O'Connor gives this structure density by saturating the story with conflicts and contrasts. Spring (vitality) contrasts with Ned's exhaustion; Ned's intention "to do wonders" with the fact that "he was as far as ever from that"; and Ned's landlords' dreams about enjoying the city with the fact that "they do not enjoy themselves." The more profound conflicts within Ned are mirrored in his being externally "slow" and cumbrous but inwardly nervous; in his being stubborn but hesitating and shy. Then follows the contrast between shy, serious Ned and his "wild light-hearted, lightheaded" nurse; and between his dream of going to Glasgow or New York and the fact that "all his fancies took flight."

The second section adds other contrasts and conflicts: between Ned and his brother; and between the father (whom Tom resembles) and the mother (whom Ned resembles). Lastly, Ned's growing sense of alienation from the environment of his youth adds more fuel to the fire: "The only unfamiliar voice, little Brigid's, seemed the most familiar. . . ."

In the first two sections, then, O'Connor establishes a series of specific conflicts to prepare the reader for his more abstract theme: "uprootedness." . . .

All the pieces of the story merge at the end as Ned and Tom analyze their uprootedness. They are alienated from their family and their culture: their father's ways are no longer theirs; the old jokes are "beginning to wear thin" (IV); and their presence flusters their cousins. They also suffer from an inner alienation. They are educated and sophisticated. Tom and Ned have outgrown something they can never return to; Ned at least has the "enamelled" memory of "a boy on a horse," of "apple-green light," of "long streaks of crimson," of a "children's picture-book" world.

Simply, they have lost the child's innocent vision; they have lost "a sort of animal instinct" (IV). Only Cait retains the quality that inspires Ned to murmur, "Child of Light, thy limbs are burning through the veil which seems to hide them" (IV). She is the mirror of "the falling rain, the rocks and hills and angry sea."

> Helmut E. Gerber, "O'Connor's 'Uprooted'," in The Explicator, Vol. XIV, No. 1, October, 1955, Item #7.

ALBERT FOWLER (essay date 1957)

[*In the excerpt below, Fowler maintains that the story "The Holy Door" best exhibits O'Connor's belief that humanity can triumph over adversity.*]

Frank O'Connor has an Irish humor that refuses to allow any one mood to dominate his stories. His zest for life in all its contradictory variety keeps him from playing the prophet of doom, and **"The Holy Door,"** longer than most of his tales, affords him more scope to develop a conviction that man can overcome the adverse and the perverse, given time to engage them. The greater part of this story deals with disasters, but O'Connor remains unimpressed with the present fashion of foreboding. Destructive elements are present in force, but he handles them as if they were only part of the picture, not the entire canvas. He does not sidestep the witch mother, the curse of the dying wife, the presage of business failure, but he keeps them in perspective.

The critical conflict of **"The Holy Door"** is waged for marital felicity by a star-crossed Charlie whose wife turns out a fool who has to be safeguarded from ignorance and hysteria by domination. The Charlie who marries her is a born worrier, full of fear for the future and forever flying after the figments of dream. The felicity he hankers for is Romeo's, and his Polly is no Juliet. Innocent, incurious, never imagining what a man does to a wife when he has her stripped, she greeted marriage with a gasp and made of it a frustration for both of them. Living in the same house with his mother, a bundle of rags and malice, was far from easy, for the mother hated the ground Charlie walked on and wished him childless for the sake of his nephew's inheritance. Wrought on by his mother's jealousy and the banter of the pub, he is terrorized by the specter of sterility to the point where he tries out the serving maid and has a son by her to prove the trouble is not all of his making.

All this is the stuff of modern literature, the fear, the self-doubt, the hatred of kin for kin, the man deluded by dream, the woman with every joint in her mind flying asunder whenever anything happens to upset her. O'Connor, however, is not victimized by his material. He does not believe with Gide that the most beautiful things are those that madness prompts and reason writes. No matter how frenetic the action becomes, no matter how charged the atmosphere, O'Connor always maintains his footing in the sane and orderly basis of life. (p. 24)

In **"The Holy Door"** O'Connor is concerned with frustration and failure, which might easily form a repetitive rhythm with the emphasis on despair, but he is careful to break into these elements with the equally powerful forces of hope, ambition and perseverance. He keeps the story to a battle from start to finish, shifting the advantage from side to side and not allowing it to remain with either one long enough to build up the fixed charm of the hypnotic. He forces both sides into motion like a referee in the ring with two boxers, breaking them apart in the clinches, guarding the one fallen on ropes or canvas, equalizing the chances and promoting the match.

O'Connor employs a sense of time and a knowledge of timing to keep the forces of despair and hope in balance. Time in his story is longer than a week or a month, long enough to ripen the fruits of patience and determination. In this respect his technique differs from that of Sartre who develops mood, which is a thing of the moment, to the point where it can be extended by meticulous care to cover a span of days. Sartre has worked on continuity till he can create the illusion that moods of melancholy, hopelessness and anguish persist for a lifetime. This illusion is based on an enormous warping of reality for literary purposes, but he is able to persuade his readers they are witnessing reality. O'Connor deals with material similar to Sartre's, material that would lend itself to treatment as mood, but instead of allowing it to lapse into an emotional state he keeps it clearly conceived in the form of problem and challenge. He does not approach his Charlie as a subject for variations on the theme of doom. Charlie remains an open question, unpredictable as all men are, not to be written off as failure till the last hour strikes, not the pawn of one mood but the product of many. O'Connor finds it more excitable to follow the career of an open question than that of a foregone conclusion. (p. 25)

There is little doubt that Sartre believes life is a tissue of suffering from beginning to end, and it is *lèse majesté* to treat suffering to anything but a tragic conclusion. According to Sartre's rules O'Connor is indulging in sentimentality and evasion. And in a certain sense **"The Holy Door"** might be considered a parody of the modern thesis of frustration as a way of life, a take-off poking fun from behind at a personality destined for failure and disgrace. Charlie is well conceived for the role of human fly, but the trouble is he is never left alone to savor the profundity of his plight in the manner of Sartre. Something keeps turning up to cut short his self-indulgence, to challenge him to another go at getting his feet off the flypaper. The timing of the humor is specially calculated to puncture the pathos at the moment when it begins to tear the heart.

It is the complexity of existence that O'Connor takes into account and that moderns like Gide and Sartre refute in favor of their rigid scheme of things. He observes that almost anything can happen in the interplay of human wills, and they insist that only one order of events is credible. He is continually reporting the unpredictable and the unforeseen, while they chronicle the fixed course of destiny.

Instead of turning a microscope on mood and searching out its every detail as Gide does, O'Connor takes in the bewildering variety of human affairs. He is by no means wedded to the heroic ending of **"The Holy Door,"** for many of his stories wind up with the scales tilted the other way. His attention is not wrapped up in any single aspect of life but includes a multitude of contradictions. By concentrating and narrowing the focus of interest, men like Gide and Sartre hypnotize the reader. They harp on one note and insist on the validity of one mood. O'Connor admits the force of a feeling of helplessness in the face of apparently insoluble problems, for he places it upstage throughout **"The Holy Door,"** but he does not allow it to stand there alone to speak its piece unchallenged. (pp. 25-6)

When after the snares and pitfalls have failed to stop this Charlie in his search and he finally finds felicity in Nora's love, he stands his ground against his mother and all her tribe:

> "Roast her over a slow fire," snapped Charlie. He was himself again, aged seventeen, a roaring revolutionary and rationalist, ready to take on the British Empire, the Catholic Church, and the Wise Woman all together. "Now listen to me, girl," he said, taking her hands. "No one is going to put speels on you. And no one is going to haunt you, either. That's only all old women's talk and we had enough of it to last us our lives. We're a match for anyone and anything . . ."

(pp. 26-7)

Albert Fowler, "Challenge to Mood in Frank

O'Connor," in Approach, No. 23, Spring, 1957, pp. 24-7.

DANIEL WEISS   (essay date 1959)

[*In the following excerpt, Weiss examines the stories "Judas" and "My Oedipus Complex" from a psychoanalytic perspective.*]

"My Oedipus Complex" is a Freudian *jeu d'esprit*, a kind of talking *id* story. Its comedy derives from the five-year-old child's innocently calling the turns in his Oedipal relationship with his mother. The father returns from the war and the boy assumes that the mother resents the interloper as much as he does. When the mother and the father both reject the child the boy is crushed by the betrayal. Finally the mother has a second child; the father in his turn is made to take second place; and he and the son make common cause.

> After a while it came to me what he was mad about. It was his turn now. After turning me out of the big bed he had been turned out himself. Mother had no consideration now for anyone but that poisonous pup, Sonny. I couldn't help feeling sorry for Father. I had been through it all myself, and even at that age I was magnanimous. I began to stroke him down and say "There! There!" He wasn't exactly responsive.
>
> "Aren't you asleep either?" he snarled.
>
> "Ah, come on and put your arm around us, can't you?" I said, and he did, in a sort of way. Gingerly, I suppose, is how you'd describe it. He was very bony but better than nothing.

It is obvious that in this story O'Connor is playing with some very simple counters, very conscious of the comic possibilities of Freud considered along broad, almost slapstick lines.

In his other story, "Judas," something very different happens. Again the over-all effect is comic, but now in the profounder sense of the word; "Judas" is the comedy of the Oedipus Complex, exploring the relationship and its ramifications, and resolving them.

In "Judas," Jerry, the young man, lives alone with his widowed mother. Being an only child, he explains, he "never knocked around the way the other fellows did." Finally, he falls for a girl, a nurse, whom he describes as a "well-educated, superior girl." He is shy of the girl and at the same time torn in his loyalty to his mother. He feels himself to be corrupt, unworthy of the girl. "Several times she asked me in, but I was too nervous. I knew I'd lose my head, break the china, use some dirty word, and then go home and cut my throat." Finally, wandering, desperate, he meets her in the street. She begins to understand his feelings about her. But in explaining her own position, and in trying to put him at his ease, she refers casually to her experiences with other young men in times past. Jerry's reaction is shock. "This was worse than appalling. This was a nightmare. Kitty, whom I had thought so angelic talking in cold blood about 'spooning' with fellows all over the house." He composes himself, finally, to accept her paradoxical behaviour; and then, since it is late, he goes home to his mother feeling extremely guilty.

With his mother, who has waited up for him, he is short to the point of brutality. But later on, in the middle of the night,

overcome by remorse, he wakes her to apologize, only to burst into tears and have her fold him in her arms.

"Judas," while it obviously deals with what is an extension of the same material that informs "My Oedipus Complex," seems to move structurally along lines dictated less by a sense of psychological determination than by a conscious artistic impulse. Yet I should like to suggest that "Judas," in respect to the psychological,—that is, the unconscious,—determination of its movement is more directed than the playfully worked out Oedipal scheme of "My Oedipus Complex."

As Freud describes the Oedipal relationships, he proposes hypothetically that at some point in his prehistory (before any systematic memory formation takes place), the child has imagined for himself a situation in which he is his mother's sole support and companion—a situation that can come about in actuality if the father dies. Added to this is the image unconsciously retained and treasured, of the mother as one's first and only love, the ideal.

After a certain point the child consciously realizes that his mother cannot become, for many reasons (because the father has, after all, prior claims and threatens to maintain them, because the mother herself rejects him, and because society frowns on it) an object of his sexual love in reality. With this realization, and with the growing awareness of the world about him, he finds other objects with whom he can, with the permission and even the approval of himself and the world, explore the possibilities of mutual sexual attraction.

But still, especially if the original Oedipal involvement is reinforced by circumstances and so survives childhood, there is an unconscious clinging to the mother image, and this clinging constitutes one of the normal and some of the abnormal factors in the determination of the young man's choice of woman. It is a choice whose governing polarities are the contradictory ones of the incestuous fixation on the mother image and the incest barrier which forbids it.

What will the girl like the girl who married dear old dad be like? First of all, and most important she will be pure, not a "doll" like the loose girls that Jerry Moynihan's friends go around with. The social equivalent of purity, being a "well-educated, superior girl," may represent this condition. She must also be sexually unattainable, a condition that makes the relationship almost impossible unless it ends in marriage. Another determinant, more remote, is the chosen woman's identification with something like the maternal function. Can she cook (very often waitresses are fatally attractive) or is she motherly toward the young or the infirm? Wealth is a good substitute for the ability to mother. Nurses are proverbially attractive and usually to men who are under their care.

As for the man, one can draw certain inferences about him. He is apt, because of his unconscious preference for the pure maternal image, to keep himself aloof, purer than his friends. He is apt, too, to make a profound distinction, which is actually only a distinction between the obverse and reverse, between women who are sexually sophisticated or downright promiscuous, and the sort of girl one marries or keeps company with. For the one he has a fear, tempered with a guilty desire, for the other a guilty desire tempered with fear. . . . More obscurely the son has mixed feelings about his mother, or for that matter, anyone's mother. Between the lines of his overt affection one can read a certain hostility and resentment. It is an impatience, compounded of guilty desire, and a frustration which defines itself consciously as an accusation of the mother for making one's own love-life impossible. In the repression of this hostility, the tendency is to turn it against oneself, to contemplate, instead of murder, suicide.

How does **"Judas"** fulfill these disinterested conditions? The comic side of the story deals with Jerry Moynihan's suicidal despair at being unable to establish an understanding relationship with the girl, Kitty, and his shock at finding out that she is more experienced in the ways of love than he thought. Because he feels his degraded feelings of lust make her avoid him, he attributes her avoiding him to the maternal virtue of purity. But the irony of the situation is heightened by his discovery that she is not so innocent. The discovery is not a comfort but a positive cause for alarm.

Thus the dilemma defines itself; Kitty must be both like and yet different from the mother, and Jerry must be both the innocent child, and not the innocent child. What precipitates the overt hostility toward the mother in contrast to the comic suicidal despair that precedes it (the story is littered with razors and penknives) is in effect the rejection of the mother brought about by his success with another woman, who can be a valid successor to his mother. Kitty, by being bold, has given him courage. She is cross with her own mother and sees her clearly. She accepts Jerry with the correct mixture of boldness and modesty, and so his mother must finally move aside.

Curious about the genesis of both these stories, I wrote to Frank O'Connor and received a thoughtfully considered reply, the gist of which I quote.

> About the story [**"Judas"**] I don't believe when I wrote it that I was even aware that it dealt with an Oedipal situation. Of course I had the same sort of intense attachment to my mother, but the chap in the story is not me . . . The nurse on the other hand is almost a straight portrait of my first girl, and she *is* a nurse and she *was* superior. I certainly hadn't read Freud, and if I knew the term it was in the way I now talk about getting to first base without ever having seen a baseball match and ignorant of what a base looks like.

> Naturally when I wrote **"My Oedipus Complex"** I knew Freud very well, and was taking pride in my iconoclasm. I always maintain that every chap who has an attractive mother and hasn't fallen in love with her and planned to murder his dad is missing one of the best things in life."

(pp. 10-14)

Daniel Weiss, "Freudian Criticism: Frank O'Connor as Paradigm," in Northwest Review, *Vol. II, No. 2, Spring, 1959, pp. 5-14.*

GERRY BRENNER (essay date 1968)

[*In the excerpt below, Brenner asserts that the most important aspect of O'Connor's short stories is the conflict between rational and irrational behavior in the characters.*]

Since an acquaintance with any short story writer is usually made through a few anthologized pieces, it is difficult to see the thematic unity and development of ideas that make the entirety of his work greater than the sum of its parts. Exposure to only **"The Drunkard," "My Oedipus Complex," "Guests of the Nation," "Judas,"** or **"Uprooted"** obstructs a clear view of O'Connor's creative virtues. The selections

often exploit the more specious aspects of his talent. Consequently he has become tagged as a humorist. And he is—a fine one. But unnoticed elements give him stature: his curious view of priestliness among the Irish laity; his probing into the themes of human loneliness and communication; his success at infusing new energy into stories about juveniles by creating not precociously passive sensibilities but active boys who get themselves into predicaments which incur both guilt and maturation; and his restoration of the storyteller's voice. But most important is his persistent sifting into the value of impulsive indiscretion and moral fecklessness in order to domesticate irrationality. And only by considering a larger sample of his work and the development of his canon can one see with some accuracy the value of this preoccupation.

The relationship between judgment and instinct, what O'Connor calls the masculine and feminine principles, penetrates all of his work. The conflicting principles are obviously an extension of the classical dialectic between reason and passion or between Neitzsche's Apollonian and Dionysian principles. Yet by grafting it to situations within the framework of the lower-middle-class fringe of Irish society, O'Connor realistically dwarfs the conflict. His treatment of the dialectic shows his leanings upon the romantic tradition by placing instinct and irrationality above judgment and rationality. So, though he asserts that mental soundness requires balancing the antinomies, he also confesses his own partiality in a rare piece of Irish understatement: "I think I like the instinctual as against the intellectual." And although he says further that "in dreams [the judgment-instinct conflict] is represented by the metaphor of father and mother," he obviously does not have the opposition functioning literally in his own work, for the father figures he creates are notoriously lacking in judgment. In fact he recognizes and espouses in the adult many of the qualities and characteristics found in adolescents, foremost among which are imprudence, irresponsibility, and egotism.

Such adolescent adulthood accounts for O'Connor's many stories which have no wider extension than their celebration of the "little hero." Many of them only incidentally treat foolhardy males, while others devote their entire focus to characters who exhibit juvenile ebullience in their reckless capacity for life. These celebratory stories—among others, **"The Majesty of the Law," "Machine-Gun Corps in Action," "The Late Henry Conran," "Fish for Friday," "Old-Age Pensioners," "Don Juan (Retired)," "The Sentry," "The Old Faith,"** and **"Androcles and the Army"**—are rendered with a gusto found elsewhere only in some of his stories of juveniles. Their *raison d' être* is their dramatization of the value of impulsive individuality. The "heroes" of these stories achieve their individuality not through mental superiority, but through mental regression. By performing an impetuous, undeliberated act, for which they oddly enough have no regret, they show themselves regressing to immature conduct.

In **"The Majesty of the Law,"** the apotheosis of old Dan Bride's individuality is founded upon his recklessness and his immature method of handling responsibilities. The story concerns Dan's hospitality to a friendly sergeant who has brought a warrant for his arrest, Dan having but slightly opened a man's head in order to end an argument. The felicity of the story is partly achieved by the adolescent reticence of both Dan and the sergeant in broaching the purpose of the sergeant's visit until he has already left once. The excesses of politeness during their long visit also enhance the story's humor: each man is guardedly not to be outdone by the other, Dan overlooking the changes which the interference of the law has effected and the sergeant drinking and attesting to the excellence of Dan's illegal whiskey. But the maturity and civility which Dan displays during their chat only heighten the effect of the story when the impulsive barbarity with which he opened a former friend's head is revealed. This contrast between Dan's even-tempered civility and his rash act of violence provides the humorous peripety of the story. But it is even more humorous and important that Dan refuses to absolve himself of the legal responsibility for his misdemeanor by paying a small fine, a civilized way of handling legal infractions. Instead he chooses to go to jail. He will serve a sentence which, he is firmly confident, will be seen as a martyr's reprisal against an unjust charge, reversing the roles of punisher-punished. Further, by choosing to be jailed, Dan will cause his accuser to suffer a defamation of character for allowing the law to interfere in what should have been a personal matter. And his defamation will forever blight both his ancestors and his progeny, a worse fate unimaginable to the Irish peasantry, who judge men neither by their merits nor rank, but by their ancestry. As Dan tells the sergeant, " '. . . nothing would give him more gratification than for me to pay [the fine]. But I'll punish him. I'll lie on bare boards for him. I'll suffer for him, sergeant, so that neither he nor any of his children after him will be able to raise their heads for the shame of it.' " Though Dan's vindictiveness is a more personal, archaic, and tribal retaliation, and therefore suits his character, it is nonetheless an uncivilized and immature way of dealing with legal problems.

But of course O'Connor refuses to scorn him. The strength of the story resides in Dan's independent responsibility to a private code of law, an unmelodramatic and psychologically interesting revenge. Dan's victory lies in what O'Connor sees as his ability to absorb completely the impersonality of public law and thereby keep the issue a personal one. His accuser, not the legal machinery, is the one who punishes, and get punished by, Dan. The upshot of the conflict between legal systems is that O'Connor celebrates the supremacy of Dan's individuality, which ignores public responsibilities, metamorphosing them into private ones. . . . By compelling his reader to applaud the majesty of Dan's personalized law, O'Connor also inveigles him into improving the impulsiveness of Dan's initial act of violence, since to accept only one act of individuality and not the other would be inconsistent: this is O'Connor's victory.

By capitalizing on the attitudes of an archaic culture, O'Connor courts a limited audience. Nonetheless, Dan's archaism metaphorically expresses the individual spirit rebelling against an impersonal world. Furthermore, O'Connor has transcended what began as an interest in such folkways as Dan's. Instead of remaining within that essentially romantic world of Syngean and Yeatsian peasants, O'Connor looked beyond its charming derring-do by subjecting it to a more realistic world. Yet his turning away from the peasantry brought him face to face with many of the same qualities found in respectable middle-class people. Hence he writes a story like **"The Mad Lomasneys"** to show that Rita Lomasney's "uncivilized" act of impulsive indiscretion—her reckless decision to marry the first of her competing suitors to arrive one day—is not something found only in peasants. Or he writes **"The Custom of the Country,"** in which a newly married girl hastily decides to go to her bigamist husband regardless of social and personal consequences. In **"Counsel for Oe-**

dipus," when a lawyer savagely exposes the misery a shrewish wife's inordinate and selfish piety has caused her husband, whom *she* is suing for separation, the husband vilifies his lawyer, irrationally shields his wife, and returns to her. **"Achilles' Heel"** tells of a bishop's inability to fire his domineering housekeeper—even though she has been proven to be the leader of a smuggling ring—because he depends upon her cooking.

Contrary both to his Irish critics who condemn the "unholy laughter" of his satire and to his academic readers who, one might surmise, balk at inklings of sentimentality, he can be more accurately viewed as treating his characters with sufficient ambivalence and detachment to satirize and to celebrate them simultaneously. To see his satire as only condemning his subjects disregards not only the values he encourages but also his rich humor. And to see him as a sentimentalist overlooks his nagging exposure of man's follies. (pp. 457-60)

To trace O'Connor's development more systematically: The clash between judiciousness and the correlatives of imprudence, impulsiveness, irrationality, and immorality marks out the central line of his short fiction. What starts in his stories as simply a celebration of individuality, initially based upon the comic rashness or boyish behavior of the Irish peasantry, later flowers into more serious ways of expressing individuality. Thus a personality cult develops into a system of values, as seen in the development of his first three story collections, O'Connor harnessing irresponsible characters to increasingly more realistic situations.

His first collection, *Guests of the Nation* (1931), adulates reckless individuals of nearly legendary stature: the quixotic old Robin Hood whose machinegun makes him so omnipotent that he participates in any vendetta or civil war that hap-

O'Connor in the late 1930s.

pens his way (**"Machine-Gun Corps in Action"**); the old man who has been hiding in his attic for five years a son who accidentally killed a man (**"Attack"**); the derring-do antics of a Civil War guerrilla with the proportions of a Cuchulain-Michael Collins combination (**"Alec"**); the profligate father who returns outraged to Ireland so that he can sue his wife for defaming his character, their son's wedding announcement having implied he was dead (**"The Late Henry Conran"**).

O'Connor withdraws from such habitually reckless characters in *Bones of Contention* (1936), his second collection. In it he celebrates the collective irresponsibilities of the peasantry who defy the abstractions of legality, as seen in **"The Majesty of the Law," "Peasants"** (acting as a derelict Anti-Defamation League, some village peasants attempt various forms of illegality—shanghai, perjury, bribery—to keep a thief from being convicted, since his conviction will blot the town's reputation forever); **"In the Train"** (thanks to the perjury of her townspeople a woman is acquitted of poisoning her husband); **"Tears—Idle Tears"** (the peasants of Ballyaindreesh collectively thwart the law from discovering a murder); **"Bones of Contention"** (an old grandmother takes the law into her hands by appropriating a friend's corpse instead of letting relations bury her); and **"The Man That Stopped"** (a peasant shrew countermands a magistrate's decree that a cataleptic be hanged as a witch and restores him to normality). But even here O'Connor can be seen capitalizing upon situations severed from actuality. By viewing responsibility as only a comic abstraction, he cannot meaningfully communicate his values of irresponsibility since he gives them no competition.

In *Crab Apple Jelly* (1944) O'Connor repeatedly achieves a satisfactory conflict between the two elements of responsibility and irresponsibility. Here he diminishes the irresponsible element by revealing it in isolated, unexpected acts of imprudence, not habitual or collective orgies. And the characters who perform them are largely respectable, middle-class people whose conduct is restricted by the responsibilities of their occupation as teacher, priest, or businessman. The central stories in the collection are **"The Mad Lomasneys," "The New Teacher"** (later retitled **"The Cheapjack"**), **"The House That Johnny Built,"** and **"The Luceys,"** all of which center around an imprudent act: respectively, a girl's decision to marry the first of her suitors to appear; a teacher's recital from a new teacher's scandalous diary, an act which he knows will lose him his own job; a businessman's proposal to a young chemist, assuming that employing her obliges her to marry him; and another businessman's precipitate vindictiveness toward his brother for refusing to help him get his son out of a jam. Besides these are **"The Bridal Night"** in which a young woman teacher goes to bed with a mad young man only to console his madness; **"Song Without Words,"** in which two monastics swap racing forms and beer and nearly succumb to the further sin of playing cards; **"The Miser,"** in which a priest, confident of extorting a generous inheritance from a dying miser who is actually penniless, is bilked; and **"Uprooted,"** a Joycean story in which (though a minor episode and one since expunged through revision) a priest confesses to his brother of having gotten a girl pregnant. By the time O'Connor had finished this collection he had achieved his sought-after realism. (pp. 461-62)

O'Connor's subsequent development first extends acts of imprudence and later gives more play to responsible characters.

The stories in *The Common Chord* (1948) show him examining how far he can push impulsive imprudence into acts of immorality without losing identification with, and admiration for, his characters. In it are related a series of immoral acts: a girl's decision to spend the night with an older man in **"Don Juan's Temptation"**; another girl's impenitent confession of having copulated with a boy she will probably never see again in **"News for the Church"**; a young bride's impulsive return to her bigamist husband in **"The Custom of the Country"**; a man's begetting a bastard to prove his virility in **"The Holy Door"**; an old man's brief coition with a country lass in **"Don Juan (Retired)"**; a priest's demonstrative affection for a friend's wife in **"The Frying Pan"**; a young wife giving birth to a former lover's child in **"Friends of the Family."** In all these stories O'Connor again restricts the imprudence of his characters' actions by seeing their immoral acts as isolated, untypical episodes performed by normally responsible characters. Since the characters are not habitual immoralists O'Connor retains identification with them.

In *Traveller's Samples* (1951) he widens his focus by shifting to stories about juveniles. Still, by treating their world of betrayal and guilt as he does, he is essentially observing their immature conduct and lack of judgment. Like one boy's seduction by a young siren (**"The Man of the House"**), or another boy's sampling of his father's porter (**"The Drunkard"**), or a third boy's surreptitious exchange of Christmas stocking gifts (**"The Thief"**), their acts are unpremeditated and imprudent, resembling those of their adult counterparts. O'Connor also continues to show his interest in instinctive indiscretion, trafficking in more immorality in **"The Lady of the Sagas," "The Masculine Principle,"** and **"Darcy in the Land of Youth."**

In *Traveller's Samples* one can also see the beginnings of a more serious line of development and one that invites more thorough examination. In this volume O'Connor indicates his awareness both of the limitations of extolling imprudence and of the need to recognize and examine the virtues of responsible characters. These preoccupations characterize his stories of the last decade, nearly a dozen of his uncollected stories, and the new stories in *More Stories by Frank O'Connor* (1954) and *Domestic Relations* (1957). (pp. 462-63)

O'Connor's more recent concerns show him drawing away from the flagrant but approved immoralists of *The Common Chord.* Instead of starting with immoralists, many of his stories will give fuller dramatization to the conflict between instinct and judgment in which instinctive immorality eventually wins out, but not quite as easily as in previous stories, and only at the cost of becoming respectable. In this category, for example, can be included **"The Sorcerer's Apprentice," "Lonely Rock," "Unapproved Route," "The Little Mother," "The Paragon,"** and **"The Masculine Principle."**

"The Sorcerer's Apprentice" is told through thirtyish Una MacDermott, unable to bring herself to marry Jimmy Foley, who has courted her for five years. After another of their frequent rows, she goes off to Dublin to stay with a girl friend who introduces her to Denis O'Brien. Poor, plain, plump, forty-five, and legally separated from his wife, he advises her that her trouble with Jimmy stems from her unwillingness to take a chance: " '. . . you have to take a chance. There's no such thing in marriage as absolute security. . . . It's a gamble, however you do it. Sooner or later you'll have to take a chance, and you should take it before you get too set in your ways.' " He further advises her not to throw her judgment out the window, " 'But you've used your judgment, so far as it takes you, and now it won't take you any farther.' " Before Una knows it she is actively flirting with Denis and then one night wakes to find herself in bed with him. When she realizes what she has done she is alarmed at her irrationality and, ironically, is disillusioned "because it had produced no effect on her." She returns to her home town later and takes up again with Jimmy, getting along well until they have another row. As a conciliatory measure she suggests spending the weekend at the seashore, and while there, entices him into spending the night with her. But in the morning Jimmy wakes with a moral hangover. Depressed herself, Una abruptly realizes that shabby Denis is really her man; she telephones him and proposes marriage.

Despite her impulsiveness and her two acts of immorality, O'Connor, while praising the relaxed conscience, does not present Una as sexually emancipated. Her unrespectable acts grow out of her frustrations with the respectably judicious behavior that has caused her to be still unmarried at thirty. She desires the moral role of wife as is emphasized by her return to Denis on the night following their coition to cook his dinner in order to see what marriage to him would be like. That her life with him will be respectably ordinary seems evident in O'Connor's presentation of Denis as a middle-aged, plump, and balding figure. By making him romantically uninteresting, O'Connor disallows the romantic interpretation that Una's passionate love for him accounts for her impulsiveness. Though an immoralist, Una is presented in such a way that O'Connor maintains identification with her because of her fundamental respectability. Her two immoral acts, the reader is made to feel confident, will be her only defections from respectable conduct.

"The Sorcerer's Apprentice" also notes the beginning of O'Connor's more concentrated focus on the judicious male as a foil to his immoralists. Jimmy Foley is O'Connor's "villain," the prudential man. Although he is recognizable in many characters of earlier stories, he receives fuller satiric treatment in O'Connor's later stories. As with his treatment of his earlier irresponsible heroes, O'Connor initially uses his villain types for their sheer comic assets; they provide fodder for his omnivorous imprudent heroes. But O'Connor's subsequent development shows his apparent awareness of having created the prudential male as only a thin comic character. Consequently he tries to reconcile imprudent and prudent characteristics so that prudent traits will not simply bear the brunt of his mockery. One can see this concern being developed in **"The Masculine Principle," "A Sense of Responsibility," "Lonely Rock," "The Paragon," "The Impossible Marriage,"** and, perhaps most clearly, in **"The Little Mother."** (pp. 463-65)

In spite of his forays into the virtues of judicious responsibility, O'Connor never abandons the instinctive urgings of individuality. His most recent development shows him regarding the clash from another frame of reference, yet one that again asserts the primacy of imprudence while being immersed in further degrees of responsible respectability. (However, he somewhat regresses to permitting his characters in their social role to assert their responsibility instead of dramatize it.) By examining imprudent clerics O'Connor tries to see how far his creative interests can be extended without, as with his immoralists, losing sympathy for his clerics and without jeering, or being jeered at, as an anticlerical writer. In his recent

stories about priests O'Connor emphasizes the need to diminish the restraint which has been imposed upon them by their occupation and their social role of authority. As noted earlier, **"Achilles' Heel,"** tells of a bishop who cannot fire his housekeeper, the leader of a smuggling ring, because he depends upon her cooking. In **"The Old Faith"** several clerics get drunk imbibing a bottle of confiscated poteen. In **"The Sentry,"** believing a sentry to have stolen onions from his garden, a priest clouts him, is later ashamed when he realizes that the sentry's story of having chased off some children might have been true, and denies knowing anything when questioned the next day by an investigating officer. In **"The Wreath"** Father Fogarty (O'Connor's most sustained character, cropping up in more than a dozen stories) and another priest permit a wreath of red roses to be buried on the coffin of a fellow clergyman even though the wreath disregards church rubric and suggests a scandalous love affair. And in **"The Mass Island"** a priest impulsively takes Father Fogarty's body to be buried across Ireland on Mass Island—where Catholics held secret services during Cromwell's time—instead of heeding the wishes of relatives.

O'Connor's rather didactic strategy in these stories appears to suggest that by focusing upon the figureheads of Irish society, and on figureheads of the judicious side of the classical dialectic between instinct and judgment, he can show even their human imprudence. Although what he describes might be considered heretical, O'Connor would retort that their heretical acts at least give them the touches of humanity necessary to make them dignified, decent fellow human beings. And by suggesting that even the clergy perform marginal acts of irrationality, O'Connor can perhaps persuade the Irish laity to let its conscience relax.

From his earliest interest in peasants' recklessness to his later interest in lower-middle-class indiscretion and immorality, and to his more recent interest in priests' imprudence, O'Connor shows a sustained assault upon the sacred grounds of judgment in an attempt to define its limitations and to exhibit the values of a more "active instinctual life." He undermines the value placed upon mature, "civilized" conduct by repeatedly deifying the imprudent hero. One might even say that to O'Connor the better part of valor is indiscretion. The radical nature of his construct of values might be more clearly understood by charting his version of the classical dialectic:

Instinct (Passion)	Judgment (Reason)
1) inherent	acquired
2) natural	artificial
3) self-expressive (-assertive)	self-repressive (-effacing)
4) impulsive	deliberative
5) imprudent	judicious
6) sinful	virtuous
7) immoral	moral

Although the instinct side of this construct enjoys general approval, such approval extends only through the first five categories, if that far, and sinful and immoral acts are prohibited both by legal and religious codes. Yet O'Connor's stories commend even sinful or immoral acts: "An Irish writer without contention is a freak of nature. All the literature that matters to me was written by people who had to dodge the censor." In his fiction the classical construct of values breaks down so that the contrasts of sin and virtue, or immorality and morality, no longer exist. His stories invalidate those contrasts by demonstrating that in some circumstances acts of sin and immorality are paradoxically both virtuous and moral, provided one consents to the romantic value of individuality. Quite simply (and sophistically), a sinful act is one of self-expression. Assuming that self-expression is good because it exhibits one's individuality, then provided an act is neither grossly perverse nor criminal, a character who commits a sin must possess the courage that acting as an individual requires; therefore, "sin" becomes transformed into a virtue. Conversely, judicious restraint is self-repressive, and by inhibiting himself O'Connor's villain has become subjected to tyrannizing abstractions that diminish individuality because they cause him to conduct himself almost at the level of unconsciousness, acting by judicious habits which cause him to live on only a minimal threshold of individuality and, hence, dignity.

O'Connor's reassessment of the classical dialectic shows him casting himself among those who approve of human beings alive to experience and willing to spurn the caution and rationality which civilization so carefully fosters. By advocating the irrationality that imprudence requires, his philosophical indebtedness to Schopenhauer, Kierkegaard, Nietzsche, and Bergson is clear. His literary forbears are also visible. Even though he disregards the romantic worship of feeling and emotion, he is in sympathy with its emphasis upon spontaneity, imagination, and the Faustian feeling that all experience is valuable. More recently, one sees the shadow of Shaw's Bergson-derived "life force" dwelling in O'Connor's stories. Other influences for anarchy are neoprimitivists like D. H. Lawrence and Liam O'Flaherty. (pp. 465-67)

The result of O'Connor's common-sensical and moral treatment of irrationality is that when it is shackled to normal circumstances and to acts which are essentially little more than imprudent, it is made respectable and valuable. By shunning grotesques, neurotics, and primitives, and by limiting himself to the marginal, temporary, and expectedly natural outbreaks of instinctual and irrational behavior, O'Connor writes of people and situations that are readily identifiable because their experience draws on the normally apprehended world, not one of mental divagations or of fantasy. In none of his characters' situations does O'Connor discover mythic or symbolically monumental significance. What he does discover is a simple but profound fact, nonetheless: the value of making concrete the originality revealed when characters react to ordinary situations as minimally irrational, as occasionally imprudent, individuals. Simply, he reclaims the commonplace by concretely observing and presenting its muted uniqueness. That he can do so through the "outmoded" techniques of nineteenth-century realism attests to his considerable talents and to his importance in an epoch of frenetic and overtaxing avant-gardism. (pp. 468-69)

> *Gerry Brenner, "Frank O'Connor's Imprudent Hero," in* Texas Studies in Literature and Language, *Vol. X, Fall, 1968, pp. 457-69.*

SHAUN O'CONNELL (essay date 1969)

[*In the review of* A Set of Variations *excerpted below, O'Connell argues that O'Connor primarily focuses on his characters' behavioral patterns rather than on stylistic presentation.*]

Though [O'Connor] talks a great deal about the strategy of the short story—and his widow tells us that there was no end to his fiddling with his own stories—he really does not seem so concerned with aesthetic design for its own sake as, say, is Nabokov who describes the clash in a work of fiction as not between the characters, but, as in a chess problem, between the author and his readers. In O'Connor's stories the primary clash *is* between the characters; his interest in design is not, it seems, so much an abstract concern with the various possible patterns of presentation for a short story, but a deep concern with the ways in which people get caught in slight variations of the same basic patterns, the nets which Joyce's Dedalus flew by, the fetters of "home," "fatherland" and "church."

Joyce flew past those nets by committing himself to a craft which wholly renewed itself, utterly changed, with each work. O'Connor's stories [in *A Set of Variations*] are much as they were in his first collection—tight, realistic, fondly-ironic, dominated by a perfectly suited voice, neatly turned from exposition through development to drama, his "three necessary elements" of the short story. Joyce was a butterfly, O'Connor a spider who built many similar but subtly different webs. Fittingly enough, the *things* each of these writers saw were related to the *ways* in which they saw. Joyce portrays his countrymen, in *Dubliners,* as walking dead, self-evident symbols of stultification which justified his desire to be artistically free. O'Connor too sees life in Ireland as mean, brutish and dull, but he sees more than this, more to it than did Joyce in his stories. There are hints of fulfillment, touches of love, possibilities of peace in O'Connor's Ireland. For, he seems to say, however bad things might be there, where might an Irishman—one not an artist as he and Joyce—go to be happier? In **"The American Wife"** Elsie tries to get her husband to leave Ireland for America, but, like other O'Connor characters, he realizes he'd be unhappy there.

> They knew they belonged to a country whose youth was always escaping from it, out beyond that harbor, and that was middle-aged in all its attitudes and institutions. Of those that remained, a little handful lived with defeat and learned fortitude and humor and sweetness . . .

Escape for an artist might be salvation, but for Tom it would be a capitulation. His Cork is a structured sadness, not a brown death like Joyce's Dublin. To show that inner-life of narrow range and small satisfactions, O'Connor mastered the art of minor variations, perfectly suited his method to his subject, his style to his purpose.

Of that obstructive trinity—home, fatherland and church—O'Connor's characters are at once most constricted and most liberated by the variations of family-life within the home. In **"A Set of Variations on a Borrowed Theme,"** old Kate Mahoney, a widow, decides to take in children to raise money for support so she won't have to live with her own married daughters. But it's more than money. "Motherhood was the only trade Kate knew, . . . she felt the older she got the better she practiced it." Sadly, perhaps, she can conceive or pursue no other mode of fulfillment beyond family-life. But—and this is O'Connor's fine point—her acceptance of this new network of restrictions leads her out far beyond the nets of conventionalism. For she comes to tell Jimmy, one of her new children, that he should never feel ashamed of himself for being illegitimate. "Strange notions from a respectable woman . . ." she thinks. She sadly watches Jimmy seek out, in his drunken father and his choice of girlfriends, a normal pattern of family-life denied him, in part by herself; she watches her own daughters recoil in jealousy from their mother's new "family." Thus, each seeks fulfillment in a family pattern which compromises those patterns others try to erect. But artfulness and love win out. An artist in a human mode, Kate creates something out of nothing, another family. Her daughters wonder,

> How could a woman who was already old take the things the world had thrown away and out of them fashion a new family, dearer to her than the old and finer than any she had known?

To ask the question that way is to make evident the answer. Kate loves most what she has been able to create beyond the restrictions of the conventionally acceptable. In another story, **"The Impossible Marriage,"** a couple are mocked by their neighbors because, though married, they live apart, caring for their widowed mothers. When the husband dies, never having truly lived with his wife, the mockers come to see how wrong they had been, how real the seemingly mock-marriage was, how happy had been the wife, herself now a widow, who had, like Kate, turned a sham family—as seen in the eyes of those whose fears made them cling for support to conventions—into the real thing. O'Connor's people try to make family patterns out of the little that is left for them to work with, like Cloone, in **"Androcles and the Army,"** who lives in "an atmosphere of intense domesticity" with his lions. They don't always make it, though. In **"Public Opinion"** a doctor has to give up his 17-year-old housekeeper after the townspeople start whispering about the rotting side of beef he buried: they think it might be a patient! "A town like this can bend iron," the doctor says. But, whether they make it or not, whether the circumstances surrounding their efforts are solemn or silly; whether they stay at home, go into the larger families of politics or the church, O'Connor's people seek out unique family patterns, patterns which set them at odds with others' patterns of convention. (pp. 610-12)

> Shaun O'Connell, "A Net of Revelations," in The Massachusetts Review, *Vol. X, No. 3, Summer, 1969, pp. 610-13.*

JOYCE CAROL OATES (essay date 1969)

[*Oates is an American novelist, short story writer, and critic who is perhaps best known for her novel* them *(1969), which won a National Book Award. As a critic, Oates has written on remarkably diverse authors and is respected for her individuality and erudition. In the excerpt below, she characterizes O'Connor as a writer of moderate passion whose stories are charmingly told but marred by an uncompelling sameness.*]

A Set of Variations is a big collection of stories by Frank O'Connor. . . . It contains stories chosen by his widow from the work he did between 1957 until his death in 1966, and it is not likely to alter his reputation in any way. O'Connor is a gentler Chekhov; in his hands we never worry, we admire people for their charming limitations, their absolute paralysis within certain outmoded institutions like the Catholic Church, we assume that character is fate, the countryside is fate, the decrees of the Bishop's housekeeper are fate; we enjoy good, sometimes remarkable, story-telling for its own sake. O'Connor has no ideas and no hatreds. His passions are mild. His technical concerns are unexciting. It was his intention to create a book of short stories that had its own unity, stories arranged in an "ideal ambiance" that would strengthen and illuminate one another: hence the title, which is not a very good title, *A Set of Variations.* In reading these stories

I was often charmed and a glimmer of something—disorder, terror—would come to me, as if excited by the fiction itself, but this was a mistake, for O'Connor is not concerned with the extremes of either joy or grief, but with ordinary life assessed in an ordinary way. There are flawless stories here, and yet I have difficulty in remembering them—it is as if O'Connor, because of the very dexterity of his writing, created stories of a certain satisfying sameness, populated by people of a certain satisfying sameness, a self-enclosed world we need to acknowledge but not to explore. (pp. 538-39)

> *Joyce Carol Oates, in a review of "A Set of Variations," in* The Hudson Review, *Vol. XXII, No. 3, Autumn, 1969, pp. 538-39.*

MURRAY PROSKY (essay date 1971)

[*In the following excerpt, Prosky discusses the importance of morality in O'Connor's stories.*]

In a literature dominated by the absurd man, the little man, or the uprooted man, the impressive Irish contribution seems to be in proportion to centuries of historical experience. The Danes, the Normans and the English have all in their turn dominated Ireland. All too often the foreigner has been a superior organization man while the native Irish remained stubbornly, if often foolishly, independent. It is interesting to conjecture how far the Irish hatred for their foreign conquerors has paralleled their distrust for the abstract notions of conduct which they were forced to submit to. Certainly the major Irish authors of the twentieth century have professed a fierce loathing for abstract systems of thought, though it would seem as though they were inadvertently replacing foreign abstractions with active ones. Joyce opposed God, Mother, and Country; Yeats contemptuously denied the abstract intellect for bodily wisdom; Synge listened for the instinctive wisdom of tramps and fishermen. O'Connor belongs to this tradition, but he is more concerned with ordinary human conduct and its consequences than with a way of saying or perceiving. Consequently, O'Connor emphasizes the moral and social basis of the short story, that it represents "submerged population groups," that its aim is to stimulate the moral imagination.

The characteristic shape of his short stories, what I call a pattern of diminishing certitude, enables O'Connor to focus on the antecedents and consequences of human action in a manner that is inherently dramatic. His stories suggest that human conduct can either brutalize or humanize the universe. The more his characters sacrifice humility, compassion and humor for rigid abstractions, the more inhumane and terrifying the effect. As the moral basis for action becomes increasingly abstract, as inhuman ideals begin to replace human realities, the more a character's sense of individual identity is contracted or destroyed. When the voice of man, however imperfect, can no longer be heard, then the world becomes a terrifying mechanism. The essential tragedy of Gogol's "Overcoat," O'Connor stressed in *The Lonely Voice,* is when men lose their natural sympathy and can no longer hear or respond to the pathetic voice of Akekey Akakievich when he says, "I am your brother." It is at this point that the universe becomes inimical to man. Where sympathy fails, so does human certainty and as a consequence of the resulting sense of isolation, man seems an insignificant speck of dust. Quite appropriately, O'Connor prefaces his study of the short story with Pascal's reaction to a mechanical and unresponsive universe: "The eternal silence of those infinite spaces terrify me." O'Connor's recognition of the infinite spaces caused by action and judgment based on inhuman abstractions is the moral basis of the pattern of diminishing certitude. It is a pattern, as this study will demonstrate, which occurs quite early in his career in **"Guests of a Nation"** (1931) and persists with increasing depth and spontaneity through *Domestic Relations* (1957). . . . (pp. 311-12)

From the very beginning of the title story of O'Connor's first major collection, *Guests of a Nation* (1931), he juxtaposes two forms of contradictory behavior. One is instinctive and directly related to responses between man and man, the other is abstract and mechanical. Buonaparte, Noble, and the old woman cannot help but respond genially to the two Englishmen, Hawkins and Belcher. Both are good-natured individuals whose personal qualities and actions seem in no way foreign or antagonistic to their Irish captors, with the significant exception of Jeremiah Donovan. The old woman could hardly begrudge housing two prisoners of war when they seemed more like guests than enemies. Belcher, who later reveals a special affection for the hearth, gallantly helps with the chores. Though he isn't much for conversation he is a good hand at cards. Hawkins talks too much to be a good cardplayer, but he has a superior knowledge of the country which is both embarrassing and flattering to his hosts. He also picked up a number of Irish dances, a compliment that could not be returned, "because our lads at that time did not dance foreign dances on principle." Buonaparte is well aware of the ironies and the tragic implications of this statement which he makes at the very beginning of his narration. He has already evaluated the effects of the execution of Belcher and Hawkins on himself and knows that part of the blame lay in allowing all his humane and instinctual responses to be violated for an abstract principle. Whatever common ground had been established by the Englishmen and their Irish counterparts had been sacrificed to some abstract code of retribution. Everything that Belcher and Hawkins do reiterates the voice of Gogol's poor copying clerk, "I am your brother." Every denial of sympathy and compassion for the sake of some vague, abstract code of justice or national honor creates those infinite and terrifying spaces.

The pattern of diminishing certitude emerges from every sacrifice of human sympathy to abstract principles. Looking back, Buonaparte realizes that his world was comprehensible as long as human action was scaled to human experiences. At the time he sees no reason why he and Noble should guard the Englishmen. They were in no way dangerous and they had no desire to escape. On the other hand, Jeremiah Donovan, Buonaparte's immediate superior, is more inclined to regard them as prisoners of war. Donovan is typical of so many of O'Connor's characters who fail to achieve a balanced perspective of themselves or others because of their rigidity or obstinacy. Unlike the other characters in the story, Donovan is repressed and anti-social. "He reddened when you talked to him, tilting from toe to heel and back, and looking down all the time at his big farmer's feet." The very qualities that Donovan is admired for, "he was a fair hand at documents," indicate how much more foreign he is to his countrymen than Belcher or Hawkins. Completely insensitive to human nature, he permits Noble and Buonaparte to treat the Englishmen as guests rather than hostages. When Buonaparte discovers that they are to be executed, he is furious with Donovan for not warning him in the first place. Unfortunately,

Buonaparte realizes that Donovan would never understand. . . . (pp. 312-13)

Buonaparte's sense of certainty diminishes as his estimation of what is reasonable or justified is swept aside by Donovan's sense of duty. His bewilderment increases as the abstract notions of duty and retribution conflict with his personal affections. O'Connor very skillfully orchestrates the absurdity of beliefs that have no relation to human experience. The old woman believes that the entire war started because, "the Italian Court stole the heathen divinity out of the temple in Japan." Noble believes in God and an afterlife but he is incapable of convincing Hawkins who is an atheist and a Marxist idealist. Hawkins maintains that the war is just another way that the capitalists, aided and abetted by the priests, preserve their power while keeping the people blind to injustice. Donovan believes in duty and with mechanical rigidity acts in accordance with his belief. By the end of the story, the murder of Belcher and Hawkins for duty's sake makes about as much sense as all the other beliefs, including the old woman's superstitious mutterings about hidden powers. Clearly, O'Connor is not particularly concerned with the claims of one belief over another, but with their effects on human conduct. What distinguishes Donovan from the rest of the characters is his inability to put aside artificial principles when they conflict with emotional sympathies. Even Donovan is vaguely aware of this conflict since the executions are performed in darkness with as little publicity as possible.

The final scene emphasizes Buonaparte's sense of tragic isolation and insignificance. Unlike Noble and the old woman he cannot pray. His reaction to the execution alters his moral universe. Buonaparte's sense of self diminishes as the terrifying spaces grow larger:

> Noble says he saw everything ten times the size, as though there were nothing in the whole world but that little patch of bog with the two Englishmen stiffening into it, but with me it was as if the patch of bog where the Englishmen were was a million miles away, and even Noble and the old woman, mumbling behind me, and the birds and the bloody stars were all far away, and I was somehow very small and very lost and lonely like a child astray in the snow. And anything that happened me afterwards, I never felt the same about again.

His loss of certitude is metaphorically emphasized by the allegorical darkness which envelops the entire episode. Ironically, Buonaparte's transition to maturity coincides with his perception of human frailty, that men are like lost children. (pp. 313-14)

In **"Uprooted"** O'Connor uses two brothers to dramatize the strain and anguish caused by the unnatural pursuit of a way of life that violates one's natural impulses. Ned Keating is very contemptuous of his peasant background and, after years of struggling for an education, is now a teacher in Dublin. Nevertheless, he is dissatisfied, and dreams of worlds more suitable to his temperament. Ned's intense awareness of himself combined with the strain of his effort to separate himself from his past, makes him too wary of impulses beyond his control. "He did not drink, smoked little, and saw dangers and losses everywhere." When his fancy takes flight, when he thinks he would like to be a laborer in Glasgow or New York so that he would once and for all find out what all his ideals meant, he patiently and cautiously withdraws. In effect, Ned's desperate determination to free himself from his past now prevents him from opening himself up to whatever life offers: "And his nature would continue to contract about him, every ideal, every generous impulse another mesh to draw his head down tighter to his knees till in ten years' time it would tie him hand and foot." One of the central ironies of the story is that Ned's brother Tom, a priest, is much more alive to the instinctual life and much less concerned with abstract ideals. But because he's a priest all his impulses to embrace life to the full are contracted. By the end of the story, Ned, who has always envied Tom's superior education and training, realizes that he too is hunted down by his own nature. The qualities that Ned envies are those which Tom would like to overcome or eliminate. (pp. 316-17)

The occasion for **"Uprooted"** is the decision by both brothers to visit their family for the Easter weekend. Back home nothing has changed. The Keating family and the peasants that live in this rural hamlet by the sea seem to live their lives according to an uninterrupted and unchanging rhythm. Whereas Ned is trying to discover a "scheme of life" in books or dreams of strange cities, these people are in no way alienated from themselves or their natural surroundings. Their awareness of life exists in the blood that runs through their veins, in the sea, in the constant drizzle and in the smell of salt and turf. Because these people have not been uprooted their lives flow from sea to blood to statement to action in one uninterrupted movement. Even Ned is impressed by the harmony between this way of life and the world which surrounds it: "It seemed to Ned that he was interrupting a conversation that had been going on since his last visit, and that the road outside and the sea beyond it, and every living thing that passed before them, formed a pantomime that was watched endlessly and passionately from the darkness of the little cottage."

Sea, turf, wind and rain are at the roots of the lives of these people and Ned, because of his ideals, and Tom, because of his orders, are both uprooted. The disparity between Ned and Tom's way of life and that of the peasants is emphasized when Tomas, their father, takes them to Carriganassa, presumably to introduce Ned to Cait Deignan. Cait is not as outspoken as her sister Delia who has been to Dublin and disparages the countryside. Ned is immediately attracted to Cait, but even then his reaction to her is more abstract than impulsive, as he finds himself murmuring, "Child of Light, thy limbs are burning through the veil that seems to hide them." Cait's blushes illuminate the beauty and vitality of her nature. For a moment, when she shares her shawl with Ned to protect him from the rain as they cross the field to the boat that will take the Keatings home, Ned experiences a momentary release from his circumscribed life: "The rain was a mild, persistent drizzle and a strong wind was blowing. Everything had darkened and grown lonely and, with his head in the blinding folds of the shawl, which reeked of turf-smoke, Ned felt as if he had dropped out of Time's pocket."

By the next morning the sense of exultation and release that Ned experienced the previous day is gone. Tom, who obviously was attracted to Cait, urges Ned to marry her. For the first time Ned realizes that Tom, in his own way, is as lonely and isolated as he. Though Ned abhors the idea of returning to teach rows of "pinched little city faces" in Dublin, he realizes that he cannot remain and marry Cait. Cait represents a way of life that is more attractive than he had ever realized, but he knows that he is no longer rooted in it. Outside his parents' house Ned sees a boy on a horse all bathed in a magical

light and realizes with more despair than ever what he had left behind:

> He unbolted the half-door, went through the garden and out on to the road. There was a magical light on everything. A boy on a horse rose suddenly against the sky, a startling picture. Through the apple-green light over Carriganassa ran long streaks of crimson, so still they might have been enamelled. Magic, magic, magic! He saw it as in a children's picture-book with all its colours intolerably bright; something he had outgrown and could never return to, while the world he aspired to was as remote and intangible as it had seemed even in the despair of youth.

Both Ned and Tom suffer because by choice and chance they lead lives that contradict the laws of their own being. Unlike the peasants of Carriganassa they no longer live in a world that is an extension of their own natures. And, ironically, it is at the point where both recognize the loneliness of the other that they seem most like brothers. (pp. 317-18)

The necessity for rationalizing the changes that occur to us, since it requires some form of accommodation to a set of circumstances that we are not familiar with, can be seen in **"The Genius."** Here a rather precocious Larry refuses to acknowledge the fact that an older girl took a liking to him in school because he reminded her of her younger brother who had been killed in an accident. But in **"The Study of History,"** Larry Delaney is terrified by infinite possibilities, but especially the notion that he may have been another child in another family. His harmless game of imagining what he may have been had his mother married the wealthy Mr. Riordan or his father married May Cadogan, becomes a nightmare after he meets the real May and her son Gussie. How slight an alteration of circumstances would have threatened his present identity (he does not consider that his present identity would not have existed) terrifies him. While innocently imagining himself to be Gussie, now that he has a real model, he is suddenly terrified by the possibility and for a moment he loses grip of himself:

> For the first time the charm did not work. I had ceased to be Gussie, all right, but somehow I had not become myself again, not any self that I knew. It was as though my own identity was a sort of sack I had to live in, and I had deliberately worked my way out of it, and now I couldn't get back again because I had grown too big for it. . . . I tried to play a counting game; then I prayed, but even the prayer seemed different, as though it didn't belong to me at all. I was away in the middle of empty space, divorced from mother and home, and everything permanent and familiar.

Like Buonaparte, in **"Guests of the Nation,"** Larry's experience of infinite possibilities is accompanied by a terrifying loss of both certainty and identity.

O'Connor's short stories begin with the painful consequences of prejudices and principles inherited by a nation because of a combination of its past history and present ideals. From, as G. B. Saul put it, "history fictionalized" in **"Guests of a Nation,"** he moves to individual histories and their consequences, such as in **"In the Train,"** and **"Uprooted."** In the period since World War II, he explores the roots of individual conduct in domestic relations and principally in the attitudes and reactions of children. Like Larry Delaney in **"The Study of History,"** O'Connor makes us aware of our uncertain position in a vague and at times terrifying universe. With the expansion of consciousness one becomes increasingly bewildered and isolated. Yet, ironically, it is this sense of isolation that is the shared experience of all humanity from childhood to old age. O'Connor's perception of this pattern of diminishing certitude is central to his aim of the short story as he conceived it, "to stimulate the moral imagination." From the moral child confused by passions and events, such as Helena and Buonaparte, he moves to the bewilderment experienced by real children. His profound understanding of the confusing circumstances surrounding our all too fragile existence is the source of the moral and humane perspective he has achieved. He does not assume a superior position to his characters. Though he is sympathetic, he is not sentimental. He admired Hemingway's short stories for their precise structure, but he could not appreciate his detachment. His own estimation of himself as a nineteenth century liberal and a nineteenth century realist again emphasizes the primacy of his moral perspective. But if we are to admire Frank O'Connor it will not be because of his good intentions, but because he was capable of echoing Akakey Akakievich's desperate cry, "I am your brother," into the twentieth century without sacrificing the demands of his art. (pp. 320-21)

> Murray Prosky, "The Pattern of Diminishing Certitude in the Stories of Frank O'Connor," in Colby Library Quarterly, Vol. IX, No. 6, June, 1971, pp. 311-21.

JAMES H. MATTHEWS   (essay date 1976)

[Matthews is the author of Frank O'Connor (1976) and Voices: A Life of Frank O'Connor (1985). In the following excerpt taken from the earlier work, he assesses the strengths and weaknesses of several of O'Connor's short story collections.]

The stories of **Bones of Contention** are typical of O'Connor's writing in the 1930s. By his own admission he was "fumbling for a style." Having found the exuberant romanticism of **Guests of the Nation** unproductive, he drew back his sights from the nation at large to smaller and less colorful social groups. The characters of these stories are not soldiers or lovers; they are peasants, drunken musicians, and tired old men. The narrative voice is casual and direct, calling attention to the persons in the story rather than to itself. Such phrases as "for as the old man said to me of him," or "as they all said," create in the story **"Peasants,"** for example, the impression of a story overheard, almost like gossip, from the peasants themselves about the "unpleasant memories" left behind by a former priest. **"Orpheus and His Lute,"** the hilarious account of the drinking habits of the Irishtown Brass and Reed Band, is told entirely as a *shanachie* tale. . . . For a writer so young these stories are surprisingly trim in form. What moral "comment" there is emerges from a natural and mature balancing of sympathy and judgment.

Though by no means its best story, the title story ["**Bones of Contention**"] is indicative of the prevailing manner of the entire volume. The very phrase "bones of contention," suggests low-grade dissension, not revolution; the struggles within all of the stories are, for the most part, isolated, petty, and spontaneous. Set in Cork and narrated by the grandson of the central figure, **"Bones of Contention"** concerns the monumental and eminently funny feud that erupts when a stubborn, hard-drinking, opinionated old woman insists upon supervising the funeral of an old friend. The cliché title serves as ironic com-

ment on the whole affair, for it is over a corpse that the "battle" is waged. The triviality of it all does not diminish the intensity of the conflict, so that all the fiery words and contentious bitching serve only to upset a normally serene community. (pp. 51-2)

O'Connor's struggle in **Bones of Contention** is primarily with himself, a struggle for a suitable style and for genuine concerns.

The finest single story in **Bones of Contention, "Michael's Wife,"** contains no provincial edginess or verbal squabbling. Irony is noticeably quiet and, above all, the sense of occasion is carried by highly evocative description. In his best stories O'Connor provides just enough physical background to give a particular incident locality. Dan Bride, the old man of **"Majesty of the Law,"** fits securely into his rough-hewn, almost archaic environment. Helena, the felon of **"In the Train,"** is placed in momentary relief by the description of Farranchreesht. The sense of total occasion crystallizes both stories, completing for a hesitant instant the incomplete puzzle of life. **"Michael's Wife"** is like the dramatic lyrics of ancient Irish poetry because of the way O'Connor merges the presentation of Irish place with the drama of an Irish person. It is not lyrical, as some critics have argued, just because of the descriptive language. It is lyrical because the sound of the voice is heard within a supremely resonant environment. And it is dramatic because its occasion is so immediate that the voice is at once discreet and expansive.

"Michael's Wife" is probably the most perfect illustration of O'Connor's theory of collaboration. In it he does indeed grab the reader by the lapels, dragging him into the center of the story. (pp. 56-7)

As satisfying as it is, **Bones of Contention** is more or less of a piece. By the time he produced his third volume of stories O'Connor had not only explored the limits of his medium but had begun to expand them. The stories of the late thirties and early forties, many of which were originally published in *The Bell*, are consistently fine. Consequently, **Crab Apple Jelly**, published in 1944, is at once the most varied and the most disciplined single volume he was to produce. As its title implies, the volume is both sweet and tart, entertaining and serious. It contains some of the savage criticism of Irish life apparent in *Dutch Interior;* O'Connor was adamant that Ireland begin to look beyond its own shoreline. However, he does not cast blame or seek causes. His humanism accepts people for what they are. If there is a unity in the volume it is not a preconceived campaign, just a natural unity of manner and tone.

The first story, **"Bridal Night,"** is powerfully impressionistic, and though it has more emotional impact than most of his stories, it is hardly sentimental. What strikes the reader is not just emotion, but the aptness of emotion. (p. 59)

O'Connor's so-called "lyrical" stories leave little doubt about the power of his prose to evoke highly poetic visual images. One of the most intriguing of these is **"Uprooted,"** a story about two brothers, a teacher and a priest, both frustrated by the present and cut off from the past. Ned Keating, the teacher, is bored in Dublin by routine and judicious patterns. Tom, the more spontaneous and vigorous of the two, is a curate in Wicklow. Together they visit their home in the west. O'Connor's descriptions and conversational exchanges are forthright and swift. The momentum of the story is fierce, disallowing deep speculation. Neither of the brothers has time to think, time to be nostalgic, or time to regret. They are bustled about, sharing hospitable drinks and meeting forgotten relations. On the island home of their mother's people they enjoy the company of young people. Ned enjoys a moment of physical attraction:

> Everything had darkened and grown lonely, and with his head in the blinding folds of the shawl which reeked of turfsmoke and his arm about Cait, Ned felt as if he had dropped out of Time's pocket.
>
> (pp. 60-1)

The end of the story is sullen; the next morning the brothers share in drowsy recollection their distraught night. Ned is troubled by Cait, of course, and the shadowy possibility of marriage. Tom's turmoil is more profound, suggesting a false vivacity the day before. . . . O'Connor locates both men in the "subjunctive"—Tom for his vicarious experience of human relationship and Ned for his reticence toward love. The committed priest thinks of what might have been and the uncommitted teacher of what might be, but rather than go back on choices once made they simply fall back into "Times pocket." As the two brothers leave home, the reader gets the distinct feeling that he is watching the final uprooting of the two men in a moment of suspended time. In the "magical light" of dawn over Cariganassa, Ned's loss is the loss of childhood, of an intolerably vivid world. His future is as "remote and intangible" as Tom's is futile and lonely. The lyrical moment is the uprooting itself, the suspending of human personality between the irremediable past and the intractable future, between promise and regret. (pp. 61-2)

O'Connor once said that "An Irish writer without contention is a freak of nature. All the literature that matters to me was written by people who had to dodge the censor." The sexual repression of middle-class Irish life provided more than one Irish writer ready material for fiction. Even as the "in" Irish writer was expected to attack the clergy, so he was expected to "shock" Irish readers with a little sex, or to expose ruthlessly the sexual blight of a parochial society. O'Connor avoided both subjects until *Crab Apple Jelly,* refusing to wage a token war, to stoop to rhetoric. Later he was censored and to some he is only remembered for that. **"The Mad Lomasneys"** is one of his earliest and one of his most successful stories about the strange way of love among the Irish. The relationship of Ned Lowry and Rita Lomasney engages O'Connor's singular attention in the story from their first, awkward encounter as adolescents to their strained and unfortunate parting. Rita is an independent, rather rash girl, with a manner best described as audacious and a voice that seems to laugh casually at life. Ned is rather unperturbably automatic, though also "clever . . . precise and tranquil." But O'Connor is not just juxtaposing the predictable and the unpredictable. He is carefully accenting the subtle games played by the middle class. Consequently, much of the story takes the same dramatic form as **"The Luceys,"** so that despite a lapse of time the effect is intensely immediate. (p. 65)

The stories of *Crab Apple Jelly* represent the refinement of O'Connor's technique of exploiting the "tone of a man's voice, speaking." He didn't see life steadily or whole; he heard it in bits and snatches. . . . Nowhere is his attention to voices more evident than in **"The Long Road to Ummera,"** a simple tale about an old woman's eccentric wish to be buried in the mountain home of her people. By his own admission the main voices were those of his own father and grandmother. The story begins: "Always in the evenings you saw her shuffle up the road. . . . " The narrator is personal and informal, speaking about his own neighbors, not about strangers. Thomas Flanagan takes this fidelity to the community to be contradictory to O'Connor's theory of the "lonely voice." . . . The voice is lonely though it speaks within the community; O'Connor's voice is lonely not in spite of his fidelity to the community but because of it. (pp. 68-9)

Before the appearance of **"The Drunkard," "Christmas Morning,"** and **"My Oedipus Complex"** he used first-person narration sparingly, and then generally as an interlocutor retelling a story told to him. The involvement of the narrator in **"The Long Road to Ummera"** or **"Peasants"** is genuine but not personal. However, one of the best stories in *The Common Chord,* **"Judas,"** is the hilarious account by a settled bachelor of his first courtship; whether it was also his last we can only guess. He chuckles at his naive fantasies and foolish antics. But he fails to comprehend what the reader can't miss—his tragic dependence on his mother. O'Connor had listened to Irish life with brutal honesty. What he found was that people make themselves miserable, that they delude themselves, that they act in silly, indiscreet, or even vicious ways in spite of everything they know to the contrary. When he turned to situations closer to himself, his honesty still prevailed. He resisted the temptations of misanthropy and self-indulgence by adhering strictly to the limitations of his aesthetic: he was an observer, not a judge or an exhibitionist. (pp. 69-70)

A Set of Variations, twenty-seven stories written mostly in the 1960s, is not his best collection but it does suggest that in the last few years of his life Frank O'Connor had returned to whatever it was that produced the stories of the 1930s. Throughout the volume he is turning old sod, sifting through old themes, returning to old loyalties. However, the book is hardly the work of a tired old man resurrecting past glories. Rather, it is the work of one whose hand is steady, whose eye is keen, and whose voice is clear. As a whole, *A Set of Variations* has a range of interest and style comparable to *Crab Apple Jelly.* The domestic relations are mainly adult relations. In fact, there are more stories about old people and about death than in any previous volume. But O'Connor could never be grim or morbid; his humor is as wry as ever. (p. 75)

Scanning the entire course of Frank O'Connor's literary career, one is above all impressed by a remarkable unity of purpose working through a maze of conflicting impulses. He is a person of fierce sympathies. His idealism was often too buoyant, his bitterness often too heavy. But when it came to his writing he was a model of discipline and control. What this indicates, I think, is that . . . he never really ceased to be a romantic, by which he meant a way of seeing things, a style of life at once impulsive and searching. He rejected the romantic aesthetic, which he saw as the sentimental indulgence of the trite emotion, the reliance on the nostalgic or rhetorical generality. Likewise, he rejected the realistic way of seeing things—the "sensible" compromise, the cynical indifference to human needs, or the sterile, academic appraisal of life. But he completely affirmed the realistic aesthetic—the careful manner and sensitive frankness that are the trademarks of his writing from first to last.

Unquestionably, O'Connor's early writing represents some of his very finest work. His early stories and essays are especially impressive for the exuberance of their concerns and the unpretentious clarity of their style. His first volume, *Guests of the Nation,* was mainly about the insurrection. The energy

O'Connor (left) and friend John Kelleher at Duleek, County Meath, 1950.

of the entire volume emanates equally from O'Connor's unrestrained youthfulness and his idealistic fervor. That he later repudiated this early mode of writing does not repudiate its idealism. The violence of **"Guests of the Nation"** is a fresh, even creative sort of thing; but for him to have indulged it would have been to stagnate. Though he moved away from violence, he nevertheless continued for some time to operate within a context of youthful vigor.

All in all, the story of Frank O'Connor is the story. Invariably, his imagination forced itself through the picturesque, the historical and the abstract to some story, some point of vivid impact. For him human dignity and rationality inevitably yield to the sudden impulse, to the unpredictable and passing moment. O'Connor believed that it is "not for nothing that some of the great storytellers . . . have been tramps." . . . To O'Connor a story, whether it was about the Nun of Beare, Michael Collins, the Rock of Cashel, or those "displaced persons" of Cork, was nothing less than a "lyric cry in the face of destiny."

Everything he wrote displays his improvising and contending spirit, but his stories speak most eloquently of his lonely struggle for integrity and freedom. If any single attitude consistently looms large in O'Connor's work, it is a distrust of human reason, a suspicion of the abstract or the unnatural. Yet ironically, the principal strategy of his stories is contain-

ment, a deliberate scaling down of issues, situations and techniques. Simplicity requires conscious discipline and superb control—it's hard to be easy. . . . When all is said, his stories will stand as his most enduring contribution to modern literature and to Irish life. (pp. 89-90)

> *James H. Matthews, in his* Frank O'Connor, *Bucknell University Press, 1976, 94 p.*

MAURICE WOHLGELERNTER   (essay date 1977)

[*Wohlgelernter is a Polish-born American critic and author of* Frank O'Connor: An Introduction *(1977). In the following excerpt taken from that book, he analyzes the war stories in* Guests of the Nation.]

[Some] of O'Connor's public experiences, first in the guerilla war and then in the Civil War, serve as a clear inspiration to some sixteen stories, most of which appear in his collection *Guests of the Nation.* In these stories, he argues the meaning of these experiences, seeking to express, artistically, the reaction of his countrymen to the agonies at the birth of their nation.

This collection, O'Connor carefully notes, was originally written "under the influence of the great Jewish story teller Isaac Babel," by which, he means, of course, Babel's *Red Cavalry.* Yet that O'Connor, who read widely in European literature, should, of all authors, come under the influence of Babel is not, on further reflection, at all surprising. For, in both these collections, we perceive "the writer's intention to create a form which shall in itself be shapely and autonomous and at the same time unusually responsible to the truth of external reality, the truth of things and events." The truth of the events, it should be added, inescapably contains moral issues with which both artists were, personally, deeply involved.

One of the prime moral issues for many in war, we know, is not whether one can endure being killed, but whether one can endure killing. Though neither Babel nor O'Connor could endure killing, they were, nevertheless, greatly interested in the impulse to violence which seems innate in all men. (pp. 31-2)

O'Connor, like Babel, [placed] . . . war and peace, violence and repose, side by side to show man's unending dilemma in having to choose between the two, though fascinated by both. (p. 33)

Not only does war reveal to man the "unreality" of his fascination with violence, but also, O'Connor suggests in many of the stories in *Guests of the Nation,* war shows man how removed the real is from the ideal; however widening is the gap between what actually is happening or has happened to his hopes and plans and what he thought he was fighting for. This situation troubled O'Connor terribly. . . . (pp. 33-4)

Far more disillusioning for O'Connor than the ever-widening gap between the ideal and the real, resulting, in part, from a war that was a "cruel," silly thing, is the fact that many of his countrymen also lost the meaning of honor, decency, and fair play. And nowhere is this more powerfully revealed than in **"Guests of the Nation."** (p. 35)

This tale touches the reader not only because of its intrinsic beauty and power but also because it shows O'Connor's understanding of man's nature, especially when man loses all sense of self and his humanity. Above all, it has a universality, the ultimate achievement in fiction, because it transcends the bounds of time and space. . . . "Duty," as O'Connor projects it in the stories, becomes a shield for monstrous acts of evil—and all because of man's failure to see as O'Connor does what abstract terms or forces, or even dispassionate governments, can do, and often actually succeed in doing to his moral nature. Reading **"Guests of the Nation,"** the sensitive reader actually feels "lost" and "astray in the snow."

But not every narrator in O'Connor's war stories, one must hasten to add, is led astray. Nor is every character bedevilled by his own inhumanity and coldness. Nor does every protagonist feel the dark power of melancholy surging within him. There are forces in the lives of men which help them retain their humanity, sanity, and probity. One such force in man is, of course, love. (pp. 35-6)

[In] all of his stories, O'Connor's humor consists essentially of his rare ability to see simultaneously the dual aspects of life—good and evil, love and hate, peace and war, the beautiful and the ugly. In other words, his humor in the "synthetical fusion of opposites, the gift of saying two things in one, of showing shine and shadow together." (p. 38)

[The] disgust with all that he saw happening to his country and countrymen may well explain why O'Connor, like, say, Yeats and Joyce and O'Casey, "had long ago decided that Ireland was morally bound to live up to his expectations." That may also explain why these giants carried on a life-long lover's quarrel with their country, with its "introverted religion" and "introverted politics." But since Ireland, for them, never did live up to their expectations, they were at ease with it only in their poems, plays, and stories. In them, they could weep and laugh, often doing both simultaneously.

And if O'Connor, like some of his contemporaries, found the political life of his country difficult to bear, it is clearly evident that in his stories of war and revolution he was, at least artistically, at ease. And these stories, on careful reading, are irresistibly interesting, precisely because "O'Connor loved those from whom he was alienated." Loving them, he naturally placed them prominently in his art. (p. 40)

What O'Connor observed and then recorded in his stories about the servants of God and the servants of the servants of God, such as their housekeepers, is rich in understanding, meaning, and humor. That he had early renounced his formal relationship with religion did not prejudice him, in his extended writings, against the Irish clergy. In point of fact, it gave him a certain objectivity not always available to the committed. These servants—bishops, parish priests, and curates—appear in O'Connor's stories as subject to the same strains and stresses in all their dedication to the "higher" life as those involved in the "lower" life. And the description of the priests that finally emerges from these stories, therefore, contains a keen insight not only into the Irish priest's professional posture but also his own personality. At times these two elements in his nature are in a conflict which gives added meaning to the artistic quality of the tales. (p. 50)

Maurice Wohlgelernter, in his Frank O'Connor: An Introduction, *Columbia University Press, 1977, 222 p.*

RICHARD J. THOMPSON (essay date 1978)

[*In the excerpt below, Thompson examines O'Connor's first*

four short story collections and observes that his best work is marked by a strong moral quality and a longing to regain something lost.]

Frank O'Connor's first four volumes are the real achievements in the Irish short story after the form crystallized a generation before in *The Untilled Field* and *Dubliners.* O'Connor deserves to be recognized not only as an artist who synthesized the ruralism and anecdotalism of Moore with the urbanity and psychological penetration of Joyce, but also as the mediator of the provincialism of the *seanachai* and the internationalism running from Ó Faoláin to Higgins. The purpose here is to examine the special flavor and manner of those four volumes—thereafter O'Connor's work declines in merit and distinction—in order to weigh his artistic importance. The volumes in question are *Guests of the Nation* (1931), *Bones of Contention* (1936), *Crab Apple Jelly* (1944), and *The Common Chord* (1947).

O'Connor was a dogged craftsman, a perfectionist, an indefatigable rewriter and self-second-guesser—all habits he shared with James Joyce, as he did a devotion to deep learning of diverse sorts. Yet O'Connor branded Joyce as "the first of the Ph.D. novelists." *Dubliners* was to him an example of how not to write short stories, for it preferred characterization over a quality that O'Connor thought prime: incident, which he called theme. (p. 65)

O'Connor's work is characterized by a yearning to recapture something lost—primal order or an older decency that has been overridden by social duty or, perhaps, a childhood of ineffable simplicity and trust. Ultimately, like Seán O'Casey, O'Connor is an Oedipist who discerns a better world before the advent of striving and grief. His longing for order, decency and love suggests his intense moralism which, along with a tone of unshakable equanimity, gives his stories their principal trademark. O'Connor says in *An Only Child* that, while he did not believe in the immortality of his own soul, he did believe in that of some souls, doubtless his mother's, and so "perhaps it was the thought of these [souls] that turned me finally from poetry to story-telling, to the celebration of those who for me represented all I should ever know of God." But these very characteristics engender his worst faults—a lack of complexity, occasionally muddy and ill-conceived plots, and a cloying nostalgic cheerfulness, what Walter Allen has called O'Connor's persistent stance of "What an interesting little boy I once was!" Temperamentally, O'Connor's vision was directed backwards to the time, recounted in his autobiography, when he was Michael O'Donovan from Blarney Lane. "Look back to look forward," he writes in his dedication to *The Backward Look.* And since his tendency is Oedipal, the habitual frame of reference in his stories is the family.

We observe the common chord tugging us ever toward the safety of womb and tomb in stories like **"The Long Road to Ummera,"** in which an old woman values her place of burial over her earthly home; or, more clearly yet, **"The Bridal Night"** in which a demented young man is lulled in the nightlong embrace of a Madonna-like neighbor who serves simultaneously as his wife and mother before he is put in the insane asylum. In **"The Babes in the Woods,"** young Terry loses his benefactor-aunt when he publicly states, within the hearing of the aunt's boyfriend, what he secretly hopes: that she is his mother. In the end he is comforted by an older child, the maternal Florry:

When she put her arms around him he fell asleep,

but she solemnly remained holding him fast to her. Then she fell asleep too and didn't notice the evening train going up the valley. It was all lit up. The evenings were drawing in.

In an ending reminiscent of Joyce's "A Painful Case," the dynamic phallic train going up the valley churns on, but the peaceful child slumbers securely in Florry's fertile arms. Oblivion, a parent's reassuring arms, painless ceasing upon the midnight air, trains that carry one—usually back—from present pain: these are the regular images of O'Connor's stories. The yearning for Oedipal escape is clear in the early stories such as **"After Fourteen Years"**: "And the train took him ever farther and farther away . . . " and **"The Procession of Life,"** in which the prostitute tells the constable: "I'm finding him a place to sleep—the poor child is perished with the cold. Leave him to me, constable. I'll look after him for the night," to the later ones like **"Judas"**: "I went to her and she hugged me and rocked me as she did when I was only a nipper," and **"The Masculine Principle,"** in which a father finally finds the son he never had in the sire of his daughter's bastard. The final words of **"The Grand Vizier's Daughter"**—"Oh daddy, I'll never do it again! Daddy, come back to me! Come back!"—sum up the sense of lost innocence and parental longing which runs through his *oeuvre*.

O'Connor's early stories—the greatest of which is **"Guests of the Nation,"** which I will take up shortly—have a toughness and bite, an undertone of repressed or potential violence—as in **"In the Train," "The Majesty of the Law,"** and **"The Luceys"**—that he unfortunately neglected later. The stories after World War II, or at least after his fourth collection in 1947, begin to grow formulaic; many appeared in *The New Yorker,* whose editors seem to have encouraged the formula. These stories often retreat from the horror and absurdity of life that one finds in his most mature stories and substitute instead puckish charm, mannered humor, quaint local color, predictable warmth, and general blandness. O'Connor grew at once too gentle—so that the successes of his later work lie mainly in slapstick, as in the Bishop of Moyle stories—and too sanguine, self-parodying, and "important," as if Yeats's warranty that he was doing for Ireland what Chekhov had done for Russia had finally begun to sink in.

What are his particular trademarks? As a young writer, O'Connor spotlights sadness and agony; constantly, he announces a text at the beginning of a story and then illustrates it fictionally. The young O'Connor hears mainly the melancholy, long, withdrawing roar of life. In fact, an evocation of melancholy crowns the endings of as many stories as do those forlorn trains, and melancholy itself is the presiding humor and the omnipresent condition of consciousness. . . . (pp. 65-7)

One of the most typical and successful of O'Connor's stories, if one were to choose from among the nearly 200 that he wrote, is **"Guests of the Nation,"** correctly called by Brian Cleeve "in a sense the seminal story of modern Irish literature." The story has as theme the centuries-old enmity between Ireland and Britain, and it is most typical of O'Connor because it illustrates the loss of fellow-feeling and basic decency that follows from the imposition of political dogma. Like several of O'Connor's early, and best, stories, **"Guests of the Nation"** is based on the author's personal experience, in this case on the Republican side during the Troubles. (pp. 69-70)

From its opening sentence, the natural, congenial, narrative voice that was to become O'Connor's chief triumph is at work. Big and doomed Belcher shifts his legs out of the ashes "at dusk" as his fellow hostage, little 'Awkins, lights the lamp and produces the cards; the narrator and Noble join the others at the table and complete the renewed human community from whose midst division is excluded, for all four are "chums." Belcher's and 'Awkins's Englishness is in this context unimportant and accidental; the narrator assures us that he has "never seen in my short experience two men that took to the country as they did." All four are simply men, merged in the egalitarian ritual of the game. Two of them have low-comedy names (Belcher's would appear later in Lucky's monologue in *Waiting for Godot*) and the Irish pair, who are in turn idealistic and gulled, are dubbed, just as comically, Noble and Bonaparte. O'Connor's prelapsarian world is violated by the assertiveness of the IRA chieftain, Jeremiah Donovan, an outsider, a watcher among players, a farmer among townsmen, a keeper of documents among men of imagination, a "supervisor" who "comes out with the usual rigmarole about doing our duty and obeying our superiors." What Donovan, whose name mordantly caricatures O'Connor's own and that of the great Fenian Jeremiah O'Donovan Rossa, personifies—a churlish hierarchical ideology that subverts natural impulse—will become O'Connor's object of scorn in his main stories.

Unlike the reader, the narrator, Bonaparte, fails for a time to see the execution of Belcher and 'Awkins coming, for Bonaparte is gentle and thinks that one doesn't shoot one's "chums." The author skilfully suppresses the gravity of official murder, the horror of an-eye-for-an-eye "justice" and its jolting effect on Bonaparte, until the very end. But Bonaparte's parochial mind, trained not to oppose, begins to suspect after he tells Noble at bedtime of Donovan's intention to execute the English. The sentence, "After we had been in bed about an hour he asked me did I think we ought to tell the Englishmen," nicely hints at the discomfiture of the tossing, mulling rebels. Just when Noble and Bonaparte begin to detect that their commitment to revolution undermines their devotion to the larger pattern of human responsibility, the reader's own appreciation of the story's implications begins to grow. He sees in the running argument between the value denouncing 'Awkins and the "Hadam and Heve" affirming Noble a miniature of the entire British-Irish dispute, and he sees in "the old woman of the house" a varicosed Countess Cathleen full of superstitious and pagan notions about Jupiter Pluvius and how the war was started by an Italian in Japan! Deftly O'Connor moves the whole scaffold of suggestions having to do with Irish serf-mindedness, piety, matriarchy, and spiritual revolt forward to the point-zero of Bonaparte's insight into the superiority of life to politics. How affecting is Bonaparte's final realization, and how private, for here he parts company with the reflexive grief and piety of Noble and the old woman and notices what has happened in overall perspective. In doing so he posits an unwritten sequel for his life in which he will attain the widening and isolated consciousness of moral vision:

> Noble says he felt he seen everything ten times as big, perceiving nothing around him but the little patch of black bog with the two Englishmen stiffening into it; but with me it was the other way, as if the patch of bog where the two Englishmen were was a thousand miles away from me, and even Noble mumbling just behind me and the old woman and the birds and the bloody stars were all

far away, and I was somehow very small and very
lonely. And anything that ever happened me after
I never felt the same about again.

One of the most trenchant conclusions to any short story
since the deep and dark tarn silently closed over the House
of Usher, this is a perfect exemplar of O'Connor's view of the
short story as a permanently shaping moment in a character's
life rather than a novelistic record of the passage of time—a
view, incidentally, which grew more honored in the breach
as his career continued. The feeling of loss is keen and irreversible (". . . I never felt the same . . . again"), the sense
of helplessness poignant. The external universe bears mute
and eternal witness, contorted as if in pain for man's folly.
The story is a glowing accomplishment for a writer still in his
twenties, and it bristles with the narrator's uneducated, vernacular verve, with the *patois* that Kate O'Brien later saw as
O'Connor's highest glory, and with the spirit of youth and
vulnerability. In the rewritten version of **"Guests of the Nation,"** the narrator becomes more of a man of the world looking back; his rough edges are gone and the original vigor is
compromised by studied wisdom. The crossroads, the loss,
the reshaping, the repudiation of "duty," the collusion with
nature, the vernacular power and the even tenor of the voice,
are all characteristics that O'Connor carried forward from
this prototype to later stories.

The revelation that the-about-to-be-shot Belcher's wife left
him the handkerchief he used as a blindfold, the letter from
'Awkins's mother that Belcher states is in 'Awkins's pocket
in case his executioners want to write her, and Belcher's deference to 'Awkins who, still kicking, requires the *coup de
grâce* ("Give 'im 'is first. . . . I don't mind. Poor bastard, we
dunno what's 'appening to 'im now.") skirt the edge of ba-
thos. But O'Connor doesn't lose his balance. As Irish Bonaparte ties his handkerchief to that of English Belcher to complete the makeshift blindfold, an interplay of darkness and vision is set up: Bonaparte comes to participate in Belcher's
death not just as a gunman but as a newly enlightened covic-
tim whose innocence is blasted full of holes. In Belcher's
stoic, extravagant gesture lies the beginning of Bonaparte's
own disaffection and also of the courage he will need. Like
the cards that were their favorite pastime, Belcher and
'Awkins go to their revenge-death as objects in a wanton
game. Often O'Connor uses membership in a group—the Republican army in the first ten stories in *Guests of the Nation,*
the band in **"Orpheus and His Lute,"** the family in **"The
Luceys,"** the townspeople of Farranchreesht in **"In the
Train,"** the police in "The Majesty of the Law"—to signal the
loss of individual option and impulse.

The "crossroads" ending recurs in later stories in *Guests of
the Nation* (1931). In **"Nightpiece with Figures,"** an unforgettable "young nun will not pass . . . lightly from [the]
minds" of three IRA men on the run; and the appealing story
"Jo" is another variation on the point of human feeling being
more important than duty. Sometimes the device gets a kind
of running start, with years of a person's life passing as a preliminary to an act of self-discovery. This happens, for example, in the *Bones of Contention* (1936) story **"Lofty,"** where
a short-lived humility overtakes a lifelong snob after his wife
leaves him and a one-time protegé takes his place as a political force. But the most resonant use of such an ending is
found in the volume's finest story, **"In the Train."**

Based on an actual trial O'Connor had witnessed in the Central Criminal Court in Dublin, **"In the Train"** is a story that
only gradually comes clear. As the initial confusion—over
the relation of the people in the successive train cars, the relevance of Michael O'Leary, and the nature of Helena
Maguire's misdeed—slowly dissipates, the reader is heart-
ened to discover that this story is not one of O'Connor's occasional puzzlers in which the resolution is enigmatic and yet
pleased with itself. . . . Rather, what he has done, ingeniously in **"In the Train,"** is to lift the story from its expected
static setting in the courtroom and place it in the rushing
train, a dynamic locale that stresses both the divisiveness of
the townspeople, sitting stolidly as they are in four different
cars, and also their common motion and inability to detrain
until reunited again in their hometown. Union and division,
independence and reliance, instinct and tribal law, are played
off against one another constantly in each "smoky compartment that jolted and rocked its way across Ireland."

Thus, the events of the story follow "in the train" of the action at the trial where Helena was declared not guilty, because the villagers lied for her, and follow also "in the train"
of the enduring sentiment of country people against informing. The reactions of the four separate clusters of passengers—the gentle police sergeant and his shrewish wife, the
four policemen, the group of peasants, and Helena with her
inebriated new acquaintance—are as automatic as the behavior of metal shavings pursuing a passing magnet. As the
groups move about and interact, the private losses that prey
on them slowly emerge: the sergeant's wife's failure to buy a
hat in the city and the sergeant's regret at not giving her a
life in the great world; the drunk's loneliness without the
"sincere" Michael O'Leary; Delancey's frustrated desire to
move to Waterford; climactically, Helena's loss of Cady Driscoll whom it is now too late to marry, her youth having been
squandered on the boorish husband her family forced upon
her. Just as her new blouse will be worn beneath her shawl,
her new life will be lived in opprobrium, among the human
herd now stirred up against her, like the cats who attack the
policeman in Delancey's anecdote.

"The law is truly a remarkable phenomenon," the slightly
"squiffy" sergeant points out to Helena; and he surely refers
to the law of Farranchreest, according to which Helena will
be given "the hunt" by the villagers who have controverted
the formal law of the city. As they approach their own village, which seems "like the flame-blackened ruin of some
mighty city," the sergeant strikes a note of separation: " 'Tis
time we were all getting back to our respective compartments." Temporarily forced to conform to city standards, the
villagers have ignored their citizenly duty and decently lied;
but for them, and so for Cady Driscoll, Helena is now a
marked woman. Her life has been in decline since the judge
freed her and she bought the blue blouse "on the way down
from the court." At the end, confronting her own image in
the train window, watching the little cottages "stepping down
through wet and naked rocks to the water's edge," Helena detects that she has gone from one misfortune to a worse: ". . .
she could only wonder at the force that had caught her up,
mastered her and thrown her aside." The wording and imagery owe something to Yeats's "Leda and the Swan" and
crown Helena's insight into the conflicting claims of wisdom
and appetite. **"In the Train"** is one of O'Connor's most
haunting stories. The author neatly balances the lowly and
bleak life of the village and its provincial police against the
bright lights of the law affirming city and its lofty magistrates.
The train of time careers along the parallel tracks of actuality
and possibility. (pp. 70-4)

The thinnest and tartest of O'Connor's four volumes is *Crab Apple Jelly* (1944). Here he veers away from his origins as storyteller in the manner of Daniel Corkery and Isaac Babel and sounds the stark moral depths that so impressed him in the work of a writer to whom his mentor Corkery had introduced him—Chekhov. It is the individualistic moralism of Chekhov and his affirmation of life in a world of decrease that impressed O'Connor, as well as Chekhov's facility for keeping atmosphere and characterization independent of one another and in the most artful proportion. What O'Connor said of the great Russian applies as well to himself: "He always writes as a moralist, but his morality is no longer the morality of the group, it is the short story writer's morality of the lonely individual soul." In *Crab Apple Jelly*, O'Connor's themes become the Chekhovian ones of loneliness (**"Song Without Words"**), aberration (**"The Bridal Night"**), death-yearning (**"The Long Road to Ummera"**), lives wasted and opportunities missed (**"Uprooted"**).

"The Bridal Night" is a major, brief effort, a gem. The crazed Denis's need to hold his idealized lady not only in his thoughts but in his arms abed to keep at bay the banshees of madness illustrates the universally shared terror of things slipping away, of the mind's dark night. The reader concurs with Denis's aggrieved mother's remark about the sacrificial Winnie that "no one would say the bad word about her" after her night of offering Denis consolation. The temptation to scandal-mongering is thwarted by the sacramental power of human contact: "From that day to the day she left us there did no one speak a bad word about what she did. . . . Isn't it a strange thing and the world as wicked as it is . . . ?" In the end, the implacable earth spins on, darkness having "fallen over the Atlantic, blank grey to its farthest reaches." The bad word of the town and the backdrop of uncaring nature mock man's pathetic liaisons, the charade of his bridal nights.

The Good Priest, based loosely on O'Connor's longtime friend Father Tim Traylor, is a stock figure in several O'Connor stories; he makes an appearance in **"The Star That Bids the Shepherd Fold"** as the young French-speaking curate Father Devine, who, as the Good Priest often does, outsmarts—here in collusion with a German ship captain—the agents of repression. The story is a warm-up for the more elegiac one that follows. **"The Long Road to Ummera,"** first published in *The Bell* in October, 1940, opens with one of the loveliest paragraphs in O'Connor's work:

> Always in the evenings you saw her shuffle up the road to Miss O's for her little jog of porter, a shapeless lump of a woman in a plaid shawl faded to the colour of snuff that dragged her head down on her bosom where she clutched its folds in one hand, a canvas apron and a pair of men's boots without laces. Her eyes were puffy and screwed up into tight little buds of flesh and her rosy old face, that might have been carved out of a turnip, was all crumpled with blindness. The old heart was failing her, and several times she would have to rest, put down the jug, lean against the wall, and lift the weight of the shawl off her head. People passed: she stared at them humbly: they saluted her: she turned her head and peered after them for minutes on end. The rhythm of life had slowed down in her till you could scarcely detect its faint and sluggish beat.

The reader cares immediately about this shuffling woman, weighted down yet determined to go her own timeless way to the end of the road. The sentences grow fragmentary and the words collapse to breathless monosyllables as her spirit flags. A dominant theme of this story, and of others in *Crab Apple Jelly*, is the necessity of pride and the price one pays for self-esteem. In these stories we find O'Connor's sympathies at their widest and his style at its most suggestive and poetic—plangent and moving, yet not "melancholy." (pp. 74-6)

Cultural transition figures in the other principal stories in *Crab Apple Jelly;* **"The Luceys," "Uprooted,"** and **"The Mad Lomasneys."** In the first, Tom and Ben Lucey carry on their sibling rivalry by remote control through their sons. Tom has long been envious of Ben's better brain, so he takes pains to provide his son Peter with an education that will guarantee Peter's social welfare; the easier-going Ben has no such anxieties about his own son, Charley, but he belittles Peter to his brother when Peter embezzles from his employer. Tom Lucey's unrelenting enmity for his brother is just as rigid and merciless as the contempt he expresses toward his son after his crime. Tom sticks to the ancient ways of spite and revenge as if they were principled. . . . He is probably O'Connor's chiefest eccentric, an Olympian, thought queer by the town, fond of old books, callous toward the alcoholic wife whose malady he no doubt contributed to, a hater of weakness, an opponent of the breezy slang of the day that would call a six-pence coin a "tanner." He is, in short, an anachronism, an embittered draper expecting and never getting the homage once accorded the capitalist who now must live in an egalitarian society that he detests. This is one of O'Connor's favorite strategies—to set the anachronistic character down in the midst of an updated social ambience. Usually the character fails. In **"The Mad Lomasneys,"** Ned Lowry loses the capricious girl he loves because he is too completely a scion of the decorous Hayfield-Hourigans, too much an ancestor worshipper, to keep up with the impulsive "chancer" Rita.

In **"Uprooted,"** the sons are expected to compensate for the sins of the father. Old Tomas "had the gumption" and won the daughter of the O'Donnells, though they were "stiff" to him because he owned no land. To save family face, his two sons have had to go east and make something of themselves, but Ned Keating, having "fought his way through the college into a city job," is now a disappointed man. His eyes are "already beginning to lose their eagerness." He is tired of Dublin and thinks longingly of Glasgow and New York; he cannot wed the sensuous, desirable Cait, for to do so would mean going back, would mean another landless Keating buckling under to another Carriganassa heiress. By mischance Ned has spiritually uprooted himself—he cannot go home because, as he tells his brother at the end, "We made our choice a long time ago and we can't go back on it now." Ned is lost in a social time warp, the past "outgrown" and the future "remote and intangible," another anachronism who, like Tom Lucey and Ned Lowry and many another O'Connor protagonist, is impaled on his own imperious pride.

The stories in O'Connor's fourth collection, *The Common Chord* (1948), show not a deepening sense of sympathy or of social complexity as does *Crab Apple Jelly*, but a new push by his heroes and heroines in the direction of personal freedom. Having gone through a phase of understanding their problems in *Crab Apple Jelly*, his characters now proceed to assert their independence, at least temporarily, from authority and "duty." The two opening stories in the collection are illustrative. In the first, **"News for the Church,"** Father Cassi-

dy humiliates the errant convent-school teacher guilty of for-
nication, "stripping off veil after veil of romance leaving her
with nothing but a cold, sordid, cynical adventure like a bit
of greasy meat on a plate." His brow-beating leads in the end
to her outcry:

> "But you're making it sound so beastly," she
> wailed.

> "And wasn't it?" he asked with lips pursed and
> brows raised.

> "Ah, it wasn't, father," she said earnestly. "Honest
> to God, it wasn't.

> At least, at the time I didn't think it was."

That carnal love can be not only pleasurable but tender is
news for the Church indeed, but it fails to make a lasting impression on Cassidy, who trudges on "heavy policeman's
feet" to watch the chastened girl leave "under the massive
fluted columns of the portico." He is a successor of all those
fierce upholders of "duty" in the early O'Connor stories, and
although he has forced the girl into collapse, it is *she* who has
taught the Church that "Honest to God, it wasn't."

The title of the second story, **"The Custom of the Country,"**
refers to the sexual inhibition of Irish womanhood. When
Anna fails to convert her heathen Englishman to Irish Catholicism, she "converts" herself to heathen Englishness and,
pregnant, decides to decamp for England to practice bigamy
with the already married Ernest. In doing so she follows the
other custom of the country, that of fleeing Mammy, in whatever form Mammy may lurk. And, really, the longest and
most ambitious story in **The Common Chord, "The Holy
Door,"** hardly differs in its central declaration. Charlie Cashman struggles to extract himself from the disagreeable control of his scorpion-like mother and his untouchable first
wife. At times he has to cope with the contumely of the town
and especially that of his first wife's family. But, most of all,
Charlie has to free himself from his own sexual ineptness. The
holy door in its primary sense refers to a consecrated place
in Rome, "opened once every seven years," to which childless
pilgrims go to pray for fecundity. Unabashed, O'Connor en-
larges the image to include the sliding confessional door of
Fr. Ring (another Good Priest), Polly's bolted bedroom door,
and the ardor-arousing iron gates of life.

Full of self-doubt about his sexual prowess, Charlie is a convenient victim for his mother's murderous barbs. Mrs. Cashman is one of O'Connor's last great eccentric creations. When
Charlie first marries Polly, she taunts him about Polly's fal-
lowness and, thus, his own impotency: "Many a better cake
than she didn't rise." After Polly's death and Charlie's taking
up with her best friend, Nora, Mrs. Cashman delivers her verdict of Nora's potential as Charlie's second wife: "That's the
hand that'll never rock a cradle for you." In a frenzy of sexual
anxiety, Charlie blurts out his proposition to Nora that they
"have the honeymoon first and the marriage after." It is a
pretty phrase but an infelicitous strategy. But the story is
never allowed to slip over into farce, for Charlie's maturation
gradually occurs. He sees what he really wants—the somatic
Nora—and goes after her despite all opposition, including
Nora's. Here in Charlie's final colloquy with the fearful Nora
is the story's climax:

> "But what'll you do if your mother puts spells on
> me?" [Nora] asked in a dazed tone, putting her
> hand to her forehead.

"Roast her over a slow fire," snapped Charlie. He
was his own man again; aged seventeen, a roaring
revolutionary and rationalist, ready if necessary to
take on the whole blooming British Empire and the
Catholic Church.

The cry of the independent spirit is heard in O'Connor's best
stories, capping the last stage of his growth. His early championing of decent human contact and the deepening social
understanding of his middle years culminates in **The Common Chord.** (pp. 77-80)

> *Richard J. Thompson, "A Kingdom of Commoners:
> The Moral Art of Frank O'Connor," in* Eire-
> Ireland, *Vol. XIII, No. 4, Winter, 1978, pp. 65-80.*

GORDON BORDEWYK   (essay date 1978)

*[In the following excerpt, Bordewyk evaluates several of
O'Connor's stories and separates them into four subject categories: war, religion, childhood, and love.]*

O'Connor was primarily a short story writer. Writing well
over 100 stories and publishing 13 collections in his lifetime,
he demonstrates his craftsmanship most clearly in this genre.
Deborah Averill notes that the characters of his stories are
searching for human relationships as an antidote to isolation.
They are also characters in search of meaning, sometimes
succeeding, occasionally failing. In the stories, O'Connor develops themes of community and communion through narrative incidents which often revolve around a conventional
quest motif. . . . Not fond of symbols or intellectual abstractions, O'Connor finds wonder and magic in the ordinary,
mundane, common circumstances of daily life. This concern
with the fundamental qualities of everyday existence and the
search for significance is evident in the four major groups into
which his stories cluster: stories of war, of religion, of youth
and of marriage. We will examine how the quest for meaning
changes the lives of his characters in the four groups of stories.

Most of O'Connor's wartime stories are contained in his first
collection, **Guests of the Nation.** It is not coincidental that
these stories cluster together in a single volume, because
O'Connor always was concerned with the unity of a story
collection. . . . While **Guests of the Nation** is not limited to
stories of war, wartime tales comprise its core. The title story
["Guests of the Nation"] is one of the most familiar and perhaps the most frequently anthologized of O'Connor's tales.
It concerns two English prisoners, Hawkins and Belcher,
who are being guarded by Irish troops. The Englishmen
adapt readily to the Irish environment, enjoying the pleasures
of companionship without a thought of escape. When the
Irish guards learn that their wards must be shot as a military
reprisal, they are shocked and distressed because they have
come to know the pair as friends who are not markedly different from them. Both the English and Irish soldiers have
found meaning for their lives in their friendship, not in the
impersonal abstractions of conquest or nationalism. After
Hawkins and Belcher are killed, the narrator states, "And
anything that ever happened to me after I never felt the same
about again." The tale is moving in its elegant simplicity. Not
only does it contrast the ways men face death—the fevered
protestations of Hawkins and the laconic resignation of Belcher—but it also suggests the dehumanizing impact of war.
The ironic title emphasizes the fact that Belcher and Hawkins
become chums with their captors, their hosts, who are forced

to abandon friendship and shoot the Englishmen who represent "the enemy." The title also suggests that culpability for war's consequences is not limited to the soldiers who give or carry out orders, but extends to the entire nation which sanctions the war.

"Nightpiece with Figures" is another story about war. Three comrades sit in a barn conversing softly, tensely anticipating some undefined danger. An old nun, Sister Alphonsus, comes to the barn to give them food and to chat with them about the past. A young nun dressed in black also comes to the barn, and she stirs a buried emotion in the soldiers when she says that, despite the disunity in the country, Ireland will outlive its informers. The men respond to the patriotic fervor of the young nun who is a symbol of a new nationalist Ireland. Sister Aphonsus, a Fenian, claims that the girl is too passionate and impatient, but the men have been changed:

> They are all happy as though some wonderful thing had happened to them, but what the wonderful thing is they could not say, and with their happiness is mixed a melancholy as strange and perturbing, as though life itself and all the modes of life were inadequate. It is not a bitter melancholy like the melancholy of defeat, and in the morning when they take to the country roads again, it will have passed.
>
> But the memory of the young nun will not pass so lightly from their minds.

The story closes with this tableau. The lives of the soldiers have been changed by their chance meeting with the nun who reinforces their belief that Ireland is a noble country. They have found meaning not in empty symbols or abstractions but in the person of the nun who represents faith and loyalty for their cause.

Human contact as a necessary antidote to wartime isolation is thematically developed in **"September Dawn."** The story concerns the disbanding of a column of volunteer soldiers and the retreat of the leaders, Keown and Hickey, who spend their first night at the home of Hickey's old aunt. Her dreams of independence had been shattered by Parnell's death and she is alienated and disillusioned. Keown drinks too much whiskey before retiring and wakes up terrified of the wind; released from the pressure of battle, he retreats into a youthful fear of natural forces. Hickey, normally more stoic and ascetic than Keown, responds to his furlough by sneaking out of bed at dawn and kissing Sheela, the kitchen girl. Like the young nun in **"Nightpiece with Figures,"** Sheela becomes an emblem of Ireland to the war-weary soldier. Exhausted from the pressure of rebellion and disgusted with his non-generative and unsatisfying isolation, Hickey needs to establish a human relationship to restore himself. The story ends with an overly lyrical crescendo:

> as she rose he took her in his arms and kissed her. She leaned against his shoulder in her queer silent way, with no shyness. And for him in that melancholy kiss an ache of longing was kindled, and he buried his face in the warm flesh of her throat as the kitchen filled with the acrid smell of turf; while the blue smoke drifting through the narrow doorway was caught and whirled headlong through grey fields and dark masses of trees upon which an autumn sun was rising.

Despite the romanticism of this final scene, the story sensi-

tively develops the theme of simple and natural emotions as a corrective to the acquired sterility of war. (pp. 37-40)

O'Connor's stories of war do not attempt to convey the sweep and motion of battle. They do not try to stimulate patriotism or examine the causes and motivations of conflict. The tales probe the human consequences of conflict, raising questions about the effects of war on ordinary individuals. Although the results are not uniform, the general effect is isolation or alienation which must be countered.

A second major group of stories concerns religion. As a major component of people's lives and as an institution which molds opinion and behavior, the church has stimulated the imagination of Irish authors for several generations. O'Connor's stories of war are generally not politically motivated and his stories of religion do not spring from dogmatic impulse. He is neither an apologist for the church nor a bitter anti-cleric; he adopts whatever attitude seems appropriate to his narrator.

"The Old Faith" is a whimsical portrait of the priesthood. Bishop Gallogly visits the ruins of the cathedral at Kilmulpeter and reads a history of St. Mulpeter prepared by Father Devine. The Mulpeter legend is composed of the raw materials of myth:

> It seemed that like most of the saints of that remote periods, St. Mulpeter had put to sea on a flagstone and floated ashore in Cornwall. There the seven harpers of the King had been put to death through the curses of the Druids and the machinations of the King's unfaithful wife. St. Mulpeter miraculously restored them to life, and through the great mercy of God, they were permitted to sing a song about the Queen's misbehavior, which resulted in St. Mulpeter turning her into a pillar-stone and converting the King to the one true faith.

Father Devine is impressed by the legend of Mulpeter, but the bishop remains unaffected by the account. At the bishop's residence for dinner that night, the priests begin drinking and exchanging stories of the fairies to the distaste of Father Devine. After dinner the priests go walking until one by one they drop from drink, imagining themselves in the clutches of fairies—a historical regression in Devine's view. The tale develops contrasts between the past and the present—with the past represented as being less affected, more simple, spontaneous and natural. The story weaves the strands of folk myths, saints' legends and contemporary religion. Essentially, superstition, belief in legends and religious faith are presented as equivalent routes to meaning. The story, however, develops the theme in a very tentative and lighthearted manner. (pp. 40-1)

"News for the Church" is another story about the role of religion as-enforcer of traditional social institutions, especially marriage. Known for his easy confessions, Father Cassidy becomes stern with a 19-year-old girl who confesses to sleeping with a man. Never having participated fully in life, he feels manipulated by the girl who had to tell someone about her affair, selecting a priest as the most convenient auditor. He probes the details of her experience, making it seem sordid and cheap. As he watches the girl leave the church with a burden of guilt, he chuckles and almost winks at the statue of Saint Anne, the patroness of marriageable girls. Cassidy has never known the pleasure of carnal love and feels cheated by the casual liberty and freedom of the girl. He is able to find meaning only through vicarious participation in the lives of people on the other side of the confessions booth.

Not all of O'Connor's religious stories are about the priesthood; some deal with individual manifestations of faith. Dan Turner in **"This Mortal Coil"** is a committed atheist who is penalized by society for his convictions. Tessie Bridie believes that Dan is the answer to her prayers for a husband, but he refuses to accept the church to satisfy her. When she decides to marry a more pious man, he unsuccessfully attempts suicide. On his second attempt, he "sees the light" and decides that life is worth living. In Irish culture, religious observance or the lack of it is a strong social determinant. Those without faith are convinced that church members do not share their misery or doubts; those who are believers avoid contact with atheists. Atheism in O'Connor's Ireland is an alienating and ostracizing position; as a character searches for satisfying relationships, he is almost compelled to faith as an antidote to isolation. Dan Turner's extremism is contrasted to the narrator's moderate lack of faith. The narrator is able to get along well in the mainstream of society because he does not flaunt his doubts or carry them to extremes—he is adaptable to custom and compromise. But his atheism is still an alienating force because when Turner has converted at the end of the story, he avoids the narrator and his former companions at all costs because of their lack of a "proper faith."

"My First Protestant" is perhaps O'Conner's most sensitive and ambiguous story about religion. Although faith is the ostensible theme, the primary movement in the story is the search for human rather than spiritual communion by the narrator and Winifred Jackson. Winifred comes from a Protestant family and she embodies the kind of spontaneity that O'Connor admires. Dan, the narrator, says: "That was what I liked in her, her capacity for quick, spontaneous intimacies without any element of calculation in them." Winifred meets Dan in the Catholic home of the Dalys' where she is seeing Joe Daly and Dan is seeing Marie. Although Winifred is not committed to her parents' faith, she resents Joe's refusal to marry until she converts to Catholicism. Joe's concern with this ritual does not spring from genuine conviction—he is quite indifferent toward faith—but is motivated by his pragmatic worry about the success of his business if the custom is not observed. Although Joe wants her to give up her faith and risk offending her parents, he would not be willing to do the same for her. Once again religion becomes a social force which inhibits human bonding. When Winifred and Joe break their engagement, Dan begins to neglect his attendance at Mass because of his distaste for the narrowness of religion and the alienation it produces. He begins to frequent the quays on Sunday mornings with a growing group of educated men known as "The Atheists' Club." Winifred marries another man who dies after a few years, and one Sunday Dan is surprised to see her leaving Mass. She explains that her parents are no longer alive to object and that she has become Catholic for the sake of her children. Essentially the story deals with the theme of unfulfilled love. Dan and Winifred have been searching for meaning in life, but their quest has led to divergent responses. Winifred, as a mother, has turned to Catholicism to compensate for what she has missed in life; Dan has abandoned his faith because he feels it has inhibited his search. He concludes the story with these words: "I thought how strange it was that the same thing should have blown us in opposite directions. A man and a woman in search of something are always blown apart, but it's the same wind that blows them."

Like his stories of war, O'Connor's religious stories are not didactic. It is the human consequences of any situation that intrigue O'Connor, and these tales are no exception. The possibilities of faith, the consequences of atheism, the abuses of religious power and the foibles of the clergy are some of his religious themes. They suggest an author who is detached from the struggles of belief, sensing that religion provides a potential route in the quest for meaning. Well aware of the possible dangers of religion, he neither endorses nor rejects religious faith; instead, he uses religion as another means of developing his motif of the quest.

A third major topic of the stories is childhood. These tales are variously nostalgic, cynical, bittersweet and optimistic. O'Connor's predominant attitude about youth is not easily defined, because his fictional treatment varies from story to story. The tales deal with the process of maturation and, like the adult characters, children in the stories are engaged in a quest for a meaning and growth.

"First Confession" examines a religious milestone in the life of a seven-year-old boy. Jackie is terrified about the severity of his sins and is afraid of the punishment he anticipates. Not fully understanding the physical arrangement of the confessional, he climbs onto a shelf to see if the priest is listening to him. When he falls, the priest consoles him and listens to him confess his daydreams about murdering his grandmother and sister. Sympathetically the tale develops the terror religion instills in the boy and juxtaposes that dread against the compassion of the priest who gives him only three Hail Mary's as penance.

Some of the stories develop themes of youthful discrimination between illusion and reality. Maturity requires the ability to distinguish actuality from appearance, but loss of innocence is the price paid for this knowledge. **"The Man of the World"** is about a young boy, Larry, who goes to Jimmy Leary's house for a holiday. Larry narrates the nostalgic anecdote some 40 years after it occurs. Older and more sophisticated than Larry, Jimmy acts as a voyeuristic mentor to the younger boy when he proposes that they watch the bedroom of a newly married couple. Seeing the man and woman prepare for bed and say their devotions, Larry is suffused by a mystical feeling: "at that moment everything had changed for me, how, beyond us watching the young married couple from ambush, I had felt someone else watching us, so that at once we ceased to be the observers and became the observed." The narrator realizes that the situation has been a different type of initiation from the one intended by Jimmy, but he does not dwell on his youthful naivete. He concludes the story with Jimmy's ironic admonition not to judge the situation by that evening; sometimes the show is much better. (pp. 42-4)

Some of O'Connor's young characters are disturbed about changes in their family life, such as the usurpation of a familiar role. **"The Pretender"** is about the disruption of Michael's life by the intrusion of Denis Corby into his family. Another usurper is Larry's father in **"My Oedipus Complex."** While his father had been away at war, Larry was the center of his mother's attention and every morning he would climb into bed with her to discuss his plans for the day. When his father returns from the conflict, he supplants Larry as the central object of the mother's concern. Larry's jealousy sparks a period of open rivalry and competition between father and son which is terminated only when a brother, Sonny, is born. Then Larry and his father reconcile in a mutual feeling of exclusion, the baby supplanting them both. The subtlety of the story and its gentle comedy create a tone which is suitable for the story's theme of the necessary fluidity of male roles within a family and the centrality of the mother as a source of strength and vitality.

Some of the stories exemplify the movement toward independence from family. **"Masculine Protest,"** like **"My Oedipus Complex,"** sketches a process of alienation from the mother when Denis is chagrined to discover that his mother will not be home for his birthday, reinforcing his impression that she does not care for him. He decides to run away to Dublin, after withdrawing his postal savings, but he has chosen an inauspicious day because the Post Office is closed. After bicycling to a town 12 miles distant, he meets a friendly bartender who pays his busfare home. His father greets Denis on his return and they never mention the incident to Denis' mother. Nor does he feel the need to run away again. The Irish mother is the center of her family and when she fails to fulfill her expected role, the males are alienated. Denis experiences bonding with other men—his father and the bartender—as a result of their shared alienation, resulting from their unsuccessful search for comfort in their family life.

In his stories of childhood, O'Connor does not dwell on the superficial pleasures of youth or the sentimental attractions of nostalgia. He sympathetically, and sometimes ironically, develops the quest for maturity, independence, experience or stability that motivates his young characters.

The fourth major group of stories deals with love and marriage. These tales are about characters who look for meaning through mature relationships. **"The Custom of the Country"** is about a bigamist, Ernest Thompson. He cannot persuade Anna Martin to abandon her inhibitions and make love to him. The plot has a complication similar to that in **"My First Protestant;"** Anna's mother insists that Ernest convert to Catholicism before he marries Anna, so he plunges into instruction enthusiastically. On their honeymoon, Anna learns that her "new husband" is already married and the father of two children. After he has returned to his home in England, she discovers that she is pregnant and she is not disturbed, but pleased. Her relationship with Ernest, despite its unorthodox nature, has lifted her above the commonness of her surroundings. Supported by her romantic fantasies of nobility, her quest for meaning, although unsuccessful by traditional standards, has proved fruitful for the idealistic girl. Her illegitimate child becomes emblematic of her temporary, but significant, love.

Another tale about multiple love relationships is **"A Torrent Dammed"** Tom Looney opens a chemist's shop in a small town, but he cannot draw much trade away from Gorman, his chief competitor. Gorman is lazy, lethargic and unambitious, but he is a member of the town's social structure, not an outsider like Looney. Maudie Moynihan falls in love with Tom because of his ambition. She teaches him about the customs and traditions of the town so that he can act accordingly. Whatever he tries, however, seems to fail until he meets Hilda Doherty. He is initially attracted to her because of her father's wealth, and after they are engaged his business begins growing. When Hilda falls off a horse and is hospitalized, Maudie visits the shop with her friend Kitty. Tom moves to Dublin and, in a surprising conclusion, marries Kitty. Love relationships and marriage are sometimes used as vehicles for social and economic success, but O'Connor does not endorse this pragmatic approach. He has closer affinities to characters who act on natural impulse rather than calculated strategy.

The narrator says a man really needs three women: one for stability, another for sympathy, and a third for inspiration. Tom marries Kitty because of the inspiration she provides.

Spontaneity and a willingness to take risks are presented as positive attributes in two final stories of the marriage group. **"After Fourteen Years"** has little narrative action. Nicholas Coleman arrives in his hometown after a long absence, apprehensive and thinking that he will be back in the city the next day. He goes to the convent to see Marie, his former lover who has become a nun. They converse at length about people and places from their past. She seems settled and devoted to her routine in the convent. Nicholas is settled too, and although he is exposed to life in the city, his participation in it is primarily vicarious. Life has passed both characters by because they opted for a stable rather than a vulnerable course of existence. The story ends on a note of regret as Nicholas listens to the metallic clicking of the train taking him back to the city. (pp. 45-6)

O'Connor's stories of war, religion, childhood and love are related by a shared questing motif. Characters look for happiness and meaning in the circumstances of their daily lives. While their search is not always successful, the fact that they keep examining life, questioning it and seeking its significance is the important matter. Those who have resigned themselves to their situations, whether through complacency or regret, are alienated from the vibrancy and excitement of life. Those who are not content with a routine have the potential to find meaning through relationships with other people. (p. 47)

Gordon Bordewyk, "Quest for Meaning: The Stories of Frank O'Connor," in Illinois Quarterly, *Vol. 41, No. 2, Winter, 1978, pp. 37-47.*

ROGER CHATALIC (essay date 1979)

[*In the excerpt below, Chatalic analyzes several of O'Connor's most important stories and maintains that O'Connor's themes derive from his conception that each individual is essentially alone in an indifferent universe.*]

O'Connor's storywriting probably took its direction from his association with [Irish writer Daniel] Corkery. He read the latter's *A Munster Twilight* as early as 1916. Corkery later introduced him to the tradition in which he was writing, viz. that established in Ireland, under the influence of nineteenth-century Russian fiction, by Moore's *The Untilled Field* and Joyce's *Dubliners*. In this same tradition O'Connor in turn took his place, claiming Turgenev as his "hero among writers". He did for the Irish provincial town what Moore had done for the Irish countryside and Joyce for the Irish capital. Corkery also introduced him to Browning, whose verse he admired all his life, and whose dramatic monologues helped him to shape his conception of his art. He has pointed out that he wrote the war stories in *Guests of the Nation* under the influence of the Soviet Jewish writer Isaac Babel, whose *Red Cavalry* came out in English in 1929, but apart from some technical devices like the use of the narrative present, the resemblance is not striking. As Thomas Flanagan remarks, O'Connor chiefly responded to a similarity in his situation and Babel's—"young slum intellectuals swept into revolutions which overturned their societies and their inner world". His mature work, at any rate, moved away from the "romanticism of violence" and the over-poetic style he later criticized in Babel. It also departed from the cold naturalism and self-conscious formal elaboration of Joyce, whose influence may be discerned in stories like **"In the Train"**. It found its keynote in a realism that tried to "unite the idealism of Yeats with the naturalism, the truthfulness of Joyce": a gently satiric, humorous realism, which may owe something to the writer's familiarity with Gaelic literature . . . and yet fraught with emotion, never far removed from pathos; a realism less candid than O'Flaherty's, and less intellectually sophisticated than O'Faolain's.

O'Connor's themes stem from his vision of modern man as the individual reduced to his private lights in a dark universe which is apt to make him feel, like the protagonist of **"Guests of the Nation"**, "somehow very small and very lost and lonely like a child astray in the snow". His sense of "the terror of the human soul alone with nature and the night", of "the mystery of human existence, of humanity faced with the spectacle of infinity", made him imagine life as "a warm vivacious lighted house in the midst of night and snow". In his stories he celebrates the virtues of the familiar, of warm intimacy, companionship and love. At the same time he shows himself aware that it behoves man to hold his own against the external chaos, and keep his house "warm", "vivacious" and "lighted". Reacting against the modern dissolution of humanism, he celebrates the individual's capacity to overcome his limitations by his subjective energy. This means that, to quote his own judgment of Chekhov, he writes "as a moralist, but his morality is no longer the morality of a group; it is the short-story writer's morality of the lonely individual soul".

His most conspicuous theme is Ireland. He tried to minimize its significance for him:

> I prefer to write about Ireland and Irish people merely because I know to a syllable how everything in Ireland can be said; but . . . only language and circumstance are local and national; all the rest is, or should be, part of the human condition, and as true for America and England as it is for Ireland.

Yet this (disingenuous ?) claim to universality amounts really to an admission that his imagination was tied to his home-

O'Connor with American poet Robert Frost in Ripton, Vermont, 1952.

land. As one of his friends remarks: "It is hard to imagine him writing about something else". He wrote about the Irish in war and in love, about Irish life in the country, in cities and small towns, about Irish clerics, Irish children, and Irishmen abroad, etc . . . Above all, as he himself emphasized, he wrote about "the Irish middle class Catholic way of life, with its virtues and its faults . . . ". His work offers a wide-ranging, if sometimes partial, picture of post-revolutionary Ireland.

He claimed to have written about his country "without any of the picturesqueness of early Irish writing which concentrated on colour and extravagance", and "out of a nationalism that had achieved its results and was ready to look at everyday things with a new respect": he saw himself "turning away from the public to the private thing". Such statements throw light on his deeper imaginative interests, but hardly allow for several aspects of his picture, especially the caustic, satirical bias he gave it in reaction to his country's socio-political drift. He was not above delighting in "colour and extravagance", as one may see, for instance, in **"The Long Road to Ummera"** or **"The Miracle"**, which are reminiscent of his admiration for Synge, and Somerville and Ross. And even his early work is not free of concern for the "public thing". His war stories often read like indictments of the inhumanity to which Irish nationalists were led by romanticizing abstractions and violence. His stories of rural Ireland raise the question of the nation's identity, centered as they are on the opposition between traditional peasant mores and the law, police and judiciary, of the new bourgeois order. His fiction of the forties and the fifties is highly concerned with exposing what he called "the death-in-life of the Nationalist Catholic establishment": it pictures a choking, provincial Ireland of small towns and sleepy cities, debilitated by ignorance and prejudice, dominated by a vulgar, sectarian middle class, and ridden by an intolerant, obscurantist priesthood. He was led to focus his anger more particularly on his mother country's fiercely puritanical attitude to love and sex, and her invidious treatment of unmarried mothers and illegitimate children. Even his stories of childhood often expose failings of Irish life. On the whole, O'Connor's vision of Ireland can hardly be said to spring from a readiness to look at everyday things with respect, or from "a nationalism that had achieved its results"; but rather from one that felt itself betrayed. As several commentators have suggested, it is charged with the feelings of a "disappointed lover".

If O'Connor's vision of Ireland turns "away from the public to the private thing", it is by avoiding the communal and deliberately seeking the personal—"romantic, individualistic, intransigent". For that reason, O'Connor's Ireland, at once home and earthly hell, also stands, as he claims, for his vision of the world at large. He inclined to view short-story protagonists as "outlawed figures wandering about the fringes of society", or submerged in "a society that has no sign-posts, a society that offers no goals and no answers", thus revealing a yearning for one that would. It is significant that he warmly admired Trollope. While it cannot be said that all his characters clearly answer such descriptions, it is true that many appear alienated from their group by their failure or refusal to conform to its norms and conventions. Several, like Stevie in **"My Da"**, have to become exiles to realize themselves. Others, like Evelyn in **"The Masculine Principle"**, find that, no more than Helena in **"In the Train"**, or indeed O'Connor himself in real life, could they fulfil themselves away from home. This points to a major conflict in the writer. He celebrates the moral and spiritual independence of figures like Anna in **"The Custom of the Country"**, who rebels against her society's mores; like the boy in **"Old Fellows"**, who finds in his imagination the strength to conquer his terror of the dark and reach his home by himself; or like the old woman in **"The Long Road to Ummera"**, who, by the sheer force of her personal vision, overcomes all obstacles to have herself buried in her faraway mountain village. But he also shows himself aware that such courses lead away from the security of the familiar, that the quest for personal integrity is apt to contradict the need for social integration, and—whatever his delight in reckless individuality or quixotic triumph—that self-realization also demands a lucid recognition of life's harder realities. Many of his stories are stories of disillusionment, which show their heroes frustrated, if not always shattered, by forces that violate their personality or nature: they often present experience as a painful thing that fosters nostalgia for childhood innocence and, ultimately, the bliss of the maternal womb.

O'Connor's fiction expresses a search for inner balance. He conceived of psychic life as the opposition of two principles: the masculine (judgment, conscience) and the feminine (instinct, emotion, fantasy), and felt that, like dreams, works of art answered their creator's need to reconcile these two principles in himself. This opposition clearly underlies the central conflict of many of his stories, for instance that of the priest and his parishioners in **"Peasants"**, of Rita and Ned in **"The Mad Losmaneys"**, or, as emphasized by the title, of Jim and Evelyn in **"The Masculine Principle"**. O'Connor tentatively acknowledged a preference for "the instinctual as against the intellectual", which can be recognized in his treatment of romantic characters like Charlie Cashman, and his interest in youthful heroes whose spontaneity is yet unspoiled, or in priests like Devine or Fogarty (as opposed to Jackson) whose emotional, imaginative nature frets under the discipline of their calling. But in other stories—**"The Mad Losmaneys"**, **"The Cheapjack"**—, he shows the necessity of a balance between the two. Ironically, in **"The Wreath"**, it is the judicious Jackson who has to extricate the imprudent Devine from his predicament.

O'Connor seldom touches overtly in his stories upon the metaphysical bearing of his vision. He does so, however, in **"Guests of the Nation", "This Mortal Coil"** and **"Don Juan's Temptation"**. He writes about the protagonist of the latter:

> He had woken up from a nice, well-ordered, intelligible world to find eternity stretching all round him and no one, priest or scientist, who could explain it to him. And with that awakening had gone the longing for companionship and love which he had not known how to satisfy, and often he had walked for hours, looking up at the stars and thinking that if only he could meet an understanding girl it would all explain itself naturally.

Characteristically, Gussie's temptation takes the form of a yearning for some ideal or faith, "something bigger than life that would last beyond death". This suggests that, symmetrically, his girl's "conversion" is an attempt, after the collapse of her simple "optimism", to stand up to the mystery of experience by forging her own values and trusting to her own judgment. The individual's need to assert his freedom, however rashly, to live out his imagination of himself, and triumph by his inner light over the limiting pressures of his circumstances, remains, for all O'Connor's claim to being a "realist", his most characteristic and essentially romantic theme.

His narrative technique and style can also be related to his central concern with human desolation. He felt that "literature is communication", that "it lifts the burden of solitude and puts us in contact with other minds". And although he once declared himself "cursed at birth with a passion for techniques", and has recently been praised by O'Faolain as "the finest craftsman in the art of the short story that Ireland has produced", he objected to the cult of form for its own sake, because to him it meant turning one's back on the reader. Deliberately eschewing detachment, symbolism, and modernistic devices, he sought "the conversational movement of prose, the casual, sinuous, evocative quality that distinguishes it from poetry and is intended to link author and reader in a common perception of the object". (pp. 192-97)

O'Connor's greatest technical originality was his attempt to recover in his fiction what he called the "narrative impulse", i.e. the spontaneous vigour of oral storytelling. It has been suggested that he thus tried, like Moore before him, to relate himself to the Irish oral tradition. (pp. 197-98)

His concern with the narrative impulse bore on his techniques of composition. Reacting against the modern short story's addiction to poetry and atmosphere on the one hand, to scenic over-concentration on the other, he insisted that a story should have a dramatic subject, statable in four lines, and comparable in its movement to the bending of an iron bar. Except for a few early sketches, his own fictions deal, if not always with such violent action as **"Guests of the Nation"**, at least with striking incidents, like Fogarty's tacit recognition of his love for Una in **"The Frying Pan"**. He knew that a good story, having its principle in some "glowing centre of action", often had to be handled, for the sake of intensity, in "one quick scene, combining exposition and development"—as **"The Majesty of the Law"** or **"News for the Church"**. Yet he was also aware of the danger, that by sacrificing exposition and narrative to drama, he might deprive the reader of the information necessary for his imagination to work. His rewriting of **"First Confession"** shows that he preferred to "isolate the exposition in the first four paragraphs and allow the development to take place in three scenes or five", which implied a re-evaluation of narrative and chronology (cf. the final versions of **"The Mad Losmaneys"** and **"The Luceys"**). While Chekhov held that "it is better to say not enough than to say too much", O'Connor wrote: "If I have to choose between too much and too little, I prefer too much". His insistence on clarity and logic, which sometimes led him to over-explicitness, reveals his need to put down his awe of life's mystery.

The store he set on the tone of the speaking voice depended on the strong aural quality of his imagination. He observed that his impressions of people mainly came from their wording of things—"the cadence of their voices, the sort of phrases they'll use", and he felt that "everybody speaks an entirely different language". This made him a master of natural, colloquial dialogue. He makes his characters speak an easy vernacular, sometimes dialectal, sometimes slangy, which he deftly modulates according to their social conditions. He also shows himself very alert to the emotional rhetorics of individual voices, giving liveliness to his pages by having them converse more or less tangentially, by questions and exclamations, as in the opening scene of **"The Long Road to Ummera"**. In his best stories he defines the conflicts of the characters in terms of their linguistic idiosyncrasies. . . . (pp. 198-99)

But of course, O'Connor's cultivation of the speaking voice lies chiefly in his treatment of his narrators. In his stories of childhood, the point of view is that of an adult reporting what, as a rule, was originally for him an excruciating experience. He now presents it humorously, from a comfortable distance, but yet in close, warm sympathy with his remembered young self. He achieves this double focus by speaking as much as he can the language that was his at the time of the action (cf. **"The Pretender"**). Several of O'Connor's early stories are told by well defined narrators, often shown addressing a listener who stands for the author (**"The Bridal Night"**) in a colloquial dialectal idiom. In later stories like **"The Holy Door"**, the teller becomes hard to identify, at once dramatically present and elusive. He speaks in a familiar, animated, sometimes testy, sometimes jocular tone; implying that he is a neighbour of the protagonists, with remarks such as: "That was no joke in *our* church"; and yet enjoying an omniscient narrator's privilege to enter the characters' private minds—for instance, in **"The Holy Door"**, mostly Charlie's, but also others', like Polly's during her wedding night. This inconsistency seems to reflect the writer's conflicting attitudes to his world: his anxiety to be integrated in it, and yet to escape its limitations. It shows him, as in his stories of childhood, trying to draw on the resources of both "instinct" and "judgment" to overcome his dread of alien realities.

As Vivian Mercier has remarked, O'Connor is a writer who would have to be included in a representative anthology of the world's short stories. If he has been comparatively ignored by academic critics, it is probably because his work can be readily enjoyed without the help of commentators. He shared in the reaction against modernistic experiment in fiction, against those whom he called "university" writers, and tried to remain a popular "natural" one.

This, of course, does not mean that he is without depth. Like many other contemporaries, he sought in his creation a remedy against existential anxiety—a sort of substitute for religion. By exalting individualistic self-realization in warm human intimacy, and seeking it for himself in his art, he tried to overcome his terror of the eternal silence of infinite spaces. (pp. 199-200)

> *Roger Chatalic "Frank O'Connor and the Desolation of Reality," in* The Irish Short Story, *edited by Patrick Rafroidi and Terence Brown, Humanities Press, Inc., 1979, pp. 189-201.*

JAMES H. MATTHEWS (essay date 1980)

[*In the excerpt below, Matthews explains how O'Connor's experiences in the Irish Civil War shaped the stories in* Guests of the Nation.]

The fifteen stories which eventually came together in **Guests of the Nation** were conceived in O'Connor's mind as a unified volume, somewhat in the manner of Corkery's *A Munster Twilight* and Joyce's *Dubliners,* even more in the manner of George Moore's *The Untilled Field,* the book which he believed contributed a new simplicity of form and style to the prose fiction of the Irish literary movement. Based on Turgenev's *Sportsman's Sketches* Moore's volume of stories seemed to span, in the mind of the young Frank O'Connor, the gap between poetry and realism. (p. 74)

The first three stories of **Guests of the Nation** concern the struggle with Britain—from the Easter Rising to the Treaty.

The next eight stories deal exclusively with the Civil War, while the final four stories, which seem somewhat out of place, are set in ambiguous time before or after the times of violence and national upheaval. Offhandedly, O'Connor called it his "war book" in a letter . . . with an equally casual reference to Isaac Babel's *The Red Cavalry,* which had just been translated. That Babel's stories made an impression on the young O'Connor is without question. He found them compelling in a disturbing way; he had been reading Russian fiction for some time, but this book spoke a new sensibility. Babel's war stories contained violence mingled with elegance and lyricism. "My First Goose" and "The Death of Dolgushov," two stories about the effect of outright brutality on sensitive individuals, undoubtedly touched a close nerve in O'Connor, whose own war memories still plagued him—not what had happened so much as how he had reacted. In Babel's stories he saw another way to span realism and poetry, to redirect intense moral concerns through stringent esthetic form. O'Connor was not so much influenced by the violence as by the manner of the stories—control, brevity, objectivity, and a lyrical apprehension of human problems.

Intense as his response to Babel was, O'Connor actually relied more heavily on another Russian for the conception of his own war stories. Turgenev's *Sportsman's Sketches* remained O'Connor's model for a volume of stories—each story discreet and whole, yet related by some thematic ambiance to the other stories in the volume. What unity **Guests of the Nation** possessed was more of tone than of theme, however, for inevitably O'Connor's mind gravitated from idea to situation, from theme to character. For a storyteller like O'Connor, life is a highly fragile and personal affair unified not by grand abstractions but by the inconvenient, elusive, and diverse patterns etched by common humanity across the surface of events. Invariably, his imagination forced itself through the picturesque, the historical, or the abstract to some situational flash point, some point of vivid impact where story becomes a "lyric cry in the face of destiny."

The violence and idealism of the events of 1916 to 1923 created in Ireland a mood of national hysteria. At least that was the voice heard by O'Connor trying to capture those events in prose six years after. In fact, the two extremes between which **Guests of the Nation** vacillates are hysteria and melancholy, between thoughtless act and numbed thoughtfulness. Benedict Kiely detected in these stories a "genuine bliss-was-it-in-that-dawn-to-be-alive romanticism," an adolescent enjoyment of the guns, the ambushes, the flying-columns. Indeed, this hysterical romanticism swirls across the surface of all but the last four stories.

"Jumbo's Wife," "Alec," and **"Machine-Gun Corps in Action"** are examples of the romanticized violence of the sort O'Connor found in Isaac Babel. In these stories war exposes the folly and weakness of character as well as the normal responses of people under pressure. Situation dominates character and the voice is blurred. The stories fail, not because O'Connor idealized violence, but because he failed to control its comic energy.

However, the next story in the volume, **"Laughter,"** delivers a more clearly realized comic story from an equally absurd misadventure. Boys playing soldier find all the ingredients of a daring ambush—revolvers, Mills bombs, trenchcoats, and dark alleys. The story is the fictional account of the poem "Ambush," written in 1924 about the time O'Connor, Sean O'Faolain, Sean Hendrick, and Vincent O'Leary tried to sabotage a Free State convoy. After the explosion the boys flee; in the "sweet sensation of flight" the main character, Stephen,

> heard beside him something that was like sobbing, the throaty sobbing of hysteria, and had almost given way to his surprise and consternation before he realised what it was. Not sobbing, but chuckling, a quiet contented chuckling, like a lover's laughter in a dark lane. In spite of himself he found the mirth contagious, and chuckled too. There was something strange in that laughter, something out of another world, inhuman and sprightly, as though some gay spirit were breathing through them both.

At that instant O'Connor captures the human dimension of the violence he has taken as his subject, the strange ways men react to hazard and death. Situation reveals character and the voice is momentarily clear. The playful and derisive laughter which follows Alec's opening anecdote about a harelip gives way to the uneasy laughter of hysteria.

However, in this story the hysteria is controlled; thematic tragedy gives way to the comic twist of character. An old woman emerges from "the gloom of an archway" and comes toward the fleeing boys. Stanton and Nolan (Hendrick and O'Faolain) continue but Cunningham and Stephen (O'Leary and O'Donovan) stop to speak. "They were above the city now, and it lay far beneath them in the hollow, a little bowl of smudgy, yellow light." The old woman asks if it was shooting she heard "below be the cross." With "wild, happy eyes" Cunningham replies that it wasn't shooting at all only a deaf old woman in a shop below spending a winter night, "blowing paper bags!" A laugh shakes her frail body and she hails the "young devil" disappearing with his comrade "under the gloom of the trees." The laughter of this survivor persists in the face of hysteria and gloom, the two extremes between which young O'Donovan/O'Connor ran his course.

"Attack," the second story of the volume, was more than likely written during the summer of 1929 before O'Connor's holiday. If such stories as "September Dawn" and "Nightpiece with Figures" represent O'Connor's lyrical voice, then "Attack" represents his objective, detached voice. It shows especially how he built a story (or in those years improvised one) not from an idea but from an incident. The attack of the story provides the situation, the place and time, the reason for the narrator and his comrade to be where they are. Two young rebels intend to attack a police barracks two hours after midnight. The ostensible enemy is the British, particularly the police who manned the garrisons tucked at the edge of so many villages in West Cork. But the real enemies are fear and loneliness with which the "peasants" in these isolated pockets are forced to live. Since it is only nine when they approach the area, they are obliged to take shelter in a nearby farmhouse. At this point Lomasney tells Owen—who like most of O'Connor's narrators is a good listener—a story about the family living in the farmhouse ahead. It is a story about a boy who loved a girl, struck and killed the "waster" she was married to, and was sent off to America by his friends. "We were frightened of the law in those days," Lomasney admits. That was five years before and no word from Paddy since. The narrator observes that he was moved by the tale mostly because it diverted his thoughts from the barracks below.

Actually, in the diversion lies the gist of the story. The atmosphere inside the cottage is what O'Connor is interested in and not the mission of destruction. The two rebels are intruders in the life of this Irish-speaking couple. During the night they discover the source of old Kiernan's defensiveness—Paddy, their son, hiding "bearded, emaciated, half-savage" in the loft. Indeed the diversion becomes the story, not as an unexpected twist or surprise but the unknown lurking just below the surface of all human affairs. Had O'Connor ended the story there it would have been merely a sentimental story of coincidence. Instead he focuses his attention on Lomasney who assumes command of the situation by instructing the old man to take the boy to the village and allow him simply to turn up. After the attack the police won't be worrying about him anyway. "That's what we're out for." The story is neither about the attack nor the discovery of a boy but the passage to maturity achieved by Lomasney, hardly more than a boy himself.

As surely as violence and hysteria, along with their safety valve of comic hilarity, dominate the surface of *Guests of the Nation,* a more serious and thoughtful voice operates below that surface, a voice of compassion and bitterness. After all, war is not a normal situation, at least not for amateur warriors. The humor of "Laughter" and "Machine-Gun Corps in Action" is the comedy of disorder, of natural nervous tension in the face of violent death. O'Connor distrusted the cold, organizational mind of the professional soldier, for whom fear and disorder have been disciplined away. If romantic hysteria, nervous laughter, and chaotic fear represent natural responses of plain people to the stress of war, then disillusionment, accompanied by loneliness and melancholy, emerges just as naturally from the violence and stress. After "hysteria" the other word used throughout the volume more than might be normally expected is "melancholy."

Although *Guests of the Nation* carries no dedication (unlike the rest of O'Connor's books), it is most certainly for Sean Hendrick, by whose side O'Connor spent most of his battle time in 1921 and 1922, running dispatches for Erskine Childers and turning out publicity sheets on a commandeered printing press. War was a romance, a love affair for them both, second only to their love affair with language and literature. So O'Connor began writing his war stories to capture something of the romance and the agony of the whole affair. In May of 1929, O'Connor wrote a story (probably rewritten from an earlier Cork draft) entitled "September Dawn," which was given the inscription "To Sean Hendrick" when published in July in the *Dublin Magazine.* The story seems to crystallize those fundamental beliefs he had come to terms with in the Civil War, particularly his belief in the manifold richness of human life and his distrust of grand abstractions. It also represented a breakthrough in terms of technique, an indication of that delicate merging of romanticism and realism which gives his finest fiction a special edge. "September Dawn" is at once highly personal and severely objective. (pp. 75-80)

"September Dawn" is the centerpiece of *Guests of the Nation* not for its theme but its voice. The lyricism of O'Connor's adolescent poems has by now been distilled into the poetic realism of a man looking back on the time of his passage to maturity. The romance of war with its tragic violence and comic disarray has been diverted to a melancholy acceptance of love and friendship. The hysteria of death has become the melancholy of life. The process of the boys in the story is the process reflected in the entire volume from adolescence, fumbling and fearful, to slightly less naive manhood. **"Nighpiece with Figures,"** the story immediately preceding **"September Dawn,"** ends with three boys in a darkened barn, silent after an elusive young nun's soft Gaelic farewell:

> with their happiness is mixed a melancholy as strange and perturbing, as though life itself and all the modes of life were inadequate. It is not a bitter melancholy like the melancholy of defeat, and in the morning, when they take to the country roads again, it will have passed.

The memory of the young nun lingers with the boys; it also lingers into the next story.

The young Irish-speaking girl of **"September Dawn"** is no less mysterious to the romantic young warriors:

> Her appearance had a peculiar distinction that was almost beauty. Very straight and slender she was with a broad face that tapered to a point at the chin, a curious unsmiling mouth, large, sensitive nostrils, and wide-set, melancholy eyes.

For those in a dishevelled flying column love is only a fleeting chance. After disbanding their column, because they "want to live for Ireland, not die for it"—and sticking together they would all die—Hickey and Keown beat a haphazard retreat from Mallow toward the safety of the mountains of West Cork. Their frantic journey is devoid of glory or romance. They snatch bits of food on the run, not daring to stop. At nightfall they are in the vicinity of Hickey's aunt and make for the cottage. A girl is there, helping the old lady with the housework. To frightened, lonely young patriots on the run even a momentary romance would suffice to fill the emptiness.

As in most of the stories in *Guests of the Nation* the setting appears as natural and unobtrusive. From the flat, densely populated area around Mallow the two boys flee the encircling ring of enemy troops, almost like animals, instinctively toward the safety of the wilds. But place is never the primary dimension in an O'Connor story. Some of the stories in the volume take place in or near Cork City with its wet streets, quays, steep hills, pubs, churches, lanes, and shops. Most of the actual fighting stories are set in the countryside outside Cork, in the rugged mountains around Macroom or the gentle hills around Mallow. Setting for O'Connor emerges as a complement to the voice of the story; setting is atmosphere. Most of the stories are wrapped in darkness, casting the disarray and desolation in silhouetted relief. Even time is vague, for the historical moment dominates natural time.

"It was late September of the finest autumn that had been known for years." The story opens with that blunt statement. The retreat of Hickey and Keown is made even more treacherous by the oblique brilliance of the autumn sun and the yellowing leaves. In this last gasp of summer the "shafts of sunlight" cast exaggerated shadows. Not the normal desultory mist of the Irish countryside, the night is remote and shadowy. The winds of the equinox which blow so steadily in the south of Ireland shake loose the leaves and keep the two tired lads edgy throughout the night. In this autumnal transition they are suspended between fear and melancholy. Hickey, sleepless and thoughtful, realizes "that his life was a melancholy, aimless life, and that all this endless struggle and concealment was but so much out of an existence that would mean little anyhow." He thinks of the girl in the big house to whom he wanted to wave but didn't out of the fear of dis-

covery. That "desire for some human contact" now returns "with all the dark power of nocturnal melancholy surging up beneath it; the feeling of his own loneliness, his own unimportance, his own folly." The swirling wind wakes Keown who imagines in hysterical terror that their pursuers have come. Only Hickey's fist silences his snivelling. The point is that the swirling politics of violence intrude even into this serene and natural setting.

In the gathering half-light before dawn Hickey smokes a cigarette and watches at the window. As the grey fog hugging the yard below lifts, "minute by minute," Hickey perceives

> all about him broken slates, with straw and withered leaves that rustled when the wind blew them about. The mist cleared farther, and he saw the trees looking much barer than they had looked the day before, with broken branches and the new day showing in great, rugged patches between them. . . . Light, a cold, wintry, forbidding light suffused the chill air. The birds were singing.

The natural passage from verdant summer to desolate winter occurs as a shadow line as indecipherable as the dawn. Below in the kitchen Hickey finds Sheela returning with a bucket of turf. "They scarcely spoke." In the light of the "newborn flame" he kisses her and

> for him in that melancholy kiss an ache of longing was kindled, and he buried his face in the warm flesh of her throat as the kitchen filled with the acrid smell of turf; while the blue smoke drifting through the narrow doorway was caught and whirled headlong through grey fields and dark masses of trees upon which an autumn sun was rising.

Grotesques and silhouettes caught in the death-dealing hysteria of war find a hope as barren as the autumn dawn, a life-affirming melancholy that pervades the entire volume. The encroaching chill and darkness of winter signal an end of summer, but in the fleeting human contact lies a minimal hope for a new beginning.

As the emotional center of the volume **"September Dawn"** mediates the numbed thoughtfulness of the first and last stories with the thoughtless frenzy of the intervening stories. Its betweenness is the emotional condition of passage, and in the poignant layering of national transition and personal growth lies the lonely voice. The volume begins in war and ends in a temporal vacuum resembling peace. The man in **"After Fourteen Years"** could be visiting Bantry at almost any historical moment, for history pales in the face of personal considerations. He could just as well be going back after forty years, because life for him has settled into polite encrustation; it is settled and there is nothing to hope for. The same can be said for Henry Conran whose death was reported prematurely, and yet perhaps not, for he seems more dead than alive anyway. Death weighs heavily on **"The Sisters"** as well, a story about two sisters living alone, one of whom cares for the other and then dies suddenly leaving the "mad" sister on her own. These three stories about the process of aging and natural death fit the prevailing silhouette of death in the preceding war stories. Whereas the war stories concern the particular change from adolescence to maturity, these stories deal with the general reality of passing from one condition in life to another. But they share with the entire volume a sense of return, a backward look at once melancholy and hopeful.

The final story of the volume returns to the crisis of adolescence. **"The Procession of Life"** ties together much of the volume, both in tone and theme. The voice is a male voice looking back on the confusion and anxiety of growing up. What encloses the young hero of the story is his provincial Cork environment in general, his brutal father in particular. Larry's beloved mother has been dead almost a year; his obstinate father, on the night in question, has locked him out of the house. . . . Alternately elated and miserable, he wanders along the quays, which are "lonely and full of shadows", until he finds a watchman's sentry box. "The river made a clucking, lonely sound against the quay wall." Larry is adrift and lonely, seeking some measure of human contact, but the grizzled old watchman chases him away when a lady of the night appears. The scene is a portrait of loneliness: three of the loneliest creatures imaginable huddled at one of those places of futility which one still finds on just about any public work site in Ireland. To Larry the woman seems a "magical creature." Her perfume he finds "overpowering and sweet." At the same time the watchman falls under her spell. The old and the young, the bitter and the naive share a radical lonesomeness. The woman's touch sends "a shiver of pleasure through him" and the watchman's competitive reproof cowers him. A constable resolves the stand-off by sending the woman away to meet him later. Whiskey and cigarettes warm three men of the night. At the end of the story Larry disobeys the policeman's order to stay with the old man and returns home jaunty and confident and ready to defy his surly father. It is another "playboy of the western world" perhaps; generation after generation echoing the same lonely voice, adolescence, maturity, and old age improvising solace in the face of cold separation.

Seeking to capture in his own volume of stories something of the unity of Turgenev, Moore, and Joyce, O'Connor gave special force to the stories that open and close *Guests of the Nation.* The lonely voice of **"The Procession of Life"** circles the entire volume, signaling the passage from hysterical romance to melancholy realism. It stands somewhat apart from the rest of the volume in terms of treatment, yet complements the overall ambiance. Curiously, it represents the kind of story for which O'Connor later became famous, the Larry Delaney story of childhood and adolescence. The voice is lyrical but not altogether personal; although there are distinct autobiographical overtones, O'Connor's natural reserve discourages too facile identification. Loneliness is embodied rather than indulged, and in the detached, backward look characteristic of nearly every story in the volume, the voices generate a life of their own.

Likewise, the title story that opens the volume stands apart. There is nothing else quite like it in O'Connor's work; its brilliance and integrity are beyond question. In **"Guests of the Nation"** O'Connor backs away from chauvinism and hysteria far enough to allow a glimpse of the characters' tragic impotence, but not so far as to miss their emotional vibrations. Thrown together by the vagaries of war, three Irish rebels and their two English hostages come to personal terms over cards and share a momentary truce in conversation. But national priorities take precedence over individual loyalties; abstract retribution undermines concrete friendship. After "assassinating" the two helpless hostages the hero-narrator finds himself in a melancholy vacuum: "It is so strange what you feel at such moments, and not to be written afterwards. . . . I was somehow very small and very lonely. And anything

that ever happened to me after I never felt the same about again."

O'Connor has not indicted the rebels nor their cause; neither has he vindicated violence. Rather he has isolated its horrible effects at the moment of impact. For him human dignity and rationality inevitably yield to the sudden impulse, to the unpredictable and passing moment. So although there is nothing quite like it in the rest of O'Connor's writing, **"Guests of the Nation"** contains these qualities which are unmistakably O'Connor's—it is simple, it possesses tight narrative design and lively drama, and it carries sparse revelations in language direct and alive. Most of all, the story embodies that "lyric cry in the face of destiny." (pp. 80-6)

In **"Guests of the Nation"** as in few of his other earlier stories, O'Connor rises above mere contrivance and literary fumbling to voice the sort of primary affirmation which he himself insisted was vital to great literature. (p. 87)

> *James H. Matthews, "Women, War, and Words: Frank O'Connor's First Confessions," in* Irish Renaissance Annual I, *Vol. I, 1980, pp. 73-112.*

RUTH SHERRY   (essay date 1980)

[*In the following excerpt, Sherry explores O'Connor's treatment of cultural differences between modern Ireland and traditional, rural Gaelic Ireland in the collection* Guests of the Nation.]

O'Connor's concern for the problem of modern Ireland's relation to Gaelic Ireland is one which is reflected in a number of his short stories, especially ones written in the 1930s and the beginning of the 1940s; it was during the earlier part of his career that he was most preoccupied with this problem and its significance for him as a writer. In time he did arrive at his own resolution of the conflicting aspects of the issue. Viewing O'Connor's position in political terms, one can see him as a representative of the first generation of modern Irish writers for whom the British were no longer the essential enemy; the significant conflicts were now to be found within Ireland herself. The stories in which O'Connor explores the relationship between modern Ireland and traditional, rural, Gaelic Ireland are varied, some comic, others sombre. What they have in common is a tendency to define the relationship between the two Irelands as one of opposition. The two worlds generally cannot be integrated, yet for individual characters this opposition is a matter of internal conflict, divided loyalties, unfulfillable aspirations, an opposition leading even to tragedy.

O'Connor's first collection of short stories, **Guests of the Nation,** generally expresses a rather mixed view of its main subject, the Civil War. Some of the stories reflect a youthful love of adventure and sense of vitality, but often they see absurdity or viciousness given licence under the name of patriotism. One story, **"The Patriarch"**, describes the experience of a Cork child who comes under the influence of a much older 'patriot' (significantly corrupted to 'patriarch' in the lanes of Cork) and grows up to take his mentor's place when the old man becomes too feeble to continue his participation in the struggle.

The opening section of the story satirizes deliciously the kind of ignorant nationalistic enthusiasm which assumes that everything Gaelic is also patriotic and idealistic. The 'Patriarch', a shopkeeper, pure 'townie', offers free sweets to any child who can speak a few words of Irish, a language he himself doesn't know and can't learn. The protagonist, Dermod, eager for the reward, pesters his Irish-speaking grandmother (clearly derived from O'Connor's own grandmother) to teach him a few sentences, but the earthy songs and sayings she produces have no connection with the Patriarch's sentimental dreams.

> When he saw me, the Patriarch began to speak in his vivid and moving way about Holy Ireland, and about the beautiful tongue in which our fathers had sent down their message of undying hatred to children forgetful of their fame. . . . I was induced to sing an Irish chorus that I had picked up from my grandmother. The old man listened in an almost ecstasy . . .
>
> I translated literally as I had heard my grandmother do:
>
> 'O, my wife and my children and my little spinning-wheel. My couple of pounds of flax each day not spun-two days she's in bed for one she's about the house, and Oh, may the dear God help me to get rid of her!'
>
> 'Are you sure you have the meaning right, *a ghile?*' he asked at last.
>
> 'That's what my grandmother says,' I replied, feeling the next word would make me weep . . .
>
> 'I have it . . . 'Tis England he means. The bad wife in the house. That's it—I have it all straightened out now. You have to have them songs interpreted for you. The pounds of flax she didn't spin are all the industries she ruined on us. England, the bad wife—ah, how true it is. Dark songs for a people in chains.

The comic and satirical tone of the opening later modulates into a more solemn mood. The story traces Dermod's growth to manhood, where he and his generation act out, in the Troubles, the consequences of the old man's principles. Dermod retains his affection for the Patriarch, but loses his reverence for him as the old man reverts to childishness and dies as fanatically devoted to the obscure St Rita of Cascia as he once was to Dark Rosaleen. As a whole the story outlines the familiar process of disillusionment and growing up away from one's early heroes which O'Connor in his own life experienced in relation to Corkery, who presided over his early patriotic education.

Several stories written in the next few years focus on the conflict between modern and traditional Ireland. In some of these stories the Irish language is not specifically at issue, but the traditional values they are concerned with derive from a culture which was certainly Gaelic. **"Peasants"**, a story more purely comic than **"The Patriarch"**, deals with traditionalists who are indifferent to the modern legal system, derived as it is from Roman and English law. They continue to operate with centuries-old, heroic notions of honour, loyalty, and retribution.

When a young man, Michael John Cronin, steals the funds of 'the Carricknabreena Hurling, Football and Temperance Association', the other members are prepared to cope with his action by reminding themselves and everyone else in the village of all his worthless relatives and ancestors generations back. By 'naming' him in this way they reaffirm the stability and continuity of the communal order, which depends, as in all tradition-based communities, upon fixed roles and identities for all members. Michael John is to be punished in the accepted way by a kind of banishment—his relatives collect money to send him to America, and justice will thus be done without reference to any outside authority.

This highly satisfactory solution is thwarted by the parish priest, Father Crowley, a comparative newcomer who sees himself to be in a power struggle with 'the long-tailed families' of the village. He is determined that Michael John must be prosecuted. For the villagers this prospect implies the betrayal of one of their own to outsiders, and involves holding not only Michael John, but all his relatives and indeed the whole village, up to the scorn of the rest of the world. 'The like of this had never been heard of in the parish before. What? Put the police on a boy and he in trouble?'

The comedy of the story depends upon the confrontation of these two unquestioned systems of value, each held with Bergsonian rigidity, Michael John restores the money, thus cancelling the crime according to traditional views; then the villagers propose that, even if Father Crowley feels obliged to turn the boy over to the police, he should later rescue him by 'giving him a character' in court; finally they offer the priest a contribution, like a blood-price, 'to cover the expense and trouble to yourself'. All these stratagems are rejected with increasing vituperation by Father Crowley.

Although the story treats comically the villagers' inability to see beyond their inherited assumptions, in the end the traditional values are vindicated. Michael John must serve a short term in prison, but Father Crowley is soon driven away from Carricknabreena by the hostility of his parishioners. When Michael John emerges from prison, his neighbours feel that he must be recompensed for his trouble. Using this money he sets himself up in business, and, taking on the role of a gombeen man, becomes a curse to the village, a result which is blamed upon the priest. This ironic ending refutes the official legal system's premise that punishment produces reform; the older system of banishing the offender to America at least got him out of the place.

The conflict in **"Peasants"** depends upon the situation of an isolated community which has been rooted in one place for centuries. The very title ('peasant' is not a neutral term in Ireland) reflects both the priest's scornful attitude toward the country people and the fact that these families have been tied to one plot of land for generations, a situation in which people *must* live together forever afterward. In such circumstances abstract modes of punishment like brief imprisonment are futile. The only sensible way of dealing with so anti-social an element as Michael John is to get rid of him altogether.

It is perhaps unexpected that a city-born-and-bred writer should show so sympathetic an insight into an essentially rural frame of mind, even though the sympathy is coloured by irony in **"Peasants"**. O'Connor's experiences in the Civil War had however brought him into touch with the Irish-speaking country of West Cork, and his later occupation as a librarian in Sligo, Wicklow and Cork often sent him travelling into the countryside in the course of his work.

> It made me realize that I was a townie and would never be anything else. In the best of the houses I visited—usually the houses of people who had been prominent in the Troubles—the people were better related to the wild countryside about them than I

am to the tame city about me. Seeing them in Cork in their uncouth clothes with their uncouth accents was one thing; seeing them on their own farms was another thing entirely, and it made me conscious of my own uncouthness rather than theirs. But those families were few, and the total effect of the country on me was one of depression.

Despite this ambivalence O'Connor seems to have derived from these experiences a more than conventional sympathy with traditional ways of thinking.

The tenacity of traditional concepts of justice and resistance to modern law in isolated communities is the subject matter of several other stories written at about the same time as **"Peasants"**. **"Tears, Idle Tears"**, a rather inferior piece of work, tells of a village which covers up an accidental death for the benefit of a policeman who might be inclined to view it as a crime. In contrast to **"Peasants"**, **"Tears, Idle Tears"** presents resistance to the law as rather ridiculous. The main point of the story is however the solidarity of the villagers, who retain all possible affection for the sergeant at the same time that they plot to deceive him.

"The Majesty of the Law" is a much finer story, and is one of O'Connor's best-known; also essentially comic, it perhaps gives greater hope for the integration of the traditional and modern worlds than do the other stories considered here. A police sergeant goes to visit Dan, an old man living alone in the hills. At the end of the visit the sergeant reveals for the first time his real purpose in coming. Dan has refused to pay a fine imposed as a result of a quarrel with a neighbour, and willingly agrees to go to prison. Dan is following a strategy which derives from an ancient heroic code of pride and shame. ' "I'll punish him. I'll lie on bare boards for him. I'll suffer for him . . . so that neither he nor any of his children will be able to raise their heads for the shame of it" '. The device of using one's own suffering to shame one's enemy is of course not dead; hunger strikes and many other forms of passive resistance are based on it and have in particular been associated with Irish Republicanism. Yeats roots the strategy in antiquity in 'The King's Threshold', where the sufferer, like Dan, emerges victorious.

Dan is conscious of himself as the survivor of a way of life which is on the verge of extinction. His conversation with the sergeant consists largely of a lament for the loss of old medicines, old ways of making whisky, old songs.

> 'Every art has its secrets, and the secrets of distilling are being lost the way the old songs were lost. When I was a boy there wasn't a man in the barony but had a hundred songs in his head, but with people running here, there, and everywhere, the songs were lost . . . Men die and men are born, and where one man drained another will plow, but a secret lost is lost forever'.

The sergeant in this story is a figure caught between the two worlds. He is a representative of the alien legal system which forbids the distilling of poteen, but in many ways his sympathies are with the old man rather than with the new system. Most of the story consists in fact of a description of a sensitive and ceremonious exchange of courtesies between the two men, host and guest. The obligations of the traditions of hospitality are accepted by both, to the point that each disowns his convictions out of courtesy; Dan defends the law against illegal distilling and the sergeant proclaims that the law was a mistake.

To the extent that the policeman shares the virtues of hospitality with Dan, he represents a continuation of the old order in the modern world, but if he is to be courteous, he must defy the very laws he represents, drinking on duty and accepting an illegal bottle as a gift. The new order has not succeeded in integrating the old traditions into its institutions, even though they are still respected by individuals. Dan, in the end, is the comic victor who employs the prescriptions of the new law in the service of the old, the title of the story referring directly to Dan's traditional code and ironically to the modern one. But Dan is an old man who has never married, and therefore does not imply any future; the sergeant by contrast has a wife and children (who incidentally 'run here, there, and everywhere') and the ultimate triumph of the new institutions is thereby suggested. Dan is furthermore faintly corrupted; for company he feels he should offer 'two handsomely decorated cups, the only cups he had, which, though chipped and handleless, were used at all only on very rare occasions; for himself he preferred his tea from a basin'. One feels that his basin, and 'the seats of the chairs [which] were only slices of log, rough and round and thick as the saw had left them', are more authentic expressions of the old man's nature than the half-understood cups—yet the desire to give the best to the visitor is pure enough.

"In the Train" treats the traditional moral code much more harshly than the stories previously considered. Helena Maguire is guilty of murder, but her 'peasant' neighbours will not testify against her in the courts, and she is acquitted. They plan, nevertheless, to use their own method of punishing her—'to give her the hunt' and drive her from her own village as Father Crowley was driven from Carricknabreena. The framework of the story is a journey between the city where the trial was held and the remote village to which murderer, witnesses and policemen are all returning. In the train they are all in a suspended state, relieved of the demands made by the places at the extreme ends of the journey. The policemen are able to share illegal liquor with the villagers, and the villagers are able to chatter with the woman they will reject and drive away, but as the train nears its destination they separate once again into their own parties, police on one side, witnesses on the other, and the murderer left alone and despairing.

During the journey there is much discussion about the relative value of the village, Farranchreest, and the city; in this story modern Ireland is represented most forcefully by the wife of the police sergeant, an unpleasant woman who feels superior to everyone else by virtue of her middle-class town upbringing: ' "I was educated in a convent and play the piano; my father was a literary man and yet I am compelled to associate with the lowest types of humanity." ' She is hardly a recommendation for modern Ireland, and yet by contrast with the punishment the murderer will receive, a conviction in the court would seem almost a kindness. The murder itself appears incidental, insignificant by comparison to the larger conflict between what is represented by town and village. If Dan in **"The Majesty of the Law"** is one of those perfectly related to the wild countryside around him, **"In the Train"** suggests why O'Connor as a young librarian nevertheless found the countryside depressing.

The conflicts between old and new which interest O'Connor are not confined to matters of law and justice. **"In the Train"** emphasizes the real power which remains in traditional communities, but in **"The Bridal Night"** O'Connor's subject is

O'Connor at Cashel in Ireland, 1964.

rather the vulnerability of those still left in remote Irish-speaking districts. This story is probably the finest of those considered here, and the one which offers the most subtle treatment of the problem under discussion. The narrator, a visitor to a lonely Irish-speaking district, meets an old woman who tells him of her one son, Denis, who has been in an asylum in Cork for many years. Denis fell in love with Winnie Regan, a well-off girl from a town who came to the place as a schoolteacher, but the love was a hopeless one and he went mad because of it. Winnie, who did not intend to encourage him, was nevertheless sorry for him and, to calm him, lay beside him the night before he was to be taken away. Although she risked her reputation by doing so, she earned the respect of the local people and became a kind of heroine. The old woman tells the stranger her story, praises Winnie, and mourns for her son.

The story has an ancient, almost Greek, feeling about it in its sense of the inevitability of suffering, especially the suffering of the innocent and helpless. It reflects the classical sense of love as a curse, a form of madness. The old woman, Mrs Sullivan, reflects the traditional representations of Ireland as an old woman, Kathleen ni Houlihan, mourning the loss of her sons; but whereas Kathleen ni Houlihan conventionally mourns sons lost to the British or gone into exile, here the loss is caused by something else, the intrusion of the towns into traditional districts. Winnie is a *stranger* in this place, with a different language, a different education, and, of course, money. The gap between her world and Denis's is so great

that Mrs Sullivan is resigned to the impossibility of there being any match between her and Denis.

Winnie is an ambiguous figure in the story. She is the outsider, part of the new native ruling class (that is, the Catholic middle class) which has replaced the Anglo-Irish and the British, but her intentions are beyond reproach. Winnie has learned Irish, even if it is only 'book Irish', and as Mrs Sullivan says, ' "She came here of her own choice, for the great liking she had for the sea and the mountains." ' The story acknowledges a strange unity and sympathy which extends from Winnie and her world to that of the Sullivans. Her independence and lack of conventionality, established early in the story by her habit of sitting and reading or writing in the cove in isolation, are the same characteristics which give her the capacity to make her gesture of sympathy with Denis, and she is then in turn accorded the honour of the people of the place.

Yet there is some ambivalence in Mrs Sullivan's account of her. One cannot blame Winnie for Denis's hopeless passion and madness, yet everything his mother says reflects her sense of Denis's goodness and worth; why isn't he good enough for Winnie? ' "A quiet, good-natured boy and another would take pity on him, knowing he would make her a fine steady husband, but she was not the sort, and well I knew it from the first day I laid eyes on her." ' Denis's madness, after all, consists *only* in being a poor country boy who falls in love with a town girl who has money. The loss of Denis for the old woman is not only the loss of a son, but of her whole family, any chance of grandchildren, as expressed in her remembering the old song, 'Lonely rock is the one wife my children will know'; by extension, the gradual death of the Gaeltacht is implicit.

There is thus a tension between acceptance of the situation, resignation, and a feeling of its inevitability on the one hand; and a sense of frustration, regret and rebellion on the other. One might also ask what the effect is of Mrs Sullivan's telling the story to the stranger, himself presumably a representative of Winnie's world. 'Town Irish' travel often enough, after all, to the isolated places—frequently, like their prototype Synge, with the motive of learning Irish and the way of life associated with it—but they *are* town people, as O'Connor acknowledged himself to be. They do not come without bringing change; they rarely settle and become integrated into a Gaeltacht community, and they thus inevitably stand in ambiguous relationship to the culture which they both value and reject. Mrs Sullivan kisses Winnie's hands as the people used to kiss the hands of the old aristocrats, and it is Winnie, with her money, education, mobility and courage, who has all the potential for action in the situation. Denis and his mother are merely acted upon.

"Uprooted" treats an experience which has become increasingly common in Ireland—the movement of population from rural places to towns. A Kerry boy, Ned, has deliberately chosen to leave home, and has achieved his ambition of becoming a schoolteacher in Dublin. Yet he is vaguely, but deeply, dissatisfied. He returns for a long weekend to his old home, in company with his brother Tom who is a priest. The Kerry landscape is described with a colour and vividness not common in O'Connor's stories, which are not usually given to much physical description.

Very little happens by way of plot. Ned and Tom visit friends and relatives; Ned sees the beauty of the countryside with new eyes, and is tempted to remain at home and marry a local girl. But when his brother Tom expresses dissatisfaction with his own life as a priest, and urges Ned to accept the fulfillment that is ready at hand, Ned does not feel able to do so. ' "We made our choice a long time ago. We can't go back on it now." '

The Kerry world to which Ned and Tom return is described in terms of timelessness; even those things which have in fact changed seem as timeless and familiar as the others: 'The only unfamiliar voice, little Brigid's, seemed the most familiar of all'. But Ned has committed himself to a world in which things must and do change. As he says to Tom, ' "I suppose we must only leave it to time. Time settles everything." '

The impulse which first drove Ned away from his home was one connected with his love of books, which were meaningless to his father. The world of Ned's childhood was one of poverty, with no books, learning, or aspiration—essentially a world with some remnants of art, in the old songs still sung, but a world without the life of the mind, even if the life of the heart was satisfied in it. In the conversation at home, all intellectual curiosity is directed to the question of whose car it was that just went up the road. Having perceived these limitations in the place of his birth, Ned cannot return to it, but the visit home seems to show him, for the first time, some of the beauty of what he has lost. The story expresses the general modern experience of longing for older and simpler modes of life, while at the same time recognizing that they are no longer re-ally available to modern people. The conclusion of the story, which presents traditional Ireland at its most appealing, also gives O'Connor's most explicit statement of the relationship between old Ireland and new Ireland:

> There was a magical light on everything. A boy on a horse rose suddenly against the sky, a startling picture. Through the apple-green light over Carriganassa ran long streaks of crimson, so still they might have been enamelled. Magic, magic, magic! He saw it as in a children's picture-book with all its colours intolerably bright; something he had outgrown and could never return to, while the world he had aspired to was as remote and intangible as it had seemed even in the despair of youth.

Ned's plight is the plight of modern Ireland generally as O'Connor tended to see it: full of aspiration, on the way to something great, but not yet arrived at a state which offered adequate recompense for the irrevocable loss of the old beauties. Significantly, Ned's move to Dublin, like O'Connor's own when he became a librarian in Dublin in 1929, is related to his love of books. In Ned's case, as in O'Connor's own, this love is not appreciated by a father with a great love of the drink. Even in his farewell to Kerry, Ned in his imagination must relate it to a book, though only a child's picture book.

The almost surrealistic use of colour in the passage quoted above may not be merely decorative. O'Connor is not a writer who relies very heavily on symbolism, any more than on visual description. Here, however, one may want to note that the red and green prominent in the ending of the story have appeared earlier, in a description of Ned's life in Dublin, where 'along the edge of the canal . . . the trees become green again and the tall claret-coloured houses are painted on the quiet surface of the water'. The pairing of red and green is of course often associated with Ireland, and was fixed in this significance for literary purposes by Joyce. Perhaps by using them here O'Connor is suggesting that both Dublin and the Kerry Coast are, equally, aspects of Ireland and the Irish experience, however much the gap between the two worlds leads to difficulty for individuals and even whole communities.

"The Long Road to Ummera" insists on the need for respect for the old ways, even from those who find them irrelevant for modern town life, and illustrates the power the old ways may have even over those who would prefer to ignore them. The story is also O'Connor's apology to the grandmother he rejected as a child. The main character, Abby, a snuff-taking, porter-drinking shawlie, is clearly modelled on her. Although she appears to be a negligible figure in her life in Cork City, Abby takes on heroic proportions in the tenacity of her devotion to her dead husband and the countryside she was forced to leave when he died.

Abby tries to extract from her son Pat, a comfortable Cork businessman, a promise that he will take her back to Ummera for her burial, along the same road she took with him when they left. Pat tries to dismiss her memories of dead people and a dead life as insignificant in modern Cork, but when she makes her own arrangements to be taken home to Ummera and dies on the way, Pat is forced to bow to the superior strength of her conviction, and takes her the rest of the road himself. When Pat mocks her interest in the dead, Abby retorts, ' "Isn't there more of us there than here?" ' Her conviction of the existence of 'us', dead or alive, conveys a sense of human unity and solidarity lacking in Pat's middle-class Cork world.

Abby's belief in the continuing reality of the dead is dramatized by her speaking the phrases of traditional Irish poetry when she is convinced her dead husband has come to lead her away:

> 'Ah, Michael Driscoll, my friend, my kind comrade, you didn't forget me after all the long years . . . They tried to keep me away, to make me stop among foreigners in the town, but where would I be without you and all the old friends? Stay for me, my treasure, stop and show me the way . . . Be easy now, my brightness, my own kind loving comrade . . . After all the long years I'm on the road to you at last.'

Although Abby has to go to extremes to elicit respect for her convictions from her son, she finds a natural sympathy in the old women around her in the hospital where she dies and in the Irish-speaking priest who reassures her when she is ill. She is thus seen as representing a world which, if dying, is not yet dead, one which still can exact tribute from the modern town dweller, rising to magnificence in its eloquence.

"The Old Faith", a slight but amusing story, describes how a bishop and a group of priests, under the influence of a confiscated bottle of poteen, begin exchanging stories about the fairies. To the horror of the one cosmopolitan sceptic in the group, they appear to give the tales full credence. Although the story is wholly comic, O'Connor is clearly on the side of the 'old believers' rather than that of the modern sceptic, and he associates 'the old faith' with a richer and warmer humanity than that represented by the more orthodox priest.

Taken together, these stories demonstrate that O'Connor saw Gaelic Ireland as still a significant element in modern Ireland, one with more moral force than may be immediately apparent. Although a few stories emphasize negative aspects of this heritage, most of them treat it and those who hold it with respect, even love. But the ultimate survival of Gaelic Ireland is nowhere assumed by these stories. However strongly some of them appeal for understanding of the Gaelic world, in other pieces of writing at about the same time O'Connor drew clear boundaries to the extent of his commitment to Gaelic Ireland. (pp. 37-50)

> Ruth Sherry, "Frank O'Connor and Gaelic Ireland," in Irish Studies, Vol. 1, 1980, pp. 35-59.

DENIS DONOGHUE (essay date 1981)

[*Donoghue is an Irish critic and editor. In the excerpt below, he offers a favorable review of O'Connor's* Collected Stories.]

O'Connor was always a storyteller. Any of his stories might begin, as one of them, **"The Late Henry Conran,"** does: " 'I've another little story for you,' said the old man." He never pretended that words came directly from the voice that spoke them, but he wrote his stories, changed them, gave them a different emphasis, a different phrasing, mainly to enhance the reader's sense of listening to a storyteller's voice. In O'Connor's stories the truth of a character is in the telling, the voice, the rhythm. (p. 3)

Of the several constituents of a short story, O'Connor was most tender toward characterization. Never indifferent to plots and actions, he was more interested in a twist of character than in a turn of events. His stories are always implicit in the characters to whom they happen. Circumstance may be fate, but only if fate is indistinguishable from character: Chances and coincidences are allowed to bring out only what is already in the character. The narrator produces the story, discloses the truth a character could not disclose for himself. The character performs his truth, short of knowing it. Often the narrator is in the center of the story, or close enough to the center to see the value of what happens there. He is not required to be gifted beyond the talent of seeing the relation between a character and what he does or suffers. That is enough. O'Connor never fusses with omniscient narrators: Enough is better than too much.

The **Collected Stories** brings together 67 stories, a collection so choice that it would be nice to know who made it. No editor is named. (pp. 3, 28)

O'Connor's strength, in the best of these stories, is his generosity. Knowing what duress means, and the penury of experience available to most people, he has always wanted to do his best for them, to show the quirky doggedness practiced by people who live on the margin. He was not a satirist. Among his contemporaries in Irish fiction, Sean O'Faolain and Liam O'Flaherty are far harder than O'Connor in their accounts of modern Ireland. Among his juniors, Mervyn Wall and James Plunkett have a sense of Ireland far more astringent than O'Connor's. A genial man, O'Connor set his geniality aside only under extreme provocation, and he longed to return to his native mood. He was hard only on people who were soft on themselves.

If he has a weakness—and who has none?—it is a tendency to mistake whimsicality for charm. Like J. M. Synge and other Irish writers, O'Connor wrote an English that remembered the Irish it displaced. Many of his phrases, like Synge's, are translated from the Irish into an English which they render more exotic than their occasion can well sustain. Synge-songs are hard things to control, their charm is insidious. In the weaker stories, like **"Song Without Words,"** what corresponds to the exotic dialect is a whimsical relation to the characters and events. Reading **"Song Without Words,"** it is hard to avoid thinking of O'Connor's Brother Arnold and Brother Michael as leading eventually to Bing Crosby and Barry Fitzgerald in "Going My Way," and to their sickening charm.

But it is a minor blemish, all told. At his best, there is no one like O'Connor; at his best, as in **"The Bridal Night," "The Long Road to Ummera," "Peasants," "The Majesty of the Law"** and another dozen stories just as good as these. . . . In sober moods I enjoy **"The Majesty of the Law"** more than any other story of O'Connor's, not only for its humor but, more than that, for its delicacy and tact. When the policeman leaves Dan Bride's house, the long conversation over, and then comes back as if he had forgotten to mention a minor matter hardly worth mentioning (to serve a warrant), I can hardly distinguish between his tact and O'Connor's.

Walter Benjamin says in his essay on Leskov that people think of a storyteller as someone who has come from afar. O'Connor's best stories put the same thought into our heads; how far, in some imaginative sense, he has had to travel to achieve such wisdom and to accomplish it with such flair. (p. 28)

> Denis Donoghue, " 'I've Another Little Story for You', " in The New York Times Book Review, September 28, 1981, pp. 3, 28.

FURTHER READING

Casey, Daniel J. "The *Seanachie's* Voice in Three Stories by Frank O'Connor." *Anglo-Irish Studies* 3 (1977): 96-107.
  Contends that O'Connor incorporated folk storytelling techniques into his short fiction in 1934 in order to extol unsophisticated country characters. Casey uses the stories "Peasants," "In the Train," and "The Majesty of the Law" as examples.

Crider, J. R. "Jupiter Pluvius in 'Guests of the Nation'." *Studies in Short Fiction* 23, No. 4 (Fall 1986): 407-11.
  Discusses the significance of the mythical god Jupiter Pluvius in the story "Guests of the Nation."

Flanagan, Thomas. "Frank O'Connor, 1903-1966." *The Kenyon Review* XXVIII, No. 4 (September 1966): 439-55.
  Personal reminiscence of O'Connor, as well as an appreciative critical evaluation of his work.

Matthews, James H. " 'Magical Improvisation': Frank O'Connor's Revolution." *Eire-Ireland* X, No. 4 (July 1975): 3-13.
  Examines the influence of the Irish Revolution on O'Connor's short fiction.

————. *Voices: A Life of Frank O'Connor.* New York: Atheneum, 1985, 450 p.
  In-depth biography.

Peterson, Richard F. "Frank O'Connor and the Modern Irish Short Story." *Modern Fiction Studies* 28, No. 1 (Spring 1982): 53-67.
  Explores O'Connor's influence on the modern Irish short story.

Saul, George Brandon. "A Consideration of Frank O'Connor's Short Stories." *Colby Library Quarterly* VI, No. 8 (December 1963): 329-42.
  Surveys O'Connor's short story collections, concluding that his prevailing virtues are honesty, poetic lyricism, and "a genuine sort of wise innocence."

Sheehy, Maurice, ed. *Michael/Frank: Studies on Frank O'Connor.* New York: Alfred A. Knopf, 1969, 203 p.
  Collection of tributes to O'Connor by writers who knew him personally and professionally, including Richard Ellmann, Wallace Stegner, and Brendan Kennelly.

Steinman, Michael. "Frank O'Connor at Work: 'The Genius'." *Eire-Ireland* XX, No. 4 (Winter 1985): 23-42.
  Traces the development of the story "The Genius" through its numerous revisions to reveal O'Connor's approach to fiction writing.

Storey, Michael L. "The Guests of Frank O'Connor and Albert Camus." *Comparative Literature Studies* 23, No. 3 (Fall 1986): 250-62.
  Compares in detail O'Connor's "Guests of the Nation" and Camus's "The Guest."

Tomory, William. *Frank O'Connor.* Boston: Twayne, 1980, 198 p.
  Biographical and critical study focusing on O'Connor's short fiction.

Whittier, Anthony. "The Art of Fiction XIX: Frank O'Connor." *The Paris Review* 5, No. 17 (Autumn-Winter 1957): 43-64.
  Interview with O'Connor in which he comments on his themes, writing techniques, literary influences, involvement with the Abbey Theatre, and experiences in the Irish Republican Army.

Alice Walker

1944-

American novelist, short story writer, essayist, poet, critic, editor, and author of children's books.

An acclaimed writer whose novel *The Color Purple* won both the American Book Award and the Pulitzer Prize in fiction in 1983, Walker is regarded as an exceptional writer of short stories. Influenced by such literary and cultural figures as feminist Gloria Steinem, Harlem Renaissance novelist and folklorist Zora Neale Hurston, and Colombian Nobel Laureate Gabriel García Márquez, Walker delineates in her stories the striving of black women for spiritual wholeness and political autonomy. Viewing the African-American woman as a symbol of hope and resurrection for humanity, Walker stresses the importance of bonds between women in contending with racism and sexism. Although most commentators categorize her writings as feminist, Walker prefers to describe her works and social convictions as "womanist." She defines this term as "a woman who loves other women. . . . Appreciates and prefers woman's culture, woman's emotional flexibility . . . and woman's strength. . . . *Loves* the spirit. . . . Loves herself. *Regardless.*" While some critics fault Walker's work for displaying a polemical tone and an excess of negative portraits of black males, most applaud her lyrical prose and skill in rendering beauty, grace, and dignity in the lives of ordinary individuals.

Much of Walker's fiction is informed by her Southern background. She was born in Eatonton, Georgia, a rural town where most blacks worked as tenant farmers. At age eight she was blinded in her right eye when an older brother accidentally shot her with a BB gun. Because her parents did not have access to an automobile, Walker did not receive medical attention until several days after the accident, and the resulting scar tissue that completely covered her eye remained until it was surgically removed when she was fourteen years old. Walker spent most of her childhood withdrawn from others because of her disfigurement and began writing poetry to combat her loneliness. She commented later that due to this incident, she "began to really see people and things, to really notice relationships and to learn to be patient enough to care about how they turned out." Upon graduating from high school with honors in 1961, Walker won a scholarship to Spelman College in Atlanta, where she became involved in the civil rights movement and participated in several sit-ins at local business establishments. In 1963, she transferred to Sarah Lawrence College in New York City, graduating from there in 1965. She spent the following summer in Mississippi as an activist and teacher and met her future husband Melvyn Leventhal, a Jewish civil rights attorney. Walker and Leventhal married in 1967 in New York City and resumed their activist work in Mississippi, becoming the first legally married interracial couple to reside in Jackson, the state capital.

In her first collection of short fiction, *In Love and Trouble: Stories of Black Women,* Walker features Southern women from disparate social and economic backgrounds who are involved with uncaring, often brutal men. The eponymous narrator of "Roselily," for example, is a poor mother of four children who is about to marry a devout black Muslim from

Chicago. As Roselily ponders her impending marriage, she observes her future husband's disdain for her rustic ways and questions his true intentions. Realizing that she is using marriage to escape her squalid environment, Roselily foresees that the union would yield "a lifetime of black and white. Of veils. . . . Not dead, but exalted on a pedestal." In "Her Sweet Jerome," an uneducated but prosperous beautician imagines that her indifferent husband is unfaithful, but discovers that his "mistress" is a collection of books about black nationalism. Walker addresses one of her most prevalent themes—the means by which past tragedies influence present situations—in "The Child Who Favored Daughter." This story centers on an embittered elderly black man who kills his daughter after discovering her relationship with a white man. The crime has deeper implications, however, for the murdered woman bore a striking resemblance to her father's beloved sister, named Daughter. Through flashbacks to his adolescence and early adulthood, the man recalls both his devotion to Daughter and his feelings of betrayal when she became the mistress of his employer. Daughter eventually returns home physically incapacitated and mentally ill, and her ensuing suicide affects her brother's future relationships with women. Barbara Christian stated: " 'The Child Who Favored Daughter' lyrically analyzes two constraints of convention which, when fused, are uniquely opposed to the growth of black women. For it merges the impact of racism, not only on society but on the person, with the threat woman's sexuality represents to patriarchal man."

Many critics noted a striking difference between the stories in *In Love and Trouble* and those in Walker's next volume, *You Can't Keep a Good Woman Down*. The latter collection features black women who are oppressed but not defeated in their attempts to take control of their lives. Exploring a multitude of themes, including love, fame, and the value of friendships, Walker expounds her womanist philosophy as well in addressing such issues as pornography and rape. In the poignant tale "A Sudden Trip Home in the Spring," a young Southern woman, a student at a Northern university, returns home for the funeral of her father, whom she regarded as a weak man. During her visit, she unexpectedly discovers strength and dignity in her older brother and grandfather. In "Advancing Luna—and Ida B. Wells," one of the longest stories in the volume, Walker combines fact and fiction to investigate sexual politics within the civil rights movement and document the history and tragic consequences of interracial rape. The story is set in Georgia, during the summer of 1965, where the unnamed black narrator and Luna, a Jewish woman, meet and become close friends while registering rural blacks to vote. Their relationship is jeopardized years later when Luna reveals she was raped by a fellow activist but remained silent because her attacker was a black man. While the narrator sympathizes with her friend's dilemma, she subconsciously doubts Luna's accusation, recalling the innumerable deaths of black men unjustly accused of raping white women throughout American history. In her confusion, the narrator embarks on an imaginary discourse with Ida B. Wells, a black journalist and social reformer who led a national antilynching campaign during the 1890s. The story concludes on an ambiguous note as the two women go their separate ways, and the narrator is unable to resolve her feelings toward her friend. While *You Can't Keep a Good Woman Down* is generally considered Walker's masterpiece in the short story genre, Katha Pollitt faulted Walker's portrayal of black women in the collection as "too partisan." She stated: "[The] black woman is *always* the most sympathetic character. [The stories] are also too unfocused, too full of loose ends and unanswered questions and of characters that are half odd and interesting individuals and half political or narrative conveniences."

Discussion of Walker's fiction often centers upon what many critics consider her negative portrayals of black males. David Bradley has noted: "Black men in Alice Walker's fiction . . . seem capable of goodness only when they become old . . . , or paralyzed and feminized. . . . If they are not thus rendered symbolically impotent, they are figures of malevolence." Walker herself stated in an interview following the publication of her first novel, *The Third Life of Grange Copeland,* that "not enough credit has been given to the black woman who has been oppressed beyond recognition. Her men have actually encouraged this oppression and insisted on it." Yet, while Walker's short stories and novels may commonly feature uncaring and abusive black men, critics have acknowledged that many of her male characters recognize and attempt to rectify their misdeeds. J. Charles Washington asserted in an essay on *In Love and Trouble* that "Walker's works demonstrate her love for her people, both men and women. . . . [These] works are predicated on the belief that man is inherently good and that, therefore, if flaws in his character exist, through the use of art that educates they can

be removed and the personality restored to health. Rather than being a sign of enmity toward Black men, then, her criticism of them and of Black women is the strongest reflection of this love."

(For further information on Walker's life and career, see *Contemporary Literary Criticism,* Vols. 5, 6, 9, 19, 27, 46, 58; *Contemporary Authors,* Vols. 37-40, rev. ed.; *Contemporary Authors New Revision Series,* Vols. 9, 27; *Something about the Author,* Vol. 31; *Dictionary of Literary Biography,* Vols. 6, 33; and *Concise Dictionary of American Literary Biography, 1968-1988.*)

PRINCIPAL WORKS

SHORT FICTION

In Love and Trouble: Stories of Black Women   1973
You Can't Keep a Good Woman Down   1981

OTHER MAJOR WORKS

Once (poetry) 1968
The Third Life of Grange Copeland (novel) 1970
Revolutionary Petunias (poetry) 1973
Meridian (novel) 1976
Good Night Willie Lee, I'll See You in the Morning (poetry) 1979
The Color Purple (novel) 1982
In Search of Our Mothers' Gardens: Womanist Prose (essays) 1984
Horses Make a Landscape Look More Beautiful (poetry) 1985
Living by the Word: Selected Writings, 1973-1987 (essays) 1988
The Temple of My Familiar (novel) 1989

CAROLYN FOWLER   (essay date 1974)

[*In the review excerpted below, Fowler discusses the strengths and weaknesses of stories from* In Love and Trouble.]

Alice Walker is an exceptionally good writer. More than that, she has the artist's insight into the quiet dramas enacted in the inner lives of those who are anonymous and ineffable: most of us. All of which adds up to a young writer of great promise and great potential.

The promise—and the potential—are manifest in Ms. Walker's first volume of short stories, **In Love and Trouble: Stories of Black Women.** The stories take in a wide spectrum of the black woman's experience in America. We are afforded glimpses of the young rural Southern woman without a husband (**"Roselily," "Strong Horse Tea"**), the bored, upper class educated housewife who wanders into a love affair with a stranger (**"Really, Doesn't Crime Pay?"**), the deeply religious old woman who "stood with eyes uplifted in her Sunday-go-to-meeting clothes" (**"The Welcome Table"**), the black campus co-ed strangely relating to the strange white professor of French (**"We Drink the Wine in France"**), the conjuring tradition (**"The Revenge of Hannah Kemhuff"**).

I have the impression that the author has first-hand knowledge of many of the different life-styles she portrays in these stories. But love is not at issue in all of them. Rather, the authentic Heart of a Woman at the core of most of them shines through to pierce the surface of our caring. Yet, it is always the poignant, sad and unfulfilled heart, and primarily as it manifests itself in the rural South, which is revealed to us. The one story not set in blackamerica (**"The Diary of an African Nun"**) does show the same lonely biding visible in most of the other women portrayed, but would probably have been better situated in a subsequent volume. And Ms. Walker's talent for affecting our sensitivities is often badly served by the tinge of cynicism she projects into many of her dénouements. All of which goes to say that *In Love and Trouble* is a book of great sensitivity, but a sensitivity not yet completely, fully realized.

Yet, these stories do succeed for the most part in creating a mood on which the reader is transposed to a state of being which, for want of more precise labels, we may call the esthetic experience. Thus, they hover in the vague no-man's-land where poetry pervades the atmosphere and obliges the world of reason to yield before the spiritual realities of the soul's yearning after more than it has. So it is that almost all of these stories focus on the most intimate reaches of the inner lives of the characters. But the purity of the esthetic experience is often marred by obvious contrivances, as in the story which opens the collection (**"Roselily"**—an unfortunate choice for first place, perhaps). Roselily stands beside the vaguely outlined figure of the man who will take her from her rural southern past and roots into the big city with her illegitimate children, and snatches of her conflicting thought alternate with the minister's recitation of the marriage ceremony. The device soon becomes tedious, and the experiencer of the story (the reader) soon becomes in spite of himself the critical observer of the writer's craft.

The extraordinary perceptiveness (extraordinary for one so young . . .) is at times marred in a different way by what appears to be the author's axe to grind against nationalists and post-civil rights revolutionaries. The internal validity of the story can suffer as a result, as it does in **"Her Sweet Jerome,"** an amalgam of two different life-styles in blackamerica. Jerome becomes what we might call the Sweetman Revolutionary. But somehow the whole circumstance of his life and his relationship with his woman don't run true to type. (For the type does exist; e.g., the "parttime revolutionary" who, to paraphrase Don Lee, "talks black and sleeps white," or the polygamous revolutionary, busy getting back to African cultural patterns, who wants his women to join forces and Support him if they really Believe.) On the other hand, a story such as **"Everyday Use"** makes a far more effective statement in pointing out that authentic black culture becomes selfconscious and artificial when its artifacts are worshiped for their own sake and not used as they were intended, or when the attempt to rediscover one's cultural roots with the remote African past in effect destroys a cultural continuity established here in America. (pp. 59-60)

One approaches *In Love and Trouble* expecting . . . to see the portrayal of black womanhood. And this is what is primarily portrayed. One has but to compare the treatment of rural southern black women in Jean Toomer's *Cane,* which also pierces through to essential aspiration, to sense the difference in treatment. There seems after all to be something illusively feminine about the woman writer's presentation of her material. However, that cannot be the most important statement to be made because, in both cases, the end effect

is a glimpse of essential human aspiration. What one really has then is a specificity in time, place, culture and sex which transcends itself and speaks of the human situation, a combination which literature, when it is truly that, almost always is. The vignette **"The Flowers,"** two pages long and a scene so reminiscent of the poem "Between the World and Me" by Richard Wright (but somehow painted with a woman's touch), tells of a young girl who, while blithely picking flowers, stumbles upon the skeleton of a lynched man:

> Myop began to circle back to the house, back to the peacefulness of the morning. It was then she stepped smack into his eyes. Her heel became lodged in the broken ridge between brow and nose, and she reached down quickly, unafraid, to free herself. It was only when she saw his naked grin that she gave a little yelp of surprise. . . .
>
> Myop gazed around the spot with interest. Very near where she'd stepped into the head was a wild pink rose. As she picked it to add to her bundle she noticed a raised mound, a ring, around the rose's root. It was the rotted remains of a noose, a bit of shredding plowline, now blending benignly into the soil. Around an overhanging limb of a great spreading oak clung another piece. Frayed, rotted, bleached, and frazzled—barely there—but spinning restlessly in the breeze. Myop laid down her flowers.
>
> And the summer was over.

Here we see Ms. Walker's talent for short, effective final statement which, by its silent commentary, shouts through the heavens of an overwhelming human inner transformation. The situation is blackamerican, the character living it is female, but the real commentary here is on the End of Innocence, portrayed in images which both sexes and most races of sensitized mankind should be able to relate to.

In Love and Trouble then is a book uneven at the edges but solid at the core, and one which leads us to expect truly significant work from this young black woman writer, as a woman, as a black woman and as a writer simply, but with the artist's eye, perceiving and portraying the soul of man. (pp. 61-2)

> *Carolyn Fowler, "Solid at the Core," in Freedom-ways, Vol. 14, No. 1, first quarter, 1974, pp. 59-62.*

MEL WATKINS (essay date 1974)

[*In the excerpt below, Watkins comments on Walker's use of black myths and Southern folk traditions in* In Love and Trouble *and places her stories in the tradition of Zora Neale Hurston.*]

[In **"Everyday Use,"** a story included in *In Love and Trouble*], Wangero Leewanika Kemanjo . . . formerly just plain Dee—returns with her city boyfriend, Hakim-a-barber, to a small Southern town to visit her mother and homely, barely literate sister. She takes Polaroid shots of the family, always with the dingy house, clay front yard or cow in the background and, when they sit down to eat, her boyfriend spurns the collards, chitlins and pork.

Later she insists on taking a handcarved top and dasher from the churn, in which milk is still clabbering, to use as a centerpiece for her alcove table and asks for some quilts, handstitched by her grandmother, to hang in her apartment. Her mother refuses to give her the quilts because they have been promised to her sister as a wedding gift. Irate at the thought of "priceless" artifacts actually being used on a bed, Dee leaves in a huff, scorning her mother and sister for not understanding *their* heritage.

Told from the mother's point of view, this tale of an urbanized daughter's return to the family and folkways she has left behind is an ironic, touching and humorous fictional encounter. **"Everyday Use"** is typical of the short stories and brief character sketches included in this impressive collection.

Alice Walker has focused her fictional eye on the black woman, her loves and, as the blues idiom puts it, her 'bukes and scorns. Other stories treat themes such as a wife's ambivalence as she prepares to leave her Southern home to accompany her husband to Chicago on their wedding night, the degeneration of the marriage of a potentially talented writer and her plodding, insensitive husband, a woman driven half mad by her younger husband's obsession with what she thinks is another woman, and the revenge by hoodoo, of an aging woman on a white social worker who had refused her aid during the Depression. And, like the lyrics of good blues, these stories are terse, ironic and humorous. Alice Walker writes efficiently and economically, and the shorter pieces here, even when thin as fiction, are often prose poems. (pp. 40-1)

In this collection, Miss Walker is moving without being maudlin, ironic without being gimmickery. *In Love and Trouble* is not the major work one might have expected after [*The Third Life of Grange Copeland*], but it is a delight to read, reminicsent in its use of black myth and Southern folkways of Zora Neale Hurston's work (one story is dedicated to Miss Hurston). Some of these tales are small gems. (p. 41)

Mel Watkins, "In Love and Trouble," in The New York Times Book Review, *March 17, 1974, pp. 40-1.*

JOHN F. CALLAHAN   (essay date 1974)

[*In the following excerpt, Callahan offers an appreciative review of* In Love and Trouble.]

Reading Alice Walker is like hearing John Coltrane's *Alabama*. Each bites into strange Southern fruit and finds a sweetness almost as unbearable as the bitterness of violence, humiliation and oppression. As Walker's character Grange Copeland says after his granddaughter's birth: " 'Out of all kinds of shit comes something clean, soft and sweet smellin'.' " Pain and joy, tenderness and power, helplessness and cruelty flow through her writing and are beautiful because of the wholeness of her talent.

In Walker's hands wholeness is an all-inclusive, open-ended theme. Pointing beyond human guilt, it suggests that an oppressed people's first step away from helplessness is to take responsibility for their actions toward each other. Asked in a 1973 interview about her "preoccupations," Walker said simply: "I am preoccupied with the spiritual survival, the survival *whole* of my people. But beyond that, I am committed to exploring the oppressions, the insanities, the loyalties, and the triumphs of black women. . . . Next to them, I place the old people—male and female—who persist in their beauty in spite of everything." (p. 21)

In Love and Trouble is a collection of Alice Walker's fiction written between 1967 and 1973. The title expresses the condition of black women in the blues tradition. *In Love and Trou-*

ble: a Southern voice—sensuous and sad, slow and strong. The language conjures images of black women working and suffering and loving while they tell their stories with music.

The stories evoke magnificently diverse lives from the same rural Southern roots. In **"The Child Who Favored Daughter,"** a black father cuts off his daughter's breasts because of her affair with a white boy. Unable to distinguish his daughter from his dead sister, he assaults her with a rage always checked in front of white people who are the cause of his oppression. The horror is bearable only because of Walker's images fusing nature and the girl's inner world and because of the ebb and flow of blues rhythms in the story's voice. In Walker's prose the facts are always stark; the essential quality of sympathy comes partly from reverberations of Jean Toomer and Zora Neale Hurston in her folk voices.

"Everyday Use" is about a woman choosing which of her daughters to give a quilt pieced in the old way by her mother. The older daughter, Dee (now Wangero Leewanika Kemanjo), comes back home with her Muslim man and demands the quilt because *she* understands the black "heritage." Maggie, the other daughter, has stayed south; she's been promised her grandma's quilt for her wedding. . . . Passionately moved by Maggie's genuine kinship with tradition, her mama declares allegiance. Maggie will get the quilt. (pp. 21-2)

In Love and Trouble is full of other challenging and movingly realized stories. Two root-workers in **"The Revenge of Hannah Kemhuff "** gain revenge for an old woman by working so shrewdly on the fear and guilt of the white woman who did Hannah wrong that she unwittingly turns a potion's magic against herself until she dies of it. **"The Welcome Table"** shows us an old, stubborn black woman who, having been lifted bodily out of a white church, has a vision of Jesus highstepping down the highway with her until she dies of ecstasy and exhaustion. **"Strong Horse Tea"** is about a "not pretty," "nobody" woman with no husband and a sick baby boy. She waits for the white doctor until the baby is almost dead. When no one comes, she turns to Aunt Sarah, an old black herb doctor. "The child's dying," Aunt Sarah tells her, and the only possible remedy is horse piss while it's still warm and steaming. Rannie Toomer goes out in a thunderstorm, fetches the strong horse tea, puts her mouth to a shoe to keep the medicine from leaking, and runs home not knowing her Baby Snooks is already dead. . . . We see tradition in **"To Hell With Dying,"** a story directly out of Walker's childhood. For years its narrator participated in "revivals" of Mr. Sweet, a diabetic, alcoholic old man who periodically seemed on the verge of dying. When he's 90, the girl, now a woman of 24 doing a Ph.D. up north, can't revive him anymore. He dies, but his steel guitar passes to the young woman. As she hums "Sweet Georgia Brown," her kinship with the old man becomes whole in her heart.

Alice Walker's power as a writer is exactly that power she has felt in Jean Toomer. "He is both feminine and masculine in his perceptions." Alice Walker is Ruth, and she is Grange Copeland. She is old Mr. Sweet and the girl who revives him. As I've heard Michael Harper say as he reads his poems and those of the neglected Sterling Brown: "I been down so long that down don't bother me." The *essentials* of Alice Walker's passionate black tradition and talent are contained in the last stanza of "Alice," Harper's poem for her:

And for this I say your name: Alice,
my grandmother's name, your name,

conjured in snake-infested field
where Zora Neale welcomed you
   home,
and where I speak from now
on higher ground of her risen
black marker where you have written
your name in hers, and in mine.

(p. 22)

John F. Callahan, "Reconsideration: The Higher Ground of Alice Walker," in The New Republic, Vol. 171, No. 11, September 14, 1974, pp. 21-2.

CHESTER J. FONTENOT   (essay date 1977)

[*Fontenot is an American critic, editor, and dramatist who has written several books on African-American literature, including* Studies in Black Literature: Black American Prose Theory (*1983*). *In the following excerpt, Fontenot analyzes Walker's short story "The Diary of an African Nun" and compares its theme of cultural duality to W. E. B. Dubois's concept of "double-consciousness," a psychological state among black intellectuals in which they experience thoughts and emotions that are at once complementary and contradictory to their social surroundings.*]

[The double-consciousness of which W. E. B. Dubois writes], "this sense of always looking at one's self through the eyes of others, of measuring one's soul by the tape of a world that looks on in amused contempt and pity," produces two warring factions: To be an American and a Black person. The struggle between these two unreconciled strivings threatens to plunge the Black American, in particular the Black artist, into a sort of half-way house, where the artist is neither accepted as a part of the American literary tradition, nor as a Black artist worthy of critical attention. (p. 192)

[Alice Walker's] **"The Diary of An African Nun"** is a supreme statement of the dilemma. Though this short story is only six pages in length, it contains material for a novella. It is divided into six parts and is set in an African mission school in Uganda, where an African woman has rejected her traditional tribal religion for Christianity. Walker begins Part I by introducing things which are not only foreign to African culture, but which also suggest tension between the "true" spirituality of African culture and the materialistic underpinnings of European culture. (p. 193)

Just as the Europeans question her commitment to the Catholic Church, so does the Black nun feel uneasy about her rejection of African traditional religion and values. She repeats her vows to the Catholic Church, but cannot help remembering the colonization of her people by Europeans. She says that, "I was born in this township, a village 'civilized' by American missionaries." . . . Walker's usage of quotations around the word "civilized" emphasizes the irony in her using the term. The things which one would call civilized are all materialistic. The first part of the story ends as the nun gazes at the Rewenzori mountains; she tells us that they "show themselves only once a year under the blazing heat of spring." . . . It is at this time that the snow, which is a false covering, melts and reveals the true nature of the mountains. The nun, like the mountains, is within a sort of superstructure which inhibits natural growth.

Part two seems to suggest the ultimate irony of an oppressed group—that is, the oppressed sees himself or herself through the eyes of the oppressor and seeks to assimilate into the soci-

ety the oppressor has set up. Once the oppressed achieves this goal, he or she realizes two things: 1) The alien society does not want him or her to be a part of it, and it will never provide the means by which the oppressed can function as a full member of that society; and 2) the oppressed realizes that he or she really doesn't want to become a part of the dominant society. . . . The oppressed is halfway between the world of the oppressor and that of the oppressor, yet belongs to neither. But the important thing to consider is that to reach a vantage point from where the oppressed can become conscious of his or her predicament requires that the oppressed distance himself or herself from the socio-cultural milieu which confronts him or her. The African nun reaches this ironic stance when she recalls the way she became a nun. (pp. 193-94)

Part three [develops her position towards her new-found faith and culture]. . . . Walker's language suggests a tension between Christianity and African pagan worship. This tension leads her to question her position in the mission school and finally toward her belief in Christ. (p. 194)

Moreover, she contrasts the down-to-earth sensuality of African tribal religion with the aloofness of Christianity. The nun longs to be "within the black circle around the red, glowing fire, to feel the breath of love hot against my cheeks, the smell of love strong about my waiting thighs! . . ." If we compare the imagery of snow which covers up the natural passions to the habit the nun wears which covers up her body, we can see that the contrast between the snow and habit on one hand and the mountains and the nun's body on the other further develops this tension. Walker concludes this part of the short story in an almost blasphemous manner. She adopts an ironical tone toward the stereotypical way in which we think of Christ. The nun, thinking about the price she pays for rejecting the sensuous African rituals, tries to move Christianity in the direction of African tribal religion. . . . (pp. 194-95)

Part four is dominated by the life and vitality of the African people. . . .

Walker contrasts the African images of sexuality—through describing the ritual lovers dance—with the *a*sexual nature of Christianity. Perhaps this suggests that European civilization is somewhat artificial. There are sins on both the Christian side, which sins against the flesh in preference of a transcendental existence, and on the African side, which sins against the eternal, spiritual world in preference of a continued reenactment of the creation. The lack of sexuality indicates that the European values are a superstructure which covers the African nun, like the snow covers the mountains, until spring, which represents a psychological revival.

Part five reveals the nun's psychological plight. Walker revives the metaphor of spring as the vitality of African culture as opposed to the harshness of European culture (symbolized as winter snow). Perhaps this imagery also suggests the fixed nature of African culture—its durable quality in contrast to the temporary or superficial nature of European culture (the snow melts every spring). It seems that the nun isn't really talking about Christianity as a belief, but as a way of attaining certain things which she couldn't get through African pagan worship. (p. 195)

The nun sees Christianity as a sort of material salvation for her people. She knows that it is spiritually decadent, yet the African people must function in a Christian world. Hence,

Christianity becomes a way of teaching her people a conscious lie to further their own ends—survival.

The last section of the short story reveals the nun's paradoxical stance toward what she is doing. . . . In short, she must walk the tight rope between the two worlds without becoming a part of either, for to become a part of the European world is to die a spiritual death, and to become a part of the African world condemns her to a material death.

If we allegorize the story, we can say that the plight of the African nun is that of the Black intellectual or middle-class . . . , who find themselves caught between two worlds which are at once complementary and contradictory. The conclusion the nun comes to is that one must be aware of the situation in which one places himself or herself by assuming an alien perspective which contradicts that of his or her native culture. "Civilization" can become something that Blacks can utilize in their struggle for independence, but to do so, they need leaders (much like Dubois' talented tenth) who can teach the masses to put the intricacies of civilization to constructive use. In this way, Black people will be able to see their involvement with American civilization as simply a way of surviving. The adoption of American values by Black Americans on one hand, and of American literary conventions by Black artists on the other, can be seen by analogy as the snow which covers the mountains and as the African nun's habit. This process would move the problem from a psychological predicament to a conscious manipulation of American civilization, and could, therefore, make progress toward lessening the agony Black Americans feel in having to deal with a double-consciousness. (pp. 195-96)

> *Chester J. Fontenot, "Alice Walker* 'The Diary of an African Nun' *and Dubois' Double Consciousness," in* Journal of Afro-American Issues, *Vol. 5, No. 2, Spring, 1977, pp. 192-96.*

ANNE Z. MICKELSON (essay date 1979)

[*In the following excerpt, Mickelson provides a feminist analysis of* In Love and Trouble.]

Without question, [Alice Walker's] fiction shows a dedicated engagement with the resources, capacities, infirmities, realities, consciousness, and spiritual health of black people—particularly women. The collection of short stories *In Love & Trouble,* presents a varied gallery of black women and their moves: to self-discovery; to tentative, uncompleted exploration; to disillusionment; to recognition of their own worth; to rage, peace, death, life. The author's moral attitudes are explicit, though she does not assault our sensibilities by peremptory treatment of the moral situations discussed. Though occasionally she steps into her own story a little unnecessarily to develop an already established attitude on the part of the reader (**"The Revenge of Hannah Kemhuff "**), the total effect of the work is a sense of precise language which consistently emphasizes the different ways in which women (and men) take action to attain dignity.

The women in these stories do not always have a chance or a choice, but the moral force of many of the stories depends on characterization which portrays the women as living refutations of passivity. If these stories possess something in common, it is the fight against resignation, victimization, loneliness, despair, stasis, "the odor of corruption" which Joyce said hovered over his Dubliners. In effect, this constitutes, for

the most part, an underlying theme which links such different women as Roselily; the narrator of **"Really, Doesn't Crime Pay?"**; the homely hairdresser (**"Her Sweet Jerome"**); Hannah Kemhuff . . . and others. Together with this linking, there is a scope of vision which moves from one woman to another, each time picking up a particular segment of the black woman's experience.

The author is always concerned with women, what happens to them, why it happens. The problem of marriage and the varying expectations of women are handled with intelligence and expert craftsmanship. There is often expressed bitterness against men—a continuing theme for the writer, as in her lines:

> Whoever he is, he is not worth
> all this.
> Don't you agree?
> And I will never
> unclench my teeth long enough
> to tell him so.
>
> ("Did This Happen to Your Mother?
> Did Your Sister Throw Up a Lot?")

"Roselily" is the story of a woman whose name suggests the grafting on of a new identity. An unmarried mother of four, she weds a stern convert to the Muslim religion, knowing that before her is a life of veils and robes. Against the background drone of the platitudinous marriage ceremony, the woman's body itches to be free of voile and satin; she remembers her body bare to the sun. Under the gauze of the wedding veil, her fingers knot and unknot, paralleling thoughts on where she is going, the kind of life that will be hers, and the identity of the man she is marrying. She knows that the man standing next to her, clasping her hand in his "iron" grip, is the price of respectability, the price for having her children free of the "detrimental wheel." He is the way to a new life. What kind of life, she asks herself? Babies? Her hands will be full? Full of what? We realize how limited her choices have been, how little chance at living she has had. Whether she will have any chance now is all left in doubt.

The wife in **"Really, Doesn't Crime Pay?"** has no such difficulty in sorting out her emotions. Intelligent, creative, she tells us precisely in diary form what her husband expects of her. She is to cream, scent, anoint, and deck her body. For diversion, she is to shop, and for fulfillment she is to bear a child. As for writing, the husband Ruel is firm in his disapproval: *"No wife of mine is going to embarrass me with a lot of foolish, vulgar stuff "* (author's italics). Like the Muslim husband in **"Roselily,"** Ruel wants babies so that his wife's hands will be full, and like Roselily, but more eloquently, the wife asks: full of what?

Instead of lengthy character description, the author's few vivid sentences acquaint us with the terrible emotional and intellectual impoverishment of the woman's life, in order to make us understand why she becomes such an easy victim to her lover, a young black writer, Mordecai Rich. Though her intelligence warns her that anyone who views other people's confusions with such a cold eye cannot have much heart, she blooms emotionally and intellectually under his praise of her work—and her body. He represents life, escape. The denouement is swift. The lover leaves; there is a long absence, and one day, sitting in a doctor's office, she picks up a magazine and sees his picture. He is serious-looking, newly-bearded, and the story under his name is hers, the one he once read and praised. There is a caption below the picture stating that the author will soon issue a new book: *The Black Woman's Resistance to Creativity in the Arts.*

The author does not hover over her character. In a few swift strokes, she shows her breaking down, then some weeks later, gathering herself together to exercise a free choice. Like Ellison's invisible man, she will yes her husband to death—creaming, softening skin and body, shopping for more and more clothes, assuring him that the baby will be conceived. Secretly, she works out her fate by undermining her husband's plan. She takes the pill religiously. Her consciousness of freedom is not illusory. Soon, she realizes, when both husband and she are quite tired of the sweet, sweet smell of her body and the softness of those creamed hands, she will leave—leave without once looking back at her doll's house. We are aware of the psychic damage of so much attention paid to revenge, but also aware that in order to exercise free choice in working out her destiny, she is doing what seems psychologically necessary at the moment.

The unwanted, unloved, rejected woman is treated in several stories with sympathy, but with a truthfulness to individual experience. **"Her Sweet Jerome"** pictures a middle-aged, ugly hairdresser whose family is what is known as "colored folks with money." Knowing herself secretly jeered, taunted and laughed at all her life by the women whom she beautifies, she cannot resist a school teacher ten years younger than herself, "so little and cute and young." She tells herself she will not rest until he and she are Mr. and Mrs. Jerome Franklin Washington the third, *"and that's the truth."* Given her character's aim, the writer adapts her art to meet the exigency of the human nature she portrays. The woman masochistically submits to beatings and her husband's contemptuous ignoring of her, until she finds out she has a rival. Consumed with jealousy, she questions, hunts, prowls down every street to find "the woman." Finally, she discovers who her rival is. Stacked under the bed are dozens of books on the black revolutionary movement. Her satisfaction is to set them on fire—a fire which symbolically matches the bonfire within her.

Not all the stories are of bleak marriage relationships. Some evoke the racial scene, such as **"The Welcome Table,"** in which a stubborn, poor, black woman is ejected from a white church. Undaunted, she walks down the long road secure in the knowledge that her beloved Jesus is walking right by her side. After all, he looks exactly like the picture of him she has seen in a white lady's Bible for whom she had worked. Pouring out her life to him, she finally collapses and dies, his smile filling her with ecstasy and exultation. The woman never strikes us as an abstract figure with a delusion, but as one of the old, lonely ones whom society has forgotten. Later, her neighbors speculate why she had walked so far: maybe she had some relatives a few miles away.

Another story which evokes the relations between the races is **"The Revenge of Hannah Kemhuff."** It recalls Tolstoy's comment that a writer can invent anything, but it is impossible to invent psychology. Hannah Kemhuff wants justice for the insult to her spirit and body, and for the misery she had suffered from the white woman who refused her relief when she and her children were starving. The husband who deserted her has already been dealt with by God. He and his new woman were swept to their death in a flood. Two root workers assure Hannah that her spirit can be mended, and proceed to mix a potion. Demonstrating how the power of

suggestion can work, Walker shows the white woman so fearful of the potion's magic that she aids in her own physical and psychological destruction.

The neglected, suffering black woman who is "not anybody much" becomes the theme of **"Strong Horse Tea."** Rannie is not married, not pretty, lives in a cold, drafty cabin and has only one thing in the world—her baby Snooks, and he is dying. At first, rejecting old Sarah's "swamp magic," she begs the white postman to summon the doctor for her. At last, realizing that the doctor is not coming, and told bluntly by old Sarah that Snooks is dying, she races out to the pasture for the strong horse tea, warm from the mare—the only thing, Sarah tells her, which will save the baby. (pp. 154-58)

Not all the stories are somber. There is a delightful insight into the common sense and humor of black country people in **"Everyday Use,"** in which the mother makes a choice concerning her concept of "tradition." She is a large, big-boned woman who has always done a man's work, and whose education stopped at the second grade. "Don't ask me why," she says briefly, "in 1927 colored asked fewer questions than they do now." Though she sometimes fantasizes being on the Johnny Carson show, and told what a fine woman she is, she laughs at her fantasies, for she has a true sense of her own worth. When her daughter Dee comes home with her black Muslim man, calling herself Wangero Leewanika Kemanjo, and informs her mother that she wants the quilt pieced by her grandmother because only she understands its tradition, the mother reacts with keen appraisal of the circumstances. She is sympathetic to the other daughter, self-effacing Maggie, who has stayed home and has been promised the quilt for her wedding, yet is ready to give up the quilt to her more aggressive sister, assuring her mother that she needs no tangible evidence of tradition. She can remember her grandmother without the quilt. Maggie gets the quilt, and the writer ends the story with language whose rhythm suggests the satisfactory tempo of the mother's life: "After we watched the car dust settle I asked Maggie to bring me a dip of snuff. And then the two of us sat there just enjoying, until it was time to go in the house and go to bed."

My own favorite among the stories is the one which Langston Hughes enjoyed: **"To Hell with Dying."** Tradition, love, the past, joy of living, a sense of black people as complete, healthy, undiminished, are all blended to convey the sense of the narrator's enrichment of her life through Mr. Sweet. For as many years as the narrator had remembered, Mr. Sweet, a family friend, has made a ritual of dying. He had been their childhood companion—a perfect companion, for he had the ability to be drunk and sober at the same time. The narrator, now a Ph.D. candidate, gets a telegram telling her that ninety-year-old Mr. Sweet is dying and could she please drop everything to come to his bedside? Of course she could, and does. He had been her first beau, and her tribute to him is "Sweet Georgia Brown" plucked out on the guitar he had left her.

One criterion of the good short story is its truthfulness to individualistic experience. Alice Walker's short stories always make us comprehend rationally the emotions and actions of the women she writes about. When a symbol is used, in a way consistent with the story's scope and form, it ties the episodes to the story with organic unity. Though in **"The Revenge of Hannah Kemhuff"** the ending seems unnecessarily tacked on, and we are aware that we are being patterned in a certain way to intensify our moral perceptiveness, this tendency is avoided in the other stories. The net result of the stories is an explicit comment on human nature, which is adequately sustained and suggests not only Walker's identification with her characters, but a genuine love for them. (pp. 159-60)

> Anne Z. Mickelson, "Winging Upward—Black Women: Sarah E. Wright, Toni Morrison, Alice Walker," in her Reaching Out: Sensitivity and Order in Recent American Fiction by Women, *The Scarecrow Press, Inc., 1979, pp. 112-74.*

BARBARA CHRISTIAN   (essay date 1981)

[*Christian is an American critic specializing in fiction written by African-American women. She is the author of* Black Women Novelists: Development of a Tradition, 1892-1976 (*1980*) *and* Black Feminist Criticism: Perspectives on Black Women Writers (*1985*). *In the following excerpted essay, she illustrates the resilience of Walker's heroines in* In Love and Trouble.]

[*In Love and Trouble*] is introduced by two seemingly unrelated excerpts, one from *The Concubine* by the contemporary West African writer, Elechi Amadi, the other from *Letters to a Young Poet* by the early 20th century German poet, Rainer Maria Rilke. In the first excerpt, Amadi described the emotional state of the young girl, Ahurole, who is about to be engaged. She is contrary, boisterous at one time, sobbing violently at another. Her parents conclude that she is "unduly influenced by *agwu,* her personal spirit," a particularly troublesome one. Though the excerpt Walker chose primarily describes Ahurole's *agwu,* it ends with this observation: "Ahurole was engaged to Ekwueme when she was 8 days old."

The excerpt from Rilke beautifully summarizes a view of the living, setting up a dichotomy between the natural and the social order:

> . . . people have (with the help of conventions) oriented all their solutions toward the easy and toward the easiest side of the easy, but it is clear that we must hold to what is difficult; everything in nature grows and defends itself in its own way, and is characteristically and spontaneously itself, seeks at all costs to be so against all opposition.
>
> (*In Love,* epigraph)

How are these two excerpts from strikingly different traditions related and why are they the preludes, the tone-setters to a volume of short stories about black women?

I am coordinating a seminar on the works of Alice Walker. We have read and discussed *Once,* Walker's first volume of poetry, and the *The Third Life of Grange Copeland,* her powerful first novel. The tension in the class has steadily risen. Now we are approaching **In Love and Trouble.** There is a moment of silence as class starts. Then one of the black women, as if bursting from an inexplicable anger says: "Why is there so much pain in these books, especially in this book?" I know this student; her life has much pain in it. She is going to school against all odds, in opposition to everything and everyone, it would seem. She is conscious of being black; she is struggling, trying to figure out why her relationships as a woman are so confused, often painful. She repeats her question adding a comment—"What kind of images are these to expose to—(pause)?" To whom, she will not say. "I don't want to see this, know this." There is more anger, then si-

lence. But she is riveted on the stories in this and other class sessions and insists on staying in this class. (p. 21)

Who are the characters in these stories? What happens to them? More to the point, what do they do that should cause this young black woman, and many others like her to be so affected? What have they or she to do with *agwu* or with Rilke's words?

In these 11 stories, Walker's protagonists share certain external characteristics that at first might seem primarily descriptive. All are female, all are black, most are Southern, all are involved in some critical relationship to lover, mother, father, daughter, husband, woman, tradition, God, nature that causes them some discomfort. But the external characteristics so easily discerned, are not emblems. They are far more complex and varied. The words, *Southern black woman,* as if they were a sort of verbal enchantment, evoke clusters of contradictory myths, images, stories, meanings according to different points of view. Who is a Southern black woman? To a white man, those words might connote a mammy, a good looking wench, or Dilsey, as it did to Faulkner. To a white woman it might connote a servant, a rival, or a wise indefatigable adviser, as it did to Lillian Hellman. To a black man, it might connote a charming, soft-spoken, perhaps backward woman, or a religious fanatic and a vale of suffering as it did to Richard Wright. But what does *being* a Southern black woman mean to her, or to the many that are her? (p. 22)

Focal to Walker's presentation is the point of view of individual black Southern girls or women who must act out their lives in the web of conventions that is the South—conventions that they may or may not believe in, may or may not feel at ease in, conventions that may or may not help them to grow. And because societal conventions in the South have much to do with the conduct of relationships—man and woman, young and old, black and white, our female protagonists, by their very existence, must experience and assess them. So naturally, Walker's women are in love and trouble. However, unlike Toomer's women in *Cane,* who too are restricted by their race, sex, and origins, Walker's women are not silent. Her women are not presented through a perceptive male narrator, but through the private voices of their imaginations or through their dearly paid for words or acts.

The way in which Walker uses point of view, character is not mere technique, but an indication of how free her protagonists are to be themselves within the constraints of convention. If they cannot act, they speak. If they cannot speak they can at least imagine, their inferiority being inviolate, a place where they can exercise autonomy, be who they are. Through act, word or dream, they naturally seek to be "characteristically and spontaneously" themselves. In order to defend the selves they know they are, they must hold to what is difficult, often wishing, however that they were not so compelled. As all natural things, they must have themselves—even in conflict. So their *agwu,* their personal spirits are troubled, as they strain against their restraints. And their acts, words dreams take on the appearance, if not of madness, of contrariness.

What specifically are some of the conventions that so restrict them, causing their spirits to be troubled even as they seek love? It is interesting to me that the stories from this volume my students found most disturbing take place within the imagination of the character. And that often that character mentally sees herself as different from her external self. She

Walker at age six in Eatonton, Georgia.

sees a different self—a dangerous self, as if a reflection in a mirror.

Roselily is such a character. The form of her story, itself a marriage ceremony, is a replica of the convention, the easy solution to which she has been oriented. As a poor black woman with four illegitimate children, she is, it seems, beyond redemption. Thus, her wedding day, attended as it is by satin voile, and lily of the valley, is from any number of viewpoints a day of triumph. But *she,* how does she see it? Walker does not use "I," the first person point of view, but the pronoun "She" throughout this marriage ceremony, as if Roselily is being seen from an external point of view. . . . It is as if even in Roselily's mind, the being who wonders about, questions this day of triumph, is both herself, and yet not herself.

Troubled, though feeling she should not be troubled, Roselily's meditation on the words of the ceremony is intensely focused, almost fixated on images of entrapment. . . . Yet because of her condition, she feels she should not feel this way. She should want: "Respect, a chance to build. Her children at last from underneath the detrimental wheel." What she feels is—trapped in her condition—trapped in her deliver from that condition. (pp. 23-4)

She comes from a Southern black community, poor, Christian, rural, its tradition held together by "cemeteries and the long sleep of grandparents mingling in the dirt." . . . But she must be poor, she must work in a sewing plant—work from which no growth will occur, work only for the purpose of sur-

vival. Here she must be a mother, preferably within the confines of marriage, where her sensuality will be legitimatized and curbed. But even without marriage she must be a mother. Tradition decrees it. Here the responsibility of her children's fathers are minimized, their condition as restricted as hers except they have mobility, can drive by "waving or not waving." Here the quality of suffering is legitimatized by Christianity, as rooted in sorrow as the graves of her grandparents. Here there is nothing new, as the cars on the highway whiz by, leaving behind a lifestyle as rooted in the past as the faces at this country wedding. (p. 24)

To the man she is marrying, God is Allah, the devil is the white man, and work is building a black nation. But he cannot abide the incorrect ways of Roselily's community, their faith in a white Christian God and their tolerance of sensuality. Just as the old women in the church feel that he is "like one of their sons except that he had somehow got away from them," he feels that this community is black except that it had gotten away from its blackness. For him, a veiled black woman in his home is a sign of his righteousness, and in marrying Roselily he is redeeming her from her backward values. With him, she will have black babies to people the nation.

Whether Southern or Northern, traditional or modern, rural or urban, convention confines Roselily to a role, a specific manifestation of some dearly held principle. As a result, her *agwu,* though expressed only in her dreaming, is even more troubled by change. For even as she glimpses possibilities, she is left with the same vision of confinement. She can only dream that "she wants to live for once. But doesn't quite know what that means. Wonders if she has ever done it. If she ever will." Not even the *I do* that she must speak in order to accept the delivery from her condition is allowed, in this story, to interrupt the dreaming. She does not speak aloud. Her dreaming is as separate from her external behavior, as this Mississippi country church is from her future home. . . . But at least she can, in her imagination, know her confinement to be troublesome and recognize in a part of herself that this change is not the attainment of *her* fulfillment.

As the first story in this volume, Roselily's meditation on her condition touches major themes that will be explored in most of the others. Distinctions between the shells of convention, to which people are usually oriented, and the marrow of a living, functional black tradition is examined in most of these stories in terms of the span and degree of freedom afforded the black woman. Like **"Roselily," "Really, Doesn't Crime Pay"** focusses on the limited image of black femaleness within Southern tradition. Only now the image is no longer a "pleasant" one but a black and middle class one as modified by the sweet smelling idealizations of the Southern lady. (pp. 24-5)

To all appearances, for that is what counts, Myrna [in **"Really, Doesn't Crime Pay"**] has succeeded in ways that Roselily had not. Myrna, after all is married to Reul (Rule), an ambitious Southern black man, who wants her to have babies that he will support, and who insists on keeping her expensively dressed and scented. But, although Reul and Roselily's new husband are worlds apart, they agree on basic tenets: that the appearance and behavior of their wives mirror the male's values, and that their women stay at home and have babies. Both women must, in their physical make-up, be the part. . . . But while Roselily does not know what she *wants* to do, when she is rested, Myrna knows that she wants to write, must write.

As in **"Roselily,"** **"Really, Doesn't Crime Pay"** takes place within the imagination of the character. But while Roselily dreams during her wedding, Myrna's imagination is presented through her entries in her writing notebook. Unlike Roselily then, whose critical musings never move beyond her interior, Myrna's break for freedom lies in trying to express herself in words. However, like Roselily, as Myrna confronts the conventions she is expected to adhere to, she also experiences discomfit within her *agwu*.

As is often true with Walker's stories, the first few sentences succinctly embodies the whole:

> September 1961
> page 118
> I sit here by the window in a house with a 30 year mortgage looking down at my Helena Rubenstein hands. . . . And why not? Since I am not a serious writer, my nails need not be bitten off. My cuticles need not have jagged edges.

These first lines not only tell us that Myrna's story will be told through her entries in her writing notebook, we also begin to realize that she knows her value is perceived to be in her appearance and social position, not in her creativity. And because she has no external acknowledgement of her value as a writer, she, with some irony, doubts her own ability. (p. 25)

As a result of her own doubts, constantly reinforced by her husband, magazines, billboards, other women, doctors, Myrna is open, both sexually and artistically to Mordecai, an artiste. He rips her off on both counts precipitating the mental breakdown and her aborted murder of her husband that we see developing in her entries.

The presentation of entries, which begin with September 1961, go back in time and finally move beyond that date, is crucial to Myrna's story. For when we meet her, she has already tried to write and been rebuffed by her husband. She has been ripped off by Mordecai, has attempted murder, has been confined to a mental institution and has eventually been returned to her husband. Like Caroline Gilman's *The Yellow Wallpaper,* the entries that make up the substance of this story express the anger and rage, in madly logical terms, which drive the house-prisoned woman writer crazy.

But the story goes beyond that impotent rage. Having tried the madness of murder and failed, Myrna concocts a far more subtle way, contrariness rather than madness, to secure her freedom. Now she says yes to everything, the smiles, the clothes, sex, the house, until she has yessed her husband to fatigue. She triumphantly tells us that "the women of the community feel sorry for him to be married to such a fluff of nothing." and she confides that "he knows now that I intend to do nothing but say *yes* until he is completely exhausted." Cunningly, she secretly takes "the Pill," insuring her eventual triumph over him. But it is her discovery of the magnificence of the manipulation of words that brings her to a possible resolution of her troubled *agwu.* Like Ralph Ellison's nameless narrator's grandfather in *Invisible Man,* she yesses them to death, though in a peculiarly female way.

In saying *yes* to mean *no* Myrna uses the manipulative power of the word and secures some small victory. But it is a victory achieved from the position of weakness, for she has no alternative. Like countless Southern belles, she has found that directness based on self-autonomy is ineffectual and that successful strategies must be covert. Such strategies demand patience, self-abnegation, falsehood. Thus at the end of this story, Myrna has yet to act: "When I am quite, quite tired of the sweet, sweet smell of my body, and the softness of these Helena Rubenstein hands, I will leave him and this house."

What happens then when a black woman goes against convention, transgresses a deeply felt taboo, and says *No* directly and aloud? In perhaps the most powerful, certainly the most violent story of this volume, the woman in **"The Child Who Favored Daughter,"** speaks practically one word in the entire story, "No." By saying "No" with such firmness she resists convention, insisting on the inviolability of her *agwu*.

This story is as important in the light it sheds on the black men in other stories, Reul, and Roselily's Muslim husband, as it is in its own right. Moving back and forth between the imaginations of the woman and her father, it presents in almost cinematic rhythm, a black male and female point of view. In committing the most damnable act for a black woman, falling in love with a white man, the Child who favored Daughter sorely touches the vulnerability of the black man who has felt the whips of racism. To a compelling degree, Reul's desire that Myrna be feminine and Roselily's husband's insistence that she be pure and sheltered are related to these men's need to be on par with the white man. . . . Racism . . . has the effect, not only of physically and economically restricting these men, but also of reinforcing their need to imitate the oppressor's conventions in order to match his worth.

But **"The Child Who Favored Daughter,"** though encompassing the sexist results of racism, goes beyond them. For it is based on an apparently universal ambivalence men have toward the sexuality of their female kin, especially their daughters. Thus, it begins with an epigraph, the equivalent of which is found in every culture:

> That my daughter should
> fancy herself in love
> with *any* man
> How can this be?
>
> Anonymous

And only a few words later, Walker underlines the result of such a sentiment. Succinctly defining *patriarch,* while exposing its absurdity, she introduces the father in this story in conceptual terms: *"Father, judge, giver of life."*

Walker juxtaposes points of view of the Child and her Father by using the parts of this definition, *judge, giver of life,* as pivotal areas of contrast. As Father, the man judges his daughter based on one piece of evidence, a letter she has written to her white lover. As in **"Really, Doesn't Crime Pay,"** the written word takes on immense significance as proof of the woman's autonomy outside the realm of the man's kingdom. In an indelible way, the Child's written words are proof not only of her crime against her Father and societal conventions, but also of her consciousness in committing it. . . .

Her Father . . . is mesmerized by the letter itself, for it is both a proclamation of her separateness from him, and, ironically, a judgment on his life. The words he selects to remember from the letter heighten our sense of his vulnerability: ' "Jealousy is being nervous about something that has never, and probably won't ever, belong to you." '

Again, as in **"Roselily,"** although we are inside the characters' psyches, Walker uses the third person. . . . But here, its usage has a different effect; for unlike Roselily, neither the Child nor her Father are presenting a different self to the world. Rather the "She" and "He" used in the absence of personalized names give the characters an archetypal quality, as if the Child stands not only for this individual black woman, but for all daughters who have transgressed against their father's law; and the Father stands not only for this bitter black man, but for all fathers who have been sinned against by their daughters.

That particular interpretation of the Child's act is organic to the story since the Father, not the Child defines himself as a patriarch. The Child does not see him as Father but as *her* father. There are other men who exist besides him; other laws that also govern. Her act proclaims this. Her words in the letter make it clear that she cannot be owned. It is precisely this difference in their interpretation of their roles that causes his *agwu* to be so agonized that it inflicts trouble on hers.

To the man in this story, he is Father, she is Daughter, a possessive relationship that admits no knowledge of any individual histories or desires. It is true that he clings to an individual history, his sense of his first betrayal by a woman who he loves. But that apparently individual story leads us back to the archetypal, for this woman is his sister, is called "Daughter," the original Daughter, rather than a particular name. Her image blots out all individualized details in other women, until all women, especially those who are "fragmented bits of himself," are destined to betray him. (pp. 26-8)

The Father's perception of himself as the *"giver of life"* is juxtaposed in the story to the keen awareness of his sister and daughter's sexuality, vital and beyond his control. He is affected by their sensual bodies, naturally capable of giving life, his daughter's "slight, roundly curved body," his sister, "honey, tawny, wild and sweet." His ambivalence toward that part of them that he can never have, that part of them that will naturally take them away from him, intensifies the physical feeling of betrayal he imagines has been dealt him by women.

"Father, judge, giver of life," yet he cannot control it. Has he created it? Walker uses, throughout this story, images of Nature which overwhelm his senses: "the lure of flower smells," the busy wasps building their paper houses, the flower body of the Child. All around the Father life escapes his control, in much the same way that his daughter's body and her will overpowers him. Like Nature, his sister, and daughter, are "flowers who pledge no allegiance to banners of any man." As he will burn the wasps' paper houses down "singeing the wings of the young wasps before they get a chance to fly or to sting him," he must protect himself from "the agony of unnameable desire" caused by his sensuous wayward daughter.

If he cannot control the life he has given, then he must take it back. The violence the Father inflicts on his Daughter, for he literally cuts off her sexual organs in biblical fashion ("If their right hand offend thee, cut it off") confirms his own sexual desire for her. It also underscores his fear of her proclaimed autonomy, her independence from him, which is based on her sexuality. In destroying her sexually, he is destroying that unknowable part of himself that he feels is slipping out of his control:

> . . . he draws the girl away from him *as one pulling off his own arm* and with quick slashes of his knife leaves two bleeding craters the size of grapefruit on her bronze chest (emphasis mine).

This Father kills *his* Daughter, not with the phallic gun, but with a knife, the instrument used in sacrificial blood ritual. He sacrifices her, to his definition of himself, what he and therefore she should be. And the brutality of his act also suggests that he must doubly kill her since he cannot attack the other object of his rage, her white lover. He kills in one blow, his desire for her and his long-frustrated rage at the white man. No longer can the white man despoil his sister or his daughter, for they no longer exist; no longer must he love what he cannot control. (pp. 28-9)

The Father's troubled *agwu* stands in contrast to the child's throughout this ballad of a tale. Her *agwu* is threatened from without; but it is not troubled within. Like Nature, she must be herself, grow and defend herself in her own way, not as defined by her father nor society. She must have herself even though she has learned that "it is the fallen flower most earnestly hated, most easily bruised," and that she has been that fallen flower the moment her father presumed to give her life. . . . So she accepts her father's beating, rising from it strong-willed and resolved, and she cannot, will not deny that she loves whom she loves. It is her composure, paradoxically her contrariness, and her lack of torment which echoes for the father the original daughter's preference for the Other, worse—her complete indifference to his pained love. Thus, her ability to be so surely herself results in her destruction. Her inner spirit and her outer actions are as one, she is a woman. To her Father though, she must act and speak as a Child, though she may think as a woman, for then her sexuality will not be a danger to him.

"The Child Who Favored Daughter" lyrically analyzes two constraints of convention which, when fused, are uniquely opposed to the growth of black women. For it merges the impact of racism, not only on society but on the person, with the threat woman's sexuality represents to patriarchal man. One feeds the other, resulting in dire consequences for the black woman who insists on her own autonomy, and for whom love, the giver of life, knows "nothing of master and slave." For such a woman strikes at the heart of hierarchy, which is central to racism and sexism, two variants of the patriarchal view of life. (p. 29)

The old woman in **"The Welcome Table"** exemplifies the *agwu* that, though troubled from without, is aware of what is necessary for its fullness and tranquility. Her story is about her relationship to God which, for her, is above and beyond any conventions to which people have oriented their solutions. In contrast to the young flower heroines of this volume, she is described in nature imagery that expresses endurance rather than sensuality, "She was angular and lean as the color of poor gray Georgia earth, beaten by king cotton and the extreme weather." Rather than smelling of flowers, she smells of "decay and musk—the fermenting scent of onionskins and rotting greens."

Again, Walker uses the third person, "She" and "They," rather than the first person "I." This time she uses it so that we can hear both the old woman's mind and those opposed to her *agwu*, so that we can experience the contrast in spirit. For what she must do is prepare herself to be welcomed into the arms of her Jesus. For that overwhelming reason, she goes to the big white church without any regard for the breach of Southern convention she is committing. All that she is concerned with is the "singing in her head." In contrast they see her act as contrariness. For *they see her* as black and old, doubly terrifying to them because one state awaits them all, and the other frightens them. So they are able to throw her out of *their* church even as they beseech their God, according to convention, for protection and love. . . .

On one hand the white congregation does not see the old woman as worthy enough to enter their church, precisely because she is black and old, yet, they relate to her in familiar terms for exactly the same reasons. Their confusion about how they are to react to her unconventional act is expressed in their uncertainty about whether they addressed her in the traditional familiar terms, "Auntie," or "Grandma." Their emphasis on this point is characteristic of the contradictions inherent in the white South's relation to its black folk. The old woman on the other hand is clear about her actions. She ignores them, is clearly *bothered* by these people who claim familial ties with her, yet know her or care about her not at all. In ignoring the conventions, she exposes the tradition of black and white familial ties as nothing more than form. All the sacred words of this tradition are brought into question by her simple act. "God, mother, country, earth, church. It involved all that and well they knew it." (p. 30)

It is significant, too, that the white men, all of whom seem younger than the old black woman, are the ones who express this confusion. It is the white women who are clear about their true relationship to this old black woman, for they do not idealize it. From their point of view, in her coming to their church, this old black woman challenges the very thing that gives them privilege. Both they and she are women—but they are white, their only claim to the pedestal on which they so uneasily stand. They know they can only hold their position if that pedestal is identified with the very essence of Southern convention, and that this old woman, and others like her, are literally and symbolically the bodies upon which that pedestal rests. Just as sexism is reinforced by racism in **"The Child Who Favored Daughter,"** so in **"The Welcome Table"** racism distorts the natural relationship that should exist between woman and woman, and mutes the respect, according to convention and nature, that the young should have for the old. (pp. 30, 70)

One stereotypical image of the Southern black woman is that of the fanatically religious old mammy so in love with a white Jesus that she becomes the white man's pawn. **"The Welcome Table"** obliterates that image as it probes the depth of black Southern tradition. For this old woman cracks the conventional shell of white Southern Christianity, and penetrates the whiteness of Jesus's face to "the candle glowing behind it," for she insists on the validity of her own faith and tradition, and on the integrity of her relationship with her God. Walker further reinforces the integrity of a black Christian tradition, of which Southern black women were the heralds, by dedicating her composition of her spiritual in prose form to Clara Ward, the great black gospel singer. For, like the slaves in their spirituals, the old black woman in **"The Welcome Table"** makes Christianity her own, going beyond its European images to its truth as it applies to her. It is her spirit that "walked without stopping."

This old woman's act, and the acts, words, even dreams of so many of Walker's protagonists in [*In Love and Trouble*] appear to others, sometimes even to themselves, as manifestations of the innate contrariness of black women. The term, *contrary,* is used more often and with greater emphasis in Afro-American culture than it is in white culture. In fact, blacks often use it as if they all suffer from it. Yet behind their use of the word itself is a grudging respect for, sometimes even a gleeful identification with, a resistance to authority.

However, Walker's analysis of the contrariness of her main characters goes beyond the concept of unfocussed rebellion. Her women behave as if they are contrary, even mad, in response to a specific convention that restricts them, and they pay a price for their insistence on retaining their integrity. (p. 70)

Walker insists on probing *both* the white society and the black community's definition of black women. For in both worlds, words such as *contrariness* or a troublesome *agwu* are used to explain away many seemingly irrational acts of women, without having to understand them as appropriate responses. Her protagonists often discover that since they are black they are perceived by whites as "the other," or since they are women they are perceived by men as "the other." In either world they are not the norm. Their deviant behavior, then, is expected and therefore need not be understood.

That is why the excerpt from Amadi's *The Concubine* sets the tone so precisely for this volume, for Ahurole's contrariness, even in a black culture not yet affected by racism, is explained away as natural. Her life as an African woman is planned for her, regardless of her personality, desires, or development. And such a plan is so rooted in tradition, that Ahurole is allowed in her society to have this one outlet, which will neither change her situation or cause others to question it.

Yet Ahurole's story is not the story of Roselily, Myrna, The Child or the Old Woman. For these black women must not only bear the traditional definitions of women in their culture, they must confront, as well, the sexist myths of another race which oppresses them. The conventions that they are expected to hold to, are not even the conventions of their own communities, but ones imposed on them. It is no wonder then that these women seem mad whenever they insist on being "spontaneously and characteristically" themselves, . . .

These stories act out Rilke's words, for they show that there is no possibility for any living being to be whole unless she can be who she is. More disturbing they show that no matter how she might want to appear, no matter what conventions are imposed on her, no matter how much she resists herself, she will oppose those who inflict trouble on her. In the final analysis then, these stories are about the most natural law of all, that all living beings must love themselves, must try to be free—that spirit will eventually triumph over convention, no matter what the cost. (p. 71)

Barbara Christian, "The Contrary Women of Alice Walker," in The Black Scholar, *Vol. 12, No. 2, March-April, 1981, pp. 21-30, 70-1.*

KATHA POLLITT   (essay date 1981)

[*Pollitt is an American poet and critic. In the following excerpt, she praises Walker's willingness to explore controversial topics in* You Can't Keep a Good Woman Down, *yet faults the author's polemicism and tendency to depict all black women as victims of racism and sexual domination.*]

Like the Victorians, we consider certain subjects fit for fiction and others too hot to handle. Unlike the Victorians, however, we don't know we think that—we're too busy congratulating ourselves on our sexual frankness to see that there might be other sorts of blindness and prudery. Nowhere is this more clearly demonstrated than in the contemporary short story. Anyone browsing among a recent year's worth of American magazines might reasonably conclude that short fiction is by definition a medium in which white middle-class writers express elegiac and seemly sentiments about such noncontroversial topics as divorce and the deaths of relatives, and that when those same writers want to talk about what is *really* on their minds they turn to journalism—as have, many think, their readers.

For this reason I give Alice Walker, the noted black poet and novelist, much credit for daring to engage in fictional terms (well, quasi-fictional terms, more on that later) some of the major racial-sexual-political issues of our time. **"Advancing Luna—and Ida. B. Wells"** examines the rape of a white civil rights worker by a black civil rights worker from the point of view of the black woman who is the victim's best friend. **"The Abortion"** dissects the complex effect on a black middle-class marriage of the wife's abortion. **"Coming Apart"** and **"Porn"** deal with male sado-masochistic sexual fantasies, as experienced by puzzled and insulted wives and girlfriends.

Its important, frankly political, semi-taboo subject matter should automatically make *You Can't Keep a Good Woman Down* fascinating to anyone, black or white, with his head not completely entrenched in the sand. Miss Walker has, moreover, at least one priceless literary gift: that of sounding absolutely authoritative. . . . Then too, she has a watchful eye for such quirky, small details as the church pew, "straight and spare as Abe Lincoln lying down," lugged up from the rural South to decorate an East Village living room, or the "overdressed" Mai Tais in an Alaskan bar: "in addition to the traditional umbrella, there were tiny snowshoes."

These qualities give edge and sparkle to the more conventional stories, the ones in which Miss Walker has imagined herself into one version or other of the spunky, tough, irrepressible "good woman" of the title. I was not surprised, perhaps, but I was charmed by **"Nineteen Fifty-Five,"** in which we hear an old black blues singer (read Big Mama Thornton) contemplate the young white rock-and-roll singer (read Elvis Presley) who has risen to stardom by singing her song (read "Hound Dog"). Equally vivid, and a little more unusual, is **"Fame,"** in which a crotchety, vain and brilliant old black writer receives an award—her 111th literary honor—from a collection of academic toadies she takes great pleasure in privately despising.

These comparatively modest stories, though, are outweighed by those that are at once more overtly political and more stylistically innovative. But as Miss Walker aims for more, she achieves less. These latter stories occupy a sort of middle ground between personal statement, political parable, conventional story and vaguely experimental fiction—and this is not a comfortable place for short stories to find themselves. As fiction, they must be about particular people, but as parable they must be about people as types. As personal statement, or as conventional fiction, they lead us to think we are hearing the voice of the author; the experimental techniques that Miss Walker employs subvert that assumption by calling our attention to the author as inventory and manipulator of every aspect of what we are reading.

Perhaps in order to cover over these conflicts, Miss Walker has relied heavily on the use of an elaborately detached, sardonic, flat-sounding prose style. But this tone is completely wrong for these stories: they are too partisan (the black woman is *always* the most sympathetic character). They are also too unfocused, too full of loose ends and unanswered questions and of characters that are half odd and interesting individuals and half political or narrative conveniences.

I never believed for a minute, for instance, that the black woman narrator [of **"Advancing Luna—and Ida B. Wells"**] was really the best friend of poor Luna, who allowed herself to be raped by a black man in Georgia rather than scream and possibly precipitate a lynching. A friend would have felt some human sympathy, along with however much political angst, or, if not, would have had to confront this lack. Instead, Luna, the person, is quickly bundled offstage, dismissed in irritating irony-laden tones for playing at poverty, for radical chic-ness, for wanting to reduce human complexities to politics—all qualities, as it happens, that are shared by the narrator. Why? So that Miss Walker can spend the rest of the story on disjointed sections with pretentious titles like "Afterwords, Afterwards, Second Thoughts" and "Luna: Ida B. Wells—Discarded Notes" that put forward a confused welter of thoughts and feelings about interracial rape, including the unhelpful suggestion that it is paid for by the F.B.I. (pp. 9, 15)

Those who admired Miss Walker's previous work, in particular her fine novel *Meridian,* and her earlier volume of short stories, *In Love and Trouble,* will know that her strengths lie elsewhere. As a storyteller she is impassioned, sprawling, emotional, lushly evocative, steeped in place, in memory, in the compelling power of narrative itself. A lavishly gifted writer, in other words—but not of this sort of book. (p. 15)

> Katha Pollitt, "Stretching the Short Story," in The New York Times Book Review, *May 24, 1981, pp. 9, 15.*

MARGE PIERCY (essay date 1981)

[*An acclaimed novelist, poet, and former political activist, Piercy is best known as the author of* Vida (1980), *a novel chronicling the breakdown and demise of the American radical movement of the 1960s. The following excerpt is taken from a review of* You Can't Keep a Good Woman Down *in which Piercy praises Walker for her creative range and artistic control.*]

In *You Can't Keep a Good Woman Down,* Alice Walker reveals her mastery and her scope. These are rich enjoyable stories. A number of them are funny, but concede nothing for their humor. They do not condescend, diminish, take cheap shots. They show no less humanity and depth than the serious stories, and our distance from the characters is usually no greater.

Nonetheless **"Nineteen Fifty-five,"** for instance, made me laugh out loud several times in a small plane being tossed around in turbulent weather to the extent that the other passengers began glaring at me nervously. It is about a black singer named Gracie Mae (she reminded me of Big Mama Thornton) whose song is bought by the manager of a white male singer, who also buys up all the copies of her record. The white male singer (who is a thinly disguised and unsympathetically treated Elvis) goes on to great riches but never understands the song.

Because he feels guilty about using her material, the white singer keeps giving her presents, while always trying to understand the song that has made him. He even attempts to share his success with Gracie Mae by taking her on the "Tonight Show" with him. But the audience wants the prettied up imitation, not vast and earthy and very black Gracie Mae.

The whole story is a fascinating exploration of the relationship between original black musicians and the white pop music that takes their work and exploits it commercially. The style is racy and colloquial. Here's Gracie Mae talking:

> And then I see this building that looks like if it had a name it would be The Tara Hotel. Columns and steps and outdoor chandeliers and rocking chairs. Rocking chairs? Well, and there's the boy on the steps dressed in a dark green satin jacket like you see folks wearing on TV late at night, and he looks sort of like a fat dracula with all that house rising behind him, and standing beside him there's this little white vision of loveliness that he introduces as his wife.

"The Lover," amusing in a quieter vein, is about a black poet at a writers' colony such as MacDowell, "a woman who, after many tribulations in her life, few of which she ever discussed even with close friends, had reached the point of being generally pleased with herself." It concerns a wholly calculated love affair.

"Petunias" is a short story just half a page long, completely chilling. It is hard to imagine a more economical piece of prose narrative. Like many of these stories, it is perfect to perform aloud. A companion piece is **"Elethia,"** less than four pages long but setting out a whole social world, both past and present in all its grotesque horror. (p. 11)

Not all the stories work. **"Coming Apart"** is a piece whose point of view on pornography moves me but which doesn't make it as a story. The husband and wife are stick figures, and the happy ending feels forced. Both **"Porn"** and **"Advancing Luna—and Ida B. Wells"** are stories that also focus on sexual politics, in both cases in the context of the civil rights movement and the days of common if painfully difficult interracial romances. Both, however, are fleshed out and move by subtle and surprising turns.

If I had to select one adjective for these stories, I would say sophisticated in the best sense of the word. These are stories from a woman who has under her control as a writer a wide range of material, from the lives of the ordinary poor to the lives of artists and academics, from political organizers to well-heeled businessmen, and who can enter their experiences with sympathy but without sentimentality. She can look at an experience from top, from bottom, from the black side, from the white side, and observe how reality changes. In all of Walker's fiction one can feel a keen and supple intelligence. (p. 14)

> *Marge Piercy, "The Little Nuances of History," in* Book World—The Washington Post, *May 31, 1981, pp. 11, 14.*

CAROLYN NAYLOR   (essay date 1982)

[In the following excerpt, Naylor lauds Walker's skill in fusing history and fiction in the stories "Advancing Luna—and Ida B. Wells," "Coming Apart," and "Porn" from You Can't Keep a Good Woman Down.*]*

Alice Walker, in her latest collection of short stories entitled *You Can't Keep a Good Woman Down,* has achieved a fusion between history and fiction which elevates the genre into an exciting, new experimental mode.

In the complex, masterful, though unresolved story, **"Ad-** **vancing Luna—and Ida B. Wells,"** Alice Walker combines fictional histories of a black woman (the first person narrator) and of Luna, a white woman, both workers in the Civil Rights Movement in Georgia with the motif which records the history of lynching black men for rape. The narrator and Luna become good friends and Luna, when comfortable in the friendship, reveals that she was raped by Freddie Pye, a black man, during the summer of 1965; the theme of rape now dominates the story, estranging the two women. Luna, aware of Southern history, has told no one of the assault. The narrator has a moment of womanly empathy with her—in tune with her intuitive, feminist sense that a violation of one woman is a violation of all women, regardless of race—but subsequently finds herself on the defensive, remembering the horrors that ensue when a white woman accuses a black man of rape, and angered by the alleged power of white women. Luna's memory is that of her lonely attempt to maintain her silence in spite of the degradation she has experienced, and she emerges as one white woman who is not in complicity with the perverted and brutal forces of American racial history.

As the narrator wrestles with her feelings and with her responsibility as a writer, an imaginary dialogue takes place with Ida B. Wells. Ida B. Wells (1862-1931) was a black woman who organized and led an anti-lynching crusade, and through her efforts as a speaker and writer spent most of her life denouncing the horror of lynching. Parts of Wells' book, *A Red Record,* trace the political reasons why white men, threatened by the growing power of black men, used spurious arguments (the last being danger to white women) to justify and perpetuate lynching. The narrator identifies Wells as muse, mentor, and "avenging angel," and acknowledging the guilt of some black men and the pathology implicit in the rationalization of rape as a means of getting back at the white man, wrestles with her need to tell the truth and confront the possibility of Wells' "retribution." Ida B. Wells, by this artistic turn, becomes at once an historical figure and fictional character, a move which underscores the conflict between racial loyalty, historical urgency and truth.

The story is unresolved ostensibly because Freddie Pye and Luna are still alive as is the narrator, but in reality, the "unresolved ending" testifies to the complexity and irresolution of all the histories—Afro-American, white American, feminist—which have converged at this moment. Thus, the truth of this "convergence" remains partially explored and unresolved. (p. 84)

"Coming Apart" and **"Porn"** are companion stories that explore the violence and brutality which define and characterize pornography. Walker in **"Coming Apart"** intertwines excerpts about pornography from the writings of Audre Lorde, Luisah Teish and Tracy A. Gardner with her own fictional voice. The evolution of the wife's "womanist" consciousness reflects her preoccupation with these three authors. (Walker says that "womanist" approximates "black feminist.") The wife's growing sensitivity is the center of a story about her husband's preoccupation with pornography and the resulting stasis in his personality. Again the history of violence against black people is alluded to, this time identified as part of the foundation of pornography. It is Tracy Gardner's essay that explicitly links the brutality of lynching in which white men annihilate black men (and women) with the obscene and inhuman treatment of women in porn.

The persistence of the wife in exposing her husband to the

voices of Lorde, Teish and Gardner and to his own racial and sexual dishonesty moves the story to a point where their potential for mutual redemption is seen. She ceases to "fake" response; he begins to envision *her* body during love-making, not the bodies in porn magazines.

In **"Porn"** the lover, attempting to increase intimacy, "shares" his pornography collection with his mate. Contrary to his expectations, he loses her, for she is unable to clear her mind of the perversity of pornographic intent and the dehumanization contained in the images. In **"Coming Apart,"** husband and wife do come apart momentarily and the potential for reconciliation is revealed. In **"Porn,"** the opposite occurs, and all that remains of a satisfying relationship is mutual distraction and unspoken rejection; for she is distracted by her inability to fantasize and he by concern for where her mind is; and their bodies are literally unable to contain one another. (pp. 84-5)

Just as the dynamic surrounding rape is the weapon held over black men and women (and white women), the brutality and dehumanization implicit in pornography hangs over all women. The violence associated with rape and pornography finally underscores the de facto violence in the anti-abortion/pro-life stand. What Alice Walker manages to do is to tie the delicate knots of intuition and insight into a revelation of how historical and social complicity are used to en-

Minnie Lou and Willie Lee Walker, Alice Walker's parents, in Georgia during the 1930s.

trap and to oppress. It is my feeling that the short story is an especially appropriate vehicle to do what she has done.

You Can't Keep a Good Woman Down is a tribute to all the women who have nurtured intuition and insight in silence. It is a powerful, evocative collection which must be read. (p. 85)

> *Carolyn Naylor, in a review of "You Can't Keep a Good Woman Down," in* The Black Scholar, *Vol. 13, Nos. 2 & 3, Spring, 1982, pp. 84-5.*

MELVIN DIXON　(essay date 1982)

[*Dixon is an American dramatist and critic. In the following excerpt, he appraises Walker's use of personal experiences in* You Can't Keep a Good Woman Down *and contends that her stories force readers to examine oppression and alienation in their own lives.*]

[***You Can't Keep A Good Woman Down***] is remarkable for the way the author merges ideology and personal experience into fiction. In these pages there is an indomitable spirit, an inspiring defiance and combativeness. Walker wrestles with the demons of male sexual domination and white racism, but also with the ambivalent legacy of the sixties.

The central character in each story reaches for some brief creative moment when individual pain can be transformed into healing images and communicated through art: singing for Traynor and Gracie Mae Still, sculpture and drawing for Sarah Davis, or simply making petunias blossom in the often hostile soil of the south. The close proximity of Walker's life and art brings certain risks—characters may not achieve the life that the author's experience or ideas attributes to them. ***You Can't Keep A Good Woman Down*** delights and moves us with its insights and calm understatement in the opening story, **"Nineteen Fifty-five,"** and in **"A Sudden Trip Home in the Spring."** Yet, several undigested events in **"The Lover"** and in **"The Abortion,"** which read more like autobiography or essay than fiction, put us at a distance. But Walker is a writer so thoroughly committed to probing the depths of personal responsibility and the necessity of art in people's lives that I am always eager to follow her explorations, whether or not they succeed. (pp. 9-10)

Walker is at her best when she shows how art requires us to examine hurt, oppression and sexual alienation. In **"A Sudden Trip Home in the Spring,"** for example, Sarah Davis leaves her cloistered, posh New York women's college to attend her father's funeral in Georgia. Sarah is an aspiring artist, yet she cannot draw black men: "she could not bear to trace defeat onto blank pages." At home in Georgia, Sarah confronts the strength she had failed to perceive in her father, her militant preacher brother, and her venerable grandfather. The defeat Sarah imagined in others had been hers all along. When she returns north she must come to more responsible terms with being the only black student at the prestigious college. Sarah learns that art requires full living and emotional commitment, which is exactly what Traynor [in **"Nineteen Fifty-five"**] lacked. Sarah must cultivate her garden wherever she may be, grow revolutionary petunias, if necessary.

Alice Walker has always been a courageous writer. She has always exposed the most painful and most personal details in the lives of her characters endeavoring, like the author herself, to come to terms with being an artist, a black artist, a black woman artist all at *once*. (p. 10)

Melvin Dixon, in a review of "You Can't Keep a Good Woman Down," in The American Book Review, *Vol. 4, No. 4, May-June, 1982, pp. 9-10.*

HOUSTON A. BAKER, JR. AND CHARLOTTE PIERCE-BAKER (essay date 1985)

[*A noted critic, poet, and educator, Baker has contributed scholarly interpretations of black literature to anthologies and such periodicals as* Phylon, Black World, *and the* Virginia Quarterly Review. *In addition, he is the editor of critical surveys of African, Caribbean, and black American literature. In the essay excerpted below, Baker and his wife Charlotte analyze Walker's story "Everyday Use" and contend that its quilt-making motif best expresses Walker's talent for illuminating beauty and cultural significance in commonplace objects.*]

A patch is a fragment. It is a vestige of wholeness that stands as a sign of loss and a challenge to creative design. As a remainder or remnant, the patch may symbolize rupture and impoverishment; it may be defined by the faded glory of the already gone. But as a fragment, it is also rife with explosive potential of the yet-to-be-discovered. Like woman, it is a liminal element between wholes.

Weaving, shaping, sculpting, or quilting in order to create a kaleidoscopic and momentary array is tantamount to providing an improvisational response to chaos. Such activity represents a nonce response to ceaseless scattering; it constitutes survival strategy and motion in the face of dispersal. A patchwork quilt, laboriously and affectionately crafted from bits of worn overalls, shredded uniforms, tattered petticoats, and outgrown dresses stands as a signal instance of a patterned wholeness in the African diaspora.

Traditional African cultures were scattered by the European slave trade throughout the commercial time and space of the New World. The transmutation of quilting, a European, feminine tradition, into a black women's folk art, represents an innovative fusion of African cloth manufacture, piecing, and appliqué with awesome New World experiences—and expediencies. The product that resulted was, in many ways, a double patch. The hands that pieced the master's rigidly patterned quilts by day were often the hands that crafted a more functional design in slave cabins by night. The quilts of Afro-America offer a *sui generis* context (a weaving together) of experiences and a storied, vernacular representation of lives conducted in the margins, ever beyond an easy and acceptable wholeness. In many ways, the quilts of Afro-America resemble the work of all those dismembered gods who transmute fragments and remainders into the light and breath of a new creation. And the sorority of quiltmakers, fragment weavers, holy patchers, possesses a sacred wisdom that it hands down from generation to generation of those who refuse the center for the ludic and unconfined spaces of the margins.

Those positioned outside the sorority and enamored of wholeness often fail to comprehend the dignity inherent in the quiltmakers' employment of remnants and conversion of fragments into items of everyday use. Just as the mysteries of, say, the blues remain hidden from those in happy circumstances, so the semantic intricacies of quiltmaking remain incomprehensible to the individualistic sensibility invested in myths of a postindustrial society. All of the dark, southern energy that manifests itself in the conversion of a sagging cabin—a shack really—into a "happy home" by stringing a broom wire between two nails in the wall and making the joint jump, or that shows itself in the "crazy quilt" patched from crumbs and remainders, seems but a vestige of outmoded and best-forgotten customs. (pp. 706-13)

Southern black women have not only produced quilts of stunning beauty, they have also crafted books of monumental significance, works that have made them appropriately famous. In fact, it has been precisely the appropriation of energy drawn from sagging cabins and stitched remainders that has constituted the world of the quiltmakers' sorority. The energy has flowed through such women as Harriet Brent Jacobs, Zora Neale Hurston, and Margaret Walker, enabling them to continue an ancestral line elegantly shared by Alice Walker. (pp. 713-14)

The quilt as interpretive sign opens up a world of *difference,* a nonscripted territory whose creativity with fragments is less a matter of "artistic" choice than of economic and functional necessity. "So much in the habit of sewing something," says Walker's protagonist in the remarkable novel *The Color Purple,* "(that) I stitch up a bunch of scraps, try to see what I can make."

The Johnson women, who populate the generations represented in Walker's short story **"Everyday Use,"** are inhabitants of southern cabins who have always worked with "scraps" and seen what they could make of them. . . . The guardians of the Johnson homestead when the story commences are the mother—"a large, big-boned woman with rough, man-working hands"—and her daughter Maggie, who has remained with her "chin on chest, eyes on ground, feet in shuffle, ever since the fire that burned the other house to the ground" ten or twelve years ago. The mood at the story's beginning is one of ritualistic "waiting": "I will wait for her in the yard that Maggie and I made so clean and wavy yesterday afternoon." The subject awaited is the other daughter, Dee. Not only has the yard (as ritual ground) been prepared for the arrival of a goddess, but the sensibilities and costumes of Maggie and her mother have been appropriately attuned for the occasion. The mother daydreams of television shows where parents and children are suddenly—and pleasantly—reunited, banal shows where chatty hosts oversee tearful reunions. In her fantasy, she weighs a hundred pounds less, is several shades brighter in complexion, and possesses a devastatingly quick tongue. She returns abruptly to real life meditation, reflecting on her own heroic, agrarian accomplishments in slaughtering hogs and cattle and preparing their meat for winter nourishment. She is a robust provider who has gone to the people of her church and raised money to send her light-complexioned, lithe-figured, and ever-dissatisfied daughter Dee to college. Today, as she waits in the purified yard, she notes the stark differences between Maggie and Dee and recalls how the "last dingy gray board of the house (fell) in toward the red-hot brick chimney" when her former domicile burned. Maggie was scarred horribly by the fire, but Dee, who had hated the house with an intense fury, stood "off under the sweet gum tree . . . a look of concentration on her face." A scarred and dull Maggie, who has been kept at home and confined to everyday offices, has but one reaction to the fiery and vivacious arrival of her sister: "I hear Maggie suck in her breath. 'Uhnnnh,' is what it sounds like. Like when you see the wriggling end of a snake just in front of your foot on the road. 'Uhnnnh'."

Indeed, the question raised by Dee's energetic arrival is whether there are words adequate to her flair, her brightness, her intense colorfulness of style which veritably blocks the sun. She wears "a dress so loud it hurts my eyes. There are yellows and oranges enough to throw back the light of the sun. I feel my whole face warming from the heat waves it throws out." Dee is both serpent and fire introduced with bursting esprit into the calm pasture that contains the Johnsons' tin-roofed, three-room, windowless shack and grazing cows. She has joined the radical, black nationalists of the 1960s and 1970s, changing her name from Dee to Wangero and cultivating a suddenly fashionable, or stylish, interest in what she passionately describes as her "heritage." (pp. 714-16)

But in her stylishness, Dee is not an example of the indigenous rapping and styling out of Afro-America. Rather, she is manipulated by the style-makers, the fashion designers whose semiotics the French writer Roland Barthes has so aptly characterized. "Style" for Dee is the latest vogue—the most recent fantasy perpetuated by American media. When she left for college, her mother had tried to give her a quilt whose making began with her grandmother Dee, but the bright daughter felt such patched coverings were "old-fashioned and out of style." She has returned at the commencement of **"Everyday Use,"** however, as one who now purports to know the value of the work of black women as holy patchers.

The dramatic conflict of the story surrounds the definition of holiness. The ritual purification of earth and expectant atmosphere akin to that of Beckett's famous drama ("I will wait for her in the yard that Maggie and I made so clean and wavy yesterday afternoon.") prepare us for the narrator's epiphanic experience at the story's conclusion.

Near the end of **"Everyday Use,"** the mother (who is the tale's narrator) realizes that Dee (a.k.a., Wangero) is a *fantasy* child, a perpetrator and victim of: "words, lies, other folks's habits." The energetic daughter is as frivolously careless of other peoples' lives as the fiery conflagration that she had watched ten years previously. Assured by the makers of American fashion that "black" is currently "beautiful," she has conformed her own "style" to that notion. Hers is a trendy "blackness" cultivated as "art" and costume. She wears "a dress down to the ground . . . bracelets dangling and making noises when she moves her arm up to shake the folds of the dress out of her armpits." And she says of quilts she has removed from a trunk at the foot of her mother's bed: "Maggie can't appreciate these quilts! She'd probably be backward enough to put them to everyday use." "Art" is, thus, juxtaposed with "everyday use" in Walker's short story, and the fire goddess Dee, who has achieved literacy only to burn "us with a lot of knowledge we didn't necessarily need to know," is revealed as a perpetuator of institutional theories of aesthetics. (Such theories hold that "art" is, in fact, defined by social institutions such as museums, book reviews, and art dealers.) Of the two quilts that she has extracted from the trunk, she exclaims: "But they're 'priceless.' " And so the quilts are by "fashionable" standards of artistic value, standards that motivate the answer that Dee provides to her mother's question: " 'Well,' I said, stumped. 'What would *you* do with them?' " Dee's answer: "Hang them." The stylish daughter's entire life has been one of "framed" experience; she has always sought a fashionably "aesthetic" distance from southern expediencies. . . . Her concentrated detachment from the fire, which so nearly symbolizes her role vis-à-vis the Afro-American community (her black friends

"worshipped . . . the scalding humor that erupted like bubbles in lye") is characteristic of her attitude. Her goals include the appropriation of exactly what *she* needs to remain fashionable in the eyes of a world of pretended wholeness, a world of banal television shows, framed and institutionalized art, and polaroid cameras—devices that instantly process and record experience as "framed" photograph. Ultimately, the framed polaroid photograph represents the limits of Dee's vision.

Strikingly, the quilts whose *tops* have been stitched by her grandmother from fragments of outgrown family garments and quilted after the grandmother's death by Aunt Dee and her sister (the mother who narrates the story) are perceived in Dee's polaroid sensibility as merely "priceless" works of an institutionally, or stylishly, defined "art world." In a reversal of perception tantamount to the acquisition of sacred knowledge by initiates in a rite of passage, the mother/narrator realizes that she has always worshipped at the altars of a "false" goddess. As her alter ego, Dee has always expressed that longing for the "other" that characterizes inhabitants of oppressed, "minority" cultures. Situated in an indisputably black and big-boned skin, the mother has secretly admired the "good hair," full figure, and well-turned (i.e., "whitely trim") ankle of Dee (Wangero). Sacrifices and sanctity have seemed in order. But in her epiphanic moment of recognition, she perceives the fire-scarred Maggie—the stay-at-home victim of southern scarifications—in a revised light. When Dee grows belligerent about possessing the quilts, Maggie emerges from the kitchen and says with a contemptuous gesture of dismissal: "She can have them, Mama. . . . I can 'member Grandma Dee without quilts." The mother's response to what she wrongly interprets as Maggie's hang-dog resignation before Dee is a radical awakening to godhead:

> When I looked at her . . . something hit me in the top of my head and ran down to the soles of my feet. Just like when I'm in church and the spirit of God touches me and I get happy and shout. I did something I never had done before: hugged Maggie to me, then dragged her on into the room, snatched the quilts out of Miss Wangero's hands and dumped them into Maggie's lap.

Maggie is the arisen goddess of Walker's story; she is the sacred figure who bears the scarifications of experience and knows how to convert patches into robustly patterned and beautifully quilted wholes. As an earth-rooted and quotidian goddess, she stands in dramatic contrast to the stylishly fiery and other-oriented Wangero. The mother says in response to Dee's earlier cited accusation that Maggie would reduce quilts to rags by putting them to everyday use: " 'She can always make some more,' I said. 'Maggie knows how to quilt.' " And, indeed, Maggie, the emergent goddess of New World improvisation and long ancestral memory, does know how to quilt. Her mind and imagination are capable of preserving the wisdom of grandmothers and aunts without material prompts. . . . (pp. 716-18)

In order to comprehend the transient nature of all wholes, one must first become accustomed to living and working with fragments. Maggie has learned the craft of fragment weaving from her women ancestors: "It was Grandma Dee and Big Dee who taught her how to quilt herself." The conjunction of "quilt" and "self " in Walker's syntax may be simply a serendipitous accident of style. Nonetheless, the conjunction works magnificently to capture the force of black woman's quilting in **"Everyday Use."** Finally, it is the "self," or a version of humanness that one calls the Afro-American self, that must, in fact, be crafted from fragments on the basis of wisdom gained from preceding generations.

What is at stake in the world of Walker's short story, then, is not the prerogatives of Afro-American women as "wayward artists." Individualism and a flouting of convention in order to achieve "artistic" success constitute acts of treachery in **"Everyday Use."** For Dee, if she is anything, *is* a fashionable denizen of America's art/fantasy world. She is removed from the "everyday uses" of a black community that she scorns, misunderstands, burns. Certainly, she is "unconventionally" black. As such, however, she is an object of holy contempt from the archetypal weaver of black wholeness from tattered fragments. Maggie's "Uhnnnh" and her mother's designation "Miss Wangero" are gestures of utter contempt. Dee's sellout to fashion and fantasy in a television-manipulated world of "artistic" frames is a representation of the *complicity of the clerks.* Not "art," then, but use or function is the signal in Walker's fiction of sacred creation.

Quilts designed for everyday use, pieced wholes defying symmetry and pattern, are signs of the scarred generations of women who have always been alien to a world of literate words and stylish fantasies. . . . The asymmetrical quilts of southern black women are like the offcentered stomping of the jazz solo or the innovative musical showmanship of the blues interlude. They speak a world in which the deceptively shuffling Maggie is capable of a quick change into goddess, an unlikely holy figure whose dues are paid in full. Dee's anger at her mother is occasioned principally by the mother's insistence that paid dues make Maggie a more likely bearer of sacredness, tradition, and true value than the "brighter" sister. "You just don't understand," she says to her mother. Her assessment is surely correct where institutional theories and systems of "art" are concerned. The mother's cognition contains no categories for framed art. The mother works according to an entirely different scale of use and value, finally assigning proper weight to the virtues of Maggie and to the ancestral importance of the pieced quilts that she has kept out of use for so many years. Smarting, perhaps, from Dee's designation of the quilts as "old-fashioned," the mother has buried the covers away in a trunk. At the end of Walker's story, however, she has become aware of her own mistaken value judgments, and she pays homage that is due to Maggie. The unlikely daughter is a *griot* of the vernacular who remembers actors and events in a distinctively black "historical" drama.

Before Dee departs, she "put on some sunglasses that hid everything above the tip of her nose and her chin." Maggie smiles at the crude symbolism implicit in this act, for she has always known that her sister saw "through a glass darkly." But it is the mother's conferral of an ancestral blessing (signaled by her deposit of the quilts in Maggie's lap) that constitutes the occasion for the daughter's first "real smile." Maggie knows that it is only communal recognition by elders of the tribe that confers ancestral privileges on succeeding generations. The mother's holy recognition of the scarred daughter's sacred status as quilter is the best gift of a hard-pressed womankind to the fragmented goddess of the present.

At the conclusion of **"Everyday Use,"** which is surely a fitting precursor to *The Color Purple,* with its sewing protagonist and its scenes of sisterly quilting, Maggie and her mother relax in the ritual yard after the dust of Dee's departing car

has settled. They dip snuff in the manner of African confreres sharing cola nuts. The moment is past when a putatively "new" generation has confronted scenes of black, everyday life. A change has taken place, but it is a change best described by Amiri Baraka's designation for Afro-American music's various styles and discontinuities. The change in Walker's story is the "changing same." What has been reaffirmed at the story's conclusion is the value of the quiltmaker's motion and strategy in the precincts of a continuously undemocratic South.

But the larger appeal of **"Everyday Use"** is its privileging of a distinctively woman's craft as *the* signal mode of confronting chaos through a skillful blending of patches. (pp. 718-20)

A formerly "patched" separateness of woman is transformed through fabric craft into a new unity. Quilting, sewing, stitching are bonding activities that begin with the godlike authority and daring of women, but that are given (as a gift toward community) to men. . . . The heavenly city of quilted design is a form of unity wrested by the sheer force of the woman quiltmaker's will from chaos. As a community, it stands as both a sign of the potential effects of black women's creativity in America, and as an emblem of the effectiveness of women's skillful confrontation of patches. Walker's achievement as a southern, black, woman novelist is her own successful application of the holy patching that was a staple of her grandmother's and great-grandmother's hours of everyday ritual. **"Everyday Use"** is, not surprisingly, dedicated to "your grandmama": to those who began the line of converting patches into works of southern genius. (p. 720)

> *Houston A. Baker, Jr. and Charlotte Pierce-Baker, "Patches: Quilt and Community in Alice Walker's 'Everyday Use',"* in The Southern Review, *Louisiana State University, Vol. XXI, No. 3, Summer, 1985, pp. 706-20.*

J. CHARLES WASHINGTON   (essay date 1988)

[*In the essay excerpted below, Washington disputes charges of critics who have noted an excess of negative portrayals of black men in Walker's fiction.*]

Now that the controversy over Alice Walker's Pulitzer Prize-winning novel *The Color Purple* has subsided, it might be worthwhile to re-examine her fiction, specifically, the short stories, in an attempt to resolve the issue of her purported attack on Black males. In particular, her critics charged her with presenting a grossly negative image of Black men, who were portrayed as mean, cruel, or violent, entirely without redeeming qualities. In a review of the film of the novel, the *Washington Post* of February 5, 1986 stated: "But what is being heatedly discussed is the characterization of Black males as cruel, unaffectionate, domineering slap-happy oafs." Gloria Steinem, a major source of these discussions, writes in the June 1982, issue of *MS.* magazine, that "a disproportionate number of her (Walker's) hurtful, negative reviews have been by Black men."

This "disproportionate number" is significant, but only because, according to Trudier Harris, "black women critics have . . . been reluctant to offer . . . criticisms of it." The reason for this reluctance, Harris explains, is that "To complain about the novel is to commit treason against Black women writers, yet there is much in it that deserves complaint." With a tone that reveals the high degree of distress and frustration she feels, Harris complains not only about the negative, unrealistic and stereotypical portraits of Black men and women the novel presents, but also about its overall thematic development. . . . (p. 23)

Though this charge came about primarily as a result of the novel, negative male characters appeared in Walker's work long before its publication. Her first novel, *The Third Life of Grange Copeland,* published in 1970, some 13 years before *Purple,* is a good example, yet many of those who cried the loudest seem to have taken no notice of this work. Perhaps the best-known voice in the chorus of Walker critics belongs to novelist David Bradley (author of *The Chaneysville Incident*). Interestingly, he does not object to the male images in *Purple,* but in a long article written for the June 8, 1984, issue of the *New York Times Magazine* [see Further Reading list], he expresses dismay at "some of the things" he finds in Walker's collection of essays *In Search of Our Mothers' Gardens,* which lends further support to the criticism and controversy the novel aroused and, because of his reputation as a novelist and critic, gives his article a quasi official stamp of approval:

> But there is much that dismays me. Some of these things can be written off as polemical excess. . . . But other excesses are more troubling because they form, it seems, a pattern indicating Alice Walker has a *high level of enmity toward Black men* [emphasis added].

As part of his support for this contention, Bradley cites Walker's "dismissal and disdain" of individual Black male writers such as Richard Wright and Jean Toomer.

An examination of Walker's works reveals what many of her critics have failed to see: that they also contain positive Black male images. Bradley, in the *New York Times Magazine* piece, comments on the positive types of Black male characters he has observed:

> Black men in Alice Walker's fiction . . . seem capable of goodness only when they become old like Grange Copeland, or paralyzed and feminized, like Truman Held. If they are not thus rendered symbolically impotent, they are figures of malevolence, like Ruth's murderous father, Brownfield. . . .

However, depending on how one looks at them, that is, the moral/social standard one uses, there are other positive male characters in Walker's fiction who do not fall into these categories. In contrast to the negative label connoting characters who are inherently evil, positive as used here means that there is within them the potential for growth, development and change. This is not to say, however, that they are without human flaws. Such characters are found in several of the short stories in Walker's first collection *In Love and Trouble.* Her presentation of both negative and positive Black male images, then, would seem to indicate that she is not carrying a feminist banner (or "womanist," her term for a Black feminist) with which she intentionally flagellates Black men.

Having established that Walker hates Black men, and apparently well versed in Freudian psychology, it seems natural that Bradley would locate the cause of Walker's enmity within her family, that is, in her hatred for her father. Similar to his handling of Walker's alleged dismissal of Toomer, however, Bradley chooses particular words of Walker to prove *his* point, when the truth is otherwise. Building his case against her, he cites her disparaging remarks about Toomer the man, which moreover had to do with racism not sexism, while de-

emphasizing her favorable remarks about his work. In fact, what Walker does in *Mothers' Gardens* is castigate Toomer for his racial ambivalence, while praising his work highly, concluding with: "*I love it (Cane) passionately;* could not possibly exist without it."

Similarly, Bradley presents only half the truth regarding Walker's feelings about her father, ignoring the significance of the change in them that occurred later in her life. For though in her youth she did harbor strong resentment against her father, blaming him for her family's poverty, as an adult she came to realize that "he was a poor man exploited by the rural middle-class rich, like millions of peasants the world over."

The charge against Walker cannot be supported, for it is based on far too simplistic a view of an artist. Though her work is woman-centered, its wider focus is on the struggle of Black people—men and women—to re-claim their own lives. . . . Her exclusive concentration on what used to be called the weaker sex who, if no longer as weak as they once were, are still the most oppressed in society does not mean that she is anti-male, but that she has less time and energy to devote to exploring more fully the problems of men or the common causes of the oppression of both. (pp. 24-6)

It is clear that Walker's commitment to women has nothing to do with sex at all. And the same can be said of the homophobia that fuels the controversy. On the contrary, both have everything to do with power—women's gain and men's loss of it. For their own empowerment and control of their own destiny, women must commit themselves to each other and to creating their own identity. The failure "to define ourselves," Audre Lorde writes in *Sister Outsider,* is that "we will be defined by others—for their use and to our detriment." Homophobia, the handmaiden of sexism, becomes a useful tool in men's efforts to define and control women. Additionally, Lorde writes, "the red herring of lesbian baiting is being used . . . to obscure the true face of facism/sexism."

Far from being a purely emotional reaction, homophobia reveals itself to have a political dimension, seen in the efficacious role it plays in maintaining power or the status quo. Frequently it is used by some men who attempt to rule Black women by fear, who threaten them with emotional rejection. . . . Ishmael Reed, the novelist who has rightfully often decried the degeneration of Black males in American society, is not above this kind of emotional blackmail if, faced with competition from a Black female, it contributes to his own personal gain. Complaining that he had sold only eight thousand copies of his last book, Reed is reported to have said, "if he had been a *black lesbian poet* [emphasis added] he would have sold many more."

This complex nexus of cause and effect, of power struggles and political ploys underlying the often turbulent relations between Black men and women lies at the heart of Walker's works. Out of it emerges the negative criticism she has received. It is inevitable that she would arouse hostility, for in her struggle to help Black men and women overcome the oppression that binds them, she refuses to be intimidated or ruled by anything other than her own conscience. (pp. 27-8)

Walker's works tell us a great deal about the lives of Black people, and it is ironic that her reward has often been controversy and harsh criticism. Her persistence in the face of it springs from her commitment to truth and honesty. Like most Black artists concerned about freeing Black people from their past mistakes, she too believes that "the truth shall set you free." In *Black Women Writers,* Barbara Christian writes that "there is a sense in which the 'forbidden' in the society is consistently approached by Walker as a possible route to truth." In contrast to many Black writers who are reluctant to criticize Black males because they fear it will exacerbate an already precarious situation between Black men and women, the "forbidden" Walker exposes is the role Black men, both the positive and negative types, have played in the oppression of Black women.

Examples of the purely negative type of Black male abound in Walker's work, among them the men in *The Color Purple;* however, as mentioned, one of the most glaring examples is the younger Grange Copeland, hero of *The Third Life,* of whom Barbara Christian writes in *Black Women Writers:* "Grange Copeland hates himself because he is powerless, as opposed to powerful, the definition of maleness for him. His reaction is to prove his power by inflicting violence on the women around him." The cyclical nature of this phenomenon is seen in the life of Grange's son Brownfield, perhaps the most monstrous character in all of Walker's fiction, who brutalizes his children and his wife and then murders her.

The role played by the positive type of Black male found in *In Love and Trouble* is no less destructive on the lives of Black women, for it often means only a change in the kind of violence inflicted; that is, emotional violence predominates over the physical kind. But there is a major difference in the men who cause the oppression, and it is this distinction which allows us to label them positive rather than negative and which supplies the hope that change is possible. While the men in *Purple* and *Third Life* shock us with their unspeakable cruelty and violence not only because they are fully aware of their immoral behavior but also because they often revel in and enjoy inflicting pain, the men in *In Love and Trouble* are never monsters of this type. On the contrary, they are at all times human beings who reveal a variety of human strengths and weaknesses.

The positive classification also depends on the perspective from which one views them. For instance, Ruel, the antagonist/husband in **"Really, Doesn't Crime Pay,"** who fails to recognize his wife's ambition to write or her need for her own identity because he only sees her as a housewife is, in my view, not a negative character. A product of the social mores of his time stemming from the morally sanctioned patriarchal tradition which fostered them, he is as much a victim as his wife of a seemingly permanent mind-set in society which neither of them created and which will bind them until they realize that they must set themselves free. Similarly, while it may be considered immoral by some, a man who marries for money, in this case at the invitation of the female, as Jerome Washington does in **"Her Sweet Jerome,"** is no more negative than a woman who does the same. To label him such would require applying to him the same pernicious double standard of which women have always been victim.

A second significant cause of the oppression of the Black women in these stories, as it relates to their interaction with Black men, is their mistaken definition of themselves as women. Their own blindness about themselves and about what they can and must do for themselves is given strong emphasis, which is another important sign that Walker is searching for the truth, and that her interest is in finding causes, not assessing blame. The female protagonist of **"Really, Doesn't Crime Pay,"** for example, is spiritually and emo-tionally imprisoned by her husband's limited definition of her humanity and sits waiting deliverance from her life of useless dissipation, completely unaware that what she desires most lies within her own power—that, in other words, she must be the agent of her own deliverance. Such behavior on the women's part does not correlate with positive male characters. It does mean, however, that the men's behavior is no worse than that of the women, their alleged victims. They are in fact equally responsible for their problems and for the suffering they inflict on each other. (pp. 28-30)

[Many] of the women in *In Love and Trouble* share culpability in their own downfall, and this fact plays an important part in softening the negative image of their Black men. For though it is not always the case, and a man or woman must bear responsibility for his/her immoral behavior no matter what the circumstances, the men's role in the oppression of these women is often aided by the women's contribution to or willful participation in—sometimes, even, a masochistic invitation of—their own victimization.

The variety of problems and character types found in these stories is perhaps the most convincing evidence of Walker's preoccupation with presenting the full range of Black humanity—"the survival whole" of her people—as seen in the individual lives of her characters. To reiterate, what we are seeing, then, is not a common theme of oppression, but a multiplicity of themes based on the individuals' responses to it. Like her female characters, the Black male characters are shown to be individual human beings. Regarding them as such, one will find among them several positive Black male images or characters, which is the thesis of this essay. Because most of the stories have female protagonists and male antagonists, in such a case the selection of stories has to be based on those in which the male antagonists are sufficiently developed to give a substantial view of their characters. From this group, two have been selected for examination: **"Really, Doesn't Crime Pay"** and **"To Hell with Dying."** (pp. 30-1)

"Really, Doesn't Crime Pay" takes place within the pages of Myrna's writing notebook. "Myrna" is never used within the story itself. To identify her, the name appears in parentheses only as an undertitle.

On the surface, the notebook entries tell about Myrna's desire to be a writer and her dissatisfaction with her life as a housewife. Spending her days in idleness and useless dissipation—she does not have to work—she falls prey to a young Black charlatan or amateur writer, Mordecai Rich, who seduces and then abandons her, leading to an emotional breakdown. One day while sitting in the doctor's office, she discovers that he has published under his own name one of her stories that she had given him. Later that night while in bed, she attempts to murder her husband Ruel, who had ridiculed her desire to be a writer, insisting instead that she have a child and become a housewife.

On a deeper level, the story is a tragedy about a young Black woman who has talent but who lacks the understanding, courage and know-how to break the restrictions placed on her and to create the meaningful identity she craves and needs. Her insecurity about her talent and her own self-worth resulting in extreme self-hatred, leads to her victimization by Mordecai and to her attempted murder of her husband, whom she blames for her plight and to whom she transfers her frustration and hatred.

Myrna's entries in her notebook are significant in revealing her character and exposing the tragic nature of her situation. Walker skillfully establishes the interrelatedness of the literary elements of theme, character and plot. Allowing us to see inside Myrna's head and heart, we observe more than twenty years of rage and anger bottled up there, which is more than enough to drive anyone mad. Since the entries in her notebook are both the plot as well as samples of her writing, what they also allow us to see is not only the quality of her writing and the sensitivity and talent required to produce it, but also the tragic waste of them and her life due to her failure to act or to attempt to solve the dilemma she faced. (pp. 31-2)

Walker never lets the reader forget that Myrna is conscious or fully aware of her acts. In fact, it is this awareness on her part that makes her appear less sympathetic, and the man with whom she commits adultery less villainous, in the readers' eyes. . . . What increases the antipathy toward her even more, however, is her use of her week-long sexual encounter with Mordecai, unknown to her husband, of course, as a way of striking back at him for his failure to recognize her need: "I gloat over this knowledge. Now Ruel will find out that I am not a womb without a brain that can be bought with Japanese bathtubs and shopping sprees."

Putting all her hope for a change in her life in Mordecai, she declares, "The moment of my deliverance is at hand." He abandons her, however, and soon thereafter she begins to reveal signs of an emotional breakdown. As her condition worsens, Ruel tells her she acts as if her mind is asleep, to which she makes the mental notes: "Nothing will wake it but a letter from Mordecai telling me to pack my bags and fly to New York." Clearly, this indicates the confusion in her mind about what change is needed to bring about the happiness she craves. This change is not an external one, although new scenes, sights and surroundings would no doubt help alleviate her mental depression. What she actually requires is a fundamental modification in the way she thinks about herself. Thus, it is not Ruel alone who needs to know that she is not "a womb without a mind," but she too must realize that she has the capability of being both "womb" and "brain"—both a housewife and artist; in separating the two or failing to see the alternative available to her, she commits the same kind of error that Ruel makes. Complementing this confusion in her mind is another serious mistake on her part: her lack of self-involvement in changing her condition. And so she sits waiting for deliverance, expecting Mordecai to do for her what only she can do for herself.

That Walker sees the solution to Myrna's problems as one of her own making is found in *Mothers' Garden,* in the author's analysis of the escape route by which Black women have traditionally sought and succeeded in securing their spiritual survival. This route, based on an intuitive sense which enabled them to know how to get what they needed, was their flexibility combined with an enormous capacity for work: this enabled them to be both worker and creator, both wife and artist. Using her mother, who bore and raised eight children, as an example, Walker first explains that many of the stories she writes are her mother's stories; then she adds:

> But the telling of these stories . . . was not the only way my mother showed herself as an artist. . . . My mother adorned with flowers whatever shabby house we were forced to live in. And not just your typical straggly country stand of zinnias, either. She planted ambitious gardens . . . with over fifty

different varieties of plants that bloom(ed) profusely from early March until late November.

The conclusion of this anecdote illustrates the enormous will and energy required to maintain the garden:

> Before she left home for the fields, she watered her flowers, chopped up the grass, and laid out new beds. When she returned from the fields she might divide clumps of beds, dig a cold pit, uproot and replant roses, or prune branches from her taller bushes or trees—until night came and it was too dark to see.

With this as the norm, one can see how far from it Myrna is. Not compelled to work to support herself, her life of ease, which would have given her ample time for self-development, cannot be compared to the lives of drudgery of the generation of Black women to which Walker's mother belongs. Myrna's easy life is of little consequence, however, for in addition to her fragile emotional nature and her blindness about the deeper cause of her problem, she lacks the pragmatism which would have enabled her to find a solution to her problem. Without it, acting instead in response to her feelings of self-hatred, she continues to destroy the life she has by contemplating suicide and by commiting cruelty against her husband. Interestingly, no critic, male or female, has commented on the cruelty and violence this female character inflicts on her husband, actions which make her no less negative than some of the males in Walker's works. After release from the hospital, where she has recovered from her breakdown, she resumes her life of uselessness and idleness. She also continues to deceive her husband, who still hopes for the birth of a child, by religiously taking birth control pills. Illustrating her enjoyment of the pain she inflicts on him, it is, she says, "the only spot of humor in my entire day when I am gulping that little yellow tablet. . . ." Her spiritual death, then, is seen not only in these acts of cruelty, but also in her refusal to give birth to life. As for her sterility and failure to come to grips with her life, she says:

> I go to the new shopping mall *twice a day now* [emphasis added]; once in the morning and once in the afternoon, or at night. I buy hats I would not dream of wearing, or even owning.

(pp. 33-6)

Ruel, Myrna's husband, is cast in the traditional mold. A solid, lower middle-class type, he is a 40-year old Korean war veteran who works in a store and raises a hundred acres of peanuts. Steady, immovable and unchanging like the earth he cultivates, he clings to life in the same small southern town in which he was born and reared. In fact, he has traveled beyond its confines only once when he went off to war. Though he claims the experience broadened him, especially his two months of European leave, it did not change him or affect his thinking in any fundamental way. Because his character had already been shaped by the values of a Southern tradition hundreds of years old, the brief, passing moment in Europe did not—indeed, could not—penetrate the deeper core of his being. . . . Ruel's ideas of what married life entails, that is, the fixed roles that marriage partners must play, . . . are the same ones he learned in childhood, passed down to him from his father. It must be noted, however, that these values are not limited to the South, for they are the foundation of the patriarchal tradition known and practiced throughout the world.

Men of this type do not permit their wives to work, as he does not, even though in his case, it may mean that he has to work two jobs to supply his wife with the things he thinks she needs or wants. Not just a reflection of the male ego, this social pattern is in keeping with the men's expectation that the freedom and time it gives their women will enable them to more easily perform their "duty" as wives and mothers. Seeing this duty as the only appropriate one for a female, Ruel naturally thinks that his wife's writing is "a lot of foolish vulgar stuff" and that she is "peculiar" for wanting to do it. This "unnatural" desire of hers is a threat to him, for its exposure to the public will cause him embarrassment. Conversely, the traditional role he urges on her will confirm his normalcy and masculinity. And so, whenever she mentions the subject of writing, "he brings up having a baby or going shopping. . . ."

When Mordecai Rich appears, Ruel is slightly jealous but does not feel threatened. How could he be disturbed by such "a skinny black tramp," when he, Ruel, is all an ideal husband should be, which is how he sees himself. However, it is his preoccupation with himself, with his own needs and self-image, that blinds him to the needs of his wife. Failing to see his own shortcomings, he readily dismisses the signs of her distress because he cannot see that she has a problem. Failing to do so, he would never believe that he might possibly be implicated in its cause. For this reason too, he only begins to notice her and to feel that something is wrong with his life after Mordecai abandons her and the signs of her oncoming nervous breakdown are too obvious to be ignored.

What we see in this couple, then, is an identically matched pair of individuals with an interesting kind of incompatibility that renders them incapable of helping each other. Both, therefore, share the blame for the deterioration or destruction of their relationship. In both individuals, the root of the problem is not immorality, but fundamental character flaws. In Ruel's case, it is his selfishness or egocentrism based on his belief that what is good or right for him is also good enough for his wife. It must be re-emphasized, however, that his behavior, which is typical of many men everywhere and therefore universal, has its basis in the mores of the patriarchal tradition, a tradition which regrettably makes little allowance for the spiritual needs of women.

Because he is a plain, common, everyday type who is unaware of any other tradition or set of values and therefore blameless, Ruel is not a negative character. In contrast to his wife, even his faults are virtues. For though he is preoccupied with his own image and his own life, it is devoted to and expressive of his love for her. Therefore, he is never cruel, brutal or violent. Rather, his life is characterized by hard work, as he struggles to provide her with a decent home to live in and other material possessions she needs or wants. Mindful of his role and image as provider, he feels ashamed of the wooden house he purchased for his wife, with its toilet in the yard. Constantly trying to improve their life, he dreams of a better home for her, telling her, "One day we'll have a new house of brick, with a Japanese bath." Finally, it is ironic that what Myrna considers his greatest fault, his insistence that she have a child, is in fact the greatest expression of his love for her, since he believes, as most men and women do, that a child will cure her illness and provide her with the self-fulfillment she needs.

It is not only his moral fiber and love that establishes Ruel as a positive male image, but also his innocence. All of these qualities produce the sympathy we feel for him. Such a solid,

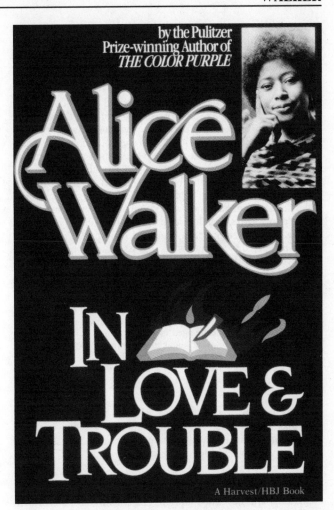

Cover of Walker's short story collection In Love & Trouble.

respectable person could not be the monster his wife makes him out to be. Such a decent person does not deserve to be the cuckhold she makes of him or the victim of the cruel tricks she plays on him. Even after Myrna's attempt to murder him, it is clear that he never understands her, or the real source of their problem. Rather, Ruel blames Mordecai. . . . After Myrna's recovery, Ruel makes repeated attempts to impregnate her, never once suspecting that she is deliberately thwarting conception of the child he desperately wants. When she fails to become pregnant, he sends her to a gynecologist. When this step also fails to produce the desired result, he finally learns one irrelevant fact: irrelevant because it will not change him either: As Myrna says, "He knows now that I intend to say yes until he is completely exhausted."

Lacking knowledge of himself and therefore incapable of changing, Ruel faces a hopeless situation. But what he represents is an important part of what Walker wishes to show us. Even such basically good men as Ruel are often unwitting contributors to the destruction of relationships between Black men and women. (pp. 36-9)

As David Bradley notes in his *New York Times Magazine* article [see Further Reading list], Walker's stories with older men protagonists (in their sixties onward) contain overwhelmingly positive Black male images. This change results

421

from a major shift in theme. Sexual or marital relations between Black men and women, with all the attendant stress
and pain they entail, are not the central focus. Rather, the author's interest is in presenting the experiences of the old as
a legacy for the young. . . . (p. 39)

Because many of Walker's stories are based on her own experiences (or, vicariously, on those of her mother), those about
older men are a necessary part of the evidence that shows she
does not hate Black men. How could she, after having learned
in her youth the kindness and love these men are capable of
giving? If she views younger men with less charity than she
extends the older ones, it is because she sees the Black male's
development as having a predictable, unchanging pattern.
That is, their aggressiveness and penchant for violence begins
in the adult years, reaches its peak in the middle years and
recedes in the later years. In Bradley's *New York Times Magazines* article, she comments on this phenomenon by saying,
"One theory is that men don't start to mature until they're
40;" and then she amplifies her point by explaining:

> I knew both my grandfathers, and they were just
> doting, indulgent, sweet old men. I just loved them
> both and they were crazy about me. However, as
> young men, middle-aged men, they were . . . bru-
> tal. One grandfather knocked my grandmother out
> of a window. He beat one of his children so severly
> that the child had epilepsy. Just a horrible, horrible
> man. But when I knew him, he was a sensitive, con-
> siderate man.

The point, then, is that because Walker understands Black
men and knows what they are capable of, she can criticize
younger men without hating them and praise older men for
the positive image, which is their legacy.

The one story of this kind in *In Love and Trouble* is **"To Hell
with Dying,"** the first story Walker ever wrote, her first published one, and her "most autobiographical." . . . Described
by Walker as a story "about an old man saved from death
countless times by the love of his neighbor's children," it is
as much, if not more, about what the old man's love does for
the neighbor's female child, who narrates the story. And
since it is about love, it is much more about life than death,
as the title indicates.

At the beginning of the story the main character, Mr. Sweet
Little, is about 70; the unnamed female child narrator is
about 4; at the end, he is 90, and she is 24. In the span of twenty years, the living out of a lifetime love affair occurs as he
moves from old age to death, and she from early childhood
to adulthood.

As the story begins, when she is still a young child, the relationship between them has the aura of a sexual relationship
between a man and a woman. Walker creates this sexual feeling, which shimmers just beneath the surface of the story,
apart from but parallel to the poetic language. It remains only
a feeling, however, because the love between the old man and
young girl is pure and wholesome.

The plot itself is simple. Mr. Sweet, a diabetic and alcoholic,
periodically falls ill, sinking so low that everyone believes he
is dying. Each time, however, he is revived or saved by the
ministrations of the narrator, who, taken to his home by her
parents, climbs on his bed and kisses and hugs him. This ritual, which her older brothers and sisters had performed before
her, was always initiated by her father's call, "To hell with
dying, man; these children want Mr. Sweet." These revivals

occurred when Mr. Sweet was in his 70s. In his 80s, he lived
a peaceful life and was no longer threatened by death. The
narrator had grown up and was away from home studying
at the university. When he was 90, she was summoned home
because Mr. Sweet was again near death. As she had so often
done in childhood, she tried to save him, but this time he did
die, leaving her with the gift of his spirit and with the realization that he had been her first love.

In any relationship, sexual or otherwise, what is important
is the giving, co-equally and unreservedly. However, if Mr.
Sweet gives more than the narrator, which seems to be the
case, that is entirely appropriate; for far more important than
the needs of the old man, whose life is nearly over, are those
of the young girl, whose life is just beginning. What he gives
her, among other things, and what she needs at this stage of
her life, is a sense of her own self-worth, of her own self-
esteem. He makes her feel that she is physically attractive
and, significantly, has the power to control her own destiny.

Because Mr. Sweet's frightening bouts with death always occurred when he was in bed and usually at night or early
morning, it was necessary for the girl to exercise her healing
powers there. This structuring of the situation, which conjures up the thought of the restorative powers of sex, contributes to the feeling of a sexual relationship between them. The
physical contact between them also strengthens this feeling:
" 'To hell with dying . . .' was my cue to throw myself upon
the bed and kiss Mr. Sweet all around the whiskers and under
the eyes and around the collar of his nightshirt were he
smelled so strongly of all sorts of things. . . . " This particular healing event, which the narrator recalls as the first time
she actually remembered participating in one of Mr. Sweet's
"revivals," occurred when she was seven, an age at which she
would have been conscious of sex and sexual differences. A
final detail of this ritual is its privacy and intimacy: "My parents would leave the room to just the three of us [her brother
was with her, although she invariably did the reviving]; Mr.
Sweet . . . would be propped up in bed . . . with me sitting
and lying on his shoulder and along his chest." Her sexual
awakening and love are further seen in her wish that she had
been old enough to be the woman Mr. Sweet had really loved
but lost when he was forced to marry his wife, Miss Mary.

There is a strong connection between the sexual mood, the
plot and the general theme of solutions to problems in relationships between Black men and women. This relationship
between the little girl and the old man, which bears such a
strong resemblance to and contains all the usual ingredients
of normal man/woman relationships except for sex, acts as
a model for those in which sex is the primary—in many cases,
the only—factor. The conclusion to be drawn or the lesson
it teaches is nothing new but bears repeating. If men and
women would base their relationship on love above all else,
these relationships might be much more successful. The sexual ingredient could only increase this likelihood by cementing
the bond between them because it would be an addition to,
not a substitute for, the love they already have for each other.

The gift of love the girl gave the old man, reflected in the numerous times she retrieved him from the brink of death, was
matched in kind by gifts he gave her. First, his response to
her, which may not have been as miraculous as it seems, gave
her a tremendous sense of power. Usually occurring during
or after his bouts of drinking, these frequent brushes with
death may have been attributable to the alcohol, in combination with his diabetes, or to the self-pity induced by it. They

may also have been a plea for attention or love, especially after his wife died. That they were not entirely spontaneous, that their cause was more emotional than physical, is seen because they were often preceded by certain recognizable signs, such as his crying while playing his guitar. On one occasion, as he was leaving the narrator's house after having displayed the tell-tale signs, her mother noted that "we'd better sleep light that night for probably we'd have to go over to Mr. Sweet before daylight. And we did."

Whatever the cause, the attacks appeared to be real, so real, in fact, that the doctor was usually called. Other than as part of what makes the story intriguing, however, the reality or cause of them is not important. What is significant is the mystery of death, paralleling Walker's comment that the events of the story are not real, only the love. More specifically, she shows us a way of conquering death or giving it a human dimension by treating it as a normal part of life. To get the point across, she gives us a child's perspective of death as an ordinary event, even fun, which has an ordinary cure, love. In contrast is the usual adult perspective of death as something horrible, and based on their supposed superior knowledge of causes and cures, they presume to exert control over it but cannot. In the end they are as confounded and perplexed as ever by its mystery.

The certainty of death's arrival, even though the threat of it had occurred no less than ten times, and of the narrator's ability to thwart it, set her and her family apart from the rest of the community: "All the neighbors knew to come to our house if something was wrong with Mr. Sweet . . . ." This responsibility placed great stress on the young girl, for, as she says, "these deaths upset me fearfully, and the thought of how much depended on me . . . made me nervous." It should be noted, however, that the fear she expresses is more of failure than of death itself. But she did not fail, and the success she always had, as well as the feeling of power and accomplishment it gave her, served to increase her feeling of self-esteem; at the same time, the "fun" and love she associated with the revivals helped remove her fear of death. (pp. 40-4)

In addition, Mr. Sweet also helped increase the girl's sense of self-esteem by making her feel that she was physically attractive. While this is important generally, it was particularly so to a young girl, whose fate was decided by the beauty of face and body, as well as by her own attitude toward it. The blemish she possessed, a low hairline, which may have led her to have negative feelings about herself, was removed by the power of Mr. Sweet's touch, quite by accident, it seems. . . . Through the power of his voice, as well as his overall attitude toward and treatment of her, he did even more to make her feel physically attractive. . . . (p. 44)

What made Mr. Sweet so likeable to the narrator as a child was his difference from other adults she knew. . . . This difference affected her because Mr. Sweet's behavior gave her a more positive image of adults, specifically, males, than the ones she had usually known. The children also liked him because he was capable of becoming one of them, treating them as if they were equals. An expert guitar player who loved to sing, sometimes, when he was "feeling good," he would dance around the yard and play with them. . . . Not only did Mr. Sweet's actions help increase the children's tolerance for adults, but the fact that he, their ideal playmate, was an old man also helped remove the barrier between youth and old age: "We never felt anything of Mr. Sweet's age when we

played with him. We loved his wrinkles and would draw some on our brows to be like him." As a boy, the narrator's brother was most affected by the positive image of Mr. Sweet: "What he would do while I talked to Mr. Sweet was pretend to play the guitar, in fact pretend that he was a young version of Mr. Sweet. . . . "

Uncertainty exists about the effect Mr. Sweet's drinking had on his bouts with death and about its effect on his life in general. There is no doubt, however, that the children considered it a plus: "His ability to be drunk and sober at the same time made him an ideal playmate. . . . " The fact that her mother "never held his drunkenness against him" also seems to suggest that she did not consider him immoral for doing it. Moreover, while it may have been a reflection of some flaw in his character, it was not an overwhelmingly controlling force in his life. Though he did often give in to it, he always remained its master. . . . (pp. 44-5)

A stronger, more ominous force operated on his life, but it did not destroy him completely either: "Mr. Sweet had been ambitious as a boy, wanted to be a doctor or lawyer or sailor, only to find that black men fare better if they did not. Since he could not become one of these things he turned to fishing as his only earnest career. . . . " What this suggests about his character is that he is a man who remained spiritually alive in spite of the racism he faced, over which he had no control. The spiritual aliveness, symbolized by his love of and ability to create music . . . enabled him to recognize and take advantage of other alternatives. From these, he made his own choice, which meant that, as with his drinking, he controlled his life. Moreover, he had learned early the uselessness of blaming fate for his problems and accepted responsibility for his own actions, for in most cases fate had nothing to do with them. He, not fate, had impregnated Miss Mary and therefore had had to marry her, even though he had been in love with another woman. He was not sure that Joe Lee, her "baby," was his own child, but he accepted the consequences of his actions, as she defended them, and did what he had to do by marrying her.

Finally, his tendency to remain in control of his own life is seen in his relationship to death. He was able to defeat death so often, which is perhaps the most important of his gifts to the narrator, because he was not ready to die. Her mother invariably shed tears whenever Mr. Sweet lay dying, the narrator states, "although she knew the death was not necessarily the last one *unless Mr. Sweet really wanted it to be*" [emphasis added]. (pp. 45-6)

On his ninetieth birthday, Mr. Sweet decided that he was ready to die, but not before he gave the narrator, who rushed home to see him, his final gifts of love. Perhaps the most valuable of these is the beauty of his dying. Shorn of ugliness and fear because of the kind of man he was and by the closeness to him of those who loved and cared for him, it occurs "in a shack overgrown with yellow roses" making the "air heavy and sweet and very peaceful." Having successfully performed the revival ritual so many times in the past, though now a grown woman and aware her effort must surely fail, the narrator, transported back to those earlier times, is tempted to try it again. But, and here is noted another valuable lesson this dying brings, it will be a vain attempt. This lesson is brought home to her by the realization of the passage of time and hence the inevitability of death, reflected in the faces of her own parents, "who also looked old and frail." Her father is a willing participant, intoning the familiar line he had uttered so many times before. She, too, does her part, as Mr. Sweet does his, tracing her hairline with his finger. But it did not work this time, because Mr. Sweet had made up his mind that he was ready to die: "I closed my eyes when his finger halted above my ear, his hand stayed cupped around my cheek. When I opened my eyes, sure that I had reached him in time, his were closed."

After his death his final gift to her was his spirit, symbolized by his guitar. "He had asked them months before to give it to me; he had known that even if I came next time he would not be able to respond in the old way." Ironically unaware of his importance to her, the narrator states that Mr. Sweet gave her his guitar because "he did not want to feel that my trip home had been for nothing." On the contrary, the significance of his life and death, which she now fully realizes, is summed up in the final paragraph of the story:

> The old guitar! I plucked the strings, hummed "Sweet Georgia Brown." *The magic of Mr. Sweet lingered still in the cool steel box* [emphasis added]. Through the window I could catch the fragrant delicate scent of tender yellow roses. The man on the . . . bed . . . had been my first love.
>
> (pp. 46-7)

The moral emphasis found in Alice Walker's works reveals her adherence to two different but similar traditions of art, the classical Greek and the ancient African, both of which form the basis of the Afro-American or Black Aesthetic. The Greeks had confidence in the immense power of art "as a molding or formative agent in developing human feelings and motivations;" and according to Leopold Senghor, "all African art has at least three characteristics: that is, art is functional, collective and committing or committed." Thus, Walker's works demonstrate her love for her people, both men and women, for, reflecting the ideals of both of these traditions, these works are predicated on the belief that man is inherently good and that, therefore, if flaws in his character exist, through the use of art that educates they can be removed and the personality restored to health. Rather than being a sign of enmity toward Black men, then, her criticism of them and of Black women is the strongest reflection of this love. She gives praise where praise is due; however, her strong moral sense, courage and commitment to truth and honesty will not allow her to shrink from criticizing where criticism is due, in order that future improvement can be made. This look toward the future, seen in her desire to bring harmony between men and women by improving human character, echoes the most distinctive ideal of the classical tradition—

"to complete human potentiality in the light of the highest standard of excellence or nobility." (pp. 47-8)

> *J. Charles Washington, "Positive Black Male Images in Alice Walker's Fiction," in* Obsidian: Black Literature in Review, *Vol. III, No. 1, Spring, 1988, pp. 23-48.*

FURTHER READING

Bradley, David. "Novelist Alice Walker Telling the Black Women's Story." *The New York Times Magazine* (8 January 1984): 25-37.

An extensive biographical profile of Walker, interspersed with critical analyses of her work.

Gilbert, Harriett. Review of *You Can't Keep a Good Woman Down*, by Alice Walker. *New Statesman* 104, No. 2680 (30 July 1982): 21.

Brief critical assessment. Gilbert places several of Walker's stories in the tradition of fiction published in the *New Yorker*.

Ingoldby, Grace. "Fall Out." *New Statesman* 108, No. 2791 (14 September 1984): 32.

Praises Walker's characterizations in *You Can't Keep a Good Woman Down*.

Peden, William. "The Black Explosion: 'All Things Considered, the Field Is Opening Up More and More'." In his *The American Short Story: Continuity and Change, 1940-1975*, pp. 134-47. Boston: Houghton Mifflin Co., 1975.

Brief survey of short fiction written by Walker and other African-American authors.

Steinem, Gloria. "Alice Walker: Do You Know This Woman? She Knows You." In her *Outrageous Acts and Everyday Rebellions*, pp. 259-75. New York: Holt, Rinehart and Winston, 1983.

A feminist appreciation of Walker's literary career. Includes a biographical section outlining Walker's childhood in rural Georgia and her years as a civil rights activist in Mississippi.

Washington, Mary Ellen. "An Essay on Alice Walker." In *Sturdy Black Bridges: Visions of Black Women in Literature*, edited by Roseann P. Bell, Bettye J. Parker, Beverly Guy-Sheftall, pp. 133-49. Garden City, NY: Anchor Books, 1979.

Overview of Walker's work. Washington portrays her as an apologist and spokesperson for black women and examines the author's preoccupation with her subject matter.

Short Story Criticism

Indexes

Literary Criticism Series
Cumulative Author Index

SSC Cumulative Nationality Index

SSC Cumulative Title Index

This Index Includes References
to Entries in These Gale Series

Contemporary Literary Criticism

Presents excerpts of criticism on the works of novelists, poets, dramatists, short story writers, scriptwriters, and other creative writers who are now living or who have died since 1960. Cumulative indexes to authors and nationalities are included, as well as an index to titles discussed in the individual volume.

Twentieth-Century Literary Criticism

Contains critical excerpts by the most significant commentators on poets, novelists, short story writers, dramatists, and philosophers who died between 1900 and 1960. Cumulative indexes to authors, nationalities, and titles discussed are included in each new volume.

Nineteenth-Century Literature Criticism

Offers significant passages from criticism on authors who died between 1800 and 1899. Cumulative indexes to authors, nationalities, and titles discussed are included in each new volume.

Literature Criticism from 1400 to 1800

Compiles significant passages from the most noteworthy criticism on authors of the fifteenth through eighteenth centuries. Cumulative indexes to authors, nationalities, and titles discussed are included in each new volume.

Classical and Medieval Literature Criticism

Offers excerpts of criticism on the works of world authors from classical antiquity through the fourteenth century. Cumulative indexes to authors, titles, and critics are included in each volume.

Short Story Criticism

Compiles excerpts of criticism on short fiction by writers of all eras and nationalities. Cumulative indexes to authors, nationalities, and titles discussed are included in each new volume.

Children's Literature Review

Includes excerpts from reviews, criticism, and commentary on works of authors and illustrators who create books for children. Cumulative indexes to authors, nationalities, and titles discussed are included in each new volume.

Contemporary Authors Series

Encompasses five related series. *Contemporary Authors* provides biographical and bibliographical information on more than 92,000 writers of fiction, nonfiction, poetry, journalism, drama, motion pictures, and other fields. Each new volume contains sketches on authors not previously covered in the series. *Contemporary Authors New Revision Series* provides completely updated information on active authors covered in previously published volumes of *CA*. Only entries requiring significant change are revised for *CA New Revision Series*. *Contemporary Authors Permanent Series* consists of updated listings for deceased and inactive authors removed from the original volumes 9-36 when these volumes were revised. *Contemporary Authors Autobiography Series* presents specially commissioned autobiographies by leading contemporary writers. *Contemporary Authors Bibliographical Series* contains primary and secondary bibliographies as well as analytical bibliographical essays by authorities on major modern authors.

Dictionary of Literary Biography

Encompasses three related series. *Dictionary of Literary Biography* furnishes illustrated overviews of authors' lives and works and places them in the larger perspective of literary history. *Dictionary of Literary Biography Documentary Series* illuminates the careers of major figures through a selection of literary documents, including letters, notebook and diary entries, interviews, book reviews, and photographs. *Dictionary of Literary Biography Yearbook* summarizes the past year's literary activity with articles on genres, major prizes, conferences, and other timely subjects and includes updated and new entries on individual authors. A cumulative index to authors and articles is included in each new volume.

Concise Dictionary of American Literary Biography

A six-volume series that collects revised and updated sketches on major American authors that were originally presented in *Dictionary of Literary Biography*.

Something about the Author Series

Encompasses two related series. *Something about the Author* contains heavily illustrated biographical sketches on juvenile and young adult authors and illustrators from all eras. *Something about the Author Autobiography Series* presents specially commissioned autobiographies by prominent authors and illustrators of books for children and young adults.

Yesterday's Authors of Books for Children

Contains heavily illustrated entries on children's writers who died before 1961. Complete in two volumes.

Literary Criticism Series
Cumulative Author Index

This index lists all author entries in the Gale Literary Criticism Series and includes cross-references to other Gale sources. References in the index are identified as follows:

AAYA: *Authors & Artists for Young Adults,* Volumes 1-2
CAAS: *Contemporary Authors Autobiography Series,* Volumes 1-10
CA: *Contemporary Authors* (original series), Volumes 1-129
CABS: *Contemporary Authors Bibliographical Series,* Volumes 1-3
CANR: *Contemporary Authors New Revision Series,* Volumes 1-28
CAP: *Contemporary Authors Permanent Series,* Volumes 1-2
CA-R: *Contemporary Authors* (revised editions), Volumes 1-44
CDALB: *Concise Dictionary of American Literary Biography,* Volumes 1-4
CLC: *Contemporary Literary Criticism,* Volumes 1-57
CLR: *Children's Literature Review,* Volumes 1-20
CMLC: *Classical and Medieval Literature Criticism,* Volumes 1-4
DLB: *Dictionary of Literary Biography,* Volumes 1-90
DLB-DS: *Dictionary of Literary Biography Documentary Series,* Volumes 1-7
DLB-Y: *Dictionary of Literary Biography Yearbook,* Volumes 1980-1988
LC: *Literature Criticism from 1400 to 1800,* Volumes 1-12
NCLC: *Nineteenth-Century Literature Criticism,* Volumes 1-26
SAAS: *Something about the Author Autobiography Series,* Volumes 1-8
SATA: *Something about the Author,* Volumes 1-57
SSC: *Short Story Criticism,* Volumes 1-5
TCLC: *Twentieth-Century Literary Criticism,* Volumes 1-35
YABC: *Yesterday's Authors of Books for Children,* Volumes 1-2

Apollinaire, Guillaume
    1880-1918 .... **TCLC 3, 8**
    See also Kostrowitzki, Wilhelm Apollinaris
    de

Appelfeld, Aharon 1932- .... **CLC 23, 47**
    See also CA 112

Apple, Max (Isaac) 1941-........ **CLC 9, 33**
    See also CANR 19; CA 81-84

Appleman, Philip (Dean) 1926-..... **CLC 51**
    See also CANR 6; CA 13-16R

Apuleius, (Lucius) (Madaurensis)
    125?-175?.................. **CMLC 1**

Aquin, Hubert 1929-1977......... **CLC 15**
    See also CA 105; DLB 53

Aragon, Louis 1897-1982....:.. **CLC 3, 22**
    See also CA 69-72; obituary CA 108;
    DLB 72

Arbuthnot, John 1667-1735.......... **LC 1**

Archer, Jeffrey (Howard) 1940- .... **CLC 28**
    See also CANR 22; CA 77-80

Archer, Jules 1915- .... **CLC 12**
    See also CANR 6; CA 9-12R; SAAS 5;
    SATA 4

Arden, John 1930- .... **CLC 6, 13, 15**
    See also CAAS 4; CA 13-16R; DLB 13

Arenas, Reinaldo 1943- .... **CLC 41**

Aretino, Pietro 1492-1556 .... **LC 12**

Arguedas, Jose Maria
    1911-1969 .... **CLC 10, 18**
    See also CA 89-92

Argueta, Manlio 1936-........... **CLC 31**

Ariosto, Ludovico 1474-1533........ **LC 6**

Aristophanes
    c. 450 B. C.-c. 385 B. C. ...... **CMLC 4**

Arlt, Roberto 1900-1942 .... **TCLC 29**
    See also CA 123

Armah, Ayi Kwei 1939-........ **CLC 5, 33**
    See also CANR 21; CA 61-64

Armatrading, Joan 1950-.......... **CLC 17**
    See also CA 114

Arnim, Achim von (Ludwig Joachim von
    Arnim) 1781-1831 .... **NCLC 5**

Arnold, Matthew 1822-1888 ...... **NCLC 6**
    See also DLB 32, 57

Arnold, Thomas 1795-1842 ...... **NCLC 18**
    See also DLB 55

Arnow, Harriette (Louisa Simpson)
    1908-1986 .... **CLC 2, 7, 18**
    See also CANR 14; CA 9-12R;
    obituary CA 118; SATA 42, 47; DLB 6

Arp, Jean 1887-1966............... **CLC 5**
    See also CA 81-84; obituary CA 25-28R

Arquette, Lois S(teinmetz) 1934-
    See Duncan (Steinmetz Arquette), Lois
    See also SATA 1

Arrabal, Fernando 1932- ...... **CLC 2, 9, 18**
    See also CANR 15; CA 9-12R

Arrick, Fran 19??- .... **CLC 30**

Artaud, Antonin 1896-1948 .... **TCLC 3**
    See also CA 104

Arthur, Ruth M(abel) 1905-1979.... **CLC 12**
    See also CANR 4; CA 9-12R;
    obituary CA 85-88; SATA 7;
    obituary SATA 26

Artsybashev, Mikhail Petrarch
    1878-1927 .... **TCLC 31**

Arundel, Honor (Morfydd)
    1919-1973 .... **CLC 17**
    See also CAP 2; CA 21-22;
    obituary CA 41-44R; SATA 4;
    obituary SATA 24

Asch, Sholem 1880-1957 .... **TCLC 3**
    See also CA 105

Ashbery, John (Lawrence)
    1927- ... **CLC 2, 3, 4, 6, 9, 13, 15, 25, 41**
    See also CANR 9; CA 5-8R; DLB 5;
    DLB-Y 81

Ashton-Warner, Sylvia (Constance)
    1908-1984 .... **CLC 19**
    See also CA 69-72; obituary CA 112

Asimov, Isaac 1920-.... **CLC 1, 3, 9, 19, 26**
    See also CLR 12; CANR 2, 19; CA 1-4R;
    SATA 1, 26; DLB 8

Astley, Thea (Beatrice May)
    1925- .... **CLC 41**
    See also CANR 11; CA 65-68

Aston, James 1906-1964
    See White, T(erence) H(anbury)

Asturias, Miguel Angel
    1899-1974 .... **CLC 3, 8, 13**
    See also CAP 2; CA 25-28;
    obituary CA 49-52

Atheling, William, Jr. 1921-1975
    See Blish, James (Benjamin)

Atherton, Gertrude (Franklin Horn)
    1857-1948 .... **TCLC 2**
    See also CA 104; DLB 9

Atwood, Margaret (Eleanor)
    1939- .... **CLC 2, 3, 4, 8, 13, 15, 25, 44;
                                          SSC 2**
    See also CANR 3, 24; CA 49-52; SATA 50;
    DLB 53

Aubin, Penelope 1685-1731? .... **LC 9**
    See also DLB 39

Auchincloss, Louis (Stanton)
    1917- .... **CLC 4, 6, 9, 18, 45**
    See also CANR 6; CA 1-4R; DLB 2;
    DLB-Y 80

Auden, W(ystan) H(ugh)
    1907-1973 ..... **CLC 1, 2, 3, 4, 6, 9, 11,
                                          14, 43**
    See also CANR 5; CA 9-12R;
    obituary CA 45-48; DLB 10, 20

Audiberti, Jacques 1899-1965 ...... **CLC 38**
    See also obituary CA 25-28R

Auel, Jean M(arie) 1936-.......... **CLC 31**
    See also CANR 21; CA 103

Austen, Jane 1775-1817.... **NCLC 1, 13, 19**

Auster, Paul 1947-............... **CLC 47**
    See also CANR 23; CA 69-72

Austin, Mary (Hunter)
    1868-1934 .... **TCLC 25**
    See also CA 109; DLB 9

Avison, Margaret 1918-......... **CLC 2, 4**
    See also CA 17-20R; DLB 53

Ayckbourn, Alan 1939- .... **CLC 5, 8, 18, 33**
    See also CA 21-24R; DLB 13

Aydy, Catherine 1937-
    See Tennant, Emma

Ayme, Marcel (Andre) 1902-1967... **CLC 11**
    See also CA 89-92; DLB 72

Ayrton, Michael 1921-1975......... **CLC 7**
    See also CANR 9, 21; CA 5-8R;
    obituary CA 61-64

Azorin 1874-1967 .... **CLC 11**
    See also Martinez Ruiz, Jose

Azuela, Mariano 1873-1952........ **TCLC 3**
    See also CA 104

"Bab" 1836-1911
    See Gilbert, (Sir) W(illiam) S(chwenck)

Babel, Isaak (Emmanuilovich)
    1894-1941 .... **TCLC 2, 13**
    See also CA 104

Babits, Mihaly 1883-1941 .... **TCLC 14**
    See also CA 114

Bacchelli, Riccardo 1891-1985 ..... **CLC 19**
    See also CA 29-32R; obituary CA 117

Bach, Richard (David) 1936-....... **CLC 14**
    See also CANR 18; CA 9-12R; SATA 13

Bachman, Richard 1947-
    See King, Stephen (Edwin)

Bacovia, George 1881-1957 .... **TCLC 24**

Bagehot, Walter 1826-1877 ...... **NCLC 10**
    See also DLB 55

Bagnold, Enid 1889-1981.......... **CLC 25**
    See also CANR 5; CA 5-8R;
    obituary CA 103; SATA 1, 25; DLB 13

Bagryana, Elisaveta 1893-........ **CLC 10**

Bailey, Paul 1937-............... **CLC 45**
    See also CANR 16; CA 21-24R; DLB 14

Baillie, Joanna 1762-1851 .... **NCLC 2**

Bainbridge, Beryl
    1933-....... **CLC 4, 5, 8, 10, 14, 18, 22**
    See also CA 21-24R; DLB 14

Baker, Elliott 1922- .... **CLC 8**
    See also CANR 2; CA 45-48

Baker, Russell (Wayne) 1925-...... **CLC 31**
    See also CANR 11; CA 57-60

Bakshi, Ralph 1938-............. **CLC 26**
    See also CA 112

Bakunin, Mikhail (Alexandrovich)
    1814-1876 .... **NCLC 25**

Baldwin, James (Arthur)
    1924-1987 ..... **CLC 1, 2, 3, 4, 5, 8, 13,
                                          15, 17, 42, 50**
    See also CANR 3; CA 1-4R;
    obituary CA 124; CABS 1; SATA 9;
    DLB 2, 7, 33; DLB-Y 87;
    CDALB 1941-1968

Ballard, J(ames) G(raham)
    1930- .... **CLC 3, 6, 14, 36; SSC 1**
    See also CANR 15; CA 5-8R; DLB 14

Balmont, Konstantin Dmitriyevich
    1867-1943 .... **TCLC 11**
    See also CA 109

Balzac, Honore de
    1799-1850 .... **NCLC 5; SSC 5**

Author Index

Coover, Robert (Lowell)
    1932- . . . . CLC 3, 7, 15, 32, 46
    See also CANR 3; CA 45-48; DLB 2;
    DLB-Y 81

Copeland, Stewart (Armstrong)
    1952- . . . . CLC 26
    See also The Police

Coppard, A(lfred) E(dgar)
    1878-1957 . . . . TCLC 5
    See also YABC 1; CA 114

Coppee, Francois   1842-1908 . . . . . . TCLC 25

Coppola, Francis Ford   1939- . . . . CLC 16
    See also CA 77-80; DLB 44

Corcoran, Barbara   1911- . . . . CLC 17
    See also CAAS 2; CANR 11; CA 21-24R;
    SATA 3; DLB 52

Corman, Cid   1924- . . . . CLC 9
    See also Corman, Sidney
    See also CAAS 2; DLB 5

Corman, Sidney   1924-
    See Corman, Cid
    See also CA 85-88

Cormier, Robert (Edmund)
    1925- . . . . CLC 12, 30
    See also CLR 12; CANR 5, 23; CA 1-4R;
    SATA 10, 45; DLB 52

Corn, Alfred (Dewitt III)   1943- . . . . . CLC 33
    See also CA 104; DLB-Y 80

Cornwell, David (John Moore)
    1931- . . . . CLC 9, 15
    See also le Carre, John
    See also CANR 13; CA 5-8R

Corso, (Nunzio) Gregory   1930- . . . CLC 1, 11
    See also CA 5-8R; DLB 5, 16

Cortazar, Julio
    1914-1984 . . . . . CLC 2, 3, 5, 10, 13, 15,
                                              33, 34
    See also CANR 12; CA 21-24R

Corvo, Baron   1860-1913
    See Rolfe, Frederick (William Serafino
    Austin Lewis Mary)

Cosic, Dobrica   1921- . . . . CLC 14
    See also CA 122

Costain, Thomas B(ertram)
    1885-1965 . . . . CLC 30
    See also CA 5-8R; obituary CA 25-28R;
    DLB 9

Costantini, Humberto   1924?-1987 . . . CLC 49
    See also obituary CA 122

Costello, Elvis   1955- . . . . CLC 21

Cotter, Joseph Seamon, Sr.
    1861-1949 . . . . TCLC 28
    See also DLB 50

Couperus, Louis (Marie Anne)
    1863-1923 . . . . TCLC 15
    See also CA 115

Cousteau, Jacques-Yves   1910- . . . . . . CLC 30
    See also CANR 15; CA 65-68; SATA 38

Coward, (Sir) Noel (Pierce)
    1899-1973 . . . . CLC 1, 9, 29, 51
    See also CAP 2; CA 17-18;
    obituary CA 41-44R; DLB 10

Cowley, Malcolm   1898-1989 . . . . CLC 39
    See also CANR 3; CA 5-6R; DLB 4, 48;
    DLB-Y 81

Cowper, William   1731-1800 . . . . . . NCLC 8

Cox, William Trevor   1928- . . . . . . CLC 9, 14
    See also Trevor, William
    See also CANR 4; CA 9-12R

Cozzens, James Gould
    1903-1978 . . . . CLC 1, 4, 11
    See also CANR 19; CA 9-12R;
    obituary CA 81-84; DLB 9; DLB-Y 84;
    DLB-DS 2; CDALB 1941-1968

Crabbe, George   1754-1832 . . . . . . NCLC 26

Crane, (Harold) Hart
    1899-1932 . . . . TCLC 2, 5
    See also CA 104; DLB 4, 48

Crane, R(onald) S(almon)
    1886-1967 . . . . CLC 27
    See also CA 85-88; DLB 63

Crane, Stephen
    1871-1900 . . . . TCLC 11, 17, 32
    See also YABC 2; CA 109; DLB 12, 54, 78;
    CDALB 1865-1917

Craven, Margaret   1901-1980 . . . . . . CLC 17
    See also CA 103

Crawford, F(rancis) Marion
    1854-1909 . . . . TCLC 10
    See also CA 107; DLB 71

Crawford, Isabella Valancy
    1850-1887 . . . . NCLC 12

Crayencour, Marguerite de   1903-1987
    See Yourcenar, Marguerite

Creasey, John   1908-1973 . . . . CLC 11
    See also CANR 8; CA 5-8R;
    obituary CA 41-44R

Crebillon, Claude Prosper Jolyot de (fils)
    1707-1777 . . . . LC 1

Creeley, Robert (White)
    1926- . . . . CLC 1, 2, 4, 8, 11, 15, 36
    See also CANR 23; CA 1-4R; DLB 5, 16

Crews, Harry (Eugene)
    1935- . . . . CLC 6, 23, 49
    See also CANR 20; CA 25-28R; DLB 6

Crichton, (John) Michael
    1942- . . . . CLC 2, 6, 54
    See also CANR 13; CA 25-28R; SATA 9;
    DLB-Y 81

Crispin, Edmund   1921-1978 . . . . CLC 22
    See also Montgomery, Robert Bruce

Cristofer, Michael   1946- . . . . CLC 28
    See also CA 110; DLB 7

Crockett, David (Davy)
    1786-1836 . . . . NCLC 8
    See also DLB 3, 11

Croker, John Wilson   1780-1857 . . NCLC 10

Cronin, A(rchibald) J(oseph)
    1896-1981 . . . . CLC 32
    See also CANR 5; CA 1-4R;
    obituary CA 102; obituary SATA 25, 47

Cross, Amanda   1926-
    See Heilbrun, Carolyn G(old)

Crothers, Rachel   1878-1953 . . . . TCLC 19
    See also CA 113; DLB 7

Crowley, Aleister   1875-1947 . . . . TCLC 7
    See also CA 104

Crowley, John   1942-
    See also CA 61-64; DLB-Y 82

Crumb, Robert   1943- . . . . CLC 17
    See also CA 106

Cryer, Gretchen   1936?- . . . . CLC 21
    See also CA 114, 123

Csath, Geza   1887-1919 . . . . TCLC 13
    See also CA 111

Cudlip, David   1933- . . . . CLC 34

Cullen, Countee   1903-1946 . . . . TCLC 4
    See also CA 108, 124; SATA 18; DLB 4,
    48, 51

Cummings, E(dward) E(stlin)
    1894-1962 . . . . CLC 1, 3, 8, 12, 15
    See also CA 73-76; DLB 4, 48

Cunha, Euclides (Rodrigues) da
    1866-1909 . . . . TCLC 24
    See also CA 123

Cunningham, J(ames) V(incent)
    1911-1985 . . . . CLC 3, 31
    See also CANR 1; CA 1-4R;
    obituary CA 115; DLB 5

Cunningham, Julia (Woolfolk)
    1916- . . . . CLC 12
    See also CANR 4, 19; CA 9-12R; SAAS 2;
    SATA 1, 26

Cunningham, Michael   1952- . . . . CLC 34

Currie, Ellen   19??- . . . . CLC 44

Dabrowska, Maria (Szumska)
    1889-1965 . . . . CLC 15
    See also CA 106

Dabydeen, David   1956?- . . . . CLC 34
    See also CA 106

Dacey, Philip   1939- . . . . CLC 51
    See also CANR 14; CA 37-40R

Dagerman, Stig (Halvard)
    1923-1954 . . . . TCLC 17
    See also CA 117

Dahl, Roald   1916- . . . . CLC 1, 6, 18
    See also CLR 1, 7; CANR 6; CA 1-4R;
    SATA 1, 26

Dahlberg, Edward   1900-1977 . . . CLC 1, 7, 14
    See also CA 9-12R; obituary CA 69-72;
    DLB 48

Daly, Elizabeth   1878-1967 . . . . CLC 52
    See also CAP 2; CA 23-24;
    obituary CA 25-28R

Daly, Maureen   1921- . . . . CLC 17
    See also McGivern, Maureen Daly
    See also SAAS 1; SATA 2

Daniken, Erich von   1935-
    See Von Daniken, Erich

Dannay, Frederic   1905-1982
    See Queen, Ellery
    See also CANR 1; CA 1-4R;
    obituary CA 107

D'Annunzio, Gabriele   1863-1938 . . . . TCLC 6
    See also CA 104

Dante (Alighieri)
    See Alighieri, Dante

Danziger, Paula   1944- . . . . CLC 21
    See also CLR 20; CA 112, 115; SATA 30,
    36

Dario, Ruben   1867-1916 . . . . TCLC 4
    See also Sarmiento, Felix Ruben Garcia
    See also CA 104

Author Index

Esenin, Sergei (Aleksandrovich)
1895-1925 .... **TCLC 4**
See also CA 104

Eshleman, Clayton 1935-.......... **CLC 7**
See also CAAS 6; CA 33-36R; DLB 5

Espriu, Salvador 1913-1985........ **CLC 9**
See also obituary CA 115

Estleman, Loren D. 1952- .... **CLC 48**
See also CA 85-88

Evans, Marian 1819-1880
See Eliot, George

Evans, Mary Ann 1819-1880
See Eliot, George

Evarts, Esther 1900-1972
See Benson, Sally

Everett, Percival L. 1957?- .... **CLC 57**
See also CA 129

Everson, Ronald G(ilmour) 1903-... **CLC 27**
See also CA 17-20R

Everson, William (Oliver)
1912-.................. **CLC 1, 5, 14**
See also CANR 20; CA 9-12R; DLB 5, 16

Evtushenko, Evgenii (Aleksandrovich) 1933-
See Yevtushenko, Yevgeny

Ewart, Gavin (Buchanan)
1916-.................. **CLC 13, 46**
See also CANR 17; CA 89-92; DLB 40

Ewers, Hanns Heinz 1871-1943 ... **TCLC 12**
See also CA 109

Ewing, Frederick R. 1918-
See Sturgeon, Theodore (Hamilton)

Exley, Frederick (Earl) 1929-.... **CLC 6, 11**
See also CA 81-84; DLB-Y 81

Ezekiel, Tish O'Dowd 1943-....... **CLC 34**

Fagen, Donald 1948-............. **CLC 26**

Fair, Ronald L. 1932-............. **CLC 18**
See also CANR 25; CA 69-72; DLB 33

Fairbairns, Zoe (Ann) 1948- .... **CLC 32**
See also CANR 21; CA 103

Fairfield, Cicily Isabel 1892-1983
See West, Rebecca

Fallaci, Oriana 1930-............. **CLC 11**
See also CANR 15; CA 77-80

Faludy, George 1913-............. **CLC 42**
See also CA 21-24R

Farah, Nuruddin 1945-............ **CLC 53**
See also CA 106

Fargue, Leon-Paul 1876-1947 ..... **TCLC 11**
See also CA 109

Farigoule, Louis 1885-1972
See Romains, Jules

Farina, Richard 1937?-1966........ **CLC 9**
See also CA 81-84; obituary CA 25-28R

Farley, Walter 1920- .... **CLC 17**
See also CANR 8; CA 17-20R; SATA 2, 43;
DLB 22

Farmer, Philip Jose 1918-....... **CLC 1, 19**
See also CANR 4; CA 1-4R; DLB 8

Farrell, J(ames) G(ordon)
1935-1979 .... **CLC 6**
See also CA 73-76; obituary CA 89-92;
DLB 14

Farrell, James T(homas)
1904-1979 .... **CLC 1, 4, 8, 11**
See also CANR 9; CA 5-8R;
obituary CA 89-92; DLB 4, 9; DLB-DS 2

Farrell, M. J. 1904-
See Keane, Molly

Fassbinder, Rainer Werner
1946-1982 .... **CLC 20**
See also CA 93-96; obituary CA 106

Fast, Howard (Melvin) 1914- ...... **CLC 23**
See also CANR 1; CA 1-4R; SATA 7;
DLB 9

Faulkner, William (Cuthbert)
1897-1962 .... **CLC 1, 3, 6, 8, 9, 11, 14,
18, 28, 52; SSC 1**
See also CA 81-84; DLB 9, 11, 44;
DLB-Y 86; DLB-DS 2

Fauset, Jessie Redmon
1884?-1961............... **CLC 19, 54**
See also CA 109; DLB 51

Faust, Irvin 1924-................. **CLC 8**
See also CA 33-36R; DLB 2, 28; DLB-Y 80

Fearing, Kenneth (Flexner)
1902-1961 .... **CLC 51**
See also CA 93-96; DLB 9

Federman, Raymond 1928- ...... **CLC 6, 47**
See also CANR 10; CA 17-20R; DLB-Y 80

Federspiel, J(urg) F. 1931-........ **CLC 42**

Feiffer, Jules 1929-............. **CLC 2, 8**
See also CA 17-20R; SATA 8; DLB 7, 44

Feinstein, Elaine 1930-........... **CLC 36**
See also CAAS 1; CA 69-72; DLB 14, 40

Feldman, Irving (Mordecai) 1928-.... **CLC 7**
See also CANR 1; CA 1-4R

Fellini, Federico 1920-............ **CLC 16**
See also CA 65-68

Felsen, Gregor 1916-
See Felsen, Henry Gregor

Felsen, Henry Gregor 1916- .... **CLC 17**
See also CANR 1; CA 1-4R; SAAS 2;
SATA 1

Fenton, James (Martin) 1949-...... **CLC 32**
See also CA 102; DLB 40

Ferber, Edna 1887-1968............ **CLC 18**
See also CA 5-8R; obituary CA 25-28R;
SATA 7; DLB 9, 28

Ferlinghetti, Lawrence (Monsanto)
1919?-.......... **CLC 2, 6, 10, 27**
See also CANR 3; CA 5-8R; DLB 5, 16;
CDALB 1941-1968

Ferrier, Susan (Edmonstone)
1782-1854 .... **NCLC 8**

Feuchtwanger, Lion 1884-1958 ..... **TCLC 3**
See also CA 104; DLB 66

Feydeau, Georges 1862-1921...... **TCLC 22**
See also CA 113

Ficino, Marsilio 1433-1499 .... **LC 12**

Fiedler, Leslie A(aron)
1917-.................. **CLC 4, 13, 24**
See also CANR 7; CA 9-12R; DLB 28, 67

Field, Andrew 1938-............ **CLC 44**
See also CANR 25; CA 97-100

Field, Eugene 1850-1895 .... **NCLC 3**
See also SATA 16; DLB 21, 23, 42

Fielding, Henry 1707-1754 .... **LC 1**
See also DLB 39

Fielding, Sarah 1710-1768.......... **LC 1**
See also DLB 39

Fierstein, Harvey 1954-.......... **CLC 33**
See also CA 123

Figes, Eva 1932-................. **CLC 31**
See also CANR 4; CA 53-56; DLB 14

Finch, Robert (Duer Claydon)
1900-....................... **CLC 18**
See also CANR 9, 24; CA 57-60

Findley, Timothy 1930-.......... **CLC 27**
See also CANR 12; CA 25-28R; DLB 53

Fink, Janis 1951-
See Ian, Janis

Firbank, Louis 1944-
See Reed, Lou
See also CA 117

Firbank, (Arthur Annesley) Ronald
1886-1926 .... **TCLC 1**
See also CA 104; DLB 36

Fisher, Roy 1930-................ **CLC 25**
See also CANR 16; CA 81-84; DLB 40

Fisher, Rudolph 1897-1934 .... **TCLC 11**
See also CA 107; DLB 51

Fisher, Vardis (Alvero) 1895-1968.... **CLC 7**
See also CA 5-8R; obituary CA 25-28R;
DLB 9

FitzGerald, Edward 1809-1883 .... **NCLC 9**
See also DLB 32

Fitzgerald, F(rancis) Scott (Key)
1896-1940 .... **TCLC 1, 6, 14, 28**
See also CA 110, 123; DLB 4, 9; DLB-Y 81;
DLB-DS 1

Fitzgerald, Penelope 1916-..... **CLC 19, 51**
See also CA 85-88; DLB 14

FitzGerald, Robert D(avid) 1902-... **CLC 19**
See also CA 17-20R

Fitzgerald, Robert (Stuart)
1910-1985 .... **CLC 39**
See also CANR 1; CA 2R;
obituary CA 114; DLB-Y 80

Flanagan, Thomas (James Bonner)
1923-.................. **CLC 25, 52**
See also CA 108; DLB-Y 80

Flaubert, Gustave
1821-1880 .... **NCLC 2, 10, 19**

Fleming, Ian (Lancaster)
1908-1964 .... **CLC 3, 30**
See also CA 5-8R; SATA 9

Fleming, Thomas J(ames) 1927- .... **CLC 37**
See also CANR 10; CA 5-8R; SATA 8

Fletcher, John Gould 1886-1950 ... **TCLC 35**
See also CA 107; DLB 4, 45

Flieg, Hellmuth
See Heym, Stefan

Flying Officer X 1905-1974
See Bates, H(erbert) E(rnest)

Fo, Dario 1929-.................. **CLC 32**
See also CA 116

Follett, Ken(neth Martin) 1949- .... **CLC 18**
See also CANR 13; CA 81-84; DLB-Y 81

Fontane, Theodor 1819-1898 ..... **NCLC 26**

Foote, Horton 1916-............. CLC 51
See also CA 73-76; DLB 26

Forbes, Esther 1891-1967......... CLC 12
See also CAP 1; CA 13-14;
obituary CA 25-28R; SATA 2; DLB 22

Forche, Carolyn 1950-........... CLC 25
See also CA 109, 117; DLB 5

Ford, Ford Madox 1873-1939 ... TCLC 1, 15
See also CA 104; DLB 34

Ford, John 1895-1973............ CLC 16
See also obituary CA 45-48

Ford, Richard 1944-.............. CLC 46
See also CANR 11; CA 69-72

Foreman, Richard 1937-.......... CLC 50
See also CA 65-68

Forester, C(ecil) S(cott)
1899-1966 .... CLC 35
See also CA 73-76; obituary CA 25-28R;
SATA 13

Forman, James D(ouglas) 1932- .... CLC 21
See also CANR 4, 19; CA 9-12R; SATA 8,
21

Fornes, Maria Irene 1930-........ CLC 39
See also CA 25-28R; DLB 7

Forrest, Leon 1937- .... CLC 4
See also CAAS 7; CA 89-92; DLB 33

Forster, E(dward) M(organ)
1879-1970 .... CLC 1, 2, 3, 4, 9, 10, 13,
15, 22, 45
See also CAP 1; CA 13-14;
obituary CA 25-28R; DLB 34

Forster, John 1812-1876 .... NCLC 11

Forsyth, Frederick 1938-...... CLC 2, 5, 36
See also CA 85-88

Forten (Grimke), Charlotte L(ottie)
1837-1914 .... TCLC 16
See also Grimke, Charlotte L(ottie) Forten
See also DLB 50

Foscolo, Ugo 1778-1827.......... NCLC 8

Fosse, Bob 1925-1987............. CLC 20
See also Fosse, Robert Louis

Fosse, Robert Louis 1925-1987
See Bob Fosse
See also CA 110, 123

Foster, Stephen Collins
1826-1864 .... NCLC 26

Foucault, Michel 1926-1984 .... CLC 31, 34
See also CANR 23; CA 105;
obituary CA 113

**Fouque, Friedrich (Heinrich Karl) de La
Motte** 1777-1843 .... NCLC 2

Fournier, Henri Alban 1886-1914
See Alain-Fournier
See also CA 104

Fournier, Pierre 1916- .... CLC 11
See also Gascar, Pierre
See also CANR 16; CA 89-92

Fowles, John (Robert)
1926- .... CLC 1, 2, 3, 4, 6, 9, 10, 15, 33
See also CANR 25; CA 5-8R; SATA 22;
DLB 14

Fox, Paula 1923-................ CLC 2, 8
See also CLR 1; CANR 20; CA 73-76;
SATA 17; DLB 52

Fox, William Price (Jr.) 1926- ..... CLC 22
See also CANR 11; CA 17-20R; DLB 2;
DLB-Y 81

Frame (Clutha), Janet (Paterson)
1924- .... CLC 2, 3, 6, 22
See also Clutha, Janet Paterson Frame

France, Anatole 1844-1924 .... TCLC 9
See also Thibault, Jacques Anatole Francois

Francis, Claude 19??-............ CLC 50

Francis, Dick 1920- ...... CLC 2, 22, 42
See also CANR 9; CA 5-8R

Francis, Robert (Churchill)
1901-1987 .... CLC 15
See also CANR 1; CA 1-4R;
obituary CA 123

Frank, Anne 1929-1945 .... TCLC 17
See also CA 113; SATA 42

Frank, Elizabeth 1945-........... CLC 39
See also CA 121, 126

Franklin, (Stella Maria Sarah) Miles
1879-1954 .... TCLC 7
See also CA 104

Fraser, Antonia (Pakenham)
1932- .... CLC 32
See also CA 85-88; SATA 32

Fraser, George MacDonald 1925-.... CLC 7
See also CANR 2; CA 45-48

Frayn, Michael 1933-...... CLC 3, 7, 31, 47
See also CA 5-8R; DLB 13, 14

Fraze, Candida 19??- .... CLC 50
See also CA 125

Frazer, Sir James George
1854-1941 .... TCLC 32
See also CA 118

Frazier, Ian 1951-............... CLC 46

Frederic, Harold 1856-1898...... NCLC 10
See also DLB 12, 23

Fredman, Russell (Bruce) 1929-
See also CLR 20

Fredro, Aleksander 1793-1876..... NCLC 8

Freeling, Nicolas 1927- .... CLC 38
See also CANR 1, 17; CA 49-52

Freeman, Douglas Southall
1886-1953 .... TCLC 11
See also CA 109; DLB 17

Freeman, Judith 1946-........... CLC 55

Freeman, Mary (Eleanor) Wilkins
1852-1930 .... TCLC 9; SSC 1
See also CA 106; DLB 12

Freeman, R(ichard) Austin
1862-1943 .... TCLC 21
See also CA 113; DLB 70

French, Marilyn 1929-........ CLC 10, 18
See also CANR 3; CA 69-72

Freneau, Philip Morin 1752-1832.. NCLC 1
See also DLB 37, 43

Friedman, B(ernard) H(arper)
1926- .... CLC 7
See also CANR 3; CA 1-4R

Friedman, Bruce Jay 1930-.... CLC 3, 5, 56
See also CANR 25; CA 9-12R; DLB 2, 28

Friel, Brian 1929-.............. CLC 5, 42
See also CA 21-24R; DLB 13

Friis-Baastad, Babbis (Ellinor)
1921-1970 .... CLC 12
See also CA 17-20R; SATA 7

Frisch, Max (Rudolf)
1911-........ CLC 3, 9, 14, 18, 32, 44
See also CA 85-88; DLB 69

Fromentin, Eugene (Samuel Auguste)
1820-1876 .... NCLC 10

Frost, Robert (Lee)
1874-1963 ... CLC 1, 3, 4, 9, 10, 13, 15,
26, 34, 44
See also CA 89-92; SATA 14; DLB 54

Fry, Christopher 1907-....... CLC 2, 10, 14
See also CANR 9; CA 17-20R; DLB 13

Frye, (Herman) Northrop 1912- .... CLC 24
See also CANR 8; CA 5-8R

Fuchs, Daniel 1909-............ CLC 8, 22
See also CAAS 5; CA 81-84; DLB 9, 26, 28

Fuchs, Daniel 1934-.............. CLC 34
See also CANR 14; CA 37-40R

Fuentes, Carlos
1928-......... CLC 3, 8, 10, 13, 22, 41
See also CANR 10; CA 69-72

Fugard, Athol 1932-... CLC 5, 9, 14, 25, 40
See also CA 85-88

Fugard, Sheila 1932- .... CLC 48
See also CA 125

Fuller, Charles (H., Jr.) 1939-...... CLC 25
See also CA 108, 112; DLB 38

Fuller, (Sarah) Margaret
1810-1850 .... NCLC 5
See also Ossoli, Sarah Margaret (Fuller
marchesa d')
See also DLB 1, 59, 73; CDALB 1640-1865

Fuller, Roy (Broadbent) 1912-.... CLC 4, 28
See also CA 5-8R; DLB 15, 20

Fulton, Alice 1952-............... CLC 52
See also CA 116

Furphy, Joseph 1843-1912........ TCLC 25

Futrelle, Jacques 1875-1912 ...... TCLC 19
See also CA 113

Gaboriau, Emile 1835-1873 ...... NCLC 14

Gadda, Carlo Emilio 1893-1973 .... CLC 11
See also CA 89-92

Gaddis, William
1922-........ CLC 1, 3, 6, 8, 10, 19, 43
See also CAAS 4; CANR 21; CA 17-20R;
DLB 2

Gaines, Ernest J. 1933-...... CLC 3, 11, 18
See also CANR 6, 24; CA 9-12R; DLB 2,
33; DLB-Y 80

Gale, Zona 1874-1938 .... TCLC 7
See also CA 105; DLB 9

Gallagher, Tess 1943-............. CLC 18
See also CA 106

Gallant, Mavis
1922-........... CLC 7, 18, 38; SSC 5
See also CA 69-72; DLB 53

Gallant, Roy A(rthur) 1924- .... CLC 17
See also CANR 4; CA 5-8R; SATA 4

Gallico, Paul (William) 1897-1976 ... CLC 2
See also CA 5-8R; obituary CA 69-72;
SATA 13; DLB 9

Grendon, Stephen   1909-1971
See Derleth, August (William)

Greve, Felix Paul Berthold Friedrich
1879-1948
See Grove, Frederick Philip
See also CA 104

Grey, (Pearl) Zane   1872?-1939 ..... TCLC 6
See also CA 104; DLB 9

Grieg, (Johan) Nordahl (Brun)
1902-1943 .... TCLC 10
See also CA 107

Grieve, C(hristopher) M(urray)   1892-1978
See MacDiarmid, Hugh
See also CA 5-8R; obituary CA 85-88

Griffin, Gerald   1803-1840 .... NCLC 7

Griffin, Peter   1942- .... CLC 39

Griffiths, Trevor   1935- .... CLC 13, 52
See also CA 97-100; DLB 13

Grigson, Geoffrey (Edward Harvey)
1905-1985 .... CLC 7, 39
See also CANR 20; CA 25-28R;
obituary CA 118; DLB 27

Grillparzer, Franz   1791-1872 ..... NCLC 1

Grimke, Charlotte L(ottie) Forten   1837-1914
See Forten (Grimke), Charlotte L(ottie)
See also CA 117, 124

Grimm, Jakob (Ludwig) Karl
1785-1863 .... NCLC 3
See also SATA 22

Grimm, Wilhelm Karl   1786-1859 .. NCLC 3
See also SATA 22

Grimmelshausen, Johann Jakob Christoffel
von   1621-1676 .... LC 6

Grindel, Eugene   1895-1952
See also CA 104

Grossman, Vasily (Semenovich)
1905-1964 .... CLC 41
See also CA 124

Grove, Frederick Philip
1879-1948 .... TCLC 4
See also Greve, Felix Paul Berthold
Friedrich

Grumbach, Doris (Isaac)
1918- .... CLC 13, 22
See also CAAS 2; CANR 9; CA 5-8R

Grundtvig, Nicolai Frederik Severin
1783-1872 .... NCLC 1

Grunwald, Lisa   1959- .... CLC 44
See also CA 120

Guare, John   1938- .... CLC 8, 14, 29
See also CANR 21; CA 73-76; DLB 7

Gudjonsson, Halldor Kiljan   1902-
See Laxness, Halldor (Kiljan)
See also CA 103

Guest, Barbara   1920- .... CLC 34
See also CANR 11; CA 25-28R; DLB 5

Guest, Judith (Ann)   1936- ...... CLC 8, 30
See also CANR 15; CA 77-80

Guild, Nicholas M.   1944- .... CLC 33
See also CA 93-96

Guillen, Jorge   1893-1984 .... CLC 11
See also CA 89-92; obituary CA 112

Guillen, Nicolas   1902-1989 ...... CLC 48
See also CA 116, 125

Guillevic, (Eugene)   1907- .... CLC 33
See also CA 93-96

Gunn, Bill   1934-1989 .... CLC 5
See also Gunn, William Harrison
See also DLB 38

Gunn, Thom(son William)
1929- .... CLC 3, 6, 18, 32
See also CANR 9; CA 17-20R; DLB 27

Gunn, William Harrison   1934-1989
See Gunn, Bill
See also CANR 12, 25; CA 13-16R

Gurney, A(lbert) R(amsdell), Jr.
1930- .... CLC 32, 50, 54
See also CA 77-80

Gurney, Ivor (Bertie)   1890-1937 ... TCLC 33

Gustafson, Ralph (Barker)   1909-.... CLC 36
See also CANR 8; CA 21-24R

Guthrie, A(lfred) B(ertram), Jr.
1901- .... CLC 23
See also CA 57-60; DLB 6

Guthrie, Woodrow Wilson   1912-1967
See Guthrie, Woody
See also CA 113; obituary CA 93-96

Guthrie, Woody   1912-1967 .... CLC 35
See also Guthrie, Woodrow Wilson

Guy, Rosa (Cuthbert)   1928-..... CLC 26 13
See also CANR 14; CA 17-20R; SATA 14;
DLB 33

Haavikko, Paavo (Juhani)
1931- .... CLC 18, 34
See also CA 106

Hacker, Marilyn   1942- .... CLC 5, 9, 23
See also CA 77-80

Haggard, (Sir) H(enry) Rider
1856-1925 .... TCLC 11
See also CA 108; SATA 16; DLB 70

Haig-Brown, Roderick L(angmere)
1908-1976 .... CLC 21
See also CANR 4; CA 5-8R;
obituary CA 69-72; SATA 12

Hailey, Arthur   1920- .... CLC 5
See also CANR 2; CA 1-4R; DLB-Y 82

Hailey, Elizabeth Forsythe   1938-... CLC 40
See also CAAS 1; CANR 15; CA 93-96

Haley, Alex (Palmer)   1921-...... CLC 8, 12
See also CA 77-80; DLB 38

Haliburton, Thomas Chandler
1796-1865 .... NCLC 15
See also DLB 11

Hall, Donald (Andrew, Jr.)
1928- .... CLC 1, 13, 37
See also CAAS 7; CANR 2; CA 5-8R;
SATA 23; DLB 5

Hall, James Norman   1887-1951 ... TCLC 23
See also CA 123; SATA 21

Hall, (Marguerite) Radclyffe
1886-1943 .... TCLC 12
See also CA 110

Hall, Rodney   1935- .... CLC 51
See also CA 109

Halpern, Daniel   1945- .... CLC 14
See also CA 33-36R

Hamburger, Michael (Peter Leopold)
1924- .... CLC 5, 14
See also CAAS 4; CANR 2; CA 5-8R;
DLB 27

Hamill, Pete   1935- .... CLC 10
See also CANR 18; CA 25-28R

Hamilton, Edmond   1904-1977....... CLC 1
See also CANR 3; CA 1-4R; DLB 8

Hamilton, Gail   1911-
See Corcoran, Barbara

Hamilton, Ian   1938- .... CLC 55
See also CA 106; DLB 40

Hamilton, Mollie   1909?-
See Kaye, M(ary) M(argaret)

Hamilton, (Anthony Walter) Patrick
1904-1962 .... CLC 51
See also obituary CA 113; DLB 10

Hamilton, Virginia (Esther)   1936-... CLC 26
See also CLR 1, 11; CANR 20; CA 25-28R;
SATA 4; DLB 33, 52

Hammett, (Samuel) Dashiell
1894-1961 .... CLC 3, 5, 10, 19, 47
See also CA 81-84

Hammon, Jupiter   1711?-1800? .... NCLC 5
See also DLB 31, 50

Hamner, Earl (Henry), Jr.   1923- ... CLC 12
See also CA 73-76; DLB 6

Hampton, Christopher (James)
1946- .... CLC 4
See also CA 25-28R; DLB 13

Hamsun, Knut   1859-1952....... TCLC 2, 14
See also Pedersen, Knut

Handke, Peter   1942- .. CLC 5, 8, 10, 15, 38
See also CA 77-80

Hanley, James   1901-1985 ... CLC 3, 5, 8, 13
See also CA 73-76; obituary CA 117

Hannah, Barry   1942- .... CLC 23, 38
See also CA 108, 110; DLB 6

Hansberry, Lorraine (Vivian)
1930-1965 .... CLC 17
See also CA 109; obituary CA 25-28R;
DLB 7, 38; CDALB 1941-1968

Hansen, Joseph   1923-............. CLC 38
See also CANR 16; CA 29-32R

Hansen, Martin   1909-1955 .... TCLC 32

Hanson, Kenneth O(stlin)   1922-.... CLC 13
See also CANR 7; CA 53-56

Hardenberg, Friedrich (Leopold Freiherr) von
1772-1801
See Novalis

Hardwick, Elizabeth   1916- .... CLC 13
See also CANR 3; CA 5-8R; DLB 6

Hardy, Thomas
1840-1928 ... TCLC 4, 10, 18, 32; SSC 2
See also CA 104, 123; SATA 25; DLB 18,
19

Hare, David   1947- .... CLC 29
See also CA 97-100; DLB 13

Harlan, Louis R(udolph)   1922-..... CLC 34
See also CANR 25; CA 21-24R

Harling, Robert   1951?-............ CLC 53

Harmon, William (Ruth)   1938-..... CLC 38
See also CANR 14; CA 33-36R

Nichols, John (Treadwell) 1940- .... **CLC 38**
See also CAAS 2; CANR 6; CA 9-12R;
DLB-Y 82

Nichols, Peter (Richard) 1927- ... **CLC 5, 36**
See also CA 104; DLB 13

Nicolas, F.R.E. 1927-
See Freeling, Nicolas

Niedecker, Lorine 1903-1970.... **CLC 10, 42**
See also CAP 2; CA 25-28; DLB 48

Nietzsche, Friedrich (Wilhelm)
1844-1900 .... **TCLC 10, 18**
See also CA 107

Nievo, Ippolito 1831-1861 .... **NCLC 22**

Nightingale, Anne Redmon 1943-
See Redmon (Nightingale), Anne
See also CA 103

Nin, Anais 1903-1977... **CLC 1, 4, 8, 11, 14**
See also CANR 22; CA 13-16R;
obituary CA 69-72; DLB 2, 4

Nissenson, Hugh 1933- .... **CLC 4, 9**
See also CA 17-20R; DLB 28

Niven, Larry 1938- .... **CLC 8**
See also Niven, Laurence Van Cott
See also DLB 8

Niven, Laurence Van Cott 1938-
See Niven, Larry
See also CANR 14; CA 21-24R

Nixon, Agnes Eckhardt 1927- ...... **CLC 21**
See also CA 110

Nkosi, Lewis 1936- .... **CLC 45**
See also CA 65-68

Nodier, (Jean) Charles (Emmanuel)
1780-1844 .... **NCLC 19**

Nordhoff, Charles 1887-1947...... **TCLC 23**
See also CA 108; SATA 23; DLB 9

Norman, Marsha 1947- .... **CLC 28**
See also CA 105; DLB-Y 84

Norris, (Benjamin) Frank(lin)
1870-1902 .... **TCLC 24**
See also CA 110; DLB 12, 71;
CDALB 1865-1917

Norris, Leslie 1921- .... **CLC 14**
See also CANR 14; CAP 1; CA 11-12;
DLB 27

North, Andrew 1912-
See Norton, Andre

North, Christopher 1785-1854
See Wilson, John

Norton, Alice Mary 1912-
See Norton, Andre
See also CANR 2; CA 1-4R; SATA 1, 43

Norton, Andre 1912- .... **CLC 12**
See also Norton, Mary Alice
See also DLB 8, 52

Norway, Nevil Shute 1899-1960
See Shute (Norway), Nevil
See also CA 102; obituary CA 93-96

Norwid, Cyprian Kamil
1821-1883 .... **NCLC 17**

Nossack, Hans Erich 1901-1978 ..... **CLC 6**
See also CA 93-96; obituary CA 85-88;
DLB 69

Nova, Craig 1945- .... **CLC 7, 31**
See also CANR 2; CA 45-48

Novak, Joseph 1933-
See Kosinski, Jerzy (Nikodem)

Novalis 1772-1801 .... **NCLC 13**

Nowlan, Alden (Albert) 1933- ...... **CLC 15**
See also CANR 5; CA 9-12R; DLB 53

Noyes, Alfred 1880-1958 .... **TCLC 7**
See also CA 104; DLB 20

Nunn, Kem 19??- .... **CLC 34**

Nye, Robert 1939- .... **CLC 13, 42**
See also CA 33-36R; SATA 6; DLB 14

Nyro, Laura 1947- .... **CLC 17**

Oates, Joyce Carol
1938- ..... **CLC 1, 2, 3, 6, 9, 11, 15, 19,
33, 52**
See also CANR 25; CA 5-8R; DLB 2, 5;
DLB-Y 81

O'Brien, Darcy 1939- .... **CLC 11**
See also CANR 8; CA 21-24R

O'Brien, Edna 1932-.... **CLC 3, 5, 8, 13, 36**
See also CANR 6; CA 1-4R; DLB 14

O'Brien, Fitz-James 1828?-1862.. **NCLC 21**
See also DLB 74

O'Brien, Flann
1911-1966 .... **CLC 1, 4, 5, 7, 10, 47**
See also O Nuallain, Brian

O'Brien, Richard 19??- .... **CLC 17**
See also CA 124

O'Brien, (William) Tim(othy)
1946- .... **CLC 7, 19, 40**
See also CA 85-88; DLB-Y 80

Obstfelder, Sigbjorn 1866-1900.... **TCLC 23**
See also CA 123

O'Casey, Sean
1880-1964 .... **CLC 1, 5, 9, 11, 15**
See also CA 89-92; DLB 10

Ochs, Phil 1940-1976............. **CLC 17**
See also obituary CA 65-68

O'Connor, Edwin (Greene)
1918-1968 .... **CLC 14**
See also CA 93-96; obituary CA 25-28R

O'Connor, (Mary) Flannery
1925-1964 ... **CLC 1, 2, 3, 6, 10, 13, 15,
21; SSC 1**
See also CANR 3; CA 1-4R; DLB 2;
DLB-Y 80; CDALB 1941-1968

O'Connor, Frank
1903-1966 .... **CLC 14, 23; SSC 5**
See also O'Donovan, Michael (John)
See also CA 93-96

O'Dell, Scott 1903- .... **CLC 30**
See also CLR 1, 16; CANR 12; CA 61-64;
SATA 12; DLB 52

Odets, Clifford 1906-1963 .... **CLC 2, 28**
See also CA 85-88; DLB 7, 26

O'Donovan, Michael (John) 1903-1966
See O'Connor, Frank
See also CA 93-96

Oe, Kenzaburo 1935- .... **CLC 10, 36**
See also CA 97-100

O'Faolain, Julia 1932- .... **CLC 6, 19, 47**
See also CAAS 2; CANR 12; CA 81-84;
DLB 14

O'Faolain, Sean 1900- ..... **CLC 1, 7, 14, 32**
See also CANR 12; CA 61-64; DLB 15

O'Flaherty, Liam 1896-1984 ..... **CLC 5, 34**
See also CA 101; obituary CA 113; DLB 36;
DLB-Y 84

O'Grady, Standish (James)
1846-1928 .... **TCLC 5**
See also CA 104

O'Hara, Frank 1926-1966 ..... **CLC 2, 5, 13**
See also CA 9-12R; obituary CA 25-28R;
DLB 5, 16

O'Hara, John (Henry)
1905-1970 ...... **CLC 1, 2, 3, 6, 11, 42**
See also CA 5-8R; obituary CA 25-28R;
DLB 9; DLB-DS 2

O'Hara Family
See Banim, John and Banim, Michael

O'Hehir, Diana 1922-............. **CLC 41**
See also CA 93-96

Okigbo, Christopher (Ifenayichukwu)
1932-1967 .... **CLC 25**
See also CA 77-80

Olds, Sharon 1942-............. **CLC 32, 39**
See also CANR 18; CA 101

Olesha, Yuri (Karlovich)
1899-1960 .... **CLC 8**
See also CA 85-88

Oliphant, Margaret (Oliphant Wilson)
1828-1897 .... **NCLC 11**
See also DLB 18

Oliver, Mary 1935-............. **CLC 19, 34**
See also CANR 9; CA 21-24R; DLB 5

Olivier, (Baron) Laurence (Kerr)
1907- .... **CLC 20**
See also CA 111

Olsen, Tillie 1913- .... **CLC 4, 13**
See also CANR 1; CA 1-4R; DLB 28;
DLB-Y 80

Olson, Charles (John)
1910-1970 ..... **CLC 1, 2, 5, 6, 9, 11, 29**
See also CAP 1; CA 15-16;
obituary CA 25-28R; CABS 2; DLB 5, 16

Olson, Theodore 1937-
See Olson, Toby

Olson, Toby 1937- .... **CLC 28**
See also CANR 9; CA 65-68

Ondaatje, (Philip) Michael
1943- .... **CLC 14, 29, 51**
See also CA 77-80; DLB 60

Oneal, Elizabeth 1934-
See Oneal, Zibby
See also CA 106; SATA 30

Oneal, Zibby 1934-.............. **CLC 30**
See also Oneal, Elizabeth

O'Neill, Eugene (Gladstone)
1888-1953 .... **TCLC 1, 6, 27**
See also CA 110; DLB 7

Onetti, Juan Carlos 1909- .... **CLC 7, 10**
See also CA 85-88

O'Nolan, Brian 1911-1966
See O'Brien, Flann

O Nuallain, Brian 1911-1966
See O'Brien, Flann
See also CAP 2; CA 21-22;
obituary CA 25-28R

Visconti, Luchino 1906-1976 . . . . . . **CLC 16**
See also CA 81-84; obituary CA 65-68

Vittorini, Elio 1908-1966 . . . . . . **CLC 6, 9, 14**
See also obituary CA 25-28R

Vizinczey, Stephen 1933- . . . . **CLC 40**

Vliet, R(ussell) G(ordon)
1929-1984 . . . . **CLC 22**
See also CANR 18; CA 37-40R;
obituary CA 112

Voight, Ellen Bryant 1943- . . . . **CLC 54**
See also CANR 11; CA 69-72

Voigt, Cynthia 1942- . . . . **CLC 30**
See also CANR 18; CA 106; SATA 33, 48

Voinovich, Vladimir (Nikolaevich)
1932- . . . . **CLC 10, 49**
See also CA 81-84

Von Daeniken, Erich 1935-
See Von Daniken, Erich
See also CANR 17; CA 37-40R

Von Daniken, Erich 1935- . . . . **CLC 30**
See also Von Daeniken, Erich

Vonnegut, Kurt, Jr.
1922- . . . . **CLC 1, 2, 3, 4, 5, 8, 12, 22, 40**
See also CANR 1; CA 1-4R; DLB 2, 8;
DLB-Y 80; DLB-DS 3

Vorster, Gordon 1924- . . . . **CLC 34**

Voznesensky, Andrei 1933- . . . **CLC 1, 15, 57**
See also CA 89-92

Waddington, Miriam 1917- . . . . **CLC 28**
See also CANR 12; CA 21-24R

Wagman, Fredrica 1937- . . . . **CLC 7**
See also CA 97-100

Wagner, Richard 1813-1883 . . . . **NCLC 9**

Wagner-Martin, Linda 1936- . . . . **CLC 50**

Wagoner, David (Russell)
1926- . . . . **CLC 3, 5, 15**
See also CAAS 3; CANR 2; CA 1-4R;
SATA 14; DLB 5

Wah, Fred(erick James) 1939- . . . . . . **CLC 44**
See also CA 107; DLB 60

Wahloo, Per 1926-1975 . . . . **CLC 7**
See also CA 61-64

Wahloo, Peter 1926-1975
See Wahloo, Per

Wain, John (Barrington)
1925- . . . . **CLC 2, 11, 15, 46**
See also CAAS 4; CANR 23; CA 5-8R;
DLB 15, 27

Wajda, Andrzej 1926- . . . . **CLC 16**
See also CA 102

Wakefield, Dan 1932- . . . . **CLC 7**
See also CAAS 7; CA 21-24R

Wakoski, Diane
1937- . . . . . . **CLC 2, 4, 7, 9, 11, 40**
See also CAAS 1; CANR 9; CA 13-16R;
DLB 5

Walcott, Derek (Alton)
1930- . . . . **CLC 2, 4, 9, 14, 25, 42**
See also CANR 26; CA 89-92; DLB-Y 81

Waldman, Anne 1945- . . . . **CLC 7**
See also CA 37-40R; DLB 16

Waldo, Edward Hamilton 1918-
See Sturgeon, Theodore (Hamilton)

Walker, Alice
1944- . . . . . . **CLC 5, 6, 9, 19, 27, 46, 58;
SSC 5**
See also CANR 9, 27; CA 37-40R;
SATA 31; DLB 6, 33; CDALB 1968-1988

Walker, David Harry 1911- . . . . **CLC 14**
See also CANR 1; CA 1-4R; SATA 8

Walker, Edward Joseph 1934-
See Walker, Ted
See also CANR 12; CA 21-24R

Walker, George F. 1947- . . . . **CLC 44**
See also CANR 21; CA 103; DLB 60

Walker, Joseph A. 1935- . . . . **CLC 19**
See also CANR 26; CA 89-92; DLB 38

Walker, Margaret (Abigail)
1915- . . . . **CLC 1, 6**
See also CANR 26; CA 73-76; DLB 76

Walker, Ted 1934- . . . . **CLC 13**
See also Walker, Edward Joseph
See also DLB 40

Wallace, David Foster 1962- . . . . **CLC 50**

Wallace, Irving 1916- . . . . **CLC 7, 13**
See also CAAS 1; CANR 1; CA 1-4R

Wallant, Edward Lewis
1926-1962 . . . . **CLC 5, 10**
See also CANR 22; CA 1-4R; DLB 2, 28

Walpole, Horace 1717-1797 . . . . **LC 2**
See also DLB 39

Walpole, (Sir) Hugh (Seymour)
1884-1941 . . . . **TCLC 5**
See also CA 104; DLB 34

Walser, Martin 1927- . . . . **CLC 27**
See also CANR 8; CA 57-60; DLB 75

Walser, Robert 1878-1956 . . . . **TCLC 18**
See also CA 118; DLB 66

Walsh, Gillian Paton 1939-
See Walsh, Jill Paton
See also CA 37-40R; SATA 4

Walsh, Jill Paton 1939- . . . . **CLC 35**
See also CLR 2; SAAS 3

Wambaugh, Joseph (Aloysius, Jr.)
1937- . . . . **CLC 3, 18**
See also CA 33-36R; DLB 6; DLB-Y 83

Ward, Arthur Henry Sarsfield 1883-1959
See Rohmer, Sax
See also CA 108

Ward, Douglas Turner 1930- . . . . **CLC 19**
See also CA 81-84; DLB 7, 38

Warhol, Andy 1928-1987 . . . . **CLC 20**
See also CA 89-92; obituary CA 121

Warner, Francis (Robert le Plastrier)
1937- . . . . **CLC 14**
See also CANR 11; CA 53-56

Warner, Rex (Ernest) 1905-1986 . . . . **CLC 45**
See also CA 89-92; obituary CA 119;
DLB 15

Warner, Sylvia Townsend
1893-1978 . . . . **CLC 7, 19**
See also CANR 16; CA 61-64;
obituary CA 77-80; DLB 34

Warren, Mercy Otis 1728-1814 . . . **NCLC 13**
See also DLB 31

Warren, Robert Penn
1905-1989 . . . **CLC 1, 4, 6, 8, 10, 13, 18,
39, 53; SSC 4**
See also CANR 10; CA 13-16R; SATA 46;
DLB 2, 48; DLB-Y 80

Washington, Booker T(aliaferro)
1856-1915 . . . . **CLC 34**
See also CA 114, 125; SATA 28

Wassermann, Jakob 1873-1934 . . . . . **TCLC 6**
See also CA 104; DLB 66

Wasserstein, Wendy 1950- . . . . **CLC 32**
See also CA 121

Waterhouse, Keith (Spencer)
1929- . . . . **CLC 47**
See also CA 5-8R; DLB 13, 15

Waters, Roger 1944-
See Pink Floyd

Wa Thiong'o, Ngugi
1938- . . . . **CLC 3, 7, 13, 36**
See also Ngugi, James (Thiong'o); Ngugi wa
Thiong'o

Watkins, Paul 1964- . . . . **CLC 55**

Watkins, Vernon (Phillips)
1906-1967 . . . . **CLC 43**
See also CAP 1; CA 9-10;
obituary CA 25-28R; DLB 20

Waugh, Auberon (Alexander) 1939- . . . **CLC 7**
See also CANR 6, 22; CA 45-48; DLB 14

Waugh, Evelyn (Arthur St. John)
1903-1966 . . . **CLC 1, 3, 8, 13, 19, 27, 44**
See also CANR 22; CA 85-88;
obituary CA 25-28R; DLB 15

Waugh, Harriet 1944- . . . . **CLC 6**
See also CANR 22; CA 85-88

Webb, Beatrice (Potter)
1858-1943 . . . . **TCLC 22**
See also CA 117

Webb, Charles (Richard) 1939- . . . . . . **CLC 7**
See also CA 25-28R

Webb, James H(enry), Jr. 1946- . . . . **CLC 22**
See also CA 81-84

Webb, Mary (Gladys Meredith)
1881-1927 . . . . **TCLC 24**
See also CA 123; DLB 34

Webb, Phyllis 1927- . . . . **CLC 18**
See also CANR 23; CA 104; DLB 53

Webb, Sidney (James)
1859-1947 . . . . **TCLC 22**
See also CA 117

Webber, Andrew Lloyd 1948- . . . . **CLC 21**

Weber, Lenora Mattingly
1895-1971 . . . . **CLC 12**
See also CAP 1; CA 19-20;
obituary CA 29-32R; SATA 2;
obituary SATA 26

Wedekind, (Benjamin) Frank(lin)
1864-1918 . . . . **TCLC 7**
See also CA 104

Weidman, Jerome 1913- . . . . **CLC 7**
See also CANR 1; CA 1-4R; DLB 28

Weil, Simone 1909-1943 . . . . **TCLC 23**
See also CA 117

Weinstein, Nathan Wallenstein 1903?-1940
See West, Nathanael
See also CA 104

Author Index

SSC Cumulative Nationality Index

SSC Cumulative Title Index

Title Index

Title Index

Title Index

8254

8254